The Theory of Corporate Finance

The Theory of Corporate Finance

Jean Tirole

Princeton University Press
Princeton and Oxford

Published by Princeton University Press,
41 William Street, Princeton, New Jersey 08540

In the United Kingdom: Princeton University Press,
3 Market Place, Woodstock, Oxfordshire OX20 1SY

Library of Congress Cataloguing-in-Publication Data

Tirole, Jean.
The theory of corporate finance / Jean Tirole.
p. cm.
Includes bibliographical references and index.
ISBN-13: 978-0-691-12556-2 (cloth: alk. paper)
ISBN-10: 0-691-12556-2 (cloth: alk. paper)
1. Corporations—Finance. 2. Business enterprises—Finance.
3. Corporate governance. I. Title.

HG4011.T57 2006
338.4′3′001—dc22 2005052166

British Library Cataloguing-in-Publication Data

A catalogue record for this book is available from the British Library

This book has been composed in LucidaBright and
typeset by T&T Productions Ltd, London

Printed on acid-free paper ∞
www.pup.princeton.edu

Printed in the United States of America

1 2 3 4 5 6 7 8 9 10

à Naïs, Margot, et Romain

Contents

Acknowledgements xi

Introduction 1

Overview of the Field and Coverage of the Book 1

Approach 6

Prerequisites and Further Reading 7

Some Important Omissions 7

References 10

I An Economic Overview of Corporate Institutions 13

1 Corporate Governance 15

1.1 Introduction: The Separation of Ownership and Control 15

1.2 Managerial Incentives: An Overview 20

1.3 The Board of Directors 29

1.4 Investor Activism 36

1.5 Takeovers and Leveraged Buyouts 43

1.6 Debt as a Governance Mechanism 51

1.7 International Comparisons of the Policy Environment 53

1.8 Shareholder Value or Stakeholder Society? 56

Supplementary Section

1.9 The Stakeholder Society: Incentives and Control Issues 62

Appendixes

1.10 Cadbury Report 65

1.11 Notes to Tables 67

References 68

2 Corporate Financing: Some Stylized Facts 75

2.1 Introduction 75

2.2 Modigliani–Miller and the Financial Structure Puzzle 77

2.3 Debt Instruments 80

2.4 Equity Instruments 90

2.5 Financing Patterns 95

2.6 Conclusion 102

Appendixes

2.7 The Five Cs of Credit Analysis 103

2.8 Loan Covenants 103

References 106

II Corporate Financing and Agency Costs 111

3 Outside Financing Capacity 113

3.1 Introduction 113

3.2 The Role of Net Worth: A Simple Model of Credit Rationing 115

3.3 Debt Overhang 125

3.4 Borrowing Capacity: The Equity Multiplier 127

Supplementary Sections

3.5 Related Models of Credit Rationing: Inside Equity and Outside Debt 130

3.6 Verifiable Income 132

3.7 Semiverifiable Income 138

3.8 Nonverifiable Income 141
3.9 Exercises 144
References 154

4 Some Determinants of Borrowing Capacity 157

4.1 Introduction: The Quest for Pledgeable Income 157
4.2 Boosting the Ability to Borrow: Diversification and Its Limits 158
4.3 Boosting the Ability to Borrow: The Costs and Benefits of Collateralization 164
4.4 The Liquidity–Accountability Tradeoff 171
4.5 Restraining the Ability to Borrow: Inalienability of Human Capital 177

Supplementary Sections

4.6 Group Lending and Microfinance 180
4.7 Sequential Projects 183
4.8 Exercises 188
References 195

5 Liquidity and Risk Management, Free Cash Flow, and Long-Term Finance 199

5.1 Introduction 199
5.2 The Maturity of Liabilities 201
5.3 The Liquidity–Scale Tradeoff 207
5.4 Corporate Risk Management 213
5.5 Endogenous Liquidity Needs, the Sensitivity of Investment to Cash Flow, and the Soft Budget Constraint 220
5.6 Free Cash Flow 225
5.7 Exercises 229
References 235

6 Corporate Financing under Asymmetric Information 237

6.1 Introduction 237
6.2 Implications of the Lemons Problem and of Market Breakdown 241
6.3 Dissipative Signals 249

Supplementary Section

6.4 Contract Design by an Informed Party: An Introduction 264

Appendixes

6.5 Optimal Contracting in the Privately-Known-Prospects Model 269
6.6 The Debt Bias with a Continuum of Possible Incomes 270
6.7 Signaling through Costly Collateral 271
6.8 Short Maturities as a Signaling Device 271
6.9 Formal Analysis of the Underpricing Problem 272
6.10 Exercises 273
References 280

7 Topics: Product Markets and Earnings Manipulations 283

7.1 Corporate Finance and Product Markets 283
7.2 Creative Accounting and Other Earnings Manipulations 299

Supplementary Section

7.3 Brander and Lewis's Cournot Analysis 318
7.4 Exercises 322
References 327

III Exit and Voice: Passive and Active Monitoring 331

8 Investors of Passage: Entry, Exit, and Speculation 333

8.1 General Introduction to Monitoring in Corporate Finance 333
8.2 Performance Measurement and the Value of Speculative Information 338

8.3 Market Monitoring 345
8.4 Monitoring on the Debt Side: Liquidity-Draining versus Liquidity-Neutral Runs 350
8.5 Exercises 353
References 353

9 Lending Relationships and Investor Activism 355

9.1 Introduction 355
9.2 Basics of Investor Activism 356
9.3 The Emergence of Share Concentration 366
9.4 Learning by Lending 369
9.5 Liquidity Needs of Large Investors and Short-Termism 374
9.6 Exercises 379
References 382

IV Security Design: The Control Right View 385

10 Control Rights and Corporate Governance 387

10.1 Introduction 387
10.2 Pledgeable Income and the Allocation of Control Rights between Insiders and Outsiders 389
10.3 Corporate Governance and Real Control 398
10.4 Allocation of Control Rights among Securityholders 404
Supplementary Sections
10.5 Internal Capital Markets 411
10.6 Active Monitoring and Initiative 415
10.7 Exercises 418
References 422

11 Takeovers 425

11.1 Introduction 425
11.2 The Pure Theory of Takeovers: A Framework 425
11.3 Extracting the Raider's Surplus: Takeover Defenses as Monopoly Pricing 426
11.4 Takeovers and Managerial Incentives 429
11.5 Positive Theory of Takeovers: Single-Bidder Case 431
11.6 Value-Decreasing Raider and the One-Share–One-Vote Result 438
11.7 Positive Theory of Takeovers: Multiple Bidders 440
11.8 Managerial Resistance 441
11.9 Exercise 441
References 442

V Security Design: The Demand Side View 445

12 Consumer Liquidity Demand 447

12.1 Introduction 447
12.2 Consumer Liquidity Demand: The Diamond–Dybvig Model and the Term Structure of Interest Rates 447
12.3 Runs 454
12.4 Heterogenous Consumer Horizons and the Diversity of Securities 457
Supplementary Sections
12.5 Aggregate Uncertainty and Risk Sharing 461
12.6 Private Signals and Uniqueness in Bank Run Models 463
12.7 Exercises 466
References 467

VI Macroeconomic Implications and the Political Economy of Corporate Finance 469

13 Credit Rationing and Economic Activity 471

13.1 Introduction 471
13.2 Capital Squeezes and Economic Activity: The Balance-Sheet Channel 471
13.3 Loanable Funds and the Credit Crunch: The Lending Channel 478
13.4 Dynamic Complementarities: Net Worth Effects, Poverty Traps, and the Financial Accelerator 484
13.5 Dynamic Substitutabilities: The Deflationary Impact of Past Investment 489
13.6 Exercises 493
References 495

14 Mergers and Acquisitions, and the Equilibrium Determination of Asset Values 497

14.1 Introduction 497
14.2 Valuing Specialized Assets 499
14.3 General Equilibrium Determination of Asset Values, Borrowing Capacities, and Economic Activity: The Kiyotaki–Moore Model 509
14.4 Exercises 515
References 516

15 Aggregate Liquidity Shortages and Liquidity Asset Pricing 517

15.1 Introduction 517
15.2 Moving Wealth across States of Nature: When Is Inside Liquidity Sufficient? 518
15.3 Aggregate Liquidity Shortages and Liquidity Asset Pricing 523
15.4 Moving Wealth across Time: The Case of the Corporate Sector as a Net Lender 527
15.5 Exercises 530
References 532

16 Institutions, Public Policy, and the Political Economy of Finance 535

16.1 Introduction 535
16.2 Contracting Institutions 537
16.3 Property Rights Institutions 544
16.4 Political Alliances 551
Supplementary Sections
16.5 Contracting Institutions, Financial Structure, and Attitudes toward Reform 555
16.6 Property Rights Institutions: Are Privately Optimal Maturity Structures Socially Optimal? 560
16.7 Exercises 563
References 567

VII Answers to Selected Exercises, and Review Problems 569

Answers to Selected Exercises 571
Review Problems 625
Answers to Selected Review Problems 633

Index 641

Acknowledgements

While bearing my name as sole author, this book is largely a collective undertaking and would not exist without the talent and generosity of a large number of people.

First of all, this book owes much to my collaboration with Bengt Holmström. Many chapters indeed borrow unrestrainedly from joint work and discussions with him.

This book benefited substantially from the input of researchers and students who helped fashion its form and its content. I am grateful to Philippe Aghion, Arnoud Boot, Philip Bond, Giacinta Cestone, Gilles Chemla, Jing-Yuang Chiou, Roberta Dessi, Mathias Dewatripont, Emmanuel Farhi, Antoine Faure-Grimaud, Daniel Gottlieb, Denis Gromb, Bruno Jullien, Dominique Olié Lauga, Josh Lerner, Marco Pagano, Parag Pathak, Alessandro Pavan, Marek Pycia, Patrick Rey, Jean-Charles Rochet, Bernard Salanié, Yossi Spiegel, Anton Souvorov, David Sraer, Jeremy Stein, Olga Shurchkov, David Thesmar, Flavio Toxvaerd, Harald Uhlig, Michael Weisbach, and several anonymous reviewers for very helpful comments.

Jing-Yuang Chiou, Emmanuel Farhi, Denis Gromb, Antoine Faure-Grimaud, Josh Lerner, and Marco Pagano in particular were extremely generous with their time and gave extremely detailed comments on the penultimate draft. They deserve very special thanks. Catherine Bobtcheff and Aggey Semenov provided excellent research assistance on the last draft.

Drafts of this book were taught at the Ecole Polytechnique, the University of Toulouse, the Massachusetts Institute of Technology (MIT), Gerzensee, the University of Lausanne, and Wuhan University; I am grateful to the students in these institutions for their comments and suggestions.

I am, of course, entirely responsible for any remaining errors and omissions. Needless to say, I will be grateful to have these pointed out; comments on this book can be either communicated to me directly or uploaded on the following website:

http://www.pupress.princeton.edu/titles/8123.html

Note that this website also contains exercises, answers, and some lecture transparencies which are available for lecturers to download and adapt for their own use, with appropriate acknowledgement.

Pierrette Vaissade, my assistant, deserves very special thanks for her high standards and remarkable skills. Her patience with the many revisions during the decade over which this book was elaborated was matched only by her ever cheerful mood. She just did a wonderful job. I am also grateful to Emily Gallagher for always making my visits to MIT run smoothly.

At Princeton University Press, Richard Baggaley, my editor, and Peter Dougherty, its director, provided very useful advice and encouragement at various stages of the production. Jon Wainwright, with the help of Sam Clark, at T&T Productions Ltd did a truly superb job at editing the manuscript and typesetting the book, and always kept good spirits despite long hours, a tight schedule, and my incessant changes and requests.

I also benefited from very special research environments and colleagues: foremost, the Institut d'Economie Industrielle (IDEI), founded within the University of Toulouse 1 by Jean-Jacques Laffont, for its congenial and stimulating environment; and also the economics department at MIT and the Ecole Nationale des Ponts et Chaussées (CERAS, now part of Paris Sciences Economiques). The friendly encouragement of my colleagues in those institutions was invaluable.

My wife, Nathalie, and our children, Naïs, Margot, and Romain, provided much understanding, support, and love during the long period that was needed to bring this book to fruition.

Finally, may this book be a (modest) tribute to Jean-Jacques Laffont. Jean-Jacques prematurely passed away on May 1, 2004. I will always cherish the memory of our innumerable discussions, over the twenty-three years of our collaboration, on the topics of this book, economics more generally, his many projects and dreams, and life. He was, for me as for many others, a role model, a mentor, and a dear friend.

Introduction

This introduction has a dual purpose: it explains the book's approach and the organization of the chapters; and it points up some important topics that receive insufficient attention in the book (and provides an inexhaustive list of references for additional reading). This introduction will be of most use to teachers and graduate students. Anyone without a strong economics background who is finding it tough going on a first reading should turn straight to Chapter 1.

Overview of the Field and Coverage of the Book

The field of corporate finance has undergone a tremendous mutation in the past twenty years. A substantial and important body of empirical work has provided a clearer picture of patterns of corporate financing and governance, and of their impact for firm behavior and macroeconomic activity. On the theoretical front, the 1970s came to the view that the dominant Arrow–Debreu general equilibrium model of frictionless markets (presumed perfectly competitive and complete, and unhampered by taxes, transaction costs, and informational asymmetries) could prove to be a powerful tool for analyzing the pricing of claims in financial markets, but said little about the firms' financial choices and about their governance. To the extent that financial claims' returns depend on some choices such as investments, these choices, in the complete market paradigm of Arrow and Debreu, are assumed to be contractible and therefore are not affected by moral hazard. Furthermore, investors agree on the distribution of a claim's returns; that is, financial markets are not plagued by problems of asymmetric information. Viewed through the Arrow–Debreu lens, the key issue for financial economists is the allocation of risk among investors and the pricing of redundant claims by arbitrage.

Relatedly, Modigliani and Miller in two papers in 1958 and 1963 proved the rather remarkable result that under some conditions a firm's financial structure, for example, its choice of leverage or of dividend policy, is irrelevant. The simplest set of such conditions is the Arrow–Debreu environment (complete markets, no transaction costs, no taxes, no bankruptcy costs).[1] The value of a financial claim is then equal to the value of the random return of this claim computed at the Arrow–Debreu prices (that is, the prices of state-contingent securities, where a state-contingent security is a security delivering one unit of numéraire in a given state of nature). The total value of a firm, equal to the sum of the values of the claims it issues, is thus equal to the value of the random return of the firm computed at the Arrow–Debreu prices. In other words, the size of the pie is unaffected by the way it is carved.

Because we have little to say about firms' financial choices and governance in a world in which the Modigliani–Miller Theorem applies, the latter acted as a detonator for the theory of corporate finance, a benchmark whose assumptions needed to be relaxed in order to investigate the determinants of financial structures. In particular, the assumption that the size of the pie is unaffected by how this pie is distributed had to be discarded. Following the lead of a few influential papers written in the 1970s (in particular, Jensen and Meckling 1976; Myers 1977; Ross 1977), the principal direction of inquiry since the 1980s has been to introduce agency problems at various levels of the corporate structure (managerial team, specific claimholders).

1. For more general conditions, see, for example, Stiglitz (1969, 1973, 1974) and Duffie (1992).

This shift of attention to agency considerations in corporate finance received considerable support from the large empirical literature and from the practice of institutional design, both of which are reviewed in Part I of the book. Chapters 1 and 2 offer introductions to corporate governance and corporate financing, respectively. They are by no means exhaustive, and do not do full justice to the impressive body of empirical and institutional knowledge that has been developed in the last two decades. Rather, these chapters aim at providing the reader with an overview of the key institutional features, empirical regularities, and policy issues that will motivate and guide the subsequent theoretical analysis.

The theoretical literature on the microeconomics of corporate finance can be divided into several branches.

The first branch, reviewed in Part II, focuses entirely on the incentives of the firm's *insiders*. Outsiders (whom we will call investors or lenders) are in a principal–agent relationship with the insiders (whom we will call borrowers, entrepreneurs, or managers). Informational asymmetries plague this agency relationship. Insiders may have private information about the firm's technology or environment (adverse selection) or about the firm's realized income (hidden knowledge);[2] alternatively outsiders cannot observe the insiders' carefulness in selecting projects, the riskiness of investments, or the effort they exert to make the firm profitable (moral hazard). Informational asymmetries may prevent outsiders from hindering insider behavior that jeopardizes their investment.

Financial contracting in this stream of literature is then the design of an incentive scheme for the insiders that best aligns the interests of the two parties. The outsiders are viewed as passive cash collectors, who only check that the financial contract will allow them to recoup on average an adequate rate of return on their initial investment. Because outsiders do not interfere in management, the split of returns among them (the outsiders' return is defined as a residual, once insiders' compensation is subtracted from profit) is irrelevant. That is, the Modigliani–Miller Theorem applies to outside claims and there is no proper security design. One might as well assume that the outsiders hold the same, single security.

Chapter 3 first builds a fixed-investment moral-hazard model of credit rationing. This model, together with its variable-investment variant developed later in the chapter, will constitute the workhorse for this book's treatment. It is then applied to the analysis of a few standard themes in corporate finance: the firm's temptation to overborrow, and the concomitant need for covenants restricting future borrowing; the sensitivity of investment to cash flow; and the notion of "debt overhang," according to which profitable investments may not be undertaken if renegotiation with existing claimants proves difficult. Third, it extends the basic model to allow for an endogenous choice of investment size. This extension, also used in later chapters, is here applied to the derivation of a firm's borrowing capacity. The supplementary section covers three related models of credit rationing that all predict that the division of income between insiders and outsiders takes the form of inside equity and outside debt.

Chapter 4 analyzes some determinants of borrowing capacity. Factors facilitating borrowing include, under some conditions, diversification, existence of collateral, and willingness for the borrower to make her claim illiquid. In each instance, the costs and benefits of these corporate policies are detailed. In contrast, the ability for the borrower to renegotiate for a bigger share of the pie reduces her ability to borrow. The supplementary section develops the themes of group lending and of sequential-projects financing, and draws their theoretical connection to the diversification argument studied in the main text.

Chapter 5 looks at multiperiod financing. It first develops a model of liquidity management and shows how liquidity requirements and lines of credit for "cash-poor" firms can be natural complements to the standard solvency/maximum leverage requirements imposed by lenders. Second, the chapter shows that the optimal design of debt maturity and the "free-cash-flow problem" encountered by cash-rich firms form the mirror image of the "liquidity

2. The distinction between adverse selection and hidden knowledge is that insiders have private information about exogenous (environmental) variables at the date of contracting in the case of adverse selection, while they acquire such private information after contracting in the case of hidden knowledge.

shortage problem" faced by firms generating insufficient net income in the short term. In particular, the model is used to derive comparative statics results on the optimal debt maturity structure. It is shown, for example, that the debt of firms with weak balance sheets should have a short maturity structure. Third, the chapter provides an integrated account of optimal liquidity and risk management. It first develops the benchmark case in which the firm optimally insulates itself from any risk that it does not control. It then studies in detail five theoretical reasons why firms should only partially hedge. Finally, the chapter revisits the sensitivity of investment to cash flow, and demonstrates the possibility of a "soft budget constraint."

Chapter 6 introduces asymmetric information between insiders and outsiders at the financing stage. Investors are naturally concerned by the prospect of buying into a firm with poor prospects, that is, a "lemon." Such adverse selection in general makes it more difficult for insiders to raise funds. The chapter relates two standard themes from the contract-theoretic literature on adverse selection, market breakdown, and cross-subsidization of bad borrowers by good ones, to two equally familiar themes from corporate finance: the negative stock price reaction associated with equity offerings and the "pecking-order hypothesis," according to which issuers have a preference ordering for funding their investments, from retained earnings to debt to hybrid securities and finally to equity. The chapter then explains why good borrowers use dissipative signals; it again revisits familiar corporate finance observations such as the resort to a costly certifier, costly collateral pledging, short-term debt maturities, payout policies, limited diversification, and underpricing. These dissipative signals are regrouped under the general umbrella of "issuance of low-information-intensity securities."

Chapter 7, a topics chapter, first analyzes the two-way interaction between corporate finance and product-market competition: how do market characteristics affect corporate financing choices? How do other firms, rivals or complementors, react to the firm's financial structure? Direct (profitability) and indirect (benchmarking) effects are shown to affect the availability of funds as well as financial structure decisions (debt maturity, financial muscle, corporate governance).

The chapter then extends the class of insider incentive problems. While the standard incentive problem is concerned with the possibility that insiders waste resources and reduce average earnings, managers can engage in moral hazard in other dimensions, not so much to reduce their efforts or generate private benefits, but rather to alter the very performance measures on which their reward, their tenure in the firm, or the continuation of the project are based. We call such behaviors "manipulations of performance measures" and analyze three such behaviors: increase in risk, forward shifting of income, and backward shifting of income.

The second branch of corporate finance addresses both *insiders' and outsiders' incentives* by taking a less passive view of the role of outsiders. While they are disconnected from day-to-day management, outsiders may occasionally affect the course of events chosen by insiders. For example, the board of directors or a venture capitalist may dismiss the chief executive officer or demand that insiders alter their investment strategy. Raiders may, following a takeover, break up the firm and spin off some divisions. Or a bank may take advantage of a covenant violation to impose more rigor in management. Insiders' discipline is then provided by their incentive scheme *and* the threat of external interference in management.

The increased generality brought about by the consideration of outsiders' actions has clear costs and benefits. On the one hand, the added focus on the claimholders' incentives to control insiders destroys the simplicity of the previous principal–agent structure. On the other hand, it provides an escape from the unrealism of the Modigliani–Miller Theorem. Indeed, claimholders must be given proper incentives to intervene in management. These incentives are provided by the return streams attached to their claims. The split of the outsiders' total return among the several classes of claimholders now has real implications and *security design* is no longer a trivial appendix to the design of managerial incentives.

This second branch of corporate finance can itself be divided into two subbranches. The first, reviewed in Part III, analyzes the *monitoring* of management by one or several securityholders (large shareholder, main bank, venture capitalist, etc.). As we just discussed, the monitors in a sense are insiders themselves as they must be given proper incentives to fulfill their mission. The material reviewed in Part III might therefore be more correctly described as the study of financing in the presence of multiple insiders (managers plus monitors). We will, however, maintain the standard distinction between nonexecutive parties (the securityholders, some of which have an active monitoring role) and executive officers. But we should keep in mind the fact that the division between insiders and outsiders is not a foregone conclusion.

Chapter 8 investigates the social costs and benefits of passive monitoring, namely, the acquisition, by outsiders with purely speculative motives, of information about the value of assets in place; and it shows how they relate to the following questions. Why are entrepreneurs and managers often compensated through stocks and stock options rather than solely on the basis of what they actually deliver: profits and losses? Do shareholders who are in for the long term benefit from liquid and deep secondary markets for shares?

The main theme of the chapter is that a firm's stock market price continuously provides a measure of the value of assets in place and therefore of the impact of managerial behavior on investor returns.

In Chapter 9, by contrast, active monitoring curbs the borrower's moral hazard (alternatively, it could alleviate adverse selection). Monitoring, however, comes at some cost: mere costs for the monitors of studying the firms and their environment, monitors' supranormal profit associated with a scarcity of monitoring capital, reduction in future competition in lending to the extent that incumbent monitors acquire superior information on the firm relative to competing lenders, block illiquidity, and monitors' private benefits from control.

Part IV develops a control-rights approach to corporate finance. Chapter 10 analyzes the allocation of formal control between insiders and outsiders. A firm that is constrained in its ability to secure financing must allocate (formal) control rights between insiders and outsiders with a view to creating pledgeable income; that is, control rights should not necessarily be granted to those who value them most. This observation generates a rationale for "shareholder value" as well as an empirically supported connection between firms' balance-sheet strength and investors' scope of control. The chapter then shows how (endogenously) better-informed actors (management, minority block shareholders) enjoy (real) control without having any formal right to decide; and argues that the extent of managerial control increases with the strength of the firm's balance sheet and decreases with the (endogenous) presence of monitors. Finally, Chapter 10 analyzes the allocation of control rights among different classes of securityholders. While the paradigm reviewed in Part III already generated conflicts among the securityholders by creating different reward structures for monitors and nonmonitors, this conflict was an *undesirable* side-product of the incentive structure required to encourage monitoring. As far as monitoring was concerned, nonmonitors and monitors had congruent views on the fact that management should be monitored and constrained. Chapter 10 shows that conflicts among securityholders may arise *by design* and that control rights should be allocated to securityholders whose incentives are least aligned with managerial interests when firm performance is poor.

Chapter 11 focuses on a specific control right, namely, raiders' ability to take over the firm. As described in Chapter 1, this ability is determined by the firm's takeover defense choices (poison pills, dual-vote structures, and so forth), as well as by the regulatory environment. In order not to get bogged down by country- and time-specific details, we first develop a "normative theory of takeovers," identifying their two key motivations (bringing in new blood and ideas, and disciplining current management) and studying the social efficiency of takeover policies adopted by the firms. The chapter then turns to the classical theory of the tendering of shares in takeover contests and of the free-rider problem, and studies firms' choices of poison pills and dual-class voting rules.

A third branch of modern corporate finance, reviewed in Part V, takes into account the existence of *investors' clienteles* and thereby returns to the classical view that securityholders differ in their preferences for state-contingent returns. For instance, it emphasizes the fact that individual investors as well as corporations attach a premium to the possibility of being able to obtain a decent return on their asset portfolio if they face the need to liquidate it. Chapter 12 therefore studies consumer liquidity demand. Consumers who may in the future face liquidity needs value flexibility regarding the date at which they can realize (a decent return on) their investment. It identifies potential roles for financial institutions as (a) liquidity pools, preventing the waste associated with individual investments in low-yield, short-term assets, and (b) insurers, allowing consumers to smooth their consumption path when they are hit by liquidity shocks; and argues that the second role is more fragile than the first in the presence of arbitrage by financial markets. It then studies bank runs. Finally, the chapter argues that heterogeneity in the consumers' preference for flexibility segments investors into multiple clienteles, with consumers with short horizons demanding safe (low-information-intensity) securities and those with longer horizons being rewarded through equity premia for holding risky securities.

Part VI analyzes the implications of corporate finance for *macroeconomic activity and policy*. Much evidence has been gathered that demonstrates a substantial impact of liquidity and leverage problems on output, investment, and modes of financing. As we will see, the agency approach to corporate finance implies that economic shocks tend to be amplified by the existence of financial constraints, and offers a rationale for some macroeconomic phenomena such as credit crunches and liquidity shortages. Economists since Irving Fisher have acknowledged the role of credit constraints in amplifying recessions and booms. They have distinguished between the "balance-sheet channel," which refers to the influence of firms' balance sheets on investment and production, and the "lending channel," which focuses on financial intermediaries' own balance sheets. Chapter 13 sets corporate finance in a general equilibrium environment, enabling the endogenous determination of factor prices (interest rates, wages). It also shows that transitory balance-sheet effects may have long-term (poverty-trap) effects on individual families or countries altogether, and investigates the factors of dynamic complementarities or substitutabilities.

Capital reallocations (mergers and acquisitions, sales of property, plants and equipment) serve to move assets from low- to high-productivity uses, and, as emphasized in several chapters, may further be driven by managerial discipline and pledgeable income creation concerns. Chapter 14 endogenizes the resale value of assets in capital reallocations. It first focuses on specialized assets, which can be resold only within the firm's industry. Their resale value then hinges on the presence in the industry of other firms that have (a) a demand for the assets and (b) the financial means to purchase them. A central focus of the analysis is whether firms build too much or too little "financial muscle" for use in future acquisitions. Second, the chapter studies nonspecialized assets, which can be redeployed in other industries, and looks at the dynamics of credit constraints and economic activity depending on whether these assets are or are not the only stores of value in the economy.

Chapter 15 investigates the very existence of stores of value in the economy, as these stores of value condition the corporate sector's ability to meet liquidity shocks in the aggregate. It builds on the analysis of Chapter 5 to derive individual firms' demand for liquid assets and then looks at equilibrium in the market for these assets. It is shown that the private sector creates its own liquidity and that this "inside liquidity" may or may not suffice for a proper functioning of the economy. A shortage of inside liquidity makes "outside liquidity" (existing rents, government-created liquidity backed by future taxation) valuable and has interesting implications for the pricing of assets.

Laws and regulations that affect the borrowers' ability to pledge income to their investors, and more generally the many public policies that influence corporate profitability and pledgeable income (tax, labor and environmental laws, prudential regulation, capital account liberalization, exchange rate management, and so forth) have a deep impact on the firms' ability to secure funding and on their design of financial structure and governance. Chapter 16 defines "contracting institutions" as referring to the public policy environment at the time at which borrowers, investors and other stakeholders contract; and "property rights institutions" as referring to the resilience or time-consistency of these policies. Chapter 16 derives a "topsy-turvy principle" of policy preferences, according to which for a widespread variety of public policies, the relative preference of heterogeneous borrowers switches over time: borrowers with weak balance sheets have, before they receive funding, the highest demand for investor-friendly public policies, but they are the keenest to lobby to have these policies repudiated once they have secured financing. This principle is applied to public policies affecting the legal enforcement of collateral, income, and control rights pledges made by borrowers, and is shown to alter the levels of collateral, the maturity of debts, and the allocation of control. The chapter then shows that borrowers exert externalities (mediated by the political process) through their design of financial structures. Finally, it studies the emergence of public policies in an environment in which policies are set by majority rule.

The book contains a large number of exercises. While some are just meant to help the reader gain familiarity with the material, many others have a dual purpose and cover insights derived in contributions that are not surveyed or little emphasized in the core of the text; a few exercises develop results not available in the literature. I would like to emphasize that solving exercises is, as in other areas of study, a key input into mastering corporate finance theory. Students will find many of these exercises challenging, but hopefully eventually rewarding. With this perspective, the reader will find in Part VII answers and hints to most exercises as well as a few review questions and exercises. Also see the website for the book at http://www.pupress.princeton.edu/titles/8123.html, where these exercises, answers, and some lecture transparencies are available for lecturers to download and adapt for their own use, with appropriate acknowledgement.

Approach

While tremendous progress has been made on the theoretical front in the past twenty years, the lack of a unified framework often disheartens students of corporate finance. The wide discrepancy of assumptions across papers not only lengthens the learning process, but it also makes it difficult for outsiders to identify the key economic elements driving the analyses. This diversity of modeling approaches is a natural state of affairs and is even beneficial for a young, unexplored field, but is a handicap when we try to take stock of our progress in understanding corporate finance.

The approach taken here obeys four precepts. The first is to stick as much as possible to the same modeling choices. The book employs a single, elementary model in order to illustrate the main economic insights. While this unified apparatus does not do justice to the wealth of modeling tools encountered in the literature, it has a pedagogic advantage in that it economizes the reader's investment in new modeling to study each economic issue. Conceptually, this *controlled experiment* highlights new insights by minimizing modifications from one chapter to the next. (The supplementary material in Chapter 3 discusses at some length some alternative modeling choices.)

Second, the exposition aims at simplifying modeling as much as possible. I will try to indicate when this involves a loss of generality. But hopefully it will become clear that the phenomena and insights are robust to more general assumptions. In this respect, I will insist as much as possible on deriving the optimal structure of financing and corporate governance, so as to ensure that the institutions we derive are robust; that is, by exhausting contracting possibilities, we check that the incentive problems we focus on cannot be eliminated.

Third, original contributions have been reorganized and sometimes reinterpreted slightly, for a couple of reasons. First, it is common (and natural!) that authors do not realize the significance of their contributions at the time they write their articles; consequently, they may motivate the paper a bit narrowly, without fully highlighting the key insights that others will subsequently build on. Relatedly, a textbook must take advantage of the benefits of hindsight. Second, the book represents a systematic attempt at organizing the field in a coherent manner. Original articles are often motivated by a specific application: dividend policy, capital structure, stock issues, stock repurchases, hedging, etc.; while such an application-driven approach is natural for research purposes, it does not fit well with a general treatment of the field since the same model would have to be repeated several times throughout a book that would be structured around applications. I do hope that the original authors will not take offense at this "remodeling" and will rather see it as a tribute to the potency and generality of their ideas.

Fourth, the book is organized in a "horizontal" fashion (by theoretical themes) rather than a "vertical" one (with a division according to applications: debt, dividends, collateral, etc.). The horizontal approach is preferable for an exposition of the theory because it conveys the unity of ideas and does not lead to a repetition of the same material in multiple locations in the book. For readers more interested in a specific topic (say, for empirical purposes), this approach often requires combining several chapters. The links indicated within the chapters should help perform the necessary connections.

Prerequisites and Further Reading

The following chapters are by and large *self-contained.* Some institutional and empirical background is supplied in Part I. This background is written with the perspective of the ensuing theoretical treatment. For a much more thorough treatment of the institutions of corporate finance, the reader may consult, for example, Allen, Brealey, and Myers (2005), Grinblatt and Titman (2002), or Ross, Westerfield, and Jaffe (1999).

Very little knowledge of contract theory and information economics is required. Familiarity with these fields, however, is useful in order to grasp more advanced topics (again, we will stick to fairly elementary modeling). The books by Laffont (1989) and Salanié (2005) offer concise treatments of contract theory. A more exhaustive treatment of contract theory will be found in the textbooks by Bolton and Dewatripont (2005) and Martimort and Laffont (2002). Shorter treatments can be found in the relevant chapters in Kreps (1990), Mas Colell, Whinston, and Green (1995), and Fudenberg and Tirole (1991, Chapter 7 on mechanism design). At a lower level, Milgrom and Roberts (1992) will serve as a useful motivation and introduction. Let us finally mention the survey by Hart and Holmström (1987), which offers a good introduction to the methodology of moral hazard, labor contracts, and incomplete contracting, and that by Holmström and Tirole (1989), which covers a broader range of topics and is nontechnical.

Similarly, no knowledge of the theory of corporate finance is required. Two very useful references can be used to complement the material developed here. Hart (1995) provides a much more complete treatment of a number of topics contained in Part IV, and is highly recommended reading. Freixas and Rochet (1997) offers a thorough treatment of credit rationing and, unlike this book, covers the large field of banking theory.[3] Further useful background reading in corporate finance can be found in Newman, Milgate, and Eatwell (1992), Bhattacharya, Boot, and Thakor (2004), and Constantinides, Harris, and Stulz (2003). Finally, the reader can also consult Amaro de Matos (2001) for a treatment at a level comparable with that of this book.

Some Important Omissions

Despite its length, the book makes a number of choices regarding coverage. Researchers, students, and instructors will therefore benefit from taking a broader perspective. Without any attempt at exhaustivity and in no particular order, this section indicates a few areas in which the omissions are particularly glaring, and includes a few suggestions for further reading.

Empirics

As its title indicates, the book focuses on theory. Some of the key empirical findings are reviewed in Chapters 1 and 2 and serve as motivation in later chapters. Yet, the book falls short of even paying an appropriate tribute to the large body of empirical results established in the last thirty years, let alone of providing a comprehensive overview of empirical corporate finance.

3. Another reference on the theory of banking is Dewatripont and Tirole (1994), which is specialized and focuses on regulatory aspects.

As in other fields of economics, some of the most exciting work involves tying the empirical analysis closely together with theory. I hope that, despite its strong theoretical bias, empirical researchers will find the book useful in their pursuit of this endeavor.

Theory

The book either does not cover or provides insufficient coverage of the following topics.

Taxes. To escape the Modigliani–Miller irrelevance results, researchers, starting with Modigliani and Miller themselves, first turned to the impact of taxes on the financial structure. Taxes affect financing in several ways. For example, in the United States and many other countries, equity is taxed more heavily than debt at the corporate level, providing a preference of firms for leverage.[4] The so-called "static tradeoff theory," first modeled by Kraus and Litzenberger (1973) and Scott (1976), used this fact to argue that the firms' financial structure is determined by a tradeoff between the tax savings brought about by leverage and the financial cost of the enhanced probability of bankruptcy associated with high debt. The higher the tax advantages of debt, the higher the optimal debt–equity ratio. Conversely, the higher the nondebt tax shields, the lower the desired leverage.[5] Taxes also affect payout choices; indeed, much empirical work has investigated the tax cost for firms of paying shareholders in dividends rather than through stock repurchases, which may bear a lower tax burden.[6]

For two reasons, the impact of taxes will be discussed only occasionally. First, the effects are usually conceptually straightforward, and the intellectual challenge is by and large the empirical one of measuring their magnitude. Second, taxes are country- and time-specific, making it difficult to draw general conclusions.[7]

Bubbles. Asset price bubbles, that is, the wedge between the price of financial claims and their fundamental,[8] have long been studied through the lens of aggregate savings and intertemporal efficiency.[9]

Some recent work was partly spurred by the dramatic NASDAQ bubble of the late 1990s, the accompanying boom in initial public offerings (IPOs) and seasoned equity offerings (SEOs), and their collapse in 2000–2001. Relative to the previous literature on bubbles, this new research further emphasizes the impact of bubbles on entrepreneurship and asset values. An early contribution along this line is Allen and Gorton (1993), in which delegated portfolio management, while necessary to channel funds from uninformed investors to the best entrepreneurs, creates agency costs and may generate short horizons[10] and asset price bubbles. Olivier (2000) and Ventura (2004) draw the implications of bubbles that are attached to investment and to entrepreneurship per se, respectively; for example, in Ventura's paper, the prospect of surfing a bubble at the IPO stage relaxes entrepreneurial financing constraints.

Bubbles matter for corporate finance for at least two reasons. First, and as was already mentioned, they may directly increase investment either by altering its yield or by relaxing financial constraints. Second, they create additional stores of value in an economy that may be in need of such stores. Chapter 15 will demonstrate that the existence of stores of value may facilitate firms' liquidity management. This may create another channel of complementarity between bubbles and investments. The research on the interaction between price bubbles and corporate

4. In order to avoid concluding that firms should issue only debt, and no equity, early contributions assumed that bankruptcy is costly. Because more leverage increases the probability of financial distress, equity reduces bankruptcy costs. (Bankruptcy costs, unlike taxes, will be studied in the book.)

5. These predictions have received substantial empirical support (see, for example, Mackie-Mason 1990; Graham 2003). There is a large literature on financial structures and the tax system (Swoboda and Zechner 1995). A recent entry is Hennessy and Whited (2005), who derive a tax-induced optimal financial structure in the presence of taxes on corporate income, dividends, and interest income (as well as equity flotation costs and distress costs).

6. See Lewellen and Lewellen (2004) for a study of the tax benefits of equity under dividend distribution and share repurchase policies.

7. For similar reasons, we will not enter into the details of bankruptcy law, which are highly country- and time-specific. Rather, we will content ourselves with theoretical considerations (in particular in Chapter 10).

8. Fundamentals are defined as the present discounted value of payouts estimated at the consumers' intertemporal marginal rate of substitution.

9. On the "rational bubble" front, see, for example, Tirole (1985), Weil (1987), Abel et al. (1989), Santos and Woodford (1997), and, for an interesting recent entry, Caballero et al. (2004a). Another substantial body of research has investigated "irrational bubbles" (see, for example, Abreu and Brunnermeier 2003; Scheinkman and Xiong 2003; Panageas 2004).

10. See Allen et al. (2004) for different implications (such as overreactions to noisy public information) of short trading horizons.

finance is still in its infancy and therefore is best left to future surveys.

Behavioral finance. An exciting line of recent research relaxes the rationality postulate that dominates this book. There are two strands of research in this area (see Baker et al. (2005), Barberis and Thaler (2003), Shleifer (2000), and Stein (2003) for useful surveys).

One branch of the behavioral corporate finance literature assumes irrational *entrepreneurs or managers.* For example, managers may be too optimistic when assessing the marginal productivity of their investment, the value of assets in place, or the prospects attached to acquisitions (see, for example, Roll 1986; Heaton 2002; Shleifer and Vishny 2003; Landier and Thesmar 2004; Malmendier and Tate 2005; Manove and Padilla 1999). They then recommend value-destroying financing decisions, investments, or acquisitions to their board of directors and shareholders.

In contrast, the other branch of behavioral corporate finance postulates irrrational *investors* and limited arbitrage (see, for example, Sheffrin and Statman 1985; De Long et al. 1990; Stein 1996; Baker et al. 2003). Irrational investors induce a mispricing of claims that (more rational) managers are tempted to arbitrage. For example, managers of a company whose stock is largely overvalued may want to acquire a less overvalued target using its own stocks rather than cash as a means of payment. Managers may want to engage in market timing by conducting SEOs when stock prices are high (see, for example, Baker and Wurgler (2002) for evidence of such market timing behavior). Conglomerates may be a reaction to an irrational investor appetite for diversification, and so forth.

As Baker et al. (2005) point out, the two branches of the literature have drastically different implications for corporate governance: when the primary source of irrationality is on the investors' side, economic efficiency requires insulating managers from the short-term share price pressures, which may result from managerial stock options, the market for corporate control, or an insufficient amount of liquidity (an excessive leverage) that forces the firm to return regularly to the capital market. By contrast, if the primary source of irrationality is on the managers' side, managerial responsiveness to market signals and limited managerial discretion are called for.

Wherever the locus of irrationality, the behavioral approach competes with alternative neoclassical or agency-based paradigms. For example, the managerial hubris story for overinvestment is an alternative to several theories that will be reviewed throughout the book, such as empire building and private benefits (Chapter 3), strategic market interactions (Chapter 7), herd behavior (Chapter 6), or posturing and signaling (Chapter 7). Similarly, market timing, besides being a rational manager's reaction to stock overvaluation, could alternatively result from a common impact of productivity news on investment (calling for equity issues) and stock values,[11] or from the presence of asset bubbles (see references above).

Despite its importance, there are several rationales for not covering behavioral corporate finance in this book (besides the obvious issue of overall length). First, behavioral economic theory as a whole is a young and rapidly growing field. Many modeling choices regarding belief formation and preferences have been recently proposed and no unifying approach has yet emerged. Consequently, modeling assumptions are still too context-specific. A theoretical overview is probably premature.

Second, and despite the intensive and exciting research effort in behavioral economics in general, behavioral corporate finance theory is still rather underdeveloped relative to its agency-based counterpart. For example, I am not aware of any theoretical study of governance and control rights choices that would be the pendant to the theory reviewed in Parts III and VI of the book in the context of irrational investors and/or managers. For instance, and to rephrase Baker et al.'s (2005) concern about normative implications in a different way, we may wonder why managers have discretion (real authority) over the stock issue and acquisitions decisions if shareholders are convinced that their own beliefs are correct. Arbitrage of mispricing often requires

11. See, for example, Pastor and Veronesi (2005). Tests that attempt to tell apart a mispricing rationale often focus on underperformance of shares issued relative to the market index (e.g., Gompers and Lerner 2003).

shareholders' consent, which may not be forthcoming if the latter have the posited overoptimistic beliefs.

International finance. Inspired by the twin (foreign exchange and banking) crises in Latin America, Scandinavia, Mexico, South East Asia, Russia, Brazil, and Argentina (among others) in the last twenty-five years, another currently active branch of research has been investigating the interaction among firms' financial constraints, financial underdevelopment, and exchange rate crises. Theoretical background on financial fragility at the firm and country levels can be found in Chapters 5 and 15, respectively, but financial fragility in a current-account-liberalization context will not be treated in the book.[12]

Financial innovation and the organization of the financial system. Throughout the book, financial market inefficiencies, if any, will result from agency issues. That is, transaction costs will not impair the creation and liquidity of financial claims. See, in particular, Allen and Gale (1994) for a study of markets with an endogenous securities structure.[13]

References

Abel, A., G. Mankiw, L. Summers, and R. Zeckhauser. 1989. Assessing dynamic efficiency: theory and evidence. *Review of Economic Studies* 56:1–20.

Abreu, D. and M. Brunnermeier. 2003. Bubbles and crashes. *Econometrica* 71:173–204.

Allen, F. and D. Gale. 1994. *Financial Innovation and Risk Sharing.* Cambridge, MA: MIT Press.

Allen, F. and G. Gorton. 1993. Churning bubbles. *Review of Economic Studies* 60:813–836.

Allen, F., R. Brealey, and S. Myers. 2005. *Principles of Corporate Finance*, 8th edn. New York: McGraw-Hill.

Allen, F., S. Morris, and H. Shin. 2004. Beauty contests and iterated expectations in asset markets. Mimeo, Wharton School, Yale and London School of Economics.

Amaro de Matos, J. 2001. *Theoretical Foundations of Corporate Finance.* Princeton University Press.

Baker, M. and J. Wurgler. 2002. Market timing and capital structure. *Journal of Finance* 57:1–32.

12. Some of the earlier contributions are reviewed in Tirole (2002). A inexhaustive sample of more recent references includes Caballero and Krishnamurthy (2004a,b), Pathak and Tirole (2005), and Tirole (2003).

13. Also, while occasionally using simple market microstructure models (see Chapters 8 and 12), the book will not look at the large literature on the determinants of this microstructure and the liquidity of primary and secondary markets (as in, for example, Pagano 1989).

Baker, M., R. Ruback, and J. Wurgler. 2005. Behavioral corporate finance: a survey. In *Handbook of Corporate Finance: Empirical Corporate Finance* (ed. E. Eckbo), Part III, Chapter 5. Elsevier/North-Holland.

Baker, M., J. Stein, and J. Wurgler. 2003. When does the market matter? Stock prices and the investment of equity-dependent firms. *Quarterly Journal of Economics* 118: 969–1006.

Barberis, N. and R. H. Thaler. 2003. A survey of behavioral finance. In *Handbook of the Economics of Finance* (ed. G. Constantinides, M. Harris, and R. Stulz). Amsterdam: North-Holland.

Bhattacharya, S., A. Boot, and A. Thakor (eds). 2004. *Credit, Intermediation and the Macroeconomy.* Oxford University Press.

Bolton, P. and M. Dewatripont. 2005. *Introduction to the Theory of Contracts.* Cambridge, MA: MIT Press.

Caballero, R. and A. Krishnamurthy. 2004a. A "vertical" analysis of monetary policy in emerging markets. Mimeo, MIT and Northwestern University.

——. 2004b. Smoothing sudden stops. *Journal of Economic Theory* 119:104–127.

Caballero, R., E. Farhi, and M. Hammour. 2004. Speculative growth: hints from the US economy. Mimeo, MIT and Delta (Paris).

Constantinides, G., M. Harris, and R. Stulz (eds). 2003. *Handbook of the Economics of Finance.* Amsterdam: North-Holland.

De Long, B., A. Shleifer, L. Summers, and R. Waldmann. 1990. Positive feedback investment strategies and destabilizing rational speculation. *Journal of Finance* 45:379–395.

Dewatripont, M. and J. Tirole. 1994. *The Prudential Regulation of Banks.* Cambridge, MA: MIT Press.

Duffie, D. 1992. The Modigliani–Miller Theorem. In *The New Palgrave Dictionary of Money and Finance*, Volume 2, pp. 715–717. Palgrave Macmillan.

Freixas, X. and J.-C. Rochet. 1997. *Microeconomics of Banking.* Cambridge, MA: MIT Press.

Fudenberg, D. and J. Tirole. 1991. *Game Theory.* Cambridge, MA: MIT Press.

Gompers, P. and J. Lerner. 2003. The really long-run performance of initial public offerings: the pre-Nasdaq evidence. *Journal of Finance* 58:1355–1392.

Graham, J. R. 2003. Taxes and corporate finance: a review. *Review of Financial Studies* 16:1075–1129.

Grinblatt, M. and S. Titman. 2002. *Financial Policy and Corporate Strategy*, 2nd edn. McGraw-Hill Irwin.

Hart, O. 1995. *Firms, Contracts, and Financial Structure.* Oxford University Press.

Hart, O. and B. Holmström. 1987. The theory of contracts. In *Advances in Economic Theory, Fifth World Congress* (ed. T. Bewley). Cambridge University Press.

Heaton, J. 2002. Managerial optimism and corporate finance. *Financial Management* 31:33–45.

Hennessy, C. A. and T. Whited. 2005. Debt dynamics. *Journal of Finance* 60:1129–1165.

Holmström, B. and J. Tirole. 1989. The theory of the firm. In *Handbook of Industrial Organization* (ed. R. Schmalensee and R. Willig). North-Holland.

Jensen, M. and W. R. Meckling. 1976. Theory of the firm, managerial behaviour, agency costs and ownership structure. *Journal of Financial Economics* 3:305–360.

Kraus, A. and R. Litzenberger. 1973. A state-preference model of optimal financial leverage. *Journal of Finance* 28:911–922.

Kreps, D. 1990. *A Course in Microeconomic Theory.* Princeton University Press.

Laffont, J.-J. 1989. *The Economics of Uncertainty and Information.* Cambridge, MA: MIT Press.

Landier, A. and D. Thesmar. 2004. Financial contracting with optimistic entrepreneurs: theory and evidence. Mimeo, New York University and HEC, Paris.

Lewellen, J. and K. Lewellen. 2004. Taxes and financing decisions. Mimeo, MIT.

Mackie-Mason, J. 1990. Do taxes affect financing decisions? *Journal of Finance* 45:1417–1493.

Malmendier, U. and G. Tate. 2005. CEO overconfidence and investment. *Journal of Finance*, in press.

Manove, M. and J. Padilla. 1999. Banking (conservatively) with optimists. *RAND Journal of Economics* 30:324–350.

Martimort, D. and J.-J. Laffont. 2002. *The Theory of Incentives: The Principal–Agent Model*, Volume 1. Princeton University Press.

Mas Colell, A., M. Whinston, and J. Green. 1995. *Microeconomic Theory.* Oxford University Press.

Milgrom, P. and J. Roberts. 1992. *Economics, Organization and Management.* Englewood Cliffs, NJ: Prentice Hall.

Modigliani, F. and M. Miller. 1958. The cost of capital, corporate finance, and the theory of investment. *American Economic Review* 48:261–297.

——. 1963. Corporate income taxes and the cost of capital: a correction. *American Economic Review* 53:433–443.

Myers, S. 1977. The determinants of corporate borrowing. *Journal of Financial Economics* 5:147–175.

Newman, P., M. Milgate, and J. Eatwell (eds). 1992. *The New Palgrave Dictionary of Money and Finance.* London: Macmillan.

Olivier, J. 2000. Growth-enhancing bubbles. *International Economic Review* 41:133–151.

Pagano, M. 1989. Endogenous market thinness and stock price volatility. *Review of Economic Studies* 56:269–287.

Panageas, S. 2004. Speculation, overpricing, and investment: theory and empirical evidence. Mimeo, Wharton School.

Pastor, L. and P. Veronesi. 2005. Rational IPO waves. *Journal of Finance* 60:1713–1757.

Pathak, P. and J. Tirole. 2005. Pegs, risk management, and financial crises. Mimeo, Harvard University and IDEI.

Roll, R. 1986. The hubris hypothesis of corporate takeovers. *Journal of Business* 59:197–216.

Ross, S. 1977. The determination of financial structure: the incentive signalling approach. *Bell Journal of Economics* 8: 23–40.

Ross, S., R. Westerfield, and J. Jaffe. 1999. *Corporate Finance*, 5th edn. New York: McGraw-Hill.

Salanié, B. 2005. *The Economics of Contracts*, 2nd edn. Cambridge, MA: MIT Press.

Santos, M. and M. Woodford. 1997. Rational asset pricing bubbles. *Econometrica* 65:19–38.

Scheinkman, J. and W. Xiong. 2003. Overconfidence and speculative bubbles. *Journal of Political Economy* 111: 1183–1219.

Scott, J. 1976. A theory of optimal capital structure. *Bell Journal of Economics* 7:33–54.

Sheffrin, H. and M. Statman. 1985. Explaining investor preference for cash dividends. *Journal of Financial Economics* 13:253–282.

Shleifer, A. 2000. *Inefficient Markets: An Introduction to Behavioral Finance.* Oxford University Press.

Shleifer, A. and R. Vishny. 2003. Stock market driven acquisitions. *Journal of Financial Economics* 70:295–311.

Stein, J. 1996. Rational capital budgeting in an irrational world. *Journal of Business* 69:429–455.

——. 2003. Agency, information and corporate investment. In *Handbook of the Economics of Finance* (ed. G. Constantinides, M. Harris, and R. Stulz). Amsterdam: North-Holland.

Stiglitz, J. 1969. A re-examination of the Modigliani–Miller Theorem. *American Economic Review* 59:784–793.

Stiglitz, J. 1973. Taxation, corporate financial policy and the cost of capital. *Journal of Public Economics* 2:1–34.

——. 1974. On the irrelevance of corporate financial policy. *American Economic Review* 64:851–866.

Swoboda, R. and J. Zechner. 1995. Financial structure and the tax system. In *Handbook in Operations Research and Management Science: Finance* (ed. R. Jarrow, V. Maksimovic, and B. Ziemba), Volume 9, Chapter 24. Amsterdam: North-Holland.

Tirole, J. 1985. Asset bubbles and overlapping generations. *Econometrica* 53:1071–1100.

——. 2002. *Financial Crises, Liquidity, and the International Monetary System.* Princeton University Press.

——. 2003. Inefficient foreign borrowing: a dual- and common-agency perspective. *American Economic Review* 93: 1678–1702.

Ventura, J. 2004. Economy growth with bubbles. Mimeo, Centre de Recerca en Economia Internacional, Universitat Pompeu Fabra.

Weil, P. 1987. Confidence and the real value of money in an overlapping generations economy. *Quarterly Journal of Economics* 102:1–21.

PART I

An Economic Overview of Corporate Institutions

1
Corporate Governance

In 1932, Berle and Means wrote a pathbreaking book documenting the separation of ownership and control in the United States. They showed that shareholder dispersion creates substantial managerial discretion, which can be abused. This was the starting point for the subsequent academic thinking on corporate governance and corporate finance. Subsequently, a number of corporate problems around the world have reinforced the perception that managers are unwatched. Most observers are now seriously concerned that the best managers may not be selected, and that managers, once selected, are not accountable.

Thus, the premise behind modern corporate finance in general and this book in particular is that corporate insiders need not act in the best interests of the providers of the funds. This chapter's first task is therefore to document the divergence of interests through both empirical regularities and anecdotes. As we will see, moral hazard comes in many guises, from low effort to private benefits, from inefficient investments to accounting and market value manipulations, all of which will later be reflected in the book's theoretical construct.

Two broad routes can be taken to alleviate insider moral hazard. First, insiders' incentives may be partly aligned with the investors' interests through the use of performance-based incentive schemes. Second, insiders may be monitored by the current shareholders (or on their behalf by the board or a large shareholder), by potential shareholders (acquirers, raiders), or by debtholders. Such monitoring induces interventions in management ranging from mere interference in decision making to the threat of employment termination as part of a shareholder- or board-initiated move or of a bankruptcy process. We document the nature of these two routes, which play a prominent role throughout the book.

Chapter 1 is organized as follows. Section 1.1 sets the stage by emphasizing the importance of managerial accountability. Section 1.2 reviews various instruments and factors that help align managerial incentives with those of the firm: monetary compensation, implicit incentives, monitoring, and product-market competition. Sections 1.3–1.6 analyze monitoring by boards of directors, large shareholders, raiders, and banks, respectively. Section 1.7 discusses differences in corporate governance systems. Section 1.8 and the supplementary section conclude the chapter by a discussion of the objective of the firm, namely, whom managers should be accountable to, and tries to shed light on the long-standing debate between the proponents of the stakeholder society and those of shareholder-value maximization.

1.1 Introduction: The Separation of Ownership and Control

The governance of corporations has attracted much attention in the past decade. Increased media coverage has turned "transparency," "managerial accountability," "corporate governance failures," "weak boards of directors," "hostile takeovers," "protection of minority shareholders," and "investor activism" into household phrases. As severe agency problems continued to impair corporate performance both in companies with strong managers and dispersed shareholders (as is frequent in Anglo-Saxon countries) and those with a controlling shareholder and minority shareholders (typical of the European corporate landscape), repeated calls have been issued on both sides of the Atlantic for corporate governance reforms. In the 1990s, study groups (such as the Cadbury and Greenbury committees in the United Kingdom and the Viénot committee in

France) and institutional investors (such as CalPERS in the United States) started enunciating codes of best practice for boards of directors. More recently, various laws and reports[1] came in reaction to the many corporate scandals of the late 1990s and early 2000s (e.g., Seat, Banesto, Metallgesellschaft, Suez, ABB, Swissair, Vivendi in Europe, Dynergy, Qwest, Enron, WorldCom, Global Crossing, and Tyco in the United States).

But what is corporate governance?[2] The dominant view in economics, articulated, for example, in Shleifer and Vishny's (1997) and Becht et al.'s (2002) surveys on the topic, is that corporate governance relates to the "ways in which the suppliers of finance to corporations assure themselves of getting a return on their investment." Relatedly, it is preoccupied with the ways in which a corporation's insiders can credibly commit to return funds to outside investors and can thereby attract external financing. This definition is, of course, narrow. Many politicians, managers, consultants, and academics object to the economists' narrow view of corporate governance as being preoccupied solely with investor returns; they argue that other "stakeholders," such as employees, communities, suppliers, or customers, also have a vested interest in how the firm is run, and that these stakeholders' concerns should somehow be internalized as well.[3] Section 1.8 will return to the debate about the stakeholder society, but we should indicate right away that the content of this book reflects the agenda of the narrow and orthodox view described in the above citation. The rest of Section 1.1 is therefore written from the perspective of shareholder value.

1. In the United States, for example, the 2002 Sarbanes-Oxley Act, and the U.S. Securities and Exchange Commission's and the Financial Accounting Standards Board's reports.

2. We focus here on corporations. Separate governance issues arise in associations (see Hansmann 1996; Glaeser and Shleifer 2001; Hart and Moore 1989, 1996; Kremer 1997; Levin and Tadelis 2005) and government agencies (see Wilson 1989; Tirole 1994; Dewatripont et al. 1999a,b).

3. A prominent exponent of this view in France is Albert (1991). To some extent, the German legislation mandating codetermination (in particular, the Codetermination Act of 1976, which requires that supervisory boards of firms with over 2,000 employees be made up of an equal number of representatives of employees and shareholders, with the chairperson—a representative of the shareholders—deciding in the case of a stalemate) reflects this desire that firms internalize the welfare of their employees.

1.1.1 Moral Hazard Comes in Many Guises

There are various ways in which management may not act in the firm's (understand: its owners') best interest. For convenience, we divide these into four categories, but the reader should keep in mind that all are fundamentally part of the same problem, generically labeled by economists as "moral hazard."

(a) *Insufficient effort.* By "insufficient effort," we refer not so much to the number of hours spent in the office (indeed, most top executives work very long hours), but rather to the allocation of work time to various tasks. Managers may find it unpleasant or inconvenient to cut costs by switching to a less costly supplier, by reallocating the workforce, or by taking a tougher stance in wage negotiations (Bertrand and Mullainathan 1999).[4] They may devote insufficient effort to the oversight of their subordinates; scandals in the 1990s involving large losses inflicted by traders or derivative specialists subject to insufficient internal control (Metallgesellschaft, Procter & Gamble, Barings) are good cases in point. Lastly, managers may allocate too little time to the task they have been hired for because they overcommit themselves with competing activities (boards of directors, political involvement, investments in other ventures, and more generally activities not or little related to managing the firm).

(b) *Extravagant investments.* There is ample evidence, both direct and indirect, that some managers engage in pet projects and build empires to the detriment of shareholders. A standard illustration, provided by Jensen (1988), is the heavy exploration spending of oil industry managers in the late 1970s during a period of high real rates of interest, increased exploration costs, and reduction in expected future oil price increases, and in which buying oil on Wall Street was much cheaper than obtaining it by drilling holes in the ground. Oil industry managers also invested some of their large amount of cash into noncore industries. Relatedly, economists have long conducted event studies to analyze the reaction of stock prices to the announcement

4. Using antitakeover laws passed in a number of states in the United States in the 1980s and firm-level data, Bertrand and Mullainathan find evidence that the enactment of such a law raises wages by 1–2%.

of acquisitions and have often unveiled substantial shareholder concerns with such moves (see Shleifer and Vishny 1997; see also Andrade et al. (2001) for a more recent assessment of the long-term acquisition performance of the acquirer–target pair). And Blanchard et al. (1994) show how firms that earn windfall cash awards in court do not return the cash to investors and spend it inefficiently.

(c) *Entrenchment strategies.* Top executives often take actions that hurt shareholders in order to keep or secure their position. There are many entrenchment strategies. First, managers sometimes invest in lines of activities that make them indispensable (Shleifer and Vishny 1989); for example, they invest in a declining industry or old-fashioned technology that they are good at running. Second, they manipulate performance measures so as to "look good" when their position might be threatened. For example, they may use "creative" accounting techniques to mask their company's deteriorating condition. Relatedly, they may engage in excessive or insufficient risk taking. They may be excessively conservative when their performance is satisfactory, as they do not want to run the risk of their performance falling below the level that would trigger a board reaction, a takeover, or a proxy fight. Conversely, it is a common attitude of managers "in trouble," that is, managers whose current performance is unsatisfactory and are desperate to offer good news to the firm's owners, to take excessive risk and thus "gamble for resurrection." Third, managers routinely resist hostile takeovers, as these threaten their long-term positions. In some cases, they succeed in defeating tender offers that would have been very attractive to shareholders, or they go out of their way to find a "white knight" or conclude a sweet nonaggression pact with the raider. Managers also lobby for a legal environment that limits shareholder activism and, in Europe as well as in some Asian countries such as Japan, design complex cross-ownership and holding structures with double voting rights for a few privileged shares that make it hard for outsiders to gain control.

(d) *Self-dealing.* Lastly, managers may increase their private benefits from running the firm by engaging in a wide variety of self-dealing behaviors, ranging from benign to outright illegal activities. Managers may consume perks[5] (costly private jets,[6] plush offices, private boxes at sports events, country club memberships, celebrities on payroll, hunting and fishing lodges, extravagant entertainment expenses, expensive art); pick their successor among their friends or at least like-minded individuals who will not criticize or cast a shadow on their past management; select a costly supplier on friendship or kinship grounds; or finance political parties of their liking. Self-dealing can also reach illegality as in the case of thievery (Robert Maxwell stealing from the employees' pension fund, managers engaging in transactions such as below-market-price asset sales with affiliated firms owned by themselves, their families, or their friends),[7] or of insider trading or information leakages to Wall Street analysts or other investors.

Needless to say, recent corporate scandals have focused more on self-dealing, which is somewhat easier to discover and especially demonstrate than insufficient effort, extravagant investments, or entrenchment strategies.

1.1.2 Dysfunctional Corporate Governance

The overall significance of moral hazard is largely understated by the mere observation of managerial misbehavior, which forms the "tip of the iceberg." The submerged part of the iceberg is the institutional response in terms of corporate governance, finance, and managerial incentive contracts. Yet, it is worth reviewing some of the recent controversies regarding dysfunctional governance; we take the United States as our primary illustration, but the universality of the issues bears emphasizing. Several forms of dysfunctional governance have been pointed out:

Lack of transparency. Investors and other stakeholders are sometimes imperfectly informed about

5. Perks figure prominently among sources of agency costs in Jensen and Meckling's (1976) early contribution.

6. Personal aircraft use is one of the most often described perks in the business literature. A famous example is RJR Nabisco's fleet of 10 aircraft with 36 company pilots, to which the chief executive officer (CEO) Ross Johnson's friends and dog had access (Burrough and Helyar 1990).

7. Another case in point is the Tyco scandal (2002). The CEO and close collaborators are assessed to have stolen over $100 million.

the levels of compensation granted to top management. A case in point is the retirement package of Jack Welch, chief executive officer (CEO) of General Electric.[8] Unbeknownst to outsiders, this retirement package included continued access to private jets, a luxurious apartment in Manhattan, memberships of exclusive clubs, access to restaurants, and so forth.[9]

The limited transparency of managerial stock options (in the United States their cost for the company can legally be assessed at zero) is also a topic of intense controversy.[10] To build investor trust, some companies (starting with, for example, Boeing, Amazon.com, and Coca-Cola) but not all have recently chosen to voluntarily report stock options as expenses.

Perks[11] are also often outside the reach of investor control. Interestingly, Yermack (2004a) finds that a firm's stock price falls by an abnormal 2% when firms first disclose that their CEO has been awarded the aircraft perk.[12] Furthermore, firms that allow personal aircraft use by the CEO underperform the market by about 4%. Another common form of perks comes from recruiting practices; in many European countries, CEOs hire family and friends for important positions; this practice is also common in the United States.[13]

Level. The total compensation packages (salary plus bonus plus long-term compensation) of top executives has risen substantially over the years and reached levels that are hardly fathomable to the public.[14] The trend toward higher managerial compensation in Europe, which started with lower levels of compensation, has been even more dramatic.

Evidence for this "runaway compensation" is provided by Hall and Liebman (1998), who report a tripling (in real terms) of average CEO compensation between 1980 and 1994 for large U.S. corporations,[15] and by Hall and Murphy (2002), who point at a further doubling between 1994 and 2001. In 2000, the annual income of the average CEO of a large U.S. firm was 531 times the average wage of workers in the company (as opposed to 42 times in 1982).[16]

The proponents of high levels of compensation point out that some of this increase comes in the form of performance-related pay: top managers receive more and more bonuses and especially stock options,[17] which, with some caveats that we discuss later, have incentive benefits.

Tenuous link between performance and compensation. High levels of compensation are particularly distressing when they are not related to performance, that is, when top managers receive large amounts of money for a lackluster or even disastrous outcome (Bebchuk and Fried 2003, 2004). While executive compensation will be studied in more detail in Section 1.2, let us here list the reasons why the link between performance and compensation may be tenuous.

First, the compensation package may be poorly structured. For example, the performance of an oil company is substantially affected by the world price of oil, a variable over which it has little control. Suppose that managerial bonuses and stock options are not indexed to the price of oil. Then the managers can make enormous amounts of money when the price of oil increases. By contrast, they lose little from the lack of indexation when the price of oil

8. Jack Welch was CEO of General Electric from 1981 to 2001. The package was discovered only during divorce proceedings in 2002.

9. Similarly, Bernie Ebbers, WorldCom's CEO borrowed over $1 billion from banks such as Citigroup and Bank of America against his shares of WorldCom (which went bankrupt in 2001) and used it to buy a ranch in British Columbia, 460,000 acres of U.S. forest, two luxury yachts, and so forth.

10. In the United States grants of stock options are disclosed in footnotes to the financial statements. By the mid 1990s, the U.S. Congress had already prevented the Financial Accounting Standards Board from forcing firms to expense managerial stock options.

11. Such as Steve Jobs's purchase of a $90 million private jet.

12. As Yermack stresses, this may be due to learning either that corporate governance is weak or that management has undesirable characteristics (lack of integrity, taste for not working hard, etc.). See Rajan and Wulf (2005) for a somewhat different view of perks as enhancing managerial productivity.

13. Retail store Dillard's CEO succeeded in getting four of his children onto the board of directors; Gap's CEO hired his brother to redesign shops and his wife as consultant. Contrast this with Apria Healthcare: in 2002, less than 24 hours after learning that the CEO had hired his wife, the board of directors fired both.

14. For example, in 1997, twenty U.S. CEOs had yearly compensation packages over $25 million. The CEO of Traveler's group received $230 million and that of Coca-Cola $111 million. James Crowe, who was not even CEO of WorldCom, received $69 million (*Business Week*, April 20, 1998).

15. Equity-based compensation rose from 20 to 50% of total compensation during that period.

16. *A New Era in Governance*, McKinsey Quarterly, 2004.

17. For example, in 1979, only 8% of British firms gave bonuses to managers; more that three-quarters did in 1994. The share of performance-based rewards for British senior managers jumped from 10 to 40% from 1989 to 1994 (*The Economist*, January 29, 1994, p. 69).

plummets, since their options and bonuses are then "out-of-the money" (such compensation starts when performance—stock price or yearly profit—exceeds some threshold), not to mention the fact that the options may be repriced so as to reincentivize executives. Thus, managers often benefit from poor design in their compensation schemes.

Second, managers often seem to manage to maintain their compensation stable or even have it increased despite poor performance. In 2002, for example, the CEOs of AOL Time Warner, Intel, and Safeway made a lot of money despite a bad year. Similarly, Qwest's board of directors awarded $88 million to its CEO despite an abysmal performance in 2001.

Third, managers may succeed in "getting out on time" (either unbeknownst to the board, which did not see, or did not want to see, the accounting manipulations or the impending bad news, or with the cooperation of the board). Global Crossing's managers sold shares for $735 million. Tenet Health Care's CEO in January 2002 announced sensational earnings prospects and sold shares for an amount of $111 million; a year later, the share price had fallen by 60%. Similarly, Oracle's CEO (Larry Ellison) made $706 million by selling his stock options in January 2001 just before announcing a fall in income forecasts. Unsurprisingly, many reform proposals have argued in favor of a higher degree of vesting of managerial shares, forcing top management to keep shares for a long time (perhaps until well after the end of their employment),[18] and of an independent compensation committee at the board of directors.

Finally, managers receive large golden parachutes[19] for leaving the firm. These golden parachutes are often granted in the wake of poor performance (a major cause of CEO firing!). These high golden parachutes have been common for a long time in the United States, and have recently made their way to Europe (witness the $89 million golden parachute granted to ABB's CEO).

The Sarbanes–Oxley Act (2002) in the United States, a regulatory reaction to the previously mentioned abuses, requires the CEO and chief financial officer (CFO) to reimburse any profit from bonuses or stock sales during the year following a financial report that is subsequently restated because of "misconduct." This piece of legislation also makes the shares held by executives less liquid by bringing down the lag in the report of sales of executive shares from ten days to two days.[20]

Accounting manipulations. We have already alluded to the manipulations that inflate company performance. Some of those manipulations are actually legal while others are not. Also, they may require cooperation from investors, trading partners, analysts, or accountants. Among the many facets of the Enron scandal[21] lie off-balance-sheet deals. For example, Citigroup and JPMorgan lent Enron billions of dollars disguised as energy trades. The accounting firm Arthur Andersen let this happen. Similarly, profits of WorldCom (which, like Enron, went bankrupt) were assessed to have been overestimated by $7.1 billion starting in 2000.[22]

Accounting manipulations serve multiple purposes. First, they increase the apparent earnings and/or stock price, and thereby the value of managerial compensation. Managers with options packages may therefore find it attractive to inflate earnings. Going beyond scandals such as those of Enron, Tyco, Xerox,[23] and WorldCom in the United States and Parmalat in Europe, Bergstresser and Philippon (2005) find more generally that highly incentivized CEOs exercise a large number of stock options during years

18. The timing of exercise of executives' stock options is documented in, for example, Bettis et al. (2003). They find median values for the exercise date at about two years after vesting and five years prior to expiration.

19. Golden parachutes refer to benefits received by an executive in the event that the company is acquired and the executive's employment is terminated. Golden parachutes are in principle specified in the employment contract.

20. See Holmström and Kaplan (2003) for more details and an analysis of the Sarbanes–Oxley Act, as well as of the NYSE, NASDAQ, and Conference Board corporate governance proposals.

21. For an account of the Enron saga and, in particular, of the many off-balance-sheet transactions, see, for example, Fox (2003). See also the special issue of the *Journal of Economic Perspectives* devoted to the Enron scandal (Volume 12, Spring 2003).

22. Interestingly, one WorldCom director chaired Moody's investment services, and it took a long time for the rating agency to downgrade WorldCom.

23. A restatement by the Securities and Exchange Commission reduced Xerox's reported net income by $1.4 billion over the period 1997–2001. Over that period, the company's CEO exercised options worth over $20 million.

in which discretionary accruals form a large fraction of reported earnings, and that their companies engage in higher levels of earnings management.

Second, by hiding poor performance, they protect managers against dismissals or takeovers or, more generally, reduce investor interference in the managerial process. Third, accounting manipulations enable firms not to violate bank covenants, which are often couched in terms of accounting performance.[24] Lastly, they enable continued financing.[25]

When pointing to these misbehaviors, economists do not necessarily suggest that managers' actual behavior exhibits widespread incompetency and moral hazard. Rather, they stress both the potential extent of the problem and the endogeneity of managerial accountability. They argue that corporate governance failures are as old as the corporation, and that control mechanisms, however imperfect, have long been in place, implying that actual misbehaviors are the tip of an iceberg whose main element represents the averted ones.

1.2 Managerial Incentives: An Overview

1.2.1 A Sophisticated Mix of Incentives

However large the scope for misbehavior, explicit and implicit incentives, in practice, partly align managerial incentives with the firm's interest. Bonuses and stock options make managers sensitive to losses in profit and in shareholder value. Besides these explicit incentives, less formal, but quite powerful implicit incentives stem from the managers' concern about their future. The threat of being fired by the board of directors or removed by the market for corporate control through a takeover or a proxy fight, the possibility of being replaced by a receiver (in the United Kingdom, say) or of being put on a tight leash (as is the case of a Chapter 11 bankruptcy in the United States) during financial distress, and the prospect of being appointed to new boards of directors or of receiving offers for executive directorships in more prestigious companies, all contribute to keeping managers on their toes.

Capital market monitoring and product-market competition further keep a tight rein on managerial behavior. Monitoring by a large institutional investor (pension fund, mutual fund, bank, etc.), by a venture capitalist, or by a large private owner restricts managerial control, and is generally deemed to alleviate the agency problem. And, as we will discuss, product-market competition often aligns explicit and implicit managerial incentives with those of the firm, although it may create perverse incentives in specific situations.

Psychologists, consultants, and personnel officers no doubt would find the economists' description of managerial incentives too narrow. When discussing incentives in general, they also point to the role of intrinsic motivation, fairness, horizontal equity, morale, trust, corporate culture, social responsibility and altruism, feelings of self-esteem (coming from recognition or from fellow employees' gratitude), interest in the job, and so on. Here, we will not enter the debate as to whether the economists' view of incentives is inappropriately restrictive.[26] Some of these apparently noneconomic incentives are, at a deeper level, already incorporated in the economic paradigm.[27] As for the view that economists do not account for the possibility of benevolence, it should be clear that economists are concerned with the study of the residual incentives to act in the firm's interests over and beyond what they would contribute in the absence of rewards and monitoring. While we would all prefer not to need this sophisticated set of

24. See Section 2.3.3 for a discussion of covenants.

25. For example, WorldCom, just before bankruptcy, was the second-largest U.S. telecommunications company, with 70 acquisitions under its belt.

26. For references to the psychology literature and for views on how such considerations affect incentives, see, for example, Bénabou and Tirole (2003, 2004, 2005), Camerer and Malmendier (2004), Fehr and Schmidt (2003), and Frey (1997).

27. For example, explicit or implicit rules mandating "fairness" and "horizontal equity" can be seen as a response to the threat of favoritism, that is, of collusion between a superior and a subordinate (as in Laffont 1990). The impact of morale can be partly apprehended through the effects of incentives on the firm's or its management's reputation (see, for example, Tirole 1996). And the role of trust has in the past twenty years been one of the leitmotivs of economic theory since the pioneering work of Kreps et al. (1982) (see, for example, Kreps 1990). Economists have also devoted some attention to corporate culture phenomena (see Carrillo and Gromb 1999; Crémer 1993; Kreps 1990). Economists may not yet have a fully satisfactory description of fairness, horizontal equity, morale, trust, or corporate culture, but an *a priori* critique of the economic paradigm of employee incentives as being too narrow is unwarranted, and more attention should be devoted to exactly what can and cannot be explained by the standard economic paradigm.

explicit and implicit incentives, history has taught us that even the existing control mechanisms do not suffice to prevent misbehavior.

1.2.2 Monetary Incentives

Let us first return to the managerial compensation problem and exposit it in more detail than was done in the introduction to the chapter.

The compensation package.[28] A typical top executive receives compensation in three ways: salary, bonus, and stock-based incentives (stock, stock options). The salary is a fixed amount (although revised over time partly on the basis of past performance). The risky bonus and stock-based compensations are the two incentive components of the package.[29] They are meant to induce managers to internalize the owners' interests. Stock-based incentives, the bulk of the incentive component, have long been used to incentivize U.S. managers. The compensation of executives in Germany or in Japan has traditionally been less tied to stock prices (which does not mean that the latter are irrelevant for the provision of managerial incentives, as we later observe). Everywhere, though, there has been a dramatic increase in equity-based pay, especially stock options. For example, in the United States, the *sensitivity* of top executives pay to shareholder returns has increased tenfold between the early 1980s and late 1990s (see, for example, Hall and Liebman 1998; Hall 2000).

Needless to say, these compensation packages create an incentive to pursue profit-maximization only if the managers are not able to undo their incentives by selling the corresponding stakes to a third party. Indeed, third parties would in general love to offer, at a premium, insurance to the managers at the expense of the owners, who can no longer count on the incentives provided by the compensation package they designed. As a matter of fact, compensation package agreements make it difficult for managers to undo their position in the firm through open or secret trading. Open sales are limited for example by minimum-holding requirements while secret trading is considered insider trading.[30] There are, however, some loopholes that allow managers to undo some of their exposure to the firm's profitability through less strictly regulated financial instruments, such as equity swaps and collars.[31]

28. See, for example, Smith and Watts (1982) and Baker et al. (1988) for more detailed discussions of compensation packages.

29. More precisely, *earnings-related compensation* includes bonus and performance plans. Bonus plans yield short-term rewards tied to the firm's yearly performance. Rewards associated with performance plans (which are less frequent and less substantial than bonus plans) are contingent on earnings targets over three to five years. Many managerial contracts specify that part or all of the bonus payments can be transformed into stock options (or sometimes into phantom shares), either at the executive's discretion or by the compensation committee. (Phantom shares are units of value that correspond to an equivalent number of shares of stock. Phantom stock plans credit the executive with shares and pay her the cash value of these shares at the end of a prespecified time period.) This operation amounts to transforming a safe income (the earned bonus) into a risky one tied to future performance. *Stock-related compensation* includes stock options or stock appreciation rights, and restricted or phantom stock plans. Stock options and stock appreciation rights are more popular than restricted or phantom stock plans, which put restrictions on sale: in 1980, only 14 of the largest 100 U.S. corporations had a restricted stock plan as opposed to 83 for option plans. Few had phantom stock plans, and in about half the cases these plans were part of a bonus plan, and were therefore conditional on the executive's voluntarily deferring his bonus. Stock appreciation rights are similar to stock options and are meant to reduce the transaction costs associated with exercising options and selling shares.

30. Securities and Exchange Commission (SEC) rules in the United States constrain insider trading and short selling.

31. An interesting article by Bettis et al. (1999) documents the extent of these side deals.

Equity swaps and collars (among other similar instruments) are private contracts between a corporate insider (officer or director) and a counterparty (usually a bank). In an equity swap, the insider exchanges the future returns on her stock for the cash attached to another financial instrument, such as the stock market index. A collar involves the simultaneous purchase of a put option and sale of a call option on the firm's shares. The put provides the insider with insurance against firm's stock price decreases, and the call option reduces the insider's revenue from a price increase.

In the United States, the SEC, in two rulings in 1994 and 1996, mandated reporting of swaps and collars. Bettis et al. argue that the reporting requirements have remained ambiguous and that they have not much constrained their use by insiders (despite the general rules on insider trading that prohibit insiders from shorting their firm's stock or from trading without disclosing their private information).

Swaps and collars raise two issues. First, they may enable insiders to benefit from private information. Indeed, Bettis et al. show that insiders strategically time the purchase of these instruments. Swap and collar transactions occur after firms substantially outperform their benchmarks (by a margin of 40% in 250 trading days), and are followed by no abnormal returns in the 120 trading days after the transaction. Second, they provide insurance to the insiders and undo some of their exposure to the firm's profitability and thereby undo some of their incentives that stocks and stock options were supported to create. Bettis et al. estimate that 30% of shares held by top executives and board members in their sample are covered by equity swaps and collars.

While there is a widespread consensus in favor of some linkage between pay and performance, it is also widely recognized that performance measurement is quite imperfect. Bonus plans are based on accounting data, which creates the incentive to manipulate such data, making performance measurement systematically biased. As we discuss in Chapter 7, profits can be shifted backward and forward in time with relative ease. Equity-based compensation is less affected by this problem provided that the manager cannot sell rapidly, since stock prices in principle reflect the present discounted value of future profits. But stock prices are subject to exogenous factors creating volatility.

Nevertheless, compensation committees must use existing performance measures, however imperfect, when designing compensation packages for the firm's executives.

Bonuses and shareholdings: substitutes or complements? As we saw, it is customary to distinguish between two types of monetary compensation: bonuses are defined by current profit, that is, accounting data, while stocks and stock options are based on the value of shares, that is, on market data.

The articulation between these two types of rewards matters. One could easily believe that, because they are both incentive schemes, bonuses and stock options are substitutes. An increase in a manager's bonus could then be compensated by a reduction in managerial shareholdings. This, however, misses the point that bonuses and stock options serve two different and complementary purposes.[32]

A bonus-based compensation package creates a strong incentive for a manager to privilege the short term over the long term. A manager trades off short- and long-term profits when confronting subcontracting, marketing, maintenance, and investment decisions. An increase in her bonus increases her preference for current profit and can create an imbalance in incentives. This imbalance would be aggravated by a reduction in stock-based incentives, which are meant to encourage management to take a long-term perspective. Bonuses and stock options therefore tend to be complements. An increase in short-term incentives must go hand in hand with an increase in long-term incentives, in order to keep a proper balance between short- and long-term objectives.

The compensation base. It is well-known that managerial compensation should not be based on factors that are outside the control of the manager.[33] One implication of this idea is that managerial compensation should be immunized against shocks such as fluctuations in exchange rate, interest rate, or price of raw materials that the manager has no control over. This can be achieved, for example, by indexing managerial compensation to the relevant variables; in practice, though, this is often achieved more indirectly and only partially through corporate risk management, a practice that tends to insulate the firm from some types of aggregate risks through insurance-like contracts such as exchange rate or interest rate swaps (see Chapter 5 for some other benefits of risk management).

Another implication of the point that managerial compensation should be unaffected by the realization of exogenous shocks is relative performance evaluation (also called "yardstick competition"). The idea is that one can use the performance of firms facing similar shocks, e.g., firms in the same industry facing the same cost and demand shocks, in order to obtain information about the uncontrollable shocks faced by the managers. For example, the compensation of the CEO of General Motors can be made dependent on the performance of Ford and Chrysler, with a better performance of the competitors being associated with a lower compensation for the executive. Managers are then rewarded as a function of their *relative* performance in their peer group rather than on the basis of their absolute performance (see Holmström 1982a).[34] There is some controversy about the extent of *implicit*

32. This discussion is drawn from Holmström and Tirole (1993).

33. The formal version of this point is Holmström's (1979) sufficient statistic result according to which optimal compensation packages are contingent on a sufficient statistic about the manager's unobserved actions. See Section 3.2.5 for more details.

34. A cost of relative-performance-evaluation schemes is that they can generate distorted incentives, such as the tendency to herding; for example, herding has been observed for bank managers (perhaps more due to implicit rather than explicit incentives), as it is sometimes better to be wrong with the rest of the pack than to be right alone.

As Keynes (1936, Chapter 12) said, "Worldly wisdom teaches that it is better for reputation to fail conventionally than to succeed unconventionally."

relative performance evaluation (see, for example, Baker et al. 1988; Gibbons and Murphy 1990), but it is fairly clear that relative performance evaluation is not widely used in *explicit* incentive schemes (in particular, managerial stock ownership).

Bertrand and Mullainathan (2001) provide evidence that there is often too little filtering in CEO compensation packages, and that CEOs are consequently rewarded for "luck." For example, in the oil industry, pay changes and changes in the price of crude oil correlate quite well, even though the world oil price is largely beyond the control of any given firm; interestingly, CEOs are not always punished for bad luck, that is, there is an asymmetry in the exposure to shocks beyond the CEO's control. Bertrand and Mullainathan also demonstrate a similar pattern for the sensitivity of CEO compensation to industry-specific exchange rates for firms in the traded goods sector and to mean industry performance. They conclude that, roughly, "CEO pay is as sensitive to a lucky dollar as to a general dollar," suggesting that compensation contracts are poorly designed.

As Bertrand and Mullainathan note, it might be that, even though oil prices, exchange rates, and industry conditions are beyond the control of managers, investors would like them to forecast these properly so as to better tailor production and investment to their anticipated evolution, in which case it might be efficient to create an exposure of CEO compensation to "luck." Bertrand and Mullainathan, however, show that better-governed firms pay their CEOs less for luck; for example, an additional large shareholder on the board reduces CEO pay for luck by between 23 and 33%.

This evidence suggests that the boards in general and the compensation committees in particular often comprise too many friends of the CEOs (see also Bertrand and Mullainathan 2000), who then de facto get to set their executive pay. We now turn to why they often gain when exposed to "luck": their compensation package tends to be convex, with large exposure in the upper tail and little in the lower tail.

Straight shares or stock options? Another aspect of the design of incentive compensation is the (non)linearity of the reward as a function of performance. Managers may be offered stock options, i.e., the right to purchase at specified dates stocks at some "exercise price" or "strike price."[35] These are call options. The options are valueless if the realized market price ends up being below the exercise price, and are worth the difference between the market price and the exercise price otherwise. In contrast, managerial holdings of straight shares let the manager internalize shareholder value over the whole range of market prices, and not only in the upper range above the exercise price.

Should managers be rewarded through straight shares or through stock options?[36] Given that managers rarely have a personal wealth to start with and are protected by limited liability or, due to risk aversion,[37] insist on a base income, stock options seem a more appropriate instrument. Straight shares provide management with a rent even when their performance is poor, while stock options do not. In Figure 1.1(a), the managerial reward when the exercise or strike price is P^S and the stock price is P at the exercise date is $\max(0, P - P^S)$ for the option; it would be P for a straight share. Put another way, for a given expected cost of the managerial incentive package for the owners, the latter can provide managers with stronger incentives by using stock options. This feature explains the popularity of stock options.

Stock options, on the other hand, have some drawbacks. Suppose that a manager is given stock options to be (possibly) exercised after two years on the job; and that this manager learns after one year that the firm faces an adverse shock (on which the exercise price of the options is not indexed), so that "under normal management" it becomes unlikely that the market price will exceed the strike price at the exercise date. The manager's option is then "under water" or "out of the money" and has little value unless the firm performs remarkably well during the remaining year. This may encourage management to take substantial risks in order to increase the

35. In the United States, stock option plans, when granted, are most often at-the-money options.

36. As elsewhere in this book, we ignore tax considerations. Needless to say, these may play a role. For example, in the United States (and at the time of writing, accounting rules are likely to change in the near future), stock options grants, unlike stock grants, create no accounting expense for the firm.

37. There is a large literature on hedging by risk-averse agents (see, for example, Anderson and Danthine 1980, 1981).

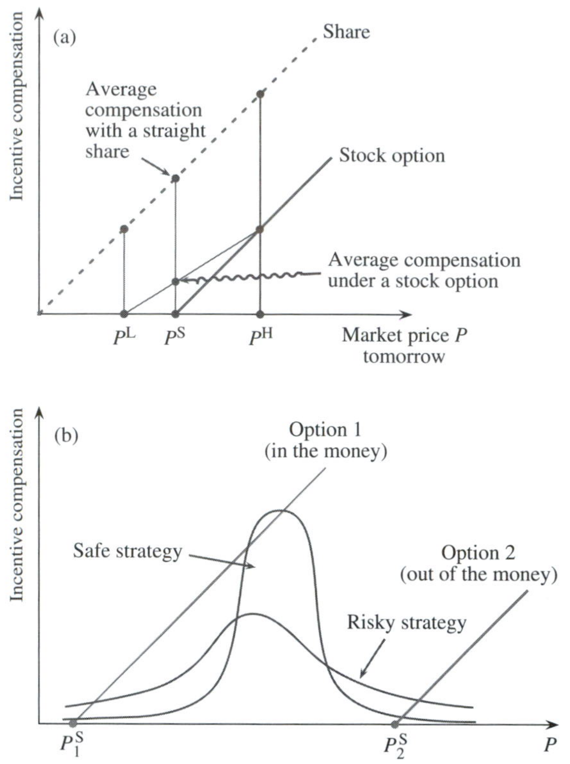

Figure 1.1 Straight shares and stock options. (a) Expected rents (P^L: low price (option "out of the money"); P^S: strike price; P^H: high price (option "in the money")). (b) Risk preferences under a stock option.

value of her stock options. (In Chapter 7, we observe that such "gambling for resurrection" is also likely to occur under implicit/career-concern incentives, namely, when a poorly performing manager is afraid of losing her job.) This situation is represented in Figure 1.1(b) by stock option 2 with high strike price P_2^S. That figure depicts two possible distributions (densities) for the realized price P depending on whether a safe or a risky strategy is selected. The value of this out-of-the money option is then much higher under a risky strategy than under a safe one.[38] The manager's benefit from gambling is much lower when the option is in the money (say, at strike price P_1^S in the figure).[39]

Another issue with "underwater options" relates to their credibility. Once the options are out of the money, they either induce top management to leave or create low or perverse incentives, as we just saw. They may be repriced (the exercise price is adjusted downward) or new options may be granted.[40] To some extent, such *ex post* adjustments undermine *ex ante* incentives by refraining from punishing management for poor performance.[41]

In contrast, when the option is largely "in the money," that is, when it looks quite likely that the market price will exceed the exercise price, a stock option has a similar incentive impact as a straight share but provides management with a lower rent, namely, the difference between market and exercise price rather than the full market price.

The question of the efficient mix of options and stocks is still unsettled. Unsurprisingly, while stock options remain very popular, some companies, such as DaimlerChrysler, Deutsche Telekom, and Microsoft, have abandoned them, usually to replace them by stocks (as in the case of Microsoft).

The executive compensation controversy. There has been a trend in executive compensation towards higher compensation as well as stronger performance linkages. This trend has resulted in a public outcry. Yet some have argued that the performance linkage is insufficient. In a paper whose inferences created controversy, Jensen and Murphy (1990) found a low sensitivity of CEO compensation to firm performance (see also Murphy 1985, 1999). Looking at a sample of the CEOs of the 250

38. Whether the manager is better off under the risky strategy depends on her risk aversion. However, if (a) the manager is risk neutral or mildly risk averse and (b) the risky strategy is a mean-preserving spread or more generally increases risk without reducing the mean too much relative to the safe strategy, then the manager will prefer the risky strategy.

39. In the figure, option 1 is almost a straight stock in that it is very unlikely that the option turns out to be valueless.

40. Consider, for example, Ascend Communications (*New York Times*, July 15, 1998, D1). In 1998, its stock price fell from $80 to $23 within four months. The managerial stock options had strike prices ranging up to $114 per share. The strike price was reduced twice during that period for different kinds of options (to $35 a share and to $24.50, respectively).

41. At least, if the initial options were structured properly. If repricing only reflects general market trends (after all, more than half of the stock options were out of the money in 2002), repricing may be less objectionable (although the initial package is still objectionable, to the extent that it would have rewarded management for luck).

For theories of renegotiation of managerial compensation and its impact on moral hazard, see Fudenberg and Tirole (1990) and Hermalin and Katz (1991). See also Chapter 5.

largest publicly traded American firms, they found that (a) the median public corporation CEO holds 0.25% of his/her firm's equity and (b) a $1,000 increase in shareholder wealth corresponds on average to a $3.25 increase in total CEO compensation (stock and stock options, increase in this and next year's salary, change in expected dismissal penalties). This sounds tiny. Suppose that your grocer kept 0.3 cents out of any extra $1 in net profit, and gave 99.7 cents to other people. One might imagine that the grocer would start eating the apples on the fruit stand. Jensen and Murphy argue that CEO incentives not to waste shareholder value are too small.

Jensen and Murphy's conclusion sparked some controversy, though. First, managerial risk aversion and the concomitant diminishing marginal utility of income implies that strong management incentives are costly to the firm's owners. Indeed, Haubrich (1994) shows that the low pay-performance sensitivity pointed out by Jensen and Murphy is consistent with relatively low levels of managerial risk aversion, such as an index of relative risk aversion of about 5. Intuitively, changes in the value of large companies can have a very large impact on CEO performance-based compensation even for low sensitivity levels. Second, the CEO is only one of many employees in the firm. And so, despite the key executive responsibilities of the CEO, other parties have an important impact on firm performance. Put another way, overall performance results from the combined effort and talent of the CEO, other top executives, engineers, marketers, and blue-collar workers, not to mention the board of directors, suppliers, distributors, and other "external" parties. In the economic jargon, the joint performance creates a "moral hazard in teams," in which many parties concur to a common final outcome. Ignoring risk aversion, the only way to properly incentivize all these parties is to promise each $1,000 any time the firm's value increases by $1,000. This is unrealistic, if anything because the payoff must be shared with the financiers.[42] Third, the work of Hall and Liebman (1998) cited earlier, using a more recent dataset (1980 to 1994), points to a substantial increase in performance-based compensation, which made Jensen and Murphy's estimates somewhat obsolete. They find that the mean (median) change in CEO wealth is $25 ($5.30) per $1,000 increase in firm value.

1.2.3 Implicit Incentives

Managers are naturally concerned about keeping their job. Poor performance may induce the board to remove the CEO and the group of top executives. The board either voluntarily fires the manager, or, often, does so under the implicit or explicit pressure of shareholders observing a low stock price or a low profit. Poor performance may also generate a takeover or a proxy fight, or else may drive a fragile firm into bankruptcy and reorganization. Finally, there is evidence that the fraction of independent directors rises after poor performance, so that top management is on a tighter leash if it keeps its position (Hermalin and Weisbach 1988). As we will see, there is substantial normative appeal for these observations: efficient contracting indeed usually requires that poor performance makes it less likely that managers keep their position (Chapters 6, 7, and 11), more likely that they be starved of liquidity (Chapter 5), and more likely that they surrender control rights or that control rights be reshuffled among investors towards ones who are less congruent with management, i.e., debtholders (Chapter 10).

There is a fair amount of evidence that executive turnover in the United States is correlated with poor performance, using either stock or accounting data (see Kojima (1997, p. 63) and Subramanian et al. (2002) for a list of relevant articles). The sensitivity of CEO removal to performance is higher for firms with more outside directors (Weisbach 1988) and smaller in firms run by founders (Morck et al. 1989). Thus, a tight external monitoring and a less complacent board are conducive to managerial turnover after a poor performance.

42. Suppose a "source" (i.e., an outside financier) brings $(n-1)$ thousand dollars to the firm for any $1,000 increase in firm value, so that the n parties responsible for the firm's overall performance receive $1,000 each. First, this financing source would be likely not to be able to break even, since the n insiders would be unable to pay out money in the case of poor performance. Second, the n insiders could collude against the source (e.g., borrow one dollar to receive n dollars from the source).

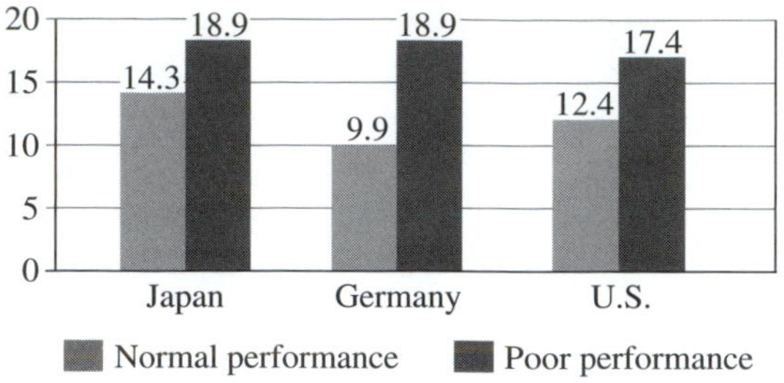

Figure 1.2 Top executive turnover and stock returns. *Source:* built from data in Kaplan (1994a,b).

Perhaps more surprisingly in view of the substantial institutional differences, the relationship between poor performance and top executive turnover is similar in the United States, Germany, and Japan: see Figure 1.2, drawn from the work of Kaplan. More recent research (see, for example, Goyal and Park 2002) has confirmed the dual pattern of an increase in forced executive turnover in the wake of poor performance and of an increased sensitivity of this relationship when there are few insiders on the board.

The threat of bankruptcy also keeps managers on their toes. Even in the United States, a country with limited creditor protection and advantageous treatment of managers during restructurings,[43] 52% of financially distressed firms experience a senior management turnover as opposed to 19% for firms with comparably poor stock performance but not in financial distress (Gilson 1989).

Are explicit and implicit incentives complements or substitutes? The threat of dismissal or other interferences resulting from poor performance provides incentives for managers over and beyond those provided by explicit incentives. Explicit and implicit incentives are therefore substitutes: with stronger implicit incentives, fewer stocks and stock options are needed to curb managerial moral hazard. While this substitution effect is real,[44] the strengths of implicit and explicit incentives are codetermined by sources of heterogeneity in the sample and so other factors (analyzed in Chapters 4 and 6 of this book), impact the observed relationship between implicit and explicit incentives (the survey by Chiappori and Salanié (2003) provides an extensive discussion of the need to take account of unobserved heterogeneity in the econometrics of contracts).

First, consider the heterogeneity in the intensity of financial constraints. A recurrent theme of this book will be that the tighter the financing constraint, the more concessions the borrower must make in order to raise funds. And concessions tend to apply across the board. Concessions of interest here are reductions in performance-based pay and in the ability to retain one's job after poor performance, two contracting attributes valued by the executive. Thus, a tightly financially constrained manager will accept both a lower level of performance-based rewards and a smaller probability of keeping her job after a poor performance (see Section 4.3.5), where the probability of turnover is determined by the composition of the board, the presence of takeover defenses, the specification of termination rights (in the case of venture capital or alliance financing) and other contractual arrangements. The heterogeneity in the intensity of financial constraints then predicts a positive comovement of turnover under poor performance and low-powered incentives. Implicit and explicit incentives then appear to be complements in the sample.

Second, consider adverse selection, that is, the existence of an asymmetry of information between the firm and its investors. Investors are uncertain about the likely performance of the executive. An executive who is confident about the firm's future prospects knows that she is relatively unlikely to achieve a poor performance, and so accepting a high turnover in the case of poor performance is less costly than it would be if she were less confident in her talent or had unfavorable information about the firm's prospects. Thus, the confident executive is willing to trade

43. Under U.S. law's Chapter 11, which puts a hold on creditor claims, the firm is run as a going concern and no receiver is designated.

44. Gibbons and Murphy (1992) analyze the impact of implicit incentives on optimal explicit incentive contracts in a different context. They posit career concerns *à la* Holmström (1982b): successful employees receive with a lag external offers, forcing their firm to raise their wage to keep them. Their model has a fixed horizon (and so does not apply as it stands to the executive turnover issue); it shows that implicit and explicit incentives are indeed substitutes: as the employee gets closer to retirement, career concerns decrease and the employer must raise the power of the explicit incentive scheme. Gibbons and Murphy further provide empirical support for this theoretical prediction.

off a high performance-based reward against an increased turnover probability in the case of poor performance (see Chapter 6). By contrast, less confident managers put more weight on their tenure and less on monetary compensation. The prediction is then one of a negative covariation between turnover in the case of poor performance[45] and low-powered incentives. Put differently, implicit and explicit incentives come out as being substitutes in the sample.[46]

Interestingly, Subramanian et al. (2002) find that, in their sample, CEOs with greater explicit incentives also face less secure jobs.

1.2.4 Monitoring

Monitoring of corporations is performed by a variety of external (nonexecutive) parties such as boards of directors, auditors, large shareholders, large creditors, investment banks, and rating agencies. To understand the actual design of monitoring structures, it is useful to distinguish between two forms of monitoring, active and speculative, on the basis of two types of monitoring information, prospective and retrospective.

Active monitoring consists in interfering with management in order to increase the value of the investors' claims. An active monitor collects information that some policy proposed or followed by management (e.g., the refusal to sell the firm to a high bidder or to divest some noncore assets) is value-decreasing and intervenes to prevent or correct this policy. In extreme cases, the intervention may be the removal of current management and its replacement by a new management more able to handle the firm's future environment. Active monitoring is *forward looking* and analyzes the firm's past actions only to the extent that they can still be altered to raise firm value or that they convey information (say, about the ability of current management) on which one can act to improve the firm's prospects.

45. Note that this is indeed a *conditional* probability: confident managers are less likely to reach a poor performance.

46. The theoretical model in Subramanian et al. (2002) emphasizes a third consideration by making learning from performance about talent sensitive to managerial effort. Then a high-powered incentive scheme, by increasing effort, also increases the informativeness of performance. This increased informativeness, if turnover is otherwise unlikely due to switching costs, in turn may raise turnover. Put differently, the manager is more likely to be found untalented if she exerts a high effort and fails.

The mechanism by which the change is implemented depends on the identity of the active monitor. A large shareholder may sit on the board and intervene in that capacity. An institutional investor in the United States or a bank holding a sizeable number of the firm's shares as custodian in Germany may intervene in the general assembly by introducing resolutions on particular corporate policy issues; or perhaps they may be able to convince management to alter its policy under the threat of intervention at the general meeting. A raider launches a takeover and thereby attempts to gain control over the firm. Lastly, creditors in a situation of financial distress or a receiver in bankruptcy force concessions on management.

While active monitoring is intimately linked to the exercise of control rights, *speculative monitoring* is not. Furthermore, speculative monitoring is partly *backward looking* in that it does not attempt to increase firm value, but rather to measure this value, which reflects not only exogenous prospects but also past managerial investments. The object of speculative monitoring is thus to "take a picture" of the firm's position at a given moment in time, that is, to take stock of the previous and current management's accomplishments to date. This information is used by the speculative monitor in order to adjust his position in the firm (invest further, stay put, or disengage), or else to recommend or discourage investment in the firm to investors. The typical speculative monitor is the stock market analyst, say, working for a passive institutional investor, who studies firms in order to maximize portfolio return without any intent to intervene in the firms' management.

But, as the examples above suggest, it would be incorrect to believe that speculative monitoring occurs only in stock markets. A short-term creditor's strategy is to disengage from the firm, namely, to refuse to roll over the debt, whenever he receives bad news about the firm's capacity to reimburse its debt. Or, to take other examples, an investment bank that recommends purchasing shares in a company or a rating agency that grades a firm's public debt both look at the firm's expected value and do not attempt to interfere in the firm's management in order to raise this value. They simply take a picture of the firms' resources and prospects in order to formulate their advice.

Another seemingly unusual category of speculative monitoring concerns legal suits by shareholders (or by attorneys on behalf of shareholders) against directors. Like other instances of speculative monitoring, legal suits are based on backward-looking information, namely, the information that the directors have not acted in the interest of the corporation in the past; per se they are not meant to enhance future value, but rather to sanction past underperformance. Two kinds of legal suits are prominent in the United States: class-action suits on behalf of shareholders, and derivative suits on behalf of the corporation (that is, mainly shareholders, but also creditors and other stakeholders to the extent that their claim is performance-sensitive), which receives any ensuing benefits.

While the mechanism of speculative monitoring and its relationship with active monitoring will be explored in detail in Part III of this book, it is worth mentioning here that speculative monitoring does discipline management in several ways. Speculative monitoring in the stock market makes the firm's stock value informative about past performance; this value is used directly to reward management through stock options and, indirectly, to force reluctant boards to admit poor performance and put pressure on or remove management. Speculative monitoring by short-term creditors, investment banks, or rating agencies drains liquidity from (or restricts funding to) poorly performing firms. Either way, speculative monitoring helps keep managers on their toes.

A second and important point is that monitoring is performed by a large number of other "eyeballs": besides stock analysts, rating agencies assess the strength of new issues. Auditors certify the accounts, which in part requires discretionary assessments such as when they evaluate illiquid assets or contingent liabilities. A long-standing issue has resurfaced with the recent scandals. These eyeballs may face substantial *conflicts of interest* that may alter their assessment (indeed, many reform proposals suggest reducing these conflicts of interest). For example, a bank's analysts may overhype a firm's stocks to investors in order to please the firm from which the investment banking branch tries to win business in mergers and acquisitions and in security underwriting.[47]

Accountants may face similar conflicts of interest if they also, directly or indirectly, act as directors, brokers, underwriters, suppliers of management or tax consulting services, and so forth.[48] Unsurprisingly, a number of countries (e.g., United States, United Kingdom, Italy) have moved from self-regulation of the accounting profession to some form of government regulation. In the United States, the Sarbanes–Oxley Act of 2002 created a regulatory body[49] to set rules for, inspect, and impose penalties on public accounting firms.[50]

1.2.5 Product-Market Competition

It is widely agreed that the quality of a firm's management is not solely determined by its design of corporate governance, but also depends on the firm's competitive environment. Product-market competition matters for several reasons. First, as already mentioned, close competitors offer a yardstick against which the firm's quality of management can be measured. It is easier for management to attribute poor performance to bad luck when the firm faces very idiosyncratic circumstances, say, because it is a monopoly in its market, than when competitors presumably facing similar cost and demand conditions are doing well. There is no arguing that

47. For example, Merrill Lynch was imposed a $100 million penalty by the New York Attorney General (2002) when internal emails by analysts described as "junk" stocks they were pushing at the time. Merrill Lynch promised, among other things, to delink analyst compensation and investment banking (*Business Week*, October 7, 2002). In the same year, Citigroup, or rather its affiliate, Salomon Smith Barney, was under investigation for conflicts between stock research and investment banking activities.

48. In 2001, nonaudit fees make up for over 50% of the fees paid to accounting firms by 28 of the 30 companies constituting the Dow Jones Industrial Average. The California Public Employees' Retirement System (CalPERS) announced that it would vote against the reappointment of auditors who also provide consulting services to the firm.

49. The Public Company Accounting Oversight Board, overseen by the SEC.

50. DeMarzo et al. (2005) argue that self-regulation leads to lenient supervision. Pagano and Immordino (2004), building on Dye (1993), explicitly model management advisory services as bribes to auditors and study the optimal regulatory environment under potential collusion between firms and their auditors. They show that good corporate governance reduces the incentive to collude and calls for more demanding auditing standards.

this benchmarking is used, at least implicitly, in the assessment of managerial performance.

Actually, product-market competition improves performance measurement even if the competitors' actual performance is not observed.[51] The very existence of product-market competition tends to filter out or attenuate the exogenous shocks faced by the firm. Suppose the demand in the market is high or the cost of supplies low. The management of a firm in a monopoly position then benefits substantially from the favorable conditions. It can either transform these favorable circumstances into substantial monetary rents if its compensation is very sensitive to profits, or it can enjoy an easy life while still reaching a decent performance, or both. This is not so for a competitive firm. Suppose, for instance, that production costs are low. While they are low for the firm, they are also low for the other firms in the industry, which are then fierce competitors; and so the management is less able to derive rents from the favorable environment.

Another related well-known mechanism through which product-market competition affects managerial incentives is the bankruptcy process. Management is concerned about the prospect of bankruptcy, which often implies the loss of the job and in any case a reduction in managerial prerogatives. To the extent that competition removes the cosy cash cushion enjoyed by a monopolist, competition keeps managers alert.[52]

While competition may have very beneficial effects on managerial incentives, it may also create perverse effects. For example, firms may gamble in order to "beat the market." A case in point is the intensely competitive market for fund management. Fund managers tend to be obsessed with their ranking in the industry, since this ranking determines the inflow of new investments into the funds and, to a lesser extent due to investor inertia, the flow of money out of the fund. This may induce fund managers to adopt strategies that focus on the ranking of the fund relative to competing funds rather than on the absolute return to investors.

It should also be realized that competition will never substitute for a proper governance structure. Investors bring money to a firm in exchange for an expected return whether the firm faces a competitive or protected environment. This future return can be squandered by management regardless of the competitiveness of the product market. And indeed, a number of recent corporate governance scandals (e.g., Barings, Credit Lyonnais, Gan, Banesto, Metallgesellschaft, Enron, WorldCom) have occurred in industries with relatively strong competition. Similarly, the reaction of the big three American automobile manufacturers to the potential and then actual competition from foreign producers was painfully slow.

1.3 The Board of Directors

The board of directors[53] in principle monitors management on behalf of shareholders. It is meant to define or, more often, to approve major business decisions and corporate strategy: disposal of assets, investments or acquisitions, and tender offers made by acquirers. It is also in charge of executive compensation, oversight of risk management, and audits.

51. This argument is drawn from Rey and Tirole (1986), who, in the context of the choice between exclusive territories and competition between retailers, argue that competition acts as an insurance device and thus boosts incentives. Hermalin (1992) and Scharfstein (1988) study the impact of product-market competition on the agency cost in a Holmström (1979) principal–agent framework.

52. Aghion et al. (1999) develop a Schumpeterian model in which management may be unduly reluctant to adopt new technologies, and show that a procompetition policy may improve incentives in those firms with poor governance structures.

53. We will here be discussing the standard board structure. There are, of course, many variants. One variant that has received much attention is the German two-tier board. For instance, AGs (*Aktiengesellschaften*) with more than 2,000 employees have (a) a management board (*Vorstand*) with a leader (*Sprecher*) playing somewhat the role of a CEO and meeting weekly, say, and (b) a supervisory board (*Aufsichtsrat*) meeting three or four times a year, appointing members of the Vorstand, and approving or disapproving accounts, dividends, and major asset acquisitions or disposals proposed by the Vorstand. The Vorstand is composed of full-time salaried executives with fixed-term contracts, who cannot be removed except in extreme circumstances, a feature that makes it difficult for an outsider to gain control over the firm.

Firm managers cannot be members of the Aufsichtsrat. Half of the members of the Aufsichtsrat are nonexecutive representatives of the shareholders, and half represents employees (both employee delegates and external members designated by trade unions). The shareholders' representatives are nonexecutives but they are not independent in the Anglo-Saxon sense since they often represent firms or banks with an important business relationship with the firm. The chairman is drawn from the shareholders' representatives, and breaks ties in case of a deadlock. For more detail about the German two-tier system, see, for example, Charkham (1994, Chapter 2), Edwards and Fischer (1994), Kojima (1997, Section 4.1.2), and Roe (2003).

Lastly, it can offer advice and connections to management. To accomplish these tasks, boards operate more and more often through committees such as the compensation, nominating, and audit committees. Boards have traditionally been described as ineffective rubber-stampers controlled by, rather than controlling, management. Accordingly, there have recently been many calls for more accountable boards.[54]

1.3.1 Boards of Directors: Watchdogs or Lapdogs?

The typical complaints about the indolent behavior of boards of directors can be found in Mace's (1971) classic book. Directors rarely cause trouble in board meetings for several reasons.

Lack of independence. A director is labeled "independent" if she is not employed by the firm, does not supply services to the firm, or more generally does not have a conflict of interest in the accomplishment of her oversight mission. In practice, though, directors often have such conflicts of interest. This is most obvious for insiders sitting on the board (executive directors), who clearly are simultaneously judge and party.[55] But nonexecutive directors are often not independent either. They may be handpicked by management among friends outside the firm. They may be engaged in a business relationship with the firm, which they worry could be severed if they expressed opposition to management. They may belong to the same social network as the CEO.[56] Finally, they may receive "bribes" from the firm; for example, auditors may be asked to provide lucrative consultancy and tax services that induce them to stand with management.

In the United States, as in France, the chairman of the board (who, due to his powers, exercises a disproportionate influence on board meetings) is most often the firm's CEO, although the fraction of large corporations with a split-leadership structure has risen from an historical average of about one-fifth to one-third in 2004.[57] Nonexecutive chairmen are much more frequent in the United Kingdom (95% of all FTSE 350 companies in 2004) and in Germany and in the Netherlands (100% in both countries), which have a two-tier board.

An executive chairmanship obviously strengthens the insiders' hold on the board of directors. Another factor of executive control over the board is the possibility of mutual interdependence of CEOs. This factor may be particularly relevant for continental Europe and Japan, where cross-shareholdings within broadly defined "industrial groups" or keiretsus in Japan creates this interdependence. But, even in the United States, where cross-shareholdings are much rarer, CEOs may sit on each others' boards (even perhaps on each others' compensation committees!).

Insufficient attention. Outside directors are also often carefully chosen so as to be overcommitted.

---

54. In France, the corporate governance movement is scoring points, partly due to the increase in foreign shareholdings (70% of stock market value, but only 13% of the seats on the boards in 1997) and to privatizations. Firms publicize their compliance with the 1995 Viénot report setting up a code of behavior for boards. Yet, the corporate governance movement is still in its infancy. There are very few independent directors. A Vuchot-Ward-Howell study (cited by *La Tribune*, March 10, 1997) estimated that only 93 directors among the 541 directors of the largest publicly traded French corporations (CAC40) are independent (although French firms widely advertise "outside directors" as "independent directors"). Many are part of a club (and often went to the same schools and issued from the same corps of civil servants) sitting on each other's boards. The composition of board committees is not always disclosed. And general assemblies are still largely perfunctory, although minority shareholder movements are developing and recent votes demonstrate (minority) opposition to managerial proposals in a number of large companies.

55. The argument that is sometimes heard that insiders should be board members (implying: with full voting rights) in order to bring relevant information when needed is not convincing, since insiders without voting rights could participate in part or all of the board meetings.

56. Kramarz and Thesmar (2004) study social networks in French boardrooms. They identify three types of civil-service related social networks in business (more than half of the assets traded on the French stock market are managed by CEOs issued from the civil service). They find that CEOs appoint directors who belong to the same social network. Former civil servants are less likely to lose their job following a poor performance, and they are also more likely than other CEOs to become director of another firm when their own firm is doing badly.

Bertrand et al. (2004) investigates the consequences of French CEOs' political connections. There is a tight overlap between the CEOs and cabinet ministers, who often come from the same corps of civil servants or more generally belong to the same social networks associated with the Ecole Polytechnique or the Ecole Nationale d'Administration. Bertrand et al. find that firms managed by connected CEOs create more (destroy fewer) jobs in politically contested areas, and that the quid pro quo comes in the form of a privileged access to government subsidy programs.

57. According to a September 2004 study by Governance Metrics International, a corporate governance rating agency based in New York (cited in Felton and Wong 2004). Among the firms that have recently separated the roles of chairman and CEO are Dell, Boeing, Walt Disney, MCI, and Oracle.

Many outside directors in the largest U.S. corporations are CEOs of other firms. Besides having a full workload in their own company, they may sit on a large number of boards. In such circumstances, they may come to board meetings (other than their own corporation's) unprepared and they may rely entirely on the (selective) information disclosed by the firm's management.

Insufficient incentives. Directors' compensation has traditionally consisted for the most part of fees and perks. There has often been a weak link between firm performance and directors' compensation, although there is a trend in the United States towards increasing compensation in the form of stock options for directors.[58]

Explicit compensation is, of course, only part of the directors' monetary incentives. They may be sued by shareholders (say, through a class-action suit in the United States). But, four factors mitigate the effectiveness of liability suits. First, while courts penalize extreme forms of moral hazard such as fraud, they are much more reluctant to engage in business judgements about, say, whether an investment or an acquisition *ex ante* made good economic sense. Judges are not professional managers and they have limited knowledge of past industry conditions. They therefore do not want to be drawn into telling managers and directors how they should run their companies. Since corporate charters almost always eliminate director liability for breaches of duty of care, it is difficult for shareholders and other stakeholders to bring a suit against board members. Second, firms routinely buy liability insurance for their directors.[59] Third, liabilities, if any, are often paid by the firms, which indemnify directors who have acted in good faith. Fourth, plaintiff's lawyers may be inclined to buy off directors (unless they are extremely wealthy) in order to settle. Overall, for Black et al. (2004), as long as outside directors refrain from enriching themselves at the expense of the company, the risk of having to pay damages or legal fees out of their own pocket is very small in the United States,[60] as well as in other countries such as France, Germany, or Japan, where lawsuits are much rarer.

This undoing of the impact of liability suits has two perverse effects: it makes directors less accountable, and, in the case of indemnification by the firm, it deters shareholders from suing the directors since the fine paid in the case of a successful suit comes partly out of their pocket.

Avoidance of conflict. Except when it comes to firing management, it is hard even for independent directors to confront management; for, they are engaged in an ongoing relationship with top executives. A conflictual relationship is certainly unpleasant. And, perhaps more fundamentally, such a relationship is conducive neither to the management's listening to the board's advice nor to the disclosure to the board of key information.

In view of these considerations, it may come as a surprise that boards have any effectiveness. Boards actually do interfere in some decisions. They do remove underperforming managers, as we discussed in Section 1.2. They may also refuse to side with management during takeover contests. A well-known case in point is the 1989 RJR Nabisco leveraged buyout (LBO) in which a group headed by the CEO made an initial bid and the outside directors insisted on auctioning off the company, resulting in a much more attractive purchase by an outsider.

It should be realized, though, that the cosy relationship between directors and management is likely to break down mainly during crises. Directors

58. Yermack (2004b), looking at 766 outside directors in Fortune 500 firms between 1994 and 1996, estimates incentives from compensation, replacement, and opportunity to obtain other directorships. He finds that these incentives together yield 11 cents per $1,000 increase in firm value (shareholder wealth) to an outside director. Thus, performance-based incentives are not negligible for outside directors even though they remain much lower than those for CEOs (e.g., $5.29 per $1,000 increase in firm value for the median CEO in 1994, as reported by Hall and Liebman (1998)).

59. As well as officers (these insurance policies are labeled directors and officers (D&O) insurance policies).

60. It was a shock to directors when ten former executive directors of WorldCom agreed to pay a total of $18 million from their own savings and ten former Enron directors paid $13 million (still, the insurance companies are expected to pay out the bulk of the money: $36 million for WorldCom and $155 million for Enron *The Economist*, January 15, 2005, p. 65). It is hard to predict whether this indicates a new trend, as these cases involved extreme misbehaviors.

D&O insurance policies are less prevalent in Europe because of the lower probability of lawsuits, but they are likely to become very widespread as lawsuits become more common.

are then more worried about liability and more exposed to the spotlight. Furthermore, their relationship with management has shorter prospects than during good times. And, indeed, directors have historically been less effective in preventing management from engaging in wasteful diversification or in forcing it to disgorge excess cash than in removing underperforming managers. Relatedly, there is evidence that decreases in the share price lead to an increase in board activity, as measured by the annual number of board meetings (Vafeas 1999).

Bebchuk and Fried (2004) offer a scathing view of board behavior. They argue that most directors choose to collude with CEOs rather than accomplish their role of guardian of shareholders' interests. Directors dislike haggling with or being "disloyal" to the CEO, have little time to intervene, and further receive a number of favors from the CEO: the CEO can place them on the company's slate, increasing seriously their chance of reelection, give them perks, business deals (perhaps after they have been nominated on the board, so that they are formally "independent"), extra compensation on top of the director fee, and charitable contributions to nonprofit organizations headed by directors, or reciprocate the lenient oversight in case of interlocking directorates. A key argument of Bebchuk and Fried's book is that the rents secured by directors for the CEO involve substantial "camouflage"; that is, these rents should be as discrete or complex as possible so as to limit "outrage costs" and backlash. This camouflage yields inefficient compensation for officers. For example, compensation committees[61] fail to filter out stock price rises or general market trends and use conventional stock-option plans (as discussed in Section 1.2); and they grant substantial ability to managers to unload their options and shares. They also grant large cash payments in the case of an acquisition, generous retirement programs, and follow-on consulting contracts. Directors also happily acquiesce to takeover defenses.[62]

61. Despite their independence (in the United States, and unlike for some other committees, such as the nomination committee, directors sitting on the compensation committee are mostly independent directors).

62. Another example of "camouflaged rent" is the granting of executive loans, now prohibited by the 2002 Sarbanes-Oxley Act.

1.3.2 Reforming the Board

The previous description of indolent boards almost smacks of conspiracy theory. Managers carefully recommend for board nomination individuals who either have conflicts of interest or are overcommitted enough that they will be forced to rubber-stamp the management's proposals at the board meetings. And managers try to remove incentives to monitor by giving directors performance-insensitive compensation and by insuring them against liability suits, and "bribe" them in the various ways described in Bebchuk and Fried's book. Most of these managerial moves must, of course, be approved by the board itself, but board members may find their own benefit to colluding with management at the expense of shareholders.

While there is obviously some truth in this description, things are actually more complex for a couple of reasons.

Teammates or referees? As we observed, board members may actually be in an uncomfortable situation in which they attempt to cooperate with top executives while interfering with their decisions. Such relationships are necessarily strenuous. These different functions may sometimes conflict. The advisory role requires the directors be supplied with information that the top management may be unwilling to disclose if this information is also used to monitor and interfere with management.[63]

Knowledge versus independence? Parties close to the firm, and therefore susceptible to conflict of interest, are also likely to be the best informed about the firm and its environment. Similarly, professional managers are likely to be good monitors of their peers, even though they have an undue tendency to identify with the monitored.

What link from performance to board compensation? Providing directors with stock options rather than fixed fees goes in the right direction, but, for the same reasons as for managers, stock options have their own limitations. In particular, if managers go for a risky strategy that reduces investor value but

63. Adams and Ferreira (2003) build a model of board composition based on this premise and show that, in some circumstances, a management-friendly board may be optimal.

raises the value of their stock options, directors may have little incentive to oppose the move if they themselves are endowed with stock options. Similarly, directors' exposure to liability suits has costs. While the current system of liability insurance clearly impairs incentives, exposing directors fully to liability suits could easily induce them to behave in a very conservative fashion or (for the most talented ones) to turn down directorial jobs.

With these caveats in mind, there is still ample scope for board reform. Save a few legal and regulatory rules (such as the 1978 New York Stock Exchange rule that listed firms must have audit committees made up of nonexecutives), directors and managers faced few constraints in the composition and governance of boards. New regulations and laws may help in this respect, but, as usual, one must ask whether government intervention is warranted; in particular, one should wonder why the corporate charter designers do not themselves draw better rules for their boards, and, relatedly, why more decentralized solutions cannot be found, in which shareholders force (provided they have the means to) boards to behave better. That is, with better information of and coordination among shareholders, capital market pressure may be sufficient to move boards in the right direction.

In this spirit, several study groups produced codes of good conduct or of best practice for boards (e.g., the 1992 Cadbury report in the United Kingdom and the 1995 Viénot report in France). Abstracts from the Cadbury report are reproduced at the end of this chapter. Among other proposals, the Cadbury report calls for (a) the nomination of a recognized senior outside member where the chairman of the board is the CEO,[64] (b) a procedure for directors to take independent professional advice at the company's expense, (c) a majority of independent directors (namely, nonexecutive directors free from business relationship with the firm), and (d) a compensation committee dominated by nonexecutive directors and an audit committee conferred to nonexecutive directors, most of whom should be independent. In contrast, the Cadbury report recommends against performance-based compensation of directors.

Table 1.1 Compliance of U.S. companies with a few CalPERS criteria in 1997. *Source:* Analysis by the *The New York Times* (August 3, 1997) of data compiled by Directorship from the 861 public companies on the Fortune 1000 list. "Independent" here means "composed of outside directors."

Has outside chairman	5%
Only one insider on the board	18%
Some form of mandatory retirement for directors	18%
Independent nominating committee	38%
Fewer than 10% of directors over 70	68%
Independent governance committee	68%
No retired chief executive on the board	82%
Independent ethics committee	85%
Independent audit committee	86%
A majority of outside directors on the board	90%
Independent compensation committee	91%

In the United States, the largest public pension fund, CalPERS, with $165.3 billion in assets in August 2004, drew in the mid 1990s a more ambitious list of 37 principles of good practice for a corporate board, 23 "fundamental" and 14 "ideal." CalPERS would like the companies to consider the ideal principles, such as a limit on the number of directors older than 70, but has stated it would be more open-minded on these principles than on the fundamental ones. CalPERS monitors the companies' compliance (in spirit, if not the letter) with these principles and publicizes the results, so as to generate proxy votes for companies that comply least. As of 1997, most firms failed to comply with a substantial number of CalPERS criteria, although some of these criteria were usually satisfied by most corporations (see Table 1.1).

While the CalPERS list is stringent and some of its criteria controversial, it illustrates well the investors' current pressure for more accountable boards.

More recently, in the wake of the many corporate scandals at the turn of the century, expert recommendations regarding the board of directors have been bolder. For example, they suggest regular meetings of the board or specific committees in the absence of executives, a policy already adopted by a

64. The UK Combined Code (the successor to the Cadbury Code) states that chairmen should be independent at the time of appointment.

number of corporations.[65] Such meetings promote truth telling and reduce individual directors' concern about the avoidance of conflict with management. A number of experts have also recommended self-evaluation of boards; for example, at regular intervals the director with the worst "grade" would be fired.[66] There have also been calls for strict limits (e.g., three) on the number of board mandates that a director can accept, for limited director tenures, and for a mandatory retirement age.

Monetary incentives have also been put forward. The directors' compensation would be more systematically related to the firm's stock value. Here the recommendation is for directors to hold a minimum number of shares in the firm.[67]

Some experts[68] have proposed a direct or intermediated (through an ombudsman) access of whistleblowers to independent directors. This is probably a good suggestion, although it has one flaw and its impact is likely to be limited for two reasons. The drawback of whistleblowing is that companies react to its threat by (a) intensively screening employees in order to pick those who are likely to prove "loyal," and (b) reducing information flows within the firm, which reduces the benefit of whistleblowing in terms of transparency and accountability.[69] Second, employees have relatively low incentives to blow the whistle. If discovered by the company (even formal anonymity does not guarantee that there will not be suspicion about the source of information), they will probably be fired. And whistleblowers notoriously have a hard time finding a new job in other firms, who fear that they will blow the whistle again.[70] In particular, employers routinely check prospective employees' litigation record. The proposal of letting whistleblowers have a direct or indirect access to independent directors is therefore likely to be most effective when (a) the sensitive information is held by a number of employees, so that whistleblower anonymity can really be preserved, and (b) the directors can check the veracity of the information independently, that is, without resorting to the whistleblower. Lastly, it must be the case that directors pay attention to the information that they receive from the whistleblower (the Enron board failed to follow up on allegations by a whistleblower). For this, they must not be swamped by tons of frivolous whistleblowing messages; and, of course, they must have incentives to exercise their corporate governance rights.

Lastly, the Sarbanes–Oxley Act (2002) in the United States requires the audit committee to hire the outside auditor and to be composed only of directors who have no financial dealing with the firm. It also makes the board more accountable for misreporting.

A Few Final Comments

Scope of codes. First, codes are not solely preoccupied with boards of directors. They also include, for example, recommendations regarding reporting (auditor governance, financial reporting), executive

65. Korn/Ferry International (2003) estimated that in 2003 87% of U.S. Fortune 1000 boards held Executive Sessions without their CEO present. By contrast, only 4% of Japanese boards gather without the CEO present.

66. In 2003, 29% of U.S. boards (41% in Asia Pacific) conducted individual director evaluation reviews (Korn/Ferry International 2003).

67. An example often cited by the proponents of this view is that of G. Wilson, who was for twelve years director of the Disney Corporation and held no share of Disney despite a personal wealth exceeding $500 million!

68. See, for example, *Getting Governance Right*, McKinsey Quarterly, 2002.

69. More generally, a cost of using informers is that it destroys trust in social groups, as has been observed in totalitarian regimes (e.g., in Eastern Germany, where people were concerned that family members or friends would report them to the Stasi).

70. Consider the example of Christine Casey, who blew the whistle on Mattel, the toy manufacturer, which reported very inflated sales forecasts to its shareholders (see, for example, *The Economist*, January 18, 2003, p. 60). Some managers kept two sets of figures, and consistently misled investors. In February 1999, Ms. Casey approached a Mattel director. After being screamed at by executives and basically demoted, in September 1999, she telephoned the SEC. She ended up resigning, filed an unsuccessful lawsuit against Mattel, and in 2003 was still without a job.

Zingales (2004) reviews the (rather bleak) evidence on what happens to whistleblowers after they have denounced management and after they quit their firm. To counteract the strong incentives not to blow the whistle, he proposes that whistleblowers receive a fraction (say, 10%) of all fees and legal awards imposed on the company (with, of course, some punishments for frivolous whistleblowing and a requirement to denounce to the SEC rather than in public). Such rewards already exists for people who help the U.S. government to recover fraudulent gains by private agents at its expense (whistleblowers are entitled to between 15% and 30%).

Friebel and Guriev (2004) argue that internal incentives are designed so as to limit whistleblowing. In their theoretical model, division managers may have evidence that top managers are inflating earnings. Top management, however, provides lower-level managers with a pay structure similar to theirs so as to make them allies. Friebel and Guriev thus provide an explanation for the propagation of short-term incentives in corporate hierarchies.

Table 1.2 Some recent codes of good governance.

	Independent directors?	Separation of chairman–CEO roles?	Rotation of external auditor?	Frequency of financial reporting?	'Comply or explain' requirement?	Selected country-specific governance issues
Brazil						
CVM Code (2002)	As many as possible	Clear preference for split	Not covered	Quarterly	No	Adoption of IAS/U.S. GAAP[1] Fiscal boards[1] Tag-along rights[1]
France						
Bouton Report (2002)	At least one-half of board	No recommendation	Regularly, for lead auditors	No recommendation given	No	Dual statutory auditors
Russia						
CG Code (2002)	At least one-quarter of board	Split required by law	Not covered	Quarterly	No	Managerial boards
Singapore						
CG Committee (2001)	At least one-third of board	Recommended	Not covered	Quarterly	Yes	Disclosure of pay for family members of directors/CEOs
United Kingdom						
Cadbury Code (1992)	Majority of nonexecutive directors	Recommended	Periodically, for lead auditors	Semiannually	Yes	
Combined Code (2003)	At least one-half of board	Clear preference for split	Not covered[2]	Semiannually, per listing rules	Yes	
United States						
Conference Board (2003)	Substantial majority of board	Separation is one of three acceptable options	Recommended for audit firm[3]	Quarterly, as required by law	No	

Source: Coombes and Wong (2004).

1. IAS, International Accounting Standards; GAAP, generally accepted accounting principles; fiscal boards are akin to audit committees, but members are appointed by shareholders; tag-along rights protect minority shareholders by giving them the right to participate in transactions between large shareholders and third parties.

2. In the United Kingdom, the accounting profession's self-regulatory body requires rotation of lead audit partner every seven years. Combined Code recommends that companies annually determine auditor's policy on partner rotation.

3. Sarbanes-Oxley Act requires rotation of lead audit *partner* every five years. Circumstances that warrant changing auditor *firm* include audit relationship in excess of ten years, former partner of audit firm employed by company, and provision of significant nonaudit services.

compensation, shareholders voting, or antitakeover defenses. Second, they are now commonplace. As of 2004, fifty countries had their own code of governance, emanating from regulators, investor associations, the industry itself, or supranational organizations. They differ across countries as shown by Table 1.2, which reports some key features of a few recently drawn codes.

Do codes matter? Codes are only recommendations and have no binding character. Probably the main reason why they seem to have an impact is that they educate the general public, including investors. To the extent that they are drawn by expert and independent bodies they carry (real) authority in indicating the conditions that are conducive to efficient governance. They further focus the debate on pointing at some "reasonable" or "normal" practices, a deviation from which ought to be explained. For example, it is often asserted that the 1992 Cadbury Code of Best Practice, by pointing at the cost of conflating the positions of chairman of the board and CEO, was instrumental in moving the fraction of the top U.K. companies that operated a separation from 50 to 95% in 2004. In performing this educative role, the codes finally may help the corresponding practices enjoy the "network externalities" inherent in familiar institutions: investors, judges, and regulators in charge of enforcing the laws gain expertise in the understanding of the meaning and implications of most often used charters; contractual deviations by individual firms therefore run the risk of facing a lack of familiarity by these parties.

Do codes suffice? Unlike codes, corporate laws do have a binding impact on the design of corporate charters, even though the exact nature of the regulatory constraint is subject to debate as courts are sometimes willing to accept contractual innovations in corporate charters in which the parties opt out of the legal rules and set different terms.[71] In the long-standing normative debate on contractual freedom in corporate law, there is relative agreement on the usefulness of corporate law as creating a default point that lowers the cost of contracting for all parties who do not want to spend considerable resources into drafting agreements.[72] Legal experts in contrast disagree on the desirability of the compulsory nature of the law. Advocates of deregulation, such as Easterbrook and Fischel (1989), argue that one size does not fit all and that a mandatory law at the very least prevents contractual innovations that would benefit all parties; they may further argue that existing rules need not be optimal even in the set of rigid rules. Others are opposed to permitting shareholders to opt out from the mandatory core of corporate law. Arguments in favor of keeping corporate law mandatory include: the absence of some concerned parties at the initial bargaining table (see Chapter 11 of this book); the possibility that inefficient governance allows managers to change the rules of the game along the way thanks to investors' apathy;[73] and the possibility that asymmetric information at the initial contracting stage engenders dissipative costs (see Chapter 6).

Even if it is not mandatory, corporate law matters for roughly the same reasons that codes are relevant. First, the transaction costs of contracting around the default point may be substantial. Second, there are the "network externalities" alluded to above in the context of codes. In particular, abiding by the statutes provides for a more competent enforcement by the legal infrastructure. These network externalities could, of course, suggest an equilibrium focus on contractual provisions that differ from existing rules; but the existence of transaction costs (the first argument) tends to make the rule a focal point.

Finally, note that a state or a country's codes and legal rules matter most when firms cannot choose where to incorporate and/or be listed. Competition among codes and legal rules[74] encourages international convergence towards standards that facilitate the corporations' access to financing (although, as will be studied in Chapter 16, firms' interests with respect to the regulatory environment may not be aligned).

1.4 Investor Activism

Active monitors intervene in such matters as the firm's strategic decisions, investments, and asset sales, managerial compensation, design of takeover defenses, and board size and composition. We first describe various forms of investor activism, leaving aside takeovers and bank monitoring, which will be discussed in latter sections. We then point to a number of limitations of investor activism.

1.4.1 Investor Activism Comes in Many Guises

Active monitoring requires control. As will be stressed in Part IV of this book, monitoring per se does not alter corporate policy. In order to implement new ideas, or to oppose bad policies of managers, the active monitor must have *control.* Control can come in two forms:[75] formal and real. Formal control is enjoyed by a family owner with a majority of voting shares, by headquarters over divisions in a conglomerate, or by a venture capitalist with explicit control rights over a start-up company. Formal control thus enables a large owner to, directly

71. On the role of courts, see, for example, Coffee (1989).

72. On this, see, for example, Ayres and Gertner (1989, 1992). Easterbrook and Fischel (1989), among others, point out that the story that corporate law is there to provide off-the-shelf terms for parties who want to economize on contracting costs is incomplete in that the default rules could be designed alternatively by law firms, corporate service bureaus, or investment banks. They argue nonetheless that the supply of default rules has the nature of a public good, if only because the court system can develop a set of precedents on how to deal with contract incompleteness.

73. Bebchuk (1989) emphasizes that the questions of contractual freedom in the initial charter and in midstream (after the charter has been drawn) are different. The amendment process is imperfect, as the shareholders's insufficient incentive to become informed may not preclude value-decreasing amendments.

74. There is a large literature on competition between legal environments. See, for example, Bar-Gill et al. (2003) and Pagano and Volpin (2005c) and the references therein.

75. This dichotomy is an expositional oversimplification. Actual control moves more continuously than suggested by the dichotomy.

Table 1.3 Ownership of common stock (as a percentage of total outstanding common shares in 2002) for (a) all equity and (b) listed equity.

<table>
<tr><th></th><th colspan="4">(a)</th><th colspan="4">(b)</th></tr>
<tr><th></th><th>U.S.</th><th>Japan</th><th>France</th><th>Germany</th><th>U.K.</th><th>Japan</th><th>France</th><th>Germany</th></tr>
<tr><td>Banks and other financial institutions</td><td>2.3</td><td>9.0</td><td>12.1</td><td>10.5</td><td>12.6</td><td>7.42</td><td>12.6</td><td>33.5</td></tr>
<tr><td>Insurance companies</td><td>7.3</td><td>4.3</td><td rowspan="2">4.5</td><td rowspan="2">9.9</td><td>19.9</td><td>7.32</td><td rowspan="2">7.0</td><td rowspan="2">7.4</td></tr>
<tr><td>Pension funds</td><td>16.9</td><td>5.4</td><td>15.6</td><td>5.62</td></tr>
<tr><td>Mutual funds</td><td>19.5</td><td>1.9</td><td>5.9</td><td>11.3</td><td>4.5</td><td>6.58</td><td>19</td><td>4.6</td></tr>
<tr><td>Households</td><td>42.5</td><td>14.0</td><td>19.5</td><td>14.7</td><td>14.3</td><td>16.84</td><td>6.5</td><td>22.9</td></tr>
<tr><td>Nonfinancial business</td><td>n.a.</td><td>43.7</td><td>34.3</td><td>34.2</td><td>0.8</td><td>38.12</td><td>20.2</td><td>11.7</td></tr>
<tr><td>Government</td><td>0.7</td><td>14.0</td><td>4.5</td><td>2.7</td><td>0.1</td><td>4.12</td><td>3.6</td><td>1.9</td></tr>
<tr><td>Foreign</td><td>10.6</td><td>7.7</td><td>19.2</td><td>16.6</td><td>32.1</td><td>13.98</td><td>31.2</td><td>18.1</td></tr>
</table>

This table was assembled by David Sraer. The details of its construction can be found in an appendix (see Section 1.11.1).

and unencumbered (except perhaps by fiduciary duties), implement the changes he deems necessary. In contrast, real control is enjoyed by a minority owner who persuades other owners, or at least a fraction of them sufficient to create a dissenting majority, of the need for intervention. The extent to which a minority owner is able to convince other owners to move against management depends on two factors: ease of communication and of coalition-building with other investors, and congruence of interest among owners. The degree of congruence is determined by the active monitor's reputation (is he competent and honest?), by the absence of conflict of interest (will the monitor benefit from control in other ways than his fellow shareholders?), and by his stake in the firm (how much money will the monitor lose in case of a misguided intervention?). The latter factor explains why minority block shareholders are often described (a bit abusively) as having a "control block" even though they do not formally control the firm, and why dissidents in proxy contests are less trusted if their offer is not combined with a cash tender offer.

Proxy fights. In a proxy contest, a stockholder or a group of stockholders unhappy with managerial policies seeks either election to the board of directors with the ultimate goal of removing management, or support by a majority of shareholders for a resolution on a specific corporate policy. Sometimes, the *threat* of a proxy contest suffices to achieve the active monitor's aims, and so the contest need not even occur. For example, active monitors may use a political campaign to embarrass directors and force them to remove the CEO; or they may meet with directors or management and "convince" them of the necessity to alter their policies.

Proxy fights are an important element of corporate discipline in the United States. For example, in 1992–1993, financial institutions claimed the scalps of the CEOs of American Express, Borden, General Motors, IBM, Kodak, and Westinghouse. They also pressed for smaller boards and a larger fraction of outside directors, and forced large pay cuts on the bosses of ITT, General Dynamics, and U.S. Air (*The Economist*, August 19, 1996, p. 51). Proxy fights are associated with low accounting earnings, but, perhaps surprisingly, seem to have little relationship with the firm's stock returns (see de Angelo 1988; de Angelo and de Angelo 1989; Pound 1988).

As we discussed, the existence and success of proxy fights depend not only on whether the initiator is trusted by other shareholders,[76] but also on their cost and feasibility. The competition between management (who can use corporate resources) and dissidents must be fair. And shareholders must be able to communicate among themselves. Until 1992, U.S. regulations made it very difficult for institutional investors (many of whom typically own a small piece

76. Proxy votes may be ineffective if the dissenters do not succeed in building a majority. For example, in 2003, Disney was able to ignore in large part a proxy vote in which about 40% of the votes were cast against management.

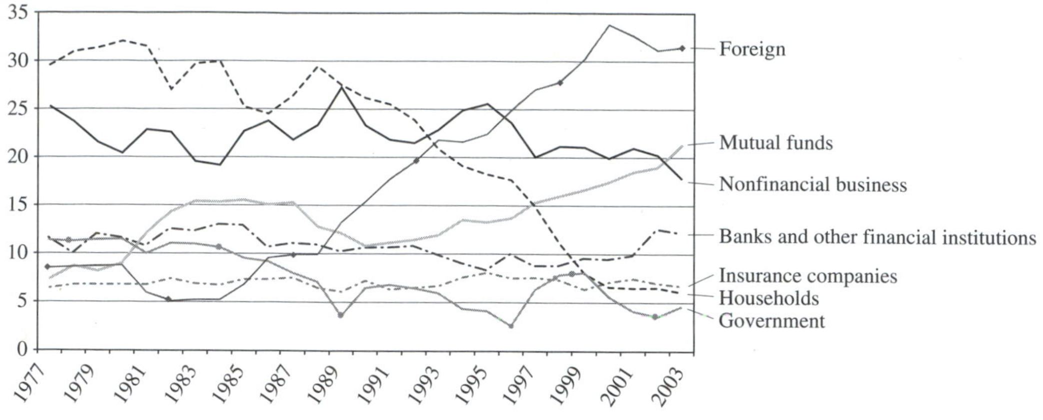

Figure 1.3 Evolution of listed-equity ownership by sectors in France (1977–2003). (Assembled by David Sraer.)

of the firm, as we will see) to communicate. A 1992 SEC rule change has allowed freer communication. Furthermore, the 1992 new SEC rules have lowered the cost of a proxy fight from over \$1 million to less than \$5,000 (*The Economist*, January 29, 1994, p. 24 of a survey on corporate governance).

Proxy fights are rare in many other countries, and almost unheard of in Japan, where general assemblies tend to be perfunctory.

1.4.2 Pattern of Ownership

Investor activism is intimately linked to the structure of ownership. A brief review of this structure (in the context of publicly held companies) is therefore in order.

Table 1.3 looks at the ownership of common stock for listed and unlisted companies. It shows that, as of 2002, countries differ substantially as to who owns equity. In the United States, households and institutional investors other than banks hold most of the shares.[77] Households (other than owners of family firms) have much lower stockholdings in France, Germany,[78] and Japan.

Table 1.3(b), for the same year, specializes to *listed companies*. Note that foreign ownership is substantially higher, indicating that foreign equity portfolios tend to specialize in listed companies.

Figures 1.3 and 1.4 describe the intertemporal evolution of listed-equity ownership in France and the United Kingdom, respectively.

Institutional investors do not all have the same incentives to monitor, as we will later discuss. It is therefore interesting to have a closer look at the decomposition of shareholdings among these investors. Table 1.4 describes this decomposition for the United States in 2004.

Pension funds play a much more minor role in other countries such as France, Germany, Italy, or Japan; in these countries, they are quasi-nonexistent, because retirement benefits are publicly funded on a pay-as-you-go basis (as in France), or because pension funds are just a liability item on the firms' balance-sheet and do not stand as independent investors (as in Germany).

The absence or weakness of pension funds is not the only characteristic of non-Anglo-Saxon countries. As we will see, *ownership concentration* is substantial. Also, *cross-shareholdings* among firms is widespread, as shown by the ownership share of nonfinancial business. There is a complex web of

77. We here focus on the ownership of common stock. Needless to say, the ownership pattern for assets in general may be quite different. For example, U.S. banks held almost no equity due in part to the prohibition contained in the 1933 Glass-Steagall Act, an act passed by Congress prohibiting commercial banks to participate in investment banking or to collaborate with full-service brokerage firms (this act was repealed in 1999). In contrast, their market share of total assets among U.S. financial institutions in 1994 was 28.7% (as opposed to 15.3% for insurance companies, 14.6% for private pension funds, 7.1% for public pension funds, 9.5% for mutual funds, 3.5% for money market funds, and 21.3% for other institutions). *Source:* Board of Governors of the Federal Reserve System, Flow of Funds Accounts 1995, cited by Sametz (1995).

78. For further information about the ownership of German corporations, see Franks and Mayer (2001).

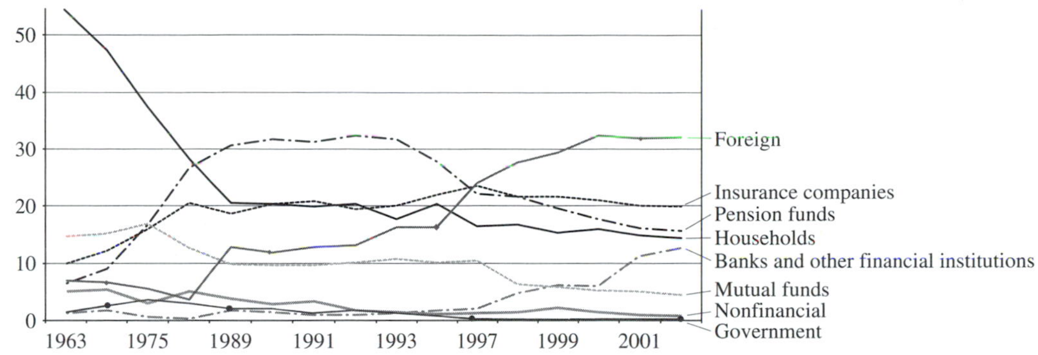

Figure 1.4 Evolution of listed-equity ownership by sectors in the United Kingdom (1963–2002). (Assembled by David Sraer.)

Table 1.4 Institutional investors' equity holdings as a percentage of the total U.S. equity market by category. (IEH, institutional equity holdings ($ billion); TEM, total equity market.)

Type of institution	IEH	TEM (%)
Banks	213.7	1.8
Commercial Banking	3.5	0.0
Savings Institutions	29.1	0.2
Banks, personal trusts and estates	181.1	1.5
Insurance companies	861.2	7.3
Life Insurance companies	708.9	6.0
Other Insurance companies	152.3	1.3
Pension funds	2015.0	17.0
Private pension funds	1096.7	9.2
State and local government retirement funds	869.8	7.3
Federal government retirement funds	48.5	0.4
Investment companies	2394.8	20.2
Mutual funds	2188.0	18.4
Closed-end funds	33.7	0.3
Exchange-traded funds	98.2	0.8
Brokers and dealers	74.9	0.6
All institutions	5484.7	46.2

This table was assembled by David Sraer. The details of its construction can be found in an appendix (see Section 1.11.2).

Table 1.5 Average percentage of shares owned by firms in the keiretsu divided by total outstanding shares in 1992. *Source:* Kojima (1997, p. 57).

Mitsui	19.3%
Mitsubishi	38.2%
Sumitomo	28%
Fuyo	16.9%
Sanwa	16.7%
Dai-ichi Kangin	14.2%

cross-participations within loosely defined or more structured industrial groups. For example, Table 1.5 reproduces findings of a study of the Japanese Fair Trade Commission summarizing cross-shareholdings in the major Japanese industrial groups.

Another interesting international difference relates to the *size of the stock market.* Anglo-Saxon countries have well-developed stock markets; the capitalizations of the U.S. and U.K. stock markets in June 1996 made up about 90% and 120% of their respective GDPs (gross domestic products). With some exceptions (e.g., Japan and Switzerland), other stock markets are smaller (under 40% of GDP in France; Germany and Italy around the same date); for example, many relatively large German firms choose to remain private.

Ownership concentration. There are also wide variations in the concentration of shares across countries.

In the majority of publicly listed Italian firms, for example, one shareholder holds above 50% of the shares (Franks et al. 1996). Family-owned firms there play an important role, as they do in France, Germany, and Sweden (see Table 1.6). Using a sample of 5,232 listed firms in 13 countries, Faccio and Lang (2002) provide a systematic analysis of ownership in Western Europe, pointing out the wide diversity of

Table 1.6 The identity of controlling owners in Europe (%) (1996–2000).

Country	France	Germany	Italy	Sweden	U.K.
Widely held	14	10	13	39	63
Family	65	64	60	47	24
Identified families	26	27	39	23	12
Unlisted firms	39	38	20	24	11
State	5	6	10	5	0
Widely held corporation	4	4	3	0	0
Widely held financial	11	9	12	3	9
Miscellaneous	1	3	1	6	3
Cross-holdings	0	2	1	0	0
Number of firms	607	704	208	245	1953

Source: Faccio and Lang (2002). Reprinted from *Journal of Financial Economics*, Volume 65, M. Faccio and L. Lang, The ultimate ownership of Western European corporations, pp. 365–395, Copyright (2002), with permission from Elsevier. A detailed description can be found in an appendix (see Section 1.11.3).

institutions (dual-class shares, cross-holdings, pyramidal structures[79]) and concentration. They find that 54% of European firms have only one controlling owner and that more than two-thirds of the family-controlled firms have top managers from the controlling family. Widely held firms account for 37% of the sample and family-controlled ones for 44%.

Similarly, Claessens et al. (2000) investigate the ownership structure of 2,980 publicly traded firms in nine East Asian countries (see, in particular, Table 1.7). In all countries, control vastly exceeds what would be predicted by cash-flow rights and is enhanced through pyramid structures and cross-holdings between firms. In their sample, more than two-thirds of the firms are controlled by a single shareholder, and about 60% of the firms that are not widely held are managed by someone related to the family of the controlling shareholder. There are significant variations across countries, though: for example, corporations in Japan are often widely held while those in Indonesia and Thailand are mainly family owned.

In contrast, ownership concentration is much smaller in Anglo-Saxon countries. For example, the mean and the median of the "three-shareholder concentration ratio," namely, the fraction of ownership by the three largest shareholders, for the largest listed firms, are 0.19 and 0.15 for the United Kingdom, 0.34 and 0.68 for France, and 0.48 and 0.50 for Germany (La Porta et al. 1998).

Ownership is extremely dispersed in the United States. While Shleifer and Vishny (1986) report that above 50% of the Fortune 500 firms have at least one shareholder holding a block exceeding 5%, large blocks are relatively rare (except, of course, in the case of leveraged buyouts or family-held firms). The median largest shareholder has only 9% of the firm's equity, and a number of moderate size block shareholders typically coexist; 20% (respectively, 15%) of firms traded on the New York Stock Exchange, the Amex, and the over-the-counter market have a nonofficer (respectively, officer) holding more than 10% of shares (Barclay and Holderness 1989). Institutional investors often hold (individually) a very small amount of the firm's stock; for example, in 1990, the most visible "active investor," CalPERS, reportedly held less than 1% of the firms it invested in (Kojima 1997, p. 22).

Stable holdings versus active portfolio management. Another point of departure among countries is the degree of stability of stock holdings.

Simplifying somewhat, Japanese and German investors have traditionally been in for the long haul, while Anglo-Saxon investors reshuffle their portfolios frequently. Institutional investors dominate liquidity trading in the United States. Mutual funds

79. Pyramids refer to the indirect control of one corporation by another that does not totally own it.

Table 1.7 The identity of controlling owners in Asia (%) (1996).

Country	Hong Kong	Japan	Korea	Malaysia	Singapore	Taiwan	Thailand
Widely held	7	79.8	43.2	10.3	5.4	26.2	6.6
Family	66.7	9.7	48.4	67.2	55.4	48.2	61.6
State	1.4	0.8	1.6	13.4	23.5	2.8	8
Widely held corporation	19.8	3.2	6.1	6.7	11.5	17.4	15.3
Widely held financial	5.2	6.5	0.7	2.3	4.1	5.3	8.6
Number of firms	330	1240	345	238	221	141	167

Source: Claessens et al. (2000). Reprinted from *Journal of Financial Economics*, Volume 58, S. Claessens, S. Djankov, and L. Lang, The separation of ownership and control in East Asian corporations, pp. 81–112, Copyright (2000), with permission from Elsevier. A detailed description can be found in an appendix (see Section 1.11.3).

and actively managed pension funds hold their shares, on average, for 1.9 years (Kojima 1997, p. 84). In contrast, shareholdings are very stable in Japan. Kojima (1997, p. 31) assesses that, for a typical Japanese firm, about 60% of shareholdings are stable. In Japan, business corporations (which hold substantial amounts of stocks through cross-shareholdings) and financial institutions view themselves as engaged in a long-term relationship with the firms they invest in.[80] Table 1.8 confirms the low turnover rate for corporate and institutional investors.

Table 1.8 Stock trading by type of investor in terms of average percentage turnover rates (for the years 1990–92).

Life and casualty insurance companies	sales	4.9
	purchases	5.0
Business corporations	sales	8.5
	purchases	8.4
Banks	sales	12.3
	purchases	12.8
Individuals	sales	24.9
	purchases	24.7
Foreigners	sales	61.4
	purchases	65.1
Investment trusts	sales	65.3
	purchases	64.9

Source: Kotaro (1995, p. 15) and Economic Planning Agency White Papers (1992).

1.4.3 The Limits of Active Monitoring

For all its benefits, investor activism encounters a number of limits, studied in Chapters 9 and 10 and grouped below in four categories.

Who monitors the monitor? Active monitors are in charge of mitigating the agency problem within the firms they invest in. The same agency problem, however, often applies, with a vengeance, to the monitors themselves. In particular, pension and mutual funds have a very dispersed set of beneficiaries and no large shareholder! Coffee (1991) argues that there are very few mechanisms holding U.S. institutional money managers accountable: most face no threat of hostile takeover or proxy fights; pension funds have no debt and therefore face less pressure to generate profits than ordinary corporations; and executive compensation is hard to design, as well as constrained by the regulatory framework (compensation is a function of assets under management rather than an incentive compensation based on the fund's capital appreciation, which is contrary to federal securities laws).

Thus, monitoring may be impaired by the fact that monitors may not act in the interest of the beneficiaries. Corporate managers usually argue, in this respect, that institutional investors are too preoccupied by short-term profit, presumably because the managers of pension and mutual funds are keen to keep their positions and to manage larger funds. Some corporate managers also complain that the institutions' managers monitoring them have limited managerial competency.

80. See Aoki (1984, 1990), Aoki and Patrick (1995), Kotaro (1995), and Kojima (1994, 1997) for discussions of long-term financial relationships in Japan.

Congruence with other investors. Even if the agency problem between the active monitor and its beneficiaries is resolved (say, because the two coincide, as in the case of a large private owner), the active monitor does not internalize the welfare of other investors and therefore may not monitor efficiently. This may give rise to:

Undermonitoring. A pension fund owning 1 or 2% of a corporation has vastly suboptimal incentives to acquire strategic information and launch a proxy fight, as it receives only 1 or 2 cents per dollar it creates for the shareholders. Substantial free riding may thus be expected, for example, when institutional ownership is very dispersed.

Collusion with management. Relatedly, a monitor may enter into a quid pro quo with management or be afraid of retaliation in case it dissents (for example, noncooperative fund managers in a proxy fight may not be selected to manage the firm's pension plan).

Self-dealing. Large blockholders monitoring a firm may use their private information to extract rents from the firm through transactions with affiliated firms and the like. How much they can extract depends on the strength of legal enforcement of shareholders rights as well as on the (non)existence of other large shareholders who are not made part of the sweet deals and can denounce the abuse.

Cost of providing proper incentives to the monitor. Again, leaving aside agency problems within the monitor, several authors, most notably Coffee (1991), Porter (1992), and Bhide (1993a), have argued that only "long-term players" are good monitors. Their basic idea is that investors have little incentive to create long-run value improvement (exert voice) if they can easily exit by reselling their shares at a fair price. They further argue that illiquidity, promoted, say, by privately placed equity, large blocks with limited marketability, taxes on realized capital gains, or equity with limited resale rights (letter stocks), would enhance the quality of monitoring, and they point at the long-term, stable relationships in Japan and Germany between the investors and the corporations they invest in.[81] These authors recognize that illiquidity is costly to the institutional investors but they argue that this cost is limited for some institutional investors such as pension funds. While Chapter 9 will qualify the view that active monitoring requires a long-term involvement, the point that properly structuring the active monitor's incentives may entail some illiquidity costs is valid.

Perverse effects on the monitorees. While monitoring is generally beneficial, it does not come without side effects for the monitoree. There may be overmonitoring and a reduction in initiative (see Chapter 9), and the firm's managers may become overly preoccupied by short-run news that will determine their tenure in the firm. They may then devote much time to manipulating short-term earnings (see Chapter 7) and trying to secure the cooperation of the largest institutional investors.

Legal, fiscal, and regulatory obstacles. A number of authors, most notably Roe (1990), Coffee (1991), and Bhide (1993a), have emphasized the legal, fiscal, and regulatory impediments to investor activism in the United States, and argued that U.S. regulators have discouraged efficient governance.

First, stockholders who sit on a firm's board are exposed to SEC and class-action suits.[82] Furthermore, an individual or a group that possesses "control" of a company is deemed an "affiliate" and faces volume and holding-period restrictions on reselling shares;[83] Section 16(b) of the Securities Exchange Act of 1934 stipulates that any gain that an officer, director, or 10% holder of a security receives on purchases or sales of the security within six months of an earlier purchase or sale must be paid back to the corporation. These rules create illiquidity, which add to the natural illiquidity of big blocks. These are therefore particularly costly for mutual funds, which face redemptions and therefore must be able to sell.

Another rule affecting institutional control is the diversification rule. In order to receive favorable tax

81. With respect to this last point, it should be noted that these contributions were written in the late 1980s to early 1990s when the "GJ" model (for "Germany–Japan") was fashionable. The economic evolution of the 1990s made observers much less keen on endorsing this model, and more keen (probably too keen) on embracing the Anglo-Saxon paradigm.

82. Section 20 of 1934 Securities Exchange Act.

83. Securities Act of 1933.

treatment as a diversified fund, a pension fund or mutual fund cannot hold more than 10% of the stock of any firm (even though a holding above 10% may be small relative to the fund's total managed assets, so that the rule has no virtue in terms of diversification and prudential regulation!). It is therefore not surprising that U.S. institutional investors hold small fractions of shares of individual firms so as to avoid restrictions on short-term (insider) trading and receive favorable tax treatment, and that they avoid sitting on boards.

While the details of regulation are country- and time-specific, it should be borne in mind that they can have a nonnegligible impact on corporate governance.

1.5 Takeovers and Leveraged Buyouts

One of the most controversial aspects of corporate governance, and certainly one that varies most across countries, is the market for corporate control. The explosion of hostile takeovers and of leveraged buyouts (LBOs) in the United States in the 1980s[84] has been perceived with awe, horror, and admiration. In Japan and continental Europe, where acquisitions are usually negotiated with management, they represent the worst of an American capitalism based on greed and myopia. In Anglo-Saxon countries, in contrast, many view them as an original mode of corporate governance that substitutes efficient teams for entrenched, money-wasting managers (Manne 1965).[85]

Although they are divided on the topic, economists are in agreement on many of the costs and benefits of takeovers (reviewed in Chapter 11), and hold much more dispassionate views on the topic than practitioners and laymen. On the managerial side, takeovers may be needed to keep managers on their toes, if the board and general assembly are ineffective monitors and thus traditional corporate governance fails. But, as for other forms of incentive based on the termination of employment, they may induce managers to act "myopically" and boost their short-term performance at the expense of the long-term one. On the corporate policy front, takeovers may put in place a new managerial team with fresh ideas on how to run the firm and less keen on sticking to former strategy mistakes. But they may also let a value-reducing raider gain control from uncoordinated shareholders. Finally, takeovers may shatter implicit contracts with other stakeholders. Chapter 11 will therefore study private and social inefficiencies arising in the market for corporate control.

Let us begin with three salient features of the U.S. corporate environment of the 1980s. First, while definitely smaller than that of the subsequent merger wave (see below), the volume of mergers and acquisitions was very high by historical standards during the decade. Indeed, 143 of the 1980 Fortune 500 firms had become acquired by 1989. About $1.3 trillion changed hands in the 1980s. Of course, most acquisitions were or looked "friendly" (it is hard to measure the extent to which negotiated acquisitions are influenced or driven by the threat of a takeover); out of 3336 transactions that occurred in 1986, only 40 were hostile[86] and 110 corresponded to tender offers unopposed by management. Yet the size of some hostile takeovers, their wide media coverage, the personality characteristics of the participants,[87] and the anxiety of managers (few keep their job after a successful raid, so that one of a manager's worst nightmares is to become the target of a takeover bid) all concurred to draw substantial attention to the phenomenon.

84. There are several excellent reviews of the takeover and LBO boom of the 1980s, including Bhagat et al. (1990), Holmström and Kaplan (2001, 2003), Kaplan (1993), Milgrom and Roberts (1992, Chapter 15), and the papers by Shleifer and Vishny, Jensen, Jarrell et al., and Scherer in the 1988 symposium of the *Journal of Economic Perspectives*.

85. This view is, of course, far from being uniform. For example, Peter Drucker, a leading management guru, argued in 1986 that "there can be absolutely no doubt that hostile takeovers are exceedingly bad for the economy." He characterized the high leverage of acquired companies as "severely impairing the company's potential for economic performance." And he condemned the sell-off of the most valuable parts of the acquired businesses (see Bhide 1993b).

86. "Hostile" refers to the fact that the raider invites shareholders to accept the offer whether the board recommends it or not.

87. Bosses under siege, and raiders such as Boone Pickens, Goldsmith, Perelman, Campeau, and Icahn became almost household names. Books about hostile acquisitions, such as *Barbarians at the Gate* by B. Burrough and J. Helyar (New York: Harper & Row, 1990) relating the $25 billion takeover of RJR Nabisco by KKR (a spectacular takeover which started as a management buyout (MBO), but in which management ultimately lost to KKR, who paid more than twice the price prevailing before the bidding war began), turned into bestsellers.

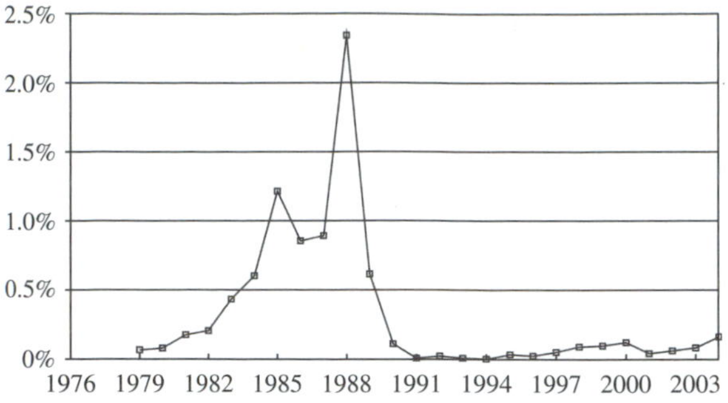

Figure 1.5 Going private volume as percentage of average total stock market value 1979–2003. *Source:* Holmström and Kaplan (2001) and S. Kaplan (personal communication, 2005).

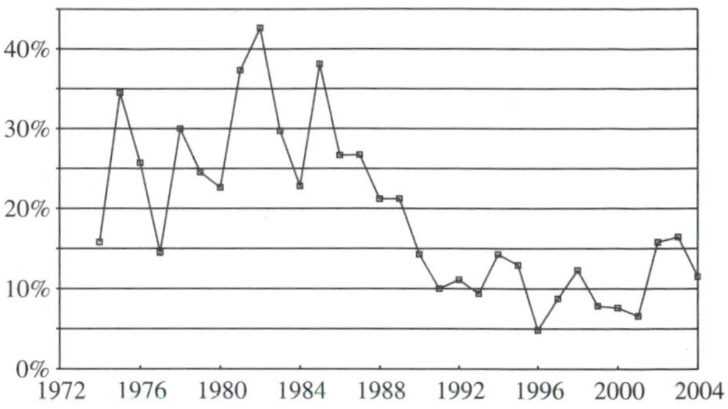

Figure 1.6 Contested tender offers as percentage of total 1974–2004. *Source:* Holmström and Kaplan (2001) and S. Kaplan (personal communication, 2005).

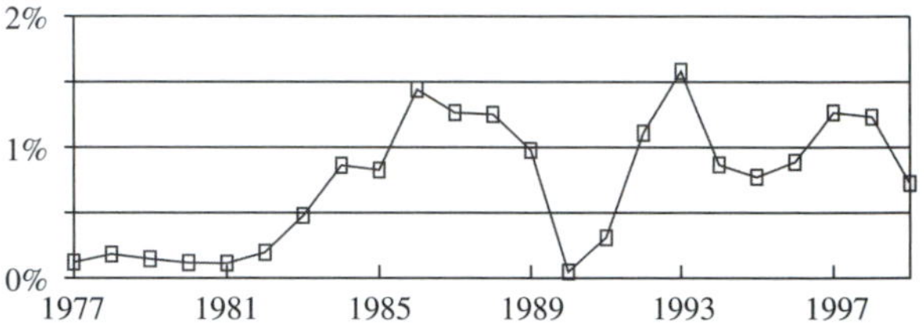

Figure 1.7 Noninvestment grade bond volume (as a percentage of average total stock market capitalization) 1977–1999. *Source:* Holmström and Kaplan (2001).

Second, many publicly traded firms were turned back private through leveraged buyouts, especially management buyouts (see Figure 1.5).

Third, corporate leverage increased substantially during the decade. Firms bought back their own shares, and sometimes put them into Employee Stock Ownership Plans. Furthermore, and associated with the takeover and LBO wave, a new form of public debt, namely, risky or junk bonds, appeared and grew remarkably fast: $32.4 billion of junk bonds were issued in 1986, and the stock of junk bonds had swollen to $175 billion by the fall of 1988 (Stigum 1990, p. 100).

The trend stopped around 1989–1990. The junk bonds used for LBOs and takeovers, especially those issued in the second half of the decade, started defaulting. A number of Savings and Loans, who had been big buyers of junk bonds, went bankrupt.[88] The creator of junk bonds (Michael Milken) and his employer (the investment bank Drexel-Burnham-Lambert, which subsequently went bankrupt) were sued and found guilty of a number of misdemeanors and criminal offenses (insider trading, stock manipulation, fraud, falsified records). Hostile takeovers declined (see Figure 1.6).

While the risky bond market recovered around 1992–1993 (see Figure 1.7), it was then much less related to mergers and acquisitions.

Simultaneously, the popularity of LBOs had waned. Buyouts of public corporations fell from $60 billion in 1988 to $4 billion in 1990 (W. T. Grimm's Mergerstat Review 1991). Takeovers in general collapsed in 1990. Most states had by then put in place restrictive antitakeover laws, partly under the pressure of the Business Roundtable (composed of the CEOs of the 200 largest U.S. corporations).

It should be noted, though, that the volume of mergers and acquisitions was substantially higher in the 1990s than in the 1980s. The recent merger wave,[89] culminating in the 1998–2001 period, was the largest in American history and associated with high stock valuations and the use of equity as a form of payment; but more takeover defenses were in place than in the 1980s. What died out in the 1990s were hostile takeovers.[90]

88. The difficulties faced by the S&Ls did not stem from junk bonds, but with the interest rate shock of the late 1970s, and several mistakes of prudential regulators in the 1980s. However, the S&L disaster added to the general negative feelings about junk bonds.

89. Documented, for example, in Moeller et al. (2003).

90. Meanwhile, hostile takeovers have gained a bit more prominence in Europe, where they have traditionally been very rare. British-based Vodafone's 2000 takeover of the German company Mannesmann for $183 billion, for example, attracted much attention, caused several

Lastly, firms tried to accomplish internally very much what takeovers and LBOs were about. Cost-cutting and leanness became fashionable through concepts such as reengineering, downsizing, focus, and EVA.[91] Share repurchases allowed firms to increase their leverage. And proxy fights such as those led by institutional investors and facilitated by the 1992 new SEC rules provides a substitute mechanism for interfering with management when takeover defenses and antitakeover laws made it difficult to acquire control by purchasing a large number of shares. Before discussing these phenomena, we first review some of the institutional innovations of the decade.

1.5.1 Takeover Bids and Defenses

Although it is generally preceded by a purchase of a "toehold" by the potential acquirer, a takeover process really starts with a tender offer, that is, with an invitation to buy the firm's shares at an announced price. The offer may concern part or all of the stock. And it may be conditional on a certain number of shares being effectively tendered, the idea being that the bidder is often interested in the shares only if he obtains a controlling stake. The bid may also be multitiered, that is, specify a different price for shares beyond some threshold level, or may offer a uniform price for all shares (multitier offers are allowed in the United States, but British raiders cannot pay less to minority shareholders once 30% of the shares have been acquired).

While hostile takeovers have long been part of the American corporate scene, there has been a phenomenal volume of such takeovers in the 1980s, with a peak in 1988–1989. They have been particularly prominent in such industries as oil and gas, mining and minerals, banking and finance, and insurance. Jensen (1988) has argued that takeovers facilitate exit and cash disgorgement in slow-growth industries, where management refuses to unwind its empire and uses the available cash, where there is any, to engage in wasteful diversifications. Relatedly, Morck et al. (1990) find that firms in industries with low ratios of market value of securities over the accounting value of assets (that is, with low "Tobin's Qs") are more likely to be the target of takeover bids.

Management reacted not only by lobbying for restrictive antitakeover laws,[92] but also by adopting (or by convincing shareholders or the board to adopt) takeover defenses. Takeover defenses (which will also be studied in Chapter 11) come in many guises and are sometimes quite ingenious. (See Jarrell et al. (1988) and Malatesta (1992) for more detailed discussions.)

Some defenses, called corporate charter defenses, just *make it technically difficult for the raider to acquire control*. With a *staggered board*, only a fraction of members rather than all directors are up for reelection in a given year, so that a successful raider has to wait for some time after the acquisition to acquire full control. Under a *supermajority rule*, a raider needs $x\%$ of the votes in order to effect a merger or another significant corporate reorganization, such as large asset sales, where x may be 80 or 90 rather than 50 (as it would be under a simple majority rule). *Fair price clauses* attempt to force an acquirer to offer a premium for all shares by imposing a very stringent supermajority clause (nearing shareholder unanimity) unless a high and uniform price is offered for all shares (where "high," for example, means that the bid must exceed the highest share price during the preceding year). Another variation on the supermajority rule consists in placing a number of shares in an Employee Stock Ownership Plan (ESOP). To the extent that employees will vote with management in the event of a takeover (which is likely), ESOPs make it more difficult for a raider to gain control.[93] In the same spirit, *differential voting rights* provide privileged voting rights

law suits, and created a public debate about the large golden parachutes for Mannesmann executives (including 31 million euros for its chairman).

91. EVA refers to "economic value added," a technique promoted by management consulting companies such as Stern Stewart, and which consists in imputing a cost of capital to guide internal investment decisions. See Rogerson (1997) for more detail.

92. For a description of the main antitakeover laws (control share laws, fair price laws, and freeze-out laws), see, for example, Malatesta (1992).

Comment and Schwert (1995) express skepticism about the deterrence effect of antitakeover laws and argue that the collapse of the market for corporate control at the end of the 1980s is due to other factors, such as the recession and the resulting credit crunch. They find, however, that takeover premia paid by raiders are higher when target firms are protected by state laws or by poison pills.

93. See, for example, Pagano and Volpin (2005a) for the deterrent effect of ESOPs in hostile takeover attempts. Dhillon and Ramirez

to shares that are held for an extended period (and so the raider cannot benefit from the corresponding privileges); and *dual-class recapitalizations* provide management or family owners with more votes than would be warranted by their shares. Still another way for a firm to deter takeovers is to change its state of incorporation and *move to a state with tougher antitakeover statutes.*

A second group of takeover defenses amount to diluting the raider's equity, often at the expense of the corporation. The idea is to make the firm less attractive to the raider, perhaps at the cost of making the firm less attractive to anybody else as well. *Scorched-earth policies* consist in selling, possibly at a low price, assets which the raider is particularly keen on acquiring, either because they would create synergies with his own operations or because they would generate a steady flow of cash that would help finance the often highly leveraged acquisition (relatedly, management may try to increase leverage or reduce the amount of corporate cash that can be enjoyed by a potential raider). Entering *litigation* against the raider may also prove an effective deterrent. For, even if the raider is reasonably confident of winning the case, the very cost of litigation may make the prey much less desirable.

Lastly, a wide variety of *poison pills* have been conceived. Poison pills generally refer to special rights of the target's shareholders to purchase additional shares at a low price or sell shares to the firm at a high price conditionally, say, on a raider acquiring a certain fraction of the target's shares. That is, poison pills are call or put options for the target shareholders that have value only in case of a hostile takeover. Poison pills thus reduce the value of equity in the event of a takeover. Popular poison pills include flip-over plans, which, inter alia, allow the shareholder to buy shares in the surviving or merged firm at a substantial discount, say 50%.[94]

To complete this brief description, let us also mention two common practices used by managers, once the takeover process has started, to repel raiders at the expense of shareholder value. Managers sometimes look for a *white knight*, namely, an alternative acquirer with a friendlier attitude vis-à-vis current management and willing to bid up the price; the presence of the white knight may discourage the raider (who, remember, has to find the funds for the takeover attempt) and the firm may end up being sold at a relatively low price to the white knight. Perhaps the most controversial defense of all is the practice of *greenmail* (or targeted block stock repurchases), through which management, using company money, purchases at a premium the raider's block of the target's stock. Greenmail can be viewed as a form of collusion between management and the raider at the expense of other shareholders.

Let us conclude this discussion of takeover institutions and strategies with a puzzle (that will be discussed in Part IV of the book). Leaving aside statutory defenses, which lie outside the firm's control, one may question the process through which corporate charter (supermajority amendments, fair price clauses, staggered boards, changes in the state of incorporation) and other defenses (greenmail, litigation against the raider, poison pills) come about. The former require ratification by the shareholders, while the latter are subject to board approval without shareholder ratification. In view of the substantial conflict of interest faced by management in such matters and of the fact that greenmail and the adoption of poison pills are usually greeted by a negative stock price reaction,[95] it is not *a priori* clear why boards exert so little control and why corporate charter defenses are so often approved by shareholders. This rubber-stamping of managerial

(1994) point out that ESOPs, like many other antitakeover devices, have two effects: a reduction in the occurrence of takeovers and an increase in the relative bargaining power of the firm vis-à-vis the raider (see Chapter 11 for a study of these two effects); using the 1989 Delaware court decision on Polaroid's ESOP, establishing the legality of ESOPs as a takeover defense, Dhillon and Ramirez find that the overall stock price reaction upon the announcement of an ESOP tended to be positive over their sample period, consistent with the relative bargaining power effect, but that, after the Delaware court decision, it was strongly negative for those firms that were already subject to takeover speculation, consistent with the managerial entrenchment hypothesis.

94. The term "flip-over" refers to the fact that formally the plans are call options given as dividends to the target shareholders. The shareholder can exercise these options at a high price in the case of a takeover and the firm can redeem these options at a nominal fee before a bid or acquisition. The impediment resides mainly in the flip-over provision, which gives old shareholders the right to dilute the firm after a takeover.

95. See, for example, Jarrell et al. (1988) and Malatesta (1992) for reviews of the evidence.

proposals in the matter of takeover defenses raises the question of whether they increase incumbent shareholders' wealth (for one thing, they may force the raider to bid a higher price: on this see Chapter 11), or whether this is just another illustration of managerial entrenchment and poor corporate governance.

1.5.2 Leveraged Buyouts

Roughly speaking, a leveraged buyout (LBO) consists in taking a firm private by purchasing its shares and allocating them to a concentrated ownership composed of management, a general partner, and other investors (the limited partners or LBO fund). Due to the dearth of equity of the owners, the new entity is highly leveraged. Typically, top-level managers (either incumbent managers, often under the threat of a takeover, or a dissenting team) ally with an LBO specialist who brings equity of his own and also finds investors to cofinance the LBO. An LBO involving current management is called a management buyout (MBO).[96] Either way, the coalition acquires the outstanding shares and divides equity in roughly the following fashion: management receives 10–30%,[97] and the buyout partnership, namely, the LBO specialist (who sits on the board) and the investors, pick up the remainder. An LBO specialist such as KKR (Kohlberg–Kravis–Roberts) as a general partner typically has 20% of the nonexecutive shares while the limited partners purchase the remaining 80%.[98]

The flip side of concentrated ownership is that the coalition must also issue a substantial amount of debt. Leverage ratios in LBOs were as high as 20:1 in the 1980s (and fell below 5:1 in the 1990s; typical debt-to-equity LBO ratios have only been 40–60% in recent years). In Kaplan's (1990) sample, the average ratio of long-term debt over debt plus equity for firms subject to a buyout was about 20% before the buyout and 85% after completion of the buyout.

Substantial managerial stock ownership is all the more important as the LBO sponsor usually has a very lean structure. The sponsor intervenes actively in key strategic decisions, but must operate arm's-length vis-à-vis everyday operating choices. Jensen's (1989a) survey of LBO partnerships finds an average staff of 13 professionals and 19 nonprofessionals in an LBO partnership. The world's largest LBO partnership, KKR, had 16 professionals and 44 additional employees.[99]

Typically, banks provide two types of loan: long-term senior loans with maturity of, say, seven years, and short-term loans that are used as bridges until junk bonds are issued. Junk bonds are public debt which is junior to bank debt in several respects: they are unsecured and include few covenants; their principal is not amortized before maturity; and their maturity, ten years, say, exceeds that of bank loans. Junk bonds are evidently risky and are often renegotiated (towards reduced interest payments, stretched-out maturities, and equity-for-debt swaps). In 1986, they were held mainly by mutual funds (32%), insurance companies (32%), pension funds (12%), individuals (12%), and thrifts (8%).[100]

The proclaimed virtues of the buyout partnership arrangement are (a) stronger monetary incentives for the firm's managers relative to those of a publicly traded corporation,[101] (b) active monitoring taken seriously, in which the general partner has both the incentives and the means of intervention, and (c) high leverage, which forces management and the partnership to work out cost reductions and improvements in efficiency, and to sell divisions (possibly in the form of MBOs with the managers of these divisions!).

It is worth emphasizing that buyout partnerships do not function as conglomerates. For example, KKR,

96. The ownership pattern much resembles the financing of start-ups by venture capitalists, described in Chapter 2. There are a couple of differences, though. In particular, start-ups generate lower income, and are therefore not much leveraged, while LBOs often concern firms with steady cash flows and are highly leveraged.

97. The median management equity ownership of the post-buyout companies in the Kaplan and Stein (1993) sample of MBOs was 22.3% (as opposed to 5% in the pre-buyout entities).

98. All shares are owned by the private equity group. The sharing rule just alluded to governs the split of the capital gains once the investment is exited.

99. Interestingly, it took over companies with large headquarters, sometimes exceeding 5,000 employees.

100. S. Rasky, "Tracking junk bond owners," *The New York Times*, December 7, 1986, cited in Perry and Taggart (1993).

101. Jensen (1989a,b) estimates that in the 1980s the average CEO in an LBO firm receives \$64 per \$1,000 increase in shareholder value, as opposed to \$3 for the average Fortune 1000 firm.

a well-known general partner in LBOs,[102] keeps its companies[103] separate. The companies thus operate as stand-alone entities and do not cross-subsidize each other. As a matter of fact, cross-subsidization is prohibited by the statutes of the partnership. The LBO sponsor must ask its institutional investors for permission to transfer any cash from one LBO division to another. And LBO funds must return capital from exited investments to the limited and general partners and are not allowed to reinvest the funds.

Another point worth noting is that KKR sticks to the companies for five to ten years before exiting. This gives it nonnegligible incentives to invest for the long run. When successful, it resells its share to another large investor or takes the company public again. As is the case for a venture capitalist, these exit options allow KKR to free equity to invest in new ventures (on this, see Chapter 9).[104]

Concerning leverage, LBO targets have to generate large and steady cash flows in order to service the high debt payments. Thus LBOs can be successful only for mature industries with these cash-flow characteristics. Examples of such industries that have been mentioned in the literature are oil and gas, mining and chemicals, forest products, broadcasting, tobacco, food processing, and tyres.[105] Still, there have been a number of defaults, mainly for the deals that took place in the second half of the decade. Kaplan and Stein (1993) analyze a sample of 124 large MBOs completed during the 1980s. Of the 41 deals completed between 1980 and 1984, only one defaulted on its debt; in contrast, 22 of the 83 deals put together between 1985 and 1989 defaulted. Kaplan and Stein find that the MBOs put together in the second half of the decade were characterized by (a) high purchase prices (relative to cash flows), (b) riskier industries, (c) smaller and more secured positions held by banks, and substantial junk bond financing, and (d) more up-front payments to management and deal makers. In a nutshell, the MBOs became riskier during the decade. As Kaplan and Stein note, this evidence is consistent with loose statements about an "overheated buyout market" and "too much financing chasing too few good deals" in the second half of the decade, but it does not quite explain why financial markets made such mistakes.

LBOs are, most likely, a circumscribed phenomenon. Most observers (including Jensen) agree that they can apply only to firms with specific characteristics, namely, strong and predictable cash flows. As will be emphasized in Chapter 5, it would be a mistake, for example, to burden firms in growth industries (in which investment needs exceed the cash flows) with high levels of debt; similarly, debt may be a dangerous form of finance for firms with risky cash flows. Rappaport (1990) further argues that the "reliquification objective" implies that LBOs are a transitory form of organization. LBO sponsors and limited partners want to be able to cash out, in the form of a return to public corporation status or negotiated sales, in order to be able to invest in new firms (sponsors) or to face their liquidity needs (institutions). Not only do most LBO limited-partnership agreements have a limited duration (often ten years), but the exit option is often exercised before the end of the partnership. Rappaport cites a Kidder Peabody study on 90 initial public offerings (IPOs) for buyout corporations between 1983 and 1988, in which 70% of the companies were taken public within three years of their LBO date.

1.5.3 The Rise of Takeovers and the Backlash: What Happened?

There are several competing hypotheses for what happened in the 1980s in the United States. None of these hypotheses is a satisfactory explanation by itself, but all offer some insights about the events.[106]

102. KKR is not only known for spectacular takeovers such as the RJR Nabisco one. It has also rewarded its investors (wealthy individuals, commercial banks, pension funds) over a span of 20 years with a 23.5% annual return, compared with around 15% for the stock market index (S&P 500) (*The Economist*, August 2, 1997, p. 77).

KKR itself has been very profitable. Its profits do not come solely from the capital gains on its equity investments (merchant banker activity). As an agent for the investors, it receives a 1.5% management fee, a retainer fee for monitoring performance, and a fee for servicing on boards of directors (agency activity). Lastly, it receives a 1% fee after the deals are completed (investment banking activity). See Kaufman et al. (1995, Chapter 10).

103. That is, 15 in April 1991, with combined revenues $40 billion.

104. The exit may be fully planned in the original deal; for example, the limited partnership may be limited to last ten years.

105. One-third of the LBOs in the manufacturing sector between 1978 and 1988 took place in the food and tobacco industries. Seventy percent of LBOs in the nonmanufacturing sector concerned retail trade and services (Rappaport 1990).

106. A more complete, and very useful discussion, of the hypotheses can be found in Holmström and Kaplan (2001, 2003).

Hypothesis 1: Decline of corporate governance. The first possibility, stressed by Jensen (1984, 1988, 1989a,b) and Jensen and Ruback (1983) among others, is that the previous system of corporate governance was basically broke. The lack of monitoring by the board and large shareholders was, of course, nothing new in 1980, but it may have been particularly costly in a period of excess liquidities, i.e., in a period in which managers had substantial amounts of cash to spend. According to Jensen, entrenched managers refused (and were not forced by boards) to disgorge their excess cash flow and rather invested it in unattractive projects. Furthermore, international competition, deregulation and technological change implied that a number of firms had to exit or downsize. The proponents of this hypothesis thus argue that the capital market substituted for a deficient corporate governance, and helped fire inefficient managers, allocate corporate cash to its most efficient uses, and create an efficient exit.

Hypothesis 2: Financial innovation. Another and complementary hypothesis, also often associated with Jensen, holds that LBOs created a new and superior form of corporate governance for mature industries. High-powered executive compensation, "external management" by active monitors such as KKR, and high leverage all created, according to Jensen, better incentives for efficiency.[107] The financing of these LBOs was facilitated by the development of a junk bond market during the decade. The fact that few industries are good candidates for LBOs and the decline of LBOs in the 1990s imply that this explanation has only limited scope.

Hypothesis 3: Break-up of conglomerates. According to this hypothesis, takeovers targeted the conglomerate empires built in the 1960s and 1970s. These conglomerates had proved unmanageable, but managers did not want to reduce the size of their empires through "bust-ups" (sales of divisions to other companies) and "spin-offs" (transformations of divisions into independent companies). An external intervention was called for that had to downsize these conglomerates and make them focus on their core business.[108]

A variant of this hypothesis demonstrates the lenient enforcement of antitrust statutes under the Republican administrations of the 1980s. This relaxation of competition policy resulted in new opportunities for horizontal and vertical mergers. In this variant, the driver for the bust-ups is not the lack of focus of the existing conglomerates, but rather the nonrealization of "synergies" (understand: exploitation of market power) under the existing structures.

There are a number of other hypotheses for the takeover wave of the 1980s, including speculative excesses and transfers from employees, the bondholders, and the Treasury (to which we come back shortly).

What is the *verdict for the 1980s?*

Large gain for target shareholders. The winners were without doubt the target shareholders. While estimates differ and also vary with the type of takeover,[109] a 30% premium is definitely in the ballpark.

Neutral outcome for the acquirer. Most estimates show that the bidders neither gained nor lost, or else that they lost slightly in value (see Kaplan (1997) for a review). There are several possible explanations for this fact. The first is consistent with the notion that takeovers create value and is based on Grossman and Hart's (1980) free-riding argument (see Chapter 11). According to this argument, a raider cannot offer less than the post-acquisition value of the firm and have the target shareholders tender their shares; for, it would then be optimal for an individual shareholder to refuse to tender his shares and to enjoy the higher value of the post-acquisition firm. But if all shareholders behave this way, the raider cannot acquire control and the value-increasing changes are never implemented. While the free-rider problem is important and certainly contributes to explaining low returns for the acquirers, it depicts only an extreme case and there is every reason to believe that a raider should be able to make some profit (see

107. Kaplan (1989) provides evidence of improvements in operating profits in a sample of leveraged buyouts pulled together in the 1980s.

108. See, for example, Bhagat et al. (1990) and Kaplan and Weisbach (1992). Kaplan (1997), reviewing the evidence, argues that there was no deconglomeration in the 1980s in the United States. But there was, perhaps, unwinding of bad diversification.

109. For example, Kaplan and Stein find a 43% premium for their sample of MBOs.

Chapter 11). So, another argument seems needed if we want to explain the neutral or negative effect of takeovers on the acquirers' value. One possibility, less consistent with the view that takeovers are value enhancing, is that acquirers themselves are agents and misuse the resources entrusted to them. And, indeed, acquisitions are a quick and easy way for managers to expand the scope of their control and build empires.[110]

Where does the overall gain come from? Takeovers are associated with an increase in total value (target plus acquirer). Somehow, investors must believe that gains will result from the change in control. Where do these gains come from? Again, there are two possible views on this. The antitakeover view asserts that they primarily result from transfers from stakeholders (laid-off employees, expropriated bondholders and Treasury, consumers hurt by the merged firms' market power) to shareholders. There is little evidence that takeovers reduce wages and generate unemployment,[111] although they may do so in particular instances: the takeover of TWA by Icahn implied wage losses for unionized workers (Shleifer and Summers 1988). More likely, white-collar employees may be laid off when a merger leads to a cut in redundant headquarters personnel. In any case, the transfers from employees to shareholders do not seem commensurate with the overall gain to shareholders.[112] Several papers have similarly studied the possibility the increased leverage could have hurt the bondholders, or the Treasury due to tax shields (see Jarrell et al. 1988). These studies too conclude that these effects are small on average (although they can be significant in specific transactions). All these studies combined suggest that the pro-takeover view, according to which takeovers are efficiency enhancing, must have at least some validity for the 1980s (see below for a contrast with the 1990s). It is quite possible that takeovers indeed prevented some managers from wasting free cash flow and forced some exit or curtailments in excess capacity. And it seems that takeovers did not have a large negative impact on long-term investments such as R&D expenditures (see, for example, Hall 1990).

Contrast with subsequent mergers and acquisitions. As discussed above the merger wave that peaked in the 1998–2001 period was the largest in American history. It differs from that of 1980s not only through its reduced emphasis on hostile takeovers: it also seems to have led to wealth destruction. Moeller et al. (2003) estimate that, from 1998 through 2001, shareholders of acquiring firms lost $240 billion and that this loss was not offset by a larger gain by shareholders of the target firms. Indeed, the combined loss when adding the targets' gains was still $134 billion.

How meaningful is the overall-gain test? Suppose that it is established empirically that a sizeable fraction of the net gains from takeovers to shareholders does not come from transfers from other stakeholders. This still does not quite settle the takeover debate for two reasons. First, there are hidden benefits and costs of takeovers that may not be properly accounted for. On the benefit side, those managers whose firm ends up not being taken over may still operate value enhancements through fear that inaction would trigger a takeover. Such benefits from the "contestability" of the managerial position may be hard to measure. On the cost side, the possibility of takeovers creates incentives to underinvest in unobservable long-term investments. Takeovers may also induce managers to engage in costly defenses or to focus most of their attention on producing good earnings reports or looking for white knights (see Chapters 7 and 11). Such costs are also hard to measure. A second issue is that of the reference point. In particular, one must ask whether the benefits of takeovers cannot be achieved in other ways, for example, through improved corporate governance and whether these alternative ways would not generate the same costs as takeovers. More theoretical and

110. Shleifer and Vishny (1988). Morck et al. (1990) point out that half of the announcements of takeovers are greeted with a negative stock price reaction from the bidder's shareholders. Behavioral hypotheses (in terms of managerial hubris) have also been offered to explain the lack of profits of acquirers: see the introduction to the book for references to the behavioral literature.

111. Bhagat et al. (1990) and Lichtenberg and Siegel (1990) find a limited impact of hostile takeovers on employment (except, perhaps, for redundant white-collar employees).

112. For a review of the evidence, see Kaplan (1997), who further points out that many firms that did not undergo a takeover laid off workers over the 1980s and early 1990s; for example, General Motors and General Electric reduced the workforce by over 200,000 and 100,000, respectively.

empirical work is needed in order to have a better assessment of the benefits and costs of takeovers.[113]

1.6 Debt as a Governance Mechanism

Our discussion so far has largely focused on the impact of shareholders in corporate governance. We now turn to that of debt claims.

1.6.1 Debt as an Incentive Mechanism

Leaving aside the possible tax advantages of debt, which are sometimes an important consideration in the design of financial structures but are country- and time-specific, debt is often viewed as a disciplining device, especially if its maturity is relatively short. By definition, debt forces the firm to disgorge cash flow. In so doing, it puts pressure on managers in several related ways (the theoretical foundations and implications of these informal arguments will be studied in Chapters 3, 5, and 10).

• By taking cash out of the firm, it prevents managers from "consuming" it. That is, it reduces their ability to turn their "free cash flow" into lavish perks or futile negative net present value investments.

• Debt incentivizes the company's executives. Managers must contemplate their future obligation to repay creditors on time, and therefore must pay attention to generate cash flows beyond the future debt repayments or else enhance their firm's prospect so as to facilitate future issues of claims. Absent such efforts, they may become cash-strapped and be unable to sink even desirable reinvestments. This threat of illiquidity has a positive disciplining effect on management.

At the extreme, the firm may be liquidated in the context of a bankruptcy process, leading to an increase in the probability of termination of employment, frustration, and stigma for the managers who led the firm to its end.[114]

• Under financial distress, but in the absence of liquidation, the nonrepayment of debt puts the creditors in the driver's seat. Roughly speaking, creditors acquire control rights over the firm. They need not formally acquire such rights. But they hold another crucial right: that of forcing the firm into bankruptcy. This threat indirectly gives them some control over the firm's policies.

As we will later discuss, management is not indifferent as to who exercises control over their firms: different claimholders, through the cash-flow rights attached to their claims, have different incentives when interfering with the firm's management. In particular, debtholders tend to be more "conservative" than equityholders, as they get none of the upside benefits and in contrast suffer from downside evolutions. They are therefore more inclined to limit risk, especially by cutting investment and new projects.[115]

• Finally, when the managers hold a substantial amount of claims over the firm's cash flow, debtholding by investors has the benefit of making managers by and large residual claimants for their performance. An (extreme) illustration of this point arises when an entrepreneur's borrowing needs are relatively small and there is enough guaranteed future income (collateral, or certain cash flow) to repay the corresponding debt. Then, issuing debt to investors implies that any increase in the firm's profit goes to the entrepreneur. Put differently, the entrepreneur fully internalizes the increase in profit brought about by her actions, and so faces the "right incentives" to minimize cost and maximize profit.

1.6.2 Limits to Debt as a Governance Mechanism

Throughout this book, we will also emphasize that debt is by no means a panacea. There are several

113. Despite obvious selection biases, clinical analyses may also shed some light about value creation and destruction in mergers and acquisitions. For example, the analysis of two acquisitions in Kaplan et al. (1997) sheds some light on the potential pitfalls: lack of understanding of the target by the managers of the acquiring firm, failure to realize synergies, diversion of the acquiring firm's management's attention, complexity of compensation design, and so forth.

114. In Zwiebel (1996), managers choose debt as a commitment to produce high profits in the short run. The bankruptcy process is viewed as facilitating managerial turnover in the case of poor performance, relative to equity-based channels of managerial turnover (takeovers, or dismissal via the board, or a proxy fight). Issuing debt or distributing dividends (or, more generally, any policy that makes a liquidity crisis in the case of poor performance more likely) therefore increases sensitivity of turnover to poor performance and makes shareholders more comfortable with current management.

115. At the extreme, debtholders are more keen on liquidating a firm than shareholders: for the former, a bird in the hand—the value of liquidated assets—is worth two in the bush—the uncertain prospect of full repayment.

reasons why this is so; this section emphasizes two such reasons.

Cost of illiquidity. The flip side of threatening management with a shortage of future cash flow is that cash disgorgements may actually end up depriving the firm from the liquidities it needs to finance ongoing projects and start on new ones, since the firm's cash flow and reinvestment needs are affected by uncertainty that lies beyond the reach of managerial control: input prices may rise, competitors may enter the market, projects may face hardships over which managers have no control, and so forth. Furthermore, risk management opportunities may be limited; that is, the firm may not be able to insure at a reasonable cost against these exogenous shocks.

The firm, when facing an adverse shock to its cash flow or its reinvestment needs, could, of course, return to the capital market and raise funds by issuing new securities (bonds, bank debt, equity), as stressed, in particular, by Myers (1977). For several reasons, though, returning to the capital markets is unlikely to provide enough liquidity. First, issuing new securities in good conditions may take time and liquidity needs, for example, for paying employees and suppliers, may be pressing. Second, and more fundamentally,[116] the capital market may be reluctant to refinance the firm. They will not be able to recoup fully the benefits attached to refinancing as some of these benefits will necessarily go to insiders. Furthermore, they may be uncertain about the firm's prospects and the value of existing assets, and therefore worry about adverse selection—the possibility that securities have low value. Consequently, debt claims, especially of short maturity, expose the firm to the risk of liquidity associated with credit rationing in the refinancing market.

Bankruptcy costs. At the extreme, the firm's inability to repay the debt coupons may push it into bankruptcy. Bankruptcy processes vary substantially across the world, but to fix our ideas, it may be useful to take the U.S. case as an illustration (with the caveat that the U.S. bankruptcy institutions are particularly lenient on managers as compared with other countries). There are two main forms of bankruptcy. Under Chapter 7, the firm's assets are liquidated by a court-appointed trustee; the priority of claims (who is paid first?) is respected.[117] Firms rarely file bankruptcy under Chapter 7 directly, however. Rather, they use Chapter 11, which allows for a workout in which a reorganization plan is designed and thus liquidation is at least temporarily avoided.[118] Indeed, it may be the case that the firm is unable to pay its debt, but has a positive ongoing value for investors as a whole. To let the firm continue, it is then necessary for creditors to make concessions, for example, by forgiving some of their debt and taking equity in exchange.[119] Management is then given six months (or more if the bankruptcy judge extends the period) to formulate a reorganization plan. Creditors can propose their own plan afterwards. A reorganization plan must be approved by a qualified majority (e.g., one-half in number, two-thirds in amount).[120] In the absence of approval, creditors can finally force the firm into entering Chapter 7.

Chapter 11 is often heralded by its proponents as enabling firms to design plans that let them continue if they have valuable assets or prospects; its critics, in contrast, argue that management, equityholders, and junior, unsecured creditors have the ability to delay the resolution, at great cost to senior creditors. They further argue that the bankruptcy process is not as strong a disciplining device as it should be. Gilson (1990), based on a study of 111 U.S. firms, reports that 44% of CEOs (and 46% of directors) are still in place four years after the start of the bankruptcy

116. Note that the two reasons are related. Suppose, for example, that information about the firm's state is widely available. Then it should not take long to raise cash by issuing new securities. It is in part because investors are uncertain about the firm's prospects and the value of existing assets that they need time to analyze the firm's condition and that it takes time to issue securities.

117. The "Absolute Priority Rule" (APR) distributes the firm's payoffs according to priority. In particular, junior claimholders receive nothing until senior claimholders are fully paid.

118. Under Chapter 11, all payments to creditors are suspended (automatic stay), and the firm can obtain additional financing by granting new claims seniority over existing ones. A number of proposals have been made in the literature to replace Chapter 11, deemed too slow in removing inefficient management, by a new bankruptcy procedure that would still facilitate the renegotiation of existing claims (see, in particular, Bebchuk 1988; Aghion et al. 1992).

119. Exchange offers are only one of the actions that can be taken to reorganize the company. Others include asset sales, reduced capital expenditures, and private debt restructuring.

120. See Asquith et al. (1994) and Gertner and Scharfstein (1991) for empirical evidence and theoretical considerations relative to workouts.

process. Even if managers must cope with stricter covenants and often more powerful monitoring (by a large block shareholder) after bankruptcy, the process still proves relatively lenient towards them.

Workouts are desirable if they serve to protect stakeholders (including employees) who would suffer from a liquidation, and are undesirable if their main function is to hold up senior creditors and delay a liquidation that is socially efficient.

The workout *process* may fail for several reasons.

Transaction costs. It is difficult to bring to the bargaining table many groups of stakeholders. Even leaving aside employees and fiscal authorities, who have claims over the firm, a number of claimholders with very dissonant objectives must be induced to engage in serious bargaining: holders of debt claims with various covenants, maturities, degree of collateralization, and trade creditors (just think of the number of trade creditors involved in the bankruptcy of a large retailer!). Other stakeholders may have a stake in the firm without having formal claims over its cash flow. For example, if a supplier of Boeing or Airbus is about to go bankrupt, then the airplane manufacturer may bend over backwards and enter into a long-term supply agreement in order to keep the supplier afloat. This example illustrates the fact that even parties without an existing claim in the firm may need to be brought to the bargaining table.

Bargaining inefficiencies. Bargaining between the various parties may be inefficient—the Coase Theorem may not apply—for a variety of reasons. Prominent among them is asymmetric information, between insiders and outsiders and among outsiders.[121] Each party may be reluctant to enter a deal in which it suspects that other parties are willing to sign because it is favorable to them. Relatedly, some bargaining parties may attempt to hold up other parties by delaying the resolution.[122] Their ability to do so depends on the specifics of the bankruptcy process. A unanimity rule, applied either within a class of claimholders or across classes of claimholders, aims at protecting all claimholders; but it gives each individual claimholder or each class of claimholders the ability to hold up the entire reorganization process: they can threaten not to sign up and wait until they are bought out at a handsome price. This is why bankruptcy processes often specify only qualified majorities.[123]

Costs of the bankruptcy process can be decomposed into two categories:

Direct costs include the legal and other expenses directly attached to the process. Most studies have found that direct costs are relatively small, a few percent of market value of equity plus book value of debt (see, for example, Warner 1977; Altman 1984; Weiss 1990).

Indirect costs, associated with managerial decisions in anticipation of or during bankruptcy, are much harder to define and to measure; but they seem to be much more substantial than direct costs. In principle, bankruptcy costs may include the actions, such as gambling, taken by incumbent management in order to avoid entering the bankruptcy process, and the costs of cautious management during the process.[124]

1.7 International Comparisons of the Policy Environment

The book will emphasize the many contractual concessions firms make to investors in order to boost pledgeable income and raise funds: covenants, monitoring structures, control rights, board composition, takeover defenses, financial structure, and so forth. Bilateral and multilateral agreements between firms and their investors do not occur in an institutional vacuum, though. Rather, the firms' ability to

121. Asymmetric information between insiders and outsiders is stressed, for example, in Giammarino (1989).

122. Free riding was first emphasized in Grossman and Hart (1980).

123. The debate between unanimity and qualified majority rules has a long-standing counterpart in international finance. In particular, many sovereign bonds are issued under New York law, which requires unanimity for renegotiation (i.e., agreement to forgive some of the debt). In contrast, sovereign bonds issued under U.K. law specify only a qualified majority for approval of a deal renegotiated with the issuing country. Proponents of the New York law approach argue that it is precisely because renegotiations are difficult that discipline is imposed on the government. Critics, in contrast, point at the holdups and inefficiencies brought about by the unanimity rule. Much more detailed descriptions and analyses of the debate can be found in, for example, Eichengreen and Portes (1997, 2000) and Bolton and Jeanne (2004).

124. We refer to Senbet and Seward (1995) for a discussion of these as well as for a broader survey of the bankruptcy literature.

commit to return funds to their investors depends on a policy environment that is exogenous to individual firms. As defined in Chapter 16, "contracting institutions" refer to the laws and regulations that govern contracts and contract enforcement, as well as, more broadly, to the other policy variables such as taxes, labor laws, and macroeconomic policies that affect pledgeable income and value.[125] Contracting institutions vary substantially across countries, and so, as a result, do financial development and corporate governance.[126]

An active line of research, initiated by La Porta, Lopez-de-Silanes, Shleifer, and Vishny (1997, 1998, 1999, 2000),[127] studies the relationship between countries' legal structures and corporate finance. La Porta et al. consider two broad legal traditions. *Common law*, which prevails in most English-speaking countries, emphasizes judiciary independence, reactivity to precedents, and limited codification. *Civil law*, in contrast, stresses codification (e.g., the Napoleonic and Bismarckian codes) and is historically more associated with politically determined careers for judges (judges have only recently gained their independence in France, for example); furthermore, its more centralized determination makes it easier for interest groups to capture it than under common law. There are three broad subcategories of civil law: French, German, and Scandinavian. Both common law and civil law have spread through conquest, colonization, import, or imitation.[128]

La Porta et al. derive some interesting correlations between legal systems and investor protection. They measure investor protection through a list of qualitative variables: e.g., one-share–one-vote, proxy by mail allowed, judicial venue for minority shareholders to challenge managerial decisions, preemptive rights for new issues of stocks, ability to call extraordinary shareholders' meetings, in the case of *shareholder protection*; and creditors' consent to file for reorganization, inability for the debtor to retain administration of property during a reorganization, ability for secured creditors to gain possession of that security, respect of priority rules in bankruptcy, in the case of *creditor protection*. Shareholder rights are then aggregated in an "antidirector rights index," and creditor rights in a "creditor rights index."

A key finding is that the protection of shareholders is strongest in common law countries, weakest in French-style civil law countries, with German- and Scandinavian-style law countries somewhere in between.[129]

As one would expect, the extent of investor protection impacts the development of financial markets. Indeed, the work of La Porta et al. was partly motivated by country-specific observation. La Porta et al. (1997) documented a positive covariation between shareholder protection and the breadth of the equity market.[130] For example, in Italy (French-origin civil law system) (see Pagano et al. 1998), companies rarely go public, and the voting premium (the price difference between two shares with the same cash-flow rights but different voting rights) is much larger than in the United States (a common law country).[131] Similarly, Germany's stock market capitalization is rather small relative to GDP.

More generally, common law countries have the highest ratio of external capital (especially equity) to GDP. (But, as Rajan and Zingales (2003) note, legal origins alone cannot explain why, in 1913, the ratio of stock market capitalization over GDP was twice as high in France as in the United States.) Common law countries also have the largest numbers of firms undergoing IPOs. The reader will find in Rajan and Zingales (2003) both a series of measures of countries'

125. Chapter 16 will further study "property rights institutions," referring to the permanence of the contracting institutions and the time-consistency of government policies.

126. This section briefly reviews some of the empirical work on comparative corporate governance. As we discussed in this chapter, there is also a large institutional literature comparing the main financial systems (see, for example, Allen and Gale 2000, Part 1; Berglöf 1988; Charkham 1994; Kindelberger 1993).

127. See also La Porta, Lopez-de-Silanes, and Shleifer (1999).

128. Glaeser and Shleifer (2002) argue that the foundations for English and French common and civil laws in the twelfth and thirteenth centuries were reactions to the local environments.

129. The exception to this rule is that *secured* creditors are best protected in German- and Scandinavian-origin legal systems.

130. Pagano and Volpin (2005b) also find a positive covariation, although a weaker one, for their panel data. They show, in particular, that the dispersion in shareholder protection has declined since the La Porta et al. study, in that the La Porta et al. measures of shareholder protection have substantially converged towards the best practice in the 1993–2002 interval.

131. Premia commanded by voting shares are 5.4% for the United States, 13.3% in the United Kingdom, 29% in Germany, 51.3% in France, and 81.5% in Italy (compilation by Faccio and Lang (2002) of various studies).

financial development[132] as well as a discussion of the relevance of such measures.

Relatedly, we would also expect systems with poor investor protection to resort to substitute mechanisms. La Porta et al. (1998) consider two such mechanisms. One is the use of bright-line rules, such as the possibility of mandatory dividends in countries with poor shareholder protection. More importantly, one would expect such countries to have a more concentrated ownership structure, since such a structure creates incentives for high-intensity monitoring and curbs managerial misbehavior (see Chapter 9). La Porta et al. (1998, Table 8) indeed find a sharply higher concentration of ownership in countries with French-style civil law.[133]

La Porta, Lopez-de-Silanes, and Shleifer (1999) more generally document that large firms in non-Anglo-Saxon countries are typically controlled by large resident shareholders or a group of shareholders. Looking at the top 20 firms in each country as ranked by market capitalization of common equity at the end of 1995, they show that, on average, 36% are "widely held," 31% "family controlled," 18% "state-controlled," and 15% in "residual categories" (defining categories is no straightforward task; see their paper for details). Quite crucially, widely held firms are much more common in countries with a good investor protection; for example, all top 20 firms in the United Kingdom and 16 out of the top 20 firms in the United States are widely held.[134] A similar picture emerges for medium-size firms. Specific evidence on the control of European firms can be found in the book edited by Barca and Becht (2002), whose findings (summarized by Becht and Mayer) confirm the sharp contrast between continental Europe and Anglo-Saxon countries. Control is concentrated in Europe not only because of the presence of large investors, but also by the absence of significant holdings by others. In the United States and the United Kingdom, in contrast, the second and third shareholders are often not noticeably smaller than the first.

Davydenko and Franks (2004) make similar observations on the debt side using a sample of small firms defaulting in their bank debt in France, Germany, and the United Kingdom. Of the three countries, France clearly exhibits the weakest protection of creditor rights: court-administered procedures are mandated by law to pursue the preservation of the firm as a going concern and the maintenance of employment; and, in the case of liquidation, even secured lenders rank behind the state and the employees in terms of priority. By contrast, U.K. secured creditors can impose the privately contracted procedure specified by the debt contract and they receive absolute priority in recovering their claims. Davydenko and Franks indeed find that medium recovery rates for creditors are 92% in the United Kingdom, 67% in Germany, and 56% in France.[135] The theory developed in Section 4.3 predicts that French firms will want to offer more collateral in order to make up for the shortage in pledgeable income. Davydenko and Franks show that collateralization (in particular of receivables) is high in France.

This analysis raises a number of interesting questions. First, the relative convergence between common and civil law systems makes it unlikely that legal origins by themselves can explain the current differences in corporate governance and financial institutions, between, say, the United States and the United Kingdom on the one hand, and continental Europe on the other. Some source of hysteresis must be involved that preserves systems with strong (weak) investor protection. This brings us to a second point: legal institutions, and more broadly contracting institutions, are endogenous; they are fashioned by political coalitions, which themselves depend, among other things, on financial outcomes (see Chapter 16). A case in point is the emergence of stricter antitakeover legislation in the United States in the wake of the hostile takeover wave of the 1980s. The broader theme of a political determination of

132. For example, equity issues over gross fixed capital formation for the corporate sector, deposits over GDP for the banking sector, stock market capitalization, or number of companies listed related to GDP.

133. They also find that large economies and more equal societies have a lower ownership concentration.

134. While La Porta et al. attribute dispersed ownership in the United States to good investor protection, Roe (1994) in contrast emphasizes populist regulatory impediments to concentrated ownership in that country.

135. Their sample covers the 1996–2003 period, except for France (1993–2003 period).

corporate finance institutions is developed at length by, for example, Roe (2003).[136,137]

Remark (determinants of institutions). La Porta et al.'s correlation between legal system and investor protection is revisited in Acemoglu et al. (2001), who look at European colonization and argue that the mode of settlement, more than the legal system, had a bigger impact on contracting institutions. They divide colonies into two broad categories: those (Africa, Central America, Caribbean, South Asia) where the Europeans had little interest in settling—perhaps due to high mortality rates—and developed "extractive institutions," which allowed little protection for private property and few checks and balances against government expropriation; and those in which Europeans settled in larger numbers (United States, Canada, Australia, New Zealand) and therefore developed institutions that were far more protective of private property. There is, of course, a correlation between the British Empire and the latter category.[138]

1.8 Shareholder Value or Stakeholder Society?

The corporate governance debates reviewed in this chapter are framed in terms of shareholder value; as we noted in the introduction to this chapter, economists, and for that matter much of the legal framework, have always asserted, on the grounds that prices reflect the scarcity of resources, that management should aim at maximizing shareholder wealth. To many noneconomists, economists in this respect appear "oblivious to redistributional issues," "narrow-minded," or "out of touch with social realities." A widespread view in politics and public opinion is that corporations should serve a larger social purpose and be "responsible," that is, they should reach out to other stakeholders and not only to shareholders.

1.8.1 The Corporate Social Responsibility View

An economist would rephrase the position of the proponents of the stakeholder society as the recommendation that management and directors internalize the externalities that their decisions impose on various groups. Examples of such externalities and concomitant duties toward stakeholders, according to the proponents of the stakeholder society, can be found in the following list.

Duties toward employees. Firms should refrain from laying off workers when they make sizeable profits (the "downsizing" move of the 1990s and events such as the January 1996 laying off of 40,000 employees by a record-profit-making AT&T and the $14 million annual compensation of its chairman created uproars on the left and the right of the American political spectrum); firms should also protect minorities, provide generous training and recreational facilities, and carefully monitor safety on the job.

Duties toward communities. Firms should refrain from closing plants in distressed economic areas except when strictly necessary; in normal times they should contribute to the public life of its communities.

Duties toward creditors. Firms should not maximize shareholder value at the expense of creditor value.

Ethical considerations. Firms ought to protect the environment even if this reduces profit. They should refrain from investing in countries with oppressive governments, or with weak protection of or respect for the minorities (child labor, apartheid, etc.). Firms should not evade taxes, or bribe officials in less developed countries, even when such behavior raises profit on average.

---

136. See also Krosner and Strahan (1999) on bank branching regulation, Hellwig (2000) on corporate governance regulation, and Rajan and Zingales (2003), who argue that incumbent firms may be leading opponents to reforms facilitating financial development.

The endogeneity of political institutions is, of course, a broader theme in economics: see Laffont (2000) (other theoretical books emphasizing the political determination of policy include Dixit (1996), Laffont and Tirole (1993), and Persson and Tabellini (2000)).

137. Corporate governance systems may also be forced to converge if companies can cross-list in jurisdictions (countries) with better shareholder protection or engage in cross-border merger and acquisition activity. The literature on convergence towards best practice corporate governance includes Coffee (1999), Gilson (2001), and Pagano and Volpin (2005c).

138. The impact of extractive institutions as upsetting existing ones is further explored in Acemoglu et al. (2002), who attempt to account for a reversal of prosperity after the sixteenth century between the then poor (United States, Canada, Australia, etc.) and rich (India, China, Incas, Aztecs, etc.) colonies.

Many managers view their role within society in an even broader sense (satisfaction of consumer wants, support of the arts, political contributions, etc.) than suggested by this list.

According to Blair (1995, p. 214), even in the United States, which traditionally has been much less receptive to the stakeholder society idea than most other developed countries (especially outside the Anglo-Saxon world), "by the late 1960s and early 1970s corporate responsiveness to a broad group of stakeholders had become accepted business practice." Charitable contributions, divestitures from (apartheid-practicing) South Africa, and paid leave for employees engaging in public service activities, for example, became commonplace and were upheld by the courts. The consensus for some internalization of stakeholder welfare partly broke down in the 1980s. Proponents of shareholder value gained influence. Yet, the hostile takeover wave of that decade sparked an intense debate as to whether the increase in shareholder wealth associated with the takeover did not partly come to the detriment of employees and communities (see, for example, Shleifer and Summers 1988).

The popularity of the stakeholder society view in the public is to be contrasted with the strong consensus among financial economists that maximizing shareholder value has major advantages over the pursuit of alternative goals. A particularly influential advocate of the shareholder-value approach has been Milton Friedman (1970).[139]

Economists have long argued in favor of a proper internalization of externalities. And certainly the vast majority of them have no objections to the goals advanced by the proponents of the stakeholder society. A scientific debate therefore focuses on how to achieve these goals, rather than on the goals themselves.

1.8.2 What the Stakeholder Society Is and What It Is Not

Some management gurus have surfed the stakeholder society wave and have argued that "stakeholding" makes commercial sense. In a nutshell, the recommendation is to treat employees fairly through job security, training facilities, etc. The reasoning is that, by building a reputation for fairness, the firm will be able to attract the most talented employees and to induce them to invest in the firm, as the employees will know that they are engaged in a long-term relationship with the firm and that their firm-specific investments will be rewarded. This argument can, of course, be extended to, say, suppliers and communities, who are inclined to offer lower prices or larger subsidies, respectively, to a more trustworthy firm.

Such recommendations smack of social responsiveness; but in fact they are about shareholder value: intertemporal value maximization often trades off short-run sacrifices (investments) for the prospect of higher long-term profits.[140] Treating stakeholders fairly in order to raise intertemporal

139. "In a free-enterprise, private-property system, a corporate executive is an employee of the owners of the business. He has direct responsibility to his employers. That responsibility is to conduct the business in accordance with their desires, which generally will be to make as much money as possible while conforming to the basic rules of the society, both those embodied in law and those embodied in ethical custom. Of course, in some cases his employers may, of course, have a different objective. A group of persons might establish a corporation for an eleemosynary purpose—for example, a hospital or a school. The manager of such a corporation will not have money profit as his objective but the rendering of certain services.

"Of course, the corporate executive is also a person in his own right. As a person, he may have many other responsibilities that he recognizes or assumes voluntarily—to his family, his conscience, his feelings of charity, his church, his clubs, his city, his country. He may feel impelled by these responsibilities to devote part of his income to causes he regards as worthy, to refuse to work for particular corporations, even to leave his job, for example, to join his country's armed forces. If we wish, we may refer to some of these responsibilities as 'social responsibilities.' But in these respects he is acting as a principal, not an agent; he is spending his own money or time or energy, not the money of his employers or the time or energy he has contracted to devote to their purposes. If these are 'social responsibilities,' they are the social responsibilities of individuals, not of business.

"The stockholders or the customers or the employees could separately spend their own money on the particular action if they wished to do so. The executive is exercising a distinct 'social responsibility,' rather than serving as an agent of the stockholders or the customers or the employees, only if he spends the money in a different way than they would have spent it.

"But if he does this, he is in effect imposing taxes, on the one hand, and deciding how the tax proceeds shall be spent, on the other.

"Here the businessman—self-selected or appointed directly or indirectly by stockholders—is to be simultaneously legislator, executive and jurist. He is to decide whom to tax by how much and for what purpose, and he is to spend the proceeds—all this guided only by general exhortations from on high to restrain inflation, improve the environment, fight poverty and so on and on."

140. To again quote from Friedman (1970), who is highly critical of the stakeholder society concept: "Of course, in practice the doctrine of social responsibility is frequently a cloak for actions that are justified on other grounds rather than a reason for those actions.

profit is not what the stakeholder society is about. Rather, *the "socially responsible corporation" is one that consciously makes decisions that reduce overall profits.*[141]

Similarly, we do not classify actions whose primary interest is to restore the firm's public image under the corporate social responsibility heading. It is perhaps no coincidence that multinationals, and in particular ones that, for good or bad reasons, have a poor public image (tobacco, oil, pharmaceutical companies), have eagerly embraced the concepts of corporate social responsibility and sustainable development and created senior executive positions in charge of the firm's social responsibility.

Before discussing the implementation of the stakeholder society, let me address the issue of what the concept exactly refers to. On the one hand, the stakeholder society may refer to a *broad mission of management.* According to this view, management should aim at maximizing the sum of the various stakeholders' surpluses (adopting an utilitarian approach); and, if management is not naturally inclined to do so, incentives should be designed that induce management to account for the externalities imposed on all stakeholders. On the other hand, the stakeholder society may refer to the *sharing of control by stakeholders,* as is, for example, the case for codetermination in Germany.[142] Presumably, the two notions are related; for instance, it would be hard for a manager to sacrifice profit to benefit some stakeholder if a profit-maximizing raider can take over the firm and replace her, unless that very stakeholder can help the manager deter the takeover (see Pagano and Volpin 2005a).[143] In what follows, we will take the view that the stakeholder society means both a broad managerial mission and divided control.

We focus on optimal contracting among stakeholders (including investors) and wonder whether managerial incentives and a control structure can be put in place that efficiently implement the concept of stakeholder society. Another layer of difficulty is added by the existence of a regulatory environment that restricts the set of contracts that can be signed among stakeholders. Interestingly, countries such as France, Germany, and Japan, which traditionally are more sympathetic to the stakeholder society than the United States and the United Kingdom, also have legal, regulatory, and fiscal environments that are assessed by most economists as creating weaker governance systems (see Section 1.7).

As in other areas of contract law, a hard question is, why does one need a law in the first place? Couldn't the parties reach efficient agreements by themselves, in which case the role of courts and of the government is to enforce private contracts and not to reduce welfare by constraining feasible agreements? For example, why can't a mutually agreeable contract between investors and employees allow employee representation on the board, stipulate reasonable severance pay for laid-off workers, and create incentives that will induce management to internalize the welfare of employees, thus substituting for an enlarged fiduciary duty by the management

"To illustrate, it may well be in the long run interest of a corporation that is a major employer in a small community to devote resources to providing amenities to that community or to improving its government. That may make it easier to attract desirable employees, it may reduce the wage bill or lessen losses from pilferage and sabotage or have other worthwhile effects. Or it may be that, given the laws about the deductibility of corporate charitable contributions, the stockholders can contribute more to charities they favor by having the corporation make the gift than by doing it themselves, since they can in that way contribute an amount that would otherwise have been paid as corporate taxes.

"In each of these and many similar cases, there is a strong temptation to rationalize these actions as an exercise of 'social responsibility.' In the present climate of opinion, with its wide spread aversion to 'capitalism,' 'profits,' the 'soulless corporation' and so on, this is one way for a corporation to generate goodwill as a by-product of expenditures that are entirely justified in its own self-interest.

"It would be inconsistent of me to call on corporate executives to refrain from this hypocritical window-dressing because it harms the foundations of a free society. That would be to call on them to exercise a 'social responsibility'! If our institutions, and the attitudes of the public make it in their self-interest to cloak their actions in this way, I cannot summon much indignation to denounce them. At the same time, I can express admiration for those individual proprietors or owners of closely held corporations or stockholders of more broadly held corporations who disdain such tactics as approaching fraud."

141. Interestingly, in the 1960s and 1970s, U.S. courts accommodated socially responsible activities such as donations to charities by arguing that short-run diversion of shareholder wealth may be good for the shareholders "in the long-run." Courts thereby avoided conceding that directors did not have a primary duty to maximize shareholder wealth (see Blair 1996, p. 215).

142. Porter (1992) argues in favor of board representation of customers, suppliers, financial advisors, employees, and community representatives.

143. In this sense, there may be some consistency in the German corporate governance system between shared control, the absence or small level of managerial stock options, and the inactivity of the takeover market.

toward employees, legal restrictions on layoffs, or mandated collective bargaining?

Besides the standard foundations for the existence of laws (transaction-costs benefits of standard form contracts well understood by all parties, *ex post* completion of a (perhaps rationally) incomplete contract by judges in the spirit of the original contract, contract writing under asymmetric information or under duress, etc.), a key argument for regulatory intervention in the eyes of the proponents of the stakeholder society has to do with tilting the balance of bargaining power away from investors and toward stakeholders. This position raises the questions of whether redistribution is best achieved through constraining feasible contractual arrangements (as opposed to through taxation, say), and whether regulation even serves its redistributive goals in the long run, to the extent that it may discourage investment and job creation and thereby end up hurting employees' interests.

Whatever its rationale, regulatory intervention in favor of stakeholder rights plays an important role in many countries. Thus, besides the normative question of whether laws protecting stakeholders can be justified on efficiency grounds, the positive question of how such laws actually emerge is also worthy of study. Clearly, political economy considerations loom large in the enacting of pro-stakeholder regulations. In this respect, one may also be suspicious of the motives behind the endorsement of the stakeholder society concept by some managers, to the extent that they do not propose to replace shareholder control by a different, but strong, governance structure. That is, the stakeholder society is sometimes viewed as synonymous with the absence of effective control over management. (That the shareholder–stakeholder debate neglects the role of management as a party with specific interests has been strongly emphasized by Hellwig (2000), who discusses extensively the "political economy" of corporate governance.)

1.8.3 Objections to the Stakeholder Society

Four different arguments can be raised against a stakeholder-society governance structure. The first, which will be developed in Chapter 10, is that giving control rights to noninvestors may discourage financing in the first place. For example, suppose the community of "natural stakeholders" is composed of management and employees, who do not have the funds to pay for investment themselves, and that the investors are concerned that they will not be able to recoup their investment in the firm if they share control with the stakeholders; that is, there may not be enough "pledgeable income" that the stakeholders can credibly promise to pay back when they have a say in the governance structure. The stakeholders probably will then want to hand control over to the investors, even in situations in which control by investors reduce total surplus. "Shareholder value" may be the only way to obtain the required money.

The second and third objections are developed in a bit more detail in the supplementary section. The second objection is also relative to the governance structure. The issue with the sharing of control between investors and natural stakeholders is not only that it generates less pledgeable income and therefore less financing than investor control, but also that it may create inefficiencies in decision making. On many decisions, investors and natural stakeholders have conflicting objectives. They may not converge to mutually agreeable policies. In particular, deadlocks may result from the sharing of control.

The third issue with the concept of stakeholder society is managerial accountability. A manager who is instructed to maximize shareholder value has a relatively well-defined mission; her performance in this mission—stock value or profit—is relatively objective and well-defined (even though this book will repeatedly emphasize the substantial imperfections in performance measurement). In contrast, the socially responsible manager faces a wide variety of missions, most of which are by nature unmeasurable. Managerial performance in the provision of positive externalities to stakeholders is notoriously ill-defined and unverifiable. In such situations managerial incentives are known to be poor (see Dewatripont et al. 1999b).

Concretely, the concern is that the management's invocation of multiple and hard-to-measure missions may become an excuse for self-serving behavior, making managers less accountable. For example, an empire builder may justify the costly acquisition

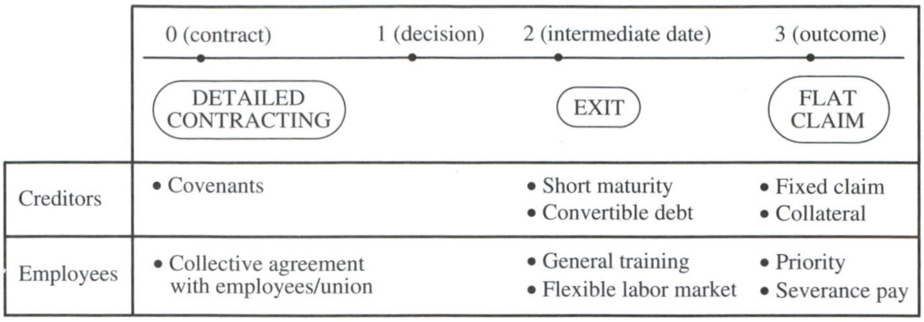
0 (contract)
1 (decision)
2 (intermediate date)
3 (outcome)
DETAILED CONTRACTING
EXIT
FLAT CLAIM
Creditors
• Covenants
• Short maturity
• Convertible debt
• Fixed claim
• Collateral
Employees
• Collective agreement with employees/union
• General training
• Flexible labor market
• Priority
• Severance pay

Figure 1.8 Protecting noncontrolling stakeholders.

of another firm on the grounds that this acquisition will save a few jobs. Or a manager may select a costly supplier officially on the grounds that this supplier has a better environmental policy, while actually entering in a sweet deal with a friend or reciprocating a favor. As a last example, an inefficient manager may install antitakeover defenses on the grounds that employees must be protected against potential layoffs implemented by a profit-maximizing raider.

The fourth argument is that a successful popular push for corporate social responsibility de facto imposes a tax on business, whose proceeds escape control by political process. While there are sometimes good reasons to subtract public policy from political pressures by handing it over to less politically accountable bodies such as independent agencies and nongovernmental organizations, it is not obvious that social goals are best achieved by directors and officers eager to pander to their own constituencies (in particular, their customers and policy makers who affect their firm's stake).

1.8.4 The Shareholder-Value Position

Proponents of the maximization of shareholder value (hopefully) do not object to the goals of the stakeholder society. Rather, they disagree on how these goals are to be reached. Implicit in their position is the view that externalities are best handled through the contractual and legal apparatus, rather than through some discretionary action by the firm's officers and directors. Shareholders can substantially expropriate creditors by picking risky moves, or by disgorging cash and assets, leaving the creditors with an empty shell? Then, creditors should (and actually do on a routine basis—see Chapter 2) insist on a set of covenants that will protect them against expropriation. Maximization of value can come at the expense of the firm's workforce? Then, employees and unions should enter collective agreements with the firm specifying rules for on-the-job safety, severance pay, and unemployment benefits.[144] And so forth.

We just saw that it is important to use the contractual apparatus in order to reduce the externalities imposed by the choices of the controlling shareholders. There are *two ways of creating contractual protections* for the noncontrolling stakeholders. The first is to circumscribe the action set available to the controlling stakeholder by ruling out those actions that are more likely to involve strong negative externalities on other stakeholders; this reduction in the size of the action set involves transaction and flexibility costs, but it may still create value. The second is to make the claims of noncontrolling stakeholders as insensitive to biased decision making as possible. This idea is illustrated in Figure 1.8 for the case of creditors and employees.

As we discuss in Chapter 2, debt contracts impose a large number of positive and negative covenants, which can be summarized as defining the action set for shareholders. Making the creditors' claim less sensitive to shareholders' actions has two aspects: *flat claims* and *exit options*. First, the creditors' final claim is often a fixed nominal claim; and collateral further helps limit the creditors' potential losses in the case of nonreimbursement of the debt. Second, debt contracts often provide creditors with exit

144. This position underlies the use of layoff taxes and experience rating (see Blanchard and Tirole (2004, 2005) for a policy discussion and an optimal mechanism approach, respectively).

options that can be exercised before the value of the claim's payout is realized. This is most evident in the case of short-term debt, which gives debtholders the choice between rolling over the debt and getting out if bad news accrues; debt that is convertible into equity protects debtholders against excessive risk taking by shareholders. Debt contracts thus often limit the creditors' exposure to biased decision making by shareholders.

The same logic can be applied to the protection of employees. Let us here focus on the exit options. Exit options are, of course, facilitated by the firm's policies with respect to general training, vesting of retirement plans, and so forth. But quite importantly, exit options for employees as well as their welfare when they are laid off depend heavily on a variable over which the employment contract between the firm and its employees has no control, namely, the firm's economic environment and the flexibility of the labor market. While being laid off is always quite costly to a worker, this cost is currently much higher in a country like France, which has high unemployment (in particular, long-term unemployment) and low mobility for a variety of reasons (such as close family ties and the fiscal environment[145]), than in Anglo-Saxon economies, where it is currently easier for laid-off workers to find a job of comparable quality. One could therefore conjecture that one of the reasons why shareholder value is currently less controversial in Anglo-Saxon countries than in continental Europe is that the externalities exerted by shareholder control on employees are smaller in the former.

Of course, proponents of shareholder value recognize that contracts are imperfect. They then point at the role of the legal environment. Courts can fill in the details of imprecise or incomplete contracts as long as they abide by the spirit of the original contracts. And, in the case of externalities not covered by any private contract (as is the case, for instance, with diffuse pollution externalities), courts (in reaction to lawsuits), or regulators (say, through environmental taxation), can substitute for the missing contracts.

The counterargument to this last point is that the legal and regulatory framework is itself imperfect. It sometimes lags the collective will (if such a thing exists). And it is often influenced by intense interest group lobbying (see, for example, Pagano and Volpin 2005b). So, when laws are "suboptimal," managers may need to substitute for the required reforms (but, as noted above, nothing guarantees that they will better represent the "collective will" than the courts or legislators).

While incentive and control considerations plead in favor of shareholder value and against social responsibility,[146] shareholder-value maximization is, of course, very much a second-best mandate. In view of some imperfections in contracts and the laws, extremist views on shareholder value are distasteful. It implies, for instance, that management should bribe dictators or government officials in less developed countries when this practice is not sanctioned in the firm's home country; or that firms should have little concern for the environment when environmental taxes are thwarted by intense lobbying or measurement problems. New forms of intervention should then be designed in order to reconcile shareholder value and social responsibility in such instances of contract failure, although it should be recognized that proper incentives are then hard to design.

Green funds (investing in businesses that exert efforts to protect the environment) or more broadly ethical funds and consumer boycotts have attempted to do just that. They are interesting and well-meaning attempts at substituting for an imperfect regulation of externalities, but have their own limitations. (a) One limitation is that both investors and consumers have poor information: incentives provided by individual investors and consumers require these actors to be well-informed about the actual facts as well as to be capable of interpreting these facts (for example, the social and economic impacts of a policy are often misunderstood). Presumably, trustworthy informational intermediaries are needed to guide their choice. (b) Another limitation

145. For example, high real estate transaction taxes have traditionally reduced owners' mobility. Similarly, for nonowners, laws related to rentals have made the rental market rather illiquid.

146. An early exponent of this view was Berle himself. He argued that "you cannot abandon emphasis on the view that business corporations exist for the sole purpose of making profits for their stockholders until such time as you are prepared to offer a clear and reasonably enforceable scheme of responsibilities to someone else" (1932, cited by Blair 1995).

is free riding in the (costly) production of sanctions against socially irresponsible firms: as the evidence shows, a nonnegligible fraction of investors are willing to accept a slightly lower rate of return in order to avoid funding firms that behave in an unethical way. Most are, however, unlikely to be willing to take a low rate of return, in the same way that households are indignant when a park or an old neighborhood is converted into luxury condominium buildings but rush to acquire the resulting units.

Supplementary Section

1.9 The Stakeholder Society: Incentives and Control Issues

This supplementary section, which draws in part on Tirole (2001), develops the analysis of Section 1.8.3 on the implementation of the stakeholder society in a little more detail.

1.9.1 Monetary Incentives

To implement the stakeholder society, managerial incentives should be designed so as to align the managers' incentives with the sum of the stakeholders' surpluses rather than just the equityholders' surplus. We thus consider sequentially the provision of explicit and implicit incentives.

As discussed in this chapter, managerial incentives that explicitly emphasize shareholder value are provided through bonuses and stock options that encourage management to devote most of its effort to enhancing profitability and favor this objective when trading off the costs and benefits of alternative decisions. Similarly, managerial incentives that would explicitly emphasize stakeholder value would be provided by rewarding management on the basis of some measure of the aggregate welfare of the stakeholders (including investors). The key issue here is whether such a measure of aggregate welfare is readily available. I would argue that it is harder to measure the firm's contribution to the welfare of employees, of suppliers, or of customers than to measure its profitability. For one thing, there is no *accounting* measure of this welfare, although in some examples one can find imperfect proxies, such as the number of layoffs.[147] For another thing, there is no *market* value of the impact of past and current managerial decisions on the future welfare of stakeholders; that is, there is no counterpart to the stock market measurement of the value of assets in place, since the employment, supply, or other relationships with the firm are not traded in liquid markets, unlike the shareholder relationship. (Besides, if a measure of the impact of managerial decisions upon stakeholders' welfare were available (which I do not believe to be the case), then there would be no objection to shareholder value since the firm could be forced to internalize the externalities through contracts specifying that the firm will compensate the stakeholders for the externalities!)

Relatedly, to avoid giving management a blank check to pursue whatever policy pleases it, management could be made subject to an enlarged fiduciary duty: stakeholders could take management to court and try to demonstrate that managerial actions do not follow the mandate of the stakeholder society. An enlarged fiduciary duty would therefore be an attempt to make management accountable for the welfare of stakeholders.

Those familiar with the difficulty of implementing the restricted concept of fiduciary duty toward shareholders will easily imagine the limitations of an enlarged fiduciary duty. In a nutshell, management can almost always rationalize any action by invoking its impact on the welfare of *some* stakeholder. An empire builder can justify a costly acquisition by a claim that the purchase will save a couple of jobs in the acquired firm; a manager can choose his brother-in-law as supplier on the grounds that the latter's production process is environmentally friendly.

In the absence of a reliable measure of stakeholders' welfare that could be incorporated into a formal compensation contract, managers could still receive profit-based compensation as under the paradigm of shareholder value. Unfortunately, multitask explicit incentives theory (e.g., Holmström and Milgrom 1991) has taught us that designing pay

147. And their duration. A clever aspect of the experience rating system for layoff taxes is that the amount paid by the company depends on the level of benefits received by the employee it laid off, and so firing someone who remains unemployed for two years is much more costly than firing someone who will find a job the next day.

that is sensitive to the performance of a single task leads to a neglect of the other tasks.[148] We therefore infer that the stakeholder society is likely to be best promoted through *flat* managerial compensation, that is, through a fixed wage rather than performance-based incentives. There is in this respect some consistency between the lenient views in the French, German, and Japanese populations toward the stakeholder society and the historically low power of the managerial incentive schemes in these countries.[149]

1.9.2 Implicit Incentives and Managerial Missions

The previous discussion raises the issue of what management will maximize under flat explicit incentive schemes. The optimistic view is that management will choose what is best for society, that is, will maximize the sum of the stakeholders' surpluses. This view is sometimes vindicated: consider caritative organizations. Such organizations by definition aim at raising the welfare of the poor, of the hungry, or at providing access to cultural services to a broad audience, to give a few examples. Profit-maximizing behaviors would obviously defeat the purpose of such organizations. The key to success for caritative organizations is to empower idealistic employees who will derive private benefits from promoting social welfare.

While this paradigm works relatively well in some contexts, it would, however, be naive to trust it can be transposed to general environments. Most economic agents indeed place their own welfare above that of society. Thus, we cannot assume that managers facing flat compensation schemes will maximize the total surplus. Their incentives are then generally governed by their career concerns. The existence of multiple missions associated with the welfare of each stakeholding group suggests an investigation of the economics of multitask career concerns (which are actually the incentives faced by politicians, bureaucrats, and most employees, who have little performance-related pay).

Implicit incentives stem from an economic agent's desire to signal characteristics, such as ability, to what is broadly called the agent's "labor market," namely, whoever will in the future take actions that reflect beliefs about these characteristics and will impact the agent's welfare: board of directors, potential employers, voters, and so forth (Holmström 1999). Implicit incentives substitute (imperfectly) for explicit ones in environments in which performance cannot be well-described *ex ante*, but can be better assessed after the fact due to the accrual of new information.[150]

Implicit incentives are less proficient than explicit ones simply because the link from performance to reward cannot be fully controlled by a contract. This is particularly the case in a multitask environment. Indeed, multitasking impairs informal incentives just as it impairs formal ones (Dewatripont et al. 1999a,b). One reason is that managerial performance becomes noisier when the manager pursues multiple missions; the absence of "focus" on a specific task is therefore costly. Another reason is that multitasking may give rise to "fuzzy missions," that is, to situations in which the agent's labor market no longer knows which missions the agent is trying to pursue (although it tries to infer them by looking at what the agent has done best). The manager then does not know along which lines he will be evaluated. This uncertainty can be shown to further reduce the agent's incentives.

We are thus led to the view that the design of (explicit and implicit) managerial incentives for the stakeholder society is a particularly complex issue. This conclusion should not come as a surprise. After all, governments may be the ultimate stakeholder-society organizations, since they are instructed to balance the welfares of many different interest groups. It is well-known that proper incentives for bureaucrats and politicians are hard to design.

148. Unlike Sinclair-Desgagne (1999), we assume that the nonmonetary dimension cannot be subjected to an audit. Otherwise, in some circumstances, it may be possible to provide high-powered multitask incentives (as Sinclair-Desgagne shows) through a combination of compensation based on the monetary dimension together with an audit of the other tasks when monetary performance is high.

149. As discussed in the text of the chapter, entrepreneurial incentive schemes have become more high-powered in the last decade in non-Anglo-Saxon countries as well.

150. More technically, a missing "deciphering key" does not allow the contracting parties to describe at the contracting stage the meaning of a "good performance"; it is only later when the uncertainty unfolds that it becomes clearer what a good performance means.

1.9.3 The Costs and Benefits of Shared Control: Lessons from Input Joint Ventures for the Stakeholder Society

We now come to the second aspect of the stakeholder society: the control structure. The stakeholder society is unlikely to be promoted by the undivided control structure that prevails under the shareholder-value paradigm. Nor is it likely to be sustainable if control goes entirely to nonfinanciers; for, consider undivided control by other stakeholders such as employees or customers. Such control structures are not mirror images of shareholder control. Employee or customer control makes it difficult to protect investors by contractual means. While covenants can restrict the payment of dividends to shareholders (so as to prevent shareholders from leaving creditors and other stakeholders with an empty shell), it is much harder to prevent employees or customers from paying themselves large "dividends" when they have control. For this point, the distinction between "natural stakeholder" (management, employees, customers, etc.) and "stakeholder by design" (the investors) is crucial. Dividends paid to shareholders are highly visible and verifiable; dividends paid to natural stakeholders may not be: employees may enjoy large perks and customers may select gold-plated designs. The partial lack of control over dividends in kind severely impairs the effectiveness of governance structures in which investors are not represented.

Let us therefore discuss the sharing of control among stakeholders in the form of a generalized codetermination.[151] To help us think through alternative control structures, let us use the analogy of the organization of a production process with multiple users needing a common input. This input can be manufactured by a third party, either a not-for-profit or a for-profit corporation, controlled by players that are independent from the users (structural separation); or by one of the users, who then sells it to the other users (vertical integration); or else by a specific-purpose entity controlled jointly by the users (joint venture or association). For example, an electricity transmission network may be controlled by a distribution company or a generator (vertical integration), a group of users (joint venture), or an independent organization (not-for-profit as in the case of an independent system operator, or for-profit as in the case of a transmission company).

We can gain some insights into the costs and benefits of shared control from looking at the familiar case of a production of a joint input and apply them to the corporate governance debate. Indeed, input joint ventures are quite common: credit card associations such as Visa and MasterCard,[152] some stock exchanges, Airbus, research and farm cooperatives, telecommunications, biotechnology, and automobile alliances are all examples of joint ventures. Joint ventures, partnerships, and associations can be viewed as instances of stakeholder societies to the extent that players with conflicting interests share the control. But it should also be noted that the first argument in favor of shareholder value, the dearth of pledgeable income (see Section 1.8.3), may not apply to them: partners in joint ventures can more easily bring capital than employees in a corporation; the need for borrowing from independent parties is therefore much reduced. In other words, self-financing by the users of the input of a joint venture implies that the dearth of pledgeable income is not a key factor here.

An interesting lesson drawn from the work of Hansmann (1996) and from much related evidence is that the heterogeneity of interests among the partners of a joint venture seriously impedes the joint venture's efficacy. As one might expect, conflicts of interest among the partners create mistrust and lead to deadlocks in decision making.[153]

151. We focus here on the sharing of all major control rights among stakeholders. Alternatively, multiple control rights could be shared among stakeholders, but some could be allocated fully to specific shareholders. In some circumstances, the two can be closely related: different stakeholders may threaten to hurt each other substantially through the exercise of their proprietary control rights; the parties must then cooperate on a global deal as if they shared all control rights. A case in point is the failed attempt in the mid 1990s by Mr. Schrempp, the chairman of Daimler-Benz, to take advantage of a newly passed law in Germany offering firms the possibility of limiting the payments to sick employees. The board of directors took back the decision a few days later because the envisioned restructuring of Daimler-Benz required the cooperation of employees. The chairman, up to that time a strong proponent of shareholder value, declared that he would never mention the phrase shareholder value again.

152. MasterCard became for-profit in 2003.

153. These deadlocks can be attributed primarily to asymmetries of information, but sometimes may stem from limited compensation abilities of some of the parties. This is where the Coase Theorem fails.

Appendixes

1.10 Cadbury Report

Report of the Committee on the Financial Aspects of Corporate Governance

Introduction

1. The Committee was set up in May 1991 by the Financial Reporting Council, the London Stock Exchange, and the Accountancy profession to address the financial aspects of corporate governance.

2. The Committee issued a draft report for public comment on 27 May 1992. Its final report, taking account of submissions made during the consultation period and incorporating a Code of Best Practice, was published on 1 December 1992. This extract from the report sets out the text of the Code. It also sets out, as Notes, a number of further recommendations on good practice drawn from the body of the report.

3. The Committee's central recommendation is that the boards of all listed companies registered in the United Kingdom should comply with the Code. The Committee encourages as many other companies as possible to aim at meeting its requirements.

4. The Committee also recommends:

   (a) that listed companies reporting in respect of years ending after 30 June 1993 should make a statement in their report and accounts about their compliance with the Code and identify and give reasons for any areas of non-compliance;

   (b) that companies' statements of compliance should be reviewed by the auditors before publication. The review by the auditors should cover only those parts of the compliance statement which relate to provisions of the Code where compliance can be objectively verified (see note 14).

5. The publication of a statement of compliance, reviewed by the auditors, is to be made a continuing obligation of listing by the London Stock Exchange.

6. The Committee recommends that its sponsors, convened by the Financial Reporting Council, should appoint a new Committee by the end of June 1995 to examine how far compliance with the Code has progressed, how far its other recommendations have been implemented, and whether the Code needs updating. In the meantime the present Committee will remain responsible for reviewing the implementation of its proposals.

7. The Committee has made clear that the Code is to be followed by individuals and boards in the light of their own particular circumstances. They are responsible for ensuring that their actions meet the spirit of the Code and in interpreting it they should give precedence to substance over form.

8. The Committee recognises that smaller listed companies may initially have difficulty in complying with some aspects of the Code. The boards of smaller listed companies who cannot, for the time being, comply with parts of the Code should note that they may instead give their reasons for non-compliance. The Committee believes, however, that full compliance will bring benefits to the boards of such companies and that it should be their objective to ensure that the benefits are achieved. In particular, the appointment of appropriate non-executive directors should make a positive contribution to the development of their businesses.

The Code of Best Practice

1. The Board of Directors

1.1. The board should meet regularly, retain full and effective control over the company and monitor the executive management.

1.2. There should be a clearly accepted division of responsibilities at the head of a company, which will ensure a balance of power and authority, such that no one individual has unfettered powers of decision. Where the chairman is also the chief executive, it is essential that there should be a strong and independent element on the board, with a recognised senior member.

1.3. The board should include non-executive directors of sufficient calibre and number for their views to carry significant weight in the board's decisions. (Note 1.)

1.4. The board should have a formal schedule of matters specifically reserved to it for decision to ensure that the direction and control of the company is firmly in its hands. (Note 2.)

1.5. There should be an agreed procedure for directors in the furtherance of their duties to take independent professional advice if necessary, at the company's expense. (Note 3.)

1.6. All directors should have access to the advice and services of the company secretary, who is responsible to the board for ensuring that board procedures are followed and that applicable rules and regulations are complied with. Any question of the removal of the company secretary should be a matter for the board as a whole.

2. Non-executive Directors

2.1. Non-executive directors should bring an independent judgement to bear on issues of strategy, performance, resources, including key appointments, and standards of conduct.

2.2. The majority should be independent of management and free from any business or other relationship which could materially interfere with the exercise of their independent judgement, apart from their fees and shareholding. Their fees should reflect the time which they commit to the company. (Notes 4 and 5.)

2.3. Non-executive directors should be appointed for specified terms and reappointment should not be automatic. (Note 6.)

2.4. Non-executive directors should be selected through a formal process and both this process and their appointment should be a matter for the board as a whole. (Note 7.)

3. Executive Directors

3.1. Directors' service contracts should not exceed three years without shareholders' approval. (Note 8.)

3.2. There should be full and clear disclosure of directors' total emoluments and those of the chairman and the highest-paid UK director, including pension, contributions and stock options. Separate figures should be given for salary and performance-related elements and the basis on which performance is measured should be explained.

3.3. Executive directors' pay should be subject to the recommendations of a remuneration committee made up wholly or mainly of non-executive directors. (Note 9.)

4. Reporting and Controls

4.1. It is the board's duty to present a balanced and understandable assessment of the company's position. (Note 10.)

4.2. The board should ensure that an objective and professional relationship is maintained with the auditors.

4.3. The board should establish an audit committee of at least three non-executive directors with written terms of reference which deal clearly with its authority and duties. (Note 11.)

4.4. The directors should explain their responsibility for preparing the accounts next to a statement by the auditors about their reporting responsibilities. (Note 12.)

4.5. The directors should report on the effectiveness of the company's system of internal control. (Note 13.)

4.6. The directors should report that the business is a going concern, with supporting assumptions or qualifications. (Note 13.)

Notes

These notes include further recommendations on good practice. They do not form part of the Code.

1. To meet the Committee's recommendations on the composition of sub-committees of the board, boards will require a minimum of three non-executive directors, one of whom may be the chairman of the company provided he or she is not also its executive head. Additionally, two of the three non-executive directors should be independent in the terms set out in paragraph 2.2 of the Code.
2. A schedule of matters specifically reserved for decision by the full board should be given to directors on appointment and should be kept up to date. The Committee envisages that the schedule would at least include:
   (a) acquisition and disposal of assets of the company or its subsidiaries that are material to the company;
   (b) investments, capital projects, authority levels, treasury policies and risk management policies.

   The board should lay down rules to determine materiality for any transaction, and should establish clearly which transactions require multiple board signatures. The board should also agree the procedures to be followed when, exceptionally, decisions are required between board meetings.
3. The agreed procedure should be laid down formally, for example in a Board Resolution, in the Articles, or in the Letter of Appointment.
4. It is for the board to decide in particular cases whether this definition of independence is met. Information about the relevant interests of directors should be disclosed in the Directors' Report.
5. The Committee regards it as good practice for non-executive directors not to participate in share option schemes and for their service as non-executive directors not to be pensionable by the company, in order to safeguard their independent position.
6. The Letter of Appointment for non-executive directors should set out their duties, term of office, remuneration, and its review.
7. The Committee regards it as good practice for a nomination committee to carry out the selection process and to make proposals to the board. A nomination committee should have a majority of non-executive directors on it and be chaired either by the chairman or a non-executive director.
8. The Committee does not intend that this provision should apply to existing contracts before they become due for renewal.
9. Membership of the remuneration committee should be set out in the Directors' Report and its chairman should be available to answer questions on remuneration principles and practice at the Annual General Meeting. Best practice is set out in PRO NED's Remuneration Committee Guidelines published in 1992.
10. The report and accounts should contain a coherent narrative, supported by the figures of the company's performance and prospects. Balance requires that setbacks

should be dealt with as well as successes. The need for the report to be readily understood emphasises that words are as important as figures.

11. The Committee's recommendations on audit committees are as follows:

    (a) They should be formally constituted as sub-committees of the main board to whom they are answerable and to whom they should report regularly; they should be given written terms of reference which deal adequately with their membership, authority and duties; and they should normally meet at least twice a year.

    (b) There should be a minimum of three members. Membership should be confined to the non-executive directors of the company and a majority of the non-executives serving on the committee should be independent of the company, as defined in paragraph 2.2 of the Code.

    (c) The external auditor and, where an internal audit function exists, the head of internal audit should normally attend committee meetings, as should the finance director. Other board members should also have the right to attend.

    (d) The audit committee should have a discussion with the auditors at least once a year, without executive board members present, to ensure that there are no unresolved issues of concern.

    (e) The audit committee should have explicit authority to investigate any matters within its terms of reference, the resources which it needs to do so, and full access to information. The committee should be able to obtain outside professional advice and if necessary to invite outsiders with relevant experience to attend meetings.

    (f) Membership of the committee should be disclosed in the annual report and the chairman of the committee should be available to answer questions about its work at the Annual General Meeting.

    Specimen terms of reference for an audit committee, including a list of the most commonly performed duties, are set out in the Committee's full report.

12. The statement of directors' responsibilities should cover the following points:

    - the legal requirements for directors to prepare financial statements for each financial year which give a true and fair view of the state of affairs of the company (or group) as at the end of the financial year and of the profit and loss for that period;
    - the responsibility of the directors for maintaining adequate accounting records, for safeguarding the assets of the company (or group), and for preventing and detecting fraud and other irregularities;
    - confirmation that suitable accounting policies, consistently applied and supported by reasonable and prudent judgements and estimates, have been used in the preparation of the financial statement;
    - confirmation that applicable accounting standards have been followed, subject to any material departures disclosed and explained in the notes to the accounts. (This does not obviate the need for a formal statement in the notes to the accounts disclosing whether the accounts have been prepared in accordance with applicable accounting standards.)

    The statement should be placed immediately before the auditors' report which in future will include a separate statement (currently being developed by the Auditing Practices Board) on the responsibility of the auditors for expressing an opinion on the accounts.

13. The Committee notes that companies will not be able to comply with paragraphs 4.5 and 4.6 of the Code until the necessary guidance for companies has been developed as recommended in the Committee's report.

14. The company's statement of compliance should be reviewed by the auditors in so far as it relates to paragraphs 1.4, 1.5, 2.3, 2.4, 3.1 to 3.3 and 4.3 to 4.6 of the Code.

1.11 Notes to Tables

1.11.1 Notes to Table 1.3

Sources: (a) Federal Reserve, Banque de France, Bank of Japan, and Eurostat; (b) Bank of England, Banque de France, Bank of Japan, and Eurostat. Data are not available for (a) the United Kingdom or (b) the United States.

Construction for both parts is as follows.

United States. 1. *Sources:* Federal Reserve of the United States, Flow of Funds Accounts of the United States (Release of December 9, 2004), Level Tables, Table L.213 (http://www.federalreserve.gov/releases/zl/Current/zlr-4.pdf).

2. *Details:* Corporate equities are shares of ownership in financial and nonfinancial corporate businesses. The category comprises common and preferred shares issued by domestic corporations and U.S. purchases of shares issued by foreign corporations, including shares held in the form of American depositary receipts (ADRs); it does not include mutual fund shares. Data on issuance and holdings of corporate equities are obtained from private data-reporting services, trade associations, and regulatory and other federal agencies. Purchases of equities by the households and nonprofit organizations sector are found as the residual after the purchases of all other sectors have been subtracted from total issuance. *Construction:* "insurance companies" = "life insurance companies" + "other insurance companies"; "banks and other financial institutions" =

"commercial banking" + "saving institutions" + "bank and personal trusts and estate" + "brokers and dealers"; "mutual funds" = "mutual funds" + "closed-end funds" + "exchange-traded funds"; "pension funds" = "private pension funds" + "state and local government retirement funds" + "federal government retirement funds."

France. 1. *Sources:* Banque de France, Comptes Nationaux Financiers, Séries Longues, Accès par Opération, Encours, Actif: F5I Actions et Autres Participations hors titre d'OPCVM, 2002 (http://www.banque-france.fr/fr/stat_conjoncture/series/cptsnatfinann/html/tof_ope_fr_encours_actif.htm).

2. *Construction:* "insurance companies" + "pension funds" = "sociétés d'assurance et fonds de pension"; "mutual funds" = "autres intermédiaires financiers"; "banks and other financial institutions" = "sociétés financières" − "autres intermédiaires financiers" − "sociétés d'assurance et fonds de pension."

Germany. 1. *Sources:* Eurostat, Comptes des patrimoines, Actifs financiers, Actions et autres participations, à l'exclusion des parts d'organismes de placement collectif, 2002 (http://europa.eu.int/comm/eurostat/).

2. *Construction:* see France.

Japan. 1. *Sources:* Bank of Japan, Flow of Funds (Annual Data (2002)/Financial assets and liabilities), Column AP (shares and other equity) (http://www2.boj.or.jp/en/dlong/flow/flow12.htm#01).

2. *Construction:* "banks and other financial institutions" = "financial institutions" − "insurance" − "pension total" − "securities investment trust."

(b) *Sources:* National Statistics Bureau of the U.K., 2002 Share Ownership Report, Table A: Beneficial Ownership of U.K. Shares, 1963–2002 (http://www.statistics.gov.uk/downloads/theme_economy/ShareOwnership2002.pdf).

2. *Description:* contains details on the beneficial ownership of U.K. listed companies as at December 31, 2002. The survey uses data downloaded from the CREST settlement system to assign shareholdings to National Accounts sectors.

3. *Construction:* "mutual funds" = "unit trust" + "investment trust" + "charities"; "banks and other financial institutions" = "banks" + "other financial institutions"; "pension funds" = "insurance companies"; "insurance companies" = "insurance"; "mutual funds" = "securities investment trust."

1.11.2 Notes to Table 1.4

Sources: Federal Reserve of the United States, Flow of Funds Accounts of the United States (Release of December 9, 2004), Level Tables, Table L.213 (http://www.federalreserve.gov/releases/zl/Current/zlr-4.pdf). *Other financial institutions:* includes securities held by brokers and security dealers investing on their own account rather than for clients; venture capital companies; unauthorized investment trusts; unauthorized unit trusts; and other financial institutions not elsewhere specified.

1.11.3 Notes to Tables 1.6 and 1.7

Description of Table 1.6: ultimate control of publicly traded firms. Data relating to 5,232 publicly traded corporations are used to construct this table. The table presents the percentage of firms controlled by different controlling owners at the 20% threshold. Data are collected at various points in time between 1996 and 2000, depending on countries. Controlling shareholders are classified into six types:

Family. A family (including an individual) or a firm that is unlisted on any stock exchange.

Widely held financial institution. A financial firm (SIC 6000-6999) that is widely held at the control threshold.

State. A national government (domestic or foreign), local authority (county, municipality, etc.), or government agency.

Widely held corporation. A nonfinancial firm, widely held at the control threshold.

Cross-holdings. The firm Y is controlled by another firm, which is controlled by Y, or directly controls at least 20% of its own stocks.

Miscellaneous. Charities, voting trusts, employees, cooperatives, or minority foreign investors.

Companies that do not have a shareholder controlling at least 20% of votes are classified as widely held.

Description of Table 1.7: assembled data for 2,980 publicly traded corporations (including both financial and nonfinancial world) and supplemented with information from country-specific sources. In all cases, the ownership structure was collected as of the end of fiscal year 1996 or the closest possible date. This table presents result defining control on a 20% threshold of ownership.

References

Acemoglu, D., S. Johnson, and J. Robinson. 2001. The colonial origins of comparative development: an empirical investigation. *American Economic Review* 91:1369–1401.

——. 2002. Reversal of fortune: geography and institutions in the making of the modern world income distribution. *Quarterly Journal of Economics* 117:1231–1294.

Adams, R. and D. Ferreira. 2003. A theory of friendly boards. Mimeo, Stockholm School of Economics.

Aghion, P., O. Hart, and J. Moore. 1992. The economics of bankruptcy reform. *Journal of Law, Economics, & Organization* 8:523–546.

Aghion, P., M. Dewatripont, and P. Rey. 1999. Competition, financial discipline, and growth. *Review of Economic Studies* 66:825–852.

Albert, M. 1991. *Capitalisme contre Capitalisme*. Paris: Seuil.

Allen, F. and D. Gale. 2000. *Comparing Financial Systems*. Cambridge, MA: MIT Press.

Altman, E. 1984. A further empirical investigation of the bankruptcy cost question. *Journal of Finance* 39:1067–1089.

Anderson, R. W. and J. P. Danthine. 1980. Hedging and joint production: theory and illustrations. *Journal of Finance* 35:487–498.

——. 1981. Cross hedging. *Journal of Political Economy* 89: 1182–1196.

Andrade, G., M. Mitchell, and E. Stafford. 2001. New evidence and perspectives on mergers. *Journal of Economic Perspectives* 15:103–120.

Aoki, M. 1984. Shareholders' non-unanimity on investment financing: banks vs individual investors. In *The Economic Analysis of the Japanese Firm* (ed. M. Aoki). Elsevier.

——. 1990. Toward an economic model of the Japanese firm. *Journal of Economic Literature* 28:1–27.

Aoki, M. and H. Patrick. 1995. *The Japanese Main Bank System: Its Relevance for Developing and Transforming Economies*. Oxford: Clarendon Press.

Asquith, P., R. Gertner, and D. Scharfstein. 1994. Anatomy of financial distress: an examination of junk-bond issuers. *Quarterly Journal of Economics* 109:625–658.

——. 1992. Strategic contractual inefficiency and the optimal choice of legal rules. *Yale Law Journal* 101:729–73.

Baker, G., M. Jensen, and K. Murphy. 1988. Compensation and incentives: practice vs theory. *Journal of Finance* 43: 593–616.

Bar-Gill, O., M. Barzuza, and L. Bebchuk. 2003. The market for corporate law. Discussion Paper 377, John M. Olin Center for Law, Economics, and Business, Harvard Law School.

Barca, F. and M. Becht. 2002. *The Control of Corporate Europe*. Oxford University Press.

Barclay, M. and C. Holderness. 1989. Private benefits from control of public corporations. *Journal of Financial Economics* 25:371–395.

Bebchuk, L. 1988. A new approach to corporate reorganizations. *Harvard Law Review* 101:775–804.

——. 1989. The debate on contractual freedom in corporate law. *Columbia Law Review* 89:1395–1415.

Bebchuk, L. and J. Fried. 2003. Executive compensation as an agency problem. *Journal of Economic Perspectives* 17: 71–92.

——. 2004. *Pay without Performance: The Unfulfilled Promise of Executive Compensation*. Cambridge, MA: Harvard University Press.

Becht, M., P. Bolton, and A. Roell. 2002. Corporate governance and control. In *Handbook of the Economics of Finance* (ed. G. Constantinides, M. Harris, and R. Stulz). Amsterdam: North-Holland.

Bénabou, R. and J. Tirole. 2003. Intrinsic and extrinsic motivation. *Review of Economic Studies* 70:489–520.

——. 2004. Incentives and prosocial behavior. Mimeo, Princeton University and IDEI.

——. 2005. A cognitive theory of identity. Mimeo, Princeton University and IDEI.

Berglöf, E. 1988. *Owners and Their Control over Corporations: A Comparison of Six Financial Systems*. Ministry of Industry, Stockholm.

Bergstresser, D., and T. Philippon. 2005. CEO incentives and earnings management. *Journal of Financial Economics*, in press.

Berle, A., Jr. and G. Means. 1932. *The Modern Corporation and Private Property*. Chicago: Commerce Clearing House.

Bertrand, M. and S. Mullainathan. 1999. Is there discretion in wage setting? *RAND Journal of Economics* 30:535–554.

——. 2000. Agents with and without principals. *American Economic Review Papers and Proceedings* 90:203–208.

——. 2001. Are CEOs rewarded for luck? The ones without principals are. *Quarterly Journal of Economics* 116:901–932.

Bertrand, M., F. Kramarz, A. Schoar, and D. Thesmar. 2004. Politically connected CEOs and political outcomes: evidence from France. Mimeo, University of Chicago, MIT and CREST-INSEE.

Bettis, J. C., J. M. Bizjak, and M. Lemmon. 1999. Insider trading in derivative securities: an empirical examination of the use of zero-cost collars and equity swaps by corporate insiders. Mimeo, Arizona State University.

——. 2003. The cost of employee stock options. Mimeo, Arizona State University.

Bhagat, S., A. Shleifer, and R. Vishny. 1990. Hostile takeovers in the 1980s: the return of corporate specialization. *Brookings Papers on Economic Activity: Microeconomics*, pp. 1–72. Brookings Institution Press.

Bhide, A. 1993a. The hidden costs of stock market liquidity. *Journal of Financial Economics* 34:31–52.

——. 1993b. The causes and consequences of hostile takeovers. In *The New Corporate Finance: Where Theory Meets Practice* (ed. D. Chew), pp. 502–535. New York: McGraw-Hill.

Black, B., B. Cheffins, and M. Klausner. 2004. Outside directors and lawsuits: what are the real risks? *McKinsey Quarterly* 4:71–77.

Blair, M. 1995. *Ownership and Control: Rethinking Corporate Governance for the Twenty-First Century*. Washington, D.C.: Brookings Institution.

Blanchard, O. J. and J. Tirole. 2004. Redesigning the employment protection system. *De Economist* 152:1–20.

——. 2005. The optimal design of labor market institutions: a first pass. Mimeo, MIT and University of Toulouse.

Blanchard, O. J., F. Lopez-de-Silanes, and A. Shleifer. 1994. What do firms do with cash windfalls? *Journal of Financial Economics* 36:337–360.

Bolton, P. and O. Jeanne. 2004. Structuring and restructuring sovereign debt: the role of seniority. Mimeo, Princeton University.

Burrough, B. and J. Helyar. 1990. *Barbarians at the Gate.* New York: Harper & Row.

Cadbury Report. 1992. *The Financial Aspects of Corporate Governance.* Burgess Science Press.

Camerer, C. and U. Malmendier. 2004. Behavioral organizational economics. Mimeo, Caltech and Stanford University.

Carrillo, J. and D. Gromb. 1999. On the strength of corporate cultures. *European Economic Review* 43:1021–1037.

Charkham, J. 1994. *Keeping Good Company: A Study of Corporate Governance in Five Countries.* Oxford University Press.

Chiappori, P. A. and B. Salanié. 2003. Testing contract theory: a survey of some recent work. In *Advances in Economics and Econometrics: Theory and Applications, Eighth World Congress of the Econometric Society* (ed. M. Dewatripont, L. Hansen, and S. Turnovsky), pp. 115–149. Cambridge University Press.

Claessens, S., S. Djankov, and L. Lang. 2000. The separation of ownership and control in East Asian corporations. *Journal of Financial Economics* 58:81–112.

Coffee, J. 1989. The mandatory/enabling balance in corporate law: an essay on the judicial role. *Columbia Law Review* 89:1618–1691.

——. 1991. Liquidity versus control: the institutional investor as corporate monitor. *Columbia Law Review* 91: 1277–1368.

——. 1999. The future as history: the prospects for global convergence in corporate governance and its implications. *Northwestern University Law Review* 93:641–708.

Comment, R. and W. Schwert. 1995. Poison or placebo? Evidence on the deterrence and wealth effects of modern antitakeover measures. *Journal of Financial Economics* 49: 3–44.

Coombes, P. and S. Wong. 2004. Why codes of governance work. In *A New Era in Governance*, pp. 48–53. McKinsey Quarterly.

Crémer, J. 1993. Corporate culture and shared knowledge. *Industrial and Corporate Change* 2:351–386.

Davydenko, S. and J. Franks. 2004. Do bankruptcy codes matter? A study of defaults in France, Germany and the UK. Mimeo, London Business School.

De Angelo, H. and L. de Angelo. 1989. Proxy contests and the governance of publicly held corporations. *Journal of Financial Economics* 23:29–59.

De Angelo, L. 1988. Managerial competition, information costs, and corporate governance: the use of accounting performance measures in proxy contests. *Journal of Accounting and Economics* 10:3–36.

DeMarzo, P. M., M. Fishman, and K. Hagerty. 2005. Self-regulation and government oversight. *Review of Economic Studies* 72:687–706.

Dewatripont, M., I. Jewitt, and J. Tirole. 1999a. The economics of career concerns. Part I. Comparing information structures. *Review of Economic Studies* 66:183–198.

——. 1999b. The economics of career concerns. Part II. Application to missions and accountability of government agencies. *Review of Economic Studies* 66:199–217.

Dhillon, U. and G. Ramirez. 1994. Employee stock ownership and corporate control: an empirical study. *Journal of Banking and Finance* 18:9–26.

Dixit, A. 1996. *The Making of Economic Policy.* Cambridge, MA: MIT Press.

Dye, R. 1993. Auditing standards, legal liability, and auditor wealth. *Journal of Political Economy* 101:887–914.

Easterbrook, F. and D. Fischel. 1989. The corporate contract. *Columbia Law Review* 89:1416–1448.

Edwards, J. and K. Fischer. 1994. *Banks, Finance and Investment in Germany.* Cambridge University Press.

Eichengreen, B. and R. Portes. 1997. Managing financial crises in emerging markets. Paper for the Federal Reserve Bank of Kansas City's annual economics conference, Jackson Hole, August 28–30.

——. 2000. Debt restructuring with and without the IMF. Paper for the International Financial Institutions Advisory Committee, Washington, D.C.

Faccio, M. and L. Lang. 2002. The ultimate ownership of Western European corporations. *Journal of Financial Economics* 65:365–395.

Fehr, E. and K. Schmidt. 2003. Theories of fairness and reciprocity. Evidence and economic applications. In *Advances in Economics and Econometrics* (ed. M. Dewatripont, L. P. Hansen, and S. Turnovsky), Volume 1, pp. 208–257. Cambridge University Press.

Felton, R. and S. Wong. 2004. How to separate the roles of chairman and CEO. *McKinsey Quarterly* 4:59–69.

Fox, L. 2003. *Enron: The Rise and Fall.* John Wiley & Sons.

Franks, J. and C. Mayer. 2001. The ownership and control of German corporations. *Review of Financial Studies* 14: 943–977. (Reprinted in *Governance and Ownership* (ed. R. Watson, K. Keesey, S. Thompson, and M. Wright). Cheltenham: Edward Elgar.)

Franks, J., C. Mayer, and L. Renneboog. 1996. The role of large share stakes in poorly performing companies. Mimeo, London Business School.

Frey, B. 1997. *Not Just for the Money—An Economic Theory of Personal Motivation.* Cheltenham: Edward Elgar.

Friebel, G. and S. Guriev. 2005. Earnings manipulation and internal incentives. Mimeo IDEI, Toulouse, and New Economic School, Moscow.

Friedman, M. 1970. The social responsibility of business is to increase its profits. *The New York Times Magazine*, September 13.

Fudenberg, D. and J. Tirole. 1990. Moral hazard and renegotiation in agency contracts. *Econometrica* 58:1279–1320.

Gertner, R. and D. Scharfstein. 1991. A theory of workouts and the effects of reorganization law. *Journal of Finance* 46:1184–1222.

Giammarino, R. 1989. The resolution of financial distress. *Review of Financial Studies* 2:25–47.

Gibbons, R. and K. Murphy. 1990. Relative performance evaluation for chief executive officers. *Industrial and Labor Relations Review* 43(special issue):305–515.

——. 1992. Optimal incentive contracts in the presence of career concerns: theory and evidence. *Journal of Political Economy* 100:468–505.

Gilson, R. 2001. Globalizing corporate governance: convergence of form or function. *American Journal of Comparative Law* 49:329–357.

Gilson, S. 1989. Management turnover and financial distress. *Journal of Financial Economics* 25:241–262.

——. 1990. Bankruptcy, boards, banks, and blockholders: evidence on changes in corporate ownership and control when firms default. *Journal of Financial Economics* 27: 355–387.

Glaeser, E. and A. Shleifer. 2001. Not for profit entrepreneurs. *Journal of Public Economics* 81:99–115.

——. 2002. Legal origins. *Quarterly Journal of Economics* 117:1193–1229.

Goyal, V. K. and C. W. Park. 2002. Board leadership and CEO turnover. *Journal of Corporate Finance* 8:49–66.

Grossman, S. and O. Hart. 1980. Takeover bids, the free rider problem, and the theory of the corporation. *Bell Journal of Economics* 11:42–64.

Hall, B. H. 1990. The impact of corporate restructuring on industrial research and development. *Brookings Papers on Economic Activity: Microeconomics*, pp. 85–124. Brookings Institution Press.

——. 2000. What you need to know about stock options. *Harvard Business Review* 78:121–129.

Hall, B. and J. Liebman. 1998. Are CEOs really paid like bureaucrats? *Quarterly Journal of Economics* 113:653–691.

Hall, B. and K. Murphy. 2002. Stock options for undiversified executives. *Journal of Accounting and Economics* 33:3–42.

Hansmann, H. 1996. *The Ownership of Enterprise*. New Haven, CT: Yale University Press.

Hart, O. and J. Moore. 1989. Default and renegotiation: a dynamic model of debt. Mimeo, MIT and LSE. (Published in *Quarterly Journal of Economics* (1998) 113:1–42.)

——. 1996. The governance of exchanges: members' cooperatives versus outside ownership. *Oxford Review of Economic Policy* 12:53–69.

Haubrich, J. 1994. Risk aversion, performance pay, and the principal-agent problem. *Journal of Political Economy* 102:258–276.

Hellwig, M. 2000. On the economics and politics of corporate finance and corporate control. In *Corporate Governance: Theoretical and Empirical Perspectives* (ed. X. Vives), Chapter 3, pp. 95–134. Cambridge University Press.

Hermalin, B. 1992. The effects of competition on executive behavior. *RAND Journal of Economics* 23:350–365.

Hermalin, B. and M. Katz. 1991. Moral hazard and verifiability: the effects of renegotiation in agency. *Econometrica* 59:1735–1753.

Hermalin, B. and M. Weisbach. 1988. The determinants of board composition. *RAND Journal of Economics* 19:589–606.

Holmström, B. 1979. Moral hazard and observability. *Bell Journal of Economics* 10:74–91.

——. 1982a. Moral hazard in teams. *Bell Journal of Economics* 13:324–340.

——. 1982b. Managerial incentive problems: a dynamic perspective. In *Essays in Economics and Management in Honor of Lars Wahlbeck*. Swedish School of Economics, Helsinki. (Reprinted in 1999 in *Review of Economic Studies* 66:169–182.)

Holmström, B. and S. Kaplan. 2001. Corporate governance and merger activity in the United States: making sense of the 1980s and 1990s. *Journal of Economic Perspectives* 15: 121–144.

——. 2003. The state of U.S. corporate governance: what's right and what's wrong. *Journal of Applied Corporate Finance* 15(3):8–20.

Holmström, B. and P. Milgrom. 1991. Multi-task principal-agent analyzes: incentive contracts, asset ownership, and job design. *Journal of Law, Economics, & Organization* 7(Special Issue):24–52.

Holmström, B. and J. Tirole. 1993. Market liquidity and performance monitoring. *Journal of Political Economy* 101: 678–709.

Jarrell, G., J. Brickley, and J. Netter. 1988. The market for corporate control: the empirical evidence since 1980. *Journal of Economic Perspectives* 2:49–68.

Jensen, M. 1984. Takeovers: folklore and science. *Harvard Business Review* November–December:109–121.

——. 1988. Takeovers: their causes and consequences. *Journal of Economic Perspectives* 2:21–48.

——. 1989a. The eclipse of the public corporation. *Harvard Business Review* 67:61–74.

——. 1989b. Active investors, LBOs, and the privatization of bankruptcy. *Journal of Applied Corporate Finance* 2(1): 35–44.

Jensen, M. and W. R. Meckling. 1976. Theory of the firm, managerial behaviour, agency costs and ownership structure. *Journal of Financial Economics* 3:305–360.

Jensen, M. and K. Murphy. 1990. Performance pay and top management incentives. *Journal of Political Economy* 98: 225–264.

Jensen, M. and R. S. Ruback. 1983. The market for corporate control: the scientific evidence. *Journal of Financial Economics* 11:5–50.

Kaplan, S. 1989. The effects of management buyouts on operating performance and value. *Journal of Financial Economics* 24:217–254.

——. 1994a. Top executives, rewards and firm performance: a comparison of Japan and the U.S. *Journal of Political Economy* 102:510–546.

——. 1994b. Top executives, turnover and firm performance in Germany. *Journal of Law, Economics, & Organization* 10:142–159.

Kaplan, S. and J. Stein. 1993. The evolution of buyout and financial structure in the 1980s. *Quarterly Journal of Economics* 108:313–357.

Kaplan, S. and M. Weisbach. 1992. The success of acquisitions: evidence from divestitures. *Journal of Finance* 47: 107–138.

Kaplan, S., M. Mitchell, and K. Wruck. 1997. A clinical exploration of value creation and destruction in acquisitions: organization design, incentives, and internal capital markets. In *Mergers and Productivity* (ed. M. Mitchell and K. Wruck). National Bureau of Economic Research.

Kaufman, A., L. Zacharias, and M. Karson. 1995. *Managers vs. Owners: The Struggle for Corporate Control in American Democracy.* Oxford University Press.

Keynes, J. M. 1936. *The General Theory of Employment, Interest and Money.* London: Macmillan.

Kindelberger, C. 1993. *A Financial History of Western Europe*, 2nd edn. Oxford University Press.

Kojima, K. 1994. An international perspective on Japanese corporate finance. RIEB DP45, Kobe University.

——. 1997. *Corporate Governance: An International Comparison.* Hajime Printing.

Korn/Ferry International. 2003. *30th Annual Board of Directors Study.* New York.

Kotaro, T. 1995. *The Japanese Market Economic System: Its Strengths and Weaknesses.* Tokyo: LTCB International Library Foundation.

Kramarz, F. and D. Thesmar. 2004. Beyond independence: social networks in the boardroom. Mimeo, CREST-INSEE.

Kremer, M. 1997. Why are worker cooperatives so rare? NBER Working Paper 6118.

Kreps, D. 1990. Corporate culture and economic theory. In *Perspectives on Positive Political Economy* (ed. J. Alt and K. Shepsle), pp. 90–143. Cambridge University Press.

Kreps, D., P. Milgrom, J. Roberts, and R. Wilson. 1982. Rational cooperation in the finitely repeated prisoner's dilemma. *Journal of Economic Theory* 27:245–252.

Kroszner, R. S. and Strahan, P. E. 1999. What drives deregulation? Economics and politics of the relaxation of bank branching restrictions. *Quarterly Journal of Economics* 114:1437–1467.

Laffont, J. J. 1990. Analysis of hidden gaming in a three level hierarchy. *Journal of Law, Economics, & Organization* 4: 301–324.

——. 2000. *Incentives and Political Economy.* Clarendon Lectures. Oxford University Press.

Laffont, J. J. and J. Tirole. 1993. *A Theory of Incentives in Procurement and Regulation.* Cambridge, MA, and London: MIT Press.

La Porta, R., F. Lopez-de-Silanes, and A. Shleifer. 1999. Corporate ownership around the world. *Journal of Finance* 54:471–517.

La Porta, R., F. Lopez-de-Silanes, A. Shleifer, and R. Vishny. 1997. Legal determinants of external finance. *Journal of Finance* 52:1131–1150.

——. 1998. Law and finance. *Journal of Political Economy* 106:1113–1155.

——. 1999. The quality of government. *Journal of Law Economics and Organization* 15:222–279.

——. 2000. Investor protection and corporate governance. *Journal of Financial Economics* 58:3–27.

Levin, J. and S. Tadelis. 2005. Profit sharing and the role of professional partnerships. *Quarterly Journal of Economics* 120:131–171.

Lichtenberg, R. and D. Siegel. 1990. The effect of takeovers on the employment and wages of central office and other personnel. *Journal of Law and Economics* 33:383–408.

Mace, M. 1971. *Directors: Myth and Reality.* Boston, MA: Harvard Business School.

Malatesta, P. 1992. Takeover defences. In *The New Palgrave Dictionary of Money and Finance* (ed. P. Newman, M. Milgate, and J. Eatwell). London: Macmillan.

Manne, H. 1965. Mergers and the market for corporate control. *Journal of Political Economy* 73:110–120.

Milgrom, P. and J. Roberts. 1992. *Economics, Organization and Management.* Englewood Cliffs, NJ: Prentice Hall.

Moeller, S., F. Schlingemann, and R. Stulz. 2003. Wealth destruction on a massive scale? A study of acquiring-firm returns in the recent merger wave. Mimeo, Southern Methodist University.

Morck, R., A. Shleifer, and R. Vishny. 1989. Alternative mechanisms for corporate control. *American Economic Review* 79:842–852.

——. 1990. Do managerial objectives drive bad acquisitions? *Journal of Finance* 45:31–48.

Murphy, K. 1985. Corporate performance and managerial remuneration: an empirical analysis. *Journal of Accounting and Economics* April:11–42.

——. 1999. Executive compensation. In *Handbook of Labor Economics* (ed. O. Ashenfelter and D. Card), Volume 3b, Chapter 38, pp. 2485–2563. Amsterdam: Elsevier.

Myers, S. 1977. The determinants of corporate borrowing. *Journal of Financial Economics* 5:147–175.

Pagano, M. and G. Immordino. 2004. Optimal auditing standards. Mimeo, University di Napoli Federico II.

Pagano, M. and P. Volpin. 2005a. Workers, managers, and corporate control. *Journal of Finance* 60:841–868.

——. 2005b. The political economy of corporate governance. *American Economic Review* 95:1005–1030.

——. 2005c. Shareholder protection, stock market development, and politics. Marshall Lecture, European Economic Association, Amsterdam, August 27.

Pagano, M., F. Panetta, and L. Zingales. 1998. Why do companies go public? An empirical analysis. *Journal of Finance* 53:27–64.

Perry, K. and R. Taggart. 1993. The growing role of junk bonds in corporate finance. In *The New Corporate Finance: Where Theory Meets Practice* (ed. D. Chew), pp. 279–287. New York: McGraw-Hill.

Persson, T. and G. Tabellini. 2000. *Political Economics: Explaining Economic Policy*. Cambridge, MA: MIT Press.

Porter, M. 1992. Capital disadvantage: America's failing capital investment system. *Harvard Business Review* 70:65–82.

Pound, J. 1988. Proxy contest and the efficiency of shareholder oversight. *Journal of Financial Economics* 20:237–265.

Rajan, R. and J. Wulf. 2005. Are perks really managerial excess? *Journal of Financial Economics*, in press.

Rajan, R. and L. Zingales. 2003. The great reversals: the politics of financial development in the 20th century. *Journal of Financial Economics* 69:5–50.

Rappaport, A. 1990. The staying power of the public corporation. *Harvard Business Review* 68:96–104.

Rey, P. and J. Tirole. 1986. The logic of vertical restraints. *American Economic Review* 76:921–939.

Roe, M. 1990. Political and legal restraints on ownership and control of public companies. *Journal of Financial Economics* 27:7–42.

——. 1994. *Strong Managers, Weak Owners: The Political Roots of American Corporate Finance*. Princeton University Press.

——. 2003. *Political Determinants of corporate governance: Political Context, Corporate Impact*. Oxford University Press.

Rogerson, W. 1997. Intertemporal cost allocation and managerial investment incentives: a theory explaining the use of economic value added as a performance measure. *Journal of Political Economy* 105:770–795.

Sametz, A. 1995. An expanded role for private pensions in U.S. corporate governance. *Journal of Applied Corporate Finance* 8(2):97–110.

Scharfstein, D. 1988. Product market competition and managerial slack. *RAND Journal of Economics* 19:392–403.

Senbet, L. and J. Seward. 1995. Financial distress, bankruptcy and reorganization. In *Finance* (ed. R. A. Jarrow, V. Maksimovic, and W. Ziemba), pp. 921–961. New York: Elsevier Science.

Shleifer, A. and L. Summers. 1988. Breach of trust in hostile takeovers. In *Corporate Takeovers: Causes and Consequences* (ed. A. J. Auerbach). University of Chicago Press.

Shleifer, A. and R. Vishny. 1986. Large shareholders and corporate control. *Journal of Political Economy* 94:461–488.

——. 1988. Value maximization and the acquisition process. *Journal of Economic Perspectives* 2:7–20.

——. 1989. Managerial entrenchment: the case of management-specific investment. *Journal of Financial Economics* 25:123–139.

——. 1997. A survey of corporate governance. *Journal of Finance* 52:737–783.

Sinclair-Desgagne, B. 1999. How to restore higher-powered incentives in multitask agencies. *Journal of Law, Economics, & Organization* 15:418–433.

Smith, C. and R. Watts. 1982. Incentive and tax effects of executive compensation plans. *Australian Journal of Management* 7:139–157.

Stigum, M. 1990. *The Money Market*, 3rd edn. Burr Ridge, IL: Irwin.

Subramanian, N., A. Chakraborty, and S. Sheikh. 2002. Performance incentives, performance pressure and executive turnover. Mimeo, Brandeis University.

Tirole, J. 1994. The internal organization of government. *Oxford Economic Papers* 46:1–29.

——. 1996. A theory of collective reputations, with applications to the persistence of corruption and to firm quality. *Review of Economic Studies* 63:1–22.

——. 2001. Corporate governance. *Econometrica* 69:1–35.

Vafeas, N. 1999. Board meeting frequency and firm performance. *Journal of Financial Economics* 53:113–142.

Warner, J. 1977. Bankruptcy, absolute priority, and the pricing of risky debt claims. *Journal of Financial Economics* 4: 239–276.

Weisbach, M. S. 1988. Outside directors and CEO turnover. *Journal of Financial Economics* 20:431–460.

Weiss, L. 1990. Bankruptcy resolution: direct costs and violation of priority of claims. *Journal of Financial Economics* 27:285–214.

Wilson, J. Q. 1989. *Bureaucracy: What Government Agencies Do and Why They Do It*. New York: Basic Books.

Yermack, D. 2004a. Flights of fancy: corporate jets, CEO perquisites, and inferior shareholder returns. Mimeo, New York University.

——. 2004b. Remuneration, retention, and reputation incentives for outside directors. Mimeo, New York University.

Zingales, L. 2004. Want to stop corporate fraud? Pay off those whistle-blowers. AEI-Brookings Joint Center Policy Matters Sunday, January 18, 2004. Page B02. (Available at http:// www.aei-brookings.org /dailyregreport /archives / 010019.php.)

Zwiebel, J. 1996. Dynamic capital structure under managerial entrenchment. *American Economic Review* 86:1197–1215.

2

Corporate Financing: Some Stylized Facts

2.1 Introduction

One of the goals of corporate finance theory is to help predict or advise on security issues and payout policies at various stages of a firm's life cycle. There is much discretion involved in specifying a security's cash-flow rights, control rights, and other rights (collateral, options) and the contingencies under which these rights are triggered and exercised. As for corporate governance in Chapter 1, the purpose of this selective review of corporate financing and payout policies is to guide the later theoretical construct and to enable future feedback concerning the accuracy of its predictions.

This chapter offers a succinct description of the financing of firms, focusing on their main financial instruments: debt and equity, in their different varieties.

2.1.1 A Wide Variety of Claims

The simplest form of debt is a claim to a predetermined level on the firm's income. Equityholders receive any profit, that is, are "residual claimants," beyond that level. On the other hand, if debt is not repaid, shareholders receive nothing and debtholders are entitled to the existing income. The view of debt and equity as claims with concave and convex return structures, respectively, is represented in Figure 2.1 for some arbitrary reimbursement level D.

Note that debt in a highly leveraged or "undercapitalized" firm (D high) resembles equity in a modestly leveraged or "well-capitalized" one (D low), in that in both cases claimholders are basically residual claimants at all income levels. Thus, securities that are labeled one way (e.g., debt) may have cash-flow features (and, as we will later see, functions) that are more characteristic of another type of securities (e.g., equity).

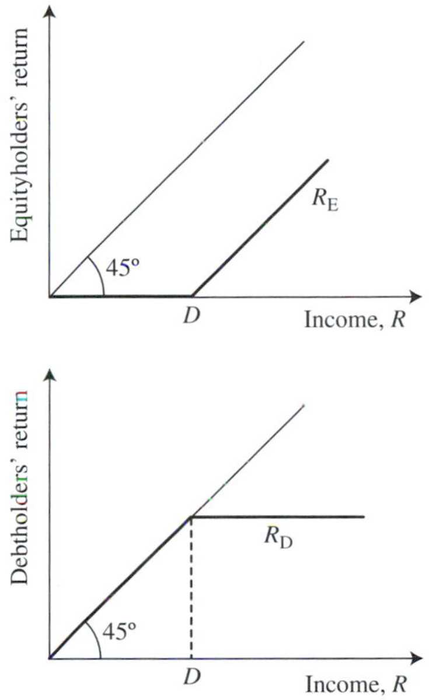

Figure 2.1

This elementary description of financial claims is a useful starting point, but it is oversimplistic. In particular, it ignores the following considerations:

- The firm is usually an ongoing entity, which produces a stream of returns rather than a single one. The one-dimensional representation of Figure 2.1 is at best a condensed view of the stream of returns attached to the claim.

- Who holds the claim in general matters. Corporate governance, for example, depends on whether equity is held by "insiders" (managers, entrepreneurs) or by "outsiders"; on whether share ownership among outsiders is concentrated in the hands of one or a couple of main shareholders or is spread among many shareholders; and on whether debt is held by a large player (such as a bank) or by dispersed investors.

• Claims are not simply defined by their attached returns streams. Claimholders also receive control rights, that is, the right to make decisions, whose scope is either specified in advance or is defined by default (residual rights of control), in circumstances that are defined contractually. For example, shareholders usually have control rights as long as debt covenants are satisfied, but debtholders acquire some control rights in case of violation of these covenants.

• Income (R) may be hard for outsiders to verify in the case of small entrepreneurs. Medium and large firms in contrast usually have a fairly reliable accounting structure, although accounting manipulations may enable managers to shift reported income between years (for instance, through the choice of date of recognition of expenses and revenue), and more generally to distort the overall picture of earnings performance and capabilities.

• Debt may be decomposed into ordinary debt and *secured debt*. When debt is not fully reimbursed, secured debtholders do better than ordinary debtholders as they can seize the assets used as collateral as part of their lending contract.

• The debt–equity dichotomy does not do justice to the richness of claims encountered in the corporate world. Rather than giving a comprehensive description of the many existing claims,[1] here we shall describe a few of the most common intermediate claims between debt and equity.

First, one must distinguish between *senior debt* and *subordinated* or *junior debt*. In the case of default, more senior debtholders are reimbursed first; holders of subordinated debt are then repaid if enough is left, as they have priority over equityholders. Junior debt must therefore deliver a higher yield than senior debt in order to compensate for the higher risk of default. Figure 2.2 depicts the returns attached to subordinated debt when the firm must pay D to senior debtholders and d to junior debtholders. The return schedule for subordinated debt is neither convex nor concave. For d large, subordinated debt resembles equity: a severely undercapitalized (that is, highly leveraged) firm is unlikely

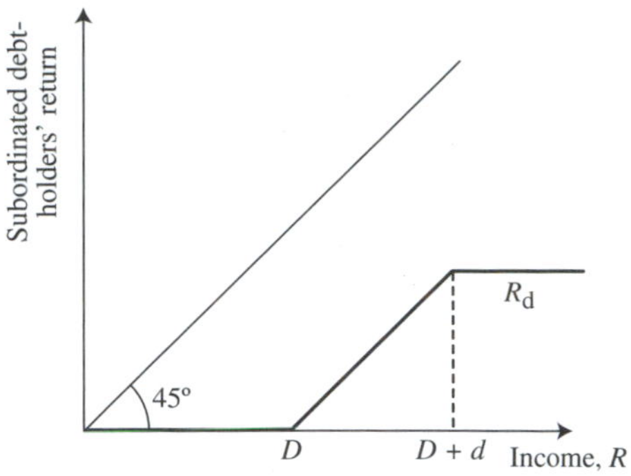

Figure 2.2

to produce much income for its shareholders, so the holders of subordinated debt are almost residual claimants once senior debt is reimbursed. Conversely, for small amounts of senior debt D, the preferences of junior debtholders resemble those of ordinary debtholders.

Another common intermediate claim is (*cumulative*) *preferred stock*. Preferred stock is like debt in that its holders are entitled to a fixed, predetermined repayment. Unlike debt, the firm is not obliged to pay back this specified amount, and thus nonrepayment does not trigger default. However, the firm cannot pay a dividend on (common) stock unless the cumulative (past and current) payments due to preferred stockholders have been made. Preferred stockholders are thus senior to (common) stockholders. Also, while common stocks usually carry voting rights, preferred stockholders often do not have voting rights. They thus have little control over the firm. Their claim is junior to debt, and so for a financial structure made of debt, preferred stock, and equity the returns attached to preferred stocks are also depicted by Figure 2.2 in a single-period context. However, in an ongoing context, preferred stock gives the firm more flexibility on the repayment schedule than subordinated debt.

Subordinated debt and preferred stocks are instances of *mezzanine finance*, that is, of investments that occupy a middle-level position between common equity and senior debt in the firm's capital structure. Mezzanine investments[2] (with exceptions: preferred stocks are usually publicly traded)

1. See, for example, Allen et al. (2005) for more details. Finnerty (1993) provides an overview of some sixty recently introduced types of (debt and equity) security.

2. See Willis and Clark (1993) for more on mezzanine finance.

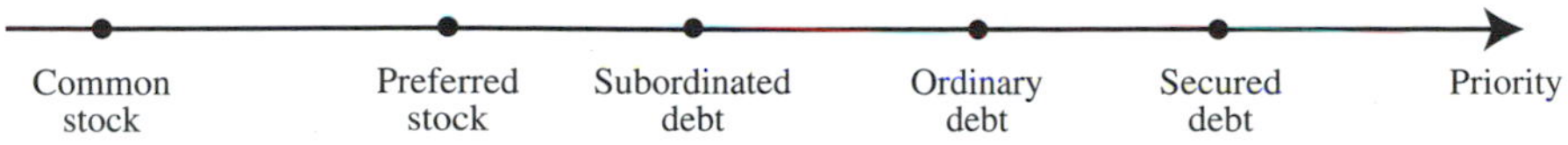

Figure 2.3 Priority structure.

generally are privately placed[3] and often include equity participations in the form of warrants[4] and stock appreciation rights.[5]

The priority structure of the main claims described so far is summarized in Figure 2.3.

A last major intermediate claim is *convertible debt*, one of the many claims that take the form of an option, which the holders can elect to exercise if circumstances are favorable. Convertible debt is basically debt, except that its holders can exchange it for the firm's shares at some predetermined conversion rate.[6] The holders of convertible debt may exercise this option and acquire shares, for instance, if the firm's prospects become favorable, or if for a given expected income of the firm the riskiness of the firm's income has increased due to changes in the environment or to managerial choices (well-diversified holders of a convex, respectively concave, claim like, respectively dislike, risk). Indeed, Jensen and Meckling (1976), among others, have argued that the convertibility option protects debtholders against excessive risk taking by the firm. To see why, consider a corporate move that does not affect the firm's expected profit, but increases its riskiness.[7] For example, the firm may put all its eggs in the same basket by investing in a single risky activity, or by refraining from hedging against market risk (e.g., foreign exchange, interest rate, or raw material risk). Risk-neutral or well-diversified investors benefit from this increase in risk if they hold a convex claim, and they lose if their claim's return profile is concave. In this sense, (diversified) equityholders like (mean-preserving) increases in risk while debtholders dislike such increases in risk. Indeed, equityholders may gain even if the increase in riskiness reduces total investor value (value of debt plus equity), the case of a mean-decreasing increase in risk. For this reason, debtholders are particularly wary of decisions that affect riskiness. To protect themselves against abusive risk taking by the corporation, debtholders may demand covenants that force the firm to exert care; but it may be difficult to force the firm to hedge adequately and so the debtholders may be further protected by a convertibility option: a move that enriches shareholders to the detriment of debtholders is then undone if the latter have the option to convert their claim into an equity claim.

2.2 Modigliani–Miller and the Financial Structure Puzzle

Why do we care about the firms' financial structure? The short answer is that insiders as well as outsiders (commercial banks, investment banks, rating agencies, venture capitalists, equityholders, etc.) devote a lot of attention to its design. But we must also ask whether this attention is warranted. As a matter of fact, economists were stunned when, in two articles in 1958 and 1961, Modigliani and Miller came up with the following rather striking and somewhat counterintuitive result. Under some conditions, the total value of the firm—that is, the value of all claims over the firm's income—is independent of the financial structure. That is, the level of debt, the split of debt into claims with different levels of collateral and different seniorities in the case of bankruptcy, dividend distributions, and many other characteristics or policies relative to the financial structure have no impact on total value. In other words, decisions concerning the financial structure affect only how

3. A private placement is an issue that is offered to a single or to a few investors. In the United States, private placements do not have to be registered with the SEC.

4. A warrant is a long-term call option, that is, an option to buy the security at a specific exercise price on or before a specified exercise date.

5. Stock appreciation rights are stock options which enable their holder to receive the capital gain relative to the exercise price without supplying cash.

6. A convertible bond resembles a package of a bond and a warrant (a warrant is an option to buy shares at a set price on or before a given date). The difference is that the payment to buy the shares is in cash in the case of a warrant, and in a bond in the case of a convertible.

7. In the sense of a mean-preserving spread (i.e., second-order stochastic dominance).

the "corporate pie" (the statistical distribution of income that the firm generates) is shared, but has no effect on the total size of the pie. Thus, an increase in debt or a dividend distribution dilutes the debtholders' claim and benefits the shareholders, but the latter's gain exactly offsets the former's loss.

To illustrate this point, consider the simple debt-equity structure of Figure 2.1, and assume that investors are risk neutral.[8] Let V_E and V_D denote the values of equity and debt for debt repayment D. Then the total value,

$$V_E + V_D = \mathcal{E}(\max(0, R - D)) + \mathcal{E}(\min(R, D)) = \mathcal{E}(R),$$

is independent of D, where $\mathcal{E}(\cdot)$ denotes the expectation with respect to the distribution of the random variable R.[9]

Add to this result the observation that efficient corporate policies should aim at maximizing the size of the corporate pie: any increase in the firm's total value brought about by a change in policy can be divided among the claimholders in a way that makes everyone better off.[10] Modigliani and Miller's conclusion then follows: the financial structure is irrelevant. Managers and investors might as well devote their time to more useful tasks and simplify their financial structure by issuing a single claim, which could be labeled "100% equity" or "equity without debt" (this is the claim depicted by the 45° line in Figure 2.1). The firm would then become an "all-equity firm."

Similarly, the payout policy (dividends and share repurchases/issuance) has no impact on firm value. To illustrate this, consider an all-equity firm, again with risk-neutral investors. Time is discrete: $t = 0, 1, 2, \dots$. In each period t, a random net revenue R_t accrues; then a per-share dividend d_t is paid, the number of shares is adjusted from n_{t-1} to n_t, and an investment I_t is sunk.[11] Consider, for each t, a given (state-contingent) investment policy I_t, as well as an (also state-contingent) choice of dividend d_t and number of shares n_t ($n_t < n_{t-1}$ in the case of share repurchases, $n_t > n_{t-1}$ when new shares are issued). Let P_t denote the price of a share at the end of period t (after the dividend payment) and β the discount factor.

By arbitrage,

$$P_t = \beta\mathcal{E}[d_{t+1} + P_{t+1}].$$

Furthermore, at date t, there is an accounting equality between the sum of revenue and amount raised in the capital market (this amount is negative for share repurchases) and the sum of dividend and investment:

$$R_t + P_t(n_t - n_{t-1}) = n_{t-1}d_t + I_t.$$

The total value of shares in the firm at the end of period t is therefore

$$\begin{aligned} V_t \equiv n_t P_t &= \beta n_t \mathcal{E}[d_{t+1} + P_{t+1}] \\ &= \beta\mathcal{E}[R_{t+1} - I_{t+1} + (n_{t+1} - n_t)P_{t+1} + n_t P_{t+1}] \\ &= \beta\mathcal{E}[R_{t+1} - I_{t+1} + V_{t+1}] \\ &= \mathcal{E}\Big[\sum_{\tau \geqslant 1} \beta^\tau (R_{t+\tau} - I_{t+\tau})\Big] \end{aligned}$$

by induction. Thus, the value of claims on the firm depends only on its "real" characteristics—investment policy and net income—and not on the dividend and capital market choices.

It is only recently that economists have started developing a better understanding of the role of the financial structure. And, although the theory of corporate finance is still evolving, it is fair to say that considerable progress has been made. To examine whether the business community's close attention to the financial structure is warranted, economists have questioned the idea that the size of the pie is exogenously determined. At an abstract level, one can analyze the matter in the following terms. Whenever managerial decisions cannot be perfectly specified contractually, the incentives given to those who pick those decisions affect the firm's income (the

8. The Modigliani–Miller irrelevance result is much more general than this. In particular, it holds even if investors are risk averse (the proof then employs "state-contingent prices").

9. Risk neutrality is not required for the result. Intuitively, with risk-averse investors, one can still define "state-contingent prices," that is, the prices of 1 unit of income in the various states of nature, and apply this equality to the sum of the values of equity and debt.

Also, the notation for expectations will be $E[\cdot]$ in the rest of the book. We use another notation here in order to avoid a confusion with equity.

10. Unless the winners do not have enough money, or more generally means of exchange, to compensate the losers (on this, see Chapter 3).

11. The investment, together with previous investments, will generate a random income R_{t+1} through a production function that we do not need to describe here.

size of the pie) and therefore the split of the pie matters. To clarify this point, consider the numerous decisions taken by the firm's "insiders," namely, the entrepreneurial or managerial team. As discussed in Chapter 1, there is no *a priori* reason why insiders have proper incentives to maximize total firm value. Casual observation suggests that managers do not always exert enough care in their choice of projects or in their supervision of divisions and subsidiaries; that they may waste corporate funds to build empires; that they sometimes select policies because they are easy to implement or will not jeopardize a comfortable managerial position; that some divest resources to indulge in perks (luxurious headquarters, entertainment expenses, corporate jets); or that they may select suppliers or employees on grounds (e.g., friendship) other than efficiency.

Such hazards have been known for a long time, and "governance structures" have been put in place that limit (but do not eliminate) deviations from profit maximization. As discussed in Chapter 1, there are roughly three ways of preventing insiders' misbehavior. First, some contractual constraints can be imposed on managers in the form of covenants and other clauses in financial deals. However, covenants by nature can be based only on public and therefore coarse information, and have their limits. Second, claimholders and managers can agree to build strong or "high-powered" managerial incentives to maximize profit. As pointed out in Chapter 1, though, the provision of high-powered incentives to entrepreneurial or managerial teams is costly, and is unlikely per se to achieve perfect congruence between insiders' and outsiders' interests. It is important that such incentives, if any, be complemented by monitoring and occasional intervention by outsiders: deviations from profit maximization may be detected by outsiders, who can put the firm back on track if they have the authority to do so. Because monitoring is partly a public good for claimholders and therefore is likely to generate free riding, a ubiquitous pattern in efficient corporate financing is the implicit or explicit delegation of monitoring to one or several claimholders with large enough stakes in the firm to induce them to monitor managerial policies, and with a contractual right to interfere if management goes awry. The monitoring patterns differ in their intensity and in the nature of the monitors' claims. Again from Chapter 1, we know that monitors may have debt claims (commercial banks and insurance companies, investment banks), equity claims (large shareholder, such as a pension fund, another corporation, a venture capital firm, or an LBO specialist), or no claim at all (rating agencies, whose incentives are purely based on their reputation to grade corporations accurately).

Our presentation of the main stylized facts about corporate financing emphasizes informational and control issues, which we feel are central to a good understanding of the matter. This does not mean that other considerations, such as tax or clientele effects, are irrelevant. *Tax considerations* influence the choice of financial structure. In particular, debt usually enjoys tax advantages relative to equity; relatedly, junk bonds, which are highly risky bonds, may be issued partly to avoid the corporate income tax that is borne by equity. Taking advantage of the imperfections of the tax system is a consummate and perennial exercise for financial experts (as well as for other experts), but its details are often country- and time-specific, so we will ignore them here.[12] Another important consideration is the presence of *clientele effects* in the supply side of loans. Many financial intermediaries (banks, insurance companies, pension funds, mutual funds) are subject to regulatory requirements, which penalize them for holding certain types of asset or even prohibit them from doing so.[13] The motivation for such controls is that financial intermediaries are subject to moral hazard just like nonfinancial companies, the effect of which is explored further in Chapter 13. Issuers of claims respond, of course, to the fact that financial intermediaries (the main purchasers of the claims) have for regulatory reasons higher demands for certain classes of claims.

A third consideration relates to the *enforcement of financial contracts*. We will mostly assume that such contracts are enforced. In practice, bankruptcy law may not always respect agreements and may

12. See the introduction to the book for a few references on the impact of taxes on financial structures.

13. For more institutional details as well as for a comparison between the governance structures of nonfinancial and financial companies, see Chapters 2 and 3 in Dewatripont and Tirole (1994a).

reshuffle the claims. For example, some bankruptcy laws are prejudiced against secured debt and do not fully allocate the collateral to secured debtholders. Bankruptcy laws can therefore have an impact on the financial structure of firms.[14]

The chapter is organized as follows. Section 2.3 considers debt claims and classifies them along several dividing lines: public versus private, secured versus unsecured, high- versus low-intensity monitoring, priority, covenants. Section 2.4 performs a similar analysis with respect to equity claims. Section 2.5 looks at the firm's actual financial choices, and asks the following questions: How are new investments financed? What are the determinants of leverage? Which firms are financially constrained? How are financial structures affected by business cycle-related fluctuations and by the firm's profit realizations?

2.3 Debt Instruments

A prospective borrower faces a number of choices. First, the firm must choose from whom to borrow. It can apply for a bank loan, place debt privately with institutions such as life insurance companies, issue bonds to the public at large, or use still other forms of credit such as trade credit (that is, credit from suppliers). Second, the firm can issue short-term (possibly rolled over) debt or long-term debt. Third, it can restrict its flexibility in future decision making and transfer some control rights to lenders through the writing of covenants. Fourth, it can pledge assets as collateral. And, fifth, the firm can establish a structure of priority among debt instruments in case of default.

A typical debt liability specifies:[15]

- the amount of borrowing (the principal), the term (maturity), the rate of interest, the scheduling (whether the amount borrowed is due only at maturity or a specified portion of the issue is retired each year—the case of a "sinking fund" requirement), and possibly other conditions (indexation, call provision,[16] etc.);
- a mechanism for transmitting timely, credible information to the lender(s);
- warranties (in which the borrower confirms in writing the accuracy of information about the legal status of the firm, its financial statements, the absence of pending or threatened litigation against it, the absence of previous lien on the collateral or of unpaid taxes, etc.);
- affirmative covenants, which force the borrower to take actions that protect the lender(s);
- negative covenants, which place restrictions on the borrower's ability to take decisions that hurt the lender(s); and
- default and remedy conditions, which specify the circumstances under which the lender(s) can terminate the lending relationship and their rights in such circumstances.

Debt issuance and management is thus a complex operation, and we stress only a few of its key features in this section.

2.3.1 Debt Maturity, Security, and Liquidity

(a) *Collateral.* In business parlance, lenders may lend "against assets" or "against cash flow." Lending against cash flow simply means that their lending is "unsecured," that is, not backed by assets, so that the expectation of recovering money is purely based on the assessment that the borrower will be able to generate enough cash flow. Lending against assets means that the lenders are partially protected against nonrepayment of interest or principal by a pledge of assets. That is, the lenders can repossess (seize) the specified assets in case of default. Lending is then "secured."

14. For example, Biais and Malécot (1996) argue that the low protection of creditors under the 1985 French bankruptcy law (which was reformed in 1994) and the concomitant reluctance of creditors to lend long is one of the factors explaining why French firms had more short-term debt than their American or British counterparts. French bankruptcy law still offers poor protection even to secured creditors because privately-agreed-upon procedures must be overruled by the court, which by law must favor continuation and employment over other alternatives, and because the state and the employees have priority over secured creditors in the case of liquidation.

15. See, for example, Greenbaum and Thakor (1995) for details about the way loans are structured.

16. A call provision granted to the issuer is the right for the issuer to retire the issue earlier than the stated maturity. This option is valuable because if the market interest rates fall, the issuer can retire the issue and refinance at a lower rate. The issuer must, of course, pay a higher interest rate in exchange for this privilege. Conversely, a right granted to the lender to accelerate payments or the collection of the entire loan somewhat protects the lender against default to the extent that it gives him an exit option when he receives signals of an impending default.

Various assets can be pledged: accounts receivables from trade customers,[17] inventories, real estate, equipment, or the managers' personal property. Guarantees from a government or from banks (letters of credit) can also play the role of collateral.

We will see in Chapter 4 that the pledging of assets substantially increases the availability of credit, although it comes with a number of costs (transaction costs, which are substantial, as well as other costs). For this reason, a substantial fraction of commercial and industrial lending is made on a secured basis.

(b) *Trading and liquidity.* It is customary to distinguish between public and private placements. Public bonds are issued on a "primary market" either directly by the issuer or more commonly through an underwriter (securities firm, investment bank, etc.). They are then traded in a "secondary market."[18] In contrast, private placements and bank loans are usually not traded after their issuance, although there has lately been a move toward transforming the corresponding claims into "securities" (that is, claims that are widely traded), a process called "securitization."

The chief determinant of whether a claim can be easily traded in a secondary market (is "liquid") is the symmetry of information among investors about the value of the claim. Suppose that the owner of a claim has more information about its value than prospective buyers of the claim. Buyers are then concerned by the "lemons problem": while the seller may have personal reasons to sell the claim (e.g., liquidity needs), he may also sell the claim because he knows that the claim is not worth much. The buyers are accordingly distrustful, and exchange is unlikely to occur in situations of large asymmetries of information (Akerlof 1970). This theoretical view sheds light on why some claims are liquid and others are not. As we will see, public bonds are usually fairly safe from default by the borrower. There is therefore little asymmetry of information among market participants about the value of public bonds, and public bonds are quite liquid.[19] In contrast, we will see that bank loans and privately placed debt have higher probabilities of default and may involve substantial asymmetries of information between the initial lenders and the prospective buyers in a secondary market. It is therefore not surprising that the securitization of such claims has remained limited.

(c) *Maturities.* Borrowing can be short or long term. Definitions of what short and long term mean are, of course, subjective, and depend on the instrument. For instance, public bonds with maturity under five years are labeled short term and those over twelve years long term. Bank loans under one year (which constitute roughly half of the bank loans) are short term and those over one year long term.

Short-term credit includes the following three items:

Loan commitments and lines of credit granted by commercial banks to borrowers. A loan commitment specifies a maximum loan amount, the commitment's period, and the terms of the loan (a commitment fee to be paid up front, as well as possibly a fee on unused balance; and the interest rate, often a fixed markup over a market rate of interest).

Commercial paper, the only publicly traded short-term debt. Commercial paper has had a very low default rate over the last forty years; it is unsecured, although its quality is increasingly enhanced

17. Alternatively, accounts receivables may be "factored" rather than pledged. That is, they are sold at a discount from their face value to a factoring company which then collects the payments. The supplier or trade creditor then receives cash which can be used to reduce the amount of borrowing, rather than be pledged as collateral when receivables are not factored (for an examination of the similarities and differences between the roles of cash and collateral for the availability of credit, see Chapter 4).

Similarly, the value of assets stemming from commercial transactions may be enhanced by bank guarantees (bankers' acceptances or letters of credit) granted by the buyer's bank (such guarantees are, for example, often used to finance foreign trade). The supplier's bank is then willing to provide an immediate payment to the supplier for the goods delivered in exchange for the enhanced trade credit, namely, the bankers' acceptance, because the claim on the buyer has become almost riskless. (Indeed, bankers' acceptances are widely traded and their interest rate in the market tracks closely the international cost of money to borrowers, LIBOR (the London Interbank Offered Rate on Eurodollar deposits traded between banks, that is, the interest rate corresponding to almost default-free transactions).)

18. Bonds are usually traded "over the counter" (on the OTC market), that is, through bilateral exchanges via dealers rather than in a centralized exchange as in the case of major stocks.

19. Note that the important property of bonds here is not the fact that default is unlikely, but rather its implication that information about their value is fairly symmetric. Indeed, while one might believe that low default rates make bonds pretty riskless, changes in market interest rates induce important fluctuations in their price (if they are not indexed on the market rate). So, the general rule is that symmetric information about a claim makes it more liquid regardless of its riskiness.

by "backup lines of credit" from a bank. Those backup lines of credit do not guarantee repayment by the bank to the holders of commercial paper in case of borrower default, but they provide liquidity enhancement to the borrower and therefore reduce the probability of default.[20]

Trade credit, that is, borrowing from suppliers. Trade credit is an important source of short-term financing at the individual firm level. In 1991, U.S. manufacturing firms had 13.7% of their total assets in accounts receivable and 7.4% in accounts payable. Trade credit is even more significant in some other countries (the same numbers for Japan were 24% and 13%).[21] It is typically very expensive: for instance, about 80% of the U.S. firms offer their products on terms called "2-10 net 30," which means that the buyer must pay within 30 days, but receives a 2% discount if payment occurs within 10 days. The 2% price increase over the remaining 20 days corresponds to a 37.24% annual interest rate![22]

Firms in general would prefer to be granted long-term credit because short-term credit forces them to return repeatedly to their bank or to the credit market for new money and exposes them to the risk of refusal and to the necessity of selling assets at distress prices or of cutting down on their activity. On the other hand, short-term borrowing has two key benefits: first, it returns more funds to the lenders and thus facilitates financing in the first place; second, precisely because it forces firms to return occasionally to their lenders, short-term borrowing imposes more discipline on the borrowers (the theoretical underpinnings for this argument will be examined in Chapters 5 and 6).

Long-term credit corresponds to bank loan agreements and to long-term privately or publicly placed debt. Long-term credit agreements are much more elaborate than short-term ones and involve a number of covenants. This brings us to the design of loans, to which we will turn in Section 2.3.3.

2.3.2 Credit Analysis

When contemplating short-term and especially long-term lending, lenders perform a credit analysis along several directions. They analyze the borrower's financial data (capital structure, cash flow statements, liquidity, etc.). They estimate the market and liquidation values of assets. They also look at the capability and character of the entrepreneur or top management. Bankers refer to the "five Cs of credit": character and capacity (capability), capital, collateral, and coverage (the first four Cs were just described, the fifth is simply the existence of insurance against death or disability of a key person): see Section 2.7 for more details. Chapters 3–6 will analyze the role of capital, collateral, and capability and character.

Credit analyses are also performed by third parties who do not lend to the firm. Predominant among

20. The maturity of commercial paper is often lower than one month, although it can extend to nine months. This short maturity implies that it is often rolled over. A bank line of credit is basically an insurance policy for the borrower/issuer as it allows the latter to pay back the outstanding commercial paper without having to sell off assets at "fire sale" (low) prices in case adverse market conditions or bad news about the issuer make it difficult to roll over the commercial paper.

Commercial paper in practice is meant to have low credit risk. (For this reason, only 22% of the commercial paper in the United States is issued by industrial companies, financial companies accounting for the bulk of the issues.) A clear description of the mechanics of commercial paper is Chapter 22 of Stigum (1990).

21. Rajan and Zingales (1995) report accounts payable for large firms equal to 15% of assets in the United States, 11.5% in Germany, and 17% in France. See Petersen and Rajan (1997) for an in-depth study of trade credit in the United States.

More recent numbers for the United States can be found in Frank and Goyal (2003), who more generally provide evidence about broad patterns of financing activity. They report for 1998 and for 7,301 U.S. industrial firms a percentage of book value of total assets equal to 17.7% for receivables and 10.4% for account payables.

22. Several explanations have been proposed as to why trade credit is widely observed given the high cost to the buyer. Some (e.g., Smith 1987) view it as a means for the supplier to distinguish between high- and low-risk buyers, and to learn useful information for their future relationship. Others have suggested that the underlying collateral (the products shipped, if they have not yet been resold) has higher value for the supplier than for a bank, but this does not explain why the interest rate on trade credit is much larger than that on bank loans. Brennan et al. (1988) offer a price discrimination explanation for trade credit. Wilner (1994) links the higher rate of interest on trade credit with the suppliers' poor bargaining position in a renegotiation following default: because the suppliers care much about the continuation of their relationship with the buyers, they make more concessions than banks in renegotiation. Biais and Gollier (1997) argue that suppliers may have private information about the riskiness of their clients, which implies that trade credit, if extended, provides a favorable signal about the credit quality of the clients and allows the latter to get cheap complementary financing from banks, which in turn has value to the suppliers in the context of ongoing trade relationships. Finally, Burkart and Ellingsen (2004) trace the informational superiority of trade creditors over banks to the knowledge that the transfer of the input has taken place. They argue on the basis of their theoretical model that trade credit should have a short maturity as it loses its advantage when the illiquid input is transformed into liquid output.

these are rating agencies. Their main raison d'être is that credit analysis is costly and, when claimholders are dispersed (as is usually the case for a public bond), it is efficient to centralize credit analysis in a single entity (or a small number of entities). Issuers of bonds or of commercial paper, by paying fees to rating agencies for being graded, in a sense solve the collective action problem faced by prospective bondholders.[23] One may wonder why rating agencies can have any reliability given they do not put their own money into the borrowing firm and that, even worse, they are paid by the very companies that they rate, which, of course, creates a conflict of interest. The answer is that they care about their reputation for measuring and disclosing accurately the riskiness of the claim. A good rating is worth more to an issuer if the previous issues which were given the same rating by the rating agency have had a good track record. Thus a rating agency which has the reputation for not trying to please its issuing clients can actually command higher fees from them.

Ratings are based on criteria similar to those used by banks for their credit analysis. The rating agency looks at the borrower's capital, cash flow, liquidity (including the existence of resources to meet unexpected cash demands), capability, and at the firm's line of business. What they emphasize more depends on various characteristics of the issue, in particular its maturity. For example, the main focus for commercial paper (which, recall, is very short-term public debt) is the borrower's liquidity, that is, how easy it is for the borrower to come up with cash to repay the maturing commercial paper.

While there are a number of private rating agencies, the market is still dominated by the two best known, Moody's and Standard & Poor's (S&P), which suggests that reputation is a very worthwhile asset and a strong barrier to entry. Ratings are sometimes also prepared by agencies or organizations in charge of controlling the asset quality of financial intermediaries and are then employed for prudential regulation, i.e., to verify the capital adequacy of the financial intermediary.[24]

Rating agencies use grades to measure the credit worthiness of issuers and securities. For example, S&P gives the following grades (in descending order): AAA, AA, A, BBB, BB, B, CCC, CC, C (and D for a firm in default); Moody's has a very similar notation. The grade reflects an estimate of the likelihood of default. For example, the cumulative default rate over the first ten years of a bond's life was 0.1% for an AAA rated bond and 31.9% for a B rated bond in Altman's (1989) sample. It is also customary to define a coarser partition, with "investment grade securities" being those with grades above BBB, and "below investment grade securities" or "junk bonds" being the others. As an approximation, only investment grade securities are issued, so securities below investment grade are mainly downgraded investment grade securities.[25] Needless to say, ratings, while useful, are not perfect, if only because agency problems may creep into decisions of credit-rating agencies as well (for example, they may devote insufficient resources to analyzing a security issue or they may strategically delay recognizing their past mistakes).

Lastly, like bondholders, trade creditors face a collective action problem with respect to the credit analysis of borrowers. A trade borrower often faces several dispersed lenders and it may be excessively costly for each to conduct a credit analysis. Unsurprisingly, trade creditors do rely on external ratings. Besley and Osteryoung (1985) cite a survey showing that 69% of U.S. firms use credit ratings supplied by mercantile agencies when determining credit limits for their clients.

2.3.3 The Writing of Debt Agreement Covenants

As discussed in more detail in Section 2.8, covenant writing is an important step in the lending process.

23. In the past, rating agencies collected fees from investors rather than from the issuer; but this, of course, gave rise to free riding among investors.

24. For example, in the United States, the National Association of Insurance Commissioners in 1990 issued guidelines creating six quality categories, NAIC-1 through NAIC-6, for privately placed debt. Only the top two grades, NAIC-1 and NAIC-2, correspond to investment grade ratings from major rating agencies. Investments by insurance companies in privately placed debt of below NAIC-3 quality are heavily penalized. Consequently, an important source of funding for below NAIC-3 borrowers dried up almost instantaneously. See, for example, Carey et al. (1993) and Emerick and White (1992) for more details about the guidelines (known as Rule 144A) and about their impact.

25. In the United States, below investment grade securities represented less than 4% of corporate debt in 1977. Even in the aftermath of the junk bond explosion of the 1980s, only one-quarter of the 23% of corporate debt rated below investment grade had been issued as junk bonds.

Covenants can be found to various extents in bank loan agreements, in privately placed debt agreements, and in public bonds issues. Their details depend not only on the nature of the lenders, but also on the maturity and other specificities of the claim.

It is customary to distinguish between positive and negative covenants. Positive covenants stipulate actions the borrower must take, while negative covenants put restrictions on managerial decisions. I do not find this standard distinction very enlightening: a positive covenant specifying an action may be viewed as a negative covenant prohibiting the opposite action. For instance, the obligation of maintaining assets in good repair and working order, a positive covenant, can be alternatively stated as the prohibition of letting the company's assets wear and tear. We will depart from tradition by offering a taxonomy more in line with economic considerations, which suggest two rationales for covenants.

To understand the first rationale for covenants, it is useful to recall that managers and shareholders are in control of the firm as long as the covenants are not violated.[26] Managers and shareholders often have incentives to take actions that jeopardize the payment of interest and principal to lenders (we will later divide such actions into two sets). These actions redistribute wealth from lenders to managers and mainly shareholders. Note that the fact that the actions redistribute wealth per se is not a motivation for the existence of covenants. Such actions may reduce the value of debt and increase that of equity, and yet have no impact on the total value of the firm following the Modigliani–Miller logic. Tolerating such actions through the absence of covenants lowers the value of debt, but may have no overall effect:[27] to the extent that the actions are anticipated, the *ex ante* price of bonds and equity reflects the transfer that will take place *ex post*, so that total investor value (the value of debt plus that of equity) is still the same. It is only to the extent that managers and shareholders may have incentives to take actions that reduce total firm value that covenants have a role. Thus, the first role of covenants is to prevent managers and shareholders from taking value-reducing actions that could be privately optimal because they expropriate debtholders.

The second role of covenants is to define the circumstances under which different classes of claimholder (equityholders or debtholders) receive the right to intervene in management.[28] The threat of external intervention in management is best viewed as part of the incentive package offered to insiders. As Chapter 10 will show, it may be optimal to confer control rights on shareholders in good times and on debtholders in the case of mediocre performance. The transfer of control is triggered by the nonpayment of interest or principal or by a covenant violation. This yields the second rationale for the existence of covenants. Further, to the extent that shareholders and managers are hurt by a transfer of control to debtholders, the former have incentives to manipulate the (mainly financial) measures of performance defined by this type of covenant. A further set of covenants can, however, be introduced to limit such manipulations.

Thus, our taxonomy of covenants highlights two rationales. We further divide the two sets into two subsets each.

2.3.3.1 Covenants Meant to Prevent Value Reduction (The "Conflict View")

As discussed above, the divergence of preferences between shareholders and debtholders may induce the former, when they are in control, to take actions that are meant to benefit them to the detriment of the latter. They may be willing to sacrifice total value to achieve this goal. For convenience, we subdivide the actions into two subsets depending on whether they involve an increase in the riskiness of the firm's cash flow.

Actions not increasing risk. We first consider actions that reduce the value of existing debt without

26. In principle, the shareholders, perhaps through the board of directors, are in control. In practice, asymmetric information between insiders and outside shareholders introduces an important distinction between formal authority, held by shareholders, and real or effective authority, often enjoyed by managers. For more details on this idea, see Chapter 10.

27. Unless borrowers and lenders find it easier to value debt when debt is associated with a standard set of covenants.

28. This rationale in a sense is more primitive than the first one, because it explains why claims with conflicting interests are created. The possibility of redistribution among claims, and therefore the first rationale for covenants, would disappear if there were a single claim.

per se increasing the riskiness of the firm's income flow. Covenants put restrictions on *payments* to shareholders. Payments can take different forms: cash dividend,[29] share repurchase,[30] or "affiliated transactions" (in which the firm engages in loss-making transactions, e.g., through generous transfer prices, with another unit also owned by the shareholders). Excessive payments may leave the debtholders with an "empty shell."[31]

Second, covenants impose limitations on *further indebtedness*. The issuance of new debt dilutes the value of existing debt (the reader may want to check this for the simple financial structure displayed in Figure 2.1); accordingly, limits on the amount of new debt are generally set by a covenant. Dilution is particularly strong if the new debt is either secured or senior to the current debt. It is therefore not surprising that additional covenants cover new secured or senior debt: limitations on liens; positive covenants forcing the firm to pay taxes (the government often acquiring a claim senior to that of creditors in the case of unpaid taxes) or, in the United States, to contribute to the Pension Benefit Guarantee Corporation (again, the debts to the Guarantee Corporation are senior to those of creditors); and covenants restricting leases (long-term noncancelable rental agreements may acquire some seniority, e.g., one year's lease payment, over other creditors' claims).

Actions increasing risk ("asset substitution"). As mentioned earlier, shareholders, with their convex claim, benefit from increased risk taking while debtholders, with their concave claim, are hurt. Of course, and as we noted earlier, debtholders are partially protected against gambling if their claim is convertible into equity, as they can switch to equity if the firm's income becomes riskier. But most debt claims are not convertible. Covenants are then meant to protect debtholders against increases in risk. Examples include covenants prohibiting investments into new lines of business, earmarking the loan for specified purposes, or limiting the growth of the firm; and covenants requiring life or casualty insurance for key personnel or setting minimum standards of coverage against interest rate or exchange rate risk.

It is clear that such actions, whether they increase risk or not, need not reduce total value. But each has the potential of doing so. Let us give a few examples. (i) Large payments to shareholders seriously decapitalize the firm and make it more likely that the firm will face liquidity problems or that control will be transferred to debtholders in the near future (see below). This may either demotivate the managers or induce them to "gamble for resurrection" (see, for example, Dewatripont and Tirole 1994a,b), creating value losses. (ii) Unpaid taxes in general involve late payment penalties, generating a value loss for the firm. (iii) Shareholders may benefit from issuing new debt to finance a new investment with negative net present value (NPV) simply because the loss to current and diluted debtholders exceeds the NPV loss. (iv) Risk taking may create a value loss, and yet raise the value of equity.

We now turn to the second rationale for covenants.

2.3.3.2 Covenants Defining Control Rights (The "Control View")

Shift of control in the case of mediocre performance. Some financial covenants are meant to transfer control to debtholders in the case of mediocre performance. One encounters covenants linked with the firm's (long-term) solvency. These covenants are expressed both in relative and absolute value. For example, total debt cannot exceed a fraction of total assets (leverage constraint). Or the firm's net worth (an accounting measure of equity, expressed as the difference between the book value of assets and that of liabilities) must exceed some minimum level. Interestingly, covenants also require a minimum amount of liquidity, even for long-term

29. See, for example, Smith and Warner (1979) for a description of the mathematical formulae limiting dividend distribution.

30. Share repurchases are an alternative to dividend distributions. In a share repurchase, the firm buys back its own stock and thus hands money back to shareholders (there are several modalities; see, for example, Brealey and Myers (1988, pp. 359, 360) for more details).

31. Spin-offs may be a way of expropriating debtholders. An example is Marriott Corp.'s 1992 attempt to split into two companies, a service company called Marriott International and a real-estate company called Host Marriott, a smaller and riskier concern to whom all of Marriott Corp.'s debts would have been assigned. Unsurprisingly, the initial stock market reaction at the announcement of the split was a rise of 21% of Marriott's stock price; and a bondholder lawsuit for fraud quickly ensued (*Washington Post*, November 18, 1992).

loans; for instance, the firm's working capital[32] is required to exceed some minimal level. Liquidity requirements are meant to guarantee that the firm will be able to face its short-term obligations. One may wonder why so much attention is paid to liquidity measures, since the fundamental issue is always that of the firm's solvency: for, a firm that momentarily lacks money can always make the shortfall through borrowing if its solvency is not in question. In this sense, liquidity problems are always solvency problems. Yet, and as bankers well know, solvency problems are often signaled by liquidity problems. Hence, the rationale for separate covenants on minimum liquidity.

The shift of control does not quite mean that debtholders start running the firm; they may do so occasionally if the firm is bankrupt and a receiver defending their interests is put in charge of the firm, or if they swap their debt for equity. But, more often, they will exert control indirectly by threatening not to refinance or to apply the default and remedy conditions (for example, the possibility for a bank to accelerate the collection of its entire loan) when a covenant is violated.[33] They can then impose a change in corporate policy, impose new covenants, renegotiate the claims, etc.

Completing the control view. This shift-of-control mechanism is more effective if two conditions are satisfied. First, the lenders must be well-informed in order to be able to detect a covenant violation and to properly exercise the power they have in that contingency. Second, the firm should not be able to fictitiously satisfy financial covenants through accounting manipulations.

Informational covenants. The need for lenders to be informed rationalizes a new class of covenants. Among these are covenants requiring the firm to report to the lender(s) a number of variables on a regular basis, covenants specifying extensive rights of inspection of facilities and books by the lender(s), and, in the case of a bank lender, the requirement that the firm's principal checking accounts be maintained with the bank.

Covenants limiting accounting manipulations. Financial covenants, to be effective, should not be easily manipulable. To the extent that their violation transfers part of the control to debtholders, managers and shareholders have incentives to use "creative" accounting in order to satisfy the financial covenants if needed. This motivates the existence of a further class of covenants that are meant to give credence to financial covenants. First, the lender(s) and the borrower must agree on an accounting method, in general the Generally Accepted Accounting Principles (GAAP) in the United States. But GAAP still leaves a substantial discretion. Covenants are then used to reduce this discretion by limiting instruments for creative accounting. Consider, for example, measures of the firm's solvency. The firm may have an incentive to sell assets whose market price exceeds the historical or book value, in order to increase the firm's measured net worth or to decrease measured leverage (as the cash received exceeds the accounting value of the assets on the balance sheet). The real net worth or leverage is not affected by the operation, but solvency covenants may no longer be violated. Consequently, loan agreements often prohibit the sale of more than a specified fraction (10%, 15%, or more) of the assets, or else require that the proceeds be used to pay down the debt.[34]

Another concern of borrowers is that the firm's real solvency be concealed through "off-balance-sheet activities" (recall from Chapter 1 that off-balance-sheet activities were prominent in some recent scandals in Europe and the United States). In particular, some liabilities are not incurred at present and in a noncontingent way. They are then recorded "off-balance." For example, a loan commitment promised against a fee to a borrower is off balance sheet for the bank issuing the commitment. The off-balance-sheet liabilities of a nonfinancial company include, for instance, leasing arrangements, consignment stocks

32. As measured, say, by the ratio of "current assets" (assets that will normally be turned into cash within a year) to current liabilities (liabilities that will normally be repaid within a year).

33. The borrower usually has a "cure period" of a few weeks to satisfy the covenant if the latter is violated. Because the deterioration of a financial ratio may be due to a bad realization of the environment such as a temporary shortfall in earnings rather than to managerial misbehavior, it makes sense to give the firm a chance to reestablish compliance with the agreement.

34. Another reason to limit the sale of assets may be that the proceeds of the sale could be used to buy new assets or enter new activities that would increase the riskiness of the firm's income (recall the "conflict view" of the rationale for covenants).

for dealers (who repay the manufacturer from sales), or an asset sale and repurchase agreement (which is similar to a loan, as the difference between the buyback price and the selling price constitutes de facto an interest payment). While not all off-balance-sheet financing need concern lenders, some arrangements may make the income statement and/or the balance sheet look better than they really are and help de facto breach loan or bond covenants without formally violating them. Consider, for example, a lease (long-term rental agreement) set up, as is often the case, so that lease payments are small at the start and larger later on. Suppose further that the lease specifications make cancellation costly. Then the firm's net worth is overstated as the corresponding future liabilities are off balance sheet. As another illustration, consider a firm's pledge to rescue a subsidiary if the latter gets into financial distress. This contingent liability is not recorded on the balance sheet, but is quite real. Unsurprisingly, covenants attempt to limit balance-sheet manipulations by the firm.[35]

2.3.3.3 Bankruptcy Process

Covenant violation generates trouble for the borrower. So does, of course, default. In the case of default, creditors or other interested parties, if they do not choose to roll over or forgive some of their claims, may force bankruptcy.[36] We will not discuss bankruptcy procedures both for conciseness and because the laws as well as the extent of their enforcement by courts are necessarily country- and time-specific. Let us just list a few well-known points. First, creditors are compensated according to some priority rule in the case of liquidation. For example, in the United States, (1) administrative expenses of the bankruptcy process are paid first, then come (2) unpaid taxes or debts to government agencies (e.g., the Pension Benefit Guarantee Corporation), (3) some wage claims (up to some ceiling), (4) secured and senior creditors, (5) junior creditors, (6) preferred shares, and, last, (7) equityholders. Second, many bankruptcy processes do not end up with a liquidation, although the threat of liquidation is important in the renegotiation or reorganization process. Third, secured and senior creditors obviously fare better than other creditors in liquidation. In the United States, secured creditors receive about 31% of their claims, senior creditors 36%, and unsecured creditors 8% (Brealey and Myers 1988, p. 742). For overviews of the issues with the current bankruptcy laws and for some policy suggestions, we refer the reader to, for example, Aghion et al. (1992), Bebchuk (1988), and White (1989).

2.3.4 The Overall Picture: Two Dichotomies in the Credit Market

2.3.4.1 Duality on the Lending Side

Simplifying a bit, lenders can be split into two groups, depending on the concentration of claimholdings.

Sophisticated (concentrated, well-informed) lenders, also called relationship investors, include banks and institutional investors (e.g., life insurance companies) investing in private placements. The corresponding loans are extended by one or a few lenders, who are heavily involved in the writing of the loan, the monitoring of the covenants, and the renegotiation in case of covenant violation.

Dispersed lenders include public bondholders and trade creditors. They are numerous and face a free-rider problem. That is, they individually have suboptimal incentives to invest in information collection and monitoring of the borrower.

The empirical evidence shows that claims issued to sophisticated and dispersed lenders differ in a number of respects.

(a) *Screening.* It is customary to say that sophisticated investors perform more *ex ante* monitoring (that is, more screening or more credit analysis)

35. Our rendition of the writing of covenants is, of course, not exhaustive. For example, there are covenants restricting the purchase of claims (e.g., stocks) in other companies. Such covenants have several of the rationales discussed above: preventing the firm from engaging in self-dealing transactions with related companies, avoiding asset substitution, and increasing the transparency of financial covenants, the latter rationale being related to the issue of double gearing in prudential regulation (see, for example, Chapter 3 in Dewatripont and Tirole 1994a).

36. There is some controversy over whether creditors are well-protected by bankruptcy proceedings. In the United States (where most bankruptcy filings are made voluntarily by firm managers), Chapter 11 allows managers to remain in control and to have six months to propose a reorganization plan. The resulting procedure and the possibility of modifying priorities may enable managers to impose an unfavorable renegotiation plan to some groups of creditors.

before extending a loan. We must, of course, be careful not to take this view for granted; after all, while public bondholders perform little screening themselves, their demand for bonds on the primary market depends on the assessment or the mere presence of sophisticated agents such as rating agencies and underwriters, who have their reputations at stake. Thus, such sophisticated agents may go some way toward solving the bondholders' collective action problem and perform some of the role performed by banks and institutional investors in the case of private placements.

Yet, there is a widespread feeling that banks and institutional investors receive more information and access to management than those provided to investors in public markets.[37] Also, the illiquidity of bank loans and private placements demonstrates a superiority of the sophisticated investors' information over that of other investors.

(b) *Covenants.* Debt issued to sophisticated investors involves more and tighter covenants than public debt.[38] Commercial paper has very few covenants, and its long-term counterpart, public debt, has mainly negative covenants, while for both bank and nonbank private debt, affirmative and negative covenants are common.

(c) *Seniority/security/maturity.* There is a wide range of maturities from overnight (or even sometimes intraday) loans to very-long-term borrowing such as the 1996 successful 100-year bond issue by IBM.[39] Table 2.1 reviews the average maturities for a large sample of U.S. firms.

Loan maturity varies with the types of assets that are being financed. As Hart and Moore (1989) observe, assets tend to be matched with liabilities. Long-term loans are often used for fixed-asset acquisitions (property, machinery, etc.), while short-term loans tend to be used for working capital purposes (payroll needs, inventory financing, smoothing of seasonal imbalances). Thus the maturity of loans adjusts to the durability of the underlying collateral (if any).

Table 2.1 Maturity and priority structure of fixed claims in the United States. *Source:* Barclay and Smith (1996, Table 3). Reprinted with permission from Blackwell Publishing Ltd, Oxford.

	Percentage of total fixed claims	
	Mean	Median
Maturity		
More than one year	0.69	0.80
More than two years	0.56	0.65
More than three years	0.46	0.51
More than four years	0.39	0.39
More than five years	0.32	0.28
Priority		
Capitalized leases	0.11	0.00
Secured debt	0.40	0.31
Ordinary debt	0.38	0.21
Subordinated debt	0.10	0.00

Bank debt or privately placed debt tends to be secured and senior. Public bonds are rarely secured and are sometimes subordinated. It is also customary to distinguish the two forms of debt on the basis of maturity: bank debt often has shorter maturities. While banks indeed play a major role in providing short-term credit to firms, things are in fact a bit more complex here. First, there are forms of dispersed debt, such as commercial paper and trade credit, which have a very short maturity. Second, banks and institutional investors also issue long-term credits.[40] On the whole, James (1987) reports average maturities for the United States equal to 5.6 years for bank debt, 15.3 years for nonbank private debt, and 18 years for publicly listed debt, while Light and White (1979) report an average maturity of 35 days for commercial paper.

(d) *Renegotiation in the case of covenant violation (or nonrepayment).* According to conventional wisdom as well as some evidence, the renegotiation of

37. See, for example, Emerick and White (1992), who show how borrowers with very low or no credit ratings may still be able to obtain low-interest-rate credit from sophisticated investors, which suggests the existence of superior information acquisition.

38. See Kahan and Tuckman (1993) for a comparison of covenants for privately placed debt and public bonds. See also Smith and Warner (1979) and Carey et al. (1993).

39. IBM then borrowed $850 million in 100-year bonds.

40. For example, in the United States, insurance companies have played a major role in funding less creditworthy firms through long-term credits (five- to twenty-year debt).

covenants is easier when debt is held by sophisticated investors.[41] Asquith et al. (1994) show that 80% of the U.S. companies under distress restructure their bank debt through direct renegotiation (see also Gilson et al. 1990). Relatedly, Hoshi et al. (1990, 1991) find that Japanese firms that are in a "main-bank" coalition (*keiretsu*) invest and sell more after the onset of distress.

The ease of renegotiation may be due either to the concentration of claims or to better information of investors in the case of sophisticated lenders. It may be difficult to renegotiate with many investors, although some mechanisms are designed so as to achieve coordination among dispersed investors (nomination of a bond trustee who acts on behalf of the multitude of bondholders, possibility for the firm to offer new securities in exchange for bonds in order to lower its debt obligations).

(e) *Default and liquidity.* With the (minor) exception of junk bonds, public debt (commercial paper, public bonds) is rarely defaulted.[42] As explained above, this implies that there is little asymmetry of information among investors as to their value and that it can be widely traded in financial markets. In contrast, bank loans and privately placed debts do default (or are renegotiated under the threat of liquidation) with nonnegligible probability. There is asymmetric information among investors about their value, and the corresponding claims are much less liquid than commercial paper and public bonds.

(f) *Certification.* There is some evidence that the existence of a stake of a sophisticated investor in a firm helps the firm raise complementary funding, which suggests that the stake conveys favorable information about the creditworthiness of the firm. For example, firms raise more money in an initial public offering of shares when they have bank loans (James and Weir 1991). Also related is the evidence that the announcement of a bank loan grant raises the firm's stock price (Lummer and McConnell 1989).

(g) *Issue costs.* Issue costs (transaction costs, disclosure costs) are large for commercial paper and public debt and small for bank or nonbank private debt. In particular, issuing public bonds in the United States requires the firm to disclose key financial data, which may be a major disincentive if the firm's equity is not publicly traded (and therefore few of these data are public knowledge).

2.3.4.2 Duality on the Borrowing Side

Symmetrically to lenders, borrowers can approximately be split into two groups, depending on the riskiness of the debt they issue: high-quality borrowers tend to be well-capitalized, large, and highly rated by credit-rating agencies; conversely, low-quality (risky) issuers tend to be poorly capitalized, small, and unrated by credit-rating agencies.[43]

The two types of borrower have quite different borrowing patterns, which will later figure prominently in the theoretical analysis:

- High-quality borrowers have more long-term debt. The short-term indebtedness of large firms in the United States (recall that quality and size are strongly correlated) is 13% against 29% for small firms. The corresponding numbers in Germany are 39.5% and 55.9% (Gertler and Gilchrist 1994).
- High-quality borrowers can more easily obtain a loan commitment from a bank (Avery and Berger 1991) or issue commercial paper.[44] For this reason and the previous one, they manage their liquidity needs more easily than risky borrowers.
- High-quality borrowers can borrow (long) by issuing public debt while risky borrowers cannot. Risky borrowers must borrow from sophisticated investors.
- Unsurprisingly in view of the previous observations, high-quality borrowers suffer little and hardly reduce their investments, if at all, during a credit

41. Note that the ease of renegotiation is a mixed blessing. On the one hand, renegotiation enhances the efficiency of *ex post* outcomes; for example, it can prevent liquidation in situations in which continuation is socially optimal. On the other hand, it weakens the power of *ex ante* incentives. The firm is less concerned about the possibility of a covenant violation and the concomitant threat if it knows that the covenants will be renegotiated. That is, the prospect of renegotiation reduces discipline. For more on this, see Burkart et al. (1996), as well as the discussion of the soft budget constraint in Section 5.5.

42. For example, Stigum (1990, p. 1037) observed that only five issuers of commercial paper had defaulted in the United States during a period of fifteen years.

43. Indeed, "fewer that 25 of the over 400 industrial U.S. companies rated investment-grade by Standard & Poor's Corporation had total assets of less than $500 million as of year-end 1991" (Emerick and White 1992).

44. Commercial paper, which, recall, is unsecured short-term public debt, is mainly issued by firms with AAA or AA credit ratings.

crunch. A credit crunch is triggered by a decrease in banks' and other intermediaries' loanable funds (either because of a decrease in the intermediaries' capitalization or because of a tightening of prudential regulation or of monetary policy). Because risky borrowers are dependent on such funds, they are substantially hurt by a credit crunch. Also, bank loans to small manufacturing firms fall relative to bank loans to large firms when "money is tight" (Gertler and Gilchrist 1993; Oliner and Rudebusch 1993).

- The restrictiveness of loan covenants is inversely related to the credit quality of the borrower (Carey et al. 1993). Small borrowers also post more collateral than high-grade borrowers (Berger and Udell 1990).

2.4 Equity Instruments

Our treatment of equity financing will be a bit briefer than that of debt financing since we have already covered some of the material in Sections 1.4 and 1.5 on active monitoring by large shareholders and takeovers, respectively. We here emphasize the life cycle of equity financing from start-up and alliance financing to the initial public offering (IPO) or sale, and from there on to seasoned equity offerings. On the equity side, one central theme is, as in the case of debt, the role of delegated monitoring in alleviating the hazards attached to dispersed ownership. Since we have already reviewed the role of large shareholders, boards, and the market for corporate control in Chapter 1, we here focus on that of venture capitalists and alliance partners as illustrations of equity financing in the early stages of a firm's life (another important form of private equity with covenants with regards to the exit mechanism that are reminiscent of those for venture capital is shareholder agreements, including joint ventures[45]). We then discuss the mechanisms for issuing equity in Section 2.4.2.

2.4.1 Privately Held Equity and Sophisticated Investors: The Case of Start-up Financing

As in the case of debt, companies may need to sell their equity to some large, sophisticated investor. Three prominent classes of such investors in the case of privately held companies are venture capitalists, large customers, and leveraged buyout (LBO) specialists. As a rule of thumb, venture capitalists (venture capital partnerships, investment institutions, or wealthy individuals) and large customers provide finance for young, high-risk firms, while LBOs often concern mature firms with rather predictable cash flows. While LBO entities are highly leveraged and venture capital start-ups carry little or no debt, venture capital and LBO deals have several features in common, including high-intensity monitoring by concentrated outside equity holdings and high-powered incentives (small cash salary and substantial equity holding) for insiders. We discussed LBOs in the context of takeovers (see Section 1.5), and, not to repeat ourselves, we here focus on venture capital and large customer financing.

2.4.1.1 Venture Capital

Venture capital is used to finance start-up companies, often in high-tech industries (software, biotechnology. For instance, Apple, Compaq, Genentech, Google, Intel, Lotus, and Microsoft initially received venture capital), but also in other industries (for example, Federal Express and People Express started with venture capital). Further, venture capitalists specialize in highly risky projects (they fail to recoup their investments in many of the selected firms, but make spectacular profits on a few). Venture capitalists take concentrated equity positions[46] in the company they finance as well as seats on the board of directors. They carefully structure deals and monitor the firm. They also bring expertise and industry contacts.

(a) *Structure of deals.*[47] Like sophisticated creditors (see Section 2.3.3), venture capitalists devote much attention to the structure of deals. Screening

45. See Chemla et al. (2004).

46. In the case of a venture capital partnership, the lead venture capitalist or general partner (who performs most of the monitoring) has an average equity stake of 19% while limited partners have an average equity stake of 15%.

Our discussion of venture capital focuses on the American environment. For a discussion of the financing of high-tech start-ups in Europe, see Adam and Farber (1994).

47. For more on deal writing, see Gompers (1995), Case 9-288-014 of the Harvard Business School (1987), and Sahlman (1990). The reader will find much interesting evidence on venture capital contracts in Gompers and Lerner (1999, 2001) and Lerner (2000).

of firms is intense (a tiny fraction of proposals received are funded), and conditions imposed on firms are drastic. Venture capital deals usually include:

• A very detailed outline of the various stages of financing (e.g., seed investment, prototype testing, early development, growth stage, etc.). At each stage the firm is given just enough cash to reach the next stage.

• The right for the venture capitalist to unilaterally stop funding at any stage. That is, the venture capitalist may need no justification to stop funding. Less universally, the venture capitalist may further have a put provision, namely, a right to demand repayment of all or some of the already invested capital.[48]

• The right for the venture capitalist to demote or fire the managers if some key investment objective is not met, and a noncompete clause for key employees.

• The right to control future financing. Venture capitalists have preemptive rights to participate in new financing and have registration rights.[49]

• Often, the venture capitalist's ownership of preferred stock (often convertible into common stock), that is, of a claim senior to the manager's claim in liquidation. Eighty percent of venture capital deals in Kaplan and Strömberg's (2003) sample had the venture capitalist hold convertible preferred stocks (Sahlman (1990) and Gompers (1998) report similar findings).

• Some covenants such as the obligation to purchase life insurance for key employees.

• An exit mechanism for the venture capitalist. The expectation is that at some stage, the firm (if it has survived all previous stages) will go public and will sell shares in an IPO to other investors (e.g., pension funds, insurance companies, individual investors) and that the venture capitalist will sell part or all of her shares; or else the start-up will be purchased by a large firm.

Kaplan and Strömberg (2003) study a sample of 213 venture capital investments in the late 1990s. They document that the venture capitalists' rights (cash flow, board, voting, liquidation, and others) are often contingent on verifiable measures of financial and nonfinancial performance. An example of a financial performance measure is EBIT (earnings before interest and taxes). Nonfinancial performance measures include patent grants (or, for a pharmaceutical product, Federal Drug Administration approval), actions to be taken, or the founder remaining in the firm. Following on a good performance, the entrepreneur retains or obtains more control rights and the venture capitalist may then content himself with cash-flow rights. Conversely, a poor performance may lead to a double penalty for the entrepreneur: her financial stake in the start-up depreciates and the venture capitalist retains his control rights or acquires new ones. Selecting a subsample of 67 companies, Kaplan and Strömberg (2004) further show that, in more risky companies (entrepreneurs who are inexperienced or have failed in the past, companies whose operations are harder to observe, etc.), venture capitalists receive more control rights, have a greater ability to liquidate upon poor performance, entrepreneurs receive more contingent compensation, and financing in a given round is more contingent.

(b) *Certification and reputational capital.* Venture capitalists care about their reputational capital for (at least) two reasons (see Barry et al. 1990; Sahlman 1990; Megginson and Weiss 1991). First, a number of other parties—such as limited partners, input suppliers, providers of later-stage financing—piggyback on the venture capitalist's monitoring of the firm. A reputation for careful monitoring thus enhances the prospects of the venture. Second, if the start-up undergoes an IPO, the venture capitalist's good reputation (as in the case of a bank loan, see Section 2.3.4.1) reduces the underpricing of the firm's share at the IPO. (As one would expect, underpricing is particularly low if the venture capitalist keeps an equity position beyond the IPO to signal the quality of the new issue.) These two benefits for the firm from the venture capitalist's good reputation enable the latter to obtain a better deal from the borrower.

(c) *Comparison with sophisticated debtholders.* Debt financing is not an attractive alternative for the types of firm usually financed by venture capital.

48. Bank loan agreements usually allow the bank to collect the entire loan, that is, to accelerate its payment, only if certain covenants are violated.

49. In contrast, bank loan agreements mainly limit dilution of debt through issuance of equal priority or more senior debt (see Section 2.3.3).

First, ideas are not good collateral (recall that debt financing is often secured). Second, many such firms do not generate positive cash flows for quite a while and any short-term debt obligation could lead the firm into bankruptcy. Accordingly, such firms resort to equity financing. It is nonetheless interesting to compare the two types of financing. Venture capital deals combine several features of debt contracts with sophisticated creditors (high-intensity screening and monitoring, careful attention to the timing of funding, some control over future financing, seniority of claims, some covenants, certification) with the usual prerogatives of equity (such as a fuller right to control financing or the right to demote or fire managers). Simplifying a bit, venture capital deals involve more control rights for the financier and fewer covenants than private debt agreements.

2.4.1.2 Alliance with a Large Customer

For R&D firms, contracting with a large customer offers an alternative to venture capital financing. Indeed, research alliances surpassed public offerings in the 1990s as the dominant source of financing for biotechnology firms (Lerner and Merges 1998). A biotechnology company often enters into a research agreement with a pharmaceutical (or larger biotechnology) firm. The latter's primary role at the research stage is to provide financing; its role in production expands gradually as the project moves to the development and the marketing and sales stages. The biotechnology company is rewarded through royalties from licensing, including from the license to the partner, if the project is completed successfully.

The principal–agent relationship between the pharmaceutical company and the biotechnology unit (the R&D firm) is fraught with moral hazard. First, some dimensions are related to multitasking, as the R&D firm may juggle several research projects, including ones with other partners or on its own. Second, biotechnology companies' researchers often have academic objectives (publications requiring disclosure, reputation for a research orientation that enables the employment of postdocs, etc.) that may clash with a given project's profitability concerns. Third, reputational concerns (vis-à-vis academia or future partners) may prevent a researcher from admitting that the project is unlikely to succeed and therefore from suggesting termination.

Lerner and Malmendier (2004) study biotechnology research collaborations. Almost all such contracts in their sample specify termination rights. These may be conditional on specific events (50% of the contracts in their sample of 584 biotechnology research agreements) or at the complete discretion of the financier (39%). The financing firm may in the case of termination acquire broader licensing rights than it would have in the case of continuation. These broad licensing rights can be viewed as costly collateral pledging that both increase the income of the financier and boost the R&D firm's incentive to reach a good performance on the project.[50] Lerner and Malmendier's empirical finding is that such an assignment of termination and broad licensing rights is more likely when it is hard to specify a lead product candidate in the contract (and so entrepreneurial moral hazard is particularly important) and when the R&D firm is highly constrained financially.

2.4.2 Initial and Seasoned Public Offerings

It is customary to identify *four stages* of equity financing. In the first stage, equity is held by one or several entrepreneurs. These entrepreneurs may in a second stage raise equity capital from a small number of investors through a private placement; alternatively, they may have a privileged relationship with a bank. In a third stage (which most firms do not get to) the firm goes public in an initial public offering (IPO). Lastly, it may then conduct secondary or seasoned public offerings (SPOs). IPOs and SPOs have a strong business cycle component and are much more frequent during upswings.

2.4.2.1 The Going-Public Decision

Going public is *costly*. First, firms must supply detailed information on a regular basis to regulators and investors. This involves transaction costs as well as possibly disclosure of strategic information to product market rivals.[51] Second, the firm must pay

50. See Section 4.3.4 for the theoretical foundations of this assertion. See also Review Problem 10 for a modeling of some of the arguments.

51. Yosha (1995) argues that firms with sensitive R&D information should remain private.

substantial underwriting and legal fees. In the United States, the commissions paid to investment bankers have converged in the late 1990s to 7% of the transaction for 90% of the IPOs (Chen and Ritter 2000); they are lower in other countries.[52] A company that goes public usually issues a fixed number of shares at some prespecified price. Shares are rationed if there is excess demand at the offer price. It is well documented (Ibbotson 1975; Ritter 1987) that IPOs with a preset price are underpriced in that the shares are traded on the secondary market shortly after the IPO at a premium of 15–20% on average relative to their offer price. During 1990–1998, companies going public in the United States left $27 billion on the table, a sum twice as large as the $13 billion fees paid to investment bankers (Loughran and Ritter 2002). A standard explanation for this underpricing phenomenon is the existence of a "winner's curse" in such offerings (Rock 1986).[53] Third, the insiders (entrepreneur, venture capitalist if any) have superior information about the prospects of the firm,[54] especially if the firm has low visibility and no track record. The insiders may therefore be reluctant to sell shares at a discount when they are unable to demonstrate to investors that the firm indeed has excellent prospects. Fourth, new investors often demand control rights, especially in countries with a poor enforcement of minority rights; entrepreneurs, however, may want to retain control for themselves or within the family. As a matter of fact, family firms still dominate the corporate landscape around the world (see Section 1.4).

Firms derive several *benefits* from going public. First, going public enables firms to tap new sources of finance and to enable the firm's growth. Relatedly, it enables the firm to be less reliant on financing by a single bank or a venture capitalist; by diversifying its sources of finance, it is better protected against a "holdup" by the key financier. Second, going public facilitates exit; it allows the entrepreneurs and large shareholders to diversify their portfolios (see Pagano 1993); relatedly, it enhances the liquidity of their claims (see Chapter 9). Third, going public creates a relatively objective measure of the value of assets in place, which can be used for managerial compensation purposes (see Chapter 8). Fourth, going public may help discipline managers through the channel of takeovers.[55] On the other hand, it may reduce the intensity of monitoring by creating a more dispersed ownership structure, which has costs as well as benefits (such as the promotion of officers' initiative (Burkart et al. 1997)). Lastly, the firm's listing on a stock exchange enhances name recognition; this may help the firm not only to find new investors, but also to improve its relationship with other potential stakeholders such as trading partners or creditors.

There are few empirical investigations of the decision to go public. Pagano et al. (1998), on Italian data, show that firms in industries in which other firms have a high market-to-book ratio are more likely to go public. This may be due either to the possibility that the increased availability of funds associated with public listing is more attractive to firms with high growth prospects (this reason does not seem plausible for the Italian sample, as investment and

52. Chen and Ritter analyze several factors that may be conducive to high commissions: importance of buying underwriter prestige, possibility of tacit or explicit collusion, incentive provided to the underwriter to credibly certify the issue, nonprice competition.

"Legal fees" include registration fees, taxes, fees for legal and accounting services, and so forth. See Eckbo and Masulis (1995) for an earlier review of the empirical evidence on the magnitude of those fees.

53. Suppose that some investors have superior information about the prospects of the company than others, but that they may not buy the whole issue (because of regulatory constraints, risk aversion, etc.). The less informed investors should realize that they receive more shares when the informed investors are unwilling to buy, that is, when the company's prospects are low, and that they are rationed when prospects are high. Hence, the only way to attract less informed investors is to sell shares at the discount. (The IPO underpricing is only about 4% in France, where a mechanism resembling more a standard auction without rationing is used.) The winner's curse effect seems to be weaker when the existence of a bank loan signals that prospects are high.

Interestingly, underpricing is also smaller when the offering's underwriter guarantees the proceeds from the entire issue to the company—the method of firm commitment—than when the underwriter only offers "best efforts" to place the issue. The underwriter may well "certify" the issue better in the former case than in the latter case, in which its stake is lower. On the other hand, it might be that the higher underpricing under a best-efforts contract is due to a sample selection bias—best-efforts contracts are used mainly for smaller, speculative issues (therefore prone to substantial winner's curses)—rather than to a weaker certification by the underwriter. (See, for example, Eckbo and Masulis (1992), Hanley and Ritter (1992), Loughran and Ritter (2002), Ritter (2003), and Ritter and Welch (2002) for more information on IPOs.)

54. See Chapter 6 as well as Chemmanur and Fulghieri (1999).

55. See Chapter 11. Zingales (1995) further argues that free riding by small shareholders may help extract more surplus from prospective acquirers.

profitability decrease after the IPO) or to the possibility that firms go public in hot (high-value) markets (see Section 2.5 for a discussion of market timing). A second finding is that larger companies are more likely to go public. A third finding is that, even controlling for firm characteristics and the reduction in leverage after the IPO, firms borrow from a larger number of banks and experience a reduction in the cost of bank credit after the IPO, perhaps due to the increase in transparency or to the availability of new sources of capital. Lastly, and unsurprisingly in view of the low level of investor protection in Italy,[56] the Italian stock market is much smaller relative to the size of the economy than the American one. Relatedly, the typical Italian firm going public is eight times as large and six times as old as the typical firm going public in the United States.

A few studies (e.g., Anderson and Reeb (2003) for the United States and Sraer and Thesmar (2004) for France) attempt to analyze the relative profitability of family firms. Family firms run by their founder(s) unsurprisingly tend to be very profitable. The question is more whether firms that are run by heirs or by a professional manager hired by the family who has retained control over the firm[57] do less well than widely held firms.[58] On the one hand, one might expect heirs not to be the most appropriate choice for management (indeed, the founder may want to sacrifice wealth in order for the family to keep the benefits of control). On the other hand, the founder may have superior information about prospects and may want to keep the firm private when these are excellent. Thus, even ignoring other effects, it is not clear what we should expect.

Sraer and Thesmar (2004) use a panel of 750 corporations listed on the French stock exchange from 1994 through 2000. On that stock market, two-thirds of the firms exhibit a significant family ownership; among these, almost 50% are still managed by their founder, 30% by a heir of the founder, and 20% by a professional CEO. Consistently with previous studies on U.S. data, Sraer and Thesmar find that family ownership is associated with both higher economic and market performance. Lower wages in family firms seem to explain an important part of these higher performances. Sraer and Thesmar provide evidence consistent with the fact that, because of their different time horizons, family firms have a comparative advantage in enforcing implicit insurance contracts with their labor force. A surprising fact is that heir-managed firms do as well (in terms of return on equity or return on assets) as firms run by founders or by professional managers, and better than widely held corporations. As Sraer and Thesmar note, though, there are potential biases stemming from both the impact (alluded to above) of private information on the decision to go public and from the fact that badly managed heir-controlled firms tend to disappear or else surrender control under financial hardship.[59]

2.4.2.2 The Equity Issue Process and the Role of Underwriters

There are several flotation methods.[60] The most common way of raising equity in the United States is to use an underwriter. The underwriter may guarantee the proceeds of the shares in case of undersubscription; the underwriter can then sell the unsold shares at a lower, but not at a higher, price than the price stated in the public offering. This is the "firm commitment" contract institution. The risk borne by the underwriter is limited, though, if, as is often the case, the price is fixed shortly before the offering. By contrast, under a "best efforts" contract, the underwriter does not bear the risk of offer failure; and the offer is withdrawn if a minimum sales level is not

56. An indicator of the poor investor protection in Italy is the very high premium attached to shares with voting rights relative to shares with the same cash-flow rights but no voting rights (see Zingales 1994).

57. For example, among automobile manufacturers, Peugeot has been managed by heirs, and Fiat and BMW by professional managers.

58. In Burkart et al.'s (2003) theoretical model, a founder chooses between selling the firm, in which case it becomes widely held and is run by a professional manager, and keeping control over it, which gives the founder the option between a professional manager and a heir to run the firm. They assume that heirs are less competent than professional managers and argue that transforming the firm into a widely held company is optimal when the legal protection is high. With lower investor protection, ownership concentration is called for. Heir-managed firms, which avoid a separation of ownership and control, arise in their model when investor protection is very poor.

59. Looking for such biases, they nonetheless argue that their approach may actually underestimate the performance of heir-controlled firms relative to widely held firms, as heir-controlled firms are performing better than all other firms one year before returning private.

60. See, for example, Eckbo and Masulis (1995) and Hanley and Ritter (1992) for more extensive discussion of flotation methods.

reached within a specified amount of time. In the 1980s, firm commitment issues accounted for the bulk of SPOs of common stock in the United States, and for about 60% of IPOs. The remaining 40% of IPOs, corresponding mainly to smaller, more speculative issuers, were conducted under best-efforts contracts (Ritter 1987).

Underwriters often play the dual role of stock analysts. They subsequently issue recommendations to investors regarding the value of the securities that they have helped float.[61] Indeed, the underwriter most often implicitly commits to provide analyst coverage in the aftermarket. Conversely, even "independent" or "nonaffiliated" analysts, who have not underwritten the specific security that they are assessing (or other securities issued by the firm), may later on assist with other public offerings.[62] There is a widespread feeling that this dual role creates a conflict of interest, so that analysts have incentives to issue positive recommendations so as to please issuers and obtain future underwriting contracts.[63] In the United States, a settlement between regulators and major brokerage firms made the latter pay a fine of $1.4 billion for biased and misleading recommendations. This incentive to please issuers must be traded off against that to maintain a reputation for reliable assessments. Research has been investigating the differentials in conflict of interest.[64]

There are other ways of issuing equity, such as private placements and direct issues. A potentially important alternative to tapping new investors is to issue shares to existing shareholders through the institution of rights offers. Indeed, in North America and in Europe, existing shareholders have by law the first right of refusal to purchase a new issue of common stock. A rights offer consists in offering shares first to existing shareholders, often at a 15–20% discount under the current market price. Rights offers have become rare in the United States, but they are more common in Europe and in Japan.

Still another way of issuing equity is to transform other securities (as in the case of an equity for debt swap) or cash into equity, or to issue securities that can later be converted into equity (convertible debt, warrants, stock options). Employee stock ownership and direct reinvestment plans automatically transform employee compensation and shareholder dividends, respectively, into shares. As noted by Eckbo and Masulis (1995) in the United States, such schemes may have substituted for rights offers.

2.5 Financing Patterns

This section documents firms' financing patterns. Firms finance operating expenditures and investments in roughly two ways: (a) *retentions*, which we define as the difference between post-tax income and total payments to investors. Total payments to investors include payouts to shareholders (dividends, share repurchases), and payments to creditors (principal and interest) and to other securityholders; and (b) *return to the capital market*, that is, the issuing of new shares and bonds and the securing of new loans or trade credit.

Chapters 5 and 6 will stress the risk inherent to capital market refinancing. Unless the firm draws on a previously-contracted-for credit line or more generally is able to use some already secured source of financing, the refinancing process is confronted with investors' reluctance to lend funds whose proceeds they will imperfectly appropriate. Refinancing thus exposes the firm to the risk of being unable to

61. In the United States, they must wait 25 days to issue such recommendations.

62. While underwriters have an incumbency advantage for future offerings, a nonnegligible fraction of issuers do switch underwriters. Krigman et al. (2001), on a U.S. sample in the mid 1990s, find that 30% of the firms completing a secondary equity offering within three years after their IPO switched lead underwriter. Noting that most of the switchers do not report a dissatisfaction with their IPO underwriter, they suggest two possible explanations for this phenomenon. First, firms that started with less-well-known underwriters may "graduate" to higher-reputation ones. Second, they may "buy" additional analyst coverage from the new lead underwriter.

63. Much of the research builds upon information supplied by the company's management. The brokerage firms' revenue from providing advice to institutional investors and others is indirect. First, they receive money from future investment banking contracts with companies that are covered. Second, brokerage firms receive trading commissions from institutional investors, who if they own such shares in a company do not want the brokerage firm to publicly issue a "sell" recommendation.

64. Michaely and Womack (1999), on a sample of 1990–1991 U.S. IPOs, find that lead underwriters issue more optimistic recommendations and that the market reacts less to their recommendations. Bradley et al. (2004), on a "bubble period" sample of 1997–1998 U.S. IPOs, do not find any difference in market reaction between affiliated and nonaffiliated analysts, which they interpret as evidence that affiliated analysts have superior information or that nonaffiliated analysts are also very eager to please the company.

Table 2.2 Average financing of nonfinancial enterprises, as a percentage of total financing sources, 1970–1985. *Source:* Mayer (1990).

	Canada	Finland	France	Germany	Italy	Japan	U.K.	U.S.
Retentions	54.2	42.1	44.1	55.2	38.5	33.7	72.0	66.9
Capital transfers	0.0	0.1	1.4	6.7	5.7	0.0	2.9	0.0
Short-term securities	1.4	2.5	0.0	0.0	0.1	n.a.	2.3	1.4
Loans	12.8	27.2	41.5	21.1	38.6	40.7	21.4	23.1
Trade credit	8.6	17.2	4.7	2.2	0.0	18.3	2.8	8.4
Bonds	6.1	1.8	2.3	0.7	2.4	3.1	0.8	9.7
Shares	11.9	5.6	10.6	2.1	10.8	3.5	4.9	0.8
Other	4.1	6.9	0.0	11.9	1.6	0.7	2.2	−6.1
Statistical adjustment	0.8	−3.5	−4.7	0.0	2.3	n.a.	−9.4	−4.1

finance positive net present value (NPV) continuation projects or growth prospects.[65]

The section is organized as follows. Section 2.5.1 documents sources of finance. Section 2.5.2 discusses some key theoretical principles and empirical findings relative to payout policies, or equivalently retentions. Finally, Section 2.5.3 studies seasoned equity and debt offerings.

2.5.1 Sources of Corporate Finance

Several studies (see, in particular, Borio 1990; Corbett and Jenkinson 1994; Eckbo and Masulis 1995; Kojima 1994; Kotaro 1995; Mayer 1988; Rajan and Zingales 1995, 2003) have documented the sources of finance in different countries. Figure 2.4 and Table 2.2 illustrate some typical findings for the 1980s, due to Mayer (1988, 1990).

In all countries, internal financing (retained earnings) constitutes the dominant source of finance. Bank loans usually provide the bulk of external financing, well ahead of new equity issues, which account for a small fraction of new financing in all major OECD countries.[66] One difference among countries is the role of bond financing. Bond markets play a minor role except in North America.[67]

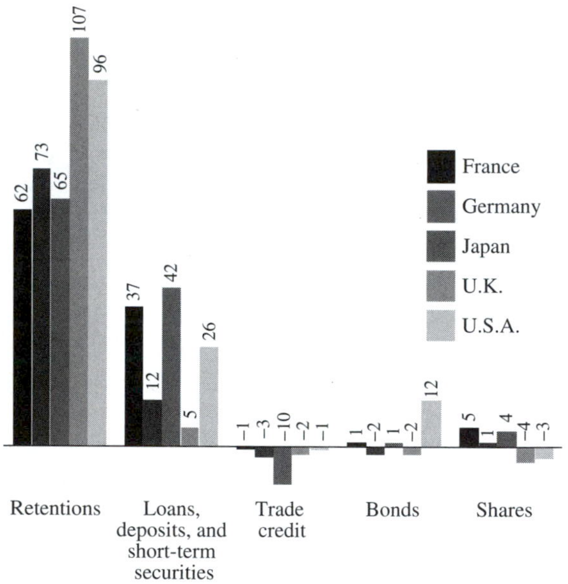

Figure 2.4 Reprinted from *European Economic Review*, Volume 32, C. Mayer, New issues in corporate finance, pp. 1167–1189, Copyright (1988), with permission from Elsevier.

The 1980s have even witnessed net retirements of equity in the United States. This does not mean that the volume of equity issues was negligible relative to that of debt issues. Indeed, Rajan and Zingales (1995) report that, in their sample of U.S. firms and for the 1984–1986 period, equity issuance amounted to 65% of external financing; equity reduction, though, accounted for 68% of external financing, and so the net equity issuance was negative and basically all external financing was debt

65. As will be discussed in Chapter 5, this agency-based feature is absent in the classic Arrow–Debreu competitive equilibrium model, which assumes that firms' income is fully pledgeable to investors and so firms incur no cost when relying solely on refinancing in the capital market when needed.

66. These numbers are, of course, net, aggregate numbers. They hide substantial differences among firms; for example, equity financing may be important for start-up firms.

67. Although large European firms now have access to Eurobonds and syndicated bank loans. See also Table 2.5 below, in which bonds represent the bulk of the "Securities other than stocks" category.

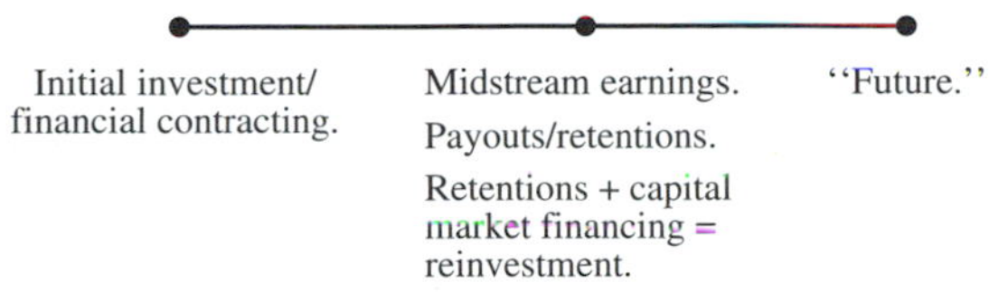

Figure 2.5

financing (primarily long-term debt issuance minus long-term debt reduction, as net short-term debt issuances were negligible).[68] The U.S. picture for the period differs a little from that for other countries over the same period. There was no equity reduction in Japan and almost none in the United Kingdom; furthermore, net equity issuance accounted for 23% and 68% of external financing in these two countries (in which external financing formed 33% and 16% of total financing, respectively). More recent data confirm the relatively minor role of equity issues in capital formation. Rajan and Zingales (2003) report that the fraction of gross fixed-capital formation raised via equity in 1999 was 12% in the United States, 9% in the United Kingdom and France, 8% in Japan, and 6% in Germany.[69]

These data should not, of course, lead us to naively overemphasize the role of "internal" financing. After all, "retentions" are cash that shareholders consent to leave in the firm for the latter to reinvest, while "equity issuances" are cash that shareholders also give to the firm for reinvestment purposes. Either way, and in a first analysis, this is cash handed over by shareholders to the firm. The difference between the two sources of finance will therefore need to be investigated in the book (see, in particular, the various discussions of the sensitivities of investment to cash flow).

2.5.2 Payout Policy and Leverage

As discussed above, there are two broad sources of financing: retentions and new securities' issues (or new loans). Because new securities' issues are hard or costly to arrange, retentions play an important

Table 2.3

	Firm should retain more of its earnings if	Firm should pay out more of its earnings if
growth opportunities are	high	low
correlation of date-1 and date-2 profitabilities is	high	low
financial constraint at date 0 is	weak	tight
earnings are	small	large

role (Section 2.5.1). Yet, investors expect dividends (or share repurchases), principal, and interest, and so there is a tradeoff between retaining earnings within the firm so as to achieve continuation and growth and the need to attract investors by promising payouts to shareholders and debt repayment to creditors.[70]

To study the two key issues related to total payments to investors (payouts and debt repayments), namely, their *level* (how much?) and *structure* (what kind?), it is convenient to envision the simplified timeline in Figure 2.5 for the firm's life cycle.

The tradeoff we just alluded to refers to the tradeoff at the initial stage, "stage 0," at which the firm aims at attracting funds in sufficient quantity without jeopardizing its liquidity position midstream, at "stage 1" (more generally, the tradeoff would arise at each refinancing stage).

(a) *Payment level.* How much of the midstream earnings should be returned to investors? Intuition (to be confirmed in subsequent chapters) suggests some determinants of the payout level: see Table 2.3.

The evidence seems largely consistent with the predictions of Table 2.3. A caveat, though: the evidence presented below is incomplete. In particular, while the predictions refer to the total payment (dividend/share repurchases + principal and interest + other payments to investors), some of the evidence refers only to the dividend or the debt component of the payment. Because the determinant in question may also affect the structure of payments (e.g., the

68. External financing over the period was typically small: computed as the ratio of the net external financing to the sum of cash flow from operations and net external financing, it amounted to 14% over 1984–1986.

69. These refer to funds raised through both initial equity offerings and seasoned equity issues.

70. See Allen and Michaely (2004) for an exhaustive survey of corporate payout policies.

debt/equity ratio), it might be that the other component(s) move in the other direction.

Growth opportunities. Given the difficulties associated with returning to the capital market, the firm should pay out less when midstream reinvestment needs are high.

There is indeed much evidence that growth opportunities[71] are correlated with a lower dividend distribution (Fama and French 2001) and a lower leverage (Myers 1984).

Serial correlation of profits. The serial correlation of profits is related to growth opportunities, since, if high profits midstream are a signal of persistently high demand or low product-market competition and therefore of high future profitability, it may make sense not to distribute them and to reinvest in the firm (Poterba 1988).

Financial constraints. Recall the tradeoff between pleasing investors through high payments and promoting the firm's long-term growth through retentions. Financially constrained firms must try harder to attract funds and therefore must increase their payment ratio. There is indeed evidence that financially unconstrained firms take on low debt burdens (Hubbard 1998).

Earnings size. Intuitively, firms with low earnings midstream, controlling for growth opportunities, should distribute less than those with high earnings since a lower payment-to-earnings ratio is required in order to achieve a given level of retentions. This theoretical prediction may be less compelling than the others, though, since firms with low profits may also be financially constrained, which as we indicated above would suggest high payouts, an effect that would be further amplified by a serial correlation of profits.

The list in Table 2.3 is, of course, incomplete. For example, the derived payment policy may depend on the extent of date-0 moral hazard, as, for example, when the midstream earnings are sensitive to date-0 managerial choices. A policy of reinvesting a sizeable fraction of the profits provides management with an incentive to boost these earnings. That is, a lower payment ratio in the case of high earnings reduces moral hazard. Thus, the sensitivity of retentions to earning should increase when date-0 moral hazard increases (see Section 5.5). In the same vein, large payouts may not be advisable when management can easily reinvest earnings as they accrue and thereby hide them temporarily from investors. Lower payment ratios then incentivize management to recognize the earnings. Relatedly, firms may have an easier time secretly reinvesting money when cash flows are high (see Dow et al. 2003; Philippon 2003).

71. Empirically, growth opportunities are often proxied by the ratio of market value of assets to book value of assets.

Table 2.4 Leverage in different industries. Measures of corporate net worth by industry in the United States, 1985.

Industry	Ratio of net worth to total assets	Ratio of debt to equity
All industries	0.32	2.11
Agriculture, forestry, and fishing	0.32	2.12
Mining	0.45	1.21
Construction	0.28	2.52
Manufacturing	0.45	1.20
Transportation and public utilities	0.40	1.50
Wholesale and retail trade	0.29	2.49
Services	0.31	2.25
Finance, insurance, and real estate	0.26	2.90
Commercial banks	0.08	11.00
Savings banks[1]	0.04	28.00

Source: U.S. Internal Revenue Service, White (1991).
1. Mutual savings banks plus savings and loan associations.

(b) *Payment structure: the determinants of financial structure.* So far, we have discussed only total payment to investors. Should this payment take the form of a fixed, predetermined payment to debtholders or a more flexible payout to shareholders? This raises the question of the firm's desired financial structure, to which we now turn our attention.

We have seen that some firms (financed by venture capital) do not contract debt liabilities. In contrast, others, following an LBO, may have debt–equity ratios of 10 or 20. Some publicly traded companies have similarly high debt–equity ratios because of the

Table 2.5 International comparison of financial structures.

	France	Germany	U.K.	Italy	U.S.	Japan
Securities other than stocks	7.3	2.3	10.6	2.3	15.6	8.0
Credit	24.3	43.2	30.7	32.1	10.0	39.5
short term	6.7	12.2	—	—	—	—
long term	17.5	31.0	—	—	—	—
Stocks	52.9	40.7	53.0	49.4	45.6	28.0
listed	17.1	—	—	—	—	—
nonlisted	30.8	—	—	—	—	—
Trade credit	15.5	8.2	5.7	12.5	8.0	17.9

Source: David Thesmar, personal communication. Table built from Eurostat, Federal Reserve Board, Bank of Japan; year 2002; fraction of total liabilities of nonfinancial corporations; fractions may not add to 100 since some lines have been omitted, to ease readability. "Securities other than stocks" are basically bonds. Also "Trade credit" is not netted out with trade credit on the other side of the balance sheet.

low cash-flow risk: for instance, banks[72] and, before the deregulation of the 1980s and especially the 1990s, public utilities (such as telephone, electricity, gas companies).[73] Bradley et al. (1984) find that U.S. telecommunications and gas and electricity companies had ratios of book value of long-term debt to book value of long-term debt plus market value of equity of 51.5% and 53%, respectively (as opposed to 29.1% for an average contemporary U.S. firm).

Measures of leverage vary substantially across studies for several reasons. For example, comprehensive samples include large numbers of small firms, which presumably are more levered than larger ones; and so leverage ratios are higher than in studies focusing on smaller samples (for example, that of listed firms). For the same reason, studies that report nonweighted means are likely to report higher leverage than those that compute weighted averages. Another reason why statistics vary widely is that studies differ in the period they cover and that leverage is time-dependent (for instance, it depends on the business cycle). Table 2.4 (due to White, who reports on a very large, nonweighted 1985 sample of U.S. firms) depicts the ratio of equity over debt plus equity in the left column and the ratio of debt to equity in the right column; a typical debt–equity ratio in this sample lies around 2.

The aggregate market-based average ratio has been remarkably stable in the United States at around 0.32 over the past half-century in the United States (Frank and Goyal 2004).

Table 2.5 (based on national accounts, and therefore weighting firms by their size, leading to lower measures of leverage) provides more recent data for France, Germany, and the United Kingdom.

Key findings about the empirical determinants of leverage are:[74]

(i) Firms that are safe (e.g., utilities before the deregulation), produce steady cash flows, and have easily redeployable assets that they can pledge as collateral (e.g., aircraft for airline companies or real estate) can afford high debt–equity ratios.

(ii) In contrast, risky firms, firms with little current cash flows, and firms with intangible assets (e.g., with substantial R&D and advertising) tend to

72. Banks are fairly riskless both because of tight prudential regulation (which, incidentally, offers a number of analogies with the analysis of covenants in Section 2.3.3) and because of deposit insurance and of the expectation that formally uninsured deposits will benefit from an implicit governmental guarantee in the case of distress. Currently, international standards impose, among other requirements, a minimum ratio of equity over (risk-weighted) assets of 8% for banks.

73. Anglo-Saxon utilities used to be regulated under the so-called cost-of-service or rate-of-return regulation, which by and large guaranteed them a safe return. The introduction of higher-powered schemes (price caps, sliding scale plans, etc.) in the 1990s made them riskier, and leverage accordingly decreased.

Regulated utilities traditionally faced little upside and especially downside risk, as regulators allowed rate increases when the utility performed poorly and strove to capture the rent through rate cuts or other means if the firm became very profitable. One substantial difference with LBOs, however, is that managerial incentives were weak. In the United States, top managers of utilities received definitely fewer bonuses and stock options than their nonregulated counterparts (see, in particular, Joskow et al. 1993), who, in turn and as we saw in Chapter 1, have much weaker incentives than managers in LBOs.

74. See Allen et al. (2005), Frank and Goyal (2004), Harris and Raviv (1992), Masulis (1988), and Titman and Wessels (1988).

have low leverage. Companies whose value consists largely of intangible growth options (high market-to-book ratios and heavy R&D spending) have significantly lower leverage ratios than companies whose value is represented primarily by tangible assets.

Remark (share repurchases and dividends). Equity payouts come in two forms: dividends and share repurchases. Share repurchases have grown substantially over the years. In particular, distributions associated with open market repurchase programs in the United States grew from $15.4 billion to $113 billion between 1985 and 1996 while dividends grew from $67.6 billion to $141.7 billion (Jagannathan et al. 2000).

In a frictionless world, the choice between the two would be neutral. It is therefore not immediately clear why firms pay so much attention to the split. Lintner (1956) postulated that dividends distribute "permanent cash flows" while repurchases distribute "temporary ones." This postulate seems more driven by the desire to account for the observed smoothness of dividends and the related observation that repurchases are very volatile (large during booms and low during recessions) than by theoretical considerations.

The world, however, is not frictionless. Taxes may differentiate the two.[75] Also, employee stock options (which, recall from Chapter 1, grew substantially in the last two decades) do not perfectly adjust for the distribution of dividends; that is, the value of options decreases when the stock goes ex dividend, which creates an incentive for management to push for share purchases (Jolls 1998).

(c) *Sensitivity of investment to cash flow.* A number of papers relate cash flow and investment. A standard finding is that firms with more cash on hand and less debt invest more, controlling for investment opportunities.[76] There are questions about what this relationship means. Were the firms at the initial financing stage ("stage 0" in our simplified timeline), more cash would ease financial constraints and therefore would indeed boost investment, as we will see in the next chapter. However, sensitivity of investment to cash flow is demonstrated in samples of ongoing concerns ("stage 1" in the timeline). One must then ask, why isn't any extra cash simply returned to investors? It may be, as we noted above, that the retention of some of the extra cash rewards management for good performance.

An alternative hypothesis is that corporate governance is far from perfect. A few papers indeed point in this direction. Blanchard et al. (1994) study large cash windfalls from legal settlements unrelated to the firm's ongoing line of business. They show that firms' acquisitions increase with these cash windfalls. Lamont (1997) shows that shocks to the price of crude oil has a substantial impact on nonoil investments of companies with an oil stake. Clearly, managers are not responsible for the oil price increase and therefore are not being rewarded for the extra cash flow.[77] Lastly, Philippon (2003) finds that investments of firms with bad governance are more cyclical than those of firms with good governance.

A more controversial finding, due to Fazzari et al. (1988), is that firms that are more financially constrained exhibit a higher sensitivity of investment to cash flow. The theory is actually rather ambiguous as to whether this should be the case.[78] Using a different approach to measuring financial constraints, Kaplan and Zingales (1997) in contrast find that *less* financially constrained firms exhibit a greater sensitivity of investment to cash flow.

2.5.3 Seasoned Financing

Let us now turn to the second broad source of refinancing: firms can conduct seasoned equity offerings (SEOs), issue new bonds, or borrow from banks.

(a) *Informational impact of SPOs and borrowing.* A well-established fact is the average permanent

75. See, for example, Jagannathan et al. (2000) for the United States. Dividends and share repurchases are treated the same at the corporate level, but repurchases had a tax advantage at the individual tax level (which was reduced by the tax reform in 1986).

See Grullon and Ikenberry (2000) for an overview of what is known about stock repurchases.

76. See the surveys by Hubbard (1998) and Stein (2003), and the many references therein.

77. Unless they are being rewarded for accurately forecasting the oil price increase. But this possibility would apply only to those managers who invested more than average in oil production. In any case, the hypothesis of a poor governance in the oil industry is to be entertained in view of the independent evidence collected by Bertrand and Mullainathan (see Section 1.4).

78. See Kaplan and Zingales (1997, 2000) and Chapter 3 for the case of initial financing and Chapter 5 for the case of an ongoing concern.

Table 2.6 Impact of financing on stock price.
Source: Eckbo and Masulis (1995).

Type of security offered	Flotation method	Type of issuer: Industrial	Utility
Common stock	Firm commitment	−3.1 (216)	−0.8 (424)
	Standby rights	−1.5 (32)	−1.4 (84)
	Rights	−1.4 (26)	−0.2 (27)
Preferred stock	Firm commitment	−0.78* (14)	0.1* (249)
Convertible preferred stock	Firm commitment	−1.4 (53)	−1.4 (8)
Convertible bonds	Firm commitment	−2.0 (104)	n.a.
	Rights	−1.1 (26)	n.a.
Straight bonds	Firm commitment	−0.3* (210)	−0.13* (140)
	Rights	0.4* (11)	n.a.

Reprinted from *Handbook in Operations Research and Management Science: Finance*, Volume 9, E. Eckbo and R. Masulis, Seasoned equity offerings: a survey, Copyright (1995), with permission from Elsevier. Average two-day abnormal common stock returns and average sample size (in parenthesis) from studies of announcements of SPOs by NYSE/AMEX listed U.S. companies. Returns are weighted average by sample size of the returns reported by the respective studies (all returns *not* marked with a "*" are significantly different from 0 at the 5% level).

fall in stock price of about 3% in the wake of an announcement of a seasoned equity issue (Asquith and Mullins 1986). (The price decrease is much less pronounced for public utilities: −0.68% as opposed to −3.25% for the 1963–1980 period in the United States, according to Masulis and Korwar (1986). It is also interesting to note that there were more common stock offerings by utilities than by industrial firms during that period, even though utilities are only a small fraction of stock market capitalization. The price decrease is also smaller in Japan (see Kang and Stulz 1994).)

In contrast, the firm's stock price rises when a bank loan agreement is announced (James 1987) although the effect seems to be driven mainly by the successful renegotiation of existing bank loans (Lummer and McConnell 1989).

There is little impact of straight debt offerings on stock prices (Eckbo 1986). Table 2.6 reports Eckbo and Masulis's (1995) summary of existing evidence for industrial firms and public utilities in the United States.

Other and related stylized facts are that the stock price increases with an announcement of higher dividends, decreases with an equity for debt swap, and increases with a debt for equity swap.

(b) *Market timing.* The link between financing and the business cycle is one of the best-documented facts in corporate finance:

(i) Bank finance is countercyclical (see Bernanke et al. 1994); firms which can afford to issue public debt in economic booms often turn to banks to meet their financing requirements during recessions. The percentage of long-term bank loans that are unsecured varies inversely with business conditions.

(ii) Firms with strong balance sheets may extend more trade credit to weaker firms and issue more commercial paper in a recession.[79] Commercial paper and bank loans move in opposite directions (Kashyap et al. 1993). Loanable funds are smaller in recessions, while there is a countercyclical demand for short-term credit.[80]

(iii) Smaller and medium-sized firms, who rely more on banks, are more affected than larger firms by business cycle-related fluctuations (Gertler and Gilchrist 1994).

(iv) Equity issues are more frequent in upswings of business cycles, both in absolute terms and relative to debt issues.[81]

(v) The negative stock price reaction to common stock issues is smaller during expansions.

(vi) Equity issues are also more frequent after an increase in the firm's own stock value.

Particularly striking is equity market timing: firms issue shares at high prices and repurchase them at low prices. Conversely, firms tend to repurchase

79. See Calomiris et al.'s (1995) study of the U.S. slowdown of 1989–1992.

80. For more on the transmission mechanism, see, for example, Bernanke and Blinder (1992), Kashyap and Stein (2000), and Kashyap et al. (1993).

81. See Eckbo and Masulis (1995) for a review of the evidence. Relatedly, stock repurchases tend to follow a decline in stock prices.

shares when values are low. This is supported by both empirical evidence (see Baker and Wurgler (2002) for a survey and Baker et al. (2003)) and survey evidence (Graham and Harvey 2001). Relatedly, corporate investment and stock market values are positively correlated both in time-series and cross-section analyses; and high stock market values such as those of the late 1990s are conducive to mergers and acquisitions in which deals are for stocks rather than cash.[82]

An interesting question is why firms time the market so carefully. There are several hypotheses in this respect.[83]

Marginal productivity. Standard neoclassical economies can partly account for a correlation between high market values and high investment. Good news about the marginal productivity of capital or low interest rates (triggered, say, by large savings rates) raises the value of firms and at the same time the profitability of new investments. If, furthermore, new investments are financed through new equity issues, then there is a close relationship between market values and equity issues (see, for example, Pastor and Veronesi 2005). The relationship is likely to be weaker, though, if to finance the new investments, debt issues or retentions—perhaps associated with high current cash flows which signal high future ones—are used instead. Note that the Modigliani–Miller Theorem unfortunately does not provide much help in predicting which source of finance is tapped.

Lower adverse selection during booms. It may be the case that adverse selection is smaller during booms, as refinancing is then more likely to be driven by new investment opportunities rather than by the desire to issue overvalued shares. Choe et al. (1993) indeed show that the negative price response to seasoned common stock offerings is significantly lower during booms. So, to the extent that firms cannot issue only debt if they want to avoid the hazards associated with higher leverage ratios, issuing equity in good times may be a wise strategy.

82. See Shleifer and Vishny (2003), who argue that managers attempt to arbitrage incorrect stock market valuations.

83. This is not meant to be exhaustive. For example, the existence of abundant liquidity in good times (see Chapter 15) may encourage more investment.

Bubbles. A couple of theoretical papers show that investment through share issues is particularly profitable in high-bubble times (Olivier 2000; Ventura 2005). Such rational-bubble models thus predict a strong correlation between equity issues and high market valuations.

Irrational markets. Several authors have lately argued that managers wait for market exuberance to issue shares. Managers who know the value of their firms better than investors and are incentivized by stock options to raise the firm's shareholder value should indeed recommend equity issues during booms and equity purchases during recessions to their board and shareholders. Note that in this argument the irrationality of investors may not stem per se from their lack of knowledge of the firm's true value (unless they fail to recognize the macroeconomic pattern of correlation), but rather in their failing to understand the adverse selection they face.

Whatever the reason, market timing is likely to have permanent effects on firms' capital structure, as documented by Baker and Wurgler (2002). And it is likely to have a differentiated impact on firms (Baker et al. (2003) find empirical support for the idea that firms that are most dependent on equity—young, highly leveraged, high cash-flow volatility, low cash-flow firms—exhibit a stronger correlation between stock prices and subsequent investment).

2.6 Conclusion

The purpose of this chapter has been to give a concise overview of corporate financing. The theoretical analysis will build on a number of themes that have become evident in this chapter, namely, the key role played by information and incentives in general, and by capital, liquidity, value of collateral, and external monitoring more specifically.

Appendixes

The following two texts are rather representative of the business world's approach to loan agreements. The first describes the five Cs of credit analysis mentioned in Section 2.3.2. The second provides a detailed description of loan covenants.

2.7 The Five Cs of Credit Analysis

The text in this section is from a Harvard Business School note on acquiring bank credit.

When asked how a banker evaluates a borrower's creditworthiness, one is likely to hear about the "five Cs of credit analysis": the character, capacity, capital, collateral, and coverage of potential borrowers. Below, we discuss what these five Cs refer to and how they are analyzed.

Character. For many bankers, character determines if a small business loan will be approved at all. The potential trouble involved in dealing with questionable characters—noncooperation with the bank, fraud, litigation, and write-offs—are a significant deterrent. The time, legal expense, and opportunity costs incurred due to a problem loan far outweigh the potential interest income derived. (This factor, however, is less important with larger companies managed by a team of individuals.)

Capacity. Capacity refers to the borrower's ability to operate the business and successfully repay the loan. An assessment of capacity is based on management experience, historical financial statements, products, market operations, and competitive position.

Capital structure. A bank draws comfort from a capital structure with sufficient equity. Equity serves as a layer of capital to draw upon in the course of operations so as to protect the bank's exposure. Bankers also view equity as an indication of the borrower's commitment to his business. They derive greater comfort from knowing that the borrower has much to lose if his business loses.

Collateral. Collateral is the bank's claim on the borrower's assets in case the business defaults on the loan or files for bankruptcy. The bank's secured interest generally gives it a priority over other creditors in claiming proceeds from liquidated assets. The bank may also require that the borrower pledge as collateral personal assets outside of the business. For bankers, collateral is security and an alternative source of repayment beyond cash flow.

Coverage. Coverage refers simply to business insurance or "key-man" insurance which is often required when management ability is concentrated in a few individuals. In the event of the death or disability of a key manager, such coverage ensures that the bank will be repaid if the business cannot meet its obligations.

2.8 Loan Covenants

The text in this section is from Zimmerman (1975).

Loan agreements are a source of confusion and misunderstanding to many bankers. Frequently, the reader of loan agreements is not aware of their objectives and limitations, and, furthermore, is bewildered by the legal jargon of the numerous qualifying clauses.

Essential to the creation of effective loan agreements are the affirmative and negative covenants, which specify what the borrower must and must not do to comply with the agreement. The thrust of this paper is to facilitate the understanding and use of covenants in loan agreements. The use of covenants will be discussed in detail following an overview of the purpose, characteristics, and basic composition of loan agreements.

Purpose of Loan Agreements

Large amounts of time, effort, and money are spent in the development and implementation of loan agreements. They provide protection and communication for the parties involved and a general stability for the loan relationship through greater understanding among the parties. Further, should the borrower have other long-term debt, the loan agreement coordinates any legal or procedural interface with the debt and its associated creditors.

Where several banks are participating in a large credit, the loan agreement specifies the rules which govern the loan administration, and the responsibilities and liabilities of each bank.

As a major objective, the lender is interested in protecting its loan and assuring timely repayment. Through the loan agreement, the bank creates a clear understanding with the borrower as to what is expected of it. In doing so, the bank establishes its control of the relationship and provides for several basic functions to effect that control.

The lender attempts to ensure regular and frequent communication with the borrower by using certain covenants in the loan agreement. The communication results in an up-to-date assessment of the borrower's financial situation and its general management philosophy.

When the bank requires that the borrower maintain certain financial ratios, it is accomplishing several objectives. On the surface these covenants provide triggers or early-warning signals of trouble, which will allow the bank to take rapid remedial action. The borrower is made aware of where the minimum performance cutoffs are. However, the banker is also helping the borrower set reasonable goals in terms of financial conditions and growth. In some cases a "growth formula" is created which states that until a specified set of financial conditions is met, the borrower may not be eligible for further debt.

All these controls—required ratios, ratio goals, required actions, and forbidden actions—may seem arbitrary or restrictive; but applied wisely, they are not. The process lets all parties know where they stand, thus reducing the number of unknowns or uncertainties in the loan relationship.

Characteristics of Loan Agreements

When asked to describe the salient characteristics of loan agreements, most bankers will use adjectives such as "long" or "dull" or "confusing." While many agreements may be thus described, other definitions are certainly more informative.

The loan agreement is one of the most important loan documents in that it provides the basis for the entire banking relationship, establishing intents and stating expectations. It relates all the basic loan documents to one another and creates the means of control and lines of communication which are important in protecting all parties involved.

It follows that only three main courses of action are open to the bank in the event of default by the borrower. The account officer may waive, either temporarily or permanently, the condition which has been violated. This is frequently done in the case of financial ratios, although too lax an attitude in this respect can lead to a loss of control and an ineffective covenant and/or loan agreement. An alternative is for the banker to have the agreement rewritten to make it more viable. The rewrite is also a tactic used to obtain a much tighter hold over the borrower, if needed, by using as a bargaining tool the bank's legal right to call the loan. The third, and most drastic, approach for the bank is, of course, to declare the borrower in default, call the loan, and, if necessary, file suit against the borrower.

The implications of the nature of a loan agreement are extremely important. As an example, assume that a loan has been made on an unsecured basis and one covenant forbids the pledging of assets to anyone. This is obviously an attempt to maintain the strength of the bank's unsecured position in the event of liquidation. However, let us further assume that in violation of the agreement, the borrower pledges its assets to another lender. The bank certainly retains its option to call the loan, but the other lender holds the security. If the bank does call the loan, forcing liquidation, it remains an unsecured creditor vying for those assets which remain after satisfaction of the first lienholder.

The loan agreement, then, is not a substitute for security. If a loan should be secured in the absence of an agreement, then security should be taken with one. In fact, a loan agreement is not a substitute for anything. If the situation does not satisfy the five Cs of a loan decision—character, capacity, capital, conditions, and collateral—then the loan should not be made.

Composition of a Loan Agreement

There are seven basic sections of standard loan agreements, any of which may be modified, depending upon the purpose of the loan.

- *The loan.* This section describes the loan by type, size of commitment, interest rate, repayment schedule, and security taken, if any. Also specified are all participants and their roles plus terms of participation if more than one lender is involved. Any definitions of financial accounting or legal terminology to be used in the agreement are stated here.

- *Representations and warranties of borrower.* Basically, this section is an attestation to the lender that certain statements are true. For instance, the borrower may warrant that it is a corporation, that is entering into the agreement legally, that financial statements supplied to the bank are true, and that no material change has occurred since their preparation. The company may attest to the nature of its business, that it does own its assets as represented, and that it currently is not under litigation. In other words, the company reaffirms in writing all those things about its current state of existence which have been known or assumed throughout the negotiations.

- *Affirmative covenants.* In contrast to the warranties, which attest to existing fact, affirmative covenants state what action or event the borrower must cause to occur or exist in the future.

- *Negative covenants.* Negative covenants state what action or event the borrower must prevent from occurring or existing in the future.

- *Conditions of lending.* This section states that, prior to the lending of any money, all documents and notes must be in proper form, that both the borrower's and the bank's counsel must approve the entire arrangement, and that the borrower's auditor, or at least its chief financial officer, must certify current compliance with all conditions of the loan agreement.

- *Events of default.* Conditions which will be considered events of default are specifically stated. Such conditions might be delinquent payment, misrepresentation, insolvency proceedings, change in ownership, or other occurrences which could jeopardize the company's viability and/or the bank's position. All covenant violations are considered events of default, although many are designed to be used in correcting a situation rather than in calling the loan. In any event of default, timing is crucial. For instance, it may be that default does not occur until a covenant has been violated for thirty consecutive days.

- *Remedies.* The remedies section spells out what the bank may do in the event of default. The bank's rights may include several potential actions, but always include the right to accelerate payments, a term which means to call the loan. Timing is important. The borrower may have a certain amount of time to correct the default prior to the enforcement of a remedy. In a credit with several participating banks, the remedies section also defines procedures for calling the loan. For example, the agreement may require banks representing 70% of the commitment to call the loan.

Approach to the Covenant Package

Prior to writing a set of covenants for a loan agreement it is necessary to have a systematic approach to developing them. One must ask questions ranging from an assessment of basic objectives and risks to types of protection and remedy which must be provided to ensure the successful attainment of the objectives.

Since covenants are the heart of a loan agreement, setting the objectives is a process very similar to that of defining those for the total agreement. The bank is obviously hoping to be repaid on a timely basis, but, as a secondary set of objectives, would like to maintain or improve upon the financial position, cash flow, growth progression, and general financial condition of the borrower. Once goals have been set for the mutual benefit and protection of all parties, the lender must reassess the risks involved from a point of view different from that in the initial loan decision.

Determination of Risk

No longer is the lender looking for a yes/no decision. The aim at this point is to define the risks involved and to determine their magnitude. The account officer needs to ask, What conditions or events could block the accomplishment of my objectives? In other words, Where is the loan vulnerable? Weaknesses may lie in poor cash flow, thin net worth, or other financial statements items. It may be that the industry is volatile and highly subject to strikes or public fancy. Perhaps the company is small or it has a short track record, so that much of the loan decision is based upon projections.

Whatever the risks, it is now the task of the loan agreement writer to prevent or minimize the consequences of those risks as well as possible, in a form which remains as flexible as possible.

Scope of Covenants

The lender's effort to safeguard the loan against known and unknown risks will take the form of loan covenants. In asking what triggers exist and what actions may reasonably be taken and enforced once a risk materializes, the scope of potential covenants is almost limitless. Triggers may range from financial ratios and limits on financial statement accounts to restrictions on corporate, or even management, activities.

Furthermore, methods of treating a specific item are quite flexible in order to obtain the appropriate coverage. For example, it is possible to restrict a financial statement item to a minimum or maximum of

- a fixed dollar amount;
- a dollar amount increase or decrease per time period;
- a percentage of total assets, tangible net worth, or some independent indicator;
- a percentage change per time period.

As a special case, businesses subject to seasonal variances may have the above modifications fluctuate with the peaks and troughs of the cycle to more closely approximate actual conditions.

With so many potential requirements and restrictions, however, it becomes evident that the key to an effective loan agreement is not to see how many activities or conditions can be covered: it is to obtain the most protection in the simplest, most efficient manner.

Simplicity and Efficiency

To devise a simple and efficient network of covenants, it is imperative that the writer have a thorough understanding of the company, its management, and loan-associated risk in conjunction with a realistic attitude. This combination will result in covenants which allow the borrower maximum flexibility within the constraints necessary to provide the bank maximum protection.

(1) The borrower will maintain an adequate cash flow.

(2) The borrower will maintain a ratio of cash flow to current maturities of long-term debt of 1.5 to 1 on a fiscal-year basis.

The necessity for a realistic attitude dictates that a covenant also be such that the borrower is able to comply with it and the lender is willing to enforce it. Should either of these conditions not be met, a covenant may be frequently waived, thereby losing its psychological and, perhaps, legal control.

The essence of a loan agreement covenant is that it is simple, well-defined, measurable, risk-reducing, efficient, and reasonable. In short, it is the creative development of protection in the loan situation. As an aid to the direct application of these principles, a working guide to the construction of loan agreement covenants follows.

Working Guide for Loan Agreement Covenants[84]

Functional Objectives

The key objectives are described as follows:

• *Full disclosure of information.* To make competent, ongoing lending decisions, the account office must have an intimate understanding of the borrower. Full disclosure also aids the lender in maintaining regular contact with the borrower and close control over the loan relationship.

• *Preservation of net worth.* The borrower's basic financial strength and ability to support debt and absorb downturns

84. Only the first section of the working guide is reproduced here.

lie in its net worth. The purpose of related covenants is to assure the growth and continued strength of that net worth.

• *Maintenance of asset quality.* Asset value represents two major factors of importance to the lender: earning power and liquidation value. In either case, it is to the bank's advantage to require high standards of asset quality.

• *Maintenance of adequate cash flow.* In the case of normal repayment of a loan, the lender is repaid from the borrower's cash flow. In such cases, it is imperative that the lender closely monitor the cash flow and attempt to maintain its quality.

• *Control of growth.* As a definite drain upon cash flow, working capital, fixed assets, management energies, and capital funds, excessive growth has been recognized as the cause of numerous charge-offs and bad loans in the past few years. It is obviously in the interest of both banker and borrower to maintain growth in an orderly fashion although the two parties rarely see eye to eye on this matter. The bank's objective is to reach a clear understanding with the borrower on the limits of its growth.

• *Control of management.* In any loan situation, but particularly if the loan is unsecured, the success of the total relationship depends heavily upon the borrower's management. The bank then hopes to ensure the continuing quality of management.

• *Assurance of legal existence and concept of going concern.* The purpose of devising covenants such as these is to ensure the banks of a viable entity which may produce the conditions necessary to repay its loan.

• *Provision for bank profit.* Banks lend money in return for an expected profit, and are therefore interested, not only in protecting the principal amount of the loan, but also the profit, whether it be interest, servicing income, or other.

References

Adam, M. C. and A. Farber. 1994. *Le Financement de l'Innovation Technologique: Théorie Economique et Expérience Européenne.* Paris: Presses Universitaires de France.

Aghion, P., O. Hart, and J. Moore. 1992. The economics of bankruptcy reform. *Journal of Law, Economics, & Organization* 8:523–546.

Akerlof, G. 1970. The market for "lemons": qualitative uncertainty and the market mechanism. *Quarterly Journal of Economics* 84:488–500.

Allen, F. and R. Michaely. 2004. Payout policy. In *Corporate Finance: Handbook of the Economics of Finance* (ed. G. Constantinides, M. Harris, and R. Stulz), pp. 337–429. Amsterdam: North-Holland.

Allen, F., R. Brealey, and S. Myers. 2005. *Principles of Corporate Finance*, 8th edn. New York: McGraw-Hill.

Altman, E. 1989. Measuring bond mortality and performance. *Journal of Finance* 44:909–922.

Anderson, R. and D. Reeb. 2003. Founding-family ownership and firm performance: evidence from the S&P 500. *Journal of Finance* 58:1301–1328.

Asquith, P. and D. W. Mullins, Jr. 1986. Seasoned equity offerings. *Journal of Financial Economics* 15:61–89.

Asquith, P., R. Gertner, and D. Scharfstein. 1994. Anatomy of financial distress: an examination of junk bond issuers. *Quarterly Journal of Economics* 109:625–658.

Avery, R. and A. Berger. 1991. Loan commitments and bank risk exposure. *Journal of Banking and Finance* 15:173–192.

Baker, M. and J. Wurgler. 2002. Market timing and capital structure. *Journal of Finance* 57:1–32.

Baker, M., J. Stein, and J. Wurgler. 2003. When does the market matter? Stock prices and the investment of equity-dependent firms. *Quarterly Journal of Economics* 118: 969–1006.

Barclay, M. and C. Smith. 1996. On financial architecture: leverage, maturity and priority. *Journal of Applied Corporate Finance* 8(4):4–17.

Barry, C., C. Muscarella, J. Peavy, and M. Vetsuyens. 1990. The role of venture capital in the creation of public companies. *Journal of Financial Economics* 27:447–471.

Bebchuk, L. 1988. A new approach to corporate reorganizations. *Harvard Business Review* 101:775–804.

Berger, A. and G. Udell. 1990. Collateral, loan quality and bank risk. *Journal of Monetary Economics* 25:21–42.

Bernanke, B. and A. Blinder. 1992. The Federal Funds Rate and the channels of monetary transmission. *American Economic Review* 82:901–921.

Bernanke, B., M. Gertler, and S. Gilchrist. 1994. The financial accelerator and the Flight to quality. National Bureau of Economic Research, Working Paper 4789.

Besley, S. and J. Osteryoung. 1985. Survey of current practices in establishing trade credit limits. *Financial Review* February:70–82.

Biais, B. and C. Gollier, C. 1997. Trade credit and credit rationing. *Review of Financial Studies* 10:903–937.

Biais, B. and J. F. Malécot. 1996. Incentives and efficiency in the bankruptcy process: the case of France. The World Bank, PSD Occasional Paper 23.

Blanchard, O. J., F. Lopez-de-Silanes, and A. Shleifer. 1994. What do firms do with cash windfalls? *Journal of Financial Economics* 36:337–360.

Borio, C. 1990. Patterns of corporate finance. Bank for International Settlements, Basel, Working Paper 27.

Bradley, M., G. Jarell, and H. Kim. 1984. On the existence of an optimal capital structure: theory and evidence. *Journal of Finance* 39:857–878.

Bradley, D., B. Jordan, and J. Ritter. 2004. Analyst behavior following IPOs: the "bubble period" evidence. Mimeo, Clemson University.

Brealey, R. and S. Myers. 1988. *Principles of Corporate Finance*, 3rd edn. McGraw-Hill.

Brennan, M. and A. Thakor. 1990. Shareholder preferences and dividend policy. *Journal of Finance* 45:993–1019.

Brennan, M., V. Maksimovic, and J. Zechner. 1988. Vendor financing. *Journal of Finance* 43:1127–1141.

Burkart, M. and T. Ellingsen. 2004. In-kind finance: a theory of trade credit. *American Economic Review* 94:569–590.

Burkart, M., D. Gromb, and F. Panunzi. 1996. Debt design, liquidation value, and monitoring. Mimeo, MIT.

——. 1997. Large shareholders, monitoring and the value of the firm. *Quarterly Journal of Economics* 112:693–728.

Burkart, M., F. Panunzi, and A. Shleifer. 2003. Family firms. *Journal of Finance* 58:2167–2202.

Calomiris, C., C. Himmelberg, and P. Wachtel. 1995. Commercial paper and corporate finance: a microeconomic perspective. *Carnegie-Rochester Series on Public Policy* 42: 203–250.

Carey, M., S. Prowse, J. Rea, and G. Udell. 1993. Recent developments in the market for privately placed debt. *Federal Reserve Bulletin* February:77–92.

Chemla, G., M. Habib, and A. Ljungqvist. 2004. An analysis of shareholder agreements. Mimeo, Imperial College, London, University of Zurich, and New York University.

Chemmanur, T. J. and P. Fulghieri. 1999. A theory of the going-public decision. *Review of Financial Studies* 12:249–279.

Chen, H. C. and J. Ritter. 2000. The seven percent solution. *Journal of Finance* 55:1105–1132.

Choe, H., R. Masulis, and V. Nanda. 1993. Common stock offerings across the business cycle: theory and evidence. *Journal of Empirical Finance* 1:3–31.

Corbett, J. and T. Jenkinson. 1994. The financing of industry, 1970–1989: an international comparison. CEPR DP 948.

Dewatripont, M. and J. Tirole. 1994a. *The Prudential Regulation of Banks.* Cambridge, MA: MIT Press.

——. 1994b. A theory of debt and equity: diversity of securities and manager–shareholder congruence. *Quarterly Journal of Economics* 109:1027–1054.

Dow, J., G. Gorton, and A. Krishnamurthy. 2003. Equilibrium asset prices under imperfect corporate control. National Bureau of Economic Research, Working Paper 9758.

Eckbo, B. E. 1986. Valuation effects of corporate debt offerings. *Journal of Financial Economics* 15:119–151.

Eckbo, E. and R. Masulis. 1992. Cost of equity issuance. In *The New Palgrave Dictionary of Money and Finance* (ed. P. Newman, M. Milgate, and J. Eatwell), Volume 1, pp. 496–499. London: Macmillan.

——. 1995. Seasoned equity offerings: a survey. In *Handbook in Operations Research and Management Science: Finance* (ed. R. Jarrow, V. Maksimovic, and B. Ziemba), Volume 9. Amsterdam: North-Holland.

Emerick, D. and W. White. 1992. The case for private placements: how sophisticated investors add value to corporate debt issuers. *Journal of Applied Corporate Finance* 5(3):83–91.

Fama, E. and K. French. 2001. Disappearing dividends: changing firm characteristics or lower propensity to pay? *Journal of Financial Economics* 60:3–43.

Fazzari, S., R. G. Hubbard, and B. C. Petersen. 1988. Financing constraints and corporate investment. *Brookings Papers on Economic Activity* 1:141–195.

Finnerty, J. 1993. An overview of corporate securities innovation. In *The New Corporate Finance: Where Theory Meets Practice* (ed. D. Chew). New York: McGraw-Hill.

Frank, M. Z. and V. K. Goyal. 2003. Testing the pecking order of capital structure. *Journal of Financial Economics* 67: 217–248.

——. 2004. Capital structure decisions: which factors are reliably important? (February 11, 2004). EFA 2004 Maastricht Meetings Paper 2464; Tuck Contemporary Corporate Finance Issues III Conference Paper.

Gertler, M. and S. Gilchrist. 1993. The role of credit market imperfections in the monetary transmission mechanism. *Scandinavian Journal of Economics* 95:43–64.

——. 1994. Monetary policy, business cycle and the behavior of small business firms. *Quarterly Journal of Economics* 109:309–340.

Gibson, S., J. Kose, and L. Lang. 1990. Troubled debt restructuring: an empirical study of private reorganization of firms in default. *Journal of Financial Economics* 27:315–353.

Gompers, P. 1995. Optimal investment, monitoring, and the staging of venture capital. *Journal of Finance* 50:1461–1489.

——. 1998. An examination of convertible securities in venture capital investments. Harvard Business School, Working Paper.

Gompers, P. and J. Lerner. 1999. *The Venture Capital Cycle.* Cambridge, MA: MIT Press.

——. 2001. *The Money of Invention: How Venture Capital Creates New Wealth.* Boston, MA: Harvard Business School Press.

——. 2003. The really long-run performance of initial public offerings: the pre-Nasdaq evidence. *Journal of Finance* 58:1355–1392.

Graham, J. and C. Harvey. 2001. The theory and practice of corporate finance: evidence from the field. *Journal of Financial Economics* 60:187–243.

Greenbaum, S. and A. Thakor. 1995. *Contemporary Financial Intermediation.* Fort Worth, TX: Dryden Press, Harcourt Brace College Publishers.

Grullon, G. and D. Ikenberry. 2000. What do we know about share repurchases? *Journal of Applied Corporate Finance* 13(1):31–51.

Hanley, K. and J. Ritter. 1992. Going public. In *The New Palgrave Dictionary of Money and Finance* (ed. P. Newman, M. Milgate, and J. Eatwell), Volume 2, pp. 248–255. London: Macmillan.

Harris, M. and A. Raviv. 1988. Corporate control contests and capital structure. *Journal of Financial Economics* 20: 55–88.

Hart, O. and J. Moore. 1989. Default and renegotiation: a dynamic model of debt. Mimeo, MIT and LSE. (Published in *Quarterly Journal of Economics* (1998) 113:1–42.)

Harvard Business School. 1987. Note on financial contracting: deals. Case 9-288-014, rev. 1989.

——. 1990. Note on acquiring bank credit. Case 9-391-010, prepared by P. Bilden.

——. 1991. Note on bank loans. Case 9-291-026, prepared by S. Roth, rev. 1993.

Hoshi, T., A. Kashyap, and D. Scharfstein. 1990. The role of banks in reducing the costs of financial distress in Japan. *Journal of Financial Economics* 27:67–88.

——. 1991. Corporate structure, liquidity and investment: evidence from Japanese industrial groups. *Quarterly Journal of Economics* 106:33–60.

Hubbard, R. 1998. Capital-market imperfections and investment. *Journal of Economic Literature* 36:193–225.

Ibbotson, R. 1975. Price performance of common stock new issues. *Journal of Financial Economics* 2:235–272.

Jagannathan, M., C. P. Stephens, and M. S. Weisbach. 2000. Financial flexibility and the choice between dividends and stock repurchases. *Journal of Financial Economics* 57: 355–384.

James, C. 1987. Some evidence on the uniqueness of bank loans. *Journal of Financial Economics* 19:217–235.

James, C. and P. Weir. 1991. Borrowing relationships, intermediation, and the cost of issuing public securities. *Journal of Financial Economics* 28:149–172.

Jensen, M. and W. Meckling. 1976. Theory of the firm: managerial behavior, agency costs, and capital structure. *Journal of Financial Economics* 3:305–360.

Jolls, C. 1998. Stock repurchases and incentive compensation. National Bureau of Economic Research, Working Paper 6467.

Joskow, P., N. Rose, and A. Shepard. 1993. Regulatory constraints on CEO compensation. *Brookings Papers on Economic Activity, Microeconomics*, pp. 1–58. Brookings Institution Press.

Kahan, M. and B. Tuckman. 1993. Private vs public lending: evidence from covenants. Mimeo, New York University.

Kang, J. K. and R. Stulz. 1994. How different is Japanese corporate finance? An investigation of the information content of new securities issues. National Bureau of Economic Research, Working Paper 4908.

Kaplan, S. and P. Strömberg. 2003. Financial contracting theory meets the real world: an empirical analysis of venture capital contracts. *Review of Economic Studies* 70:281–315.

Kaplan, S. and P. Strömberg. 2004. Characteristics, contracts, and actions: evidence from venture capitalist analyses. *Journal of Finance* 59:2177–2210.

Kaplan, S. N. and L. Zingales. 1997. Do investment-cash flow sensitivities provide useful measures of financing constraints? *Quarterly Journal of Economics* 112:169–216.

——. 2000. Investment-cash flow sensitivities are not valid measures of financing constraints. *Quarterly Journal of Economics* 115:707–712.

Kashyap, A. and J. Stein. 2000. What do a million observations on banks say about the transmission of monetary policy? *American Economic Review* 90:407–428.

Kashyap, A., J. Stein, and D. Wilcox. 1993. Monetary policy and credit conditions: evidence from the composition of external finance. *American Economic Review* 83:78–98.

Kojima, K. 1994. An international perspective on Japanese corporate finance. RIEB DP45, Kobe University.

Kotaro, T. 1995. *The Japanese Market Economy System: Its Strengths and Weaknesses.* Tokyo: LTCB International Library Foundation.

Krigman, L., W. Shaw, and K. Womack. 2001. Why do firms switch underwriters? *Journal of Financial Economics* 60: 245–284.

Lamont, O. 1997. Cash flow and investment: evidence from internal capital markets. *Journal of Finance* 52:83–109.

Lerner, J. 2000. *Venture Capital and Private Equity: A Casebook.* New York: John Wiley.

Lerner, J. and U. Malmendier. 2004. Contractibility and the design of research agreements. Mimeo, Harvard University and Stanford University.

Lerner, J. and R. Merges. 1998. The control of technology alliances: an empirical analysis of the biotechnology industry. *Journal of Industrial Economics* 46:125–156.

Light, J. and W. White. 1979. *The Financial System.* Homewood, IL: Irwin.

Lintner, J. 1956. Distribution of incomes of corporations among dividends, retained earnings, and taxes. *American Economic Review* 46:97–113.

Loughran, T. and J. Ritter. 2002. Why don't issuers get upset about leaving money on the table in IPOs? *Review of Financial Studies* 15:413–444.

Lummer, S. L. and J. J. McConnell. 1989. Further evidence on the bank lending process and the reaction of the capital-market to bank loan agreements. *Journal of Financial Economics* 25:99–122.

Masulis, R. 1988. *The Debt/Equity Choice.* Cambridge, MA: Ballinger Publishing Company.

Masulis, R. and A. Korwar. 1986. Seasoned equity offerings. An empirical investigation. *Journal of Financial Economics* 15:91–117.

Mayer, C. 1988. New issues in corporate finance. *European Economic Review* 32:1167–1189.

Mayer, C. 1990. Financial systems, corporate finance, and economic development. In *Asymmetric Information, Corporate Finance, and Investment* (ed. G. Hubbard). National Bureau of Economic Research, University of Chicago Press.

Megginson, W. and K. Weiss. 1991. Venture capitalist certification in initial public offerings. *Journal of Finance* 46: 879–903.

Michaely, R. and K. Womack. 1999. Conflict of interest and the credibility of underwriter analyst recommendations. *Review of Financial Studies* 12:653–686.

Miller, M. and F. Modigliani. 1961. Dividend policy, growth and the valuation of shares. *Journal of Business* 34:411–433.

Modigliani, F. and M. Miller. 1958. The cost of capital, corporate finance, and the theory of investment. *American Economic Review* 48:261–297.

Myers, S. C. 1984. The capital structure puzzle. *Journal of Finance* 39:575–592.

Oliner, S. and G. Rudebusch. 1993. Is there a bank credit channel to monetary policy? Mimeo, Federal Board of Governors.

Olivier, J. 2000. Growth-enhancing bubbles. *International Economic Review* 41:133–151.

Pagano, M. 1993. The flotation of companies on the stock market: a coordination failure model. *European Economic Review* 37:1101–1125.

Pagano, M., F. Panetta, and L. Zingales. 1998. Why do companies go public? An empirical analysis. *Journal of Finance* 53:27–64.

Pastor, L. and P. Veronesi. 2005. Rational IPO waves. *Journal of Finance* 60:1713–1757.

Petersen, M. and R. Rajan. 1997. Trade credit: theory and evidence. *Review of Financial Studies* 10:661–691.

Philippon, T. 2003. Corporate governance over the business cycle. Mimeo, New York University.

Poterba, J. 1988. Coments on Fazzari, Hubbard and Petersen. *Brookings Papers on Economic Activity*, pp. 200–204. Brookings Institution Press.

Rajan, R. and L. Zingales. 1995. What do we know about capital structure? Some evidence from international data. *Journal of Finance* 50:1421–1460.

——. 2003. The great reversals: the politics of financial development in the 20th century. *Journal of Financial Economics* 69:5–50.

Ritter, J. 1987. The cost of going public. *Journal of Financial Economics* 19:269–282.

——. 2003. Investment banking and securities issuance. In *Handbook of the Economics of Finance* (ed. G. Constantinides, M. Harris, and R. Stulz). Amsterdam: North-Holland.

Ritter, J. and I. Welch. 2002. A review of IPO activity, pricing, and allocations. *Journal of Finance* 57:1795–1828.

Rock, K. 1986. Why new issues are underpriced. *Journal of Financial Economics* 15:187–212.

Sahlman, W. 1990. The structure and governance of venture-capital organizations. *Journal of Financial Economics* 27: 473–521.

Shleifer, A. and R. Vishny. 2003. Stock market driven acquisitions. *Journal of Financial Economics* 70:295–311.

Smith, C. and J. Warner. 1979. On financial contracting: an analysis of bond covenants. *Journal of Financial Economics* 7:117–161.

Smith, J. 1987. Trade credit and informational asymmetry. *Journal of Finance* 42:863–872.

Sraer, D. and D. Thesmar. 2004. Performance and behavior of family firms: evidence from the French stock market. Mimeo, CREST, INSEE.

Stein, J. 2003. Agency, information and corporate investment. In *Corporate Finance: Handbook of the Economics of Finance* (ed. G. Constantinides, M. Harris, and R. Stulz), pp. 111–165. Amsterdam: North-Holland.

Stigum, M. 1990. *The Money Market*, 3rd edn. New York: Irwin.

Titman, S. and R. Wessels. 1988. The determinants of capital structure choice. *Journal of Finance* 43:1–19.

Ventura, J. 2004. Economy growth with bubbles. Mimeo, Centre de Recerca en Economia Internacional, Universitat Pompeu Fabra, and CEPR.

White, M. 1989. The corporate bankruptcy decision. *Journal of Economic Perspectives* 3:129–152.

White, L. 1991. *The S&L Debacle: Public Policy Lessons for Bank and Thrift Regulation.* Oxford University Press.

Willis, J. and D. Clark. 1993. An introduction to mezzanine finance and private equity. In *The New Corporate Finance: Where Theory Meets Practice* (ed. D. Chew). New York: McGraw-Hill.

Wilner, B. 1994. The interest rates implicit in trade credit discounts. Mimeo, Kellogg School, Northwestern University.

Yosha, O. 1995. Information, disclosure costs and the choice of financing source. *Journal of Financial Intermediation* 4: 3–20.

Zimmermann, C. 1975. An approach to writing loan agreement covenants. In *Journal of Commercial Bank Lending*, pp. 213–228.

Zingales, L. 1994. The value of the voting right: a study of the Milan Stock Exchange. *Review of Financial Studies* 7: 125–148.

——. 1995. Inside ownership and the decision to go public. *Review of Economic Studies* 62:425–448.

PART II

Corporate Financing and Agency Costs

3

Outside Financing Capacity

3.1 Introduction

> A would-be borrower is said to be *rationed* if he cannot obtain the loan that he wants even though he is willing to pay the interest that the lenders are asking, perhaps even a higher interest. In practice such credit rationing seems to be commonplace: Some borrowers are constrained by fixed lines of credit which they must not exceed under any circumstances; others are refused loans altogether. As far as one can tell, these rationing phenomena are more than the temporary consequences of short-term disequilibrium adjustment problems. Indeed they seem to inhere in the very nature of the loan market.

This quotation from Bester and Hellwig (1987) is a good description of the puzzle of credit rationing. Why are lenders not willing to raise interest rates if the demand for loans exceeds their supply at the prevailing rates? One possible explanation is that interest rate ceiling regulations prevent such adjustment toward market equilibrium; however, such regulations have mostly been phased out and credit rationing is still a key feature of loan markets.

In the last thirty years, economists, following the impetus of Jaffee and Russell (1976), Keeton (1979), and Stiglitz and Weiss (1981), have come to the view that credit rationing is actually an equilibrium phenomenon driven by the asymmetry of information between borrowers and lenders. They have used both moral hazard and adverse selection arguments to explain why a lender would not want to raise interest rates even if the borrower were willing to pay higher rates, and why loans markets are personalized (there is usually no organized market for a standard commodity named "2-year loan at 10% interest rate") and clear through quantities (credit limits) as well as through prices (interest rates).

Both explanations start from the observation that a higher interest rate reduces the borrower's stake in the project: an interest rate increase has no effect on the borrower in the event of bankruptcy as long as the borrower is protected by limited liability. But it lowers the borrower's income in the absence of bankruptcy. The moral-hazard explanation is that this reduced stake may demotivate the borrower, induce her to pursue projects with high private benefits, or to neglect the project in favor of alternative activities, or even (in extreme cases) engage in outright fraud. That is, an increase in the interest rate may lower the probability of reimbursement indirectly through reduced performance.[1] The adverse selection explanation is that, in a situation where lenders cannot directly tell good and bad borrowers apart, higher interest rates tend to attract low-quality borrowers; for, low-quality borrowers are more likely to default on their loan and therefore are less affected by a rise in the interest rate than high-quality borrowers. Lenders may then want to keep interest rates low in order to face a better sample of borrowers.

This chapter analyzes credit rationing and the role of net worth. It emphasizes the moral-hazard

1. This moral-hazard explanation emphasizes the reduction in profit (technically speaking, in the sense of first-order stochastic dominance). Stiglitz and Weiss (1981) consider a different form of moral hazard. They observe that if the contract between the borrower and the lenders is a standard debt contract and if the lenders cannot observe the riskiness of the project chosen by the borrower, the borrower may have an incentive to choose an excessively risky project at the cost of sacrificing expected profit. Hart (1985) criticized this approach and observed that the conflict of interest between borrower and lenders relative to the choice of project riskiness could be solved by replacing the debt contract by profit sharing. To reintroduce divergent preferences between the two parties, one can either assume that the profit is costly to verify or completely unverifiable (see the descriptions of the costly state verification and of the nonverifiable income models in the supplementary section) or else introduce the form of moral hazard considered in this chapter. See Section 7.2.3 for models with both forms of moral hazard.

explanation, leaving the adverse selection explanation for Chapter 6. Section 3.2 develops the simplest model of credit rationing and uses it to illustrate the role of net worth. In this model, an "entrepreneur" or a "borrower" does not have enough money to finance a fixed-size project and must therefore resort to outside funding. The project may "succeed" and generate some income or "fail" and produce nothing. A key feature of this model is that lenders face an agency problem as the borrower may mismanage the project. She may take a private benefit and thereby reduce the probability that the project succeeds. The private benefit is inefficient in that its value to the borrower is smaller than the foregone profit; yet the borrower, who receives the entire private benefit and only part of the profit, may choose to enjoy the private benefit. The borrower must then keep a sufficient stake in the outcome of the project in order to have an incentive not to waste the money. Consequently, the project's income cannot be fully pledged to outside investors, which in turn implies that the project may not receive financing even if the expected income when the manager behaves exceeds the investment cost, that is, even if the project has positive net present value (NPV). That is, there may be credit rationing.

This first analysis points up some determinants of credit rationing. Borrowers with little cash on hand, with large private benefits from misbehaving, and whose performance conveys little information about managerial choices (in the technical sense of a low likelihood ratio) are more likely to see their positive-NPV projects turned down by the capital market.

It is also shown that investors optimally write covenants preventing the borrower from issuing in the future and without their approval claims on the firm's income, even if these new claims are junior to, and therefore do not directly dilute, theirs in bankruptcy. Because new claims alter managerial incentives, they may indirectly dilute the initial investors' stake anyway. Finally, Section 3.2 takes a first look at the sensitivity of investment to cash flow. While we argue that this question is best addressed in a dynamic setup (see Chapter 5), the basic model gives us some first insights as to whether investment can be predicted to increase with cash flow and whether this effect is likely to be more pronounced for firms with weak balance sheets.

Section 3.3 uses this basic model to illustrate the phenomenon of debt overhang, according to which the borrower may not be able to raise new funds for a profitable project if she has already committed future income linked with existing assets and if he cannot renegotiate some "debt forgiveness" or more generally some "claim forgiveness" or "claim dilution" with initial investors.

Banks, financial markets, and rating agencies generally feel that firms should not lever beyond some maximum level, called the debt capacity. Section 3.4 derives a rationale for debt capacity (or, more generally, borrowing capacity) and studies its determinants. In contrast with Section 3.2, which analyzes a fixed-size investment model, Section 3.4 views investment as a continuous variable, and shows that the firm's productive investments are optimally set equal to a given multiple of its equity. Equivalently, because investments are equal to equity plus leverage, this finding can be interpreted as the existence of a maximum leverage or gearing ratio.

The continuous investment extension serves another purpose besides the derivation of the outside financing capacity. It is also a convenient modeling device which will allow us to tackle in a simple way more complex issues related to choices of firm size such as diversification (Chapter 4), growth prospects (Chapter 5), asset repurchases (Chapter 14), the investment cycle (Chapter 14), as well macroeconomic models requiring an aggregation across borrowers (Chapters 13 and 14).

Because in the basic model, the project either succeeds or fails, and delivers nothing in the latter alternative, any claim is but a share to income in the case of success under limited liability. Put differently, it does not generate a diversity of claims such as debt and equity. "Debt capacity" is an abuse of terminology (it really is an "outside financing capacity") in that the outsiders' claim can but need not be interpreted as debt: if the profit in the case of success is 10, a claim of 4 can be interpreted either as a 40% equity stake, or as a risky debt claim with nominal value 4 which is defaulted upon in the case of failure. We later capture one feature of debt, namely, its priority over equity by introducing a leftover value of the assets in the case of failure. We show that it is optimal for investors to have priority in the case of default and for the entrepreneur to be the residual claimant (Chapter 5 will investigate another feature of debt, namely, the borrower's promise to pay fixed amounts to investors as a going concern, i.e., before liquidation; and Chapter 10 will connect debtholders' control rights with their cash-flow rights).

By focusing on a simple model of credit rationing, we do not do full justice to the corporate finance literature, which has developed a wide array of models with a similar flavor. For the sake of completeness, the supplementary section studies three broad classes of models that, through more sophisticated modeling, have aimed at deriving an interpretation of the "leftover claim" of outside investors as a standard debt claim.

3.2 The Role of Net Worth: A Simple Model of Credit Rationing

3.2.1 The Fixed-Investment Model

Variants of the following entrepreneurial model[2] will be used in the following: an entrepreneur (also called the "insider" or the "borrower," "she") has a project. This project requires a fixed investment I. The entrepreneur initially has "assets" ("cash on hand" or "net worth") $A < I$. For the moment we interpret these assets as being cash or liquid securities that can be used toward covering the cost of investment. (We will later explore the possibility that these assets be illiquid. For example, they might be equipment or premises that are needed for the implementation of the project.) The entrepreneur's cash can either be invested in the project or used for consumption. To implement the project the entrepreneur must borrow $I - A$ from lenders. (We will later observe that we can ignore the possibility that the entrepreneur consumes some of the cash and borrows more than $I - A$.)

Project. If undertaken, the project either succeeds, that is, yields verifiable income $R > 0$, or fails, that is, yields no income. The probability of success is denoted by p. The project is subject to moral hazard. The entrepreneur can "behave" ("work," "exert effort," "take no private benefit") or "misbehave" ("shirk," "take a private benefit");[3] or, equivalently, the entrepreneur chooses between a project with a high probability of success and another project which ceteris paribus she prefers (is easier to implement, is more fun, has greater spinoffs in the future for the entrepreneur, benefits a friend, delivers perks, is more "glamorous," etc.) but has a lower probability of success.[4]

Behaving yields probability $p = p_{\mathrm{H}}$ of success and no private benefit to the entrepreneur, and misbehaving results in probability $p = p_{\mathrm{L}} < p_{\mathrm{H}}$ of success and private benefit $B > 0$ (measured in units of account) to the entrepreneur.[5] In the "effort interpretation," B can also be interpreted as a disutility of effort saved by the entrepreneur when shirking. Let $\Delta p \equiv p_{\mathrm{H}} - p_{\mathrm{L}}$.

Preferences and the loan agreement. Both the borrower and the potential lenders (or "investors") are risk neutral.[6] For notational simplicity, there is no time preference; the rate of return expected by investors (which is also the riskless rate, due to risk neutrality) is taken to be 0.[7] The borrower is protected by limited liability, and so her income cannot take negative values.

Lenders behave competitively in the sense that the loan, if any, makes zero profit. That is, we have in mind that several prospective lenders compete for issuing a loan to the borrower, and that, if the most attractive loan offer made a positive profit, the borrower could turn to an alternative lender and offer

2. This specific model is taken from Holmström and Tirole (1997). But its main idea can be found in various forms in many anterior papers.

3. See Exercise 3.20 for the continuous-effort version of the model.

4. Note that, for simplicity, we treat the entrepreneur as a unitary actor. There is an interesting question as to how moral hazard and incentives propagate down within the corporate hierarchy. Pagano and Volpin (2005) assume that benefits accrue to all company insiders, and not only to managers; in their model, managers need workers' cooperation to produce and therefore share benefits with employees.

5. For example, in the biotechnology alliance financing discussed in Section 2.4.2, the private benefit might be the entrepreneur's benefit from working on other projects (with other partners or on her own). The shift in attention then reduces the probability of success of the project under consideration.

6. Exercise 3.2 generalizes this analysis to allow for entrepreneurial risk aversion. Exercise 3.12 considers risk-averse investors.

7. The investors have rate of time preference equal to 0, which is also the market rate of interest.

to switch for a slightly lower interest rate.[8] We use the plural "lenders" even though a single lender may turn out to finance the entire loan, because we want to emphasize that lending is a passive and anonymous activity in the theories reviewed in Part II.

Let us turn to the loan contract. A contract first stipulates whether the project is financed.[9] If so, it further specifies how the profit is shared between the lenders and the borrower. The borrower's limited liability will imply that both sides receive 0 in the case of failure (the gross payoffs are the *ex post* monetary payoffs and take no account of past investments and private benefit). Intuitively, there is no point in specifying a positive transfer from the lenders to the borrower, as such a transfer can only weaken incentives, while it has no insurance benefit under risk neutrality. This property will be proved more rigorously and is here taken for granted. In the case of success, the two parties share the profit R; R_b goes to the borrower and R_l to the lenders.[10] To sum up, we posit an incentive scheme for the entrepreneur of the following form: R_b in the case of success, 0 in the case of failure.

The zero-profit constraint for the lenders can be written as

$$p_H R_l = I - A,$$

assuming that the loan agreement induces the borrower to behave (which under our assumptions will be the case). The rate of interest ι is given by

$$R_l = (1+\iota)(I-A) \quad \text{or} \quad 1+\iota = 1/p_H.$$

So, unless $p_H = 1$, the nominal rate of interest ι reflects a default premium and exceeds the expected rate of return (called r in Part VI and here normalized to 0) demanded by investors.

We summarize the timing in Figure 3.1.

We assume that the project is viable only in the absence of moral hazard. That is, the project has positive NPV if the entrepreneur behaves,

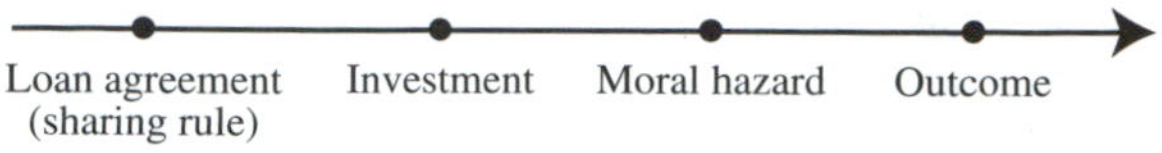

Figure 3.1

$$p_H R - I > 0, \tag{3.1}$$

but negative NPV, even if one includes the borrower's private benefit, if she does not,

$$p_L R - I + B < 0. \tag{3.2}$$

It is easy to see that inequality (3.2) implies that no loan that gives an incentive to the borrower to misbehave will be granted. Indeed, rewrite (3.2) as

$$[p_L R_l - (I - A)] + [p_L R_b + B - A] < 0.$$

So, in the case of misbehavior, either the lenders must lose money in expectation, or the borrower would be better off using her cash for consumption, or both.

3.2.2 The Lenders' Credit Analysis

Because the project has negative NPV in the case of misbehavior, the loan agreement must be careful to preserve enough of a stake for the borrower in the enterprise. The borrower faces the following tradeoff once the financing has been secured: by misbehaving, she obtains private benefit B, but she reduces the probability of success from p_H to p_L. Because she has stake R_b in the firm's income (she receives R_b in the case of success and 0 in the case of failure), the borrower will therefore behave if the following "incentive compatibility constraint" is satisfied:

$$p_H R_b \geqslant p_L R_b + B \quad \text{or} \quad (\Delta p) R_b \geqslant B. \tag{IC$_b$}$$

From this incentive compatibility constraint we infer that the highest income in the case of success that can be pledged to the lenders without jeopardizing the borrower's incentives is

$$R - \frac{B}{\Delta p}.$$

The *(expected) pledgeable income* is then

$$\mathcal{P} = p_H\left(R - \frac{B}{\Delta p}\right).$$

8. See Exercise 3.13 for the extension of the model to lender market power.

9. "Random financing" contracts, in which the borrower brings equity in exchange for a probability between 0 and 1 of being financed may in some cases be optimal when the investment size is fixed (as it is here) or more generally in the presence of indivisibilities or increasing returns to scale (see Exercise 3.1). For simplicity, we focus on deterministic contracts.

10. The lenders' net payoff is thus $R_l - (I - A)$ in the case of success, and $-(I - A)$ in the case of failure. The borrower's net payoff is thus $R_b - A$ in the case of success, and $-A$ in the case of failure, to which, in both cases, must be added a private benefit B if shirking occurs.

Because the lenders must break even in order to be willing to finance the project, a necessary condition for the borrower to receive a loan is that the expected pledgeable income exceed the lenders' initial outlay:

$$\mathcal{P} \equiv p_{\mathrm{H}}\left(R - \frac{B}{\Delta p}\right) \geqslant I - A, \qquad (\mathrm{IR}_{\mathrm{l}})$$

where "IR_{l}" stands for the lenders' individual rationality constraint (which we will also often call the "breakeven constraint" or the "participation constraint"). Thus a necessary condition for financing to be arranged is

$$A \geqslant \bar{A} = p_{\mathrm{H}}\frac{B}{\Delta p} - (p_{\mathrm{H}}R - I). \qquad (3.3)$$

To make things interesting, we will assume that

$$\bar{A} > 0 \iff p_{\mathrm{H}}R - I < p_{\mathrm{H}}\frac{B}{\Delta p}, \qquad (3.4)$$

otherwise even a borrower with no wealth of her own would be able to obtain credit. Condition (3.4) says that the NPV is smaller than the minimum expected rent that must be left to the borrower to provide her with an incentive to behave.

Thus, *the borrower must have enough assets in order to be granted a loan.* Note that, if $A < \bar{A}$, the project has positive NPV and yet is not funded. With insufficient assets, the entrepreneur must borrow a large amount and therefore pledge a large fraction of the return in the case of success. The entrepreneur then keeps only a small fraction of the monetary gain and is demotivated. The two parties cannot find a loan agreement that both induces effort (which requires a high compensation for the borrower in the case of success) and allows the lenders to recoup their investment. There is *credit rationing.* A rationed borrower may be willing to give a high fraction of the return to the lenders,[11] which here is equivalent to be willing to pay a high interest rate. But the lenders do not want to grant such a loan.

Conversely, if $A \geqslant \bar{A}$, the entrepreneur is able to secure financing, and so condition (3.3) is both a necessary and a sufficient condition for financing. The entrepreneur offers claim R_{l} to competitive investors so as not to leave them with a surplus:

$$p_{\mathrm{H}}R_{\mathrm{l}} = I - A.$$

11. This will be the case if A is small.

Her stake,

$$R_{\mathrm{b}} = R - R_{\mathrm{l}} = R - \frac{I - A}{p_{\mathrm{H}}} \geqslant R - \frac{I - \bar{A}}{p_{\mathrm{H}}} = \frac{B}{\Delta p}, \qquad (3.5)$$

then induces her to behave.

As the conventional wisdom goes, "one only lends to the rich." The threshold $\bar{A}$ has a natural interpretation. As noted earlier, the term $p_{\mathrm{H}}B/\Delta p$ is nothing but the minimum expected monetary payoff to be left to the borrower to preserve incentives; it will be called the *agency rent.* The borrower must make an initial contribution at least equal to $\bar{A}$ so as to reduce the agency rent net of the initial downpayment A to at most the monetary profit $p_{\mathrm{H}}R - I$ of the project.

Using the breakeven condition for the lenders ($p_{\mathrm{H}}R_{\mathrm{l}} = I - A$), the borrower obtains net utility or payoff (where "net" means that we subtract the consumption utility, A, that the entrepreneur would get by not undertaking the project):

$$U_{\mathrm{b}} = \begin{cases} 0 & \text{if } A < \bar{A}, \\ p_{\mathrm{H}}R_{\mathrm{b}} - A = p_{\mathrm{H}}(R - R_{\mathrm{l}}) - A & \\ \qquad = p_{\mathrm{H}}R - I & \text{if } A \geqslant \bar{A}. \end{cases} \qquad (3.6)$$

As could have been expected from the zero-profit condition for the lenders, *the borrower receives the entire social surplus or net present value if the project is funded.*[12]

So, the borrower's utility jumps up at $A = \bar{A}$. While the discontinuity is an artefact of the rigidity of the level of investment, the fact that 1 unit of assets may be worth more than 1 to the borrower in a situation of asymmetric information is quite general. Indeed, in the continuous investment version of this model to be developed in Section 3.4, we will see that for the borrower *assets or net worth have a shadow value exceeding* 1.

Determinants of credit rationing. To sum up, two factors may make a firm credit-constrained in this model:[13]

(i) low amount of cash on hand (low A);

12. This property holds only in equilibrium. Were the entrepreneur to deviate and misbehave, the entrepreneur's (off-the-equilibrium-path) utility would exceed the smaller (off-the-equilibrium-path) NPV (at least for A close to $\bar{A}$), since the lenders would lose money.

13. The market interest rate, here normalized at 0, is another determinant of the strength of the balance sheet. More generally, the pledgeable income must exceed the investors' outlay times $(1 + r)$,

(ii) high agency cost, where the agency cost can be measured, fixing the project's NPV, $p_H R$, by the combination of the private benefit B and the likelihood ratio $\Delta p / p_H$.

The entrepreneur's ability to borrow is limited by the nonpledgeability of some $(p_H B / \Delta p)$ of the value to investors. Here moral hazard is determined by two factors: the private benefit B that the entrepreneur can enjoy by misbehaving, and the extent to which the verifiable performance reveals such misbehavior. The informativeness of the performance variable regarding effort is defined by the likelihood ratio $(\Delta p / p_H) = (p_H - p_L)/p_H$.[14] This ratio measures the proportional reduction in the probability of success when the entrepreneur misbehaves and is therefore also a measure of the marginal productivity of effort by the borrower. The higher the likelihood ratio, the more informative about effort choice the outcome is ("the better the performance measurement"), and the easier the access to outside financing (in the sense that the minimum net worth $\bar{A}$ decreases). In the model of this section, the pledgeable income never exceeds $p_H R - B$, since the entrepreneur can always take her private benefit B, but may be much smaller when performance measurement is poor, i.e., the likelihood ratio is low.

In practice, the agency cost is influenced not only by the project's and the entrepreneur's characteristics, but also by the surrounding legal, regulatory, and corporate environment. Countries with strong investor protection limit the managers' ability to squander investor money and thereby exhibit lower agency costs; relatedly, the firms' ability to cross-list in jurisdictions with good shareholder protection is expected to reduce their agency cost and therefore to facilitate financing.[15]

Remark (full investment of entrepreneurial assets). We have assumed that the borrower invests her entire wealth. However, it is easy to see that this is an optimal choice for the borrower. Would the borrower want to consume $c \leqslant A$ and invest only $A - c$? If the project is still funded, the borrower still obtains the entire social surplus $p_H R - I$. On the other hand, it becomes more difficult to obtain a loan. Now, the entrepreneur's initial assets must exceed $\bar{A} + c$ in order for the project to be funded. Therefore the entrepreneur cannot gain by not investing her entire wealth in the project.[16]

Remark (high-powered incentive scheme). Earlier we claimed that risk neutrality implies that the absence of reward for the entrepreneur in the case of failure involves no loss of generality. Suppose, more generally, that the entrepreneur receives R_b^S in the case of success and R_b^F in the case of failure, where

$$p_H R_b^S + (1 - p_H) R_b^F \geqslant p_L R_b^S + (1 - p_L) R_b^F + B$$
$$\iff \quad (\Delta p)(R_b^S - R_b^F) \geqslant B$$

in order to discourage the entrepreneur from misbehaving. The investors' income is then

$$p_H(R - R_b^S) + (1 - p_H)(-R_b^F) \leqslant p_H\left(R - \frac{B}{\Delta p}\right) - R_b^F \leqslant \mathcal{P}.$$

Rewarding the entrepreneur in the case of failure implies a uniform upward shift in her minimum incentive-compatible pay structure and an overall reduction in what can be pledged to investors (note the analogy with the previously considered case of an initial consumption c). By contrast, the entrepreneur's utility, provided that she can secure funding, is not affected: because the investors break even, the entire surplus goes to the entrepreneur, who receives

$$U_b = p_H R - I,$$

regardless of the choice of R_b^F. We thus conclude that rewarding the entrepreneur in the case of failure cannot raise her utility, but can compromise financing.

---

where r is the rate of interest:

$$p_H\left(R - \frac{B}{\Delta p}\right) \geqslant (1 + r)(I - A).$$

Thus, keeping the investment cost I fixed, an increase in the rate of interest r is equivalent to a decrease in the cash on hand.

14. The likelihood ratio is often defined as p_H / p_L. The two notions are obviously equivalent.

15. See, for example, the empirical confirmations by Doidge et al. (2004), Miller (1999), Pagano et al. (2001), and Reese and Weisbach (2002).

16. This reasoning relies, of course, on the borrower's putting equal weight on current and future consumption. If the borrower had immediate consumption needs, she would put some of A aside for consumption. We invite the reader to extend the analysis to the more general specification in which the borrower consumes c_0 at the start and c_1 after the outcome is realized, and has utility the expectation of $u_0(c_0) + u_1(c_1)$, where the functions $u_0(\cdot)$ and $u_1(\cdot)$ are increasing and concave. (The basic insights are unaltered. See also Exercise 3.2.)

Remark (value and investor value). Because the essence of corporate finance is that investors cannot appropriate the full benefit attached to the investments they enable, we must distinguish two slices in the overall cake: that for the insiders and the rest for the outsiders (the decomposition must be finer if there are multiple categories of each). In this book, "value" or "total value" refers to the total cake, while "investor value" refers to the investors' slice; in the barebones model of this section, these two values are pR and pR_1 for probability of success p once the investment has been sunk (of course, one needs to subtract I and $I - A$, respectively, if one wants to obtain the corresponding net or *ex ante* magnitudes). The empirical literature often uses the phrase "value" for what we call here "investor value," but this should not create confusion.

Remark (risk taking). Moral hazard here refers to the possibility that the borrower takes an action that reduces investor value (and total value as well). There is no risk taking. We will come back to risk taking in subsequent chapters, but the reader may want to consult Exercises 3.15, 3.16, and 4.15 for three simple ways of introducing risk taking in the context of this simple model.

3.2.3 Do Investors Hold Debt or Equity?

We interpreted the loan agreement as a profit-sharing contract. It turns out that with two levels of profit, 0 and R, the lenders' claim can be thought of as being either debt or equity: put differently, there is here no difference between risky debt and equity. The debt interpretation goes as follows: the borrower must reimburse R_1 or else go bankrupt. In the case of reimbursement the borrower keeps the residual $R - R_1$. Alternatively, the two parties can define shares in an all-equity venture. The entrepreneur and the investors hold fractions R_b/R and R_1/R, respectively, of equity. These are called "inside equity" and "outside equity."

This feature of the two-outcome model is both a weakness and a strength. A serious weakness is that it cannot, as it stands, account for the richness of existing securities; but we will show how to extend it in order to generate a more realistic diversity of claims. A strength of this modeling is that it will enable us to analyze a number of key ideas without being held back by the need to specify whether one is analyzing debt, equity, or an alternative claim. Some readers may find it surprising that a lack of predictive power relative to the structure of outside claims may constitute a strength. To clarify this point, it is worth pointing out that many phenomena in corporate finance have wider scope than that defined by the context in which they were discovered. Let us provide some illustrations in support of this view:

(a) As we will study in Chapter 5, Easterbrook (1984) and Jensen (1986) have argued that it is optimal to require cash-rich firms to pay out income on a regular basis, thereby forcing them to return to the capital market. The payment takes the form of a dividend in Easterbrook and of a short-term debt obligation in Jensen. The starting point for both analyses, namely, the desire to pump free cash flow out of the firm, is the same.

(b) The foundations for the soft-budget-constraint problem, also studied in Chapter 5, do not rely on outside claims being debt or equity. While it is usually analyzed in the context of specific assumptions on the financial structure, its logic is quite general.

(c) The literatures on monitoring of a firm by a large shareholder and by a bank holding debt claims have much in common. They are both concerned with the monitor's incentive to supervise and with the impact of monitoring on the firm's behavior.

(d) The idea of using dispersed claimholders to extract rents from third parties (see Chapters 7 and 11) has been developed in separate literatures on debt and on equity.

Thus, abstracting in a first step from the complex issues associated with the diversity of outside claims may generate a better focus on, and a more rigorous analysis of the fundamentals of such phenomena. A richer analysis can then be obtained from the introduction of further modeling features that motivate a diversity of outside claims.

3.2.4 Dilution and Overborrowing

Recall from Section 2.3.3 (see also Fama and Miller 1972) that debt contracts include negative covenants

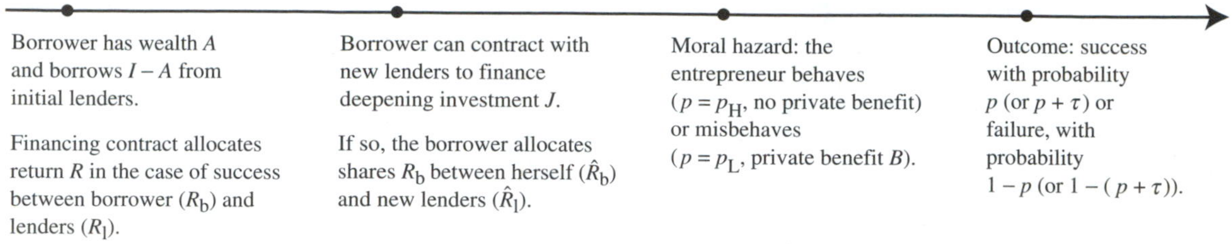
Borrower has wealth A and borrows $I-A$ from initial lenders.
Financing contract allocates return R in the case of success between borrower (R_b) and lenders (R_l).
Borrower can contract with new lenders to finance deepening investment J.
If so, the borrower allocates shares R_b between herself ($\hat{R}_b$) and new lenders ($\hat{R}_l$).
Moral hazard: the entrepreneur behaves ($p=p_H$, no private benefit) or misbehaves ($p=p_L$, private benefit B).
Outcome: success with probability p (or $p+\tau$) or failure, with probability $1-p$ (or $1-(p+\tau)$).

Figure 3.2

prohibiting the dilution of creditors' claims through the issue of new securities, especially ones with equal or higher seniority. There are two basic reasons for such covenants. First, creditors obviously do not want the borrower to issue claims that have a higher or the same seniority as theirs, as this reduces the amount they can collect if the firm defaults. Second, and more subtly, the issue of new securities may alter managerial incentives and the size of the pie.

Let us illustrate the second reason in our simple context. Consider the borrowing contract above in which the lenders take claim R_l in the case of success and the borrower an incentive-compatibility claim $R_b \geqslant B/\Delta p$. Now suppose that there is an opportunity for a "deepening investment." This investment costs an extra J and increases the probability of success uniformly by τ. That is, the probability of success becomes $p_H + \tau$ if the entrepreneur behaves and $p_L + \tau$ if the entrepreneur misbehaves.[17] Assume that this deepening investment is inefficient in that its net cost C_1 is positive, or put differently the expected increase in profit is smaller than J:

$$C_1 \equiv J - \tau R > 0.$$

The timing goes as in Figure 3.2.

We assume away any negative covenant prohibiting further borrowing and so the borrower can contract with new lenders.[18] However, in the case of new financing, initial lenders are not formally diluted in that they keep their stake R_l in success when the borrower contracts with new lenders. So the first motivation for inserting a covenant that prohibits the issuing of new securities is absent.

Note first that it is not in the interest of the borrower to contract with new investors if this results in the same effort, i.e., in no taking of private benefit. Intuitively, the new investment reduces total value by C_1, and so someone must lose in the process. Because the value of the initial investors' claim is increased (to $(p_H+\tau)R_l$) if the borrower still behaves, either the entrepreneur or the new investors must lose, which is impossible because the losing party would refuse to write the second financing contract. So assume that the new financing contract disincentivizes the borrower. This reduced incentive results in a second cost:

$$C_2 \equiv (\Delta p)R - B > 0.$$

As described in the timing, let $\hat{R}_b$ and $\hat{R}_l$ denote the new stake of the borrower and the stake of the new lenders, with

$$\hat{R}_b + \hat{R}_l = R_b.$$

Assuming that the new lenders are competitive, then

$$(p_L + \tau)\hat{R}_l = J.$$

The entrepreneur gains from overborrowing if and only if

$$(p_L + \tau)\hat{R}_b + B > p_H R_b,$$

or, using the breakeven condition for the new investors,

$$[(p_L + \tau)R_b - J] + B > p_H R_b.$$

After some manipulations, this condition becomes

$$[p_H - (p_L + \tau)]R_l > C_1 + C_2.$$

This necessary and sufficient condition for the deepening investment to be financed has a simple

17. This additivity property is convenient because it separates the incentive compatibility constraint from the impact of the new investment.

18. More generally, the division of the pie ($R_l + R_b = R$) is not made contingent on the event of a deepening investment.

interpretation. The right-hand side is the total cost of refinancing: direct cost plus incentive cost. The left-hand side of the inequality is the *externality* on the initial investors. Thus the total cost must be smaller than the loss of value for the initial investors.

When the borrower's balance sheet (as measured by A, say) improves, R_b increases, R_l decreases, and so this inequality is less likely to be satisfied. Put differently, in the absence of negative covenant, *overborrowing is more likely to happen with weak borrowers.*

Let us conclude this analysis of overborrowing with a few remarks. First, overborrowing in this situation can alternatively be avoided by forcing the entrepreneur not to dilute her own claim; this requirement is usually included in compensation contracts, although there have been attempts to evade it through derivative contracts (see Section 1.2.2). Second, the financing contracts need not be signed sequentially: simultaneous contracts also give rise to an overborrowing problem (see Bizer and DeMarzo 1992; Segal 1999). Third, the overborrowing problem arises with a vengeance in the context of sovereign borrowing, in which it is hard to specify a limit on indebtedness of the sovereign, if only because there are many different ways for a government to add new liabilities (see Bolton and Jeanne (2004) for an analysis of sovereign borrowing with the possibility of dilution). Finally, *in a multiperiod financing context, uncoordinated lending further leads to excessively short maturity structures of debt*, as investors scramble to obtain priority over other investors (see Exercise 5.9).

3.2.5 Boosting the Ability to Borrow: Reputational Capital and Capability

Recall from Chapter 2 that lenders do not only look at tangible assets such as cash, land, and equipment. Ceteris paribus, they are more likely to issue a loan if the borrower has a good reputation, as was stressed in particular by Diamond (1991). The role of this intangible capital is easily analyzed in the credit rationing model.

Suppose, for example, that the borrower has less attractive opportunities for misbehavior, in that the private benefit B from misbehaving is reduced to $b < B$.[19] This may have several interpretations. Along the lines of the "effort interpretation" of moral hazard, one might imagine that the project falls well within the core competency of the entrepreneur and therefore demands less attention or supervision of the subordinates: the task is just easier for the entrepreneur. Alternatively, one could imagine that the entrepreneur has less attractive outside options (focusing on other, separate projects of her own) or opportunities for fraud and embezzlement (e.g., it is harder to buy inputs at an inflated price from a friend or family).

With reduced scope for moral hazard, the asset threshold is accordingly lower: from equation (3.3),

$$\bar{A}(b) < \bar{A}(B),$$

where

$$\bar{A}(\beta) \equiv p_H \frac{\beta}{\Delta p} - (p_H R - I),$$

and thus

$$\bar{A}(B) - \bar{A}(b) = \frac{p_H}{\Delta p}(B - b) > 0.$$

In this sense, a "more reliable borrower" (that is, a borrower who has a lower private benefit from misbehaving) is more likely to obtain a loan.

How does this fit with the idea that a good reputation helps raise external finance? Suppose now that the private benefit (B or b) is not directly observed by the lenders, who only have the borrower's track record at their disposal. That is, the lenders know whether the borrower's past projects have been successful or whether past loans have been reimbursed. They use this information to update their beliefs about the reliability of the borrower. A better track record is an (imperfect) indicator of good reliability, that is, in our example, of a low private benefit from misbehaving.

Consider an entrepreneur who got a loan for a first project, and may in the future have new projects that will also call for outside financing. Let us further assume that these future projects are not yet well-defined, and focus on short-term finance. (Chapter 5 will analyze long-term loans.) In this situation, the entrepreneur should adopt a long-term perspective.

19. We could alternatively analyze the impact of a higher probability of success or of changes in other variables, with similar insights. The focus on the private benefit allows a cleaner analysis because changes in the private benefit keep the NPV of the project constant.

That is, she should not content herself with comparing the private benefit and the monetary payoff attached to the first project; she should also take into account the fact that a current success will bring two further benefits:

A *retained-earnings benefit*: even under symmetric information between the parties about the entrepreneur's reliability, a current success helps the entrepreneur build up net worth. This net worth has a shadow value; a unit of income is valued above 1 by the entrepreneur if there is a probability of credit rationing in the future. This benefit is studied in Exercise 3.11.

A *reputational benefit*: if, furthermore, the lenders have incomplete information about the entrepreneur's reliability, their updating of beliefs about this reliability confers an extra benefit on the entrepreneur in the case of success. Reputation complements net worth in reducing the probability of future credit rationing.[20]

An implication of the existence of this reputational benefit is that an unreliable borrower who would have no incentive to behave were her unreliability known to the lenders may have an incentive to behave today in order to get a loan tomorrow. The analysis of the situation becomes more complex once we realize that lenders are unlikely to be fools and understand that unreliable borrowers may have an incentive to masquerade as reliable ones. A proper study of reputational capital requires some (at least intuitive) understanding of dynamic games with incomplete information (see Exercise 6.3). We hope that the idea that reputational capital can substitute for net worth to thwart credit rationing is clear enough. There is indeed empirical evidence that reputation helps borrowers to obtain credit as well as better terms (see, for instance, Banerjee and Duflo's (2000) study of the Indian software industry).

Remark (information sharing). The impact of reputational capital is stronger, the more widely the information about borrower performance is disseminated. Padilla and Pagano (2000) observe that information sharing among lenders reinforces the borrowers' incentives to perform and argue that this may account for the fact that lenders (banks, finance companies, and retailers) spontaneously provide information about past defaults, delays in payment, current debt exposure, and riskiness of their borrowers to credit bureaus and credit-rating agencies, and therefore to their competitors. They develop a model in which lenders may share information even when this may encourage consumer poaching and thus enhanced *ex post* competition.

3.2.6 Making Efficient Use of Information to Reduce the Agency Cost

A basic theoretical result in the economics of agency, due to Holmström (1979), states that making economic agents accountable for events over which they have no control does not help with moral-hazard problems and generally worsens incentives. Roughly speaking, one should try to use the most informative or precise measurement of the agent's economic activity, or what is called in statistics a "summary" or "sufficient statistic."[21] This result underlies much of the thinking about managerial compensation, for example, the quest for good metrics to reward employees (based on customer satisfaction, reduction of unit costs, sales, etc.) or division managers (like EVA (economic value added) or balanced scorecard methods). More to the point for our context, it offers theoretical foundations for the use of benchmarking. Benchmarking, also called relative performance evaluation, consists in comparing the performance of, say, a firm with that of similar firms, to better assess managerial accomplishments. For example, a car producer's good financial performance is less indicative of good management if other car producers also do well than if the automobile industry is in a

20. Things are actually a bit more complicated than this dual benefit suggests: the reputational benefit depends on the borrower's equilibrium behavior (which itself depends on the retained-earnings benefit) and not only on the reputational one. Technically, if the retained-earnings benefit is strong enough to induce a high-private-benefit entrepreneur to behave, then success brings no reputational benefit.

21. A good introduction to sufficient statistics is Chapter 9 of DeGroot (1970). Suppose that one observes two variables x and y, and that one is trying to infer a third, unobservable variable z. The joint distribution of x and y, given z, is $f(x, y \mid z)$. The variable x is a sufficient statistic for (x, y) if the posterior distribution of z conditional on the observation of x and y depends only on x. To recognize sufficient statistics, a necessary and sufficient condition is the factorization criterion, that is, the existence of functions g and h such that $f(x, y \mid z) = g(x, y)h(x, z)$. A simple computation then shows that the distribution of z conditional on x and y does not depend on y.

recession. Or, a high price fetched by the stock of a software or biotechnology start-up company in an initial public offering (IPO) is not foolproof evidence of good entrepreneurship and careful venture capital monitoring if this price is reached during a stock price bubble.

We will come back a few times in this book to the issue of the quality of performance measurement and how it affects the ability to receive financing.[22] Let us just observe that in our context, the ability to raise financing is enhanced by conditioning entrepreneurial compensation on the performance measure with the highest available likelihood ratio.[23]

Let us provide a first illustration of this principle.

Benchmarking. A possible reinterpretation of our model is that there are three states of nature.

(i) Favorable state (probability p_L). The environment is sufficiently favorable that the project will succeed regardless of the entrepreneur's effort.

(ii) Unfavorable state (probability $1 - p_H$). The environment is harsh and the project will fail even if the entrepreneur does her best.

(iii) Intermediate state (probability $\Delta p = p_H - p_L$). Success is not guaranteed, but is reached provided the entrepreneur exerts effort.

Of course, no one *ex ante* knows which state prevails. The financing and effort decisions are chosen in the ignorance of the state of nature.[24]

Suppose now that one will learn *ex post* whether the state was favorable or not (i.e., intermediate or unfavorable), say, by looking at a less promising firm in the same industry that succeeds only if circumstances are favorable. Consider the following compensation scheme:

- the entrepreneur receives 0 if the state is favorable;
- the entrepreneur otherwise receives R_b in the case of success and 0 in the case of failure.

The incentive constraint is still

$$(\Delta p)R_b \geqslant B \tag{IC$_b$}$$

since the entrepreneur's stake is still R_b in the state of nature in which she affects profit. The pledgeable income, however, has increased since one no longer pays the entrepreneur for being lucky: now the maximal pledgeable income is

$$p_H R - (\Delta p)\Big[\min_{\{IC_b\}} R_b\Big] = p_H R - B,$$

where $[\min_{\{IC_b\}} R_b]$ denotes the smallest reward R_b that ensures incentive compatibility.

Next, let us assume that the firm's performance can be compared with that of an identical firm facing the same state of nature. Assuming that the entrepreneur in the other firm behaves, then "success" in the other firm provides information that the state is either favorable or intermediate, while "failure" in the other firm reveals an unfavorable state. Then, conditional on the entrepreneur failing, one learns either that she was unlucky or that she failed because she misbehaved. In this case, the pledgeable income cannot be increased by benchmarking if one abides by the entrepreneur's limited liability:[25] when

22. See, for example, Section 4.4 and Chapter 9.

23. For example, it would never come to one's mind to condition the entrepreneur's compensation on the weather in Bali, on the outcome of the soccer World Cup, or on other "irrelevant" variables. Why? Let us be a bit more technical here. In the notation of footnote 21, let (x, y) denote the verifiable state of nature (which includes, but is not limited to, the firm's profit $x \in \{0, R\}$), on which the entrepreneur's reward R_b can be conditioned. Thus, let $R_b(x, y)$ denote the state-contingent compensation specified by the financing contract. Suppose that the firm's profit x is a sufficient statistic for (x, y) when assessing the entrepreneur's effort, which we will here call $z \in \{L, H\}$ (see footnote 21 for the definition of a sufficient statistic). The density of the verifiable state (x, y) for a given effort z can be factorized: $f(x, y \mid z) = g(x, y)h(x, z)$. Thus for a choice of effort $z \in \{L, H\}$, the entrepreneur's expected reward is

$$\int_x \int_y R_b(x, y)g(x, y)h(x, z)\,dx\,dy = \int_x \hat{R}_b(x)h(x, z)\,dx,$$

where $\hat{R}_b(x) \equiv \int_y R_b(x, y)g(x, y)\,dy$.

So, a contract that rewards the entrepreneur solely as a function for profit $(\hat{R}_b(x))$ can do at least as well as a more general contract. And, in general, it can do better (in our context, it does strictly better in particular if $\int_y R_b(0, y)g(0, y) > 0$ and if a strictly positive borrower payoff in the case of success jeopardizes financing). Added risk is bad when the limited liability constraint is binding (and would be bad if the agent were risk averse even if she is not protected by limited liability).

24. Information accrues *ex post* through profit realization. Still the state is not learned *ex post* in the basic model.

25. Benchmarking could become relevant again in this example if we relaxed the limited liability constraint by introducing reputational concerns such as a stigma that affects future borrowing or other future relationships of the borrower or else costly nonmonetary penalties (jail or costly collateral pledging as in Chapter 4). Then, the observation that both entrepreneurs fail implies that the state of nature was unfavorable and so stigmas and/or nonmonetary penalties are not in order, unlike the situation in which only one entrepreneur fails (which implies that she misbehaved).

the entrepreneur fails, she already receives 0. On the other hand, it would be optimal to punish the entrepreneur harshly when she fails and the benchmark firm succeeds.[26]

3.2.7 Sensitivity of Investment to Cash Flow: A First Look

Recall from Section 2.5 the empirical finding that investment is sensitive to cash flow. An interesting issue is whether this "investment–cash flow sensitivity" increases with the extent to which the firm is financially constrained. Fazzari et al. (1988) use *a priori* measures of financial constraints and find that the sensitivity of investment to cash flow is particularly large for firms that have trouble raising external funds (for example, firms facing high agency costs). Kaplan and Zingales (1997) argue that there is no theoretical basis for this relationship and present empirical evidence that differs from that of Fazzari et al.

Although the model in this chapter is static while the empirical evidence relates to ongoing concerns (multistage financing is studied in Chapter 5), it can shed some light on the debate. We can imagine that cash on hand A includes the cash flow accruing from the firm's previous activity and see how investment reacts to a small change in the cash flow.[27]

There is a sense in which Fazzari et al. (1988) are right on the theoretical front: the firms whose investment is boosted by a small increase in cash flow are the marginal firms, i.e., those whose cash on hand A lies just below $\bar{A} = I - \rho_0$, where ρ_0 denotes the pledgeable income:

$$\rho_0 \equiv p_{\mathrm{H}}\left(R - \frac{B}{\Delta p}\right) = p_{\mathrm{H}}R - \frac{p_{\mathrm{H}}B}{\Delta p}.$$

Firms with more cash or a lower agency cost do not modify their investment behavior as their investment was already unconstrained.

Suppose, however, that firms are heterogeneous in the two dimensions: cash A and pledgeable income ρ_0 (we normalize the investment I to be the same for all). Assume for simplicity that these two variables are independently distributed (there is no reason for this to be the case: for example, firms with higher pledgeable income may have been able to invest more in the past and be richer today). Let $G(A)$ denote the (continuous) cumulative distribution of cash among firms in the economy, with density $g(A)$. Because only firms with cash on hand A satisfying $\rho_0 \geqslant I - A$ receive financing, aggregate investment among firms with pledgeable income ρ_0 is

$$\mathcal{I}(\rho_0) \equiv [1 - G(I - \rho_0)]I.$$

Now, consider a small, uniform increase in cash δA for all firms. Then, investment among firms characterized by ρ_0 increases by

$$\delta\mathcal{I}(\rho_0) = g(I - \rho_0)I\delta A.$$

And so

$$\frac{\partial}{\partial \rho_0}(\delta\mathcal{I}(\rho_0)) = -g'(I - \rho_0)I\delta A.$$

If the density is decreasing ($g' < 0$), the sensitivity of investment to cash flow is higher for firms with a *low* agency cost (a high ρ_0) as in Kaplan and Zingales; intuitively, the cutoff $\bar{A}$ for firms with a low agency cost is low, and so with a decreasing density there are a lot of marginal firms. With an increasing density ($g' > 0$), the sensitivity of investment to cash flow is higher for firms with a *high* agency cost (a low ρ_0), as in Fazzari et al. Thus, unless one has more precise information about the actual heterogeneity of firms, it is difficult to predict how the sensitivity of investment to cash flow varies with an *a priori* measure of financial constraints (a proxy for (minus) ρ_0).

26. This is one aspect in which a "limited liability model" differs from a "risk-aversion model." In the rest of Section 3.2, we might as well have assumed that the entrepreneur is very risk averse at her subsistence level, normalized at zero consumption, that is, her utility falls very quickly at that level. Suppose at the extreme that the entrepreneur gets $-\infty$ when receiving a negative income. Then, provided that $p_{\mathrm{H}} < 1$ (the entrepreneur may behave and be unlucky), it would not be optimal to set rewards below the subsistence level.

27. This thought experiment in a sense consists in looking at a single period of an ongoing firm that engages in short-term borrowing from investors. There are two reasons why this is only a first step toward an understanding of the sensitivity of investment to cash flow. First, if the firm anticipates that it may be credit-constrained tomorrow, the shadow value of 1 unit of profit at the end of the period exceeds 1, as it may help overcome financing problems in the future. More importantly, this shadow value may vary with current investment. Second, the description of the financial arrangements as a sequence of short-term borrowing contracts misses important long-term financing features (credit lines, debt-equity ratio, maturity structure of debt, etc.) that have an important impact on financial constraints (see Chapter 5).

3.3 Debt Overhang

Following Myers (1977), a number of contributions have studied situations in which a borrower is debt-ridden and unable to raise funds for an otherwise profitable project. The borrower is then said to suffer from debt overhang. The framework just developed suggests two possible interpretations of debt overhang. The first interpretation pursued below is a mere reinterpretation of the credit rationing analysis above: previous investors' collateral claim on the firm's assets reduces the net worth to below the threshold asset level for financing the new investment. Furthermore, the new project overall produces too little pledgeable income and so investment does not take place even if previous investors are willing to renegotiate their claim. The second and more interesting interpretation, and that stressed by the literature, emphasizes the need for renegotiating past liabilities in order to enable new investments.

3.3.1 Decrease in Net Worth

First, the borrower may have a positive-NPV project that would be financed in the absence of any previous debt obligation, but is denied financing due to such an obligation. Namely, suppose that (i) the entrepreneur has A in cash or collateral, but owes D from previous borrowing to a group of investors whom we will call the "initial investors," (ii) the initial investors have insisted on a covenant specifying that the borrower cannot raise more funds without their consent, and (iii) the borrower's assets A are pledged to the initial investors as collateral in case of default. If[28]

$$A > \bar{A} > A - D \geqslant 0,$$

the project would have been financed in the absence of previous borrowing but is not undertaken, since investors as a whole, that is, the initial investors and new investors (who can, of course, be the initial investors themselves), cannot recoup the cost of their investment $(I - A)$ plus the previous debt obligation (D) while they can receive D by seizing the collateral. More precisely, suppose the borrowers, the initial investors, and the new investors enter an agreement so as to finance the project. Because initial investors can secure themselves D by seizing the collateral, they must receive an expected payment at least equal to D under this agreement. Because the pledgeable income net of the investment cost is equal to

$$p_{\rm H}\left(R - \frac{B}{\Delta p}\right) - I,$$

new investors obtain at most

$$p_{\rm H}\left(R - \frac{B}{\Delta p}\right) - I - D + A = A - D - \bar{A} < 0,$$

which contradicts the fact that rational investors must at least break even.

3.3.2 Lack of Renegotiation[29]

Second, and more interestingly, suppose that

(i) the project is sufficiently profitable to attract funds even if the borrower has zero net worth,

$$\bar{A} < 0;$$

(ii) the borrower has previously been granted a long-term loan and is due to reimburse D "at the end," that is, when the outcome of the project (if financed) occurs;

(iii) this long-term debt obligation is contractually *senior* to any claim that the borrower might issue (a senior claim is a claim that must be paid before the borrower or any other claimholder receives any money);

(iv) the borrower has no cash ($A = 0$); and

(v) the debt overhang problem is sufficiently serious as not to be overcome by the expected profitability of the new project, or, put differently, the "slack" in pledgeable income, $-\bar{A}$, is smaller than what has to be paid back to previous investors, $p_{\rm H}D$, if the project is funded:

$$\bar{A} + p_{\rm H}D > 0.$$

28. Recall that

$$\bar{A} = p_{\rm H}\frac{B}{\Delta p} - (p_{\rm H}R - I)$$

is the minimum net worth to obtain financing.

29. The notion that renegotiation breakdowns generate debt overhang is central to Myers's (1977) original analysis, and also underlies that in Hart and Moore (1995) and Bhattacharya and Faure-Grimaud (2001). We will describe the debt overhang situation as one in which a new investment cannot be financed solely because renegotiation with previous debtholders proves infeasible. Debt overhang is generally described in the literature as a situation in which a firm may not be able to continue because it cannot renegotiate with its creditors. It is clear that the two situations are formally equivalent. The act of spending money to let a distressed firm continue is equivalent to an investment.

Because the borrower has no cash, initial investors receive nothing if the project is not financed. So, they are willing to participate in the financing of the project as long as they break even on this investment. For example, they can forgive existing debt, finance the investment I, and demand the entire cash-flow rights attached to external shares, that is, $R - B/\Delta p$ in the case of success. The initial investors then obtain

$$p_{\mathrm{H}}\left(R - \frac{B}{\Delta p}\right) - I = -\bar{A} > 0.$$

The borrower is willing to go along with this arrangement, which allows her to continue and obtain rent $p_{\mathrm{H}}B/\Delta p$ in expectation rather than 0 if the project is not financed.

Suppose next that the initial investors have no cash and thus cannot directly finance the investment I. The borrower then needs to turn to new investors. Are the latter willing to finance the project? Because the initial debt is senior, and because the borrower needs to keep a minimum stake in the firm in order to commit to behave, at most

$$R - \frac{B}{\Delta p} - D$$

can be pledged to new investors in the case of success (and 0 in the case of failure). New investors are willing to enter an agreement to finance the project if and only if

$$p_{\mathrm{H}}\left(R - \frac{B}{\Delta p} - D\right) \geqslant I$$

or

$$\bar{A} + p_{\mathrm{H}}D \leqslant 0,$$

which contradicts assumption (v).

To sum up, *the borrower cannot raise funds from new investors if she does not renegotiate some debt forgiveness from initial investors.* If renegotiation with initial investors is infeasible, gains from trade between the borrower and the community of investors may not be realized. Renegotiation breakdown creates debt overhang.

The possibility of debt overhang is often invoked in contexts in which "initial investors" stand for "corporate bondholders." It is often thought that because they are dispersed, and despite the existence of some coordinating mechanisms (nomination of a bond trustee, possibility for the firm to offer new securities in exchange for the bonds), bondholders have trouble renegotiating their claim when the borrower faces distress and requires some debt forgiveness.

In contrast, let us assume that initial investors are able to act collectively and renegotiate their initial claims. Because $\bar{A} < 0$, we know that there exists some renegotiated arrangement that is agreeable to all parties (borrower, initial investors, new investors), who would all get nothing if they failed to reach an agreement. Suppose, for example, that the initial investors accept a reduction in the face value of the debt from D to $d < D$, where

$$\bar{A} + p_{\mathrm{H}}d = 0.$$

Then new investors receive

$$\left(R - \frac{B}{\Delta p} - d\right)$$

in the case of success and are therefore willing to invest, since

$$p_{\mathrm{H}}\left(R - \frac{B}{\Delta p} - d\right) = I$$

is equivalent to their breakeven constraint (3.3):

$$p_{\mathrm{H}}\left(R - \frac{B}{\Delta p}\right) = I - \bar{A}.$$

Initial investors benefit from forgiving some of their claim as they now get

$$p_{\mathrm{H}}d = -\bar{A} > 0.$$

Lastly, the borrower can undertake the project and obtains rent $p_{\mathrm{H}}B/\Delta p > 0$.

Debt renegotiation thus allows the project to be undertaken and all parties to share the resulting gains from trade. How these gains from trade are actually shared depends, of course, on the relative bargaining power of the borrower and the initial investors (the new investors being assumed to be competitive and thus to just break even). The arrangement described above corresponds to the renegotiation that is most favorable to the initial investors. But, by varying continuously the relative bargaining power of the borrower and initial investors, one can generate any level of debt forgiveness from $D - d$ (the most favorable to initial investors) to D (the least favorable to them).

3.4 Borrowing Capacity: The Equity Multiplier

3.4.1 The Continuous-Investment Model

The continuous-investment model of this section is the polar opposite of the fixed-investment one. The fixed-investment model depicts a situation in which returns are sharply decreasing beyond some investment level. In contrast, we now assume that there are constant returns to scale in the investment technology. An investment $I \in [0, \infty)$ yields income RI, proportional to I, in the case of success, and 0 in the case of failure. The borrower's private benefit from misbehaving is also taken to be proportional to investment. As before, the borrower has a choice between behaving, in which case she derives no private benefit and the probability of success is p_H, and misbehaving, that is, enjoying private benefit BI, and reducing the probability of success to $p_L = p_H - \Delta p < p_H$. (One can also analyze the intermediate case of a continuous investment with general decreasing returns to scale (see Exercise 3.5).)

The borrower initially has cash A, and must therefore borrow $I - A$ to finance a project of size I. A loan agreement specifies that the lenders (who as before are assumed to make no profit) and the borrower receive 0 each in the case of failure, and R_l and R_b, respectively, in the case of success, where $R_l + R_b = RI$.

As in Section 3.2, we assume that investment has positive NPV (net present value), here per unit of investment, if the borrower behaves,

$$p_H R > 1, \tag{3.7}$$

but negative NPV otherwise,

$$1 > p_L R + B, \tag{3.8}$$

so that unless one can control the agency problem the investment cannot be funded. We also make an assumption that guarantees that the equilibrium investment is finite:

$$p_H R < 1 + \frac{p_H B}{\Delta p}. \tag{3.9}$$

Like inequality (3.5) in Section 3.2, inequality (3.9) has a simple interpretation: the expected net revenue per unit of investment, $p_H R - 1$, is lower than the per-unit agency cost, $p_H B/\Delta p$.

Finally, we keep assuming that the capital market is competitive. The analysis is very similar when the borrower faces a lender with market power, except that the resulting investment scale is smaller (see Exercise 3.13).

3.4.2 The Lenders' Credit Analysis

Following the steps of Section 3.2, the incentive compatibility and the breakeven conditions are

$$(\Delta p) R_b \geqslant BI \tag{IC$_b$}$$

and

$$p_H(RI - R_b) \geqslant I - A. \tag{IR$_l$}$$

In equilibrium, competitive lenders make no profit on the contract that is most advantageous for the borrower; the borrower's net utility is therefore equal to the social surplus brought about by the investment:

$$U_b = (p_H R - 1)I. \tag{3.10}$$

From (3.10) it is optimal for the borrower to invest as much as possible. The upper bound on investment and in turn her borrowing capacity ("outside financing capacity" or "debt capacity") are determined by constraints (IC$_b$) and (IR$_l$). Substituting (IC$_b$) into (IR$_l$), we obtain

$$I \leqslant kA, \tag{3.11}$$

where

$$k = \frac{1}{1 - p_H(R - B/\Delta p)} > 1. \tag{3.12}$$

The denominator of k is positive from (3.9). Furthermore, conditions (3.7) and (3.8) imply that $(\Delta p)R > B$, and therefore that the denominator of k is smaller than 1. This is important: the fact that $k > 1$ shows that the borrower can lever her wealth, k being the multiplier.

The multiplier is smaller, the higher the private benefit (B) and the lower the likelihood ratio ($\Delta p/p_H$, fixing p_H and thus the profitability of the investment), which are our two measures of the agency cost.

Conditions (3.7) and (3.10) furthermore imply that it is optimal for the borrower to invest k times her cash A, that is, to borrow $d = (k - 1)$ times her level of cash, where

$$d = \frac{p_H(R - B/\Delta p)}{1 - p_H(R - B/\Delta p)}. \tag{3.13}$$

The maximum loan, dA, is called "*borrowing capacity*."[30]

Another important concept (which will be used, for example, in computing the value of retained earnings in a dynamic context) is the *shadow value v of equity (here cash)*. The entrepreneur derives gross utility $v > 1$ from one more unit of equity. Letting $U_b^g \equiv A + U_b$ denote the borrower's gross utility, and using (3.10) and (3.11), we have

$$U_b^g \equiv vA, \tag{3.14}$$

where the shadow value of equity is

$$v = \frac{p_H B/\Delta p}{1 - p_H(R - B/\Delta p)} > 1. \tag{3.15}$$

As one would expect (in the relevant range defined by (3.7)–(3.9)), the borrowing capacity increases with per-unit income R and decreases with the extent of the moral-hazard problem (measured by the borrower's private benefit or the inverse of the likelihood ratio). The shadow value of equity increases with per-unit income R and also with the extent of the moral-hazard problem.[31]

Finally, let us introduce some notation that will be used repeatedly throughout the book. Let

$$\rho_1 \equiv p_H R$$

denote the expected payoff per unit of investment and

$$\rho_0 \equiv p_H\left(R - \frac{B}{\Delta p}\right)$$

denote the expected pledgeable income per unit of investment. Assumptions (3.7) and (3.9) can be rewritten as

$$\rho_1 > 1 > \rho_0.$$

The equity multiplier is then

$$k = \frac{1}{1 - \rho_0}, \tag{3.11$'$}$$

the debt capacity per unit of net worth

$$d = \frac{\rho_0}{1 - \rho_0}, \tag{3.12$'$}$$

and the borrower's gross utility

$$U_b^g = vA = \frac{\rho_1 - \rho_0}{1 - \rho_0} A. \tag{3.14$'$}$$

The borrower's net utility can then be written as

$$U_b^n = U_b = U_b^g - A = \frac{\rho_1 - 1}{1 - \rho_0} A = (\rho_1 - 1)I,$$

as one could have expected.

Remark (factors that keep the investment bounded). Condition (3.9) (the condition that the pledgeable income per unit of investment is smaller than 1) was needed in order to keep the investment finite in this constant return to scale environment. Such a condition is no longer needed if the price of output and therefore the revenue in the case of success is not fixed but rather depends on, say, industry investment. An increase in per-firm investment then lowers the market price, reducing both value and pledgeable income (see Exercise 3.17 for more detail).

Remark (sensitivity of investment to cash flow). Let us briefly return to the sensitivity of investment to cash flow. In the variable-investment model,

$$\frac{\partial}{\partial \rho_0}\left(\frac{\partial I}{\partial A}\right) = \frac{1}{(1 - \rho_0)^2} > 0,$$

and so firms with a low agency cost, which are therefore less financially constrained, exhibit a higher sensitivity. Intuitively, such firms have a high multiplier and their investment is therefore more sensitive to available cash.

3.4.3 Collateral Values: Outside Debt and the Maximal Incentives Principle

We now return to the indeterminacy of the financial structure (debt or equity) discussed earlier. It turns out that this indeterminacy was an artefact of the absence of profit in the case of failure.[32]

Thus, assume that, for investment size I, the profit is $R^S I$ in the case of success and $R^F I$ in the case of failure, where R^F is now positive. $R^F I$ can be thought of as the salvage value of assets and

$$RI \equiv (R^S - R^F)I$$

30. Note also that the "gearing ratio" $g = d/k = p_H R - p_H B/\Delta p$ is less than 1, and that the debt-over-inside-equity ratio is equal to d.

31. The shadow value is here constant with wealth A. With a decreasing-returns-to-scale technology, v depends on wealth and $v'(A) < 0$: the marginal wealth enables less and less profitable marginal investments as wealth increases (see Exercise 3.5).

32. The clearest illustration of this point is for the variable-investment model, which is why we treat this here. The same point can be made in a slightly different form (as some indeterminacy may remain) in the fixed-investment version (see Exercise 3.18).

as the increase in profit brought about by success. One would expect R^{F} to be larger when secondary asset markets are liquid.[33]

The model is otherwise the same as in the rest of Section 3.4: the private benefit (BI in the case of misbehavior, 0 otherwise) is also proportional to investment.

The generalization of the condition that the NPV per unit of investment is positive while the pledgeable income per unit of investment is negative ($p_{\mathrm{H}}R > 1 > p_{\mathrm{H}}(R - B/\Delta p)$) is

$$p_{\mathrm{H}}R + R^{\mathrm{F}} > 1 > p_{\mathrm{H}}\left(R - \frac{B}{\Delta p}\right) + R^{\mathrm{F}}.$$

A contract specifies an investment level I and a sharing rule, or equivalently a reward for the entrepreneur for each performance level: $\{R_{\mathrm{b}}^{\mathrm{S}}, R_{\mathrm{b}}^{\mathrm{F}}\}$, with $R_{\mathrm{b}}^{\mathrm{S}}, R_{\mathrm{b}}^{\mathrm{F}} \geqslant 0$ due to limited liability.

The optimal contract maximizes the entrepreneur's expected compensation,

$$U_{\mathrm{b}} = \max_{\{R_{\mathrm{b}}^{\mathrm{S}}, R_{\mathrm{b}}^{\mathrm{F}}, I\}} \{p_{\mathrm{H}}R_{\mathrm{b}}^{\mathrm{S}} + (1 - p_{\mathrm{H}})R_{\mathrm{b}}^{\mathrm{F}} - A\},$$

subject to two constraints (that will turn out to be binding at the optimum): the entrepreneur's incentive constraint,

$$(\Delta p)(R_{\mathrm{b}}^{\mathrm{S}} - R_{\mathrm{b}}^{\mathrm{F}}) \geqslant BI,$$

and the investors' breakeven constraint,

$$p_{\mathrm{H}}(R^{\mathrm{S}}I - R_{\mathrm{b}}^{\mathrm{S}}) + (1 - p_{\mathrm{H}})(R^{\mathrm{F}}I - R_{\mathrm{b}}^{\mathrm{F}}) \geqslant I - A.$$

To show that the investors' breakeven constraint is binding, note that, if it were not, then the entrepreneur could increase $R_{\mathrm{b}}^{\mathrm{S}}$ and $R_{\mathrm{b}}^{\mathrm{F}}$ by an equal and small amount without affecting the incentive compatibility constraint. This uniform increase in compensation would raise the entrepreneur's payoff. As is now familiar, we conclude that the investors receive no surplus, and so (by substituting the breakeven constraint into the objective function) the entrepreneur's utility is equal to the NPV:

$$U_{\mathrm{b}} = (p_{\mathrm{H}}R + R^{\mathrm{F}} - 1)I.$$

Because the NPV per unit of investment is positive, the entrepreneur therefore chooses the highest possible investment.

Next, note that the incentive constraint is binding (otherwise, the optimal investment would be infinite, which would violate the two constraints combined).

Lastly, suppose that $R_{\mathrm{b}}^{\mathrm{F}} > 0$ at the optimum. And consider a small increase $\delta R_{\mathrm{b}}^{\mathrm{S}} > 0$ in managerial compensation in the case of success together with a small decrease $\delta R_{\mathrm{b}}^{\mathrm{F}} < 0$ in the case of failure that keeps the investors' profitability constant:

$$p_{\mathrm{H}}\delta R_{\mathrm{b}}^{\mathrm{S}} + (1 - p_{\mathrm{H}})\delta R_{\mathrm{b}}^{\mathrm{F}} = 0.$$

This small change (which is feasible only if $R_{\mathrm{b}}^{\mathrm{F}} > 0$) also keeps the objective function constant. But the incentive constraint is now slack, a contradiction. We thus conclude that at the optimum

$$R_{\mathrm{b}}^{\mathrm{F}} = 0.$$

Hence, an all-equity firm cannot be optimal: in the absence of debt, the entrepreneur would receive $R^{\mathrm{F}}I$ times her share of stocks in the firm, and therefore would be rewarded even in the case of failure. By contrast, investors' holding debt $D \geqslant R^{\mathrm{F}}I$ is an optimal financial structure. Using the fact that the two constraints are binding, the borrowing capacity is given by

$$R^{\mathrm{F}}I + p_{\mathrm{H}}\left(R - \frac{B}{\Delta p}\right)I = I - A$$

or

$$I = \frac{A}{1 - [p_{\mathrm{H}}(R - B/\Delta p) + R^{\mathrm{F}}]}. \tag{3.16}$$

Predictions. The variable-investment model of this section is, of course, much too simplistic to provide even a stylized account of capital structure and investment. It, however, delivers three interesting preliminary insights.

• *Firms with lower agency costs borrow more.* As in Section 3.2.2, the firm's outside financing capacity is higher, the lower the agency cost as measured either by the private benefit B or by (the inverse of) the likelihood ratio $\Delta p/p_{\mathrm{H}}$ (keeping p_{H} and therefore profitability constant).

• *The investors' holding safe debt plus some equity maximizes the entrepreneur's stake in the project and thereby her incentives.* (We will investigate the generality of this insight in Section 3.5.)

Decomposing the investors' claim into safe debt (which repays $R^{\mathrm{F}}I$) and risky equity (which repays in

33. Several chapters in this book (primarily Chapter 14) will investigate the determinants of asset prices in secondary markets.

expectation $p_H[R - B/\Delta p]I$), the leverage ratios,

$$\frac{\text{debt}}{\text{total equity}} = \frac{R^F I}{p_H R I} = \frac{R^F}{p_H R}$$

and

$$\frac{\text{debt}}{\text{outside equity}} = \frac{R^F I}{p_H(R - B/\Delta p)I} = \frac{R^F}{p_H(R - B/\Delta p)},$$

are both constant in this simple-minded model.

• *Credit rationing is more binding for firms with less tangible assets or assets that have a lower value in liquidation* (there is indeed substantial evidence in this direction: see Chapter 2). To see this, let us decrease the value of tangible assets while keeping the NPV per unit of investment constant: that is, keeping other parameters constant, let us consider a decrease from R^F to $\hat{R}^F$ ($\hat{R}^F < R^F$) of the per-unit salvage value and an increase from p_H to $p_H + \tau$ ($\tau > 0$) of the probability of success such that

$$\hat{R}^F + (p_H + \tau)R = R^F + p_H R.$$

In order to keep the agency problem invariant (so as not to interfere with the first prediction), let us assume that the probability of success in the case of misbehavior becomes $p_L + \tau$. The borrower's incentive compatibility constraint is then unchanged as

$$[(p_H + \tau) - (p_L + \tau)](R_b^S - R_b^F) = (\Delta p)(R_b^S - R_b^F).$$

The analysis is unchanged and the new investment becomes

$$\hat{I} = \frac{A}{1 - [(p_H + \tau)(R - B/\Delta p) + \hat{R}^F]} < I.$$

Thus, ceteris paribus, tangible assets facilitate financing.[34]

3.4.4 Going Forward

This chapter offered a first glance at the basic conflict between value and pledgeable income. When pressed to produce returns to attract investors, borrowers first offer them a large debt repayment or a higher share of profits (Section 3.2). This policy is, however, limited by entrepreneurial moral hazard and must be supplemented by costly "concessions." Technically, with competitive investors, the total value (NPV) goes to the entrepreneur, who aims at maximizing this value subject to the constraint that the pledgeable income be sufficient to enable the investors to recoup their investments. The resulting policy (charter, covenants, governance structure, etc.) therefore sacrifices value to generate enough pledgeable income if the breakeven constraint condition is binding.

The variable-investment model of Section 3.4 pointed at such an elementary concession: a limited investment size. Indeed, with constant returns to scale, it would be optimal for the firm to grow without bounds, but pleasing investors requires a limited size (all the more so, as we have seen, as the agency problem is important and as assets are intangible). The rest of the book will provide further illustrations of the idea that entrepreneurs must sometimes "bend over backwards" in order to attract investors: costly collateral pledging, restricted exit options, short maturity structures, enlisting of active and speculative monitors, allocations of control rights to equityholders and debtholders, limits on takeover defenses, and so forth.

34. Rather than increase the probability of success, we could have increased the payoff R in the case of success. Then investment would have been invariant (see equation (3.16)). As increases in the value of the risky component are in general associated with both types of changes, the conclusion that tangible assets facilitate financing is robust.

Supplementary Sections

3.5 Related Models of Credit Rationing: Inside Equity and Outside Debt

This supplementary section reviews three classic, alternative models of credit rationing. These models are a bit more complex than the basic credit rationing model developed in this chapter and this supplementary section is accordingly more technical than the text. They are not relegated to the supplementary section because they are deemed "less important." Rather, the reader should recall from the introduction that we want to conduct controlled experiments throughout the book. Using the same simple and tractable model throughout allows us to concentrate on the key insights of the theory without getting bogged down by extraneous modeling changes. This is the motivation for setting these models aside. It should furthermore be borne in mind that these

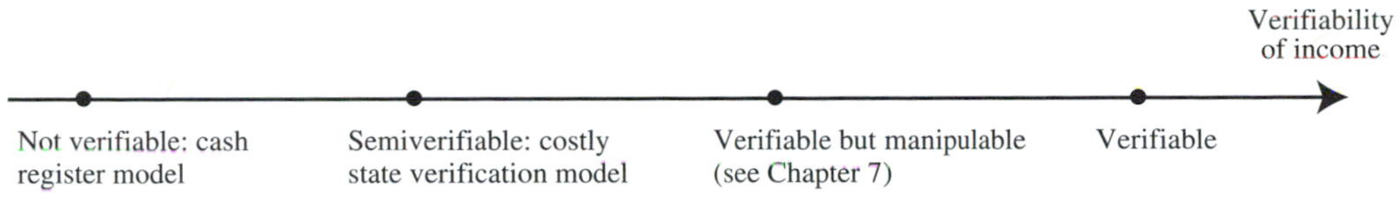

Figure 3.3

models yield pretty much the same insights as our basic model. While this supplementary section can be skipped without adverse consequences for the comprehension of the rest of the book, students intending to specialize in corporate finance should thoroughly learn these alternative models.

Two assumptions are shared by the three models reviewed in the supplementary section and by the moral-hazard model developed in the text.

(a) The entrepreneur can divert some of the income.[35] Hence, only part of the project's income can be pledged to investors, and so positive-NPV projects may not be financed.

(b) Investors are passive. Their claim is thus defined as a "leftover" once the entrepreneur's optimal incentive scheme is derived.

The point of departure between the models is the form of diversion that is presumed. The scope for diversion is determined by what is presumed with regard to the verifiability of income. This chapter has adopted a polar assumption, namely, that of a fully verifiable income. Figure 3.3 presents some alternative assumptions.

In the other polar case, the entrepreneur can divert money as she wants. One may then wonder why the entrepreneur would ever repay her loans and therefore why lenders would bring in money in the first place. For example, in the two-outcome model, the entrepreneur can appropriate R in the case of success and pretend that the project has failed, thus repaying nothing to the lenders. Anticipating this "strategic default," the lenders would not want to invest. Repayment must then be motivated by some other consideration. The lenders' foreclosing on the entrepreneur's assets (held as hostages) is an important but obvious example. A perhaps more interesting motivation for repayment in the context of unverifiable income, and a motivation that has been emphasized in the literature, is the threat that the entrepreneur's future projects not be financed.

In between these two polar cases lies the influential costly state verification (CSV) model, in which the borrower cannot steal money from the firm (unlike in the nonverifiable income model), but only a costly audit reveals the firm's income to the lenders. To economize on audits, the lenders and the borrower can agree to let the borrower report on the realized income. However, the lenders cannot just trust the borrower to report truthfully and must at least occasionally engage in the costly auditing process in order to verify that the borrower does not underreport income.

Lastly, one can maintain the assumption that the firm's income is verifiable (there is a reliable accounting structure), so that the firm's accounts truthfully reflect its cash position. However, the *significance* of this cash position is unclear if the entrepreneur can manipulate income, for example, by shifting income across accounting periods.

Little attention has been devoted to assessing the empirical relevance of the various assumptions on the verifiability of firm income. This is all the more unfortunate since, as we have seen, a wide range of hypotheses have been entertained. The nonverifiability of income is perhaps most plausible for a small enterprise. For example, a farmer or a shopkeeper who can arrange sales that are not recorded by invoices can divert money. They then literally steal money from the firm. Most firms, however, have proper accounts and it may then be difficult for insiders to steal from the cash register. On the other hand, lenders may not know exactly how much there is in the firm. While the firm's cash and investments in marketable assets are readily verifiable, the value

35. The moral-hazard model can be viewed as one in which the entrepreneur can divert money. Namely, the diversion activity involves a deadweight loss equal to $(\Delta p)R_{\rm l} - [B - (\Delta p)R_{\rm b}] = (\Delta p)R - B$, that is, the difference between the money lost by investors and the (monetary equivalent of the) net gain for the borrower when she misbehaves.

of the firm's other (tangible or intangible) assets in general is revealed to outsiders only after a costly audit. It has been argued in the literature that this audit ought to be interpreted as a bankruptcy process. Lastly, another useful paradigm is that of verifiable but manipulable income, reviewed in Chapter 7; while it seems very relevant for many firms, it has unfortunately been studied much less than the other three paradigms and little yet is known about its properties.

As we shall see, a key result that is common to all three models reviewed in the supplementary section is that they all structure the entrepreneur's incentive problem so that her claim optimally takes the form of an equity claim and the lenders' that of a fixed payment. In other words, these models predict a combination of *inside equity and outside (risky) debt.*

From principal–agent theory, we know that the agent's optimal incentive scheme in general does not take the form of "inside equity." Therefore, a fair amount of structure must be imposed on the agency relationship in order to generate a standard debt contract for the lenders. Consequently, the theories described below are often criticized for their lack of robustness; it is also pointed out that they do not account for the diversity of capital structures that characterize modern corporations, and that even small firms sometimes admit outside equity (for example, venture capital). Such criticisms are well-taken, but, left unqualified, they miss the point of these modeling exercises; for, the purpose of such exercises is not to show that the standard debt contract should be the unique outside claim in a wide range of circumstances, but rather to identify forces that make standard debt an appealing instrument, leaving the relaxation of the assumptions and the derivation of more realistic corporate financing modes to further modeling effort.

3.6 Verifiable Income

For continuity of exposition, we start with the least departure from the model in the text. The first approach to standard debt contracts employs the verifiable income paradigm and draws on the logic of *maximal insider incentives*. Namely, a standard debt contract for outsiders makes the borrower residual claimant for the marginal income above the debt repayment level and, *under some conditions*, provides the entrepreneur with maximal incentives to exert effort.

Two remarks are in order here. First, residual claimancy exposes the borrower with substantial risk, and so borrower risk neutrality must be assumed in order not to introduce a tradeoff between incentives and insurance.[36] Second, a standard result in incentive theory is that full incentives are provided when the agent receives at the margin one dollar whenever profit increases by one dollar, that is, when the agent pays a fixed amount to the principal and is "residual claimant" for the remaining profit. This is not quite so under a debt contract; under a standard debt contract, the borrower is residual claimant for income only when income exceeds the repayment level; she receives nothing at the margin as long as income lies below the repayment level. This is why we added the qualifier "under some conditions."

Innes (1990) analyzes the verifiable income model for a continuum of effort levels, and, more interestingly, for a continuum of outcomes. The firm's income R is now a random variable distributed over an interval $[0, \bar{R}]$ according to the distribution $p(R \mid e)$, where $e \geqslant 0$ is the entrepreneur's effort level. The borrower's disutility of effort function $g(e)$ satisfies the standard assumptions:

$$g' > 0, \quad g'' > 0,$$
$$g(0) = 0, \quad g'(0) = 0, \quad g'(\infty) = \infty.$$

In particular, this cost function is convex and the assumptions on its derivative guarantee that the borrower's optimal effort is strictly positive and finite.

We assume that a higher effort raises income in the sense of the monotone (log) likelihood ratio property (MLRP):

$$\frac{\partial}{\partial R}\left[\frac{\partial p(R \mid e)/\partial e}{p(R \mid e)}\right] > 0.$$

36. As is well-known, lenders in general should bear some of the risk faced by a risk-averse agent. See, for example, Mirrlees (1975), Holmström (1979), and Shavell (1979) for general considerations on the principal–agent model, and Lacker (1991) for an application to financing.

This condition says that a higher income "signals" a higher effort (see, for example, Holmström (1979) and Milgrom (1981) for more details on MLRP).

We maintain the assumptions of verifiable income, limited liability for the borrower and risk neutrality on both sides, and that the lenders demand a rate of return equal to 0. Let $w(R)$ denote the borrower's reward when the realized income is R. Let us make the following assumption.

Assumption (monotonic reimbursement):

$$R - w(R) \quad \textit{is nondecreasing for all } R. \tag{M}$$

Innes motivates this assumption by the possibility that the borrower secretly adds cash into the firm's accounts. Suppose that $R_1 < R_2$, but $R_1 - w(R_1) > R_2 - w(R_2)$. Then when the realized income is R_1, the borrower could borrow $(R_2 - R_1)$ from a third party and increase her reward by $w(R_2) - w(R_1) > R_2 - R_1$; and so the borrower could repay the third party and make a surplus from the transaction. The reimbursement would then be the same, namely, $R_2 - w(R_2)$, for both realizations of income and would thus be nondecreasing.

Let us now consider the problem of maximizing the borrower's utility (i.e., the NPV under a competitive capital market) subject to the incentive compatibility constraint (as depicted by the borrower's first-order condition with respect to her effort choice), the lenders' breakeven condition and the monotonicity constraint.

Program I:

$$\max_{\{w(\cdot),e\}} \left\{ \int_0^{\bar{R}} w(R) p(R \mid e)\, \mathrm{d}R - g(e) \right\}$$

s.t.

$$\int_0^{\bar{R}} w(R) \frac{\partial p(R \mid e)}{\partial e}\, \mathrm{d}R = g'(e), \tag{IC$_\mathrm{b}$}$$

$$\int_0^{\bar{R}} [R - w(R)] p(R \mid e)\, \mathrm{d}R = I - A, \tag{IR$_\mathrm{l}$}$$

$$R - w(R) \quad \text{is nondecreasing for all } R. \tag{M}$$

As is usual in principal–agent models, most of the interesting insights are derived from the maximization with respect to the managerial compensation schedule $w(\cdot)$. Letting μ and λ denote the (nonnegative) multipliers of the constraints (IC$_\mathrm{b}$) and (IR$_\mathrm{l}$), and *ignoring in a first step the monotonicity constraint*, the Lagrangian of Program I is

$$\mathcal{L} = \int_0^{\bar{R}} w(R) \left[1 + \mu \frac{\partial p(R \mid e)/\partial e}{p(R \mid e)} - \lambda \right] p(R \mid e)\, \mathrm{d}R - g(e) - \mu g'(e) + \lambda \left[\int_0^{\bar{R}} R p(R \mid e)\, \mathrm{d}R - I + A \right].$$

It is therefore linear in $w(R)$ for all R (this is, of course, due to risk neutrality).

Let us begin with a thought experiment and impose the extra constraint that lenders have limited liability, $w(R) \leqslant R$ for all R. This assumption, which we will later dispense with, is less natural than borrower's limited liability since investors could at the contracting date put assets (e.g., Treasury bonds) into escrow and therefore credibly commit to pay rewards exceeding the firm's income. Under this lenders-limited-liability assumption, the solution would be

$$w(R) = \begin{cases} R & \text{if } 1 + \mu \dfrac{\partial p(R \mid e)/\partial e}{p(R \mid e)} > \lambda, \\[2ex] 0 & \text{if } 1 + \mu \dfrac{\partial p(R \mid e)/\partial e}{p(R \mid e)} < \lambda. \end{cases}$$

Assume that the shadow price μ of the incentive constraint is strictly positive.[37] Then, MLRP implies that there exists a threshold level of income R^* such that

$$w(R) = \begin{cases} R & \text{if } R > R^*, \\ 0 & \text{if } R < R^*. \end{cases}$$

The borrower's reward and the reimbursement are depicted in Figure 3.4.[38]

The solution thus generalizes the maximal insider incentive principle: the borrower receives nothing for $R < R^*$ and the firm's entire income for $R > R^*$.[39] Note, though, that the reimbursement pattern is unfamiliar in that the lenders' claim is valueless in good states of nature.

After this thought experiment, let us come back to Program I. We leave it to the reader to check

37. If the incentive constraint is not binding, the optimal effort in Program I is then the first-best effort, given by

$$g'(e) = \int_0^{\bar{R}} R \frac{\partial p(R \mid e)}{\partial e}\, \mathrm{d}R.$$

38. If rewards in excess of income were allowed, the solution would be degenerate with $w(R) = 0$ for $R < \bar{R}$ and a spike at $\bar{R}$ (or with a discrete number of outcomes, a reward only when the income is the highest possible one).

39. Such contracts are called "live or die" contracts in the literature.

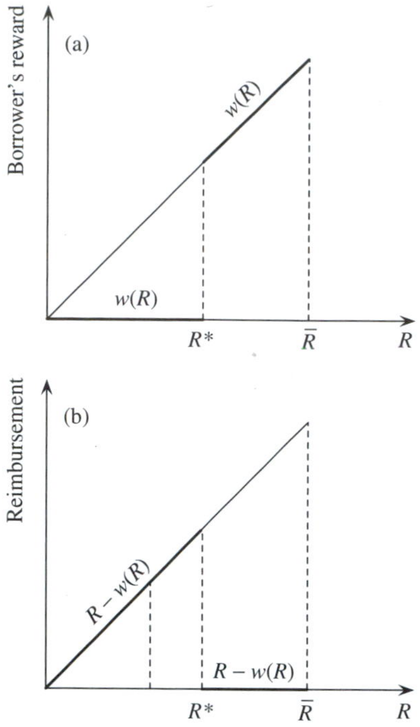

Figure 3.4

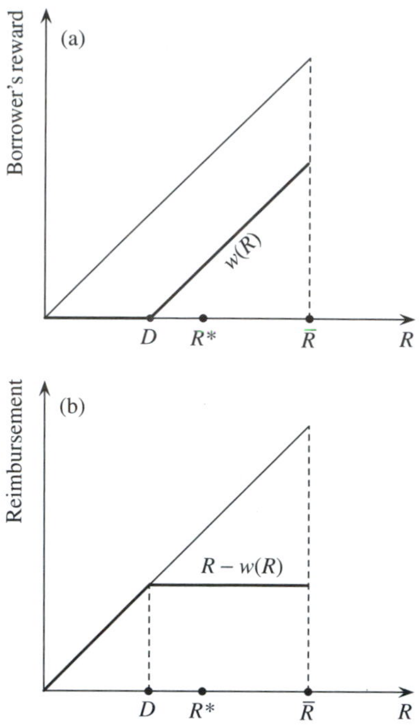

Figure 3.5

that adding the monotonic reimbursement constraint to Program I[40] yields the solution depicted in Figure 3.5.

Intuitively, the optimal reimbursement scheme subject to the monotonicity constraint (depicted in Figure 3.5(b)) approximates as closely as possible the optimal reimbursement scheme (depicted in Figure 3.4(b)) in the absence of this constraint. Note also that under the monotonicity constraint the assumption of limited liability on the lenders' side no longer bites: the borrower receives nothing for low incomes, and since the reward cannot grow faster than the firm's income from the monotonicity constraint, the reward can never exceed the firm's income. The assumption of limited liability on the lenders' side thus need not be made if monotonicity of reimbursement is imposed.

The Innes derivation of a standard debt contract relies on strong assumptions (risk neutrality, monotonic reimbursement), but it illustrates nicely the fact that debt contracts have good incentives properties, provided that the borrower's discretion consists in raising or decreasing income. Leaving aside borrower risk aversion, to which we turn next, there are, however, several caveats. First, a debt contract is less appropriate when the borrower's discretion also involves a choice of riskiness, a case which we will discuss in Chapter 7. Second, a debt contract may not be optimal if the borrower learns information after the contract is signed and before the borrower chooses her effort: a debt contract offers poor incentives to work in bad states of nature, as shown by Chiesa (1992). (Chiesa's point also applies to the other models reviewed in this supplementary section.)

Risk aversion. We have assumed that the entrepreneur and the lenders are both risk neutral. Does the debt optimality result carry over to, say, entrepreneurial risk aversion?[41] When the entrepreneur is risk averse, the optimal contract must, besides satisfying the lenders' breakeven constraint, aim at two targets: effort inducement and insurance.

40. Monotonicity implies that the function $R \to R - w(R)$ is differentiable almost everywhere, and so $(\mathrm{d}/\mathrm{d}R)[R - w(R)] \geqslant 0$ almost everywhere. It also implies that the reimbursement schedule has no downward jump (unlike that depicted in Figure 3.4(b)).

41. Some of the results reviewed next carry over to investor risk aversion as well. See the papers cited below.

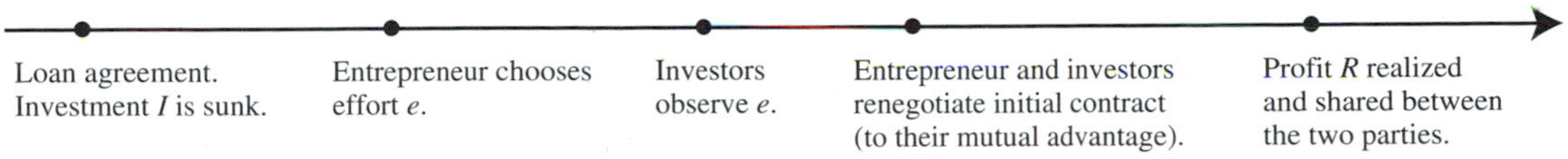

Figure 3.6

As is well-known (see, for example, Holmström 1979), these two goals are, in general, in conflict. Insuring the entrepreneur against variations in profit makes her unaccountable, and results in a low level of effort.

The literature, though, has identified a case in which there is no conflict between the two targets. Namely, this literature assumes that the investors observe the entrepreneur's effort before the profit is realized and that renegotiation then takes place.[42]

The investors' observing the entrepreneur's effort turns out to substantially improve what incentive schemes can achieve.[43]

Hermalin and Katz (1991). Let us begin with the work of Hermalin and Katz. Assume, for simplicity, that investors are risk neutral, while the entrepreneur is risk averse, with a separable utility function:

$$U_{\mathrm{b}} = \int_0^{\bar{R}} u(w(R))p(R \mid e)\,\mathrm{d}R - g(e),$$

where u is increasing and concave.

Unlike Innes, Hermalin and Katz do not need to assume that the likelihood ratio is monotone or that the investors' payoff is monotonic in profit. But they make the following two assumptions.

Assumption (entrepreneur's unlimited liability):

$$w(R) \gtrless 0 \quad \textit{for all } R.$$

Assumption (entrepreneur-offer renegotiation). *At the renegotiation stage (see Figure 3.6), the entrepreneur makes a take-it-or-leave-it contract offer* $(\tilde{w}(\cdot))$. *If the investors (who at that point have observed effort) accept, the new contract is in force. Otherwise, the initial contract* $(w(\cdot))$ *still prevails.*[44]

It is simple to see that the first-best outcome can then be implemented through a *debt contract.*[45]

The first-best outcome refers to the hypothetical situation in which effort would be observed, and so there is no incentive compatibility constraint.

Program II:

$$\max_{\{w(\cdot),e\}} \left\{ \int_0^{\bar{R}} u(w(R))p(R \mid e)\,\mathrm{d}R - g(e) \right\}$$

s.t.

$$\int_0^{\bar{R}} [R - w(R)]p(R \mid e)\,\mathrm{d}R = I - A. \qquad (\mathrm{IR_l})$$

The solution to this program yields full insurance (all the risk is borne by risk-neutral investors, none by the risk-averse entrepreneur),

$$w(R) = w^* = E(R \mid e^*) + A - I \quad \text{for all } R,$$

42. "Renegotiation" means that both parties agree to alter the initial contract to their mutual advantage; the initial contract is perfectly enforceable if any party wants it to be enforced.

43. Two points here for the more technically inclined reader.

First, the original as well as general result in this line of research is due to Maskin (1977). He shows that, under very weak assumptions, the prospect of sharing information about the noncontractible dimensions (here effort) enables parties to achieve what they could have achieved if this shared information were also received by an impartial judge. In a nutshell, courts do not need to observe what the parties observe. It suffices that the parties be given proper incentives to reveal what they know, in a sort of "*adversarial hearing.*" The contribution of the papers to be discussed shortly is, among other things, to link Maskin's so-called "Nash implementation" literature with the principal–agent model with renegotiation, and to derive some concrete implications relative to debt contracts.

Second, it is crucial that the parties observe effort and renegotiate *before* the profit is realized. In particular, if the entrepreneur's utility function is separable in effort and reward (as we will assume here), then effort no longer affects the entrepreneur's von Neumann–Morgenstern utility function once profit is realized, and so the level of effort can no longer be elicited through a Maskin adversarial hearing scheme.

For further discussion of these and related issues, see, for example, Hart and Moore (1999), Maskin and Tirole (1999), and Tirole (1999).

44. See Edlin and Hermalin (2000, 2001) for extensions of the Hermalin and Katz analysis to situations with shared bargaining power.

45. Again, for the more technically inclined reader, note that we did not allow for a more general message space. We look at a particular form of initial contract (a wage schedule) that does not involve general messages from both parties, as more general contracts would call for. Here the *ex post* messages are created by the renegotiation process: the offer of a new wage schedule by the entrepreneur, and the acceptance or refusal decision of the investors. This is, of course, inconsequential: because the optimal allocation is attained, more general contracts could not do better.

where $E(R \mid e) = \int_0^{\bar{R}} Rp(R \mid e)\,dR$ is the expected profit, and a first-best effort level e^* given by

$$e \text{ maximizes } \{u(w^*) - g(e)\}$$
$$\text{s.t. } E(R \mid e) - w^* = I - A,$$

or, equivalently,

$$e^* \text{ maximizes } \{u(E(R \mid e) + A - I) - g(e)\}.$$

Now consider the case in which effort is not verifiable by a court, but is observed by the investors before the profit accrues. At the renegotiation stage, for an arbitrary effort e chosen by the entrepreneur, the entrepreneur will offer a contract $\tilde{w}(\cdot) = \{w(R)\}_{R\in[0,\bar{R}]}$ so as to solve the following program.

Program III:

$$\max_{\{\tilde{w}(\cdot)\}} \left\{ \int_0^{\bar{R}} u(\tilde{w}(R))p(R \mid e)\,dR - g(e) \right\}$$

s.t.

$$\int_0^{\bar{R}} [R - \tilde{w}(R)]p(R \mid e)\,dR \geqslant \hat{V}(e),$$

where

$$\hat{V}(e) \equiv E(R \mid e) - \int_0^{\bar{R}} w(R)p(R \mid e)\,dR$$

is the investors' expected income under the initial contract.

Note that Program III coincides with Program II provided that

$$\hat{V}(e) = I - A.$$

It therefore suffices to find an initial contract such that, regardless of the effort choice, the investors' expected income is equal to $I - A$. This is achieved by a riskless debt contract in which the entrepreneur must reimburse

$$D \equiv I - A.$$

(The risk-free character of this form of debt is due to the entrepreneur's unlimited liability. With limited liability, a debt contract is risky for the lender: it pays only R whenever $R < D$. And so a low effort reduces the investors' status quo utility $\hat{V}(e)$ in the renegotiation process.)

We thus derive Hermalin and Katz's result: the incentive and insurance problems separate. A debt contract makes the entrepreneur residual claimant (i.e., eliminates any externality of effort choice on the investors' welfare), and therefore provides her with optimal incentives. The debt contract is, however, very risky for the borrower; but renegotiation shifts the entire risk to the risk-neutral investors.[46]

Remark (varying the bargaining power in renegotiation). That a debt contract cum renegotiation results in the first-best outcome does not generalize to arbitrary renegotiation processes. Suppose, for example, that the investors, rather than the entrepreneur, make a take-it-or-leave-it renegotiation offer. The entrepreneur's reservation value in renegotiation is

$$\hat{U}(e) = \int_0^{\bar{R}} u(R - D)p(R \mid e)\,dR - g(e).$$

Because the entrepreneur obtains no surplus from the renegotiation, she chooses effort so as to maximize $\hat{U}(e)$, rather than $[u(E(R \mid e) - I + A) - g(e)]$. On the other hand, renegotiation still results in full insurance for the entrepreneur.

Dewatripont, Legros, and Matthews (2003). In a sense Dewatripont et al. combine the models of Innes and Hermalin and Katz. Like the latter, they allow risk aversion and confer upon renegotiation the task of creating efficient risk sharing (full insurance if the investors are risk neutral). But they share with Innes the presumption that the entrepreneur does not have unlimited liability and so a debt contract does not insulate investors against risk and therefore against externalities induced by the entrepreneur's effort choice.

Dewatripont et al. make the following assumptions (the first three are borrowed from Innes and

46. It is crucial that the investors observe the effort. Were the investors not to observe effort, then renegotiation would potentially take place under asymmetric information about the effort choice. Indeed, equilibrium behavior results in an asymmetry of information at the renegotiation stage and in inefficient renegotiation. To see this, suppose, for example, that the entrepreneur in equilibrium selects the efficient effort e^* for certain. Then the investors agree to fully insure the entrepreneur at wage equal to $E(R \mid e^*) - \hat{V}(e^*)$. But full insurance then induces the entrepreneur to select the lowest possible effort. The equilibrium is then in mixed strategies (at least for the optimal contract).

For more detail about contract renegotiation when the effort is not observed by the investors, see Fudenberg and Tirole (1990), Ma (1991, 1994), and Matthews (1995). Matthews (2001) analyzes this asymmetric-information renegotiation under the limited liability and monotonicity assumptions made here.

General results on contract design with renegotiation under *symmetric* information can be found in Maskin and Moore (1999) and Segal and Whinston (2002).

the fourth from Hermalin and Katz):

(i) Entrepreneur's limited liability.
(ii) Monotonicity of the investors' claim.
(iii) Monotone likelihood ratio property.
(iv) Entrepreneurial risk aversion (let us assume for simplicity that investors are risk neutral).

For these assumptions, a central result of their paper[47] is that under entrepreneur-offer renegotiation (the entrepreneur makes a take-it-or-leave-it offer at the renegotiation stage), *the optimal contract is again a debt contract.*

Renegotiation clearly leads to full insurance. Hence, we only need to worry about the equilibrium level of effort. The first point to note is that there is always underprovision of effort: the entrepreneur does not internalize the impact of her effort on the investors' pre-renegotiation (equal to post-renegotiation) utility,

$$\hat{V}(e) = \int_0^{\bar{R}} [R - w(R)] p(R \mid e)\, \mathrm{d}R$$
$$\equiv \int_0^{\bar{R}} R_1(R) p(R \mid e)\, \mathrm{d}R.$$

Now

$$\hat{V}'(e) = \int_0^{\bar{R}} \left[R_1(R) \frac{p_e(R \mid e)}{p(R \mid e)} \right] p(R \mid e)\, \mathrm{d}R$$
$$= \operatorname{cov}\left(R_1(R), \frac{p_e(R \mid e)}{p(R \mid e)} \right),$$

using the well-known property of the likelihood ratio that its mean is equal to 0.[48] Because p_e/p is increasing and has mean 0, its covariance with a nondecreasing function is positive, and so

$$\hat{V}'(e) \geqslant 0.$$

47. Dewatripont et al. also show that there is no loss of generality in considering contracts in which the investors exercise an option after observing the entrepreneur's effort (this, of course, does not imply that only contracts in this class can implement the optimum. Indeed, the renegotiated debt contract studied below involves post-effort "messages" from both parties and does not belong to this class. By contrast, convertible debt does). The intuition is that, by not allowing a post-effort message by the entrepreneur, one minimizes the size of the set of her possible deviations. By contrast, including a message (an option since this is the only message) sent by the investors is important, because it keeps the entrepreneur on her toes.

48. Let $P(\cdot)$ denote the cumulative distribution of the density $p(\cdot)$:

$$\int_0^{\bar{R}} \frac{p_e}{p} p\, \mathrm{d}R = \int_0^{\bar{R}} p_e\, \mathrm{d}R = \frac{\mathrm{d}}{\mathrm{d}e}(P(\bar{R}) - P(0))$$
$$= \frac{\mathrm{d}}{\mathrm{d}e}(1 - 0) = 0.$$

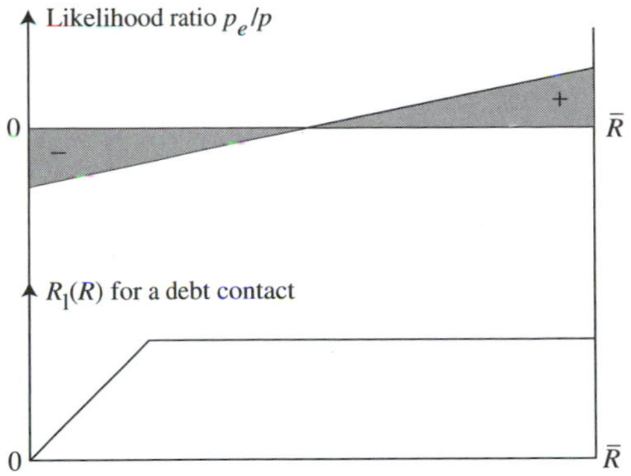

Figure 3.7

Actually, as p_e/p is strictly increasing and $R_1(\cdot)$ cannot in general be constant without violating the entrepreneur's limited liability constraint,[49]

$$V'(\hat{e}) > 0.$$

This means that at the margin, entrepreneurial effort exerts a strictly positive externality on the investors. Because the equilibrium effort is necessarily privately optimal for the entrepreneur, the effort is socially suboptimal.

In order to *minimize the externality* of the entrepreneur's effort choice on investors' welfare (that is, in order to make the entrepreneur as accountable as possible), one must give as much income as possible to investors for low profit and as little as possible for high profit, subject to $R_1(\cdot)$ being nondecreasing. Simple computations show that this is obtained for a debt contract. The intuition is provided in Figure 3.7.

That is, a debt contract maximizes entrepreneurial incentives, although it in general results in inefficiently low effort relative to the first best. Hence, it yields the preferred outcome, given that renegotiation results in efficient risk sharing.

Like Hermalin and Katz's, Dewatripont et al.'s result relies on the entrepreneur's having the full bargaining power in the renegotiation process. Dewatripont et al. show that the entrepreneur may exert an effort above the first-best level under a debt contract when the investors have bargaining power

49. The investors would receive a constant $R_1 = I - A$; and so, if $I > A$ and the minimum profit is 0, the entrepreneur must have a negative income for low profits.

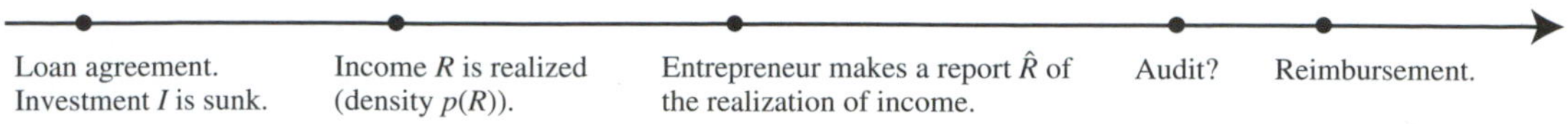

Figure 3.8

in the renegotiation process.[50] Interestingly and relatedly, the investors may be made worse off by a higher effort choice by the entrepreneur. While they are made better off by such a choice in the absence of renegotiation (from the monotonicity of their claim), a higher effort also strengthens the entrepreneur's status quo point in the renegotiation, which may hurt the investors if the latter have the bargaining power.

3.7 Semiverifiable Income

This section reviews the costly state verification (CSV) model of Townsend (1979), Diamond (1984), and Gale and Hellwig (1985).[51] While the earlier literature posited, rather than derived, specific financial structures, Townsend's contribution was the first to obtain a financial structure from an optimization problem, and therefore from primitive assumptions.

As we discussed earlier, the CSV model presumes that diversion of income takes the form of hiding income rather than enjoying a private benefit or reducing one's effort. The lenders can perfectly verify income, but only by incurring an audit cost K.[52] This cost is borne by the lenders, since the borrower (optimally) invests her net worth A in the project—as in the moral-hazard, verifiable-income model—and no longer has money to pay for the audit cost. Given borrower's net worth A and investment cost I, the lenders must invest $I - A$ in the project. This investment yields a random income R distributed on $[0, \infty)$, say, according to density $p(R)$. This income is costlessly observed by the borrower. Note that we do not introduce any moral-hazard conditioning the distribution of R; for, the semiverifiability of income already creates scope for diversion. The timing of the CSV model is described in Figure 3.8.

The revelation principle[53] states that, in designing the loan agreement, there is no loss of generality involved in focusing on contracts that require the entrepreneur to report income, and, furthermore, that the contract can be structured, again without loss of generality, so that the entrepreneur has an incentive to report the true realized income ($\hat{R} = R$).

A *contract* specifies for each report $\hat{R}$ a probability $y(\hat{R}) \in [0, 1]$ of no audit, and nonnegative rewards $w_0(\hat{R}, R)$ and $w_1(\hat{R}, R)$ in the absence and presence of audit; note that the investors' return R_l can depend only on the report in the absence of audit: $w_0(\hat{R}, R) = R - R_l(\hat{R})$, and can be made contingent on the true income as well when an audit takes place.

For an arbitrary contract, let

$$w(R) \equiv y(R)w_0(R, R) + (1 - y(R))w_1(R, R)$$

denote the borrower's expected reward when realized income is R.

A *standard debt contract* specifies a debt level D, no audit if D is repaid, and an audit and no reward

50. It is still the case that debt provides the greatest incentives. Debt may induce the entrepreneur to work too hard in order to lower the probability that the realized output is low.

On the other hand, the first best can often be achieved through a different type of contract in conformity with the general results of Maskin (1977) in the absence of renegotiation, and of Maskin and Moore (1999) and Segal and Whinston (2002) in the presence of renegotiation. The limited liability, monotonicity, and no-third-party assumptions, however, put a limit on what can be achieved through elicitation schemes. Dewatripont et al. show that either the first best is implementable, or, if it is not, debt is an optimal contract.

51. See also Williamson (1986). As in the rest of this chapter, this section presumes "universal risk neutrality." In Townsend (1979), the borrower may be risk averse. Two-sided risk aversion is studied in Krasa and Villamil (1994) and Winton (1995).

Winton (1995) also introduces multiple investors by assuming that (a) each investor can invest less than the total funding need ($I - A$) and (b) investors conduct separate audits. One of his main results is that an absolute-priority rule is optimal even with symmetric lenders, in particular, because it avoids a complete duplication of verification costs.

52. Diamond (1984) interprets K as a nonpecuniary penalty imposed on the borrower rather than as an audit cost. One possible interpretation is that the debtor goes to jail if she does not repay her debt. Lacker (1992) provides a different interpretation of the nonmonetary cost. In his model, the optimal contract is a debt contract in which the borrower transfers collateral which she values more than the lenders (see Section 4.3) in the case of default. We will stick to the audit cost interpretation for the purpose of the exposition.

53. See, for example, Fudenberg and Tirole (1991, Chapter 7) for a presentation of the revelation principle and of mechanism design.

if it is not. So, $y(R) = 1$ if $R \geqslant D$ and $y(R) = 0$ if $R < D$, and $w(R) = \max(R - D, 0)$.

The optimal contract maximizes the borrower's expected income subject to the incentive constraint that the borrower reports the truth and the break-even constraint for the investors.

Program IV:

$$\max_{\{y(\cdot),w_0(\cdot),w_1(\cdot,\cdot)\}} \left\{ \int_0^\infty w(R)p(R)\,dR \right\}$$

s.t.

$$w(R) = \max_{\hat{R}}\{y(\hat{R})w_0(\hat{R},R) + (1 - y(\hat{R}))w_1(\hat{R},R)\}, \tag{IC$_b$}$$

$$\int_0^\infty [R - w(R) - [1 - y(R)]K]p(R)\,dR \geqslant I - A. \tag{IR$_l$}$$

Note that, since (IR_l) will be binding at the optimum and thus can be added to the objective function, Program IV is equivalent to that of minimizing the expected audit cost

$$\left[\int_0^\infty [1 - y(R)]p(R)\,dR\right]K$$

subject to (IC_b) and (IR_l).

The following assumption substantially simplifies the analysis and, as we will see, underlies the optimality of a standard debt contract.

Assumption (deterministic audit):

$$y(R) = 0 \text{ or } 1 \text{ for all } R.$$

The deterministic audit assumption divides the set of feasible incomes into two regions $\mathcal{R}_0$ and $\mathcal{R}_1$ (such that $\mathcal{R}_0 \cap \mathcal{R}_1 = \varnothing$ and $\mathcal{R}_0 \cup \mathcal{R}_1 = [0, \infty)$), labeled respectively the no-audit and the audit regions. The assumption further implies that the reimbursement, $R - w(R)$, is constant over the no-audit region; indeed, suppose that the reimbursement is higher for R' than for R, where R' and R both belong to $\mathcal{R}_0$. For income R', the borrower would be better off pretending income is R and reimbursing less. The lenders, who do not audit when reported income is R, are then unable to detect misreporting. So, the reimbursement, D say, is constant over $\mathcal{R}_0$. And $\mathcal{R}_0 \subseteq [D, \infty)$. The same reasoning also implies that the reimbursement for an R in $\mathcal{R}_1$ cannot exceed D: if it did, then $R - w(R) > D$ and the borrower would be better off reporting an income in $\mathcal{R}_0$.

Let us now show that *for any contract satisfying* (IC_b) *and* (IR_l), *there exists a standard debt contract that does at least as well for the borrower.* The proof is in two steps. First, we show that for an arbitrary contract, there exists a first debt contract that pays out more to lenders at a smaller audit cost. Second, we show that there exists a second debt contract for which the lenders break even and which involves an even smaller audit cost. These two steps imply that, comparing the second debt contract to the initial contract, both the audit cost and the lenders' payoff are (weakly) smaller in the second debt contract and therefore the borrower is (weakly) better off under the second debt contract than under the initial contract.

So consider an arbitrary contract (which is incentive compatible and individually rational for the lenders). Let $\mathcal{R}_0$ and $\mathcal{R}_1$ denote the no-audit and audit regions and let D denote the repayment in the no-audit region. We know that $\mathcal{R}_0 \subseteq [D, \infty)$. Construct a first debt contract, in which the repayment is D as well. Its no-audit and audit regions are defined by $\mathcal{R}_0^* = [D, \infty)$ and $\mathcal{R}_1^* = [0, D)$. The borrower receives nothing in the latter, no-audit region. Because $\mathcal{R}_0 \subseteq \mathcal{R}_0^*$, the expected audit cost is smaller under this first debt contract. Let us next show that repayment to lenders is (weakly) larger under the new debt contract. For $R \in \mathcal{R}_0$, this repayment is the same, namely, D. For $R \in \mathcal{R}_1 \cap \mathcal{R}_0^*$, the repayment is at most D under the initial contract and equal to D under the new debt contract. For $R \in \mathcal{R}_1 \cap \mathcal{R}_1^*$, the lenders' payoff is $R - K$ under the new debt contract and therefore cannot be larger under the initial contract. This concludes the first step of the proof.

The second step is straightforward. Suppose that the first debt contract leaves a strictly positive surplus to the lenders (it cannot leave a negative surplus from the first step of the proof and from the fact that they at least break even under the initial contract). Then, there exists $D' < D$ such that the lenders' expected net payoff

$$[1 - P(D')]D' + \int_0^{D'} Rp(R)\,dR - P(D')K - (I - A)$$

is equal to 0 (where $P(\cdot)$ denotes the cumulative distribution corresponding to density $p(\cdot)$). This second debt contract, with nominal debt D', involves a lower audit cost than the first debt contract

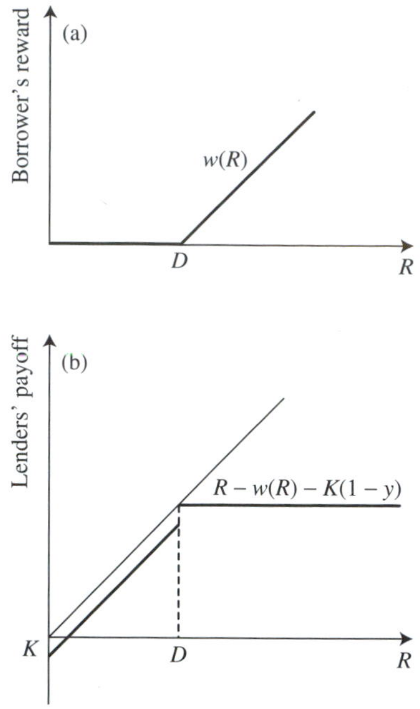

Figure 3.9

$(P(D')K < P(D)K)$ and leaves no surplus to the lenders. It is therefore preferred by the borrower to the initial contract. This concludes the proof of Townsend's classic result.

The state-contingent payoffs under a standard debt contract with debt D are depicted in Figure 3.9.

Random audits. Townsend (1979) pointed out that a debt contract is in general no longer optimal when random audits (a standard feature of taxation and insurance institutions) are allowed. We refer the reader to Mookherjee and P'ng (1989) for a general analysis of random audits (see also Border and Sobel 1987). We here content ourselves with an illustration of the benefit of random audits for the two-outcome case. Suppose that the project yields R^{S} (in the case of success) or R^{F} (in the case of failure), where $R^{\mathrm{S}} > R^{\mathrm{F}} > 0$. The pledgeable income is maximized, and the probability of an audit minimized, if the full income in the case of failure goes to the lenders when the borrower reports a failure and there turns out to be no audit (this can be seen most clearly from condition (3.18) below). For a given debt level D such that $R^{\mathrm{F}} < D < R^{\mathrm{S}}$, incentive compatibility is ensured by a probability of no audit y^{F} in the case of a report of the low income, where

$$R^{\mathrm{S}} - D = y^{\mathrm{F}}(R^{\mathrm{S}} - R^{\mathrm{F}}). \tag{3.17}$$

Thus, to the extent that the debt level is smaller than the higher income, there is no need to audit with probability 1. Since the optimal deterministic audit would have $y^{\mathrm{F}} = 0$, we conclude that a random audit economizes on audit costs.

If p denotes the probability of R^{S}, then the break-even condition for the lenders is

$$pD + (1 - p)[R^{\mathrm{F}} - (1 - y^{\mathrm{F}})K] = I - A. \tag{3.18}$$

Renegotiation. Gale and Hellwig (1989) observe that, to the extent that audit is not a mechanical exercise triggered by the report, the threat to audit in the case of a small report may not be credible. They conclude that the possibility of renegotiation undoes the optimality of standard debt contracts and reduces welfare.

The basic insight is that the audit's raison d'être is to induce truthful reporting and therefore that the audit no longer serves a purpose once the borrower has reported her income. The borrower and the lenders are then tempted to renegotiate in order to economize on the audit cost if the contract specifies that the firm is audited for the report made by the borrower. However, the anticipation of the absence of audit after renegotiation undermines the borrower's incentive to report truthfully.[54]

To obtain some intuition as to why renegotiation is an issue, consider a standard debt contract with debt level D and suppose that the borrower is expected to pay back D whenever $R \geqslant D$. Suppose that the borrower says that she is not able to repay D but offers to repay $D - K$. The lenders should then be happy to forgo the audit and receive $D - K$ because they will never receive more if they audit. On the other hand, such debt forgiveness cannot be equilibrium behavior either, since the borrower then has an incentive to ask for debt forgiveness even when $R > D$. As this rather loose reasoning suggests, the equilibrium analysis is complex and requires a good knowledge of the theory of dynamic

54. Renegotiation is always welfare-reducing when the initial contract is complete, as is the case in Townsend's analysis. Renegotiation only adds further constraints to the mechanism design.

games with incomplete information. A full analysis thus lies outside the scope of these notes.[55]

Interpretation of the CSV model. Although the CSV model is elementary, its interpretation requires some thinking through. An implicit assumption is that the borrower can withdraw nothing from the cash register before the audit, but can fully withdraw the residual income after repayment if there has been no audit. One interpretation of the model is that the borrower can actually steal the income, but cannot consume it and must refund it if an audit takes place. An alternative interpretation is that the entrepreneur can, over time, transform the hidden income into (utility-equivalent) perks; the entrepreneur can enjoy these perks only if the firm is not shut down. The audit decision is then interpreted as a bankruptcy process, in which the lenders recoup the value of the assets in the firm.[56]

3.8 Nonverifiable Income

Let us conclude this review of alternative models of credit rationing with the polar case in which the borrower's income cannot be observed even through an audit. That is, the borrower can consume this income with complete impunity. As we observed, the borrower's incentive to repay can then only result from a threat of termination or nonfinancing of future projects. Bolton and Scharfstein (1990) and Hart and Moore (1989) (with Bolton and Scharfstein (1996) and Gromb (1994) extending their analysis) have constructed such models in which the borrower repays under the threat of termination.

There are two dates. The date-1 investment I yields income R_1 with probability p and 0 with probability $1 - p$ (as for the CSV model, to which this model is somewhat akin as we will see, there is no need to introduce a dependence of p on entrepreneurial effort since the nonverifiability of income allows for strategic nonrepayment and therefore for moral hazard). At date 2, the initial investment, if not terminated, yields expected income R_2 to the entrepreneur. Since date 2 is the last period in this model, the entrepreneur repays nothing at date 2 (as long as return 0 belongs to the support of the distribution of the second-period income, which we will assume). Thus we may as well treat R_2 as if it were a deterministic private benefit of continuation for the entrepreneur. If the project is liquidated at the end of date 1, the lenders receive liquidation value L, $0 \leqslant L < I - A$, the entrepreneur receives nothing at date 2 (in some contributions, L is equivalently interpreted not as the liquidation value, but rather as the savings associated with not incurring a second-period investment yielding R_2). Assume $L < R_2$, so liquidation is inefficient. Lastly, we will assume for expositional simplicity that there is no discounting between dates 1 and 2.

Let us now look for an optimal contract, that is, the contract that maximizes the borrower's expected payoff subject to incentive compatibility and to the constraint that the investors break even. The entrepreneur obviously repays nothing when the first-period income is equal to 0. Let $y_0 \in [0, 1]$ denote the probability of continuation when there is no repayment at date 1 (so $1 - y_0$ is the probability of termination). Consider a contract that specifies a repayment equal to $D \leqslant R_1$ when the first-period income is R_1, together with a probability y_1 of continuation if D is repaid.

The payment of D when the first-period income is R_1 must be incentive compatible, or

$$R_1 - D + y_1 R_2 \geqslant R_1 + y_0 R_2 \iff (y_1 - y_0) R_2 \geqslant D.$$

In words, the increase in the probability of termination due to nonrepayment must offset the loss in income D for the entrepreneur.

55. Another relevant contribution is that of Krasa and Villamil (2000). They assume, among other things, that the investors cannot commit to spend the fixed inspection cost. The investors thus decide whether to enforce the initial contract after observing the entrepreneur's payment. The key result is that enforcement must then be deterministic and the optimal time-consistent contract is a simple debt contract.

56. Chang (1993) builds a model of payout policy that is closely related to both the moral-hazard model in the text and the CSV model. There are three dates rather than two. Investment and financing occur at date 0. Some random income accrues at date 1, which is observed solely by the manager. The manager selects an allocation of this income between a payout to investor and a low-yield reinvestment (called in the paper "over-consumption" or "on-the-job spending"). This reinvestment increases date-2 income, but by less than a date-1 dividend of the same magnitude; in contrast it yields a private benefit at date 1. It is then optimal to link compensation to the payout so as to avoid excessive reinvestment. Chang derives conditions under which the optimal contract can be implemented through a debt contract, according to which investors can seize control when the contractually specified payment to investors is not made at date 1 and have then incentives to pay an audit cost in order to measure the date-1 income.

The optimal contract thus solves the following program.

Program V:

$$\max_{\{y_0,y_1,D\leqslant R_1\}} \{p(R_1 - D + y_1R_2) + (1-p)(y_0R_2)\}$$

s.t.

$$(y_1 - y_0)R_2 \geqslant D, \qquad (\text{IC}_\text{b})$$

$$p[D + (1-y_1)L] + (1-p)(1-y_0)L \geqslant I - A. \quad (\text{IR}_\text{l})$$

To avoid considering multiple cases, let us assume that R_1 is "sufficiently large" so that the constraint $D \leqslant R_1$ is not binding. (We will later provide a condition for this to be the case.) We first note that the breakeven constraint (IR_l) is binding. Otherwise, the debt D could be lowered while keeping the two constraints satisfied (and (IR_l) implies that D cannot be equal to 0 since $L < I - A$).

Second, note that $y_1 = 1$ (there is no liquidation in the case of repayment); for, assume that $1 > y_1 > y_0$. Increase y_1 by a small amount $\varepsilon > 0$, and raise D by εL so as to keep (IR_l) satisfied. Note that the incentive constraint remains satisfied as $R_2 > L$. The borrower's utility increases by $p(R_2 - L)\varepsilon > 0$. In words, liquidating in the case of repayment is bad both for efficiency (liquidation is always inefficient) and for incentives.

Third, the incentive constraint must be binding. Note that y_0 must be lower than 1 in order for it to be satisfied (there would never be a repayment if there were no threat of liquidation in the case of nonrepayment). If the incentive constraint is not binding, raise y_0 by a small $\varepsilon > 0$, and increase D by $\varepsilon L(1-p)/p$, so as to keep (IR_l) satisfied. The borrower's welfare increases by

$$-p\left[\frac{\varepsilon L(1-p)}{p}\right] + (1-p)\varepsilon R_2 = (1-p)(R_2 - L)\varepsilon > 0.$$

Using these results, we conclude that $y_1 = 1$ and D and y_0 solve

$$(1 - y_0)R_2 = D \qquad (3.19)$$

and

$$pD + (1-p)(1-y_0)L = I - A. \qquad (3.20)$$

And so the probability of liquidation in the absence of repayment is

$$1 - y_0 = \frac{I - A}{pR_2 + (1-p)L}. \qquad (3.21)$$

Following Bolton and Scharfstein and Hart and Moore, we have thus formalized the idea that *the threat of termination provides incentives for repayment when income is nonverifiable.*

Some interesting comparative statics results emerge from (3.21). Termination is less likely in the case of nonrepayment if

- the value of continuing (R_2) increases (the borrower then has more to lose from being terminated and the probability of termination can be reduced),
- the liquidation value L increases (the lenders obtain more money when liquidating and therefore can liquidate less often and still recoup their investment),
- the probability p of first-period success increases (the lenders are then repaid often), and
- the borrower's net worth A increases.

Povel and Raith (2004) extend Bolton and Scharfstein's model by allowing for a noncontractible choice of investment level in the first period. In their model, the date-1 revenue is continuous and takes value $\theta z(J) + [I - J]$, where θ is a random variable, $J \leqslant I$ is the actual investment secretly chosen by the entrepreneur, $z(J)$ the concave production function, and $I - J$ the noninvested funds (which are not diverted). Because a debt contract maximizes the entrepreneur's incentive to take risk, the entrepreneur ends up investing all the funds that are made available to her by the investors ($J = I$). And so debt remains the optimal contract.[57]

Relationship to the CSV model. This model is closely related to the CSV model. In both cases lenders cannot be repaid (at least if the lowest possible income is 0) unless they undertake some wasteful action. The counterpart to the audit cost K in the CSV model is the waste in second-period value, $R_2 - L$, in the nonverifiable income model. Indeed, in the two-outcome case, the incentive constraints (3.17) (taken for $R^\text{S} = R$ and $R^\text{F} = 0$) and (3.19) are identical. There are some differences between the two models, though. The cost of the wasteful activity

57. Povel and Raith also consider various extensions in which entrepreneurial moral hazard takes different forms. For example, they show that a simple debt contract may no longer be optimal when the entrepreneur chooses how much effort to exert or the project's riskiness rather than how much of the funds to invest.

(audit, liquidation) is borne by the lenders in the CSV model and by the borrower in the nonverifiable income model. In a world in which some agent (here, the borrower) is cash constrained, who bears the cost matters, which accounts for a small discrepancy between the breakeven conditions (3.18) and (3.20). We should also point out that the CSV model is notoriously difficult to extend to a multiperiod context (see Chang 1990; Snyder 1994; Webb 1992), while the nonverifiable income model can be more straightforwardly extended (see Gromb 1994).

Relationship to costly collateral pledging. The next chapter will argue that firms can boost pledgeable income and facilitate financing by pledging collateral in the case of default. Collateral pledging serves two purposes. First, it incentivizes management to repay investors. Second, it boosts pledgeable income. But collateral pledging is costly to the extent that lenders may value the collateral less than the borrower and so transferring it to lenders involves a deadweight loss. The Bolton–Scharfstein model can be viewed as a special case of costly collateral pledging. The collateral is the date-2 project. The lenders' gain, L from "seizing the collateral," i.e., taking the control over the decision to continue away from the borrower, is lower than the value, R_2, accruing to the borrower when continuing at date 2.

Renegotiation. As for the CSV model, there has been some discussion of the impact of renegotiation in the literature on nonverifiable income.

Consider first renegotiation *after* "liquidation" has taken place. For such renegotiation to make sense, one must adopt the interpretation of "liquidation" as the "nonfinancing of a second-period investment $I_2 = L$ that allows the borrower to receive expected income R_2 in period 2," and not as a (possibly piecewise) resale of the firm's assets. Even though financing the second-period investment increases total surplus by $R_2 - L$, no such financing occurs unless it is specified by the initial contract. The lenders do not want to bring in money at date 2 since they will not be repaid anything. So, a contract that specifies liquidation is *renegotiation proof* in the two-period model. Incidentally, it is no longer renegotiation proof with more than two periods, as was shown by Gromb (1994). For example, at date 2 the lenders may anticipate to be repaid at the end of date 2 through the threat of noncontinuation at date 3. Gromb characterizes the equilibrium outcomes with renegotiation.[58]

Second, consider renegotiation after the termination decision has been made (the borrower has defaulted, and the draw of the random variable has indicated liquidation), but before it is implemented. Suppose that the borrower at that point in time offers to the lenders a bribe slightly above L for not liquidating. Although this offer demonstrates that the borrower has strategically defaulted (otherwise, she would have no money), the lenders should be eager to accept. This in turn encourages strategic default and undermines the efficiency of the debt contract.[59]

Notice again the analogy with the CSV model. In both cases, a wasteful action (audit, liquidation) by the lenders serves as an incentive device in order to induce the borrower to pay out income. Once this income has been paid, though, the wasteful action no longer serves a purpose and the parties are better off renegotiating to avoid the corresponding efficiency loss. The prospect of renegotiation, however, *ex ante* eliminates incentives to pay out income, and reduces welfare overall. We again refer the reader to the original articles for more details about the impact of renegotiation.

Relation to the sovereign debt literature. The strategic default literature is closely linked to that on sovereign borrowing in international finance. Repayment of debt by the sovereign responds to two incentives: international sanctions and the future cost of being shut down from the international capital market after default. A subliterature, starting with Bulow and Rogoff (1989a,b), assumes away sanctions and focuses on the incentives provided by exclusion. In this literature, future refinancing (or the lack

58. To do so, he rules out retained earnings by the borrower (an assumption labeled the "fresh tomato assumption," by reference to the hypothesis that the borrower is not able to carry over resources for investment in future periods). He shows that even a monopoly lender may make no profit when the horizon is long. The intuition for this result is that if the lender enjoys a rent from continuation the borrower can safely default as the lender will always be eager to renegotiate after termination.

59. The extent of renegotiation as well as the sharing of the *ex post* gains from trade may depend on the number of lenders. See Bolton and Scharfstein (1996) for an analysis of the impact of lender dispersion on the optimal contract.

thereof) must be self-sustaining rather than contracted upon. The basic mechanism is otherwise similar to the Bolton–Scharfstein mechanism, in that lenders cannot appropriate any of the current return and count solely on the nonrefinancing threat to recoup their investment. Bulow and Rogoff consider an infinite-horizon, symmetric-information model in which (a) the sovereign can decide not to reimburse and (b) the sovereign can save, and (c) the rate of growth of the economy is smaller than the rate of interest. They show that no lending is feasible as the borrower always prefers to default (and save some of the concomitant extra income).

Several contributions have shown that borrowing may be feasible in more general no-sanction environments. First, Hellwig and Lorenzoni (2004) show that when the rate of growth in the absence of sovereign borrowing exceeds the rate of interest, then sovereign debt borrowing is feasible, even though incentive-compatible repayments still require borrowing levels below the first-best level. Intuitively, exclusion from borrowing is a stronger threat when the rate of growth is large relative to the rate of interest. Second, an outright exclusion, in which the defaulting sovereign cannot even save, makes it particularly costly for the sovereign to repudiate its debt. Again, some sovereign debt may then be issued in equilibrium (Kehoe and Levine 1993; Kocherlakota 1996). Finally, standard "type-based" reputation models (see, for example, Kreps et al. 1982) would deliver some equilibrium borrowing.

3.9 Exercises

Exercise 3.1 (random financing). Consider the fixed-investment model of Section 3.2. We know that if $A \geqslant \bar{A}$, where

$$I - \bar{A} = p_{\mathrm{H}}\left(R - \frac{B}{\Delta p}\right),$$

it is both optimal and feasible for the borrower to sign a contract in which the project is undertaken for certain. We also noted that for $A < \bar{A}$, the borrower cannot convince investors to undertake the project with probability 1. With $A > 0$, the entrepreneur benefits from signing a "random financing contract," though.

(i) Consider a contract in which the borrower invests $\hat{A} \in [0, A]$ of her own money, the project is financed with probability x, and the borrower receives R_{b} in the case of success and 0 otherwise. Write the investors' breakeven condition.

(ii) Show that (provided the NPV, $p_{\mathrm{H}}R - I$, is positive) it is optimal for the borrower to invest

$$\hat{A} = A.$$

How does the probability that the project is undertaken vary with A?

Exercise 3.2 (impact of entrepreneurial risk aversion). Consider the fixed-investment model developed in this chapter: an entrepreneur has cash amount A and wants to invest $I > A$ into a project. The project yields $R > 0$ with probability p and 0 with probability $1 - p$. The probability of success is p_{H} if the entrepreneur works and $p_{\mathrm{L}} = p_{\mathrm{H}} - \Delta p$ ($\Delta p > 0$) if she shirks. The entrepreneur obtains private benefit B if she shirks and 0 otherwise. Assume that

$$I > p_{\mathrm{H}}\left(R - \frac{B}{\Delta p}\right).$$

(Suppose that $p_{\mathrm{L}}R + B < I$; so the project is not financed if the entrepreneur shirks.)

(i) In contrast with the risk-neutrality assumption of this chapter, assume that the entrepreneur has utility for consumption c:

$$u(c) = \begin{cases} c & \text{if } c \geqslant c_0, \\ -\infty & \text{otherwise.} \end{cases}$$

(Assume that $A \geqslant c_0$ to ensure that the entrepreneur is not in the "$-\infty$ range" in the absence of financing.)

Compute the minimum equity level $\bar{A}$ for which the project is financed by risk-neutral investors when the market rate of interest is 0. Discuss the difference between $p_{\mathrm{H}} = 1$ and $p_{\mathrm{H}} < 1$.

(ii) Generalize the analysis to risk aversion. Let $u(c)$ denote the entrepreneur's utility from consumption with $u' > 0$, $u'' < 0$. Conduct the analysis assuming either limited liability or the absence of limited liability.

Exercise 3.3 (random private benefits). Consider the variable-investment model: an entrepreneur ini-

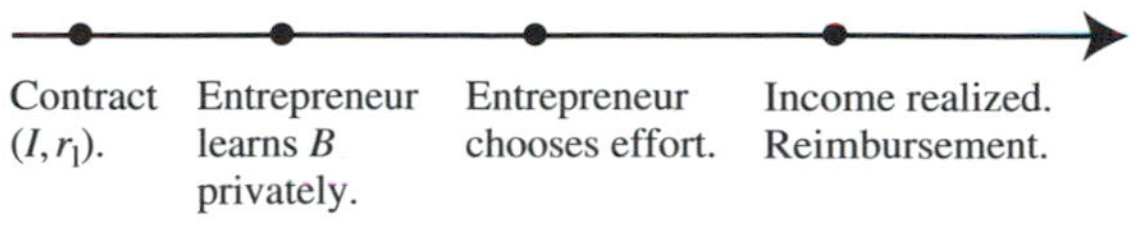

Figure 3.10

tially has cash A. For investment I, the project yields RI in the case of success and 0 in the case of failure.

The probability of success is equal to $p_H \in (0,1)$ if the entrepreneur works and $p_L = 0$ if the entrepreneur shirks. The entrepreneur obtains private benefit BI when shirking and 0 when working. The per-unit private benefit B is unknown to all *ex ante* and is drawn from (common knowledge) uniform distribution F:

$$\Pr(B < \hat{B}) = F(\hat{B}) = \hat{B}/R \quad \text{for} \quad \hat{B} \leqslant R,$$

with density $f(\hat{B}) = 1/R$. The entrepreneur borrows $I - A$ and pays back $R_l = r_l I$ in the case of success. The timing is described in Figure 3.10.

(i) For a given contract (I, r_l), what is the threshold B^*, i.e., the value of the private per-unit benefit above which the entrepreneur shirks?

(ii) For a given B^* (or equivalently r_l, which determines B^*), what is the debt capacity? For which value of B^* (or r_l) is this debt capacity highest?

(iii) Determine the entrepreneur's expected utility for a given B^*. Show that the contract that is optimal for the entrepreneur (subject to the investors breaking even) satisfies

$$\tfrac{1}{2}p_H R < B^* < p_H R.$$

Interpret this result.

(iv) Suppose now that the private benefit B is observable and verifiable. Determine the optimal contract between the entrepreneur and the investors (note that the reimbursement can now be made contingent on the level of private benefits: $R_l = r_l(B)I$).

Exercise 3.4 (product-market competition and financing). Two firms, $i = 1, 2$, compete for a new market. To enter the market, a firm must develop a new technology. It must invest (a fixed amount) I. Each firm is run by an entrepreneur. Entrepreneur i has initial cash $A_i < I$. The entrepreneurs must borrow from investors at expected rate of interest 0. As in the single-firm model, an entrepreneur enjoys private benefit B from shirking and 0 when working. The probability of success is p_H and $p_L = p_H - \Delta p$ when working and shirking.

The return for a firm is

$$R = \begin{cases} D & \text{if both firms succeed in developing the technology (which results in a duopoly),} \\ M & \text{if only this firm succeeds (and therefore enjoys a monopoly situation),} \\ 0 & \text{if the firm fails,} \end{cases}$$

where $M > D > 0$.

Assume that $p_H(M - B/\Delta p) < I$. We look for a Nash equilibrium in contracts (when an entrepreneur negotiates with investors, both parties correctly anticipate whether the other entrepreneur obtains funding). In a first step, assume that the two firms' projects or research technologies are independent, so that nothing is learned from the success or failure of the other firm concerning the behavior of the borrower.

(i) Show that there is a cutoff $\underline{A}$ such that if $A_i < \underline{A}$, entrepreneur i obtains no funding.

(ii) Show that there is a cutoff $\bar{A}$ such that if $A_i > \bar{A}$ for $i = 1, 2$, both firms receive funding.

(iii) Show that if $\underline{A} < A_i < \bar{A}$ for $i = 1, 2$, then there exist two (pure-strategy) equilibria.

(iv) The previous questions have shown that when investment projects are independent, product-market competition makes it *more difficult* for an entrepreneur to obtain financing. Let us now show that when projects are correlated, product-market competition may *facilitate financing* by allowing financiers to benchmark the entrepreneur's performance on that of competing firms.

Let us change the entrepreneur's preferences slightly:

$$u(c) = \begin{cases} c & \text{if } c \geqslant c_0, \\ -\infty & \text{otherwise.} \end{cases}$$

That is, the entrepreneur is infinitely risk averse below c_0 (this assumption is stronger than needed, but it simplifies the computations).

Suppose, first, that only one firm can invest. Show that the necessary and sufficient condition for investment to take place is

$$p_H\left(M - \frac{B}{\Delta p}\right) - c_0 \geqslant I - A.$$

(v) Continuing on from question (iv), suppose now that there are two firms and that their technologies are *perfectly correlated* in that if both invest and both entrepreneurs work, then they both succeed or both fail. (For the technically oriented reader, there exists an underlying state variable ω distributed uniformly on $[0,1]$ and common to both firms such that a firm always succeeds if $\omega < p_L$, always fails if $\omega > p_H$, and succeeds if and only if the entrepreneur works when $p_L < \omega < p_H$.)

Show that if

$$p_H D - c_0 \geqslant I - A,$$

then it is an equilibrium for both entrepreneurs to receive finance. Conclude that product-market competition may facilitate financing.

Exercise 3.5 (continuous investment and decreasing returns to scale). Consider the continuous-investment model, with one modification: investment I yields return $R(I)$ in the case of success, and 0 in the case of failure, where $R' > 0$, $R'' < 0$, $R'(0) > 1/p_H$, $R'(\infty) < 1/p_H$. The rest of the model is unchanged. (The entrepreneur starts with cash A. The probability of success is p_H if the entrepreneur behaves and $p_L = p_H - \Delta p$ if she misbehaves. The entrepreneur obtains private benefit BI if she misbehaves and 0 otherwise. Only the final outcome is observable.) Let I^* denote the level of investment that maximizes total surplus: $p_H R'(I^*) = 1$.

(i) How does investment $I(A)$ vary with assets?

(ii) How does the shadow value v of assets (the derivative of the borrower's gross utility with respect to assets) vary with the level of assets?

Exercise 3.6 (renegotiation and debt forgiveness). When computing the multiplier k (given by equation (3.12)), we have assumed that it is optimal to specify a stake for the borrower large enough that the incentive constraint (IC_b) is satisfied. Because condition (3.8) implies that the project has negative NPV in the case of misbehavior, such a specification is clearly optimal when the contract cannot be renegotiated. The purpose of this exercise is to check in a rather mechanical way that the borrower cannot gain by offering a loan agreement in which (IC_b) is not satisfied, and which is potentially renegotiated before the borrower chooses her effort. While there is a more direct way to prove this result, some insights are gleaned from this pedestrian approach. Indeed, the exercise provides conditions under which the lender is willing to forgive debt in order to boost incentives (the analysis will bear some resemblance to that of liquidity shocks in Chapter 5, except that the lender's concession takes the form of debt forgiveness rather than cash infusion).[60]

(i) Consider a loan agreement specifying investment I and stake $R_b < BI/\Delta p$ for the borrower. Suppose that the loan agreement can be renegotiated after it is signed and the investment is sunk and before the borrower chooses her effort. Renegotiation takes place if and only if it is mutually advantageous. Show that the loan agreement is renegotiated if and only if

$$(\Delta p)RI - \frac{p_H BI}{\Delta p} + p_L R_b \geqslant 0.$$

(ii) Interpret the previous condition. In particular, show that it can be obtained directly from the general theory. Hint: consider a fictitious, "fixed-investment" project with income $(\Delta p)RI$, investment 0, and cash on hand $p_L R_b$.

(iii) Assume for instance that the entrepreneur makes a take-it-or-leave-it offer in the renegotiation (that is, the entrepreneur has the bargaining power). Compute the borrowing capacity when $R_b < BI/\Delta p$ and the loan agreement is renegotiated.

(iv) Use a direct, rational expectations argument to point out in a different way that there is no loss of generality in assuming $R_b \geqslant BI/\Delta p$ (and therefore no renegotiation).

Exercise 3.7 (strategic leverage). (i) A borrower has assets A and must find financing for an investment $I(\tau) > A$. As usual, the project yields R (success) or 0 (failure). The borrower is protected by limited liability. The probability of success is $p_H + \tau$ or $p_L + \tau$, depending on whether the borrower works or shirks, with $\Delta p = p_H - p_L > 0$. There is no private benefit when working and private benefit B when shirking. The financial market is competitive and the expected rate of return demanded by investors is equal to 0. It is never optimal to give incentives to shirk.

60. The phenomenon of debt renegotiation has been analyzed in a number of settings: see, for example, Bulow and Rogoff (1989a,b), Eaton and Gersovitz (1981), Fernandez and Rosenthal (1990), Gale and Hellwig (1989), Gromb (1994), Hart and Moore (1989, 1995), and Snyder (1994).

The investment cost I is an increasing and convex function of τ (it will be further assumed that $p_H R > I(0)$, that in the relevant range $p_H + \tau < 1$, and that $I'(0)$ is "small enough" so as to guarantee an interior solution). Let τ^*, A^*, and τ^{**} be defined by

$$I'(\tau^*) = R,$$

$$[p_H + \tau^*]\left[R - \frac{B}{\Delta p}\right] = I(\tau^*) - A^*,$$

$$I'(\tau^{**}) = R - \frac{B}{\Delta p}.$$

Can the borrower raise funds? If so, what is the equilibrium level τ of "quality of investment"?

(ii) Suppose now that there are two firms (that is, two borrowers) competing on this product market. If only firm i succeeds in its project, its income is (as in question (i)), equal to R (and firm j's income is 0). If the two firms succeed (both get hold of "the technology"), they compete *à la* Bertrand in the product market and get 0 each. For simplicity, assume that the lenders observe only whether the borrower's income is R or 0, rather than whether the borrower has succeeded in developing the technology (showoffs: you can discuss what would happen if the lenders observed "success/failure"!).

So, if $q_i \equiv p_i + \tau_i$ denotes the probability that firm i develops the technology (with $p_i = p_H$ or p_L), the probability that firm i makes R is $q_i(1 - q_j)$. (This assumes implicitly that projects are independent.)

Consider the following timing. (1) Each borrower simultaneously and secretly arranges financing (if feasible). A borrower's leverage (or quality of investment) is *not* observed by the other borrower. (2) Borrowers choose whether to work or shirk. (3) Projects succeed or fail.

- Let $\hat{\tau}$ be defined by

$$I'(\hat{\tau}) = [1 - (p_H + \hat{\tau})]R.$$

  Interpret $\hat{\tau}$.
- Suppose that the two borrowers have the same initial net worth A. Find the lower bound $\hat{A}$ on A such that $(\hat{\tau}, \hat{\tau})$ is the (symmetric) Nash outcome.
- Derive a sufficient condition on A under which it is an equilibrium for a single firm to raise funds.

(iii) Consider the set up of question (ii), except that borrower 1 moves first and publicly chooses τ_1. Borrower 2 may then try to raise funds (one will assume either that τ_2 is secret or that borrower 1 is rewarded on the basis of her success/failure performance; this is in order to avoid strategic choices by borrower 2 that would try to induce borrower 1 to shirk). Suppose that each has net worth $\tilde{A}$ given by

$$\tilde{q}\left[(1 - \tilde{q})R - \frac{B}{\Delta p}\right] = I(\tilde{q} - p_H) - \tilde{A},$$

where $\tilde{q}$ satisfies

$$I'(\tilde{q} - p_H) = (1 - \tilde{q})R - \frac{B}{\Delta p}.$$

- Interpret $\tilde{q}$.
- Show that it is optimal for borrower 1 to choose $\tau_1 > \tilde{q} - p_H$.

Exercise 3.8 (equity multiplier and active monitoring). (i) Derive the equity multiplier in the variable-investment model. (Reminder: the investment $I \in [0, \infty)$ yields income RI in the case of success and 0 in the case of failure. The borrower's private benefit from misbehaving is equal to BI. Misbehaving reduces the probability of success from p_H to $p_L = p_H - \Delta p$. The borrower has cash A and is protected by limited liability. Assume that $\rho_1 = p_H R > 1$, $\rho_0 = p_H(R - B/\Delta p) < 1$ and $1 > p_L R + B$. The investors' rate of time preference is equal to 0.) Show that the equity multiplier is equal to $1/(1 - \rho_0)$.

(ii) Derive the equity multiplier with active monitoring: the entrepreneur can hire a monitor, who, at private cost cI, reduces the entrepreneur's private benefit from shirking from BI to $b(c)I$, where $b(0) = B$, $b' < 0$. The monitor must be given incentives to monitor (denote by R_m his income in the case of success). The monitor wants to break even, taking into account his private monitoring cost (so, there is "no shortage of monitoring capital").

- Suppose that the entrepreneur wants to induce level of monitoring c. Write the two incentive constraints to be satisfied by R_m and R_b (where R_b is the borrower's reward in the case of success).
- What is the equity multiplier?
- Show that the entrepreneur chooses c so as to maximize

$$\max_c \left\{\frac{\rho_1 - 1 - c}{1 - \rho_0 + (p_H/\Delta p)[b(c) + c - B]}\right\}.$$

Exercise 3.9 (concave private benefit). Consider the variable-investment model with a concave private benefit. The entrepreneur obtains $B(I)$ when shirking and 0 when behaving, where $B(0) = 0$, $B' > 0$, $B'' < 0$ (and $B'(0)$ large, $\lim_{I\to\infty} B'(I) = B$, where $p_H(R - B/\Delta p) < 1$).

(i) Compute the borrowing capacity.

(ii) How does the shadow price v of the entrepreneur's cash on hand vary with A?

Exercise 3.10 (congruence, pledgeable income, and power of incentive scheme). The credit rationing model developed in this chapter assumes that the entrepreneur's and investors' interests are *a priori* dissonant, and that incentives must be aligned by giving the entrepreneur enough of a stake in the case of success.

Suppose that the entrepreneur and the investors have indeed dissonant preferences with probability x, but have naturally aligned interests with probability $1-x$. Which prevails is unknown to both sides at the financing stage and is discovered (only) by the entrepreneur just before the moral-hazard stage.

More precisely, consider the fixed-investment model of Section 3.2. The investors's outlay is $I - A$ and they demand an expected rate of return equal to 0. The entrepreneur is risk neutral and protected by limited liability. With probability x, interests are dissonant: the entrepreneur obtains private benefit B by misbehaving (the probability of success is p_L) and 0 by behaving (probability of success p_H). With probability $1 - x$, interests are aligned: the entrepreneur's taking her private benefit B coincides with choosing probability of success p_H.

(i) Consider a "simple incentive scheme" in which the entrepreneur receives R_b in the case of success and 0 in the case of failure. R_b thus measures the "power of the incentive scheme."

Show that it may be optimal to choose a low-powered incentive scheme if preferences are rather congruent (x low) and that the incentive scheme is necessarily high-powered if preferences are rather dissonant (x high).

(ii) Show that one cannot improve on simple incentive schemes by presenting the entrepreneur with a menu of two options (two outcome-contingent incentive schemes) from which she will choose once she learns whether preferences are congruent or dissonant.

Exercise 3.11 (retained-earnings benefit). An entrepreneur has at date 1 a project of fixed size with characteristics $\{I^1, R^1, p_H^1, p_L^1, B^1\}$ (see Section 3.2). This entrepreneur will at date 2 have a different fixed size project with characteristics $\{I^2, R^2, p_H^2, p_L^2, B^2\}$, which will then require new financing. So, we are considering only a short-term loan for the first project. Retained earnings from the first project can, however, be used to defray part of the investment cost of the second project. Assume that all the characteristics of the second project are known at date 1 except B^2, which is distributed on $[\underline{B}^2, \bar{B}^2]$ according to the cumulative distribution $F(B^2)$. Assume for simplicity that $\underline{B}^2 > \Delta p^2 (p_H^2 R^2 - I^2)/p_H^2$. The characteristics of the second project become common knowledge at the beginning of date 2.

(i) Compute the shadow value of retained earnings. (Hint: what is the entrepreneur's gross utility in period 2?)

(ii) Show that it is possible that the first project is funded even though it would not be funded if the second project did not exist and even though the entrepreneur cannot pledge at date 1 income resulting from the second project.

Exercise 3.12 (investor risk aversion and risk premia). One of the key developments in the theory of *market* finance has been to find methods to price claims held by investors. Market finance emphasizes state-contingent pricing, the fact that 1 unit of income does not have a uniform value across states of nature. This book assumes that investors are risk neutral, and so it does not matter how the pledgeable income is spread across states of nature. This assumption is made only for the sake of computational simplicity, and can easily be relaxed.

Consider a two-date model of market finance with a representative consumer/investor. This consumer has utility of consumption $u(c_0)$ at date 0, the date at which he lends to the firm, and utility of consumption $u(c(\omega))$ at date 1, date at which he receives the return from investment. There is macroeconomic uncertainty in that the representative consumer's date-1 consumption depends on the state of nature ω. The state of nature describes both what happens in this particular firm and in the rest of the economy (even though aggregate consumption is independent of the outcome in this particular firm to the extent that the firm is atomistic, which we will assume).

Suppose that the entrepreneur works. Let S denote the event "the project succeeds" and F the event "the project fails." Let

$$q_S = E\left[\frac{u'(c(\omega))}{u'(c_0)} \;\middle|\; \omega \in S\right]$$

and

$$q_F = E\left[\frac{u'(c(\omega))}{u'(c_0)} \;\middle|\; \omega \in F\right].$$

The firm's activity is said to covary positively with the economy (be "procyclical") if $q_S < q_F$, and negatively (be "countercyclical") if $q_F < q_S$.

Suppose that

$$p_H q_S + (1 - p_H) q_F = 1.$$

(i) Interpret this assumption.

(ii) In the fixed-investment model of Section 3.2 (and still assuming that the entrepreneur is risk neutral), derive the necessary and sufficient condition for the project to receive financing.

(iii) What is the optimal contract between the investors and the entrepreneur? Does it involve maximum punishment ($R_b = 0$) in the case of failure? How would your answer change if the entrepreneur were risk averse? (For simplicity, assume that her only claim is in the firm. She does not hold any of the market portfolio.)

Exercise 3.13 (lender market power). (i) *Fixed investment.* An entrepreneur has cash amount A and wants to invest $I > A$ into a (fixed-size) project. The project yields $R > 0$ with probability p and 0 with probability $1 - p$. The probability of success is p_H if the entrepreneur works and $p_L = p_H - \Delta p$ ($\Delta p > 0$) if she shirks. The entrepreneur obtains private benefit B if she shirks and 0 otherwise. The borrower is protected by limited liability and everyone is risk neutral. The project is worthwhile only if the entrepreneur behaves.

There is a single lender. This lender has access to funds that command an expected rate of return equal to 0 (so the lender would content himself with a 0 rate of return, but he will use his market power to obtain a superior rate of return). Assume

$$V \equiv p_H R - I > 0$$

and let $\bar{A}$ and $\hat{A}$ be defined by

$$p_H\left[R - \frac{B}{\Delta p}\right] = I - \bar{A}$$

and

$$p_H \frac{B}{\Delta p} - \hat{A} = 0.$$

Assume that $\bar{A} > 0$ and that the *lender* makes a take-it-or-leave-it offer to the borrower (i.e., the lender chooses R_b, the borrower's compensation in the case of success).

- What contract is optimal for the lender?
- Is the financing decision affected by lender market power (i.e., compared with the case of competitive lenders solved in Section 3.2)?
- Draw the borrower's *net* utility (i.e., net of A) as a function of A and note that it is nonmonotonic (distinguish four regions: $(-\infty, \bar{A})$, $[\bar{A}, \hat{A})$, $[\hat{A}, I)$, $[I, \infty)$). Explain.

(ii) *Variable investment.* Answer the first two bullets in question (i) (lender's optimal contract and impact of lender market power on the investment decision) in the variable-investment version. In particular, show that lender market power reduces the scale of investment. (Reminder: I is chosen in $[0, \infty)$. The project yields RI if successful and 0 if it fails. Shirking, which reduces the probability of success from p_H to p_L, yields private benefit BI. Assume that $p_H R > 1 > p_H(R - B/\Delta p)$. Hint: show that the two constraints in the lender's program are binding.)

Exercise 3.14 (liquidation incentives). This exercise extends the fixed-investment model of Section 3.2 by adding a signal on the profitability of the project that (a) accrues after effort has been chosen, and (b) is privately observed. (The following model is used as a building block in a broader context by Dessi (2005).)

An entrepreneur has cash A and wants to invest $I > A$ into a project. The project yields R (success) or 0 (failure) at the end. An intermediate signal reveals the probability y that the project will succeed, with $y = \bar{y}$ or $\underline{y}$ ($\bar{y} = \underline{y} + \Delta y$ and $\Delta y > 0$). The probability, p, that $y = \bar{y}$ depends on the entrepreneur's effort. If the entrepreneur behaves, then $p = p_H$ and the entrepreneur receives no private benefit. If the entrepreneur misbehaves, then $p = p_L$

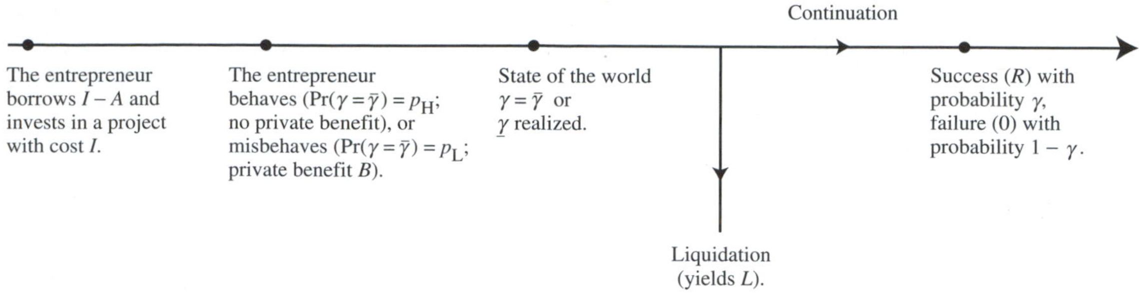

Figure 3.11

and the entrepreneur receives private benefit B. Investors and entrepreneur are risk neutral and the latter is protected by limited liability. The competitive rate of return is equal to 0.

Introduce further an option to liquidate after the signal is realized but before the final profit accrues. Liquidation yields L, and L is entirely pledgeable to investors.

One will assume that

$$\bar{\gamma}R > L > \underline{\gamma}R,$$

so that it is efficient to liquidate if and only if the signal is bad; and that

$$p_H\bar{\gamma}R + (1 - p_H)L > I$$

(which will imply that the NPV is positive).

Figure 3.11 summarizes the timing.

(i) Suppose first that γ is verifiable. Argue that the entrepreneur should be rewarded solely as a function of the realization of γ. What is the pledgeable income? Show that the project is financed if and only if $A \geqslant \bar{A}$, where

$$p_H\left(\bar{\gamma}R - \frac{B}{\Delta p}\right) + (1 - p_H)L = I - \bar{A}.$$

(ii) Suppose now that γ is observed only by the entrepreneur. This implies that the entrepreneur must be induced to tell the truth about γ. Without loss of generality, consider an incentive scheme in which the entrepreneur receives R_b in the case she announces $\gamma = \bar{\gamma}$ (and therefore the project continues) *and* the final profit is R, L_b if she announces $\gamma = \underline{\gamma}$ (and therefore the project is liquidated), and 0 otherwise.

Show that the project is funded if and only if

$$A \geqslant \bar{A} + \underline{\gamma}\frac{B}{(\Delta p)(\Delta \gamma)}.$$

Exercise 3.15 (project riskiness and credit rationing). Consider the basic, fixed-investment model (the investment is I, the entrepreneur borrows $I - A$; the probability of success is p_H (no private benefit) or $p_L = p_H - \Delta p$ (private benefit B), success (failure) yields verifiable profit R (respectively 0)). There are two variants, "A" and "B," of the projects, which differ only with respect to "riskiness":

$$p_H^A R^A = p_H^B R^B, \quad \text{but } p_H^A > p_H^B;$$

so project B is "riskier." The investment cost is the same for both variants and, furthermore,

$$p_H^A - p_L^A = p_H^B - p_L^B.$$

Which variant is less prone to credit rationing?

Exercise 3.16 (scale versus riskiness tradeoff). Consider an entrepreneur with a project of variable investment I. The entrepreneur has initial wealth A, is risk neutral, and is protected by limited liability. Investors are risk neutral and demand a rate of return equal to 0.

The project comes in two versions:

Risky. The project costs I and ends up (potentially) productive only with probability $x < 1$. The timing goes as follows. (a) The scale of investment I is selected. (b) After the investment has been sunk, news accrues as to the profitability of the project. With probability $1 - x$, the project stops and yields 0. With probability x, the project continues (without any need for reinvestment). In the latter case, (c) the entrepreneur chooses an effort; good behavior confers no private benefit on the entrepreneur and yields subsequent probability of success p_H; misbehavior confers private benefit BI and yields probability of success p_L. Finally, (d) the outcome accrues: success yields RI and failure 0.

Safe. The investment cost, XI with $X > 1$, is higher for a given size I. But the project is always productive ("$x = 1$"). The moral hazard and outcome stages are as in the case of a risky choice.

We will assume that the contract aims at inducing good behavior. Letting

$$\rho_1 \equiv p_H R \quad \text{and} \quad \rho_0 \equiv p_H\left(R - \frac{B}{\Delta p}\right),$$

one will further assume that $x > 1/\rho_1$ and $X < \rho_1$.

Assume that entrepreneur and investors contract on which version will be selected.

(i) Show that the risky version is chosen if and only if

$$xX \geqslant 1.$$

(ii) Interpret this condition in terms of a "cost of bringing 1 unit of investment to completion."

Exercise 3.17 (competitive product market interactions). There is a mass 1 of identical entrepreneurs with the variable-investment technology described in Section 3.4. The representative entrepreneur has wealth A, is risk neutral, and is protected by limited liability.

Denote the average investment by I and the individual investment i (in equilibrium $i = I$ by symmetry but we need to distinguish the two in a first step in order to compute the competitive equilibrium). A project produces Ri units of goods when successful and 0 when it fails. The probability of success is p_H in the case of good behavior (the entrepreneur receives no private benefit) and $p_L = p_H - \Delta p$ in the case of misbehavior (the entrepreneur then receives private benefit Bi). Assume that it is optimal to induce the entrepreneur to behave.

The market price of output is $P = P(Q)$, with $P' < 0$, where Q is aggregate production (with $P(Q)$ tending to 0 as Q goes to infinity, to ensure that aggregate investment is finite). Finally, the shocks faced by the firms are independent (there is no industry-wide uncertainty) and the risk-neutral investors demand a rate of return equal to 0.

Show that the equilibrium is unique. Compute the equilibrium level of investment. (Hint: distinguish two cases, depending on whether A is large or small.)

Exercise 3.18 (maximal incentives principle in the fixed-investment model). Pursue the analysis of Section 3.4.3, but for the fixed-investment model of Section 3.2: the investment cost I is given and the income is either R^S or R^F (instead of R or 0), where $R^S > R^F > 0$. We assume that

$$R^F < I - A,$$

so the project cannot be straightforwardly financed by bringing in net worth A and pledging the lower income R^F to lenders. Let

$$R \equiv R^S - R^F$$

denote the increase in income from the low to the high level. Show that the debt contract is optimal, but unlike in the variable-investment case it may not be uniquely optimal.

Exercise 3.19 (balanced-budget investment subsidy and profit tax). This exercise shows that a balanced-budget public policy that is not based on information that is superior to investors' does not boost pledgeable income and therefore outside financing capacity (unless there are externalities among firms: see Exercise 3.17). This general point is illustrated in the context of the variable-investment model: an entrepreneur has cash amount A and wants to invest $I > A$ into a (variable size) project. The project yields $RI > 0$ with probability p and 0 with probability $1 - p$. The probability of success is p_H if the entrepreneur works and $p_L = p_H - \Delta p$ ($\Delta p > 0$) if she shirks. The entrepreneur obtains private benefit BI if she shirks and 0 otherwise. The borrower is protected by limited liability and everyone is risk neutral. The project is worthwhile only if the entrepreneur behaves. Competitive lenders demand a zero expected rate of return. Assume that the NPV is positive:

$$\rho_1 \equiv p_H R > 1,$$

but

$$\rho_0 \equiv p_H\left(R - \frac{B}{\Delta p}\right) < 1.$$

The government has two instruments: a subsidy s per unit of investment, and a proportional tax t on the final profit.

The government must set (s, t) so as to balance its budget. Show that the government's policy is neutral:

$$I = \frac{A}{1-\rho_0} \quad \text{and} \quad U_b = (\rho_1 - 1)I$$

for any (s, t), where U_b is the entrepreneur's utility.

Exercise 3.20 (variable effort, the marginal value of net worth, and the pooling of equity). In the fixed-investment model, the shadow price of entrepreneurial net worth is equal to 0 almost everywhere and is infinite at the threshold $A = \bar{A}$. A more continuous response arises when the entrepreneur's effort is continuous rather than discrete. The object of this exercise is to show that the shadow price is positive and *decreasing in* A in the range in which the entrepreneur is able to finance her project but must borrow from investors. It then applies the analysis to the internal allocation of funds between two divisions.

An entrepreneur has cash A and wants to invest $I > A$ into a fixed-size project. The project yields R with probability p and 0 with probability $1 - p$. Reaching a probability of success p requires the entrepreneur to sink (unobservable) effort cost $\frac{1}{2}p^2$ (there is no private benefit in this version). The borrower is risk neutral and is protected by limited liability. Investors are risk neutral and the market rate of interest is 0. Assume that $\sqrt{2I} < R < 1$.

(i) Note that, had the borrower no need to borrow ($A \geqslant I$), the borrower's net utility would be

$$U_b = V^* = \tfrac{1}{2}R^2 - I,$$

independently of A.

(ii) Find the threshold $\bar{A}$ under which the project is not funded. (Hint: write the pledgeable income as a function of the entrepreneur's reward R_b in the case of success. Argue that one can focus attention on the values of R_b that exceed $\frac{1}{2}R$. Do not forget that the NPV must be nonnegative.)

Letting $V(A)$ denote the NPV in the region in which the entrepreneur's project is financed. Show that the shadow price of net worth, $V'(A)$, satisfies

$$V'(A) > 0,$$
$$V'(I) = 0,$$
$$V''(A) < 0.$$

(iii) Following Cestone and Fumagalli (2005), consider two entrepreneurs, each with net worth A. They will each have a project described as above, but with random investment cost. For simplicity, one of them will face investment cost I_H and the other I_L, where

$$I_L - A < \tfrac{1}{4}R^2 < I_H - A,$$

but it is not known in advance who will face which investment cost (each is equally likely to be the lucky entrepreneur). Investment costs, however, will become publicly known before the investments are sunk. Assume that

$$\tfrac{3}{8}R^2 > I_H,$$

so that the only binding constraint for financing in question (ii) is the investors' breakeven constraint; and that

$$\tfrac{1}{2}R^2 > (I_L + I_H) - 2A,$$

and so both projects can be financed by pooling resources. Do the entrepreneurs, behind the veil of ignorance, want to pool their resources and commit to force the lucky firm to cross-subsidize the unlucky one? (Hint: show that under pooling, and, if both invest, the net worth is split so that both entrepreneurs have the same stake in success.)

Exercise 3.21 (hedging or gambling on net worth?). Froot et al. (1993) analyze an entrepreneur's risk preferences with respect to net worth. In the notation of this book, the situation they consider is summarized in Figure 3.12.

The entrepreneur is risk neutral and protected by limited liability. The investors are risk neutral and demand a rate of return equal to 0.

At date 0, the entrepreneur decides whether to insure against a date-1 income risk

$$r = A_0 + \varepsilon,$$

where $\varepsilon \in [\underline{\varepsilon}, \bar{\varepsilon}]$, $E[\varepsilon] = 0$, and $A_0 + \underline{\varepsilon} \geqslant 0$.

For simplicity, we allow only a choice between full hedging and no hedging (the theory extends straightforwardly to arbitrary degrees of hedging). Hedging (which wipes out the noise and thereby guarantees that the entrepreneur has cash on hand A_0 at date 1) is costless.

After receiving income, the entrepreneur uses her cash to finance investment I and must borrow $I - A$ from investors, with $A = A_0$ in the case of hedging and $A = A_0 + \varepsilon$ in the absence of hedging (provided that $A \leqslant I$; otherwise there is no need to borrow).

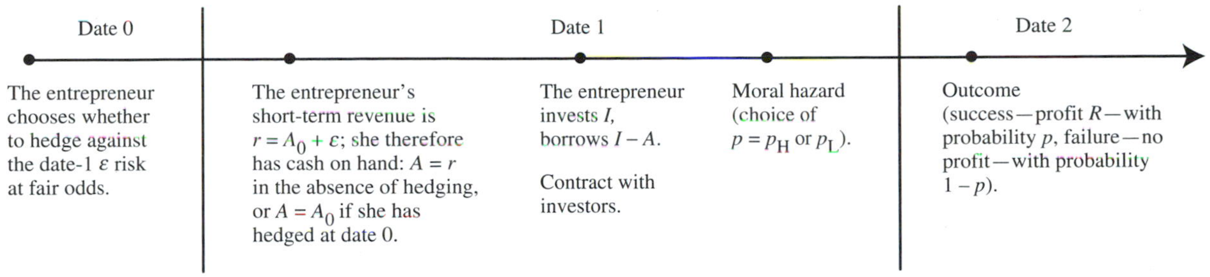
Date 0
Date 1
Date 2
The entrepreneur chooses whether to hedge against the date-1 ε risk at fair odds.
The entrepreneur's short-term revenue is r = A0 + ε; she therefore has cash on hand: A = r in the absence of hedging, or A = A0 if she has hedged at date 0.
The entrepreneur invests I, borrows I − A.
Contract with investors.
Moral hazard (choice of p = pH or pL).
Outcome (success—profit R—with probability p, failure—no profit—with probability 1 − p).

Figure 3.12

Note that there is no overall liquidity management as there is no contract at date 0 with the financiers as to the future investment.

This exercise investigates a variety of situations under which the entrepreneur may prefer either hedging or "gambling" (here defined as "no hedging").

(i) *Fixed investment, binary effort.* Suppose that the investment size is fixed (as in Section 3.2), and that the entrepreneur at date 1, provided that she receives funding, either behaves (probability of success p_H, no private benefit) or misbehaves (probability of success p_L, private benefit B). As usual, the project is not viable if it induces misbehavior and has a positive NPV ($p_H R > I > p_L R + B$, where R is the profit in the case of success). Let $\bar{A}$ be defined (as in Section 3.2) by

$$p_H\left(R - \frac{B}{\Delta p}\right) = I - \bar{A}.$$

Suppose that ε has a wide support.

Show that the entrepreneur

- hedges if $A_0 \geqslant \bar{A}$,
- gambles if $A_0 < \bar{A}$.

(ii) *Fixed investment, continuous effort.* Suppose, as in Exercise 3.20, that succeeding with probability p involves an unverifiable private cost $\frac{1}{2}p^2$ for the entrepreneur (so, effort in this subquestion involves a cost rather than the loss of a private benefit). (Assume $R < 1$ to ensure that probabilities are smaller than 1.)

Write the investors' breakeven condition as well as the NPV as functions of the entrepreneur's stake, R_b, in success. Note that one can focus without loss of generality on $R_b \in [\frac{1}{2}R, R]$. Assume that $I - A_0 < \frac{1}{4}R^2$ and that the support of ε is sufficiently small that the entrepreneur always receives funding when she does not hedge (and *a fortiori* when she hedges). This assumption eliminates the concerns about financing of investment that were crucial in question (i).

Show that the entrepreneur hedges.

(iii) *Variable investment.* Return to the binary effort case ($p = p_H$ or p_L), but assume that the investment I is variable (as in Section 3.4). The income is RI in the case of success and 0 in the case of failure. The private benefit of misbehaving is $B(I)$ with $B' > 0$. Assume that the size of investment is always constrained by the pledgeable income and that the optimal contract induces good behavior.

Show that the entrepreneur

- hedges if $B(\cdot)$ is convex;
- is indifferent between hedging and gambling if $B(\cdot)$ is linear;
- gambles if $B(\cdot)$ is concave.

(iv) *Variable investment and unobservable income.* Suppose that the investment size is variable and that the income from investment $R(I)$ is unobservable by investors (fully appropriated by the entrepreneur) and is concave. Suppose that it is always optimal for the entrepreneur to invest her cash on hand.

Show that the entrepreneur hedges.

(v) *Liquidity and risk management.* Suppose, in contrast with Froot et al.'s analysis, that the entrepreneur can sign a contract with investors at date 0. Show that the entrepreneur's utility can be maximized by insulating the date-1 volume of investment from the realization of ε, i.e., with full hedging, even in situations where gambling was optimal when funding was secured only at date 1.

References

Banerjee, A. and E. Duflo. 2000. Reputation effects and the limits of contracting: a study of the Indian software industry. *Quarterly Journal of Economics* 115:989–1017.

Bester, H. and M. Hellwig. 1987. Moral hazard and credit rationing: an overview of the issues. In *Agency Theory, Information, and Incentives* (ed. G. Bamberg and K. Spremann). Heidelberg: Springer.

Bhattacharya, S. and A. Faure-Grimaud. 2001. The debt hangover: renegotiation with noncontratible investment. *Economics Letters* 70:413–419.

Bizer, D. and DeMarzo, P. 1992. Sequential banking. *Journal of Political Economy* 100:41–61.

Bolton, P. and O. Jeanne. 2004. Structuring and restructuring sovereign debt: the role of seniority. Mimeo, Princeton University.

Bolton, P. and D. Scharfstein. 1990. A theory of predation based on agency problems in financial contracting. *American Economic Review* 80:93–106.

——. 1996. Optimal debt structure with multiple creditors. *Journal of Political Economy* 104:1–26.

Border, K. and J. Sobel. 1987. Samurai accountant: a theory of auditing and plunder. *Review of Economic Studies* 54: 525–540.

Bulow, J. and K. Rogoff. 1989a. A constant recontracting model of sovereign debt. *Journal of Political Economy* 97: 155–178.

——. 1989b. Multilateral negotiations for rescheduling developing country debt: a bargaining theoretic framework. In *Analytical Issues in Debt* (ed. J. Frenkel, M. Dooley, and P. Wickham). Washington, D.C.: IMF.

Cestone, G. and C. Fumagalli. 2005. The strategic impact of resource flexibility in business groups. *RAND Journal of Economics* 36:193–214.

Chang, C. 1990. The dynamic structure of optimal debt contracts. *Journal of Economic Theory* 52:68–86.

——. 1993. Payout policy, capital structure, and compensation contracts when managers value control. *Review of Financial Studies* 6:911–933.

Chiesa, G. 1992. Debt and warrants: agency problems and mechanism design. *Journal of Financial Intermediation* 2: 237–254.

DeGroot, M. 1970. *Optimal Statistical Decisions*. New York: McGraw-Hill.

Dessi, R. 2005. Start-up finance, monitoring and collusion. *RAND Journal of Economics* 36:255–274.

Dewatripont, M., P. Legros, and S. Matthews. 2003. Moral hazard and capital structure dynamics. *Journal of the European Economic Association* 1:890–930.

Diamond, D. 1984. Financial intermediation and delegated monitoring. *Review of Economic Studies* 51:393–414.

Diamond, D. 1991. Monitoring and reputation: the choice between bank loans and directly placed debt. *Journal of Political Economy* 99:689–721.

Doidge, C., A. Karolyi, and R. Stulz. 2004. Why are foreign firms listed in the U.S. worth more? *Journal of Financial Economics* 71:205–238.

Easterbrook, F. 1984. Two-agency-cost explanations of dividends. *American Economic Review* 74:650–659.

Eaton, J. and M. Gersovitz. 1981. Debt with potential repudiations: theoretical and empirical analysis. *Review of Economic Studies* 48:289–309.

Edlin, A. S. and B. Hermalin. 2000. Contract renegotiation and options in agency. *Journal of Law, Economics, & Organization* 16:395–423.

——. 2001. Implementing the first best in an agency relationship with renegotiation: a corrigendum. *Econometrica* 69:1391–1395.

Fama, E. and M. Miller. 1972. *The Theory of Finance*. New York: Holt, Rinehart and Winton.

Fazzari, S., R. G. Hubbard, and B. C. Petersen. 1988. Financing constraints and corporate investment. *Brookings Papers on Economic Activity* 1:141–195.

Fernandez, R. and R. Rosenthal. 1990. Strategic models of sovereign-debt renegotiations. *Review of Economic Studies* 57:331–350.

Froot, K., D. Scharfstein, and J. Stein. 1993. Risk management: coordinating corporate investment and financing policies. *Journal of Finance* 48:1629–1658.

Fudenberg, D. and J. Tirole. 1990. Moral hazard and renegotiation in agency contracts. *Econometrica* 58:1279–1320.

——. 1991. *Game Theory*. Cambridge, MA: MIT Press.

Gale, D. and M. Hellwig. 1985. Incentive-compatible debt contracts: the one-period problem. *Review of Economic Studies* 52:647–663.

——. 1989. Repudiation and renegotiation: the case of sovereign debt. *International Economic Review* 30:3–31.

——. 1994. Renegotiation in debt contracts. PhD thesis, Ecole Polytechnique, Paris.

Hart, O. 1985. A comment on Stiglitz and Weiss. Mimeo, MIT.

Hart, O. and J. Moore. 1989. Default and renegotiation: a dynamic model of debt. Mimeo, MIT and LSE. (Published in *Quarterly Journal of Economics* (1998) 113:1–42.)

——. 1995. Debt and seniority: an analysis of the role of hard claims in constraining management. *American Economic Review* 85:567–585.

——. 1999. Foundations of incomplete contracts. *Review of Economic Studies* 66:115–138.

Hellwig, C. and G. Lorenzoni. 2004. Bubbles and private liquidity. Mimeo, UCLA and MIT.

Hermalin, B. and M. Katz. 1991. Moral hazard and verifiability: the effects of renegotiation in agency. *Econometrica* 59:1735–1753.

Holmström, B. 1979. Moral hazard and observability. *Bell Journal of Economics* 10:74–91.

Holmström, B. and J. Tirole. 1997. Financial intermediation, loanable funds, and the real sector. *Quarterly Journal of Economics* 112:663–692.

Innes, R. 1990. Limited liability and incentive contracting with ex ante action choices. *Journal of Economic Theory* 52:45–67.

Jaffee, D. and T. Russell. 1976. Imperfect information, uncertainty, and credit rationing. *Quarterly Journal of Economics* 90:651–666.

Jensen, M. 1986. Agency costs of free cash flow, corporate finance and takeovers. *American Economic Review* 76:323–329.

Kaplan, S. N. and L. Zingales. 1997. Do investment-cash flow sensitivities provide useful measures of financing constraints? *Quarterly Journal of Economics* 112:169–216.

Keeton, W. R. 1979. *Equilibrium Credit Rationing.* New York and London: Garland.

Kehoe, T. and D. Levine. 1993. Debt-constrained asset markets. *Review of Economic Studies* 60:865–888.

Kocherlakota, N. 1996. Implications of efficient risk sharing without commitment. *Review of Economic Studies* 63:595–609.

Krasa, S. and A. Villamil. 1994. Optimal contracts with costly state verification: the multilateral case. *Economic Theory* 4:167–187.

——. 2000. Optimal contracts when enforcement is a decision variable. *Econometrica* 68:119–134.

Kreps, D., P. Milgrom, J. Roberts, and R. Wilson. 1982. Rational cooperation in the finitely repeated prisoner's dilemma. *Journal of Economic Theory* 27:245–252.

Lacker, J. 1991. Why is there debt? *Economic Review, Federal Reserve Bank of Richmond* 77(4):3–19.

——. 1992. Collateralized debt as the optimal contract. Mimeo, Federal Reserve Bank of Richmond.

Lacker, J. and J. Weinberg. 1989. Optimal contracts under costly state verification. *Journal of Political Economy* 97: 1345–1363.

Ma, C. A. 1991. Adverse selection in a dynamic moral hazard. *Quarterly Journal of Economics* 106:255–275.

——. 1994. Renegotiation and optimality in agency contracts. *Review of Economic Studies* 61:109–130.

Maskin, E. 1977. Nash equilibrium and welfare optimality. Mimeo, MIT. (Published in *Review of Economic Studies* (1999) 66:23–38.)

Maskin, E. and J. Moore. 1999. Implementation and renegotiation. *Review of Economic Studies* 66:39–56.

Maskin, E. and J. Tirole. 1999. Unforeseen contingencies and incomplete contracts. *Review of Economic Studies* 66:83–114.

Matthews, S. 1995. Renegotiation of sales contracts. *Econometrica* 63:567–590.

——. 2001. Renegotiating moral hazard contracts under limited liability and monotonicity. *Journal of Economic Theory* 97:1–29.

Milgrom, P. 1981. Good news and bad news: representation theorems and applications. *Bell Journal of Economics* 12: 380–391.

Miller, D. 1999. The market reaction to international cross-listings: evidence from depositary receipts. *Journal of Financial Economics* 51:103–123.

Mirrlees, J. 1975. The theory of moral hazard and unobservable behaviour. Part I. Mimeo, University of Oxford. (Published in *Review of Economic Studies* (1999) 66:3–21.)

Mookherjee, D. and I. P'ng. 1989. Optimal auditing, insurance and redistribution. *Quarterly Journal of Economics* 104:399–415.

Myers, S. 1977. Determinants of corporate borrowing. *Journal of Financial Economics* 5:147–175.

Padilla, J. and M. Pagano. 2000. Sharing default information as a borrower discipline device. *European Economic Review* 44:1951–1980.

Pagano, M. and P. Volpin. 2005. Shareholder protection, stock market development, and politics. Presented as the Marshall Lecture European Economic Association meeting, Amsterdam, August 27, 2005.

Pagano, M., O. Randl, A. A. Roell, and J. Zechner. 2001. What makes stock exchanges succeed? Evidence from cross-listing decisions. *European Economic Review* 45:770–782.

Povel, P. and M. Raith. 2004. Optimal debt with unobservable investments. *RAND Journal of Economics* 35:599–616.

Reese, W. and M. Weisbach. 2002. Protection of minority shareholder interests, cross-listings in the United States, and subsequent equity offerings. *Journal of Financial Economics* 68:65–104.

Segal, I. 1999. Contracting with externalities. *Quarterly Journal of Economics* 114:337–388.

Segal, I. and M. Whinston. 2002. The Mirrlees approach to mechanism design with renegotiation (with applications to hold-up and risk-sharing). *Econometrica* 70:1–45.

Shavell, S. 1979. Risk sharing and incentives in the principal and agent relationship. *Bell Journal of Economics* 10:55–73.

Snyder, C. 1994. Income shifting, slack constraints, and long-term financial contracts. In "Buyers, suppliers, competitors: the interaction between a firm's horizontal and vertical relationships," Chapter 2. PhD thesis, MIT.

Stiglitz, J. and A. Weiss. 1981. Credit rationing in markets with imperfect information. *American Economic Review* 71:393–410.

Tirole, J. 1999. Incomplete contracts: where do we stand? *Econometrica* 67:741–781.

Townsend, R. 1979. Optimal contracts and competitive markets with costly state verification. *Journal of Economic Theory* 21:417–425.

Webb, D. 1992. Two-period financial contracts with private information and costly state verification. *Quarterly Journal of Economics* 107:1113–1123.

Williamson, O. 1986. Costly monitoring, financial intermediation, and equilibrium credit rationing. *Journal of Monetary Economics* 18:159–179.

Winton, A. 1995. Costly state verification and multiple investors: the role of seniority. *Review of Financial Studies* 8:91–123.

4

Some Determinants of Borrowing Capacity

4.1 Introduction: The Quest for Pledgeable Income

This chapter refines the analysis of Chapter 3 by analyzing several factors that increase or reduce the ability to borrow. The fixed-investment variant of Section 3.2 taught us that socially worthwhile projects may not be undertaken because the investors can only be offered a piece of the total cake. Thus, they are reluctant to get involved if they have to finance a major portion of the outlay. The variable-investment variant of Section 3.4 hinted at a theme that will recur throughout this book: for contracting choices of interest,[1] there is a trade-off between value (social surplus, NPV) and pledgeable income (value to investors). An entrepreneur is willing to sacrifice value to raise pledgeable income and thereby secure financing. The total size of the cake is thereby reduced, but if the fraction of the cake that is returned to investors is increased sufficiently, financing becomes more likely. The quest for pledgeable income took a simple form in Section 3.4, namely, a limit on the scale of investment, but the principle of a sacrifice of value to boost pledgeable income will be seen to have broad applicability and to explain a number of our financial institutions. The chapter offers some first illustrations.

Section 4.2 offers a simple presentation of the diversification argument, that is, the possibility for the borrower to pledge her payoff on a project as "collateral" for another, independent project. Such "cross-pledging" can be achieved either through a contract in which the former claim is promised as collateral to the holders of liabilities in the latter project, or by integration of the activities within a single firm, in which liabilities are not "earmarked" to a specific division, but rather joint to all divisions. We analyze the conditions under which diversification alleviates the incentive problem and point at some limits to diversification.

Section 4.3 studies the pledging of real assets as a (partial) guarantee enjoyed by the investors in the case of default. It identifies some factors that make some assets good collateral and studies costs associated with the use of physical assets as collateral. It shows, in particular, that collateral should generally be pledged contingent on poor performance, and that borrowers with weak balance sheets should pledge more collateral if the relationship between borrower and lenders is fraught with moral hazard.

Section 4.4 analyzes the optimal liquidity of the entrepreneur's stake in the firm. Intuitively, letting the entrepreneur cash in earlier rather than later creates a valuable option value: it may be that the entrepreneur faces profitable investment opportunities in new projects or that she needs money for personal reasons before the outcome of the project is realized. A liquid entrepreneurial claim thus raises value; however, by giving the entrepreneur a chance to exit before the performance in the project is known increases the agency cost and therefore reduces the pledgeable income. Section 4.4 investigates the circumstances under which the entrepreneur's claim can indeed be made liquid.

Section 4.5 shows that borrowing may be hampered if the borrower can force renegotiation of the initial loan agreement by threatening not to complete the project. This potential "holdup" problem is particularly serious when the entrepreneur is indispensable to the completion of the project, and when her outside opportunities have become attractive relative to her inside prospects.

1. The choice would be a no-brainer if a contractual choice increased both the value and the pledgeable income relative to another contractual choice: the increased pledgeable income would facilitate financing, and the increased value, which, recall, is appropriated by the borrower under competitive lending, would be more attractive to the borrower.

Lastly, the supplementary section investigates the rationales for group lending, which turn out to be closely related to some of the themes of this chapter. The supplementary section argues that group lending may be an attempt either to use social capital as collateral or to use peer monitoring in order to reduce agency costs.

4.2 Boosting the Ability to Borrow: Diversification and Its Limits

The computation of the equity multiplier in Section 3.4 was conducted under the assumption that the probability of success is independent of the scale of the investment. As we will observe, this implicitly assumed that if an expansion in the scale of "the project" actually stands for an increase in the number of projects, then the projects' outcomes are perfectly correlated (conditional on the effort that is exerted on them).[2] This formalization depicted a polar case in which there are no benefits to diversification.

However, as Diamond (1984) has forcefully argued,[3] diversification may bring substantial incentive benefits when projects are independent. Intuitively, the borrower can *cross-pledge* the incomes of various projects. That is, she can use the income she receives on a successful project as *collateral* for other projects. Such cross-pledging is useless when projects are correlated, because, when a project fails, the collateral posted for this project (the income from other projects) is valueless.

We analyze the incentive benefits from diversification in the cases of two independent projects and of a large number of such projects.[4] We then point at some limits to the diversification argument.

4.2.1 The Benefits of Diversification: The Case of Two Projects

Let us consider two independent and identical projects with fixed investment size I. That is, the two projects are as described in Section 3.2. Projects succeed (yield R) or fail (yield 0). The probability of success is p_H if the entrepreneur behaves (but then receives no private benefit) and p_L if she misbehaves (and receives private benefit B). Let $2A$ denote the entrepreneur's initial wealth, that is, A per project. The borrower is risk neutral and protected by limited liability. The lenders are risk neutral and demand an expected rate of return equal to 0.

If both projects are funded, then the borrower can work on both, shirk on both, or work on either of them. There can also be four outcomes: both projects succeed, they both fail, or only one of them succeeds. It is clear that two projects are undertaken only if the incentive scheme induces the borrower to work on both projects. Otherwise, the borrower would be better off undertaking one project or none.

4.2.1.1 Project Financing

Let us begin with the benchmark of stand-alone financing for each project. Project financing refers to the provision of funding for a given, well-identified project. The analysis is then that of Section 3.2 for

2. One way to think about the case of perfect correlation is to introduce a latent random variable ω that is, say, uniformly distributed on $[0, 1]$ and that is realized after the borrower's choice of efforts on the various projects. If $0 \leqslant \omega < p_L$, then a project succeeds even if the borrower shirked on the project. If $\omega \geqslant p_H$, a project fails even if the borrower worked on the project. Lastly, if $p_L \leqslant \omega < p_H$, a project succeeds if and only if the borrower worked on the project. Note that the latent variable is the same for all projects.

The model with multiple projects with sizes $I_1, \dots, I_n$ and private benefits $B_1, \dots, B_n$ can then be shown to be equivalent to a model with a single project with size $I = \sum_i I_i$ and private benefit $B = \sum_i B_i$. Heuristically, the pledgeable income is the same in the case of multiple projects and of a single, large project.

The reader might intuit that the borrower has more leeway for misbehavior in the case of multiple projects, as she has other alternatives (shirk on some projects and work on others) to working on all projects than shirking on all projects. This intuition, however, is misleading because these "partial deviations" are perfectly detected whenever they might be beneficial. Indeed, suppose $\omega < p_L$ (respectively, $\omega \geqslant p_H$). Then all projects succeed (respectively, fail) regardless of effort and the borrower would be better off shirking on all projects. And if $p_L \leqslant \omega < p_H$, some projects succeed and some fail, proving unambiguously that the borrower has deviated from the strategy of zealousness on all projects. Thus, if the borrower receives nothing in such situations, the best strategy for the borrower is, as in the case of a single project, either to work (on all projects) or to shirk (on all projects). Even with multiple projects, there is a single relevant incentive constraint (work or shirk).

In contrast, the case of independent projects can be represented by a set of independent random variables $\{\omega_i\}_{i=1,\dots,n}$ with the same distribution as ω.

3. See, for example, Cerasi and Daltung (2000), Matutes and Vives (1996), Williamson (1986), and Yanelle (1989) for contributions that make use of Diamond's argument.

4. Similar expositions of the Diamond argument can be found in Holmström (1993) and Hellwig (2000).

each project taken in isolation. The borrower receives R_b in the case of success and 0 in the case of failure of a given project, independently of what happens in the borrower's other activity. As usual, the incentive constraint for a given project is

$$(\Delta p)R_b \geqslant B,$$

and the per-project financing condition is that the pledgeable income exceeds the investors' initial outlay:

$$p_H\left(R - \frac{B}{\Delta p}\right) \geqslant I - A$$

or

$$A \geqslant \bar{A}.$$

This condition can be interpreted as a capital or net worth requirement. If $A < \bar{A}$, project financing is not viable.

Note that project financing does not make full use of the borrower's potential liability. When project 1, say, fails, then with conditional probability p_H (which is the prior probability under statistical independence of the two projects), project 2 is successful and returns R_b to the entrepreneur. Even under limited liability the entrepreneur's income on the first project can be brought down to $[-R_b]$ (conditional on the second project succeeding) rather than 0. We now make use of this observation.

4.2.1.2 Cross-Pledging

Let us now bring the two projects under a single roof (a "firm"), or at least allow joint liability between the two projects, so that the income on one project is used as collateral for the other project. Let R_2, R_1, R_0 denote the borrower's reward when the number of successful projects is 2, 1, 0, respectively. A risk-neutral borrower cares only about her expected reward, and thus the loan agreement should be structured so as to provide the borrower with maximal incentives for a given expected reward

$$p_H^2 R_2 + 2p_H(1 - p_H)R_1 + (1 - p_H)^2 R_0.$$

Intuitively, this requires that the borrower be rewarded only when the two projects are successful, namely, $R_2 > 0$, $R_1 = R_0 = 0$ (or, more precisely, there always exists *one* optimal incentive scheme which rewards the borrower only in the case of full success). Showing this formally is a simple exercise, which we leave to the reader,[5] who can also consult Section 4.7 for a closely related result. Note that $R_1 = 0$ corresponds to full cross-pledging (contrast this with project financing, under which $R_1 = R_b > 0$, where R_b is the entrepreneur's compensation in the case of success in a given project).

Taking this feature of the incentive scheme for granted, the condition that guarantees that the borrower prefers to work on both projects to working on neither is

$$p_H^2 R_2 - 2B \geqslant p_L^2 R_2$$

or

$$(p_H + p_L)R_2 \geqslant 2\frac{B}{\Delta p}. \tag{4.1}$$

Note that this condition implies that the borrower also prefers to work on both projects to working on a single one: by shirking on the second project, say, the borrower reduces the probability of full success by p_H (the probability that the first project succeeds) times Δp (the reduction in the second project's probability of success). And thus the second incentive constraint can be written as

$$p_H(\Delta p)R_2 \geqslant B. \tag{4.2}$$

Since $p_H > \frac{1}{2}(p_H + p_L)$, this second constraint (4.2) is automatically satisfied if the first, (4.1), is.

Let us now compute the expected pledgeable income. It is equal to the expected return on the projects, $2p_H R$, minus the minimum expected payoff to the borrower, $p_H^2 R_2$, that is consistent with incentive compatibility. From (4.1) the latter is

$$p_H^2 R_2 = \frac{2p_H^2 B}{(p_H + p_L)\Delta p} = 2(1 - d_2)\frac{p_H B}{\Delta p},$$

5. There are two incentive constraints. First, the borrower must prefer to work on both projects to working on a single one, and so

$$p_H^2 R_2 + 2p_H(1 - p_H)R_1 + (1 - p_H)^2 R_0 - 2B$$
$$\geqslant p_H p_L R_2 + (p_H + p_L - 2p_H p_L)R_1 + (1 - p_H)(1 - p_L)R_0 - B.$$

She must also prefer working on both projects to working on none, and so

$$p_H^2 R_2 + 2p_H(1 - p_H)R_1 + (1 - p_H)^2 R_0 - 2B$$
$$\geqslant p_L^2 R_2 + 2p_L(1 - p_L)R_1 + (1 - p_L)^2 R_0.$$

It then suffices to show that for a given $\{R_2, R_1, R_0\}$ satisfying these two inequalities, there exists R_2' such that $\{R_2', 0, 0\}$ also satisfies the two inequalities and provides the entrepreneur with the same expected compensation:

$$p_H^2 R_2' = p_H^2 R_2 + 2p_H(1 - p_H)R_1 + (1 - p_H)^2 R_0.$$

where

$$d_2 \equiv \frac{p_L}{p_L + p_H} \in (0, \tfrac{1}{2})$$

is an agency-based measure of economies of diversification into two independent projects. Letting $2A$ denote the borrower's initial net worth (so, A is her per-project cash on hand), the two projects can be funded if

$$2p_H R - 2(1 - d_2)\frac{p_H B}{\Delta p} \geqslant 2I - 2A,$$

or

$$p_H\left[R - (1 - d_2)\frac{B}{\Delta p}\right] \geqslant I - A, \qquad (4.3)$$

or

$$A \geqslant \bar{\bar{A}}, \quad \text{with } \bar{\bar{A}} \equiv I - p_H\left[R - (1 - d_2)\frac{B}{\Delta p}\right] < \bar{A}.$$

Thus, cross-pledging facilitates financing.

Role of correlation. The benefits from cross-pledging come from the diversification effect. We have assumed that projects were independent. Suppose, in contrast, that the two projects are perfectly correlated. Then, condition (3.3) implies that they can both be funded if and only if

$$p_H\left[R - \frac{B}{\Delta p}\right] \geqslant I - A \quad \text{or} \quad A \geqslant \bar{A}.$$

In words, there is no cost to project financing if projects are perfectly correlated. Or, put differently, the effect of diversification, that is, of the independence of the two projects, is tantamount to a reduction of the private benefit from B to $(1 - d_2)B$. Because of the independence of the two projects, the borrower can pledge his income on a project as collateral for the other project, were the second project to fail. Thus *project finance*, namely, a mode of financing that establishes (unrelated) claims on individual projects, *is here suboptimal* unless $d_2 = 0$, that is, unless there are no economies of diversification. We refer to Exercise 4.4 for the study of arbitrary (positive or negative) correlation between the two projects.

Variable investment size. In the case of fixed investment sizes, the benefit from diversification takes the form of a facilitated access to financing. Conditional on getting financing, the total NPV $(2(p_H R - I))$ is, of course, unchanged. With variable investment sizes, the extent of financing, rather than the access to financing, is the issue. Then diversification increases the borrowing capacity and therefore the NPV (see Exercise 4.10).

4.2.2 The Benefits of Diversification: A Large Number of Projects

The previous diversification result extends straightforwardly to n independent projects.

For the purpose of this section, let us assume that

$$p_H R - I < B.$$

The reader will check that a borrower with net worth nA can finance the n projects if and only if

$$p_H\left[R - (1 - d_n)\frac{B}{\Delta p}\right] \geqslant I - A. \qquad (4.4)$$

where

$$d_n = \frac{p_L(p_H^{n-1} - p_L^{n-1})}{p_H^n - p_L^n}$$

increases with n (note that $d_1 = 0$). In the limit as n tends to infinity, d_n converges to p_L/p_H and the financing condition converges to

$$p_H R - B \geqslant I - A. \qquad (4.5)$$

That is, in the limit the pledgeable income per project is equal to $p_H R - B$. Intuitively, with a large number of independent projects, shirking on a non-negligible fraction of projects is necessarily detected by the law of large numbers. And so the highest rent that the entrepreneur can grab is her private benefit B on each project.

In this model, increasing the number of projects raises the pledgeable income per project and alleviates incentive problems, but does not fully eliminate credit rationing. Recall that positive-NPV projects satisfy $p_H R \geqslant I$ and that we assumed that

$$p_H R - I < B.$$

For a given total net worth of the borrower, her net worth per project A tends to 0 as n tends to infinity and thus (4.5) is violated. In other words, a borrower with a finite net worth cannot undertake an arbitrarily large number of positive-NPV projects. Thus net worth still plays a role even with a large number of projects.

In contrast, Diamond (1984) showed that a borrower who can avail herself of a large number of projects is never credit rationed, and thus faces no capital (or leverage) requirement. Where does this discrepancy in results come from? Here the borrower can always divert nB in private benefits. So, her rent necessarily grows proportionally with the number of projects.

Alternatively, we could have assumed away private benefits and called B the disutility of working on a project, with the disutility of shirking being normalized at 0. In this "Diamond formulation," a project has positive NPV if $p_H R \geqslant I + B$, as the disutility of effort must be counted as a cost of the project. (In contrast, in the basic formulation the borrower does not take her private benefit.) The incentive conditions remain the same as in the private benefit model, and thus the only difference between the two formulations is the definition of a positive-NPV project. Condition (4.5) then shows that in the Diamond formulation, the borrower can undertake an arbitrarily large number of positive-NPV projects provided that her cash on hand is nonnegative.

This unboundedness and the related lack of capital requirement differentiate the Diamond formulation from the one considered here. But the main message—diversification boosts borrowing capacity—is the same in both formulations.

Remark (optimality of the standard debt contract). Diamond shows that a *debt contract* with investors achieves the social optimum with a large number of projects. Suppose (somewhat informally) that in our formulation (i) there is a continuum of independent projects and (ii) $p_H R - I > B$, so we are in a situation in which the borrower can undertake an infinite number of projects without any initial net worth. Assume indeed that the borrower has no initial net worth ($A = 0$), and let the borrower issue a debt contract in which she must reimburse $D = I$ (we normalize the mass of projects to one). Investors are willing to purchase this debt claim if and only if the probability of default is equal to 0.

Let us first check that the borrower prefers behaving on all projects to shirking on all. The "law of large numbers"[6] implies that the firm's total income is $p_H R$ in the former case and $p_L R$ in the latter case. As $p_H R > I > p_L R$, the borrower's residual claims are $p_H R - I$ and 0, respectively. So, the borrower prefers working on all projects if and only if $p_H R - I > B$, which we have assumed in order to guarantee that the borrower needs no capital to undertake a large number of projects.

More generally, it is easy to check that the borrower does not benefit from working on a fraction of projects and shirking on the remaining fraction. Suppose the borrower works on a fraction κ of projects. Either $\kappa p_H R + (1 - \kappa) p_L R < I$, and then there is default and the borrower would be better off shirking on all projects; or $\kappa p_H R + (1 - \kappa) p_L R \geqslant I$, and then

$$\frac{d}{d\kappa}[\kappa p_H R + (1 - \kappa)(p_L R + B)] = (\Delta p)R - B > 0,$$

and so, if $\kappa < 1$, the borrower, who receives the firm's incremental income once debt is fully reimbursed, is better off increasing κ.

The logic of the argument is clear: a debt contract makes the borrower *residual claimant* of profits whenever there is no default. So she has proper incentives to work as long as she does not choose to default (we employ "choose" on purpose, because the law of large numbers implies that there is no surprise as to whether default occurs).

4.2.3 Limits to Diversification

While the point that diversification can alleviate incentive problems and lower capital requirements is an important one, it should be realized that there are in practice a number of obstacles to diversification.

Endogenous correlation. The key to the diversification argument is that projects are independent, so that if one fails another is still likely to succeed and the latter's income is thus good collateral for the former. An important implicit assumption of the diversification argument is that the borrower cannot alter the independence through project choice; for, the borrower has an incentive to choose correlated projects ("asset substitution"). Intuitively, the correlation destroys the value of "collateral," and cross-pledging then is useless.

To illustrate this, consider the contract obtained in the case of two projects

$$\{R_2 = 2B/[(\Delta p)(p_H + p_L)],\ R_1 = R_0 = 0\}.$$

Suppose that the manager can choose two independent projects or two perfectly correlated projects,

6. Interpreted very loosely. See Diamond (1984) and Hellwig (2000) for more careful treatments, with a finite number of projects going to infinity.

but that the investors are unable to tell whether the projects are independent or correlated. By choosing correlated projects rather than independent ones, the borrower obtains

$$U_b^c = p_H R_2 > U_b^i = p_H^2 R_2,$$

where "c" stands for "correlated projects" and "i" for "independent projects," and so diversification does not occur.

This point, which is related to the discussion of "asset substitution" in Chapter 7, should not surprise the reader. The borrower's claim is an equity claim, and is therefore convex in realized income. The borrower's incentive structure makes her risk loving (even though her intrinsic preferences exhibit risk neutrality). Under correlation, the probabilities of 2, 1, and 0 successes are $(p_H, 0, 1 - p_H)$, while they are $(p_H^2, 2p_H(1 - p_H), (1 - p_H)^2)$ in the case of independent projects. Correlation therefore induces a mean-preserving spread of the distribution. And, as is well-known, risk lovers benefit from a mean-preserving spread.

Similarly, consider Diamond's debt contract, which, recall, implements the optimum with a large number of projects. Assume again that the borrower can choose between independent projects and correlated projects. Then

$$U_b^c = p_H(R - I) > U_b^i = p_H R - I,$$

so the borrower prefers correlation.

The theoretical concern expressed here underlies much of corporate risk management and of prudential reforms attempting to measure a bank's "value at risk." The covariance among activities of a firm or of a financial institution such as a bank, or of a division thereof, is often hard to measure. Financial innovation, in particular the development of derivatives, such as swaps, futures, and options, has created new opportunities for insurance against external shocks (such as interest rate or exchange rate shocks). This in principle should alleviate incentive problems by protecting managers from shocks they have no control over and thereby making them more accountable.[7] On the other hand, derivatives and other financial products can be used in the opposite direction to *increase* rather than decrease risk; and it often proves difficult for outsiders to estimate the risk pattern of a firm's or a division's portfolio. Consequently, boards of directors or chief executive officers are concerned about a division or a trader losing fortunes through nondiversified portfolios. Similarly, bank depositors (or rather their representatives, namely, the banking supervisors) are worried about failure of nondiversified banks and have been actively designing methods for measuring the riskiness of a portfolio so as to better tailor capital requirements to this riskiness.

Core business competency. Another obvious obstacle to diversification is that the borrower often has expertise only in limited sectors. Expanding within the realm of the core business may not substantially improve diversification as new activities are subject to the same industry-wide shocks as existing ones. On the other hand, diversification outside the core business activities generates inefficiencies (which can easily be modeled in our framework by introducing, say, new and independent projects with increasing stand-alone capital requirements).[8] In such situations, diversification need not boost debt capacity.

Limited attention. To the extent that diversification goes together with an increase in the number of projects, there is some concern that the borrower cannot handle that many projects. The borrower can, of course, expand and delegate the supervision of these projects to other agents, but this introduces further agency problems. Therefore, there exists a cost to diversifying through expansions.[9]

Remark (the diversification discount). A number of empirical studies, starting with Wernerfelt and Montgomery (1988), have shown that diversification

7. See Holmström (1979), Shavell (1979), as well as Section 3.2.6. Loosely stated, the "sufficient statistic theorem" states that an agent's reward should depend only on variables over which she has control.

8. A number of observers believe that the diversification of the U.S. Savings and Loans away from residential mortgages and toward commercial real estate, instalment loans, credit card loans, and corporate securities increased rather than decreased their probability of failure (this diversification was allowed by regulators in the early 1980s in response to the serious hardships then faced by the S&Ls).

9. There is a large literature on the "span of control" and the incentive cost associated with bigger hierarchies. See, for example, Calvo and Wellisz (1978, 1979), Aghion and Tirole (1997), and the references therein.

is associated with low firm value. This observation raises questions about the direction of causality (is diversification the cause of the diversification discount?) and, relatedly, as to why diversification is still so widespread despite the popularity of refocusing. Is diversification the outcome of inefficient empire building and, if so, why are boards of directors and shareholders so complacent toward managerial recommendations in this respect? Or do diversified firms simply differ from specialized ones in a number of characteristics, as several studies have indicated? For example, Villalonga (2004a,b) shows that diversified firms are present in industries with a low Tobin's q[10] and have a lower percentage of their stock owned by institutions and insiders; she argues that the diversification discount cannot be attributed to diversification itself.

We have little to say about the possibility of empire building at this stage of the book.[11] More generally, the Diamond argument is too simplistic to address the empirical evidence regarding diversification; yet it is interesting to look at its consequences. Its logic implies that it is silent about the return expected by uninformed investors: the latter receive the market rate of return regardless of the entrepreneur's diversification decision. So a diversification discount, if any, must apply to total investor shares, which in this barebones model, also include the entrepreneur's shares (or insiders' and informed investors' shares in a broader model). Consider moving from one project to two in the model above. There are several reasons why the added project may reduce profitability: the second project may have a lower return than the first (for instance, the payoff in the case of success is lower: $R_2 \leqslant R_1$; this is the core business competency argument); the avoidance of asset substitution requires costly monitoring (endogenous correlation argument); or the second project may divert managerial attention from the first (limited attention argument). In each case, the second project reduces average profitability, and yet the entrepreneur may want to undertake it if she has enough funds or the agency cost is low enough.[12] While this exercise shows how a diversification discount may arise from corporate heterogeneity rather than a poor investment pattern, it is somewhat unsatisfactory as it misses the broader discussion of the various relevant dimensions of heterogeneity that would be needed for both a better theoretical understanding of diversification and a more structured estimation of the discount and its underpinnings.

4.2.4 Sequential Projects: The Build-up of Net Worth

Section 4.7, in the supplementary section, investigates the case of a sequence of two projects, project 1 at date 1 and project 2 at date 2.[13] The key difference with the case of two "simultaneous projects" analyzed in Section 4.2.1 is that the outcome (success or failure) in the first project is realized before the investment in the second project needs to be sunk. The new feature is that the investment in the second project can be made contingent on the first project's outcome. In particular, the optimal contract may threaten the entrepreneur with nonrefinancing if the first project fails even though the projects are independent and so there is no learning about the second project's profitability from first-period performance. In the (constant-returns-to-scale) variable-investment context, the main results of that section can be summarized in the following way:

(i) The entrepreneur cannot do better through long-term contracting than entering a sequence of short-term contracts in which the investors are reimbursed only on the current project and break even in each period (no cross-pledging). The entrepreneur receives nothing and does not invest in the second project if she fails in the first period.

10. Tobin's q is equal to the market value of a firm's assets divided by the replacement value of these assets.

11. Managerial rents do grow with firm size in our model, suggesting that the borrower would push for a larger empire. The question is therefore why investors would let the borrower sacrifice investor value to increase her own managerial rent. In Chapter 10, we will discuss reasons why managers often get their own way.

12. It is, furthermore, easy to build examples in which diversified firms have a lower percentage of stocks held by insiders (due to the fact that they have to borrow more).

13. The analysis carries over to an arbitrary number of projects.

(ii) The first-period investment is larger than it would be in the absence of a follow-up project. The threat of not being able to finance the second project acts as disciplining device and alleviates date-1 moral hazard. Put differently, the fact that \$1 of entrepreneurial net worth at date 2 is worth more than \$1 to the entrepreneur due to credit rationing makes the entrepreneur more eager to behave at date 1.

(iii) Stakes are increasing: the date-2 investment in the case of date-1 success is larger than the date-1 investment.

(iv) The entrepreneur has a higher utility in the sequential-project case, as the lower agency cost boosts borrowing capacity.

(v) Project correlation need no longer reduce the entrepreneur's utility due to a learning effect: the second-period project's dimension can be made contingent on the first-period outcome, which is then informative about the date-2 prospects.

4.3 Boosting the Ability to Borrow: The Costs and Benefits of Collateralization

In the previous sections, "assets" or "net worth" referred to some form of cash that the borrower was able to put up front to defray part of the cost of investment. Some other assets cannot be used up front to participate in the financing, and yet are "quasi-cash." Suppose for instance that the entrepreneur has no cash but, as a leftover of a previous activity, will deliver some accounts receivables to a buyer, resulting for the entrepreneur in riskless profit A. So total profit will be $R + A$ in the case of success of the current project and A in the case of failure. Obviously, the entrepreneur can pledge this riskless profit A to the lenders, and everything is *as if* the entrepreneur had cash A today. Or, to emphasize the same point, suppose that the entrepreneur has no cash today, but that the investment I is used to purchase equipment or commercial real estate, that is used for the project and will after completion of the project be resold at some riskless price A. This resale value can be pledged as collateral to the lenders and is quasi-cash.

More generally, the ability to pledge productive assets may help raise external finance. This section makes a few points concerning the link between collateral and loan agreements.

4.3.1 Redeployability

We start with the straightforward point that the option to use a productive asset for other purposes outside the firm helps raise external finance. Suppose that we extend the fixed-investment framework of Section 3.2 to allow for the possibility of learning that the investment could have superior alternative uses. More precisely, let I be spent to purchase some productive asset such as land or equipment. After the investment is sunk but before the entrepreneur starts working on the project, a public signal accrues that indicates whether the project is viable:

- with probability x, the project is viable and its characteristics are as described in Section 3.2 (so, the model of Section 3.2 corresponds to $x = 1$);
- with probability $1 - x$, the parties learn that the project will not deliver any income (at least under current management), regardless of the entrepreneur's effort (for example, there might turn out to be no demand for the corresponding product or perhaps the entrepreneur will prove to be an incompetent manager of the assets).

In the second situation, labeled "distress," the asset can be sold to a third party at some exogenous price $P \leqslant I$ (this value of collateral in the case of distress is here taken as exogenous: see the discussion below). A high resale price P corresponds to a highly redeployable asset. By contrast, a specialized asset should fetch a low resale price. Commercial real estate is one of the most redeployable assets, even though resale implies a loss. At the opposite extreme lie highly specific investments such as a die (or, more generally, custom-made equipment) or the personnel's human capital investment into the project. Some equipment with well-organized second-hand markets, such as buses and airplanes, may lie in between.

The timing of this extension of the basic model is summarized in Figure 4.1.

With a positive probability of distress ($x < 1$) and with asset specialization ($P < I$), the condition for a

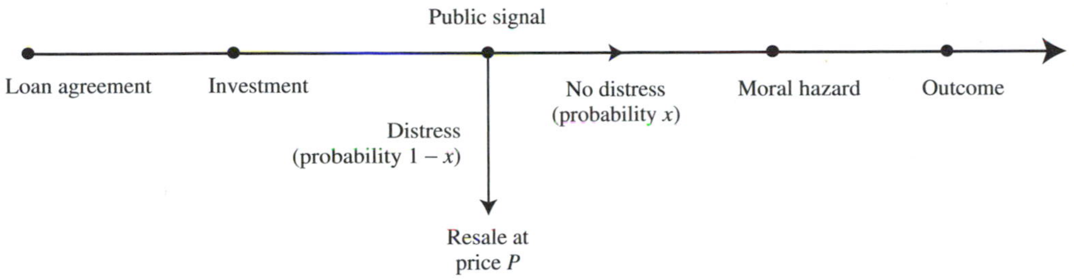

Figure 4.1

positive NPV becomes more stringent,

$$xp_{\mathrm{H}}R + (1-x)P > I,$$

and thus condition (3.1) becomes

$$x(p_{\mathrm{H}}R - I) > (1-x)(I-P). \tag{4.6}$$

That is, the expected profit must dominate the expected capital loss associated with distress. An increase in redeployability, that is, a decrease in the resale discount, $I-P$, of course, makes it more likely that the project be a positive-NPV one.

Assuming (4.6) holds and turning to the lenders' credit analysis, we compute the pledgeable income. Obviously, *it is optimal to pledge the full amount of the resale price in the case of distress to the lenders before committing part of the income R obtained in the case of success.* This results from the fact that pledging the resale value has no adverse incentive effect,[14] while profit sharing reduces the entrepreneur's stake when there is no distress. Accordingly, one possible interpretation of what happens in distress is that the firm goes bankrupt and the lenders seize the collateralized asset.

A necessary and sufficient condition for the project to be funded (the modification of condition (3.3)) is that the pledgeable income exceed the lenders' initial outlay:

$$xp_{\mathrm{H}}\left(R - \frac{B}{\Delta p}\right) + (1-x)P \geqslant I - A. \tag{4.7}$$

The threshold asset level $\bar{A}$, above which the project is funded, is given by condition (4.7) satisfied with equality; it decreases with the redeployability of the asset (as stressed, for example, in Williamson (1988)).[15] That redeployability of assets helps a firm to borrow may explain why a Silicon Valley firm has a hard time borrowing long term and borrows at high spreads over comparable-maturity Treasuries when it can borrow, while a gas pipeline company can borrow more easily and at much lower spreads.

4.3.2 Equilibrium Determination of Asset Values

The analysis of the previous subsection took the resale price P as given. One can broaden the study by investigating the demand side (who are the buyers?) and equilibrium considerations (how is the demand P determined by the interaction of supply and demand in the second-hand asset market?). Several important themes emerge from this broader agenda.

Fire sale externalities and the possibility of surplus-enhancing cartelization. Suppose that multiple firms want to put similar assets on the market when in distress. The competition between them brings down the price P. This has two effects. First, for a given investment level, assets fetch a lower price in the case of distress and so are less valuable than if a single firm disposed of its assets. This is the familiar profit-destruction effect of competition. Second, and more

14. Actually, it would even have a positive incentive effect if the entrepreneur could influence the probability of distress (which is exogenous here).

15. Furthermore, $\bar{A}$ increases with the probability of distress as long as the resale price does not exceed the pledgeable income ($P \leqslant p_{\mathrm{H}}(R - B/\Delta p)$). (Checking the validity of the assumption requires an equilibrium model of the determination of P (see, for example, Chapter 14).)

The ability to resell the asset at a high price here boosts borrowing capacity. This need not always be so if the lenders cannot prevent the borrower from reselling the assets. The borrower may then be more tempted to sell the asset in order to consume the proceeds or finance new, possibly negative NPV, investments if the asset fetches a high resale price (see, for example, Myers and Rajan 1998). Checking whether the asset is not resold for such purposes may be more difficult for assets that may need to be traded for portfolio reasons. (In Chapter 7, we will discuss a different, but related, theme called asset substitution.)

interestingly, the reduction in resale value aggravates credit rationing, and so investment declines. While the first effect, around the competitive equilibrium, amounts to a transfer between sellers and buyers, the latter effect creates a reduction in total surplus.

This raises two issues. First, could the firms not gain from colluding *ex ante* and committing to put only a fraction of the distressed assets on the market? This restraint has a cost and a benefit for the firms. The cost is that they lose the resale price on the distressed assets that they withhold. The benefit (which is a cost to buyers) is that withholding raises the market price P. It turns out that, in the case of a large number of firms and under the maintained hypothesis that assets kept in a distressed firm are worthless, firms are better off cartelizing (i.e., agreeing on a policy of restraint) if and only if the elasticity of demand for the assets is greater than 1.

Second, could cartelization increase total social surplus (buyers' surplus plus sellers' surplus)? In the absence of credit rationing, the answer would be an unambiguous "no": at the margin 1 unit of withheld assets has value $P > 0$ to the buyer and has opportunity cost 0 for the seller (since there is no alternative use of the assets inside the firm). Thus, any withholding would involve a deadweight loss. Not necessarily so under credit rationing: as we noted, the investment expansion creates economic wealth. Total surplus increases, if (fixing the pledgeable income) the NPV is sufficiently large, that is, if the agency cost (measured by the difference between the NPV and the pledgeable income) is large, and the elasticity of demand exceeds 1. This result, as well as that on the elasticity of demand, is demonstrated in Exercise 4.16.

Before connecting those results to a standard debate, though, let us issue the following caveat. Even when cartelization increases total surplus, it does not generate a Pareto-improvement. Indeed, buyers suffer from the increase in price in the resale market. This raises the issue of whether cartelization is an efficient policy to redistribute income toward the corporate sector. The general point illustrated here is that under credit rationing the marginal investment has high profitability, and so any policy that boosts pledgeable income has the potential to increase total surplus. Another such policy consists in subsidizing investment; while it may create moral hazard, it does not lead to an *ex post* inefficient allocation of assets, unlike cartelization. So, even if one ignores distributional issues and focuses on total surplus maximization, boosting pledgeable income may conceivably be achieved through less costly public policies than allowing cartelization.

The deflationary impact of simultaneous sales of assets by firms in distress is sometimes evoked in the context of banking and financial intermediation. During a severe recession, banks and other financial intermediaries often dispose of their assets (real estate, securities, etc.), which lowers the price that they can demand for these assets.[16] For example, it is not uncommon for commercial real estate in big cities to rapidly lose half of its value as a result of fire sales by financial intermediaries. Unsurprisingly, the latter sometimes attempt (perhaps with the help of the central bank as a cartel ring master) to reduce their asset sales in a concerted manner. As we have noted, this strategy pays off only when the elasticity of demand for the relevant assets is sufficiently large.

Corporate mergers and acquisitions markets. The discussion so far has ignored the fact that the buyers of assets are often themselves corporations. Thus buyers and not only sellers face financial constraints. This raises the question of whether the buyers have enough "financial muscle" to purchase the assets.

Another set of issues relates to the possibility that there may be few buyers. Put differently, the equipment, buildings, or intellectual property portfolio of the firm in distress may be exploitable by and therefore of interest to only one or a couple of potential buyers. The resale price is then determined through bargaining.

We treat these issues and others in Chapter 14.

4.3.3 The Costs of Asset Collateralization

As discussed in Section 4.3.1, pledging assets helps the borrower raise funds. Yet, the discussion there was incomplete in that there was no real difference between the firm's *ex post* income and the *ex post*

16. The consequence may be a lower ability to borrow *ex ante*, as formalized above, or a shortage of liquidity, as formalized in Chapter 5.

value of its assets, except for the fact that the assets had value even when income was low. Indeed, the borrower and the lenders had the same marginal rate of substitution between assets and cash; in other words entitlements to cash and to assets were substitute means of transferring income back to the lender. The optimal policy took the form of a pledging of assets rather than income to the lenders: incentive considerations require punishing the borrower in the case of poor performance, and so if poor performance means no or little income, the only possible punishment is the seizing of the assets.

But, somehow, we ought to come up with a *cost* of pledging assets as well as a benefit. In this respect the literature on credit rationing has emphasized that assets may have a lower value for the lenders than for the borrower (Bester 1985, 1987; Besanko and Thakor 1987; Chan and Kanatas 1985).[17] There are at least seven broad reasons for the existence of a deadweight loss attached to collateralization.

(i) There may be *ex ante* and *ex post transaction costs* involved in including liens into loan contracts, in recovering the collateralized assets in default, and in selling the asset to third parties (writing costs, brokerage fees, taxes, or judiciary costs). For example, countries differ in the efficiency and honesty of their courts. Slow trials and uncertainty about how much lenders will recoup in the judiciary process may make them discount the value of collateral, reducing both the borrower's ability to raise funds, and destroying value even if the borrower succeeds in securing a loan.[18]

(ii) The borrower may derive *benefits from ownership* that a third party would not enjoy. For example, the borrower may attach sentimental value to her family house that is mortgaged. Similarly, for a piece of equipment, the borrower may have acquired through *learning by doing or investment in human capital* specific skills to operate this equipment while a would-be acquirer needs to start from scratch and attaches a lower value to the equipment. Or there may be synergies with other productive assets that remain under the entrepreneur's possession.

(iii) Relatedly, *some assets are very hard to sell.* In particular, licensing trade secrets and know-how is quite difficult to the extent that the prospective licensee must know enough in order to be interested in securing a license, but may want to use the (legally unprotected) idea without paying once he has the information (Arrow 1962).

(iv) Alternatively, one may introduce *differential prospects of future credit rationing for the lenders and the borrower.* Suppose the lenders will not be credit rationed in the future while the borrower may be. The borrower, as we have seen, attributes a shadow value in excess of 1 to a unit of retained earnings while the lender does not. (This need not be the case. Lenders may themselves be exposed to credit rationing. See Chapter 13.) It may then be optimal not to confiscate all the borrower's assets in the case of failure even if the borrower is risk neutral.

(v) Contrary to what has been assumed, the borrower may be *risk averse.* Pledging her remaining resources (e.g., a house) in case of bankruptcy may inflict too large a cost on the borrower, given that bankruptcy may result from bad luck and not only from moral hazard.

(vi) The pledging of an asset may induce very *suboptimal maintenance* of the asset by the borrower, if maintenance cannot be carefully specified as part of the loan agreement. This moral-hazard problem is particularly acute when the borrower may receive signals that distress is imminent. Then, the probability that the asset will be transferred to the lenders is high, so that investment in maintenance is privately unprofitable for the borrower. Similarly, the entrepreneur may be unwilling to make follow-on investments into how better to utilize a piece of equipment if there is a nonnegligible probability that it will be reclaimed. It may then be desirable not to use the asset as collateral even if the value of the asset is identical for the borrower and for the lenders. For more on this, see Exercise 4.1.

17. Lacker (1991, 1992) finds conditions under which the optimal contract between a borrower and lenders is a collateralized debt contract, assuming, in particular, that the borrower values the collateral goods more highly than do the lenders.

18. See Jappelli et al. (2005) for Italian and cross-country evidence. For example, credit is harder to obtain in Italian provinces with long trials and large judicial backlogs.

(vii) Lastly, and a more subtle point, assets may come with an *attached managerial rent*, as noted by Holmström (1993). Suppose that the lenders cannot operate the assets themselves. They must then resort to a manager to operate the assets when they seize them. If these assets are again subject to moral hazard in the future, the manager brought in may need to be given a rent in order to behave (this rent is the analog of the term $p_H B/\Delta p$, but applied to future periods). By contrast, the entrepreneur need not concede this rent if she keeps the assets and operates them herself. We conclude that the lenders apply a discount, namely, the managerial rent, to the assets while the entrepreneur does not. (We will come back to this idea more formally in Chapter 14.)

4.3.4 Costly Collateral, Contingent Pledges, and the Strength of the Balance Sheet

Let us therefore posit the existence of a wedge in valuations of collateral, and assume the following:

- The borrower has no cash initially, so that the full investment I is defrayed by the lenders. The investment is used to purchase an asset.
- The asset is used in production, but still has a residual value after income is realized. This residual value is A for the entrepreneur and $A' \leqslant A$ for the lenders (so, there is a deadweight loss of $A - A'$ if the asset is seized).[19] Thus the collateral studied in this subsection is one (such as equipment acquired for, or intellectual property produced by, this project) that would not exist in the absence of funding and investment. By contrast, the next subsection will look at preexisting collateral (such as a family house).

A loan agreement specifies how income is shared in the case of success (as earlier), as well as possibly a contingent right for the lenders to seize the asset. More formally, let R_b and R_l denote the borrower's and the lenders' incomes in the case of success ($R_b + R_l = R$), and let y_S and y_F denote the probabilities that the borrower keeps the asset in the cases of success or failure.

Using the lenders' zero-profit condition and the assumption that the project can be financed only if the borrower is induced to behave, the borrower's utility (gross or net, since she has no cash on hand) is equal to the social surplus from undertaking the project, that is, the expected monetary profit (including the residual value of the asset in its most efficient use) minus the deadweight loss associated with the transfer of the asset to the lenders:

$$\begin{aligned} U_b &= p_H(R_b + y_S A) + (1 - p_H) y_F A \\ &= p_H R - I + A \\ &\quad - [p_H(1 - y_S) + (1 - p_H)(1 - y_F)](A - A'). \end{aligned} \tag{4.8}$$

The optimal loan agreement maximizes U_b subject to the constraints that the borrower be willing to behave and that the lenders break even:

$$(\Delta p)[R_b + (y_S - y_F)A] \geqslant B \tag{IC$_b$}$$

and

$$p_H[R_l + (1 - y_S)A'] + (1 - p_H)(1 - y_F)A' \geqslant I. \tag{IR$_l$}$$

The incentive constraint (IC$_b$) says that the increase in the borrower's expected payoff (income plus increased probability of keeping the asset) associated with good behavior exceeds the private benefit of misbehaving. The "individual rationality" constraint (IR$_l$) requires that the lenders recoup their investment I on average.

As explained in Section 3.2.2, a good measure of the borrower's strength or creditworthiness is her level of pledgeable cash $p_H(R - B/\Delta p)$ compared with investment I. We can therefore measure the strength of the balance sheet in various ways: (minus) the investment level I, or the agency cost (private benefit B, inverse of the likelihood ratio $\Delta p/p_H$ for a given p_H). (Furthermore, if the borrower had some initial cash on hand $\tilde{A}$ that could contribute to defray the investment cost I (so the right-hand side of (IR$_l$) would become $I - \tilde{A}$), the borrower's balance-sheet strength would also increase with this level of cash $\tilde{A}$.) We now perform some comparative statics with respect to the strength of the balance sheet. As the strength of the balance sheet decreases, one observes successively three different regimes.[20]

19. Section 4.3.4 closely follows Holmström (1993).

20. The derivative of the Lagrangian with respect to y_S is positive if that with respect to R_b or that with respect to y_F is. Depending on the values of the parameters, some of the three regimes may not exist.

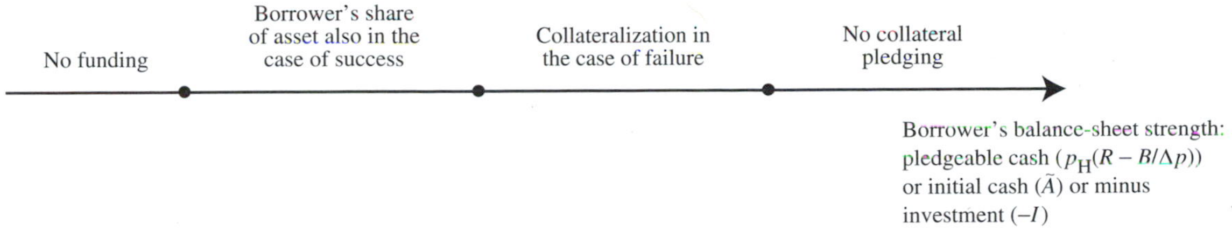

Figure 4.2 Only weak borrowers pledge collateral.

(i) *Strong balance sheet: no collateral:* $\{y_S = y_F = 1, R_b > 0\}$. The borrower always keeps the asset. Because the marginal rate of substitution between asset and money is higher for the borrower than for the lenders, it is optimal for the borrower to pledge money first. This no-collateral regime holds as long as the pledgeable income allows the lenders to recoup their investment, that is, as long as $p_H R - p_H B/\Delta p \geqslant I$.

(ii) *Intermediate balance sheet: collateral in the case of failure:* $\{y_S = 1, y_F \leqslant 1, R_b \geqslant 0\}$. If the asset is to be pledged, it is better to pledge it in the case of failure because this has attractive incentive properties.

(iii) *Weak balance sheet: borrower's share of asset in the case of success:* $\{y_S \leqslant 1, y_F = 0, R_b = 0\}$. The borrower's only compensation is a share of the asset (that is, here, some probability of keeping it) only in the case of success.

This theory predicts that *weak borrowers pledge more collateral than strong borrowers*, the intuition being that collateral pledging makes up for a lack of pledgeable cash. In other words, weak borrowers must borrow against assets and cash and not only against cash. The expression of the borrower's utility implies that the borrower prefers pledging as little collateral as possible. Therefore, the regime that prevails is the one that pledges the least collateral in expectation and yet is consistent with the incentive constraint (IC_b) and the breakeven constraint (IR_l). This implies that the prevailing regime is as depicted in Figure 4.2.

This testable implication of the moral-hazard model is to be contrasted with that of the adverse-selection model (see Section 6.3). There, we will show that when the borrower has private information about her firm's prospects at the date of contracting, only a strong borrower (namely, a borrower with a high probability of success) pledges collateral.

Lastly, it is important to stress the key role of *contingent pledging.* Transferring money to investors is by assumption more efficient than transferring assets, and so incentives are best provided by giving the entrepreneur a contingent share in the assets than a contingent share in income. The intuition for the results obtained above in this respect can be obtained by comparing the pledgeable incomes under noncontingent and contingent collateral pledges. That is, we simplify the analysis above by comparing only $\{y_S = y_F = 0\}$ with $\{y_S = 1, y_F = 0\}$.

Under a noncontingent collateralization of the assets, the pledgeable income is

$$p_H\left(R - \frac{B}{\Delta p}\right) + A'.$$

With a contingent collateralization, the incentive constraint is

$$(\Delta p)(R_b + A) \geqslant B,$$

and so, if $A < B/\Delta p$, say (assets do not suffice to provide incentives), the pledgeable income is

$$\begin{aligned} p_H\left[R - \left(\frac{B}{\Delta p} - A\right)\right] &+ (1 - p_H)A' \\ &= p_H\left(R - \frac{B}{\Delta p}\right) + A' + p_H(A - A'). \end{aligned}$$

A similar rationale will underlie the optimality of a contingent allocation of control rights (see Section 10.2.3).

Multiple assets. Suppose now that the investment I is used to purchase two equipments. These two assets have, say, the same residual values $A_1 = A_2$ to the borrower, and different residual values, $A_1' > A_2'$, say, to the lenders. That is, asset 1 is more redeployable than asset 2. We invite the reader to check, following the steps of the previous argument, that *the borrower pledges the more redeployable asset first.*

4.3.5 Pledging Existing Wealth

The previous subsection analyzed a discrete model of costly collateral pledging, in which collateral corresponded to the leftover value of the project's investment. This subsection develops a related framework, a variant of which will be used in Section 6.3. We assume here that the amount pledged is a continuous variable (this modification is inconsequential since the ability to "pledge stochastically" in the previous subsection de facto made the pledge a continuous variable). More interestingly, the collateral corresponds to the borrower's existing (non-project-related) wealth. For example, it could be the borrower's family house or shares in other ventures. The analysis and conclusions are strongly analogous to the previous ones, although the treatment of the borrower's participation constraint is different: the borrower, having no wealth of her own, was always willing to undertake the project in the previous subsection. This may not be so if she has to pledge her own wealth; the borrower would not want to simultaneously receive no reward for success and lose existing wealth through collateral pledges. Accordingly, region (iii) in Section 4.3.4 cannot exist.

Suppose that the entrepreneur can pledge an arbitrary amount C,

$$0 \leqslant C \leqslant C^{\max},$$

conditional on failing (we will later check that conditional collateral dominates unconditional collateral). Investors value collateral C at βC, where $\beta < 1$, when they seize it.[21]

The borrower's net utility, as usual, is equal to the NPV. The NPV is equal to its value in the absence of collateral, $p_{\mathrm{H}}R - I$, minus the deadweight loss associated with collateral pledging. This deadweight loss is equal to $(1-\beta)C$ times the probability, $1-p_{\mathrm{H}}$, that the firm fails. And so

$$U_{\mathrm{b}} = p_{\mathrm{H}}R - I - (1-p_{\mathrm{H}})(1-\beta)C.$$

The NPV is maximized when $C = 0$; the borrower will therefore not pledge collateral unless she needs to. Thus, if A denotes the borrower's cash on hand and $A \geqslant \bar{A}$, where

$$p_{\mathrm{H}}\left(R - \frac{B}{\Delta p}\right) = I - \bar{A},$$

then $C = 0$.

By contrast, firms with weaker balance sheets, i.e., $A < \bar{A}$, need to pledge collateral in order to raise funds.[22] Under collateral pledging, the incentive constraint becomes[23]

$$(\Delta p)(R_{\mathrm{b}} + C) \geqslant B,$$

since the borrower loses both her reward R_{b} and the collateral when she fails (her stake is just larger).

The investors' breakeven condition becomes

$$p_{\mathrm{H}}(R - R_{\mathrm{b}}) + (1-p_{\mathrm{H}})\beta C \geqslant I - A,$$

or, using the incentive compatibility constraint,

$$p_{\mathrm{H}}\left(R - \frac{B}{\Delta p}\right) + p_{\mathrm{H}}C + (1-p_{\mathrm{H}})\beta C \geqslant I - A.$$

Note that the pledging of collateral raises pledgeable income both directly (term $(1-p_{\mathrm{H}})\beta C$) and indirectly through the reduction in entrepreneurial reward (term $p_{\mathrm{H}}C$).[24] To minimize the deadweight loss, the borrower pledges the minimum amount of collateral that allows investors to break even:

$$C(A) = \frac{(I-A) - p_{\mathrm{H}}(R - B/\Delta p)}{p_{\mathrm{H}} + (1-p_{\mathrm{H}})\beta}.$$

Note that $C(A)$ is a decreasing function of A: among firms that pledge collateral, those with the weakest balance sheet pledge more collateral.

Finally, we claimed that conditional pledges dominate unconditional ones. Suppose that the borrower pledges C regardless of the final outcome. Then the deadweight loss is higher for a given amount of collateral and the NPV becomes

$$\hat{U}_{\mathrm{b}} = p_{\mathrm{H}}R - I - (1-\beta)C.$$

---

21. The dichotomous example of Section 4.3.4 corresponds to $C = (1-y_{\mathrm{F}})A$ and $\beta = A'/A$.

22. We assume that $C^{\max}$ is small enough that the NPV remains positive even if the borrower pledges all assets:

$$p_{\mathrm{H}}R - I - (1-p_{\mathrm{H}})(1-\beta)C^{\max} \geqslant 0.$$

23. A different way of writing this constraint is

$$p_{\mathrm{H}}R_{\mathrm{b}} + (1-p_{\mathrm{H}})(-C) \geqslant p_{\mathrm{L}}R_{\mathrm{b}} + (1-p_{\mathrm{L}})(-C) + B.$$

24. This latter term (and the validity of the analysis) rests on the condition that $R_{\mathrm{b}} \geqslant 0$, which we will assume (this is guaranteed by imposing $B/\Delta p \geqslant C^{\max}$). For large amounts of collateral, it is no longer possible to substitute collateral for reward, since the latter would become negative and violate limited liability.

The incentive compatibility constraint is

$$(\Delta p)R_b \geqslant B,$$

and the investors' breakeven condition is

$$p_H(R - R_b) + \beta C \geqslant I - A.$$

When $A < \bar{A}$, the amount of collateral is

$$\hat{C}(A) = \frac{(I - A) - p_H(R - B/\Delta p)}{\beta} = \frac{p_H + (1 - p_H)\beta}{\beta} C(A) > C(A).$$

Intuitively, cash is more cheaply transferred than assets. Thus, not only is the deadweight loss higher for a given amount of collateral, but there is also a need for a larger collateral. And so the conditional pledge dominates the unconditional one.[25]

Remark (loan size and collateral requirement). This analysis presumes a single "margin" for concessions, namely, costly collateral pledging. Adding other margins yields interesting covariations. For example, Exercise 4.17 looks at a variable investment size. As the agency cost decreases (B, or, keeping p_H constant, $p_H/\Delta p$ decreases), the firm expands and borrows more (the investment size I increases) and pledges less collateral.[26] Interestingly, Boot et al. (1991) find empirically that larger loans have lower collateral requirements.

More generally, it would be interesting to let collateral be codetermined with other corporate finance patterns. Another finding of Boot et al. (1991) is that loans of longer maturities have less collateral. As the next chapter will show, the optimal maturity of liabilities is longer for firms with stronger balance sheets. Because such firms can also afford pledging less collateral, this other finding of Boot et al. also makes a lot of sense.

4.3.6 Executive Turnover as Costly Collateral Pledging

At a broad level of abstraction, the asset that is being pledged by the entrepreneur in the case of poor performance need not be a physical asset. The pledge could refer to any transfer or action that brings a benefit to investors and a larger cost to the entrepreneur. In particular, the entrepreneur may post her job as collateral, either directly as a commitment to quit in the case of poor performance, or, more plausibly, indirectly through institutional changes that make it easier for investors to dismiss the manager: an increase in the number of outsiders on the board, removal of takeover defenses, termination rights granted to the venture capitalist, and so forth.

Investors benefit from the ability to remove the manager because they may find another manager with a higher productivity or lower private benefits. Executive turnover, however, may involve a deadweight loss as discussed above: the new manager will enjoy a rent, which will be received neither by the entrepreneur nor by the investors. Hence, the cost to the incumbent entrepreneur of being removed may well exceed the benefit to the investors.

What does this analogy[27] imply for the executive turnover pattern? First, turnover should be more likely following poor performance, in the same way collateral is more likely to go to investors following poor performance; this is indeed the case in practice (see Section 1.2.3). Second, turnover is negatively correlated with explicit incentives, in the same way as the entrepreneur receives nothing when collateral is seized. This prediction of a positive covariation between explicit and implicit incentives is also supported by empirical evidence.

4.4 The Liquidity–Accountability Tradeoff

We have assumed that the entrepreneur's compensation is delayed until the consequences of her management (the final profit) are realized. As is intuitive and will be confirmed in the analysis below, it was indeed optimal to proceed in this way in the environment that has been analyzed until now: the more delayed the compensation, the larger the volume of information available, and thus the more precise the assessment of the entrepreneur's performance. In reality, entrepreneurial compensation accrues progressively and not only at the "end." For one thing,

25. As noted in the previous footnote, this assumes that the levels of collateral are small enough that with conditional pledging R_b remains positive.

26. As A increases, the firm expands and pledges less collateral, but it is harder to get any prediction on net borrowing $I - A$.

27. The formal treatment of the analogy requires adding a second period (as in Section 4.7 below, but without a second-period investment) and is left to the reader.

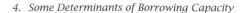

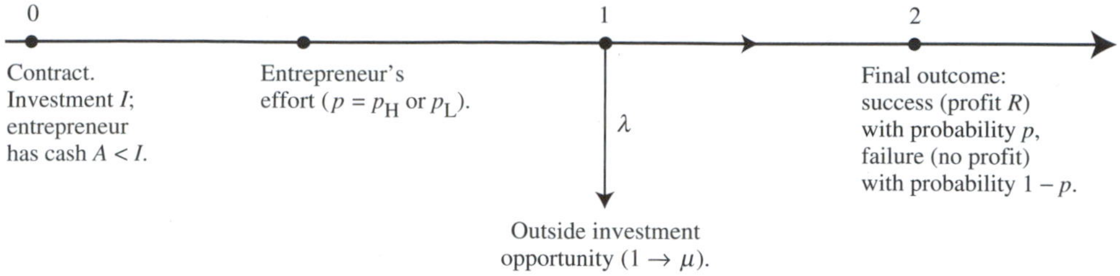

Figure 4.3

the entrepreneur needs to consume along the way, and would therefore like to spread her compensation over time. This section investigates a related reason, namely, that the entrepreneur may want to cash out in order to undertake new and profitable activities.

Letting the entrepreneur cash out before her performance is clearly ascertained aggravates moral hazard. There is in general a tradeoff between liquidity and accountability. The problem of dealing with the imperfection in performance measurement at the entrepreneur's exit date is compounded when the investors cannot verify whether the entrepreneur indeed faces attractive outside investment opportunities. This lack of observability creates scope for "strategic exit." The option of exiting early further aggravates the moral-hazard problem because an early exit allows the entrepreneur to escape the sanction attached to a poor performance.

The theme of this section is an old one in corporate finance and corporate law. As Coffee (1991) notes, "American law has said clearly and consistently since at least the 1920s that those who exercise control should not enjoy liquidity and vice versa." In the policy debate, the existence of a tradeoff between liquidity and accountability has been a focal object of debate primarily at the level of active monitors. In a nutshell (we will come back to this theme in Chapter 9), it has often been argued that the institutional investors in the United States enjoy much more liquidity than their Japanese and European counterparts and therefore are much less prone to monitoring ("exercise voice"). Note, though, that they have easier access to information and to judicial action against corporate insiders, which lowers the cost of limited monitoring relative to their European and Japanese counterparts.

To unveil some implications of the liquidity-accountability tradeoff and its limits, let us generalize the fixed-investment model of Section 3.2 to allow for the possibility that the entrepreneur enjoys an attractive new investment opportunity at an intermediate date, which is after the project has been financed and the investment sunk but before the outcome is realized.[28] This new investment opportunity is fleeting; in particular, it disappears if it is not taken advantage of when the profit on the initial project accrues. The timing is described in Figure 4.3.

As usual, we assume that the entrepreneur's cash A is insufficient to finance the initial investment I. There is moral hazard: the entrepreneur enjoys no private benefit if she behaves (in which case the probability of success is p_H) and private benefit $B > 0$ if she misbehaves (the probability of success is then p_L). The project yields R if successful and 0 if it fails. This final outcome (R or 0) is obtained *whether or not the entrepreneur takes advantage of the new investment opportunity.* Investors and the entrepreneur are risk neutral, and the latter is protected by limited liability. We assume that the investment would be financed in the absence of new reinvestment opportunities:

$$p_H\left(R - \frac{B}{\Delta p}\right) \geqslant I - A.$$

The new feature is the possible existence of an outside investment opportunity for the entrepreneur. We will say that the entrepreneur faces a "liquidity shock" if such an opportunity arises. The rationale for this terminology is that the model

28. The model is a simplified version of the one in Aghion et al. (2004), to which we refer for more detail. There is also a large literature on the liquidity-control tradeoff for active monitors (see Section 9.4).

admits alternative interpretations in which the entrepreneur needs money at the intermediate stage for reasons other than new investment opportunities. More generally, the marginal value of the entrepreneur of having cash available at the intermediate date is high. It might be that the entrepreneur is ill, or wants to send her children to college, or to acquire a property.

When a new investment opportunity arises, which happens with probability λ, the entrepreneur (who, it can be shown, has optimally invested all her wealth A in the initial investment) can only rely on the amount r_b that she can contractually withdraw at the intermediate date to reinvest in the new venture. We assume that the entrepreneur receives μr_b when investing r_b, where $\mu > 1$. None of this return is pledgeable to the investors.[29]

Consider the following class of contracts. The entrepreneur receives

- r_b at the intermediate date, and nothing at the final date, in the case of a liquidity shock;
- R_b in the case of success (and 0 in the case of failure) when the final outcome is realized and nothing at the intermediate stage, in the absence of a liquidity shock.

This "menu" deserves several comments. First, the type of compensation is contingent on the presence or absence of a liquidity shock. This raises no problem when the existence of a liquidity shock is verifiable by the investors. As we already observed, though, this need not be the case, and it must then be the case that the entrepreneur indeed finds it privately optimal to choose *full exit* (take r_b) when facing a liquidity shock and *full vesting* (wait and receive R_b in the case of success) in the absence of a liquidity shock.

Second, one may wonder whether this full exit/full vesting menu is not too restrictive, in that one could find better schemes. In particular, one might in the case of a liquidity shock allow for "*partial vesting*" (the entrepreneur receives some performance-contingent delayed compensation together with some cash r_b at the intermediate date with an option to convert this cash into additional shares). It turns out that under risk neutrality, partial vesting, and actually arbitrary, schemes do not improve on the limited class considered above in case (a) below, and may not improve in case (b); and that in the case of possible improvement in (b) it suffices to consider partial vesting schemes. We will solve for the optimal mechanism and will point it out if the latter involves partial vesting.

Third, the reader may wonder where the amount r_b comes from, given that the firm generates no cash at the intermediate date, of which the entrepreneur could keep some fraction. This is a matter of implementation. When computing the optimal state-contingent allocation, one need only know that r_b will have to be paid *in some way* by the investors and therefore must be subtracted from pledgeable income. Only thereafter comes the question of implementation. One possibility, although not the most realistic one in our context, is that the investors initially bring more than $I - A$: liquidity, in the form of Treasury bonds, say, is hoarded so as to be able to honor the contract with the entrepreneur in the case of exit. Alternatively, and as will later be emphasized, securities can be issued at the intermediate date (that pay off in the case of eventual success). This dilution of initial claimholders allows the firm to raise sufficient cash to compensate the entrepreneur at the exit date.

(a) *Verifiable liquidity shock.* Let us begin with the benchmark case in which the liquidity shock is observable by the investors. There is then a single dimension of moral hazard: the entrepreneur must be induced to behave. Intuitively, all incentives are provided by the contingent compensation that the entrepreneur receives when she does not exit. This intuition is confirmed by the analysis of the incentive compatibility constraint:

$$\lambda\mu r_b + (1-\lambda)p_H R_b \geqslant \lambda\mu r_b + (1-\lambda)p_L R_b + B. \quad (\text{IC}_b)$$

That is, with probability λ, the entrepreneur cashes out and reinvests, obtaining μr_b. Because r_b cannot be made contingent on profit, it has no impact on the entrepreneur's effort decision. All incentives are provided by the share R_b held in delayed compensation in the absence of a liquidity shock. Indeed, the incentive compatibility constraint can be rewritten as

$$(1-\lambda)(\Delta p)R_b \geqslant B.$$

29. See Exercise 4.5 for the extension to partly pledgeable return.

This is but the incentive constraint obtained in Section 3.2 in the absence of a liquidity shock ($\lambda = 0$) except that the entrepreneur's stake R_b must be magnified since the incentive sanction will bite only with probability $1 - \lambda$.

The pledgeable income is the maximal expected income that can be pledged to the investors without destroying incentives. *For a given* r_b, this pledgeable income is equal to the firm's expected income, $p_H R$, minus the minimum expected compensation that must be given to the entrepreneur to preserve incentives:

$$p_H R - \Big\{\lambda r_b + (1-\lambda) p_H \min_{\{R_b \text{ satisfying } (\mathrm{IC_b})\}} R_b\Big\} = p_H\Big(R - \frac{B}{\Delta p}\Big) - \lambda r_b.$$

Thus, everything is as if the entrepreneur contributed not A but $[A - \lambda r_b]$, since she gets a fixed amount r_b with probability λ.

The social surplus (NPV), which, because of the competitiveness of the financial market, goes to the entrepreneur, is

$$U_b = \mathrm{NPV} = p_H R - I + \lambda(\mu - 1) r_b. \tag{4.9}$$

Thus more liquidity (a higher r_b) increases the borrower's net utility U_b. Of course, the catch is that more liquidity reduces the pledgeable income. So, in the optimal contract, r_b will be set at the highest possible level consistent with having enough pledgeable income to fund the investment:

$$r_b = r_b^*,$$

where

$$p_H\Big(R - \frac{B}{\Delta p}\Big) - \lambda r_b^* = I - A;$$

for, it is optimal to set

$$R_b^* = \frac{B}{(1-\lambda)\Delta p}$$

so as to maximize the liquidity of the entrepreneur's claim. Intuitively, the entrepreneur values income more early than late and so it is optimal to minimize delayed compensation once incentives are sufficient.[30]

30. To prove this more formally, maximize U_b subject to ($\mathrm{IC_b}$) and the financing constraint:

$$p_H(R - R_b) - \lambda r_b \geqslant I - A.$$

Note also that r_b^* increases with A. And so an entrepreneur with a stronger balance sheet enjoys more liquidity.

(b) *Nonverifiable liquidity shock and strategic exit.* When at date 1 only the entrepreneur knows whether she faces a liquidity shock, moral hazard becomes multidimensional. The entrepreneur now has the option to "misrepresent" the existence or nonexistence of a liquidity shock. Furthermore, the two forms of moral hazard interact. The entrepreneur, if she decides to misbehave, may well want to strategically exit before the consequences of her behavior are discovered. The investors' inability to verify the existence of a liquidity shock thus aggravates the incentive problem. The agency cost is accordingly raised.

To simplify the exposition, we will assume in the rest of the section that

$$p_L = 0.$$

This assumption implies that, were the entrepreneur to misbehave, the entrepreneur would indeed want to cash out early even when she has no new investment opportunity: the delayed claim, $p_L R_b$, would then be valueless. More generally, a small probability of success in the case of misbehavior induces strategic exit. And so the entrepreneur's payoff in the case of misbehavior becomes

$$[\lambda\mu + 1 - \lambda] r_b + B$$

(the multiplier μ applies only in the case of a liquidity shock). The incentive constraint is now

$$\lambda\mu r_b + (1-\lambda) p_H R_b \geqslant [\lambda\mu + 1 - \lambda] r_b + B \tag{$\mathrm{IC_b}$}$$

or

$$(1-\lambda)[p_H R_b - r_b] \geqslant B. \tag{$\mathrm{IC_b'}$}$$

Because $p_L = 0$, one verifies that the nonverifiability of the liquidity shock aggravates moral hazard, as this constraint can be rewritten as

$$(1-\lambda)[(\Delta p) R_b - r_b] \geqslant B. \tag{$\mathrm{IC_b''}$}$$

In a sense, the entrepreneur can avail herself of r_b even in the absence of a liquidity shock, and the performance-contingent compensation must accordingly be higher powered.

Does the entrepreneur have an incentive to select correctly in the menu when she behaves? The incentive constraint (IC_b') relative to the effort choice implies that $p_H R_b > r_b$, and so the entrepreneur strictly prefers the delayed compensation when facing no liquidity shock. In contrast, we will need to investigate whether the entrepreneur has an incentive to cash out in the case of a liquidity shock, that is, whether

$$\mu r_b \geqslant p_H R_b. \tag{4.10}$$

Let us ignore this constraint for the moment.

The NPV *for a given* r_b is unchanged by the possibility of strategic exit. It is

$$U_b = p_H R - I + \lambda(\mu - 1) r_b.$$

In contrast, the agency cost has increased; that is, the pledgeable income is now reduced to

$$\begin{aligned} p_H R - \Big\{\lambda r_b + (1-\lambda) p_H \min_{\{R_b \text{ satisfying } (\mathrm{IC}_b)\}} R_b\Big\} &= p_H\left(R - \frac{B}{\Delta p}\right) - r_b \\ &< p_H\left(R - \frac{B}{\Delta p}\right) - \lambda r_b \end{aligned}$$

when $r_b > 0$.

Again it is optimal to provide the entrepreneur with as much liquidity as is consistent with the financing constraint. So

$$r_b = r_b^{**} < r_b^{*},$$

with

$$p_H\left(R - \frac{B}{\Delta p}\right) - r_b^{**} = I - A.$$

Delayed compensation is then given by (IC_b') taken with equality

$$R_b = R_b^{**} = \frac{B + (1-\lambda) r_b^{**}}{(1-\lambda)\Delta p} > R_b^{*}.$$

The possibility of strategic exit hurts the entrepreneur since from (IC_b') we see that she will be allowed to enjoy less liquidity than she would otherwise. Her stake in the firm is made less liquid in order to prevent her from shirking and exiting.

Lastly, we must return to the neglected constraint (4.10). If

$$\mu r_b^{**} \geqslant p_H R_b^{**},$$

then the ignored constraint (4.10) is indeed satisfied. The optimal scheme is then our menu of a full exit option (r_b^{**}) and a fully vested option (R_b^{**} in the case of success). If instead the constraint is not satisfied, as is the case when the firm has a weak balance sheet (A is low), then the liquid claim is too small to make full exit attractive enough even in the case of a liquidity shock.[31] It is easy to show that the *structure* of the incentive scheme must be changed slightly and that the entrepreneur's claim involves *partial vesting*:

- the entrepreneur receives some "baseline," illiquid share R_b^0 in the case of success (with value $p_H R_b^0$);
- the entrepreneur further receives cash r_b^{**} at the intermediate date, which she has the option to convert into extra shares paying ΔR_b in the case of success, with total stake $R_b \equiv R_b^0 + \Delta R_b$ if she elects this conversion option.

The entrepreneur's utility ($p_H R - I + \lambda(\mu - 1) r_b^{**}$) is unchanged. Only the composition of the compensation package is altered.[32]

To sum up, the (quite plausible) unobservability of the liquidity shock makes it harder for the entrepreneur to receive a liquid claim. It implies more *vesting* (a more delayed payoff for the entrepreneur).

In practice, contracts often have clauses for accelerating vesting—the entrepreneur can cash faster—in certain contingencies. These contingencies may either be direct performance measures (income,

31. The ignored constraint can be rewritten as

$$(\mu - 1) r_b^{**} \geqslant \frac{B}{(1-\lambda)}.$$

32. To show this, note that the added constraint cannot increase the value of the program. So we just need to show that one can do as well as when one ignores the constraint. The incentive constraint relative to the effort choice under the partial vesting scheme is

$$\lambda[\mu r_b^{**} + p_H R_b^0] + (1-\lambda) p_H R_b \geqslant [\lambda\mu + 1 - \lambda] r_b^{**} + B.$$

The pledgeable income is, using this constraint satisfied with equality,

$$p_H R - \left[\lambda(r_b^{**} + p_H R_b^0) + (1-\lambda)\left(r_b^{**} + \frac{B - \lambda p_H R_b^0}{1-\lambda}\right)\right] = p_H\left(R - \frac{B}{\Delta p}\right) - r_b^{**}.$$

Thus, the pledgeable income depends only on r_b^{**}. The entrepreneur must find it privately optimal to convert the cash into shares when there is no liquidity shock and to exit when there is one:

$$\mu r_b^{**} \geqslant p_H(\Delta R_b) \geqslant r_b^{**}.$$

Thus it suffices to choose ΔR_b in the interval defined by these two inequalities (which is consistent with $\Delta R_b \leqslant R_b$ since we are in the case $\mu r_b^{**} < p_H R_b^{**}$ by assumption). Because ΔR_b has no impact on the NPV and the pledgeable income, we have shown that this simple change in the structure of compensation allows us to satisfy the *ex post* revelation constraints at no cost.

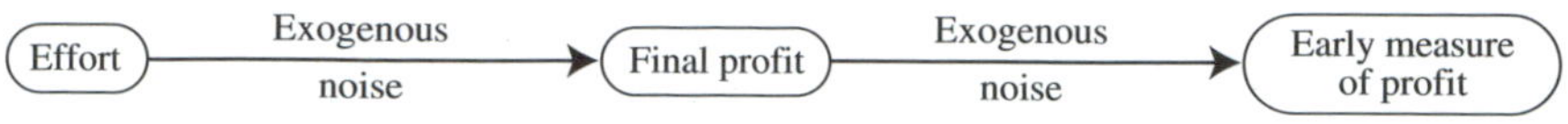

Figure 4.4

patents, etc.) or result from market monitoring. We now turn to the latter possibility.

(c) *Facilitating exit through speculative monitoring and the reverse pecking order.* As we have seen, the cost of liquidity is that it makes the entrepreneur less accountable since she can "get away with a poor performance." Ideally, one would want to have an early assessment or "picture" of the entrepreneur's performance and thereby be able to measure it before the profit actually accrues. Chapter 9 will emphasize the key role played by financial markets in the measurement of the value of assets in place. The buyers of claims in the firm are incentivized to assess their value; the price fetched by the securities in a public offering, for example, conveys useful information about the likely performance of the firm.

Chapter 9 will stress the use of market monitoring as a way to filter out at any point in time some of the future exogenous noise that garbles the assessment of performance. Here we want to abstract completely from this consideration and assume rather that an early signal is available that is a noisy version of final performance. That is, the final profit is a superior way of assessing the entrepreneur's performance. In technical terms, the profit is a "sufficient statistic" or "summary" for the pair of observables (profit, signal) when trying to infer effort.[33] Crudely speaking, there is nothing to be learned from the signal when one already knows the profit (see Figure 4.4 for a schematic).

The fact that the signal is a garbled version of the final profit implies that, in the absence of a liquidity shock ($\lambda = 0$), the signal should just be ignored, and the compensation entirely based on the best measure of performance, namely, profit.

We will later interpret this signal as the price fetched in an initial public offering (IPO) or other security issue; just assume for the moment that it comes "out of the blue" at the intermediate date, just after the entrepreneur learns whether she faces a liquidity shock and before she cashes out.

The signal can be "good" or "bad." Let

$$q_{\mathrm{H}} \equiv \Pr(\text{good signal} \mid \text{high effort})$$

and

$$q_{\mathrm{L}} \equiv \Pr(\text{good signal} \mid \text{low effort}).$$

Assume[34]

$$q_{\mathrm{H}} > q_{\mathrm{L}}.$$

Intuitively, and because of risk neutrality, if the entrepreneur announces that she wants to cash out (case (b)), one should (i) use the signal and (ii) give her cash $\hat{r}_{\mathrm{b}}$ only if the signal is good. For example, in the case in which the liquidity shock is not verifiable (case (b)), the incentive constraint relative to effort can now be written:

$$\lambda q_{\mathrm{H}}\mu\hat{r}_{\mathrm{b}} + (1-\lambda)p_{\mathrm{H}}R_{\mathrm{b}} \geqslant q_{\mathrm{L}}[\lambda\mu + (1-\lambda)]\hat{r}_{\mathrm{b}} + B. \tag{IC$_{\mathrm{b}}$}$$

Making the size of the liquid claim contingent on the signal ($\hat{r}_{\mathrm{b}}$ if the signal is good, 0 if it is bad) relaxes the constraint. Let

$$r_{\mathrm{b}} \equiv q_{\mathrm{H}}\hat{r}_{\mathrm{b}} \quad \text{and} \quad \theta \equiv \frac{q_{\mathrm{L}}}{q_{\mathrm{H}}} < 1.$$

The incentive constraint can be rewritten as

$$\lambda\mu r_{\mathrm{b}} + (1-\lambda)p_{\mathrm{H}}R_{\mathrm{b}} \geqslant [\lambda\mu + (1-\lambda)]\theta r_{\mathrm{b}} + B.$$

While the entrepreneur's expected utility for a given r_{b} is unchanged, the pledgeable income increases to

$$p_{\mathrm{H}}\left(R - \frac{B}{\Delta p}\right) - r_{\mathrm{b}}[1 - (1-\theta)(\lambda\mu + 1 - \lambda)],$$

and so r_{b} and the NPV are increased. In that sense, liquidity is enhanced by the existence of speculative monitoring.

Application. These ideas can be illustrated in the context of venture capital, for example. One difference with the model analyzed above is that at

33. For the concept of sufficient statistic, see Section 3.2.4.

34. Let x and y denote the probability of a good signal when the profit is R and 0, respectively, with (this is the definition of a "good signal") $x > y$. Then

$$q_{\mathrm{H}} = p_{\mathrm{H}}x + (1-p_{\mathrm{H}})y > q_{\mathrm{L}} = p_{\mathrm{L}}x + (1-p_{\mathrm{L}})y.$$

least two parties with control over the venture—the entrepreneur and the venture capitalist (the active monitor)—may each want to exit. But the broad principles stated above apply. Venture capital agreements carefully plan the conditions for their exit. For example, venture capitalists usually exit four to five years after the initial capital injection. At this time, the performance is usually still unknown (for example, it may take ten or fifteen years for a drug to go through the research and development stages, to be tested, to obtain regulatory approval, and to finally enter the market). So it is particularly important to obtain some advanced, even noisy, estimate of future profits. This "photographing" of the value of assets in place is in part synchronized with the exit mechanism. The conversion of the venture capitalist's convertible preferred stocks into common stocks is usually contingent on the value achieved at the IPO.[35]

Recall that at the beginning of the section we provided several interpretations for the way the transfer r_b is implemented. The first was the hoarding of liquidity, say, in the form of Treasury bonds, to allow the entrepreneur to cash out. This method, however, has the substantial drawback of not generating any information about the value of assets in place.

Similarly, issuing safe debt (which would be feasible if the profit in the case of failure were strictly positive) would not convey any information about the probability of success, and therefore would keep the agency cost high.

In practice, therefore, the exit mechanism is associated with the issuance of *risky securities* (say equity claims). The observation of the signal by new claimholders, however, is costly, so that incentives must be given for the production of this interim information. The riskier the claim, the more incentive the buyers of the claim have to carefully assess the value of assets in place. In the case of venture capital, the exit mechanism is indeed linked to either an IPO or a sale to a large buyer, in any case with the sale of equity.

35. The venture capitalist's reward and timing of exit depends on other parameters besides the start-up's own performance. As discussed in Section 2.5, IPOs also "time the market." For example, after the 2000 collapse of the Internet bubble, the market for IPOs dried up; venture capitalists were deprived of an exit option and could not reinvest in new start-ups.

The need for a precise assessment at the date of exit calls for a reversal of the "pecking-order hypothesis." This hypothesis, whose rationale we will investigate in Chapter 6, holds that, when issuing claims outside, firms prefer to start with relatively riskless claims and issue very risky ones only as a last resort. So they will first issue safe debt, then risky debt, then preferred stocks, and finally equity. The need to incentivize the measurement of the value of assets in place instead suggests issuing risky securities first.

4.5 Restraining the Ability to Borrow: Inalienability of Human Capital

We have until now assumed that the loan agreement between the entrepreneur and the lenders is not renegotiated. Since the agreement is Pareto-optimal, renegotiation cannot strictly improve the welfare of both sides to the agreement. Hart and Moore (1994) have argued that renegotiation may nevertheless occur if the entrepreneur is indispensable for the completion of the project. Hart and Moore's idea is that the entrepreneur can blackmail the lenders and try to obtain a bigger share of the pie by threatening not to complete the project.[36]

To illustrate in the simplest fashion how this blackmail might operate, suppose there is no moral hazard, so $B = 0$, and that the entrepreneur has no cash, so $A = 0$. Since

$$p_H R > I,$$

the (positive-NPV) project is then financed in the absence of contract renegotiation. The entrepreneur can, for example, write a debt contract specifying that D will be paid to the lenders in the case of success, where

$$p_H D = I.$$

Introducing renegotiation, Hart and Moore consider a timing similar to that in Figure 4.5.[37] The project

36. We here focus on holdups by *borrowers*. See Section 9.4 for the opposite problem of holdups by *lenders*, which refers to the relationship banker "expropriating" the entrepreneur's future surplus thanks to his superior knowledge of the firm relative to other potential lenders. Expropriation of the entrepreneur's specific investment through high interest rates is the dark side of "relationship banking." In this case, it is the investors who need to compete in order to enhance the borrower's bargaining power.

37. More precisely, Hart and Moore build a multiperiod model, in which the timing for each period is similar to that of Figure 4.5. The scope of their analysis is accordingly much broader than the account given in this section.

Figure 4.5

yields nothing if it is not completed. And, because of the absence of moral hazard, it yields R with probability p_H and 0 with probability $1 - p_H$ if it is completed.

There are two key assumptions for the analysis. First, the lenders cannot bring in a new entrepreneur to complete the project if the entrepreneur refuses to complete it; one may have in mind that part of the investment I is devoted to the acquisition of knowledge by the entrepreneur and that this knowledge is indispensable to complete the project. More generally, bringing in a new entrepreneur could substantially delay the project and/or wastefully duplicate the investment in human capital (besides, the new entrepreneur might herself blackmail the lenders if the first one is no longer available to complete the project). Note that, in contrast with physical assets, the investment in the entrepreneur's human capital cannot be seized: it is inalienable.

The second assumption is that the action of "completing the project" can be contracted upon after, but not before, the investment is incurred. Therefore, in effect, the renegotiation itself replaces effort as the source of moral hazard.

The key ingredient of the analysis is the description of the renegotiation process. Two opposite views can be held on this matter. On the one hand, one may predict that the lenders will stay put and will refuse to renegotiate. If the project has a deadline, a self-interested entrepreneur will complete the project even in the absence of renegotiation, since completing the project brings her

$$p_H(R - D) = p_H R - I > 0.$$

On the other hand, one may, following Hart and Moore, take a more optimistic view of the entrepreneur's bargaining power and argue that in this situation both sides have bargaining power, as both receive 0 in the case of noncompletion.[38] Let us assume that the lenders (respectively, entrepreneur) receive a fraction θ (respectively, $1 - \theta$) of the pie in the renegotiation. The fraction θ reflects the lenders' bargaining power. Anticipating renegotiation, the lenders are willing to invest in the firm if and only if

$$\theta(p_H R) \geqslant I.$$

Note that θ cannot exceed D/R. Otherwise, the entrepreneur would just refrain from renegotiating and complete the project, leaving only D to the lenders in the case of success.

The interesting case is when θ is smaller than D/R. Then

$$\theta(p_H R) < I,$$

and the project is not financed: although the lenders break even in the absence of renegotiation, renegotiation reduces their share in the case of success and transforms lending into a money-losing operation. The firm then suffers from credit rationing—the nonfinancing of a positive-NPV project—despite the "absence" of moral hazard.[39] This model can be viewed as one of *expropriation of the lenders' investment.*[40]

Determinants of bargaining power. We now identify some factors that reduce the borrower's bargaining power (increase θ) and thus help her obtain funding.

38. Arguably, this view may be more relevant if, for example, there is no deadline and the value, initially $p_H R$, shrinks over time due to discounting. Then the lenders can less easily stay put and make the entrepreneur responsible for destroying the value of the project.

39. Actually, the model is formally identical to one with moral hazard. It suffices to define an "equivalent private benefit" B:

$$\theta p_H R \equiv p_H\left(R - \frac{B}{\Delta p}\right).$$

The model with renegotiation (with parameter θ) and no moral hazard is equivalent to the model without renegotiation and with moral hazard (with private benefit B).

40. It thereby bears some resemblance to the models of expropriation of specific investment in the industrial organization and labor economics literatures (Grout 1984; Klein et al. 1978; Williamson 1975, 1985). It is also very similar to the model in Jappelli et al. (2005), where *ex post* the lender can refuse to pay unless brought to court, but the inefficiency of the court implies that the lenders can secure only a fraction of the final value of the assets.

One such factor is *reputation*. Reputation may operate on the *borrower*'s side. That is, the borrower may in the past have developed a reputation for not opportunistically renegotiating her loans. We refer the reader to Section 3.2.4 for a discussion of reputational capital. The *lenders* may also develop a reputation for not accepting to renegotiate. For example, a bank may lend to several such borrowers and may credibly adopt a tough stance with all of them knowing that, were it to give in to one of them, it would be in a weak bargaining position with the others.[41]

Relatedly, if completion cannot be described in a formal contract even after investment has occurred, the lenders may be worried that by forgiving some debt they would expose themselves to *further blackmail* by the entrepreneur (as do families and the police when they pay a ransom to a kidnapper). They may then want to resist the entrepreneur's blackmail in order not to appear weak.

The second factor that may affect θ is the *dispersion of lenders*. We have already mentioned the possibility that dispersion may hinder renegotiation when we discussed debt overhang. We will come back to this theme when defining the notion of a soft budget constraint in Chapter 5.

A third factor affecting the parties' bargaining power is their *outside options*.[42] We assumed above that they had none: the borrower had no substitute activity and the lenders could not replace the entrepreneur by someone else. Let us conclude this discussion by introducing outside options, starting with the entrepreneur. Suppose that the entrepreneur can obtain utility V in an alternative project (none of which can be seized by the investors), where

$$(1-\theta)p_{\mathrm{H}}R < V < p_{\mathrm{H}}R.$$

These inequalities imply two things. First, it is inefficient for the entrepreneur to abandon the project ($V < p_{\mathrm{H}}R$). Second, by exercising her outside option, the entrepreneur obtains more (V) than what he would get if this outside option were not available ($(1-\theta)p_{\mathrm{H}}R$). Put differently, to "estimate" the entrepreneur's bargaining power in renegotiation, one must look at her outside option. The investors must then lower their stake to θ' to "keep the entrepreneur on board," where

$$V = (1-\theta')p_{\mathrm{H}}R.$$

That is, the entrepreneur's outside option amounts to a redefinition of the investors' bargaining power from θ to $\theta' < \theta$. The entrepreneur's outside option here never benefits her and may hurt her, as the investors may no longer be willing to finance her project.[43]

Lastly, the entrepreneur's bargaining power is weaker when she can be replaced, possibly at a cost, by another entrepreneur to complete the project. This theme is familiar from industrial organization: a party's (here, the investors') specific investment is better protected if this party can use *ex post competition* to secure a better bargaining position.[44] In the context of our financing model, suppose that the entrepreneur is not completely indispensable; that is, the investors can, by incurring cost $c < p_{\mathrm{H}}R$, find a replacement for the entrepreneur. For example, c may stand for the cost incurred by a new entrepreneur (and compensated for by the lenders) to obtain the knowledge necessary to complete the project.

The loan agreement can specify that the lenders can seize the assets and fire the entrepreneur. In this case, the lenders will not settle for less than $p_{\mathrm{H}}R - c$, which is what they get by replacing the entrepreneur. Let θ^* be defined by

$$p_{\mathrm{H}}R - c \equiv \theta^* p_{\mathrm{H}}R \quad \text{or} \quad \theta^* \equiv 1 - \frac{c}{p_{\mathrm{H}}R}.$$

Suppose now that

$$\theta p_{\mathrm{H}}R < I < \theta^* p_{\mathrm{H}}R,$$

where θ is the lenders' bargaining power when they cannot seize the asset. Then the initial entrepreneur can find funding for the project provided she allows the lenders to seize the asset if they so desire.[45] We

41. See Kreps and Wilson (1982) and Milgrom and Roberts (1982) for a formalization of such behaviors.

42. See, for example, Osborne and Rubinstein's (1990) book for a review of models of bargaining with outside options.

43. The entrepreneur is hurt by her outside option if

$$\theta(p_{\mathrm{H}}R) \geqslant I > \theta'(p_{\mathrm{H}}R).$$

44. See Farrell and Gallini (1988) and Shepard (1987).

In practice, the replacement is often made by shareholders rather than debtholders. Recall, though, that in this basic model there is no difference between debt and equity, and so we do not have to worry about a possible dissonance between shareholders and debtholders regarding the replacement decision.

45. This contract leaves rent $\theta^* p_{\mathrm{H}}R - I > 0$ to the lenders. There are several ways for the entrepreneur to recoup this rent. First, she may

therefore conclude that *giving the lenders the right to seize the firm's assets may enable the entrepreneur to credibly commit not to expropriate the lenders.* In a sense, we are back to the idea that collateral pledging boosts debt capacity. The new insight here is simply that *the value of the collateral depends on how indispensable the entrepreneur is.*

Supplementary Sections

4.6 Group Lending and Microfinance

Borrowers with weak balance sheets (no cash, no adequate collateral, no guaranteed income streams) are unlikely to have access to sources of finance. A number of recent and apparently successful institutions have tried to strengthen the balance sheet of small borrowers by lending to groups rather than to individuals. A well-known example is the Grameen Bank in Bangladesh, but similar institutions exist in several developing countries. A comprehensive overview of institutions, incentive considerations, and empirical data in microfinance can be found in Armendáriz de Aghion and Morduch (2005).

The borrowers organize themselves in groups and each participant accepts joint responsibility for the loan. As in Section 4.2, there is cross-pledging among several projects, but here the projects are not projects of a single borrower, but rather projects of different borrowers.[46]

Group lending may at first sight seem surprising. We saw in Section 3.2.4 that a borrower should be made accountable only for outcomes that she can control. And if another borrower's performance is relevant because it conveys information and enables benchmarking, then the dependence of a borrower's reward on the other borrower's performance is generally negative; for example, if two nearby located farmers face similar climatic conditions, then benchmarking may enable the lenders to get information about whether a farmer's good or bad performance is related to effort or just luck. In that case, a farmer is at least partly compensated on the basis of relative performance. In contrast, under group lending, a borrower prefers the other borrowers to do well because of the joint liability. This supplementary section discusses the ways in which group lending can indeed strengthen the borrowers' balance sheets and thereby enable financing.

Group lending can be given two rationales, both of them closely related to themes developed in this chapter. First, group lending may make use of nonmonetary collateral, actually collateral that is per se valueless to the investors: the social capital within the group. Second, group lending may be based on peer monitoring. Members of the group may monitor the quality of the other members' projects *ex ante*, or once financing has been secured monitor each other's project management.

Both ideas will be illustrated using the context of two borrowers facing identical, fixed-investment projects (see Section 3.2). That is, each borrower has a project of size I and has limited cash on hand $A < I$. Projects succeed (yield R) or fail (yield 0). The probability of success is p_H if the entrepreneur behaves (but then receives no private benefit) and p_L if she misbehaves (and receives private benefit B). Assume universal risk neutrality and borrower limited liability.

The two projects are independent. In particular, there is no scope for benchmarking as a source of linkage between the two projects. We will assume that

$$p_H\left(R - \frac{B}{\Delta p}\right) < I - A.$$

That is, the projects cannot be financed on a stand-alone basis. Furthermore, absent other considerations, linking the two projects contractually by making one borrower's compensation contingent on the other borrower's performance cannot alleviate the financing problem (see Section 3.4.2): because projects are unrelated, such a link could only garble individual performance measurement and increase the agency cost.

ask for some "downpayment." Concretely, this may take the form of incomplete investment of the entrepreneur's equity A if we introduced some (provided that $\theta^* p_H R - I < 0$). Alternatively, the entrepreneur might specify that she keeps some share in the firm even in the event she is replaced.

46. The literature on group lending includes (but is far from being limited to) Armendáriz de Aghion (1999), Armendáriz de Aghion and Gollier (2000), Banerjee et al. (1994), Besley and Coate (1995), Ghatak and Guinnane (1999), Ghatak and Kali (2001), Laffont and N'Guessan (2000), Laffont and Rey (2000), Stiglitz (1990), and Varian (1990). See Ahlin and Townsend (2003a,b) for empirical work on selection into joint liability contracts.

(a) *Group lending: using social capital as collateral.* The theory of corporate finance focuses primarily, although not exclusively, on physical capital (assets, incomes). Capital can be given a broader meaning, some of which is relevant for our present concern. Relations among people matter substantially even in economic situations such as lending relationships. One view of group lending is that social capital can supplement an insufficient amount of physical capital and thereby facilitate financing. "Social capital" is a complex notion (see, for example, Chapter 12 in Coleman 1990), and we certainly will not do justice to it in this short section.

An important manifestation of social capital is the trust people of a group or community have in each other. Groups in which members trust each other achieve much more than other groups in which they don't. And quite importantly, members of a group value their reputation within the group, as they will be chosen for valuable interaction or given discretionary power if they are deemed trustworthy or reliable.

How can the lending relationship use this fact to increase the borrower's incentives to behave, given that misbehavior is relative to the lenders, and not to the members of the group? Under group lending, the borrower may be concerned that, if she misbehaves, not only will she be more likely to forgo the monetary reward, but also the others may then be upset and infer some "individualistic" tendency in her behavior.[47] They may question her altruism and again be reluctant to interact with her in the future (see Exercise 4.7).[48]

Let us here develop a simple version in which there is no asymmetric information about the agents' degree of altruism. Suppose that each borrower puts weight a ($a \leqslant 1$) on the other borrower's income relative to her own income. The parameter a is one of altruism (a was set equal to 0 until now).

Note that altruism has no effect if borrowers attempt to secure financing for their projects separately; for, assuming financing occurs, each borrower then correctly takes the other borrower's income as exogenous to her own behavior, and so the incentive constraint (which, recall, sets the level of the nonpledgeable income) remains:

$$(\Delta p)R_{\mathrm{b}} \geqslant B.$$

And so the projects do not receive financing.

Consider now group lending. The borrowers receive R_{b} each if *both* projects succeed and 0 otherwise. It is an equilibrium for both entrepreneurs to behave if

$$p_{\mathrm{H}}^2(R_{\mathrm{b}} + aR_{\mathrm{b}}) \geqslant p_{\mathrm{H}}p_{\mathrm{L}}(R_{\mathrm{b}} + aR_{\mathrm{b}}) + B$$

or

$$p_{\mathrm{H}}(R_{\mathrm{b}} + aR_{\mathrm{b}}) \geqslant \frac{B}{\Delta p}. \qquad (\mathrm{IC_b})$$

Crucially, the term "aR_{b}" in the incentive constraint plays the same role in the incentive constraint as did physical collateral (e.g., the family house that is turned over to investors in the case of failure) in Section 4.3. The *per-borrower* pledgeable income is now

$$p_{\mathrm{H}}R - p_{\mathrm{H}}^2\Big[\min_{\{\mathrm{IC_b}\}} R_{\mathrm{b}}\Big] = p_{\mathrm{H}}\left(R - \frac{B}{(1+a)\Delta p}\right).$$

The stronger the altruism (a), the higher the pledgeable income! In particular, if

$$p_{\mathrm{H}}\left(R - \frac{B}{(1+a)\Delta p}\right) \geqslant I - A,$$

financing becomes feasible.

(b) *Group lending: peer monitoring.* The competing rationale for group lending is, as we said, peer monitoring. Peer monitoring can occur at two stages: *ex ante* (before the investment decision) and *ex post* (after the investment decision). In either case, group lending is one way of eliciting the information that borrowers have about each other. *Ex ante*, entrepreneurs may have information about each other that is not available to lenders (as in, for example, Ghatak and Kali 2001). An entrepreneur's being willing to team up with another entrepreneur under a joint liability lending arrangement is good news about the ability or willingness of the latter to be successful.

47. Another channel of impact of social capital on lending relationships is that if the project fails and so the borrower does not pay the lenders back, the other members of the group may infer that the borrower is lazy, overly prone to favor her family or close friends, enjoys private benefits, and so on; the other members may therefore be reluctant in the future to engage in other forms of interaction with the borrower. While disclosure is an attempt to lever up social capital (in a sense, to free the lenders and borrower from the limited liability constraint), this story explains information sharing, but not group lending.

48. Che (2002) endogenizes the punishment behavior by introducing repeated interactions among group members.

Table 4.1

	good project	bad project	Bad project
Pr(success)	p_H	p_L	p_L
Private benefit	0	b	B

In other words, group lending alleviates the adverse-selection problem.[49]

Ex post, that is, after the financing has been committed, borrowers may monitor each other in a way lenders cannot mimic cheaply. For example, borrowers may have a comparative advantage in monitoring each other due to geographical proximity or a common technological expertise.

Let us consider the following mutual monitoring model (which will also be used in Chapter 9). After the investments are sunk, but before each entrepreneur's moral-hazard decision, each entrepreneur can monitor the other entrepreneur (the two monitoring decisions are made simultaneously and noncooperatively). So each entrepreneur has two roles: that of a monitor (for the other's project) and that of a monitoree (for her own project). To formalize the idea that monitoring reduces the extent of moral hazard, assume that a monitor can reduce the private benefit that can be enjoyed by the monitoree by shirking from B to $b < B$. The monitor must, however, bear an unobservable private monitoring cost $c > 0$ in order to achieve this reduction in private benefit.

An interpretation of this monitoring structure is as described in Table 4.1. Each entrepreneur will have to choose among a number of *ex ante* identical projects (the set of projects are different for the two entrepreneurs). The entrepreneur privately learns the payoffs attached to each project. There are three relevant projects: (1) the good project, which yields no private benefit and has probability of success p_H; (2) the low-private-benefit bad project, which yields private benefit b and has probability of success p_L; and (3) the high-private-benefit Bad project, which yields private benefit B and has probability of success p_L. The monitor moves first. If she incurs effort cost c, she is able to identify the other entrepreneur's high-private-benefit Bad project and thus to prevent the other entrepreneur from selecting it, say, by telling the investors about it (under group lending and in the absence of altruism and collusion, it will indeed be in the monitor's interest to report this information). But she still cannot tell the other two projects apart, and so the monitoree can still choose the low-private-benefit bad project if she wishes so. The monitor learns nothing when she does not incur the monitoring cost c; then, because the projects are still indistinguishable by the investors, the monitoree can choose any of the three projects as in the absence of monitoring (of course, the low-private-benefit bad project is then dominated for the entrepreneur and is irrelevant).

For expositional simplicity only, we will assume that

$$b = c$$

(this assumption says that moral hazard is equally strong along its two dimensions and makes the model "symmetric").

Let us investigate the conditions under which group lending and peer monitoring facilitate the entrepreneur's access to funds.[50] Suppose the entrepreneurs monitor each other and behave. A group lending contract that gives them R_b each if both projects succeed and 0 otherwise yields to each entrepreneur utility

$$p_H^2 R_b - c.$$

By failing either to monitor or to behave (but not both), an entrepreneur reduces the probability of success of the other project or of her project from p_H to p_L, and obtains

$$p_H p_L R_b = p_H p_L R_b - c + b.$$

Our first incentive compatibility constraint is therefore

$$p_H R_b \geqslant \frac{b}{\Delta p} = \frac{c}{\Delta p}.$$

49. This reduction in adverse selection can be studied using the techniques developed in Chapter 6.

50. We will assume that the entrepreneurs do not collude with each other. Extensive analyses of the impact of collusion on monitoring in corporate finance can be found in Dessi (2005) and, in the context of group lending, Laffont and Rey (2000). Laffont and Meleu (1997) emphasize the role of peer monitoring as creating possible side transfers for agents to collude in situations where other forms of side transfers are not readily available.

Note also that even if they do not collude, the two entrepreneurs might "coordinate" on an equilibrium in which they do not monitor each other.

It must also be the case that the entrepreneur does not want to misbehave on both fronts:

$$p_H^2 R_b - c \geqslant p_L^2 R_b + b$$

or

$$(p_H + p_L) R_b \geqslant \frac{b+c}{\Delta p}. \qquad (\text{IC}_b)$$

As in our study of diversification (Section 4.2), the binding constraint is the latter one (since $(p_H + p_L) < 2p_H$). Thus, the pledgeable income per project is

$$p_H R - p_H^2 \Big[\min_{\{\text{IC}_b\}} R_b \Big] = p_H R - \frac{p_H^2}{p_H^2 - p_L^2}(b+c).$$

The pledgeable income has increased relative to the case of separate financing if and only if

$$\frac{p_H^2}{p_H^2 - p_L^2}(b+c) < \frac{p_H B}{\Delta p}$$

or

$$\left(\frac{p_H}{p_H + p_L}\right)(b+c) < B.$$

Thus if the monitoring cost (equal here to the low private benefit) is low enough relative to the high private benefit, peer monitoring facilitates access to funds. Intuitively, joint liability creates an incentive for cross-monitoring provided that the monitoring cost is small. While monitoring per se is wasteful, it is worth inducing as long as it generates a substantial reduction in private benefit ($B - b$) from misbehavior and provided that funding cannot be secured under project finance (as has been assumed here). Joint liability can thus be added to our list of concessions made by borrowers in order to secure financing.

4.7 Sequential Projects

As announced in Section 4.2.4 we investigate the impact of sequentiality on borrowing capacity and NPV in the context of diversified projects. We do so in the variable-investment context, which requires a straightforward extension of Section 4.2 to this environment.

4.7.1 Benchmark: Simultaneous Diversification

As in Section 4.2, assume that the entrepreneur may undertake two independent projects and that the outcomes are realized only after efforts have been exerted (and so the financing of the second project cannot be made contingent on the outcome of the first). We, however, assume that the technology is the constant-returns-to-scale one studied in Section 3.4. We proceed rather sketchily since the analysis is almost identical to the fixed-investment one of Section 4.2.1. A project $i \in \{1, 2\}$ of size I_i yields revenue RI_i with probability p, where $p = p_H$ if the entrepreneur behaves (no private benefit) and $p = p_L$ if the entrepreneur misbehaves (private benefit BI_i). Let

$$I \equiv I_1 + I_2$$

denote the total investment.

As in Section 4.2, risk neutrality implies that it is optimal to reward the entrepreneur only when both projects succeed. Let R_b denote this reward. As in Section 4.2.1, there are two incentive constraints, but the binding one relates to misbehavior on both projects:

$$p_H^2 R_b \geqslant p_L^2 R_b + BI.$$

Hence, maximizing the NPV subject to the investors' breakeven constraint can be written as

$$U_b^{\text{simultaneous}} = \max (p_H R - 1) I$$

s.t.

$$p_H RI - p_H^2 \left[\frac{BI}{p_H^2 - p_L^2} \right] = I - A.$$

And so

$$I = \frac{A}{1 - \hat{\rho}_0},$$

where

$$\hat{\rho}_0 \equiv p_H \left[R - \frac{p_H}{p_H + p_L} \frac{B}{\Delta p} \right] = p_H \left[R - (1 - d_2) \frac{B}{\Delta p} \right],$$

using the notation of Section 4.2.1.

The entrepreneur does not want to misbehave on project i if and only if

$$p_H^2 R_b \geqslant p_H p_L R_b + BI_i,$$

or, after some manipulations,

$$\frac{p_H}{p_H + p_L} \geqslant \frac{I_i}{I} \quad \text{for } i \in (1, 2).$$

This constraint is satisfied as long as the investment is split relatively equally between the two projects (for example, it is strictly satisfied for $I_i = \frac{1}{2} I$), but not if all or most eggs are put into the same basket (as in the case when I_1, say, is close to I): benefits from diversification are largest when the investment is indeed split across projects.

4.7.2 Long-Term Finance and the Build-up of Net Worth

Let us now consider the sequential case, in which the outcome of the first project is known before investment is sunk in the second project: project 1 and its realization occur at date 1, project 2 and its realization at date 2. To make the simultaneous and sequential cases comparable, we assume that there is no discounting between the two periods. We initially assume that the first loan agreement covers only the first project, and study how the build-up of equity motivates the entrepreneur. We then analyze the optimal long-term contract and ask whether there is scope for lender commitment of future financing.

4.7.2.1 Short-Term Loan Agreements: The Increasing-Stake Result

To conduct a credit analysis in period 1, the lenders must see through the borrower's incentives to build up equity. So, they must work *backwards* and compute the borrower's gross utility in period 2 when she goes to the capital market to finance the date-2 (variable size) project with arbitrary assets A_2. In Section 3.4, we showed that this gross utility is

$$vA_2,$$

where $v > 1$ is the shadow value of equity given by equation (3.14′):

$$v = \frac{\rho_1 - \rho_0}{1 - \rho_0},$$

where

$$\rho_1 \equiv p_{\mathrm{H}}R$$

denotes the expected payoff per unit of investment, and

$$\rho_0 \equiv p_{\mathrm{H}}\left(R - \frac{B}{\Delta p}\right)$$

denotes the expected pledgeable income per unit of investment.

Consider now the date-1 project. Suppose that the corresponding loan agreement specifies (a) an investment level I_1 and (b) a sharing rule in the case of success, R_{b} for the borrower and R_{l} for the lenders.[51] As in the static case, it is easy to show that the optimal date-1 contract specifies a reward for the entrepreneur only when the project succeeds. Letting $A_1 = A$ denote the borrower's initial cash endowment, the date-1 investors' breakeven constraint is as usual given by

$$p_{\mathrm{H}}R_{\mathrm{l}} \geqslant I_1 - A. \qquad (\mathrm{IR_l})$$

The incentive constraint is slightly modified due to the existence of the shadow value of equity:

$$(\Delta p)[v(RI_1 - R_{\mathrm{l}})] \geqslant BI_1. \qquad (\mathrm{IC_b})$$

The analysis is identical to that in Section 3.4, except for the existence of this shadow value (which amounts to replacing "B" by "B/v"). The pledgeable income per unit of investment becomes

$$\tilde{\rho}_0 = p_{\mathrm{H}}\left(R - \frac{B}{v\Delta p}\right) = \rho_1 - \frac{\rho_1 - \rho_0}{v} = \rho_1 + \rho_0 - 1.$$

The date-1 debt capacity is therefore given by $I_1 = k_1 A$, where[52]

$$k_1 = \frac{1}{1 - \tilde{\rho}_0} = \frac{1}{2 - \rho_0 - \rho_1} > k = \frac{1}{1 - \rho_0}. \qquad (4.11)$$

Under short-term loan agreements, the borrower invests in period 2 if and only if she has income, that is, if and only if the first project is successful. She then invests

$$I_2^{\mathrm{S}} = kA_2^{\mathrm{S}} = \frac{A_2^{\mathrm{S}}}{1 - \rho_0},$$

where A_2^{S} is her date-2 equity in the case of date-1 success:

$$A_2^{\mathrm{S}} = RI_1 - R_{\mathrm{l}} = \frac{BI_1}{(\Delta p)v}.$$

After some computations, one finds that the (date-1) expected second-period investment is equal to the first-period investment:

$$p_{\mathrm{H}}I_2^{\mathrm{S}} = I_1.$$

Our first result is that *stakes increase over time*: conditional on proper performance, the second-period investment is $1/p_{\mathrm{H}} > 1$ times the first-period investment. The split of investment occurs only in expectations.

51. Strictly speaking, it is not necessary that the income attached to the first project be realized in period 1. In particular, it could be the case that this income accrues only in period 2. If a signal accrues at the end of date 1 that is a sufficient statistic for the probability of success and is public information, the future proceeds from the date-1 project can be sold in the marketplace, that is, *securitized*, and everything is as if the income accrued at date 1.

52. We assume that the denominator of k_1 is positive. Otherwise, the debt capacity in period 1 is infinite.

The borrower's *gross* utility under short-term loan agreements, $U_b^{g,ST}$, is

$$U_b^{g,ST} = p_H[vA_2^S] = \frac{\rho_1 - \rho_0}{2 - \rho_0 - \rho_1}A.$$

This yields a *net* borrower utility:

$$U_b^{ST} \equiv U_b^{g,ST} - A = \frac{2(\rho_1 - 1)}{2 - \rho_0 - \rho_1}A, \tag{4.12}$$

which, we check, is nothing but the NPV:

$$\text{NPV} = (\rho_1 - 1)(I_1 + p_H I_2^S)$$

since $p_H I_2^S = I_1 = A/(2 - \rho_0 - \rho_1)$.

We can draw two further conclusions from this analysis.

The prospect of follow-up projects is a disciplining device. Consequently, the first-period borrowing capacity is larger than in the absence of such projects (see (4.11)). The lenders trust the borrower more because the latter attaches a shadow value (in excess of 1) to retained earnings.

Because of the nature of a short-term loan agreement, the borrower is unable to continue if the first project fails. There is therefore *no insurance* concerning the financing of the second-period project. We now ask whether such insurance should be supplied in a long-term loan agreement.

4.7.2.2 Long-Term Loan Agreements and Credit Commitments

Suppose now that the date-1 contract between the lenders and the borrower specifies (a) the date-1 investment I_1, (b) the date-2 investment I_2 contingent on whether the first project failed or succeeded, and (c) the sharing of the first- and second-period incomes.

Obviously, the borrower is always weakly better off under a long-term contract because she can always obtain the short-term contract outcome by duplicating what would have happened under a sequence of short-term contracts. So, the question is whether the borrower can *strictly* gain by signing a long-term contract.

Let us first derive the optimal long-term contract in our constant-returns-to-scale model. Let us assume that the first-period investment is I_1, and that the first-period income is split into R_b and $R_l = RI_1 - R_b$. The second-period net utilities for the borrower are V_2^S and V_2^F, where the superscripts "S" and "F" indicate that the date-1 project succeeded or failed. Similarly, the date-2 utilities for the lenders are W_2^S and W_2^F. Without loss of generality we can assume that R_b is consumed (rather than reinvested) by the borrower: if part of R_b were reinvested, one could equivalently reallocate this part to the lenders, whose contribution towards defraying the cost of the second-period investment would increase accordingly.

We necessarily have

$$V_2^k + W_2^k = (p_H R - 1)I_2^k, \quad k = \text{S, F}. \tag{4.13}$$

Furthermore, incentive compatibility in period 2 requires that

$$V_2^k \geqslant \frac{p_H B}{\Delta p} I_2^k, \quad k = \text{S, F}. \tag{4.14}$$

Thus we want to maximize the borrower's net intertemporal utility:

$$\max U_b = p_H(R_b + V_2^S) + (1 - p_H)V_2^F - A \tag{4.15}$$

subject to (4.13), (4.14), to the incentive compatibility condition in period 1,

$$(\Delta p)(R_b + V_2^S - V_2^F) \geqslant BI_1, \tag{4.16}$$

and to the breakeven constraint,

$$p_H[RI_1 - R_b + W_2^S] + (1 - p_H)W_2^F = I_1 - A. \tag{4.17}$$

We leave it to the reader to analyze this program.[53] Solving it shows that the date-1 and date-2 investments are the same as under short-term contracting,

$$I_1 = \frac{A}{2 - \rho_0 - \rho_1}, \qquad I_2^S = \frac{I_1}{p_H}, \qquad I_2^F = 0,$$

and that the borrower's utility is also the same as under short-term contracting,

$$U_b^{g,LT} = \frac{2(\rho_1 - \rho_0)}{2 - \rho_0 - \rho_1}A = U_b^{g,ST}.$$

Thus, *the borrower obtains the same intertemporal utility as under short-term loan agreements if the technology exhibits constant returns to scale.*

53. One may proceed as follows. (i) One can show that, without loss of generality, $R_b = 0$ (the borrower might as well reinvest earnings rather than consume them). (ii) Substituting (4.13) into (4.17) to eliminate the W_2^k, one sees that (4.14) must be binding for k = S, F (otherwise, one would increase the date-2 investments). (iii) One then shows that there is no loss of generality in taking $V_2^F = I_2^F = 0$. (iv) Lastly, using (4.17) and (4.14), and showing that (4.16) is binding, one obtains $p_H I_2^S = I_1$. The conclusions then follow.

This equivalence between short- and long-term contracts which extends to an arbitrary number of projects is striking, although it relies crucially on risk neutrality.[54]

4.7.2.3 Comparison: The Impact of Sequentiality

Finally, we compare the entrepreneur's net payoffs (the NPVs) in the simultaneous and sequential cases:

$$U_{\mathrm{b}}^{\mathrm{simultaneous}} = \frac{\rho_1 - 1}{1 - \hat{\rho}_0} A < U_{\mathrm{b}}^{\mathrm{sequential}} = \frac{2(\rho_1 - 1)}{2 - \rho_0 - \rho_1} A$$

if and only if

$$1 - \hat{\rho}_0 > \frac{2 - \rho_0 - \rho_1}{2} \iff 2 > \rho_1 + \rho_0,$$

which is indeed satisfied. Thus, the entrepreneur is better off under sequential projects. Intuitively, sequentiality alleviates moral hazard: the entrepreneur cannot take her private benefit on the second project if the first project fails. By contrast, she can do so when projects are simultaneous; the disciplining threat of nonrefinancing is then empty.

We can also point at the impact of project correlation. It was argued in Section 4.2 that when projects are simultaneous, correlation reduces the pledgeable income and ultimately hurts the entrepreneur. Correlation is more of a mixed blessing in the case of sequential projects; for, a failure in the first project (which has positive probability unless $p_{\mathrm{H}} = 1$) is informative about the payoff to the second project. Put differently, correlation would generate a learning effect that is beneficial whether there is an agency problem or not. With an agency cost, it is *a fortiori* optimal not to fund the second project if the first project fails. The second project is, however, funded on a larger scale if the first project succeeds.[55]

4.7.3 Continuation versus Financial Incentives in Infinite-Horizon Models

As the previous two-period model demonstrated, managerial incentives can be provided either through the promise of continuation or the threat of termination[56] or through financial compensation. Continuation is under entrepreneurial risk neutrality a more efficient "carrot" than financial rewards whenever continuation has a positive NPV: the same incentive can then be provided at a lower cost to investors, or, conversely, the same pledgeable income is consistent with a higher entrepreneurial payoff.

The two-period setup, however, leaves aside some interesting issues. First, it provides little insight into the potentially complex dynamics of retentions and refinancing under a longer horizon. Second, in the two-period version, the obviously efficient design of incentives rewards the entrepreneur with pure continuation (no financial reward) in the first period and a purely financial reward in the second period. With an infinite horizon, continuation is always an option and always more efficient (yields a higher NPV) than a financial reward; yet, the manager must at some point cash in if successful. This dual pattern of retentions and comovement of the continuation and financial rewards incentives is addressed in two papers by DeMarzo and Fishman (2002) and by Biais, Mariotti, Plantin, and Rochet (2004), which both assume an infinite horizon $t = 0, 1, \ldots$.[57] While covering these papers lies outside the scope of this book, we can point at a few of their insights.

Biais et al. (2004) consider a stationary environment in which the per-period (recurrent) investment has a fixed size and pledgeable income in each period is smaller than the per-period reinvestment cost:

$$p_{\mathrm{H}}\left(R - \frac{B}{\Delta p}\right) < I.$$

The only element of nonstationarity may stem from a date-0 up-front investment cost I_0 which takes an arbitrary value (and therefore may largely exceed the continuation or reinvestment cost I).

54. Principal–agent theory has investigated conditions under which the optimal long-term contract between a principal and an agent can be implemented through a sequence of short-term contracts. See Chiappori et al. (1994) for a very clear exposition.

55. Under perfect correlation, and assuming that the optimal incentive scheme induces good behavior at date 1 (which is not a foregone conclusion, since the learning benefit might be stronger under misbehavior), the posterior probabilities of success under good and bad behaviors are $\hat{p}_{\mathrm{H}} = 1$ and $\hat{p}_{\mathrm{L}} = p_{\mathrm{L}}/p_{\mathrm{H}}$, respectively. And so the second-period incentive constraint following a first-period success can be written as

$$(\hat{p}_{\mathrm{H}} - \hat{p}_{\mathrm{L}})R_{\mathrm{b}} \geqslant BI_2 \iff \hat{p}_{\mathrm{H}}R_{\mathrm{b}} \geqslant \frac{p_{\mathrm{H}}BI_2}{\Delta p}.$$

The nonpledgeable income at date 2 is thus the same (for a given investment) as when the projects are independent. But the NPV, $\hat{p}_{\mathrm{H}}RI_2$, and therefore the pledgeable income are higher due to the learning effect.

56. Or, more generally, the prospect of upsizing or downsizing.

57. See also Gromb (1999) and Clementi and Hopenhayn (2002) for related work.

$0 \qquad \mathcal{U}_b^{***} \qquad \mathcal{U}_b^{**} \qquad \mathcal{U}_b^{*} \qquad \mathcal{U}_b(t) \longrightarrow$

Probability of continuation $x(t)$	$0 \leqslant \dfrac{\mathcal{U}_b}{\mathcal{U}_b^{***}} \leqslant 1$	1	1	1 (actually, $x(t+\tau) = 1$ for all $\tau \geqslant 0$)
Flow financial payment in the case of success $R_b(t)$	0	0	$\mathcal{U}_b(t) - \mathcal{U}_b^{**}$	$\dfrac{B}{\Delta p}$
Flow financial payment in the case of failure	0	0	0	0
Continuation value $\mathcal{U}_b(t+1)$	greater than $\mathcal{U}_b^{***}/\beta$ if success 0 (liquidation) if failure	greater than $\mathcal{U}_b(t)/\beta$ if success lower than $\mathcal{U}_b(t)/\beta$ if failure	$\mathcal{U}_b^{*}$ if success lower than $\mathcal{U}_b(t)/\beta$ if failure	$\mathcal{U}_b^{*}$

Figure 4.6

In each period t, the firm either continues, implying reinvestment cost I, or is liquidated. If it continues, the manager chooses effort ($p = p_H$ or p_L, where misbehavior yields an instantaneous private benefit B); finally, the date-t performance (profit R in the case of success, 0 in the case of failure) is observed at the end of period t.

The entrepreneur and the investors are risk neutral, with preferences

$$E\left[\sum_{t=0}^{\infty} \beta^t c_t\right],$$

where β is the discount factor (smaller than 1) and c_t is the agent's date-t consumption (which, for the entrepreneur, may include the private benefit B if she elects to misbehave at date t). The entrepreneur is, as usual, protected by limited liability.

As is standard in repeated-moral-hazard models (see, for example, Chiappori et al. 1994; Spear and Srivastava 1987), the optimal contract is best characterized through the state-independent expected continuation valuation of the entrepreneur. Thus, let $\mathcal{U}(t)$ denote the expected present discounted utility of the entrepreneur at date t; this value function depends on the history up to date t and turns out to be a "sufficient statistic" for the future starting at date t.

Figure 4.6 describes the optimal combination of continuation and financial incentives. It confirms that the entrepreneur is first rewarded through continuation or, equivalently, deterred by the threat of termination (or downsizing: the probability $x(t)$ of continuation can also be interpreted, when investment is continuous (but bounded above), as the fraction of assets that are not liquidated).

Indeed, as long as the value function does not exceed level $\mathcal{U}_b^{**}$, no payment is made to the entrepreneur. Payments occur only when the value function is high, that is, when the past performance has been satisfactory (intuitively, enough milestones have been reached).

Turning to the implementation of the optimal contract, Biais et al. show that it can be implemented by giving investors stocks and bonds claims and that payouts can be made contingent solely on the size of accumulated reserves $L(t)$. There exist thresholds $L^{***} < L^{**} < L^{*}$ (corresponding to value function thresholds $\mathcal{U}_b^{***} < \mathcal{U}_b^{**} < \mathcal{U}_b^{*}$) such that, in particular,

- for $L(t) \geqslant L^{*}$, stocks pay a dividend;
- for $L(t) \geqslant L^{***}$, bonds distribute their full coupon;
- for $L(t) \leqslant L^{***}$, the firm cannot meet its debt payment and enters financial distress. It is downsized by a factor $L(t)/L^{***}$ (and then keeps operating on a smaller scale if it exits distress).

The date-0 financing contract sets the initial financial cushion $L(0)$ and the entrepreneur receives shares in the firm (as in the two-period model).

DeMarzo and Fishman (2002) perform a similar analysis, but in a generalized "Bolton–Scharfstein framework" (see Section 3.8) in which the investors cannot observe the cash flows. The moral-hazard dimension then refers to the entrepreneur's concealing realized cash flow rather than taking actions that may jeopardize these cash flows. When diverting 1, the manager receives $k \leqslant 1$ (in a sense, $k = B/\Delta p$ in Biais et al., and so, even if the income is verifiable in Biais et al. and nonverifiable in DeMarzo and Fishman, the models are mathematically very similar). DeMarzo and Fishman emphasizes an implementation in terms of a long-term coupon debt and a credit line. The credit line provides flexibility for the entrepreneur to accommodate, for a limited time, the adverse shocks that may arise under a random cash flow. (We will return to credit lines in Chapters 5 and 15.)

4.8 Exercises

Exercise 4.1 (maintenance of collateral and asset depletion just before distress). This exercise analyzes the impact of the existence of a privately received signal about distress on credit rationing. Consider the model of Section 4.3.4 with $A' = A$ (so the asset has the same value for the borrower and the lender). The new feature is that the resale value of the asset is A only if the borrower invests in maintenance; otherwise the final value of the asset is 0, regardless of the state of nature. The loan agreement cannot monitor the borrower's maintenance decision (but the resale value is verifiable). So, there are two dimensions of moral hazard for the borrower. The borrower incurs private disutility $c < A$ from maintaining the asset, and 0 from not maintaining it. Assume that $p_L B/(\Delta p) \geqslant c$, and that the entrepreneur is protected by limited liability.

(i) Suppose that the borrower receives no signal about the likelihood of distress (that is, the maintenance decision can be thought of as being simultaneous with that of choosing between probabilities p_H and p_L of success). Show that the analysis of this chapter is unaltered except that the borrower's utility U_b is reduced by c.

(ii) Suppose now that with probability ξ in the case of failure the borrower privately learns that failure will occur with certainty. With probability $(1 - \xi)$ in the case of failure and with probability 1 in the case of success, no signal accrues. ($\xi = 0$ corresponds to question (i).) The signal, if any, is received after the choice between p_H and p_L but before the maintenance decision. Suppose further that the asset is pledged to the lenders only in the case of failure. Show that, if the entrepreneur is poor and c is "not too large," constraint (IC_b) must now be written

$$(\Delta p)(R_b + A) \geqslant B + (\Delta p)\xi c.$$

Interpret this inequality. Find a necessary and sufficient condition for the project to be funded.

(iii) Keeping the framework of question (ii), when is it better not to pledge the asset at all than to pledge it in the case of failure?

Exercise 4.2 (diversification across heterogeneous activities). Consider two variable-investment activities, α and β, as described in Section 3.4. The probabilities of success p_H (when working) and p_L (when shirking) are the same in both activities. The two activities are independent (as in Section 4.2). The two activities differ in their per-unit returns (R^α and R^β) and private benefits (B^α and B^β). Let, for $i \in \{\alpha, \beta\}$,

$$\rho_1^i \equiv p_H R^i > 1 \quad \text{and} \quad \rho_0^i = p_H\left(R^i - \frac{B^i}{\Delta p}\right) < 1.$$

For example, $\rho_1^\alpha < \rho_1^\beta$ but $\rho_0^\alpha > \rho_0^\beta$.

(i) Suppose that the entrepreneur agrees with the investors to *focus* on a single activity. Which activity will they choose?

(ii) Assume now that the firm invests I^α in activity α and I^β in activity β and that this allocation can be contracted upon with the investors. Write the incentive constraints and breakeven constraint.

Show that it may be that the optimum is to invest more in activity β ($I^\beta > I^\alpha$) even though the entrepreneur would focus on activity α if she were forced to focus.

Exercise 4.3 (full pledging). In Section 4.3.1, we claimed that it is optimal to pledge the full value of the resale in the case of distress before committing any of the income R obtained in the absence of distress. Prove this formally.

Exercise 4.4 ("value at risk" and benefits from diversification). This exercise looks at the impact of portfolio correlation on capital requirements. An entrepreneur has two identical fixed-investment projects. Each involves investment cost I. A project is successful (yields R) with probability p and fails (yields 0) with probability $1 - p$. The probability of success is endogenous. If the entrepreneur works, the probability of success is $p_H = \frac{1}{2}$ and the entrepreneur receives no private benefit. If the entrepreneur shirks, the probability of success is $p_L = 0$ and the entrepreneur obtains private benefit B. The entrepreneur starts with cash $2A$, that is, A per project.

We assume that the probability that one project succeeds conditional on the other project succeeding (and the entrepreneur behaving) is

$$\tfrac{1}{2}(1 + \alpha)$$

(it is, of course, 0 if the entrepreneur misbehaves on this project). $\alpha \in [-1, 1]$ is an index of correlation between the two projects.

The entrepreneur (who is protected by limited liability) has the following preferences:

$$u(R_b) = \begin{cases} R_b & \text{for } R_b \in [0, \bar{R}], \\ \bar{R} & \text{for } R_b \geqslant \bar{R}. \end{cases}$$

(i) Write the two incentive constraints that will guarantee that the entrepreneur works on both projects.

(ii) How is the entrepreneur optimally rewarded for $\bar{R}$ large?

(iii) Find the optimal compensation scheme in the general case. Distinguish between the cases of positive and negative correlation. How is the ability to receive outside funding affected by the coefficient of correlation?

Exercise 4.5 (liquidity of entrepreneur's claim). (i) Consider the framework of Section 4.4 (without speculative monitoring). In Section 4.4, we assumed that none of the value μr_b (with $\mu > 1$) obtained by reinvesting r_b was appropriated by the entrepreneur. Assume instead that $\mu_0 r_b$ is returned to investors, where $\mu_0 < 1$. For consistency, assume that investors observe whether the entrepreneur faces a liquidity shock (this corresponds to case (a) in Section 4.4). And, to avoid having to consider the correlation of activities and the question of diversification (see Section 4.2), assume that $(\mu - \mu_0)r_b$ is a private benefit that automatically accrues to the entrepreneur and therefore cannot be "cross-pledged."

There is an equivalence between rewarding success with payment R_b when there was no interim investment opportunity and rewarding success with $(1 - \lambda)R_b$ independently of interim investment opportunity. As in Section 4.4 we assume that the entrepreneur is rewarded with R_b only when there was no interim investment opportunity.

How is the liquidity of the entrepreneur's claim affected by $\mu_0 > 0$?

(ii) Suppose now that the probability of a "liquidity shock," i.e., a new investment opportunity, is endogenous. If the entrepreneur does not search, then $\lambda = 0$; if she searches, which involves private cost $\bar{\lambda}c$ for the entrepreneur, then $\lambda = \bar{\lambda}$. Rewrite the financing constraint.

Exercise 4.6 (project size increase at an intermediate date). An entrepreneur has initial net worth A and starts at date 0 with a fixed-investment project costing I. The project succeeds (yields R) or fails (yields 0) with probability $p \in \{p_L, p_H\}$. The entrepreneur obtains private benefit B at date 0 when misbehaving (choosing $p = p_L$) and 0 otherwise. Everyone is risk neutral, investors demand a 0 rate of return, and the entrepreneur is protected by limited liability.

The twist relative to this standard fixed-investment model is that, with probability λ, the size may be doubled *at no additional cost* to the investors (i.e., the project duplicated) at date 1. The new investment is identical with the initial one (same date-2 stochastic revenue; same description of moral hazard, except that it takes place at date 1) and is perfectly correlated with it. That is, there are three states of nature: either both projects succeed independently of the entrepreneur's effort, or both fail independently of effort, or a project for which the entrepreneur behaved succeeds and the other for which she misbehaved fails.

Denote by R_b the entrepreneur's compensation in the case of success when the reinvestment opportunity does not occur, and by $\mathcal{R}_b$ that when both the initial and the new projects are successful. (The entrepreneur optimally receives 0 if any activity fails.)

Show that the project and its (contingent) duplication receive funding if and only if

$$(1+\lambda)\left[p_{\mathrm{H}}\left(R-\frac{B}{\Delta p}\right)\right] \geqslant I-A.$$

Exercise 4.7 (group lending and reputational capital). Consider two economic agents, each endowed with a fixed-investment project, as described, say, in Section 3.2. The two projects are independent.

Agent i's utility is

$$R_{\mathrm{b}}^{i}+aR_{\mathrm{b}}^{j},$$

where R_{b}^{i} is her income at the end of the period, R_{b}^{j} is the other agent's income, and $0<a<1$ is the parameter of altruism. Assume that

$$p_{\mathrm{H}}\left(R-\frac{B}{(1+a)\Delta p}\right)<I-A<p_{\mathrm{H}}R.$$

(i) Can the agents secure financing through individual borrowing? Through group lending?

(ii) Now add a later or "stage-2" game, which will be played after the outcomes of the two projects are realized. This game will be played by the two agents and will not be observed by the "stage-1" lenders. In this social game, which is unrelated to the previous projects, the two agents have two strategies C (cooperate) and D (defect). The *monetary* (not the utility) payoffs are given by the following payoff matrix:

		Agent 1: C	Agent 1: D
Agent 2	C	1, 1	−2, 2
	D	2, −2	−1, −1

(the first number in an entry is agent 1's monetary payoff and the second agent 2's payoff).

Suppose $a=\frac{1}{2}$. What is the equilibrium of this game? What would the equilibrium be if the agents were selfish ($a=0$)?

(iii) Now, assemble the two stages considered in (i) and (ii) into a single, two-stage dynamic game. Suppose that the agents in stage 1 (the corporate finance stage) are slightly unsure that the other agent is altruistic: agent i's beliefs are that, with probability $1-\varepsilon$, the other agent (j) is altruistic ($a^{j}=\frac{1}{2}$) and, with probability ε, the other agent is selfish ($a^{j}=0$). For simplicity, assume that ε is small (actually, it is convenient to take the approximation $\varepsilon=0$ in the computations).

The two agents engage in group lending and receive R_{b} each if both projects succeed and 0 otherwise. Profits and payments to the lenders are realized at the end of stage 1.

At stage 2, each agent decides whether to participate in the social game described in (ii). If either refuses to participate, each gets 0 at stage 2 (whether she is altruistic or selfish); otherwise, they get the payoffs resulting from equilibrium strategies in the social game.

Let δ denote the discount factor between the two stages. Compute the minimum discount factor that enables the agents to secure funding at stage 1.

Exercise 4.8 (peer monitoring). The peer monitoring model studied in the supplementary section assumes that the projects are independent. Suppose instead that they are (perfectly) correlated. (See Sections 3.2.4 and 4.2. There are three states of nature: favorable (both projects always succeed), unfavorable (both projects always fail), and intermediate (a project succeeds if and only if the entrepreneur behaves), with respective probabilities p_{L}, $1-p_{\mathrm{H}}$, and Δp.)

(i) Replace the limited liability assumption by {no limited liability, but strong risk aversion for $R_{\mathrm{b}}<0$ and risk neutrality for $R_{\mathrm{b}}\geqslant 0$}. Show that group lending is useless and that there is no credit rationing.

(ii) Come back to the limited liability assumption and assume that

$$p_{\mathrm{H}}\left(R-\frac{B}{\Delta p}\right)<I-A.$$

Assume that $b+c<B$. Find a condition under which the agents can secure funding.

Exercise 4.9 (borrower-friendly bankruptcy court). Consider the timing described in Figure 4.7.

The project, if financed, yields random and verifiable short-term profit $r\in[0,\bar{r}]$ (with a continuous density and *ex ante* mean $E[r]$). After r is realized and cashed in, the firm either liquidates (sells its assets), yielding some known liquidation value $L>0$, or continues. Note that (the random) r and (the deterministic) L are not subject to moral hazard. If the

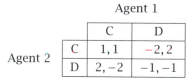

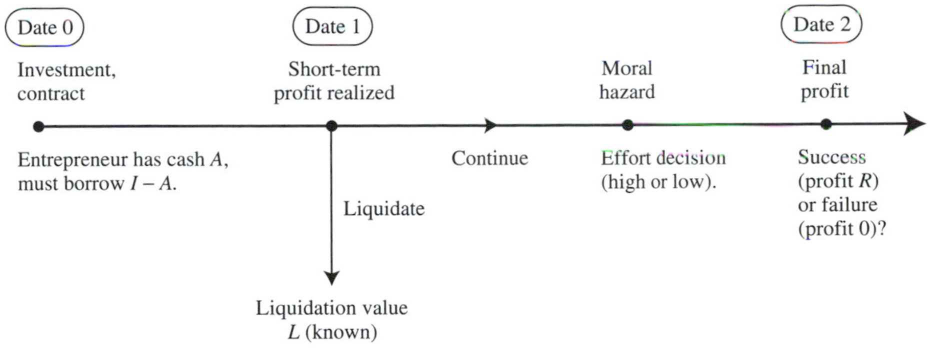

Figure 4.7

firm continues, its prospects improve with r (so r is "good news" about the future). Namely, the probability of success is $p_{\mathrm{H}}(r)$ if the entrepreneur works between dates 1 and 2 and $p_{\mathrm{L}}(r)$ if the entrepreneur shirks. Assume that $p'_{\mathrm{H}} > 0$, $p'_{\mathrm{L}} > 0$, and

$$p_{\mathrm{H}}(r) - p_{\mathrm{L}}(r) \equiv \Delta p$$

is independent of r (so shirking reduces the probability of success by a fixed amount independent of prospects). As usual, one will want to induce the entrepreneur to work if continuation obtains. It is convenient to use the notation

$$\rho_1(r) \equiv p_{\mathrm{H}}(r)R \quad \text{and} \quad \rho_0(r) \equiv p_{\mathrm{H}}(r)\left[R - \frac{B}{\Delta p}\right].$$

Investors are competitive and demand an expected rate of return equal to 0. Assume

$$\rho_1(r) > L \quad \text{for all } r \tag{1}$$

and

$$E[r] + L > I - A > E[r + \rho_0(r)]. \tag{2}$$

(i) Argue informally that, in the optimal contract for the borrower, the short-term profit and the liquidation value (if the firm is liquidated) ought to be given to investors.

Argue that, in the case of continuation, $R_{\mathrm{b}} = B/\Delta p$. (If you are unable to show why, take this fact for granted in the rest of the question.)

Interpret conditions (1) and (2).

(ii) Write the borrower's optimization program.

Assume (without loss of generality) that the firm continues if and only if $r \geqslant r^*$ for some $r^* \in (0, r)$. Exhibit the equation defining r^*.

(iii) Argue that this optimal contract can be implemented using, inter alia, a short-term debt contract at level $d = r^*$. Interpret "liquidation" as a "bankruptcy."

How does short-term debt vary with the borrower's initial equity? Explain.

(iv) Suppose that, when the decision to liquidate is taken, the firm must go to a bankruptcy court. The judge mechanically splits the bankruptcy proceeds L equally between investors and the borrower.

Define $\hat{r}$ by

$$\rho_0(\hat{r}) \equiv \tfrac{1}{2}L.$$

Assume first that

$$r^* > \hat{r}$$

(where r^* is the value found in question (ii)).

Show that the borrower-friendly court actually prevents the borrower from having access to financing. (Note: a diagram may help.)

(v) Continuing on question (iv), show that when

$$r^* < \hat{r},$$

the borrower-friendly court either prevents financing or increases the probability of bankruptcy, and in all cases hurts the borrower and not the lenders.

Exercise 4.10 (benefits from diversification with variable-investment projects). An entrepreneur has two variable-investment projects $i \in \{1, 2\}$. Each is described as in Section 3.4. (For investment level I^i, project i yields RI^i in the case of success and 0 in the case of failure. The probability of success is p_{H} if the entrepreneur behaves (and thereby gets no private benefit) and $p_{\mathrm{L}} = p_{\mathrm{H}} - \Delta p$ if she misbehaves (and then obtains private benefit BI^i). Universal risk neutrality prevails and the entrepreneur is protected

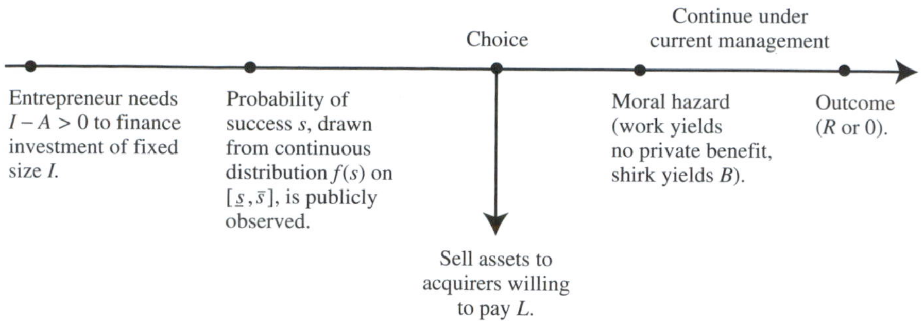

Figure 4.8

by limited liability.) The two projects are *independent* (not correlated). The entrepreneur starts with total wealth A. Assume

$$\rho_1 \equiv p_H R > 1 > \rho_0 \equiv p_H\left(R - \frac{B}{\Delta p}\right)$$

and

$$\rho_0' \equiv p_H\left(R - \frac{p_H}{p_H + p_L}\frac{B}{\Delta p}\right) < 1.$$

(i) First, consider project finance (each project is financed on a stand-alone basis). Compute the borrower's utility. Is there any benefit from having access to two projects rather than one?

(ii) Compute the borrower's utility under cross-pledging.

Exercise 4.11 (optimal sale policy). Consider the timing in Figure 4.8.

The probability of success s is not known initially and is learned publicly after the investment is sunk. If the assets are not sold, the probability of success is s if the entrepreneur works and $s - \Delta p$ if she shirks (in which case she gets private benefit B). Assume that the (state-contingent) decision to sell the firm to an acquirer can be contracted upon *ex ante*. It is optimal to keep the entrepreneur (not sell) if and only if $s \geqslant s^*$ for some threshold s^*. (Assume in the following that s has a wide enough support and that there are no corner solutions. Further assume that, conditional on not liquidating, it is optimal to induce the entrepreneur to exert effort. If you want to show off, you may derive a sufficient condition for this to be the case.) As is usual, everyone is risk neutral, the entrepreneur is protected by limited liability, and the market rate of interest is 0.

(i) Suppose that the entrepreneur's reward in the case of success (and, of course, continuation) is $R_b = B/\Delta p$. Assuming that the financing constraint is binding, write the NPV and the investors' breakeven constraint and show that

$$s^* = \frac{(1+\mu)L}{R + \mu(R - B/\Delta p)}$$

for some $\mu > 0$. Explain the economic tradeoff.

(ii) Endogenize $R_b(s)$ assuming that effort is to be encouraged and show that indeed $R_b(s) = B/\Delta p$ for all s. What is the intuition for this "minimum incentive result"?

(iii) Suppose now that s can take only two values, s_1 and s_2, with $s_2 > s_1$ and

$$s_2\left(R - \frac{B}{\Delta p}\right) > \max(L, I - A).$$

Introduce a first-stage moral hazard (just after the investment is sunk). The entrepreneur chooses between taking a private benefit B_0, in which case $s = s_1$ for certain, and taking no private benefit, in which case $s = s_2$ for certain. Assume that financing is infeasible if the contract induces the entrepreneur to misbehave at either stage. What is the optimal contract? Is financing feasible? Discuss the issue of contract renegotiation.

Exercise 4.12 (conflict of interest and division of labor). Consider the timing in Figure 4.9.

The entrepreneur (who is protected by limited liability) is assigned two simultaneous tasks (the moral-hazard problem is bidimensional):

- The entrepreneur chooses between probabilities of success p_H (and then receives no private benefit) and p_L (in which case she receives private benefit B).
- The entrepreneur is in charge of overseeing that the asset remains attractive to external buyers

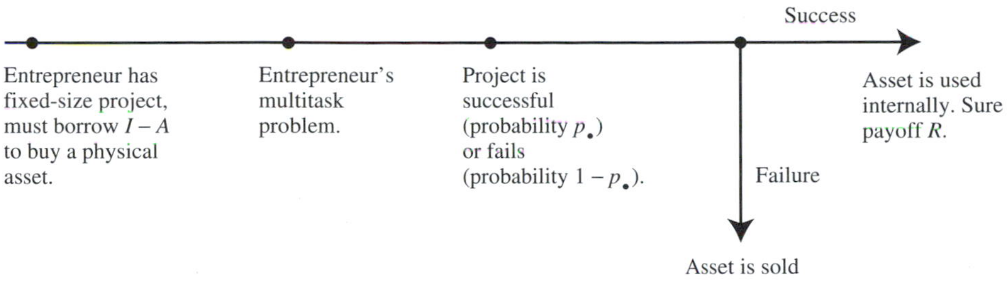

Figure 4.9

in the case where the project fails and the asset is thus not used internally. At private cost c, the entrepreneur maintains the resale value at level L. The resale value is 0 if the entrepreneur does not incur cost c. The resale value is observed by the investors if and only if the project fails.

Let R_b denote the entrepreneur's reward if the project is successful (by assumption, this reward is not contingent on the maintenance performance); $\hat{R}_b$ is the entrepreneur's reward if the project fails and the asset is sold at price L; last, the entrepreneur (optimally) receives nothing if the project fails and the asset is worth nothing to external buyers.

The entrepreneur and the investors are risk neutral and the market rate of interest is 0. Assume that to enable financing the contract must induce good behavior in the two moral-hazard dimensions.

(i) Write the three incentive compatibility constraints; show that the constraint that the entrepreneur does not want to choose p_L and not maintain the asset is not binding.

(ii) Compute the nonpledgeable income. What is the minimum level of A such that the entrepreneur can obtain financing?

(iii) Suppose now that the maintenance task can be delegated to another agent. The latter is also risk neutral and protected by limited liability. Show that the pledgeable income increases and so financing is eased.

Exercise 4.13 (group lending). Consider the group lending model with altruism in the supplementary section, but assume that the projects are perfectly correlated rather than independent. What is the necessary and sufficient condition for the borrowers to have access to credit?

Exercise 4.14 (diversification and correlation). This exercise studies how necessary and sufficient conditions for the financing of *two projects* undertaken by the same entrepreneur vary with the projects' correlation. The two projects are identical, taken on a stand-alone basis. A project involves a fixed investment cost I and yields profit R with probability p and 0 with probability $1-p$, where the probability of success p is chosen by the entrepreneur for each project: p_H (no private benefit) or $p_L = p_H - \Delta p$ (private benefit B).

The entrepreneur has wealth $2A$, is risk neutral, and is protected by limited liability. The investors are risk neutral and demand rate of return equal to 0.

In the following questions, assume that, conditional on financing, the entrepreneur receives R_k when $k \in \{0, 1, 2\}$ projects succeed, and that $R_0 = R_1 = 0$ (this involves no loss of generality).

(i) *Independent projects.* Suppose that the projects are uncorrelated. Show that the entrepreneur can get financing provided that

$$p_H\left[R - \left(\frac{p_H}{p_H + p_L}\right)\frac{B}{\Delta p}\right] \geqslant I - A.$$

(ii) *Perfectly correlated projects.* Suppose that the shocks affecting the two projects are identical. (The following may, or may not, help in understanding the stochastic structure. One can think for a given project of an underlying random variable ω uniformly distributed in $[0, 1]$. If $\omega < p_L$, the project succeeds regardless of the entrepreneur's effort. If $\omega > p_H$, the project fails regardless of her effort. If $p_L < \omega < p_H$, the project succeeds if and only if she behaves. In the case of independent projects, ω_1 and ω_2 are independent and identically distributed (i.i.d.). For perfectly correlated projects, $\omega_1 = \omega_2$.) Show that the two projects can be financed if and

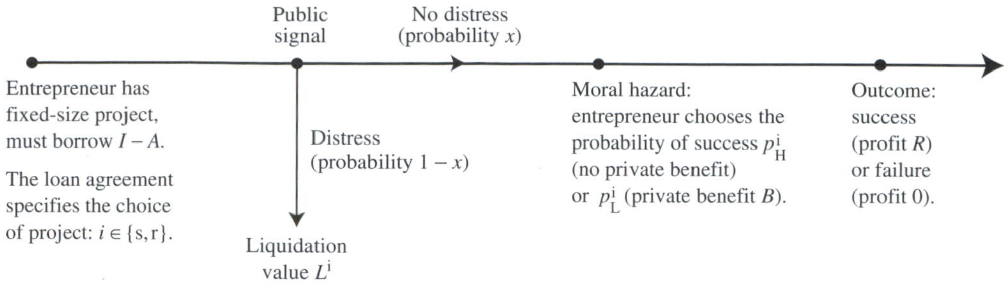

Figure 4.10

only if

$$p_H\left(R - \frac{B}{\Delta p}\right) \geqslant I - A.$$

(iii) *Imperfectly correlated projects.* Suppose that with probability x the projects will be perfectly correlated, and with probability $1 - x$ they will be independent (so $x = 0$ in question (i) and $x = 1$ in question (ii)). Derive the financing condition. What value of x would the entrepreneur choose if she were free to pick the extent of correlation between the projects: (a) before the projects are financed, in an observable way; (b) after the projects are financed?

Exercise 4.15 (credit rationing and bias towards less risky projects). This exercise shows that a shortage of cash on hand creates a bias toward less risky projects. the same proposition in the context of a tradeoff between collateral value and profitability. The timing, depicted in Figure 4.10, is similar to that studied in Section 4.3.

The entrepreneur must finance a fixed-size project costing I, and has initial net worth $A < I$. If investors consent to funding the project, investors and entrepreneurs agree, as part of the loan agreement, on which variant, i = s (safe) or r (risky) is selected. A public signal accrues at an intermediate stage. With probability x (independent of the project specification), the firm experiences no distress and continues. The production is then subject to moral hazard. The entrepreneur can behave (yielding no private benefit and probability of success p_H^i) or misbehave (yielding a private benefit B and probability of success p_L^i); success generates profit R. One will assume that

$$p_H^s - p_L^s = p_H^r - p_L^r \equiv \Delta p > 0.$$

With probability $1 - x$, the firm's asset must be resold, at price L^i with $L^i < p_H^i R$.

We assume that two specifications are equally profitable but the risky project yields a higher long-term profit but a smaller liquidation value (for example, it may correspond to an off-the-beaten-track technology that creates more differentiation from competitors, but also generates little interest in the asset resale market):

$$L^s > L^r$$

and

$$(1 - x)L^s + xp_H^s R = (1 - x)L^r + xp_H^r R.$$

The entrepreneur is risk neutral and protected by limited liability, and the investors are risk neutral and demand a rate of return equal to 0.

(i) Show that there exists $\bar{A}$ such that for $A > \bar{A}$, the entrepreneur is indifferent between the two specifications, while for $A < \bar{A}$, she strictly prefers offering the safe one to investors.

(ii) What happens if the choice of specification is not contractible and is to the discretion of the entrepreneur just after the investment is sunk?

Exercise 4.16 (fire sale externalities and total surplus-enhancing cartelizations). This exercise endogenizes the resale price P in the redeployability model of Section 4.3.1 (but with variable investment). The timing is recapped in Figure 4.11.

The model is the variable-investment model, with a mass 1 of identical entrepreneurs. The representative entrepreneur and her project of endogenous size I are as in Section 4.3.1. In particular, with probability x the project is viable, and with probability $1-x$ the project is unproductive. The assets are then resold to "third parties" at price P. The shocks faced by individual firms (whether productive or not) are

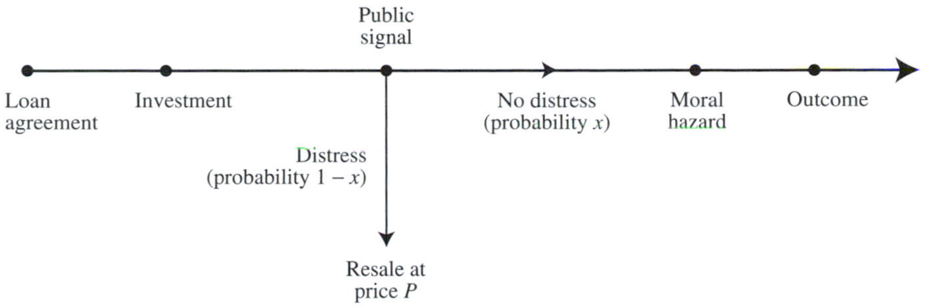

Figure 4.11

independent, and so in equilibrium a fraction x of firms remain productive, while a volume of assets $J = (1 - x)I$ (where I is the representative entrepreneur's investment) has become unproductive under their current ownership.

The third parties (the buyers) have demand function $J = D(P)$, inverse demand function $P = P(J)$, gross surplus function $S(J)$ with $S'(J) = P$, net surplus function $S^{\mathrm{n}}(P) = S(J(P)) - PD(P)$ with $(S^{\mathrm{n}})' = -J$. Assume $P(\infty) = 0$ and $1 > x\rho_0$.

(i) Compute the representative entrepreneur's borrowing capacity and NPV.

(ii) Suppose next that the entrepreneurs *ex ante* form a cartel and jointly agree that they will not sell more than a fraction $z < 1$ of their assets when in distress.

Show that investment and NPV increase when asset sales are restricted if and only if the elasticity of demand is greater than 1:

$$-\frac{P'J}{P} > 1.$$

Check that this condition is not inconsistent with the stability of the equilibrium (the competitive equilibrium is stable if the mapping from aggregate investment I to individual investment i has slope greater than -1).

(iii) Show that total (buyers' and firms') surplus can increase when z is set below 1.

Exercise 4.17 (loan size and collateral requirements). An entrepreneur with limited wealth A finances a variable-investment project. A project of size $I \in \mathbb{R}$ if successful yields $R(I)$, where $R(0) = 0$, $R' > 0$, $R'' < 0$, $R'(0) = \infty$, $R'(\infty) = 0$. The probability of success is p_{H} if the entrepreneur behaves (she then receives no private benefit) and $p_{\mathrm{L}} = p_{\mathrm{H}} - \Delta p$ if she misbehaves (she then receives private benefit BI).

The entrepreneur can pledge an arbitrary amount of collateral with cost $C \geqslant 0$ to the entrepreneur and value $\phi(C)$ for the investors with $\phi(0) = 0$, $\phi' > 0$, $\phi'' < 0$, $\phi'(0) = 1$, $\phi'(\infty) = 0$.

The entrepreneur is risk neutral and protected by limited liability and the investors are competitive, risk neutral, and demand a rate of return equal to 0.

Assume that the first-best policy does not yield enough pledgeable income. (This first-best policy is $C^* = 0$ and I^* given by $p_{\mathrm{H}}R'(I^*) = 1$. Thus, the assumption is $p_{\mathrm{H}}[R(I^*) - BI^*/\Delta p] < I^* - A$.)

Assume that the entrepreneur pledges collateral only in the case of failure (on this, see Section 4.3.5), and that the investors' breakeven constraint is binding. Show that as A decreases or the agency cost (as measured by B or, keeping p_{H} constant, $p_{\mathrm{H}}/\Delta p$) increases, the optimal investment size decreases and the optimal collateral increases.

References

Aghion, P. and J. Tirole. 1997. Formal and real authority in organizations. *Journal of Political Economy* 105:1–29.

Aghion, P., P. Bolton, and J. Tirole. 2004. Exit options in corporate finance: liquidity vs incentives. *Review of Finance* 3:327–353.

Ahlin, C. and R. Townsend. 2003a. Using repayment data to test across models of joint liability lending. Mimeo, University of Chicago.

——. 2003b. Selection into and across credit contracts: theory and field research. Mimeo, University of Chicago.

Armendáriz de Aghion, B. 1999. On the design of a credit agreement with peer monitoring. *Journal of Development Economics* 60:79–104.

Armendáriz de Aghion, B. and C. Gollier. 2000. Peer group formation in an adverse selection model. *Economic Journal* 110:632–643.

Armendáriz de Aghion, B. and J. Morduch. 2005. *The Economics of Microfinance.* Cambridge, MA: MIT Press.

Arrow, K. 1962. Economic welfare and the allocation of resources for invention. In *The Rate and Direction of Incentive Activity: Economic and Social Factors* (ed. R. Nelson). Princeton University Press.

Banerjee, A., T. Besley, and T. W. Guinnane. 1994. The neighbor's keeper: the design of a credit cooperative with theory and test. *Quarterly Journal of Economics* 109:491–515.

Besanko, D. and A. Thakor. 1987. Collateral and rationing: sorting equilibria in monopolistic and competitive credit markets. *International Economic Review* 28:671–689.

Besley, T. and S. Coate. 1995. Group lending, repayment incentives and social collateral. *Journal of Development Economics* 46:1–18.

Bester, H. 1985. Screening vs. rationing in credit markets with imperfect information. *American Economic Review* 75:850–855.

——. 1987. The role of collateral in credit markets with imperfect information. *European Economic Review* 31:887–899.

Biais, B., T. Mariotti, G. Plantin, and J. C. Rochet. 2004. Dynamic security design. Mimeo, IDEI.

Boot, A., A. Thakor, and G. Udell. 1991. Secured lending and default risk: equilibrium analysis and monetary policy implications. *Economic Journal* 101:458–472.

Calvo, G. A. and S. Wellisz. 1978. Supervision, loss of control, and the optimal size of the firm. *Journal of Political Economy* 86:943–952.

——. 1979. Hierarchy, ability, and income distribution. *Journal of Political Economy* 87:991–1010.

Cerasi, V. and S. Daltung. 2000. The optimal size of a bank: costs and benefits of diversification. *European Economic Review* 44:1701–1726.

Chan, Y. and G. Kanatas. 1985. Asymmetric valuations and the role of collateral in loan agreements. *Journal of Money, Credit and Banking* 17:84–95.

Che, Y.-K. 2002. Joint liability and peer monitoring under group lending. *Contributions to Theoretical Economics* 2(1), Article 3. (Available at http://www.bepress.com/bejte/contributions/vol2/iss1/art3.)

Chiappori, P. A., I. Macho, P. Rey, and B. Salanié. 1994. Repeated moral hazard: memory, commitment, and the access to credit markets. *European Economic Review* 38:1527–1553.

Clementi, G. L. and H. Hopenhayn. 2002. A theory of financing constraints and firm dynamics. Mimeo, Rochester University.

Coffee, J. 1991. Liquidity versus control: the institutional investor as corporate monitor. *Columbia Law Review* 91:1277–1368.

Coleman, J. 1990. *Foundations of Social Theory.* The Belknap Press of the Harvard University Press.

DeMarzo, P. and M. Fishman. 2002. Optimal long-term contracting with privately observed cash flows. Working Paper, Northwestern University.

Dessi, R. 2005. Start-up finance, monitoring and collusion. *RAND Journal of Economics* 36:255–274.

Diamond, D. 1984. Financial intermediation and delegated monitoring. *Review of Economic Studies* 51:393–414.

Farrell, J. and N. Gallini. 1988. Second-sourcing as a commitment device: monopoly incentives to attract competition. *Quarterly Journal of Economics* 103:673–694.

Ghatak, M. and T. W. Guinnane. 1999. The economics of lending with joint liability: a review of theory and practice. *Journal of Development Economics* 60:195–228.

Ghatak, M. and R. Kali. 2001. Financially interlinked business groups. *Journal of Economics and Management Strategy* 10:591–619.

Gromb, D. 1994. Renegotiation in debt contracts. PhD thesis, Ecole Polytechnique, Paris.

Grout, P. 1984. Investments and wages in the absence of binding contracts: a Nash bargaining approach. *Econometrica* 52:449–460.

Hart, O. and J. Moore. 1994. A theory of debt based on the inalienability of human capital. *Quarterly Journal of Economics* 109:841–880.

Hellwig, M. 2000. Financial intermediation with risk aversion. *Review of Financial Studies* 67:719–742.

Holmström, B. 1979. Moral hazard and observability. *Bell Journal of Economics* 10:74–91.

——. 1993. *Y. Jahnsson Lectures.* Delivered in Helsinki.

Jappelli, T., M. Pagano, and M. Bianco. 2005. Courts and banks: effect of judicial costs on credit market performance. *Journal of Money, Credit, and Banking* 37:223–244.

Klein, B., R. Crawford, and A. Alchian. 1978. Vertical integration, appropriable rents and the competitive contracting process. *Journal of Law and Economics* 21:297–326.

Kreps, D. and R. Wilson. 1982. Reputation and imperfect information. *Journal of Economic Theory* 27:253–279.

Laffont, J. J. and M. Meleu. 1997. Reciprocal supervision, collusion and oranizational design. *Scandinavian Journal of Economics* 99:519–540.

Laffont, J. J. and T. N'Guessan. 2000. Group lending with adverse selection. *European Economic Review* 44:773–784.

Laffont, J. J. and P. Rey. 2000. Collusion and group lending with moral hazard. Mimeo, IDEI.

Matutes, C. and X. Vives. 1996. Competition for deposits, fragility, and insurance. *Journal of Financial Intermediation* 5:184–216.

Milgrom, P. and J. Roberts. 1982. Predation, reputation and entry deterrence. *Journal of Economic Theory* 27:280–312.

Myers, S. and R. Rajan. 1998. The paradox of liquidity. *Quarterly Journal of Economics* 113:733–739.

Osborne, M. and A. Rubinstein. 1990. *Bargaining and Markets.* San Diego, CA: Academic Press.

Shavell, S. 1979. Risk sharing and incentives in the principal and agent relationship. *Bell Journal of Economics* 10:55–73.

Shepard, A. 1987. Licensing to enhance demand for new technologies. *RAND Journal of Economics* 18:360–368.

Spear, S. and S. Srivastava. 1987. On repeated moral hazard with discounting. *Review of Economic Studies* 54:599–617.

Stiglitz, J. 1990. Peer monitoring and credit markets. *World Bank Economic Review* 4:351–366.

Varian, H. 1990. Monitoring agents with other agents. *Journal of Institutional and Theoretical Economics* 146:153–174.

Villalonga, B. 2004a. Diversification discount or premium? New evidence from the business information tracking series. *Journal of Finance* 59:479–506.

Villalonga, B. 2004b. Does diversification cause the "diversification discount"? *Financial Management* 33:5–27.

Wernerfelt, B. and C. Montgomery. 1988. Tobin's *q* and the importance of focus in firm performance. *American Economic Review* 78:246–250.

Williamson, O. 1975. *Markets and Hierarchies: Analysis of Antitrust Implications.* New York: Free Press.

——. 1985. *The Economic Institutions of Capitalism.* New York: Free Press.

——. 1988. Corporate finance and corporate governance. *Journal of Finance* 43:567–592.

Williamson, S. 1986. Costly monitoring, financial intermediation and equilibrium credit rationing. *Journal of Monetary Economics* 18:159–179.

Yanelle, M. O. 1989. The strategic analysis of intermediation. *European Economic Review* 33:294–304.

5

Liquidity and Risk Management, Free Cash Flow, and Long-Term Finance

5.1 Introduction

As ongoing entities, firms are concerned that they may in the future be deprived of the funds that would enable them to take advantage of exciting growth prospects, strengthen existing investments, or simply stay alive. Such liquidity shortages reflect an inadequacy between available resources and refinancing needs. Available resources in turn depend on the difference between the firm's income and "total payment to investors" (payouts—defined as payments to shareholders, namely, dividends and share repurchases—plus debt repayments).

For example, firms that generate a decent income but contract substantial short-term liabilities may experience a liquidity shortage. A key feature of a firm's capital structure is therefore the impact of its composition on the sequencing of payments to investors. Short-term debt, by forcing the firm to disgorge cash, and putable securities, by allowing their holders to accelerate payments if certain covenants are violated,[1] exacerbate liquidity problems, while long-term debt and equity give the firm more breathing room, as do preferred stocks, a form of debt whose payments can be postponed in time.[2]

Besides liabilities and payouts, the potential for liquidity shortages also depends on income and its availability. For example, even in the absence of payments to investors, a liquidity shortage is quite predictable for those firms, such as R&D start-ups, that do not generate income for a while after their inception. Income availability also depends on income variability, which in turn can be decreased or increased by diversification choices and by corporate risk management.

Unsurprisingly, liquidity planning is central to the practice of corporate finance and consumes a large fraction of chief financial officers' (CFOs') time. Income, payments to investors, and risk management are all endogenous. This chapter's task is to build an integrated account of their determinants and to rationalize some key empirical regularities discussed in Section 2.5; for instance, (i) firms with good growth prospects might be expected to take less debt for fear of compromising future investment, and (ii) highly indebted firms are more likely to borrow on a short-term and secured basis going forward.

Chapters 3 and 4 focused on a single-stage (fixed- or variable-investment) financing. This chapter analyzes multistage financing, starting with a study of corporate liquidity demand. It models liquidity demand in a straightforward way. The novelty relative to Chapters 3 and 4 is the introduction of an intermediate date (date 1) between the financing stage (date 0) and the realization of the outcome (date 2). At that intermediate date the borrower, who may or may not produce an intermediate income, experiences a liquidity shock that needs to be withstood in order for the firm to continue and possibly succeed. A simple interpretation of this liquidity shock is as a reinvestment need (an investment cost overrun), but it can be equivalently thought of as being a new investment opportunity or else a shortfall in earnings at the intermediate stage, in which case a new external cash infusion is needed in order to cover operating expenses.

1. For example, in 1995, the downgrading of KMart's debt put the company on the brink of a bankruptcy filing, as a further downgrade would have triggered the put of $550 million in bonds, and banks had demanded covenants limiting the acceleration of payments, thus making it impossible for the firm to honor the put option. In the end, KMart reportedly paid putable bondholders $98 million to abandon their put option.

2. As long as dividends are not paid to shareholders: preferred stocks are senior relative to common stocks.

The question then arises as to how the firm can face this liquidity demand if it has little or no cash at the intermediate stage (it is "cash poor"), or, if it is "cash rich," but its intermediate income has been previously committed through, say, short-term debt liabilities contracted at date 0. It must then return to the capital market and issue new securities at date 1. However, this generally proves insufficient. Indeed, we show that the borrower should not wait until the liquidity shock occurs to secure funds to withstand it. While she may be able to convince investors to renegotiate and let their claims be diluted through a new security issue if the expected return from continuation (relative to date-1 liquidation) exceeds the agency cost, the logic of credit rationing extends to the reinvestment stage as long as investors are unable to capture the entire social benefits from continuation. In our model, provided that there is moral hazard after the liquidity shock is withstood, the borrower must keep a minimum stake in the firm in order to have incentives to manage the firm properly, which prevents pledging the firm's full value to new investors.

Thus, the borrower ought to anticipate that she will perhaps not be able to raise enough funds on the capital market to withstand the shock. It is therefore optimal for the borrower to hoard reserves either in the form of liquid securities that can be resold when the need occurs or in the form of a credit line secured from a financial institution for a cash-poor firm,[3] or in the form of retentions for a cash-rich firm. Even though the borrower is risk neutral, the hoarding of reserves is best viewed as an *insurance mechanism.* Due to credit rationing at the interim stage, the value of funds for the borrower is higher in bad states than in good ones. Reserves indeed provide an efficient cross-subsidy from good states to bad ones; for example, the borrower pays a commitment fee for the right to be able to draw on a credit line that has value only if the borrower cannot obtain funds at the interim stage, that is, in bad states of nature.

Section 5.2 provides the basics of liquidity management in the context of the fixed-investment model. Assuming, in a first stage, that the intermediate cash flow, if any, is entirely determined by events not controlled by management, it identifies the rationale of credit lines for cash-poor firms and of retentions for cash-rich ones. It also endogenizes the maturity structure of liabilities and derives the theoretical predictions relative to the empirical regularities discussed above. Section 5.3 extends the analysis to a variable investment size in order to identify a liquidity–scale tradeoff.

Section 5.4 shows how corporate risk management is part of the overall liquidity management planning, and offers some guiding principles for efficient risk management. It first shows that the rationale for hedging is to prevent the firm's continuation and reinvestment policy from being perturbed by shocks that are exogenous to the firm. While the firm optimally insulates itself completely from these shocks in the benchmark, the subsequent analysis identifies five reasons, besides transaction costs associated with hedging contracts, why partial hedging is preferable: serial correlation of shocks, market power, aggregate risk, asymmetric information, and managerial incentives.

Section 5.5 extends the basic model of Sections 5.2 and 5.3 by assuming that the firm's cash flow in part

3. There is a wide variety of loan commitments in practice. All specify the maximum loan amount, the terms under which the loan will be made, and the commitment's period. The borrower usually pays an up-front fee to obtain the commitment as well as fees on unused commitment balance (e.g., 25 or 50 basis points per year). The borrower is free to fully or partially "take down" the loan up to the maximum loan specified in the agreement, at an interest rate usually set at a markup above a market interest rate (e.g., a fixed add-on over the prime rate; for example, the borrower can borrow up to the specified maximum amount at LIBOR plus 50 basis points, where LIBOR is the London Interbank Offered Rate). Banks also often require that the borrower keep deposits (at below market rate) with the bank (these are the compensating balance requirements).

Loan commitments are pervasive in bank lending, with over 75% of commercial and industrial loans at large U.S. banks being take-downs under commitments (Veitch 1992). We refer to the book by Greenbaum and Thakor (1995) for further details on loan commitments.

Early theoretical work on loan commitments includes Thakor et al. (1981), Boot et al. (1987), Thakor and Udell (1987), and Greenbaum et al. (1989, 1991). These papers, as we will, view loan commitments as insurance against the borrower's deterioration in credit worthiness. For instance, Boot et al. (1987) analyze the case of a firm that may or may not be able to enter a standard debt agreement with prospective lenders in the future. The cause of credit rationing in their paper is the borrower's privy information about future prospects (associated with an unobserved investment decision in their model). They show that a loan commitment setting a low borrowing rate may eliminate the welfare distortion due to credit rationing. This chapter sets up a simpler framework in which loan commitments arise even in the absence of asymmetric information at the refinancing stage. It fully endogenizes the cause of credit rationing and the optimal long-term contract.

reflects managerial decisions and not solely extraneous uncertainty. For incentives reasons, the amount of liquidity available to the firm should then increase with the realized cash flow; that is, reinvestment should be sensitive to cash flow (which corresponds well to the empirical tests of the sensitivity of investment to cash flow, which are performed on ongoing entities and demonstrate a positive association between reinvestment and cash flow). There is, however, no theoretical ground for assuming that this sensitivity decreases with the strength of the firm's balance sheet.

While Sections 5.2–5.4 emphasize the point that the capital market may *ex post* rationally, but inefficiently, deny funds to the firm, Section 5.5 also studies the opposite phenomenon of a capital market that is too lenient with the borrower. When the liquidity shock is endogenous, that is, depends on the borrower's behavior, it may be optimal to let the firm fail even for moderate liquidity shocks. The prospect of failure then acts as a disciplining device for the borrower, and induces her to better control liquidity needs. Once the need for liquidity accrues, however, it may no longer be optimal for the capital market to adhere to this tough stance. Indeed, if the expected return from continuation exceeds the agency cost, the borrower can successfully renegotiate the initial agreement and obtain more funds. This is the phenomenon of the soft budget constraint. We then show how the soft-budget-constraint problem may arise whenever more general news about poor past performance accrues at the intermediate stage.

Following Easterbrook (1984) and Jensen (1986, 1989), Section 5.6 focuses on cash-rich firms, defined as firms with cash inflows exceeding their efficient reinvestment needs or opportunities. Such firms have excess liquidity that must be "pumped out" in order not to be used on wasteful projects, unwarranted diversifications, perks, and so forth. Jensen's (1989) list of industries with potential free-cash-flow problems includes steel, chemical, television and radio broadcasting, brewing, tobacco, and wood and paper products.

Overall, the liquidity-shortage and free-cash-flow problems are two sides of the same coin. The key issue in the design of long-term financing is to ensure that, at intermediate stages, the right amount of money is available for the payment of operating expenses and for reinvestment and the right amount is paid out to investors. Whether this results in a net inflow (the liquidity-shortage case) or outflow (the free-cash-flow case) is important for the comprehension of corporate financing, but is a pure convention as far as economic principles are concerned. And, indeed, we merely reinterpret the liquidity-shortage model in order to obtain its flip side, the free-cash-flow model.

The exposition in this chapter is based in part on joint work (in particular, Holmström and Tirole 1998, 2000) and numerous discussions with Bengt Holmström.

5.2 The Maturity of Liabilities

5.2.1 Basics

We depart from the previous sole focus on solvency by introducing the possibility that, during the implementation of the project (of size I), the firm be hit by an adverse shock and be required to plow in some extra cash in order to be able to pursue the project. A firm has two ways of facing urgent liquidity needs if it lacks funds (either because it generates no cash in the short run (a "cash-poor firm") or because it generates enough income in the short-run to cover reinvestment needs ("cash-rich firm") but pays out part or all of this income and therefore has limited retentions). The first is to secure some source of cash before the liquidity shock occurs. For example, the firm may "overborrow" and keep liquid assets such as Treasury bills on its balance sheet in order to be able to absorb the shock by selling these assets when needed. Alternatively, the firm may secure a line of credit with a lender (usually a bank). In contrast, the second approach consists in waiting for the shock to occur to start raising funds.

As explained in the introduction, the wait-and-see approach generates excessive liquidity problems. That is, there are situations where the firm would be rescued under an optimal contract but neither initial lenders nor new lenders want to participate even in a coordinated rescue. This is due to the fact that the borrower's stake is incompressible, that is, a concession by the borrower (in the form of a reduction of her stake) creates moral hazard and is

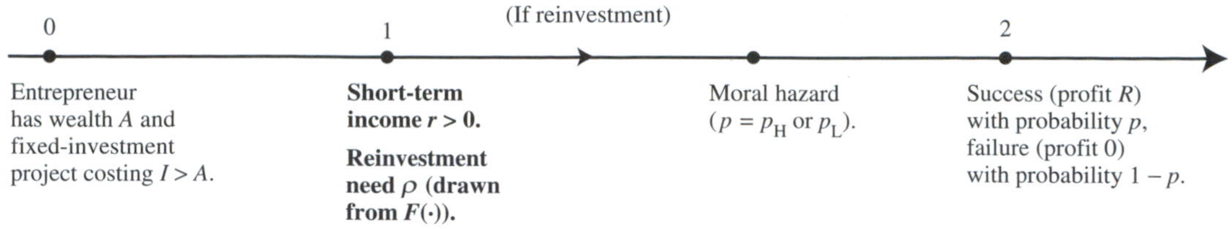

Figure 5.1

unacceptable to lenders. So, the lenders do not internalize the loss incurred by the borrower when the project is stopped, and yet the borrower is unable to propose a concession to induce them to internalize this externality.

Consider the setup of Section 3.2, except that there is an intermediate date at which income accrues and some reinvestment need is realized. As indicated in Figure 5.1, the entrepreneur at date 0 has wealth A and borrows $I - A$, where I is the fixed cost of investment.

At date 1, the investment yields deterministic and verifiable income $r \geqslant 0$. Continuation, though, requires reinvesting an amount ρ, where ρ is *ex ante* unknown and has cumulative distribution function $F(\rho)$ with density $f(\rho)$ on $[0, \infty)$. The realization of ρ is learned at date 1. Note that we here assume that the date-1 income is deterministic while the reinvestment need is random. The important assumption is that at least one of the two is random.

If the firm does not reinvest ρ, then the firm is liquidated. The liquidation value is 0. If the firm reinvests ρ, then the firm yields, at date 2, R with probability p and 0 with probability $1 - p$, where $p = p_H$ if the entrepreneur behaves (and then gets no private benefit) and $p = p_L = p_H - \Delta p$ if the entrepreneur misbehaves (in which case she receives private benefit B).

The entrepreneur and the investors are risk neutral, the entrepreneur is protected by limited liability, and the investors demand a rate of return equal to 0.

Thus, the model is nothing but an extension of the basic fixed-investment one in Section 3.2. We have just added an intermediate income r and a reinvestment need ρ (the bold type in Figure 5.1). (Put differently, the model of Section 3.2 corresponds to the special case $r = 0$ and F being a spike at $\rho = 0$.) We assume that there exists in the economy a store of value that yields the consumers' rate of interest (0 here). That is, 1 unit invested at date 0 delivers a return of 1 unit at date 1 (Chapter 15 will investigate the reasonableness of this assumption). We now give a *heuristic* description of the optimal contract.

Suppose in a first step that the initial contract can specify whether the firm continues or liquidates for each value of ρ (as we will see, it actually does not matter whether the realized value of ρ is verifiable, as long as there is no use that can be made of the date-1 cash flow besides reinvesting it and distributing it to investors). Intuitively, it is optimal to continue whenever it is cheap to do so:

$$\rho \leqslant \rho^*,$$

where ρ^* is a cutoff.

As is now familiar to the reader, competition among investors deprives them of a surplus, and so the borrower's utility is equal to the NPV. Assuming, as usual, that the optimal contract induces the high effort in the case of continuation and noting that the probability of continuation is $\Pr(\rho \leqslant \rho^*) = F(\rho^*)$, the borrower's net utility is

$$U_b(\rho^*) = [r + F(\rho^*) p_H R] - \left[I + \int_0^{\rho^*} \rho f(\rho)\, d\rho\right],$$

where the first bracket represents expected revenue and the second bracket total investment (initial investment plus expected reinvestment).

Ensuring good behavior in the case of continuation suggests giving to the entrepreneur, at date 2, R_b in the case of success and 0 in the case of failure, where

$$(\Delta p) R_b \geqslant B.$$

Furthermore, there is no loss of generality in assuming that the entrepreneur receives nothing at date 1. Suppose she receives $r_b > 0$. Then the contract could eliminate this short-term compensation and increase R_b by δR_b, so that the expected total reward remains constant: $F(\rho^*)p_H\delta R_b = r_b$. If anything, this substitution alleviates moral hazard in the case of continuation. And the suppression of the date-1 compensation does nothing to the date-1 income (which we took to be exogenous, an assumption we relax in Section 5.5).

The pledgeable income, $\mathcal{P}$, deflated by the investors' initial outlay, $I - A$, is therefore

$$\mathcal{P}(\rho^*) - (I - A) = \left[r + F(\rho^*)\left[p_H\left(R - \frac{B}{\Delta p}\right)\right]\right] - \left[I + \int_0^{\rho^*} \rho f(\rho)\,d\rho - A\right],$$

since the entrepreneur no longer has cash and so the reinvestment must be paid out of either the investors' pocket or date-1 revenue.

Taking derivatives in U_b and $\mathcal{P}$, the key insights are as follows:

- The NPV (U_b) is increasing in the cutoff ρ^* as long as $\rho^* < p_H R$, and is decreasing thereafter. Intuitively, one would want to salvage an investment when the cost, ρ, of a rescue is smaller than the expected payoff, $p_H R$, of continuing.
- By contrast, the pledgeable income increases with ρ^* for $\rho^* < p_H(R - B/\Delta p)$ and decreases thereafter. This is again intuitive: investors have to bear the cost, ρ, of salvaging the investment and can put their hands on at most $p_H(R - B/\Delta p)$ given that the entrepreneur must be given incentives to behave in the case of continuation.

We are then led to consider three cases. Depending on the strength of the balance sheet, there may be (i) an efficient amount of liquidation, (ii) an over-optimal amount of liquidation to satisfy investors, or (iii) no funding at all:

(i) $\mathcal{P}(p_H R) \geqslant I - A$.

In this case, the "first-best cutoff" $\rho^* = p_H R$, which maximizes U_b, leaves sufficient income to investors. The contract then specifies, say, no compensation r_b at date 1 for the entrepreneur, and a reward R_b in the case of continuation and success at date 2.[4]

(ii) $\mathcal{P}(p_H R) < I - A \leqslant \mathcal{P}\left(p_H\left(R - \frac{B}{\Delta p}\right)\right)$.

The optimal contract then specifies[5] $r_b = 0$ and $R_b = B/\Delta p$. The entrepreneur receives nothing at the intermediate date and, in the case of continuation, receives the lowest compensation, $R_b = B/\Delta p$, that is incentive compatible. Intuitively, the entrepreneur can be paid in two currencies: cash and continuation. Cash payments are just transfers and do not affect the NPV (as long as incentive compatibility obtains); as long as $\rho < p_H R$, continuation is a more efficient currency since continuation increases the NPV.

The cutoff $\rho^* \in [p_H(R - B/\Delta p), p_H R]$ is then given by[6]

$$r + F(\rho^*)\left[p_H\left(R - \frac{B}{\Delta p}\right)\right] = I + \int_0^{\rho^*} \rho f(\rho)\,d\rho - A.$$

Figure 5.2 illustrates the determination of the cutoff in this region. The pervasive logic of credit rationing applies not only to the choice of initial investment, but also to the continuation decision. In order to be able to invest more *ex ante*, the borrower accepts a level of reinvestment below the *ex post* efficient level ($\rho^* < p_H R$). The intuition is that, because incentives must be preserved, the borrower cannot pledge to the lenders the entire benefit of the reinvestment decision. Also, ρ^* exceeds the per-unit pledgeable income $p_H(R - B/\Delta p)$, which is the level that maximizes the borrowing capacity. A small increase in ρ^* at that level induces only a second-order decrease in

4. More generally, r_b and R_b are given by the investors' breakeven condition:

$$r - r_b + F(p_H R)[p_H(R - R_b)] = I + \int_0^{p_H R} \rho f(\rho)\,d\rho - A,$$

as long as $R_b \geqslant B/\Delta p$ and $r_b \geqslant 0$.

5. Here there is no indeterminacy. A positive r_b reduces ρ^*, which in turn reduces U_b.

6. An early paper emphasizing the role of the insiders' stake and the absence of maximization of the firm's value to investors in the optimal choice of an interim policy, such as continuation and restructuring, is Chang (1992). In that paper, the interim decision consists in restructuring the firm, thereby imposing a cost on insiders. It is shown that restructuring occurs less often than it would if investors had noncontingent control rights over the restructuring decision and therefore chose to restructure the firm whenever this increased the firm's interim value.

Here, abandoning the project (the analog of restructuring in Chang's paper) maximizes the investors' interim value whenever $\rho > p_H[R - B/\Delta p]$. However, abandoning imposes a cost on the entrepreneur, namely, the loss of rent $p_H B/\Delta p$. The firm continues in a broader set of circumstances than would maximize the investors' interim value, in the same way as restructuring occurs less often than would be the case if one maximized the investors' interim value in Chang's paper. Chang studies the implications for the allocation of control rights. We focus on those for liquidity management.

See also Dasgupta and Sengupta (2005) for a recent contribution to this literature.

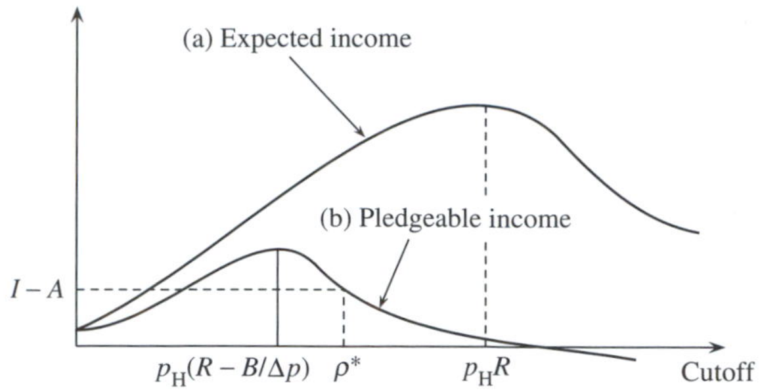

Figure 5.2 Optimal continuation policy:
(a) $U_b + I = r + F(\rho^*)[p_H R] - \int_0^{\rho^*} \rho f(\rho)\,d\rho$;
(b) $\mathcal{P}(\rho^*) = r + F(\rho^*)[p_H(R - B/\Delta p)] - \int_0^{\rho^*} \rho f(\rho)\,d\rho$.

debt capacity, and a first-order gain in the efficiency of *ex post* refinancing.

(iii) $\mathcal{P}\left(p_H\left(R - \dfrac{B}{\Delta p}\right)\right) < I - A.$

In this case, funding is not feasible. The value ρ^* that maximizes the pledgeable income ($\rho^* = p_H(R - B/\Delta p)$) does not suffice to compensate the investors for their initial outlay.

5.2.2 Term Structure of Cash-Rich Firms

Let us define a cash-rich firm as one that is meant to disgorge money at the intermediate stage: $r > \rho^*$ (in particular, $r \geqslant p_H R$ suffices to ensure that the firm is cash rich). The optimal contract can be implemented through a combination of *short-term debt*,

$$d = r - \rho^*,$$

and *long-term debt* (to be paid in the case of continuation),[7]

$$D = R - \frac{B}{\Delta p}.$$

We thus obtain a simple theory of *maturity structure*. Note further that as the strength of the balance sheet, as measured by the value of A, changes, only ρ^* changes. In particular, as A increases, ρ^* also increases (see region (ii) in Section 5.2.1; it increases only weakly in region (i)), and so d decreases. Conversely, *a weak balance sheet implies a short maturity structure* (d large).

This helps us to understand why *highly indebted firms are more likely to borrow on a short-term basis.* Highly leveraged firms can be viewed as firms with a weak balance sheet,[8] and so must accept shorter maturities.

Similarly, if we added another margin of concession in the form of costly collateral pledging (thus combining this section with the modeling in Section 4.3), one would find that firms with weak balance sheets borrow on a short-term and secured basis.

Discussion. While we emphasize the short-term debt interpretation, this payment can actually be interpreted either as a short-term debt as in Jensen (1986) or as a dividend as in Easterbrook (1984). Note, though, that the dividend interpretation must be accompanied by a covenant concerning maximal dividend distribution.[9] Otherwise, investors would want to pay dividends up to $r - \rho_0 > d$, where $\rho_0 = p_H(R - B/\Delta p)$, in order to prevent the entrepreneur from reinvesting whenever the liquidity shock exceeds the date-1 pledgeable income ρ_0. With this interpretation, we see that covenants specifying maximal amounts of dividends serve to protect the *entrepreneur* against excessive liquidation.[10]

---

7. Here, long-term debt and equity are equivalent. To obtain three different claims (short-term debt, long-term debt, equity), one can proceed as in Chapter 3 and introduce a leftover value in the case of failure at date 2.

8. Suppose that the firm already owes D_0 at date 2. The income in the case of success is then $R - D_0$. The analysis above shows that in the constrained region (ii), ρ^* decreases as D_0 increases. And so the short-term debt d increases.

Things get more complex when the initial debt is short-term debt (d_0). Then the disposable short-term debt revenue becomes $r - d_0$. The cutoff ρ^* decreases with d_0. *Total* short-term debt ($d_0 + d$) increases with d_0, but the sign of the impact on *new* short-term debt d depends on distributional assumptions.

This analysis presumes, as in Section 3.3, that initial short-term (d_0) or long-term (D_0) debts are not renegotiated. The analysis is different if initial debtholders can be brought to the bargaining table, but the general point that their presence weakens the firm's balance sheet remains.

9. In practice, dividends may also be limited because managers have some control over their level (this alternative story is more complex to analyze than the covenant one because it relies on the drivers' of managerial "real authority" (see Chapter 10 for the concept of real authority)).

10. This insight complements the standard, and important explanation for the existence of such covenants. As discussed in Chapter 2, they are usually viewed as protecting *creditors* against expropriation by the equityholders, who could use dividend distributions and share repurchases to leave long-term creditors with an "empty shell." In this part, we focus on the conflict between the entrepreneur and the securityholders, and so the introduction of conflicts among securityholders would serve no purpose.

This study focuses on the conflict between the entrepreneur and the investors concerning payments to investors out of cash-flow, without going into the details of whether the payment d must be interpreted as short-term debt or as a (constrained) dividend. That is, it is general enough to encompass the theories of Easterbrook and Jensen, but ought to be refined in order to motivate a diversity of securities. Note also that by predicting a fixed payment d, it does not do justice to the rich range of conditional payments observed in practice, that endow investors with more or less flexibility in pumping cash out of the firm: dividend, preferred dividend, putable securities, renegotiated short-term debt, short-term debt (we will return to this point in Section 5.6.2).

5.2.3 Credit Lines for Cash-Poor Firms

Suppose in contrast that the investment "takes a long time" to produce income. At the extreme, there is no short-term profit: $r = 0$.

Can the entrepreneur just "wait and see," that is, borrow I at date 0 in exchange for shares in the firm and return to the capital market at date 1 if need occurs? Let us thus assume that the entrepreneur does not plan her liquidity in advance and that the liquidity shock occurs at date 1. To raise cash on the capital market to pay ρ, the entrepreneur must issue new shares and thereby dilute historical investors.

Letting $\rho_0 \equiv p_H(R - B/\Delta p)$, and to illustrate this dilution, suppose that the entrepreneur faces a liquidity shock $\rho = \frac{1}{2}\rho_0$. The value of external shares held by initial investors is equal to ρ_0. Suppose that the number of shares is doubled.[11] That is, as many shares are sold to new investors as already exist. So the value of each share is halved. The firm thereby raises $\frac{1}{2}\rho_0 = \rho$ in cash and can withstand the liquidity shock. Are initial investors willing to let themselves be diluted? The value of their shares is, of course, reduced to $\frac{1}{2}\rho_0$. But contemplate the alternative of liquidating the investment, under which the initial investors receive nothing! Thus, initial investors are willing to accept the dilution.[12]

Similarly, to meet a liquidity shock equal to $\frac{3}{4}\rho_0$, the firm must quadruple the number of shares, and so on. But there is an upper bound to this process: investors will never pay more than the firm is worth to them. Hence, even in a frictionless capital market, the firm cannot raise more than ρ_0. Going back to the capital market at date 1 then at best allows the firm to withstand a liquidity shock of magnitude

$$\rho \leqslant \rho_0 = p_H\left(R - \frac{B}{\Delta p}\right).$$

Because the optimal financing arrangement specifies[13]

$$p_H\left(R - \frac{B}{\Delta p}\right) < \rho^* \leqslant p_H R,$$

the entrepreneur must secure a line of credit or hoard liquidity in order to face the date-1 liquidity shock.[14] We will shortly describe how to do so, but there are basically two alternatives and combinations thereof: a credit line or liquid assets of magnitude ρ^* with no right to dilute existing claimholders by issuing new claims at date 1 (so the entrepreneur borrows $I + \rho^*$); or a smaller credit line or amount of liquid assets, equal to $[\rho^* - p_H(R - B/\Delta p)]$ with a right to dilute claimholders as needed to ensure continuation. Either way, the entrepreneur must plan liquidity management.

The optimum can be implemented by a nonrevokable line of credit granted by, say, one of the lenders (a bank) at level ρ^*. It is important that this line of credit be nonrevokable (in a broad sense: see below). Otherwise the lender would have an incentive not to abide by his promise to rescue the firm if $\rho > \rho_0$, that is, if the liquidity shock exceeds the date-1 pledgeable income ρ_0. In practice, lenders often prefer to keep discretion over the extension of credit by making the line revokable, or delivering promises such as "comfort or highly confident letters," which are legally hard to enforce and are only a moral promise to provide credit. This discretion potentially has a cost to the borrower, as, whenever $\rho_0 < \rho < \rho^*$, the lender would like to renege on his promise to provide funds to the firm unless he tries to maintain a reputation for "fairness" by extending credit even when this is not strictly profitable for him (see Boot

11. Including for internal shares, so as to keep the entrepreneur's stake R_b in success constant and therefore preserve incentive compatibility.

12. Note the analogy with the incentives for debt forgiveness when there is a debt overhang (see Chapter 3).

13. Except in the nongeneric case where $\mathcal{P}(p_H(R - B/\Delta p)) = I - A$.

14. Note that if $A > 0$, the hoarding of liquidity can in part come from the retention of A (this is a matter of accounting).

et al. 1987, 1993). In practice, a bank may offer a formally revokable line of credit, but have a reputation for abiding by its promise unless the borrower has behaved in an egregious way that yet was not ruled out by a negative covenant.

We also implicitly assume that there is no concern over the lender's *ability* (as opposed to *willingness*) to abide by his commitment. However, the lender may himself face liquidity and solvency problems in the future. In practice, only well-capitalized and safe institutions are able to make a firm promise of this type (banks and some other financial institutions obviously have a comparative advantage in doing so, due to the close monitoring of their solvency and liquidity by the regulators as well as, at least for large ones, an explicit or implicit backing of their on- and off-balance-sheet liabilities by the state).

Remark (capital market frictions). Note here that the suboptimality of reinvestment under the wait-and-see policy is independent of the debt-overhang phenomenon discussed in Section 3.3. Indeed, the assumption that liquidity shocks below ρ_0 can be withstood through the dilution of existing claims implies either that lending is concentrated among a few lenders, or that the initial agreement is structured so as to facilitate renegotiation,[15] or else that the entrepreneur receives rights to dilute existing claims by issuing senior claims (as in Hart and Moore (1995)). If some claims proved difficult to renegotiate, the firm would be able to raise even less than ρ_0 by turning to the capital market at date 1, and its demand for liquidity would be even higher than that derived here.

Remark (renegotiation). Could this line of credit be renegotiated to the parties' mutual advantage once the fraction ρ is realized? First, note that if $\rho \leqslant \rho^*$, then *a fortiori* $\rho < p_H R$ and therefore it is *ex post* efficient to continue; so there is no scope for a renegotiation in which the lender would compensate the borrower for not using the credit line, as this renegotiation would reduce total surplus and therefore at least one of the parties would be strictly better off not renegotiating. Second, could the two parties both benefit from an increase in the line of credit to ρ when $\rho^* < \rho \leqslant p_H R$? Even though this increase would yield the *ex post* efficient reinvestment policy, there is no way for the borrower to compensate the lender, again because the borrower's stake is incompressible. One can show that the lender will turn down any request for an increase in the credit line.[16] So will any alternative lender (other lenders may have even less incentives to refinance, because unlike the initial lender they do not have a vested stake to lose).

Remark (role played by uncertainty about liquidity needs). We can now explain why *ex ante* uncertainty about the liquidity need is a key ingredient of the demand for liquidity. Suppose, in contrast, that ρ is deterministic. If $\rho \geqslant \rho_0 = p_H(R - B/\Delta p)$, then investors do not want to lend at date 0, since they know that they will have to cover at date 1 a liquidity shock that exceeds the income that can be pledged to them in period 2. If $\rho < \rho_0$, then the firm is always solvent at date 1, in that new claims can be issued at date 1 (that partially dilute existing ones) in order to meet the liquidity shock and continue; hence, there is no need to hoard reserves.

Again, a good way of thinking about this issue is in terms of insurance. A high liquidity shock is similar to an illness or an accident, and a low liquidity shock is similar to the absence of such a mishap. There is no scope for insurance if it is known in advance whether there will be an illness or an accident.

5.2.4 A Reinterpretation: Growth Prospects

In the basic model, the firm is liquidated if it does not meet the liquidity shock. In a straightforward reinterpretation, it continues as is, but cannot take advantage of a profitable growth opportunity if it does not come up with enough cash to reinvest.

Suppose that, at date 1, the firm still receives deterministic income r, but, in the absence of cash reinjection at date 1, continues and succeeds with probability $p = p_H$ or p_L, depending on whether the entrepreneur behaves or misbehaves at date 1. At date 1, though, the firm can raise its date-2 expected profit by reinvesting. One way of formalizing

15. See Section 5.5.3 for a discussion of factors hindering and facilitating renegotiation of claims.

16. More formally, the lender turns down the request because $\rho > \rho^* > \rho_0$.

this is to assume that the payoffs in the cases of success and failure remain R and 0, respectively, but the probability of success in the case of reinvestment becomes $p + \tau$, where $\tau > 0$ and $p = p_H$ or $p = p_L$, depending on whether the entrepreneur behaves or misbehaves. This separable form is handy as it implies that the entrepreneur's incentive compatibility constraint is not affected by the reinvestment:

$$(p_H + \tau)R_b \geqslant (p_L + \tau)R_b + B \quad \iff \quad (\Delta p)R_b \geqslant B.$$

The reinvestment cost ρ is drawn at date 1 from the cumulative distribution function $F(\rho)$ with density $f(\rho)$ on $[0, \infty)$.

It is clearly optimal to reinvest if and only if ρ is below some cutoff ρ^*. The entrepreneur's utility, equal to the NPV, is

$$U_b(\rho^*) = [r + [p_H + F(\rho^*)\tau]R] - \left[I + \int_0^{\rho^*} \rho f(\rho)\,d\rho\right].$$

As earlier, the interesting case arises when the firm is financially constrained but nonetheless can raise funds (a situation equivalent to that labeled region (ii) in Section 5.2.1); the cutoff is then given by the investors' breakeven condition:

$$r + [p_H + F(\rho^*)\tau]\left(R - \frac{B}{\Delta p}\right) = [I - A] + \int_0^{\rho^*} \rho f(\rho)\,d\rho$$

and

$$\tau\left(R - \frac{B}{\Delta p}\right) \leqslant \rho^* < \tau R.$$

The latter set of inequalities expresses the fact that reinvestment is first-best suboptimal ($\rho^* < \tau R$), but occurs whenever it boosts pledgeable income ($\rho^* \geqslant \tau[R - (B/\Delta p)]$).

In this model, growth opportunities are measured by the parameter τ. Let us look at the impact of growth opportunities on the maturity structure by differentiating the investors' breakeven condition:

$$\frac{d(d)}{d\tau} = \frac{d(r - \rho^*)}{d\tau} = -\frac{F(\rho^*)}{f(\rho^*)}\frac{R - B/\Delta p}{\rho^* - \tau(R - B/\Delta p)} < 0.$$

Thus, *firms with better growth opportunities should go for longer maturities.* Relatedly, there is substantial evidence that firms with growth opportunities have lower leverage ratios.[17]

17. See Section 2.5. Recall that equity here can be viewed as debt with a long maturity.

5.3 The Liquidity-Scale Tradeoff

The fixed-investment model is handy to illustrate the optimal term structure of debt for cash-rich firms and credit line for cash-poor ones. But, for other purposes, it is too simple, in that there is no other "margin" that the entrepreneur can trade off against liquidity. When, for example, investment size is variable, as we now assume, the entrepreneur faces a choice between a larger investment and more liquidity.[18]

This section focuses on cash-poor firms and extends the model of Section 5.2 to include a variable investment size in order to identify the liquidity-scale tradeoff (which also applies to cash-rich firms): the firm must sacrifice scale in order to benefit from more liquidity.

5.3.1 The Two-Shock Case

We consider the variable-investment model and add a liquidity shock at an intermediate stage. This liquidity shock amounts to a cost overrun that is proportional to the initial investment. To develop our intuition, let us begin with the case in which there are only two possible values for the (per-unit) liquidity shock: 0 with probability $1-\lambda$ and ρ with probability λ (see Figure 5.3). We will say that the firm is "intact" when it does not need to reinvest and "in distress" when it needs to reinvest ρ per unit of investment.

Except for this random shock, the model is identical to the variable-investment version of Section 3.4. Continuation (which is contingent on reinvesting ρI if the firm is in distress) is subject to moral hazard. The probability of success is p_H if the entrepreneur behaves and p_L if she misbehaves. The private benefit of misbehaving is BI. The project yields RI in the case of success and 0 in the case of failure. Note that we focus on policies that rescue either the entire investment or none of it in the case of distress.[19]

18. More generally, the entrepreneur would face a tradeoff between more liquidity and fewer control rights granted to investors (see Chapter 10), and so forth.

19. Quite generally, we could allow partial reinvestments. That is, a reinvestment $\rho x I$ allows the firm to salvage a fraction $x \in [0, 1]$ of the investment. In this case, the private benefit of misbehaving, BxI, is proportional to the salvaged investment xI; and so is the profit RxI in the case of success. But it turns out that one can focus without loss of generality on policies that either rescue the entire investment ($x = 1$) or rescue none ($x = 0$) in the case of distress.

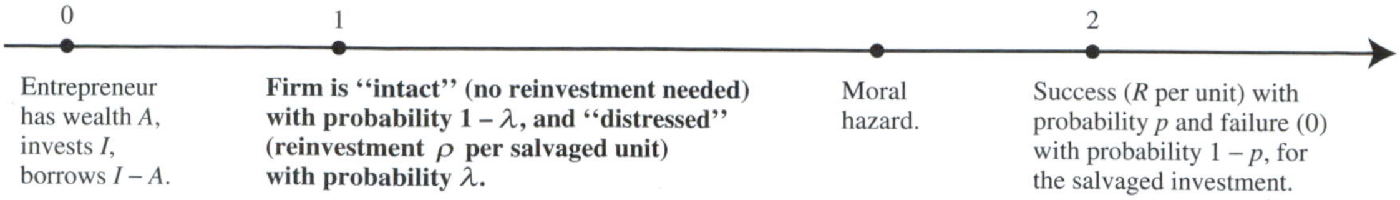

Figure 5.3

Let us assume that

$$\rho_0 \equiv p_{\rm H}\left(R - \frac{B}{\Delta p}\right)$$
$$< c \equiv \min\left\{1 + \lambda\rho, \frac{1}{1-\lambda}\right\}$$
$$< \rho_1 \equiv p_{\rm H}R.$$

This pair of inequalities (which boils down to $\rho_0 < 1 < \rho_1$ in the no-liquidity-shock case ($\lambda = 0$) of Section 3.4) will, as we will see, imply that investing has a positive NPV, but also that the entrepreneur is constrained in her borrowing.

In the case of continuation, the entrepreneur optimally receives 0 in the case of failure and $R_{\rm b}$ in the case of success, where $R_{\rm b}$ is large enough so as to incentivize her:

$$(\Delta p)R_{\rm b} \geqslant BI.$$

As in Section 3.4, making this inequality an equality maximizes the pledgeable income and thereby the entrepreneur's borrowing capacity. This implies that under continuation, an expected amount $\rho_0 I$ goes to investors at date 2.

Let us compare the two policies.

(i) *Abandon the project in the case of distress.* If the project is abandoned in the case of distress, investors receive their expected income $\rho_0 I$ only when there is no shock, that is, with probability $1 - \lambda$. On the other hand, there is no reinvestment at date 1. Thus, when the entrepreneur has initial wealth A, the investors' breakeven constraint is

$$(1-\lambda)\rho_0 I = I - A,$$

yielding investment capacity,

$$I = \frac{A}{1-(1-\lambda)\rho_0}$$

(a generalization of formula (3.12) to the case $\lambda \geqslant 0$).

The entrepreneur's utility, equal to the NPV, is

$$U_{\rm b}^0 = [(1-\lambda)\rho_1 - 1]I = \frac{(1-\lambda)\rho_1 - 1}{1-(1-\lambda)\rho_0}A$$

or

$$U_{\rm b}^0 = \left[\left(\rho_1 - \frac{1}{1-\lambda}\right)\bigg/\left(\frac{1}{1-\lambda} - \rho_0\right)\right]A.$$

Comparing this formula with that in the absence of a liquidity shock ($\lambda = 0$), the average cost of bringing 1 unit of effective or intact investment to date 2 is now $1/(1-\lambda)$ instead of 1, because the initial investment bears fruits only if there is no liquidity shock.

(ii) *Pursue the project even in the case of distress.* The decision to withstand the liquidity shock at date 1 has a cost and benefit. The cost is that the average cost of bringing 1 unit of investment intact to date 2 is $(1+\lambda\rho)$ (the date-0 cost, 1, plus the expected date-1 reinvestment cost, $\lambda\rho$). The benefit is that the project is never abandoned. The borrowing capacity is given by

$$(1+\lambda\rho)I - A = \rho_0 I$$

or

$$I = \frac{A}{(1+\lambda\rho) - \rho_0}.$$

Similarly, the entrepreneur's utility (the NPV) is

$$U_{\rm b}^1 = [\rho_1 - (1+\lambda\rho)]I$$

or

$$U_{\rm b}^1 = \frac{\rho_1 - (1+\lambda\rho)}{(1+\lambda\rho) - \rho_0}A$$

(which, again, for $\lambda = 0$, boils down to formula (3.14′) in Section 3.4).

Thus, we find a similar formula as in the alternative policy, except that the average cost of effective investment is now $(1+\lambda\rho)$.

The policy of withstanding the liquidity shock is optimal if and only if $U_{\rm b}^1 \geqslant U_{\rm b}^0$, or

$$1 + \lambda\rho \leqslant \frac{1}{1-\lambda},$$

which can be rewritten as

$$(1-\lambda)\rho \leqslant 1.$$

In words, it is optimal to withstand the liquidity

shock if

- it is low (ρ low),
- it is likely (λ high).

The first conclusion is obvious; but the second may be less so since a high probability of a liquidity shock increases both the benefit and the cost of withstanding it.

As in the case of a fixed investment size, we can draw the implications of this analysis for liquidity management. If the optimal policy is not to rescue the investment in the case of distress, nothing needs to be done at date 0 besides signing a contract and investing I. In contrast, if the optimal policy is to pursue the project even in the case of distress, the entrepreneur must be able to avail herself of the amount ρI if a shock occurs.

If $\rho > \rho_0$ (which is not inconsistent with the condition $(1-\lambda)\rho \leqslant 1$ obtained earlier), then liquidity necessarily must be planned in advance. Waiting exposes the firm to credit rationing at date 1. (As the analysis for a continuum of liquidity shock will demonstrate, this case is in a sense the "generic case.") For example, the firm may contract a credit line to the level of ρI with a bank; alternatively, it can contract for a credit line corresponding only to the shortfall $(\rho - \rho_0)I$ and also acquire the right to dilute initial investors (so as to obtain $\rho_0 I$). More on this in Section 5.3.3.

5.3.2 Continuum of Liquidity Shocks

We now generalize the analysis to a continuum of possible values for the liquidity shock. This continuous-investment, continuous-shock version will be used in the rest of the chapter.

After the (endogenous size) investment I is sunk at date 0 and before the borrower works on the project, some exogenous shock occurs at date 1 that determines a per-unit-of-investment level $\rho \in [0, \infty)$ of "cost overruns." That is, a cash infusion equal to ρI is needed in order for the project to continue. If ρI is not invested, the project is abandoned altogether and thus yields no income. As in Section 5.2, the fraction ρ is *a priori* distributed according to the continuous distribution $F(\rho)$ on $[0, \infty)$, with density $f(\rho)$. (As we already observed, the model of Section 3.4 is therefore a special case, with F being a spike at $\rho = 0$.)

Regardless of the required amount of the cash infusion, the project, if pursued, is still a project of size I, in that the income in the case of success is RI and the borrower's private benefit from misbehaving is BI. One cannot increase the size of the project after the initial stage.

The timing is summarized in Figure 5.4.

We assume that investment has positive NPV. That is, under a rule that specifies that the project is abandoned if and only if $\rho \geqslant \tilde{\rho}$ for at least some threshold $\tilde{\rho}$, the expected payoff per unit of investment is strictly positive. This positive-NPV condition under liquidity shocks is

$$\max_{\tilde{\rho}} \left\{ F(\tilde{\rho}) p_{\mathrm{H}} R - 1 - \int_0^{\tilde{\rho}} \rho f(\rho)\,\mathrm{d}\rho \right\} > 0. \tag{5.1}$$

We first look for the optimal loan agreement. The next subsection will discuss its implementation. It is easy to show that it is optimal to have a "cutoff rule" for infusing cash. There exists an optimal threshold ρ^* such that one should continue if and only if

$$\rho \leqslant \rho^*. \tag{5.2}$$

The incentive constraint in the case of continuation is the same as in the absence of a liquidity shock (see Section 3.4):

$$(\Delta p) R_{\mathrm{b}} \geqslant BI. \tag{IC$_\mathrm{b}$}$$

The breakeven condition is slightly altered by the presence of liquidity shocks:

$$F(\rho^*)[p_{\mathrm{H}}(RI - R_{\mathrm{b}})] \geqslant I - A + \int_0^{\rho^*} \rho I f(\rho)\,\mathrm{d}\rho. \tag{IR$_\mathrm{l}$}$$

That is, the lenders receive a return only if the project is pursued, which has probability $F(\rho^*)$. The left-hand side of (IR$_\mathrm{l}$) is the expected pledgeable income. Furthermore, there is a new term, representing the expected outlay on overruns, on the right-hand side. From these two constraints, we deduce the borrowing capacity (or, more precisely, the maximum investment that allows the lenders to break even):

$$I = k(\rho^*)A,$$

where

$$\begin{aligned} k(\rho^*) &= \frac{1}{1 + \int_0^{\rho^*} \rho f(\rho)\,\mathrm{d}\rho - F(\rho^*)[p_{\mathrm{H}} R - p_{\mathrm{H}} B/\Delta p]} \\ &= \frac{1}{1 + \int_0^{\rho^*} \rho f(\rho)\,\mathrm{d}\rho - F(\rho^*)\rho_0} \end{aligned} \tag{5.3}$$

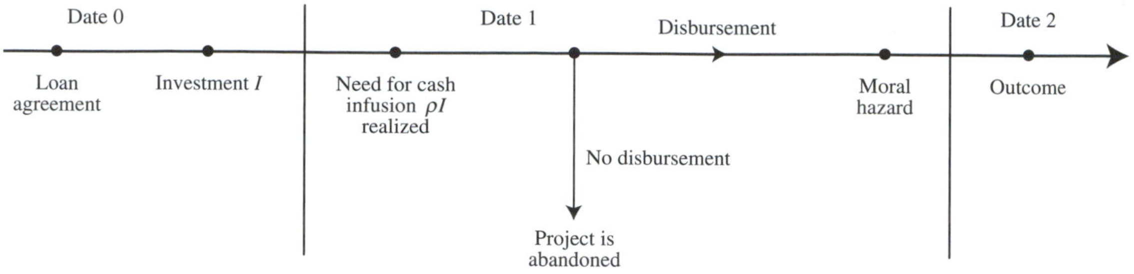

Figure 5.4

involves a straightforward modification relative to the no-liquidity-shock multiplier k. Reduced profitability implies that the multiplier is smaller than that in the absence of liquidity shocks: $k(\rho^*) < k = 1/(1-\rho_0)$. Note that the borrower's borrowing capacity is maximal when the threshold ρ^* is equal to the expected per-unit pledgeable income $\rho_0 \equiv p_{\rm H}(R - B/\Delta p)$.

Given that the competitive lenders make no profits, the borrower's net utility is as usual the social surplus brought about by the project, namely,

$$U_{\rm b} = m(\rho^*)I = m(\rho^*)k(\rho^*)A, \tag{5.4}$$

where

$$m(\rho^*) \equiv F(\rho^*)p_{\rm H}R - 1 - \int_0^{\rho^*} \rho f(\rho)\,{\rm d}\rho$$

is the margin per unit of investment.

What is the optimal continuation rule? Ideally, one would want to continue if and only if this is *ex post* efficient, that is, if and only if $\rho \leqslant p_{\rm H}R$. Indeed, $\rho^* = p_{\rm H}R$ maximizes the margin $m(\rho^*)$. However, at $\rho^* = p_{\rm H}R$, the multiplier k is decreasing in ρ^*. So one actually ought to choose a lower threshold in comparison to the *ex post* efficient one. It is easily seen from (5.3) and (5.4) that

$$U_{\rm b} = \frac{p_{\rm H}R - (1 + \int_0^{\rho^*} \rho f(\rho)\,{\rm d}\rho)/F(\rho^*)}{(1 + \int_0^{\rho^*} \rho f(\rho)\,{\rm d}\rho)/F(\rho^*) - p_{\rm H}(R - B/\Delta p)} A,$$

and so the optimal threshold minimizes the expected unit cost $c(\rho^*)$ of effective investment:

$$\rho^* \text{ minimizes } c(\rho^*) \equiv \frac{1 + \int_0^{\rho^*} \rho f(\rho)\,{\rm d}\rho}{F(\rho^*)} \tag{5.5}$$

or

$$\int_0^{\rho^*} F(\rho)\,{\rm d}\rho = 1. \tag{5.6}$$

Condition (5.6) can be obtained, for example, by integrating by parts and rewriting the expected unit cost of effective investment as

$$c(\rho^*) = \rho^* + \frac{1 - \int_0^{\rho^*} F(\rho)\,{\rm d}\rho}{F(\rho^*)}.$$

This expression also shows that *at the optimum*,[20] *the threshold liquidity shock is equal to the expected unit cost of effective investment*:[21]

$$c(\rho^*) = \rho^*.$$

This in turn implies that

$$U_{\rm b} = \frac{\rho_1 - \rho^*}{\rho^* - \rho_0} A. \tag{5.7}$$

Next, we observe that *this optimal threshold lies between the expected per-unit-of-investment pledgeable income and income*:

$$\rho_0 = p_{\rm H}\left(R - \frac{B}{\Delta p}\right) < \rho^* < \rho_1 = p_{\rm H}R. \tag{5.8}$$

This follows from the fact that the margin $m(\rho^*)$ and the multiplier $k(\rho^*)$ are both decreasing above ρ_1 and both increasing below ρ_0 (see Figure 5.5).[22] Condition (5.8) is consistent with (5.7): if ρ^* were to exceed ρ_1, the project could not be financed profitably. And if ρ^* were to be lower than ρ_0, the borrowing capacity and the borrower's utility would be infinite.

Equation (5.8) implies, as in Section 5.2.3, that a wait-and-see policy, under which the borrower tries

20. It is easy to show that $c(\cdot)$ is quasi-convex ($c''(\rho^*) > 0$ if $c'(\rho^*) = 0$).

21. Note that ρ^* is here independent of A. The constant-returns-to-scale model is a limit case in that the probability of continuation and all per-unit-of-investment variables are independent of A: all firms are alike up to a scale factor.

22. Indeed, $m(\cdot)$ is quasi-concave with a maximum at ρ_1 and $k(\cdot)$ is quasi-concave with a maximum at ρ_0.

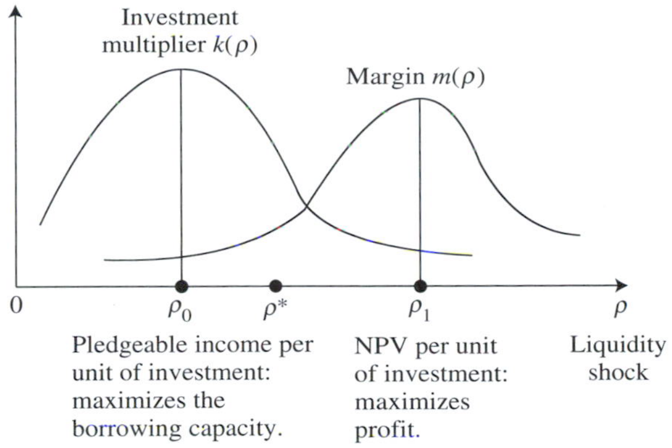

Figure 5.5

to raise funds from the lenders on the capital market at date 1 in order to cover the liquidity shock, is suboptimal. Even under perfect coordination among lenders at date 1 (there is no "debt-overhang" phenomenon), the lenders will provide new credit only if the pledgeable income exceeds the amount of reinvestment, that is, only if

$$\rho \leqslant \rho_0.$$

Because $\rho_0 < \rho^*$, it is optimal for the borrower to get more assurance against the firm's shortage of funds than is provided by a wait-and-see policy. This creates a corporate demand for liquidity.

Remark (effect of an increase in risk on liquidity hoarding). Condition (5.6) has a simple implication. An increase in the riskiness of the liquidity shock in the sense of a mean-preserving spread of F[23] raises the left-hand side of (5.6) and thus reduces the threshold ρ^*. So, the borrower should hoard more liquidity when the liquidity shock incurs a mean-preserving reduction in risk.[24]

Liquidation value. We have assumed that no money is recovered if the project is abandoned at date 1. Let us generalize the model slightly by assuming that the assets in place have a salvage value $LI \geqslant 0$, that is, L per unit of investment if the firm is liquidated at date 1. The salvage value is a monetary value that can be transferred to the lenders if the project is abandoned. We let the reader follow the steps of the previous analysis and show the following: the equity multiplier and the margin become

$$k(\rho^*) = \frac{1}{[1 - L + \int_0^{\rho^*} \rho f(\rho)\,d\rho] - F(\rho^*)(\rho_0 - L)}, \tag{5.3$'$}$$

$$m(\rho^*) = F(\rho^*)(\rho_1 - L) - \left[1 - L + \int_0^{\rho^*} \rho f(\rho)\,d\rho\right]. \tag{5.4$'$}$$

These modifications can be understood in the following way. First, there is a fictitious reduction of L in the unit cost of investment. Were the project always abandoned at date 1, the lenders would collect L and thus the net unit cost of investment would be equal to $1 - L$. Second, and with this convention, the decision to continue at date 1 implies a loss L per unit of investment. This monetary loss must be subtracted both from the expected payoff $\rho_1 = p_H R$ and from the expected pledgeable income $\rho_0 = p_H(R - B/\Delta p)$. This yields (5.3′) and (5.4′).

Next, $U_b = m(\rho^*)k(\rho^*)A$ and so the threshold ρ^* still minimizes the (modified) expected unit cost of effective investment:

$$\rho^* \text{ minimizes } c(\rho^*) \equiv \frac{1 - L + \int_0^{\rho^*} \rho f(\rho)\,d\rho}{F(\rho^*)} = \rho^* + \frac{1 - L - \int_0^{\rho^*} F(\rho)\,d\rho}{F(\rho^*)}. \tag{5.5$'$}$$

And so, at the optimum,

$$\int_0^{\rho^*} F(\rho)\,d\rho = 1 - L, \tag{5.6$'$}$$

$$c(\rho^*) = \rho^*,$$

and

$$U_b = \frac{(\rho_1 - L) - \rho^*}{\rho^* - (\rho_0 - L)} A. \tag{5.7$'$}$$

23. See, for example, Rothschild and Stiglitz (1970, 1971). The distribution $G(\rho)$ (with density $g(\rho)$, say) is a mean-preserving spread of distribution $F(\rho)$ if (i) $\int_0^\infty G(\rho)\,d\rho = \int_0^\infty F(\rho)\,d\rho$ ($\Leftrightarrow \int_0^\infty \rho g(\rho)\,d\rho = \int_0^\infty \rho f(\rho)\,d\rho$, so the means are the same), and (ii) $\int_0^{\rho^*} G(\rho)\,d\rho \geqslant \int_0^{\rho^*} F(\rho)\,d\rho$ for all ρ^*.

24. This, however, does *not* imply that the firm should hoard a lot of liquidity when uncertainty disappears: suppose that the distribution F converges to a spike at $\rho > \rho_0$. Then, the investors' breakeven condition cannot be satisfied and there is no borrowing. More generally, an empirical analysis of the impact of liquidity risk on liquidity hoarding will confront a selection bias: because continuation is akin to an option value, a decrease in the uncertainty about ρ affects pledgeable income and NPV (more on this shortly) and thereby impacts the investment size or the very existence of investment.

As the margin and the multiplier are both decreasing above $\rho_1 - L$ and increasing below $\rho_0 - L$, we have

$$\rho_0 - L < \rho^* < \rho_1 - L.$$

We can thus generalize the insight that liquidity has to be secured in advance. Under a wait-and-see strategy, the lenders (or the capital market more generally) do not want to reinvest more than the net gain of continuation, namely, $\rho_0 - L$ per unit of investment. And so the borrower should hoard liquidity at date 0.

From (5.6′), we also infer that

$$\frac{\mathrm{d}\rho^*}{\mathrm{d}L} = -\frac{1}{F(\rho^*)}.$$

That is, a unit increase in the salvage value reduces the threshold by more than 1 unit. The gap between the optimal stopping rule and the wait-and-see outcome narrows as the salvage value increases. This result will have an interesting implication when we apply the model to cash-rich firms in Section 5.6.

5.3.3 Application to Liquidity Management

We now pursue in more detail the analysis of Section 5.2 concerning whether common institutions can implement the optimal reinvestment policy.

The optimum can be implemented by a nonrevokable line of credit granted by a lender (a bank) at level $\rho^* I$. The borrower, who is always better off continuing, will always take advantage of this line of credit as long as $\rho \leqslant \rho^*$, although she will need only part of it. (In practice, lines of credit are actually often unused. Their value is essentially an option value.)

Alternatively, the lenders can grant a smaller line of credit, namely, $(\rho^* - \rho_0)I$, and give the borrower the right to dilute their claims at date 1 in order to finance the liquidity shock. The value of external claims in the case of continuation, that is, the *date-1* pledgeable income, is equal to $\rho_0 I$ and therefore the borrower can raise up to $\rho_0 I$ in a perfect capital market (by issuing new equity or new debt, depending on the interpretation given to external claims). So, overall, the borrower can gather $(\rho^* - \rho_0)I + \rho_0 I = \rho^* I$ in order to withstand the liquidity shock.

An alternative to providing a credit line for the future is for the lenders (especially if they are dispersed) to lend more money today, which the borrower will be able to use in the case of a liquidity shock. That is, the lenders can invest $I(1+\rho^*) - A$ in the firm at the start. We now observe that the lenders should not let the borrower allocate resources freely between liquid and illiquid assets (illiquid assets are here the investment), but rather should demand that a liquidity ratio (which we will define as the ratio of liquid assets over total assets) be kept equal to $\rho^*/(1+\rho^*)$ until the liquidity shock accrues. The borrower then invests I and keeps $\rho^* I$ in safe, liquid claims (which bear no interest by convention).

Monitoring overinvestment in illiquid assets. Recall from Chapter 2 that loan agreements do not focus solely on the borrower's solvency, that is, on the relationship between the firm's total indebtedness and its assets, but also strictly constrain the borrower's liquidity. For example, many loan agreements require that the borrower maintain a minimum level of working capital. To the extent that liquidity crises are ultimately solvency problems, it is not *a priori* clear why this is so. Let us bring one answer to this puzzle, and show that it may be optimal for lenders to *simultaneously* impose gearing (leverage) and liquidity ratios.

In the absence of a liquidity requirement, the borrower may want to invest more than I initially into illiquid assets. To develop our intuition for this, suppose that the borrower invests the full $I(1+\rho^*) \equiv I^*$ in illiquid assets; despite the lack of cash left for reinvestment, the project will often be continued, as the lenders, facing the fait accompli of an overinvestment in illiquid assets, have an incentive to rescue the firm as long as it is profitable for them to do so at date 1: $\rho \leqslant \rho_0$.

An interesting issue relates to whether the investors should renegotiate the borrower's compensation scheme so as to account for the unexpectedly high scale of operations. The answer to this question depends on the way the managerial compensation contract was initially drawn, namely, on whether the entrepreneur was granted a share of the final profit or a fixed bonus in the case of success (the two specifications are equivalent when the investment size is fixed, but no longer are so when investment, and therefore profit, can be scaled up or down). If the borrower owns a share in the firm's final profit, then managerial compensation scales up with investment, and the initial incentive scheme remains incentive compatible as investment increases and is not renegotiated by lenders to account for the altered firm size.

Alternatively, the entrepreneur may have been granted in the initial agreement a fixed reward for "success"; because the private benefit scales up with investment, the initial incentive scheme is then no longer incentive compatible. Lenders then offer to increase the borrower's reward in the case of "success" and so they raise the borrower's payoff in the case of success to $BI^*/\Delta p$ in order to make sure the borrower behaves.[25]

The lenders might, of course, want to claim initially that they will not put any more money into the venture, but this is not a credible commitment. Anticipating this *soft budget constraint*, the borrower may overinvest. Indeed, the borrower, who, regardless of the design of her initial compensation contract, receives expected rent $p_H B/(\Delta p)$ per unit of illiquid assets, prefers investing I^* rather than I if

$$F(\rho^*)p_H\left(\frac{B}{\Delta p}I\right) < F(\rho_0)p_H\left(\frac{B}{\Delta p}I^*\right)$$

or

$$F(\rho^*) < F(\rho_0)(1+\rho^*). \qquad (5.9)$$

Condition (5.9) is satisfied as long as B lies below some threshold: ρ_0 is decreasing in B, and, for ρ_0 just below ρ^*, (5.9) is necessarily satisfied, and it is optimal for the borrower to deviate from investment I. Because the borrower is then strictly better off overinvesting, the lender should rationally anticipate to lose money overall.[26] Hence, the rationale for a liquidity requirement.

Monitoring overhoarding of liquid assets. As mentioned earlier, lenders may also need to verify that the borrower does not underinvest in illiquid assets in order to overinsure against liquidity shocks. The analysis is contingent on several assumptions and we select a specific set of assumptions for the sole purpose of illustrating a possible incentive to underinvest in illiquid assets. Suppose (i) that the borrower can use the excess liquidity in order to withstand the liquidity shock, (ii) that the borrower and investors receive shares of the date-2 profit with share $(B/\Delta p)/R = (\rho_1 - \rho_0)/\rho_1$ held by the borrower and share $(R - B/\Delta p)/R = \rho_0/\rho_1$ held by the investors (all-equity firm), and (iii) that unused liquidity is returned to investors. Suppose further that the borrower invests $I' \leqslant I$ in illiquid assets and thus hoards liquidity equal to $\rho^* I + [I - I']$. She can then withstand liquidity shocks ρ such that

$$\rho I' \leqslant \rho^* I + [I - I'].$$

Letting $\varepsilon \equiv (I - I')/I'$, and using the all-equity-firm assumption, the borrower prefers to underinvest if and only if

$$F(\rho^* + (1+\rho^*)\varepsilon)I' > F(\rho^*)I$$

or

$$F(\rho^* + (1+\rho^*)\varepsilon) > F(\rho^*)(1+\varepsilon).$$

For small underinvestments, this condition is satisfied if and only if

$$\frac{(1+\rho^*)f(\rho^*)}{F(\rho^*)} > 1.$$

Roughly, if liquidity shocks around the threshold ρ^* are quite likely, hoarding a bit more liquidity than allowed is privately profitable for the borrower.

The borrower would always prefer underinvesting to investing I if she had a fixed claim (namely, $BI/\Delta p$ in the case of success).

5.4 Corporate Risk Management

Risk management is ranked by financial executives, CEOs, and investors as one of their most important concerns (see, for example, Rawls and Smithson 1990; Froot 1995). Firms can hedge against risk in a variety of ways. They can trade in forward/futures markets or enter swap agreements (which are over-the-counter deals that oblige two parties to exchange well-defined cash flows at specified dates) in order to cover their exposure to price variations: multinationals and financial institutions routinely obtain such

---

25. As long as

$$p_H\left(R - \frac{B}{\Delta p}\right)I^* \geqslant p_L R I^* - p_L \frac{B}{\Delta p} I$$

$$\iff \quad (\Delta p)\left(R - \frac{B}{\Delta p}\right) \geqslant p_L \frac{B}{\Delta p}\frac{\rho^*}{1+\rho^*},$$

which holds at least if p_L is small. (We here assume that the reward is not canceled when the firm succeeds and the profit is higher than what it would have been in the case of success.)

26. That the lender loses money results from the facts that the borrower deviates from investment I to obtain more than U_b, and that U_b is the maximum utility for the borrower consistent with a nonnegative profit for the lender.

insurance against currency or interest rate fluctuations, and producers or buyers of raw material or agricultural products similarly insure against price fluctuations by trading in commodity futures. Other hedging instruments include securitization, in which the issuer sells part of her portfolio of loans, assets, or intellectual property (or at least reduces the risk borne on the corresponding assets if she keeps some liability), and straight insurance against specific risks (theft, fire, death of key employee, guarantee of a financial institution against default on a claim such as a receivable, and so forth).

Corporate risk management is not driven by the desire to provide claimholders with insurance. There are two ways to see this: first, claimholders can obtain this insurance by diversifying their own portfolio; second, and relatedly, an insurance contract transfers risk from one party to another and therefore does not affect the aggregate uncertainty, which, according to standard asset pricing theory (the consumption-based capital asset pricing model), is the key driver of asset prices. By contrast, corporate risk management can be rationalized by agency-based (credit-rationing) considerations. We have seen that, even in a world of universal risk neutrality, firms ought to obtain some insurance against liquidity shocks as long as capital market imperfections prevent them from pledging the entire value of their activity to new investors. Following Froot, Scharfstein, and Stein (1993), we therefore derive an elementary explanation of corporate hedging from agency-based considerations.[27]

Froot et al. study risk management and financial structure in a sequential contracting context. In a first stage, an entrepreneur who has not yet issued securities to investors faces an uncertain short-term income. This short-term income serves, in the absence of hedging, as cash on hand for the second-stage investment; the second-stage investment is financed by resorting to borrowing from investors but, as in Chapter 3, agency costs may expose the entrepreneur to credit rationing. The entrepreneur in the first stage can choose to stabilize her short-term income, and therefore her net worth in the subsequent borrowing stage.

As Froot et al. point out, the absence of financial design in a sequential contracting context makes it difficult to make general predictions as to whether the entrepreneur should hedge. Exercise 3.21, in part adapted from Froot et al., indeed presented a number of situations in which the entrepreneur preferred either to hedge against an exogenous risk or to use this risk to gamble. For example, if the agency cost is linear in investment, hedging is optimal when the production function is strictly concave, while gambling is optimal if there are indivisibilities in investment (as is the case in the fixed-investment model of Section 3.2) and hedging does not allow the entrepreneur to reach the funding threshold of cash on hand. In the variable-investment model of Section 3.4, the entrepreneur is indifferent between hedging and gambling, and would prefer hedging (gambling) if the private benefit were convex (concave) instead of linear in investment.

When risk management is not integrated with a choice of financial structure (the entrepreneur is still residual claimant when choosing whether to hedge), risk management is a "jack of all trades and a master of none": because the level of liquidity cannot be separately controlled, the choice of its riskiness must also make up for the missing optimization of the financial structure. Indeed, hedging is always optimal in the environments presented in Exercise 3.21 under simultaneous liquidity and risk management. The following treatment therefore builds on Froot et al.'s seminal work by integrating liquidity and risk management.

5.4.1 The Rationale for Hedging

Let us assume that some shock exogenous to the firm affects the firm's date-1 net revenue, which we here normalize to 0. Let ε denote this income shock, where

$$E(\varepsilon \mid \rho) = 0.$$

For example, I might stand for a foreign investment, and ε might represent a foreign exchange risk. Let

27. Other explanations have been offered in the literature. Stulz (1984) argues that corporate hedging allows managers to obtain some insurance for their risky portfolio (stock options, etc.) against shocks that they have no control over. While this point is well-taken, Froot et al. (1993) note that managers could obtain such diversification by going to the corresponding markets themselves, and so Stulz's argument relies on a transaction cost differential. Tax reasons have also been discussed in the literature. See Mason (1995) for a more complete discussion.

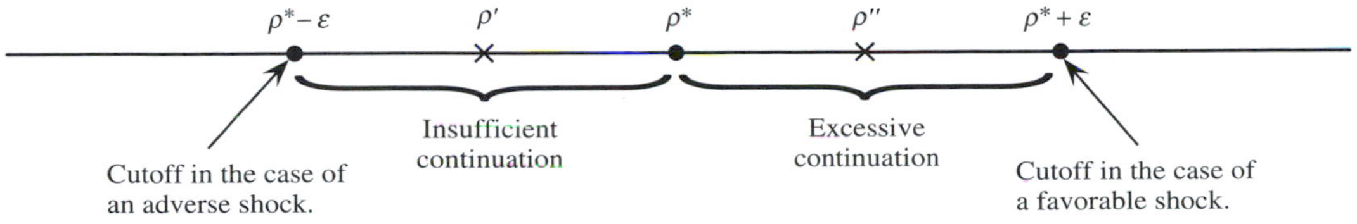

Figure 5.6

us furthermore assume that the firm can costlessly obtain insurance against this exogenous shock. As was the case for liquidity management, we envision an *ex ante* contract between borrower and investors and thereby obtain an unambiguous answer to the question: "Should the firm neutralize the cash flow variability by entering hedging arrangements?"[28]

Intuitively, a random liquidity garbles the reinvestment policy. Suppose, for example, that the shock can take values ε and $-\varepsilon$ with equal probabilities; the firm's need for a given ρ becomes $\rho+\varepsilon$ and $\rho-\varepsilon$, respectively. Relative to the deterministic reinvestment policy obtained by eliminating the shock (i.e., reinvest if and only if $\rho \leqslant \rho^*$), the firm reinvests too little in the case of an adverse shock and too much in the case of a favorable one (see Figure 5.6). For example, the firm has enough cash to continue when $\rho = \rho''$ and the income shock is favorable and not enough when $\rho = \rho' < \rho''$ and the income shock is adverse.

This reasoning is, however, too simplistic as the cutoff ρ^* itself depends on the risk management policy. Let us now provide a more rigorous proof. This proof is the same for a fixed and a variable investment. Let us, for instance, consider the variable-investment model and assume that the income shock (an earnings shortfall if it is positive, a gain if negative) is εI, proportional to investment and distributed according to an arbitrary continuous distribution.

If the firm *hedges*, then for a given amount of liquidity hoarding the threshold under which the firm can continue, ρ^*, is deterministic and the analysis of Section 5.3.2 shows that the borrower's utility is

$$U_{\rm b} = \frac{\rho_1 - c(\rho^*)}{c(\rho^*) - \rho_0} A$$

for an arbitrary threshold ρ^*.

In the *absence of corporate hedging*, the threshold is now random: if the firm hoards just enough liquidity to withstand liquidity shocks below some ρ^* when $\varepsilon = 0$, then for an arbitrary realization ε the firm can withstand liquidity shocks ρ such that[29]

$$\rho + \varepsilon \leqslant \rho^*,$$

and so the state-contingent threshold is $\rho^* - \varepsilon$. Writing (IR_1) and (5.4) as expectations with respect to the random variable ε, the reader will check that the borrower's utility in the absence of corporate hedging is

$$\hat{U}_{\rm b} \equiv \frac{\rho_1 - \hat{c}(\rho^*)}{\hat{c}(\rho^*) - \rho_0},$$

where ρ^* denotes the threshold when $\varepsilon = 0$,

$$\hat{c}(\rho^*) \equiv \frac{1 + E_\varepsilon[\int_0^{\rho^*-\varepsilon} \rho f(\rho)\,\mathrm{d}\rho]}{E_\varepsilon[F(\rho^* - \varepsilon)]},$$

and E_ε denotes an expectation with respect to ε.

Using the Arrow–Pratt Theorem (see Arrow 1965; Pratt 1964),[30] it is easy to see that, for each ρ^*, there

28. "*Ex post*," that is, once financing has been secured, borrower and investors do not have perfectly congruent views on risk management, and therefore the notion of "optimal risk management" at that point in time depends on whose standpoint one takes. Similarly, different classes of investors (e.g., debtholders and shareholders), if any, have conflicting objectives regarding risk management.

29. We here ignore the possibility of renegotiation (see Section 5.5), which arises for large ε: if $\rho \in (\rho^* - \varepsilon, \rho_0)$, then the liquidity shock is smaller than the pledgeable income and investors are willing to bring in new cash (see the treatment of the soft budget constraint). Similarly, when $\rho \in (\rho_1, \rho^* - \varepsilon)$, continuation is inefficient and investors optimally offer a bribe to the borrower for not continuing.

Two remarks are in order here. First, our analysis can be amended to reflect the possibility of renegotiation. Second, renegotiation is irrelevant if the exogenous shock ε remains small.

30. Let $H(x) \equiv 1 + \int_0^x \rho f(\rho)\,\mathrm{d}\rho$. Let us first show that H is "more convex than F," in the sense that H is a convex transform of F, that is, $H \circ F^{-1}$ is convex. A straightforward computation shows that $(H \circ F^{-1}(y))' = F^{-1}(y)$, and so $(H \circ F^{-1}(y))'' > 0$, where $y \equiv F(x)$.

Second, for a given threshold ρ^*, define $\bar{\rho}$ such that

$$F(\bar{\rho}) = E_\varepsilon[F(\rho^* - \varepsilon)].$$

That is, $\bar{\rho}$ is the certainty equivalent of the random variable $\rho^* - \varepsilon$ for function F. Because H is more convex than F, the Arrow–Pratt Theorem (which states that the risk premium is smaller for the more convex exists a $\bar{\rho}$ such that

$$c(\bar{\rho}) \leqslant \hat{c}(\rho^*),$$

which implies that

$$U_b \geqslant \hat{U}_b.$$

In words, corporate risk management lowers the expected unit cost of effective investment and adds value.[31]

Remark (substitutes to corporate hedging: alternative risk transfer). Note that insurance could be provided by means other than hedging on a market. In particular, a bank could offer a *conditional* credit line, such that the maximal amount varies one-to-one (and positively) with ε.[32] Namely, the maximal commitment is equal to $(\rho^* + \varepsilon)I$, and so the firm can withstand liquidity shocks $\rho I \leqslant (\rho^* + \varepsilon)I - \varepsilon I = \rho^* I$. In the absence of transaction costs, conditional credit lines and corporate hedging are perfect substitutes. Such contingent credit lines do exist,[33] but they are less pervasive than corporate hedging. Contingent credit lines may substitute for corporate hedging when either the insurance contract must be tailored to the borrower's specific needs (and so there is no market for the corresponding claims) or when it is difficult to write formal hedging contracts because the underlying shock cannot be well-described *ex ante* or objectively measured *ex post*. The contingent credit line must in the latter circumstances rest on the bank's reputation for abiding by its implicit promises.

In circumstances in which the risk can be insured against in deep markets, corporate hedging is likely to be a lower-transaction-cost alternative; for, and as we will see in future chapters, the credit line is only one of several variables that must be indexed to exogenous shocks such as macroeconomic shocks. (For example, managerial compensation should not depend on shocks over which managers have no control. Hence, bonuses and stock options should be indexed on currency and interest rate fluctuations and on several other exogenous risks. Similarly, the allocation of control rights among claimholders should be indexed on such variables.)

While it may be simpler to have the firm engage in corporate hedging rather than index many contracts and covenants, further study is needed before drawing such a conclusion. As a matter of fact, financing arrangements known under the heading of alternative risk transfer (ART) have developed over the years although they have still much scope for growth. Such products blend elements of corporate finance and insurance. A case in point is catastrophe bonds (cat bonds) such as the ones issued by Vivendi Universal to cover its movie studios in Los Angeles against earthquakes, or the bonds that are contingent on the occurrence of a hurricane.[34]

5.4.2 When Is Incomplete Hedging Optimal? Another Look at the Sensitivity of Investment to Cash Flow

We just obtained a stark result of *full hedging*: any exogenous income fluctuation perturbs optimal liquidity management by making the firm sometimes reinvest when the reinvestment cost is high while it sometimes is unable to reinvest for low reinvestment costs. Even leaving aside the *transaction costs* involved in entering hedging contracts (including those associated with the monitoring of the counterparty's solvency), there are several reasons why firms, or countries for that matter, should not, and actually do not in practice, fully hedge.

---

function) implies that $H(\bar{\rho}) \leqslant E_{\varepsilon}[H(\rho^* - \varepsilon)]$, and so $c(\bar{\rho}) \leqslant c(\rho^*)$, as announced.

31. As is the case for the allocation of the initial credit between liquid and illiquid assets (see Section 5.3.3), the borrower's compliance with corporate hedging must be monitored. We invite the reader to check that it may not be in the borrower's best interest to indeed purchase the associated insurance policy once she has obtained the financing for the investment and secured the associated amount of liquidity.

32. Alternatively, the firm could issue debt with interest payments indexed on the shock ε. For example, an oil producer could issue debt whose interest payment increases with the market price of oil.

33. Standby loan commitments are informal arrangements, generally backing the issue of commercial paper by large firms. Under a standby loan agreement, the bank promises to refinance the firm during disruptions in the commercial paper market (Veitch 1992). Incidentally, it is interesting to note that the usage rate on standby commitments is low relative to other categories of loan commitments (Veitch 1992).

In the area of international finance, a number of authors have proposed that reimbursement of sovereign debt be made contingent on observable shocks, such as GDP or exchange rate fluctuations, or (better as this does not give rise to government moral hazard) to world prices of raw materials and other competitive exports of the country.

34. As another example, a few years ago Michelin secured a bank credit line and an insurance facility for five years, contingent on a simultaneous fall in GDP in its various markets and in tyre sales.

(a) *Market power.* Consider the producer of a raw material (copper, oil, etc.) with market power. The market price then depends not only on uncertainty that is exogenous to the firm (e.g., demand shifts), but also on the firm's supply decisions. Thus, suppose for illustrative purposes that there are two dates, 0 and 1 (these two dates are meant to correspond to the risk-management-choice and the risk-income dates of the model). And suppose for simplicity that the firm is a monopolist in the market for the raw material. The monopolist at date 0 sells f units forward at predetermined price p^{f}. This amounts to writing an insurance contract that pays the firm at date 1 f times the (positive or negative) difference between p^{f} and the date-1 spot price. Once the monopolist has sold these f units, though, they are no longer hers, and therefore the monopolist has at date 1 decreased incentives to restrain output to keep the spot price up. From the point of view of the monopolist at date 1, output withholding raises the price on her extra production only (her inframarginal units do not include the forward sales). Forward sales overall result in an output that exceeds the monopoly output and therefore reduce revenue.[35]

Example. Suppose that the date-1 spot price is $\tilde{a}-q$, where $\tilde{a}$ is an exogenous demand shock realized at date 1 and q is output, and that the marginal cost is 0. In the absence of forward sales, the monopolist chooses q at date 1 so as to maximize $q(\tilde{a}-q)$, yielding $q=\frac{1}{2}\tilde{a}$ and a revenue that is random at date 0: $r=\frac{1}{4}\tilde{a}^2$. The expected profit is thus $\frac{1}{4}E[\tilde{a}^2]$, where $E[\cdot]$ denotes an expectation with respect to $\tilde{a}$.

Suppose now that the monopolist sells f units at price p^{f} at date 0. At date 1, the monopolist chooses an extra output q (to be added to the f units that she committed to deliver) so as to maximize $q[\tilde{a}-(q+f)]$, and so $q=\frac{1}{2}(\tilde{a}-f)$.[36] Under rational expectations, the forward price must be equal to the expected spot price:

$$p^{\mathrm{f}}=E[\tilde{a}-(q+f)]=E[\tfrac{1}{2}(\tilde{a}-f)].$$

Total (date-0 plus date-1) profit,

$$\tfrac{1}{4}(E[\tilde{a}^2]-f^2),$$

decreases with f.

More generally, forward sales reduce monopoly power, and so, in the absence of date-1 reinvestment need, it is strictly optimal not to hedge at all ($f=0$).[37] When one combines the corporate risk management motive of this chapter with the exercise of market power, the optimal degree of hedging is partial hedging.

(b) *Serial correlation of profits.* An important assumption behind the full-hedging result of Section 5.4.1 is that the date-1 profit realization conveys no information about the firm's prospects: it is a transitory shock. Suppose in contrast that a high date-1 profit is good news about date-2 profitability. For example, the price of a crop may reflect permanent shocks such as the reduction of trade barriers, the entry of competing offers, or a change in consumer preferences.

With positive serial correlation of profits, a high current profit is associated with attractive reinvestment opportunities. This suggests that the liquidity available to the borrower at date 1 should covary with the date-1 profit (so, for example, the farmer's debt contract should not be fully indexed to the price of the crop). Things are, however, more complex than this first argument suggests, because better prospects also make it easier for the borrower to return to the capital market at the intermediate stage. The *attractive-reinvestment-opportunities*

35. This reasoning is reminiscent of that underlying the "Coase conjecture," which states that a durable-good monopolist tends to create its own competition and to "flood the market" (see, for example, Tirole 1988, Chapter 1), although the setting is slightly different (the good is here nondurable).

36. We assume that the price is always positive. Otherwise,

$$q=\max\{\tfrac{1}{2}(\tilde{a}-f),0\};$$

but the gist of the analysis remains the same.

37. This basic insight must be amended a bit in the case of oligopoly. A large literature, starting with Allaz and Vila (1993), has shown that firms that compete *à la* Cournot (in quantities) partially hedge despite the absence of reinvestment need. The intuition is that forward markets induce each oligopolist to try to act as a "Stackelberg leader" and to thereby force its rivals to cut output on the spot market (see, for example, Chao et al. (2005), Creti and Manca (2005), and Willems (2005) for recent contributions to this literature). As usual, this conclusion is reversed if firms compete in prices rather than quantities (see Mahenc and Salanié 2004); under price competition, oligopolists would like to "commit" to set high prices so as to induce others to also set high prices. Buying (i.e., gambling) on the forward market is a commitment for suppliers to set high prices in the spot market.

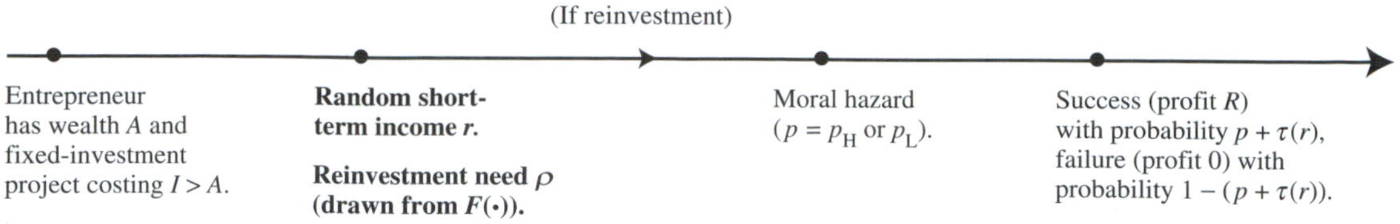

Figure 5.7

effect, however, in general dominates the *easier-refinancing effect*, and so the firm should not be fully insured against exogenous profit shocks, as we now illustrate.

Let us consider the fixed-investment model of Section 5.2, but with two twists:

- The short-term income, r, is random, with mean $\bar{r}$.
- The probability of success in the case of continuation is an increasing function of r,
$$p + \tau(r), \quad \text{with } \tau' > 0,$$
where $p = p_H$ or p_L depending on the entrepreneur's date-1 behavior. (The separable form of the probability-of-success function as usual guarantees that the incentive constraint is invariant.) We assume that the realizations of r and ρ are independent.

These twists are depicted in bold in Figure 5.7.

Let us follow the steps of Section 5.2 and determine the optimal state-contingent cutoff $\rho^*(r)$ (so continuation occurs if and only if $\rho \leqslant \rho^*(r)$). Letting $E[\cdot]$ denote expectations with respect to r, the NPV is

$$U_b = \bar{r} + E[F(\rho^*(r))[p_H + \tau(r)]R] - I - E\bigg[\int_0^{\rho^*(r)} \rho f(\rho)\,d\rho\bigg].$$

The investors' breakeven constraint similarly is

$$\bar{r} + E\bigg[F(\rho^*(r))[p_H + \tau(r)]\bigg[R - \frac{B}{\Delta p}\bigg]\bigg] \geqslant I - A + E\bigg[\int_0^{\rho^*(r)} \rho f(\rho)\,d\rho\bigg].$$

Letting μ denote the shadow price of the breakeven constraint (we assume that the constraint is binding, i.e., $\mu > 0$), the first-order condition with respect to $\rho^*(r)$ yields, for each r,

$$\rho^*(r) = \frac{[p_H + \tau(r)][R + \mu(R - B/\Delta p)]}{1 + \mu}.$$

Let us now investigate the implementation of the optimal contract. A *fully indexed debt* can be defined as a date-1 liability $d(r)$ such that

$$d(r) = d_0 + r,$$

for some constant d_0. That is, in the absence of refinancing in the capital market, a fully indexed debt insulates the firm's retained earnings against its cash-flow risk. We, however, want to allow the firm to return to the capital market: insulation of retained earnings against the cash-flow risk does not imply insulation of the reinvestment policy. The amount it can raise in the capital market at date 1,

$$[p_H + \tau(r)]\bigg(R - \frac{B}{\Delta p}\bigg),$$

is increasing with the date-1 profit as $\tau' > 0$ (this was referred to earlier as the "easier-refinancing effect"). The optimal policy is implemented when the cutoff is equal to the cash cushion plus the refinancing capacity:

$$\rho^*(r) = [r - d^*(r)] + [p_H + \tau(r)]\bigg(R - \frac{B}{\Delta p}\bigg),$$

or

$$d^*(r) = r - \frac{p_H + \tau(r)}{1 + \mu}\bigg(\frac{B}{\Delta p}\bigg).$$

In the presence of an agency cost ($B > 0$), the debt is not fully indexed. The easier-refinancing effect is at play, but the existence of a managerial rent puts a limit on what can be achieved by returning to the capital market. Put differently, *the firm should keep some of its cash flow as retained earnings*.

The source of this cash-flow sensitivity of debt is the monotonicity of managerial rents[38] with the

38. Here, this rent is $[p_H + \tau(r)](B/\Delta p)$.

resolution of uncertainty. Thus, the credit rationing problem at the seasoned offering stage is more severe, the more favorable the resolution of uncertainty. While this monotonicity is often a reasonable assumption, one can, of course, envision cases where it does not hold. To check our intuition, Exercise 5.11 considers the case of a permanent price shock P: the date-1 income is Pr (where r is now known and P is a random variable realized at date 1) and the date-2 income in the case of success is PR. The managerial rent in the case of continuation[39] is then insensitive to the state of nature. While the date-1 cash flow affects reinvestment through its informational content, there should not be any cash-flow sensitivity of retained earnings; put differently, debt due at date 1 is perfectly indexed to the output price ($d(P) = Pr - \ell_0$ for some positive ℓ_0).

When, in contrast, a high profit today announces *low* profits tomorrow (negative serial correlation, $\tau' < 0$), the conclusions are reversed. Suppose, for example, that an industry is subject to cycles and furthermore that investments made at the peak (trough) mature at the trough (peak); one possible story is that the other firms in the industry are subject to poor governance and that they invest when they have large cash flows rather than when investments are profitable. How should a (well-governed) firm behave in such an industry? By analogy with the formula above, it should retain less money in net terms when its profit grows.[40]

(c) *Aggregate risk.* Hedging markets often involve economic variables, such as interest rates or exchange rates, that respond to macroeconomic shocks. As is well-known and reflected, for instance, in the capital asset pricing model (CAPM), aggregate risk must be borne by and is optimally shared among economic agents; insuring against it therefore involves a risk premium. Put differently, economic agents cannot insulate themselves from such risks at a "fair price."

We invite the reader to return to the analysis of Section 5.4.1, focusing for simplicity on linear insurance schemes and assuming that eliminating a fraction θ of the income shock (which therefore becomes $(1-\theta)\varepsilon$ in net terms) costs $\sigma\theta$ (proportional to θ). It is easy to see[41] that it is suboptimal to fully hedge; that is, the optimal θ is less than 1. Intuitively, a small risk (θ close to, but smaller than 1) induces only small deviations from the optimal risk management and reinvestment policy, and therefore a second-order NPV loss; in contrast, the cost of this insurance is first order and proportional to θ.

We thus conclude that firms should hedge less against shocks involving larger macroeconomic risk premia.

(d) *Asymmetric information.* Asymmetric information may limit the development of hedging markets. Consider, for example, the potential market for five-year hedges against variations in the overall power prices and in zonal price differences in the U.S. electricity Midwest market. The value of such derivatives depends on very complex predictions of the evolution of supply and demand as well as of likely changes in incentive regulation for both generators and transmission grid owners.

Generators, load-serving entities, and transmission owners, who are keen on hedging their positions, may find few counterparts who have the necessary expertise. And even if some employees of financial institutions do have this expertise, their bosses probably do not and will be reluctant to let them gamble large amounts of money on such long-term derivative markets.

(e) *Incentives.* Finally, borrowers may need to be made somewhat accountable for fluctuations in an exogenous variable, because the quality of their investments depends on how well they predict the future value of this variable. For example, the oil manager of a small oil company has no impact on the oil price; however, the choice of how much to invest in oil rather than in other activities depends on her forecast of the future price of oil. In this case, insulating the borrower from fluctuations in the oil price provides poor incentives for accurate prediction and therefore for efficient investment.

Forecasting future exogenous variables can be modeled in the basic framework as a date-0 moral hazard. The next section studies the implications for liquidity management of such *ex ante* moral hazard.

39. Equal to $p_H(B/\Delta p)$.

40. This policy may be difficult to implement, especially if the firm can hide profits (see Chapter 7).

41. See Holmström and Tirole (2000) for a more rigorous proof.

There, it will be shown that borrowers should not be rewarded for good short-term performance solely through monetary compensation and that liquidity should be sensitive to cash flow. This implies, in particular, that the liquidity of an oil company should not be fully insulated from fluctuations in the stock price even if the company has no market power.

5.5 Endogenous Liquidity Needs, the Sensitivity of Investment to Cash Flow, and the Soft Budget Constraint

5.5.1 Endogenous Liquidity Shocks

Starting with Dewatripont and Maskin (1995), the economics literature has stressed the perverse incentive effects of bailouts and other insurance devices: a state-owned enterprise that knows that it will be bailed out by the government if it loses money has little incentive to reduce its costs or generate revenue.[42] A project manager who knows that the company will be keen on completing the project once large fixed costs have been sunk may "goldplate" the project or spend time on other activities. Hardening the budget constraint may therefore improve incentives.[43]

In the context of corporate financing, liquidity hoarding and credit line commitments become less attractive when liquidity shocks are endogenous, that is, when they depend on the borrower's actions. For incentive purposes, it is not optimal to commit to rescue the borrower often. The borrower has suboptimal incentives to avoid adverse shocks if she knows that she can easily raise cash to cover such shocks. In such circumstances the borrower must be kept "on a short leash." We will discuss how this can be done.

To illustrate in a stark way the point that one may want to commit to a "hard budget constraint," suppose that, after the loan agreement is signed but before the reinvestment need parameter ρ is realized, the borrower can by incurring private effort cost c prevent any cost overrun: $\rho = 0$ with probability 1 (as in Section 3.4). On the other hand, ρ is drawn from distribution $F(\rho)$ (as in this section) if the borrower does not incur this cost. Suppose further that c is small enough that it is optimal to induce the borrower to incur the cost.

Assuming for example that the firm has no date-1 income (and so is cash-poor), the optimal policy then obviously consists in letting the borrower invest I and promising never to plow back any money into the firm. In this case the borrower knows that if she does not spend c, the project will be discontinued with probability 1 (provided that the cumulative distribution F has no atom at 0). This threat obviously keeps her on her toes.

The crux of the matter is then, How can we make this hard budget constraint credible? For, we have seen that, in the case of "reasonable" overrun ($\rho \leqslant \rho_0$), the lenders have an *ex post* incentive to renege on their promise not to rescue the firm. Anticipating this, the borrower may not bother to incur cost c to prevent overruns.

5.5.1.1 A Broader Perspective

When is the firm's budget constraint likely to be soft? The basic idea of long-term financing is, as we have seen in Sections 5.2 and 5.3, that the intermediate stage (date-1) exhibits rationing of credit for reinvestment and so it is optimal for the firm to secure *ex ante* (at date 0) more liquidity than it will obtain by going to the capital market at the intermediate stage. Thus the problem is not that the capital market is too soft but rather that it is too tough at the intermediate stage. Hence, the soft-budget-constraint problem does not arise.

This need not be so, however, when information accrues at date 1 that sheds light on some activity subject to earlier (date-0) moral hazard.[44] It is then optimal to commit at date 0 to punish the entrepreneur if the information "signals" that the borrower has not acted in the lenders' interest.

---

42. See Kornai (1980) for a study of the soft budget constraint in centrally planned economies and its macroeconomic consequences.

43. Hardening the budget constraint may, however, induce short-termism, that is, a managerial focus on immediate performance, to the detriment of long-term goals, as was demonstrated by von Thadden (1995). See Chapter 7 for a study of short-termism.

44. Or to adverse selection for that matter. For example, if information accrues at date 1 that the entrepreneur is likely to be a bad borrower, notwithstanding claims to the contrary at the contracting stage, it is in general optimal to commit at date 0 to punish the firm for such bad news at date 1, in order to screen borrowers more efficiently. See Chapter 6 for a treatment of adverse selection.

The key to the soft-budget-constraint phenomenon is that monetary punishments may be limited because they are costly. In our model, the entrepreneur's incompressible stake implies that monetary punishments are limited in the case of continuation. So, *liquidation may be the only feasible punishment for the entrepreneur when bad signals about her activity accrue at date 1*. In contrast with monetary punishments, which are simple transfers from the entrepreneur to the lenders, nonmonetary punishments may be *ex post* Pareto-inefficient. The soft budget constraint arises from the fact that while the punishment serves a purpose at date 0 (it deters bad date-0 behavior), it may no longer serve a purpose at date 1. And so it is likely to be renegotiated away if it is *ex post* Pareto-inefficient.[45] In the present case, a Pareto-inefficient liquidation, namely, one that occurs for liquidity shocks below the pledgeable income, is not credible.

Two types of news about date-0 moral hazard can accrue at date 1. The first involves "bygones," namely, variables that, in the absence of considerations relative to punishing or rewarding past behavior, should have no impact on decision making because they no longer affect payoffs. Such a variable is date-1 income.[46] It does not impact the optimal date-1 policy in the absence of considerations of reward or punishment.

Variables in the second set both convey information about managerial performance and impact date-1 decision making. The level of date-1 liquidity shock, news about the prospects for date 2 in the case of continuation (say, news about the probability of success or about income in the case of success), and the level of the date-1 salvage value of the assets in the case of liquidation all belong to this second category.

In the next section, we focus on the case of an endogenous intermediate revenue in order to identify the punishment aspect and the soft budget constraint in the simplest manner. It is straightforward, though, to extend the analysis to the second set of variables (see Exercises 5.3 and 5.4). These exercises show that the results obtained in Section 5.5.2 carry over to news about date-2 prospects and about the salvage value. In particular, the soft-budget-constraint problem always arises when news is bad, that is, when performance is poor.

5.5.2 Endogenous Intermediate Income

Let us generalize the model of Section 5.3.2 by introducing an endogenous short-term revenue.[47] The investment of variable size I generates a nonnegative date-1 revenue rI. This (verifiable) date-1 income is subject to date-0 moral hazard. The distribution of the per-unit income r on an interval $[0, r^+]$ is $G(r)$ with density $g(r)$ if the entrepreneur works at date 0, and $\tilde{G}(r)$ with density $\tilde{g}(r)$ if the entrepreneur shirks at date 0. Let

$$\ell(r) \equiv \frac{g(r) - \tilde{g}(r)}{g(r)}$$

denote the likelihood ratio.[48] As usual, we assume that a high date-1 revenue signals that the entrepreneur is likely to have worked at date 0.

Monotone likelihood ratio property: $\ell(r)$ weakly increases with r.

This property implies, in particular, that the distribution of the date-1 income improves, in the sense of first-order stochastic dominance, if the entrepreneur works: $G(r) \leqslant \tilde{G}(r)$ for all r. To avoid technical difficulties, we will further assume that the likelihood ratio is constant past some level of r lower than r^+.[49]

45. The literature on mutually advantageous renegotiation is based on the same principle: an *ex ante* contract between a principal and an agent creates distortions in order to provide the agent with incentives to act in the principal's interest. Once the agent has acted, the distortion no longer serves a purpose and tends to be renegotiated away, thus reducing the agent's *ex ante* incentives. For example, in the standard moral-hazard model, the agent receives suboptimal insurance, which is then partly renegotiated away (see Fudenberg and Tirole 1990; Ma 1991). There is also a large literature, initiated by Dewatripont (1989), on renegotiation when the initial contract is plagued by adverse selection (see, for example, Hart and Tirole 1988; Laffont and Tirole 1990; Rey and Salanié 1996).

46. An almost equivalent example is a separable date-2 revenue that will accrue independently of date-1 decisions (such as liquidation versus continuation) and is publicly learned at date 1. Indeed, if the corresponding claim is securitized, it becomes a date-1 revenue for the firm.

47. The analysis in this section is modeled after that in Section 3 of Rochet and Tirole (1996). This article has quite a different purpose. It studies systemic risk generated by interbank exposures. Interbank lending is motivated by the benefits from peer monitoring among banks. The date-1 income of this section corresponds to (minus) the loss in the interbank market in Rochet and Tirole.

48. There are, of course, several equivalent ways of defining this ratio. Another common one is $g(r)/\tilde{g}(r)$.

49. In the absence of this assumption and given risk neutrality, it may be optimal to give the entrepreneur an extra rent beyond her

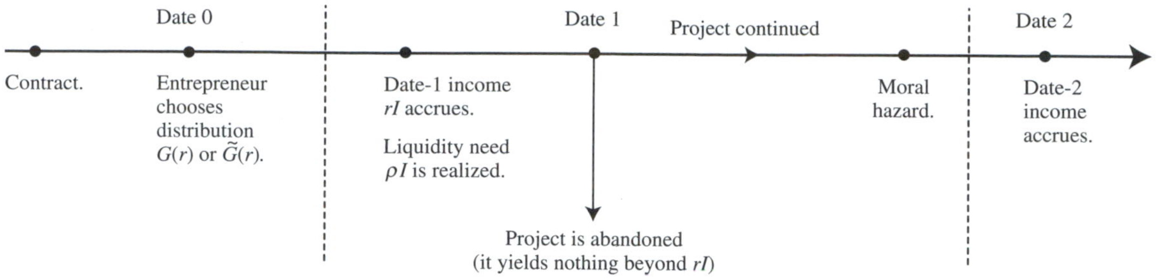

Figure 5.8

This is a purely technical assumption, which has no serious consequence for the analysis.

The entrepreneur enjoys private benefit $B_0 I$ at date 0 if she shirks, and 0 if she works. The modified timing is summarized in Figure 5.8.

As earlier, we let

$$\rho_1 = p_{\mathrm{H}} R \quad \text{and} \quad \rho_0 = p_{\mathrm{H}}\left(R - \frac{B}{\Delta p}\right)$$

denote the per-unit expected income and pledgeable income, respectively. (Recall that ρ_0 embodies the date-1 moral hazard, and so there is no need for including the corresponding incentive constraint ($\mathrm{IC_b}$) in the program below.)

Let us, in a first step, ignore the credibility issue. Letting "NSBC" stand for "no soft budget constraint," we maximize the project's NPV subject to the constraints that lenders break even and that the entrepreneur has an incentive to work at date 0. A *contract* specifies a state-contingent threshold $\rho^*(r)$ and a per-unit "extra rent" $\Delta(r)$.

A word of explanation is called for here. This per-unit extra rent is equal to the entrepreneur's expected rent per unit of investment when the state of nature is r, minus either the minimal per-unit rent, $p_{\mathrm{H}} B/\Delta p$ that is necessary to induce good behavior in the case of continuation, or 0 in the case of liquidation. So, if the entrepreneur receives $R_{\mathrm{b}} \geqslant B/\Delta p$ in the case of success at date 2, then

$$\Delta(r) = p_{\mathrm{H}}\left(R_{\mathrm{b}} - \frac{B}{\Delta p}\right).$$

And, in the case of liquidation, $\Delta(r) \geqslant 0$ represents the cash payment made to the entrepreneur at date 1.

incentive-compatible stake, entirely at the highest possible income r^+, in the form of a "spike" at r^+.

Section 3.4 showed that in the absence of date-0 moral hazard, it is optimal to set this extra rent $\Delta(r)$ equal to 0, so as to pledge as much income as is feasible to the lenders and thus to boost debt capacity. As we will see, this no longer needs to be the case in the presence of date-0 moral hazard. The flip side of punishing the entrepreneur for bad performance, that is, for a low date-1 income, by liquidating the firm even for low liquidity shocks, is that it is optimal to reward her for high date-1 income with continuation even for high liquidity shocks. But, for $\rho > \rho_1$, continuation is inefficient and it is optimal, as we will see, to convert the reward into monetary rewards and thus into extra rents $\Delta(r) > 0$.

Ignoring for simplicity the choice of investment size I, we can now write the program when there is no credibility issue.

Program NSBC:

$$\max_{\{\rho^*(\cdot),\Delta(\cdot)\geqslant 0\}} \left\{\int_0^{r^+}\left[r + F(\rho^*(r))\rho_1 - \int_0^{\rho^*(r)} \rho f(\rho)\,\mathrm{d}\rho - 1\right] g(r)\,\mathrm{d}r\right\} I$$

$$\text{s.t.} \quad \left\{\int_0^{r^+}\left[r + F(\rho^*(r))\rho_0 - \Delta(r) - \int_0^{\rho^*(r)} \rho f(\rho)\,\mathrm{d}\rho\right] g(r)\,\mathrm{d}r\right\} I \geqslant I - A \qquad (\mathrm{IR_l})$$

and

$$\left\{\int_0^{r^+} [F(\rho^*(r))(\rho_1 - \rho_0) + \Delta(r)] \times [g(r) - \tilde{g}(r)]\,\mathrm{d}r\right\} I \geqslant B_0 I, \qquad (\mathrm{IC_b'})$$

recalling that $B_0 I$ is the *date-0* private benefit of misbehaving.

Note that (IC$'_b$) can be rewritten by highlighting the role of the likelihood ratio:

$$\int_0^{r^+} [F(\rho^*(r))(\rho_1 - \rho_0) + \Delta(r)]\ell(r)g(r)\,\mathrm{d}r \geqslant B_0. \tag{IC$'_b$}$$

Letting μ and ν denote the (nonnegative) multipliers of constraints (IR$_l$) and (IC$'_b$), the necessary (and sufficient) conditions for program NSBC yield

$$\rho^*(r) = \frac{\rho_1 + \mu\rho_0 + \nu(\rho_1 - \rho_0)\ell(r)}{1+\mu}$$

and

$$\Delta(r) = 0 \quad\Rightarrow\quad \nu\ell(r) \leqslant \mu \quad\Rightarrow\quad \rho^*(r) \leqslant \rho_1,$$
$$\Delta(r) > 0 \quad\Rightarrow\quad \nu\ell(r) = \mu \quad\Rightarrow\quad \rho^*(r) = \rho_1.$$

Note that the latter inequalities imply that there is never a negative-NPV continuation ($\rho > \rho_1$). And, as we suggested earlier, there is no extra rent as long as $\rho^*(r) < \rho_1$. The explanation is that for $\rho < \rho_1$, continuation maximizes net payoff and thus it is better to reward the entrepreneur with continuation than with (nonincentive-based) cash. In contrast, for $\rho > \rho_1$, continuation is inefficient and so, if $\rho^*(r) > \rho_1$, one can improve the welfare of all parties by liquidating the firm and providing the entrepreneur with more cash.

Next, we analyze the optimal continuation rule. Because likelihood ratios are equal to 0 in expectation, one has

$$E[\rho^*(r)] = \frac{\rho_1 + \mu\rho_0}{1+\mu},$$

where $E[\cdot]$ denotes the expectation operator (with respect to density g). And so, "on average," the threshold is a convex combination of ρ_1 and ρ_0, as in the absence of date-0 moral hazard. The state-contingent threshold can be rewritten as

$$\rho^*(r) - E[\rho^*(r)] = \lambda\ell(r),$$

where

$$\lambda \equiv \frac{\nu(\rho_1 - \rho_0)}{1+\mu}.$$

Because the likelihood ratio is increasing, the continuation rule is more lenient, the higher the date-1 income.

Figure 5.9 summarizes the analysis. The coefficient λ is small when date-0 moral hazard is relatively unimportant. This arises either if the date-0

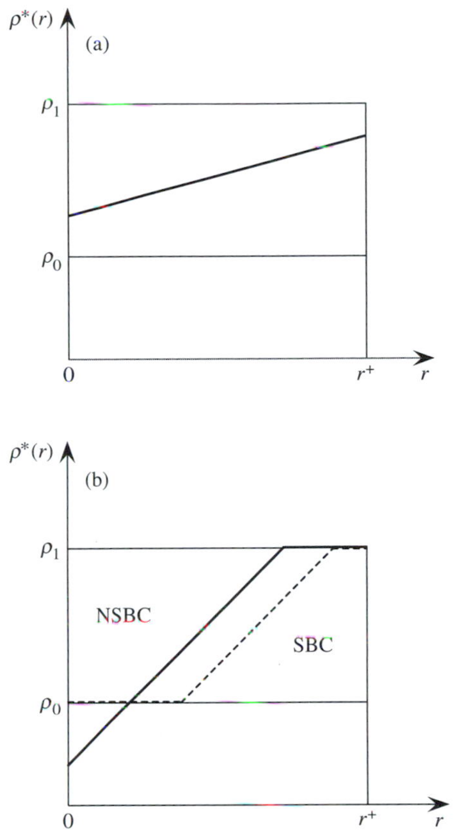

Figure 5.9 (a) λ small; (b) λ large.

per-unit-of-investment private benefit B_0 is small or if the date-1 income is mainly determined by external demand and cost shocks that lie beyond the control of the entrepreneur (and so $\ell(\cdot)$ remains close to 0: see part (a) of the figure).[50] When date-0 moral hazard is more substantial (λ large), two new phenomena can arise. First, the "constraint" $\rho^*(r) \leqslant \rho_1$ may become binding for r large. Second, $\rho^*(r)$ may fall below the pledgeable income ρ_0 for r low. The solution, ignoring renegotiation, is depicted in bold.

We are now set for a discussion of the soft budget constraint. If the entrepreneur can renegotiate Pareto-suboptimal liquidation, then the relevant program becomes

Program SBC = Program NSBC with added constraint $\rho^*(r) \geqslant \rho_0$ for all r.

50. In the latter case, though, it may become optimal to let the entrepreneur take her private benefit B_0 at date 0.

If date-0 moral hazard is small enough (λ small) so that $\rho^*(0) \geqslant \rho_0$, the soft-budget-constraint problem does not arise. If date-0 moral hazard is substantial (λ large), then $\rho^*(r) < \rho_0$ for $r < r_0$ (see Figure 5.9(b)).

We leave it to the reader to check that, for any level of investment I, the solution to Program SBC is depicted by the dashed curve in Figure 5.9(b).

Lastly, note that—and this is obviously a general property—the borrower's *ex ante* welfare is always (weakly) lower when renegotiation is feasible, since the soft-budget-constraint problem adds an extra constraint to the optimization program.

5.5.3 Keeping Commitment Credible

Several devices that might allow lenders to commit not to plow back money into the firm have been considered in the literature (in contexts that differ from the one studied here, but which have in common the need for such a commitment). Following the debt overhang literature (see Section 3.3), Hart and Moore (1995) assume that the initial lenders are *dispersed* and cannot participate in a claim restructuring;[51] and, to prevent refinancing by new investors, Hart and Moore restrict the availability of new capital by putting limits on the dilution of the claims of initial lenders. In particular, making initial lenders senior and new lenders junior strongly reduces the incentive of new lenders to provide refinancing (in the absence of renegotiation, the senior lenders' stake is another incompressible stake on top of the entrepreneur's. So there is hardly any pledgeable income).[52]

Another possibility is to create a diversity of claims with different control rights, and to give, in states of financial trouble, control to "tough" claimholders who have a strong incentive to impose abandonment of the project or risk reduction in such states. In Dewatripont and Tirole (1994), those tough claimholders are debtholders rendered conservative by their concave return stream, (outside) equityholders being softer. Berglöf and von Thadden (1994) argue that the short-term debtholders can be used to play the role of the "tough guy," with the long-term debtholders being softer. In Burkart et al. (1995), a bank receives senior, secured claims in order to have a strong incentive to liquidate the firm in case of trouble (see also Gorton and Kahn 2000).

The use of a tough claimholder with control rights in the case of financial straits can provide a hard budget constraint only if one of the following two conditions holds:

(i) either the tough claimholder is unable to renegotiate with other claimholders and the entrepreneur;
(ii) or renegotiation is feasible, but some concession can be extracted from the entrepreneur in the bargaining process through the threat of tough intervention in the case of disagreement.

It is important to note that this second possibility could not be a motivation for the diversity of claims in the model of this section. While the claimholders can obtain a concession from the entrepreneur in the form of a lower stake through the threat of abandoning the project, this concession destroys the entrepreneur's incentives sufficiently that it actually does not benefit the claimholders. The concession story can only be valid in a situation where the entrepreneur is able to make concessions that do not substantially impair her incentives.

To sum up, there is no surefire way of imposing a hard budget constraint; at this stage we mainly have at our disposal methods that in specific circumstances should, but need not, harden the budget constraint.

5.5.4 Sensitivity of Investment to Cash Flow

As discussed in Section 2.5.2, the empirical finding that firms' investments are sensitive to their cash flow can be either rationalized by optimal contracting considerations or viewed as evidence that managers take advantage of poor governance in order to engage in wasteful investments when they have the ability to do so. While both explanations seem relevant, we pursue the first one here.

---

51. This assumption is commonly made for public debt in particular. For example, building on Bulow and Shoven (1978) and White (1980), Gertner and Scharfstein (1991) emphasize the difficulty of rescheduling debt when there are many creditors.

52. As Hart and Moore show, it may be optimal to allow some dilution of existing claims because new profitable investment opportunities may arrive and need to be financed (in our model small overruns may occur even if the entrepreneur incurs cost B_0, so that it is worth allowing some reinvestment on the equilibrium path).

Recall also the debate between Fazzari et al. (1988) and Kaplan and Zingales (1997) as to whether firms with a weak balance sheet exhibit a higher sensitivity of investment to cash flow. We took a first look at this prediction in Section 3.2.7 by interpreting "cash flow" as "net worth" and observed that the theory makes no clear prediction in this regard. In that section, though, we argued that this first look has drawbacks and that firms are better viewed as ongoing entities.

The relationship

$$\rho^*(r) - E[\rho^*(r)] = \lambda\ell(r)$$

indicates that (re)investment should indeed be sensitive to cash flow: continuation or investment (in the reinterpretation in which retentions are used to finance growth prospects) are part of an optimal carrot-and-stick scheme designed to encourage the production of cash flow.[53]

The issue of whether the sensitivity of investment to cash flow increases with the intensity of financial constraints is more complex. In the case of small date-0 moral hazard (implying $\Delta(r) \equiv 0$), and letting $\hat{\rho} \equiv E[\rho^*(r)]$, the constraint ($\text{IC}_\text{b}'$) can be rewritten as

$$E_r[F(\hat{\rho} + \lambda\ell(r))\ell(r)] = \frac{B_0}{\rho_1 - \rho_0}.$$

For a uniform distribution ($F(\rho) = f \cdot \rho$) and using the fact that the expectation of the likelihood ratio is equal to 0, we obtain

$$\lambda E_r[\ell^2(r)] = \frac{B_0}{f(\rho_1 - \rho_0)} = \text{constant}.$$

The financial constraint impacts only the average liquidity in that, as earlier, a tighter financial constraint in general results in a shorter maturity structure:[54]

$$\rho^*(r \mid A) = \hat{\rho}(A) + \lambda\ell(r).$$

Thus, *for a uniform distribution, the sensitivity of investment to cash flow is independent of the financial constraint.*[55] More generally, with nonuniform distributions, the sensitivity parameter λ may increase or decrease with A. We thus conclude that no strong prediction emerges as to the relationship between financial constraint and sensitivity of investment to cash flow.

5.6 Free Cash Flow

As we discussed in the introduction to this chapter, the free-cash-flow problem faced by firms with excess liquidity is the mirror image of the liquidity shortage problem faced by cash-poor ones. While the latter must contract on the provision of liquidity beyond the level provided *ex post* by the capital market, the former must design a mechanism that forces them to pay out excess cash in the future.

We first review the relationship between the liquidity shortage and the free-cash-flow problems. The problem of preventing inefficient liquidation of cash-poor firms becomes one of preventing inefficient continuation of the cash-rich firm. This results in a theory of claim maturity. The optimal contract takes the form of a mandatory payment to claimholders at date 1. As in Section 5.2.2, this payment, which can be interpreted either as a dividend as in Easterbrook (1984)[56] or as short-term debt as in Jensen (1986), forces the borrower to pay out the excess cash and prevents her from wasting it on suboptimal reinvestments.

Section 5.6.2 goes beyond this reinterpretation of the liquidity shortage model by considering more complex settings in which a fixed payment is not optimal. As has been emphasized in the literature, rough instruments such as short-term debt then simultaneously allow some undesirable reinvestments and prevent some desirable ones. As we explain, optimal contracting requires the firm to use market information more fully in order to properly manage the firm's liquidity.

53. As discussed in Chapter 2, $\rho^*(r)$ alternatively should increase with r even in the absence of date-0 moral hazard, if the first- and second-period revenues are correlated. A simple way to introduce this learning effect in our model would be to assume that the date-2 probability of success is $p + \tau(r)$, where (i) $p = p_\text{L}$ or p_H depends, as usual, on the entrepreneur's date-1 behavior, and (ii) τ is increasing in r (see (b) in Section 5.4.2).

54. (IR_l), in the case of a uniform distribution and normalizing $f = 1$, can be rewritten as

$$\hat{\rho}\rho_0 - \tfrac{1}{2}\hat{\rho}^2 - \lambda^2 E[\tfrac{1}{2}\ell^2(r)] = I - A - \bar{r}.$$

Because λ is independent of A and $\hat{\rho} > \rho_0$, $\hat{\rho}$ increases with A.

55. The constant-returns-to-scale model, as usual, is not appropriate to study the impact of the intensity of financial constraints on the sensitivity of investment to cash flow, since all firms are scaled-up or scaled-down versions of each other (Program NSBC depends only on A/I). But suppose that I is fixed in Program NSBC (more generally, returns could be decreasing).

56. An early paper on dividends with a similar idea is Rozeff (1982).

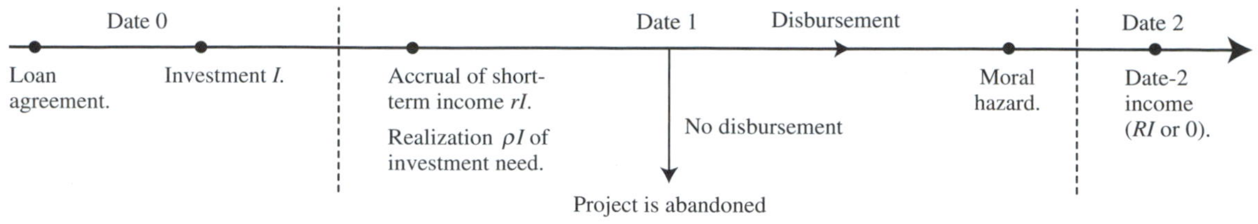

Figure 5.10

5.6.1 Optimal Claim Maturity

Let us return to the continuous-investment, continuous-shock version of Section 5.3.2, but with a short-term income (the analysis is not really new and is therefore only sketched): see Figure 5.10. Because the short-term income rI is fully pledgeable to the lenders, everything is *as if* the unit investment cost were equal to $1 - r$ instead of 1. The lenders' breakeven condition, that is, the equality between expected revenue and expected investment cost, becomes

$$rI + F(\rho^*)\rho_0 I = I - A + \left[\int_0^{\rho^*} \rho f(\rho)\,\mathrm{d}\rho\right] I$$

and so

$$k(\rho^*) = \frac{1}{1 + \int_0^{\rho^*} \rho f(\rho)\,\mathrm{d}\rho - [r + F(\rho^*)\rho_0]}. \tag{5.3''}$$

The margin (expected profit of the firm per unit of investment) becomes

$$m(\rho^*) = [r + F(\rho^*)\rho_1] - \left[1 + \int_0^{\rho^*} \rho f(\rho)\,\mathrm{d}\rho\right]. \tag{5.4''}$$

And thus the borrower's (gross) utility becomes

$$U_\mathrm{b} = m(\rho^*)k(\rho^*)A = \frac{\rho_1 - c(\rho^*)}{c(\rho^*) - \rho_0}A,$$

where the expected unit cost of effective investment, $c(\rho^*)$, is given by

$$c(\rho^*) = \frac{1 - r + \int_0^{\rho^*} \rho f(\rho)\,\mathrm{d}\rho}{F(\rho^*)}. \tag{5.5''}$$

So the optimal threshold is given by

$$\int_0^{\rho^*} F(\rho)\,\mathrm{d}\rho = 1 - r \tag{5.6''}$$

and the borrower's utility by

$$U_\mathrm{b} = \frac{\rho_1 - \rho^*}{\rho^* - \rho_0}A. \tag{5.7''}$$

It is important to note that *the short-term income, even though it is deterministic and fully pledgeable, is not equivalent to an increase in the borrower's cash on hand A*. Such an increase in equity would result in a larger investment (as is the case here), but not in a modification of the continuation rule. By contrast, condition (5.6″) shows that the larger the short-term profit, the lower the optimal threshold ρ^*. To understand this point, recall the tradeoff between increasing borrowing capacity (by choosing ρ^* close to ρ_0) and increasing the probability of continuation (by choosing ρ^* close to ρ_1). The short-term revenue (like a salvage value) makes it worth sacrificing continuation more in order to boost borrowing capacity. Lastly, note that the distinction between a short-term revenue and a salvage value is that the salvage value is obtained only if the investment is liquidated at date 1. And so the net expected date-2 profit and date-1 pledgeable income are $\rho_1 - L$ and $\rho_0 - L$ in the case of a salvage value, and ρ_1 and ρ_0 in the case of a short-term income. This explains the difference between, say, (5.7′) and (5.7″).

(a) *Liquidity management.* Let us now turn to the implementation of the optimum and thus to the claim maturity. To this purpose we make the following assumption.[57]

Free-cash-flow assumption: $r > \rho^*$. Under the free-cash-flow assumption, and given that the entrepreneur cannot steal the intermediate income, the entrepreneur would reinvest excessively if she were not asked to pay out money to investors at date 1. Namely, she would reinvest as long as $\rho \leqslant r$.

To obtain the optimal amount of reinvestment, an amount $P_1 \equiv (r - \rho^*)I$ must be pumped out of the firm, and the entrepreneur must be denied the right to dilute initial investors.

57. Of course, it must also be the case that $\rho^* > \rho_0$ (otherwise, the borrower's borrowing capacity and utility would be infinite in this constant-returns-to-scale model). Because $\mathrm{d}\rho^*/\mathrm{d}r < -1$, we must thus also assume that r is not "too large."

Remark (salvage value). The analysis is again extended straightforwardly to allow for a salvage value LI for the assets if the project is discontinued at date 1. The threshold ρ^* is then given by

$$\int_0^{\rho^*} F(\rho)\,d\rho = 1 - r - L.$$

We thus conclude that the short-term payment $P_1 = (r - \rho^*)I$ grows faster than the salvage value.

5.6.2 Liquidity Management in More General Settings

The previous section considered a somewhat special setting, in which short-term debt suffices to fine-tune the firm's cash at date 1. As one might imagine, a fixed payment at date 1 in general is unlikely to be quite the right way to manage a cash-rich firm's liquidity (neither is a fixed credit line for a cash-poor firm). More instruments are needed in order to obtain the optimal state-contingent reinvestment policy. A sizeable literature has developed that shows that with rough instruments such as short-term debt there is in general a tradeoff between allowing more undesirable reinvestments and preventing more desirable ones (see, for example, Harris and Raviv 1990; Hart and Moore 1995; Stulz 1991).[58] The literature has not yet, to the best of my knowledge, come to grips with a general theory of liquidity management. Although we will not provide such a theory, we can make a number of observations relative to it.

Investors' date-1 control of liquidity is unlikely to be optimal. One might think that date-1 control by investors provides the flexibility required when a fixed payment (or a fixed credit line) does not properly adjust the firm's liquidity. We have seen, however, that investors tend to liquidate excessively (to reinvest too little), and so investors' control is unlikely to be optimal.

58. In Harris and Raviv and Stulz, short-term debt reduces free cash flow. Hart and Moore allow a more complex management of liquidity (they allow the amount of cash used at date 1 to be contingent on the date-2 revenue, which is deterministic at date 1 in their model). They do not, however, allow the firm's liquidity to be fully contingent on the market's information about variables that are realized at date 1 and which could be obtained from the value of securities or the money raised in a security issuance.

Make full use of market information. Consider a general environment in which a number of variables besides the liquidity shock are random and are realized and publicly observed at date 1: the first-period income r, the salvage value L, the second-period expected payoff in the case of continuation ρ_1 and the date-1 pledgeable income in the case of continuation ρ_0. Suppose in a first step that these variables are verifiable by a court of law. Then the optimal contract should specify a state-contingent threshold $\rho^*(r, L, \rho_1, \rho_0)$ beyond which reinvestment does not take place. This state-contingent threshold is straightforwardly computed by generalizing the previous analysis to random payoff values (see below for an example of such a computation).

At date 1, though, only the first-period income r is directly verifiable. The implementation of the optimal state-contingent rule requires extracting the values of L, ρ_1, and ρ_0 from the capital market. The date-1 values of the securities provide such information; in this respect, we should note that a diversity of tradable securities creates more market valuations and may be able to "span" a larger state space. But reading from market valuations is not the only way to extract information about the state of nature. For example, the acceptance of an exchange offer by a secured creditor with unpaid short-term debt (that is, an offer of securities or cash in exchange for debt forgiveness) reveals information about the salvage value L of the assets that are collateralized. Similarly, the renegotiation of existing claims embodies available information at date 1.[59]

Again, our aim here is not to develop a general theory of liquidity management, but rather to point out that optimal liquidity management should make use of the wealth of information held by the capital market about current and future asset values. We now illustrate this point through an example.

5.6.2.1 An Illustration: *Ex Ante* Uncertainty about the Second-Period Income

Let us assume that there is *ex ante* uncertainty not only about the liquidity shock ρ but also about the

59. David (2001), for example, argues that the renegotiation of putable securities enables the payment to their holders to be contingent on the state of nature.

second-period income in the case of success (see Exercise 5.8 for a different illustration of the use of market valuations for liquidity management). More precisely, suppose that the second-period income is equal to RI with probability $\underline{\alpha}$ and to $(R+\Delta R)I$ (with $\Delta R > 0$) with probability $\bar{\alpha} = 1-\underline{\alpha}$. (All of our results generalize to a continuum of possible values for the income in the case of success.) The second-period income in the case of failure is always equal to 0. So, in terms of our general modeling, there is uncertainty of magnitude $p_{\mathrm{H}}\Delta R$ with regards to both ρ_0 and ρ_1. For notational simplicity, we set $L = 0$ (no salvage value).

One can show that if all variables were verifiable at date 1, the optimal liquidity management would specify two thresholds, $\underline{\rho}^*$ when the second-period income is RI and $\bar{\rho}^*$ when the second-period income is $(R+\Delta R)I$, where[60]

$$\bar{\rho}^* = \underline{\rho}^* + p_{\mathrm{H}}\Delta R.$$

As one would expect, the optimal threshold moves one-to-one with the realized increment in expected second-period income and pledgeable income.

It is clear that *short-term debt is no longer sophisticated enough to provide the firm with the appropriate amount of liquidity.* Assuming away any right for the entrepreneur to dilute initial investors, a fixed payment P_1 defines a threshold,

$$\rho^* \equiv r - P_1,$$

that is independent of the news about date-2 income.

It is also easy to illustrate in this model a tradeoff that has been highlighted repeatedly in the literature. Suppose one constrains oneself to the use of short-term debt and that the firm is not allowed to conduct a seasoned offering at date 1. The optimal level of short-term debt defines a threshold equal to the value given in (5.6″),[61] and satisfying

$$\bar{\rho}^* > \rho^* > \underline{\rho}^*.$$

So, under the restriction to liquidity management through short-term debt, the contract must trade off insufficient reinvestment in the state in which prospects are good and excessive reinvestment in the state in which the prospects are mediocre. And, indeed, at the constrained optimum, there is excessive reinvestment when $\rho \in (\underline{\rho}^*, \rho^*]$ and the second-period per-unit income in the case of success is R and insufficient reinvestment when $\rho \in (\rho^*, \bar{\rho}^*]$ and the second-period per-unit income in the case of success is $(R+\Delta R)$.

A similar point can, of course, be made for a random date-1 income, as a fixed P_1 does not pump the proper amount of money out of the firm as long as either r or ρ^* is random. This tradeoff thus suggests why (nonindexed) *debt is a more appropriate instrument for firms with safe cash flows* (regulated public utilities, banks, firms in mature industries).[62]

To let the reinvestment policy respond to future prospects, it is necessary to use market information about these prospects. There are several ways of doing so. Here is a simple way of relying efficiently on market information in the context of an unknown payoff in the case of success: force the entrepreneur to pay out

$$P_1 = [r - (\underline{\rho}^* - \rho_0)]I$$

(if P_1 is positive; otherwise contract at date 0 for a credit line at level $-P_1$); and give the entrepreneur the right to dilute at date 1 existing securities in order to withstand a liquidity shock. Because the pledgeable income is equal to $\rho_0 I$ in the mediocre state and $(\rho_0 + p_{\mathrm{H}}\Delta R)I$ in the good state,

60. We leave it to the reader to check that

$$k(\underline{\rho}^*, \bar{\rho}^*) = \frac{1}{(1-r) - \underline{\alpha}[F(\underline{\rho}^*)\rho_0 - \int_0^{\underline{\rho}^*} \rho f(\rho)\,d\rho] - \bar{\alpha}[F(\bar{\rho}^*)(\rho_0 + p_{\mathrm{H}}\Delta R) - \int_0^{\bar{\rho}^*} \rho f(\rho)\,d\rho]}$$

and

$$m(\underline{\rho}^*, \bar{\rho}^*) = \underline{\alpha}\left[F(\underline{\rho}^*)\rho_1 - \int_0^{\underline{\rho}^*} \rho f(\rho)\,d\rho\right] + \bar{\alpha}\left[F(\bar{\rho}^*)(\rho_1 + p_{\mathrm{H}}\Delta R) - \int_0^{\bar{\rho}^*} \rho f(\rho)\,d\rho\right] - (1-r).$$

61. The reader will check that

$$U_{\mathrm{b}} = \frac{(\rho_1 + \bar{\alpha}p_{\mathrm{H}}\Delta R) - \rho^*}{\rho^* - (\rho_0 + \bar{\alpha}p_{\mathrm{H}}\Delta R)}A,$$

where ρ^* is given by (5.6″).

62. Jensen and Meckling (1976) argue on different grounds that firms with safe cash flows should have more debt. They are interested in the conflict of interests between shareholders and debtholders, and observe that high debt levels may induce shareholders to pursue highly risky strategies if the riskiness of income can be easily manipulated. Note that the definitions of "safe cash flows" are not quite the same in both arguments. We use "safe" in the sense of "nonrisky" while Jensen and Meckling emphasize the absence of moral hazard in the choice of riskiness.

the entrepreneur is able to withstand shocks up to

$$rI - [r - (\underline{\rho}^* - \rho_0)]I + \rho_0 I = \underline{\rho}^* I$$

in the mediocre state and

$$rI - [r - (\underline{\rho}^* - \rho_0)]I + (\rho_0 + p_H \Delta R)I = \bar{\rho}^* I$$

in the good state. We have thus verified that the use of market information about date-2 income allows the implementation of the optimal state-contingent reinvestment policy.

It is clear that more sophisticated mechanisms are required to fine-tune the firm's liquidity when there is also uncertainty about the first-period income,[63] the salvage value, and the entrepreneur's minimum stake (which defines $\rho_1 - \rho_0$). But the general message is clear: market mechanisms can supply the information that is required to implement an optimal liquidity management policy.

5.7 Exercises

Exercise 5.1 (long-term contract and loan commitment). Consider the two-project, two-period version of the fixed-investment model of Section 3.2 and a unit discount factor. Assume, say, that the borrower initially has no equity ($A = 0$). Show the following.

(i) If $p_H(p_H R - I) + (p_H R - I - p_H B/\Delta p) \geqslant 0$, then the optimal long-term contract specifies a loan commitment in which the second-period project is financed at least if the first-period project is successful. Show that if $p_H(p_H R - I) + (p_H R - I - p_H B/\Delta p) > 0$, then the optimal long-term contract specifies that the second-period project is implemented with probability 1 in the case of first-period success, and with probability $\xi \in (0, 1)$ in the case of failure.

(ii) In question (i), look at how ξ varies with various parameters.

(iii) Is the contract "renegotiation proof," that is, given the first-period outcome, would the parties want to modify the contract to their mutual advantage?

(iv) Investigate whether the long-term contract outcome can be implemented through a sequence of short-term contracts where the first-period contract specifies that the borrower receives $\bar{A} = I - p_H(R - B/\Delta p)$ with probability 1 in the case of success and with probability ξ in the case of failure.

Exercise 5.2 (credit rationing, predation, and liquidity shocks). (i) Consider the fixed-investment model. An entrepreneur has cash A and can invest $I_1 > A$ in a project. The project's payoff is R_1 in the case of success and 0 otherwise. The entrepreneur can work, in which case her private benefit is 0 and the probability of success is p_H, or shirk, in which case her private benefit is B_1 and the probability of success p_L. The project has positive NPV ($p_H R_1 > I_1$), but will not be financed if the contract induces the entrepreneur to shirk. The (expected) rate of return demanded by investors is 0.

What is the threshold value of A such that the project is financed?

In the following, let

$$\rho_0^1 \equiv p_H\left(R_1 - \frac{B_1}{\Delta p}\right).$$

The next three questions add a prior period, period 0, in which the entrepreneur's equity A is determined. The discount factor between dates 0 and 1 is equal to 1.

(ii) In this question, the entrepreneur's date-1 (entire) equity is determined by her date-0 profit. This profit can take one of two values, a or A, such that

$$a < I_1 - \rho_0^1 < A.$$

At date 0, the entrepreneur faces a competitor in the product market. The competitor can "prey" or "not prey." The entrepreneur's date-0 profit is a in the case of predation and A in the absence of predation. Preying reduces the competitor's profit at date 0, but by an amount smaller than the competitor's date-1 gain from the entrepreneur's date-1 project not being funded.

- What happens if the entrepreneur waits until date 1 to go to the capital market?
- Can the entrepreneur avoid this outcome? You may want to think about a credit line from a

63. If this first-period income rI is random but exogenous (that is, not affected by moral-hazard or adverse-selection considerations), it suffices to distribute it, so as not to create a spurious dependence of the reinvestment policy on the particular realization of date-1 income. The optimal policy is clearly more complex if moral-hazard or adverse-selection considerations imply that the entrepreneur should be rewarded for high date-1 income by receiving more liquidity.

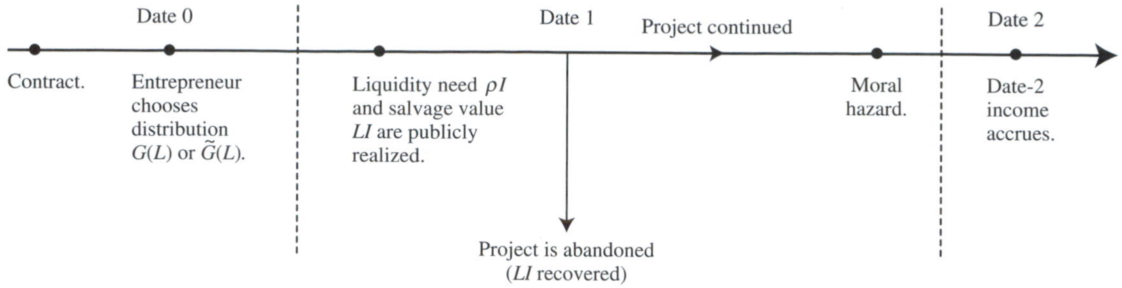

Figure 5.11

bank. Would such a credit line be credible, that is, would it be renegotiated to the mutual advantage of the entrepreneur and his investors at the end of date 0?

(iii) Forget about the competitor, but keep the assumption that the entrepreneur's date-0 profit can take the same two values, a and A. We now introduce a date-0 moral-hazard problem on the entrepreneur's side.

Assume that the entrepreneur's date-0 production involves an investment cost I_0 and that the entrepreneur initially has no cash. The entrepreneur can work or shirk at date 0. Working yields no private benefit and probability of profit A equal to $q_{\rm H}$ (and probability $1 - q_{\rm H}$ of obtaining profit a). Shirking yields private benefit B_0 to the entrepreneur, but reduces the probability of profit A to $q_{\rm L} = q_{\rm H} - \Delta q$ ($0 < q_{\rm L} < q_{\rm H} < 1$). Assume that

$$I_1 + I_0 - (q_{\rm L}A + (1 - q_{\rm L})a) > \rho_0^1.$$

- Interpret this condition.

Consider the following class of long-term contracts between the entrepreneur and investors. "The date-1 project is financed with probability 1 if the date-0 profit is A and with probability $x < 1$ if this profit is a. The entrepreneur receives $R_{\rm b} = B_1/\Delta p$ if the date-1 project is financed *and* succeeds, and 0 otherwise." Assume that such contracts are not renegotiated.

- What is the optimal probability x^*? (Assume that $(\Delta q)p_{\rm H}B_1 \geqslant (\Delta p)B_0$.)
- Assuming that $\rho_0^1 > I_1$, is the previous contract robust to (a mutually advantageous) renegotiation?

(iv) Show that the entrepreneur cannot raise sufficient funds at date 0 if renegotiation at the end of date 0 cannot be prevented, if $\rho_0^1 > I_1$, and if

$$I_0 + I_1 - (q_{\rm H}A + (1 - q_{\rm H})a) > \rho_0^1 - \left(\frac{q_{\rm H}B_0}{\Delta q}\right).$$

Exercise 5.3 (asset maintenance and the soft budget constraint). Consider the variable-investment framework of Section 5.3.2, except that the date-0 moral hazard affects the per-unit salvage value L. Date-1 income is now equal to a constant (0, say). Assets are resold at price LI in the case of date-1 liquidation. The distribution of L on $[0, \bar{L}]$ is $G(L)$, with density $g(L)$, if the borrower works at date 0, and $\tilde{G}(L)$, with density $\tilde{g}(L)$, if the borrower shirks at date 0. We assume the monotone likelihood ratio property:

$$\frac{g(L)}{\tilde{g}(L)} \text{ is increasing in } L.$$

The borrower enjoys date-0 private benefit B_0I if she shirks, and 0 if she shirks. The timing is summarized in Figure 5.11.

As usual, let $\rho_1 \equiv p_{\rm H}R$ and $\rho_0 = p_{\rm H}(R - B/\Delta p)$. And let

$$\ell(L) \equiv \frac{g(L) - \tilde{g}(L)}{g(L)}.$$

(i) Determine the optimal contract $\{\rho^*(L), \Delta(L)\}$ (where $\rho^*(L)$ and $\Delta(L)$ are the state-contingent threshold and extra rent (see Section 5.5.2)) in the absence of the soft budget constraint (that is, the commitment to the contract is credible). Show that

- $\rho^*(L) = -L + (\rho_1 + \mu\rho_0 + \nu(\rho_1 - \rho_0)\ell(L))/(1 + \mu)$ for some positive μ and ν;
- $\Delta(L) = 0$ as long as $\rho^*(L) \leqslant \rho_1 - L$;
- conclude as to when rewards take the form of an increased likelihood of continuation or cash (or both).

(ii) When would the investors want to rescue the firm at date 1 if it has insufficient liquidity? Draw $\rho^*(L)$ and use a diagram to provide a heuristic description of the soft-budget-constraint problem. Show that the soft budget constraint arises for $L \leqslant L_0$ for some $L_0 \geqslant 0$.

Exercise 5.4 (long-term prospects and the soft budget constraint). Perform the same analysis as in Exercise 5.3, with the difference that the date-0 choice of the entrepreneur does not affect the salvage value, which is always equal to 0. Rather, the date-0 moral hazard refers to the choice of the distribution of the second-period income in the case of continuation. This income is $R_L \geqslant 0$ or $R_H = R_L + R$, where $R \geqslant 0$ is a constant. The distribution of R_L, $G(R_L)$, or $\tilde{G}(R_L)$ is determined at date 0. Assume that $g(R_L)/\tilde{g}(R_L)$ is increasing in R_L. As usual, let p_H and p_L denote the probabilities of R_H when the entrepreneur works or shirks *ex post*. And let $\rho_1 \equiv p_H R$ and $\rho_0 = p_H(R - B/\Delta p)$. Assume that R_L is publicly revealed at date 1 before the continuation decision. Solve for the optimal state-contingent policy in the absence of the soft-budget-constraint problem. Show that the soft-budget-constraint problem arises (if it arises at all) under some threshold value of R_L.

Exercise 5.5 (liquidity needs and pricing of liquid assets). Consider the liquidity-needs model with a *fixed investment* and *two possible liquidity shocks*. The borrower has cash A and wants to finance a fixed-size investment $I > A$ at date 0. At date 1, a cash infusion equal to ρ is needed in order for the project to continue. If ρ is not invested at date 1, the project stops and yields nothing. If ρ is invested, the borrower chooses between working (no private benefit, probability of success p_H) and shirking (private benefit B, probability of success $p_L = p_H - \Delta p$). The project then yields, at date 2, R in the case of success and 0 in the case of failure.

The liquidity shock is equal to ρ_L with probability $(1 - \lambda)$ and to ρ_H with probability λ, where

$$\rho_L < \rho_0 < \rho_H < \rho_1,$$

where $\rho_1 \equiv p_H R$ and $\rho_0 \equiv p_H(R - B/\Delta p)$. Assume further that

$$\rho_0 - \rho_L > I - A. \tag{1}$$

There is a single liquid asset, Treasury bonds. A Treasury bond yields 1 unit of income for certain at date 1 (and none at dates 0 and 2). It is sold at date 0 at price $q \geqslant 1$. (The investors' rate of time preference is equal to 0.)

(i) Suppose that the firm has the choice between buying enough Treasury bonds to withstand the high liquidity shock and buying none. Show that it chooses to hoard liquidity if

$$(q-1)(\rho_H - \rho_0) \leqslant (1-\lambda)(\rho_0 - \rho_L) - \lambda(\rho_H - \rho_0) - I + A \tag{2}$$

and

$$(q-1)(\rho_H - \rho_0) \leqslant \lambda(\rho_1 - \rho_H). \tag{3}$$

(ii) Suppose that the economy is composed of a continuum, with mass 1, of identical firms with characteristics as described above. The liquidity shocks of the firms are perfectly correlated. There are T Treasury bonds in the economy, with $T < \rho_H - \rho_0$. Show that when λ is small, the liquidity premium $(q - 1)$ commanded by Treasury bonds is proportional to the probability of a high liquidity shock. (Hint: show that either (2) or (3) must be binding, and use (1) to conclude that (3) is binding.)

(iii) Suppose that, in the economy considered in the previous subquestion, the government issues at date 0 not only the T Treasury bonds, but also a security that yields at date 1 a payoff equal to 1 in the good state (the firms experience liquidity shock ρ_L) and 0 in the bad state (the firms experience liquidity shock ρ_H). What is the equilibrium date-0 price q' of this new asset? (Prices of the Treasury bonds and of this new asset are market clearing prices.)

Exercise 5.6 (continuous entrepreneurial effort; liquidity needs). (i) An entrepreneur with initial cash A and protected by limited liability wants to invest in a fixed-size project with investment cost $I > A$. After the investment is made, the entrepreneur chooses the probability p of success ($0 \leqslant p \leqslant 1$); the disutility of effort is $g(p) = \frac{1}{2}p^2$. (The entrepreneur enjoys no private benefit in this model.) In question (i) only, the profit is $R = 2\sqrt{I - A}$ in the case of success and 0 in the case of failure. (We assume that $R < 1$ to avoid considering probabilities of success exceeding 1. R takes an arbitrary value in question (ii).) As usual, the uninformed investors demand

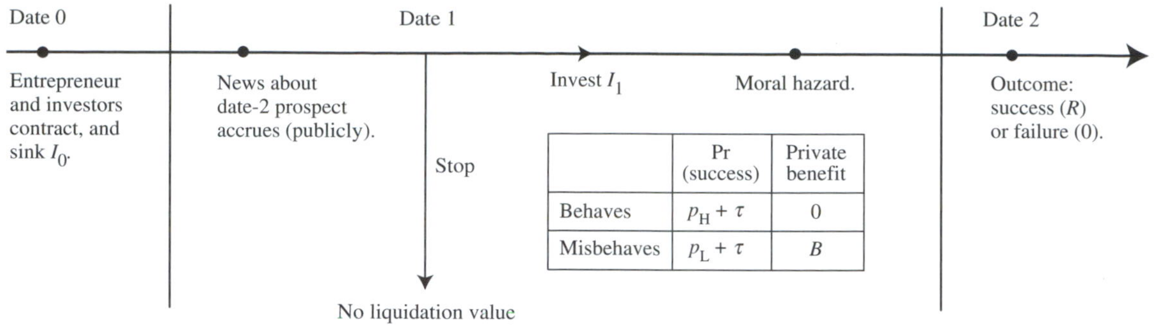

Figure 5.12

an expected rate of interest equal to 0 and everyone is risk neutral. Let R_b denote the entrepreneur's reward in the case of success.

Solve for the optimal contract (R_b). Show that

$$R_b = \tfrac{1}{2}R.$$

(ii) Now introduce an intermediate liquidity shock ρ (for a now arbitrary level A of cash on hand). The cumulative distribution of ρ is $F(\rho)$ on $[0, \infty)$ and the density $f(\rho)$. The effort decision is made *after* the value of ρ is realized and, of course, *conditional* on the choice of continuing (incurring reinvestment cost ρ). *Suppose* that the entrepreneur's stake in the case of continuation (R_b) is independent of ρ. Write the investors' breakeven condition. Write the optimization program yielding (R_b, ρ^*), where ρ^* is the cutoff liquidity shock.

Exercise 5.7 (decreasing returns to scale). Extend the treatment of Section 5.6.1 to the case of decreasing returns to scale: the payoff in the case of continuation and success is $R(I)$, with $R(0) = 0$, $R' > 0$, $R'' < 0$, $R'(0) = \infty$, and $R'(\infty) = 0$. The rest is unchanged (the short-term income is rI, the reinvestment need is ρI, and the private benefit is BI).

(i) What are the first-order conditions yielding the optimal investment level I and cutoff ρ^*?

(ii) Assuming that $r > \rho^*$, and that $(R(I)/I - R'(I))$ is increasing in I (a condition satisfied, for example, by $R(I)$ quadratic), derive the impact of the strength of the balance sheet as measured, say, by A on debt maturity.

Exercise 5.8 (multistage investment with interim accrual of information about prospects). In this chapter we have focused mostly on the case of shocks about the reinvestment need (cost overruns, say). Consider, instead, the case of news about the final profitability. In the two-outcome framework, news can accrue about either the probability of success or the payoff in the case of success. We consider both, in sequence. The investment is a multistage one: let

$$I = I_0 + I_1,$$

where I_0 is the date-0 investment and I_1 is the date-1 reinvestment. In contrast with I_0, I_1 is not incurred if the firm decides to stop. The timing is as in Figure 5.12.

As usual, the entrepreneur has initial wealth A, is risk neutral, and protected by limited liability. Investors are risk neutral. The discount rate is equal to 0. If reinvestment cost I_1 is sunk at date 1, then the firm can continue. Misbehavior reduces the probability of success by Δp, but yields private benefit B to the entrepreneur.

Assume

$$B < (\Delta p)R.$$

As announced, we consider two variants.

(a) *News about the probability of success.* R is known at date 0, but the probability of success is $p_H + \tau$ in the case of good behavior and $p_L + \tau$ in the case of misbehavior, where τ is publicly learned at the beginning of date 1. The random variable τ is distributed according to the distribution function $F(\tau)$ with density $f(\tau)$ on $[\underline{\tau}, \bar{\tau}] = [-p_L, 1 - p_H]$ (to keep probabilities in the interval $[0, 1]$). Let τ^e denote the expectation of τ.

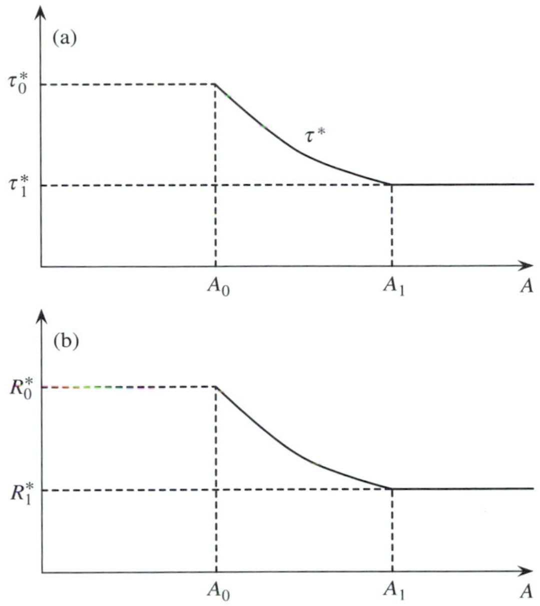

Figure 5.13

(b) *News about the payoff in the case of success.* The probabilities of success are known: p_H and p_L (normalize: $\tau = 0$). By contrast, the profit R in the case of success is drawn from distribution $G(R)$ with density $g(R)$ on $(0, \infty)$. (The profit in the case of failure is always equal to 0.)

(i) For each variant, show that there exist two thresholds, A_0 and A_1, $A_0 < A_1$, such that the first best prevails for $A \geqslant A_1$ and financing is secured if and only if $A \geqslant A_0$. Show that the continuation rules take the form of cutoffs, as described in Figure 5.13.

Determine τ_0^*, τ_1^*, R_0^*, R_1^*.

(ii) For each variant, assume that $A = A_0$. Let $y \equiv (p_H + \tau)R$ denote the expected income, and $\mathcal{R}(y)$ denote the entrepreneur's rent in the case of continuation. Show that (above the threshold y^*)

- $0 < \mathcal{R}'(y) < 1$ in variant (a);
- $\mathcal{R}$ is constant in variant (b).

Exercise 5.9 (the priority game: uncoordinated lending leads to a short-term bias). This chapter, like Chapters 3 and 4, has assumed that the firm's balance sheet is transparent. In particular, each investor has perfect knowledge of loans made by other lenders and of the firm's obligations to them.

This exercise argues that uncoordinated lending leads to financing that is too oriented to the short term. In a nutshell, lenders, by cashing out early, exert a negative externality on other lenders. Because this externality is not internalized, the resulting financial structure contains too much short-term debt.

We consider a three-period model: $t = 0, 1, 2$. The entrepreneur has no cash ($A = 0$), is risk neutral, and is protected by limited liability. At date 0, a fixed investment I is made. The project yields a known return $r > 0$ at date 1, and an uncertain return (R or 0) at date 2. Because the point is quite general and does not require credit constraints, we assume away moral hazard; or, equivalently, the private benefit from misbehaving is 0. The probability of a date 2 success is

$$p + \tau(I_1),$$

where I_1 is the date-1 deepening investment, equal to r minus the level of short-term debt repaid to lenders and the date-1 payment to the entrepreneur (the firm does not return to the capital market at date 1), and τ is an increasing and concave function (with $\tau'(0) = \infty$). Assume that $\tau'(r)R < 1$.

We assume that the entrepreneur cannot engage in "fraud," that is, cannot fail to honor the short-term debt and, if the project succeeds at date 2, the long-term debt. By contrast, obligations to lenders, and in particular I_1, cannot be verified as the firm's balance sheet is opaque.

(i) Derive the first-best investment I_1^*. Show how this allocation can be implemented by a mixture of short- and long-term debt (note that in this model without moral hazard the structure of compensation for the entrepreneur exhibits a degree of indeterminacy).

(ii) Assume that $r - I_1^* < I$ (creditors must hold long-term debt). Suppose next that financing is not transparent. Start from the first-best solution, with a large number (a continuum of mass 1) of lenders, with the representative lender owning short-term claim r_1 and contingent long-term claim R_1 on the firm.

Show that the entrepreneur has an incentive to secretly collude with any lender to increase the latter's short-term claim in exchange for a smaller long-term claim.

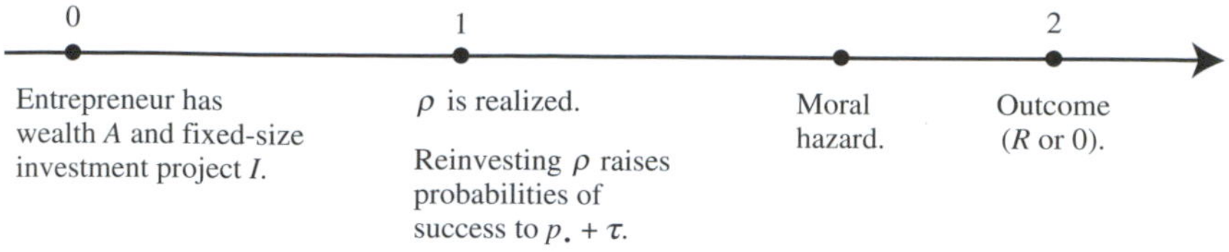

Figure 5.14

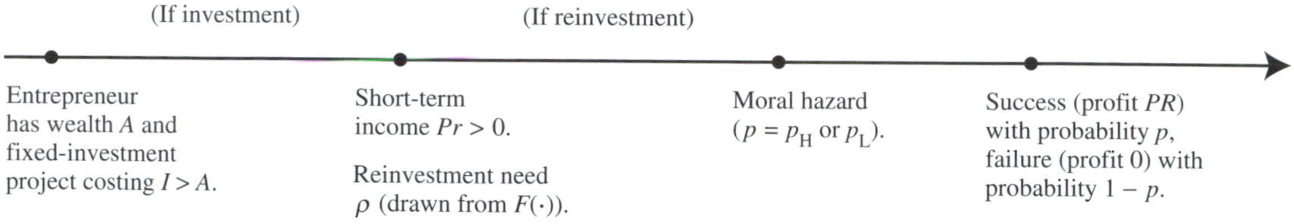

Figure 5.15

Given the constraint that financing is provided by many lenders and that the latter do not observe each other's contracts, is the indeterminacy mentioned in question (i) resolved?

Exercise 5.10 (liquidity and deepening investment). (i) Consider the fixed-investment model. The entrepreneur has cash A and can invest $I > A$ in a project. The project's return in the case of success (respectively, failure) is R (respectively, 0). The probability of success is p_{H} if the entrepreneur behaves (she then gets no private benefit) and $p_{\mathrm{L}} = p_{\mathrm{H}} - \Delta p$ if she misbehaves (in which case she gets private benefit B). In this subquestion and in the subsequent extension, one will assume that the project is viable only if the incentive scheme induces the entrepreneur to behave. The entrepreneur and the capital market are risk neutral; the entrepreneur is protected by limited liability; and the market rate of interest is equal to 0.

Let

$$\rho_1 \equiv p_{\mathrm{H}} R \quad \text{and} \quad \rho_0 \equiv p_{\mathrm{H}}[R - B/\Delta p],$$

and assume $\rho_1 > I > \rho_0$.

What is the necessary and sufficient condition for the project to be financed?

(ii) Now add an intermediate stage, in which there is an option to make a deepening investment. This investment increases the probability of success to $p_{\mathrm{H}} + \tau$ (in the case of good behavior) and $p_{\mathrm{L}} + \tau$ (in the case of misbehavior).

If the deepening investment is not made, the probabilities of success remain p_{H} and p_{L}, respectively. This deepening investment costs ρ, where ρ is unknown *ex ante* and distributed according to distribution $F(\rho)$ and density $f(\rho)$ on $[0, \infty)$. The timing is summarized in Figure 5.14.

Let $\mu \equiv \tau / p_{\mathrm{H}}$, $\hat{\rho}_1 \equiv \mu \rho_1$, and $\hat{\rho}_0 \equiv \mu \rho_0$.

Write the incentive compatibility constraint and (for a given cutoff ρ^*) the investors' breakeven condition.

(iii) What is the optimal cutoff ρ^*? (Hint: consider three cases, depending on whether

$$\rho_0[1 + \mu F(\hat{\rho}_k)] \lesseqgtr I - A + \int_0^{\hat{\rho}_k} \rho f(\rho)\,\mathrm{d}\rho,$$

with $k = 0, 1$.)

(iv) Should the firm content itself with returning to the capital market at date 1 in order to finance the deepening investment (if any)?

Exercise 5.11 (should debt contracts be indexed to output prices?). This exercise returns to optimal corporate risk management when profits are positively serially correlated (see Section 5.4.2). The source of serial correlation is now a permanent shift in the market price of output, as summarized in Figure 5.15. The model is the fixed-investment model, except that the date-1 and date-2 incomes depend on an exogenous market price P, with mean $\bar{P}$, that is realized at date 1. The realizations of P and ρ are independent.

The rest of the model is otherwise the same as in Section 5.2. Following the steps of Section 5.4.2:

(i) Determine the optimal reinvestment policy $\rho^*(P)$.

(ii) Show that, accounting for seasoned offerings, the optimal debt is *fully indexed debt*:

$$d(P) = Pr - \ell_0,$$

where ℓ_0 is a positive constant.

References

Allaz, B. and J. L. Vila. 1993. Cournot competition, forward markets and efficiency. *Journal of Economic Theory* 59: 1–16.

Arrow, K. 1965. *Aspects of the Theory of Risk Bearing.* Helsinki: Yrjö Jahnsson in Säätiö.

Berglöf, E. and E. L. von Thadden. 1994. Short-term versus long-term interests: capital structure with multiple investors. *Quarterly Journal of Economics* 109:1055–1084.

Boot, A., S. Greenbaum, and A. Thakor. 1993. Reputation and discretion in financial contracting. *American Economic Review* 83:1165–1183.

Boot, A., A. Thakor, and G. Udell. 1987. Competition, risk neutrality and loan commitments. *Journal of Banking and Finance* 11:449–471.

Bulow, J. and J. Shoven. 1978. The bankruptcy decision. *Bell Journal of Economics* 9:437–456.

Burkart, M., D. Gromb, and F. Panunzi. 1995. Security design, liquidation value, and monitoring. Mimeo, MIT.

Chang, C. 1992. Capital structure as an optimal contract between employees and investors. *Journal of Finance* 454: 1141–1158.

Chao, H. P., S. Oren, and R. Wilson. 2005. Resource adequacy via option contracts. Mimeo, Stanford University.

Creti, A. and F. Manca. 2005. Mandatory electricity contracts as competitive device. Mimeo, IDEI.

Dasgupta, S. and K. Sengupta. 2005. Financial constraints, hurdle rates, and economic activity: implications from a multi-period model. Mimeo, Hong Kong University of Science & Technology and University of Sydney.

David, A. 2001. Pricing the strategic value of putable securities in liquidity crises. *Journal of Financial Economics* 59: 63–99.

Dewatripont, M. 1989. Renegotiation and information revelation over time: the case of optimal labor contracts. *Quarterly Journal of Economics* 104:589–620.

Dewatripont, M. and E. Maskin. 1995. Credit and efficiency in centralized and decentralized economics. *Review of Economic Studies* 62:541–555.

Dewatripont, M. and J. Tirole. 1994. A theory of debt and equity: diversity of securities and manager-shareholder congruence. *Quarterly Journal of Economics* 109:1027–1054.

Easterbrook, F. 1984. Two agency-cost explanations of dividends. *American Economic Review* 74:650–659.

Fazzari, S., R. G. Hubbard, and B. C. Petersen. 1988. Financing constraints and corporate investment. *Brookings Papers on Economic Activity* 1:141–195.

Froot, K. 1995. Incentive problems in financial contracting. In *The Global Financial System* (ed. D. Crane et al.), Chapter 7. Boston, MA: Harvard Business School Press.

Froot, K., D. Scharfstein, and J. Stein. 1993. Risk management: coordinating corporate investment and financing policies. *Journal of Finance* 48:1629–1658.

Fudenberg, D. and J. Tirole. 1990. Moral hazard and renegotiation in agency contracts. *Econometrica* 58:1279–1320.

Gertner, R. and D. Scharfstein. 1991. A theory of workouts and the effects of reorganization law. *Journal of Finance* 46:1189–1222.

Gorton, G. and J. Kahn. 2000. The design of bank loan contracts. *Review of Financial Studies* 13:331–364.

Greenbaum, S. and A. Thakor. 1995. *Contemporary Financial Intermediation.* Fort Worth, TX: Dryden Press, Harcourt Brace College Publishers.

Greenbaum, S., G. Kanatas, and I. Venezia. 1989. Equilibrium loan pricing under the bank–client relationship. *Journal of Banking and Finance* 13:221–235.

——. 1991. Loan commitments and the management of uncertain credit demand. *Journal of Real Estate Finance and Economics* 4:351–366.

Harris, M. and A. Raviv. 1990. Capital structures and the informational role of debt. *Journal of Finance* 45:321–349.

Hart, O. and J. Moore. 1995. Debt and seniority: an analysis of the role of hard claims in constraining management. *American Economic Review* 85:567–585.

Hart, O. and J. Tirole. 1988. Contract renegotiation and Coasian dynamics. *Review of Economic Studies* 55:509–540.

Holmström, B. and J. Tirole. 1998. Private and public supply of liquidity. *Journal of Political Economy* 106:1–40.

——. 2000. Liquidity and risk management. *Journal of Money, Credit and Banking* 32:295–319.

Jensen, M. 1986. Agency costs of free cash flow, corporate finance and takeovers. *American Economic Review* 76:323–339.

——. 1989. Eclipse of the public corporation. *Harvard Business Review* 67:61–74.

Jensen, M. and W. R. Meckling. 1976. Theory of the firm, managerial behaviour, agency costs and ownership structure. *Journal of Financial Economics* 3:305–360.

Kaplan, S. N. and L. Zingales. 1997. Do investment-cash flow sensitivities provide useful measures of financing constraints? *Quarterly Journal of Economics* 112:169–216.

Kornai, J. 1980. *Economics of Shortage*. New York: North-Holland.

Laffont, J.-J. and J. Tirole. 1990. Adverse selection and renegotiation in procurement. *Review of Economic Studies* 57: 597–626.

Ma, A. 1991. Adverse selection in a dynamic moral hazard. *Quarterly Journal of Economics* 106:255–276.

Mahenc, P. and F. Salanié. 2004. Softening competition through forward trading. *Journal of Economic Theory* 116: 282–293.

Mason, S. 1995. The allocation of risk. *The Global Financial System* (ed. D. Crane et al.), Chapter 5. Boston, MA: Harvard Business School Press.

Pratt, J. 1964. Risk aversion in the small and in the large. *Econometrica* 32:122–136.

Rawls, W. and C. Smithson. 1990. Strategic risk management. *Journal of Applied Corporate Finance* 1:6–18.

Rey, P. and B. Salanié. 1996. Long-term, short-term, and renegotiation: on the value of commitment with asymmetric information. *Econometrica* 64:1395–1414.

Rochet, J. C. and J. Tirole. 1996. Interbank lending and systemic risk. *Journal of Money, Credit and Banking* 28:733–762.

Rothschild, M. and J. Stiglitz. 1970. Increasing risk. I. A definition. *Journal of Economic Theory* 2:225–243.

——. 1971. Increasing risk. II. Its economic consequences. *Journal of Economic Theory* 3:66–84.

Rozeff, M. 1982. Growth, beta and agency costs as determinants of dividend payout ratios. *Journal of Financial Research* 5:249–259.

Stulz, R. 1984. Optimal hedging policies. *Journal of Financial and Quantitative Analysis* 19:127–140.

——. 1991. Managerial discretion and optimal refinancing policies. *Journal of Financial Economics* 26:3–27.

Thakor, A. and G. Udell. 1987. An economic rationale for the price structure of bank loan commitments. *Journal of Banking and Finance* 11:271–289.

Thakor, A., H. Hong, and S. Greenbaum. 1981. Bank loan commitments and interest rate volatility. *Journal of Banking and Finance* 5:497–510.

Tirole, J. 1988. *The Theory of Industrial Organization*. Cambridge, MA: MIT Press.

Veitch, J. 1992. Loan commitments. In *The New Palgrave Dictionary of Money and Finance* (ed. J. Eatwell, M. Milgate, and P. Newman), Volume 2. London: Macmillan.

Von Thadden, E. L. 1995. Long term contracts, short term investment and monitoring. *Review of Economic Studies* 62:557–575.

White, M. 1980. Public policy toward bankruptcy: me-first and other priority rules. *Bell Journal of Economics* 11:550–564.

Willems, B. 2005. Cournot competition, financial option markets and efficiency. Mimeo, Katholieke Universiteit Leuven.

6

Corporate Financing under Asymmetric Information

6.1 Introduction

There is a fair amount of empirical evidence, some of it reviewed in Chapters 1 and 2, showing that securities are often issued under unequal access to information. This chapter investigates the consequences of such informational asymmetries for financing decisions.

Suppose that a firm wants to raise funds on the capital market. The standard motivation for issuing claims, and the one that has been emphasized in previous chapters, is the financing of projects: initial financing, reinvestments, and expansions associated with new projects. An alternative motivation for issuance is risk sharing. For example, a risk-averse entrepreneur may want to diversify her portfolio by selling some of her shares in the firm. Third, the issuance may be motivated by liquidity reasons: an entrepreneur or a venture capitalist may want to cash in to be able to move on to other projects; or a bank may want to securitize loans in order to increase its loanable funds. In all three cases, the issuance is motivated by the existence of gains from trade between the issuer and potential investors. A fourth motivation, though, is unrelated to the existence of gains from trade: the issuer may want to push overvalued assets to investors.

The firm may use a private placement to a small group of knowledgeable investors, conduct an initial public offering, or, if it has already gone public, a seasoned offering. When issuing (buying) new claims, the firm (its investors) should be preoccupied with two types of informational asymmetries: between the issuer and the investors, and among investors.

This chapter studies asymmetric information between insiders and investors and the concomitant lemons problem. Investors have imperfect knowledge of the firm's prospects, the value of assets in place, the value of pledged collateral, the issuer's potential private benefit, or any other firm characteristics that affect the profitability of investment. Accordingly, investors are concerned that they might purchase overvalued claims.

A standard theme of information economics is that gains from trade are often left unexploited in markets plagued by adverse selection. In a famous article, Akerlof (1970) showed how markets for used wares may shrink or even disappear when sellers are better informed about their quality than buyers. The application of this general idea to credit markets is that the issuer may raise less funds or raise funds less often when the capital market has limited access to information about the firm. *Market breakdown*, the fact that potential issuers may refrain altogether from going to the capital market or, less drastically, limit their recourse to that market, and *cross-subsidization*, which, in its most basic form, refers to good borrowers being forced, by the suspicion of low-quality borrowing, to issue high-interest debt or to substantially dilute their equity stake, are studied in Section 6.2.

While this section focuses on the simple environment in which good borrowers are unable to separate from bad ones (except, when there are assets in place, by forgoing attractive investment opportunities), it already delivers a rich set of empirical predictions, some of which historically motivated the theory in the first place.

First, adverse selection can account for the negative stock price reaction associated with equity offerings. This negative stock price reaction is not an obvious phenomenon. After all, investors may learn from an announcement of a seasoned security offering that the firm enjoys new and attractive investment opportunities. The negative stock price reaction, however, can be rationalized by the investors' concern that the issue is motivated by the desire to depart with overvalued assets. An issuer who knows that assets in place are undervalued by investors (a "good borrower") is reluctant to issue shares under terms that would be too favorable to investors. The issuer may then prefer to forgo a profitable investment opportunity (and possibly remain private in the process). Share issues are then a bad signal about firm profitability.[1] It can further be shown that the stock price reaction is less negative in good times, i.e., during booms.

Second, the analysis provides some foundation for the pecking-order hypothesis. According to Myers's (1984) and Myers and Majluf's (1984) pecking-order hypothesis,[2] firms prefer to use "internal finance" (initial equity, retained earnings) to finance their investments. If internal finance is an insufficient source of funds and external finance is required, firms first issue debt, the safest security, then hybrid securities such as convertibles, and finally, as a last resort, equity. The idea is that neither internal finance nor default-free debt suffers from the informational asymmetries and the cross-subsidization traditionally associated with external finance. If these do not suffice to meet the firm's financing needs, the firm will still strive to issue *low-information-intensity claims*, that is, claims whose valuation is the least affected by the asymmetry of information.

The pecking-order hypothesis has received substantial empirical support. The primary source of financing for mature firms (see Chapter 2) is retentions; and outside finance is mainly debt finance, since seasoned equity issues are relatively rare. Another stylized fact corroborating the pecking-order hypothesis is the absence of stock price reaction upon the announcement of a debt issue, in sharp contrast with the decline for a seasoned equity issue.

As usual, things are more complicated than is suggested by this interesting hypothesis. First, while entrepreneurial equity accumulated from previous projects is indeed free from asymmetric information problems, retained earnings are, in practice, endogenous; in particular, the management of a firm may need to convince its shareholders not to distribute large dividends and to keep cash for reinvestments. Whether shareholders are willing to go along with the management's recommendation depends, inter alia, on their belief about the relative profitability of reinjecting cash into the firm and disgorging it. So, "internal finance" is not free of informational problems. Second, what constitutes low-information-intensity financing depends on the type of information that is privy to the issuer, and thus one cannot always equate low-information-intensity financing with debt financing. Third, there are other forces, studied in this book, than asymmetric information that may introduce departures from Myers and Majluf's pecking-order hypothesis and generate alternative pecking orders. For example, cash-poor firms' viability concerns seriously limit their demand for debt finance (Chapter 5); and the entrepreneurs' and large investors' exit strategies require issuing equity or more generally "information-intensive" claims (Chapters 4 and 9). Indeed, the empirical evidence is that small, high-growth firms do not behave at all according to the pecking-order hypothesis, even though these firms are fraught with asymmetric information and therefore would be good candidates for a financing pattern fitting Myers and Majluf's pecking order (Frank and Goyal 2003). But Myers and Majluf's pecking-order hypothesis remains a good starting point for the analysis.

Finally, the analysis of Section 6.2 provides a simple rationale for market timing—the fact that equity issues are more frequent after the firm's stock price or the stock market rises. The idea is simply that in such circumstances the concerns about adverse selection may be dwarfed by the fundamentals, enabling issuers to raise equity.

The second theme borrowed from information economics (Spence 1974; Rothschild and Stiglitz 1976; Wilson 1977) is that the informed side of a market is likely to introduce or accept distortions in contracting so as to signal attributes that are

1. A similar reasoning applies to share buybacks (in 2004, companies announced plans to repurchase $230 billion of their stocks). As Dobbs and Rehm (2005) note, a share repurchase conveys several signals: (a) the management's intention not to engage in a wasteful acquisition or capital expenditure, (b) the management's confidence that the company will not need the cash to cover future expenditures, and (c) the absence of new investment opportunities. Despite the third signal, financial markets in general applaud firms' moves to buy shares back.

2. See, for example, Chapter 18 of Brealey and Myers (1988) for a presentation and Harris and Raviv (1992) for an extensive discussion.

attractive to the uninformed side of the market. More concretely, a good borrower will try to demonstrate attractive prospects to the investors by introducing distortions that are costly to her, but that would be even costlier to a bad borrower. Depending on the setting, this may mean investing too little or too late, resorting to a private placement and to the enlisting of a costly monitor, diversifying the issuer's portfolio insufficiently, underpricing claims, hoarding insufficient liquidity, distributing dividends, or resorting excessively to debt.

Section 6.3 thus studies various dissipative signals that good borrowers use in order to reassure investors and obtain good financing conditions or financing at all: costly collateral pledging, underpricing, suboptimal risk sharing, short-term finance, and hiring of a monitor.

Before proceeding, a brief discussion of the relationship of this chapter to the literature as well as some of the missing topics may be useful. (The rest of the introduction can be skipped in a first reading.)

6.1.1 Methodological Issues

While much progress has been made in the last twenty years toward the understanding of market breakdown and costly signaling, most papers in the literature make assumptions that ought to be relaxed in order to confirm the validity of the arguments. One can divide the criticisms into three categories.

Unconventional goals of the issuer. The literature has analyzed situations with two parties: the "issuer" and the "capital market." The issuer, who is better informed than the capital market, stands for "management" or a "small group of well-informed insiders." There is little difficulty in interpreting this theoretical framework in a situation where the issuer is an entrepreneur who has not yet issued claims, privately or publicly.

The interpretation, however, becomes more complex when management already faces existing claimholders.[3] This raises two issues. First, *who is in charge of financing decisions?* The literature generally assumes that the management is. This assumption is objectionable on both institutional and theoretical grounds. In practice, management ordinarily does not have formal authority (explicit control rights) over financing decisions. The venture capitalist usually controls issuances of the start-up corporation. The board of directors and shareholders review decisions such as dividend distribution, issuance of shares, sale of assets, and so forth. Neither is it *a priori* clear, from a theoretical perspective, why management, which faces a conflict of interest, should have control over its financial structure.

Yet, while the assumption that the management controls the financing does not *a priori* hold on institutional or theoretical grounds, the opposite assumption, that management has no say in financing decisions, largely oversimplifies reality. Management does, in practice, have a sizeable influence on financing decisions. Fortunately, the two viewpoints can be reconciled by introducing a distinction between formal and real authority on financing decisions. Management may not have the formal right to pick financing decisions, but, *precisely because it is superiorly informed*, it has substantial real control over such decisions.[4]

Reflecting this tension between formal rights over financial decisions conferred upon potentially uninformed parties and partial control by management, many papers, including a number of pioneering works in the area (e.g., Ross 1977; Bhattacharya 1979; Myers and Majluf 1984; Miller and Rock 1985) assume that management has the formal right to design the issuance, but internalizes other considerations besides its own welfare. Namely, it is assumed that management benefits directly when securities

3. For instance, a start-up company is partly owned by one or several venture capitalists; a publicly traded corporation already has debt and equity when undertaking a seasoned offering. A coherent interpretation of the theoretical construct then consists in assuming that (i) management and the existing claimholders are symmetrically informed, and are better informed than the new investors, and (ii) management and existing claimholders can redistribute utility among themselves through secret deals. (The need for secrecy arises from the fact that transfers between management and existing claimholders that are observed by new investors convey information about the private information held by the coalition.) Management and existing claimholders may then be viewed as a coalition of well-informed insiders. For this interpretation to hold, it must also be the case that (iii) existing claimholders for some reason (capital requirements faced by intermediaries, undiversified portfolio, or other) are not able to bring in the new funds themselves; otherwise, the new investors would infer that the issuance is overvalued and that they are being ripped off by existing claimholders, and so they would not want to purchase the new claims.

4. We will come back to formal and actual control in Chapter 10.

are highly valued by the market (Ross), or attempts to maximize the value of old (or possibly all) shareholders (Myers and Majluf, Bhattacharya), or else chooses dividends so as to manipulate the current stock price (Miller and Rock). These attempts at reconciling the facts that management has some real, but no formal, control over financing decisions are not arbitrary, although they are reduced forms. In practice, management does care about the capital market's opinion, and tries to some extent to keep its shareholders happy. Such an internalization of the opinion and welfare of others is, however, endogenous. *Management cares solely about its own well-being*, and it is only to the extent that its incentive scheme makes it sensitive to the welfare of others that such concerns may arise. It is thus desirable to build on the reduced forms considered in these papers, and to endogenize the management's degree of authority over financial decisions and its internalization of investors' preferences.

Limitations on the set of issuable securities. Most of the literature presupposes the type of security (usually equity) being issued.[5] This approach has the advantage of simplicity as it abstracts from security design. It also offers interesting insights into the information intensity of various securities and the signaling costs attached to them. It thus supplies a useful building block, although it cannot address the issue of how asymmetric information impacts on the choice of securities.

Two further caveats. The literature describes the issuance as a signaling game, that is, as a two-stage game in which, first, the informed issuer designs the claims and structures their pricing and, second, the uninformed capital market decides whether to purchase the claims. As is well-known, such games are usually plagued by a large multiplicity of (perfect Bayesian) equilibria.[6] Contributions usually derive their insights from the examination of a specific equilibrium. The literature also does not usually make full use of contracting possibilities, even if the type of security to be issued is exogenous. Technically, issuance is a "mechanism designed by an informed principal."[7] In the parlance of this theory, the issuer is the "principal," namely, the party who designs the mechanism, and the capital market the "agent."[8] For the sake of completeness and to obtain sufficient conditions for uniqueness of equilibrium in the issuance game, we will describe this approach in the supplementary section.

6.1.2 Some Limitations of this Chapter

No asymmetric information among investors. This chapter focuses on informational asymmetries between issuers and investors. Because this would require reviewing auction theory, it does not survey the large literature on asymmetries of information among investors bidding for financial claims at initial public offerings or seasoned equity offerings. A well-known paper by Rock (1986) shows that, in fixed-price offerings, underpricing is needed to compensate small, uninformed investors for the winner's curse (the fact that winning at a common value auction reveals that the other informed bidders were unwilling to pay much for the shares). Fixed-price offerings are not optimal procedures in such environments. The subsequent literature (Benveniste and Spindt 1989; Benveniste and Wilhelm 1990; Spatt and Srivastava 1991) therefore

5. For example, in Stiglitz and Weiss (1985), one of the early papers on corporate finance under asymmetric information, firms differ in their riskiness (in the sense of second-order stochastic dominance). Stiglitz and Weiss assume that lenders can offer only debt contracts, and show that the repayment probability decreases with the rate of interest offered by lenders, and that the loan market is characterized by credit rationing. However, the assumptions of the model predict that investors should instead offer equity contracts, in which case there would be no adverse selection (all firms have the same mean income) and no credit rationing (Hart 1985).

6. For studies of signaling games, see, for example, Fudenberg and Tirole (1991, Sections 8.2 and 11.2), Myerson (1991, Section 6.7), and Osborne and Rubinstein (1994, Sections 13.3 and 13.4).

7. See Myerson (1983) and Maskin and Tirole (1990, 1992). An alternative strategy for modeling a competitive capital market would consist in assuming that the competitive lenders make contract offers to the informed entrepreneur. That is, we could consider a competitive capital market *screening* the informed borrower rather than the situation in which the informed borrower *signals* to the competitive capital market (see, for example, Rothschild and Stiglitz (1976), Wilson (1977), and Hellwig (1987) for screening approaches to the description of insurance markets). The study of competitive screening is, however, complex and not yet settled.

8. This theory shows that it may be optimal to include later options for the contract designer into the design that provide the informed principal with choices to be made after the claims have been purchased. The basic idea of these options is to protect the capital market against bad surprises by confronting the issuer with an *ex post* choice (we will illustrate this rather abstract point later). Such options drastically reduce the multiplicity of equilibria, to the point that there exists a unique perfect Bayesian equilibrium of the issuance game over some range of parameters.

adopted a mechanism-design approach. Biais et al. (2002) generalize the optimal-mechanism-design approach to situations in which there is an agency problem between the underwriter and the issuer (as in Baron 1982).[9]

Investors have no informational advantage over issuers. While most informational asymmetries relate to insiders' private knowledge about assets in place and prospects, it is easy to envision situations in which the asymmetry of information operates in the reverse direction, namely, in which investors are better informed on some dimensions. For example, venture capitalists are usually better able than unseasoned entrepreneurs to assess a business model or prospects of a product. In this chapter we will simplify the analysis by assuming that insiders are better informed than investors.[10]

No signal sent to third parties. This chapter focuses on the information conveyed by the issuance to investors. For conciseness, we do not cover an interesting literature that analyzes the informational impact of financial decisions on third parties, such as product-market competitors or suppliers (see Gertner et al. 1988; Poitevin 1989; Bhattacharya and Chiesa 1995; Yosha 1995). For instance, a firm may be eager to signal to investors that the demand for its product is high, as this may allow it to obtain more financing, but still be reluctant to convey such information to potential entrants in that market, whose entry it wants to deter. In contrast, there is no tension for the firm when signaling that it has low costs simultaneously to the capital and product markets when it wants to deter potential entrants.[11]

6.2 Implications of the Lemons Problem and of Market Breakdown

A number of important insights can be gleaned from the following barebones model, in which the borrower has private information about the probability of success.

Privately-known-prospects model. A borrower/entrepreneur has no funds ($A = 0$) to finance a project costing I. The project yields R in the case of success and 0 in the case of failure. The borrower and the lenders are risk neutral, and the borrower is protected by limited liability. The interest rate in the economy is normalized at 0.

The borrower can be one of two types. A good borrower has a probability of success equal to p. A bad borrower has a probability of success q. Assume that $p > q$ and that $pR > I$ (at least the good type is creditworthy). There are two subcases, which we will treat separately:

either $pR > I > qR$
(only the good type is creditworthy),

or $pR > qR > I$
(both types are creditworthy).

The borrower has private information about her type. The capital market, which is competitive and demands an expected rate of return equal to 0, puts probabilities α and $1 - \alpha$ on the borrower being a good or a bad type, respectively. Under asymmetric information, the capital market does not know whether it faces a "p-borrower" (a good borrower) or a "q-borrower" (a bad borrower).[12] Let

$$m \equiv \alpha p + (1 - \alpha)q$$

denote the investors' prior probability of success.

Note that we have left out for the moment moral hazard in the definition of the privately-known-prospects model. The coexistence of moral hazard

9. Another well-known contribution on competition among asymmetrically informed investors is Broecker (1990), who assumes that investors receive private signals about the firm's profitability (but are still less well informed than the borrower) and compete in reimbursement rules for the borrower's business. See also Milgrom and Weber's classic paper (1982) on auctions with common values, and the large subsequent literature.

10. In Inderst and Müller (2005b), a borrower applies to a lender for a loan. The initial contract is drawn under symmetric information. The lender then acquires private, soft information about the quality of the borrower. Because the lender does not internalize the borrower's rent from being funded, the lender denies rationally, but inefficiently, credit for a range of signals. In another recent paper, Inderst and Müller (2005a) add collateral and show that this improves the efficiency of the lender's credit decision by flattening the borrower's repayment schedule.

11. There is a separate literature on the disclosure of proprietary information, arguing that private financing may make it possible to reveal information to an investor without revealing it to competitors (see Campbell 1979; Campbell and Kracaw 1980). In Bhattacharya and Ritter (1983), the firm chooses how much information to reveal; it attempts to reveal its true value to investors and does not reveal all the information that its competitors would like to learn.

12. Here we present the model in terms of a single borrower whose quality is unknown. Equivalently, the model represents a situation in which there are lots of entrepreneurs, a fraction α of which are high-quality ones, and in which investors are unable to tell borrowers apart in terms of quality.

with adverse selection is not necessary for most applications (for which one can therefore ignore private benefits, $B = 0$ in the notation of the book, and thereby remove the moral-hazard component) since adverse selection by itself creates an agency cost and a concomitant credit rationing, and triggers a number of interesting institutional responses. Ignoring moral hazard therefore simplifies the presentation. (In Application 6, however, we will add *ex post* moral hazard in the context of *ex ante* private information about the likelihood of a liquidity shock; in that application, moral hazard will generate a rent from continuation, and *ex post* credit rationing, and thereby create a cost of financing through short-maturity liabilities.) Note also that we assume that the entrepreneur has no cash on hand ($A = 0$), and so she cannot signal her trust in the project by investing her personal wealth into it. Cash on hand will play a key role in Application 8 below.

6.2.1 Market Breakdown and Cross-Subsidization

6.2.1.1 Symmetric Information

To set a benchmark, first consider financing when the investors know the project's prospects.

The good entrepreneur obtains financing. One optimal arrangement[13] for her is to secure the highest level of compensation, R_b^G in the case of success, consistent with investors' breaking even on average:

$$p(R - R_b^G) = I.$$

If $qR < I$, the bad borrower does not want to invest because, under symmetric information, she would receive the NPV, $qR - I < 0$ if she could secure funding. Besides, she cannot obtain financing anyway because the pledgeable income, qR, is smaller than the investors' outlay, I.

If $qR > I$, then the bad borrower receives funding and secures compensation R_b^B in the case of success, where

$$q(R - R_b^B) = I.$$

Clearly,

$$R_b^B < R_b^G.$$

6.2.1.2 Asymmetric Information

The symmetric-information outcome, however, is not robust to asymmetric information, as the bad borrower can, by mimicking the good borrower, derive utility qR_b^G that is greater than that (either 0 or qR_b^B) she obtains by revealing her type.[14]

Let us assume that the only feasible financial contracts are contracts that give the borrower a compensation $R_b \geqslant 0$ in the case of success and 0 in the case of failure. (The validity of this assumption will be discussed in the remark below on the optimality of contracts.) Such contracts necessarily pool the two types of borrower as each prefers receiving financing to not being funded, and conditional on being funded, prefers contracts with a higher compensation. The investors' profit for such a contract is therefore on average:

$$[\alpha p + (1 - \alpha)q](R - R_b) - I = m(R - R_b) - I.$$

No lending: $mR < I$. This case can arise only if the bad borrower is not creditworthy. It then arises whenever the probability that the borrower is a bad borrower is large enough, or

$$\alpha < \alpha^*,$$

where

$$\alpha^*(pR - I) + (1 - \alpha^*)(qR - I) = 0.$$

Because the borrower cannot receive a negative compensation ($R_b \geqslant 0$), investors lose money if they choose to finance the project. Accordingly they do not and the market breaks down.

The good borrower is therefore hurt by the suspicion that she might be a bad one. There is *underinvestment.*

13. Here there is some indeterminacy as to the way the entrepreneur is compensated: the contract can specify any reward $R_b \leqslant R_b^G$ in the case of success, together with, for example, a lump-sum payment (sign-up fee or advances) $T \geqslant 0$ such that investors break even:

$$p(R - R_b) = I + T.$$

Equivalently, the entrepreneur could receive no lump-sum payment up front and receive cash even in the case of failure.

Our choice of contract, in which the borrower receives nothing in the case of failure, will facilitate the comparison with the outcome under asymmetric information.

14. The same lack of incentive compatibility holds *a fortiori* for any of the contracts that are optimal for the good borrower under symmetric information (see the previous footnote), as the reader will check. As we will later observe, the bad borrower is least tempted to choose the good borrower's contract if the latter rewards the borrower only for a good outcome.

Lending: $mR \geqslant I$. This case corresponds either to the situation in which both types are creditworthy or to that in which the bad borrower is not creditworthy but $\alpha \geqslant \alpha^*$.[15]

The borrower's compensation R_b is then set so that investors break even *on average*:

$$m(R - R_b) = I.$$

This implies that, *ex post*, investors make money on the good type ($p(R - R_b) > I$) and lose money on the bad type ($q(R - R_b) < I$): there is *cross-subsidization.*

Note also that

$$R_b < R_b^G$$

(and $R_b > R_b^B$ if the bad borrower is creditworthy). The good borrower is still hurt by the presence of bad ones, although to a lesser extent than when the market breaks down. The good borrower must content herself with a lower compensation (i.e., a higher cost of capital) in the case of success than under symmetric information. Put differently, and interpreting the investors' share as a risky loan with nominal interest rate r such that $R - R_b = (1 + r)I$, then $r > r^G$, where r^G is the rate of interest that the good borrower could obtain under symmetric information: $R - R_b^G = (1 + r^G)I$.

When the bad borrower is not creditworthy, then the outcome is *overinvestment*, as was pointed out in particular by De Meza and Webb (1987), one of the early papers in this literature. Adverse selection (i.e., asymmetric information) reduces the quality of loans.

Remark (a measure of adverse selection). The condition

$$mR \geqslant I$$

can be rewritten as

$$\left[1 - (1 - \alpha)\left(\frac{p - q}{p}\right)\right] pR \geqslant I.$$

We can thus define an index of adverse selection:

$$\chi \equiv (1 - \alpha)\left(\frac{p - q}{p}\right).$$

In the absence of signaling possibility, the good borrowers' pledgeable income, pR, is discounted by the presence of bad borrowers. The discount is measured by the product of the probability of bad types, $1 - \alpha$, times the likelihood ratio, $(p - q)/p$.[16] This discount is the counterpart of the agency cost that obtains under moral hazard (and is equal to the product of the private benefit B divided by the likelihood ratio $(p_H - p_L)/p_H$).[17]

Alternatively, we can measure the cost incurred by the good borrower due to asymmetric information. Instead of receiving the NPV,

$$pR - I,$$

attached to her type, she receives

$$pR_b = p\left(R - \frac{I}{m}\right)$$

or, after some manipulation,[18]

$$pR_b = (pR - I) - \frac{\chi}{1 - \chi} I.$$

Remark (optimality of contracts). Whether the market breaks down or not, a good borrower is hurt by the presence of bad borrowers and therefore would like to separate from bad borrowers if she could. Could she do better than demanding some compensation R_b in the case of success and 0 in the case of failure? Relatedly, could an investor make money by offering a more sophisticated contract to the entrepreneur? The answer to these questions (which are studied in Section 6.5) turns out to be "no" when both types are creditworthy. Intuitively, lending is then efficient and so contractual innovations, keeping investor profitability constant, just amount to redistributing wealth between the good and bad borrowers. A contract that rewards the borrower only in the case of success best reflects the good borrower's comparative advantage, as she is more likely

15. The former situation can be subsumed in the latter one by setting $\alpha^* = 0$.

16. The likelihood ratio can be defined by $(p - q)/p$, $(p - q)/q$, or p/q, indifferently. That $(1 - \alpha)$ enters the measure of adverse selection comes from the fact that good borrowers cannot be distinguished from bad ones in this section. As we will see in Section 6.3, the likelihood ratio, but not the prior α, plays a role in the characterization of a separating equilibrium (the prior plays a role, however, in determining whether the separating equilibrium is unique or dominated by a pooling outcome).

17. The agency cost in the moral-hazard case was expressed in absolute terms while it is here convenient to write it as a fraction of total income so as to let the likelihood ratio appear.

18. Note that this expression holds only when financing can be secured, i.e., when $(1 - \chi)pR \geqslant I$. Under this restriction one indeed checks that $pR_b \geqslant 0$.

to succeed than the bad one. It thereby minimizes the subsidizing of the bad borrower by the good one.

By contrast, when the bad borrower is not creditworthy, the pooling allocation implies overinvestment. It would be more efficient to give a lump-sum payment to bad borrowers to "go away" and accept not to invest; this policy, however, raises concerns about its feasibility (see Section 6.5).

6.2.2 Extensions and Applications

Application 1: Market Timing

Firms tend to issue shares when stock[19] prices are high.[20] As discussed in Section 2.5, there are several possible reasons for this. A commonly advanced one is that adverse selection becomes less relevant during booms.

To see this, let us assume that the probability of success is the sum of the firm's type (p or q, good or bad) and a publicly observable shift parameter $\tau \gtrless 0$ that indexes the firm's, the industry's, or the economy's publicly observable prospects: the probabilities of success are then $p+\tau$ and $q+\tau$ for the good and bad borrowers, respectively. The condition for financing becomes

$$[\alpha(p+\tau)+(1-\alpha)(q+\tau)]R > I$$

or

$$(m+\tau)R > I.$$

Thus the better the market conditions (the larger τ is), the more likely it is that firms can obtain financing. During booms, the intrinsic value of the project becomes large relative to the lemons problem.[21] The reader will indeed check that the index χ of adverse selection is smaller when market conditions improve.

19. Note that we have not yet distinguished between risky debt and equity. See Application 3 below, though.

20. More generally, equity market timing is the practice of issuing shares at a high price and repurchasing them at a low price. Also, "market timing" sometimes refers to the attempt by borrowers to sell equity when it is overvalued. We here mean that borrowers issue equity during good times.

21. We derived this result in the case of a separable production function (additive in probabilities). More generally, an increase in the average probability of success facilitates financing.

Note also that the more general point is that credit rationing is alleviated during booms, whether it is due to adverse selection or moral hazard.

Application 2: Assets in Place, the Negative Stock Price Reaction, and the Going-Public Decision

Let us next suppose that the entrepreneur already owns a project that, without further investment, will succeed with probability p or q, yielding profit R. As before, the entrepreneur knows the probability of success while the investors put probability α on p and $(1-\alpha)$ on q. Thus, in the absence of further information (and so the investors' expectation of the probability of success is m), the assets in place are undervalued (respectively, overvalued) if the true probability of success is p (respectively, q).

For computational simplicity, we will assume that the entrepreneur initially owns all shares. But nothing is altered if she owns only a fraction of the shares. By "stock price reaction upon the announcement of an equity issue," we mean the difference between the total value of shares (whoever owns them) before and after the announcement. This notion corresponds to the approach taken by event studies in empirical work.

An equity offering may be motivated by a profitable "deepening investment" (more generally, the key feature is that one cannot contract on the cash flow generated by this investment separately from that generated by assets in place: the incomes generated by the two are intertwined or fungible[22]). At cost I, the probability of success can be raised by an amount τ such that

$$\tau R > I.$$

That is, investing is efficient for both types of borrowers. Note that we assume for the moment that the increase in profitability is uniform across types: the probability of success becomes $p+\tau$ for a good borrower and $q+\tau$ for a bad one.

The entrepreneur, however, has no cash on hand. Accordingly, the full amount I must be raised from investors. The entrepreneur must therefore issue new shares, thereby reducing the fraction of shares she owns.

A key insight is that relinquishing shares to investors is relatively less costly to the borrower with overvalued assets in place (the bad borrower) than to

22. Otherwise, it would be optimal for the good borrower to engage in project finance so as to avoid having to cross-subsidize the bad one.

the borrower with undervalued assets in place (the good borrower). Thus, if the good borrower conducts an equity offering, so does the bad one.

Let us therefore investigate the possibility of an (efficient) pooling equilibrium. The entrepreneur must offer a stake R_l in success to the investors such that

$$[\alpha(p+\tau)+(1-\alpha)(q+\tau)]R_l = I \iff (m+\tau)R_l = I,$$

where, as earlier, $m \equiv \alpha p + (1-\alpha)q$ is the prior mean probability of success. There exists a unique R_l, $0 < R_l < R$, satisfying this condition.

The good borrower, though, can guarantee herself pR by not diluting her stake.[23] Thus, she is willing to issue new shares only if

$$(p+\tau)(R-R_l) \geqslant pR \iff \tau R \geqslant \frac{p+\tau}{m+\tau}I. \quad (6.1)$$

After some manipulation, condition (6.1) can be rewritten to show that the value of investment, $\tau R - I$, must exceed some strictly positive hurdle,

$$\tau R - I \geqslant \frac{\chi_\tau}{1-\chi_\tau}I,$$

where χ_τ is the post-investment index of adverse selection,

$$\chi_\tau = \frac{(1-\alpha)[(p+\tau)-(q+\tau)]}{p+\tau} = \frac{(1-\alpha)(p-q)}{p+\tau}$$

(so $\chi_0 = \chi$).

Condition (6.1) is always satisfied if there is little adverse selection (χ_τ is close to 0) or if the deepening investment is very profitable ($\tau R/I$ is large).

We are thus led to consider two situations:

Pooling equilibrium. If condition (6.1) holds, then both types conduct an equity offering.[24] If the accrual of this deepening investment is anticipated,[25] the total value of shares *before and after* the seasoned equity offering is

$$(m+\tau)R - I.$$

There is no stock price reaction to the offering, which is perfectly anticipated and uninformative.

Separating equilibrium. More interestingly, suppose that condition (6.1) is violated. The good borrower then does not raise funds. The bad borrower still does, but under market conditions that are not as favorable as in a pooling equilibrium. Because the investors know that the equity offering reveals overvalued assets, they demand a higher stake $R_l^B > R_l$ such that

$$(q+\tau)R_l^B = I.$$

The good borrower does not want to raise funds because

$$(p+\tau)(R-R_l^B) < pR \iff \tau R < \frac{p+\tau}{q+\tau}I, \quad (6.2)$$

which holds if condition (6.1) is violated.

The announcement of a seasoned equity offering then leads to a *negative stock price reaction*. The preannouncement total value of shares is[26]

$$V_0 = \alpha[pR] + (1-\alpha)[(q+\tau)R - I].$$

After the announcement, it becomes

$$V_1 = (q+\tau)R - I.$$

Hence,

$$V_0 > V_1 \iff pR > (q+\tau)R - I.$$

But we know that

$$pR > (p+\tau)\left(R - \frac{I}{q+\tau}\right),$$

and so *a fortiori*

$$V_0 > V_1.$$

23. That this "reservation utility" depends on the borrower's type is the essential difference with the barebones model. Here, in the jargon of incentive theory, "reservation utilities are type-contingent." See Jullien (2000) for the state-of-the-art treatment of adverse selection with type-contingent reservation utilities.

24. This pooling equilibrium is not unique whenever

$$(p+\tau)I/(m+\tau) \leqslant \tau R \leqslant (p+\tau)I/(q+\tau);$$

indeed, if investors believe that an equity offering comes from a bad borrower and $\tau R \leqslant (p+\tau)I/(q+\tau)$, then the good type indeed prefers not to raise funds. However, the pooling equilibrium is the *Pareto-dominant* equilibrium (it is the best equilibrium for both the good and the bad borrower), and so we will focus on it.

Note also that if condition (6.1) holds, then the bad borrower definitely prefers to raise funds since the analogous condition for her is

$$\tau R \geqslant \frac{q+\tau}{m+\tau}I,$$

which is always satisfied.

25. Otherwise, the news of the existence of an investment opportunity by itself raises the value of shares.

26. As in the previous footnote, note that we assume that the investment opportunity is perfectly anticipated by the capital market. Otherwise, the issue of new securities could convey good news about the firm's opportunity set and the concomitant boost in share price might dominate the effect unveiled here.

Combining both cases, we see that the pooling equilibrium (condition (6.1)) is more likely to obtain if the project being financed is more valuable (τ increases or I decreases). We therefore conclude that price reaction on average should be less negative in booms.

Furthermore, and again combining the two cases, *the negative price reaction is smaller when the volume of equity offering, as measured by the amount collected in the offering,*[27] *is large.* Actually, in our example, the price reaction is 0 when both types issue shares. More generally, with a continuum of types, the price reaction is always negative, as long as some types refrain from issuing equity (see Exercise 6.5).

Remark (correlation between value of assets in place and profitability of investment). The analysis can be straightforwardly extended to allow for increases in the probability of success to be positively or negatively correlated with the value of assets in place. Let τ_G and τ_B denote the increases in the probability of success for the good and bad types, respectively. Investors know the values τ_G and τ_B, but do not know which obtains (otherwise they would also know whether the borrower is good or bad if $\tau_G \neq \tau_B$). Assume $p + \tau_G > q + \tau_B$ and so who is a "good borrower" does not vary with investment. The average increase τ is equal to $\alpha\tau_G + (1 - \alpha)\tau_B$. The condition for both types conducting a seasoned equity offering is now

$$(p + \tau_G)\left(R - \frac{I}{m + \tau}\right) \geqslant pR.$$

An increase in correlation corresponds to an increase in τ_G keeping τ constant. Thus, the good borrower is more likely to issue shares, the higher the correlation, as might have been expected.

Remark (going-public decision). Although too simplistic, this model sheds some light on the going-public decision. Think about the firm's resorting to the capital market as a process through which an entrepreneur (or more generally an entrepreneur and a close set of well-informed financiers: venture capitalist, friends, or family holding an equity-like stake) decides to tap further financing and dilute her own stake in order to expand. Then the entrepreneur will tend to remain private when optimistic about the firm's prospects. Of course, the model abstracts from many interesting issues (studied later in the book) associated with the going-public process, such as the certification by an investment banker, the acceptance of strong disclosure requirements, and possibly the loss of control over the firm. But its basic point—that entrepreneurs who feel that assets in place are undervalued by the market tend to forgo profitable investment opportunities and to remain private—is a robust one (see Chemmanur and Fulghieri 1999).

27. This amount is I in the pooling equilibrium and $(1 - \alpha)I$ on average in the separating one.

Application 3: Pecking-Order Hypothesis

An important theme in corporate finance is that adverse selection calls for the issuance of debt claims. As we discussed in the introduction, Myers (1984) and Myers and Majluf (1984) have formulated a pecking-order hypothesis that places debt as the preferred source of external financing. Recall that these authors argue that sources of financing can be ranked according to their information intensity, from low to high information intensity: (1) internal finance (entrepreneur's cash, retained earnings), (2) debt, (3) junior debt, convertibles, and (4) equity.

The pecking-order hypothesis is based on the investors' concern about the value of the claim they acquire. It is clear, for example, that *default-free debt* creates no concern for investors as to the value of their claim. We first provide conditions under which debt is indeed the preferred source of financing under asymmetric information about the firm's prospects,[28] and then discuss the robustness of the pecking-order hypothesis.

As discussed in Chapter 3, there is no distinction between debt and equity claims when the profit is either R or 0. Let us therefore add a salvage value of the assets R^F: the profit in the case of failure is $R^F > 0$ and that in the case of success is $R^S = R^F + R$, where R still denotes the profit increment. Except for the introduction of a salvage value, the model is

28. We know that under moral hazard and risk neutrality, the entrepreneur should offer a debt contract to investors so as to mitigate the moral-hazard problem (see Sections 3.4 and 3.5). We show that the same point holds under adverse selection, even when there is no moral hazard.

otherwise that of Section 6.2.1: there are no assets in place. The investment cost I must be entirely defrayed by the investors. The probability of success is p for a good borrower (probability α) and q for a bad one (probability $1-\alpha$). The prior mean probability of success is $m \equiv \alpha p + (1-\alpha)q$.

Let us assume that

$$mR^{\mathrm{S}} + (1-m)R^{\mathrm{F}} > I$$

and so there is enough pledgeable income to secure funding even when the bad borrower pools with the good one.

Let $\{R_{\mathrm{b}}^{\mathrm{S}}, R_{\mathrm{b}}^{\mathrm{F}}\}$ denote the (nonnegative) rewards of the borrower in the cases of success and failure. Assuming that the borrower receives funding, the investors' breakeven condition is

$$m(R^{\mathrm{S}} - R_{\mathrm{b}}^{\mathrm{S}}) + (1-m)(R^{\mathrm{F}} - R_{\mathrm{b}}^{\mathrm{F}}) \geqslant I.$$

The good borrower maximizes her expected payoff

$$pR_{\mathrm{b}}^{\mathrm{S}} + (1-p)R_{\mathrm{b}}^{\mathrm{F}}$$

subject to the breakeven constraint. At the optimum, the investors' breakeven condition is satisfied with equality. It can be rewritten as

$$[p-(1-\alpha)(p-q)](R^{\mathrm{S}} - R_{\mathrm{b}}^{\mathrm{S}}) + [1-p+(1-\alpha)(p-q)](R^{\mathrm{F}} - R_{\mathrm{b}}^{\mathrm{F}}) = I.$$

The good borrower's utility is then equal to

$$\begin{aligned} pR_{\mathrm{b}}^{\mathrm{S}} + (1-p)R_{\mathrm{b}}^{\mathrm{F}} &= [pR^{\mathrm{S}} + (1-p)R^{\mathrm{F}} - I] \\ &\quad - (1-\alpha)(p-q)[(R^{\mathrm{S}} - R_{\mathrm{b}}^{\mathrm{S}}) - (R^{\mathrm{F}} - R_{\mathrm{b}}^{\mathrm{F}})]. \end{aligned}$$

On the right-hand side of this equality, the first term in brackets represents the NPV of the good borrower, namely, what she would receive under symmetric information. The second term as usual refers to the adverse-selection discount.

The good borrower wants to minimize this discount while satisfying the investors' breakeven constraint.[29] Because the discount increases with $R_{\mathrm{b}}^{\mathrm{F}}$ and decreases with $R_{\mathrm{b}}^{\mathrm{S}}$, the good borrower sets

$$R_{\mathrm{b}}^{\mathrm{F}} = 0.$$

Then, $R_{\mathrm{b}}^{\mathrm{S}}$ is determined by the investors' breakeven constraint:

$$m(R^{\mathrm{S}} - R_{\mathrm{b}}^{\mathrm{S}}) + (1-m)R^{\mathrm{F}} = I.$$

To sum up this analysis, the borrower commits the entire salvage value as safe debt issued to investors. The borrower further issues risky equity with stake $R^{\mathrm{S}} - R_{\mathrm{b}}^{\mathrm{S}}$ in the case of success (and 0 in the case of failure) so as to make up for the shortfall in pledgeable income:

$$m(R^{\mathrm{S}} - R_{\mathrm{b}}^{\mathrm{S}}) = I - R^{\mathrm{F}}.$$

Thus, the firm first issues safe debt with a debt obligation D given by

$$D = R^{\mathrm{F}},$$

and, second, supplements the capital thus raised through an equity issue entitling shareholders to a fraction R_{l}/R of profits in excess of R^{F}, where

$$mR_{\mathrm{l}} = I - D.$$

Note that the borrower must issue more equity, the more acute the adverse-selection problem (the lower m is) or the higher the investment cost.

Intuitively, the borrower starts by issuing the claim that is least exposed to adverse selection, here the safe-debt claim. Doing so allows the good borrower to *minimize the cross-subsidization* with

29. Alternatively, we can use Lagrangian techniques. Let μ denote the shadow price of the investors' breakeven constraint, and $\mathcal{L}$ the Lagrangian of the program:

$$\mathcal{L} \equiv pR_{\mathrm{b}}^{\mathrm{S}} + (1-p)R_{\mathrm{b}}^{\mathrm{F}} + \mu[m(R^{\mathrm{S}} - R_{\mathrm{b}}^{\mathrm{S}}) + (1-m)(R^{\mathrm{F}} - R_{\mathrm{b}}^{\mathrm{F}}) - I].$$

Then

$$\frac{\partial\mathcal{L}}{\partial R_{\mathrm{b}}^{\mathrm{S}}} = p - \mu m \quad\text{and}\quad \frac{\partial\mathcal{L}}{\partial R_{\mathrm{b}}^{\mathrm{F}}} = (1-p) - \mu(1-m).$$

Because

$$\frac{p}{m} > 1 > \frac{1-p}{1-m},$$

necessarily,

$$\frac{\partial\mathcal{L}}{\partial R_{\mathrm{b}}^{\mathrm{F}}} \geqslant 0 \quad\text{implies that}\quad \frac{\partial\mathcal{L}}{\partial R_{\mathrm{b}}^{\mathrm{S}}} > 0,$$

and, conversely,

$$\frac{\partial\mathcal{L}}{\partial R_{\mathrm{b}}^{\mathrm{S}}} \leqslant 0 \quad\text{implies that}\quad \frac{\partial\mathcal{L}}{\partial R_{\mathrm{b}}^{\mathrm{F}}} < 0.$$

Thus we are led to consider two cases (the second is studied only for the sake of completeness): (i) $\partial\mathcal{L}/\partial R_{\mathrm{b}}^{\mathrm{F}} < 0$ (the most interesting case). Then $R_{\mathrm{b}}^{\mathrm{F}} = 0$. (ii) $\partial\mathcal{L}/\partial R_{\mathrm{b}}^{\mathrm{F}} \geqslant 0$. In this case, $\partial\mathcal{L}/\partial R_{\mathrm{b}}^{\mathrm{S}} > 0$. And so, if there is no bound on $R_{\mathrm{b}}^{\mathrm{S}}$, $R_{\mathrm{b}}^{\mathrm{S}}$ must be increased as much as possible (and $R_{\mathrm{b}}^{\mathrm{F}}$ must decrease accordingly to keep the breakeven constraint satisfied) until $R_{\mathrm{b}}^{\mathrm{F}} = 0$, in which case we are back to case (i). But it is probably more reasonable to add the constraint that $R_{\mathrm{b}}^{\mathrm{S}} \leqslant R$. Otherwise, the borrower could in the case of failure borrow R from a third party and reimburse this third party from the reward, $R_{\mathrm{b}}^{\mathrm{S}}$, received from the apparent "success." Thus, case (ii) corresponds to the uninteresting case in which $I < R^{\mathrm{F}}$, that is, the investment is "self-financing." In this case, the entrepreneur issues only safe debt. The pecking order still applies, although in a rather trivial way.

the bad borrower. The more sensitive the investors' claim to the borrower's private information, the higher the return that the investors demand from a good borrower to make up for the money they lose on the bad one. As we will observe in Section 6.3, *this principle of issuing low-information-intensity claims carries over to situations in which the good borrower has the means, and not only the incentive, to separate from the bad one.*

How robust is the debt bias to the specification of the income space? Section 6.6 considers the case of a *continuum* of possible incomes. It builds on Innes (1990, see Section 3.5) and DeMarzo and Duffie (1999).[30] It derives conditions (basically, the conditions obtained by Innes in the moral-hazard, no-adverse-selection setup)[31] under which a good borrower separates from a bad one by offering a standard debt contract.

Are low-information-intensity claims always debt claims? The debt bias principle must be qualified in four important respects:

Insurance. First, forces other than signaling may alter the nature of the securities issued. This point is well illustrated by the Leland–Pyle–Rothschild–Stiglitz model of diversification by a risk-averse entrepreneur, reviewed in Application 8. We will derive conditions under which the bad borrower obtains full insurance, and even the good borrower is partially insured. Their contracts cannot therefore be viewed as insider equity contracts.

Exit strategy. Second, and more interestingly, the issue may not only serve the "*ex post*" goal of obtaining the best possible terms for the issuer at the issuing date. The issue may also reflect an "*ex ante*" objective of providing the issuer with good incentives to create value before the issuing date. As we alluded to in Section 4.4 and will emphasize in Chapter 9, it may then be optimal for the issuer to commit to float information-intensive securities because such securities induce value measurement by the market and allow insiders to be compensated for their past performance; that is, the floating of information-intensive securities enables partial or full exit strategies.

Nature of informational asymmetry. Third, what constitutes a low-information-intensity claim depends on the form of informational asymmetry. We have seen that, when information relates to the probability of success, signaling tends to result in the issuance of a standard debt contract.

Suppose that the asymmetry of information is also related to the *riskiness* of the distribution, and that the good borrower has a less risky distribution than the bad one. Then it is clear that a debt contract may no longer reflect the good borrower's comparative advantage; for, the debt contract provides the bad borrower with a substantial rent when the income is very high.

To illustrate this point in a trivial manner, suppose that there are three possible levels of income: low, middle, and high. A good type always obtains the middle income. A bad type obtains either the low or the high income. The firm's expected income is higher for the good type. The good type then signals herself by issuing a claim that distributes everything to investors when the firm's income is either low or high, but less than the firm's income when the firm obtains the middle income. Such a claim, which may not violate the monotonicity of the investors' claim with the firm's income, does not resemble a debt claim because it distributes the firm's income to investors when income is high.

A more sophisticated illustration of the principle that low-information-intensity securities need not be debt claims is Stein's (1992) rationalization of convertible bonds as reducing the investors' exposure to low-profitability, high-risk borrowers when the former observe signals about the borrower's type after purchasing the securities.

Rent extraction. We have assumed that the entrepreneur or manager faces a competitive financial market. Investors cannot then attempt to extract the good borrower's rent. The pecking-order hypothesis

30. DeMarzo and Duffie consider a "hidden-knowledge" model rather than an "adverse-selection" one (that is, the issuer learns her information *after* the contract is signed) and look at a variable investment scale. They also make an assumption that is weaker than the monotone likelihood ratio property assumed in the appendix.

Other papers that argue that debt contracts are a natural response to adverse selection include Allen and Gale (1992) and Nachman and Noe (1994), which both use Banks and Sobel's (1987) "divinity refinement" to select pooling at a debt contract. For more on security design under adverse selection, see, in particular, Boot and Thakor (1993) and Demange and Laroque (1995).

31. For readers who have covered Section 3.5, the optimality of a debt claim for investors depends on the assumption that the investors' claim is monotonic.

actually states that the good borrower maximizes this rent by issuing low-information-intensity securities, thereby minimizing the cross-subsidization of the bad borrower.

Suppose in contrast that investors have some market power. For example, they may have control over the managerial position; or a venture capitalist or a large investor might have a smaller informational handicap vis-à-vis the borrower than other investors. Then the investors will want to extract some of the good borrower's rent. Rent extraction is best performed when the borrower's stake is least sensitive to her private information—the case of a fixed compensation[32]—that is, when the investors' stake (which is complementary to that of the borrower) is derived from *high*-information-intensity securities!

Of course, providing the borrower with a fixed stake, namely, a wage that is not contingent on performance is not desirable when the borrower must exert effort. There is then an incentive-rent extraction tradeoff (see Laffont and Tirole 1986). Furthermore, there is now scope for separation: confident borrowers will tend to select high-powered incentive schemes along the lines of the pecking-order hypothesis, while less confident ones will go for safer compensation (higher fixed wage, lower volume of stock options). To use an analogy, regulated utilities that are confident in their ability to reduce cost tend to choose price caps or sliding-scale plans rather than low-powered cost-of-service regulation.[33]

6.3 Dissipative Signals

Section 6.2 focused on environments in which good borrowers could not separate from bad ones (except by forgoing profitable investment opportunities, when there are assets in place). In practice, borrowers often try to convey the quality of the securities they issue through "dissipative signals"; these dissipative signals are the counterpart in an adverse-selection context of the "value-decreasing concessions" in the moral-hazard context. This section describes some frequently used dissipative signals, without any attempt at exhaustivity.

Application 4 considers the reduction in the asymmetry of information between borrower and lenders through the costly certification by an informed investor or other party or through a disclosure policy. Applications 5–9 then analyze how the good borrower may try to signal her residual private information (that is, the information that is still private after certification and disclosure) through financial structure choices. The key theme in those applications is that, in order to separate, the good borrower must offer contractual terms that do not appeal to a bad one and allow lenders to break when they know that they are facing a good borrower. This will lead us to the general principle that, as in the pecking-order theory, the response to the lemons problem is the issuance of low-information-intensity securities, i.e., securities for which investors are not "too exposed" to errors in their assessment of the borrower's type.[34]

Application 4: Certification

As we have seen, adverse selection in general leads to cross-subsidization or market breakdown, which are costly to good borrowers or issuers. Therefore, good issuers have an incentive to try to mitigate the investors' informational disadvantage. The asymmetry of information can be reduced through disclosure to investors of information about the firm's prospects. Another form of disclosure bears on past repayments (see Exercise 6.7, based on Padilla and Pagano (1997), on information sharing among lenders). But, while disclosure is not to be neglected, it is most effective for "hard information," that is, information that can be verified by the investors once disclosed by the issuer.[35] Disclosure is a less effective

32. Using the notation of Application 3, the borrower's utility is $\theta R_b^S + (1-\theta)R_b^F$, where $\theta \in \{p, q\}$. The derivative of this utility with respect to θ is $R_b^S - R_b^F$. And so the utility (rent) grows most slowly (actually not at all) with the borrower's type when $R_b^S = R_b^F$.

33. Yermack (1997) analyzes stock option awards to CEOs of large U.S. corporations between 1992 and 1994. He finds that the average cumulative abnormal stock return in the 50 days following the award is slightly above 2% (the award is not disclosed until several months after the fiscal year ends, so the market cannot react to the news of a more incentivized CEO). Yermack's interpretation is that managers who receive private information about impending improvements in corporate performance may influence compensation committees towards more performance-based compensation. The story is thus a bargaining analog of the compensation-menu theory just alluded to.

34. This definition of a low-information-intensity security is vague. The supplementary section gives a general and rigorous definition. Besides, what constitutes a low-information-intensity security will become clear in specific applications.

35. See Grossman (1980), Grossman and Hart (1980), Milgrom (1981), and Milgrom and Roberts (1986) for the theory of disclosure.

means of reducing informational asymmetries if the information is "soft," that is, cannot be verified by the investors.

Lending by an informed party (whether a bank, a peer, or a trade creditor) is a signal that the informed party is confident about the possibility of repayment. Such "informed lending" is therefore likely to bring along less well-informed investors.[36] Monitoring will be studied in depth in a moral-hazard context in Part III of this book. Let us here mention that similar ideas have been developed in an adverse-selection context; for example, Ghatak and Kali (2001) analyze "positive associative matching" in a world of joint liability (see also Section 4.5 of this book); when entrepreneurs are made liable for the loans issued to other entrepreneurs through cross guarantees, good borrowers have a strong incentive to associate themselves with a safe partner.

More generally, issuers can reduce informational asymmetries by borrowing from well-informed investors or by asking them to certify the quality of the issue. There is a large variety of certifying agents: underwriters,[37] rating agencies, auditors, venture capitalists. Of course, it must be the case that the certifying agent has an incentive to become well-informed about the firm's prospects and to take actions that properly convey their information to the prospective investors. The "actions" can be a rating, a report, or a subscription to the issue (or, in the case of a venture capitalist, the action of keeping a non-negligible stake in the firm).[38] And, in all cases, reputation helps keep the certifier honest (indeed, reputation is the only such incentive for a rating agency, which does not take a stake in the firm). We refer to Baron (1982), Raviv (1989), and Chapter 9 for a discussion of monitors' incentives. Here we content ourselves with a simple analysis in which the certification is modeled in reduced form as the purchase, at cost $c > 0$, of a signal that perfectly reveals the borrower's type.

Recall that in the privately-known-prospects model (without assets in place) and in the absence of certification, funding, if any, implies an entrepreneurial reward R_b in the case of success given by

$$m(R - R_b) = I,$$

where $m = \alpha p + (1 - \alpha)q$ is the prior mean probability of success. Let us assume that $mR > I$ and so funding is indeed feasible; the good borrower is then concerned by cross-subsidization.[39]

Suppose that at cost c, the borrower can have access to a reputable certifier who then provides accurate evidence regarding the quality of the project; that is, other investors will then know whether the borrower's probability of success is p or q.[40] (Note that the borrower has no cash to pay the certifier up front. One can imagine that the borrower gives the certifier shares in the firm; these shares can further ensure that the certifier will incur the monitoring cost (see Chapter 9).)

A bad borrower obviously has no incentive to pay a cost c to reveal to the capital market that the probability of success is only q. By resorting to a certifier,

A key insight of this literature is that hard information is, under weak conditions, disclosed if it is known to be held by the issuer. The intuition is that a good issuer benefits from disclosing and thus discloses. An average issuer must then disclose not to be pooled with bad ones. And so even a bad issuer can disclose. A limitation on disclosure occurs when the issuer may or may not have the hard information. An issuer with bad information may then claim not to have any information (see, for example, Tirole (1986) and Okuno-Fujiwara et al. (1990) for models with this feature).

These models assume that information once disclosed is assimilated by investors. Fishman and Hagerty (2003) study an interesting model of disclosure in which a fraction of investors do assimilate the disclosed information while the remaining fraction only observe that there has been disclosure. They show that there may be an equilibrium with no voluntary disclosure, that investors, but not issuers, should support mandatory disclosure, and that mandatory disclosure rules are more likely with regards to information that is difficult to understand.

Finally, Dewatripont and Tirole (2005) study the efficacy of communication that is neither hard nor soft in that its understanding by the receiver depends on the sender's and the receiver's efforts to communicate, which in equilibrium depend on the congruence of their objectives.

36. See, for example, Rochet and Tirole (1996a,b) for investigations of this idea in the context of interbank loans.

37. In the United States underwriters are employed in over 80% of the offerings (Smith 1977). In contrast, according to Marsh (1979), 99% of the new equity in the United Kingdom in the mid 1970s was raised through rights offers (in which current shareholders receive a right from the firm giving them an option to purchase additional shares at a prespecified price).

38. There is, for example, a large empirical literature on certification in initial public offerings. See, for example, Megginson and Weiss (1991) and the references therein.

39. What follows holds *a fortiori* in the "no lending" case. In this case, the good borrower receives 0 in the absence of certification. Hence, provided that certification is feasible (i.e., $pR \geqslant I + c$), the good borrower will be certified.

40. Exercise 6.6 allows for noisy signals about borrower quality.

a good borrower can obtain compensation $\hat{R}_b^G$ in the case of success given by

$$p(R - \hat{R}_b^G) = I + c.$$

The good borrower prefers to resort to a certifier if and only if[41]

$$\hat{R}_b^G > R_b \iff R - \frac{I+c}{p} > R - \frac{I}{m},$$

or, after some manipulation,

$$\frac{c}{I+c} < (1-\alpha)\left(\frac{p-q}{p}\right).$$

This latter condition compares the certification cost, c, expressed as a fraction of the amount of funds to be raised, $I+c$, with our measure of adverse selection χ, which, recall, is equal to the probability of a bad type, $1-\alpha$, times the likelihood ratio, $(p-q)/p$.

Chemmanur and Fulghieri (1994) argue that the cost of diversification "c" may be the lack of diversification of the certifier when the latter, unlike here, is risk averse. They consider a firm's decision to raise external finance either by placing shares privately with a risk-averse large investor such as a venture capitalist or selling shares to a wider constituency, for example, through an IPO, assuming that information acquisition is needed to raise funds. The issuer then trades off the risk premium demanded by the large investor, and the duplication of information under decentralized monitoring in a wider capital market.[42]

41. To be more precise, multiple equilibria coexist over a range of parameters, namely,

$$(1-\alpha)\left(\frac{p-q}{p}\right) \leqslant \frac{c}{I+c} \leqslant \frac{p-q}{p}.$$

Then, "no certification" and "certification of the good borrower only" are both equilibria (there also exists a third equilibrium, in which the good borrower randomizes between being certified and not being certified). The equilibrium is unique only if we focus on *Pareto-dominant* equilibria. In the range with multiple equilibria, both types are better off if the good borrower does not get certified (the "no certification" equilibrium) as the lack of certification then carries no stigma.

42. Lerner and Tirole (2005) analyze forum shopping, that is, the choice of congruence between the certifier on the one hand and the certified agent (here, the issuer) and the buyers (here, the investors) on the other. In the financial context of investment banking, relationship banking, venture capital, or ratings, the congruence is determined by the financial stake, if any, of the certifier in the issuer and by the certifier's willingness to attract future issuers' business. In the basic model, the issuer has no private information about the quality of issued securities; the issuer chooses a level of congruence as well as concessions made to investors (for example, price, collateral pledging, or control rights) and the certifier studies the quality. Issuers with *a priori* more attractive offerings choose more complacent certifiers and make fewer concessions. When the issuer has private information (that is correlated with the certifier's future assessment), then in a separating equilibrium, confident issuers (the "good borrowers") select tougher (less complacent) certifiers than under symmetric information, and also tougher ones than less confident issuers.

Application 5: Costly Collateral Pledging

This section studies the possibility of signaling by pledging collateral (Besanko and Thakor 1987; Bester 1985, 1987; Chan and Kanatas 1985).[43] It builds on the idea, already exploited in Chapter 4, that collateral is valued less highly by the lenders than by the borrower. It shows how a borrower may want to pledge collateral, even though she would not need to do so if information were symmetric. To give the gist of the argument in the simplest possible setting, we extend the privately-known-prospects model as follows: while the borrower still has no cash on hand (in the notation of previous chapters, $A = 0$), she has (a sizeable amount of) assets that can be pledged to investors. That such assets are more valuable to the borrower than to the investors (see Section 4.3 for a fuller discussion), is formalized in the usual way: a transfer of assets valued $C \geqslant 0$ by the borrower has value βC, $0 \leqslant \beta < 1$, for the investors.

Assumption 6.1. *Under symmetric information even the bad borrower does not need to pledge collateral to receive funding:*

$$0 < \tilde{V} \equiv qR - I < V \equiv pR - I.$$

Symmetric information. If the lenders knew the borrower's prospects, the borrower's utility would be equal to the project's NPV, V for the good borrower and $\tilde{V}$ for the bad one, since the project has positive NPV and the entire income is pledgeable (see Section 3.2). To obtain utility V under symmetric information, the good borrower would demand a reward R_b^G in the case of success such that lenders break even when the probability of success is p:[44]

$$p(R - R_b^G) = I.$$

Indeed, her utility would then be equal to

$$pR_b^G = pR - I = V.$$

43. See Coco (2000) for a survey of the use of collateral.

44. Again, this contract is not uniquely optimal. Any compensation scheme that lets the investors break even and does not give a negative income to the borrower in any state of nature is optimal.

Similarly, under symmetric information the bad borrower would demand R_b^B such that

$$q(R - R_b^B) = I,$$

and would obtain utility

$$qR_b^B = qR - I = \tilde{V}.$$

Note that

$$R_b^G = \frac{V}{p} \quad \text{and} \quad R_b^B = \frac{\tilde{V}}{q}.$$

Asymmetric information. As before, when the lenders do not know the borrower's type, the good borrower can no longer obtain her full information utility: if the good borrower were to get financing when demanding reward $R_b^G = V/p$, the bad borrower would want to mimic this demand and obtain utility

$$qR_b^G = qR - \frac{q}{p}I > qR - I = \tilde{V}.$$

That is, by mimicking the good borrower, the bad borrower could reduce her payment to investors and increase her own expected return. The investors, however, should anticipate this "pooling behavior" and refuse to lend since

$$[\alpha p + (1-\alpha)q](R - R_b^G) < I.$$

Can the good borrower credibly signal her type by pledging costly collateral C to be seized by the lenders in the case of failure? That is, can she offer contractual terms that do not appeal to a bad borrower and allow lenders to break even when they know that they face a good borrower? We look for a "separating equilibrium" (we will later ask whether there can be other equilibrium allocations). Consider thus the problem of choosing a reward R_b and an amount of collateral C to be pledged by the good borrower in the case of failure subject to the lenders' breaking even when the corresponding probability of success is p, and to the bad borrower's not wanting to offer contractual terms $\{R_b, C\}$. Note that we assume that the good borrower offers no collateral in the case of success; we will later check that this is indeed the case. Intuitively, posting collateral in the case of success is more costly to a good than to a bad borrower because the good borrower is more likely to succeed, and so such a bond is not a good separating device.

A bad borrower, who in equilibrium is recognized by the lenders, must obtain utility $\tilde{V}$: she cannot obtain more while being funded, and, on the other hand, she can guarantee herself $\tilde{V}$ by pledging no collateral and demanding her full-information reward R_b^B in the case of success,

$$q(R - R_b^B) = I.$$

The lenders then take no risk in lending to the borrower since at worst the borrower is a bad borrower and the lenders still break even.

So, consider the following program, which maximizes the good borrower's utility subject to the constraints that the investors break even when recognizing a good project and that the bad borrower does not want to mimic the good one:

$$\max_{\{R_b, C\}} \{pR_b - (1-p)C\}$$

$$\text{s.t.}$$

$$p(R - R_b) + (1-p)\beta C \geqslant I,$$

$$qR_b - (1-q)C \leqslant \tilde{V}.$$

Both constraints in this program must be binding. If the "mimicking constraint" that the bad borrower does not want to offer contractual terms $\{R_b, C\}$ were not binding, the good borrower would choose $R_b = R_b^G$ and $C = 0$, which, we know, would induce mimicking. The breakeven constraint must also be binding.[45]

The two constraints thus define two equations with two unknowns, yielding, after some computations,

$$R_b^* = R - \left[\frac{(1-q) - \beta(1-p)}{p(1-q) - \beta q(1-p)}\right] I > R_b^G \qquad (6.3)$$

and

$$C^* = \frac{I}{1 + q(1-p)(1-\beta)/(p-q)} > 0. \qquad (6.4)$$

It is also straightforward to show that the good borrower is better off offering these costly contractual terms and being recognized as a good type than being thought of as being a bad type:

$$pR_b^* - (1-p)C^* > pR_b^B \qquad (6.5)$$

45. Otherwise C and R_b would go to infinity while

$$\frac{dR_b}{dC} = \frac{1-q}{q},$$

but this would violate the breakeven constraint.

(which we already knew, since contractual terms $\{R_b = R_b^B, C = 0\}$ satisfy the constraints of the program).[46]

Signaling can occur here because it is *relatively* more costly for a bad borrower to pledge collateral than for a good one to. Again, the cost of pledging collateral is higher for a bad borrower, while a higher reward R_b in the case of success is valued more by a good borrower than by a bad one since $p > q$. (The reader knowledgeable in information economics will here recognize that the "Spence–Mirrlees" or "sorting" condition is satisfied.)

Determinants of collateralization. Condition (6.4) implies the following.

• The good borrower must pledge more collateral when collateral pledging becomes cheaper for the borrower ($\partial C^*/\partial\beta > 0$). That is, for β high, the borrower must pledge substantial amounts of collateral. (Recall that we have assumed that the borrower has a "sizeable amount of assets." If this is not the case, the good borrower may not be able to signal her type as well as is described here.)

• The good borrower must pledge more collateral, the stronger the asymmetry of information ($\partial C^*/\partial q < 0$). Here, keeping p constant, consider the impact of a decrease in q (keeping Assumption 6.1 satisfied, though) on the level of collateral. Investors are more concerned by the borrower's type when q is small; in contrast, C^* tends to 0 (and R_b^* to R_b^G) when q tends to p, as we would expect.

Note, however, that this positive covariation between collateralization and informational asymmetry holds under the assumption that both types are creditworthy in the absence of collateral (Assumption 6.1). Suppose in contrast that a bad borrower never succeeds: $q = 0$.[47] Then the good borrower does not need to pledge any collateral in order to signal her type. So, the positive covariation between collateralization and informational asymmetry, which is a nice testable implication of the theory, does not hold in general. Its testing requires some conditioning, whose validity may be difficult to assess empirically.

Lastly, let us note another testable implication of the theory: good borrowers pledge more collateral than bad ones (here, the bad borrower pledges no collateral at all). This testable implication is fragile as well, since we know from Section 4.4 that, under symmetric information and moral hazard, it may be the case that only a bad borrower pledges collateral; for, a borrower may need to make up for his lack of pledgeable income by offering some costly collateral. So, the positive covariation between the project's NPV and the degree of costly collateralization is contingent on the source of the agency cost (adverse selection rather than moral hazard). The empirical evidence (Berger and Udell 1990; Booth 1992) tends to support the view that good borrowers post less collateral.

Full analysis. The analysis above is incomplete in two respects.

First, we implicitly assumed that the only way for a good borrower to separate from a bad one is to offer some costly collateral in the case of failure. Could the borrower signal her type in other ways? Other departures from the symmetric-information contract are (i) a random probability of financing of the investment, (ii) a positive amount of collateral in the case of success, and (iii) a positive reward for the borrower in the case of failure. Intuitively, the borrower's offering to receive a reward in the case of failure should make the investors suspect that the borrower has a high probability of failure and thus should not be a good signaling device. Neither should a random probability of financing be, since a good borrower values undertaking the project more than a bad one. Finally, and as we have already argued, a positive collateral in the case of success is less costly to a bad type than to a good type and is thus not a good signaling device. Section 6.7 allows for the possibility of separating via means other than collateral pledging. It shows that it is indeed efficient for the good borrower to pledge collateral in

46. The good type offering $\{R_b^*, C^*\}$ and the bad type offering $\{R_b^B, 0\}$ is therefore a (perfect Bayesian) equilibrium. To complete the description of this separating equilibrium, specify, for example, that any "off-the-equilibrium-path" contract, that is, any contract that differs from these two contracts, is perceived by the capital market as emanating from the bad borrower.

47. $q = 0$ is admittedly an extreme case because the bad borrower does not strictly gain from pooling with the good borrower even in the absence of collateral pledging. But the reasoning holds more generally for q small.

the case of failure, if she wants to separate from the bad one.[48]

Second, we have not yet investigated uniqueness. There might exist other separating, pooling, or hybrid equilibria. Section 6.7 shows that the allocation $\{R_b^*, C^*\}$ for the good type and $\{R_b^B, 0\}$ for the bad type is the unique (perfect Bayesian) outcome when the capital market's prior belief that the borrower is good is lower than some threshold, that is, if and only if[49]

$$\alpha \leqslant \alpha^* \quad \text{for some } \alpha^*,\ 0 < \alpha^* < 1.$$

Remark (signaling through weak entrenchment). As was shown in Section 4.3.6, "posting one's job as collateral" is formally akin to posting more familiar forms of collateral. Assume that the manager has private information about her quality rather than about the quality of the current project. A good manager would like to convey her information to investors. Because a good manager is more likely than a bad one to deliver a high performance and see her appointment renewed, she can use a low degree of entrenchment, in the sense of a low protection against managerial turnover, to signal her quality. In practice, the composition of the board of directors and the design of takeover defenses affect the ease with which shareholders can remove existing management. Furthermore, managerial turnover is (both theoretically and empirically) associated with bad news about firm performance. In this context, a good manager, who is less likely to fail, bears a lower cost from jeopardizing her job in the case of failure than a bad one. Thus, weak protection against managerial turnover is an effective signaling device.

The previous analysis of collateral pledging showed that a good borrower both demands a higher reward R_b in the case of success and posts a higher level of collateral in the case of failure. Relabeling the variables, the analysis thus also predicts a *negative covariation between managerial equity and job protection*: a confident manager will opt both for low job protection, as we just argued, and high-powered incentives (i.e., high sensitivity of compensation to performance).[50] This prediction seems to be supported empirically; in particular, Subramanian et al. (2002) find that managers with the steeper incentives are also more likely to be fired after a poor performance.

Application 6: Short-Term Maturities

Chapter 5 showed that firms that generate too little cash flow to meet their liquidity needs do not want to adopt a wait-and-see attitude but rather should secure resources early on in order not to face credit rationing at intermediate stages. This section shows that in a situation of asymmetric information about the firm's prospects, a firm may want to signal its creditworthiness by securing less resources (liquidity) for the future than would be efficient under symmetric information. In essence, a good borrower can convey that she is confident about the firm's prospects and that she is not afraid of going back to the capital market at an intermediate stage.

Let us consider the following variant of the model of debt maturities set up in Section 5.2. At date 0 the entrepreneur has a project of fixed size I, has wealth A, and must borrow $I - A$. At date 1, the investment yields a deterministic and verifiable short-term (date-1) profit $r > 0$. With probability λ, continuation requires reinvesting ρ (the liquidation value

48. Technically, the separating allocation $\{R_b^*, C^*\}$ for the good type and $\{R_b^B, 0\}$ for the bad type is the "low-information-intensity optimum," that is, the allocation that maximizes the good borrower's utility subject to the investors' breakeven condition (or, more generally, subject to the capital market not losing money on any type) and to the bad borrower not receiving a rent.

49. Intuitively, the only way for the good type to obtain a higher utility than that of the separating allocation is to relax the mimicking constraint by letting the bad borrower obtain more than $\tilde{V}$ when mimicking. This implies, however, that the investors lose money on the bad borrower (and thus the bad borrower must pool with the good one). The cross-subsidization is, however, costly to the good borrower, as the profit made by investors on the good borrower must offset their loss on the bad borrower times the ratio $(1 - \alpha)/\alpha$ of bad to good borrowers.

Note furthermore that the good borrower can guarantee herself the separating payoff pR_b^*. (The following reasoning paraphrases that in the supplementary section for the reader who will have skipped that section.) It suffices that she offers a pair of options $\{R_b^*, C^*\}$ and $\{R_b^B, 0\}$, from which she will choose after the investors agree to finance the project. The investors are guaranteed to break even regardless of the borrower's type, since the good borrower will choose $\{R_b^*, C^*\}$ from (6.5), and the bad borrower will choose $\{R_b^B, 0\}$ from the program above. On the other hand, if α is high, it becomes optimal for the good borrower to pool with the bad one: see Section 6.7 for a description as well as for a computation of the best equilibrium for the good type.

50. This assumes that the manager does not have so much cash on hand that her number of shares allows her to control the board of directors. If this were the case (e.g., as in family firms), then high stakes would also be associated with strong entrenchment.

is equal to 0); with probability $1 - \lambda$, continuation requires no reinvestment.[51]

In the case of continuation, the firm at date 2 yields R in the case of success and 0 in the case of failure. The probability of success is p_{H} in the case of good behavior and $p_{\mathrm{L}} = p_{\mathrm{H}} - \Delta p$ in the case of misbehavior (which yields private benefit B). Moral hazard is introduced in order to create an entrepreneurial rent from continuation, or, equivalently, a cost for the entrepreneur associated with early termination. Put differently, moral hazard introduces a friction in the date-1 refinancing market. Let

$$\rho_1 \equiv p_{\mathrm{H}} R \quad \text{and} \quad \rho_0 \equiv p_{\mathrm{H}}\left(R - \frac{B}{\Delta p}\right)$$

denote the continuation NPV and pledgeable income, respectively.

Assume that

$$\min\{\rho_1, r\} > \rho > \rho_0.$$

The left inequality states that, viewed at date 1, continuation is always a positive-NPV proposition ($\rho_1 > \rho$) and that the short-term income suffices to meet the liquidity shock ($r > \rho$). The right inequality implies that in the absence of retentions (date-1 income that is not redistributed to investors) or credit line, the borrower cannot meet the liquidity shock by returning to the capital market ($\rho > \rho_0$). Finally, assume that the project cannot be financed in the absence of a positive probability of continuation,

$$I > A + r,$$

and that the project has a positive NPV,

$$r + \rho_1 - \lambda\rho > I.$$

Figure 6.1 summarizes the timing.

Symmetric information. We will consider an asymmetry of information about the probability λ of a liquidity shock. But suppose, first, that the entrepreneur and the investors are symmetrically informed, and that

$$I - A \leqslant r + \rho_0 - \lambda\rho,$$

which implies that investors are willing to finance the project even with certain continuation.

51. As usual, the entrepreneur is risk neutral and protected by limited liability; and the investors are risk neutral and demand a 0 rate of return.

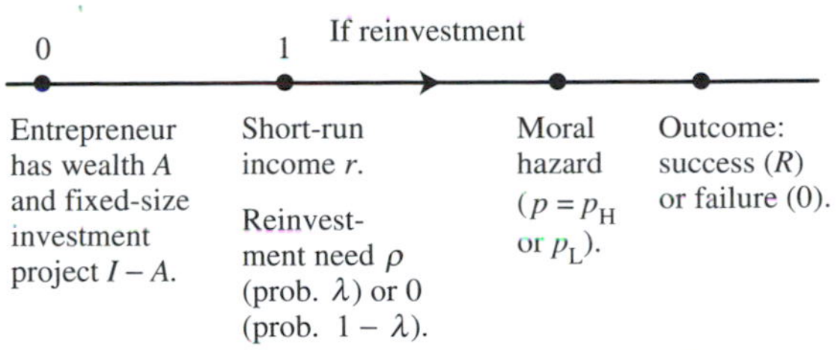

Figure 6.1

Let us show that, under symmetric information, the contract between the investors and the entrepreneur allows the latter to always bring the project to completion, and that this optimum can be implemented by a level of short-term debt

$$d \leqslant r - (\rho - \rho_0),$$

a reinvestment of remaining earnings, if any, in bonds (yielding a zero rate of interest at date 2), a reward R_{b} for the entrepreneur in the case of success, and the remaining income going to the investors at date 2.

Letting x denote the probability of continuation in the case of a shock, the NPV is

$$U_{\mathrm{b}} = r + [1 - \lambda + \lambda x]\rho_1 - \lambda x \rho - I.$$

Hence, $x = 1$ is optimal. The condition

$$d \leqslant r - (\rho - \rho_0)$$

allows continuation even in the case of a liquidity shock: the borrower can use retentions ($r - d$) together with what can be raised in the capital market (ρ_0) to meet shock ρ.

Asymmetric information. Assume now that the investors are imperfectly informed about the probability of shock. This probability is

$$\lambda \quad \text{with probability } \alpha,$$
$$\tilde{\lambda} > \lambda \quad \text{with probability } 1 - \alpha.$$

The entrepreneur knows which obtains. Assume that even the bad borrower (whose probability of a shock is $\tilde{\lambda}$) can continue with probability 1 under symmetric information:

$$I - A \leqslant r + \rho_0 - \tilde{\lambda}\rho.$$

Thus the good borrower is concerned solely by cross-subsidies to the bad one.

We focus (without loss of generality) on contracts specifying a short-term debt $d \in [0, r]$ at date 1, a reward $R_b^+ \geqslant B/\Delta p$ in the case of no shock and success, and a reward $R_b^- = B/\Delta p$ in the case of a shock, continuation, and success (R_b^+ and R_b^- are the only incomes received by the entrepreneur, who receives nothing in the case of failure or early termination). Intuitively, large rewards R_b^- (i.e., in excess of the incentive payment $B/\Delta p$) in the case of a shock, continuation, and success are relatively more attractive to the bad borrower and so will not be used by the good borrower, who has a relative preference for being rewarded more in the absence of shock. The rationale for focusing on such contracts as well as the equilibrium analysis are provided in Section 6.8. The main predictions of the model are as follows:

(i) In a separating equilibrium the bad borrower gets her symmetric-information allocation and therefore continues with probability $x = 1$. By contrast, the good borrower uses a suboptimally low probability of continuation in order to separate from the bad borrower: $x < 1$. Liquidation is as costly to her as to a bad borrower when a shock occurs but is relatively less costly overall, as the shock occurs less often.

(ii) The good borrower grants herself a higher reward R_b^+ in the absence of a shock and in the case of success than under symmetric information: because she reduces her liquidity hoarding relative to the symmetric-information case, investors are willing to increase her compensation. But, as usual, the good borrower is worse off than under symmetric information; she sacrifices continuation, which is a more efficient "currency," that is, a more efficient form of "payment" to the entrepreneur than monetary compensation (as long as $\rho < \rho_1$ and $R_b^+ \geqslant B/\Delta p$).

(iii) There exists a threshold α^* such that the separating equilibrium described above is the unique equilibrium whenever $\alpha \leqslant \alpha^*$. Other equilibria exist when $\alpha > \alpha^*$; they involve some pooling and are preferred by both types to the separating equilibrium.

Returning to the first implication, the discrete-shock model has a slightly awkward feature: the random probability of continuation in the case of a shock. This can be implemented either through a "random credit line" or, equivalently, through a "random debt": $d \geqslant r - (\rho - \rho_0)$ with probability $1 - x$ (precluding reinvestment in the case of a shock since $\rho + d > r + \rho_0$) and $d < r - (\rho - \rho_0)$ with probability x. In this sense, the debt is larger than under symmetric information (for which $x = 1$). The particular conclusion of a stochastic debt is rather unrealistic, but it is an artefact of the discrete-shock version: with a continuum of shocks (a continuous distribution $F(\rho)$ as in Chapter 5), the *short-term debt* d for the good borrower is deterministic and *larger than under symmetric information* (we leave it to the reader to demonstrate this property).

Relationship to the literature. The idea that short-term debt can be used as a signal of high-quality borrowing, which was first explored in a different context by Diamond (1991, 1993),[52] relates to a more general theme in the economics of adverse selection. Namely, (costly) short-term contracting may be a way of signaling that one is confident about the future and that one does not fear having to recontract at later stages. In Aghion and Bolton (1987), a supplier has superior information about the probability of entry of a competitor and would like to signal that this probability of entry is low in order to obtain better terms of trade when contracting today with buyers. Aghion and Bolton show that the supplier can signal to buyers that entry is unlikely by offering a contract specifying no penalty for breach if the buyer later switches to a different supplier; this is, in essence, a short-term contract. The point is that imposing no penalty for breach is less costly to the supplier when the probability of entry by a rival is small and so the "sorting condition" is satisfied. Hermalin (2002) considers a labor relationship in which a long-term contract between an employer and an employee specifying a penalty for breach induces the employer to provide general purpose on-the-job training to the employee. Hermalin shows that a worker with private information about her talent may want to signal a high talent by offering no

52. Ross (1977) also modeled debt as a signal of quality. Ross's model was not concerned with the maturity structure, but rather with the cost imposed on managers by bankruptcy. Under costly bankruptcy, issuing debt is relatively less costly for a borrower who knows that the probability of low profit is small.

penalty for breach in order to prove that she is not afraid of going back to the labor market, even though such a short-term contract deprives her of on-the-job training. In Diamond (1991), a borrower enters into a short-term borrowing contract in order to signal her creditworthiness. Diamond's model, unlike the one considered here, assumes that cash flows are not verifiable (but they are observable). Diamond shows that borrowers with high (respectively, intermediate, low) ratings use short- (respectively, long-, short-) term debt, where the rating refers to the *ex ante* probability of a good type.[53]

Finally, we have assumed, as elsewhere in this book, that entrepreneurs are rational. Landier and Thesmar (2004) study a competitive credit market in which optimistic and realistic entrepreneurs coexist. To some extent, optimistic entrepreneurs are akin to the confident borrowers (p-borrowers) of our adverse-selection model. Indeed, optimistic borrowers in Landier and Thesmar opt for shorter debt maturities than realistic entrepreneurs, as they (mistakenly) believe that they are unlikely to face difficult circumstances; relatedly, they are more willing to transfer control in such circumstances (for contingent transfers of control, see Chapter 10). Some features are different in a behavioral world, though. First, investors obviously pay the optimistic entrepreneurs "with dreams," yielding abnormally low returns to entrepreneurship (investors, however, do not benefit from the entrepreneurs' irrationality, since competition in the financial market drives investor profits to 0). Second, contracts may end up being contingent on variables that the borrower has no control over, violating a standard principle of agency theory.[54] Landier and Thesmar test their model on French entrepreneurship data and find a positive correlation between optimistic expectation errors (that they measure by comparing reported entrepreneurial expectations on future business growth and actual performance) and the use of short-term debt.

Application 7: Payout Policy

Large and well-established firms distribute a substantial fraction of their earnings in payouts (dividends and stock repurchases). For example, in 1999, U.S. corporations paid \$350 billion in dividends and repurchases, plus an extra \$400 billion on liquidation dividends associated with mergers and acquisitions. Indeed, most firms pay dividends while also raising debt or equity.

Payout behavior exhibits well-known patterns.[55] A key pattern for this chapter is that payout announcements affect stock prices and convey information beyond that contained in earnings announcements. The firm's stock price substantially increases (respectively, decreases) upon the announcement of an increase (respectively, decrease) in payout. This reaction is particularly strong for low-capitalization firms. All this suggests that dividends convey information held by the firm's insiders, but not by the stock market. This application focuses on this pattern and more generally on the *level* of payout; it thereby neglects interesting questions related to the choice of payout *structure* between dividends and share repurchases.[56]

Financial economists have repeatedly argued that dividends are used by a firm's insiders as signals. In particular, Bernheim and Wantz (1995) provide evidence that dividends are often motivated by signaling concerns rather than a disposal of free cash

53. Similar ideas have also been expressed in a screening setup, i.e., a setup in which the uninformed parties make the offers. In particular, in Michelacci and Suarez (2004), firms post employment contracts and learn the workers' abilities only after the workers have taken the job. Fixing the wage in advance has the benefit of eliminating holdup problems associated with bargaining after relationship-specific investments have been sunk by the parties. Alternatively, the firms can leave scope for recontracting or bargaining; this helps them address the adverse-selection problem, as high-ability workers, whose wage is higher under *ex post* bargaining than that of low-ability workers, may find such open-ended contracts more attractive than a fixed-wage contract. As a result, contracts tend to be too open-ended, which reduces aggregate income.

54. Namely, the sufficient statistic theorem (see Chapter 3).

55. See, for example, Allen and Michaely (1995, 2004) for exhaustive overviews and Karpoff and Thorley (1992) for a brief survey of the main facts. A large literature has been preoccupied with the firms' motivation to pay dividends, whether for signaling or for other reasons. Papers in this strand of research include Allen et al. (2000), Araujo et al. (2004), Benartzi et al. (1997), Bernheim (1991), and Healy and Palepu (1988).

56. A well-known puzzle is why corporations have traditionally favored dividends even in countries where the latter are taxed at the ordinary tax rate while share repurchases are taxed on a capital gain basis, which, combined with the ability to postpone the realization of capital gains, results in a lower effective tax rate (share repurchases caught up with dividends in the late 1990s).

Another interesting fact is that dividends are smoother (vary less over time) than share repurchases. Theories of why firms may opt for dissipative dividends include Ofer and Thakor (1987) and Hausch and Seward (1993).

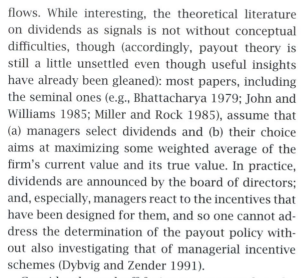

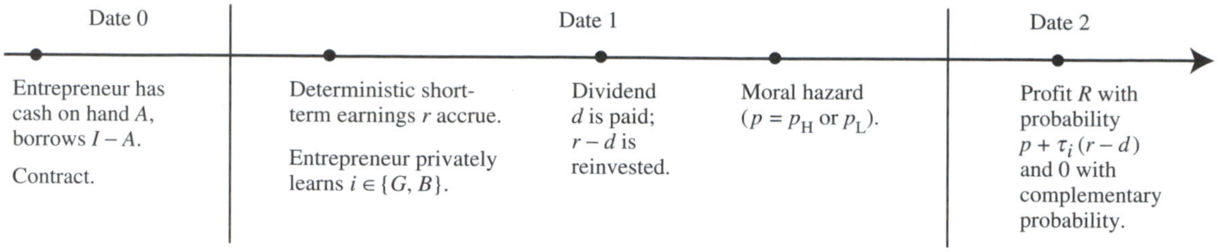

Figure 6.2

flows. While interesting, the theoretical literature on dividends as signals is not without conceptual difficulties, though (accordingly, payout theory is still a little unsettled even though useful insights have already been gleaned): most papers, including the seminal ones (e.g., Bhattacharya 1979; John and Williams 1985; Miller and Rock 1985), assume that (a) managers select dividends and (b) their choice aims at maximizing some weighted average of the firm's current value and its true value. In practice, dividends are announced by the board of directors; and, especially, managers react to the incentives that have been designed for them, and so one cannot address the determination of the payout policy without also investigating that of managerial incentive schemes (Dybvig and Zender 1991).

Consider the tradeoff facing a manager when she proposes to shareholders a level of payouts (let us call these from now on "dividends"). Managers' monetary compensation is directly affected by the payout; how much so depends on how frontloaded or backloaded the managerial compensation scheme is (that is, how aligned it is with the welfare of current versus future shareholders); for example, incentives that would be based on the long-term value of the shares would discourage managers from proposing dividends. Of course, and as was already noted, this front- or backloading is endogenous, and therefore the direct effect can be controlled through the design of the managerial compensation scheme.

Besides this direct effect, dividend distribution also has an indirect impact on managerial welfare to the extent that it conveys information about managerial performance or about the state of the firm. The distribution of dividends may be costly for several reasons (even ignoring tax considerations). First, dividends drain cash out of the firm and therefore reduce the amount that is reinvested or else used as cushion for the future (which, as we know from Chapter 5 or the previous application, are useful when there is a cost of outside finance). Second, it may be costly to gather the cash: for example, illiquid assets with value initially known only by the managers may need to be sold, securitized, or certified creating a dissipative cost. Despite these costs, managers may be under pressure to propose dividends. First, and in a logic similar to that of Application 6, managers may want to signal that they are confident that they will not need a large financial cushion in the future, making the shareholders more prone today to permit the continuation of operations or even to reinvest in the firm. Second, and as we will see in Chapter 7, managers may be keen to use dividends to demonstrate the existence/reality of cash (or valuable assets) when their job is at stake; that is, we would expect firms to disgorge more cash when there is a threat of CEO employment termination.

We will content ourselves with an analysis of dividend payments in a situation described in Figure 6.2, in which the entrepreneur learns information about the marginal benefit of investment and therefore of retained earnings. (A very similar analysis can be performed for the case in which the manager privately observes earnings.)

The model is the standard fixed-investment one. There is no asymmetry of information at the contracting date, date 0. The date-1 earnings r can be used to pay a dividend d or to reinvest J in the firm: $r = d + J$. Reinvestment increases the probability of success by $\tau_i(J)$, where $i \in \{G, B\}$ is privately learned at date 1 by the entrepreneur: $i = G$ with probability α and $i = B$ with probability $1 - \alpha$. A higher reinvestment increases the probability of success:

$$\tau_i' > 0.$$

That $i = G$ corresponds to good news about profitability can be expressed as

$$\tau_G(J) > \tau_B(J) \quad \text{for all } J.$$

For simplicity, we assume that, due to indivisibilities in the reinvestment function,

$$J \in \{0, r\}.$$

That is, it is optimal to reinvest all or none of the earnings. Let us first assume that reinvestment is useful only if $i = B$:

$$[\tau_B(r) - \tau_B(0)]R > r > [\tau_G(r) - \tau_G(0)]R.$$

Moral hazard is described as usual: the entrepreneur chooses between p_H (no private benefit) and p_L (private benefit B).

We look at the case in which the contract involves reinvestment when $i = B$ and none when $i = G$. This will be the case if α is not too large or if the benefits from reinvestment when $i = B$ are substantial.[57]

The NPV is then given by

$$\text{NPV} = \alpha[r + [p_H + \tau_G(0)]R] + (1-\alpha)[p_H + \tau_B(r)]R.$$

Let us first obtain the pledgeable income, assuming as usual that inducing effort is optimal. Let $R_b^r \geqslant B/\Delta p$ and $R_b^0 \geqslant B/\Delta p$ denote the entrepreneur's rewards in the case of success when the entrepreneur distributes dividend $d = r$ and does not distribute any dividend, respectively (the rewards in the case of failure can without loss of generality be set equal to 0). For the entrepreneur to distribute short-term profit r when $i = G$, she must be rewarded with a short-term payment r_b^r when she offers to pay dividend $d = r$. Incentive compatibility relative to dividend payment when $i = G$ requires that

$$r_b^r + [p_H + \tau_G(0)]R_b^r \geqslant [p_H + \tau_G(r)]R_b^0.$$

Conversely, the entrepreneur must choose to reinvest when $i = B$:

$$[p_H + \tau_B(r)]R_b^0 \geqslant r_b^r + [p_H + \tau_B(0)]R_b^r.$$

This latter incentive constraint will later be shown to be nonbinding for the determination of the pledgeable income. The investors' expected gross return is

$$\alpha[(r - r_b^r) + [p_H + \tau_G(0)](R - R_b^r)] + (1-\alpha)[p_H + \tau_B(r)](R - R_b^0).$$

Using the incentive constraint relative to dividend payment when $i = G$ as well as the minimum stake $B/\Delta p$ for the rewards, the pledgeable income, that is, the highest expected income that can be pledged to investors while satisfying the various incentive constraints, is

$$\mathcal{P}^* \equiv \alpha\left[r + [p_H + \tau_G(0)]R - [p_H + \tau_G(r)]\frac{B}{\Delta p}\right] + (1-\alpha)[p_H + \tau_B(r)]\left(R - \frac{B}{\Delta p}\right).$$

Let us now show that a simple incentive scheme specifying managerial equity shares s_1 and s_2 in periods 1 and 2, respectively, induces management to propose the proper state-contingent dividend.

At date 2, the entrepreneur must hold a fraction,

$$s_2 \geqslant \frac{B/\Delta p}{R},$$

of the shares in order to exert effort. Because $r_b^r = s_1 r$, the dividend is paid in state $i = G$ if

$$s_1 r + s_2[p_H + \tau_G(0)]R \geqslant s_2[p_H + \tau_G(r)]R \iff s_1 r \geqslant s_2[\tau_G(r) - \tau_G(0)]R.$$

Thus, s_1/s_2 must exceed some threshold θ^* in order to induce dividend payments:

$$\frac{s_1}{s_2} \geqslant \theta^* \equiv \frac{[\tau_G(r) - \tau_G(0)]R}{r}.$$

This threshold θ^* is lower than 1 since $r > [\tau_G(r) - \tau_G(0)]R$. Conversely, s_1/s_2 should not exceed some other threshold $\theta^{**} > 1$, otherwise there would be a dividend payment even when $i = B$:

$$\frac{s_1}{s_2} \leqslant \theta^{**} \equiv \frac{[\tau_B(r) - \tau_B(0)]R}{r}.$$

Incentives must be properly balanced.[58]

Let us now return to the computation of the pledgeable income. This upper bound on what can

57. Otherwise, the optimal (deterministic) policy would be a mandatory dividend policy ($d = r$), which is equivalent to the existence of short-term debt.

58. We cannot in general conclude whether s_1 should be larger or smaller than s_2. However, in the case in which pledgeable income is very scarce, i.e., when $\mathcal{P}^*$ is only slightly above $I - A$, then $s_1 < s_2$.

be promised to investors while preserving the entrepreneur's incentive to exert effort and to distribute dividends efficiently holds only if the ignored constraint (that relative to the absence of dividend payment when $i = B$) is satisfied. To show that $\mathcal{P}^*$ can be obtained, let

$$s_2 = \frac{B/\Delta p}{R} \quad \text{and} \quad s_1 = \theta^* s_2.$$

Then the investors' expected gross return is indeed $\mathcal{P}^*$ and because $s_1/s_2 < \theta^{**}$, the ignored constraint is indeed satisfied.

Finally, we can illustrate the *positive stock price reaction to a dividend announcement* despite the fact that a dividend signals poor reinvestment prospects, and not only a high value of assets in place. The *ex ante* value of a share is

$$V_0 = \alpha[r + [p_H + \tau_G(0)]R] + (1 - \alpha)[p_H + \tau_B(r)]R.$$

Upon announcement of a dividend, the value jumps to

$$V_1 = r + [p_H + \tau_G(0)]R.$$

Thus

$$V_1 - V_0 = (1 - \alpha)[r - [\tau_B(r) - \tau_G(0)]R],$$

and so

$$V_1 > V_0 \iff r > [\tau_B(r) - \tau_G(0)]R.$$

But

$$\tau_B(r) < \tau_G(r) \quad \text{and} \quad r > [\tau_G(r) - \tau_G(0)]R$$

by assumption. Thus, V_1 indeed exceeds V_0 (and conversely upon an announcement of no dividend).

In the case in which reinvestment is profitable only if $i = G$, the stock price reaction to a dividend announcement is *a fortiori* positive, because the dividend then signals both a high value of assets in place and a profitable reinvestment. One can also construct cases, though, in which a dividend announcement is accompanied with a negative stock price reaction. If the capital market is not uncertain about the value of assets in place, and, provided that finding new investment opportunities is not subject to managerial moral hazard and that proper managerial incentives have been designed, then a dividend is a signal that the manager was unable to find an attractive reinvestment opportunity.

Application 8: Diversification and Incomplete Insurance

Leland and Pyle (1977), in one of the pioneering papers in the signaling literature, consider a situation in which a risk-averse entrepreneur has a substantial stake (perhaps the entire stake) in her firm and wants to diversify her portfolio. The issuance of claims is thus not necessarily motivated by the desire to undertake a new project or to expand an existing one. Rather, gains from trade result from risk sharing with investors who are less exposed to the firm's specific risk or have a higher risk tolerance.

Diversification may, however, be costly due to adverse selection. To illustrate this, suppose that investors are risk neutral with respect to the firm's risk, say, because the firm's risk is idiosyncratic (i.e., is specific to the firm and not governed by economy-wide fluctuations) and can be diversified away. Under symmetric information about the firm's characteristics and in the absence of moral hazard, the entrepreneur optimally obtains full insurance and the risk attached to the firm's income is fully borne by the investors. This is, in general, not so under asymmetric information, since investors are concerned that they might be purchasing a "lemon." In a nutshell, a good borrower is willing to bear risk in order to "demonstrate" that she is confident about the firm's prospects. Although imperfect diversification has a cost, it allows a good borrower to obtain a better price for the claims she issues.

We develop the Leland–Pyle model in an optimal contracting framework similar to that of Stiglitz (1977) and Rothschild and Stiglitz (1976). We use the privately-known-prospects model (see Section 6.2), in which the entrepreneur has no initial cash ($A = 0$) and the following twists are added:

- there is no need for financing ($I = 0$), that is, the entrepreneur's resorting to investors is solely motivated by diversification or insurance concerns;
- while the investors are risk neutral, the entrepreneur is risk averse (this is the only time we invoke risk aversion in this chapter); the entrepreneur has increasing and strictly concave utility function $U(w)$, where w is her final wealth.

As in the rest of this chapter, the entrepreneur initially owns the firm entirely and issues claims to investors.

Symmetric information. Under symmetric information about her type, the good borrower would offer to receive income R_b^S in the case of success and R_b^F in the case of failure so as to maximize her utility subject to the investors' breakeven constraint:

$$\max_{\{R_b^S, R_b^F\}} \{pU(R_b^S) + (1-p)U(R_b^F)\}$$

s.t.

$$p(R - R_b^S) + (1-p)(-R_b^F) \geqslant 0.$$

As is well-known, the solution to this program provides the entrepreneur with full insurance:

$$R_b^S = R_b^F = R_b^G,$$

where

$$R_b^G = pR.$$

That is, the good entrepreneur receives a constant income equal to the firm's expected income pR.

Similarly, under symmetric information, the bad borrower contracts for a constant income R_b^B given by

$$R_b^B = qR < R_b^G.$$

To summarize the symmetric-information case, the entrepreneur sells out her entire stake in the firm at a price equal to the firm's expected income, pR for the good type and qR for the bad type.[59] The symmetric-information solution is represented by points G and B on the 45° line in Figure 6.3. This diagram depicts allocations in the space of borrower incomes $\{R_b^S, R_b^F\}$. The no-contract outcome is the point R = $(R, 0)$ and is the same for both types.

Asymmetric information. The good borrower can no longer obtain a constant income equal to R_b^G under asymmetric information. If this were so, the bad borrower could guarantee herself a rent equal to $R_b^G - R_b^B = (p-q)R$ over her symmetric-information utility by mimicking the good borrower. Investors would lose $(1-\alpha)(R_b^G - R_b^B)$ on bad borrowers, which they would need to recoup on good ones.

59. Needless to say, the entrepreneur would not sell her entire stake if we reintroduced moral hazard. We ignore moral hazard for expositional simplicity, but the conclusions are robust to its presence.

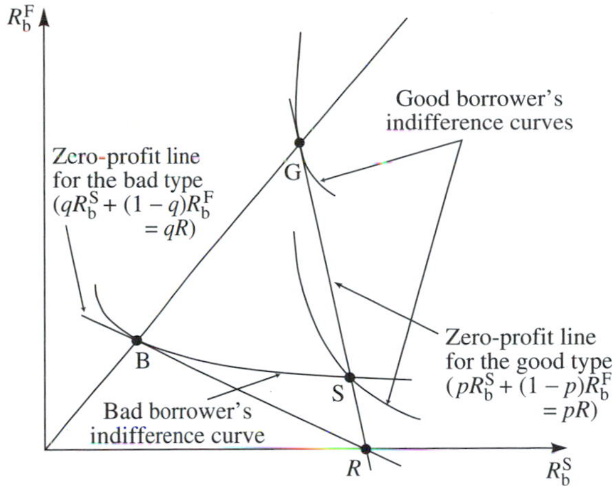

Figure 6.3

Consider now the problem of maximizing the good borrower's utility subject to the investors' breaking even on that borrower, and to the good borrower's allocation not being preferred by the bad borrower to her symmetric-information allocation (that is, to the constraint that the bad borrower obtains no rent over his symmetric-information payoff):

$$\max_{\{R_b^S, R_b^F\}} pU(R_b^S) + (1-p)U(R_b^F)$$

s.t.

$$p(R - R_b^S) + (1-p)(-R_b^F) \geqslant 0,$$

$$qU(R_b^S) + (1-q)U(R_b^F) \leqslant U(R_b^B).$$

That both constraints in this program must be binding can be inferred from Figure 6.3. The allocation $\{R_b^S, R_b^F\}$ must be below the bad borrower's indifference curve passing through point B, and below the zero-profit line corresponding to the good borrower. A key property is that the good borrower's indifference curves have higher absolute slopes than the bad borrower's indifference curves at any given point.[60] That is, the good borrower requires a higher

60. At an arbitrary point $\{R_b^S, R_b^F\}$, the slope is equal (in absolute value) to

$$\frac{p}{1-p}\frac{U'(R_b^S)}{U'(R_b^F)}$$

for the good borrower and

$$\frac{q}{1-q}\frac{U'(R_b^S)}{U'(R_b^F)}$$

for the bad borrower.

increase in her income in the case of failure for a given decrease in her income in the case of success to keep her utility constant, compared with the bad borrower. In other words, the good borrower is less eager to obtain insurance because she has a higher probability of success than a bad borrower.

The solution of the program is therefore obtained by taking the intersection of the two constraints and is depicted by point S in Figure 6.3, where "S" stands for "separating" equilibrium. It is indeed an equilibrium for the bad borrower to sell out at price R_b^B and obtain full insurance (that is, choose point B) and for the good borrower to limit her portfolio diversification to point S.[61]

The properties of the separating allocation analyzed above fit with the general theme that a good borrower tries to signal good prospects by increasing the sensitivity of her own returns to the firm's profit. She concomitantly reduces the sensitivity of the investors' return to the firm's profit relative to the symmetric-information optimum.

Determinants of diversification. Keeping p constant, when the bad borrower's probability of success q decreases, point B in Figure 6.3 moves down along the diagonal, and so point S moves away from the full insurance point G and closer to the no-insurance point $\mathrm{R} = (R, 0)$ on the investors' zero-profit line for the good borrower, and so the good borrower diversifies less.

Note also that a limited diversification is good news about the firm's prospects since only good borrowers are willing to bear the associated risk. Thus, in a more general model in which the entrepreneur initially owns a fraction of, but not the entire, equity, the news that the entrepreneur sells her entire stake in the firm generates a negative stock price reaction. Put differently, a limited equity offering creates a positive stock price reaction.

Full analysis. A direct application of the results obtained in the supplementary section shows that the allocation $\{S, B\}$, that is, S for the good borrower and B for the bad one, is "interim efficient" if and only if the proportion of good borrowers lies below some threshold α^*, where

$$0 < \alpha^* < 1.$$

Thus, the separating allocation $\{S, B\}$ with suboptimal diversification for the good borrower is the unique (perfect Bayesian) equilibrium for $\alpha \leqslant \alpha^*$.

61. To avoid the possibility that either type prefers to offer an allocation outside $\{B, S\}$, it suffices to specify that such an allocation would generate the belief that the borrower is a bad borrower.

Application 9: Underpricing

There is substantial evidence of underpricing in IPOs and SEOs.[62] There are multiple interpretations for this underpricing (see Ritter (2003) for an overview). The most common one, mentioned in the introduction to this chapter and in Section 2.4.2, refers to a specific design for selling the securities combined with asymmetric information among investors, giving rise to a concern about the "winner's curse." Another theory suggests that underpricing stems from collusion between the investment bank underwriting (and thereby certifying) the issue and institutional investors against naive entrepreneurs.[63] This section develops a signaling explanation.

Underpricing is a most primitive signaling device, used only when a good borrower does not have cheaper means of setting herself apart from a bad one.

We illustrate the possibility of underpricing in a model in which only good borrowers are creditworthy under symmetric information. The model is the privately-known-prospects model, except that we assume that the borrower initially has cash A ($A > 0$ will play an important role in the signaling behavior, as we will see), and the following.

62. See, for example, Ibbotson (1975), Ibbotson and Jaffe (1975), Ritter (1984), and Smith (1977), who provide evidence of underpricing for both unseasoned and seasoned issues. For unseasoned issues, Ibbotson found an average discount relative to the aftermarket price of 11.4%; Ibbotson and Jaffe estimate the average discount at 16.8%.

63. There is also a potential for collusion against more naive investors; for instance, in a hot market, stakes are high and investment banks' reputational constraints are less effective.

There is a large literature as well as an empirical controversy as to whether issuers and investment bankers underprice as an insurance against the threat of litigation risk. For example, Titnic (1988) indeed found that underpricing increased following the enactment of the 1933 Securities Act, which increased litigation risk. In contrast, Zhu (2004) finds an increase in IPO underpricing following the 1995 enactment of the Private Securities Litigation Reform Act, which made litigation harder. See, for example, Zhu (2004) and Lowry and Shu (2002) for a discussion of the econometric issues in measuring the impact of the litigation threat.

Assumption 6.2. *Only the good borrower is creditworthy:*

$$qR < I - A < pR.$$

That is, the pledgeable income exceeds the funding need, $I - A$, only for the good borrower.

If investors knew the borrower's type, the good type, who would be the only one to be financed, would offer to keep R_b^G in the case of success, where R_b^G is such that the issue is sold at par:[64]

$$p(R - R_b^G) = I - A.$$

Assumption 6.3. $A < qR_b^G$.

Assumption 6.3 can be interpreted in the following way. The condition $A < qR_b^G$ states that the bad borrower would be willing to commit her entire wealth in order to have access to the contractual terms obtained by the good borrower under symmetric information. This condition means that the bad type is eager to pool with the good type and will imply that the good type's utility is reduced by the asymmetry of information, or, in other words, that the good type would be strictly better off if she could disclose credible information about the quality of borrowing.

We proceed heuristically. Formal results are stated below and proved in Section 6.9. Can a good borrower get funded by offering contractual terms that are both unappealing to a bad type, who would then prefer not to be funded, and allow lenders to break even? As we have seen, such separation requires that the good borrower be less greedy than under symmetric information and thus offer $R_b < R_b^G$. The highest reward that is unappealing to a bad borrower, R_b^*, is given by

$$qR_b^* = A. \tag{6.6}$$

Note that (6.6) assumes that the borrower commits her entire wealth A. The intuition as to why this must be so is that the good borrower wants to pledge as much as possible as a signal that she is confident about future returns.

Are investors willing to finance the project when the borrower offers to bring in her entire wealth and demands a reward equal to R_b^* (or slightly less)? "Knowing" that this offer can only emanate from a good borrower, the investors' expected profit is

$$p(R - R_b^*) - (I - A) = p(R_b^G - R_b^*) > 0. \tag{6.7}$$

So, the issue is not only subscribed. It is also *underpriced*, i.e., investors more than break even. This means that there must be rationing at the issuance.[65] In a sense, the good borrower "burns money" (here in the sense of leaving money on the table) in order to signal to investors that they are buying into a high-quality loan.

Determinants of underpricing. In the range of parameters satisfying Assumptions 6.2 and 6.3, underpricing is equal to $p(R_b^G - R_b^*)$ in absolute terms and to

$$\frac{p(R_b^G - R_b^*)}{p(R - R_b^G)} = \frac{p(R_b^G - R_b^*)}{I - A} = \frac{pR - I - ((p - q)/q)A}{I - A}$$

in relative terms.

Relative underpricing decreases with the extent of adverse selection, as measured by the likelihood ratio, $(p - q)/q$. When the two types become more similar, i.e., q increases keeping p fixed (still under Assumption 6.2), the good borrower must underprice more in order to make the issue unappealing to a bad borrower.

Full analysis. The analysis above is incomplete in two respects.

First, we implicitly assumed that the good borrower separates from a bad one by demanding a lower share of the pie in the case of success. Could the good borrower distort her contractual terms in other ways so as to reduce the cost of signaling her type? The other possible departures from the symmetric-information contract are (i) a random probability of financing, (ii) providing the borrower with an *ex post* choice between funding and a

64. Again, this contract is not uniquely optimal: any contract specifying nonnegative rewards for the manager and letting investors break even will do.

65. The good borrower could equivalently publicly "burn" an amount of money equal to the left-hand side of (6.7), and then the investors would break even. Underpricing seems a more robust signaling device, though. For example, if the investors supply any noncontractible input, however tiny, that increases the probability of success, raising the investors' stake rather than purely burning money is a more efficient signaling device. Furthermore, as Allen and Faulhaber (1989) argue, underpricing reduces the probability of a lawsuit when the outcome turns out to be adverse.

lump-sum transfer without funding, and (iii) an incomplete commitment of the borrower's wealth. Intuitively, the last departure should not signal that the borrower is a good one. As for the first departure, the borrower could pay an application fee in exchange for a random chance of getting funded. But this is a less efficient signaling method than taking a lower share in the case of success and being funded with probability 1. Section 6.9 shows that the separating allocation defined by (6.7) is indeed the low-information-intensity optimum, that is, the allocation that maximizes the good borrower's utility subject to the bad borrower not receiving a rent (or more generally subject to the capital market not losing money on any type). By contrast, the second departure introduces new, pooling equilibria, as we discuss below.

Second, we have not yet investigated uniqueness. There might exist other separating, pooling or hybrid equilibria. Section 6.9 shows that the separating allocation is not the unique equilibrium outcome for any α (that is, $\alpha^* = 0$). Indeed, there exist pooling equilibria in which both types are better off than in the separating equilibrium. These pooling equilibria involve the borrower choosing after contracting with the investors between (a) investment and no lump-sum payment (the borrower is rewarded only in the case of success) and (b) no investment and a positive lump-sum payment. In a sense, the bad type (who chooses option (b)) is bribed to "go away" and not invest. The pooling equilibrium is sustained by the investors' belief that this option-contract offer is selected by both types, and so their posterior belief just after the contract is offered (but before the option is exercised) is the same as the prior belief.

As the probability of a good type converges to 0, so does the lump-sum payment and thus the pooling equilibrium converges to the separating one. Note, furthermore, that the pooling equilibrium involves no underpricing (the investors make money on the good type, but lose as much in expectation on the bad one).[66]

Intermediate signals. Good borrowers are willing to use a low IPO price in order to signal the quality of their project in Allen and Faulhaber (1989) as well. The specifics of modeling are slightly different from those described here in that (a) the entrepreneur need only finance an amount I of investment initially and will later need to finance the complementary amount J to implement the project, and (b) a public signal correlated with the entrepreneur's initial information about the quality of the project is publicly learned before the firm conducts the seasoned offering allowing to defray J.[67]

We therefore conclude that underpricing as a signal is a possibility, not a necessity.

Supplementary Section

6.4 Contract Design by an Informed Party: An Introduction

We noted that the proper modeling of the situation in which an informed party issues claims in a competitive capital market is one of contract design by an informed principal. The purpose of this section is to give an introduction to the relevant techniques and results, developed in Maskin and Tirole (1992). While the section is mathematically straightforward, it is more abstract and formal than the rest of the chapter and of the book. We focus on two potential types for the borrower, a "good type" and a "bad type"; the results derived in this section hold for an arbitrary number of types.

A borrower who attempts to raise funds from lenders has private information about some characteristic (private benefit, value of assets in place, prospects of the firm, value of collateral) that affects the lenders' payoff. The borrower may have type b or $\tilde{b}$. While the borrower knows her type, the lenders only know that this type is b with probability α and $\tilde{b}$ with probability $1 - \alpha$.

66. Namely, both types of borrower offer a contract in which they bring in A and which gives them, if investors accept, an option between (i) going ahead with the investment and receiving $\hat{R}_b \in (R_b^*, R_b^G)$ in the case of success, and (ii) refraining from investing and receiving cash payment $q\hat{R}_b (> A)$. The good borrower exercises the first option and the bad borrower the second. The investors offset their loss (which would be equal to 0 if $\hat{R}_b = R_b^*$) on the bad borrowers by a profit on the good borrowers (which would be strictly positive if $\hat{R}_b = R_b^*$):

$$\alpha[p(R - \hat{R}_b) - (I - A)] - (1 - \alpha)(q\hat{R}_b - A) = 0.$$

67. Other related models of IPO underpricing include Grinblatt and Hwang (1989) and Welch (1989).

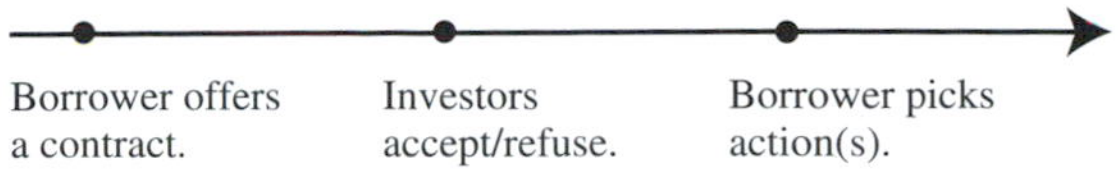

Figure 6.4

Let us, abstractly, denote the contractual terms faced by the borrower by c. Let $U_b(c)$ and $\tilde{U}_b(c)$ denote the two types' net utilities for arbitrary contractual terms c.[68] Let $U_l(c)$ and $\tilde{U}_l(c)$ denote the investors' expected profit when contractual terms are c and the borrower turns out to have type b and $\tilde{b}$, respectively.

Example (privately-known-prospects). In Section 6.2, the borrower had possible types $b = p$ and $\tilde{b} = q$. The contractual terms c were just the borrower's reward R_b^S in the case of success. More generally, they also contain the probability of investment, x, her reward in the case of failure, R_b^F, and in the absence of investment, R_b^0, even though the latter in equilibrium can be taken to be equal to 1, 0, and 0, respectively (see Section 6.5). We have

$$\begin{aligned} U_b(c) &= x[pR_b^S + (1-p)R_b^F] + (1-x)R_b^0, \\ \tilde{U}_b(c) &= x[qR_b^S + (1-q)R_b^F] + (1-x)R_b^0, \\ U_l(c) &= x[p(R - R_b^S) - (1-p)R_b^F] - (1-x)R_b^0, \\ \tilde{U}_l(c) &= x[q(R - R_b^S) - (1-q)R_b^F] - (1-x)R_b^0. \end{aligned}$$

In other applications, contractual terms also include the amount of collateralized assets, the levels of liquidity hoarded at date 0, or of the short-term debt repayment, etc. For more generality, c and $\tilde{c}$ can also be taken to be random.

Figure 6.4 describes the timing of the *issuance game.* As earlier, we assume that the borrower designs the issue and offers the associated claims to a competitive capital market. Investors purchase the claims if and only if they expect a nonnegative profit. Lastly, the borrower chooses some action(s).

A few clarifications are in order. First, we allow for post-contracting actions by the borrower in order to accommodate situations in which the borrower can waste resources (as in Chapters 3-5).[69] Second, we said that investors subscribe "if and only if they expect a nonnegative profit." The expectation should be taken relative to the updated beliefs, that is, the investors' beliefs after they observe the contract offer and thus possibly learn something about the borrower. Third, we will analyze the perfect Bayesian equilibrium (or equilibria) of the issuance game.[70]

Fourth, a "contract" can in principle be anything that the borrower sees fit to design. However, for the purpose of the analysis, it can be shown that there is no loss of generality in assuming that the borrower offers an "option contract" $(c, \tilde{c})$, that is, as many contractual terms as there are possible types. The terminology "option contract" comes from the fact that, if the investors subscribe (accept the contract), the borrower must then exercise her built-in option and choose between c and $\tilde{c}$. The choice of contractual terms is then included in the "actions" to be taken *ex post* by the borrower. It can further be shown that there is no loss of generality in assuming that the option contract is "incentive compatible," that is, that type b prefers contractual terms c to $\tilde{c}$ and type $\tilde{b}$ prefers $\tilde{c}$ to c (the reader knowledgeable in information economics will here recognize a version of the "revelation principle").

The reader may at this stage wonder why a borrower might want to offer contractual terms not only for her own type, but also for the other type, a type that she actually does not have, when she will end up choosing the contractual terms that are fitted to her own type anyway. While the reason will become clear both in the abstract treatment below and in the applications, it is worth sketching it now: while option contracts do not augment the set of equilibrium allocations relative to "simple contracts," in which the borrower offers a single contractual term (that is, the equilibrium allocations are also equilibrium

68. So, for example, if the borrower has initial cash A, and has quasi-linear preferences, the net utility is equal to the gross utility minus A.

69. We could also allow for *ex post* actions by active investors as in Parts III and IV.

70. Very roughly speaking, a perfect Bayesian equilibrium of a game is a set of strategies and beliefs such that at any stage of the game players act optimally given their beliefs at that stage (the equilibrium is "perfect") and beliefs are updated by the players according to Bayes' rule using equilibrium strategies and observed actions (the updating is Bayesian). See, for example, Fudenberg and Tirole (1991, Chapter 8) for a formal definition.

Here investors are assumed to update their beliefs about the borrower's type using the borrower's equilibrium type-contingent contract offer and the actual contract offer. The previous condition, that they subscribe if and only if they expect a nonnegative profit given their updated beliefs, is an optimization requirement.

allocations when one focuses on simple contracts), option contracts help eliminate "bad expectations." For example, the good borrower b may not be able to obtain contractual terms c by offering the simple contract c because investors may be convinced that such an offer stems from a bad borrower and that they will lose money ($\tilde{U}_\mathrm{l}(c) < 0$). However, if the good borrower appends to c another option, namely, contractual terms $\tilde{c}$, that a bad borrower prefers to c ($\tilde{U}_\mathrm{b}(\tilde{c}) > \tilde{U}_\mathrm{b}(c)$) and yet allows investors to break even ($\tilde{U}_\mathrm{l}(\tilde{c}) \geqslant 0$), then the good borrower "guarantees" that investors will not lose money regardless of their expectations, and can thus safely enjoy contractual terms c. We will come back to this idea later.

The characterization of the equilibrium (or equilibria) of the issuance game requires defining a couple of intuitive notions. Let an *allocation* be a pair of (possibly identical) type-contingent contractual terms $(c, \tilde{c})$. That is, it defines contractual terms c for type b and $\tilde{c}$ for type $\tilde{b}$. (Note that an option contract defines an allocation.)

Definition. An allocation $(c, \tilde{c})$ is *incentive compatible* if type b prefers c to $\tilde{c}$ and type $\tilde{b}$ prefers $\tilde{c}$ to c:

$$U_\mathrm{b}(c) \geqslant U_\mathrm{b}(\tilde{c}) \quad \text{and} \quad \tilde{U}_\mathrm{b}(\tilde{c}) \geqslant \tilde{U}_\mathrm{b}(c).$$

Because the borrower's type is not observed, a given type can always mimic what the other type does, and so equilibrium allocations must be incentive compatible.

Definition. An incentive-compatible allocation $(c, \tilde{c})$ is *profitable type-by-type* if

$$U_\mathrm{l}(c) \geqslant 0 \quad \text{and} \quad \tilde{U}_\mathrm{l}(\tilde{c}) \geqslant 0.$$

Definition. An incentive-compatible allocation $(c, \tilde{c})$ is *profitable in expectation* (relative to the prior beliefs) if

$$\alpha U_\mathrm{l}(c) + (1 - \alpha)\tilde{U}_\mathrm{l}(\tilde{c}) \geqslant 0.$$

An incentive-compatible allocation $(c, \tilde{c})$ that is profitable in expectation is *interim efficient* if it is Pareto-optimal for the two types of borrower in the set of incentive-compatible, profitable-in-expectation allocations.

We now ask, what can a borrower guarantee herself given that the lenders may have arbitrary expectations about her type (what she can guarantee herself evidently depends on her actual type)? The answer relies on the following definition.[71]

Definition. Utility $U_\mathrm{b}(c_0)$ for borrower type b is the *low-information-intensity optimum* for that type if c_0 maximizes type b's utility in the set of incentive-compatible, profitable-type-by-type allocations. That is, it is (part of) the solution to the following program.

Program I (type b):

$$\max_{\{c,\tilde{c}\}} U_\mathrm{b}(c)$$

s.t.

$$U_\mathrm{b}(c) \geqslant U_\mathrm{b}(\tilde{c}),$$

$$\tilde{U}_\mathrm{b}(\tilde{c}) \geqslant \tilde{U}_\mathrm{b}(c),$$

$$U_\mathrm{l}(c) \geqslant 0,$$

$$\tilde{U}_\mathrm{l}(\tilde{c}) \geqslant 0.$$

The low-information-intensity optimum $\tilde{c}_0$ for type $\tilde{b}$ is defined similarly (Program I (type $\tilde{b}$)).

The payoff pair $(U_\mathrm{b}(c_0), U_\mathrm{b}(\tilde{c}_0))$ is called the *low-information-intensity optimum.* (By abuse of terminology, we will sometimes call the allocation $(c_0, \tilde{c}_0)$ itself the low-information-intensity optimum.)

The allocation $(c_0, \tilde{c}_0)$, even though it is derived from two independent programs, is itself incentive compatible. (Suppose, for example, that type $\tilde{b}$ strictly prefers c_0 to $\tilde{c}_0$. Then the solution $(c_0, \tilde{c})$ of Program I (type b) defining c_0 satisfies the constraints of Program I (type $\tilde{b}$) defining $\tilde{c}_0$ (they are the same), and furthermore

$$\tilde{U}_\mathrm{b}(\tilde{c}) \geqslant \tilde{U}_\mathrm{b}(c_0) > \tilde{U}_\mathrm{b}(\tilde{c}_0).$$

Thus, $\tilde{c}_0$ cannot be the low-information-intensity optimum for type $\tilde{b}$ after all.)

The low-information-intensity optimum plays a key role in most of the financial economics literature on signaling. We will derive it repeatedly in the applications below. A trivial but very useful result (the following lemma) is that the borrower in equilibrium must obtain at least her low-information-intensity optimum.

71. The low-information-intensity optimum is called the "Rothschild–Stiglitz–Wilson" allocation in Maskin and Tirole (1992) after the influential papers of Rothschild and Stiglitz (1976) and Wilson (1977), in which the low-information-intensity optimum plays a central role.

Lemma 6.1. *The borrower can guarantee herself her low-information-intensity optimum* ($U_b(c_0)$ *if she has type* b, *and* $\tilde{U}_b(\tilde{c}_0)$ *if she has type* $\tilde{b}$).

Proof. Suppose the borrower offers the "option contract" $(c_0, \tilde{c}_0)$; by this, we mean that if the lenders accept the contract, the borrower picks the contractual terms c_0 or $\tilde{c}_0$. Because $(c_0, \tilde{c}_0)$ is incentive compatible, lenders know that type b will pick c_0 and type $\tilde{b}$ will pick $\tilde{c}_0$. Because $U_l(c_0) \geqslant 0$ and $\tilde{U}_l(\tilde{c}_0) \geqslant 0$ (the allocation is profitable type-by-type), lenders know that they will break even whatever their belief about the borrower's type.[72] □

The key result (due to Maskin and Tirole 1992) is the following.

Proposition 6.1.

(a) *The issuance game has a unique perfect Bayesian equilibrium if the low-information-intensity optimum is interim efficient* (*relative to prior beliefs* $(\alpha, 1-\alpha)$). *The borrower then obtains her low-information-intensity optimum* ($U_b(c_0)$ *for type* b, $\tilde{U}_b(\tilde{c}_0)$ *for type* $\tilde{b}$).

(b) *If the low-information-intensity optimum is not interim efficient, then the set of equilibrium payoffs for the two types of borrowers is the set of payoffs that result from an incentive-compatible, profitable-in-expectation allocation and* (*weakly*) *Pareto-dominate the low-information-intensity optimum.*

The uniqueness result (part (a)) is straightforward: an equilibrium allocation must be incentive compatible, and (from Lemma 6.1) must weakly Pareto-dominate the low-information-intensity optimum. It cannot, however, strictly Pareto-dominate this optimum if the latter is (interim) efficient, and so it must yield the same utilities.

Proposition 6.1 provides a mechanical way of deriving the equilibrium or equilibria of the issuance game. Let us now show that, under a very weak condition, the equilibrium can be straightforwardly characterized. Let $\tilde{c}^{\mathrm{SI}}$ denote the *symmetric information* contractual terms for the bad borrower. It solves

$$\max_{\{\tilde{c}\}} \tilde{U}_b(\tilde{c})$$
$$\text{s.t.}$$
$$\tilde{U}_l(\tilde{c}) \geqslant 0.$$

Assumption 6.4 (weak monotonic profit[73]). *Investors make a nonnegative profit if the contractual terms are those of the bad borrower under symmetric information and the borrower is a good one:*

$$U_l(\tilde{c}^{\mathrm{SI}}) \geqslant 0.$$

This assumption is in general satisfied when both types are creditworthy under symmetric information (and it is satisfied in all of our illustrations). It is always satisfied when the bad borrower is not creditworthy under symmetric information: in that case, $\tilde{c}^{\mathrm{SI}}$ is the absence of funding and thus $U_l(\tilde{c}^{\mathrm{SI}}) = 0$.

Definition. The *separating allocation* is the allocation c^* for the good borrower and the symmetric-information contractual terms $\tilde{c}^{\mathrm{SI}}$ for the bad borrower, where c^* maximizes the good borrower's payoff subject to the investors breaking even for the good borrower and to the bad borrower not preferring c^* to $\tilde{c}^{\mathrm{SI}}$:

$$\max_{\{c\}} U_b(c)$$
$$\text{s.t.}$$
$$U_l(c) \geqslant 0,$$
$$\tilde{U}_b(c) \leqslant \tilde{U}_b(\tilde{c}^{\mathrm{SI}}).$$

Note that the separating allocation is profitable type-by-type.

Lemma 6.2. *Under the weak monotonic-profit assumption, the separating allocation is the low-information-intensity optimum.*

Proof. First, note that the bad borrower's symmetric-information program has the same objective function and fewer constraints than her low-information-intensity optimum program, Program I (type $\tilde{b}$). Hence,

$$\tilde{U}_b^{\mathrm{SI}} \equiv \tilde{U}_b(\tilde{c}^{\mathrm{SI}}) \geqslant \tilde{U}_b(\tilde{c}_0).$$

72. We are a bit casual about the borrower's and the lenders' behaviors when they are indifferent. Proving that the equilibrium behavior following the offer of contract $(c_0, \tilde{c}_0)$ is indeed the one described in the proof requires taking limits of slightly perturbed contracts for which indifferences are broken (see Maskin and Tirole (1992) for the details).

73. We state the assumption for the case in which $\tilde{c}^{\mathrm{SI}}$ is unique. If there are multiple solutions to the symmetric-information program for the bad borrower, we require that $U_l(\tilde{c}^{\mathrm{SI}}) \geqslant 0$ holds for at least one of them.

Conversely, the bad borrower can guarantee herself her symmetric-information payoff even under asymmetric information; for, suppose she offers $\tilde{c}^{\text{SI}}$. From the weak monotonic-profit assumption, investors at least break even regardless of the borrower's type. Hence, they are willing to subscribe to the issue. Hence,

$$\tilde{U}_{\text{b}}(\tilde{c}_0) = \tilde{U}_{\text{b}}^{\text{SI}},$$

and $\tilde{c}_0$ can be identified with $\tilde{c}^{\text{SI}}$, without loss of generality.

Second, consider Program I (type b), yielding the low-information-intensity optimum for type b. It has the same objective function and is more constrained than the separating program. (Note that the constraint $\tilde{U}_{\text{b}}(c) \leqslant \tilde{U}_{\text{b}}(\tilde{c}^{\text{SI}})$ in the separating program is replaced by the constraint $\tilde{U}_{\text{b}}(c) \leqslant \tilde{U}_{\text{b}}(\tilde{c})$ for some $\tilde{c}$ satisfying in particular $\tilde{U}_{\text{l}}(\tilde{c}) \geqslant 0$; because $\tilde{U}_{\text{l}}(\tilde{c}) \geqslant 0$ and $\tilde{U}_{\text{l}}(\tilde{c}^{\text{SI}}) \geqslant 0$, and $\tilde{c}^{\text{SI}}$ maximizes $\tilde{U}_{\text{b}}(\cdot)$ subject to this constraint $\tilde{U}_{\text{l}}(\cdot) \geqslant 0$, $\tilde{U}_{\text{b}}(\tilde{c}) \leqslant \tilde{U}_{\text{b}}(\tilde{c}^{\text{SI}})$. Thus the constraint $\tilde{U}_{\text{b}}(c) \leqslant \tilde{U}_{\text{b}}(\tilde{c})$ for some $\tilde{c}$ satisfying $\tilde{U}_{\text{l}}(\tilde{c}) \geqslant 0$ is not looser than the constraint $\tilde{U}_{\text{b}}(c) \leqslant \tilde{U}_{\text{b}}(\tilde{c}^{\text{SI}})$. It may be tighter given that the low-information-intensity optimum also requires $U_{\text{b}}(c) \geqslant U_{\text{b}}(\tilde{c})$.) Therefore,

$$U_{\text{b}}(c^*) \geqslant U_{\text{b}}(c_0).$$

Conversely, the good borrower can guarantee herself her separating allocation payoff; for, suppose that she offers profitable-type-by-type option contract $(c^*, \tilde{c}^{\text{SI}})$. This allocation is indeed incentive compatible (by construction, $\tilde{U}_{\text{b}}(c^*) \leqslant \tilde{U}_{\text{b}}(\tilde{c}^{\text{SI}})$; furthermore, if $U_{\text{b}}(c^*) < U_{\text{b}}(\tilde{c}^{\text{SI}})$, $(c^*, \tilde{c}^{\text{SI}})$, would not be the solution to the separating program, since it would be dominated by $(\tilde{c}^{\text{SI}}, \tilde{c}^{\text{SI}})$, which satisfies the constraints of this program from the weak monotonic-profit assumption). Hence, investors accept this option contract and so $U_{\text{b}}(c^*) = U_{\text{b}}(c_0)$. □

Lemma 6.3. *Under the weak monotonic-profit assumption, there exists a threshold level α^* for prior beliefs such that the low-information-intensity optimum (that is, the separating allocation under the weak monotonic-profit assumption) is interim efficient if and only if $\alpha \leqslant \alpha^*$.*

Proof. We have seen that the good borrower can obtain her separating payoff and the bad borrower her full information payoff. Looking at the program defining the separating allocation, it is clear that the good borrower cannot obtain more than her separating payoff unless the bad borrower obtains a rent beyond her symmetric-information payoff.

Let $\hat{\mathcal{R}} \geqslant 0$ denote the bad borrower's rent above her full information utility, and define the minimal loss incurred by investors on the bad type when the latter has extra rent $\hat{\mathcal{R}}$:

$$-\mathcal{L}(\hat{\mathcal{R}}) = \max_{\{\tilde{c}\}} \tilde{U}_{\text{l}}(\tilde{c})$$

s.t.

$$\tilde{U}_{\text{b}}(\tilde{c}) \geqslant \tilde{U}_{\text{b}}^{\text{SI}} + \hat{\mathcal{R}}.$$

$\mathcal{L}(\cdot)$ is an increasing function and (as long as investors break even under the symmetric-information allocation) $\mathcal{L}(0) = 0$. Consider the following program.

Program II:

$$\max_{\{c,\hat{\mathcal{R}}\}} U_{\text{b}}(c)$$

s.t.

$$\alpha U_{\text{l}}(c) - (1-\alpha)\mathcal{L}(\hat{\mathcal{R}}) \geqslant 0,$$

$$\tilde{U}_{\text{b}}(c) \leqslant \tilde{U}_{\text{b}}^{\text{SI}} + \hat{\mathcal{R}}.$$

If $\hat{\mathcal{R}} > 0$ is strictly suboptimal, then the good borrower cannot obtain more than her low-information-intensity optimum; for, in any equilibrium of the issuance game, the investors must break even and so

$$\alpha U_{\text{l}}(c) - (1-\alpha)\mathcal{L}(\hat{\mathcal{R}}) \geqslant 0$$

must hold.

If the optimum of Program II yields $\hat{\mathcal{R}} > 0$, then the solution to Program II dominates the low-information-intensity optimum for the good borrower and yields an upper bound on the good type's (perfect Bayesian) equilibrium payoff. This upper bound is attained if the good type prefers the allocation defined by Program II to the allocation $\tilde{c}$ that minimizes the loss $\mathcal{L}(\hat{\mathcal{R}})$ incurred by investors for the bad type. (The proof of these assertions follows the steps of the proof of part (b) of Proposition 6.1.)

Lastly, it is simple to observe that if the low-information-intensity optimum is interim efficient for some belief α, it is also interim efficient for all beliefs $\alpha' < \alpha$: suppose it were not. Then, there would exist $\hat{\mathcal{R}}$ and c such that $U_b(c) > U_b(c_0)$, $\alpha' U_l(c) \geqslant (1-\alpha')\mathcal{L}(\hat{\mathcal{R}})$ and $\tilde{U}_b(c) \leqslant \tilde{U}_b^{SI} + \hat{\mathcal{R}}$. But $\hat{\mathcal{R}}$ and c satisfy these conditions *a fortiori* for α, given that $\mathcal{L}(\hat{\mathcal{R}}) > 0$. □

We summarize our results in the following proposition.

Proposition 6.2. *Suppose that the weak monotonic-profit assumption holds. Then*

(a) *the separating allocation is the low-information-intensity optimum;*

(b) *there exists a threshold α^* such that the low-information-intensity optimum is interim efficient and is thus the unique (perfect Bayesian) equilibrium payoff vector of the issuance game if and only if $\alpha \leqslant \alpha^*$.*

A few comments on this definition are in order. First, Program II is of interest even when equilibrium is not unique ($\alpha > \alpha^*$). It defines an upper bound for the payoff for the good borrower in the set of feasible payoffs. Second, although α^* is usually positive (see examples below), it may be equal to 0. This is illustrated by the privately-known-prospects model of Section 6.2.1, when the bad borrower is not creditworthy. Indeed, in that model, the low-information-intensity optimum corresponds to the no-financing allocation. We leave it to the reader to check that it is interim efficient if and only if

$$[\alpha p + (1-\alpha)q]R \leqslant I,$$

that is, for $\alpha \leqslant \alpha^*$. In this case, we had indeed proved directly (that is, without the use of part (a) of Proposition 6.1) that the equilibrium, namely, complete market breakdown, is unique.

Third, when $\alpha > \alpha^*$, there are other equilibrium outcomes than the low-information-intensity optimum. The equilibrium exhibited in Section 6.2.1 is actually the one with the highest payoff for the good type and thus solves Program II. Proposition 6.1(b) can be used to obtain the set of equilibrium payoffs, which admits this equilibrium payoff as the upper bound for the good borrower and the low-information-intensity optimum as the lower bound for both types.

Appendixes

6.5 Optimal Contracting in the Privately-Known-Prospects Model

(For the technically minded reader only.) Consider the model of Section 6.2.1. In all generality, an allocation is a probability x that the investment be made and rewards R_b^S, R_b^F, and R_b^0 in the case of success, failure, and no investment, respectively. The payoff to type $r \in \{p, q\}$ for this allocation is then

$$U_b(r) = x[rR_b^S + (1-r)R_b^F] + (1-x)R_b^0.$$

Let $\{x, R_b^S, R_b^F, R_b^0\}$ denote the good type's allocation. Incentive compatibility (the fact that the bad type can mimic the good type) implies that the bad type's utility $\tilde{U}_b$ can be related to the good type's $U_b = U_b(p)$ in the following way:

$$\tilde{U}_b \geqslant U_b - x(p-q)(R_b^S - R_b^F).$$

Using this inequality and the investor's breakeven constraint,

$$\alpha[x(pR - I) - U_b] + (1-\alpha)[\tilde{x}(qR - I) - \tilde{U}_b] \geqslant 0,$$

where $\tilde{x}$ is the probability that the bad type invests, the best allocation for the good type solves

$$\max_{\{x, R_b^S, R_b^F, R_b^0\}} U_b(p)$$

s.t.

$$\alpha x(pR - I) + (1-\alpha)\tilde{x}(qR - I) - U_b(p) + (1-\alpha)x(p-q)(R_b^S - R_b^F) \geqslant 0.$$

We leave it to the reader to show that, at the optimum of this program, $R_b^F = R_b^0 = 0$, and

- if $qR - I > 0$, then $\tilde{x} = 1$, and the pooling allocation studied in the text is the optimal allocation for the good type;
- if $qR - I < 0$, then $\tilde{x} = 0$; incentive compatibility then requires a lump-sum payment for the bad type,

$$\tilde{R}_b^0 = qR_b^S.$$

Two remarks are in order concerning this lump-sum payment. First, the borrower obviously cannot go to the investors and just ask them to pay $\tilde{R}_b^0 > 0$ in exchange for no claims at all, as the investors would just refuse. The process through which this allocation can be implemented was studied in the supplementary section: the borrower offers a menu to the investors: $\{x = 1,\ R_b^S > 0,\ R_b^F = 0,\ R_b^0 = 0\}$ for the good type and $\{x = 0,\ \tilde{R}_b^0\}$ for the bad type and only selects in the menu once the investors have accepted to finance the investment. Because the menu is incentive compatible and satisfies the investors' breakeven condition, it is an equilibrium for the investors to indeed finance the project.

Second, the lump-sum-payment policy raises the concern that the payout $\tilde{R}_b^0$ attract "fake entrepreneurs," who do not even have a project (put differently, $1 - \alpha$ could quickly become very close to 1, leading to market breakdown after all).

6.6 The Debt Bias with a Continuum of Possible Incomes

Consider the privately-known-prospects model in Application 3, but assume that the firm's income is *continuous*. The entrepreneur and the investors are risk neutral. The entrepreneur has initial assets A and wants to finance a project costing $I > A$. There is no moral hazard. The income is distributed on $[0, \infty)$ according to density $p(R)$ and cumulative distribution $P(R)$ in the case of a good borrower, and to density $\tilde{p}(R)$ and cumulative distribution $\tilde{P}(R)$ in the case of a bad borrower. The definition of what constitutes a good borrower is linked to the monotone likelihood ratio property, according to which a higher income makes it more likely that it emanates from a good borrower.

Assumption 6.5 (monotone likelihood ratio property). *$p(R)/\tilde{p}(R)$ is increasing.*

We also make the following assumption.

Assumption 6.6 (only the good borrower is creditworthy). *Under symmetric information, only the good borrower would receive funding for the project:*

$$\tilde{V} \equiv \int_0^\infty R\tilde{p}(R)\,\mathrm{d}R - I < 0 < V \equiv \int_0^\infty Rp(R)\,\mathrm{d}R - I.$$

As in the previous sections, we look for a contract between the good borrower and the investors that maximizes the good borrower's payoff subject to the investors' breaking even for that type and to the bad borrower's preferring to keep cash A rather than mimicking the good borrower in order to get funding. Let $w(R)$ denote the borrower's income when the firm's income is R. We assume that $0 \leqslant w(R) \leqslant R$; see Section 3.6 for a discussion of this (rather strong) assumption of the investors' limited liability.

So, we solve

$$\max_{\{w(\cdot)\}} \int_0^\infty w(R)p(R)\,\mathrm{d}R$$

s.t.

$$\int_0^\infty [R - w(R)]p(R)\,\mathrm{d}R \geqslant I - A,$$

$$\int_0^\infty w(R)\tilde{p}(R)\,\mathrm{d}R \leqslant A,$$

$$0 \leqslant w(R) \leqslant R.$$

Ignoring the last constraint for the moment, the Lagrangian for this linear program is

$$\mathcal{L} = \int_0^\infty \left[1 - \lambda - \mu\frac{\tilde{p}(R)}{p(R)}\right] w(R)p(R)\,\mathrm{d}R + \lambda(V + A) + \mu A,$$

where λ and μ are the (positive) multipliers of the breakeven and the mimicking constraints. Using the monotone likelihood ratio property, there thus exists a threshold R^* (such that $p(R^*)/\tilde{p}(R^*) = \mu/(1-\lambda)$) such that

$$w(R) = \begin{cases} R & \text{if } R \geqslant R^*, \\ 0 & \text{if } R < R^*. \end{cases}$$

We thus obtain, and for the same reason, the result obtained by Innes (1990) in the moral-hazard version of the model.[74]

---

74. When are the two constraints binding and when is it possible for a good borrower to separate from a bad one? Let $R^*(A)$ be defined by

$$\int_{R^*(A)}^\infty R\tilde{p}(R)\,\mathrm{d}R = A.$$

The investors' profit from a good type is then

$$V + A - \int_{R^*(A)}^\infty Rp(R)\,\mathrm{d}R,$$

whose derivative with respect to A is equal to $1 - p(R^*)/\tilde{p}(R^*)$. From the monotone likelihood ratio property, this derivative is first positive and later negative. If A is small, the good borrower cannot separate from a bad one (she may still be able to get financing if α is large enough). One can show that there exists some A^* such that the two constraints are binding and the unique optimal contract is as described in the text. For $A > A^*$, this contract is optimal but no longer unique; all optimal contracts must still resemble it in that they must

Building further on Innes and on the discussion in Section 3.6, we note that this result does not quite vindicate the pecking-order hypothesis for risky debt. (Note, incidentally, that the firm cannot issue any safe debt since the lowest possible income is equal to 0.) While investors are residual claimants in case of default ($R < R^*$), they receive nothing otherwise.

To conform with the pecking-order hypothesis, one must add Innes's monotonic reimbursement assumption, according to which the investors' return, $R - w(R)$, should not decrease with the firm's income.[75] Then, as in Section 3.6 to which we refer for more detail, the optimal contract for the good borrower is a *standard debt contract*.

6.7 Signaling through Costly Collateral

The prerequisite for this appendix, which provides a rigorous analysis of Application 5, is the reading of the supplementary section.

First, we check that the weak monotonic-payoff assumption holds. Here

$$\begin{aligned} U_1(\tilde{c}^{\mathrm{SI}}) &= p(R - R_{\mathrm{b}}^{\mathrm{B}}) - I \\ &= (p - q)(R - R_{\mathrm{b}}^{\mathrm{B}}) > 0. \end{aligned}$$

Application 5 in the text identified contractual terms with the borrower's reward $R_{\mathrm{b}}^{\mathrm{S}} = R_{\mathrm{b}}$ in the case of success and the amount of collateral $C^{\mathrm{F}} = C$ transferred to investors in the case of failure. More generally, we must allow for a reward $R_{\mathrm{b}}^{\mathrm{F}} \geqslant 0$ in the case of failure, a level of collateral C^{S} in the case of success, and a probability x of investment.[76] So Program II′ can be written

$$\max_{\{R_{\mathrm{b}}^{\mathrm{S}}, R_{\mathrm{b}}^{\mathrm{F}}, C^{\mathrm{S}}, C^{\mathrm{F}}, x, \tilde{\mathcal{R}}\}} x[p(R_{\mathrm{b}}^{\mathrm{S}} - C^{\mathrm{S}}) + (1-p)(R_{\mathrm{b}}^{\mathrm{F}} - C^{\mathrm{F}})]$$

s.t.

$$\begin{aligned} \alpha x[p(R - R_{\mathrm{b}}^{\mathrm{S}} + \beta C^{\mathrm{S}}) + (1-p)(-R_{\mathrm{b}}^{\mathrm{F}} + \beta C^{\mathrm{F}}) - I] \\ - (1-\alpha)\mathcal{L}(\tilde{\mathcal{R}}) \geqslant 0, \\ x[q(R_{\mathrm{b}}^{\mathrm{S}} - C^{\mathrm{S}}) + (1-q)(R_{\mathrm{b}}^{\mathrm{F}} - C^{\mathrm{F}})] \leqslant (qR - I) + \tilde{\mathcal{R}}. \end{aligned}$$

We leave it to the reader to check that

- $\mathcal{L}(\tilde{\mathcal{R}}) = \tilde{\mathcal{R}}$ (there is no dissipation of profit through collateral pledging in the program defining $\mathcal{L}(\cdot)$);
- there is no loss of generality involved in assuming, as we did in Section 6.3, that $x = 1$, $R_{\mathrm{b}}^{\mathrm{F}} = C^{\mathrm{S}} = 0$.

Letting $R_{\mathrm{b}}^{\mathrm{S}} = R_{\mathrm{b}}$ and $C^{\mathrm{F}} = C$, one can then show that the good type's utility increases with $\tilde{\mathcal{R}}$ if and only if[77]

$$\frac{(1-p)(q + p\alpha/(1-\alpha))}{p(1-q) - \beta q(1-p)}(1-\beta) > 1.$$

This condition is violated for $\alpha = 0$ and satisfied for α close to 1. More generally, it is satisfied for

$$\alpha > \alpha^*,$$

for some $\alpha^* \in (0, 1)$. Note, last, that α^* grows with β. One can also show that the optimal $\tilde{\mathcal{R}}$ is a nondecreasing function of α.

6.8 Short Maturities as a Signaling Device

In a separating equilibrium in Application 6, the bad type gets the symmetric-information payoff:

$$\tilde{U}_{\mathrm{b}} = r + \rho_1 - \tilde{\lambda}\rho - I.$$

The best separating allocation for the good type is given by

$$\max_{\{x, R_{\mathrm{b}}^{+}, R_{\mathrm{b}}^{-}\}} \{(1-\lambda)p_{\mathrm{H}}R_{\mathrm{b}}^{+} + \lambda p_{\mathrm{H}} x R_{\mathrm{b}}^{-} - A\}$$

s.t.

$$\begin{aligned} &(\Delta p)R_{\mathrm{b}}^{+} \geqslant B, && (\mathrm{IC}_{\mathrm{g}^+}) \\ &(\Delta p)R_{\mathrm{b}}^{-} \geqslant B, && (\mathrm{IC}_{\mathrm{g}^-}) \\ &(1-\tilde{\lambda})p_{\mathrm{H}}R_{\mathrm{b}}^{+} + \tilde{\lambda}p_{\mathrm{H}}xR_{\mathrm{b}}^{-} - A \leqslant \tilde{U}_{\mathrm{b}}, && (\mathrm{IC}_{\mathrm{bad}}) \\ &r + (1-\lambda)p_{\mathrm{H}}(R - R_{\mathrm{b}}^{+}) + \lambda x[p_{\mathrm{H}}(R - R_{\mathrm{b}}^{-}) - \rho] \\ &\qquad \geqslant I - A. && (\mathrm{IR}_1) \end{aligned}$$

The incentive constraint of the bad type ($\mathrm{IC}_{\mathrm{bad}}$) should bind. Otherwise the good type gets the symmetric-information contract with $x = 1$, $p_{\mathrm{H}}R_{\mathrm{b}}^{+} = \rho_1 - \rho_0 + \varepsilon^{+}$, and $p_{\mathrm{H}}R_{\mathrm{b}}^{-} = \rho_1 - \rho_0 + \varepsilon^{-}$, where

load reimbursements to investors onto the lower tail of the distribution.

75. This assumption is also made in DeMarzo and Duffie (1999).

76. There is no need to introduce collateral pledging in the absence of investment because this can be duplicated through a uniform increase in C^{F} and C^{S}. Similarly, there is no point introducing a payment in the absence of investment because it can be duplicated through a uniform increase in payment in the case of investment.

77. To show this, one first shows by contradiction that each constraint is binding. The two constraints then yield R_{b} and C.

$(1-\lambda)\varepsilon^+ + \lambda\varepsilon^- = r + \rho_0 - (I - A) - \lambda\rho$, and the bad type mimics the good type as

$$\begin{aligned}\tilde{U}_b - [(1-\tilde{\lambda})p_H R_b^+ + \tilde{\lambda} p_H R_b^- - A] &= (\tilde{\lambda} - \lambda)(\varepsilon^+ - \varepsilon^- - \rho) \\ &\leqslant (\tilde{\lambda} - \lambda)\left[\frac{r - (I - A) + \rho_0 - \rho}{1 - \lambda}\right] \\ &< 0,\end{aligned}$$

where the first inequality results from the definition of ε^+ and ε^-, (IR_l) and the fact that $\varepsilon^- \geqslant 0$.

This also shows that

$$(IC_{bad}) \text{ binds} \quad \Longrightarrow \quad x < 1.$$

The lender should break even, that is, (IR_l) must bind. If it is not binding, by increasing the reward in the case of success and no shock and by decreasing the probability of continuation in the case of a shock, the good type can be made better off: increase R_b^+ by δR_b^+ and decrease x by δx such that (IC_{bad}) is unchanged, i.e., $(1-\tilde{\lambda})p_H \delta R_b^+ = \tilde{\lambda} p_H \delta x R_b^-$. Then the utility of the good type is increased by $((\tilde{\lambda} - \lambda)/\tilde{\lambda}) p_H \delta R_b^+ > 0$.

Intuitively, the good type should not be rewarded too much in the case of a liquidity shock in order to decrease the utility of the bad type pretending to be a good type. If (IC_{g^-}) is not binding, decrease the reward and increase the probability of continuation in the case of a shock such that the expected value of the entrepreneur in the case of a liquidity shock is unchanged. Keeping xR_b^- unchanged, decrease R_b^- by δR_b^- and increase x by δx. The only change is that (IR_l) is not binding anymore, which is not optimal.

In the end

$$R_b^- = \frac{B}{\Delta p},$$

$$(1-\tilde{\lambda})p_H R_b^+ + \tilde{\lambda} x(\rho_1 - \rho_0) - A = \tilde{U}_b,$$

$$r + (1-\lambda)(\rho_1 - p_H R_b^+) - \lambda x(\rho - \rho_0) = I - A.$$

Implementation. We need to implement R_b^+, x, and $R_b^- = B/\Delta p$ for the good type, $\tilde{R}_b^+$ and $\tilde{R}_b^-$ for the bad type. In a sense, the good type uses a larger short-term debt to signal his type. An awkward feature of the discrete setup considered here is that refinancing for the good type is random conditional on the realization ρ of the liquidity shock. This may be implemented, for example, through $d = r$ and a random credit line equal to ρ, which could be drawn with probability x only. With a continuous distribution for the liquidity shock, one would obtain the more natural result that d is smaller than ($\tilde{d}$ is the same as) under symmetric information.

That the equilibrium is unique for α below some α^* results from the general proposition proved in the supplementary section. For $\alpha > \alpha^*$, there exist (nonseparating) equilibria Pareto-dominating the separating one. In particular, for α close to 1, the good type is better off pooling with the bad type and being able to withstand the liquidity shock for certain, at the cost of a (slightly) smaller reward than under symmetric information.

6.9 Formal Analysis of the Underpricing Problem

The prerequisite for this appendix, which extends the analysis of Application 9, is the reading of the supplementary section.

6.9.1 Low-Information-Intensity Optimum

Let us solve the separating program for the model of Application 9. First, we must consider general contractual terms c. They consist in

- a probability $x \in [0, 1]$ of funding,
- a reward $R_b^S \geqslant 0$ in the case of success,
- a reward $R_b^F \geqslant 0$ in the case of failure,
- an initial payment $\mathcal{A} \leqslant A$ by the borrower to the lenders (the borrower keeps $A - \mathcal{A}$); a negative $\mathcal{A}$ corresponds to a transfer from lenders to the borrower.

Let us solve for the low-information-intensity allocation:

$$\max_{\{x, R_b^S, R_b^F, \mathcal{A}\}} \quad U_b(c) = x[pR_b^S + (1-p)R_b^F] - \mathcal{A}$$

s.t.

$$U_l(c) = x[p(R - R_b^S) + (1-p)(-R_b^F) - I] + \mathcal{A} \geqslant 0,$$

$$\tilde{U}_b(c) = x[qR_b^S + (1-q)R_b^F] - \mathcal{A} \leqslant 0.$$

Note that $x > 0$ (otherwise, the solution would yield $U_b(c) = 0$, which is impossible since the separating, underpricing allocation derived in the text provides the good type with a strictly positive net utility). Second, one can take $R_b^F = 0$; for, if $R_b^F > 0$, then a small change $\{\delta R_b^F < 0, \ \delta R_b^S > 0\}$ such that

$p\delta R_b^S + (1-p)\delta R_b^F = 0$ does not affect $U_b(c)$ and $U_l(c)$ and reduces $\tilde{U}_b(c)$. Third, suppose that $x < 1$. Then increasing x slightly, keeping xR_b^S constant, does not affect $U_b(c)$ and $\tilde{U}_b(c)$ and increases $U_l(c)$ (since $pR > I$). So, $x = 1$ given that $\tilde{U}_b(c) = 0$ (as was shown in the text, the full information solution does not hold under asymmetric information, and so the constraint $\tilde{U}_b(c) \leqslant 0$ must be binding). Hence, we can take $x = 1$, and because $\tilde{U}_b(c) = 0$

$$qR_b^S = \mathcal{A}.$$

We conclude that the low-information-intensity optimum is the allocation derived in Section 6.3.

Equilibrium uniqueness. We saw in the supplementary section that the issuance game admits a unique (perfect Bayesian) equilibrium if and only if the low-information-intensity optimum is interim efficient. We must therefore examine Program II (see the supplementary section). First, we minimize the investors' loss $\mathcal{L}(\tilde{\mathcal{R}})$ on the bad borrower when the bad borrower has net utility $\tilde{\mathcal{R}}$:

$$\min_{\{\tilde{x},\tilde{R}_b^S,\tilde{R}_b^F,\tilde{\mathcal{A}}\}} \mathcal{L}(\tilde{\mathcal{R}}) = -[\tilde{x}[q(R-\tilde{R}_b^S) + (1-q)(-\tilde{R}_b^F) - I] + \tilde{\mathcal{A}}]$$

s.t.

$$\tilde{x}[q\tilde{R}_b^S + (1-q)\tilde{R}_b^F] - \tilde{\mathcal{A}} \geqslant \tilde{\mathcal{R}},$$

where the notation mimics that just employed. And so

$$\begin{aligned}\mathcal{L}(\tilde{\mathcal{R}}) &= -\tilde{x}(qR - I) + \tilde{\mathcal{R}} \\ &= \tilde{\mathcal{R}}\end{aligned}$$

at the optimum (since $qR < I$).

The next program is the same as that for the low-information-intensity optimum except that (i) the breakeven condition is tightened by $(1-\alpha)\tilde{\mathcal{R}}$, and (ii) the mimicking condition is relaxed by $\tilde{\mathcal{R}}$:

$$\max_{\{x,\tilde{\mathcal{R}}\}} U_b(c)$$

s.t.

$$\alpha U_l(c) - (1-\alpha)\tilde{\mathcal{R}} \geqslant 0,$$

$$\tilde{U}_b(c) \leqslant \tilde{\mathcal{R}}.$$

By the same reasoning as for the low-information-intensity program, we can content ourselves with contractual terms c specifying $R_b^F = 0$. Then one can solve this program with respect to $(xR_b^S, x, \mathcal{A})$ rather than $(x, R_b^S, \mathcal{A})$ (it is a bit simpler) and show that

$$\mathcal{A} = A$$

and

$$\text{either } qR_b^S = A \text{ or } \tilde{\mathcal{R}} > 0.$$

In sum, the good borrower can either leave no rent to the bad borrower and set

$$R_b^S = \frac{A}{q}$$

as in the separating allocation; or she can set $\tilde{\mathcal{R}} > 0$ and then R_b^S is determined by the investors' breakeven constraint:

$$\alpha[p(R - R_b^S) - (I - A)] + (1-\alpha)[-\mathcal{L}(\tilde{\mathcal{R}})] = 0,$$

where

$$\mathcal{L}(\tilde{\mathcal{R}}) = \tilde{\mathcal{R}} = qR_b^S - A.$$

And so

$$pR - I + A = \left[p + \frac{1-\alpha}{\alpha}q\right]R_b^S - \frac{1-\alpha}{\alpha}A.$$

She then gets a higher utility (whether she is a good or bad borrower) than in the separating equilibrium.

6.10 Exercises

Exercise 6.1 (privately known private benefit and market breakdown). Section 6.2 illustrated the possibility of market breakdown without the possibility of signaling. This exercise supplies another illustration. Let us consider the fixed-investment model of Section 3.2 and assume that *only the borrower knows the private benefit associated with misbehavior.* When the borrower has private information about this parameter, lenders are concerned that this private benefit might be high and induce the borrower to misbehave. In the parlance of information economics, the "bad types" are the types of borrower with high private benefit. We study the case of two possible levels of private benefit (see Exercise 6.2 for an extension to a continuum of possible types). The borrower wants to finance a fixed-size project costing I, and, for simplicity, has no equity ($A = 0$). The project yields R (success) or 0 (failure). The probability of success is p_H or p_L, depending on whether the borrower works or shirks, with $\Delta p \equiv p_H - p_L > 0$. There is no private benefit when working. The private benefit B enjoyed by the borrower when shirking is either $B_L > 0$ or $B_H > B_L$. The borrower will be labeled a "good borrower" when $B = B_L$ and a "bad borrower" when $B = B_H$. At the date of contracting, the borrower knows the level of her private benefit, while the capital market puts (common knowledge) probabilities α that the borrower is a good borrower and $1-\alpha$ that she is a bad borrower. All other parameters are common knowledge between the borrower and the lenders.

To make things interesting, let us assume that under asymmetric information, the lenders are uncertain about whether the project should be funded:

$$p_H\left(R - \frac{B_H}{\Delta p}\right) < I < p_H\left(R - \frac{B_L}{\Delta p}\right). \tag{1}$$

Assume that investors cannot break even if the borrower shirks:

$$p_L R < I. \tag{2}$$

(i) Note that the investor cannot finance only good borrowers. Assume that the entrepreneur receives no reward in the case of failure (this is indeed optimal); consider the effect of rewards R_b in the case of success that are (a) smaller than $B_L/\Delta p$, (b) larger than $B_H/\Delta p$, (c) between these two values.

(ii) Show that there exists α^*, $0 < \alpha^* < 1$, such that

- no financing occurs if $\alpha < \alpha^*$,
- financing is an equilibrium if $\alpha \geqslant \alpha^*$.

(iii) Describe the "cross-subsidies" between types that occur when borrowing is feasible.

Exercise 6.2 (more on pooling in credit markets). Consider the model of Exercise 6.1, in which the borrower has private information about her benefit of misbehaving, except that the borrower's type is drawn from a continuous distribution instead of a binary one. We will also assume that there is a monopoly lender, who makes a credit offer to the borrower. The borrower has no equity ($A = 0$).

Only the borrower knows the private benefit B of misbehaving. The lender only knows that this private benefit is drawn from an *ex ante* cumulative distribution $H(B)$ on an interval $[0, \bar{B}]$ (so, $H(0) = 0$, $H(\bar{B}) = 1$). (Alternatively, one can imagine that lenders face a population of borrowers with characteristic B distributed according to distribution H, and are unable to tell different types of borrower apart in their credit analysis.) The lender knows all other parameters. For a loan agreement specifying share R_b for the borrower in the case of success, and 0 in the case of failure, show that the lender's expected profit is

$$U_l = H((\Delta p)R_b)p_H(R - R_b) + [1 - H((\Delta p)R_b)]p_L(R - R_b) - I.$$

Show that

- the proportion of "high-quality borrowers" (that is, of borrowers who behave) is endogenous and increases with R_b;[78]
- adverse selection reduces the quality of lending (if lending occurs, which as we will see cannot be taken for granted);
- there is an externality among different types of borrower, in that the low-quality types (B large) force the lender to charge an interest rate that generates strictly positive profit on high-quality types (those with small B);
- the credit market may "break down," that is, it may be the case that no credit is extended at all even though the borrower may be creditworthy (that is, have a low private benefit). To illustrate this, suppose that $p_L = 0$ and H is uniform ($H(B) = B/\bar{B}$). Show that if
$$\frac{p_H^2}{\bar{B}}\frac{R^2}{4} < I$$
(which is the case for $\bar{B}$ large enough), no loan agreement can enable the lender to recoup on average his investment.

Exercise 6.3 (reputational capital). Consider the fixed-investment model. All parameters are common knowledge between the borrower and the investors, except the private benefit which is known only to the borrower. The private benefit is equal to B with probability $1 - \alpha$ and to b with probability α, where $B > b > 0$.

78. In this model, the loan agreement attracts all types of borrowers if it attracts any type willing to behave. It is easy to find variants of the model in which this is not the case and an increase in R_b attracts higher-quality borrowers, where "higher-quality" refers to an *ex ante* selection effect and not only to an *ex post* behavior like here.

(i) Consider first the one-period adverse-selection problem. Suppose that the borrower has assets $A > 0$ such that

$$p_{\mathrm{H}}\left(R - \frac{b}{\Delta p}\right) > I - A > \max\left[p_{\mathrm{H}}\left(R - \frac{B}{\Delta p}\right), p_{\mathrm{L}}R\right].$$

Show that the project receives funding if and only if

$$(p_{\mathrm{H}} - (1-\alpha)\Delta p)\left(R - \frac{b}{\Delta p}\right) \geqslant I - A.$$

(ii) Suppose now that there are two periods ($t = 1, 2$). The second period is described as in question (i), except that the belief $\tilde{\alpha}$ at date 2 is the posterior belief updated from the prior belief α, and that the borrower has cash A only if she has been successful at date 1 (and has 0 and is not funded if she has been unsuccessful). So, suppose that the first-period project is funded and that the borrower receives at the end of date 1 a reward A when successful and 0 when unsuccessful. The first-period funding is project finance and does not specify any funding for the second project. Suppose for notational simplicity that the private benefit is the same (B or b) in period 1 and in period 2. Let Δp_1 denote the increase in the probability of success when diligent in period 1. Assume that

$$\begin{aligned} b &< (\Delta p_1)A < B \\ &< (\Delta p_1)\left[p_{\mathrm{L}}\left(R - \frac{I - A}{p_{\mathrm{H}} - (1-\alpha_{\mathrm{S}})\Delta p}\right) + B\right] \end{aligned}$$

and

$$\begin{aligned} &(p_{\mathrm{H}} - (1-\alpha)\Delta p)\left(R - \frac{b}{\Delta p}\right) \\ &\qquad < I - A \\ &\qquad < (p_{\mathrm{H}} - (1-\alpha_{\mathrm{S}})\Delta p)\left(R - \frac{b}{\Delta p}\right), \end{aligned}$$

where $1 - \alpha_{\mathrm{S}} \equiv (1-\alpha)p_{\mathrm{L}}/((1-\alpha)p_{\mathrm{L}} + \alpha p_{\mathrm{H}})$.

A "pooling equilibrium" is an equilibrium in which the borrower's first-period effort is independent of her private benefit. A "separating equilibrium" is (here) an equilibrium in which the b-type works and the B-type shirks in period 1. A "semiseparating" equilibrium is (here) an equilibrium in which in period 1 the b-type works and the B-type randomizes between working and shirking.

- Show that there exists no pooling and no separating equilibrium.
- Compute the semiseparating equilibrium. Does this model formalize the notion of reputational capital?

Exercise 6.4 (equilibrium uniqueness in the suboptimal risk-sharing model). In the suboptimal risk-sharing model of Application 8, prove the claim made in the text that the low-information-intensity optimum depicted by {S, B} in Figure 6.3 is interim efficient if and only if the belief that the borrower is a good borrower lies below some threshold α^*, $0 < \alpha^* < 1$. (Verify the weak-monotonic-profit condition in the supplementary section, and show that α^* is in the interior of the interval $[0, 1]$.)

Exercise 6.5 (asymmetric information about the value of assets in place and the negative stock price reaction to equity offerings with a continuum of types). Consider the privately-known-prospects model of Application 2 in Section 6.2.2, but with a continuum of types. The entrepreneur already owns a project, which with probability p yields profit R and probability $1 - p$ profit 0. The probability p is private information of the borrower. From the point of view of the investors, p is drawn from cumulative distribution $F(p)$ with continuous density $f(p) > 0$ on some interval $[\underline{p}, \bar{p}]$. Assume that the distribution has monotone hazard rates:

$$\frac{f(p)}{F(p)} \quad \text{is decreasing in } p$$

and

$$\frac{f(p)}{1 - F(p)} \quad \text{is increasing in } p.$$

(This assumption, which is satisfied by most usual distributions, is known to imply that the truncated means $m^-(p)$ and $m^+(p)$ have slope less than 1:

$$0 < (m^-(p))' \equiv \frac{\mathrm{d}}{\mathrm{d}p}[E(\tilde{p} \mid \tilde{p} \leqslant p)] \leqslant 1$$

and

$$0 < (m^+(p))' \equiv \frac{\mathrm{d}}{\mathrm{d}p}[E(\tilde{p} \mid \tilde{p} \geqslant p)] \leqslant 1$$

(see, for example, An 1998).)

The model is otherwise as in Section 6.2.2. A seasoned offering may be motivated by a profitable deepening investment: at cost I, the probability of success can be raised by an amount τ such that

$$\tau R > I$$

(of course, we need to assume that $\bar{p} + \tau \leqslant 1$). The entrepreneur has no cash on hand, is risk neutral, and is protected by limited liability. The investors are risk neutral and demand a rate of return equal to 0.

(i) Show that in any equilibrium, only types $p \leqslant p^*$, for some cutoff p^*, raise funds and finance the deepening investment.

(ii) Show that $p^* > \underline{p}$ and that if $p^* < \bar{p}$, then

$$\frac{\tau R}{I} = \frac{p^* + \tau}{m^-(p^*) + \tau}.$$

Show that if the benefits from investment are "not too large," in that

$$\frac{\tau R}{I} < \frac{\bar{p} + \tau}{E[p] + \tau},$$

then indeed $p^* < \bar{p}$.

Show that if there are multiple equilibria, the one with the highest cutoff p^* Pareto-dominates (is better for all types than) the other equilibria.

(iii) Is there a negative stock price reaction upon announcement of an equity issue?

(iv) Focusing on an interior Pareto-dominant equilibrium, show that, when τ increases, the volume of equity issues increases.

Exercise 6.6 (adverse selection and ratings). A borrower has assets A and must find financing for a fixed investment $I > A$. As usual, the project yields R (success) or 0 (failure). The borrower is protected by limited liability. The probability of success is p_{H} or p_{L}, depending on whether the borrower works or shirks, with $\Delta p \equiv p_{\mathrm{H}} - p_{\mathrm{L}} > 0$. There is no private benefit when working. The private benefit enjoyed by the borrower when shirking is either b (with probability α) or B (with probability $1 - \alpha$). At the date of contracting, the borrower knows her private benefit, but the market (which is risk neutral and charges a 0 average rate of interest) does not know it. Assume that $p_{\mathrm{L}}R + B < I$ (the project is always inefficient if the borrower shirks) and that

$$p_{\mathrm{H}}\left(R - \frac{B}{\Delta p}\right) < I - A < p_{\mathrm{H}}\left(R - \frac{b}{\Delta p}\right) \qquad (1)$$

and

$$[\alpha p_{\mathrm{H}} + (1-\alpha)p_{\mathrm{L}}]\left[R - \frac{b}{\Delta p}\right] < I - A. \qquad (2)$$

(i) Interpret conditions (1) and (2) and show that there is no lending in equilibrium.

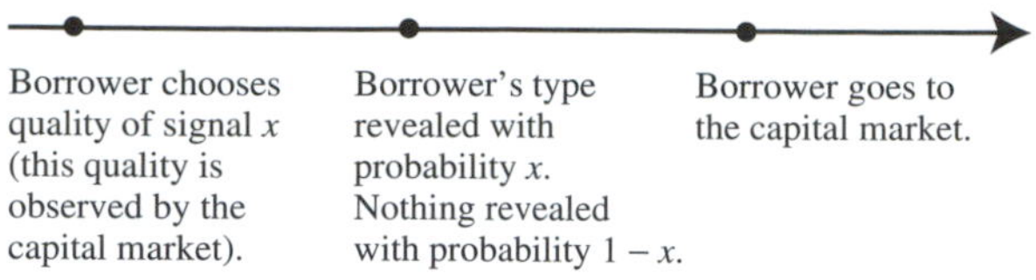

Figure 6.5

(ii) Suppose now that the borrower can at cost $r(x) = rx$ (which is paid from the cash endowment A) purchase a signal with quality $x \in [0, 1]$. (This quality can be interpreted as the reputation or the number of rating agencies that the borrower contracts with.) With probability x, the signal reveals the borrower's type (b or B) perfectly; with probability $1 - x$, the signal reveals nothing. The financial market observes both the quality x of the signal chosen by the borrower and the outcome of the signal (full or no information). The borrower then offers a contract that gives the borrower R_{b} and the lenders $R - R_{\mathrm{b}}$ in the case of success (so, a contract is the choice of an $R_{\mathrm{b}} \in [0, R]$). The timing is summarized in Figure 6.5.

Look for a pure strategy, *separating* equilibrium, that is, an equilibrium in which the two types pick different signal qualities.[79]

- Argue that the bad borrower (borrower B) does not purchase a signal in a separating equilibrium.
- Argue that the good borrower (borrower b) borrows under the same conditions regardless of the signal's realization, in a separating equilibrium.
- Show that the good borrower chooses signal quality $x \in (0, 1)$ given by

$$A = x(A - rx) + (1-x)\left[p_{\mathrm{L}}\left(R - \frac{I - A + rx}{p_{\mathrm{H}}}\right) + B\right].$$

- Show that this separating equilibrium exists only if r is "not too large."

Exercise 6.7 (endogenous communication among lenders). Padilla and Pagano (1997) and others have observed that information sharing about creditworthiness is widespread among lenders (banks,

79. One will assume that if the signal reveals the borrower's type, the investors put probability 1 on this type, even when they put weight 0 on the corresponding type after observing the quality of the signal.

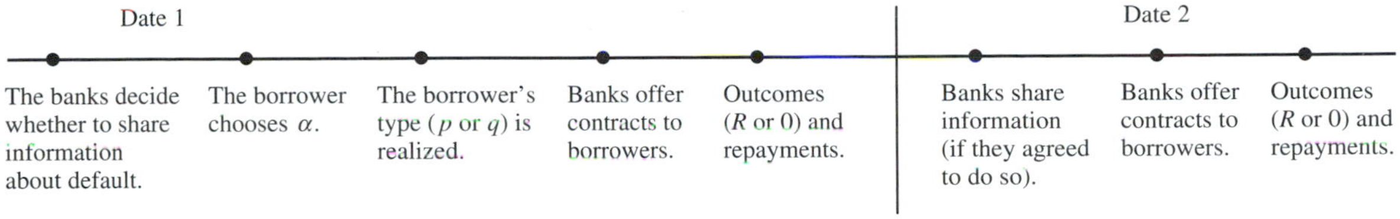

Figure 6.6

suppliers, etc.). For example, Dun & Bradstreet Information Services, one of the leading rating agencies, collects information from thousands of banks. Similarly, over 600,000 suppliers communicate information about delays and defaults by their customers; and credit bureaux centralize information about the consumer credit markets.

Padilla and Pagano (see also Pagano and Jappelli (1993) and the references therein) argue that information sharing has both costs and benefits for the banks. By sharing information, they reduce their differentiation and compete more with each other. But this competition protects their borrowers' investment and therefore enhances opportunities for lending. In a sense, the "tax rate" (the markup that banks can charge borrowers) decreases but the "tax base" (the creditworthiness of borrowers) expands. This exercise builds on the Padilla–Pagano model.

There are two periods ($t = 1, 2$). The discount factor between the two periods is δ. A risk-neutral borrower protected by limited liability has no cash on hand ($A = 0$). Each period, the borrower has a project with investment cost I. The project delivers at the end of the period R or 0. There is no moral hazard. The probability of success is p if the entrepreneur is talented (which has probability α), and q if she is not (which has probability $1 - \alpha$). We will assume that the market rate of interest in the economy is 0, that the lenders are risk neutral, and that only the good type is creditworthy:

$$pR > I > qR.$$

The date-1 and date-2 projects (if financed) are correlated and yield the same profit (they both succeed or both fail).

There are n towns. Each town has one bank and one borrower. The "local bank" has local expertise and thereby learns the local borrower's type; the other banks, the "foreign banks," learn nothing (and therefore have beliefs α that the entrepreneur is talented) at date 1. At date 2, the foreign banks learn

- only whether the borrower was financed at date 1, if there is no information sharing among banks;
- whether the borrower was financed at date 1 and whether she repaid (i.e., whether she was successful), if there is information sharing about riskiness.

In other words, information sharing is feasible on hard data (repayments), but not on soft data (assessment of ability).

Padilla and Pagano add two twists to the model. First, banks decide *ex ante* whether they will communicate information about default and they make this decision public. Second, the borrower's type may be endogenous (in which it refers more to an investment in the projects or industry than in "pure talent"): at increasing and convex cost $C(\alpha)$ $\{C' > 0,$ $C'' > 0,$ $C(0) = 0,$ $C'(0) = 0,$ $C'(1) = \infty\}$, the borrower develops a p project with probability α and a q project with probability $1 - \alpha$. C can be viewed as an investment cost and represents a nonmonetary cost borne by the borrower.

Contracts between banks and borrowers are *short-term* contracts. These contracts just specify a payment R_b for the borrower in the case of success during the period (and 0 in the case of failure). Furthermore, in each period, banks simultaneously make take-it-or-leave-it offers to borrowers. And at date 2, the incumbent bank (the bank that has lent at date 1) makes its offer after the other banks.

The timing is summarized in Figure 6.6.

(i) Suppose first that the probability α of being a p-type is exogenous (there is no borrower investment), that $[\alpha p+(1-\alpha)q]R-I+\delta(\alpha p+(1-\alpha)q)(R-I) < 0$, and that $qR - I + \delta q(R - I) < 0$. Show that the banks prefer not to share information.

(ii) Next, suppose that the borrower chooses α. Assuming that the two assumptions made in (i) still hold in the relevant range of αs (for example, $\alpha \in [0, \bar{\alpha}]$, where $\bar{\alpha}$ satisfies the conditions), show that the banks choose to share information.

Exercise 6.8 (pecking order with variable investment). Consider the privately-known-prospects model with risk neutrality and variable investment. For investment I, the realized income is either $R^{S}I$ (in the case of success) or $R^{F}I$ (in the case of failure), where $R^{S} > R^{F} \geqslant 0$. A good borrower has probability p_{H} of success when working and p_{L} when shirking; similarly, a bad borrower has probability q_{H} of success when working and q_{L} when shirking, where $p_{H} - p_{L} = \Delta p = q_{H} - q_{L}$, for simplicity. The entrepreneur's private benefit is 0 when working and BI when shirking. The entrepreneur is risk neutral and protected by limited liability; the investors are risk neutral and demand a rate of return equal to 0.

(i) Let $\tilde{U}_{b}^{SI}$ denote the bad borrower's gross utility under symmetric information.[80] Consider the problem of maximizing the good borrower's utility subject to the investors' breaking even on that borrower, to the mimicking constraint that the good borrower's terms not be preferred by the bad borrower to her symmetric-information terms, and to the no-shirking constraint. Let $\{R_{b}^{S}, R_{b}^{F}\}$ denote the (nonnegative) rewards of the good borrower in the cases of success and failure. Write the separating program.

(ii) Show that $R_{b}^{F} = 0$.

(iii) (Only if you have read the supplementary section.) Show that the separating outcome is the only perfect Bayesian equilibrium of the issuance game if and only if $\alpha \leqslant \alpha^{*}$ for some threshold α^{*}.

Exercise 6.9 (herd behavior). It is often argued that the managers of industrial companies, banks, or mutual funds are prone to herd.[81] They engage in similar investments with sometimes little evidence that their strategy is the most profitable. An economic agent may indeed select a popular strategy against her own information that another strategy may be more profitable. A number of contributions have demonstrated that herding behavior may actually be individually rational even though it is often collectively inefficient. The literature on herding behavior starts with the seminal contributions of Banerjee (1992), Bikhchandani et al. (1992), Scharfstein and Stein (1990), and Welch (1992); see Bikhchandani and Sharma (2001) for a survey of applications of this literature to financial markets.

There are several variants of the following basic argument. Consider first a sequence of agents $i = 1, 2, \ldots$ choosing sequentially between strategies A and B. Agents receive their own signals; they observe previous decisions but not the others' signals. Suppose that agents 1 and 2 have, on the basis of their own information, selected A. Agent 3, observing the first two choices, may well then select strategy A even if her own signal favors the choice of B. Agent 4, not knowing agent 3's motivation to choose A, may then also choose strategy A even if his own signal points toward the choice of B. And so forth. It may therefore be the case that all agents choose A, even though the cumulative evidence, if it were shared, would indicate that B is the best choice.

The literature also analyzes herd behavior in situations in which agents have principals (that is, they are not full residual claimants for the consequences of their choices). In particular, such agents may adopt herd behaviors because of *reputational concerns* (see Chapter 7). Suppose, for instance, that a manager's job is rather secure; herding with the managers of other firms is then likely to be attractive to the manager: if the strategy fails, the manager has the excuse that other managers also got it wrong ("it was hard to predict"). Choosing an unpopular strategy, even if one's information points in that direction, is risky, as there will be no excuse if it fails. The literature on herd behavior has also investigated the use of benchmarking by principals in *explicit incentives* (compensation contracts) rather than in implicit ones (career concerns).

Let us build an example of herding behavior in the context of the privately-known-prospects model of Section 6.2. There are two entrepreneurs, $i = 1, 2$, operating in different markets, but whose optimal

80. This utility was derived in Section 3.4.2. It is equal to

$$\left[1 + \frac{q_{H}R - 1}{1 - q_{H}(R - B/\Delta p)}\right]A$$

if $q_{H}R \geqslant 1$, and to A otherwise.

81. One of the first empirical papers on herding behavior is Lakonishok et al. (1992). The large empirical literature on the topic includes Chevalier and Ellison (1999).

strategy is correlated. There are two periods, $t = 1, 2$. Entrepreneur i can raise funds only at date $t = i$ (so they secure funding sequentially). A project yields R when it succeeds and 0 when it fails. The entrepreneurs are risk neutral and protected by limited liability; the investors are risk neutral and demand a rate of return equal to 0. The entrepreneurs have no net worth or cash initially.

The two entrepreneurs each have to choose between strategy A and B. Strategies differ in their probability of success. A borrowing contract with investors specifies both the managerial compensation R_b in the case of success (and 0 in the case of failure) and the strategy that the entrepreneur will select.[82] Crucially, entrepreneur 2 and her potential investors observe the date-1 financing contract for entrepreneur 1. Entrepreneurs, but not investors, learn the state of nature.

Consider the following stochastic structure.

Unfavorable environment (probability $1 - \alpha$*).* The probabilities of success are, with equal probabilities, $(q, 0)$ for one project and $(0, q)$ for the other, where the first element is entrepreneur 1's probability of success and the second entrepreneur 2's. So entrepreneurs necessarily choose different projects if they apply for funding.

Favorable environment (probability α*).* With probability θ, the best project is the same for both and has probability of success p; the worst project for both has probability of success r, where

$$p > \max\{q, r\}.$$

With probability $1 - \theta$, the two entrepreneurs' best strategies differ: the probabilities of success are (p, r) and (r, p), respectively, for entrepreneur 1's and entrepreneur 2's best strategy (which are A or B with equal probabilities). Thus θ is the probability of correlation of the best strategies in a favorable environment; this probability is equal to 0 in the unfavorable environment.

Let $m \equiv \alpha p + (1 - \alpha)q$ and assume that

$$qR > I.$$

Show that funding and herding (with probability $\alpha(1 - \theta)$, entrepreneur 2 chooses entrepreneur 1's best strategy even though it does not maximize her probability of success) is an equilibrium behavior as long as

$$r\left[R - \frac{I}{\theta p + (1 - \theta)r}\right] \geqslant p\left[R - \frac{I}{q}\right].$$

Note that entrepreneur 2 is on average worse off than in an hypothetical situation in which investors did not observe the strategy of entrepreneur 1 (or that in which the optimal strategies were uncorrelated).

82. One will assume therefore that the first entrepreneur cannot condition her financing contract on the later choice of strategy by the second entrepreneur.

Exercise 6.10 (maturity structure). At date 0 the entrepreneur has cash on hand A and needs to finance an investment of fixed size I. At date 1, a deterministic income r accrues; a liquidity shock must be met in order for the firm to continue. Liquidation yields nothing. The probability of success in the case of continuation depends on a date-1 effort: for a good borrower, this probability is p_H or p_L depending on whether she behaves (no private benefit) or misbehaves (private benefit B); similarly, for a bad borrower, it is q_H or q_L. We assume that

$$p_H - p_L = q_H - q_L = \Delta p,$$

and so the incentive compatibility constraint in the case of continuation is the same for both types of borrower:

$$(p_H - p_L)R_b = (q_H - q_L)R_b = (\Delta p)R_b \geqslant B,$$

where R_b is the borrower's reward in the case of success.

The borrower knows at the date of contracting whether she is a "p-type" or a "q-type." Let

$$\rho_0^G \equiv p_H\left(R - \frac{B}{\Delta p}\right) \quad \text{and} \quad \rho_0^B = q_H\left(R - \frac{B}{\Delta p}\right)$$

denote the date-1 pledgeable incomes for the good and bad types.

The liquidity shock is deterministic and equal to ρ. Information is asymmetric at date 0, but the capital market learns the borrower's type perfectly at date 1, before the liquidity shock has to be met. Assume that

$$\rho_0^G > \rho > \rho_0^B.$$

Suppose further that under symmetric information only the good borrower is creditworthy (provided that she is incentivized to behave).

Assume that $r < I - A < r + [\rho_0^G - \rho]$. Show that the good borrower can costlessly signal her type.

References

Aghion, P. and P. Bolton. 1987. Contracts as a barrier to entry. *American Economic Review* 77:388–401.

Akerlof, G. 1970. The market for lemons, qualitative uncertainty and the market mechanism. *Quarterly Journal of Economics* 84:488–500.

Allen, F. and G. Faulhaber. 1989. Signalling by underpricing in the IPO market. *Journal of Financial Economics* 23:303–323.

Allen, F. and D. Gale. 1992. Measurement distortion and missing contingencies in optimal contracts. *Economic Theory* 2:1–26.

Allen, F. and R. Michaely. 1995. Dividend policy. In *Handbooks of Operations Research and Management Science: Finance* (ed. R. Jarrow, V. Maksimovic, and W. Ziemba). Amsterdam: North-Holland.

——. 2004. Payout policy. In *Corporate Finance: Handbook of the Economics of Finance* (ed. G. Constantinides, M. Harris, and R. Stulz), pp. 337–429. Amsterdam: North-Holland.

Allen, F., A. Bernardo, and I. Welch. 2000. A theory of dividends based on tax clienteles. *Journal of Finance* 55:2499–2536.

An, M. 1998. Logconcavity versus logconvexity: a complete characterization. *Journal of Economic Theory* 80:350–369.

Araujo, A., H. Moreira, and M. Tsuchida. 2004. Do dividends signal more earnings? Getulio Vargas Foundation, RJ.

Banerjee, A. 1992. A simple model of herd behavior. *Quarterly Journal of Economics* 107:797–817.

Banks, J. and J. Sobel. 1987. Equilibrium selection in signaling games. *Econometrica* 55:647–662.

Baron, D. 1982. A model of demand for investment banking advising and distribution services for new issues. *Journal of Finance* 37:955–976.

Benartzi, S., R. Michaely, and R. Thaler. 1997. Do changes in dividends signal the future or the past? *Journal of Finance* 52:1007–1034.

Benveniste, L. and P. Spindt. 1989. How investment bankers determine the offer price and allocation of new issues. *Journal of Financial Economics* 24:343–361.

Benveniste, L. and W. Wilhelm. 1990. A comparative analysis of IPO proceeds under alternative regulatory environments. *Journal of Financial Economics* 28:173–207.

Berger, A. and G. Udell. 1990. Collateral, loan quality and bank risk. *Journal of Monetary Economics* 25:21–42.

Bernheim, D. 1991. Tax policy and the dividend puzzle. *RAND Journal of Economics* 22:455–476.

Bernheim, D. and A. Wantz. 1995. A tax-based test of the dividend signaling hypothesis. *American Economic Review* 85:532–551.

Besanko, D. and A. Thakor. 1987. Collateral and rationing sorting equilibria in monopolistic and competitive credit markets. *International Economic Review* 28:671–689.

Bester, H. 1985. Screening vs rationing in credit markets with imperfect information. *American Economic Review* 75:850–855.

——. 1987. The role of collateral in credit markets with imperfect information. *European Economic Review* 31:887–899.

Bhattacharya, S. 1979. Imperfect information, dividend policy and "the bird in the hand" fallacy. *Bell Journal of Economics* 10:259–270.

Bhattacharya, S. and G. Chiesa. 1995. Proprietary information, financial intermediation and research incentives. *Journal of Financial Intermediation* 4:328–357.

Bhattacharya, S. and J. Ritter. 1983. Innovation and communication: signalling with partial disclosure. *Review of Economic Studies* 50:331–346.

Biais, B., P. Bossaerts, and J. C. Rochet. 2002. An optimal IPO mechanism. *Review of Economic Studies* 69:117–146.

Bikhchandani, S. and S. Sharma. 2001. Herd behavior in financial markets. *IMF Staff Papers* 47:279–310.

Bikhchandani, S., D. Hirshleifer, and I. Welch. 1992. A theory of fads, fashion, custom, and cultural change as informational cascades. *Journal of Political Economy* 100: 992–1026.

Boot, A. and A. Thakor. 1993. Security design. *Journal of Finance* 48:1349–1378.

Booth, J. 1992. Contract costs, bank loans, and the cross-monitoring hypothesis. *Journal of Financial Economics* 31: 25–41.

Brealey, R. and S. Myers. 1988. *Principles of Corporate Finance*, 3rd edn. New York: McGraw-Hill.

Broecker, T. 1990. Credit-worthiness tests and interbank competition. *Econometrica* 58:429–452.

Campbell, T. 1979. Optimal investment financing decisions and the value of confidentiality. *Journal of Financial and Quantitative Analysis* 14:913–924.

Campbell, T. and W. Kracaw. 1980. Information production, market signalling, and the theory of financial intermediation. *Journal of Finance* 35:863–882.

Chan, Y. and G. Kanatas. 1985. Asymmetric valuations and the role of collateral in loan agreements. *Journal of Money, Credit and Banking* 17:84–95.

Chemmanur, T. and P. Fulghieri. 1994. Reputation, renegotiation, and the choice between bank loans and publicly traded debt. *Review of Financial Studies* 7:475–506.

——. 1999. A theory of the going-public decision. *Review of Financial Studies* 12:249–279.

Chevalier, J. and G. Ellison. 1999. Career concerns of mutual fund managers. *Quarterly Journal of Economics* 114:389–432.

Coco, G. 2000. On the use of collateral. *Journal of Economic Surveys* 14:191–214.

Demange, G. and G. Laroque. 1995. Private information and the design of securities. *Journal of Economic Theory* 65: 233–257.

DeMarzo, P. M. and D. Duffie. 1999. A liquidity-based model of security design. *Econometrica* 67:65–99.

De Meza, D. and D. Webb. 1987. Too much investment: a problem of asymmetric information. *Quarterly Journal of Economics* 102:281–292.

Dewatripont, M. and J. Tirole. 2005. Modes of communication. *Journal of Political Economy*, in press.

Diamond, D. 1991. Debt maturity structure and liquidity risk. *Quarterly Journal of Economics* 106:709–737.

——. 1993. Bank loan maturity and priority when borrowers can refinance. In *Capital Markets and Financial Intermediation* (ed. C. Mayer and X. Vives), pp. 12–35. Cambridge University Press.

Dobbs, R. and W. Rehm. 2005. The value of share buybacks. *McKinsey Quarterly* 3:55–61.

Dybvig, P. and J. Zender. 1991. Capital structure and dividend irrelevance with asymmetric information. *Review of Financial Studies* 4:201–219.

Fishman, M. and K. Hagerty. 2003. Mandatory versus voluntary disclosure in markets with informed and uninformed customers. *Journal of Law, Economics, & Organization* 19: 45–63.

Frank, M. Z. and V. K. Goyal. 2003. Testing the pecking order of capital structure. *Journal of Financial Economics* 67: 217–248.

Fudenberg, D. and J. Tirole. 1991. *Game Theory*. Cambridge, MA: MIT Press.

Gertner, R., R. Gibbons, and D. Scharfstein. 1988. Simultaneous signalling to the capital and product markets. *RAND Journal of Economics* 19:173–190.

Ghatak, M. and R. Kali. 2001. Financially interlinked business groups. *Journal of Economics & Management Strategy* 10:591–619.

Grinblatt, M. and C. Y. Hwang. 1989. Signalling and the pricing of new issues. *Journal of Finance* 44:393–420.

Grossman, S. 1980. The role of warranties and private disclosure about product quality. *Journal of Law and Economics* 24:461–483.

Grossman, S. and O. Hart. 1980. Disclosure laws and takeover bids. *Journal of Finance* 35:323–334.

Harris, M. and A. Raviv. 1992. Financial contracting theory. In *Advances in Economic Theory, Sixth World Congress* (ed. J. J. Laffont). Cambridge University Press.

Hart, O. 1985. A comment on Stiglitz and Weiss. Mimeo, MIT.

Hausch, D. and J. Seward. 1993. Signaling with dividends and share repurchases: a choice between deterministic and stochastic cash disbursements. *Review of Financial Studies* 6:121–154.

Healy, P. and K. Palepu. 1988. Earnings information conveyed by dividend initiations and omissions. *Journal of Financial Economics* 21:149–175.

Hellwig, M. 1987. Some recent developments in the theory of competition in markets with adverse selection. *European Econonomic Review* 31:319–325.

Hermalin, B. 2002. Adverse selection, short-term contracting and the underprovision of on-the-job training. *Contributions to Economic Analysis & Policy*, Bepress, 1(1), article 5.

Ibbotson, R. 1975. Price performance of common stock new issues. *Journal of Financial Economics* 2:235–272.

Ibbotson, R. and J. Jaffe. 1975. "Hot issue" markets. *Journal of Finance* 30:1027–1042.

Inderst, R. and H. Müller. 2005a. A lender-based theory of collateral. Mimeo, London School of Economics and New York University.

——. 2005b. Credit risk analysis and security design. *Journal of Finance*, in press.

John, K. and J. Williams. 1985. Dividends, dilution, and taxes: a signalling equilibrium. *Journal of Finance* 40: 1053–1070.

Jullien, B. 2000. Participation constraints in adverse selection models. *Journal of Economic Theory* 93:1–47.

Karpoff, J. and S. Thorley. 1992. Dividend announcements. In *The New Palgrave Dictionary of Money and Finance* (ed. P. Newman, M. Milgate, and J. Eatwell). London: Macmillan.

Laffont, J. J. and J. Tirole. 1986. Using cost observation to regulate firms. *Journal of Political Economy* 94:614–641.

Lakonishok, J., A. Shleifer, and R. Vishny. 1992. The impact of institutional trading on stock prices. *Journal of Financial Economics* 32:23–43.

Landier, A. and D. Thesmar. 2004. Financial contracting with optimistic entrepreneurs: theory and evidence. Mimeo, University of Chicago and ENSAE.

Leland, H. and D. Pyle. 1977. Information asymmetries, financial structure and financial intermediaries. *Journal of Finance* 32:371–387.

Lerner, J. and J. Tirole. 2005. A model of forum shopping. Mimeo, Harvard University and IDEI, University of Toulouse.

Lowry, M. and S. Shu. 2002. Litigation risk and IPO underpricing. *Journal of Financial Economics* 65:309–335.

Marsh, P. 1979. Equity rights issues and the efficiency of the UK stock market. *Journal of Finance* 34:839–862.

Maskin, E. and J. Tirole. 1990. The principal–agent relationship with an informed principal. I. The case of private values. *Econometrica* 58:379–410.

——. 1992. The principal–agent relationship with an informed principal. II. Common values. *Econometrica* 60: 1–42.

Megginson, W. and K. Weiss. 1991. Venture capitalist certification in initial public offerings. *Journal of Finance* 46: 879–903.

Michelacci, C. and J. Suarez. 2004. Incomplete wage posting. Mimeo, CEMFI, Madrid.

Milgrom, P. 1981. Good news and bad news: representation theorems and applications. *Bell Journal of Economics* 12: 380–391.

Milgrom, P. and J. Roberts. 1986. Relying on the information of interested parties. *RAND Journal of Economics* 17:18–32.

Milgrom, P. and R. Weber. 1982. A theory of auctions and competitive bidding. *Econometrica* 50:1089–1122.

Miller, M. and K. Rock. 1985. Dividend policy under asymmetric information. *Journal of Finance* 40:1031–1051.

Myers, S. 1984. The capital structure puzzle. *Journal of Finance* 39:573–592.

Myers, S. and N. Majluf. 1984. Corporate financing and investment decisions when firms have information that investors do not have. *Journal of Financial Economics* 13: 187–221.

Myerson, R. 1983. Mechanism design by an informed principal. *Econometrica* 51:1767–1797.

——. 1991. *Game Theory*. Cambridge, MA: Harvard University Press.

Nachman, D. and T. Noe. 1994. Optimal design of securities under asymmetric information. *Review of Financial Studies* 7:1–44.

Ofer, A. and A. Thakor. 1987. Theory of stock responses to alternative corporate cash disbursement methods: stock repurchases and dividends. *Journal of Finance* 42:365–394.

Okuno-Fujiwara, M., A. Postlewaite, and K. Suzumura. 1990. Strategic information revelation. *Review of Economic Studies* 57:25–47.

Osborne, M. and A. Rubinstein. 1994. *A Course in Game Theory*. Cambridge, MA: MIT Press.

Padilla, J. and M. Pagano. 1997. Endogenous communication among lenders and entrepreneurial incentives. *Review of Financial Studies* 10:205–236.

Pagano, M. and T. Jappelli. 1993. Information sharing in credit markets. *Journal of Finance* 48:1693–1718.

Poitevin, M. 1989. Financial signaling and the deep-pocket argument. *RAND Journal of Economics* 20:26–40.

Raviv, A. 1989. Alternative models of investment banking. In *Financial Markets and Incomplete Information* (ed. S. Bhattacharya and G. Constantinides), Volume 2, pp. 225–232. Lanham, MD: Rowman and Littlefield.

Ritter, J. 1984. The "hot issue" market of 1980. *Journal of Business* 57:215–240.

——. 2003. Investment banking and securities issuance. In *Handbook of the Economics of Finance* (ed. G. Constantinides, M. Harris, and R. Stulz). Amsterdam: North-Holland.

Rochet, J. C. and J. Tirole. 1996a. Controlling risk in payment systems. *Journal of Money, Credit and Banking* 28:733–762.

——. 1996b. Interbank lending and systemic risk. *Journal of Money, Credit and Banking* 28:832–862.

Rock, K. 1986. Why new issues are underpriced. *Journal of Financial Economics* 15:187–212.

Ross, S. 1977. The determination of financial structure: the incentive signalling approach. *Bell Journal of Economics* 8: 23–40.

Rothschild, M. and J. Stiglitz. 1976. Equilibrium in competitive insurance markets: an essay in the economics of imperfect information. *Quarterly Journal of Economics* 90: 629–650.

Scharfstein, D. and J. Stein. 1990. Herd behavior and investment. *American Economic Review* 80:465–479.

Smith, C. 1977. Alternative methods for raising capital: rights versus underwritten offerings. *Journal of Financial Economics* 5:273–307.

Spatt, C. and S. Srivastava. 1991. Pre-play communication, participation, restrictions, and efficiency in initial public offerings. *Journal of Financial Studies* 4:709–726.

Spence, M. 1974. *Market Signaling*. Cambridge, MA: Harvard University Press.

Stein, J. 1992. Convertible bonds as backdoor equity financing. *Journal of Financial Economics* 32:3–21.

Stiglitz, J. 1977. Monopoly, non-linear pricing and imperfect information: the insurance market. *Review of Economic Studies* 44:407–430.

Stiglitz, J. and A. Weiss. 1981. Credit rationing in markets with imperfect information. *American Economic Review* 71:393–410.

Subramanian, N., A. Chakraborty, and S. Sheikh. 2002. Performance incentives, performance pressure and executive turnover. Mimeo, Brandeis University.

Tirole, J. 1986. Hierarchies and bureaucracies. *Journal of Law, Economics, & Organization* 2:181–214.

Titnic, S. 1988. Anatomy of initial public offerings of common stock. *Journal of Finance* 443:789–822.

Welch, I. 1989. Seasoned offerings, imitation costs, and the underpricing of initial public offerings. *Journal of Finance* 44:421–450.

——. 1992. Sequential sales, learning, and cascades. *Journal of Finance* 47:695–732.

Wilson, C. 1977. A model of insurance markets with incomplete information. *Journal of Economic Theory* 16:167–207.

Yermack, D. 1997. Good timing: CEO stock option awards and company news announcements. *Journal of Finance* 52:449–476.

Yosha, O. 1995. Information disclosure costs and the choice of financing source. *Journal of Financial Intermediation* 4: 3–20.

Zhu, Y. 2004. Is IPO underpricing related to litigation risk? Evidence based on the Private Securities Litigation Reform Act of 1995. Mimeo, Michigan State University.

7

Topics: Product Markets and Earnings Manipulations

This chapter studies two underexplored but important topics in corporate finance. Section 7.1 puts the firm in its industrial context by adding the interactions with its competitors, suppliers, or clients. Needless to say, the interest is not in these interactions per se, which have been the focus of an enormous amount of literature in industrial organization, but rather in how corporate financing is affected by these interactions, and vice versa.

Section 7.2 looks at the topical issue of earnings manipulation.[1] The management's ability to garble signals received through creative accounting, timing of income recognition, and risk taking adds an extra degree of moral hazard into the managerial incentive problem. Incentive schemes, such as stock options or high-powered career concerns, that are meant to align managerial incentives with investors' interests and thus induce high performance also tend to invite management to game the incentive system.

7.1 Corporate Finance and Product Markets

We examine the interaction between corporate financing and industrial organization. A firm designing its funding level and structure (collateral, liquidity, diversification, control rights, and corporate governance, say) does so in the context of horizontal (competitors) and vertical (suppliers and customers) interactions.

Two broad questions then emerge.

(i) How do market characteristics affect corporate financing choices?

(ii) How do other firms react to a firm's financial structure? And does a firm want to alter its financial structure so as to affect the behavior of other firms? That is, can a firm use its financial structure so as to reduce product-market competition or to extract more favorable conditions from other parties in the vertical chain? For example, does leverage make a firm weak or strong against its competitors in the product market? Or can leverage be used to extract lower wages from a labor union or better terms from a supplier?[2]

We analyze these questions in sequence.

7.1.1 Impact of Competition on Financial Choices

7.1.1.1 Basics: Profit Destruction and Benchmarking Effects

Let us begin with two basic and opposite effects of competition on a firm's ability to obtain funding. First, competitive pressure reduces market power and profit, and thereby makes it more difficult for firms to receive financing. This profit-destruction effect is not specific to markets with credit rationing; that is, firms tend to be less keen on investing in the presence of rivals whether they have easy access to outside financing or not. At most, the profit-destruction effect exacerbates the lack of pledgeable income and the concomitant difficulty for the borrowers to raise funds. Second, the presence of competitors subject to similar demand and cost conditions facilitates the investors' control of the agency problem. In a nutshell, the competitors' performance brings about information that helps investors assess the circumstances under which their firm operated. This reduces the agency cost and thereby facilitates financing.

1. As discussed in Chapter 1 (see also the papers by Healy and Palepu, Lev, and Demski in the 2003 *Journal of Economic Perspectives* symposium on "Enron and conflicts of interests"), recent corporate scandals in the United States and in Europe have highlighted the pervasiveness and the scope of earnings manipulations.

2. See also Cestone (2000) for a survey of corporate financing and product-market competition.

(a) *Profit destruction.* Consider the profit-destruction effect first. A market is (potentially) served by a duopoly (the analysis generalizes straightforwardly to an arbitrary number of firms): firms $i = 1, 2$. Each of these firms must develop a new technology (or acquire know-how) in order to enter and serve the market. Thus, one can think of the market as being primarily an innovation market.

The model is the basic, fixed-investment model of Section 3.2 except for the twist that a firm's profit depends on how successful the other firm is. Namely, while a firm makes no profit if it fails to develop the new technology, its profit when its succeeds in developing it depends on whether it faces a competitor, that is, whether the other firm also succeeds. Thus the firm's profit is as follows:

$$\text{profit} = \begin{cases} M & \text{if it is the only firm to succeed,} \\ D & \text{if both firms succeed,} \\ 0 & \text{if it fails,} \end{cases}$$

where

$$M \geqslant D \geqslant 0 \quad \text{and} \quad p_{\mathrm{H}} M > I.$$

Here, M stands for "monopoly profit" and D for "duopoly profit."[3] The condition $M \geqslant D$ means that competition reduces individual profit. The condition $p_{\mathrm{H}} M > I$, where p_{H} is the probability of success in the case of good behavior, says that the NPV under monopoly is positive.[4]

The familiar agency cost affects the development process. Each entrepreneur succeeds with probability p_{H} if she behaves (in which case she receives no private benefit) and with probability $p_{\mathrm{L}} = p_{\mathrm{H}} - \Delta p$ if she misbehaves (and thereby receives private benefit B), where $\Delta p > 0$.

Each entrepreneur needs to raise $I - A$ in order to finance her project, where I is the investment cost and A her initial net worth.

To isolate the profit-destruction effect, we first rule out any possibility of benchmarking (that is, of rewards that are based not only on the firm's performance but also on that of its rival) by assuming that *the two research processes are independent*, and so investors in one firm cannot infer anything about the entrepreneur's behavior by looking at whether the other firm succeeds or fails.

Assuming, as usual, that investors can break even only if incentives are in place for the entrepreneur to behave, we look at conditions under which the two firms receive financing, or only one firm receives it.

Equilibrium in which both firms receive funding. When one's potential competitor is funded (and is induced to behave), the expected income is

$$p_{\mathrm{H}}[(1 - p_{\mathrm{H}})M + p_{\mathrm{H}} D] + (1 - p_{\mathrm{H}})[0],$$

since the firm succeeds in developing the technology with probability p_{H} and is then a monopolist with probability $1 - p_{\mathrm{H}}$ and a duopolist with probability p_{H}.

The pledgeable income is smaller, though. The entrepreneur must receive a reward R_{b} in the case of success in developing the technology[5] (and 0 in the case of failure), which ensures incentive compatibility:

$$(\Delta p) R_{\mathrm{b}} \geqslant B.$$

Thus the pledgeable income is equal to the expected income described above minus the probability of success, p_{H}, times the minimum reward, $B/\Delta p$, to be given to the entrepreneur in order to provide adequate incentives.

It is an equilibrium for both firms to receive funding if, for each firm, the pledgeable income exceeds the investors' initial outlay, or

$$p_{\mathrm{H}}\left[(1 - p_{\mathrm{H}})\left(M - \frac{B}{\Delta p}\right) + p_{\mathrm{H}}\left(D - \frac{B}{\Delta p}\right)\right] \geqslant I - A. \quad (7.1)$$

Equilibria in which only one firm receives funding. When inequality (7.1) is not satisfied, investors are unwilling to fund a firm if its rival receives funding. Let us therefore look at the possibility that only one firm receives financing. This firm is a monopolist if it succeeds; therefore the pledgeable income is

$$p_{\mathrm{H}}\left[M - \frac{B}{\Delta p}\right].$$

3. The case of an R&D race (see Schroth and Szalay (2004) for an R&D race with financial constraints) is somewhat akin, in reduced form, to $D = \frac{1}{2}M$: each receives a patent with probability $\frac{1}{2}$.

4. Otherwise, no firm in the industry would ever invest.

5. Under risk neutrality, it does not matter whether the entrepreneur receives a uniform R_{b} regardless of the performance of the competitor, or, say, gets a share θ of the firm's profit (with $\theta[(1 - p_{\mathrm{H}})M + p_{\mathrm{H}} D] = R_{\mathrm{b}}$).

Under entrepreneurial risk aversion, though, it would become strictly optimal *not* to make the reward contingent on the other firm's performance: there is no point imposing a risk on the entrepreneur that she has no control over. (This is an application of the sufficient statistic result: see Section 3.2.6.)

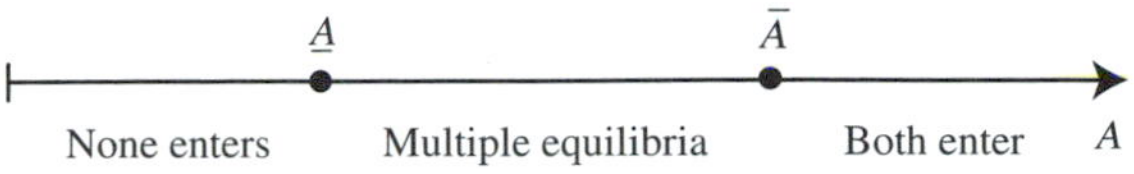

Figure 7.1

A necessary and sufficient condition for the funding of a single firm is therefore

$$p_H\left(M - \frac{B}{\Delta p}\right) \geqslant I - A$$
$$\geqslant p_H\left[(1 - p_H)M + p_H D - \frac{B}{\Delta p}\right]. \tag{7.2}$$

Note that in this case the equilibrium is indeterminate. It may be firm 1 or firm 2 that gets funded.[6] The entrepreneurs are not indifferent as to which equilibrium prevails, though. Their net utility from receiving monopoly funding is $p_H M - I > 0$; it is equal to 0 when denied funding. This suggests that, in this case, the entrepreneurs have an incentive to preempt each other and invest "too early," spending investment I before the technology is ripe. (This preemption game is analyzed in Exercise 7.4.)[7]

Summing up and letting $\bar{A}$ and $\underline{A}$ be defined by

$$p_H\left(M - \frac{B}{\Delta p}\right) = I - \underline{A}$$

and

$$p_H\left[(1 - p_H)M + p_H D - \frac{B}{\Delta p}\right] = I - \bar{A},$$

the outcome(s) are described in Figure 7.1.

(b) *Benchmarking.* Competition generally allows some benchmarking (also called relative performance evaluation) because the performance of rival firms is partly governed by common shocks to industry cost and demand. To illustrate this point in a somewhat contrived, but straightforward, manner, consider the previous model, but assume that the exogenous events that determine the firms' outcomes

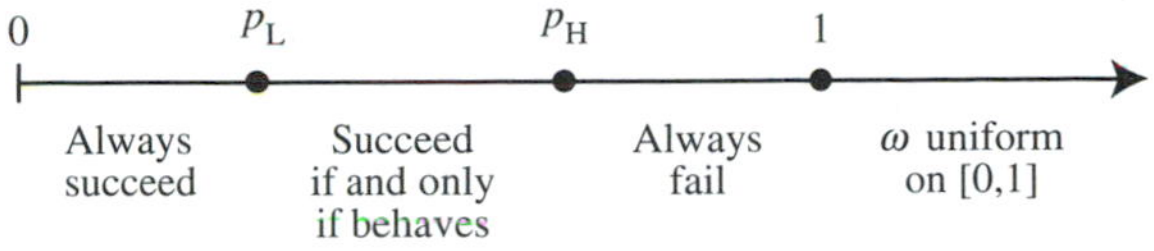

Figure 7.2

(success/failure) are the same, i.e., perfectly correlated across firms, rather than independent random variables. This "perfect correlation conditional on effort" is represented in Figure 7.2.

Here ω is a random variable distributed uniformly on $[0, 1]$. A project always succeeds if $\omega < p_L$, always fails if $\omega > p_H$, and succeeds only in the case of good behavior if $p_L < \omega < p_H$. Because ω is uniformly distributed, the probability of success is therefore equal to p_H if the entrepreneur behaves and p_L if she misbehaves. Perfect correlation means that the realization of random variable ω is the same for both firms.

Let us further, and for the sake of this argument only, replace the assumption that the entrepreneurs are risk neutral and protected by limited liability by the assumption that the entrepreneurs are risk neutral for positive incomes and infinitely risk averse for negative incomes: their utility from income w is w for $w \geqslant 0$, and $-\infty$ for $w < 0$. The two assumptions are very similar and often lead to the same conclusions. Not so in this somewhat rigged example, as we will see.

It is easy to see that an equilibrium exists in which the agency cost is eliminated by benchmarking, that is, in which the pledgeable income is the entire NPV. Define the following incentive scheme for entrepreneur i:

$$w_i = \begin{cases} a_i & \text{with } a_i \geqslant 0 \text{ if firm } i \text{ does at least as well as firm } j, \\ -b_i & \text{with } b_i > 0 \text{ if firm } i \text{ is outperformed by firm } j. \end{cases}$$

Suppose that firm j's entrepreneur is subject to such an incentive scheme and behaves in equilibrium. Then, if firm i's entrepreneur and investors agree on such an incentive scheme as well, entrepreneur i will behave. Indeed good behavior ensures that she will never be outperformed and allows her to secure a_i. Misbehavior implies that she is

6. Actually, in this game in which the entrepreneurs simultaneously look for funding sources, there also exists a mixed-strategy equilibrium, in which each entrepreneur receives funding with probability κ, such that

$$\kappa p_H\left[[1 - \kappa + \kappa(1 - p_H)]M + \kappa p_H D - \frac{B}{\Delta p}\right] = \kappa I - A.$$

7. The industrial organization literature has repeatedly stressed the incentive for preemption in such "natural monopoly" environments even in the absence of credit rationing.

outperformed, and therefore receives a very low utility ($-\infty$ here!) with probability Δp (i.e., when ω falls in the interval (p_L, p_H)).

Therefore the full expected income, $p_H D$,[8] is pledgeable and so funding is both feasible and desirable if and only if

$$p_H D \geqslant I.$$

It may even be that funding is easier under competition than under monopoly: this occurs whenever $p_H D \geqslant I$ and $p_H(M - B/\Delta p) < I - A$, that is, when the agency cost under monopoly is high (say, because B is high) and firms do not compete much (D close to M, as is the case, for example, when the two firms serve markets that are either only partly overlapping or similar).

Note, lastly, that benchmarking would be useless in this highly stylized example if we instead assumed that entrepreneurs were protected by limited liability. If entrepreneur i misbehaves, then she will be found out whenever ω takes value in the interval (p_L, p_H), because firm i fails while firm j succeeds, but then the punishment ($w_i = 0$) is no worse than it would have been in the absence of benchmarking. The conclusion that there is "no benefit from benchmarking" here is as extreme and nonrobust as the conclusion that "benchmarking fully eliminates the agency cost" under the alternative assumption of "infinite-risk-aversion-below-zero," that is, of a utility function that is equal to $-\infty$ for negative incomes. The general conclusion in less stylized models is that benchmarking reduces, but does not eliminate, the agency cost (see, for example, Exercise 7.5).

7.1.1.2 Impact of Competition on Financial Structure and Corporate Governance

So far, we have considered only the impact of competition on a firm's *ability to secure funding*. Following Aghion et al. (2000), let us extend the analysis to the impact of competition on the *terms of financing*. We make two basic points.

- Financial structure or corporate governance choices are interdependent: one firm's choice is affected by its rivals' choice in the matter.

- The quest for pledgeable income may make these choices "strategic complements" when they otherwise (i.e., in terms of NPV) would be "strategic substitutes": more discipline (in the sense of more profit-oriented behavior) in the rival firms lowers the firm's pledgeable income and calls for more discipline in order to satisfy the firm's investors.

These general statements are deliberately vague with regards to the nature of the financing "choices" made by the firms. These choices may be, for example,

- a choice of "financial muscle," which determines the firm's ability to withstand liquidity shocks,
- a refocusing on a line of business increasing one's efficiency in this line of business,
- the choice of high-powered monitoring or of vertical integration, resulting in improved corporate governance,
- relatedly, the act of granting more extensive control to investors, resulting in an enhanced concern for efficiency and profitability.

In fact, the choice may refer to any provision that (a) raises pledgeable income while (b) making the firm more competitive in the product market.

Anticipating Chapter 10, we illustrate these points in the context of the allocation of a control right. (Exercise 7.2 applies similar ideas to the firms' choice of financial muscle. More on this later.)

Let us return to the model without benchmarking (the two research processes are independent, and benchmarking is therefore useless). We assume that both firms have enough cash or pledgeable income to be attractive to investors. Therefore the issue is what kind of funding they receive rather than whether they are funded.

Let us introduce in each firm the possibility of taking an interim action that

(i) raises the probability of success uniformly by $\tau > 0$ (so the probability of success becomes $p_H + \tau$ or $p_L + \tau$, depending on the entrepreneur's behavior, if the action is taken, and remains p_H or p_L if the status quo action is selected); and

(ii) engenders a private cost $\gamma > 0$ for the entrepreneur (or more generally the insiders).

For example, the interim action could consist in firing workers or divesting a division that manage-

8. The profit in the case of success is D rather than $p_H D + (1 - p_H)M$ because the technologies are perfectly correlated and so the two firms succeed or fail at the same time.

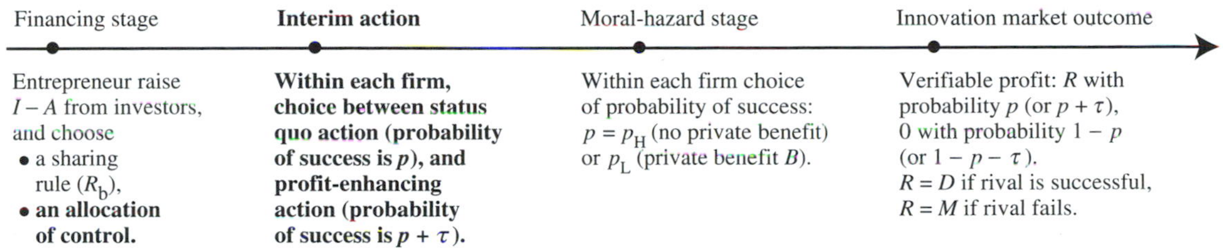
Financing stage
Interim action
Moral-hazard stage
Innovation market outcome
Entrepreneur raise $I - A$ from investors, and choose
• a sharing rule (R_b),
• an allocation of control.
Within each firm, choice between status quo action (probability of success is p), and profit-enhancing action (probability of success is $p + \tau$).
Within each firm choice of probability of success: $p = p_H$ (no private benefit) or p_L (private benefit B).
Verifiable profit: R with probability p (or $p + \tau$), 0 with probability $1 - p$ (or $1 - p - \tau$).
$R = D$ if rival is successful,
$R = M$ if rival fails.

Figure 7.3

ment is eager to run. The action (like the "status quo action") is *ex ante* indescribable, so its implementation is achieved through the allocation of the control right to a party with specific incentives to take or not take the profit-enhancing action.

We assume that

$$\gamma > \tau M, \tag{7.3}$$

which implies that the action always (i.e., even in a monopoly situation) decreases value.

The timing is described in Figure 7.3 (the new elements relative to the basic model are indicated in bold).

Two key preliminary points. First, if the control right over the interim action is granted to investors, they will choose the profit-enhancing action, since it raises the probability of success (and they receive no money in the case of failure) and they bear none of the cost γ. By contrast, and from (7.3), when in control, the entrepreneur does not choose the profit-enhancing action, since she bears the entire cost and receives only part of the benefit. Thus, the allocation of the control right matters for the actual decision making.

Second, the separability of the impacts of the exercise of the control right and of the moral-hazard choice of the entrepreneur implies that the entrepreneur's incentive constraint is not affected by the allocation of the control right: letting R_b denote the entrepreneur's reward if her firm succeeds (R_b can be chosen independently of the other firm's performance since benchmarking is useless) and 0 her reward in the case of failure, this incentive constraint is

$$(p_H - p_L)R_b \geqslant B$$

if the entrepreneur retains the control right, and

$$[(p_H + \tau) - (p_L + \tau)]R_b \geqslant B$$

if investors receive control. The invariance of the incentive constraint to the allocation of the control right obviously shortens the analysis.[9]

Because investor control reduces the NPV and therefore the entrepreneur's utility, each entrepreneur would rather not surrender control. Let us therefore find the ranges of parameters over which the entrepreneurs can secure financing with and without surrendering control to investors.

Equilibrium in which both entrepreneurs retain control. When entrepreneurs retain control, a firm's probability of success is p_H and so the expected income is

$$p_H[(1 - p_H)M + p_H D].$$

Because $R_b \geqslant B/\Delta p$, the pledgeable income is equal to the expected income minus $p_H B/\Delta p$. Hence, financing is possible if the pledgeable income exceeds the investors' initial outlay; this condition takes the same form as in the previous subsection:[10]

$$p_H\left[(1 - p_H)M + p_H D - \frac{B}{\Delta p}\right] \geqslant I - A. \tag{7.4}$$

Firms that start with a substantial amount of cash on hand (that is, condition (7.4) is satisfied) create a form of corporate governance that is unfriendly to investors (who, because of the breakeven condition, must be compensated through a higher share of profit in the case of success).

Equilibrium in which both entrepreneurs surrender control. Suppose now that

$$p_H\left[[1-(p_H+\tau)]M+(p_H+\tau)D-\frac{B}{\Delta p}\right] < I-A \tag{7.5}$$

9. It also implies that, in Figure 7.3, whether the interim action comes before or after the moral-hazard stage is irrelevant.

10. Aghion et al. call this the "shirking region." I avoid this terminology so as not to create confusion with the moral-hazard part of the model.

and

$$(p_H + \tau)\left[[1 - (p_H + \tau)]M + (p_H + \tau)D - \frac{B}{\Delta p}\right] \geqslant I - A. \quad (7.6)$$

Inequalities (7.4) and (7.5) state that, when the rival surrenders control to her investors (and therefore succeeds with probability $p_H + \tau$), there is enough pledgeable income to attract investors only if the entrepreneur surrenders control herself. In this case, and provided that the cost γ of the profit-enhancing action is not so high as to make the NPV negative,[11] then it is an equilibrium for the two entrepreneurs to surrender control. Aghion et al. call this the "bonding region."

Let us push this analysis a bit further by asking ourselves whether the corporate governance decisions (here, the allocations of control) are strategic complements or strategic substitutes. They are strategic complements (substitutes) if your retaining control makes me more (less) willing to retain control. Let $x_i = 0$ if entrepreneur i retains control and $x_i = 1$ otherwise.

As it turns out, corporate governance decisions are either (a) strategic substitutes from an NPV perspective or (b) strategic complements from a pledgeable income perspective.

(a) *Strategic substitutability from an NPV perspective.* Entrepreneur i's utility (also equal to her firm's NPV under a competitive capital market) is[12]

$$\begin{aligned} U_b^i &= \mathcal{V}^i(x_i, x_j) \\ &= (p_H + x_i\tau) \\ &\qquad \times [[1 - (p_H + x_j\tau)]M + [p_H + x_j\tau]D] \\ &\qquad - I - x_i\gamma, \end{aligned}$$

where

$$x_i, x_j \in \{0, 1\}.$$

And so

$$\frac{\partial^2 \mathcal{V}^i}{\partial x_i \partial x_j} = -\tau^2(M - D) < 0.$$

Intuitively, the cost of surrendering control, γ, is independent from competitive pressure. By contrast, raising the probability of success by τ is more advantageous if the other firm is less likely to succeed, since the monopoly profit exceeds the duopoly one. In a nutshell, the cost of surrendering control looms smaller when the payoff from good performance increases (this property holds whether or not condition (7.3) is satisfied).

(b) *Strategic complementarity from a pledgeable income perspective.* The condition that pledgeable income must exceed the investors' initial outlay is

$$\begin{aligned} \mathcal{P}^i&(x_i, x_j) \\ &= (p_H + x_i\tau) \\ &\qquad \times \left[[1 - (p_H + x_j\tau)]M + [p_H + x_j\tau]D - \frac{B}{\Delta p}\right] \\ &\geqslant I - A; \end{aligned}$$

and so

$$\frac{\partial \mathcal{P}^i}{\partial x_i} > 0 \quad \text{and} \quad \frac{\partial \mathcal{P}^i}{\partial x_j} < 0.$$

Thus, if entrepreneur i can secure financing without relinquishing control when the other entrepreneur surrenders control, she *a fortiori* can secure financing and keep control when her rival keeps control. Or, put differently, an entrepreneur who faces a tight financing constraint is more likely to surrender control if her rival also does so.[13]

This strategic complementarity may give rise to multiple equilibria. Condition (7.4) is consistent with conditions (7.5) and (7.6) holding simultaneously, and so the two equilibria studied above coexist over a range of parameters. Note further that if both equilibria coexist, then the one in which the two entrepreneurs retain control is better for both entrepreneurs ("Pareto-dominates") than the one in which they both surrender control.

7.1.1.3 Committing to Be Tough: Brander and Lewis (1986)

The analysis in Section 7.1.1.2, with a minor modification, also illustrates a well-known idea, due to Brander and Lewis (1986): *a firm may want to choose its financial structure or corporate governance so as to commit to being very competitive (aggressive) in*

11. That is,

$$U_b = \text{NPV} = (p_H + \tau)[(1 - (p_H + \tau))M + (p_H + \tau)D] - I - \gamma > 0.$$

12. Due to the symmetric structure of the model, $\mathcal{V}^i$, like the pledgeable income $\mathcal{P}^i$ defined below, is independent of i. Nonetheless, we keep the index i so as to make it clear which firm is being discussed.

13. Technically, the set of parameters for which $x_i = 1$ is needed to deliver a pledgeable income in excess of $I - A$ when $x_j = 0$ is a subset of the set of parameters for which $x_i = 1$ is needed when $x_j = 1$.

the product market, thereby deterring or limiting entry by a rival. (This section offers a good transition from the literature on the impact of competition on the ability to raise funds to the next section on commitment effects.)

Return to the timing described in Figure 7.3 and decompose the "financing stage" into two substages. Namely, firm 1 chooses its financing structure (including the allocation of control) *before*, rather than simultaneously with, firm 2.

It is easy to find parameters such that

(i) firm 2 cannot secure financing even by giving control to its investors when firm 1 gives control to its own investors,

(ii) under a simultaneous choice of financial structure, there would have been an equilibrium (actually a Pareto-dominating one, as we have just seen), in which both entrepreneurs keep the control right and receive financing, and

(iii) firm 1 selects to deter firm 2's entry by giving control to its investors.

Indeed suppose that[14]

$$\mathcal{P}^2(1,1) < I - A < \mathcal{P}^2(0,0). \tag{7.7}$$

The left-hand inequality in (7.7) implies that tough corporate governance deters entry, yielding (i). The right inequality means that both firms could have been funded under simultaneous choices of financial structure and so (ii) obtains. For the "Brander–Lewis equilibrium" to arise, we also need to ensure (iii), that is, firm 1's willingness to sacrifice control to the purpose of deterring entry:

$$(p_H + \tau)M - \gamma - I > p_H[(1 - p_H)M + p_H D] - I$$

or

$$p_H^2(M - D) > \gamma - \tau M. \tag{7.8}$$

That is, the cost of relinquishing control is $\gamma - \tau M > 0$. But, with probability p_H^2, the probability that both firms are successful when they both invest, firm 1 earns a monopoly profit rather than a duopoly one.

This analysis only conveys the spirit of the Brander–Lewis contribution. The latter actually studied the incentive to deter entry through a choice of overindebtedness in the context of Cournot competition.[15] Namely, firms 1 and 2 know that they will compete *à la* Cournot in the product market. The supplementary section covers the original Brander–Lewis model.

7.1.2 Committing through the Financial Structure

The choice of financial structure alters the incentives of those who run firms, and thereby indirectly modifies the behavior of product market rivals. The principle according to which financial and corporate governance choices can be used to affect other firms' behavior is obviously quite general, and has been developed in a variety of contexts. Let us discuss two of these.

7.1.2.1 Financial Muscle and Predation

An old theme in industrial organization and antitrust policy is that cash-rich firms can prey upon cash-poor rivals. The standard definition of predation is that the predator voluntarily loses money in the short run (relative to the short-term profit that could have been achieved with an alternative strategy) so as to kick a rival out of the market, at which point the reduction in competition will allow it to more than recoup the short-term loss in earnings (see, for example, Joskow and Klevorick 1979). The instrument of predation is usually a low price, but it could be any strategic choice that hurts the rival's bottom line and prospects: intense advertising, selective price cuts, close positioning, clever versioning, etc. In the long-purse theory of predation, the cash-poor rival exits because it can no longer secure financing for its operating or investment costs. By contrast, the predator is assumed to have "deep pockets" (a "long purse") and its existence and investments are not jeopardized by short-term losses.

14. To see that $\mathcal{P}^2(x,x)$ may be decreasing in x, note that

$$\frac{\partial}{\partial \tau}\left[(p_H + \tau)\left[[1 - (p_H + \tau)]M + (p_H + \tau)D - \frac{B}{\Delta p}\right]\right] = \frac{\mathcal{P}^2 - (p_H + \tau)^2(M - D)}{p_H + \tau}.$$

So, if, for example, $\mathcal{P}^2$ is small (corresponding, in equilibrium, to A close to I), $\mathcal{P}^2(x,x)$ decreases with x. Or, more directly, condition (7.7) can be satisfied for some choice of $I - A$ if and only if $M - (B/\Delta p) < (2p_H + \tau)(M - D)$.

15. Substantial extensions of the Brander–Lewis analysis can be found in Maksimovic (1988) and Poitevin (1989). Other papers studying financial contracting in an imperfectly competitive product market include Fulghieri and Nagarajan (1992) and Glazer (1994).

This long-purse story (articulated, for instance, by McGee (1958)), at least in its basic form in which the predator charges rock-bottom prices so as to make the prey lose money, was challenged by Telser (1966) and the Chicago School on the grounds that the prey can always receive financing after a predatory period as long as its prospects are good. That is, the prey's former losses from being preyed upon are "water under the bridge," and are therefore irrelevant. Financiers will look at the prey's prospects, not its past.

In a nutshell, Telser's critique takes an Arrow–Debreu view, under which the capital market is not marred by agency costs and so investment is driven by investment opportunities and not by forgone earnings. And, indeed, this sunk-loss argument is well-taken if firms can always obtain financing for continuation projects that have a positive NPV. In that case, money lost in the past, because it has no effect on future prospects, also has no impact on future investments and decisions. Unsurprisingly, the subsequent literature reintroduced the credit constraints that were not formalized but were implicit in the pre-Telser antitrust literature.

As a warm-up exercise, we begin with the "simple-minded long-purse story" in which the prey may in the future face credit rationing, but obtains no long-term commitment from its lenders, that is, financing occurs through a sequence of short-term borrowing (Fudenberg and Tirole 1986). The possibility that the prey be credit rationed tomorrow may induce the predator to take actions today that reduce both profits today and, in particular, lessen the prey's net worth tomorrow. We then move on to the more interesting case in which the prey, anticipating this, can (as was studied in Chapter 5) secure long-term financing and thereby attempt to discourage predation: this case has been analyzed in the strategic security design literature pioneered by Bolton and Scharfstein (1990).

Simple-minded long-purse story: short-term financing arrangements. There are two dates, $t = 0, 1$. There is no discounting between the two periods. Consider a duopoly. Firms $i = 1, 2$ are identical in all respects except the amount of wealth they have access to in order to finance investments. Firm 1 (the predator, the financially strong firm) has a large amount of wealth and never needs to go to the capital market to finance investment. Firm 2 (the prey, the financially weak firm) has just enough wealth to finance the date-0 investment.[16]

While the financially weak firm is self-financed at date 0, it will need to borrow in order to finance the date-1 investment cost. Its date-0 profit is its date-1 net worth or cash on hand.

Without loss of generality we describe date 0 in reduced form: firm 1 can take a costly action (prey) that reduces both firms' date-0 profits. In particular, firm 2's profit falls from $A > 0$ to a (we take the profit to be deterministic in order to simplify the exposition; again, there is no loss of generality here).

The second period, date 1, is described exactly as in Section 7.1.1: for each firm, the investment cost is I. Entrepreneurs then engage in moral hazard. The probability of success of the date-1 project is p_H if the entrepreneur behaves and $p_L = p_H - \Delta p$ if she misbehaves (in which case she obtains private benefit B). A firm's date-1 profit is M if it alone succeeded, D if both firms succeeded, and 0 otherwise. Let

$$C \equiv p_H D + (1 - p_H)M$$

denote the expected date-1 "competitive" profit per firm when both invest (assuming as always that incentive schemes induce good behavior). The timing is summarized in Figure 7.4.

Assume that

$$I - A < p_H\left(C - \frac{B}{\Delta p}\right) < I - a.$$

This condition says that the pledgeable income—equal to the probability of success, p_H, times the amount of revenue in the case of success, $C - B/\Delta p$, that can be promised to investors without compromising incentives—exceeds the investors' date-1 outlay in the financially weak firm if the latter has retained earnings A, but not if it only retained earnings a. Thus, assuming that the NPV is positive even under competition ($p_H C > I$), predation by firm 1 triggers firm 2's exit.

Does firm 1 find it profitable to induce exit? Firm 1 compares its date-0 cost of predation with its date-1

16. Alternatively, one could assume that it is able to secure financing for the date-0 investment, where the loan is to be repaid from date-0 profits: that is, there is no long-term financing arrangement.

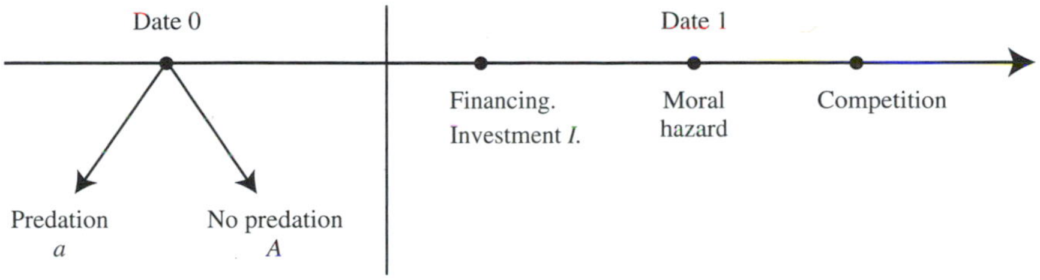

Figure 7.4

gain from monopolization. The gain from monopolization, $M - D$, is reaped only when, in the absence of exit, both firms would have been successful, that is with probability p_H^2.

Let k denote the predator's cost of predation (for example, $k = A - a$ if the cost of predation is the same for both firms, but obviously, it need not be). In the absence of discounting between dates 0 and 1, firm 1 chooses to prey if and only if

$$k < p_H^2(M - D).$$

More generally, if the prey's investment decreases with its cash on hand (as it does in corporate finance models), the predator is willing to incur losses as long as she can recoup these later on thanks to her rival's reduced scale.

Note also that the prey's potential date-1 funding contract is designed at date 1. In particular, the firm cannot contract with date-0 investors to secure a credit line that will allow it to continue even if earnings are low. Such a credit line might salvage a valuable investment at date 1 (as in Chapter 5), and crucially it might also deter date-0 predation in the first place. This brings us to the strategic security design literature.

Strategic security design (Bolton and Scharfstein): reducing the sensitivity of investment to cash flow. The simple-minded version brings credit constraints to the forefront of the analysis of predation, but has two serious shortcomings. First, as we noted, it does not allow for long-term contracting such as credit lines or long-term debt. Second, it does not make the date-0 agency costs explicit (since the prey's date-0 investment is self-financed, the two shortcomings are, as we will see, related; it becomes important to explicitly model date-0 agency costs when the firm secures long-term financing). The crucial work of Bolton and Scharfstein (1990) (see also the very careful analysis of renegotiation in Snyder (1996)) addresses these shortcomings.

The literature makes three basic points.

1. *A financially weak firm can reduce the occurrence of predation through long-term contracting with its financiers.* Intuitively, the predator feels less inclined to prey (and thereby lose money) if the prey has secured a financial cushion and therefore will probably be able to finance its reinvestment.[17] Conversely, the predator is deterred from predation if the prey has contracted a large amount of short-term debt and does not receive financing even for high earnings (this will later be called the "shallow-pocket strategy"). Either way, a reduction in the prey's sensitivity of investment to cash flow reduces the predator's incentive to prey.

2. *Financial cushions that insure the potential prey against fluctuations in revenue (and thereby deter predation) exacerbate the incentive problem within the firm.* In general, financial contracts may not be able to distinguish between losses that are due to predation and those stemming from other causes (effort, competitive environment). And so, because a shortfall in revenue may be due to managerial moral hazard and not only to the rival's predatory actions, insurance against predation also exacerbates moral hazard. In other words, there is a tension between the minimization of the rival's incentive to prey and the minimization of agency costs within the firm when investors cannot disentangle whether a low profit is due to aggressive competition or low managerial effort.

17. An alternative to a credit line to build financial muscle is to become a division of a conglomerate, as in Cestone and Fumagalli (2005). For a modeling of financial muscle in a conglomerate, see Exercise 3.20.

3. *Long-term contracts that protect against predation are credible.* That is, investors and the entrepreneur do not find it advantageous to renegotiate their agreement to their mutual advantage later on.[18] As in Chapter 5, when continuation maximizes total (entrepreneur and investor) value but reduces investors' payoff, the continuation policy is not renegotiated: either it dictates continuation, in which case there are no gains from renegotiation; or it leads to liquidation, and then the entrepreneur has no cash to compensate investors for the loss they incur if they agree to finance continuation.

Let us now investigate these points in more detail. To do so, we need to build upon the simple-minded model by explicitly describing the date-0 actions and by allowing for long-term financing. To simplify the analysis, let us assume that

- $p_H = 1$;
- furthermore, date 0 is identical to date 1 except for the private benefit from misbehaving—the latter is equal to B_0 at date 0 and B at date 1;[19]
- the financially strong firm's act of predation in a given period[20] results in 0 profits (failure) for both firms in that period;
- investors in the financially weak firm observe only that firm's profit at date 0.[21]

As earlier, the financially strong firm is self-financed. The financially weak firm signs a long-term agreement with its investors that specifies:[22]

- the probabilities z^S and z^F of refinancing (date-1 investment) in the case of date-0 success (i.e., profit D) or failure (i.e., profit 0), respectively;
- a reward R_b^i in the case of date-1 success (which assumes a date-1 reinvestment in the first place), where $i \in \{S, F\}$ indexes the date-0 outcome—for all i, R_b^i must satisfy the date-1 incentive constraint $(\Delta p)R_b^i \geqslant B$.[23]

The timing is summarized in Figure 7.5.

Let us make the following assumptions.

Assumption 7.1. *Positive-NPV investment even under duopoly in the absence of predation:*

$$D - I > 0.$$

(Recall: the probability of success in the case of good behavior is here equal to 1.)

Assumption 7.2. *Dearth of pledgeable income in the case of continuation:*[24]

$$\left(D - \frac{B}{\Delta p}\right) - I < 0.$$

Preventing predation by firm 1 at date 0 benefits firm 2 in two ways. First, its date-0 income is

18. A large literature has investigated the use of contracts with third parties as a way to commit to certain types of behavior in strategic interactions (e.g., Katz 1991). A subset of these contributions raises the question of whether such commitments are credible, i.e., whether the parties to the contract would not undo its provisions once the latter have served their objective of altering the others' behavior in the strategic interaction. Once must then assume that the parties to the contract are unable for some reason to renegotiate, or else show that renegotiation is at best inefficient, as in Caillaud et al. (1995), where renegotiation is plagued by informational asymmetries.

19. We will later assume that $B_0 < B$. This distinction between B_0 and B allows us to shorten the analysis by ensuring that date-0 incentives can be provided through the continuation policy. See below.

20. Predation can, of course, occur at date 0 only. The predator can only lose by preying at date 1 because there is no future at that date.

21. The important assumption is that a court cannot ascertain whether the absence of date-0 profit for firm 2 is due to a predatory act or to moral hazard (lack of luck is not a possible third explanation because we assumed that $p_H = 1$).

Indeed, historically, courts have had difficulties in ascertaining the occurrence of predation. Legal scholars, such as Areeda and Turner (1975), have suggested comparing the price charged by the alleged predator to its marginal cost, approximated by the average variable cost. There are several difficulties with this, leaving aside the fact that predation may be implemented through nonprice instruments. Measurability is not easy. Prices may be multidimensional and have wholesale components; marginal costs are often difficult to measure. Second, marginal cost is not necessarily the correct theoretical benchmark. On the one hand, a price above marginal cost may be predatory since the short-term profit-maximizing price may be well above marginal cost. On the other hand, prices below marginal cost may arise as part of strategies that are not meant to induce the rival's exit. They are common in markets where (a) quality is unknown, so introductory offers encourage consumers to try the product, or (b) the firms want to benefit from learning by doing and so price aggressively initially, or (c) consumers are locked into their initial consumption, so that the prospect of future profits from these "installed-base consumers" induces firms to lose money to "acquire" them, or else (d) there are network externalities and networks/firms are willing to lose money to enlist the initial group or marquee players who will attract other consumers. Bolton et al. (2000, 2001) offer a standard for financial predation. See also Tirole (1988, in particular Chapter 9) for some of the theoretical principles.

Note also that even if courts were able to measure predation cheaply and accurately, the time involved in the process might still make it impossible to base the refinancing decision on the existence or nonexistence of predation.

22. Exercise 7.7 shows that there is only a slight loss of generality in considering this class of contracts, and that the results are not qualitatively affected by our focus on this class.

23. Note that if $(\Delta p)R_b^i < B$, then there is always renegotiation to an $R_b^i \geqslant B/\Delta p$ as long as $p_H(R - B/\Delta p) > p_L R$. But even in the absence of renegotiation, the analysis generalizes.

24. Given that rent $p_H(B/\Delta p) = B/\Delta p$ must be given to the entrepreneurs, investors would not finance firm 2 at date 1 in the absence of retained earnings and long-term contracting obligations.

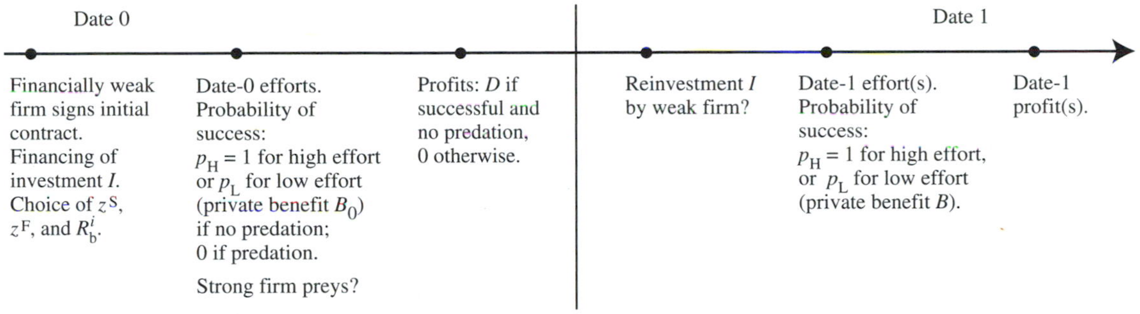

Figure 7.5

increased by D, the duopoly profit. Second, it may avoid credit rationing, which from Assumption 7.2 is a threat, and from Assumption 7.1 undesirable.

Predation deterrence constraint. To avoid predation firm 2 must choose its financial contract so that firm 1's date-0 cost of predation, D, exceed its date-1 gain from monopolization. To compute the latter, note that it is not in firm 1's interest to prey in the last period. Hence, preventing refinancing by firm 2 raises firm 1's profit from D to M. And the probability that firm 2 receives refinancing falls from z^{S} in the absence of predation to z^{F} under predation (recall that the probability of refinancing is z^{S} if firm 2's date-0 profit is D and z^{F} if it is equal to 0). The predation deterrence constraint is therefore

$$D \geqslant (z^{\mathrm{S}} - z^{\mathrm{F}})(M - D). \qquad \text{(PD)}$$

To deter predation, the weak firm's contract must make the continuation decision relatively insensitive to that firm's date-0 profit performance. Note that (PD) can be rewritten as

$$\frac{D}{M - D} \geqslant z^{\mathrm{S}} - z^{\mathrm{F}}. \qquad \text{(PD}')$$

Suppose that competition between the two firms reduces industry profit:

$$M \geqslant 2D.$$

The left-hand side of (PD′) can then take any value between 0 (extreme, Bertrand competition) and 1 (perfect tacit collusion or noncompeting goods). In the latter case, (PD′) really does not constrain the financial contract and there is little incentive to prey. By contrast, with Bertrand competition, predation can only be deterred by a performance-insensitive continuation rule (on the other hand, remaining in the market is also unattractive for firm 2).

Weak firm's date-0 incentive constraint. The weak firm's contract must also induce its entrepreneur to behave. Here, the entrepreneur's compensation is delayed. She receives R_{b}^{i} if there is reinvestment and firm 2 has profit D in the last period. Let

$$\mathcal{R}_{\mathrm{b}}^{\mathrm{S}} \equiv z^{\mathrm{S}} R_{\mathrm{b}}^{\mathrm{S}} \quad \text{and} \quad \mathcal{R}_{\mathrm{b}}^{\mathrm{F}} \equiv z^{\mathrm{F}} R_{\mathrm{b}}^{\mathrm{F}}$$

denote the expected continuation payoffs for the entrepreneur in the cases of date-0 success and failure, respectively. By misbehaving at date 0, the entrepreneur receives private benefit B_0, but reduces the probability of date-0 success by Δp (provided that the rival does not prey, i.e., if constraint (PD) is satisfied).

Hence, the incentive constraint is

$$\mathcal{R}_{\mathrm{b}}^{\mathrm{S}} - \mathcal{R}_{\mathrm{b}}^{\mathrm{F}} \geqslant \frac{B_0}{\Delta p}. \qquad \text{(IC)}$$

(a) *The no-predation benchmark.* Suppose, first, that the predator is unable to prey and so constraint (PD) is irrelevant. Let $U_{\mathrm{b}}(z^{\mathrm{S}})$ denote the NPV:

$$U_{\mathrm{b}}(z^{\mathrm{S}}) \equiv D - I + z^{\mathrm{S}}(D - I).$$

From Assumption 7.1, it increases in z^{S}.

The investors' breakeven constraint can be written as

$$U_{\mathrm{b}}(z^{\mathrm{S}}) - \mathcal{R}_{\mathrm{b}}^{\mathrm{S}} + A \geqslant 0. \qquad (\mathrm{IR_l})$$

Finally, the entrepreneur's incentive compatibility constraint is

$$\mathcal{R}_{\mathrm{b}}^{\mathrm{S}} - \mathcal{R}_{\mathrm{b}}^{\mathrm{F}} \geqslant \frac{B_0}{\Delta p}. \qquad \text{(IC)}$$

We are led to consider two cases.

Strong balance sheet. We will say that the firm has a strong balance sheet if constraints (IR_l) and (IC) do not rule out the efficient continuation policy:

$$z^\text{S} = 1.$$

Because $\mathcal{R}_\text{b}^\text{S} = z^\text{S} R_\text{b}^\text{S}$ and $R_\text{b}^\text{S} \geqslant B/\Delta p$, a necessary condition for this is

$$U_\text{b}(1) - \frac{B}{\Delta p} + A \geqslant 0,$$

that is, that A be "sufficiently large." Then $\mathcal{R}_\text{b}^\text{S}$ is given by the breakeven constraint:

$$\mathcal{R}_\text{b}^\text{S} = U_\text{b}(1) + A.$$

For this condition to also be sufficient, constraint (IC) must be satisfied, or, using the investors' breakeven condition,

$$\mathcal{R}_\text{b}^\text{F} + \frac{B_0}{\Delta p} \leqslant U_\text{b}(1) + A.$$

Because the right-hand side of the latter inequality is greater than $B/\Delta p$ and $\mathcal{R}_\text{b}^\text{F} \geqslant z^\text{F} B/\Delta p$, if $B \geqslant B_0$, which we will assume, there exists $\bar{z}^\text{F}$ such that the solution is incentive compatible for $R_\text{b}^\text{F} = B/\Delta p$ and

$$0 \leqslant z^\text{F} \leqslant \bar{z}^\text{F}.$$

Weak balance sheet. If

$$U_\text{b}(1) - \frac{B}{\Delta p} + A < 0,$$

then continuation cannot be guaranteed without violating the investors' breakeven constraint. And so

$$z^\text{S} = \bar{z}^\text{S} < 1.$$

It is then optimal to set $R_\text{b}^\text{S} = B/\Delta p$ so as to harness as much pledgeable income and generate as much continuation as possible. The probability of continuation in the case of success is given by

$$U_\text{b}(\bar{z}^\text{S}) - \mathcal{R}_\text{b}^\text{S} + A = 0,$$

or, using $\mathcal{R}_\text{b}^\text{S} = \bar{z}^\text{S}(B/\Delta p)$,

$$D - I + \bar{z}^\text{S}\left[D - I - \frac{B}{\Delta p}\right] + A = 0.$$

From Assumption 7.2, the left-hand side of this equation is decreasing in the probability of continuation. From Assumption 7.1, the equation has a unique solution in $(0,1)$. Again, if $\bar{z}^\text{S} B \geqslant B_0$, which we will assume, there exists $\bar{z}^\text{F} \in (0,1)$ such that the incentive constraint is satisfied as long as $0 \leqslant z^\text{F} \leqslant \bar{z}^\text{F}$.

(b) *Reintroducing the predation-deterrence constraint.* The best, predation-deterring financial contract is now obtained by maximizing firm 2's NPV subject to the predation-deterrence constraint (PD), the breakeven constraint (IR_l), and the incentive-compatibility (IC) constraint.

If the solution in the no-predation benchmark case satisfied (PD), then it is also the solution when predation if feasible. So, we will assume that (PD) is not satisfied by the benchmark solution. Let us begin with the case of a weak balance sheet.

Weak balance sheet. A benchmark solution $(\bar{z}^\text{S}, z^\text{F})$ satisfies (IC) if and only if

$$(\bar{z}^\text{S} - z^\text{F})\frac{B}{\Delta p} \geqslant \frac{B_0}{\Delta p}$$

and (PD) if and only if

$$(\bar{z}^\text{S} - z^\text{F})(M - D) \leqslant D.$$

These two constraints are inconsistent if

$$\frac{B_0}{B} > \frac{D}{M - D}.$$

which we will assume.

Relative to the benchmark, the weak firm's entrepreneur must reduce the sensitivity of investment to cash flow, which is proportional to $z^\text{S} - z^\text{F}$. She cannot increase z^S without violating the investors' breakeven constraint. She must thus reduce z^S below $\bar{z}^\text{S}$. Furthermore, using (IC) and (PD) satisfied with equality yields

$$\mathcal{R}_\text{b}^\text{S} - z^\text{S}\frac{B}{\Delta p} = \frac{B_0}{\Delta p} - \frac{B}{\Delta p}\left(\frac{D}{M - D}\right) > 0,$$

and so $R_\text{b}^\text{S} > B/\Delta p$. Note that continuation in the case of success is no longer an efficient currency because it induces the predator to prey; this explains why R_b^S is greater than $B/\Delta p$.

Finally, the probability of continuation in the case of success must satisfy the investors' breakeven constraint:

$$U_\text{b}(z^\text{S}) - \mathcal{R}_\text{b}^\text{S} + A = 0$$

or

$$D - I + z^\text{S}\left(D - I - \frac{B}{\Delta p}\right) - \left[\frac{B_0}{\Delta p} - \frac{B}{\Delta p}\left(\frac{D}{M - D}\right)\right] + A = 0.$$

Hence,

$$z^\text{S} < \bar{z}^\text{S}.$$

Everything is as if the balance sheet (as measured by A) had further deteriorated. The entrepreneur is forced to adopt a *shallow-pocket* (low probability of continuation) policy.

Strong balance sheet. We only sketch the case of a strong balance sheet. Under a strong balance sheet, $\bar{z}^{\mathrm{S}} = 1$ in the absence of predation threat. Reducing z^{S} (here below 1) is, as in the case of a weak balance sheet, a feasible response to deter predation.[25]

Let us use this case to illustrate another feasible response, namely, the *deep-pocket* policy. Here, a deep-pocket policy consists in raising z^{F} while keeping $z^{\mathrm{S}} = \bar{z}^{\mathrm{S}} = 1$. Maintaining incentive compatibility, however, requires raising $R_{\mathrm{b}}^{\mathrm{S}}$ and thereby violating the investors' breakeven constraint.[26] Thus, the deep-pocket policy requires finding new forms of pledgeable income and/or cash on hand. This book emphasizes the various concessions that can be made to boost pledgeable income (costly collateral, control rights, etc.).

To simplify the exposition, let us enrich the model by assuming that the entrepreneur can increase cash on hand from A to any $A' \geqslant A$ at deadweight cost $\varepsilon(A' - A) > 0$.[27] Because the entrepreneur reaches the first-best allocation when predation is not feasible, then $A' = A$ in the no-predation-threat benchmark. Because reducing z^{S} is costly, if ε is small, the entrepreneur is better off raising cash on hand so as to reduce the amount borrowed. She can then set z^{F} so as to satisfy constraint (PD),

$$(1 - z^{\mathrm{F}})(M - D) = D,$$

and set $R_{\mathrm{b}}^{\mathrm{S}}$ so as to satisfy the incentive constraint:[28]

$$R_{\mathrm{b}}^{\mathrm{S}} - z^{\mathrm{F}} \frac{B}{\Delta p} = \frac{B_0}{\Delta p}.$$

We thus conclude that it may be optimal for the entrepreneur to waste resources to find new sources of cash (or to make concessions to investors) so as to be able to increase the probability of continuation in the case of failure.

Let us conclude with Bolton and Scharfstein's third point: the financing contract between entrepreneur 2 and her lenders is *renegotiation proof.* To appreciate the relevance of this remark, note that, when $z^{\mathrm{F}} > 0$, firm 1 would not be deterred from preying if it anticipated that in the case of date-0 failure of firm 2, firm 2's entrepreneur and her investors would renegotiate and decide not to refinance continuation. To see that the entrepreneur and the investors cannot renegotiate to their mutual advantage, note that continuation is *ex post* optimal from Assumption 7.1. This is indeed the essence of predation in this model: a lack of continuation is not due to a lack of investment opportunities, but rather to a lack of internal funds. So reducing z^{F} would reduce total value or NPV (entrepreneur plus investor), and at least one of the two parties would necessarily lose—and therefore prefer the implementation of the initial contract. Thus renegotiation toward less frequent continuation will not occur.

Similarly, when $z^{\mathrm{S}} < 1$, firm 1 would be incentivized to prey if it anticipated that the probability of continuation would be renegotiated upwards in the case of success. Again, this renegotiation will not occur, but this time for a different reason. Increasing the probability of continuation would increase total value. However, investors necessarily lose when refinancing from Assumption 7.2 and the fact that the entrepreneur no longer has wealth at date 1.

Empirical work. A series of empirical papers (Phillips 1995; Chevalier 1995a,b) argue that debt weakens the competitive position of firms.[29] Chevalier (1995a,b) and Chevalier and Scharfstein (1996) study the link between balance-sheet strength and product market behavior in the U.S. supermarket industry. They measure the strength (or rather the weakness) of the balance sheet by the firm's leverage; for example, an LBO firm (a firm that results from a leveraged buyout, and therefore is highly

---

25. Constraint (PD) is violated by the benchmark solution if

$$U_{\mathrm{b}}(1) - \frac{B}{\Delta p} + \left[\frac{B_0}{\Delta p} - \frac{B}{\Delta p}\left(\frac{D}{M - D}\right)\right] + A < 0.$$

26. The assumption that $p_{\mathrm{H}} = 1$ implies that on the equilibrium path there is no date-0 failure. And so the cost of a high z^{F} in terms of pledgeable income does not correspond to a loss by investors in the case of continuation after a failure. Rather, a high z^{F} makes it harder to satisfy the (IC) constraint, which requires giving extra rents to the entrepreneur in the case of success and thereby reducing the pledgeable income.

27. One can think of a nonmonetary, *ex ante* effort that costs the entrepreneur $(1 + \varepsilon)$ per unit of cash collected.

28. A' is then given by

$$U_{\mathrm{b}}(1) - \frac{B}{\Delta p} + \left[\frac{B_0}{\Delta p} - \frac{B}{\Delta p}\left(\frac{D}{M - D}\right)\right] + A' = 0.$$

29. See, for example, MacKay and Phillips (2005) for a recent survey of the evidence.

indebted) has a weak balance sheet. Such LBOs in their sample were frequently motivated by the deterrence of takeovers rather than by product market expansion. Two notable results are as follows:

(a) Entry and expansion of non-LBO firms is more likely in markets with LBO firms. This suggests that either LBO firms are unable to expand sufficiently rapidly and thus leave more elbowroom for other firms, or these other firms attempt to prey on the weaker LBO firms. Either way the financial structure of firms seems to affect product market behavior.[30]

(b) Supermarket prices are procyclical. One possible interpretation is that financially weak firms are more fragile during recessions, which may encourage some predation.

7.1.2.2 Committing vis-à-vis Suppliers or Customers

Until now we have focused on the interaction between financial structure and product-market competition. The design of the financial structure may also be used to alter the behavior of complementors in the vertical chain, rather than that of the producers of substitutes. A series of papers (Bronars and Deere 1991; Perotti and Spier 1993; Spiegel 1996; Spiegel and Spulber 1994) has argued in various settings that leverage can be used as a commitment to be tough in bargaining over conditions of trade. This insight is usually based on the following premises:[31]

(a) the firm will in the future negotiate with a third party over, say, a transfer price;

(b) the negotiation will be conducted by the entrepreneur (or more generally by the entrepreneur and a class of investors such as shareholders, as long as other interested claimholders are not part of the renegotiation);

(c) this third party has some bargaining power in the renegotiation, perhaps because of an existing relationship or because of institutional (regulatory) constraints on bargaining processes (the one case that is excluded by this assumption is the case in which the entrepreneur has full bargaining power, i.e., is able to make a take-it-or-leave-it offer to the third party).

In the same way that a firm can use leverage or give the control right over output determination to the entrepreneur to commit to behaving aggressively in the product market (see the discussion of the Brander–Lewis model above), the firm is able to commit to being an aggressive bargainer in future negotiations by giving control to the entrepreneur in those negotiations and by designing her compensation scheme in such a way that her eagerness to reach agreement or her ability to pay is reduced. Third parties are then induced to make concessions.

The third party may be a union, from which the firm tries to extract low wages (Bronars and Deere 1991; Dasgupta and Sengupta 1993), a regulator, from whom the firm (a utility) tries to extract high regulated retail prices (Spiegel 1996; Spiegel and Spulber 1994), a government, from whom the defense contractor tries to obtain high procurement prices, a raider, whose takeover offer the incumbent management tries to raise, or, conversely shareholders, whose free-riding behavior the raider tries to limit (see Chapter 11 and Müller and Panunzi (2004)). For example, in the context of labor relations, Bronars and Deere (1991) find a positive correlation at the industry level between leverage and unionization. Matsa (2005) develops a model of optimal maturity structure similar to that in Chapter 5, but in the presence of wage bargaining at the intermediate stage. He shows that short-term debt indeed rises with the union's bargaining power. Empirically, he uses U.S. state-specific changes in labor law, namely, the enactment of right-to-work leaves, which outlaw employment contract provisions that require employees to join or financially support the union, and thereby weaken unions. Such laws are indeed associated with an increase in the maturity structure of debt.

Note the role of (b) and (c) in the reasoning: if the entrepreneur acted on behalf of herself and all investors in the renegotiation process (say, because they act in concert or realign their interests just before the negotiation), then the initial financial structure would be irrelevant. Hence, the role of assumption (b). As for (c), there would be no point changing

30. Interestingly, Zingales (1998) finds that, in the U.S. trucking industry, a firm's leverage reduces the probability that it survives an increase in competition.

31. See, however, the discussion of Chemla and Faure-Grimaud (2001) below.

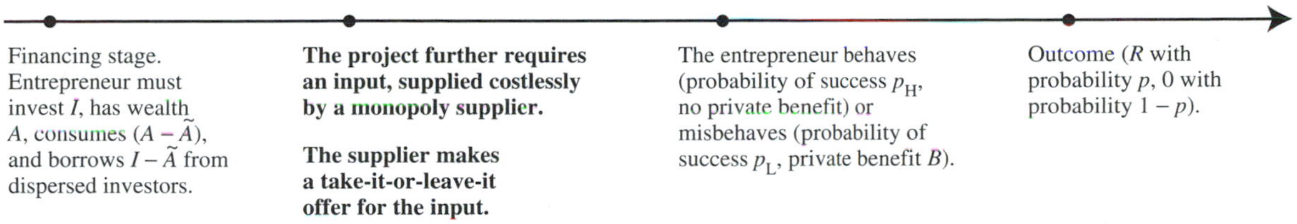
Financing stage. Entrepreneur must invest I, has wealth A, consumes $(A - \tilde{A})$, and borrows $I - \tilde{A}$ from dispersed investors.
The project further requires an input, supplied costlessly by a monopoly supplier.
The supplier makes a take-it-or-leave-it offer for the input.
The entrepreneur behaves (probability of success p_H, no private benefit) or misbehaves (probability of success p_L, private benefit B).
Outcome (R with probability p, 0 with probability $1 - p$).

Figure 7.6

the entrepreneur's objective function by altering the financial structure if the third party had no bargaining power. For example, a competitive supplier accepts the lowest price (its cost) that makes it break even, and this lowest price obtains regardless of the buyer's financial structure.

As we will see, the analysis here is closely related to those of the debt overhang (see Section 3.3) and of the soft budget constraint (see Section 5.5).

To illustrate the commitment effect, consider the situation depicted in Figure 7.6.

This is the standard fixed-investment model except for one twist: the initial investment financed by the lenders is not a sufficient enabler of the technology. A supplier will later bring, at no incremental cost to him, a key complementary input (say, a patent license) to make it possible to continue the project; in the absence of this input, the probability of success is nil. As usual, we assume that

$$p_H R > I > p_L R + B$$

(the NPV is positive if the entrepreneur behaves) and

$$p_H\left(R - \frac{B}{\Delta p}\right) \geqslant I - A$$

(there is enough pledgeable income).

To make the point in the most striking way, we assume that the supplier has full bargaining power: he will set the price for the input. This situation is most conducive to a holdup problem (see, for example, Williamson 1975). Once the investment I has been sunk, the supplier can ask for an extravagant price and basically expropriate the specific investment made by the entrepreneur and her lenders. Indeed, suppose that the entrepreneur and the initial investors acted in concert when deciding whether to accept the supplier's offer. Then the investors would be willing at date 1 to bring an amount of money equal to the pledgeable income, $p_H[R - B/\Delta p]$, that they can rescue by accepting the supplier's offer. Thus, the supplier fully expropriates the initial investors' claims in the firm, implying that the investors should at date 0 expect their initial outlay to yield no return. Hence, no investment takes place at date 0.

By contrast, assume now, as in Section 3.3, that the initial investors are dispersed and cannot take part in a renegotiation process. The supplier at date 1 offers a price for the input to the entrepreneur, who can at this point invest any of her wealth $(A - \tilde{A})$ not yet invested in the firm and/or turn to new investors.

The entrepreneur can now "trick" the supplier in the following way: she issues *senior* debt

$$D = R - \frac{B}{\Delta p}$$

to the initial investors, takes the minimum incentive-compatible stake $R_b = B/\Delta p$ in the firm, which she commits not to resell (i.e., writes a vesting provision and commits not to short-sell her stake), and, finally, keeps none of her noninvested wealth (i.e., consumes $A - \tilde{A}$). She thereby creates a debt overhang problem. New investors are unwilling to finance the firm at date 1 since the firm's income in the case of success, R, is already committed in part to the senior debtholders, $R - B/\Delta p$, with the rest, $B/\Delta p$, being needed as an incentive payment to induce the entrepreneur to behave. So, no new income can be raised by the entrepreneur in the absence of renegotiation with the initial investor. This debt overhang problem, which is usually a handicap for entrepreneurs needing to get refinancing, is an asset here because the cost of "refinancing" is fully endogenous: the supplier has no choice but to lower the price of its input to its marginal cost, here normalized at 0. At the initial stage, the entrepreneur borrows $I - \tilde{A}$ with

$$p_{\rm H}\left(R - \frac{B}{\Delta p}\right) = I - \tilde{A},$$

and consumes $A - \tilde{A} \geqslant 0$. She thereby fully extracts not only the investors' rent (as is usual in a competitive capital market), but also that of the monopoly supplier.

Note also that, were the entrepreneur to retain her noninvested wealth, $A - \tilde{A}$, until date 1, the supplier would be able to appropriate part of or all of this retained wealth. Indeed the entrepreneur has a stake, $p_{\rm H}B/\Delta p$, equal to her rent in the case of continuation. The supplier can then ask the entrepreneur to pay[32]

$$\min\left(A - \tilde{A}, p_{\rm H}\frac{B}{\Delta p}\right).$$

We thus uncover one exception to the general rule that the entrepreneur cannot lose by investing all her wealth in the firm at the initial stage as long as the contract with investors is structured properly.[33] Here, there is also a contract with a supplier, and, crucially, this contract is not yet entered into at the initial financing stage. The benefit from "committing not to be able to pay the supplier for his input" vindicates this partial consumption of the entrepreneur's equity.

Exercise 7.8 considers a very similar situation in which the third party is a customer rather than a supplier. The final payoff R in the case of success of the project is then endogenous, since it is the amount that the customer will pay for the intermediate input produced by the entrepreneur. As in the model above, the negotiation with the third party over the transfer price takes place after the initial financing stage, and so the financial structure can be used in order to extract more favorable conditions from the third party.

The exercise shows that *short-term debt is more efficient than long-term debt at capturing the customer's surplus.* To see this, suppose that the entrepreneur issues long-term debt (to be repaid after the outcome is realized) to dispersed investors, and, for simplicity, that this customer has full bargaining power in the negotiations. The customer can always wait until the outcome is realized to sign a contract, and (if the project is successful) propose to buy the good at a negligible price (0). Of course, this implies that the entrepreneur has no monetary stake in the case of success, and, anticipating this, chooses to misbehave if no contract has been signed before she chooses the effort decision. But as long as the probability of success, $p_{\rm L}$, in the case of misbehavior is positive, the customer can guarantee himself a rent.

Not so under short-term debt. If this short-term debt is not repaid, the entrepreneur's firm is liquidated. The customer then cannot play the previous waiting game, and must disburse if he is to keep his rent associated with the production of the intermediate input. Short-term debt therefore puts more pressure directly on the firm, and indirectly on the customer, than long-term debt. The reader will here note the analogy with the analysis of the *soft budget constraint* (the difference with Section 5.5 is that the customer, rather than the investors, is the victim of the soft budget constraint; but in both cases, a party with a stake in continuation is led to disburse in order to rescue the firm and prevent liquidation).

Chemla and Faure-Grimaud (2001) show that leverage may help a firm extract a high price from a customer even when the firm has price-setting power (so condition (c) above is violated) and when it can renegotiate with its investors (condition (b) is violated). Their insight is derived in the context of dynamic pricing to a consumer. As in Coase (1972), the firm does not know whether the consumer has a high or low valuation. Its optimal policy, if it could commit to a pricing policy over time and provided that the probability that the customer's valuation is high, is then to commit to a high price equal to the high valuation; unfortunately, the consumer's expectation that the monopolist will have an incentive to lower its price to the low-valuation level if the first offer is refused induces the high-valuation consumer to wait for a "price concession." That is,

32. Equivalently, if the entrepreneur borrowed less than $p_{\rm H}(R - B/\Delta p)$ from initial investors and took a larger stake than is needed to satisfy the incentive compatibility constraint, then the supplier would be able to charge a positive price.

33. See also the discussion of the Brander–Lewis model in the supplementary section.

Another and related reason why the entrepreneur may not want to invest her whole wealth in the firm arises when a raider wants to take over the firm (a raider's bid is similar to the input supplier's price). As we will see in Chapter 11, dispersed ownership may be a way of extracting the raider's rent. By contrast, if the entrepreneur keeps a large stake in the firm, this may lead to smaller takeover premia.

the monopolist's ability to lower its price tomorrow reduces its bargaining power today. Coase's durable-good monopolist model shows that a monopolist's bargaining power may be limited even if it has price-setting power.

Chemla and Faure-Grimaud introduce corporate finance into the Coase model. Leverage implies that the firm may be liquidated if it does not generate enough cash flow. Interestingly, leverage enables the monopolist to credibly charge a high price; for, if the high-valuation buyer does not purchase, no cash flow is generated and short-term debt is not repaid. The possibility of liquidation (and of a concomitant lack of price concessions in the future) induces the high-valuation buyer to accept higher offers early on. Also important is that Chemla and Faure-Grimaud allow for the possibility of renegotiation between entrepreneur and investors after the former's failure to repay her short-term debt. Because the entrepreneur values continuation more than the investors (who in Chemla and Faure-Grimaud receive a liquidation value when the firm is shut down early), the investors may well prefer not to renegotiate and to shut down the firm.[34] Finally, the strategic use of debt reduces social welfare because it exerts a negative externality on the high-valuation buyer, who is given the choice between paying a higher price or not consuming at all.

7.2 Creative Accounting and Other Earnings Manipulations

Much of the analysis in the previous chapters has looked at the provision of managerial incentives to reach higher levels of performance. For example, managerial incentives can be aligned with investors' objectives by rewarding management for superior performance, that is by linking a high compensation to a realization in the upper tail of the performance spectrum. Unfortunately, such "high-powered incentive schemes" usually imply that managerial and investor interests are no longer aligned along other dimensions of managerial activity. In particular, schemes that induce high effort create additional forms of moral hazard, in two ways:

(i) timing of income recognition, to the extent that management has leeway in moving income forward and backward in time;
(ii) risk management, as management can take actions that increase or decrease the firm's income risk.

These additional forms of moral hazard are costly for two reasons: they garble performance measurement and investors' assessment of managerial or project quality; and, as we will shortly see, they generally entail direct costs.

The leitmotiv of this section is thus that high-powered incentive schemes face a multitasking problem (they change effort, but also other behaviors), and that any move toward high-powered incentives must be accompanied with a direct control of these side effects. We start with the case of earnings manipulations and then address risk taking.

7.2.1 Earnings Manipulations

The accounting literature (see, for example, Merchant 1989; Ronen and Sadan 1981) has, over a long period, documented the many ways in which management can alter the external assessments of its firm's performance. To simplify, there are basically two categories of earnings management techniques.

Accounting methods ("cooking the books"). Even without resorting to fraud, managers have substantial discretion in their income and balance-sheet statements. That is, they enjoy flexibility even within the confines of the Generally Accepted Accounting Principles.

For example, the choice of reserves or provisions for loan losses is always subjective. When a customer does not reimburse his trade credit or when, more generally, a borrower fails to pay interest or principal on a loan, there is usually some probability that the borrower will nevertheless be able to partly or fully repay the loan in the future. Alternative hypotheses as to whether the borrower's situation will

34. The literature on Coase's durable-good model has often suggested that the monopolist's commitment power can be restored by committing to transfer a large amount of money to a third party if the monopolist lowers its price over time. The standard criticism of this argument is that such a contract with a third party is not renegotiation proof, since, once a high price has been charged, the firm and the third party are better off renegotiating away the lack of price flexibility. Chemla and Faure-Grimaud make such side-contracts (with investors as the "third party") credible by letting the entrepreneur be cash constrained and by introducing an agency problem that creates an *ex post* divergence of interests between entrepreneur and investors.

improve so that he will be in a position to reimburse have a substantial impact on the provisions to be made by the firm. More generally, estimating the value of investments that are not marked-to-market[35] involves some discretion. This discretion can be used in particular to make the firm look more profitable than it really is.[36] Of course, an underprovision only shifts loss recognition in time. Later provisions will need to be made when losses are actually realized or become impossible to hide and deny.

Another common way of shifting income across time is the choice of when a sale or expense is recorded. For example, a sale can be recorded only in January when it actually took place in December, or the reverse. This manipulation affects the assessment of the firm's performance during the year.

In the same spirit, the choice between capitalizing or expensing maintenance and investment costs shifts accounting income across time. Relatedly, a recent debate has focused on whether corporations should expense the stock options (a contingent liability) that they grant to their managers (see Chapter 1).

Lastly, there are various ways of practicing balance-sheet window dressing. For example, the firm may transfer poor investments and associated debts to nonconsolidated subsidiaries.

Such manipulations have the potential to fool the firm's investors and to distort their assessment as to whether they should interfere to change the course of action or replace the manager. And they involve direct costs. First, managerial attention may be devoted to practicing "creative accounting" and fooling investors. Second, corporate resources may be engaged in the process. For example, the firm may reduce the external accountants' investigative ardors by dangling the prospect of termination of lucrative consulting contracts.

Operating methods. Alternatively, the firm may distort its strategy in order to alter the external perception of the firm's condition. This form of posturing has direct (real) effects, and not only the indirect ones associated with the garbling of investors' information. For example, to inflate current profits, the firm may delay maintenance and reduce its inventory levels. Or it may run end-of-period sales. Instead of slashing its prices in January just after the holiday season, it can boost the previous year's profit by running a December sale at the cost of reducing overall profit. It can grant advantageous terms to its customers in exchange for their accepting to take early delivery (conversely, to delay income recognition, it may convince them to accept late shipments or to pay late).

The direct costs of such strategies are obvious: bad timing, overtime pay, production disturbances, and the like.

7.2.1.1 Managerial Myopia: The Incentive for Posturing

A common theme in corporate finance is that there are benefits to keeping management "on a tight leash" by giving investors an option to fire management, downsize the firm or more generally interfere when they perceive that performance is not adequate. We have seen several reasons why such interference may raise efficiency or at least increase pledgeable income. First, interference *ex post* sanctions past mismanagement and thus *ex ante* may act as a deterrent against such moral hazard. Second, interference may be more forward looking: inadequate past performance may well signal poor prospects. Third, interference may also help solve the adverse-selection problem studied in the previous chapter: a low-quality borrower is more reluctant to seek financing if she knows it is likely that her project or employment will be terminated before completion.

Now, the modes of intervention are diverse: a strong board (or a venture capitalist) may exercise its control rights to fire the manager[37] or restrict her

35. Some assets, such as stocks in publicly traded companies, have market values that can be and are used to estimate the gains and losses on these assets. This objectivity brought about by the existence of a market is a major argument in favor of using market values in accounting (there are drawbacks, though, as market values may make the firm's balance sheet highly volatile (see, for example, Dewatripont and Tirole (1994) on this)). The absence of marked-to-market accounting generates behaviors such as the use of lease-backs: when commercial real estate appreciates, the company may be tempted to sell its buildings and immediately lease them back, so as to allow the capital gain to show up in the accounts.

36. Or, conversely, to understate the value of its assets: see Section 7.2.2 for why managers sometimes try to play a low-key role.

37. There is substantial evidence that nonroutine management changes are associated with poor financial performance (see, for example, Weisbach 1988; Murphy and Zimmerman 1993).

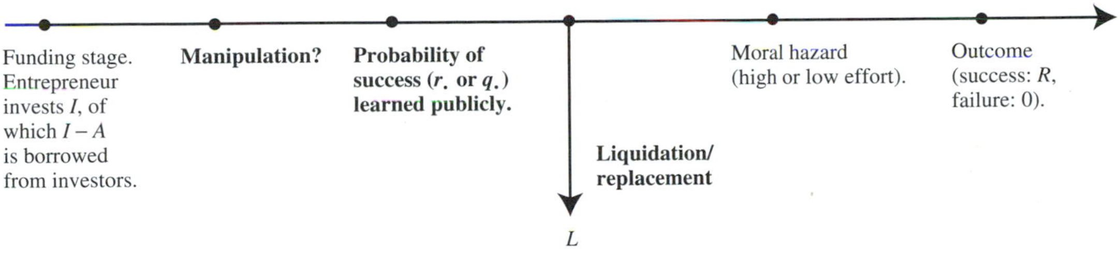

Figure 7.7

freedom. A raider may take over the firm and replace management or implement a new strategy. A bank may select not to roll over its short-term debt and therefore to confront the firm with limited liquidity.

The trouble is that management may boost short-term profit through desirable and undesirable means: when faced with the threat of firing, liquidation or merely restricted freedom, management may have an incentive to inefficiently inflate short-run performance at the cost of long-term loss that exceeds the short-term gain, a behavior often called "managerial myopia"; this behavior is rational from the manager's perspective, though: "myopia" refers to the perception of an external observer who witnesses a short-term orientation and fails to account for the agency considerations inherent in this behavior. Thus, solving one agency problem gives rise to a different one. This point has been developed in particular by Stein (1989).[38]

Consider the fixed-investment model of Section 3.2, with the new ingredient that there is some learning at an intermediate stage about the entrepreneur's ability to run the project and the concomitant opportunity to replace her (or to liquidate the project) on the basis of this information (see Figure 7.7). The manager's type, which is a synonym for the probability of success, is either $r_\bullet$ or $q_\bullet$, where the dot subscript refers to the fact that the probability of success is not solely determined by the manager's ability and is a function of later effort (high or low).

No manipulation. Let us for the moment rule out any managerial manipulation of the intermediate information received by the investors. The latter learn at the intermediate stage that the probability of success in the case of continuation $\pi_\bullet = (\pi_H, \pi_L)$ (that is, contingent on effort: π_H in the case of good behavior, π_L in the case of misbehavior) is either high ($r_\bullet = (r_H, r_L)$) or low ($q_\bullet = (q_H, q_L)$), with $r_H > q_H$ and $r_L > q_L$. At the funding stage, no one knows which prevails, and the prior on the two possibilities is $(\alpha, 1-\alpha)$:

$$\pi_\bullet = \begin{cases} r_\bullet & \text{with probability } \alpha, \\ q_\bullet & \text{with probability } 1-\alpha. \end{cases}$$

Although a number of applications involve the manipulation of short-term earnings, we will for notational simplicity assume that the signal is a pure signal, and is not linked to an intermediate profit. One can think of this signal as some balance-sheet information regarding the final payoff. The basic ideas would carry over to information revealed by a short-term profit.

For simplicity, we will also assume that the manager's "type" ($r_\bullet$ or $q_\bullet$) is orthogonal to later moral hazard. So, if r_H and q_H denote the probabilities of success in the case of good behavior, and r_L and q_L those in the case of misbehavior, then

$$r_H - r_L = q_H - q_L = p_H - p_L = \Delta p,$$

letting $p_H \equiv \alpha r_H + (1-\alpha) q_H$ and $p_L \equiv \alpha r_L + (1-\alpha) q_L$ refer to the prior beliefs that the project will succeed under good and bad behavior, respectively. Thus, regardless of the manager's type, shirking reduces the probability of success by Δp.

38. For other investigations of managerial myopia, see, for example, Darrough (1987), Narayanan (1985), and especially von Thadden (1995).

There is a closely related literature on second sourcing in procurement and regulation (see, for example, Laffont and Tirole 1988). In that literature, a franchised supplier privileges current cost reduction over long-term investment in facilities when faced with the possibility that the franchise be terminated and the facilities turned over to a new management team.

Suppose that, when it accrues, the information about the manager's type is public and, for simplicity, verifiable;[39] and that, contingent on the signal, the initial contract specifies whether management is allowed to continue or not.[40] In the case of termination, the firm generates an expected profit L that can be shared between investors and incumbent management.

Example. Suppose that the manager's replacement is another similar manager of unknown ability in the job. Then, the "liquidation" value is

$$L = p_{\mathrm{H}}\left(R - \frac{B}{\Delta p}\right).$$

For, the new management must be provided with a reward, $B/\Delta p$, in the case of success that induces the high effort. The pledgeable income is therefore equal to $p_{\mathrm{H}}[R - B/\Delta p]$.

We make the following assumption:

$$q_{\mathrm{H}}R > L. \tag{7.9}$$

Inequality (7.9) says that, ceteris paribus, even a low-ability manager would prefer to keep her job, as this yields a higher NPV than termination. Put differently, it is *ex ante* efficient for the entrepreneur to retain her job. In the example above, in which the entrepreneur is replaced by another entrepreneur with unknown ability, (7.9) is satisfied if the agency cost, and thus the rent to be left to the new entrepreneur, are high.

We will also assume that

$$I - A > \max\left\{p_{\mathrm{H}}\left(R - \frac{B}{\Delta p}\right), L\right\}, \tag{7.10}$$

while

$$I - A < \alpha r_{\mathrm{H}}\left(R - \frac{B}{\Delta p}\right) + (1-\alpha)L. \tag{7.11}$$

The first inequality (7.10) states that guarantee of either tenure (the entrepreneur always keeps her job) or termination (the entrepreneur is always fired) does not generate enough pledgeable income to attract investors. Because the incentive problem is independent of the entrepreneur's type, the entrepreneur must be rewarded at least $B/\Delta p$ for success in order to have an incentive to behave. And so the pledgeable income under guaranteed tenure is insufficient to cover the investors' initial outlay, $I - A$. By contrast, the second inequality, (7.11), which requires that

$$q_{\mathrm{H}}\left(R - \frac{B}{\Delta p}\right) < L < r_{\mathrm{H}}\left(R - \frac{B}{\Delta p}\right),$$

implies that there is enough pledgeable income to attract investors when there is termination in case of low ability, provided that the investors receive the return L in the case of termination.

Under a competitive capital market the entrepreneur's utility in case of funding is equal to the NPV:

$$U_{\mathrm{b}}(z^r, z^q) = \alpha[z^r(r_{\mathrm{H}}R) + (1-z^r)L] + (1-\alpha)[z^q(q_{\mathrm{H}}R) + (1-z^q)L] - I,$$

where z^r and z^q are the contracted-for probabilities of continuation of employment of a high- and low-ability entrepreneur, respectively. From (7.9), this utility is maximized by a guaranteed tenure:

$$z^r = z^q = 1.$$

Guaranteed tenure, however, does not attract funds (from (7.10)); and so some (contingent) termination must be conceded in order to satisfy the investors' breakeven constraint:

$$\alpha\left[z^r r_{\mathrm{H}}\left(R - \frac{B}{\Delta p}\right) + (1-z^r)L_{\mathrm{l}}^r\right] + (1-\alpha)\left[z^q q_{\mathrm{H}}\left(R - \frac{B}{\Delta p}\right) + (1-z^q)L_{\mathrm{l}}^q\right] \geqslant I - A,$$

where L_{l}^r and L_{l}^q ($\leqslant L$) are the lenders' returns in the case of termination of a high- and low-ability manager, respectively. Clearly, setting

$$L_{\mathrm{l}}^r = L_{\mathrm{l}}^q = L$$

is optimal since this relaxes the investors' breakeven constraint without altering the NPV.[41] Also, it is

39. That is, a court can ascertain the realization of this type. Alternatively, and equivalently, the type can be inferred from the market value of risky financial claims on this firm (since these values fall when the manager has low ability and increase when she has high ability).

40. Following up on the previous footnote: if the realization of the type cannot be directly ascertained by the court, a mechanism must be designed that indirectly yields the same outcome as that given by direct court verification. For example, some debt may be due at the intermediate stage, and management may be given the right to issue equity in order to repay the debt. Since the value of the equity issue grows with the manager's observed ability, the continuation decision is thus made contingent on the type. We will discuss a similar mechanism in Chapter 9.

41. By the same token, it is optimal to minimize the entrepreneur's reward in the case of continuation of employment. This property is

more efficient (in terms of maximizing both the NPV and the pledgeable income) to retain a high-ability manager:

$$z^r = 1.$$

Let $z^q = z^*$. From (7.10) and (7.11), the value $z^* \in (0, 1)$ is the smallest value[42] that satisfies the investors' breakeven constraint:

$$\alpha r_{\mathrm{H}}\left(R - \frac{B}{\Delta p}\right) + (1-\alpha)\left[z^* q_{\mathrm{H}}\left(R - \frac{B}{\Delta p}\right) + (1 - z^*)L\right] = I - A. \tag{7.12}$$

Some termination in case of low ability is the concession made by the entrepreneur to attract investors. As is familiar, the entrepreneur sacrifices value (NPV) to boost pledgeable income.

Manipulation. Until now, we have assumed that the information received by the investors at the intermediate stage lies outside the entrepreneur's control. Let us now assume that the entrepreneur can, at a cost, alter this information.

More precisely, suppose that the entrepreneur can generate the high signal $r_{\bullet}$ by (secretly) manipulating the information. This manipulation comes at a cost: the probability of success falls (uniformly) by $\tau > 0$.[43]

We distinguish two forms of manipulation:

Uninformed manipulation. The entrepreneur does not know her type when deciding whether to manipulate information (so, she learns her type at the same time as the investors in Figure 7.7).

Informed manipulation. The entrepreneur knows her type when choosing whether to manipulate the information (but learns it only after the funding stage, which therefore still occurs under symmetric information).[44]

Suppose, in the first step, that the financing contract specifies, besides the probabilities of continuation z^r and z^q for signals $r_{\bullet}$ and $q_{\bullet}$, a reward $R_{\mathrm{b}} \geqslant B/\Delta p$ in the case of continuation and success (and no payment to the entrepreneur otherwise).

Under *uninformed manipulation*, the entrepreneur decides whether to generate signal $r_{\bullet}$ for certain before learning her type. Assume throughout that it is optimal to induce the entrepreneur not to manipulate the investors' information.[45]

Under uninformed manipulation, the no-manipulation constraint is

$$z^r[(p_{\mathrm{H}} - \tau)R_{\mathrm{b}}] \leqslant [\alpha z^r r_{\mathrm{H}} + (1-\alpha) z^q q_{\mathrm{H}}]R_{\mathrm{b}}.$$

The left-hand side of this constraint is the entrepreneur's expected reward in the case of manipulation. In that case, signal $r_{\bullet}$ is generated, yielding continuation probability z^r. The average probability of success is then $p_{\mathrm{H}} - \tau$. The right-hand side accounts for the entrepreneur's not knowing her type when deciding whether to manipulate the information.

This inequality can be rewritten as

$$\frac{z^r}{z^q} \leqslant \frac{1}{1 - \tau/(1-\alpha)q_{\mathrm{H}}}. \tag{7.13}$$

Inequality (7.13) states that the probability of continuation in the case of a good signal cannot be much greater than that in the case of a bad signal. For example, when the cost of manipulation (as measured by τ) converges to 0, these probabilities must be approximately equal (given that continuation for a good signal is otherwise more appealing and so $z^r \geqslant z^q$).

Under *informed manipulation*, the entrepreneur is tempted to manipulate the information only when she learns that she is inefficient. The new no-manipulation constraint is

$$z^r[(q_{\mathrm{H}} - \tau)R_{\mathrm{b}}] \leqslant z^q[q_{\mathrm{H}} R_{\mathrm{b}}]$$

---

already embodied in the breakeven constraint by setting the investors' return at $R - B/\Delta p$ in the case of success.

42. The reader may find this "random termination contract" unrealistic. This randomness is, however, an artifact of the discrete representation of the type space. With a continuum of possible types for the entrepreneur, the optimal policy would take the form of a deterministic cutoff rule: employment would continue if and only if the entrepreneur's ability exceeds some threshold.

43. Since we will focus on policies that incentivize management not to engage in such manipulations, we do not need to specify the impact of the manipulation on L. This impact may be small or nonexistent if termination is interpreted as a liquidation and the resale of the firm's collateral; in contrast, in the replacement interpretation given in the example above, it may make sense to assume that L is reduced from $p_{\mathrm{H}}[R - B/\Delta p]$ to $(p_{\mathrm{H}} - \tau)[R - B/\Delta p]$.

44. If the entrepreneur were to learn her type before contracting with the investors, she might use dissipative signals such as a distorted continuation rule in order to reveal her type (see Chapter 6).

45. With this class of contract, it cannot be the case that the entrepreneur manipulates the information. If she did, then $z^r = z^q = z$, since the investors cannot tell the two states apart. The initial contract should instead set $z^r = z^q = z$, which provides no incentive for manipulation and yields the same continuation decision.

or

$$\frac{z^r}{z^q} \leqslant \frac{1}{1-\tau/q_H}. \tag{7.14}$$

Note that constraint (7.14) is harder to satisfy than constraint (7.13). That is, the continuation decision must be made even less signal dependent (in the sense that z^r/z^q is closer to 1) under informed manipulation. This is intuitive: the entrepreneur is more likely to want to look good and to start cheating if she knows that she will be in trouble otherwise. By contrast, under uninformed manipulation, the cost of manipulation is wastefully incurred when the entrepreneur turns out to be efficient. The relevant no-manipulation constraint, (7.13) in the case of uninformed manipulation and (7.14) in the case of informed manipulation, will be labeled (NM).

Whether manipulation is uninformed or informed, the initial contract must in general lower z^r or increase z^q—in a nutshell, make continuation less signal dependent—or both. This is reminiscent of the analysis of the predation-deterrence constraint (PD) earlier in this chapter. The difference is that the lack of responsiveness of the continuation rule is meant to alter the behavior of the entrepreneur, rather than that of a product-market rival.

The threat of manipulation may prevent the firm from receiving funding in the first place. Start from the solution ($z^r = 1$, $z^q = z^*$) as defined by equation (7.12) when there is no scope for manipulation, and suppose that the ratio $1/z^*$ does not satisfy the relevant (NM) constraint. That is,

$$\frac{1}{z^*} > \frac{1}{1-\tau/(1-\alpha)q_H}$$

under uninformed manipulation and

$$\frac{1}{z^*} > \frac{1}{1-\tau/q_H}$$

under informed manipulation.

If one keeps $z^r \equiv 1$, then z^q must be increased about z^* so as to satisfy the (NM) constraint. Increasing z^q above z^*, however, is not feasible since this reduces pledgeable income, which then becomes insufficient to cover the investors' initial outlay. Thus continuation cannot be guaranteed to a high-ability entrepreneur ($z^r < 1$).

This reduction in z^r reduces pledgeable income as $r_H[R-B/\Delta p] > L$.[46] Hence, z^q must also be brought down below z^* in order to make up for the shortfall in pledgeable income.[47]

As one could have expected, *the entrepreneur's ability to cook the books ex post may jeopardize funding ex ante.* And, even if funding is feasible, this ability reduces the NPV.

7.2.1.2 Golden Parachutes

Top managers often receive very large compensation packages when their employment is terminated. These "golden parachutes" appear particularly "obscene" when termination is motivated by poor performance. Of course, many of these packages result from the board being in cahoots (or not wanting to enter any conflict) with top management. There is also some efficiency rationale for golden parachutes. Intuitively, the "softened landing" that they offer to managers makes them less prone to engage in various venal behaviors, such as earnings manipulations, in order to keep their job. In a nutshell, proponents of golden parachutes argue that they are the price to pay for incentive compatibility.[48]

Are golden parachutes beneficial here? They are clearly costly as they reduce pledgeable income.[49] However, a golden parachute helps relax the (NM) constraint. In a sense, they create more "balanced"

46. Note, though, that $z^r < 1$ requires commitment power. Otherwise termination with some probability would not be renegotiation proof, since both parties would be better off agreeing on continuation.

47. But this still may not create enough pledgeable income. Write the (binding) (NM) constraint as $z^q = \theta z^r$ with $\theta < 1$. The derivative of the pledgeable income with respect to z^r is (with obvious notation)

$$\frac{\mathrm{d}\mathcal{P}(z^r,\theta z^r)}{\mathrm{d}z^r} = \alpha\Big[r_H\Big(R-\frac{B}{\Delta p}\Big)-L\Big]-(1-\alpha)\theta\Big[L-q_H\Big(R-\frac{B}{\Delta p}\Big)\Big].$$

Because $\mathcal{P}(1,\theta) < I-A$, satisfying the investors' breakeven constraint requires that $\mathrm{d}\mathcal{P}/\mathrm{d}z^r < 0$ (this is a necessary, but not a sufficient, condition). And so, necessarily, $p_H(R-B/\Delta p) < L$. In particular, financing cannot be secured in the example in which L is derived from replacing the manager by another one with unknown ability (then, $L = p_H(R-B/\Delta p)$).

48. Jensen (1988), in the context of takeovers, was one of the first advocates of golden parachutes, on the grounds that they help align managerial incentives with those of investors and thereby facilitate takeovers.

49. A further cost might arise if we added to the model an "*ex ante* moral hazard" problem, in which the $r_\bullet$ or $q_\bullet$ signal would result not from an exogenously determined managerial ability to accomplish the task, but from an *ex ante* "investment effort" of the entrepreneur (as, for example, in Section 5.5). The golden parachute might exacerbate this form of moral hazard.

incentives for the manager by increasing her payoff in the case of liquidation.[50] Indeed, consider (for example) the case of informed manipulation and suppose that the entrepreneur receives some amount $T \geqslant 0$ when admitting that prospects are poor, i.e., when the signal is $q_{\bullet}$.[51] The new (NM) constraint is

$$z^r[(q_H - \tau)R_b] \leqslant z^q[q_H R_b] + T, \qquad (7.15)$$

where $R_b = B/\Delta p$ in order to maximize the income that can be pledged to investors.[52]

The key question is whether it is cheaper to prevent manipulation by making tenure relatively insensitive to new information or by granting a golden parachute ($T > 0$). To answer this question, let us write the NPV (which does not depend on T),

$$\begin{aligned} U_b(z^r, z^q, T) &= \text{NPV} \\ &= \alpha[L + z^r(r_H R - L)] \\ &\quad + (1-\alpha)[L + z^q(q_H R - L)] - I, \end{aligned}$$

and the pledgeable income,[53]

$$\begin{aligned} &\mathcal{P}(z^r, z^q, T) \\ &\quad = \alpha[L + z^r[r_H(R - R_b) - L]] \\ &\qquad + (1-\alpha)[L + z^q[q_H(R - R_b) - L] - T] \\ &\quad = I - A. \end{aligned}$$

Intuitively, there are two "currencies" available for paying the manager: continuation and golden parachute. A golden parachute is just a cash transfer while the continuation policy affects the NPV. One would therefore expect a golden parachute to be used exactly when the continuation policy is an inefficient policy, that is, when continuation under poor prospects reduces the NPV.

To demonstrate this "efficient currency result," suppose that $T > 0$. Looking at the pledgeable income, a unit increase in z^q (which increases the *ex ante* utility U_b because of the assumption that $q_H R > L$, but reduces pledgeable income), must be compensated by a decrease in the golden parachute equal in absolute value to

$$\left|\frac{dT}{dz^q}\right| = L - q_H(R - R_b).$$

From (7.15), this marginal change that keeps investor income constant relaxes the (NM) constraint:

$$\begin{aligned} dz^q(q_H R_b) + dT &= dz^q[q_H R_b - L + q_H(R - R_b)] \\ &= (q_H R - L)\,dz^q > 0. \end{aligned}$$

Thus the optimal golden parachute policy is to have none:

$$T^* = 0.$$

Not so when continuation under poor prospects reduces the NPV, and not only the investor income. Suppose now that

$$q_H R < L.$$

Then, from the previous reasoning, a golden parachute is a cheaper instrument than an insensitive tenure to keep the entrepreneur from manipulating accounts. When it is optimal to fire the manager in the case of poor prospects, she is paid a golden parachute:

$$z^{q*} = 0 \quad \text{and} \quad T^* = z^r(q_H - \tau)R_b > 0.$$

Exercise 7.9 asks the reader to check this heuristic reasoning more formally.

7.2.1.3 The Importance of Commitment

We have assumed that the review and the concomitant decision over whether to retain the entrepreneur are contingent on some performance measure that is objective[54] (although manipulable) and can

50. The need for balanced managerial incentives to prevent income manipulation is a much more general theme in corporate finance, and arises even in situations where the manager's tenure or the continuation of the project are not at stake.

For example, Friebel and Guriev (2005) show how incentives for earnings manipulation depend on the structure of managerial compensation, that is on the ratio of short versus long incentives (note the analogy with the point made on payouts in Application 7 in Section 6.3). A key aspect of Friebel and Guriev's model is the presence of division managers, who may act as whistleblowers in the case of income manipulation by the CEO (in the United States, the Sarbanes–Oxley Act of 2002 has tried to make whistleblowing easier by, for example, protecting employees who provide evidence about violations of regulations). The paper shows how top managers can neutralize the incentive to blow the whistle by providing lower-level managers with short-term incentives and thereby provides an explanation for the propagation of short-term incentives (based on stock options) within the corporate hierarchy.

51. This compensation is slightly different from a golden parachute, since the latter would be received contingent on termination (in particular, when $z^r < 1$, the golden parachute would be received with positive probability even though the manager does not admit to poor prospects). The form of golden parachute considered here is more efficient because it is more effective at addressing the (NM) constraint. But it relies on our assumption that the state of nature is contractible. The analysis would not change much with the alternative formalization.

52. R_b is assumed to be the same in both states, but this involves no loss of generality.

53. So, in the previous notation, $L_l^r = L$ and $L_l^q = L - T/(1 - z^q)$.

54. In the sense of being verifiable. Note that the court, even if it does not itself observe the manager's productivity, could infer it

be contracted upon. By contrast and by the same reasoning, softer pieces of information can less easily enter the decision to fire/retain the entrepreneur. To see this, suppose that the investors have control over the tenure decision, and that they, but not the court, observe the signal.

It is then clear that manipulation must occur. Indeed, were the equilibrium separating, the investors would perfectly learn the entrepreneur's ability and so would set (*ex post*)

$$z^r = 1 \quad \text{and} \quad z^q = 0.$$

Unless they are able to develop a reputation for implementing the optimal commitment policy (z^r, z^q), the investors are too tough in the case of low ability (or too lenient in the case of high ability!). Thus, manipulation is more likely in the absence of commitment. Or, put differently, it may be worth reestablishing commitment by not giving investors the control right over the firing decision; but then the entrepreneur is never fired and funding is impossible to secure if (7.10) holds.

7.2.1.4 Relationship to the "Early Signal" Literature

Levitt and Snyder (1997) consider a moral-hazard environment that is similar in spirit to the situation described in Figure 7.7. In our terminology, an entrepreneur, after receiving funding for an investment, chooses a high or low effort. She then privately learns a signal about the probability of success of the project. Thus, the situation is similar to the "informed manipulation" case studied above in that, despite the absence of adverse selection at the *ex ante* stage, the entrepreneur acquires hidden knowledge during the relationship. Liquidation is desirable if the news is bad and continuation is optimal if the news is good. The issue, though, is to provide the entrepreneur with an incentive to disclose bad news. Levitt and Snyder analyze the outcome when investors are able or unable to commit to a liquidation policy. Let us, for conciseness, focus on the commitment case. A key result is that the investors should reward the entrepreneur for coming forward with bad news. Also, the investors optimally commit to not systematically liquidate the project when the continuation value is negative; in particular, liquidation weakens the link between the agent's effort and the project's outcome, and therefore garbles performance measurement.

through, say, the variation in the firm's stock price if this firm is traded in a public market.

7.2.2 Career Concerns

7.2.2.1 A Noncontingent-Continuation Result

We have assumed that managerial incentives to behave are exclusively monetary, e.g., come from stock options that become vested with tenure.[55] Very similar phenomena arise when managers want to keep their jobs because of the attached private benefits (perks, third-party favors, prestige).[56]

The version of the model we consider here is very similar to that described in Figure 7.7. Hence, to simplify things to the extreme, it assumes that monetary incentives are not effective at motivating the entrepreneur. Namely, make the following two modeling changes:

- The manager does not respond to all monetary incentives. That is, her utility from money is

$$U(w) = \begin{cases} w_0 & \text{if } w \geqslant w_0, \\ -\infty & \text{if } w < w_0. \end{cases}$$

The manager wants some (subsistence) income w_0 corresponding to the standard of living that she could obtain in another activity, but is not interested in money beyond that level. Consequently, any contract that with some probability will result in a wage below w_0 will not be accepted by the manager, and any reward beyond w_0 is wasted money for the investors; the manager will thus receive a fixed wage w_0. Thus, while the "career-concerns model" generically refers to situations in which economic agents are incentivized by the future gains (monetary or nonmonetary) attached to a good reputation, this section focuses on the specific incentives

55. There are also, of course, (potential) private benefits in the model; but these private benefits, which motivate the monetary incentives in the first place, are linked to misbehavior.

56. The seminal paper by Holmström (1982) on the incentives surrounding career concerns has generated a large literature on their implications, starting with the work of Holmström and Ricart i Costa (1986) on their impact on managerial investment choices. Holmström's single-effort, single-performance-measure model is extended to a general multitask environment in Dewatripont et al. (1999a,b).

provided by the desire to keep the private benefit associated with the job.

• In the case of continuation there is no moral hazard, but the manager receives a private benefit $\mathcal{B} > 0$, rather than 0 when her firm is liquidated or she is replaced.

The rest of the timing is unchanged.

Because the entrepreneur must be given wage w_0, but no incentive payment is needed, the pledgeable income becomes $p_H R - w_0$ instead of $p_H[R - B/\Delta p]$ in condition (7.10) and $\alpha r_H R + (1-\alpha)L - w_0$ instead of $\alpha r_H[R - B/\Delta p] + (1-\alpha)L$ in condition (7.11). Hence, assumptions (7.10) and (7.11) are replaced by

$$I + w_0 - A > \max\{p_H R, L\} \tag{7.12$'$}$$

and

$$I + w_0 - A < \alpha r_H R + (1-\alpha)L \tag{7.13$'$}$$

(as earlier, one possible interpretation of L is obtained by assuming that the entrepreneur is replaced by a manager with unknown ability: for example, $L = p_H R$ if the subsistence income is equal to 0).

The (NM) constraint becomes, whether manipulation is informed or uninformed,

$$z^r \mathcal{B} \leqslant z^q \mathcal{B}. \tag{NM$'$}$$

Given that continuation is more desirable for investors in the productive state (the manager does not have a relative preference for continuation in the high- versus low-productivity state because she does not respond to monetary incentives and therefore her utility is unaffected by the profit realization), they will set

$$z^r = z^q.$$

Thus, the continuation decision is no longer contingent on the information accruing regarding the entrepreneur's ability when the latter is driven solely by the desire to keep the private benefits attached to the job. First, as we just noted, the entrepreneur cares about the job's perks and therefore is not affected by the loss in profit associated with earnings manipulation. Second, golden parachutes are ineffective if keeping her job is the manager's primary incentive. Thus, investors have no instrument to induce the entrepreneur to refrain from manipulating earnings. By contrast, and as we will see when we discuss income smoothing, the entrepreneur faces a nontrivial choice when there is more than one "review period" at which the opportunity of retaining the manager is reconsidered.

7.2.2.2 Other Forms of Posturing: Gambling and Herding

The literature has considered several forms of posturing associated with risk taking and herding behaviors. Although these forms of posturing apply to managers driven by money as well as those driven by career concerns, we choose to discuss them in the latter context so as to provide examples of managers driven by career concerns facing nontrivial manipulation decisions (unlike in the situation we just described).

Risk taking. The propensity for managers to take risks when their job is endangered and to be conservative when it is relatively secure is well-known among practitioners and economists. To show why this behavior is privately optimal for the manager, consider a two-activity, two-period firm and the timing described in Figure 7.8.

The description of the firm's activities in each period is similar to that in Diamond's (1984) model of diversification (reviewed in Section 4.2). The possibility of manipulation here refers to the entrepreneur's secretly choosing the correlation (perfect or none) of the two projects.[57] We assume the following:

- The entrepreneur (and her potential replacement) do not respond to monetary incentives. Rather, they get a private benefit $\mathcal{B}$ per period of tenure.
- The entrepreneur has, as earlier, unknown ability. With probability α, she is a high-ability manager (the probability of success of a project is r); with probability $1-\alpha$, she has low ability (the probability of success is q).[58]
- The investors have the control right over the replacement of the entrepreneur by an alternative manager; there is no commitment regarding this

57. There is no need to introduce such a choice at date 1 since the manager in place has no career concerns then, and expected profit is independent of the degree of correlation.

58. Because the entrepreneur does not respond to monetary incentives, there is no point introducing moral hazard.

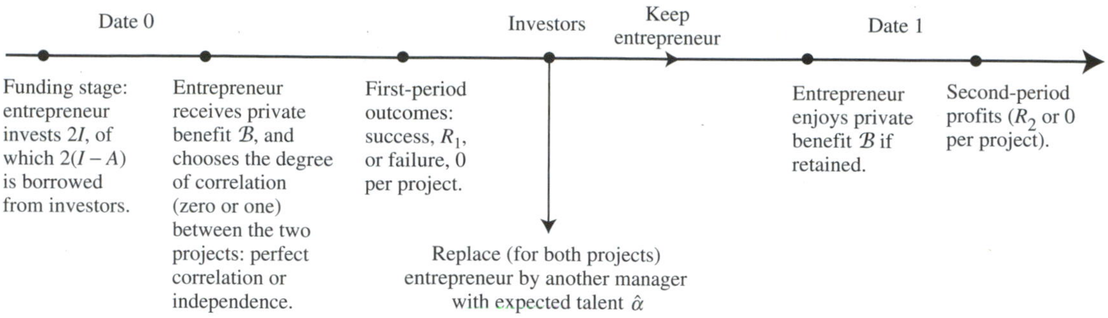

Figure 7.8

decision, and so investors just choose the manager with the highest perceived expected ability. The alternative manager's perceived expected ability is (arbitrarily) equal to $\hat{\alpha}$.

Suppose that the firm receives funding. The entrepreneur then chooses the degree of correlation (0 or 1, for simplicity) so as to maximize the probability of keeping her job.

The equilibrium behavior is summarized in Figure 7.9.

We are interested in situations in which the replacement decision is not a foregone conclusion (which it would be if the expected ability $\hat{\alpha}$ of the replacement manager were extremely high, so that a fully successful manager would be replaced anyway, or extremely low, so the incumbent manager would keep her job even after two failures).

Suppose first that the entrepreneur is expected to hedge.[59] Let α_0^{H}, α_1^{H}, and α_2^{H} denote the posterior probabilities that the incumbent manager has high ability, conditional on 0, 1, and 2 successes at date 0, where "H" stands for "hedging."[60]

For this behavior to be part of an equilibrium (and therefore to be rationally expected by the investors), the entrepreneur must not find it optimal to deviate and choose two perfectly correlated projects instead. Suppose first that

$$\hat{\alpha} < \alpha_1^{\mathrm{H}}.$$

That is, a single success out of two realizations suffices to keep the job. Because gambling increases the probability of two failures,[61] it increases the likelihood that the entrepreneur loses her job. Hence, it is indeed suboptimal for the manager to gamble. By analogy with the notion that financial options are "in the money" when things are going well (in that case, the underlying asset's price is high), we can say that the position is "*in-the-job*," that is, secure (only a disaster can lead to removal).

Suppose instead that

$$\hat{\alpha} > \alpha_1^{\mathrm{H}}.$$

Then, the entrepreneur keeps her job only if both projects succeed. But gambling augments the probability that both projects are successful.[62] The entrepreneur's position is "*out-of-the-job*," and the entrepreneur is incentivized to "gamble for resurrection." Hence, hedging is no longer an equilibrium behavior.

The search for a "gambling equilibrium" in which the investors rationally anticipate that the entrepreneur will correlate the proceeds of the two projects in an almost identical fashion, except for one quantitative point: because of gambling, the date-0 performances are less informative about the entrepreneur's ability. Thus, and as depicted in Figure 7.9,

59. "Hedging" is a slight misnomer since the term refers to the absence of correlation rather than to negative correlation. The terminology is motivated by the contrast with the gambling behavior.

60. So, using Bayes' rule:

$$\alpha_0^{\mathrm{H}} = \frac{\alpha(1-r)^2}{\alpha(1-r)^2 + (1-\alpha)(1-q)^2},$$

$$\alpha_1^{\mathrm{H}} = \frac{\alpha r(1-r)}{\alpha r(1-r) + (1-\alpha)q(1-q)},$$

$$\alpha_2^{\mathrm{H}} = \frac{\alpha r^2}{\alpha r^2 + (1-\alpha)q^2}.$$

61. This probability is $\alpha(1-r) + (1-\alpha)(1-q)$ under gambling, and $\alpha(1-r)^2 + (1-\alpha)(1-q)^2 < \alpha(1-r) + (1-\alpha)(1-q)$ under hedging.

62. This probability is $\alpha r + (1-\alpha)q$ under gambling, and $\alpha r^2 + (1-\alpha)q^2 < \alpha r + (1-\alpha)q$ under hedging.

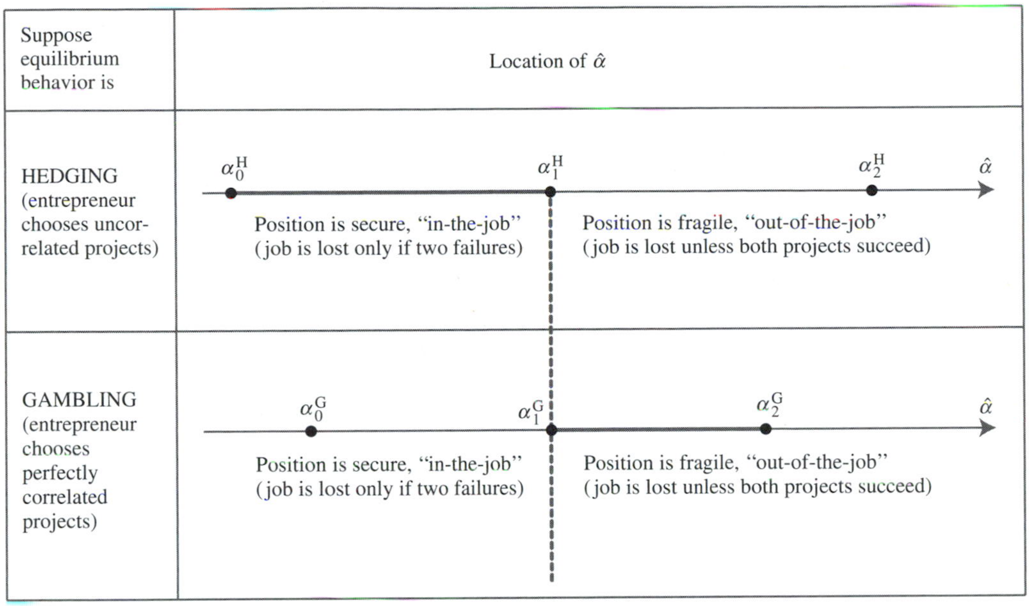

Figure 7.9

the thresholds α_0^G and α_2^G are closer to α_1^G (where "G" stands for "gambling") than were α_0^H and α_2^H.[63]

To sum up, the entrepreneur plays conservatively when her position is relatively secure, and gambles for resurrection when her position is seriously threatened. More generally, an "in-the-job" manager will be biased toward actions that reveal less about her ability (such as actions with long-term payoffs, lots of noise, no action at all, suboptimal actions where she is sure to succeed, etc.). And, as we have noted earlier, a similar insight applies to monetary-incentives-driven managers. Namely, a manager whose stock options are "in the money" tends to play safe, while one whose stock options are "out of the money" tends to gamble for resurrection in order to make these options profitable.

Empirical evidence comforts the theoretical prediction. In particular, Chevalier and Ellison (1997) analyze the portfolio choices of mutual fund managers. The latter's objective function is similar to that described in the career-concerns model. For, the year's top-rank performers attract a disproportionate share of savings in the following years. And because fees are linked to assets under management, and therefore the funds' profit is related to the volume of investments they attract, there is a strong incentive to be "among the top performers," while there is not much difference between a mediocre and an abysmal performance since in any case the fund is unlikely to attract savings later on (and may well be closed down). Chevalier and Ellison show that funds with a poor performance in the first three quarters of the year choose very risky portfolios (gamble for

---

63. More precisely,

$$\begin{aligned}\alpha_0^G &= \Pr(\text{high ability} \mid \text{two failures})\\ &= \frac{\alpha(1-r)}{\alpha(1-r)+(1-\alpha)(1-q)} > \frac{\alpha(1-r)^2}{\alpha(1-r)^2+(1-\alpha)(1-q)^2}\\ &= \alpha_0^H\end{aligned}$$

and

$$\begin{aligned}\alpha_2^G &= \Pr(\text{high ability} \mid \text{two successes})\\ &= \frac{\alpha r}{\alpha r+(1-\alpha)q} < \frac{\alpha r^2}{\alpha r^2+(1-\alpha)q^2}\\ &= \alpha_2^H.\end{aligned}$$

What about α_1^G (which is depicted as being equal to α_1^H in Figure 7.9)? Strictly speaking, the probability of one success is equal to 0 when the two projects are perfectly correlated, and so any posterior belief α_1^G is consistent with Bayes' rule. To pin down this belief in a reasonable way, we compute the posterior belief when the projects are not perfectly correlated and take the correlation to 1. Namely, suppose that the entrepreneur does not fully control the correlation. A choice of gambling results in perfect correlation with probability ρ and the absence of correlation with probability $1-\rho$ (where, presumably, ρ is close to 1). A single success then means that the two activities turned out to be uncorrelated and so

$$\alpha_1^G = \Pr(\text{high ability} \mid \text{one success}) = \alpha_1^H.$$

resurrection) while those with a good performance in these first three quarters choose a much more conservative strategy.

Herding. "Herding" refers to the behavior of managers who mimic the choices made by the rest of the industry.[64] This behavior has attracted a lot of attention in economics because it may lead to a gregarious accumulation of wrong choices and yet be individually rational. Banerjee (1992) and Bikhchandani et al. (1992) look at "social learning" models in which, at each date t, an agent makes a choice between, say, two alternatives based on her own information (signal) as well as the observation of what previous agents chose at dates $0, 1, \ldots, t-1$ on the basis of their own signals and the observation of previous agents' behaviors. From some point in time on, the current agent has seen enough choices from previous agents and therefore puts more weight on these than on her signal, which she completely discards.[65] From that point in time, all agents choose the same action. Therefore, they may herd on the wrong action, which they would not do if they observed all past signals rather than all past actions.

Scharfstein and Stein (1990) show that herding may be motivated by career concerns. In their model (as in the ones considered in this section), a manager may have high or low ability, which no one knows *ex ante*. Scharfstein and Stein assume that only high-ability managers obtain an informative signal, indeed the same one. Low-ability managers receive random signals. Because high-ability managers agree on which action is best while low-ability ones disagree, a manager under the threat of being replaced is better off mimicking what another manager chose previously, even though the late-moving manager may have the right idea while the early-moving one does not.[66]

As Scharfstein and Stein note, countervailing forces may discourage herding. For example, creativity may be a valued talent, or superstars (those whose performance is superior to that of others) may capture large rents. Another factor pushing toward differentiation is the profit incentive: if the projects result in competition between the firms in the product market, the latter are usually better off offering differentiated products. Lastly, differentiation may enable the manager to gamble.[67]

In Zwiebel's (1995) model of herd behavior, managers' *performances* rather than their actions (as in Scharfstein and Stein) are benchmarked. Managers know their own ability (but investors do not) and can select a "standard action" (or "old action") or else deviate from it. The standard action is less profitable[68] than the more innovative one, but it leads to more accurate inferences of managerial ability through relative performance evaluation: suppose that few managers are able to take the innovative action; then benchmarking is more powerful on the old action than on the innovative one. Suppose further that there is a positive cost attached to replacing the manager.

---

64. Chapter 6 already discussed the issue of herding in the context of financing under asymmetric information.

65. If the action set is finite. With a continuum of actions, one's own information in general has at least a tiny impact on one's own behavior even after observing the behavior of many other agents.

66. For example, suppose that there are two managers (whose ability is unknown, even to them) and n possible projects among which each manager must choose one (projects are not exclusive, so the two can choose the same; and there is no externality other than informational). Manager 1 privately observes a signal and then publicly picks a project. Manager 2 then receives a private signal and then publicly picks her own project. One project is profitable and the $(n-1)$ others unprofitable. The profitability of a project is revealed only in the distant future.

There are n signals. "Signal k" points to project k. Suppose that a high-ability manager's signal reveals the identity of the profitable project, while a low-ability manager receives each of the n signals with probability $1/n$ (that is, her signal is uninformative). Assume that manager 1 chooses the project corresponding to her signal (this turns out to be optimal for her). What should manager 2 do in order to maximize the investors' posterior probability that she has high ability? Suppose that in equilibrium she chooses to do the project that is suggested by her signal even though this project differs from that selected by manager 1. Then

$$\begin{aligned}\Pr(\text{manager 2 has high ability} \mid \text{different projects}) \\ &= \frac{\alpha(1-\alpha)((n-1)/n)}{2\alpha(1-\alpha)((n-1)/n) + (1-\alpha)^2((n-1)/n)} \\ &= \frac{\alpha}{1+\alpha}\end{aligned}$$

and

$$\begin{aligned}\Pr(\text{manager 2 has high ability} \mid \text{same project}) \\ &= \frac{\alpha^2 + \alpha(1-\alpha)/n}{\alpha^2 + 2\alpha(1-\alpha)/n + (1-\alpha)^2/n^2} > \frac{\alpha}{1+\alpha}.\end{aligned}$$

Hence, manager 2 would be better off ignoring her signal and mimicking manager 1's choice of project.

67. For example, while head-to-head competition in the product market leads to low profits, it also provides some hedging to firms because competitors face high input costs when the firm faces high input costs and because demands are obviously highly correlated (for more on this, see Rey and Tirole (1986)).

68. In the first-order stochastic dominance sense.

Zwiebel shows that managers with average ability choose the standard action, while those with either low or high ability choose the innovative action if they have the opportunity to do so. Intuitively, the difficulty in benchmarking performance makes the innovative action de facto riskier for the manager. Average managers are "in-the-job" due to the firing cost, and so do not want to take risks. Low-ability managers gamble for resurrection because they are "out-of-the-job." Lastly, when choosing the innovative action, high-ability managers, in Zwiebel's model, obtain a high profit and therefore do not risk being confused with low-ability ones; and so they are willing to pick the innovative action.

7.2.2.3 Income and Dividend Smoothing

A well-established fact in the accounting literature is that managers (from the CEO to lower-level division managers) smooth the earnings of their firm or unit. Thus, they may delay income recognition when things go well, and move income forward in time when they are in trouble. The latter behavior is easily understood and has been studied at length in this section. The puzzle is therefore the low-profile behavior in good times.

Fudenberg and Tirole (1995) develop an agency-based theory of income smoothing, building on the idea that managerial tenure is quite secure as long as the manager does well and her job is jeopardized when things go sour. Suppose that the manager's job is secure in the forthcoming review, but might be threatened in the future. Because continuation in the job is a nonissue today, the manager has no incentive to look particularly good today, and can even afford to hide some of her current accomplishments by delaying income recognition until later. The latter strategy makes the manager look worse today than she really is, but will boost her future performance.

Delaying income recognition in good times benefits the manager if the improvement in tomorrow's performance carries more weight in the investors' updating about the manager's ability than the associated deterioration in today's performance. Hence, the role of an *information decay* assumption: that future performance is better predicted by recent than by ancient performance. Information decay can be grasped through the following analogy: to know how a soccer player will do between ages 30 and 32, his performance between ages 25 and 30 is more informative than that between ages 20 and 25. Under information decay, the strategy of playing low key in good times increases the manager's "average" tenure in the firm.[69]

Illustration of the role of information decay. To illustrate in the simplest possible way the incentive to delay income recognition when one's job is not at stake, let us consider the extreme case in which the income initially reveals nothing about the entrepreneur's talent. For example, it could be a "legacy income" determined by the previous manager; or it could be heavily driven by exogenous uncertainty; or else the initial income could relate to a task that differs substantially from future ones (for instance, the current task might consist in reorganizing and rationalizing the firm's organization; future tasks will consist in managing growth) and so the manager's ability to perform tasks is uncorrelated over time. Exercise 7.10 allows an arbitrary correlation of ability over time.

Consider the timing in Figure 7.10.

Let us normalize the discount factor to 1, as usual. To simplify the resolution, we assume that there is no moral hazard. Managers do not respond to monetary incentives and receive a fixed wage w_0, say, equal to what they would receive outside the firm. By contrast, they enjoy a private benefit $\mathcal{B} > 0$ per period. Thus, their objective is to stay in the job as long as possible.

A manager's probability of success at date t depends on the manager's ability at the date-t task (her "current ability"). In the absence of hidden savings, a manager with high current ability succeeds with probability r, while one with low current ability succeeds with probability $q < r$.

A manager is in place at dates 1 and 2, and may or may not be retained at the end of date 2. The manager's ability is the same at dates 2 and 3 (perfect correlation), and is unrelated to that at date 1

69. Note that the manager, as in the career-concerns model above, only cares about being retained. An apparently poor short-term performance might more generally have costs, such as reduced investor trust in managerial decision making (see Chapter 10). What matters for the theory is therefore that tenure in the job be an important managerial objective.

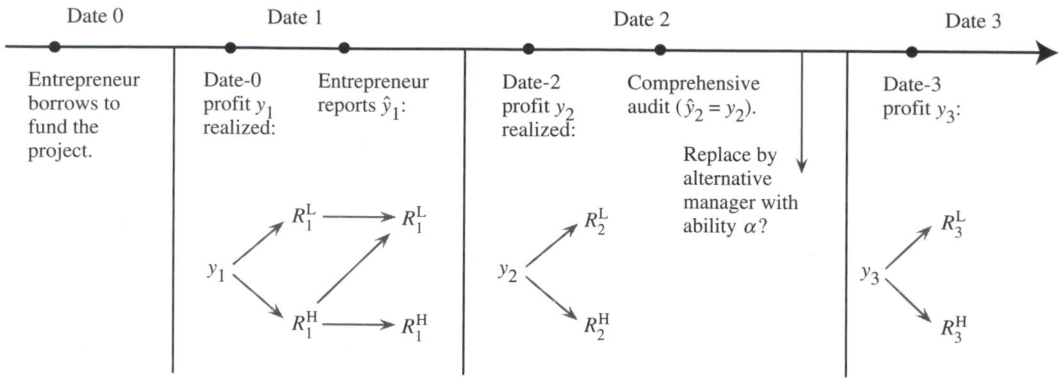

Figure 7.10

(independence). Thus, nothing can be learned from the date-1 income: $y_1 \in \{R_1^L, R_1^H\}$. The key assumptions are that

- the manager's job is secure until date 2; perhaps, the manager must be given some time, or there is no available replacement at date 1;[70]
- the date-1 income y_1 is observed only by the manager.

The manager, when having a high first-period income R_1^H, can report R_1^L and hide $R_1^H - R_1^L$ in the firm. Those hidden savings increase the probability of date-2 success ($y_2 = R_2^H$) by a uniform amount τ (so it becomes $r + \tau$ if the date-2 ability is high, and $q + \tau$ if it is low).

The date-2 income y_2, in contrast with the date-1 income, is observed by the investors. This can be given two interpretations: first, there may be a comprehensive audit at date 2; second, even in the absence of such an audit, the manager anyway has an incentive to disclose a high date-2 income (R_2^H) when income is indeed high (see below).

At date 1 no one knows the manager's ability at dates 2 and 3. Let α denote the probability that she has high ability (is talented), and

$$p \equiv \alpha r + (1 - \alpha)q.$$

If this manager is fired at date 2, the replacement manager also has probability α of being talented and therefore probability p of being successful at date 3. For simplicity, there is no switching cost. And so the manager keeps her position at the end of date 2 if and only if her updated probability α_2 of being talented exceeds α.

As long as $\tau > 0$, it is privately optimal for the incumbent manager to hide any date-1 profit:

$$\hat{y}_1 = R_1^L \quad \text{for all } y_1 \in \{R_1^L, R_1^H\}.$$

Suppose, in particular, that she did report date-1 income truthfully. Then, recalling that the *ex ante* probability of date-2 success (failure) is p (respectively, $1 - p$), the updated probability that the manager has high ability is

$$\alpha_2 = \begin{cases} \dfrac{\alpha r}{p} > \alpha & \text{in the case of date-2 success,} \\[2ex] \dfrac{\alpha(1-r)}{1-p} < \alpha & \text{in the case of date-2 failure.} \end{cases}$$

Thus, the manager retains her position if and only if she is successful at date 2. Therefore, hiding income R_1^H at date 1 is optimal, since it raises the date-2 probability of success from p to $p + \tau > p$.[71]

Of course, the optimality of the low-profile strategy (underreporting date-1 income) hinges on the fact that the entrepreneur's job is not in danger in the short term. Otherwise, the entrepreneur could well be more tempted to inflate than to deflate earnings at date 1, as we saw previously.[72]

70. Note also that y_1 here conveys no information about y_2 and y_3. There is therefore no reason to replace the manager at date 1. So, if there is at least a small cost of replacement or if the alternative manager's expected ability is lower, then replacement at date 1 is not credible.

71. More generally, the reader can check that for any equilibrium probability that the manager misreports at date 1, the manager is strictly better off misreporting. Hence, the manager always misreports.

72. A couple of papers have found empirical support for the theory outlined here. De Fond and Park (1997) find that the link between,

An extreme, but familiar, illustration of this behavior occurs when new CEOs darken the legacy of their predecessors precisely because it does not reflect badly on their own ability. In fact, it might even reflect well, i.e., if they appear to manage a great turnaround.

The idea that management has an incentive to delay income recognition and save for future (and potentially more job-threatening) times when there is currently less pressure to perform can be extended to the distribution of dividends, yielding a theory of *dividend smoothing*. Add to the model a (concave) investment function. Dividends then matter as they determine retentions and investment. To the extent that the marginal productivity of reinvestment is decreasing, distributing dividends is more costly to the firm when the actual income is low. Investors choose the dividend level but are imperfectly informed about the marginal productivity of retentions. They therefore must elicit this information in an incentive-compatible way from the manager (the manager "recommends" a dividend and makes an earnings report).

To illustrate this, generalize the previous example by introducing a date-1 reinvestment J that occurs after the date-1 income is realized. Let $\tau(J)$ denote the corresponding increase in date-2 probability of success with $\tau' > 0$, $\tau'' < 0$, $\tau(0) = 0$, $\tau'(0)(R_2^{\mathrm{H}} - R_2^{\mathrm{L}}) > 1$ (some reinvestment is desirable). Investors observe neither the date-1 income, nor the actual reinvestment. Let $d(\hat{y}_1)$ denote the dividend that is demanded by investors when the manager reports $\hat{y}_1$. The reinvestment is then[73]

$$J(y_1, \hat{y}_1) = y_1 - d(\hat{y}_1).$$

As earlier, it is easy to check that the manager keeps her job at the end of date 2 if and only if she is successful at that date. The probability of a date-2 success is

$$p + \tau(J(y_1, \hat{y}_1))$$

and so the manager wants to minimize $d(\hat{y}_1)$ regardless of her date-1 income. The equilibrium is therefore a *pooling* equilibrium in dividends at date 1.[74]

This barebones model thus predicts that when the managerial position is not threatened (that is, at date 1) the dividend is insensitive to the firm's actual income. By contrast, when the manager's job is at stake (date 2), the manager has an incentive to disclose her true income (at least if $R_2 = R_2^{\mathrm{H}}$; by implication, the income is also de facto "disclosed" when $R_2 = R_2^{\mathrm{L}}$), and thus the dividend varies with the actual income.[75] At date 2, the stock price reacts positively to earnings and dividend announcements.[76] The threat of investor intervention forces the manager to disgorge cash in the form of a dividend.[77]

Dividend smoothing has been a stylized fact in corporate finance since the work of Lintner (1956), who showed that firms by and large smooth their dividends and trigger very negative stock price reactions when they cut them. Lintner further pointed out that share repurchases (an alternative to dividends to pay out income to shareholders) provide flexibility in the payout policy (are quite large in good times and nonexistent in bad ones) and are much more volatile than dividends although he did not provide a theory for why this is so.

The model above (and its less extreme extensions[78]) only partly accounts for income and

on the one hand, current performance and predicted performance in the next period and, on the other, reported (income-decreasing) discretionary accruals goes as predicted by the theory. Kanagaretnam et al. (2003) look at banks' loan loss provisions and find that banks save earnings through such provisions in good times and lower loan loss provisions in bad times. See also Ahmed et al. (2000).

73. We assume that the date-1 income y_1 is sufficient to cover the dividend.

74. It is optimal for investors to demand dividend d^* given by (assuming that $d^* \leqslant R_1^{\mathrm{L}}$)

$$[p_1\tau'(R_1^{\mathrm{H}} - d^*) + (1 - p_1)\tau'(R_1^{\mathrm{L}} - d^*)](R_2^{\mathrm{H}} - R_2^{\mathrm{L}}) = 1,$$

where p_1 is the probability that $y_1 = R_1^{\mathrm{H}}$. Let

$$\tau \equiv p_1\tau(R_1^{\mathrm{H}} - d^*) + (1 - p_1)\tau(R_1^{\mathrm{L}} - d^*).$$

Note also that the date-3 probability of success,

$$[\alpha(r + \tau)r + (1 - \alpha)(q + \tau)q] + [1 - (p + \tau)]p = p + \alpha(1 - \alpha)(r - q)^2$$

(accounting for the possibility of replacement at date 2), is independent of the date-1 payout policy.

75. If one depicts the date-2 reinvestment as the date-1 one, the optimal dividend is such that the reinvestment is J_2^* with $\tau'(J_2^*)[R_3^{\mathrm{H}} - R_3^{\mathrm{L}}] = 1$.

76. Here, the earnings and dividend announcement convey the same information. See Fudenberg and Tirole (1995) for examples in which both announcements convey information and sequentiality trigger positive stock price reactions.

77. Other models making a similar prediction are those of Zwiebel (1996) (in which managers engage in payouts as a commitment to limit future inefficiency rather than to signal their ability) and Fluck (1999).

78. For example, if the manager responded to monetary incentives, a stock-based compensation scheme would induce her to recommend

dividend smoothing. For one thing, dividends are smoothed across states of nature rather than across time. Furthermore, like most models of dividends (see Chapter 6) it makes no distinction between dividends and share repurchases.[79]

7.2.3 Effort and Risk Taking

As we observed in Chapters 3 and 4, encouraging effort calls for rewarding management for performances in the upper tail (this is indeed what stock options attempt to achieve), but such high-powered incentives also create incentives for risk taking (often called "asset substitution" in corporate finance). Unfortunately, the analysis of this multifaceted moral-hazard problem is not well-developed. We can avail ourselves only of specific examples.

We begin with a discrete-effort, discrete-outcome version due to Biais and Casamatta (1999),[80] and then move on to a continuous-effort, continuous-outcome version first studied by Bester and Hellwig (1987).

7.2.3.1 A Discrete Version

Consider the fixed-investment model and add the following two twists:

- there are three possible payoffs: $R^{\mathrm{S}} > R^{\mathrm{M}} > R^{\mathrm{F}}$ (success, middle/intermediate, failure);
- the entrepreneur's moral hazard has two dimensions: effort (which involves a loss of private benefit and raises income) and risk taking (which increases the probabilities of R^{S} and R^{F} to the detriment of R^{M}).[81]

We return to the assumption that the entrepreneur is risk neutral and protected by limited liability. She owns a project involving an investment cost I and has cash $A < I$. Ignoring risk taking for the moment, the impact of effort is as follows.

• The entrepreneur receives private benefit B in the case of misbehavior. The three outcomes are then equally likely. The NPV is negative in the case of misbehavior:

$$\tfrac{1}{3}(R^{\mathrm{S}} + R^{\mathrm{M}} + R^{\mathrm{F}}) + B < I.$$

• In the case of good behavior, the entrepreneur receives no private benefit, and raises the probability of success and lowers the probability of failure by $\theta > 0$.[82] The NPV is then positive:

$$(\tfrac{1}{3} + \theta)R^{\mathrm{S}} + \tfrac{1}{3}R^{\mathrm{M}} + (\tfrac{1}{3} - \theta)R^{\mathrm{F}} > I.$$

Whether the entrepreneur behaves or misbehaves in this direction, she can take further actions that affect the project's outcome: namely, she can gamble and increase the probability of success by α and the risk of failure by β (and so reduce the probability of an intermediate outcome by $\alpha + \beta$). Risk taking reduces the NPV:[83]

$$\alpha(R^{\mathrm{S}} - R^{\mathrm{M}}) \leqslant \beta(R^{\mathrm{M}} - R^{\mathrm{F}}).$$

The impact of the two forms of moral hazard is summarized in Figure 7.11.

Let $R_{\mathrm{b}}^{\mathrm{S}}, R_{\mathrm{b}}^{\mathrm{M}}, R_{\mathrm{b}}^{\mathrm{F}}$ denote the borrower's (nonnegative) rewards in the case of success, intermediate profit, and failure. Intuitively, the borrower should not be rewarded in the case of failure:

$$R_{\mathrm{b}}^{\mathrm{F}} = 0;$$

for, failure is indicative of low effort and/or risk taking.[84] We leave it to the reader to check (that is, by not imposing $R_{\mathrm{b}}^{\mathrm{F}} = 0$ in the following incentive constraints) that this is indeed the case. Here, and without loss of generality, we set $R_{\mathrm{b}}^{\mathrm{F}}$ to be equal to 0.

We first assume that risk taking is to be discouraged, and later investigate when this is indeed so.

dividends that are more in line with current earnings (as long as current earnings are not too correlated with the profitability of reinvestment); see Application 7 in Section 6.3.

79. Attempts to distinguish between the two often introduce a differential tax treatment of the two policies or a differential impact on managerial wealth (because of the specific structure of stock options): see Section 2.5.2.

80. See also Alger (1999) for related modeling choices and an application to prudential regulation, as well as Gollier et al. (1997), Hellwig (1994), Hirshleifer and Thakor (1992), Palomino and Prat (2003), and Sung (1995). Biais and Casamatta further derive their model's general-equilibrium implications (see Chapter 13 for the embedding of corporate finance models in a general-equilibrium setup).

81. Technically, the former refers to a first-order-stochastic-dominance shift in income, the latter to a second-order-stochastic-dominance shift.

82. In what follows, we will naturally assume that parameters are such that all probabilities are between 0 and 1.

83. The case of pure second-order stochastic dominance (a mean-preserving spread) corresponds to an equality:

$$\alpha(R^{\mathrm{S}} - R^{\mathrm{M}}) = \beta(R^{\mathrm{M}} - R^{\mathrm{F}}).$$

But we consider a case in which risk taking has the potential to reduce NPV.

84. A more precise characterization is in terms of likelihood ratios, as in, for example, Sections 3.6 and 5.5.2.

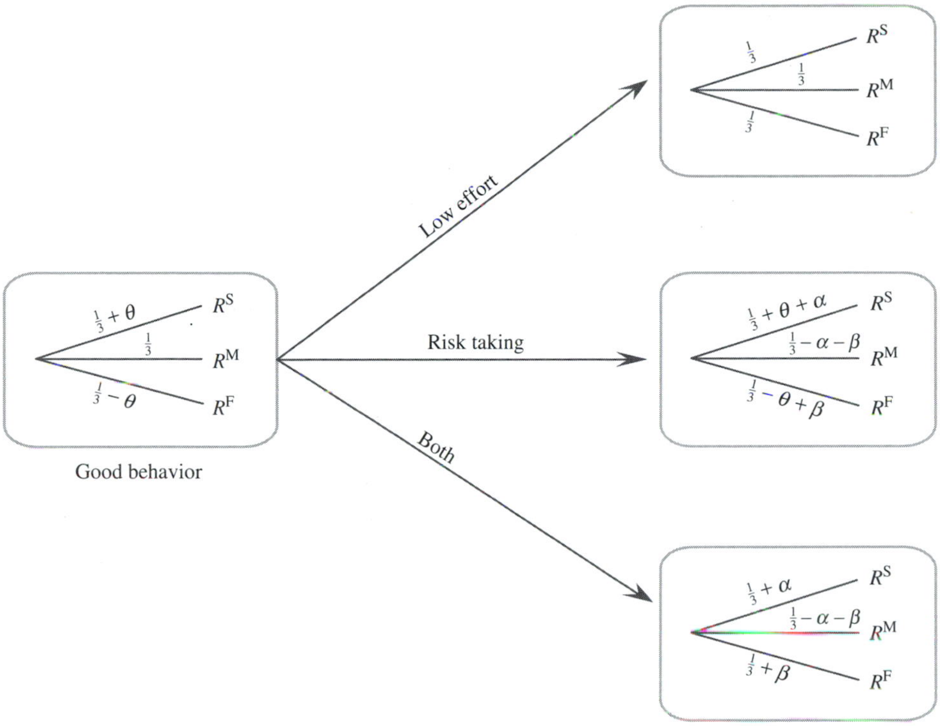

Figure 7.11

The entrepreneur's misbehavior takes several forms, and so there are *a priori* three relevant incentive constraints (see Figure 7.11).

Effort. Assuming no risk taking, the entrepreneur must be incentivized not to take the private benefit:

$$(\tfrac{1}{3}+\theta)R_b^S + \tfrac{1}{3}R_b^M \geqslant \tfrac{1}{3}R_b^S + \tfrac{1}{3}R_b^M + B$$

or

$$\theta R_b^S \geqslant B. \qquad (7.16)$$

Note that the parameter θ here plays the same role as "Δp" in the two-outcome case.

No risk taking. Next, the entrepreneur may refrain from taking a private benefit, but choose to take risk. We must therefore require that

$$(\tfrac{1}{3}+\theta)R_b^S + \tfrac{1}{3}R_b^M \geqslant (\tfrac{1}{3}+\theta+\alpha)R_b^S + (\tfrac{1}{3}-\alpha-\beta)R_b^M$$

or

$$(\alpha+\beta)R_b^M \geqslant \alpha R_b^S. \qquad (7.17)$$

Intuitively, the entrepreneur should not be paid solely in the upper tail if risk taking is to be avoided. Or, put differently, very high powered incentive schemes encourage gambling.

What about the third incentive constraint? This constraint, which states that the entrepreneur must prefer exerting effort and not taking risk to misbehaving along both moral-hazard dimensions, turns out to be redundant, due to the separability embodied in the impact of these two forms of misbehavior.[85]

If feasible, funding yields NPV, or equivalently a utility for the borrower:

$$U_b^1 \equiv (\tfrac{1}{3}+\theta)R^S + \tfrac{1}{3}R^M + (\tfrac{1}{3}-\theta)R^F - I.$$

Given the incentive-compatibility (IC) constraints (fully depicted by (7.16) and (7.17), whose conjunction determines the incentive-compatible set {IC}),

85. Namely, the third incentive constraint is

$$(\tfrac{1}{3}+\theta)R_b^S + \tfrac{1}{3}R_b^M \geqslant (\tfrac{1}{3}+\alpha)R_b^S + (\tfrac{1}{3}-\alpha-\beta)R_b^M + B,$$

which can be rewritten as

$$[\theta R_b^S - B] + [(\alpha+\beta)R_b^M - \alpha R_b^S] \geqslant 0,$$

which is implied by (7.16) and (7.17).

the pledgeable income is then

$$\begin{aligned}\mathcal{P}_1 &= (\tfrac{1}{3}+\theta)\Big(R^{\mathrm{S}} - \min_{\{\mathrm{IC}\}} R_{\mathrm{b}}^{\mathrm{S}}\Big) + \tfrac{1}{3}\Big(R^{\mathrm{M}} - \min_{\{\mathrm{IC}\}} R_{\mathrm{b}}^{\mathrm{M}}\Big)\\ &\quad + (\tfrac{1}{3}-\theta)R^{\mathrm{F}}\\ &= (\tfrac{1}{3}+\theta)\Big(R^{\mathrm{S}} - \frac{B}{\theta}\Big) + \frac{1}{3}\Big(R^{\mathrm{M}} - \frac{\alpha}{\alpha+\beta}\frac{B}{\theta}\Big)\\ &\quad + (\tfrac{1}{3}-\theta)R^{\mathrm{F}}\\ &= [U_{\mathrm{b}}^{1} + I] - (\tfrac{1}{3}+\theta)\frac{B}{\theta} - \frac{1}{3}\frac{\alpha}{\alpha+\beta}\frac{B}{\theta}.\end{aligned}$$

Funding is then feasible if and only if

$$\mathcal{P}_1 \geqslant I - A. \tag{7.18}$$

Alternatively, the contract between the entrepreneur and the investors may not attempt to avoid risk taking. It is then intuitive that the entrepreneur should be paid only in the upper tail, which is the most indicative of a high effort:

$$R_{\mathrm{b}}^{\mathrm{M}} = R_{\mathrm{b}}^{\mathrm{F}} = 0.$$

The only incentive constraint is then

$$(\tfrac{1}{3}+\theta+\alpha)R_{\mathrm{b}}^{\mathrm{S}} \geqslant (\tfrac{1}{3}+\alpha)R_{\mathrm{b}}^{\mathrm{S}} + B$$

or

$$\theta R_{\mathrm{b}}^{\mathrm{S}} \geqslant B.$$

The entrepreneur no longer needs to be rewarded for an intermediate performance.

Her utility is then

$$\begin{aligned}U_{\mathrm{b}}^{2} &= (\tfrac{1}{3}+\theta+\alpha)R^{\mathrm{S}}\\ &\quad + (\tfrac{1}{3}-\alpha-\beta)R^{\mathrm{M}} + (\tfrac{1}{3}-\theta+\beta)R^{\mathrm{F}}\\ &= U_{\mathrm{b}}^{1} - [\alpha(R^{\mathrm{S}}-R^{\mathrm{M}}) - \beta(R^{\mathrm{M}}-R^{\mathrm{F}})]\\ &< U_{\mathrm{b}}^{1}.\end{aligned}$$

The pledgeable income is

$$\begin{aligned}\mathcal{P}_2 &= (\tfrac{1}{3}+\theta+\alpha)\Big(R^{\mathrm{S}} - \frac{B}{\theta}\Big) + (\tfrac{1}{3}-\alpha-\beta)R^{\mathrm{M}}\\ &\quad + (\tfrac{1}{3}-\theta+\beta)R^{\mathrm{F}}\\ &= \mathcal{P}_1 - [U_{\mathrm{b}}^{1} - U_{\mathrm{b}}^{2}] + \Big[\frac{1}{3}\frac{\alpha}{\alpha+\beta} - \alpha\Big]\frac{B}{\theta}\end{aligned}$$

and funding is feasible if and only if

$$\mathcal{P}_2 \geqslant I - A.$$

Finally, let us investigate the optimal contract. Because risk taking reduces the NPV ($U_{\mathrm{b}}^{1} > U_{\mathrm{b}}^{2}$), the entrepreneur prefers to design incentives that induce her not to take risk, as long as funding is feasible. More precisely, we must consider two cases:

(i) If $\mathcal{P}_1 \geqslant I - A$, then the optimal contract induces the entrepreneur to exert effort and not to take risk. This contract $\{R_{\mathrm{b}}^{\mathrm{S}}, R_{\mathrm{b}}^{\mathrm{M}}, R_{\mathrm{b}}^{\mathrm{F}} = 0\}$ satisfies

$$\theta R_{\mathrm{b}}^{\mathrm{S}} \geqslant B, \tag{7.19}$$

$$(\alpha+\beta)R_{\mathrm{b}}^{\mathrm{M}} \geqslant \alpha R_{\mathrm{b}}^{\mathrm{S}}, \tag{7.20}$$

$$A \geqslant (\tfrac{1}{3}+\theta)R_{\mathrm{b}}^{\mathrm{S}} + \tfrac{1}{3}R_{\mathrm{b}}^{\mathrm{M}} - U_{\mathrm{b}}^{1}. \tag{7.21}$$

The optimal contract can be implemented through a mixture of debt and equity held by investors: let D denote the level of debt, and let $(1-x)$ denote the fraction of equity held by investors. D and x must satisfy two equations with two unknowns:

$$x(R^{\mathrm{S}} - D) = R_{\mathrm{b}}^{\mathrm{S}}$$

and

$$x(R^{\mathrm{M}} - D) = R_{\mathrm{b}}^{\mathrm{M}}.$$

Letting (7.20) be satisfied with equality,[86] it is straightforward to show that the variable thus defined satisfies[87]

$$0 < x < 1$$

and

$$R^{\mathrm{F}} < D < R^{\mathrm{M}}.$$

The implementation in this simple model is in general not unique, though. Biais and Casamatta show that alternatively the investors could hold convertible debt D with an option to convert this debt for a fraction $1-x$ of the shares. (Convertible debt has other benefits when investors observe risk taking *before* the profit is realized (see Jensen and Meckling 1976; Green 1984).)

(ii) If $\mathcal{P}_1 < I - A$, then the entrepreneur cannot secure funding while "committing" to exert effort and not to take risk. Funding may, however, be feasible if risk taking is not too costly in terms of NPV, and raises pledgeable income, i.e., if $\mathcal{P}_2 > \mathcal{P}_1$, or

$$\Big(\frac{1}{3}\frac{\alpha}{\alpha+\beta} - \alpha\Big)\frac{B}{\theta} > U_{\mathrm{b}}^{1} - U_{\mathrm{b}}^{2}.$$

86. As it would if there were another "margin" (for example, if the investment size were variable).

87. Note that

$$\frac{R^{\mathrm{S}} - D}{R^{\mathrm{M}} - D} = \frac{\alpha+\beta}{\alpha}.$$

Because

$$\alpha R^{\mathrm{S}} + \beta R^{\mathrm{F}} < (\alpha+\beta)R^{\mathrm{M}}$$

(gambling reduces the NPV), $D > R^{\mathrm{F}}$.

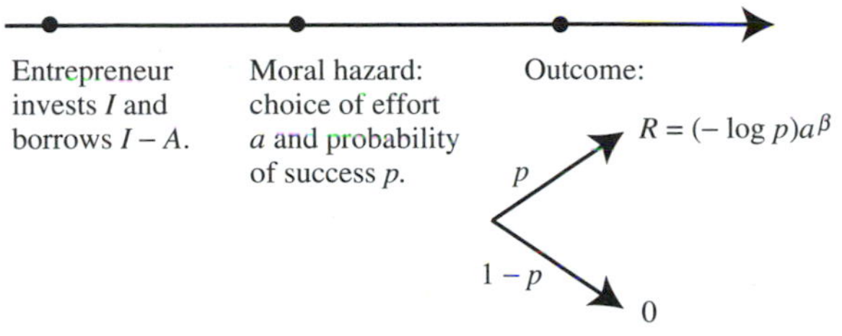

Figure 7.12

To see how this can occur, suppose that gambling hardly reduces the NPV:

$$\alpha(R^{S} - R^{M}) \simeq \beta(R^{M} - R^{F})$$

or

$$U_{b}^{1} \simeq U_{b}^{2}.$$

Then, $\mathcal{P}_2 > \mathcal{P}_1$ if and only if

$$\tfrac{1}{3} > \alpha + \beta.$$

But this inequality is automatically satisfied because of the requirement that all probabilities be nonnegative.

Hence, *if gambling involves a low cost in terms of NPV, discouraging gambling reduces the pledgeable income and makes financing more difficult.*

Note that in case (ii), the financial structure of the firm is in a sense "more levered" than in case (i) since the entrepreneur is paid solely in the upper tail. An interesting result is therefore that a reduction in net worth (A) may result in a financial structure that is more levered.[88]

(iii) Finally, if $\mathcal{P}_1$ and $\mathcal{P}_2$ are both smaller than $I - A$, there is no funding.

7.2.3.2 A Continuous Version

Bester and Hellwig (1987) build a tractable fixed-investment, continuous-effort model (see Figure 7.12).

The entrepreneur is risk neutral, is protected by limited liability, and has utility from wage w and effort a equal to $w - a$. Here, effort increases the payoff in the case of success, which is proportional to a^{β}, with $\beta < 1$. The choice of the probability of success can here be interpreted as a risk choice: a lower probability of success corresponds to a larger payoff in the case of success, as

$$R = (-\log p)a^{\beta}.$$

No-agency-cost benchmark. Suppose first that the parties can contract on a and p.[89] These variables are chosen so as to maximize the NPV:

$$\max_{\{a,p\}} \text{NPV} = p[(-\log p)a^{\beta}] - a - I,$$

yielding the first-best values.

Note that the optimal choice of p is independent of a, while the optimal choice of a depends on p,

$$a^*(p) = (\beta p(-\log p))^{1/(1-\beta)}$$

(and so $a^* = a^*(p^*)$), while

$$p^* = 1/\mathrm{e},$$

where $\log \mathrm{e} = 1$. And so

$$a^* = \left(\frac{\beta}{\mathrm{e}}\right)^{1/(1-\beta)}.$$

Agency cost. Suppose now that investors observe only the final profit, and so the reward w depends on this profit only. The initial contract can still specify the level of profit R to be reached in the case of success (by specifying $w(R') = 0$ for $R' \neq R$).[90] Thus a second-best contract sets R as well as a sharing rule specifying a reward R_b for the borrower and R_l for the lenders:

$$R = R_b + R_l.$$

Given target R and reward R_b in the case of success, the entrepreneur solves

$$\max_{\{p,a\}} \{pR_b - a\}$$

s.t.

$$(-\log p)a^{\beta} = R.$$

Using the constraint to substitute p into the objective function, the first-order condition is

$$pR_b = \frac{a}{\beta(-\log p)}.$$

The investors' breakeven constraint is then

$$pR_l \geqslant I - A$$

88. See Chapter 5 for an alternative reason why a weak balance sheet induces more leverage.

89. Actually, contracting on one of the two suffices, because R then reveals the other.

90. Given that the entrepreneur has no private information before choosing R and a, there is no point giving her discretion over the choice of R, since this discretion only serves to increase the number of possible deviations (i.e., the number of moral-hazard constraints).

or

$$pR - \frac{a}{\beta(-\log p)} \geqslant I - A.$$

The second-best optimum when there is an agency cost and the investors' breakeven constraint is binding is given by the maximization of the NPV subject to that constraint:

$$\max_{\{p,a\}}\{U_b = p(-\log p)a^{\beta} - a\}$$

s.t.

$$p(-\log p)a^{\beta} - \frac{a}{\beta(-\log p)} \geqslant I - A.$$

The analysis of the first-order conditions for this program reveals that the level of risk exceeds the first-best level, while the level of effort is suboptimal:

$$p < p^* \quad \text{and} \quad a < a^*(p).$$

To gain intuition about this result, consider the two "polar" cases in which investors hold a debt and an equity claim, respectively.

Pure-debt contract. Suppose that the entrepreneur owes a fixed amount $\mathcal{D}$ (which, due to the entrepreneur's limited liability, is paid back only in the case of success).[91] Then the entrepreneur chooses risk and effort so as to solve

$$U_b = \max_{\{p,a\}}\{p[(-\log p)a^{\beta} - \mathcal{D}] - a\},$$

and so

$$a = a^*(p).$$

Because the entrepreneur is residual claimant in the case of success, she chooses the conditionally optimal level of effort. A debt contract here provides the right incentives. By contrast, a debt contract induces the entrepreneur to take too much risk:[92] as long as $\mathcal{D} > 0$,

$$p < p^*.$$

Intuitively, the debtholders do not bear the effort cost and would like p to be as large as possible. Their concern is not internalized by the entrepreneur.

At the margin, some sharing of marginal profit with the investors is desirable. This sharing reduces the effort, which is inconsequential if a is in the neighborhood of the conditional optimum $a^*(p)$ (the loss is of second order only). And this sharing reduces risk taking.

Pure-equity contract. Conversely, suppose that investors get a fraction θ_l of profit and the entrepreneur a fraction θ_b (with $\theta_b + \theta_l = 1$).[93] The entrepreneur then solves

$$U_b = \max_{\{p,a\}}\{\theta_b p(-\log p)a^{\beta} - a\}.$$

The pure-equity contract distorts the effort decision downward,

$$a < a^*(p),$$

but it introduces no distortion in the risk choice:

$$p = p^*.$$

An increase in welfare can be achieved by giving the entrepreneur a bit more of the profit at the margin, that is by reducing θ_l and compensating this reduction by issuing some debt. Of course, this move leads to an increase in risk, but starting from the optimal value p^*, this introduces only a second-order loss.

This analysis suggests that the second-best optimum can be implemented through a mixture of debt and equity in which the firm owes an amount $\mathcal{D}$ of debt, and the entrepreneur owns a fraction θ_b of shares and therefore has utility

$$\theta_b \max\{0, p(R - \mathcal{D})\} - a.$$

Bester and Hellwig indeed show that these two instruments ($\mathcal{D}$ and θ_b) are sufficient to implement the second-best allocation.

Supplementary Section

7.3 Brander and Lewis's Cournot Analysis

Section 7.1.1.3 argued that a firm may want to choose its financial structure so as to commit to specific forms of product-market behavior (aggressivity in that section) and thereby indirectly influence

91. $\mathcal{D}$ is computed to satisfy the investors' breakeven constraint, if this is feasible.

92. To see this, one can either write the first-order condition with respect to p, or note that the cross-partial derivative of the entrepreneur's objective function with respect to p and $\mathcal{D}$ is negative (equal to -1).

93. Where the sharing rule satisfies the investors' breakeven constraint, if feasible.

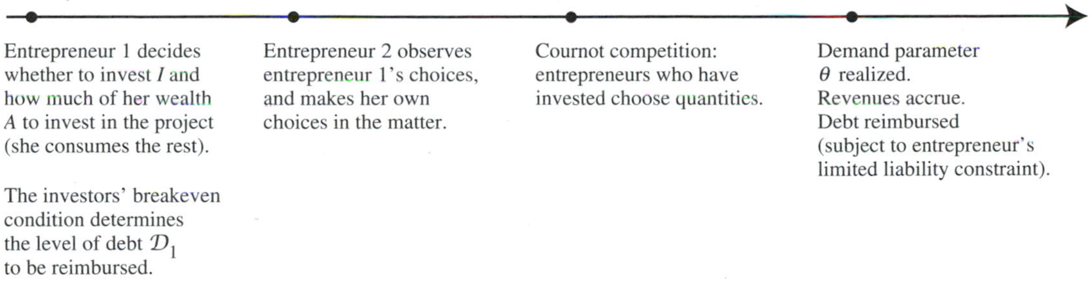

Figure 7.13

the rivals' behavior. This supplementary section describes Brander and Lewis's original analysis. In Brander–Lewis, firm i's profit, that is the combined profit of entrepreneur i and firm i's claimholders, is the standard Cournot profit with linear demand:

$$\pi_i = q_i(\theta - q_i - q_j) - I,$$

where I is the fixed investment cost and q_i is firm i's output.[94] Demand is assumed to be random. That is, the demand curve

$$Q = q_1 + q_2 = \theta - p$$

(where p is the price in the market) has a random intercept θ distributed in some interval $[\underline{\theta}, \bar{\theta}]$ according to cumulative distribution function $H(\theta)$ and density $h(\theta)$. Assume that the realization of the demand parameter θ is not known at the time at which the firms choose outputs (and, *a fortiori*, at the time at which they sink the investment cost).

Even if the entrepreneur has enough wealth to finance the investment herself ($A \geqslant I$), she may want to consume some of this wealth up front and borrow from investors by issuing debt (while keeping control over the choice of output). To see this, suppose that the entrepreneur issues debt, so she is meant to reimburse a fixed amount $\mathcal{D}_i$ *ex post*. If she is unable to reimburse $\mathcal{D}_i$, i.e., when

$$q_i(\theta - Q) < \mathcal{D}_i,$$

she is protected by limited liability and receives 0.[95] The timing of the Brander–Lewis model is depicted in Figure 7.13.

Entrepreneur i's *ex post* revenue (that is, gross of her pre-competition consumption) is

$$\int_{Q+\mathcal{D}_i/q_i}^{\bar{\theta}} [q_i(\theta - q_i - q_j) - \mathcal{D}_i] h(\theta)\, d\theta.$$

Let

$$MR_i(\theta, q_i, q_j) \equiv \theta - 2q_i - q_j$$

denote the firm's marginal revenue. The entrepreneur chooses output so as to maximize her *ex post* revenue,

$$\int_{Q+\mathcal{D}_i/q_i}^{\bar{\theta}} MR_i(\theta, q_i, q_j) h(\theta)\, d\theta = 0, \qquad (7.22)$$

while the firm as a whole (that is, internalizing the stakes of both the entrepreneur and the debtholders) would choose output so as to equate average marginal revenue to 0:

$$\int_{\underline{\theta}}^{\bar{\theta}} MR_i(\theta, q_i, q_j) h(\theta)\, d\theta = 0. \qquad (7.23)$$

The difference between (7.22) and (7.23) is illustrated in Figure 7.14. Protected by limited liability, the entrepreneur internalizes none of the lower tail of the distribution (her perceived marginal revenue is equal to 0 in this region: see part (a) of the figure). Because marginal revenue increases with demand, the first-order condition (7.22) can be depicted as in

94. We assume zero marginal costs. Alternatively, a positive marginal cost can be incorporated into the parameter θ. Also, q_i could be a strategic variable other than quantity, as long as the firms' choices remain strategic substitutes and that an increase in q_i makes profit riskier.

95. In principle, limited liability might be invoked even in the absence of debt if prices could become negative (i.e., $\underline{\theta} < Q$). But we are not interested in this possibility (which, technically, can be ruled out by assuming an upper bound of $\frac{1}{2}\underline{\theta}$ on individual outputs), because it would require a more explicit description of how these quantities are financed. We here stick to the Brander–Lewis assumption that the entrepreneur has full discretion over her quantity.

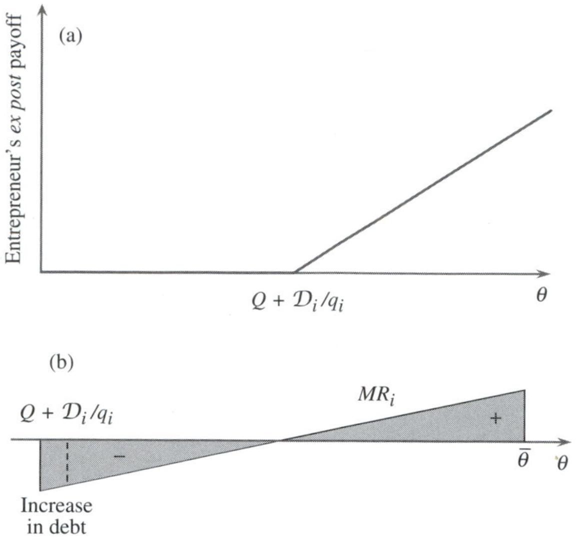

Figure 7.14 (a) Entrepreneur's incentive; (b) marginal revenue.

part (b) of the figure. When debt $\mathcal{D}_i$ increases, some of the negative realizations of the entrepreneur's marginal revenue disappear; and so to restore equality in (7.22), the entrepreneur raises output q_i. Intuitively, an increase in output increases the riskiness of the firm's revenue. Because the entrepreneur's stake is convex in the firm's revenue (Figure 7.14(a)), she has an incentive to take risk, i.e., to increase output; and the more so, the higher the level of debt. Note that this would not be so if the entrepreneur issued equity rather than debt. The entrepreneur's objective function would be $s_i[q_i(\theta - q_i - q_j)]$, where s_i is the entrepreneur's share of profit, and so q_i would be independent of the extent, $1 - s_i$, of dilution. Note also that it is important that the entrepreneur keep the control right over the choice of output. Debtholders, if they had their say in the matter, would reduce output relative to the optimal choice of the firm as a whole (entrepreneur cum debtholders) so as to reduce risk.

The strategic impact of debt is illustrated in Figure 7.15. Figure 7.15, for expositional purposes,[96] assumes that firm 2 has no debt (or, equivalently, that its debtholders and entrepreneur act in concert to choose output q_2). Firm 2's reaction function $\mathcal{R}_2^0$

96. Indeed, by the very reasoning below, firm 2, if it enters, will want to issue some debt.

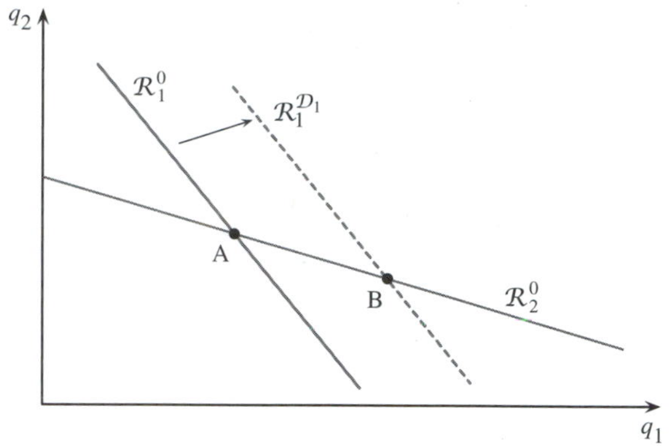

Figure 7.15

depicts the optimal choice of output for a given output q_1 of firm 1:

$$q_2 = \mathcal{R}_2^0(q_1) \quad \text{maximizes } q_2[E(\theta) - q_1 - q_2],$$

where $E(\theta)$ is the mean value of θ. That is,

$$\mathcal{R}_2^0(q_1) = \tfrac{1}{2}(E(\theta) - q_1).$$

Similarly, if firm 1 issues no debt, its reaction curve is

$$\mathcal{R}_1^0(q_2) = \tfrac{1}{2}(E(\theta) - q_2).$$

By issuing debt $\mathcal{D}_1$, though, entrepreneur 1 shifts her reaction curve $\mathcal{R}_1^{\mathcal{D}_1}$ outward, where

$$\begin{aligned}\mathcal{R}_1^{\mathcal{D}_1}(q_2) &= \tfrac{1}{2}(E(\theta \mid \theta \geqslant Q + \mathcal{D}_1/q_1) - q_2)\\ &> \tfrac{1}{2}(E(\theta) - q_2).\end{aligned}$$

Thus, the Cournot outcome if firm 2 enters shifts from A to B, with a higher firm-1 output, and lower firm-2 output and profit. In essence, entrepreneur 1 can indirectly behave as a Stackelberg leader by choosing to issue debt.[97]

So far, we have seen that for a given output q_2, say, entrepreneur 1 can commit to raise his own output by raising his debt level. The next step is to note that an expectation of a high output by firm 1 reduces the profitability of firm 2. And so firm 2 may no longer want to sink investment I.

Does entrepreneur 1 gain from committing to raise output and deter entry? From the investors'

97. A slight difference with the Stackelberg model, though, is that firm 2, if it enters, will also have an incentive to shift its reaction curve outward by issuing debt. "Stackelberg leadership" is then somewhat symmetrical.

breakeven condition, entrepreneur 1 receives the entire NPV and therefore has utility

$$U_b^1 = q_1[E(\theta) - q_1 - q_2] - I.$$

In fact, we have a Stackelberg model,[98] for which we know that entry deterrence is optimal if I is sufficiently large (so that the increase in q_1 needed to deter entry is relatively small) (see, for example, Tirole 1988, p. 317).

We have discussed only the strategic benefit of debt. The cost is clear: debt creates a divergence of objectives between the manager and the claimholders, and thus leads to quantities (or prices) that are not optimal for the firm from an *ex ante* viewpoint (keeping the strategy of the rival firm fixed in order to abstract from the beneficial strategic effect). Thus, in the Cournot game depicted in Figure 7.15, it is suboptimal to force the reaction curve as far out as possible, since at some point the marginal cost of debt exceeds its marginal benefit.

Let us make a couple of final points to conclude this discussion of the original version of Brander and Lewis. First, as long as firms compete in quantities, the "Stackelberg" incentive to issue debt carries over to situations where firms do not attempt to deter each other's entry, i.e., they accommodate each other's entry. Quantities are strategic substitutes[99] in that an expectation of a high output by one's rival reduces one's incentive to produce.[100] Thus, each firm wants to take on (a reasonable amount of[101]) debt in order to commit to be more aggressive. Thus, the Brander–Lewis result on Cournot competition is robust to the absence of intention to deter entry.

By contrast, it is sensitive to the mode of product-market competition: suppose instead that firms produce differentiated products and compete in prices. Firm i sets price p_i and then faces demand $q_i = \theta - p_i - dp_j$ (with $0 < d < 1$). Again, the demand intercept θ is random. Firm i's revenue, assuming away marginal costs, is $p_i(\theta - p_i - dp_j)$. So an increase in risk corresponds to a high price p_i. Or, put differently, debt will lead to the maximization of the firm's profit in high states of demand, which are states in which the firm wants to charge a high price. Thus, debt leads the entrepreneur to select a high price. This is advantageous, as Showalter (1995)[102] shows, when firm i accommodates entry to the extent that a high price by firm i makes it nonaggressive and induces firm j to increase its own price (prices are strategic complements). By contrast, "committing" to a high price is not a good strategy if one attempts to deter entry. Issuing debt is then suboptimal.[103]

The Brander–Spencer result is also not robust to costs of default or of illiquidity. Faure-Grimaud (2000) introduces costs of default in a Cournot model and shows that debt may make the firm less aggressive (it becomes more conservative as larger quantities increase the risk of default). Similarly, one can introduce multiperiod financing as in Chapter 5; a low level of short-term debt guarantees financial muscle and makes it less profitable for rivals to invest (see Exercise 7.2).

Finally, managerial incentive schemes may be strategically designed so as to promote tacit collusion in oligopoly (Spagnolo 2000). Comparing the situation in which the manager receives a yearly bonus proportional to profit (and therefore in the absence of risk aversion or career concerns is led to maximize the firm's present discounted value of profits) and that in which her incentives are biased toward the future (perhaps through the award of stocks or stock options), the firm may end up be-

98. At least if firm 2 is constrained to be an all-equity firm. As was noted in footnote 96, firm 2, if it enters, will itself want to issue some debt $\mathcal{D}_2$ so as to commit to a higher output and therefore force firm 1 to curtail its production back a bit. But the flavor of the analysis remains similar to Stackelberg's.

99. For more on strategic complements (upward-sloping reaction curves) and substitutes (downward-sloping reaction curves), and strategies of commitment under entry deterrence or accommodation, see Bulow et al. (1985) and Fudenberg and Tirole (1984).

100. Here, note that $MR_i(\theta, q_i, q_j)$ decreases with q_j. So, in Figure 7.15(b), the MR_i curve shifts down as q_j increases. This leads to a decrease in q_i in order to restore equality in the first-order condition (7.22).

101. As we noted, beyond some level of debt the Stackelberg strategy becomes counterproductive, because the strategic/product market benefit is offset by too big a misalignment between the entrepreneur's objective and that of her firm as a whole, and so the marginal cost of high outputs ends up exceeding the marginal benefit.

102. Showalter also looks at the case of uncertain marginal cost. There, the optimization emphasizes low-cost states (those of no default), and therefore leads to *low* prices, which are strategically disadvantageous in a situation of accommodation.

103. These conclusions are common to all games of entry deterrence and accommodation (see Fudenberg and Tirole 1984; Shapiro 1989). Here the instrument providing commitment is the choice of debt.

ing more profitable in the latter case even though the manager no longer maximizes its present discounted value; for, the managerial bias toward the future tells rival firms that the manager is not keen on undercutting and starting a price war, that is, on privileging current income at the cost of future earnings. It thereby provides these rival firms with an incentive to themselves refrain from undercutting. The strategic gain attached to softening the rivals' market behavior may well offset the loss attached to the divergence of objectives between manager and investors.

7.4 Exercises

Exercise 7.1 (competition and vertical integration). This exercise is inspired by Cestone and White (2003).

(i) A *cashless* entrepreneur ($A = 0$) considers a research project requiring a fixed investment I. When financed, the project succeeds with probability $p_{\mathrm{H}} = 1$ (for certain) if she works, and with probability $p_{\mathrm{L}} = 1 - \Delta p$ if she shirks, in which case she receives private benefit B. Regardless of the outcome, there is a verifiable salvage value $R^{\mathrm{F}} \geqslant 0$ (equipment, real estate) at the end. For the moment, there is no other firm in the market and so success brings an additional income $R = M$ (monopoly profit) on top of the salvage value. Assume that

$$R^{\mathrm{F}} + \left(M - \frac{B}{\Delta p}\right) \geqslant I. \tag{1}$$

The investment cost I includes a fixed cost $K \leqslant I$ borne by a supplier who must develop an enabling technology. There is *ex ante* a competitive supply of such suppliers, who for simplicity have enough cash to finance the entrepreneur's remaining investment cost, $I - K$, besides their own cost K. So we can formalize the supplier as a "competitive capital market" for the moment.

In exchange for his contribution (supplying the technology and providing complementary financing $I - K$ to the entrepreneur), the selected supplier receives a debt claim (the equivalent of a fixed price) and an equity stake in the entrepreneurial firm.

A *debt claim* is a payment R_1^{F} to the supplier/lender from the safe income R^{F}:

$$0 \leqslant R_1^{\mathrm{F}} \leqslant R^{\mathrm{F}}.$$

An *equity claim* is a share $\theta_1 \in [0, 1]$ of the firm's profit beyond R^{F} (here, a claim on M).

- Can the project be financed?
- Characterize the set of feasible contracts $(R_1^{\mathrm{F}}, \theta_1)$. (There is some indeterminacy, except when the inequality in (1) is an equality. Discuss informally extra elements that could be added to the model to make a debt contract strictly optimal.)

(ii) Suppose now that, after having developed the enabling technology for the entrepreneur, the supplier can, at no extra cost (that is, without incurring K again), offer the technology to a rival who is in every respect identical to the entrepreneur. If he does so, and the two downstream projects are successful, then the per-firm duopoly profit is D (on top of the salvage value R^{F}), where

$$2D < M$$

(competition destroys profit). Assume that

$$R^{\mathrm{F}} + \left(D - \frac{B}{\Delta p}\right) \geqslant I - K > R^{\mathrm{F}}. \tag{2}$$

- Note that the entrepreneur always wants to sign an exclusivity contract with the selected supplier (hint: look at the industry profit when the rival receives the enabling technology).
- In the absence of exclusivity provision (say, for antitrust reasons), look at whether the entrepreneur can obtain de facto exclusivity by choosing the debt/equity mix of the supplier properly. Assume for simplicity that $(\Delta p)(1 - \theta_1)D \geqslant B$. This will hold true in an optimal contract.

Exercise 7.2 (benefits from financial muscle in a competitive environment). This exercise extends to liquidity choices the Aghion–Dewatripont–Rey idea that pledgeable income considerations may make financial structures and corporate governance strategic complements in a competitive environment.

(i) Consider a single firm. At date 0, the entrepreneur borrows $I - A$ in order to finance a fixed-size project costing I. At date 1, the firm may need to reinvest an amount ρ with probability λ. With probability $1 - \lambda$, no reinvestment is required. In the case of continuation the entrepreneur may behave (probability of success p_H, no private benefit) or misbehave (probability of success $p_L = p_H - \Delta p$, private benefit B). Let

$$\rho_1(R) \equiv p_H R \quad \text{and} \quad \rho_0(R) \equiv p_H\left(R - \frac{B}{\Delta p}\right),$$

where R is the profit in the case of success at date 2 (the profit is equal to 0 in the case of failure).

The firm is said to have "financial muscle" if $\rho > \rho_0(R)$ and the firm chooses to withstand the liquidity shock if it occurs.

• Explain the phrase "financial muscle."

• Does the firm want to have financial muscle when $\rho > \rho_0(R)$? (Hint: consider three regions for the term $(1-\lambda)\rho_0(R) - (I - A)$: $(-\infty, 0)$, $(0, \lambda[\rho - \rho_0(R)])$, and $(\lambda[\rho - \rho_0(R)], +\infty)$.)

(ii) Suppose now that the firm (now named the incumbent) faces a potential entrant in the innovation market. The entrant is *identical* to the incumbent in all respects (parameters A, I, p_H, p_L, B and profits (see below)) *except that the entrant will never face a liquidity shock if he invests* (the entrant is therefore endowed with a better technology). Let $R = M$ denote the monopoly profit made by a firm when it succeeds and the other firm either has not invested in the first place or has invested but not withstood its liquidity shock; let

$$R = C = p_H D + (1 - p_H)M$$

(where $D < M$ is the duopoly profit) denote its expected profit when it succeeds and the other firm has invested and withstood its liquidity shock (if any). Assume that

$$\rho > \rho_1(M), \tag{1}$$

$$(1-\lambda)\rho_0(C) + \lambda\rho_0(M) > I - A > \rho_0(C), \tag{2}$$

$$(1-\lambda)\rho_1(C) + \lambda\rho_1(M) > I. \tag{3}$$

• Suppose, first, that the two firms choose their financial structures (liquidity) *simultaneously* at date 0. Show that the entrant invests and the incumbent does not.

• Suppose, second, that, at date 0, the incumbent chooses her financial structure *before* the entrant. And assume, furthermore, that

$$\rho_0(M) - \lambda\rho > I - A. \tag{4}$$

Show that the incumbent invests, while the (more efficient) entrant does not.

Exercise 7.3 (dealing with asset substitution). Consider the fixed-investment model with a probability that the investment must be resold (redeployed) at an intermediate date because, say, it is learned that there is no demand for the product. The timing is summarized in Figure 7.16.

An entrepreneur has cash A and wants to invest a fixed amount $I > A$ into a project. The shortfall must be raised in a competitive capital market. The project yields R with probability p and 0 with probability $1 - p$, provided that there is a demand for the product (which has probability x and is revealed at the intermediate stage; the final profit is always 0 if there is no demand, and so it is then optimal to liquidate at the intermediate stage). Investors and entrepreneur are risk neutral, the latter is protected by limited liability, and the market rate of interest is 0.

(i) In a first step, ignore the possibility of asset substitution. The liquidation value is $L = L_0$, and the probability of success is p_H if the entrepreneur works and $p_L = p_H - \Delta p$ if she shirks (in which case she obtains a private benefit B). Assume that the NPV of the project is positive if the entrepreneur works, and negative if she shirks.

Assume that $A \geqslant \bar{A}$, where

$$(1-x)L_0 + x p_H\left(R - \frac{B}{\Delta p}\right) = I - \bar{A} \tag{1}$$

(and that $L_0 \leqslant p_H(R - B/\Delta p)$).

• Interpret (1).

• Compute the entrepreneur's expected utility.

• What is the class of optimal contracts (or, at least, characterize the optimal contract for $A = \bar{A}$)?

(ii) Suppose now that, before the state of demand is realized, but after the investment is sunk, the entrepreneur can engage in asset substitution. She can reallocate funds between asset maintenance (value of L) and future profit (as characterized by the probability of success, say).

More precisely, suppose that the entrepreneur chooses L and

• the probability of success is $p_H + \tau(L)$ if the entrepreneur behaves and $p_L + \tau(L)$ if she misbehaves;

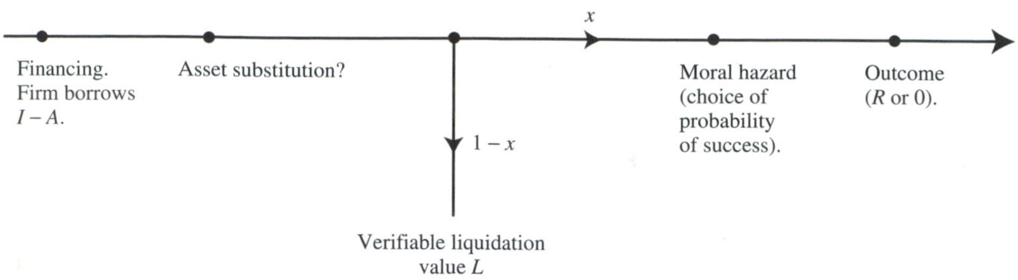

Figure 7.16

- the function τ is decreasing and strictly concave;
- $$\tau(L_0) = 0 \quad \text{and} \quad \tau'(L_0)R = -\frac{1-x}{x}; \qquad (2)$$
- the entrepreneur secretly chooses L (multitasking).

Consider contracts in which

- liquidation occurs if and only if there is no demand (hence, with probability x);
- the entrepreneur receives $r_b(L)$ if the assets are liquidated, and R_b if they are not and the project is successful (and 0 if the project fails).

Interpret (2). Compute the minimum level of A such that the threat of (excessive) asset substitution is innocuous. Interpret the associated optimal contract. (Hint: what is the optimal asset maintenance (liquidation value)? Note that, in order to induce the entrepreneur to choose this value, in the case of liquidation you may pay $r_b(L) = r_b$ if L is at the optimal level and 0 otherwise.)

Exercise 7.4 (competition and preemption). Consider the "profit-destruction model (with independent processes)" of Section 7.1.1.

As in Fudenberg and Tirole (1985), time is continuous, although both investment I and the research process and outcome are instantaneous (this is in order to simplify expressions). The actual R&D can be performed only at (or after) some fixed date t_0. The instantaneous rate of interest is r. The monopoly and duopoly profits, M and D, and the private benefit B then denote present discounted values (at interest rate r) from t_0 on. The entrepreneur's cash is worth $e^{r(t_0-t)}A$ at date t and so it grows with interest rate r and is worth A at date t_0.

Assume that

$$p_H\left(M - \frac{B}{\Delta p}\right) \geqslant I - A \geqslant p_H\left[(1-p_H)M + p_H D - \frac{B}{\Delta p}\right].$$

This condition states that if investment were constrained to occur at t_0, there would be scope for funding exactly one entrepreneur (see Section 7.1.1).

The twist is that the investment I can be sunk at any date $t \leqslant t_0$ (implying an excess expenditure of $[e^{r(t_0-t)} - 1]I$ from the point of view of date t_0 since the investment is useless until date t_0). The investment is then publicly observed.

Analyze this preemption game, distinguishing two cases depending on whether

$$p_H M \gtrless p_H\left(M - \frac{B}{\Delta p}\right) + A.$$

Exercise 7.5 (benchmarking). This exercise generalizes the benchmarking analysis of Section 7.1.1.

The assumptions are the same as in that section, except for the descriptions of risk aversion and correlation. Two firms, $i = 1, 2$, must develop, at cost I, a new technology in order to be able to serve the market. Individual profits are M for the successful firm if only one succeeds, D if both succeed, and 0 otherwise. The probability of success is p_H in the case of good behavior and p_L in the case of misbehavior (yielding private benefit B). Each entrepreneur starts with cash A.

The entrepreneurs exhibit the following form of risk aversion: their utility from income w is

$$\begin{aligned} w &\quad \text{for } w \geqslant 0, \\ (1+\theta)w &\quad \text{for } w < 0, \end{aligned}$$

where $\theta > 0$ is both a parameter of risk aversion and a measure of deadweight loss of punishment (similar to that of costly collateral pledging (see Chapters 4 and 6)).

With probability ρ, the realization of the random variable determining success/failure (see Section 7.1.1) is the same for both firms. With probability $1-\rho$, the realizations are independent for the two firms. (So Section 7.1.1 considered the polar cases $\rho = 0$ and $\rho = 1$.) No one ever learns whether realizations are correlated or not.

(i) Find conditions under which both entrepreneurs' receiving funding (and exerting effort) is an equilibrium. Describe the optimal incentive schemes.

Hints:

(a) Let $w = a_k \geqslant 0$ denote the reward of a successful entrepreneur when k $(= 1, 2)$ is the number of successful firms. Let $w = -b_k < 0$ denote the reward (really, a punishment) of an unsuccessful entrepreneur when the number of unsuccessful firms is k $(= 1, 2)$.

(b) Each entrepreneur maximizes her NPV subject to (IR_1) (the investors' breakeven condition) and (IC_b) (the entrepreneur's incentive constraint).

(c) Show that there is no loss of generality in assuming that

$$a_2 = b_2 = 0.$$

(d) Use a diagram in the (a_1, b_1)-space.

(ii) What happens when θ goes to 0 or ∞? When ρ goes to 0 or 1?

Exercise 7.6 (Brander–Lewis with two states of demand). Analyze the Brander–Lewis Cournot model with two states of demand, $\bar{\theta}$ and $\underline{\theta}$, with $\Delta\theta = \bar{\theta} - \underline{\theta} > 0$, and

$$\theta = \begin{cases} \bar{\theta} & \text{with probability } \alpha, \\ \underline{\theta} & \text{with probability } 1-\alpha. \end{cases}$$

The demand function is $p = \theta - Q$.

Let $\theta^{\mathrm{e}} \equiv \alpha\bar{\theta} + (1-\alpha)\underline{\theta}$ denote the mean. Assume that $\frac{1}{9}(\theta^{\mathrm{e}})^2 > I$.

(i) Compute the equilibrium when the two firms issue no debt.[104]

Show that both firms invest.

(ii) Next, follow Brander and Lewis in assuming that firm 1 chooses its financial structure first and picks a debt level $\mathcal{D}_1$ high enough so that when the intercept is $\underline{\theta}$, firm 1 goes bankrupt.

Note that entrepreneur 1 then ignores the bad state. Show that the new equilibrium (assuming that firm 2 enters and remains an all-equity firm) is

$$q_1 = \tfrac{1}{3}(\theta^{\mathrm{e}} + 2(1-\alpha)\Delta\theta)$$

and

$$q_2 \equiv \tfrac{1}{3}(\theta^{\mathrm{e}} - (1-\alpha)\Delta\theta).$$

(iii) Assume that firm 1 accommodates entry and that firm 2 cannot issue debt. What is the optimal level of debt $\mathcal{D}_1$ issued by entrepreneur 1?

Exercise 7.7 (optimal contracts in the Bolton–Scharfstein model). Redo the Bolton and Scharfstein analysis of Section 7.1.2, allowing for fully general contracts: the entrepreneur receives r_b^S in the case of date-0 success but no refinancing, R_b^SS in the cases of date-0 and date-1 success, and R_b^FS in the cases of date-1 success and date-0 failure (with $R_\mathrm{b}^\mathrm{SS}, R_\mathrm{b}^\mathrm{FS} \geqslant B/\Delta p$). (Under risk neutrality, there is no point rewarding failures unless it serves to deter predation. Hence, the exception R_b^FS.) Generalize the conditions (PD) and (IC) and show that $r_\mathrm{b}^\mathrm{S} = 0$ and that $R_\mathrm{b}^\mathrm{SS} \geqslant R_\mathrm{b}^\mathrm{FS}$ $(\geqslant B/\Delta p)$.

Exercise 7.8 (playing the soft-budget-constraint game vis-à-vis a customer). Consider a supplier–customer relationship with the timing as in Figure 7.17.

For simplicity, the customer is described as a self-financing entrepreneur (hence, without external investors). By contrast, the supplier is an entrepreneur who must borrow from the capital market. Thus, the context is that of the standard risk-neutral, fixed-investment model except for one twist: the payoff in the case of success, R, is determined endogenously as part of a later bargaining process with the user of the input. The customer receives gross benefit v from using the (successfully developed) input and 0 otherwise. The entrepreneur/supplier would therefore like to extract as much of v as possible from the customer.

Assume that

$$p_\mathrm{H}\left(v - \frac{B}{\Delta p}\right) \geqslant \max(I - A, p_\mathrm{L} v)$$

104. To shorten the analysis, ignore the limited liability problem that may arise for high-quantity choices. These technical problems can be eliminated by assuming that outputs cannot exceed $\frac{1}{2}\underline{\theta}$ and that $\Delta\theta$ is not too large.

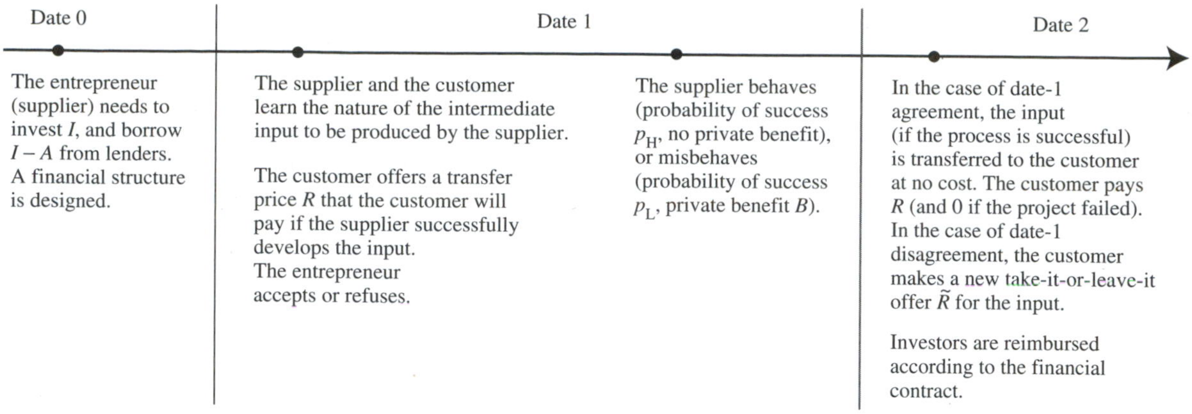

Date 0
Date 1
Date 2
The entrepreneur (supplier) needs to invest I, and borrow I − A from lenders. A financial structure is designed.
The supplier and the customer learn the nature of the intermediate input to be produced by the supplier.
The customer offers a transfer price R that the customer will pay if the supplier successfully develops the input. The entrepreneur accepts or refuses.
The supplier behaves (probability of success p_H, no private benefit), or misbehaves (probability of success p_L, private benefit B).
In the case of date-1 agreement, the input (if the process is successful) is transferred to the customer at no cost. The customer pays R (and 0 if the project failed). In the case of date-1 disagreement, the customer makes a new take-it-or-leave-it offer R̃ for the input.
Investors are reimbursed according to the financial contract.

Figure 7.17

and

$$p_L v + B < I$$

(and so, if all parties are rational, the investment will not take place if it subsequently induces the entrepreneur to misbehave). One will further assume that the input has no outside value (it is wasted if not used by the customer) and that the date-0 contract between the entrepreneur and the lenders is perfectly observed by the customer.

(i) *Long-term, nonrenegotiable debt.* Suppose, first, that the date-0 contract between the entrepreneur and her investors specifies an amount R_l of senior debt to be repaid to investors at date 2. This senior debt is purchased by investors who are unable to renegotiate their contract at any date.

Show that, when optimizing over the debt level R_l, the entrepreneur cannot obtain *ex ante* utility exceeding

$$U_b = (\Delta p)v - I.$$

(Hint: work by backward induction. What happens at date 2 if no contract has yet been signed with the customer and the project has been successful? Moving back to date 1, distinguish two cases depending on whether $p_L v \gtrless p_H(v - R_l - B/\Delta p)$.)

(ii) *Short-term, nonrenegotiable debt.* Second, assume that the entrepreneur issues an amount of short-term debt r_l and no long-term debt. This short-term debt is due at date 1 and thus the firm is liquidated if the debt is not reimbursed (again, we assume that the debt is purchased by dispersed investors who are unable to renegotiate the initial contract). Because the firm has no date-1 revenue, the customer, if he wants the supplier to continue operating, must offer to cover the debt payment r_l, besides offering a transfer price R in case of a successful development of the input. Show that the entrepreneur can obtain expected utility

$$U_b = p_H v - I.$$

(Hints: show that the customer offers $R = B/\Delta p$. Note that the entrepreneur consumes $(A + r_l) - I$ at date 0.)

Exercise 7.9 (optimality of golden parachutes). Return to the manipulation model of Section 7.2.1, with the possibility of informed manipulation. Confirm the heuristic analysis of that section through a careful analysis, allowing for general contracts (the reward R_b^r or R_b^q is contingent on the revealed information and may *a priori* exceed $B/\Delta p$; a fixed payment can be made in both states and only under revealed poor prospects: L_l^r and $L_l^q \leqslant L$; allow $q_H R$ to be larger or smaller than L).

Exercise 7.10 (delaying income recognition). Consider the timing in Figure 7.18.

Assume the following.

- The discount factor is $\delta = 1$.
- There is no moral hazard. A manager's probability of success depends only on the manager's current ability. Managers do not respond to monetary incentives and get a constant wage normalized at 0. They just get private benefit $\mathcal{B}$ per period of tenure. All incomes (y_1, y_2, y_3) go to investors.

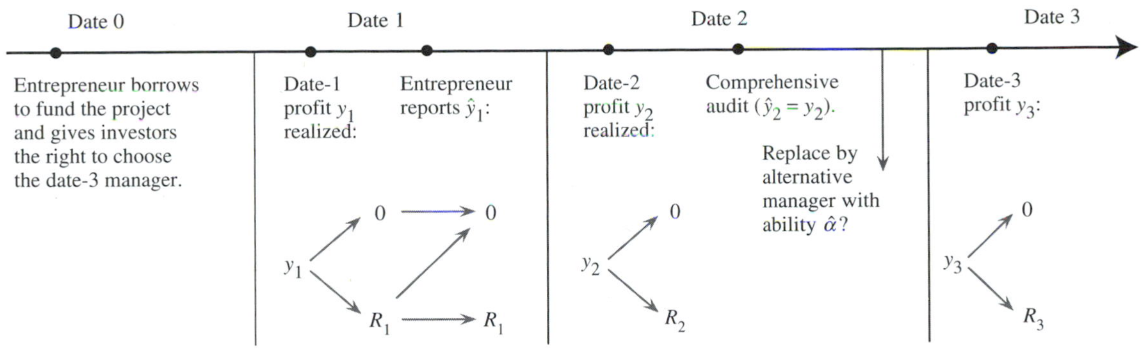

Figure 7.18

• A manager with high current ability succeeds with probability r, while one with low current ability succeeds with probability $q < r$.

• The entrepreneur's date-1 ability is high with probability α and low with probability $1 - \alpha$ (no one knows this ability). The correlation of ability between dates 1 and 2 is equal to $\rho \in [\frac{1}{2}, 1]$. That is, the entrepreneur's ability remains the same at date 2 with probability ρ. To simplify computations, assume that the manager's ability does not change between dates 2 and 3 (this assumption is not restrictive; we could simply require that the date-3 ability be positively correlated with the date-2 ability).

• At date 1, the entrepreneur privately observes the date-1 profit. If the entrepreneur has been successful ($y_1 = R_1$), she can defer income recognition. The reported profit is then $\hat{y}_1 = 0$. These savings increase the probability that $y_2 = R_2$ by a uniform amount τ ($\leqslant 1 - r$) (independent of type), presumably at a cost in terms of NPV ($R_1 > \tau R_2$).[105]

• Investors at the end of date 2 have the opportunity to replace the entrepreneur with an alternative manager who has probability $\hat{\alpha}$ of being a high-ability manager. (There is no commitment with regards to this replacement decision.) This decision is preceded by a careful audit that prevents the entrepreneur from manipulating earnings ($\hat{y}_2 = y_2$). One can have in mind a yearly report or a careful audit preceding an opportunity to replace management by a new managerial team.

105. We could also allow the entrepreneur to inflate date-1 earnings from 1 to R_1 at the cost of a reduction τ' in the probability of success at date 2 ($R_1 < \tau' R_2$). But if τ' is "not too large," there is no such incentive.

Find conditions under which a "pooling equilibrium," in which the entrepreneur keeps a low profile ($\hat{y}_1 = 0$) when successful ($y_1 = R_1$), prevails.

References

Aghion, P., M. Dewatripont, and P. Rey. 2000. Agency costs, firm behavior and the nature of competition. IDEI Working Paper 77, Toulouse.

Ahmed, A., G. Lobo, and J. Zhou. 2000. Job security and income smoothing: an empirical test of the Fudenberg and Tirole (1995) model. (Available at http://ssrn.com/abstract=24828.)

Alger, G. 1999. Moral hazard, regulation and peer monitoring. PhD Thesis, University of Toulouse 1.

Areeda, P. and D. Turner. 1975. Predatory pricing and related practices under Section 2 of the Sherman Act. *Harvard Law Review* 88:697–733.

Banerjee, A. 1992. A simple model of herd behavior. *Quarterly Journal of Economics* 107:797–817.

Bester, H. and M. Hellwig. 1987. Moral hazard and equilibrium credit rationing: an overview of the issues. In *Agency Theory, Information and Incentives* (ed. G. Bambers and K. Spremann). Heidelberg: Springer.

Biais, B. and C. Casamatta. 1999. Optimal leverage and aggregate investment. *Journal of Finance* 54:1291–1323.

Bikhchandani, S., D. Hirshleifer, and I. Welch. 1992. A theory of fads, fashion, custom, and cultural change as informational cascades. *Journal of Political Economy* 100: 992–1026.

Bolton, P. and D. Scharfstein. 1990. A theory of predation based on agency problems in financial contracting. *American Economic Review* 80:93–106.

Bolton, P., J. Brodley, and M. Riordan. 2000. Predatory pricing: strategic theory and legal policy. *Georgetown Law Journal* 88:2239–2330.

——. 2001. Predatory pricing: strategic theory and legal policy: response to critique and further elaboration. *Georgetown Law Journal* 89:2495–2529.

Brander, J. and T. Lewis. 1986. Oligopoly and financial structure: the limited liability effect. *American Economic Review* 76:956–970.

Bronars, S. and D. R. Deere. 1991. The threat of unionization, the use of debt, and the preservation of shareholder wealth. *Quarterly Journal of Economics* 106:231–254.

Bulow, J., G. Geanakoplos, and P. Klemperer. 1985. Multimarket oligopoly: strategic substitutes and complements. *Journal of Political Economy* 93:488–511.

Caillaud, B., B. Jullien, and P. Picard. 1995. Competing vertical structures: precommitment and renegotiation. *Econometrica* 63:621–647.

Cestone, G. 2000. Corporate financing and product market competition: an overview. *Giornale degli Economisti e Annali di Economia* 58:269–300.

Cestone, G. and C. Fumagalli. 2005. The strategic impact of resource flexibility in business groups. *RAND Journal of Economics* 36:193–214.

Cestone, G. and L. White. 2003. Anti-competitive financial contracting: the design of financial claims. *Journal of Finance* 58:2109–2142.

Chemla, G. and A. Faure-Grimaud. 2001. Dynamic adverse selection and debt. *European Economic Review* 45:1773–1792.

Chevalier, J. 1995a. Capital structure and product market competition: empirical evidence from the supermarket industry. *American Economic Review* 85:415–435.

——. 1995b. Do LBO supermarkets charge more? An empirical analysis of the effects of LBOs on supermarket pricing. *Journal of Finance* 50:1112–1195.

Chevalier, J. and G. Ellison. 1997. Risk taking by mutual funds as a response to incentives. *Journal of Political Economy* 105:1167–1200.

Chevalier, J. and D. S. Scharfstein. 1996. Capital-market imperfections and countercyclical markups: theory and evidence. *American Economic Review* 86:703–725.

Coase, R. 1972. Durability and monopoly. *Journal of Law and Economics* 15:143–149.

Darrough, M. 1987. Managerial incentives for short-term results: a comment. *Journal of Finance* 42:1097–1102.

Dasgupta, S. and K. Sengupta. 1993. Sunk investment, bargaining and choice of capital structure. *International Economic Review* 34:203–220.

De Fond, M. and C. Park. 1997. Smoothing income in anticipation of future earnings. *Journal of Accounting and Economics* 23:115–139.

Degeorge, F., J. Patel, and R. Zeckhauser. 1999. Earnings management to exceed thresholds. *Journal of Business* 72:1–33. (Reprinted in 2001 in *Behavioral Finance* (ed. H. M. Shefrin). Cheltenham, U.K.: Edward Elgar Publishing.)

Demski, J. 2003. Corporate conflicts of interests. *Journal of Economic Perspectives* 17:51–72.

Dewatripont, M. and J. Tirole. 1994. *The Prudential Regulation of Banks*. Cambridge, MA: MIT Press.

Dewatripont, M., I. Jewitt, and J. Tirole. 1999a. The economics of career concerns. Part I. Comparing information structures. *Review of Economic Studies* 66:183–198.

——. 1999b. The economics of career concerns. Part II. Application to missions and accountability of government agencies. *Review of Economic Studies* 66:199–217.

Diamond, D. 1984. Financial intermediation and delegated monitoring. *Review of Economic Studies* 51:393–414.

Faure-Grimaud, A. 2000. Product market competition and optimal debt contracts: the limited liability effect revisited. *European Economic Review* 44:1823–1840.

Fluck, Z. 1999. The dynamics of the management-shareholder conflict. *Review of Financial Studies* 12:379–404.

Friebel, G. and S. Guriev. 2005. Earnings manipulation and incentives in firms. Mimeo, IDEI, Toulouse, and New Economic School, Moscow.

Fudenberg, D. and J. Tirole. 1984. The fat-cat effect, the puppy-dog ploy and the lean and hungry look. *American Economic Review, Papers and Proceedings* 74:361–368.

——. 1985. Preemption and rent equalization in the adoption of new technology. *Review of Economic Studies* 52:383–402.

——. 1986. A "signal-jamming" theory of predation. *RAND Journal of Economics* 17:366–376.

——. 1995. A theory of income and dividend smoothing based on incumbency rents. *Journal of Political Economy* 103:75–93.

Fulghieri, P. and S. Nagarajan. 1992. Financial contracts as lasting commitments: the case of a leveraged oligopoly. *Journal of Financial Intermediation* 1:2–32.

Glazer, J. 1994. The strategic effects of long-term debt in imperfect competition. *Journal of Economic Theory* 62:428–443.

Gollier, C., P. F. Koehl, and J. C. Rochet. 1997. Risk-taking behavior with limited liability and risk aversion. *Journal of Risk and Insurance* 64:347–370.

Green, R. 1984. Investment incentives, debt, and warrants. *Journal of Financial Economics* 13:115–136.

Healy, P. 1985. The effect of bonus schemes on accounting decisions. *Journal of Accounting and Economics* 7:85–107.

Healy, P. and K. Palepu. 2003. The fall of Enron. *Journal of Economic Perspectives* 17:3–26.

Hellwig, M. 1994. A reconsideration of the Jensen–Meckling model of outside finance. Working Paper 9422, WWZ, Basel.

Hirshleifer, D. and A. Thakor. 1992. Managerial conservatism, project choice and debt. *Review of Financial Studies* 5:437–470.

Holmström, B. 1982. Managerial incentive problems: a dynamic perspective. In *Essays in Economics and Management in Honor of Lars Wahlbeck*. Helsinki: Swedish School of Economics. (Published in *Review of Economic Studies* (1999) 66:169–182.)

Holmström, B. and J. Ricart i Costa. 1986. Managerial incentives and capital management. *Quarterly Journal of Economics* 101:835–860.

Holthausen, R., D. Larcker, and R. Sloan. 1995. Business unit innovation and the structure of executive compensation. *Journal of Accounting and Economics* 19:279–313.

Jensen, M. 1988. Takeovers: their causes and consequences. *Journal of Economic Perspectives* 2:21–48.

Jensen, M. and W. R. Meckling. 1976. Theory of the firm, managerial behaviour, agency costs and ownership structure. *Journal of Financial Economics* 3:305–360.

Joskow, P. and A. Klevorick. 1979. A framework for analyzing predatory pricing policy. *Yale Law Journal* 89:213–270.

Kanagaretnam, K., G. Lobo, and R. Mathieu. 2003. Managerial incentives for income smoothing through bank loan loss provisions. *Review of Quantitative Finance and Accounting* 20:63–80.

Kasanen, E., J. Kinnunen, and J. Niskanen. 1996. Dividend-based earnings management: empirical evidence from Finland. *Journal of Accounting and Economics* 22:283–312.

Katz, M. 1991. Game-playing agents: unobservable contracts as precommitments. *RAND Journal of Economics* 22:307–328.

Kovenock, D. and G. Phillips. 1997. Capital structure and product market rivalry: how do we reconcile theory and evidence. *American Economic Review* 85:403–408.

Laffont, J.-J. and J. Tirole. 1988. Repeated auctions of incentive contracts, investment and bidding parity, with an application to takeovers. *RAND Journal of Economics* 19:516–537.

Lev, B. 2003. Corporate earnings: facts and fiction. *Journal of Economic Perspectives* 17:27–50.

Levitt, S. and C. Snyder. 1997. Is no news bad news? Information transmission and the role of "early warning" in the principal–agent model. *RAND Journal of Economics* 28:641–661.

Lintner, J. 1956. Distribution of incomes of corporations among dividends, retained earnings, and taxes. *American Economic Review* 46:97–113.

McGee, J. 1958. Predatory price cutting: the Standard Oil (NJ) case. *Journal of Law and Economics* 1:137–169.

MacKay, P, and G. Phillips. 2005. How does industry affect firm financial structure? *Review of Financial Studies*, in press.

Maksimovic, V. 1988. Capital structure in repeated oligopolies. *RAND Journal of Economics* 19:389–407.

Matsa, D. 2005. Evidence of strategic capital structure: how firms use debt to influence collective bargaining. Mimeo, MIT.

Merchant, K. 1989. *Rewarding Results: Motivating Profit Center Managers*. Boston, MA: Harvard Business School Press.

Müller, H. and F. Panunzi. 2004. Tender offers and leverage. *Quarterly Journal of Economics* 119:1217–1248.

Murphy, K. and J. Zimmerman. 1993. Financial performance surrounding CEO turnover. *Journal of Accounting and Economics* 16:273–316.

Narayanan, N. P. 1985. Managerial incentives for short-term results. *Journal of Finance* 40:1469–1484.

Palomino, F. and A. Prat. 2003. Risk taking and optional contracts for money managers. *RAND Journal of Economics* 34:113–137.

Perotti, E. and K. Spier. 1993. Capital structure as a bargaining tool. *American Economic Review* 83:1131–1141.

Phillips, G. 1995. Increased debt and industry product markets: an empirical analysis. *Journal of Financial Economics* 37:189–238.

Poitevin, M. 1989. Financial signaling and the deep-pocket argument. *RAND Journal of Economics* 20:26–40.

Rey, P. and J. Tirole. 1986. The logic of vertical restraints. *American Economic Review* 76:921–939.

Ronen, J. and S. Sadan. 1981. *Smoothing Income Numbers: Objectives, Means, and Implications*. Reading, MA: Addison-Wesley.

Scharfstein, D. and J. Stein. 1990. Herd behavior and investment. *American Economic Review* 80:465–479.

Schroth, E. and D. Szalay. 2004. Cash breeds success: the role of financing constraints in innovation. Mimeo, Université de Lausanne.

Shapiro, C. 1989. Theories of oligopoly behavior. In *Handbook of Industrial Organization* (ed. R. Schmalensee and R. Willig), Volume 1. Amsterdam: North-Holland.

Showalter, D. 1995. Oligopoly and financial structure: comment. *American Economic Review* 85:647–653.

Snyder, C. 1996. Negotiation and renegotiation of optimal financial contracts under the threat of predation. *Journal of Industrial Economics* 44:325–343.

Spagnolo, G. 2000. Stock-related compensation and product-market competition. *RAND Journal of Economics* 31:22–42.

Spiegel, Y. 1996. The role of debt in procurement contracts. *Journal of Economics and Management Strategy* 5:379–407.

Spiegel, Y. and D. F. Spulber. 1994. The capital structure of a regulated firm. *RAND Journal of Economics* 25:424–440.

Stein, J. 1989. Efficient capital markets, inefficient firms: a model of myopic corporate behavior. *Quarterly Journal of Economics* 104:655–669.

Sung, J. 1995. Linearity with project selection and controllable diffusion rate in continuous-time principal–agent models. *RAND Journal of Economics* 26:720–743.

Telser, L. 1966. Cutthroat competition and the long purse. *Journal of Law and Economics* 9:259–277.

Tirole, J. 1988. *The Theory of Industrial Organization*. Cambridge, MA: MIT Press.

Von Thadden, E. L. 1995. Long-term contracts, short-term investment and monitoring. *Review of Economic Studies* 62:557–575.

Weisbach, M. S. 1988. Outside directors and CEO turnover. *Journal of Financial Economics* 20:431–460.

Williamson, O. 1975. *Markets and Hierarchies: Analysis of Antitrust Implications.* New York: Free Press.

Zingales, L. 1998. The survival of the fittest or the fattest: exit and financing in the trucking industry. *Journal of Finance* 53:905–938.

Zwiebel, J. 1995. Corporate conservatism and relative compensation. *Journal of Political Economy* 103:1–25.

——. 1996. Dynamic capital structure under managerial entrenchment. *American Economic Review* 86:1197–1215.

PART III

Exit and Voice: Passive and Active Monitoring

8

Investors of Passage: Entry, Exit, and Speculation

8.1 General Introduction to Monitoring in Corporate Finance

This section provides an overview of the complex patterns of corporate monitoring. After motivating the study through a recap of the popular debate on the matter, the section introduces a key distinction between active and passive monitoring. It then discusses the attributes of a "good monitor," in particular, the incentives provided by his claims' return structure. Finally, it describes the organization of this chapter.

8.1.1 The Popular Debate

As discussed in Chapter 1, the popular press and the political debate about comparative corporate governance like to distinguish between the AS model (the Anglo-Saxon paradigm exemplified by the United States and the United Kingdom) and the GJ model (which prevails in Germany, Japan, and much of continental Europe in various forms). Empirical and theoretical research has undertaken cross-country comparisons of financial and governance systems and studied their costs and benefits.

In a nutshell, the AS model of corporate governance tends to emphasize a well-developed stock market, with strong investor protection, substantial disclosure requirements, shareholder activism (e.g., by pension funds), proxy fights, and takeovers. Banking is arm's length while the public debt market (commercial paper, bonds) may flourish. The AS model is often criticized in Europe for encouraging short-termism[1] and for preventing long-term, trust relationships between management and stakeholders from developing. In contrast, the GJ model puts banks more to the fore and, according to its proponents, encourages long-term relationships between investors and managers to the detriment of investor liquidity. Firms reputedly do relatively little shopping around for low interest rates, although some evolution to the contrary has recently been observed, for example, among German firms. Many firms stay private and the stock market is thin. Ownership is usually quite concentrated. Furthermore, in countries like France and Japan, pervasive cross-shareholdings among firms, and between firms and financial institutions (banks, insurance companies),[2] seriously limit the scope for managerial contests. The GJ system is often depicted by its critics as being collusive and as favoring entrenched managements.

This debate in part reflects the importance of monitoring in corporate governance. The prominence of monitoring mechanisms should not surprise the reader; Part II emphasized the many implications and distortions of asymmetric information (adverse selection, moral hazard) and monitoring can be seen as a way of reducing informational asymmetries between firms and investors.[3]

1. There are two possible definitions of short-termism. The first is that managers do not invest enough, because the prospect of cashing in on stock options or the fear of facing external interference or a takeover, or of being fired, make them too concerned with short-term performance (stock price, quarterly or yearly income). The second is that financial markets are too short-term oriented, in that analysts and institutional investors look for firms that will perform well in the short term but not necessarily in the long term. The argument is similar in both cases, as it implies that the incentives of corporate managers or of those, "one tier up," who analyze their performance, are too oriented toward the short term. The two forms of short-termism, furthermore, interact, as institutional short-termism puts pressure on corporate managers to "posture" and generate good short-term performance.

2. In Japan cross-ownerships are often organized within keiretsus.

3. The oversight issue may also be key to a proper definition of equity and leverage for firms and financial institutions. Although everyone would agree that short-term debt is not part of a firm's or a bank's capital, it is often suggested that a fraction of long-term debt be included in the definition of capital. (For example, international banking regulations (defined by the 1988 Basel Accord) allow subordinated debt with maturity exceeding five years to be counted, up to a limit, as "supplementary capital.") One leading interpretation of this viewpoint is that the firm or the bank is less likely to face a liquidity

8.1.2 Active and Passive Monitoring

The generic distinction between exit and voice was introduced by Hirschman (1970) in order to contrast the behaviors of organizations' members who either vote with their feet when discontented with the evolution of their organizations or stay and try to improve things.

In the context of corporate finance, the two forms of monitoring in turn correspond to the two types of information that ought to be gathered by investors in an efficient governance structure:[4]

Prospective or value-enhancing information is information that bears on the optimal course of action to be followed by the firm. It is information that ought to be collected before managerial decisions are implemented and ought to be exploited to improve decision making. These decisions may be structural (investments, spinoffs, diversification, etc.), strategic (product positioning, advertising, pricing, etc.), or related to personnel (replacement of management, downsizing, etc.).

It can be collected by an equityholder, as in the case of a venture capitalist or a large shareholder.[5] Prospective information may also be collected by debtholders, as in the case of a bank that imposes specific covenants to force or prevent a course of action, or uses the violation of a covenant to impose a change of policy by the borrower.

This form of monitoring is called *active* monitoring; it is associated with either formal or real control. Formal control exists when the monitor has control rights through, for example, a majority of seats on the board or a majority of votes at the general assembly. Real control refers to investors with minority positions who succeed in persuading a majority of the board or the general assembly to go along with a given policy.[6]

Retrospective or value-neutral or speculative information is information that has no direct bearing on future decisions and is therefore a mere measurement of past managerial performance. Acquiring speculative information may be akin to taking a picture of the value of the assets of the firm at a given point in time. (Note that "retrospective" refers to an assessment of the impact of *past* managerial choices on future profits.)

Speculative information may be acquired by equityholders, as in the case of analysts who wish to speculate by selling shares in the case of bad news and buying shares in the case of good news, but do not wish to interfere with the firm's management. It can be acquired by holders of (short-term) debt as well, as illustrated by the case of a run in the commercial paper market (for a firm) or in the interbank market (for a bank). To the extent that they vote with their feet, short-term debtholders are speculators.

In contrast with prospective information, speculative information has no value per se, as it forms the basis for *passive* (noninterventionist) monitoring. But it can serve the purpose of rewarding or punishing the management for its past behavior. For instance, an increase in the stock price associated with optimistic views about the firm's prospects benefits management through its holdings of stock options.

Several points with respect to this distinction are in order.

---

crisis if its debt is long rather than short term (see Chapter 5). An objection to this interpretation is that the enhanced liquidity would be better reflected in the liquidity rather than the solvency ratio.

An alternative interpretation is that the borrower is better monitored at the issuance date by buyers of long-term than by buyers of short-term debt, since the holders of short-term debt can usually "exit" or "run" before trouble occurs, and therefore have little incentive to monitor *ex ante* the quality of the borrower. The holders of long-term debt, according to this interpretation, have more incentives to assess the borrower's quality and to design and monitor compliance with covenants; this then "certifies" the firm, whose borrowing capacity should therefore be enhanced (which is, for example, achieved, for a bank, by raising its regulatory capital, and for a firm, by boosting the measure of its capital if lenders operate with a standard, industry-contingent target leverage ratio). We will later come back to the question of who is a good monitor.

4. These two types of information are called "strategic" and "speculative" in Holmström and Tirole (1993).

5. The threat of a proxy fight, rather than a strong presence on the board of directors, may be the conduit for shareholder intervention. CalPERS, the California Public Employees' Retirement System, draws annual lists of firms in its portfolio that it analyzes to be poor performers (relative to where they should stand if they were better managed, rather than to the market performance). It then brings its expertise and puts the case for reform to management. CalPERS, if needed, may then fight a proxy battle.

6. A venture capitalist or a takeover artist may have formal decision rights, either through previous contracting or through the acquisition of a majority of shares or both. But control is often simply real and not formal. That is, the collector of prospective information has no or limited authority and does not own a majority of shares. A case in point is the proxy fight mechanism, in which a shareholder activist (e.g., a pension fund) convinces a majority of shareholders to take action against management (see footnote 5).

(a) *Relationship to the AS–GJ debate.* The distinction between speculative and prospective information can be related to the debate on comparative corporate governance. Its critics often argue that the AS model encourages short-term profit maximization to the detriment of a long-term involvement by investors. This can be interpreted as the viewpoint that Anglo-Saxon investors exercise insufficient voice and engage in excessive speculation.

(b) *Holding period and activism.* It is tempting to identify voice with long-term involvement and exit with a short-term one. Although there is some truth in this view, as we will see in Chapter 9, we should be careful about the relevant timescale. A raider who takes over a mismanaged firm, refocuses it on its core business through spinoffs, changes management, and then resells his stake, may operate on a small timescale, that is, be a "short-term investor," and yet he exercises a substantial amount of voice because he alters in a significant way the firm's future course of action. Conversely, retrospective information can be collected by a long-term investor. A case in point is credit enhancement in the securitization of mortgages, credit card receivables, loans, and so forth. The credit enhancer "takes a picture" of the quality of the underlying assets, and certifies this quality by providing guarantees to other investors or taking a subordinate position. The issue then is not voice—the assets' returns have a life of their own—but rather the measurement of the issuer's past performance.

(c) *Dual nature of information.* Some types of information are both prospective and retrospective. In an adverse-selection context, in which the capital market has imperfect information about managerial talent, information about past managerial performance can be used both to reward or punish management and to infer whether management is likely to be fit for the firm's future challenges and thus to decide whether to keep the current management in place. Similarly, the analysis of the value of assets in place may reveal whether further investment is warranted. For example, a large lender who refuses to roll over a loan, a prestigious investment bank which refuses to underwrite an issue, or a rating agency that gives the firm a low rating, all refuse to certify the firm and may well convince other investors not to lend to the firm, resulting in lower investment or distress.

The distinction between prospective and retrospective information is somewhat cleaner in a moral-hazard context, because past and future performances are then unrelated, than in an adverse-selection context, where assessed performances across periods are linked through inferences about managerial talent.

(d) *Complements or substitutes?* Our discussion of prospective and retrospective information indicates that the two types of information perform different functions, and so both should be collected. But information collection is costly, and one may therefore wonder whether the two types of information are substitutes (the collection of speculative information reduces the marginal benefit of collecting prospective information, say) or complements (the collection of speculative information raises this marginal benefit, say). This question is central to the design of the financial system and thus to the debate on comparative corporate governance and yet it has not been investigated in detail in the literature. The next two chapters will point at some considerations relevant to the matter, but will bring no definitive answer to the question.

(e) *Rationale for delegated monitoring.* Information is basically a public good in that, once acquired by a monitor, it can be disseminated to other investors at a very low cost. Information collection is a "natural monopoly." Thus, it often makes sense to delegate the collection of specific information to a single or a small number of monitors, as was recognized by Leland and Pyle (1977), Campbell and Kracaw (1980), and Diamond (1984). Another and related implication of the public-good feature of information is that the collection of information by an investor gives rise to substantial free riding by other investors, employees (if their wage and pension claims are unsecured), trade creditors, customers, government agencies, and other stakeholders in the firm.

8.1.3 Incumbents versus Entrants: Entry into Corporate Governance

Active monitoring can be undertaken by "hired guns" (more prosaically, "enlisted or designated monitors," or "incumbents") such as a venture capitalist or a board of directors. Alternatively, it may rely on "unenlisted monitors" or "entrants," such as a raider or a proxy fight organizer. One may wonder why corporate charters and financial agreements should design mechanisms for entry into the monitoring market. Somehow, incumbent monitoring must face some limitations. Entry into monitoring may be desirable for reasons that are often similar to those underlying the benefits of entry into more familiar markets:

Ineffective monitoring. Incumbent monitors may not perform their monitoring function, say, because they collude with management. For example, collusion[7] has often been advanced as one explanation for rubber-stamping by boards of directors. Or the choices of monitors, like those of managers, may be distorted by agency problems such as career concerns. For example, they may want to stick to their earlier positive assessments of the firm even when they observe a degradation of its state.

Wrong monitor syndrome. It may be difficult to foresee in advance who will be the proper monitor in the future. The monitor's talent and the adequacy of his skills to the firm's future environments may not be known.

Liquidity needs. As Chapter 9 will emphasize, an active monitor may need to commit funds for a long period of time in order to be credible. But this active monitor may face liquidity shocks and need the invested funds for other purposes (he may also go bankrupt). In such circumstances, the active monitor may need to be replaced.

Entry into corporate monitoring is, of course, costly to the firm:

Coordination problems. Because entrants are not "enlisted" but in general appear spontaneously, there may be coordination problems among entrants. There may be duplication of information acquisition as in the case of multiple raiders. Conversely, no one may acquire the necessary information.

7. Or, more mildly, the need for directors to maintain a good ongoing relationship with managers and thereby decent access to information.

Lack of trust. A criticism often leveled at takeovers is that they prevent the development of a trust relationship between insiders (management and employees) and investors (see, in particular, Shleifer and Summers 1988). Under concentrated, long-term ownership, the large owner may be able to build a reputation for being fair to insiders and not expropriate the latter's past investments into the firm by acting opportunistically and imposing tough conditions once they have invested. Such a trust relationship may be impossible to develop in a context where entry (takeovers, proxy fights) makes monitoring more anonymous. Newcomers may then enter and renege on the previous monitor's promise to leave insiders with a rent commensurate with their investment.

Rents. (This technical point will be clarified in Chapters 9 and 11.) *Ex post* interactions with entrants is likely to cost the firm more rents than when the interaction with monitors is planned *ex ante.* The reason for this is that the *ex post* interaction generally occurs when the entrants have already acquired their information. Entrants may refrain from interacting when their information is unfavorable and enter only when they have good information. For example, a pension fund or a takeover artist may only target undervalued companies. This is to be contrasted with the case of an initial and long-term shareholder who bears the upside as well as the downside risk.

Limited investments by incumbents. Incumbent monitors have fewer incentives to invest in long-term value enhancements, that is, improvements that do not become obvious to the public until they pay off, if they know that they have a decent chance of being replaced by entrants (see Chapters 9 and 11).

8.1.4 Who Is a Good Monitor?

A somewhat unsettled issue in the literature relates to the incentive scheme that ought to be given to monitors. One illustration (among others) of this unsettledness is the old debate about whether debtholders should be senior or secured in order to have a proper incentive to monitor. The first strand in the literature (Jackson and Kronman 1979; Fama 1985; see also Calomiris and Kahn (1991) and Rey and

Stiglitz (1991) on the depositors' incentives to monitor banks provided by a first-come-first-served payment of depositors in the case of a run) argues that junior claimants have greater incentives to monitor, on the basis that their claim is more sensitive than a senior claim to managerial moral hazard (see also Exercise 9.6). The second and revisionist strand dates back to Schwartz's 1981 observation that many actual unsecured creditors appear relatively inferior monitors, while presumably superior monitors such as banks often hold short-term, secured debt. This alternative strand has developed theories as to why this may be the case (see, for example, Burkart et al. 1995; Levmore 1982; Gorton and Kahn 2000; Rajan and Winton 1995).

It should be clear, however, that there is no general answer to the question of the monitor's optimal incentive scheme. It is efficient to have different monitors collect different pieces of information, and a monitor's incentive scheme ought to depend on the type of information to be collected, on the firm's "technology" (timing of cash flows, riskiness of environment, etc.), on the existence of other monitors (to the extent that different types of information interact), and on market conditions (through the supply side of the monitoring market). For example, a simple (but perhaps misleading) guess is that a large equityholder has good incentives to monitor value enhancements (that is, managerial moral hazard that shifts the distribution of returns in the sense of first-order stochastic dominance), that a large holder of convertible, demandable, or short-term debt has good incentives to monitor risk taking (that is, managerial moral hazard that shifts the distribution of returns in the sense of second-order stochastic dominance), that a large secured claimholder has good incentives to monitor the maintenance of collateralized assets, and so forth.

The absence of general answers should not surprise us for two reasons. First, in practice, we observe a wide array of claims held by monitors. Second, monitors, although conventionally allocated to the nonexecutive side of the firm, are in part insiders. And we know from previous chapters that insiders' optimal incentive schemes depend on a variety of considerations.

8.1.5 A Recap

We can illustrate our distinctions between active and passive monitoring, and between incumbent and entrant monitoring as in Figure 8.1.

8.1.6 Chapter Outline

The chapter's main theme is that a firm's stock market price provides a measure of the value of assets in place and therefore of the impact of managerial behavior on investors' returns. It thereby creates precious information about managerial performance to the extent that managers make decisions, such as investments, whose consequences are realized only years, and sometimes decades, later.

Participants in the stock market, however, acquire costly information about the value of assets in place only if they expect to make money on this information. If the secondary market for shares is not deep, though, any attempt at buying shares, for example, will trigger a strong upward price adjustment and leave little margin for profiting from private knowledge that the firm is undervalued. By contrast, deep markets, i.e., markets with a fair amount of liquidity (nonspeculative) trading, provide substantial opportunities to speculators to conceal their trades behind liquidity trading and to benefit from their information.

This demonstrates two limits of market monitoring: first, stock market prices reflect information about the value of assets in place only to the extent that they are also garbled by other forms of uncertainty (such as liquidity trading). Second, because they may face superiorly informed speculators, shareholders who trade shares for liquidity reasons necessarily enjoy a lower return than those who can hold them for the long run. Ultimately, this cost must be borne by the issuing firm, which must issue the shares at a low price; put differently, investors who are able to keep their stocks in the long run enjoy an equity premium.

The chapter is organized as follows. Section 8.2 starts with a simple demonstration that the existence of early signals of performance reduces the agency cost and thereby increases the pledgeable income, facilitating financing. It then shows how a designated monitor can be incentivized by call or

<table>
<tr><th></th><th>Active monitoring/
prospective information</th><th>Passive monitoring/
speculative information</th></tr>
<tr><td>Incumbent monitor</td><td>Venture capitalist,
holder of unregistered securities,[1]
long-term core shareholder (noyau dur),
board of directors,
bank or life insurance company monitoring long-term loans (demands during reorganization).</td><td rowspan="2">Debt claim:
bank (short-term debt, revocable credit line, demandable debt),
commercial paper market,
interbank market.

Equity claim:
speculators (analysts),
derivative suits.

Equity-like claims:
credit enhancer,
underwriter (firm commitment contract).

Other claims:
rating agency,
underwriter
(best-efforts contract).</td></tr>
<tr><td>Entrant monitor</td><td>Raider (takeover),
proxy fight organizer.</td></tr>
</table>

1. The buyer of unregistered securities or letter stocks must write to the Security and Exchange Commission that the stocks are not bought for resale.

Figure 8.1

put options to acquire this information. It also discusses the possibility of collusion between monitor and monitoree, and the monitor's biases in information acquisition.

Section 8.3 turns to market monitoring. It first notes that stock market participants also have call and put options as they can buy or sell shares. The specificity of these call and put options, though, is that their exercise price is not fixed but rather endogenously determined: it is the market price. The section shows how speculator profit, and ultimately the market acquisition of information about the value of assets in place, is related to the depth of the market.

Information about the value of assets in place can also discipline management by severing the firm's access to cash rather than by serving as a basis for managerial compensation. To perform this function, though, passive monitoring must be performed by debtholders, since the resale of equity shares in the firm is internal to stock market participants and therefore does not drain the firm's liquidity. Section 8.4, building on Chapter 5, shows how demandable debt contracts discipline management through the threat of liquidity shortage.

8.2 Performance Measurement and the Value of Speculative Information

This section uses a straightforward extension of the fixed-investment model of Section 3.2 to obtain an elementary mechanism-design version of the Holmström and Tirole (1993) model of stock market monitoring.[8]

8. An early paper on the use of stock prices in optimal managerial incentives is Diamond and Verrecchia (1982). The starting point of that paper is that, from the sufficient statistic theorem of Holmström (1979) and Shavell (1979), "any information is of positive value if it reduces the *ex post* noise of direct estimates of an agent's level of effort." Diamond and Verrecchia assume that, after the managerial choice of effort but before income is realized, all investors exogenously observe an imperfect signal of final income, and the stock price perfectly reveals the common signal. This signal, or equivalently the stock price, is then used together with the final income to build the optimal managerial incentive scheme. In their paper, the manager's reward decreases with the stock price, because the common signal is about an exogenous, that is, action-independent, variable, which must be filtered out of the final income.

8.2.1 Introducing Early Performance Monitoring

Consider a biotech entrepreneur or a pharmaceutical company attempting to develop a molecule to cure a disease or treat its symptoms. The basic research activity will last for three or four years, after which the project, if successful heretofore, will move on to a development phase, then to a lengthy testing and regulatory approval process (say, through the Federal Drug Administration in the United States), and finally to a commercialization and marketing stage until the twenty-year patent expires (and often even after the drug gets off-patent). Clearly, the final profit made on the drug reflects much uncertainty realized years and even decades after the initial research stage: changes in regulatory standards, accrual of competing drugs, shocks to demand for the drug, changes in national health systems' organization, and so forth. The final profit is therefore a poor (by which I mean very garbled) indicator of the prospects created by the initial activity. Put differently, it very imperfectly measures the value of assets in place at the end of the research stage.

Consider, therefore, the problem of rewarding the entrepreneur or the manager for her performance during this period. It would be desirable to measure this performance early for two reasons: first, the entrepreneur or manager may need the money long before the final profit is realized; second, even if she can wait for the final profit to be realized (as will be the case in the treatment below), better incentive schemes can be tailored if some advance measure of the value of assets in place can be obtained.

The drug example illustrates a much more general point: many investment decisions bear their fruit many years and even decades after they are made. The design of managerial compensation requires obtaining performance measures that do not rely solely on accounting and income recognition.

The Holmström and Tirole paper builds on the insight of Diamond and Verrecchia in two ways. First, the stock market acquires information that is informative about value enhancement. This yields a positive relationship between managerial reward and stock price. Second, and more importantly, it assumes that information is costly to acquire. Proper incentives must then be given to speculators to acquire information, which leads to a study of the relationship between stock market liquidity and performance monitoring. The Holmström and Tirole analysis takes the stock market institution for granted, though, while the Diamond and Verrecchia paper, like this section, designs an optimal mechanism.

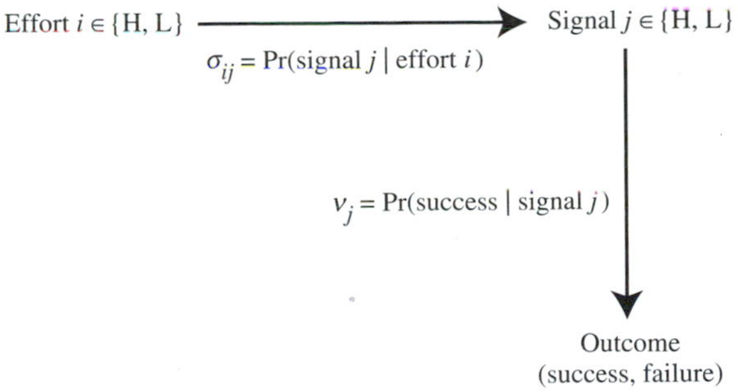

Figure 8.2

Let us start with the basic framework, which is that of Section 3.2, with an early signal of performance appended: an entrepreneur has a fixed-size project that requires investment I. The entrepreneur's cash, A, is insufficient to cover the cost of investment, $A < I$, and so the entrepreneur must borrow $I - A$ from investors. The project yields R in the case of success and 0 in the case of failure, and is subject to moral hazard. The probability of success is p_H if the entrepreneur works and $p_L = p_H - \Delta p$ if she shirks. So, the effort can be high (H) or low (L). Shirking provides private benefit B.

The new modeling feature is that, after the entrepreneurial choice of effort and before the project succeeds or fails, information can be acquired that is informative about the final outcome.

Let us assume that there are two possible signals, high (H) and low (L). (By an abuse of notation but for mnemonic reasons, we use the same notation for efforts and signals.) The (positive) probability of signal $j \in \{H, L\}$ conditional on effort $i \in \{H, L\}$ is denoted σ_{ij} (of course, $\sigma_{iH} + \sigma_{iL} = 1$ for all i). We simplify the analysis by assuming that the signal is a sufficient statistic for the final outcome (this assumption is easily relaxed). Let ν_j denote the probability of success given signal j. The sufficient statistic property means that ν_j is independent of effort. Figure 8.2 summarizes the stochastic structure.

In order for the *ex ante* probabilities of success given a high and a low effort to be equal to p_H and p_L, respectively, it must be the case that

$$p_H = \sigma_{HH}\nu_H + \sigma_{HL}\nu_L \tag{8.1}$$

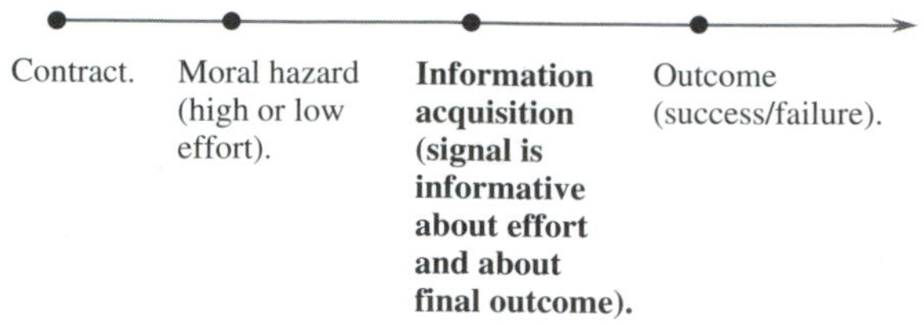

Figure 8.3

and

$$p_L = \sigma_{LH}\nu_H + \sigma_{LL}\nu_L. \tag{8.2}$$

Let us now interpret the high signal as good news about the final outcome.[9]

Assumption 8.1. *The high signal enhances the confidence in success:* $\nu_H > p_H$ *(equivalently,* $\nu_L < p_L$*).*

The timing of the extended fixed-investment model is summarized in Figure 8.3.

First we look at the benchmark in which the signal can be obtained for free and can be verified so that the entrepreneur's incentive scheme can be made directly contingent on this signal. Then we assume that information acquisition is costly and subject to moral hazard, and study information collection by an "incumbent monitor" and by an "entrant monitor" (see Section 8.1.3).

8.2.2 The Benchmark of Free Performance Monitoring

Suppose, temporarily, that the signal can be costlessly observed and verified, and so the entrepreneurial contract can depend both on the realization of the signal and on the final outcome. The optimal incentive contract, however, can be chosen so as to depend only on the realized signal. Intuitively, there is no reason to make the entrepreneur accountable for shocks she has no control over; here, for a given realization of the signal, the final outcome is totally out of the entrepreneur's control and thus her reward should not be made contingent on the realized outcome. This intuitive property results directly from the more general sufficient statistic theorem of Holmström (1979) and Shavell (1979), according to which an agent's compensation should be based only on a statistic that is "sufficient" with respect to the inference about her effort; that is, the final profit brings no information about the borrower's choice of effort to someone who already knows the signal.

Because the entrepreneur is risk neutral and protected by limited liability, and because the high (low) signal is good (bad) news for the high effort, it is clear that the entrepreneur should receive a reward R_b *in the case of a high signal* (regardless of success or failure, as we have argued), and 0 in the case of a low signal. The reward for a good signal should be sufficient to induce the entrepreneur to choose the high effort. A high effort increases the probability of a high signal from σ_{LH} to σ_{HH}, but does not enable the entrepreneur to enjoy private benefit B. And so we require that

$$(\sigma_{HH} - \sigma_{LH})R_b \geqslant B. \tag{IC$_b$}$$

As in Chapter 3, let us compute the pledgeable income. The entrepreneur's incompressible share is, in expected value,

$$\sigma_{HH}R_b = \frac{\sigma_{HH}}{\sigma_{HH} - \sigma_{LH}}B.$$

And so the necessary and sufficient condition for the entrepreneur to obtain funding is that the project's NPV net of the entrepreneur's incompressible share exceeds the investors' contribution to the initial investment:

$$p_H R - \frac{\sigma_{HH}}{\sigma_{HH} - \sigma_{LH}}B \geqslant I - A. \tag{8.3}$$

Let us compare this condition with condition (3.3) prevailing when no signal is available:

$$p_H R - \frac{p_H}{p_H - p_L}B \geqslant I - A.$$

Identities (8.1) and (8.2) imply that

$$\frac{p_H}{p_H - p_L} = \frac{\sigma_{HH}(\nu_H - \nu_L) + \nu_L}{(\sigma_{HH} - \sigma_{LH})(\nu_H - \nu_L)} > \frac{\sigma_{HH}}{\sigma_{HH} - \sigma_{LH}}.$$

We conclude that *the existence of the signal increases pledgeable income and thus facilitates funding* (the minimum entrepreneurial equity required to obtain financing is smaller). This elementary model illustrates a general point: *early signals provide information about future performance, and thus about the moral-hazard activity, that is not yet garbled by the future environmental noise* that accrues after the signal is revealed and before the final outcome is realized. Its use improves performance measurement

9. That $\nu_H > p_H$ implies that $\nu_L < p_L$ can be derived from condition (8.2) together with $\nu_H > p_L$ and $\sigma_{LH} = 1 - \sigma_{LL}$.

and de facto reduces the extent of moral hazard. Indeed, this model with a signal is equivalent to the model of Section 3.2 (without signal) but with a lower private benefit equal to

$$B_1 = \frac{\sigma_{HH}/(\sigma_{HH} - \sigma_{LH})}{p_H/(p_H - p_L)} B = \frac{\sigma_{HH}(\nu_H - \nu_L)}{\sigma_{HH}(\nu_H - \nu_L) + \nu_L} B < B.$$

Note that the coefficient of B in the first expression of B_1 is equal to the ratio of the likelihood ratios.

Remark (early measurement and NPV). In the fixed-investment model, the existence of the signal increases the pledgeable income and facilitates funding, but it does not alter the project's NPV, $p_H R - I$, also equal to the borrower's welfare in case of funding.[10] In the variable-investment model of Section 3.4, the introduction of a signal boosts debt capacity and, while it does not affect the NPV per unit of investment, raises the borrower's welfare (see Exercise 8.1).

Remark (what is the signal informative about?). A key insight is that although the signal is informative about the entrepreneur's effort, the monitor will not collect the signal in order to learn the entrepreneur's effort. Indeed, the monitor here knows for certain that the entrepreneur has worked. It is only to the extent that the signal *also* contains information about the exogenous shocks that affect the final outcome that the monitor will have an incentive to engage in costly information acquisition.[11]

Implementation. To implement the optimal incentive scheme when the signal is publicly observable but not necessarily directly verifiable by a court, one can, *for example*, let the investors' claims be publicly traded shares. (Here and below we normalize the number of shares to be one.) Their interim value is equal to $\nu_H R$ in the case of a high signal and $\nu_L R$ in the case of a low one. A fraction x of the shares is initially set aside and given to the entrepreneur if and only if the stock price is equal to $\nu_H R$. The entrepreneur receives no bonus, that is, no compensation based on realized income. (A bonus would coexist with stock options if the signal were not a sufficient statistic for managerial effort and the entrepreneur were risk averse.) Nor is the entrepreneur allowed to engage in insider trading by purchasing or selling shares not specified in the contract. The fraction of shares to be allocated to the entrepreneur in case of a high stock price is given by

$$x(\nu_H R) = R_b^*,$$

where R_b^* is the managerial reward for a high signal that makes investors break even: $p_H R - \sigma_{HH} R_b^* = I - A$. (In the case of a low stock price, the x shares are distributed among the investors.)

Note that this reward scheme is basically a *stock option*. It *gives* shares to the entrepreneur for the high realization of the stock price. A straight share, that is a noncontingent share given *ex ante* to the entrepreneur, is suboptimal here since it provides a positive reward even in the case of a low stock price. We invite the reader to go through the (slightly more complex) arithmetic of the design of stock options in which the entrepreneur's reward is linked to the appreciation in the stock price when the strike price is the stock price at the date at which the options are granted, i.e., $p_H R$. For such stock appreciation rights (SARs), the entrepreneur receives the capital gain $(\nu_H - p_H)R$ associated with a given number y of shares, without the requirement to supply cash to exercise the options. The difference with the reward scheme considered above is merely one of an accounting nature.

8.2.3 Designated Monitor

8.2.3.1 The Monitor's Option Contract

We now consider the case of an "enlisted incumbent" or "designated monitor" ("he") with costly monitoring. Let us now assume that a party who collects the signal incurs a nonobservable private cost c of doing so.[12] Furthermore, the information he

10. This would not be so if the borrower were risk averse, since the reduction in noise due to the signal would enhance the scope for insurance (see Holmström and Tirole 1993).

11. Put differently, in the absence of exogenous shock that is realized before monitoring takes place, the monitor would have no incentive to commit resources to learn an effort that he can perfectly anticipate.

12. Note that there is no asymmetry of information about the talent of the monitor (or about his cost of acquiring information). To reflect the possibility of adverse selection about the monitor, one can make use of the building blocks supplied by the literatures on delegated portfolio management (Bhattacharya and Pfleiderer 1985) and on the optimal elicitation of forecasts (Osband 1989); both literatures are concerned with the incentive scheme to be designed for a collector

collects is private, soft information. There is therefore some moral hazard in the collection of information about entrepreneurial performance. The monitor must thus be given an incentive scheme that induces him (1) to collect the information and (2) to reveal truthfully this information so that it can be used for managerial compensation purposes.[13]

There is a simple incentive scheme that induces the monitor to collect and reveal the information, and furthermore does not leave any rent (supranormal profit) to the monitor.[14] Namely, the entrepreneur can select a monitor and offer him a *stock option contract* with strike price equal to the stock price at the date at which the options are granted. The monitor has the right to purchase s^* shares at the *ex ante* par value, $p_H R$ per share (and the monitor then commits not to engage in insider trading by selling some shares or purchasing other shares).[15] The number s^* of options is given by

$$s^* \sigma_{HH}(\nu_H R - p_H R) = c. \tag{8.4}$$

The entrepreneur is rewarded as in Section 8.2.2, that is, she receives R_b^* if the monitor exercises his option (thereby triggering an increase in firm value's assessment), and receives 0 if he does not (which conveys bad news about firm value). Thus, the entrepreneur works if she expects the monitor to collect the information.

Suppose that the entrepreneur is expected to choose the high effort. If the monitor refrains from monitoring, his monitoring cost is equal to 0, but so is the value of his stock options: not knowing the signal, he still values shares at their *ex ante* par value $p_H R$, which is also the strike price. Thus the monitor is indifferent between exercising and not exercising the options, and makes no profit. If the monitor purchases the signal, then, with probability σ_{HH}, this signal is high and so shares are worth $\nu_H R$ to the monitor, resulting in a capital gain equal to $(\nu_H R - p_H R)$ per share. When the signal is low, the monitor values shares at $\nu_L R < p_H R$, and so does not exercise his options. Equation (8.4) thus states that the expected benefit from information collection is equal to its cost. It therefore also implies that the monitor receives no rent.

While the idea of providing the monitor with options to give him incentives to measure the entrepreneur's performance seems quite natural, it is not clear that one necessarily observes such arrangements frequently, at least for the acquisition of purely speculative information. (Venture capitalists or LBO fund managers typically receive 20% of the value created and structure their contracts with a number of options; for example, they generally own convertible preferred stock. However, they collect prospective as well as speculative information.) Yet one can view rolled-over short-term bank debt or revocable credit lines as options that protect the monitor (the bank) if he receives low signals about the borrower, but gives him the possibility to make money if signals are good (see Section 8.4.1).

Remark (multiplicity of equilibria under call options). There exists another equilibrium, in which the monitor does not monitor and never exercises his options, and therefore the entrepreneur shirks. Suppose that the entrepreneur shirks. Then the expected gain from monitoring is $s^* \sigma_{LH}(\nu_H R - p_H R) < c$. And because $p_L R < p_H R$, it is not worth exercising the options in the absence of monitoring.

This multiplicity can be avoided, though, by providing the monitor with put options or a mixture of put and call options (as earlier, the entrepreneur is rewarded when firm value increases). Intuitively, granting call options to the monitor makes the two effort decisions strategic complements (the

of retrospective information who has private information about his cost of collecting the information.

13. The treatment here is a modified version of Chang and Wang (1995).

14. There is no unique way of designing the optimal schemes for the entrepreneur and the monitor here. Chang and Wang (1995) offer a different one, with the same flavor: the entrepreneur is allowed to sell a fixed fraction of shares and is rewarded on the basis of the sale price.

15. The treatment here is rather loose concerning the accounting of shares in the firm. Our accounting convention is that there is a fixed number, namely, a mass 1, of shares in the firm, and so the *ex ante* (respectively, *ex post*) value of one share is $p_H R$ (respectively, either R or 0). One way to provide the entrepreneur and the monitor with the described incentives goes as follows. A fraction x of shares is set aside for the entrepreneur. These, however, become vested only if the monitor exercises his stock options; otherwise, the shares are distributed to third-party investors (who de facto have a put on the firm). Similarly, a fraction s of shares is set aside for the monitor (the proceeds, $s p_H R$, from the exercise of the call options and the shares s in the case of nonexercise can also be distributed to third-party investors). There are many equivalent accounting procedures; while the one just described is not the most natural, it makes the treatment of incentives mathematically simple.

entrepreneur has more incentive to behave if her performance is better monitored, and, with call options, the gain from monitoring is higher if the entrepreneur behaves); strategic complementarity is a well-known factor facilitating a multiplicity of equilibria in games. Put options eliminate this strategic complementarity: while the entrepreneur still has more incentive to behave when she is monitored, the gain to monitoring is now higher when the entrepreneur misbehaves.[16] Finally, and anticipating a little the study of market monitoring in Section 8.3, note that stock market participants have both call (share purchases) and put (share resales or short-sales) options.

8.2.3.2 Collusion between the Monitor and the Entrepreneur

In the parlance of organization theory, the monitor acts as a "supervisor," working for a "principal" (the other investors) and overseeing an "agent" (the entrepreneur). The supervisory activity is here meant to create a better assessment of managerial performance than is provided by accounting data. The integrity of the measurement process is not to be taken for granted. The entrepreneur has an incentive to convince the monitor in some way to supply a lenient assessment of his performance.[17]

The act of pleasing management is, of course, costly to the monitor. Suppose, for instance, that both agree at the initial date that the monitor will always exercise the call options. Under this agreement, the monitor no longer has an incentive to monitor since his information will not impact the exercise decision; the monitor therefore economizes c. The manager then shirks and obtains $R_b^* + B$ for certain, instead of $\sigma_{HH}R_b^*$ overall. The monitor loses $s^*(p_H - p_L)R$. The monitor loses less than what the entrepreneur gains if, as the reader will check, the number of call options is small, that is if the monitoring cost is small.

A mere increase in the two parties' total surplus does not suffice to generate collusion, though. In particular, collusion requires a quid pro quo. That is, the entrepreneur must be able to compensate the monitor for his sacrifice. Assuming that the entrepreneur has invested all her cash resources into the firm at the initial stage and has therefore not kept hidden reserves outside the firm in order to bribe the monitor, the entrepreneur must pay the monitor in another currency. This currency may be friendship, a symmetrical favor (for example, as when the monitor is himself an entrepreneur, whom the first entrepreneur is in charge of monitoring[18]), or else some financial resources drawn from the firm itself. The latter, "tunneling," possibility is not unrealistic, in that many of those who are *a priori* best qualified to monitor performance have some form of business relationship with the firm (lender, accountant, consultant, competitor, supplier) and thus various ways of receiving from management discrete forms of compensation drawn from corporate resources. Collusion between monitor and monitoree will be treated in more detail in Chapter 9 in the context of active monitoring; see also Exercise 8.2 for an example of collusion under speculative monitoring when the "means of exchange" takes the form of tunneling.

In contrast, anonymous market monitoring, discussed in the next section, is mostly immune to collusive activities and therefore has more integrity. This may explain why it is more frequently observed despite its drawbacks.

8.2.3.3 Excessive Speculation

The informational value of security pricing for contracting purposes stems from the fact that speculators "take a picture" of managerial performance at an early stage, before further noise garbles it. If the

16. Let us show how to avoid the multiplicity of equilibria by presenting the monitor with a choice between a call and a put rather than with a choice between a call and no investment. Let s_C and s_P denote the number of call and put options granted to the monitor. Their exercise prices are both equal to par, namely, $p_H R$. If $s_C\sigma_{HH}(\nu_H R - p_H R) + s_P\sigma_{HL}(p_H R - \nu_L R) \geqslant c$, then the monitor does indeed have an incentive to monitor provided the entrepreneur works. Furthermore, if $s_P(\sigma_{LL} - \sigma_{HL})(p_H - \nu_L) \geqslant s_C(\sigma_{HH} - \sigma_{LH})(\nu_H - p_H)$, then the monitor has even stronger incentives to monitor if the entrepreneur shirks. As earlier, the entrepreneur receives R_b^* if the monitor exercises the call option; she receives 0 if the monitor chooses the put option (or does not exercise any option).

17. See Laffont and Rochet (1997) and Tirole (1992) for surveys of the theory of collusion in organizations.

18. See Laffont and Meleu (1997) for a study of the costs of reciprocal monitoring in situations in which the colluding agents do not have access to efficient means of exchange. In corporate finance, there is some concern that CEOs sitting on each other's board may reach a "gentleman's agreement," i.e., sign a "nonaggression pact."

monitor also collects information about the subsequent uncertainty (that is, the mapping from signal to final outcome in our model), which he certainly has an incentive to do if the cost of this complementary information is small, then the stock price reflects the subsequent noise and may contain no more information about managerial performance than the final outcome itself; the speculative information is then useless for entrepreneurial compensation purposes and costly to collect to boot. *By collecting too much information, the monitor reduces the quality of performance measurement.*

This point is easy to illustrate.[19] Suppose that at cost $c + \varepsilon$, where $\varepsilon \geqslant 0$ is small, the monitor can learn not only the signal $j \in \{\mathrm{H}, \mathrm{L}\}$, but also the complementary information mapping the signal into the final outcome (see Figure 8.2). That is, at the same or slightly higher cost the monitor learns the final outcome. Faced with the option defined in Section 8.2.3.1, the monitor decides to exercise the options on the basis of the final outcome, and obtains in expectation

$$s^* p_{\mathrm{H}}(R - p_{\mathrm{H}}R) - (c + \varepsilon) > s^* \sigma_{\mathrm{HH}}(\nu_{\mathrm{H}}R - p_{\mathrm{H}}R) - c$$

(with probability p_{H}, the project will be successful; knowing this, the monitor exercises his options and realizes a capital gain of $R - p_{\mathrm{H}}R$ on the s^* shares). The options are therefore exercised with *ex ante* probability p_{H}.

More generally, it is clear that when the monitor learns the final outcome, monitoring brings no new information and the pledgeable income, which is equal to

$$p_{\mathrm{H}}R - \frac{p_{\mathrm{H}}B}{\Delta p} - (c + \varepsilon),$$

is lower than in the absence of monitoring.

Taking a broader perspective, the final outcome depends on an input that is controllable by the entrepreneur (effort) as well as on noncontrollable shocks. Ideally, one would want the monitor to oversee only the effort, so as to have the most ungarbled measurement of performance (effort). However, as we already observed, the monitor will never spend resources to learn the entrepreneur's effort, since this effort can be inferred from the incentive scheme.[20] The incentive for monitoring stems purely from the possibility of obtaining private information about the noncontrollable shocks. That is, *from the point of view of the monitor, monitoring is motivated precisely by the acquisition of information that is uninformative about entrepreneurial performance and that he should thus not acquire*! There is therefore a tradeoff: the ease with which the monitor can acquire information about noncontrollable shocks simultaneously determines the incentive to monitor and the noise in performance measurement. In other words, *the intensity of monitoring and its precision covary negatively.*

It is then not surprising that the monitor may acquire too much information, as in the example above. For example, the monitor may spend resources to obtain inside information about the likely evolution of the firm's regulatory environment or about future exogenous shocks on its demand even in contexts in which the latter should not impact on managerial decisions (they may impact on investment choices, though). For example, the future profitability of a telecom incumbent depends on the future regulatory requirements concerning the terms of local loop unbundling. An analyst may spend more time trying to anticipate this regulatory evolution than analyzing the quality of the telecom incumbent's recent investments.

Transposing this discussion to stock market monitoring (see the next section), it is sometimes asserted in the popular press that speculators may not really monitor managerial performance and may be more preoccupied with learning information that will soon become public and therefore has no informational value about the quality of management. The economic analysis provides a vindication of this argument as well as a caveat: one cannot create incentives for monitoring without tolerating the acquisition of some "useless" information. Thus the popular press is clearly right only in those instances where the information collected by speculators is

19. This insight is based on a remark of Diamond and Verrecchia (1982, p. 283).

20. As long as the entrepreneur plays a pure strategy. There would be an incentive to monitor effort even on a stand-alone basis, if the entrepreneur randomized over effort levels, or, relatedly, if the entrepreneur had hidden knowledge about her willingness to work, say, and so her action could not be perfectly predicted.

purely about exogenous shocks rather than about variables that depend on both managerial performance and exogenous shocks (e.g., learning information about the likely evolution of demand and competitive pressure to know whether the firm's past strategic decisions were right).

We saw that the monitor may acquire "*too much information*." Along the same lines, the monitor may also acquire the "*wrong information*." That is, in a context in which there are multiple measures of performance (e.g., multiple product lines or multiple yearly incomes), he may devote excessive attention to those dimensions of entrepreneurial performance on which he can learn a substantial amount of information about noncontrollable shocks. So, the allocation of monitoring effort in general is not optimal either (see Paul 1992).

8.3 Market Monitoring

8.3.1 Market Microstructure

Let us now assume that, for one of the reasons stated in the introduction to Part III, the firm cannot rely on a designated monitor. Rather, it must resort to a more anonymous market in order to obtain the retrospective information.

The simplest framework in which to study *market monitoring* is the following. Modify the model of the previous section by assuming that the identity of the monitor is (in particular *ex ante*) unknown. For simplicity, there is a single potential monitor. The monitor,[21] who may for example be the investor among many investors who at the interim stage turns out to have the relevant skills or the availability to collect the information, "appears" after the effort has been chosen. To follow common usage, we will call this monitor a "speculator."

As in Section 8.2.3, the entrepreneur must be induced to work and the monitor must have incentives to collect information. We investigate whether these incentives can be provided by a stock market institution. The crux of the analysis is that the monitor's incentives in a market context are more complex to design than those of an enlisted monitor.

Let us assume that the entrepreneur issues publicly tradable shares in the firm. Each share thus entitles its holder to a fraction of the income R in the case of success. For simplicity, short sales are prohibited. Normalizing again the number of shares to be one, and assuming that the entrepreneur's incentive scheme induces her to choose the high effort, the *ex ante* par value of a share is thus equal to $p_{\mathrm{H}}R$.

• Assume, first, that all initial investors in the firm can costlessly hold their shares until the final outcome is realized. That is, they have no liquidity needs and therefore do not derive any intrinsic benefit from reselling their shares early. Suppose then that the speculator acquires the retrospective information and that the signal is high (the speculator would not want to trade if the signal were low given that short sales are prohibited). The speculator knows that the firm is undervalued by $\nu_{\mathrm{H}}R - p_{\mathrm{H}}R > 0$ per share, and so would want to purchase shares.

21. As earlier, we here make two simplifying assumptions. First, there is a single monitor. Second, this monitor is necessarily an outsider. These two assumptions are relaxed in a different context by Fishman and Hagerty (1992), who offer an interesting study of insider trading. Their model has two types of speculators: an endogenous number of external speculators (there is free entry into speculation) and, if insider trading is allowed, the manager. The manager is assumed to receive a more precise signal than external speculators. Fishman and Hagerty therefore take as their starting point Manne's (1966) suggestion that insider trading may lead to more informationally efficient stock prices by enlisting speculators with superior monitoring ability.

As Fishman and Hagerty show, the expected gross (trading) profit of external speculators decreases when insider trading is allowed, as they then face intense competition from a superiorly informed trader; and so insider trading reduces the number of external speculators. Because the fixed costs of information acquisition by external speculators are ultimately borne by the shareholders, who face liquidity needs and must sell their shares, and by the manager (recall that external speculators make no profit on average, and so their expected gross profit from trading is equal to their fixed cost of information acquisition), insider trading creates social benefits (as Fishman and Hagerty note, this might no longer be the case if external speculators faced varying costs of acquiring information, because the decision over whether to allow insider trading would then not internalize the most efficient speculators' inframarginal rents). The impact on informational efficiency, in contrast, is ambiguous. On the one hand, insider trading adds a superiorly informed trade (and therefore increases informational efficiency): just think about the case in which external speculators are very inefficient information acquirers. On the other hand, insider trading crowds out external speculation and introduces an asymmetry among informed traders, thereby reducing competition in the asset market. Finally, the analysis, unlike that of this chapter, does not focus on the impact of speculation on managerial incentives and pledgeable income.

The analysis of disclosure by Boot and Thakor (2001) looks at the impact of the disclosure of information about the firm's prospects on the incentives of outsiders to collect information, depending on whether the disclosed information is substitute or complement with that collected by market participants.

Unfortunately for the speculator, initial investors are willing to sell their stake in the firm only if they expect to make money out of the trade. This implies that any order by the speculator can be satisfied only at price $v_H R$: in equilibrium, uninformed investors do not want to purchase at prices equal to or exceeding $p_H R$, and so any such demand must be interpreted as stemming from a speculator with good news about the firm. Hence, the speculator cannot make money out of his information. (This is a version of the "no-trade theorem" obtained by Stiglitz (1971), Kreps (1977), and Milgrom and Stokey (1982).)

In the absence of an exogenous reason for early trading, such as liquidity needs, no trade occurs and the speculator does not collect any information. In other words, even a well-functioning stock market is informationally inefficient, as in the celebrated Grossman and Stiglitz (1980) contribution.[22] Note the key difference with the case of an enlisted monitor studied in the previous section. *An enlisted monitor can be promised that he will be able to exercise his stock options at a predetermined price, namely, the ex ante par value $p_H R$. The unenlisted monitor, that is, the speculator, also has stock options (the stock market enables him to purchase tradable shares), but the strike price is now a market price and is thus endogenous.*

• In order for the speculator to benefit from his information and thus to have an incentive to collect this information, it must be the case that the price of the securities does not respond too much to the speculator's order flow. Technically, the slope of the supply curve faced by the speculator must not be infinitely steep—the securities market must be "deep."

Market depth is obtained when (a) some initial investors face liquidity needs and so an active securities market creates gains from trade, and (b) the extent of the associated supply is unknown (if the second condition fails, any order from a speculator is automatically recognized by investors or market makers). This suggests the following assumption.

Assumption 8.2 (liquidity trading).

(a) *A fraction s of initial investors are "liquidity traders": with probability $\lambda \in (0,1)$ they (all) will need to sell their shares at the interim stage (that is, before the final outcome is realized). With probability $(1-\lambda)$, none will face such liquidity needs and therefore all will behave like the other investors.*

(b) *The other investors — the "long-term investors" or the "nonliquidity traders" — have no direct information about whether there is liquidity trading.*

A few remarks about this definition are in order.

Remark (deep market). We noted that those investors who can hold shares until the final outcome—the long-term investors—should not know the exact extent of liquidity trading if they are not to infer perfectly the speculator's demand and information. This requirement is reflected in an extreme form in the assumptions that the liquidity shocks of liquidity traders are perfectly correlated and that the long-term investors do not get any direct information about the extent of liquidity trading (they may and will get some indirect information about liquidity trading through the net order flow). The perfect correlation assumption is made for computational simplicity and is obviously much stronger than needed: what is required more generally is that the long-term investors cannot infer the level of liquidity trading perfectly (from the law of large numbers, they could infer this level perfectly if there were a large number of liquidity traders with independent liquidity shocks). Put differently, the speculator's trade has a limited impact on the stock price; in this sense, the market has some "depth."

Remark (is liquidity trading "irrational"?). As will be emphasized in the discussion of the Diamond and Dybvig (1983) model in Chapter 12, liquidity trading need not be irrational. Actually, we will model it in a rational way and make use of this property for the determination of the price of initial claims. Namely, consider a three-stage timing (see Figure 8.4 below), in which initial investors purchase the securities at

22. The Grossman–Stiglitz paper is couched in the context of a competitive stock market. It was later realized that stock markets with privately informed parties are better modeled as games since an informed party is never informationally infinitesimal and thus cannot take the stock price as given. See, for example, Kyle (1989) for a discussion of modeling issues. The standard reference for the game-theoretic modeling of market microstructure is Kyle (1985). See also Kyle (1984), Admati and Pfleiderer (1988), and Laffont and Maskin (1990).

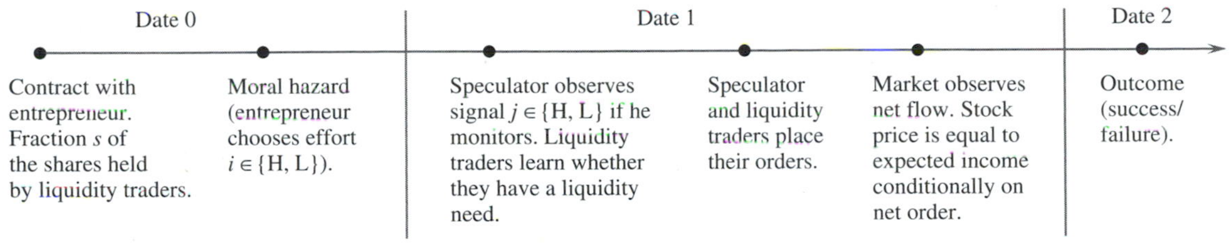

Figure 8.4

date 0, liquidity needs are realized at date 1, and the final income accrues at date 2.

Liquidity traders have utility attached to a consumption stream $\{c_0, c_1, c_2\}$ equal to

$$\begin{aligned} c_0 + c_1 &\quad \text{if they face a liquidity need at date 1,} \\ c_0 + c_1 + c_2 &\quad \text{if they do not.} \end{aligned}$$

That is, in the case of a liquidity shock they have no utility for second-period consumption (this is, of course, stronger than needed to generate sales of securities at stage 1). Long-term investors know at date 0 that their utility is always

$$c_0 + c_1 + c_2.$$

These simple preferences (or their generalization in which liquidity traders have utility $c_0 + c_1 + \theta c_2$, $0 \leqslant \theta < 1$, when facing a liquidity shock) will substantially facilitate the pricing of claims at stage 0.

Remark (exogeneity of s). We take the fraction s of liquidity traders to be an exogenous parameter. See the caveat below for a discussion of this assumption.

Let us now make the following assumption.

Assumption 8.3 (anonymous trading). *The speculator can split his order in such a way that the long-term investors (or any new investor in this market) cannot tell his order apart from those of the liquidity traders; these investors thus observe only the net order, that is the sum of the speculator's and the liquidity traders' orders.*

This assumption does not hold exactly if the speculator is forced to disclose a position exceeding some threshold or if splitting his order involves substantial transaction costs. But again, it is stronger than needed. All that is required is that the market not be able to observe the speculator's trade perfectly. The assumption that the market participants observe only the net order flow is a metaphor for a market in which market makers post bid and ask spreads and revise these in light of the observed net order flow.

Figure 8.4 describes the timing.

8.3.2 Equilibrium Behavior

Letting y and z denote the speculator's and the liquidity traders' demands for shares, the stock price P of shares is equal to the expected income conditional on total order $y + z$:

$$P = [\Pr(\text{success} \mid y + z)]R.$$

The liquidity traders' order is uninformative about the final outcome, but as we will see it plays an important role in the market's inference about the probability of success. This order is

$$z = \begin{cases} -s & \text{in the case of a liquidity shock,} \\ 0 & \text{in the absence of a liquidity shock.} \end{cases}$$

Now consider the speculator's order, assuming for the moment that it is indeed optimal for the speculator to acquire the information. It is clear that the speculator has no incentive to purchase shares if he that knows the firm is overvalued (the signal is low). When the firm is undervalued (the signal is high), he wants to purchase as many shares as is possible. But he must also be wary of not signaling his presence in the market to other investors, otherwise the price would jump to $\nu_H R$ and there would be no gain for the speculator. Given that the market observes the net order, the only way of possibly disguising one's order while purchasing shares is to purchase s shares. Table 8.1 describes the four possible states of nature.

When the speculator buys shares and there are no liquidity sales, the market knows that the speculator

Table 8.1

	High signal (probability σ_{HH})	Low signal (probability σ_{HL})
Liquidity sales (probability λ)	Stock price: P Net order: 0	Stock price: $\nu_{\mathrm{L}}R$ Net order: $-s$
No liquidity sales (probability $1-\lambda$)	Stock price: $\nu_{\mathrm{H}}R$ Net order: s	Stock price: P Net order: 0

has received favorable information and so the market price is $\nu_{\mathrm{H}}R$; conversely, when the speculator buys no shares and there are liquidity sales, the market knows that the speculator has received the low signal, and so the market price is $\nu_{\mathrm{L}}R$. In both cases the speculator's information is revealed to the market and the speculator makes no money from it.

In contrast, the market faces a nontrivial "signal extraction problem" when the net order is 0. The speculator's and liquidity traders' orders may balance either because the signal is high and there is liquidity trading, which has *ex ante* probability $\lambda\sigma_{\mathrm{HH}}$, or because the signal is low and there is no liquidity trading, which has *ex ante* probability $(1-\lambda)\sigma_{\mathrm{HL}}$. Using Bayes' rule and the fact that the stock price is equal to the expected payoff of a share, we obtain

$$P = \left[\frac{\lambda\sigma_{\mathrm{HH}}}{\lambda\sigma_{\mathrm{HH}} + (1-\lambda)\sigma_{\mathrm{HL}}}\right]\nu_{\mathrm{H}}R + \left[\frac{(1-\lambda)\sigma_{\mathrm{HL}}}{\lambda\sigma_{\mathrm{HH}} + (1-\lambda)\sigma_{\mathrm{HL}}}\right]\nu_{\mathrm{L}}R. \tag{8.5}$$

Let us compute the speculator's expected profit. With probability $\lambda\sigma_{\mathrm{HH}}$, he learns that the firm is undervalued and liquidity trading allows him to disguise his trade, which preserves some undervaluation. The amount of undervaluation is then

$$\nu_{\mathrm{H}}R - P = \left[\frac{(1-\lambda)\sigma_{\mathrm{HL}}}{\lambda\sigma_{\mathrm{HH}} + (1-\lambda)\sigma_{\mathrm{HL}}}\right][(\nu_{\mathrm{H}}-\nu_{\mathrm{L}})R].$$

That is, it is equal to the conditional probability that the firm is overvalued times the sensitivity of the true share value to the speculator's information. The speculator's expected profit is therefore

$$\pi(s) = \lambda\sigma_{\mathrm{HH}}\left[\frac{(1-\lambda)\sigma_{\mathrm{HL}}}{\lambda\sigma_{\mathrm{HH}} + (1-\lambda)\sigma_{\mathrm{HL}}}\right][(\nu_{\mathrm{H}}-\nu_{\mathrm{L}})R]s. \tag{8.6}$$

On the other hand, this profit is equal to 0 when the speculator acquires no information. This can be checked by computing the expected profit of an uninformed purchase of s shares, using Table 8.1 and equation (8.5). But this result can be obtained more easily and more intuitively by noting that an uninformed speculator is in the same position as the market and the market price is the fair price in each state of nature.

We conclude that the speculator indeed acquires information if and only if

$$\pi(s) \geqslant c,$$

where c is, as earlier, the cost of learning the signal. The speculator further obtains no rent if $s = s^{**}$, where

$$\pi(s^{**}) = c. \tag{8.7}$$

This analysis has a couple of straightforward implications.

Size of the monitor's option. The incentive scheme of the enlisted monitor of the previous section and of the unenlisted monitor of this section is qualitatively the same: it is (explicitly in the first case and implicitly in the second) an option to purchase a predetermined number of shares at a strike price. We chose the strike price to be equal to the *ex ante* par value $p_{\mathrm{H}}R$ in the case of an enlisted speculator. The strike price for the speculator is the market price, whose *ex ante* expectation is also $p_{\mathrm{H}}R$. However, the supply curve faced by the speculator is not perfectly elastic at $p_{\mathrm{H}}R$; and so, conditional on the speculator's wanting to exercise his option, the strike price (which is either P or $\nu_{\mathrm{H}}R$) is on average greater than $p_{\mathrm{H}}R$.[23] To have the same incentives to collect the information as the enlisted monitor, the speculator must be offered a larger option. It is therefore not surprising that (8.4), (8.6), and (8.7) imply

$$s^{**} > s^{*}. \tag{8.8}$$

Pledgeable income. Let us compare the pledgeable incomes under the two types of monitor. It turns out that the minimum expected entrepreneurial reward—that is, the agency cost—is the same in both cases, and so is the entrepreneur's ability to borrow.[24] This, however, is an artefact of

23. P itself may be larger or smaller than $p_{\mathrm{H}}R$.

24. Suppose that the entrepreneur is given a reward R_{b} when the stock price at date 1 is equal to $\nu_{\mathrm{H}}R$ and 0 otherwise (again, this can be interpreted as a stock option). Incentive compatibility requires that

$$(1-\lambda)(\sigma_{\mathrm{HH}} - \sigma_{\mathrm{LH}})R_{\mathrm{b}} \geqslant B,$$

since the entrepreneur receives a reward only when the monitor receives the high signal and there is no liquidity trade.

entrepreneurial risk neutrality. *The pledgeable income is strictly lower under market monitoring than with an enlisted monitor as long as the entrepreneur exhibits (even small) risk aversion.* This results from the fact that the information structure is coarser under market monitoring: the stock price is either $\nu_H R$ or P when the signal is high, and $\nu_L R$ or P when the signal is low, and it is well-known that the agency cost for a risk-averse agent increases when the information structure is garbled in the sense of Blackwell (see, for example, Grossman and Hart 1983). Thus, under entrepreneurial risk aversion the entrepreneur needs more cash on hand in order to be able to borrow. (In the variable-investment model, the entrepreneur's borrowing capacity would be reduced by the garbling of the information structure.)

This point confirms our discussion of incumbent versus entrant monitoring in Section 8.1.3. The monitor's incentive scheme is less effective under entrant monitoring, and so market monitoring must be justified by some other argument such as integrity of the monitoring process (collusion), uncertain availability of the enlisted monitor (liquidity shocks), or uncertain talent of the enlisted monitor.

Trading volume and managerial compensation. The model predicts that stock-based incentives are more desirable in liquid markets. Market liquidity enables speculators to make money on their information and therefore incentivizes them to collect information in the first place. This prediction is borne out in Garvey and Swan's (2002) study of 1,500 publicly traded U.S. corporations over the period 1992–1999. The sample exhibits wide variations in the ratio of turnover to market capitalization, which can be used as a measure of liquidity (they also use the bid–ask spread as a measure of (il)liquidity and find similar results). They find that compensation is more closely tied to shareholder wealth when the firm's shares trade more actively. By contrast, bonuses are employed in firms with a more illiquid stock market.

Equity premium. Liquidity traders are willing to pay less for the stock than long-term investors. Indeed the former each lose in expectation π/s to the speculator. Thus, if stocks are meant to attract liquidity traders, shares must be sold at a discount to compensate liquidity traders who will "lose their shirt" to the speculator. Hence, the long-term investors must earn more than the rate of interest (normalized here at 0) corresponding to their rate of time preference. Put differently, investors who are in for the long term earn an equity premium, while those who may face liquidity needs earn just a fair rate of return. There is indeed empirical evidence that the return on a given stock increases with the holding period; casual evidence to this effect is provided by bankers' classic advice not to buy stocks when having a short holding period in mind.[25]

Important caveat. By assuming an exogenous fraction s of liquidity traders, we finessed the delicate issue of how this fraction comes about. Indeed, we showed that a long-term investor is willing to pay more for a share in the firm than a liquidity trader. One may then wonder why the subscription pattern to the initial issue does not yield $s = 0$, in which case the market has no depth and the speculator has no incentive to collect information. Economic theory has not yet provided a general answer to this question (which arises more generally in the "market-microstructure" literature). Note, though, that in a general equilibrium framework, the amount of money in the economy that can be committed in the long run for certain (that is, is not subject to the possibility of liquidity trading) is limited. In equilibrium, shares attract a heterogeneous clientele (liquidity traders and long-term investors) and the partial equilibrium model of this section is consistent with the general equilibrium framework in which the composition of ownership is endogenized.[26] Furthermore, and as noted above, shares bear an equity premium (that is, yield an expected return

Thus the entrepreneur's noncompressible share is

$$\sigma_{HH}(1-\lambda)R_b = \frac{\sigma_{HH}}{\sigma_{HH}-\sigma_{LH}}B,$$

as in Section 8.2.3.

25. Amihud and Mendelson (1986a,b) find that the empirical relationship between the returns on a stock and the bid–ask spread implies a much higher trading frequency than the average one that is actually observed. Put differently, bid–ask spreads, which are determined by the trading frequency of liquidity traders, predict greater returns for the average securityholder. This observation, which fits with the theoretical prediction, stresses the importance of accounting for the heterogeneity of stockholders.

26. See Holmström and Tirole (1993) for a modest start on this question.

above the market rate, here 0) despite universal risk neutrality.

Another nagging question in this model and the broader market-microstructure literature is why liquidity traders do not hold the stock index so as to avoid selling any given stock on which they face an informational disadvantage.[27] As Subrahmanyan (1991) and Gorton and Pennacchi (1993) have pointed out, index funds protect investors who value flexibility as to the date at which they can cash in (a decent return on) maturity of their investment against better-informed players in the stock market.

Index funds have indeed grown substantially over the years, whether due to the realization that short-term holdings carry a lower yield (for the reasons exposited here), or the new demand for diversification, or more mechanically because of technical progress in running these funds.[28] The long-run tension between the investors' self-interest in diversification for both liquidity and risk-aversion reasons and the social need that individual stock prices properly reflect the value of assets in place is, in my view, a key open topic for research in finance.

8.4 Monitoring on the Debt Side: Liquidity-Draining versus Liquidity-Neutral Runs

This section is based on discussions with Bengt Holmström. It also borrows from the literature on monitoring and liquidation (e.g., Repullo and Suarez 1998) and from that on demandable debt as a disciplining device (e.g., Calomiris and Kahn 1991).[29]

8.4.1 Passive Monitoring by Debt Claims

The theory developed in Sections 8.2 and 8.3 makes no prediction as to whether passive monitoring should be performed by equityholders or holders of risky debt.

We solved for the optimal mechanism for both an enlisted monitor and market monitoring, and in both cases we showed how optimal incentives could be provided by the monitor's option to purchase stocks. Alternatively, the incentive to acquire the retrospective information could be obtained by providing the monitor with *demandable debt*. Consider enlisting a large debtholder who has a nominal claim equal to D at date 2, when the final outcome occurs. In the absence of monitoring, this debt claim has value $p_{\mathrm{H}}D$. Now, assume that the debtholder has the option to accelerate the payment and demand d at date 1 (in which case he is due nothing at date 2).[30] Suppose that

$$\nu_{\mathrm{H}}D > d > \nu_{\mathrm{L}}D, \tag{8.9}$$

so that an informed debtholder demands early repayment if and only if he receives the low signal. The debtholder indeed collects the retrospective information if and only if monitoring dominates the strategy consisting in (a) not monitoring and (b) either rolling over the debt or demanding the debt (in both cases with probability 1, since the debtholder has no information):

$$\sigma_{\mathrm{HL}}(d - \nu_{\mathrm{L}}D) \geqslant c \quad \text{and} \quad \sigma_{\mathrm{HH}}(\nu_{\mathrm{H}}D - d) \geqslant c. \tag{8.10}$$

Condition (8.10) reflects the fact that rolling over the debt has a cost in the bad state of nature, while demanding it has a cost in the good state of nature.

While the demandable debt mechanism on the debt side is the mirror image of, and is as plausible an incentive scheme for, the monitor as the stock option mechanism on the equity side, its implication for the entrepreneur's incentive scheme is *a priori* less palatable. Under debt monitoring, the entrepreneur should be rewarded if and only if the debt is not demanded. In practice, we observe that managerial incentive schemes are *directly* contingent on the value of equity, but not on whether

27. Similar issues arise when the cost of trading is a transaction cost or a tax rather than adverse selection (Constantinides 1986; Vayanos 1998).

28. Playing individual stocks has traditionally had the favor of professional and individual investors alike. For example, Keynes (1983), himself the manager of a major British insurance company and of the endowment of King's College, Cambridge (cited by Bernstein 1992, p. 48), wrote:

> I am in favor of having as large a unit as market conditions will allow ... To suppose that safety-first consists in having a small gamble in a large number of different [companies] where I have no information to reach a good judgment, as compared with a substantial stake in a company where one's information is adequate, strikes me as a travesty of investment policy.

29. See also Rey and Stiglitz (1991), Qi (1998), and Diamond and Rajan (2000). The analysis is also related to Postlewaite and Vives (1987) and Chari and Jagannathan (1988), who look at the impact of withdrawal of demandable debt by informed debtholders.

30. There is no need to specify how d is financed. It might be financed through the sale of liquidity hoarded at date 0, or, possibly, through the dilution of other securities.

debt is demanded, or for that matter on the market value of debt if debt claims are tradable. This apparent disparity with practice leads to a couple of comments.

- Debt monitoring is not inconsistent with the entrepreneur's scheme being based on the value of equity claims. For, when the large debtholder exercises his option and demands early repayment of the debt, the holders of the residual claim—the equityholders—infer that the debtholder has received the low signal and the stock price plunges. (Relatedly, empirical evidence shows that the stock price reacts positively when, for example, a bank renews a loan.) We invite the reader to check that the entrepreneur can then be rewarded properly with a stock option.

- As the next subsection argues, an important difference between monitoring on the equity and debt sides is that a run on the debt drains liquidity and therefore already hurts management by compromising new investments or continuation of old ones.

8.4.2 Passive Monitoring and Liquidity Management

An aspect that is conspicuously missing in the analysis of Sections 8.2 and 8.3 is the impact of the acquisition of retrospective information on the firm's liquidity. In the model of Section 8.2, the acquisition of retrospective information occurs at a time at which the firm's cash flow has a life of its own. That is, at that stage it has become an exogenous random variable and cannot be altered. This was meant to formalize performance monitoring in its purest form. In an ongoing firm, however, the retrospective information may impact on the firm's liquidity and (from Chapter 5) future opportunities.

There is a fundamental difference between stock market monitoring and demandable debt monitoring that cannot transpire when liquidity plays no role: *demandable debt monitoring drains the firm's liquidity while stock market monitoring does not.* A bank that demands the early payment of long-term debt or refuses to roll over short-term debt deprives the firm of liquidity. Furthermore, this source of liquidity is especially hard to replace since other investors rationally interpret the "run" as being bad news about the prospects of the firm. In contrast, the firm's liquidity is not directly affected when the speculators' information makes its stock price move up or down, although it may be indirectly affected through the informational impact on the ability to conduct a seasoned offering.

More generally, recall that the incentive of a monitor, whether an equityholder or a debtholder, to collect retrospective information is always provided by an *option* defining a choice among competing financial claims, and that the way this option is exercised is the mechanism through which the monitor's information can be truthfully elicited. A *liquidity-draining exercise* reduces the liquidity available to the firm to meet current and future liquidity shocks or reinvestment needs. A *liquidity-neutral exercise* has no such impact. A *liquidity-providing exercise*[31] is, of course, the mirror image of a liquidity-draining exercise. A bank's rolling over of the firm's short-term debt or forgiveness of its option to demand early repayment of the long-term debt can be viewed as creating liquidity relative to the situation in which it would deprive the firm of its liquidity. So, there are really two categories, which could also be labeled *liquidity-managing exercise* and *liquidity-neutral exercise.*

Rephrasing our earlier observation, a striking fact is that *monitoring by equityholders is generally liquidity neutral, while monitoring by debtholders is generally liquidity managing.* Speculation on the stock market involves mere transfers among shareholders, while a refusal to roll over short-term debt does not involve a transfer between investors. From the liquidity perspective, the proper distinction, however, is not between debt and equity, but *between long-term and short-term capital.* Consider long-term public debt and suppose that the bonds involve a substantial risk of default (which as we saw in Chapter 2 is often not the case). The speculative activity in such a market very much resembles that on a stock market. The price of bonds can move up or down without impacting the firm's liquidity.

31. An example of a liquidity-providing exercise is the conversion of a convertible bond (recall that convertible debt gives its owner the option to exchange bonds for a predetermined number of shares). The conversion wipes out the future debt payments associated with the bond. A warrant provides liquidity if the cash brought in by the investors exercising the option to purchase shares goes to the firm, and is liquidity neutral if it is distributed as a dividend.

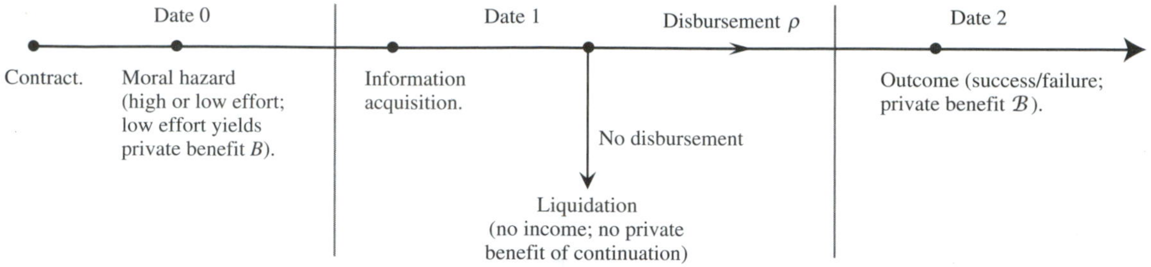

Figure 8.5

An example of a beneficial liquidity-draining exercise. Let us modify the model of Section 8.2 in two respects.

First, and as in Section 7.2.2, the entrepreneur derives no utility from income above the limited liability level (normalized at 0); this in particular implies that rewards based on securities prices are ineffective ($R_b = 0$). The entrepreneur, however, derives a private benefit $\mathcal{B}$ from the project being completed (on top of, possibly, the private benefit B derived from misbehaving at the initial stage). Second, assume that the firm, as in Chapter 5, must withstand a liquidity shock in order to complete the project. Then, a demandable debt mechanism, which induces a large debtholder to demand early repayment in case of a bad signal but not in the case of a good signal (see Section 8.4.1), provides an incentive mechanism for the entrepreneur if an early repayment prevents the firm from continuing.

The timing is summarized in Figure 8.5. For the purposes of this section, we can assume that the liquidity shock, ρ, is deterministic. If ρ is not disbursed, the project is stopped and there is no income; if ρ is disbursed, the project succeeds with probability ν_H or ν_L depending on whether the signal is good or bad. Moral hazard and the stochastic structure for signal and profit are as described in Section 8.2. Let us assume that

$$\nu_H R > \rho \geqslant \nu_L R. \tag{8.11}$$

That is, continuation is profitable (from a monetary point of view, which does not include the entrepreneur's private benefit $\mathcal{B}$ of continuation) only in the case of a good signal.[32]

The following condition will further ensure that there is enough pledgeable income for the investors provided that good incentives can be put in place:

$$\sigma_{HH}(\nu_H R - \rho) - I - c > 0. \tag{8.12}$$

Condition (8.12) says that the total cost of investment, $I + c$ (inclusive of the monitoring cost), is smaller than the income that can be obtained when continuing only for a good signal.

Consider the following financial structure. (a) The entrepreneur is allowed at date 0 to hoard an amount of liquidity (say, in Treasury bonds) equal to ρ, which she can use to meet the liquidity shock (any unused liquidity is returned to the investors). (b) As in Section 8.4.1, a potential monitor is endowed with demandable debt. This monitor has a nominal claim equal to D at date 2, together with an option of demanding d at date 1 instead (that is, then forgoing the long-term claim when exercising the short-term one), where

$$\nu_H D > d > \nu_L D, \tag{8.13}$$

and furthermore

$$\sigma_{HL}(d - \nu_L D) \geqslant c \quad \text{and} \quad \sigma_{HH}(\nu_H D - d) \geqslant c. \tag{8.14}$$

Lastly, we assume that

$$(\sigma_{HH} - \sigma_{LH})\mathcal{B} \geqslant B. \tag{8.15}$$

As earlier, (8.14) implies that the debtholder has an incentive to monitor and to demand the debt early if and only if the signal is bad. When the debtholder demands an early payment, the entrepreneur's leftover liquidity, $\rho - d$, is no longer sufficient to cover

32. An interesting subcase corresponds to $\rho = \nu_L R$. This subcase (or, more generally, the situation in which the loss of continuing in the case of a bad signal is small) is illuminating, in that the acquisition of the signal is suboptimal in the absence of managerial incentive problems, since the signal does not improve the continuation decision and is costly to acquire.

the liquidity shock ρ; besides, the investors are not willing to bring in new funds since, from (8.11), there is no monetary gain to continuation under a bad signal. Lastly, (8.15) ensures that the entrepreneur is motivated to work by the state-contingent decision rule, and (8.12), which accounts for the facts that the large debtholder must be compensated for the monitoring cost and that the entrepreneur receives no income, implies that investors can break even and so the project is funded.

We thus conclude that a demandable debt contract optimally drains the firm's liquidity while providing the creditor with an incentive to monitor.

8.5 Exercises

Exercise 8.1 (early performance measurement boosts borrowing capacity in the variable-investment model). Follow the analysis of Section 8.2.2 (publicly observable signal) and allow that the investment size is variable as in Section 3.4. Derive the entrepreneur's borrowing capacity and utility.

Exercise 8.2 (collusion between the designated monitor and the entrepreneur). Consider the fixed-investment model of Section 8.2.3 (designated monitor), but assume that the entrepreneur can, at no direct cost to her, tunnel firm resources to the monitor through, say, an advantageous supply or consulting contract that reduces the project's NPV. Namely, she can transfer an amount $T(\tau)$ to the monitor at the cost of reducing the probability of success by τ (from ν_j to $\nu_j - \tau$, where ν_j is the probability of success conditional on signal j). Assume that $T(0) = 0$, $T' > 0$, $T'(0) = R$ (a small transfer involves almost no deadweight loss), and $T'' < 0$. (Note that $T(\tau) < \tau R$ for $T(\tau) > 0$ and so tunneling is inefficient.)

By contrast, transfers from the monitor to the entrepreneur are easily detected by investors. Similarly, the entrepreneur cannot offer to share her reward without being detected.

We look at *ex post* collusion: the entrepreneur and the monitor both observe the signal $j \in \{L, H\}$ and the entrepreneur offers some level of τ against a specified option exercise behavior by the monitor.

As in the rest of this chapter, we assume that the entrepreneur is incentivized to behave. She obtains $\hat{R}_b$ if the monitor exercises his option and 0 otherwise. The monitor buys s shares at strike price $p_H R$ each if he exercises his call options.

Show that the contract studied in Section 8.2.3 is immune to tunneling if and only if s exceeds some threshold.

References

Admati, A. and P. Pfleiderer. 1988. A theory of intraday patterns: volume and price variability. *Review of Financial Studies* 1:3–40.

Amihud, Y. and H. Mendelson. 1986a. Asset pricing and the bid–ask spread. *Journal of Financial Economics* 17:224–249.

——. 1986b. Liquidity and stock returns. *Financial Analysts Journal* 42:43–48.

Bernstein, P. 1992. *Capital Ideas: The Improbable Origins of Modern Wall Street.* New York: The Free Press.

Bhattacharya, S. and P. Pfleiderer. 1985. Delegated portfolio management. *Journal of Economic Theory* 36:1–25.

Boot, A. and A. Thakor. 2001. The many faces of information disclosure. *Review of Financial Studies* 4:1021–1057.

Burkart, M., D. Gromb, and F. Panunzi. 1995. Debt design, liquidation value, and monitoring. Mimeo, Stockholm School of Economics, MIT, and Università Bocconi.

Calomiris, C. and C. Kahn. 1991. The role of demandable debt in structuring optimal banking arrangements. *American Economic Review* 81:497–513.

Campbell, T. and W. Kracaw. 1980. Information production, market signalling, and the theory of financial intermediation. *Journal of Finance* 35:863–882.

Chang, C. and Y. Wang. 1995. New security offerings as an incentive mechanism. Mimeo, Carlson School of Management, University of Minnesota.

Chari, V. and R. Jagannathan. 1988. Banking panics, information and rational expectations equilibrium. *Journal of Finance* 43:749–761.

Constantinides, G. 1986. Capital market equilibrium with transaction costs. *Journal of Political Economy* 94:842–862.

Diamond, D. 1984. Financial intermediation and delegated monitoring. *Review of Economic Studies* 51:393–414.

Diamond, D. and P. Dybvig. 1983. Bank runs, deposit insurance, and liquidity. *Journal of Political Economy* 91:401–419.

Diamond, D. and R. Rajan. 2000. A theory of bank capital. *Journal of Finance* 55:2431–2465.

Diamond, D. and R. Verrecchia. 1982. Optimal managerial contracts and equilibrium security prices. *Journal of Finance* 37:275–287.

Fama, E. 1985. What's different about banks? *Journal of Monetary Economics* 15:29–39.

Fishman, M. and K. M. Hagerty. 1992. Insider trading and the efficiency of stock prices. *RAND Journal of Economics* 23:106–122.

Garvey, G. and P. Swan. 2002. What can market microstructure contribute to explaining executive incentive pay? Liquidity and the use of stock-based compensation. Working Paper, School of Banking and Finance, Faculty of Commerce, UNSW, Sydney.

Gorton, G. and J. Kahn. 2000. The design of bank loan contracts. *Review of Financial Studies* 13:331–364.

Gorton, G. and G. Pennacchi. 1993. Security baskets and index linked securities. *Journal of Business* 66:1–27.

Grossman, S. and O. Hart. 1983. An analysis of the principal-agent problem. *Econometrica* 51:7–45.

Grossman, S. and J. Stiglitz. 1980. On the impossibility of informationally efficient markets. *American Economic Review* 70:393–408.

Hirschman, A. O. 1970. *Exit, Voice, and Loyalty.* Cambridge, MA: Harvard University Press.

Holmström, B. 1979. Moral hazard and observability. *Bell Journal of Economics* 10:74–91.

Holmström, B. and J. Tirole. 1993. Market liquidity and performance monitoring. *Journal of Political Economy* 101: 678–709.

Jackson, T. and A. T. Kronman. 1979. Secure financing and priorities among creditors. *Yale Law Journal* 89:1143.

Keynes, J. M. 1983. Letter to F. C. Scott, February 6, 1942. In *The Collected Writings of John Maynard Keynes* (ed. D. Moggridge), Volume XII, pp. 81–83. Cambridge University Press.

Kreps, D. 1977. A note on fulfilled expectations' equilibria. *Journal of Economic Theory* 14:32–43.

Kyle, A. 1984. Market structure, information, futures markets and price formation. In *International Agricultural Trade: Advanced Readings in Price Formation, Market Structure, and Price Instability* (ed. G. Storey, A. Schmitz, and A. Sarris). Boulder, CO: Westview Press.

——. 1985. Continuous auctions and insider trading. *Econometrica* 53:1315–1335.

——. 1989. Imperfect competition, market dynamics and regulatory issues. In *Financial Markets and Incomplete Information* (ed. S. Bhattacharya and G. Constantinides), Volume 2, pp. 153–161. Lanham, MD: Rowman and Littlefield.

Laffont, J.-J. and E. Maskin. 1990. The efficient market hypothesis and insider trading on the stock market. *Journal of Political Economy* 98:70–93.

Laffont, J.-J. and M. Meleu. 1997. Reciprocal supervision, collusion and organizational design. *Scandinavian Journal of Economics* 99:519–540.

Laffont, J.-J. and J. C. Rochet. 1997. Collusion in organizations. *Scandinavian Journal of Economics* 99:485–495.

Leland, H. and D. Pyle. 1977. Information asymmetries, financial structure and financial intermediaries. *Journal of Finance* 32:371–387.

Levmore, S. 1982. Monitors and freeriders in commercial and corporate settings. *Yale Law Journal* 92:49–83.

Manne, H. 1966. *Insider Trading and the Stock Market.* New York: Free Press.

Milgrom, P. and N. Stokey. 1982. Information, trade and common knowledge. *Journal of Economic Theory* 26:177–227.

Osband, K. 1989. Optimal forecasting incentives. *Journal of Political Economy* 97:1091–1112.

Paul, J. 1992. On the efficiency of stock-based compensation. *Review of Financial Studies* 5:471–502.

Postlewaite, A. and X. Vives. 1987. Bank runs as an equilibrium phenomenon. *Journal of Political Economy* 95:485–491.

Qi, J. 1998. Deposit liquidity and bank monitoring. *Journal of Financial Intermediation* 7:198–218.

Rajan, R. and A. Winton. 1995. Covenants and collateral as incentives to monitor. *Journal of Finance* 50:1113–1146.

Repullo, R. and J. Suarez. 1998. Monitoring, liquidation, and security design. *Review of Economic Studies* 11:163–187.

Rey, P. and J. Stiglitz. 1991. Short-term contracts as a monitoring device. Mimeo, INSEE, Paris, and Stanford University.

Schwartz, A. 1981. Security interests and bankruptcy priorities: a review of current theories. *Journal of Legal Studies* 10:1–37.

Shavell, S. 1979. Risk sharing and incentives in the principal and agent relationship. *Bell Journal of Economics* 10:55–73.

Shleifer, A. and L. Summers. 1988. Breach of trust in hostile takeovers. In *Corporate Takeovers: Causes and Consequences* (ed. A. Auerbach), pp. 33–56. University of Chicago Press.

Stiglitz, J. 1971. Information and capital markets. Mimeo, Stanford University.

Subrahmanyam, A. 1991. A theory of trading in stock index futures. *Review of Financial Studies* 4:17–51.

Tirole, J. 1992. Collusion and the theory of organizations. In *Advances in Economic Theory: Proceedings of the Sixth World Congress of the Econometric Society* (ed. J.-J. Laffont), Volume 2, pp. 151–206. Cambridge University Press.

Vayanos, D. 1998. Transactions costs and asset prices: a dynamic equilibrium model. *Review of Financial Studies* 11:1–58.

9

Lending Relationships and Investor Activism

9.1 Introduction

Passive monitoring is in a sense backward looking: speculative monitors assess the value of assets in place in order to best arbitrage the mispricing of securities. Active monitoring, in contrast, is forward looking: large monitors such as a firm's main bank (Hausbank), a venture capitalist, or a large blockholder intervene so as to increase the value of assets in place through investor-friendly decision making. This chapter reviews the costs and benefits of active monitoring and analyzes the private incentives to become an active monitor.

There are several reasons to be interested in active monitoring.[1] First, as we discussed in Chapters 1 and 8, the topic is central to debate on equity- versus debt-based corporate governance. Countries such as Japan, Germany, France, and more generally continental Europe, have traditionally relied on banks, and to a lesser extent large shareholders, to discipline management.[2] The legal and regulatory environment in the United States has been less well disposed toward concentrated ownership, and interference in management has put relatively more weight on takeover and proxy fights. Management has also been more likely to be incentivized through stock-based compensation than in Europe and Japan. Although these differences in governance have been vanishing lately, they are still worth noting.

Second, one would like to know when blockholdings (or, by an abuse of terminology, main bank positions) are likely to trade at a premium or at a discount. For example, Barclay and Holderness (1989) analyze block trades and show that large blocks of shares trade at a premium relative to the market price. In this respect this chapter and the next will focus on four determinants:

Monitoring cost. First, monitoring is costly. That cost by itself suggests that blockholdings should trade at a discount. Section 9.2 investigates the validity of this intuition.

Learning by lending. A large investor, through his monitoring of management, acquires private information that puts him in a superior position against competitive investors in future financing rounds.[3] Section 9.4 studies whether such "learning by lending" makes investors willing to pay a premium for large blockholdings.

Block illiquidity. Conversely, a large investor may want to disengage himself from a firm because he needs cash to meet liquidity needs. But large blockholdings may be illiquid for two reasons (moral hazard and adverse selection). First, large blocks may be subject to a standstill agreement that limits transactions or a vesting provision meant to incentivize the large investors to monitor the firms; the logic of such restrictions is that long-term investors have more incentives to oversee and interfere in the firm than investors of passage. Second, even if no such restriction is in place, potential buyers of large blocks are usually wary that their owners might be cashing out, not because of a liquidity need, but because they have learned bad news about the firm's future. Section 9.5 studies when liquidity needs of large investors generate a price discount.

Benefits from control. Lastly, large blockholdings may confer benefits from control on their owner.

1. We focus on monitoring by a financial intermediary or a large shareholder. Several strands of the literature have studied other monitors, most notably peer monitoring (see the supplementary section in Chapter 4) and trade credit (see, for example, Biais and Gollier 1997; Burkart and Ellingsen 2004; Jain 2001).

2. For a survey of relationship banking, see Boot (2000).

3. Such incumbency rents figure prominently in the work of Sharpe (1990), Rajan (1992), and Greenbaum et al. (1989), among others.

This is obvious for blockholdings with a control majority, but less so for large minority shareholders. Chapter 10 will examine when benefits from control and associated price premia are likely to exist.

Section 9.2 develops a basic model of investor activism. A monitor is given a sufficient stake in the firm to have an incentive to sink resources into overseeing managerial behavior, thereby curbing moral hazard. The enlisting of a monitor involves two basic costs: first, at the very least, the monitor must be compensated for the monitoring cost that he incurs; second, monitoring capital may be scarce and so monitors may enjoy a rent relative to other investors.

The cost of enlisting a monitor implies that firms with strong balance sheets, which have enough pledgeable income to attract financing in the absence of monitoring, prefer to borrow more cheaply from financial markets, while firms with weaker balance sheets, which must assuage the investors' concerns, have little choice but to resort to costlier intermediated finance. (By contrast, the representation of monitors as advisors who help management to formulate efficient strategies instead of preventing management from wasting corporate resources leads to the prediction that firms with strong balance sheets are those that can afford advisers.)

Section 9.2 then analyzes two other costs associated with monitoring: scope for overmonitoring and collusion. On the collusion front, monitors may adopt a lenient attitude toward management, who can reciprocate by tunneling corporate resources so as to benefit the monitors' own ventures, by offering counterfavors in kind (including friendship), and so forth. The institutional response to the threat of collusion may consist in raising the monitor's financial stake in the firm or in reducing potential conflicts of interest.

Section 9.3 asks whether large blocks are likely to emerge spontaneously in financial markets rather than through a private deal. To the extent that blockholders supply a "public good" (the monitoring of managerial behavior), the acquisition of a large stake gives rise to free riding: each shareholder would like to hold on to his share while other shareholders sell their share to a larger buyer, who would then have a sufficient stake to monitor. We investigate when blockholdings may nonetheless emerge in financial markets.

Section 9.4 studies the implications of learning by lending. It first shows that incumbent blockholders enjoy an informational rent relative to other investors. Large investors are therefore willing to pay a premium for their blockholding that reflects the future supranormal profit. Put differently, they are willing to lose money in the short run in order to acquire an informational edge over other investors, that they will be able to exploit in the future. Section 9.4 then demonstrates a cost of relationship lending: the monopoly power associated with the incumbent monitor's informational advantage gives rise to a form of holdup on managerial investment in future profitability enhancements, and therefore discourages such investment.

Section 9.5 finally analyzes another cost of monitoring: the illiquidity of the monitor's stake. The analysis here parallels that of Section 4.4 for the entrepreneur. After all, the monitor, being subject to moral hazard himself, can be viewed as an insider. His ability to exit early—before the full consequences of his monitoring performance are realized—is a disincentive to efficient monitoring. On the other hand, monitors like to plan an exit strategy because they may need funds to reinvest in other ventures or face their own liquidity shocks. The optimal contract for the monitor is more likely to be liquid (allow an early exit) if reinvestment opportunities are likely and valuable, if early performance measures (perhaps associated with an IPO) are available, and if monitoring capital is not too scarce.

9.2 Basics of Investor Activism

9.2.1 Benefit of Activism

To model the collection of prospective information, we start from the fixed-investment model of Section 3.2 and add a monitor who can intervene in order to reduce the scope for moral hazard. A risk-neutral entrepreneur with wealth A has a project costing $I > A$ and must therefore borrow $I - A$ from investors. The project yields R when it succeeds and 0 when it fails. The probability of success is p_{H} if the entrepreneur works and $p_{\mathrm{L}} = p_{\mathrm{H}} - \Delta p$ if she shirks.

Table 9.1

	good project	bad project	Bad project
Pr(success)	p_{H}	p_{L}	p_{L}
Private benefit	0	b	B

9.2.1.1 No Monitoring

In the absence of monitoring, shirking provides private benefit B. Letting R_{b} denote the entrepreneur's reward in the case of success (she receives nothing in the case of failure as she is protected by limited liability), incentive compatibility requires that

$$(\Delta p)R_{\mathrm{b}} \geqslant B. \tag{9.1}$$

Funding requires that the pledgeable income exceed the investors' investment:

$$p_{\mathrm{H}}\left(R - \frac{B}{\Delta p}\right) \geqslant I - A. \tag{9.2}$$

If this condition is satisfied, and given that the investors break even, the entrepreneur's utility is equal to the project's NPV:

$$U_{\mathrm{b}} = p_{\mathrm{H}}R - I. \tag{9.3}$$

9.2.1.2 Monitoring (With Fixed Intensity)

Let us now formalize the idea that monitoring reduces the extent of moral hazard. A straightforward way of doing so[4] is to assume that a monitor can reduce the private benefit that can be enjoyed by the entrepreneur by shirking from B to $b < B$. The monitor must, however, bear an unobservable private monitoring cost $c > 0$ in order to achieve this reduction in private benefit.

An interpretation of this monitoring structure is as described in Table 9.1. The manager will have to choose among a number of *ex ante* identical projects. The manager privately learns the payoffs attached to each project. There are three relevant projects: (1) the "good project," which yields no private benefit and has probability of success p_{H}; (2) the low-private-benefit "bad project," which yields private benefit b and has probability of success p_{L}; and (3) the high-private-benefit "Bad project," which yields private benefit B and has probability of success p_{L}.

The monitor moves first. If he incurs effort cost c, he is able to identify the high-private-benefit Bad project and thus to prevent the entrepreneur from selecting it. But he still cannot tell the other two projects apart, and so the entrepreneur, who can condition her choice of project on the existence or absence of monitoring,[5] can still choose the low-private-benefit bad project if she wishes to. The monitor learns nothing when he does not incur the monitoring cost c; then, because the projects are still indistinguishable by the investors, the entrepreneur can choose any of the three projects, as in the absence of monitoring (of course, the low-private-benefit bad project is then less attractive for the entrepreneur than the Bad project and is therefore irrelevant).

Let us assume that the entrepreneur "hires" a monitor and that the monitor's incentives induce him to monitor. The entrepreneur's private benefit from shirking is then equal to b, and so, if R_{b} denotes the entrepreneur's reward in the case of success, the entrepreneur works if and only if

$$(\Delta p)R_{\mathrm{b}} \geqslant b. \tag{9.4}$$

We can further assume that $(\Delta p)R_{\mathrm{b}} < B$; for, if $R_{\mathrm{b}} \geqslant B/\Delta p$, the entrepreneur is induced to work even in the absence of monitoring. Monitoring is then useless.

The monitor too must be provided with an incentive scheme.[6] We maintain the assumption of

4. Drawn from Holmström and Tirole (1997). The monitoring role of financial intermediaries has been studied in the theoretical literature on delegated monitoring (e.g., Besanko and Kanatas 1993; Diamond 1984, 1991; Hellwig 1991). In Admati and Pfleiderer (1994), monitoring serves to control managerial investment decisions, and in Berglöf (1994) it affects managerial replacement. Shleifer and Vishny (1986) study the incentives of potential raiders to monitor firms.

5. This sequential timing of monitoring simplifies the analysis (a similar assumption is made in Winton (1993)).

An alternative formulation consists in assuming that there are only two projects, as in Section 3.2, and that the entrepreneur chooses a project whose nature (p_{H} or p_{L}) is unknown to all, including the monitor. The monitor can then investigate at cost c, and possibly take remedial action. This class of monitoring models in general leads to equilibria in mixed strategies (see Exercise 9.5).

6. Like the borrower, the monitor is treated as a unitary actor. Put differently, the structure of incentives within the monitoring entity is left aside. Berger et al. (2005) provide empirical evidence that small banks are more willing to lend on the basis of soft information than larger ones.

universal risk neutrality, and so there is no loss of generality in assuming that the monitor receives a reward R_{m} in the case of success and 0 in the case of failure (because of limited liability). When not incurring cost c, the monitor is unable to prevent the entrepreneur from shirking, and so the incentive for monitoring is provided by an R_{m} satisfying[7]

$$(\Delta p)R_{\mathrm{m}} \geqslant c. \tag{9.5}$$

Abundance of monitoring capital assumption. Let us first assume that monitoring capital is "abundant" or "not scarce." This means that there is a large supply of monitors who are willing to invest their capital in the monitoring activity as long as they are as well-off by doing so as with any other investment.[8] They are thus willing to contribute to the firm's investment at level I_{m} such that

$$p_{\mathrm{H}}R_{\mathrm{m}} - c = I_{\mathrm{m}}. \tag{9.6}$$

The monitor then obtains no rent, and receives net payment $(p_{\mathrm{H}}R_{\mathrm{m}} - I_{\mathrm{m}})$ equal to his monitoring cost c. (In general, monitoring capital is scarce and therefore may demand a rate of return exceeding the market rate of return: see below.)

Nonmonitoring or uninformed investors are willing to fund the project if and only if

$$p_{\mathrm{H}}(R - R_{\mathrm{b}} - R_{\mathrm{m}}) \geqslant I - A - I_{\mathrm{m}}. \tag{9.7}$$

And so, using (9.4)–(9.6), the necessary and sufficient condition for the project to be funded is

$$p_{\mathrm{H}}\left(R - \frac{b}{\Delta p}\right) \geqslant I - A + c. \tag{9.8}$$

That is, monitoring reduces the agency cost from $p_{\mathrm{H}}B/\Delta p$ to $p_{\mathrm{H}}b/\Delta p$, but adds monitoring cost c. Using (9.5) and (9.6), the monitor's stake R_{m} can be chosen equal to $c/(\Delta p)$ and the monitor's investment contribution equal to

$$I_{\mathrm{m}} = \frac{p_{\mathrm{L}}c}{\Delta p}.$$

To obtain some potential role for monitoring, let us assume that the monitoring cost is small enough that monitoring increases the pledgeable income:

$$p_{\mathrm{H}}\frac{b}{\Delta p} + c < p_{\mathrm{H}}\frac{B}{\Delta p}. \tag{9.9}$$

When does the entrepreneur benefit from having a monitor? Because all investors, including the monitor, obtain no rent from their relationship with the firm, the entrepreneur's utility is equal to the project's NPV under monitoring:

$$U_{\mathrm{b}} = p_{\mathrm{H}}R - I - c. \tag{9.10}$$

We assume that the NPV is positive even in the presence of monitoring:

$$p_{\mathrm{H}}R > I + c.$$

Monitoring, as we could have expected, reduces the entrepreneur's utility by the monitoring cost, and so the entrepreneur forgoes monitoring if she can obtain funding in its absence, that is, if condition (9.2) is satisfied. On the other hand, if (9.2) is violated, the firm has no choice but to either resort to being monitored (if $c < p_{\mathrm{H}}R - I$), or forgo the project. Figure 9.1

7. Note that the monitor's certification role is jeopardized if the monitor contracts with a "protection seller" (a third-party insurer) in a credit derivative market. Under risk neutrality, the monitor and the protection seller do not obtain gains from a trade when the monitor passes the default risk on to the protection seller. When the monitor is risk averse (and $p_{\mathrm{H}} < 1$), in contrast, the monitor is tempted to offload the credit risk on to a third party, which reduces the incentive to monitor. To avoid this, the monitor's incentive constraint (9.5) must be slack and the monitor must not be "risk averse" (in order to limit the insurance gains relative to the efficiency loss in the side contract between the monitor and the protection seller). In the absence of other considerations, the monitor is better off committing never to use a credit derivative market. For more details, see Morrison (2002) (who, citing a 2000 study of the British Bankers Association, notes that the market for such credit derivatives reached \$893 billion in 2000).

8. Regardless of the monitors' net wealth, we assume that there is a well-defined amount of this wealth. This is, of course, a simplifying assumption.

In practice, investors at any point in time have a variety of (uncertain) assets, some existing but somewhat illiquid (say, real estate) and some to be derived from future earnings. Before the institutions of limited liability became widespread, it was typical for shareholders to have unlimited liability for the company's debts in case of default. This unlimited liability (which still exists in some partnerships, such as Lloyd's of London in the insurance business) is really an uncertain liability, whose cost depends not only on the firm's unpaid debts, but also on the evolution of the values of the shareholder's and other shareholders' assets, as well as on the ability of debtholders to put their hands on these wealths in case of default.

Winton (1993) builds models that depict the various costs associated with unlimited liability: the liable shareholder may have to dispose of his assets at a discount; and there may be adverse selection, in that unlimited liability shares are more attractive to investors whose assets are overappreciated, or who can more easily transfer these assets to someone else or abroad (as Winton notes, the concern about adverse selection was particularly evident in the common rule that shares could not be resold without approval of other shareholders, or else their owner has to keep residual liability after the sale). We refer to Winton's paper for the discussion of these interesting topics, and simplify our analysis by assuming that monitors' assets are known.

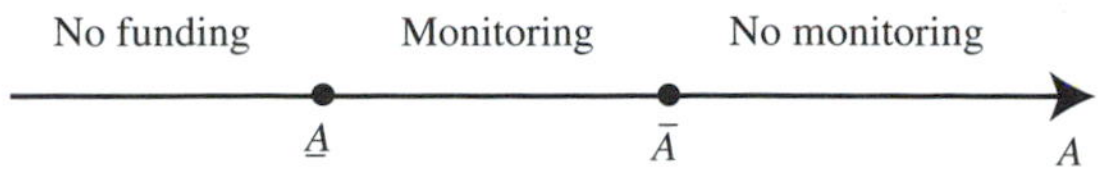

Figure 9.1 $\underline{A} = I + c - p_{\mathrm{H}}(R - b/\Delta p)$,
$\bar{A} = I - p_{\mathrm{H}}(R - B/\Delta p)$.

describes the financing pattern as a function of the entrepreneur's equity A.

That is, entrepreneurs with strong balance sheets (e.g., with $A \geqslant \bar{A}$; see Section 3.3.2 for a discussion of various notions of balance-sheet strength) borrow cheaply because they can do without monitoring, while borrowers with weaker balance sheets ($\underline{A} \leqslant A < \bar{A}$) borrow more expensively. Returning to the observations of Chapter 2, recall that strong firms (which are also often the large firms) can borrow cheaply in markets (that is, under low-intensity monitoring) and that other firms either cannot get funding or borrow at high rates from banks and other intermediaries (that is, under high-intensity monitoring). The active monitoring theory developed here suggests a reason why this may be so. James (1987) and Lummer and McConnell (1989) are among the early empirical papers demonstrating the role of banks in the reduction of agency costs. Cantillo and Wright (2000) confirm empirically that high-quality borrowers make intensive use of bond markets, while lower-quality ones resort to intermediated finance.

Link to the law-and-finance literature. Recall from Chapter 1 that La Porta et al. (1998) find that legal systems which protect investors poorly also exhibit very concentrated ownership structures. One possible interpretation for this finding is that legal systems with poor investor protection create substantial opportunities for insiders to take private benefits or tunnel corporate resources to other entities that they own. In the context of the model, the values of B and therefore of $\bar{A}$ are large. Because, under poor investor protection, the theory predicts that an increase in the extent of moral hazard in the absence of high-intensity monitoring leads to more monitoring, and because monitoring is facilitated by concentrated ownership, the theory can thus be viewed as consistent with La Porta et al.'s empirical finding. The reader may object that a poor legal infrastructure may also make it easier for the managers and the large investor to collude against other investors; the scope for collusion on the other hand calls for even more concentrated ownership, as will be demonstrated in Section 9.2.4.

Concentrated ownership versus other forms of monitoring. Concentrated ownership by a monitor with a sufficient stake improves the control of management. It, however, has costs: the cost of mere monitoring as well as other costs that will be described shortly. Thus, the governance structure must trade off the costs and benefits of concentrated ownership. Alternative ways of making managers accountable, besides direct monetary incentives, include market monitoring (Chapter 8) and takeovers (Chapter 11). Bolton and von Thadden's (1998) model predicts a more dispersed (less concentrated) ownership structure in countries (such as the United States) in which there is more active trading of shares in secondary markets and regulation facilitates takeovers. That is, in their model, monitoring through concentrated ownership and other forms of monitoring are substitutes.[9]

9.2.2 The Potential for Overmonitoring

Monitoring is useful because it reduces the scope for diversion and thereby makes borrowers more accountable to investors. Interestingly, though, monitoring can be excessive. In specific instances, a monitor may have too strong an incentive to oversee the borrower. There are three basic reasons for this.

9.2.2.1 Noninternalization of the Entrepreneur's Rent

As Pagano and Roell (1998) argue, the large monitor exerts two types of externality when deciding whether to increase the intensity of his monitoring. First, he exerts a *positive* externality on other investors. By monitoring more he makes their claims as well as his own claim more valuable; this externality is particularly strong when the monitor holds only a small fraction of the investors' total stake since he then receives only a small fraction of the value enhancements he brings about. In contrast, there is no such externality if the monitor holds all

9. This is not always the case (see Section 9.5).

the outside shares in the firm. Second, he exerts a *negative* externality on the entrepreneur, by restricting the latter's choice set in our framework. When the monitor holds all outside shares, this negative externality generates overmonitoring. It is then appropriate to reduce the monitor's incentives. The fixed-monitoring-intensity variant developed above cannot generate overmonitoring since the monitoring intensity takes only two values. If the optimal amount of monitoring is 0, then no monitor is hired and there is no overmonitoring. We therefore consider a variant with more than two intensities of monitoring:

The variable-monitoring-intensity model. To formalize the notions of undermonitoring and overmonitoring in a simple way, let us extend the monitoring model of Section 9.2.1 by introducing uncertainty about the outcome of monitoring. Namely, the monitor discovers the identity of the Bad project (the one yielding private benefit B) with probability x, and learns nothing with probability $1 - x$. The probability x of effective monitoring depends on the unverifiable effort cost or disutility of effort $c(x)$ incurred by the large monitor. We assume that this disutility of effort is increasing ($c' > 0$) and convex ($c'' > 0$), and that $c'(0) = 0$ and $c'(1) = \infty$ (so as to guarantee an interior solution when the monitor has a positive stake in the firm's success).

Let us assume without loss of generality that the borrower's reward, R_b, in the case of success is smaller than $B/\Delta p$ (otherwise, the incentive problem has been solved and monitoring is useless), and larger than $b/\Delta p$ (and thus effective monitoring prevents shirking). Assuming that monitoring capital is abundant, the project's NPV for a monitoring intensity x and the borrower's utility are identical and equal to

$$U_b = xp_HR + (1 - x)(p_LR + B) - I - c(x). \quad (9.11)$$

The level x^* of monitoring that maximizes the NPV is then given by

$$(\Delta p)R - B = c'(x^*). \quad (9.12)$$

Let us assume that at this level of monitoring, there is enough pledgeable income to pay back the investors, large and small:

$$[x^* p_H + (1 - x^*)p_L]\left[R - \frac{b}{\Delta p}\right] \geqslant I - A + c(x^*),$$

while condition (9.2) is still violated so unmonitored borrowing is infeasible.

Let us now determine the large monitor's optimal stake. Letting R_m denote the monitor's payoff in the case of success, as earlier, the monitor chooses his monitoring intensity so as to maximize

$$[xp_H + (1 - x)p_L]R_m - c(x);$$

and so

$$(\Delta p)R_m = c'(x). \quad (9.13)$$

Comparing (9.12) and (9.13) yields

$$R_m = R - \frac{B}{\Delta p}. \quad (9.14)$$

Because the entrepreneur is unable to borrow in the absence of monitoring, R_b is strictly smaller than $B/\Delta p$, and so

$$R_m < R - R_b. \quad (9.15)$$

In words, the monitor should not hold all external shares in the firm. As we explained, were the monitor to hold all external shares, a unit increase in the monitoring intensity x would exert no positive externality on other outside investors (there would be none) and would impose a negative externality—namely, the loss of $B - (\Delta p)R_b > 0$—on the entrepreneur.[10]

9.2.2.2 Killing Initiative

Alternatively, and as developed in more detail in Section 10.3, a high monitoring intensity may discourage the entrepreneur from coming up with new ideas, as argued by Burkart et al. (1997) (see also Crémer 1995; Aghion and Tirole 1997). For one thing, the monitor may make up for the entrepreneur's lack of ideas, with an obvious detrimental impact on the entrepreneur's incentive to generate ideas. But even if the monitor does not generate the

10. The potential for overmonitoring also arises in a somewhat different context in Hermalin and Weisbach (1998). In their model, the monitor is a board that tries to assess the CEO's ability (rather than to curb moral hazard as in the Pagano–Roell model) and decides whether to fire the CEO. Hermalin and Weisbach's model is a multiperiod one in which the composition of the board both reacts to past performance and affects future monitoring. To the extent that less independent boards monitor less, a decrease in the independence of the board alleviates the overmonitoring problem; relatedly, Hermalin and Weisbach's model predicts that CEO turnover is more sensitive to performance when the board is more independent. Finally, the model implies that independent directors are likely to be added to the board following poor firm performance.

ideas himself and only assesses whether the entrepreneur's proposals enhance the value for investors, overmonitoring may still occur. It may be the case that the entrepreneur no longer has incentives to come up with new projects or new courses of action if she anticipates that her proposal will be systematically modified to enhance investor value and be expunged from any private benefit for the entrepreneur. There is a tradeoff between asserting whether the entrepreneur's proposed course of action enhances investor value and rewarding the entrepreneur for her initiative.

9.2.2.3 Careful Monitoring May Aggravate the Soft-Budget-Constraint Problem

We observed in Chapter 5 that, in some situations, committing to closing the firm when performance is unsatisfactory even in circumstances in which the firm's continuation generates positive net pledgeable income may strengthen managerial discipline and force the entrepreneur to exert more effort. This tough stance may, however, not be credible, since the investors may gain more *ex post* by renegotiating and refinancing the entrepreneur. As we observed there, the dispersion of the investors may help prevent renegotiation. The absence of large monitor may contribute to make renegotiation difficult as well if the lack of information about the continuation value makes investors wary and induces them not to refinance. A lack of information may thus act as a commitment device.

9.2.3 Scarce Monitoring Capital

In general, the supply of players with *both* the expertise to monitor the entrepreneur and their own capital to invest in the firm is limited. This implies that monitoring an entrepreneur has an opportunity cost over and above the mere disutility of effort.

Absence of monitoring capital. Let us first consider the opposite polar case in which potential monitors have no capital. The selected monitor then cannot contribute to the initial investment. The monitor's stake, however, must still satisfy condition (9.5); and since $I_{\mathrm{m}} = 0$, the monitor enjoys rent

$$p_{\mathrm{H}} R_{\mathrm{m}} - c = p_{\mathrm{H}}\left(\frac{c}{\Delta p}\right) - c = \left(\frac{p_{\mathrm{L}}}{\Delta p}\right)c.$$

In comparison with the case of abundant monitoring capital, this rent decreases both the borrower's utility and the amount of income that can be pledged to the uninformed investors. On the first point, note that there is now a wedge between the borrower's utility,

$$U_{\mathrm{b}} = p_{\mathrm{H}} R - I - \left[c + \frac{p_{\mathrm{L}}}{\Delta p} c\right],$$

and the project's NPV ($p_{\mathrm{H}} R - I - c$). This wedge is, of course, equal to the monitor's rent. Similarly, the condition that the pledgeable income exceed the uninformed investor's initial outlay becomes

$$p_{\mathrm{H}}\left[R - \frac{b + c}{\Delta p}\right] \geqslant I - A.$$

The implications are the same as in the case of abundant monitoring capital. The no-monitoring region in Figure 9.1 is unaffected, while the monitoring region shrinks as $\underline{A}$ is raised by the amount, $p_{\mathrm{L}} c/(\Delta p)$, of the monitor's rent. Put differently, the entrepreneur must make up through her own cash on hand for the monitor's rent if she wants to attract uninformed investors.

General case. More generally, one may assume that monitoring capital has a shadow cost. (This shadow cost can only be determined in a general equilibrium framework (see Chapter 13).) That is, the monetary return χ on the monitor's investment contribution, defined by

$$\chi \equiv \frac{p_{\mathrm{H}} R_{\mathrm{m}}}{I_{\mathrm{m}}},$$

is intermediate between its value, $p_{\mathrm{H}}/p_{\mathrm{L}}$, when monitoring capital is abundant and the infinite level that obtains when monitors have no capital.

The monitor enjoys rent M given by

$$M \equiv p_{\mathrm{H}} R_{\mathrm{m}} - I_{\mathrm{m}} - c = \left[p_{\mathrm{L}} - \frac{p_{\mathrm{H}}}{\chi}\right]\frac{c}{\Delta p}.$$

(This "rent" is relative to what he would obtain, namely, 0, if he had no alternative use of this capital. By definition, his rent exactly reflects the opportunity cost χ of alternative investment opportunities.)

The borrower's utility is again lower than the NPV (as long as $\chi > p_{\mathrm{H}}/p_{\mathrm{L}}$) and is equal to

$$U_{\mathrm{b}} = p_{\mathrm{H}} R - I - c - M.$$

Similarly, the financing condition becomes

$$p_{\mathrm{H}}\left(R - \frac{b}{\Delta p}\right) - c - M \geqslant I - A.$$

Unsurprisingly, the project is harder to finance, the scarcer the monitoring capital (i.e., the higher χ is).

9.2.4 Other Costs Associated with Monitoring

Until now the cost of monitoring has been equal to the monitor's cost. This cost should be understood broadly, and in general exceeds the mere disutility of effort $c(x)$. Besides the scarcity of monitoring capital, there are several reasons for this.

Lack of diversification. We have assumed that the monitor is risk neutral. Suppose in contrast that the monitor is himself an entrepreneur and furthermore is risk averse, as in Admati et al. (1994). Then, providing the monitor with incentives is costly since the wedge between the rewards of the monitor in the cases of success and failure required by the provision of incentives to monitor creates a risk and destroys the monitor's insurance.[11]

Illiquidity. The monitoring activity may also have a cost in terms of liquidity. To have incentives to monitor, the monitor should not be allowed to reduce his stake in the firm's success below its initial level $c/\Delta p$ before the final outcome is revealed. For, suppose that the monitor were allowed to reduce his stake in the firm's success to $R'_{\mathrm{m}} < R_{\mathrm{m}}$, and that this privilege were not thought to impair the initial incentive to monitor. The monitor would then receive $p_{\mathrm{H}}(R_{\mathrm{m}} - R'_{\mathrm{m}})$ for the liquid shares regardless of whether he has worked or shirked (which is not observable). Assuming that these liquid shares are sold to new investors without recourse (that is, the proceeds of the sale are not put into escrow as collateral in case the project fails; in other words, the shares are really sold), then the monitor's benefit from monitoring is reduced to $(\Delta p)R'_{\mathrm{m}} < c$. And so the belief that the shares' liquidity does not impair incentives to monitor is unwarranted.

On the other hand, the monitor may encounter new and profitable investment opportunities before the outcome on this particular investment is realized. At this stage, the monitor would like to undo his position in the firm in order to reorient his investment toward these new opportunities. For example, venture capitalists typically design exit options that allow them to undo their position in order to be able to invest in new start-ups. But we observed that such liquidity or exit options may jeopardize monitoring. We come back to this topical subject at greater length in Section 9.5.

Collusion. The investor activism paradigm is that of the "three-tier hierarchy": (1) agent (entrepreneur), (2) supervisor (large monitor), (3) principal (other investors). The role of the monitor is, as for any other supervisor, to reduce the asymmetry of information between the principal and the agent. This role is endangered by the possibility of collusion. Indeed, the asymmetry of information between the principal on the one hand and the supervisor and the agent on the other is the very essence of collusion. The supervisor and the agent may take advantage of their shared privy information in order to collude against the principal; the agent may trade a more lenient supervisory activity against some favor to the supervisor.

There are three standard responses to the threat of collusion.[12] The first is to reduce the dependency of the agent's welfare on the supervisory activity in order to reduce the agent's incentives to "bribe" the supervisor. This generally results in low-powered incentives for the agent. The second is, conversely, to increase the supervisor's stake so as to make it more costly for him to collude with the agent. The third response consists in limiting the scope for "bribes." Such bribes may take various forms: tunneling, monetary transfers, counterfavor in kind, friendship, and so forth.

---

11. This is the standard "agency cost" (see, for example, Holmström (1979), or the textbooks by Bolton and Dewatripont (2004), Laffont and Martimort (2002), and Salanié (2005)). For example, suppose that the monitor's limited liability constraint is not relevant, and so we can make a comparison with the case of abundant monitoring capital studied above; for a concave utility function $u(Y-c)$ (in case of monitoring) and $u(Y)$ (in the absence of monitoring) for income Y, and for given payments $\{R^{\mathrm{S}}_{\mathrm{m}}, R^{\mathrm{F}}_{\mathrm{m}}\}$ for the monitor in the cases of success and failure, the incentive constraint is

$$p_{\mathrm{H}}u(R^{\mathrm{S}}_{\mathrm{m}} - c) + (1-p_{\mathrm{H}})u(R^{\mathrm{F}}_{\mathrm{m}} - c) \geqslant p_{\mathrm{L}}u(R^{\mathrm{S}}_{\mathrm{m}}) + (1-p_{\mathrm{L}})u(R^{\mathrm{F}}_{\mathrm{m}}),$$

and so $R^{\mathrm{S}}_{\mathrm{m}} > R^{\mathrm{F}}_{\mathrm{m}}$. Therefore the certainty equivalent of the left-hand side of the incentive constraint is smaller than $p_{\mathrm{H}}R^{\mathrm{S}}_{\mathrm{m}} + (1-p_{\mathrm{H}})R^{\mathrm{F}}_{\mathrm{m}} - c$. The monitor's participation constraint implies that the monitor's expected utility exceeds $u(0)$. The income pledgeable to the other investors (still assuming that the entrepreneur is risk neutral) is

$$p_{\mathrm{H}}\left(R - \frac{b}{\Delta p}\right) - [p_{\mathrm{H}}R^{\mathrm{S}}_{\mathrm{m}} + (1-p_{\mathrm{H}})R^{\mathrm{F}}_{\mathrm{m}}] < p_{\mathrm{H}}\left(R - \frac{b}{\Delta p}\right) - c.$$

12. See Tirole (1986) and the surveys of Tirole (1992) and Laffont and Rochet (1997).

Collusion may occur "*ex post*" or "*ex ante*." *Ex post* collusion occurs when the monitor acquires information and then makes an offer to the entrepreneur to be "cooperative," i.e., in the model of this chapter, let the entrepreneur freely choose the project rather than constraining her feasible set by ruling out the Bad project. The entrepreneur, in exchange, does a favor to the monitor. *Ex ante* collusion refers to an agreement between the two parties drawn *before* the monitor decides to acquire information. *Ex ante* collusion is more powerful in that an *ex ante* agreement allows the parties to economize on the monitoring cost c and therefore to share a bigger gain from collusion, but it may be harder to set up.[13]

Let us apply some of the general principles to the situation at hand in the context of *ex post* collusion. Dessi (2005) studies both *ex ante* and *ex post* collusion and finds that the implications discussed below apply to both situations. Because $B > (\Delta p)R_b$, the entrepreneur is better off when the monitor does not rule out the Bad project. The entrepreneur's benefit from colluding with the monitor when the latter is informed is then $B - (R_b/\Delta p)$. The monitor can collude with the entrepreneur by not ruling out the Bad project.[14] But this is costly to the supervisor who then loses $(\Delta p)R_m$ in expectation. Somehow, there must be a *quid pro quo*. As discussed above, this quid pro quo may take several forms in practice. The entrepreneur may pay a monetary bribe to the monitor. However, we have assumed that the entrepreneur has invested all her wealth in the firm; so, unless the entrepreneur has hidden wealth, it is unlikely that the bribe will take the form of a direct monetary transfer from the entrepreneur to the monitor. Friendship may motivate collusion especially if c, and therefore R_m, is small. This case is particularly relevant for boards, composed of directors who may be friendly with management and have low-powered incentives, and who may therefore be too complacent.

Lastly, and perhaps most interestingly, the entrepreneur may use corporate resources to bribe the monitor. For instance, the entrepreneur may spend time otherwise devoted to the firm to help the monitor in another activity, or else spend corporate money to benefit one of the monitor's affiliated entities. For example, a firm may select a large shareholder's subsidiary as supplier even though another supplier would have reduced cost; similarly, a firm monitored by a bank may buy from a supplier who is in distress and turns out to borrow from the same bank. A last example is supplied by consulting contracts given to the firm's auditor's consultancy division.

In the context of our model, such diversions of corporate resources can be modeled as creating a gain $G > 0$ to the monitor and reducing the probability of success uniformly by an amount $\tau > 0$. That is, the favor done to the monitor reduces the probability of success from p_H to $p_H - \tau$ if the entrepreneur works, and from p_L to $p_L - \tau$ if she shirks. The convenience afforded by the uniform reduction in the probability of success is, as already noted in this book, that it does not alter the entrepreneur's incentive constraint since $(p_H - \tau) - (p_L - \tau) = \Delta p$. That this diversion is wasteful can be expressed by $G < \tau R$.[15] We assume that any direct monetary transfer between the entrepreneur and the monitor, in contrast, can be detected by uninformed investors, and so the only means of side-payment is this tunneling of corporate resources to the monitor.

Assuming, as earlier, that $B > (\Delta p)R_b \geqslant b$, the monitor, when informed, reduces the probability of success from p_H to $p_L - \tau$ by colluding with the entrepreneur and accepting the diversion of corporate resources. Collusion therefore occurs if the monitor gains from it,

$$G \geqslant (\Delta p + \tau)R_m, \tag{9.16}$$

and if the entrepreneur gains as well,

$$B \geqslant (\Delta p + \tau)R_b. \tag{9.17}$$

13. First, the *ex ante* agreement may be compromised by asymmetric information: the entrepreneur may not know whether the monitor has the ability or time to figure out the nature of projects or whether he holds information that facilitates his discovery of payoffs (technically, the monitoring cost may be either c, or a large number and the entrepreneur does not know which prevails). The entrepreneur may then wait and see whether the monitor comes up with information that may constrain her policy. Second, the quid pro quo may be hard to synchronize: the monitor may want an immediate favor rather than a promise, which exposes the entrepreneur to future reneging by the entrepreneur.

14. For example, he can rule out the bad or the good projects instead.

15. In Dessi's (2005) richer model, the monitor is useful even if he colludes with management and the diversion is not wasteful.

Two straightforward implications follow from inequality (9.16). First, as one would expect, it is preferable to choose monitors who do not have potential conflicts of interest. In this case, a monitor to whom it is hard to transfer funds through the diversion of corporate resources (a monitor who has a low G or a high τ) is unlikely to collude with the entrepreneur.

It may, however, be hard to find such monitors who have expertise, capital, and no conflict of interest. This brings us to the second implication: preventing collusion requires raising the monitor's stake from $c/\Delta p$ to $G/(\Delta p + \tau)$ if the latter is higher (which is the case if the monitoring cost is small). The possibility of collusion may then raise the cost of monitoring (e.g., because of the scarcity of monitoring capital or because of risk aversion).

9.2.5 A Different Form of Monitoring: Advising

Venture capitalists, boards of directors, and other monitors often do not content themselves with monitoring the proposals and decisions of managers. They may also bring some expertise and advice to help the managerial team. For example, venture capitalists help recruit the managerial team, shape the strategy and business model, and set up accounting and employee compensation (Lerner 1995).

In the tradition of Holmström's (1982) formulation of moral hazard in teams, a string of contributions, including Bottazzi et al. (2005), Casamatta (2003), Hellmann (1998), Kaplan et al. (2003), Lerner and Schoar (2005), Repullo and Suarez (2000, 2004), and Schmidt (2003), have investigated such environments. The monitor's advisory activity in those models is akin to that of the entrepreneur (it raises the probability that the project is successful), and accordingly this variety of monitoring models are sometimes called "double-sided moral-hazard models."

While the monitoring model of Section 9.2.1 and the advisory models are similar in structure, they differ in a couple of (related) insights. Namely, advisory monitoring models predict the following:

- The advisor increases the NPV and so may be brought on board even in the absence of financial constraint. By contrast, a "pure monitor" in the sense of Section 9.2.1 is brought on board solely to release financial constraints, since he does not bring any value beyond ensuring that a sufficient fraction of the pie is turned back to investors.
- An entrepreneur with a *stronger* balance sheet is more likely to bring a "pure advisor" on board. An advisor is the corporate equivalent of a personal coach; access to an advisor is therefore reserved to borrowers who have the means to pay for his presence, i.e., to firms with strong balance sheets. By contrast, we saw that only firms with weak balance sheets enlist pure monitors.

We formalize the advisory role in the fixed-investment model in the context of a pure advisor (it is then straightforward to combine the advisory and monitoring functions for the monitor within the same model). An investment of size I must be financed from the entrepreneur's net worth $A < I$ and other funds. As usual, the project yields R in the case of success and 0 in the case of failure. The probability of success is $p + q$, where

- $p \in \{p_H, p_L\}$ is determined by the entrepreneur, who receives private benefit B when misbehaving (choosing probability p_L) and 0 when behaving (choosing probability p_H),
- $q \in \{q_H, q_L = 0\}$ is chosen by the monitor/advisor, if any (if there is none, then $q = q_L = 0$); the monitor incurs a nonverifiable cost $c > 0$ in order to give useful advice and thereby raise the probability of success by q_H.

The separable form postulated for the probability of success will enable us to consider the two agents' incentive constraints separately, as we will see.

Let $\Delta p \equiv p_H - p_L$ and $\Delta q \equiv q_H - q_L$. We naturally assume that the advisory activity is socially desirable:

$$(\Delta q)R \geqslant c.$$

Despite the symmetrical description of contributions to the probability of success, the entrepreneur and the monitor differ in at least one key respect: the entrepreneur owns the idea, and therefore decides whether to enlist a monitor.[16]

16. By contrast, in Holmström's (1982) original model of moral hazard in teams, the principal (here the investors) hires the two agents (here, the entrepreneur and the advisor).

9.2.5.1 No Advisor

In the absence of an advisor ($q = q_L = 0$), the treatment is the standard one. The entrepreneur's utility (when obtaining financing) is the NPV,

$$U_b^{nm} = p_H R - I,$$

and funding can be secured if and only if the pledgeable income exceeds the investors' outlay:

$$p_H\left(R - \frac{B}{\Delta p}\right) \geqslant I - A$$

or

$$A \geqslant \bar{A} = I - p_H\left(R - \frac{B}{\Delta p}\right).$$

9.2.5.2 Advisor

As in Section 9.2.1, assume that monitoring capital is plentiful, and so monitors' rent can be captured by asking them to contribute sufficiently to the investment (Exercise 9.4 verifies the robustness of the insights to monitoring capital scarcity).

In the case of success, the entrepreneur receives R_b, the monitor R_m, and the other investors $R - R_b - R_m$. All receive 0 in the case of failure.

The entrepreneur's and the monitor's incentive constraints are, respectively,[17]

$$(\Delta p)R_b \geqslant B$$

and

$$(\Delta q)R_m \geqslant c.$$

Let

$$R_m = \frac{c}{\Delta q}.$$

The contribution I_m to initial investment that is demanded from the monitor fully extracts his rent:

$$I_m = (p_H + q_H)\left(\frac{c}{\Delta q}\right) - c.$$

The entrepreneur again receives the full NPV, since neither the monitor nor the uninformed investors receive a rent:

$$U_b^m = (p_H + q_H)R_b - A = (p_H + q_H)R - I - c.$$

Note that when monitoring takes the form of advising, there can never be overmonitoring (Cestone 2004). Indeed, if monitoring capital is not scarce, and so the monitor contributes to the initial investment at the level of his future quasi-rent, it is optimal to allocate all shares not held by the entrepreneur to the monitor.[18]

9.2.5.3 Comparison

Because $(\Delta q)R > c$,

$$U_b^m > U_b^{nm}.$$

The entrepreneur prefers to avail herself of the advisory services as long as she can afford them. The key issue is whether advisory services boost or decrease pledgeable income. The pledgeable income under monitoring is

$$(p_H + q_H)\left(R - \frac{B}{\Delta p} - \frac{c}{\Delta q}\right)$$

(accounting for the fact that the monitor receives $(p_H + q_H)(c/\Delta q)$), and so financing is possible if and only if

$$(p_H + q_H)\left(R - \frac{B}{\Delta p} - \frac{c}{\Delta q}\right) \geqslant I - A - I_m$$

or

$$(p_H + q_H)\left(R - \frac{B}{\Delta p}\right) - c \geqslant I - A.$$

This last condition, taken as an equality, defines the threshold level of cash on hand, $\hat{A}$, such that the investors will let the entrepreneur hire an advisor. Thus, the pledgeable income (net of the monitor's investment contribution) increases ($\hat{A} < \bar{A}$) if and only if

$$q_H\left(R - \frac{B}{\Delta p}\right) > c.$$

This condition is not implied by that guaranteeing that monitoring increases the NPV ($q_H R > c$). We are thus led to consider two cases, depicted in Figure 9.2.

In case 2, the possibility of being monitored increases the pledgeable income, and *a fortiori* the NPV. It enhances the NPV, as well as enlarging the set of net worths for which funding is secured.

In case 1, in contrast, monitoring increases the NPV but lowers the pledgeable income. Hence, only firms with strong balance sheets (a high A) can resort to an advisor. The use of an advisor is a bit similar to an upgrading of—or extra investment in—this project; because the entrepreneur benefits from

17. Note that the two constraints are independent. For example, the monitor's constraint, $(p + q_H)R_m - c \geqslant pR_m$, does not depend on the realization of p.

18. It is weakly optimal here as long as $(\Delta q)R_m \geqslant c$. It would be strictly optimal if the monitoring intensity were continuous.

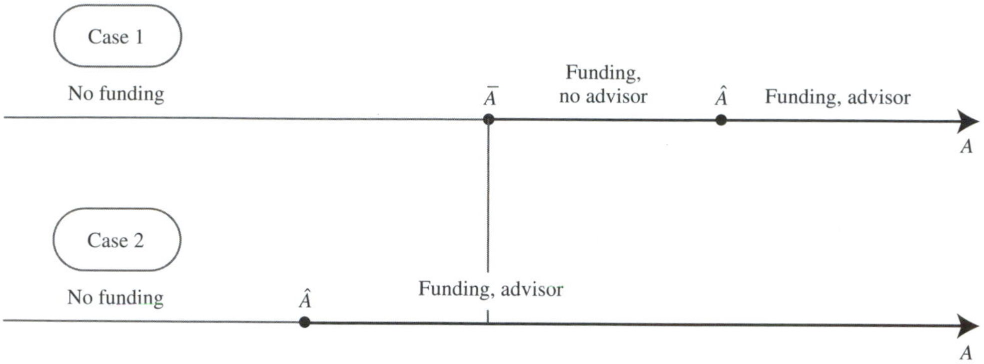

Figure 9.2 Case 1: $q_H(R - B/\Delta p) < c$. Case 2: $q_H(R - B/\Delta p) > c$.

this upgrade in the form of a higher rent, investors may not be able to put their hands on the increase in social value. This situation is reminiscent of the variable-investment model, in which an increase in the size of investment both increased the NPV and reduced the investors' profitability. Conversely, not taking on board an advisor is akin to a concession made to investors.

9.3 The Emergence of Share Concentration

As we discussed in Chapter 1, there is currently an important corporate governance debate as to whether the fiscal, legal, and regulatory environment sufficiently facilitates the emergence of large monitors. We abstract from this debate by assuming away any public restriction on or disincentive to the concentration of shares. Rather, we ask whether a large monitor will endogenously arise in an unregulated private economy. Share concentration may emerge in three ways: (a) private deal or private placement, (b) primary or seasoned offering, and (c) purchases on the secondary market.

The analysis of Section 9.2 has implicitly considered the case of a *private deal*: the entrepreneur chose a monitor (to be interpreted as a venture capitalist, an LBO specialist, a large shareholder, a bank, etc.) and then issued claims to nonmonitoring investors (junior partners, minority shareholders, other lenders, etc.). This section investigates whether a large monitor may arise endogenously through the purchase of a block of claims in a primary offering or in the secondary market. We begin with the latter possibility.

9.3.1 Tender Offer

Suppose that external shares are initially held by dispersed owners. A potential large monitor arrives and makes an unconditional and unrestricted tender offer at price P per share; that is, the large monitor stands ready to buy at price P any external share, regardless of the number of other shares tendered.

This situation gives rise to the well-known *free-rider problem* identified in Grossman and Hart (1980). Each initial owner of an outside share wishes that the other shareholders would tender their shares, since he would then benefit from the highest possible value enhancement. In general, though, individual investors are insufficiently motivated to supply the public good[19] created by share concentration. The second observation is that the large monitor in equilibrium does not acquire any share, since he must pay the *ex post* value for these shares and bears the cost of monitoring. Hence, no monitoring happens in equilibrium.

More formally, consider the *variable-monitoring-intensity* extension of Section 9.2.2.1. Let α denote the fraction of shares tendered to the large monitor. The fraction α cannot exceed the fraction $\bar{\alpha} \equiv [1 - (R_b/R)]$ of outside shares, where the entrepreneur's stake, R_b, is insufficient to generate good behavior in the absence of monitoring: $R_b < B/\Delta p$ (the case $R_b \geqslant B/\Delta p$ is, as we have seen, uninteresting, since monitoring is then irrelevant). These

19. The notion of "public good" is relative to the set of investors. As we have seen, the entrepreneur *ex post* loses from increased monitoring. Thus, share concentration may result in overmonitoring.

shares create a stake αR and an intensity of monitoring $x^*(\alpha)$ given by

$$\max_x \{[x p_{\mathrm{H}} + (1 - x) p_{\mathrm{L}}]\alpha R - c(x)\}$$

or

$$c'(x^*(\alpha)) = (\Delta p)\alpha R.$$

The intensity of monitoring is an increasing function of the fraction of shares held by the large monitor. Let

$$V(\alpha) \equiv [x^*(\alpha) p_{\mathrm{H}} + [1 - x^*(\alpha)] p_{\mathrm{L}}] R$$

denote the expected payoff of a share when the large monitor holds a fraction α of shares. $V(\alpha)$ is an increasing function of α in the interval $[0, \bar{\alpha}]$, with

$$V(0) = p_{\mathrm{L}} R$$

and

$$V(\bar{\alpha}) = [x^*(\bar{\alpha}) p_{\mathrm{H}} + [1 - x^*(\bar{\alpha})] p_{\mathrm{L}}] R.$$

Consider a tender offer P in the relevant range $[V(0), V(\bar{\alpha})]$. The number of shares tendered is $\alpha = \alpha(P)$, where

$$V(\alpha(P)) = P.$$

If the number of shares tendered were smaller than $\alpha(P)$, then the value of a share would be smaller than the tender offer and all investors would want to tender, a contradiction. Conversely, if the number of shares tendered exceeded $\alpha(P)$, the value of shares would exceed the offered price and no one would actually want to tender. Note that the fraction of shares tendered is an upward-sloping function of the price, and that the supply curve is not perfectly elastic despite the fact that investors are risk neutral.

The large monitor's profit is then

$$\alpha(P) V(\alpha(P)) - c(x^*(\alpha(P))) - \alpha(P) P = -c(x^*(\alpha(P))),$$

and is therefore negative unless $\alpha(P) = 0$, i.e., $P = V(0)$. We therefore conclude that the large investor purchases no shares.

Remark (less extreme forms of free riding). The result that the large monitor acquires no shares is, of course, extreme and only serves to illustrate the free-rider and undermonitoring phenomena. In practice, large monitors, instead of purchasing shares through a tender offer, can try to acquire shares more discretely through anonymous orders and disguise these acquisitions behind liquidity trading (see Chapter 8); in many countries large investors can indeed do so until their shareholdings reach some threshold (e.g., 5% of the shares) at which point they must publicly disclose their position. The essential difference with the previous analysis of the free-rider problem is that liquidity traders (as in Chapter 8) lose money in expectation and thereby enable the large monitor to profitably acquire some shares. In contrast, the risk-neutral (and implicitly patient) investors of our analysis fully capture any value enhancement associated with the acquisition of shares by the monitor.

Similarly, the large monitor in Admati et al. (1994) (who, as in this section, makes a tender offer) acquires some shares despite free riding by small investors, because the latter have limited risk tolerance. The monitor supplies insurance to the small investors by purchasing shares. This creates gains from trade when the monitor buys shares, and in equilibrium the monitor indeed buys some shares, albeit an insufficient amount from the point of view of investors.

9.3.2 IPO: Winner's Curse in the Absence of Asymmetric Information

(This section contains advanced material.[20])

Suppose now that the entrepreneur offers the $\bar{\alpha}$ external shares in an IPO. For expository purposes only,[21] the auction is a discriminatory auction (the generalization of the first-price auction): bidders announce a price and a maximum quantity they are willing to buy at that price; the shares are then allocated to the highest bidders by order of their bids, and the bidders pay the price they bid for the shares they acquire.

As in the previous section, there are a large number of risk-neutral small investors, who in this primary market can be called market makers or arbitrageurs.[22] These arbitrageurs stand ready to buy any amount of shares as long as the rate of return

20. The analysis in this section transposes those of Burkart et al. (1998) and Joskow and Tirole (2000) to the IPO context.

21. In the United States, IPOs often do not use discriminatory auctions.

22. The auction we consider is in no way an optimal one. We consider it only to illustrate the main point. For some results on "mecha-

they expect on these shares (which is conditional on acquiring them: see below) is nonnegative. There is also a potential monitor who is risk neutral as well. The monitoring technology is again the uncertain monitoring technology of Section 9.2.2.1.

The first point to note is that *the equilibrium bids of this IPO cannot be deterministic.* Suppose, first, that the monitor bids $P = V(0)$, that is, the value of shares when he acquires none. Either he indeed acquires no share, and so no other investor makes a (money losing) bid above $V(0)$. The monitor can then acquire all shares at a price slightly above $V(0)$ and make a profit approximately equal to $\bar{\alpha}[V(\bar{\alpha}) - V(0)] - c(x^*(\bar{\alpha})) > 0$. Or else he acquires a fraction $\alpha > 0$ at bid $P = V(0)$, but then any investor can make a positive profit by placing a bid for a single share at a price in the interval $(V(0), V(\alpha))$. Suppose, second, that the monitor bids $P = V(\hat{\alpha})$ for some $\hat{\alpha} > 0$ and acquires α shares. Either $\alpha > \hat{\alpha}$, and by the previous reasoning, any investor could increase his profit by placing a bid for one share at a price in the interval $(V(\hat{\alpha}), V(\alpha))$. Or $\alpha \leqslant \hat{\alpha}$, and then the monitor's profit is

$$\alpha[V(\alpha) - V(\hat{\alpha})] - c(x^*(\alpha)) \leqslant 0.$$

As in the case of a tender offer, free riding prevents the monitor from making a deterministic offer at a price above $V(0)$.

Let us now describe the equilibrium. *The monitor randomizes over his bid P in some interval* $[V(0), \bar{P}]$, where $\bar{P} < V(\bar{\alpha})$, according to cumulative distribution $H(P)$ with continuous density $h(P)$ (so $H(V(0)) = 0$ and $H(\bar{P}) = 1$). The monitor stands ready to buy an arbitrary number of shares at the price he bids (he does not specify a maximum quantity).

The arbitrageurs' aggregate demand for shares is downward sloping rather than perfectly elastic. Namely, the fraction of shares demanded by arbitrageurs is equal to $\bar{\alpha} - \alpha(P)$, where $\alpha(P)$, the fraction of shares acquired by the monitor in the IPO when bidding P, is an increasing function of P with $\alpha(V(0)) = 0$ and $\alpha(\bar{P}) = \bar{\alpha}$. Because of competition (free entry) and risk neutrality, each bid by an arbitrageur must have an expected payoff equal to 0.

nism design with externalities," we refer to, e.g., Jéhiel and Moldovanu (2000, 2001).

Let us compute this expected payoff *conditional on the arbitrageur receiving the corresponding share.* For bid P by the arbitrageur to be a winning bid, it must be the case that the monitor has bid some $\tilde{P} < P$. The conditional density of the monitor's bid knowing that it is lower than P is equal to $h(\tilde{P})/H(P)$ on $(V(0), P)$. The zero-expected-profit condition can therefore be written as

$$\int_{V(0)}^{P} [V(\alpha(\tilde{P})) - P] \frac{h(\tilde{P})}{H(P)} \, \mathrm{d}\tilde{P} = 0.$$

Since this condition must be satisfied for any P on $[V(0), \bar{P}]$, the derivative of its left-hand side with respect to P is also equal to 0, or

$$\frac{h(P)}{H(P)} = \frac{1}{V(\alpha(P)) - P}. \tag{9.18}$$

Condition (9.18), the investors' zero-profit condition, defines the mixed strategy $H(P)$ played by the monitor. The interesting point is the existence of a *winner's curse.* The acquisition of a share by an arbitrageur is bad news as to its value; the arbitrageur acquires the share for which he bids precisely when the monitor bids low, that is, when the monitor acquires few shares and performs little monitoring.

The monitor must be indifferent among all bids in the support of his mixed strategy. Note that $V(0)$ is in the support of H, because otherwise, the arbitrageurs would not bid prices between $V(0)$ and the greatest lower bound $\underline{P}$ of the support of H, and consequently the monitor would gain by bidding $V(0)$ instead of $\underline{P}$. Because he cannot make a profit by offering $P = V(0)$ (if he acquired some shares at this price, then arbitrageurs could make a profit by bidding just above $V(0)$), his profit must be equal to 0 for any bid on $[V(0), \bar{P}]$, or

$$\alpha(P)[V(\alpha(P)) - P] = c(x^*(\alpha(P))). \tag{9.19}$$

Equation (9.19) implies that the monitor buys shares at a discount $(V(\alpha(P)) > P)$ that is just sufficient to compensate him for his monitoring cost. The upper bound on bids, $\bar{P}$, is given by

$$\bar{\alpha}[V(\bar{\alpha}) - \bar{P}] = c(x^*(\bar{\alpha})).$$

Lastly, we have posited that the monitor wants to purchase all available shares at his bid P. This follows from the fact that his profit function is convex in the number of acquired shares for a given price per share:[23] marginal value enhancements are more profitable for the monitor, the higher his number of shares.

We conclude that the IPO, although it leaves rents neither to the monitor nor to the other investors, does not generate an optimal monitoring structure. It lies in between the tender offer and the private deal in terms of free riding.

9.4 Learning by Lending

Through their monitoring activity, large blockholders or relationship lenders curb managerial moral hazard, but they also learn private information about the firm's prospects. This section analyzes the impact of learning by lending on the pricing of large investor stakes and on managerial incentives. The informational advantage acquired by current monitoring generates future informational rents. These future rents in turn tend to be competed away (i.e., dissipated) *ex ante* through a premium paid for the "right to monitor." Crucially, this section shows that the asymmetry of information between incumbent lenders and other potential lenders enables the former to partly hold up the manager for her investments in future productivity increases, and thereby identifies a cost of relationship lending.

Let us now add a dynamic dimension to the (abundant monitoring capital) model of Section 9.2.1.[24] There are two periods, $t = 1, 2$. The discount factor between the two periods is denoted by β. For simplicity, we rule out any savings between the two dates.[25]

Date 1. Consider an entrepreneur without cash ($A = 0$), but with a project requiring investment I at date 1. This initial project is successful (yields R) with probability p, and fails (yields 0) with the complementary probability. The probability of success is p_{H} if the entrepreneur behaves and $p_{\mathrm{L}} = p_{\mathrm{H}} - \Delta p$ if she misbehaves. The private benefit of misbehaving in the absence of monitoring, B, is large enough that there is not enough pledgeable income to reimburse the initial investors. That is, an arm's-length relationship is not an option. In contrast, monitoring (which costs c to the monitor) brings down the private benefit from misbehavior to $b < B$, and generates enough pledgeable income to pay back the investment and the monitoring costs. There is no scarcity of active monitors and so, in a static context, the extra cost of enlisting an active monitor is equal to c. Let us thus assume that

$$p_{\mathrm{H}}\left(R - \frac{b}{\Delta p}\right) \geqslant I + c.$$

As shown in Section 9.2.1, this condition implies that the pledgeable income exceeds the total payment to investors (given that $A = 0$) and so the project can be financed even if there is no continuation project.[26]

Date 2. Regardless of the first-period profit, the entrepreneur is endowed with a new idea. This second project, which can be thought of as a continuation of the first, is identical to the first project, except for one thing: with probability α, the date-2 probability of success has increased uniformly by $\tau > 0$; that is, the probability of success of the second project is $p_{\mathrm{H}} + \tau$ if the entrepreneur behaves in the second period, and $p_{\mathrm{L}} + \tau$ if the entrepreneur misbehaves. Even with this improved profitability, an arm's-length relationship is still not an option at date 2; that is, the private benefit B is so large that a monitor is still needed. With probability $1 - \alpha$, these probabilities are still p_{H} and p_{L}; the second-period project is then a perfect image of the first-period one. The profit realizations (success, failure) are statistically independent across periods. We will refer to the realization

23. By the envelope theorem,

$$\frac{\mathrm{d}}{\mathrm{d}\alpha}[(p_{\mathrm{L}} + x^*(\alpha)\Delta p)\alpha R - c(x^*(\alpha))] = [p_{\mathrm{L}} + x^*(\alpha)\Delta p]R,$$

whose derivative is $(\Delta p)R[\mathrm{d}x^*/\mathrm{d}\alpha] > 0$.

24. A different model of relationship banking is developed in Scheepens (1996, Chapter 5). In Scheepens's model the borrower benefits from establishing a reputation with a bank as this increases the availability of financing later on. The initial loan may involve risky debt in order to provide the bank with an incentive to monitor.

25. Because we will assume in this section that there is enough pledgeable income and so funding is not an issue, it will not matter under symmetric information (Section 9.4.1) whether the consumer consumes or saves the compensation she earns in the case of date-1 success. The no-savings assumption, in contrast, matters (quantitatively, although presumably not qualitatively) when nonmonitoring investors are less well-informed than other parties. The level of savings by the entrepreneur and their use toward covering the date-2 investment may then, as in Chapter 6, act as signals of date-2 profitability. The no-saving assumption therefore considerably simplifies the analysis.

26. As shown in Sections 3.7, 4.8, and 5.5, in particular, making continuation contingent on performance allows managerial incentive contracts to preserve incentives while reducing current compensation, thereby increasing pledgeable income. Here, we rule out commitment to future policies, so contracting *ex ante* on contingent continuation is not a contacting option anyway.

of the probability of success as the "date-2 profitability" (since the other variables are public knowledge).

Quite importantly, we will assume that there is *no commitment* and so first-period investors' return comes from the first-period profit (if any), and the firm issues new claims in the second period. We consider three cases.

- Symmetric information: no one learns the date-2 profitability. The expected probability of success for the date-2 project is then $p_H+\alpha\tau$ or $p_L+\alpha\tau$, depending on the entrepreneur's behavior.
- Asymmetric information: the date-1 active monitor, and only the active monitor, learns the date-2 profitability.
- Endogenous profitability: the probability α of an increase in the date-2 profitability is the outcome of a date-1 investment by the entrepreneur. The entrepreneur's private cost of this investment is $D(\alpha)$. We will assume that only the active monitor observes the resulting date-2 profitability. That is, there is asymmetric information as in the previous case, but α is now endogenous.

9.4.1 Symmetric Information

Under symmetric information at date 2 (no one learns the realized date-2 profitability), the market for active monitors is competitive at dates 1 *and* 2. The entrepreneur's expected utility at date t is that period's NPV:

$$U_b(t) = p_H(t)R - (I + c),$$

where $p_H(1) = p_H$ and $p_H(2) = p_H + \alpha\tau$. And so the entrepreneur's overall utility is equal to the total NPV over the two periods, or

$$U_b = [p_H R - (I + c)] + \beta[(p_H + \alpha\tau)R - (I + c)].$$

In this symmetric-information environment, it does not matter whether the entrepreneur engages in a long-term relationship with a single active monitor, or sequentially issues a block share to an active monitor in each period. Symmetric information ensures that "Bertrand competition" among active investors operates and keeps the per-period borrowing cost $(I + c)$ at the minimum possible level.

9.4.2 Asymmetric Information

Let us now assume that only the date-1 active monitor (the "incumbent") learns the date-2 profitability (but the parameter α is still exogenous). At date 2, the incumbent and entrant monitors submit bids for the active monitoring position. In general, a "bid" is an offer by a monitor of (a) his investment contribution, and (b) his rewards in the cases of success and failure. Below, we will have the entrepreneur fix an incentive-compatible compensation scheme (part (b)), to be interpreted as the number of shares held by the large blockholder, and select the highest investment contribution offer (part (a)).

The description of the date-2 competition between the incumbent and the other potential active investors (the "entrants") is complex if we assume that the incumbent and the entrants make simultaneous offers to the entrepreneur for the active monitoring position. As observed in the literature (e.g., Rajan 1992), the equilibrium of this bidding game in general is in mixed strategies. To show this heuristically, suppose that the entrants' bid is deterministic and, if selected, yields zero profit for the monitor for probability of success[27] $q \in (p_H, p_H + \tau)$. The incumbent then overbids the entrants when the true probability is $p_H + \tau$ and underbids them (or does not bid) when the true probability is p_H. That is, an entrant is selected only if the profitability is low. This implies that the entrant loses money. This is the celebrated *winner's curse*. Next, assume that $q = p_H+\tau$. Because this bid is not matched by the incumbent when profitability is low, again the selected entrant loses money. Lastly, assume that $q = p_H$. Then it is optimal for the incumbent to bid an investment contribution corresponding to a probability of success slightly above p_H("$p_H + \varepsilon$") when the actual profitability is high. But this incumbent bidding behavior generates a profit opportunity for the entrants. By bidding a bit above the incumbent, they make a lot of money with probability α and lose a little with probability $1 - \alpha$. Hence, the equilibrium is necessarily in mixed strategies. A full treatment of this mixed-strategy equilibrium can be found in von Thadden (2004).

For the sake of simplicity, let us finesse this difficulty and assume the following sequential timing of offers by active monitors at date 2.

---

27. Technically, this means that (normalizing the active monitor's stake to be $R_m^2 = c/\Delta p$) the entrants bid the same investment contribution I_m^2 such that $q(c/\Delta p) = I_m^2 + c$.

(1) The entrepreneur defines the active monitor's stake $R_m^2 = c/\Delta p$ in the case of success (and 0 in the case of failure), and announces that the active monitor will be the bidder offering the highest investment contribution I_m^2. (There is actually no loss of generality in assuming that the stake, which must exceed $c/\Delta p$ for incentive compatibility, is exactly equal to this value.[28])

(2) New active monitors (the entrants) offer investment contributions.

(3) The incumbent active monitor then makes his offer. That is, he either matches the entrants' top offer[29] and then remains the firm's large shareholder, or he does not match it and is replaced.

(4) The residual date-2 investment, $I - I_m^2$, where I_m^2 is the highest bid, is then contributed by uninformed investors.[30]

In the bidding game, the entrants optimally bid as if the probability of success were always the lowest possible one (in this sense, our timing assumption takes the adverse-selection problem to its extreme and maximizes the incumbency rent):

$$I_m^2 = p_H R_m^2 - c$$
$$= p_H \frac{c}{\Delta p} - c.$$

For, suppose that an entrant bids a level I_m^2 corresponding to a higher expected probability of success q ($I_m^2 = qR_m^2 - c$, where $q \in (p_H, p_H + \tau)$). The entrant knows that the incumbent will match if the profitability is high and will not if the profitability is low. The entrant suffers from the winner's curse and loses money.[31]

Because the entrepreneur has no independent wealth at date 2,[32] the uninformed investors contribute the investment shortfall:

$$I_u^2 = I - I_m^2.$$

How large a stake R_u^2 they receive on average does not depend on who is assumed to win in a low-profitability state (in which the incumbent is indifferent between matching and not matching the entrant).[33] Let us assume, for example, that the incumbent always wins (for example, the auction selects the incumbent at equal bids). The stake R_u^2 is such that uninformed investors break even:

$$(p_H + \alpha\tau)R_u^2 = I_u^2.$$

The entrepreneur's date-2 utility is then[34]

$$U_b^2 = (p_H + \alpha\tau)(R - R_m^2 - R_u^2)$$
$$= [(p_H + \alpha\tau)R - I - c] - \alpha\tau\left(\frac{c}{\Delta p}\right).$$

That is, the entrepreneur's expected utility is equal to the expected NPV minus the incumbent monitor's expected rent,

$$\mathcal{R}_m^2 = \alpha\tau\left(\frac{c}{\Delta p}\right).$$

Let us now consider date-1 competition among potential large blockholders. At that date these potential active monitors are symmetrically informed and therefore perfect competitors for the block share $R_m^1 = c/\Delta p$. But the expectation of the future incumbency rent implies that they are willing to *make a generous introductory offer in order to obtain a profitable toehold*. Indeed, they are willing to contribute up to

$$I_m^1 = p_H\left(\frac{c}{\Delta p}\right) + \beta\mathcal{R}_m^2.$$

One can view the informational advantage of the incumbent active monitor as a switching cost that tends to lock the firm in with this monitor. As emphasized by the switching cost literature in industrial organization,[35] the anticipated *ex post* market power enjoyed by the incumbent provider of the service (here the monitoring service) is competed away at the *ex ante* stage through a (short-term)

28. She could set a higher stake (and, indirectly, ask for a higher investment contribution and thereby lead the large monitor to substitute for uninformed investors). But this would raise the incumbent monitor's informational rent.

29. Plus an arbitrarily small amount.

30. Following up on footnote 28, we could alternatively assume that the incumbent can bid for these as well and take a bigger stake in the firm. Note, though, that letting the incumbent do so extends the adverse-selection problem to "uninformed shares" and is not in the interest of the entrepreneur. We therefore assume that blockholdings are limited to stake $c/\Delta p$.

31. For a bid $I_m^2 = (p_H + \tau)R_m^2 - c$, whether the incumbent matches in the high-profitability state is irrelevant, and so the same conclusion holds.

32. Recall that, for the sake of simplicity, we assumed that there are no savings between dates 1 and 2.

33. Alternatively, we could have assumed that the uninformed investors bid before knowing who, between the incumbent and the entrant, wins. The equilibrium description would have been identical.

34. It is easily verified that the entrepreneur's stake exceeds $b/\Delta p$; and so the average probability of success is indeed $p_H + \alpha\tau$.

35. See Klemperer (1995) for a survey.

loss-making offer. The blockholding is initially acquired at a premium, and is later maintained at a discount.

One might conjecture that the winner's curse can be eliminated by preventing the incumbent (who after all has no comparative advantage in monitoring relative to his rivals) from competing for the block share at date 2. Note, though, that a commitment to exclude the incumbent active monitor from the second round of financing anyway is not time consistent. For, if entrants offered a contribution corresponding to probability of success $p_H + \alpha\tau$, nothing would prevent the entrepreneur from accepting an offer corresponding to a slightly higher probability from the incumbent; and this renegotiation (which would occur only if the probability of success is $p_H + \tau$) would recreate the winner's curse.

9.4.3 Holdup Cost of a Tight Relationship

Until now the "monopoly" power enjoyed by the incumbent monitor has had no inefficiency or redistributive impact. This property is special and one would in general expect *ex post* monopoly power to have some negative consequences. Let us here focus on a specific one: the ability of the active monitor to hold up (partly expropriate) the entrepreneur, who is then unable to fully benefit from the fruits of her investments. The holdup here takes a slightly unusual form. The incumbent active monitor does not formally have bargaining power vis-à-vis the entrepreneur as he is engaged in a bidding war with other prospective active monitors to keep his blockholding. But, because the latter are reluctant to bid against the incumbent, the incumbent is able to obtain supranormal date-2 profits.

Suppose therefore that the probability α of a profitability improvement is endogenous and determined at date 1 by the entrepreneur. Let $D(\alpha)$ denote the entrepreneur's date-1 (increasing and convex) private cost of generating a profitability improvement at date 2 with probability α.[36] Neither D nor α are observable by anyone but the entrepreneur.

- When the profitability increase (that is, whether the probability of success has increased by τ) is publicly observable at date 2, the entrepreneur receives the full benefit from her investments, and α solves

$$\max_{\alpha}\{-D(\alpha) + \beta\alpha\tau R\}.$$

Let α^* denote this first-best value:

$$D'(\alpha^*) = \beta\tau R. \tag{9.20}$$

- When information is still symmetric among investors, but no one observes at date 2 whether there has been a profitability increase,[37] investors (active or not) assess the returns on the date-2 financial contracts on the premise that the value of α is the equilibrium value $\hat{\alpha}$. So

$$I_m^2 = (p_H + \hat{\alpha}\tau)\left(\frac{c}{\Delta p}\right) - c$$

and

$$I_u^2 = I - I_m^2 = (p_H + \hat{\alpha}\tau)R_u^2.$$

The entrepreneur's date-2 expected utility as a function of the equilibrium value $\hat{\alpha}$ and her actual choice α (the two must coincide in equilibrium) is

$$\begin{aligned} U_b^2(\alpha, \hat{\alpha}) &= (p_H + \alpha\tau)\left(R - \frac{c}{\Delta p} - R_u^2\right) \\ &= (p_H + \alpha\tau)\left(R - \frac{I + c}{p_H + \hat{\alpha}\tau}\right). \end{aligned}$$

The entrepreneur selects α so as to maximize $-D(\alpha) + \beta U_b^2(\alpha, \hat{\alpha})$; and so

$$D'(\hat{\alpha}) = \beta\tau\left(R - \frac{I + c}{p_H + \hat{\alpha}\tau}\right) < \beta\tau R. \tag{9.21}$$

The entrepreneur underinvests in productivity improvement ($\hat{\alpha} < \alpha^*$) because she captures only the fraction of the benefits corresponding to her share in date-2 profits.

- Lastly, let us introduce *asymmetric* information and assume that the incumbent active monitor, but not the entrants, learns the realization of profitability.[38]

36. We will assume $D(0) = 0$, $D'(0) = 0$, $D'(\alpha) > 0$ for $\alpha > 0$, $D''(\alpha) > 0$, and $D(1) = \infty$.

37. Of course, the entrepreneur, when choosing α different from the equilibrium $\hat{\alpha}$ does not have the same information as investors. The situation is similar to, but a bit different from, that considered in the model of privately-known-prospects of Section 6.2, since investors here believe that the probability of success is $p_H + \hat{\alpha}\tau$ for certain. The entrepreneur does not have scope for signaling a high profitability when choosing an off-the-equilibrium path level $\alpha > \hat{\alpha}$, though.

38. We keep assuming that the entrepreneur organizes an auction between incumbent and entrants for the monitoring blockholding. We do not investigate more complex schemes.

From our previous analysis, and letting $\breve{\alpha}$ denote the new equilibrium probability,

$$I_{\mathrm{m}}^2 = p_{\mathrm{H}}\left(\frac{c}{\Delta p}\right) - c$$

and

$$I_{\mathrm{u}}^2 = I - I_{\mathrm{m}}^2 = (p_{\mathrm{H}} + \breve{\alpha}\tau)R_{\mathrm{u}}^2.$$

Simple computations show that

$$U_{\mathrm{b}}^2(\alpha, \breve{\alpha}) = (p_{\mathrm{H}} + \alpha\tau)\left(R - \frac{I + c + \breve{\alpha}\tau c/\Delta p}{p_{\mathrm{H}} + \breve{\alpha}\tau}\right)$$

and

$$D'(\breve{\alpha}) = \beta\tau\left(R - \frac{I + c + \breve{\alpha}\tau c/\Delta p}{p_{\mathrm{H}} + \breve{\alpha}\tau}\right). \tag{9.22}$$

Thus,

$$\breve{\alpha} < \hat{\alpha} < \alpha^*.$$

The first-best level of investment in profitability is obtained when the realization of profitability is observed and the capital market is competitive. Nonobservability reduces the incentive to invest. Lastly, observability by the incumbent active monitor reduces the incentive even more as others are worried about bidding against a party who is better informed; lowbidding by uninformed monitors results in a lower stake in second-period profit for the entrepreneur, who therefore has less incentive to invest in date-2 value enhancements. The informational asymmetry now has an efficiency cost in terms of fewer incentives for entrepreneurial innovation.

This analysis points to a benefit in terms of entrepreneurial initiative of an arm's-length relationship with investors (when feasible—as we have seen and as embodied in the assumptions of the analysis, an arm's-length relationship may not be an option for the borrower): in a dynamic perspective, the firm in a sense has access to a more competitive capital market in the future if it is not linked to a powerful investor today.[39]

39. An alternative way of making the capital market more competitive *ex post* is information sharing among lenders, if it can be verified that incumbent lenders do not hide information about borrowers from their competitors. See Padilla and Pagano (1997) and Exercise 6.7 for the costs and benefits of information sharing. (There is some analogy between this solution to the holdup problem and the literature in industrial organization on licensing by a supplier to (i.e., the sharing of information with) competitors as a commitment not to abuse monopoly power on a customer in the future and to thereby encourage investments by this customer (see Farrell and Gallini 1988; Shepard 1987).)

If we introduced feasible date-1 "concessions," such as costly collateral pledges or a lower investment scale, the entrepreneur might want to make such concessions so as to enable an arm's-length relationship, even though the latter would be inefficient from the point of view of date 1. This arm's-length relationship would serve to commit the entrepreneur to higher investments in date-2 profitability.

9.4.4 Arm's-Length Relationships and Firms' Ability to Refinance

Arm's-length relationships on the other hand may also have drawbacks, assuming that they are feasible. Several studies (e.g., Hoshi et al. (1990a,b, 1991) for Japan) show that firms with close ties to financial institutions are less liquidity constrained than those without such ties.

To understand why this may be so, let us return, for simplicity, to the exogenously random profitability improvement version of the model. Instead of assuming that, under perfect knowledge by the investors of the date-2 profitability, the date-2 project is always financed, let us posit that it is financed only if the probability of success has increased. So, if I_2 denotes the second-period investment (because the first project is financed, the following condition requires that the second-period investment cost exceeds the first-period cost, keeping other parameters constant),

$$p_{\mathrm{H}}\left(R - \frac{b}{\Delta p}\right) < I_2 + c < (p_{\mathrm{H}} + \tau)\left(R - \frac{b}{\Delta p}\right);$$

let us also assume that I_2 is such that an arm's-length relationship is not feasible at date 2.

If, furthermore,

$$(p_{\mathrm{H}} + \alpha\tau)\left(R - \frac{b}{\Delta p}\right) < I_2 + c,$$

an arm's-length relationship at date 1 (assuming that it is feasible) makes it impossible in the absence of a long-term contract for the firm to obtain refinancing at date 2 even by resorting to a large monitor at that date. In contrast, a date-1 active monitor who learns by monitoring enables date-2 financing with probability α. Relatedly, a number of papers, starting with James (1987), have shown that the existence or renewal of a banking relationship is associated with a positive reaction in the stock price.

However, if refinancing is a sure thing when starting with an arm's-length relationship,

$$(p_H + \alpha\tau)\left(R - \frac{b}{\Delta p}\right) > I_2 + c,$$

then the presence of an informed monitor at date 2 reduces the probability of refinancing. We thus conclude that we can rationalize the impact of arm's-length relationships on refinancing, but a richer theory is needed for crisper conclusions.[40]

9.4.5 Discussion

This treatment of holdup by a large monitor makes several strong assumptions. First, it assumes away any form of commitment. There are several issues with this lack of commitment. Coming back to the case in which date-2 financing is always optimal, the entrepreneur could better protect her investment through a long-term contract. For example, the entrepreneur could provide herself with incentives to sink $\alpha = \hat{\alpha}$ (given by (9.21)) by setting in advance the date-2 reward of the monitor (and committing to keep the incumbent monitor). The entrepreneur could further improve her incentives to invest by "backloading" her compensation and making it contingent on date-1 and date-2 successes.

A second criticism is that, in the case in which the incumbent monitor acquires private information about date-2 productivity, no use is made of the entrepreneur's own knowledge of her date-2 productivity. In particular, were the entrepreneur to observe the realization of the date-2 productivity and were she able to offer a date-2 contract to the incumbent monitor, she would be able to ask for conditions that reflect the actual productivity realization and the expropriation problem would disappear: $\alpha = \alpha^*$.[41] And, even if she did not observe this realization, she would still know what α she chose and use this to extract good terms from the incumbent monitor.[42]

Finally, we have focused on the impact of short-term contracting on managerial investments. Short-term contracting may also alter the borrower's ability to receive funds in the first place: suppose that the firm initially generates low cash flows relative to the investment cost but, provided that it receives initial financing, will later be very profitable. A monitor will be willing to lose money initially only if he is able to earn supranormal profits later on. These supranormal profits may be secured through a long-term stake, such as an equity stake, in the firm's profit.[43] In the presence of short-term contracting, though, the key to the monitor's ability to recoup his initial investment is to enjoy monopoly power in the loan market in the future (see Exercise 9.7). Interestingly, Petersen and Rajan (1994, 1995), analyzing small businesses' banking relationships in the United States around 1988–1989, show that more young firms were able to obtain external financing in concentrated local banking markets than in competitive local banking markets. The idea is that such firms have initially low cash flows and that banks, for regulatory reasons, took debt rather than equity claims; and so a concentrated local banking market offered more scope for banks to recoup initial losses in the future. Indeed, Petersen and Rajan offer evidence that banks smoothed interest rates intertemporally in concentrated markets.

9.5 Liquidity Needs of Large Investors and Short-Termism

9.5.1 The Issues

Recall that the Anglo-Saxon model of financial organization is often criticized for its lack of investor commitment (Coffee 1991; Bhide 1993: Roe 1990, 1994), and that, conversely, that prevailing in continental Europe and Japan is criticized for sacrificing investor liquidity. This section, which closely follows the lines of Section 4.4, shows that there is indeed a tradeoff between commitment and liquidity. In a

40. A further caveat is that this discussion does not allow for the long-term financing arrangements (long-term debt, equity or credit lines) considered in Chapter 5.

41. Situations with shared information make it easier to elicit the true state of the world (Maskin 1977). Here, the entrepreneur would more generally set at date 2 a *strike price* I_m^2 at which the incumbent can keep its blockholding (in case the incumbent elects not to exercise his option, the blockholding is auctioned off to the highest bidder among new monitors).

As in Maskin and Moore (1999), renegotiation would reduce the power of such schemes. For example, the incumbent monitor could strategically refuse to exercise his option when the productivity is $p_H + \tau$ and try to renegotiate with the entrepreneur.

42. Readers who are knowledgeable about contract design with correlated information will here see the link between this argument and the analysis of Crémer and McLean (1985).

43. Another way of obtaining a long-term profit is to secure a first right of refusal for future loans at predetermined high rates of interest.

nutshell, a large investor has a limited incentive to build long-term value if he can resell his stake before the impact of his monitoring is either realized or observed by the market (as in Chapter 8). In the absence of market certification of his value enhancement, this implies that the large investor must be a "long-term player." Or, using Hirschman's (1970) terminology, "exit" is inconsistent with "voice." There are, in practice, various ways of making it costly for a large investor to exit. The illiquidity of the shares (especially if shares are held privately, as in the case of letter stocks) is an obvious one. Vesting mechanisms (for example, granting extra shares or stock options if the initial shares are held beyond some prespecified length of time) are another.

Yet being a long-term player involves a substantial cost in terms of liquidity. A financial intermediary (or another firm playing the role of the monitor) may need cash to withstand its own liquidity shocks: a bank may have to honor an unusually high number of credit lines due to an industrial recession, or face an interest rate or exchange rate shock against which it is not completely hedged; it may also forgo profitable new investment opportunities if it is not able to free its assets in this firm. A parent company may similarly need to withstand its own liquidity shocks (as in Chapter 5). Venture capitalists usually insist on having an exit mechanism that enables them not to get stuck with their initial venture capital undertakings, and thereby allows them to undertake new investments.

An interim market validation or certification of the large investor's activity, on the other hand, provides a faster exit mechanism without necessarily jeopardizing monitoring. Suppose that, as in Chapter 8, some market participants collect retrospective information about the final outcome and therefore about the large investor's monitoring activity. The large investor, like the entrepreneur in Chapter 8, can then be assessed on the basis of the market's evaluation of his performance, or rather of the performance of the team composed of the large investor and the entrepreneur, and not only on the basis of the final outcome. *Passive monitoring thus provides an exit mechanism for the active monitor.*

Let us provide some illustrations of the use of speculative monitoring as an exit mechanism for the active monitor. Consider first the process of *certification.* A loan originator wants to dispose of some of its illiquid assets in order to withstand its liquidity shocks or undertake new investments. For example, by replacing risky assets by cash or cash equivalents, the financial institution relaxes its capital adequacy requirement and can thus invest in new assets. But the loan originator in general has private information about the quality of the assets to be disposed of. Typically, this loan originator—the active monitor—creates a special-purpose trust that purchases the loans and issues ("asset-backed") securities and then goes and searches for passive monitoring. There are several types of collectors of retrospective information, who often concurrently certify the quality of the loan portfolio that is being securitized: credit enhancers who provide a bank letter of credit or a cash collateral account, rating agencies,[44] independent auditors, and underwriters. At that point the asset-backed securities can be marketed to individual or institutional investors.

Another case in point is provided by venture capitalists, who may liquidate a substantial part of their holdings in a venture through an IPO or a sale to a large company. In the case of an IPO, the venture capitalist trades his shares against cash, shares in publicly traded companies, or short-term debt, which are all more liquid assets (this is called a "cash-out acquisition" (see Plummer 1987)). Alternatively, the start-up may be sold to a buyer, again providing the venture capitalist with liquidity. There is ample evidence that venture capitalists carefully plan their exit (see Black and Gilson 1998; Gompers and Lerner 1999; Lerner 1999; Sahlman 1990).

9.5.2 Modeling

Consider Figure 9.3, which describes the timing.[45] The situation is the same as in Section 9.2 except for

44. Often several agencies are involved. For example, in some cases the four main agencies, Standard & Poor's, Moody's, Fitch, and Duff and Phelps, all rate the issue.

45. The following treatment is inspired by that in Aghion et al. (2004). Kahn and Winton (1998) and Maug (1998) also emphasize the relationship between market liquidity and monitoring, but focus on small investors' liquidity demands rather than those of large blockholders/active monitors. Faure-Grimaud and Gromb (2004) and Fulghieri and Larkin (2001) are similar to Aghion et al.; they put less emphasis on mechanism design and the optimal degree of liquidity for the active monitor.

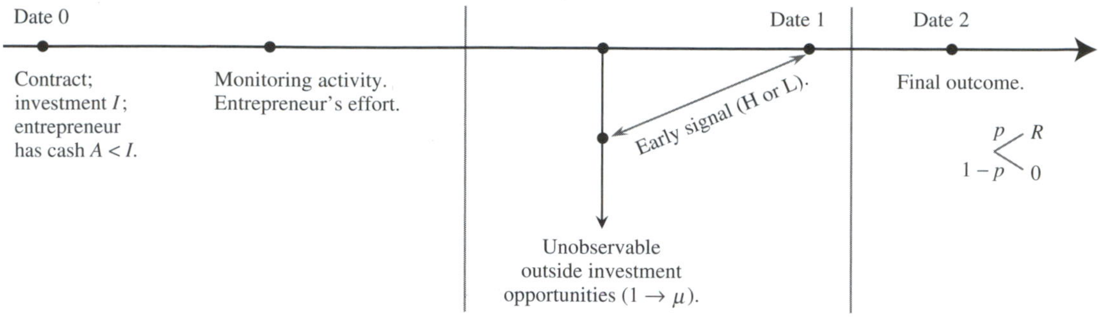

Figure 9.3

the possible presence of a liquidity shock at an intermediate stage, "date 1." As in Section 9.2, the entrepreneur, who must borrow $I - A$, needs to be monitored. Monitoring reduces the entrepreneur's private benefit of shirking from B to b, but involves private cost c for the monitor. The probability of eventual ("date 2") success is p_{H} if the entrepreneur works and p_{L} if she shirks.

At date 1, the monitor either does not face a liquidity shock, in which case he does not need money until date 2, or faces a liquidity shock. In the case of a liquidity shock, the monitor can transform an arbitrary amount of cash r_{m} (provided that it is available to him at date 1), into μr_{m}, where $\mu > 1$. The interpretation of the liquidity shock is therefore the accrual of attractive outside investment opportunities at the intermediate stage. We assume that the proceeds, μr_{m}, associated with the outside reinvestments, entirely go to the active monitor; that is, none of this return is pledgeable to those uninformed investors who have invested their money at date 0 in the firm (or to the entrepreneur for that matter). The probability of a liquidity shock is λ. The active monitor learns at date 1 whether he faces a liquidity shock. The other players never receive direct evidence on this shock.

To benefit from these attractive investment opportunities, the active monitor must be provided with liquidity at date 1. There are two issues with rewarding the monitor at date 1, though.

Imperfect performance measurement. The monitor receives (at least some of) the reward *before* the firm's final performance is realized. This limits the sanction inflicted on the monitor for poor firm performance.

We will assume that some early measure of performance is available, though (the signal accrues after the monitor learns whether he faces a liquidity shock). While this performance measure does not bring any information beyond that contained in the final payoff (the final payoff is a "sufficient statistic" to learn effort) and thus is not as good as the final performance, this "speculative information" will be used when the active monitor wants to realize his stake in the firm at date 1. More precisely, the date-1 signal is H ("high signal") or L ("low signal"). The probability of a high signal given a high (respectively, low) effort is q_{H} (respectively, q_{L}); comparing the likelihood ratios,

$$\mathcal{L}_q \equiv \frac{q_{\mathrm{H}} - q_{\mathrm{L}}}{q_{\mathrm{H}}} < \mathcal{L}_p \equiv \frac{p_{\mathrm{H}} - p_{\mathrm{L}}}{p_{\mathrm{H}}}.$$

In words, the final outcome is more informative about effort than the intermediate signal,[46] but the latter is nonetheless informative ($q_{\mathrm{H}} > q_{\mathrm{L}}$).

Strategic exit. Because the event of a liquidity shock is observable only by the monitor, the monitor can fail to monitor and claim to be facing a liquidity shock at date 1 even when he is not.

Monitoring capital is costly. In Section 9.2.3, we defined a required return χ on monitoring capital as the ratio of the active monitor's expected monetary payoff over his investment contribution. We can no longer define scarcity in those terms here, because the active monitor cares not only about how much he receives but also about *when* he receives it.

46. In Chapter 8, we assumed in contrast that the intermediate signal is a sufficient statistic and is *more* informative than the final outcome. Were we to assume this here, then providing the active monitor with a fully liquid contract (no vesting of rewards) would be optimal.

So, scarcity must be defined in terms of the active monitor's utility. In order not to confuse these two closely related concepts, we will denote by "κ" rather than "χ" the utility return on monitoring investment. Thus, if the active monitor receives gross surplus U_{m} from the contract, he is willing to contribute up to I_{m}, where

$$\kappa I_{\mathrm{m}} = U_{\mathrm{m}}.$$

Note that, necessarily,

$$\kappa \geqslant \lambda\mu + 1 - \lambda,$$

since the active monitor can always not sign a contract and enjoy return μ (with probability λ) or 1 (with probability $1-\lambda$) on the corresponding investment contribution.

Without loss of generality (see Aghion et al. 2004), the entrepreneur can offer either an "illiquid contract" in which the active monitor's stake is vested until date 2 so nothing can be withdrawn at date 1, or a "liquid contract" under which the active monitor has a choice between pulling out at date 1 and receiving r_{m} if the high signal accrues at that date (the monitor receiving nothing at date 2 if he asked to pull out at date 1), and waiting until date 2 to receive success-contingent reward R_{m}. Let us consider these two forms of contract sequentially.

Illiquid contract. Under the illiquid contract, the active monitor receives R_{m} in the case of success at date 2, 0 in the case of failure, and withdraws nothing at date 1.[47] Note that because the final payoff is a sufficient statistic, there is no point rewarding the active monitor at date 2 as a function of the date-1 signal.

To attract the active monitor, this contract must satisfy

$$p_{\mathrm{H}}R_{\mathrm{m}} - c = U_{\mathrm{m}} = \kappa I_{\mathrm{m}}. \tag{9.23}$$

The active monitor's stake R_{m} must be sufficient to induce him to monitor:

$$(\Delta p)R_{\mathrm{m}} \geqslant c. \tag{9.24}$$

47. For simplicity, we assume that the illiquid contract is not renegotiated at date 1. Midstream renegotiation of agency contracts under moral hazard reduces the attractiveness of such contracts (e.g., Fudenberg and Tirole 1990), and here would imply that the optimal contract would deliver some degree of liquidity anyway.

Conditions (9.23) and (9.24) imply that the cost of enlisting the active monitor is then

$$C = C^{\mathrm{IL}} = p_{\mathrm{H}}R_{\mathrm{m}} - I_{\mathrm{m}} = \left[\frac{p_{\mathrm{H}} - p_{\mathrm{L}}/\kappa}{p_{\mathrm{H}} - p_{\mathrm{L}}}\right]c.$$

Because $\kappa > 1$, the cost of enlisting the monitor exceeds, as in Section 9.2.3, the monitoring cost c. The borrower's utility and the pledgeable income are then

$$U_{\mathrm{b}} = p_{\mathrm{H}}R - I - C$$

and

$$\mathcal{P} = p_{\mathrm{H}}\left(R - \frac{b}{\Delta p}\right) - C,$$

respectively. The same expressions will hold in the liquid contract case as well (although, in general, the cost C of enlisting the monitor takes a different value).

Liquid contract. Suppose now that the active monitor has the choice between

- receiving r_{m} at date 1 in the case of a high signal and nothing at date 2, and
- receiving nothing at date 1 and R_{m} in the case of success at date 2.

This menu is designed so that he exercises the former option in the case of a liquidity shock and the latter option in the absence of such a shock.

Let us assume for simplicity that the probability of success when shirking, p_{L}, is small, so that if he does not monitor, the active monitor is better off receiving r_{m} than waiting for an unlikely reward R_{m} even if he has no attractive reinvestment opportunity. So his utility if he does not monitor is

$$\lambda\mu q_{\mathrm{L}}r_{\mathrm{m}} + (1-\lambda)q_{\mathrm{L}}r_{\mathrm{m}}.$$

Truthful revelation of the absence of a liquidity shock at date 1 requires that

$$p_{\mathrm{H}}R_{\mathrm{m}} \geqslant q_{\mathrm{H}}r_{\mathrm{m}}. \tag{9.25}$$

Similarly, in the case of a liquidity shock, the condition

$$\mu q_{\mathrm{H}}r_{\mathrm{m}} \geqslant p_{\mathrm{H}}R_{\mathrm{m}} \tag{9.26}$$

must be satisfied; but as we will see, inducing the active monitor to truthfully announce that he faces a liquidity shock is not constraining.

The active monitor's utility if he monitors is

$$U_{\mathrm{m}} = \lambda\mu q_{\mathrm{H}}r_{\mathrm{m}} + (1-\lambda)p_{\mathrm{H}}R_{\mathrm{m}} - c. \tag{9.27}$$

Ex ante incentive compatibility requires that

$$U_{\mathrm{m}} \geqslant (\lambda\mu + 1 - \lambda)q_{\mathrm{L}}r_{\mathrm{m}}. \tag{IC}$$

It is easy to check that this constraint is binding.[48] And so

$$U_{\mathrm{m}} = (\lambda\mu + 1 - \lambda)q_{\mathrm{L}}r_{\mathrm{m}}. \tag{9.28}$$

The cost of hiring the active monitor is

$$C = \lambda q_{\mathrm{H}}r_{\mathrm{m}} + (1-\lambda)p_{\mathrm{H}}R_{\mathrm{m}} - I_{\mathrm{m}},$$

so that, using $U_{\mathrm{m}} = \kappa I_{\mathrm{m}}$, (9.27), and (9.28),

$$\begin{aligned} C &= \left[-\lambda(\mu-1)q_{\mathrm{H}} + \left(1-\frac{1}{\kappa}\right)(\lambda\mu+1-\lambda)q_{\mathrm{L}}\right]r_{\mathrm{m}} + c \\ &= \mathcal{C}r_{\mathrm{m}} + c. \end{aligned} \tag{9.29}$$

Because $\kappa \geqslant \lambda\mu + 1 - \lambda$, the coefficient $\mathcal{C}$ of r_{m} in the expression of C is always positive when the intermediate signal is uninformative ($q_{\mathrm{H}} = q_{\mathrm{L}}$). But it becomes negative for $q_{\mathrm{H}}/q_{\mathrm{L}}$ sufficiently large.

Assume for simplicity that $p_{\mathrm{L}} = 0$, so that $C^{\mathrm{IL}} = c$. (The case p_{L} positive, but small, is almost identical.)

If $\mathcal{C} > 0$, then the unconstrained optimum has $r_{\mathrm{m}} = 0$. And so a *lower bound* on C is c. This implies that the optimal contract is illiquid. In contrast, if $\mathcal{C} < 0$, then r_{m} should be "as large as possible." Given (IC), it is then clear that (9.25) is binding (and that (9.26) is not). And so, from (9.27) and (9.28),

$$[\lambda\mu + 1 - \lambda][q_{\mathrm{H}} - q_{\mathrm{L}}]r_{\mathrm{m}} = c. \tag{9.30}$$

Hence, provided that

$$\lambda(\mu-1)q_{\mathrm{H}} > \left(1-\frac{1}{\kappa}\right)(\lambda\mu+1-\lambda)q_{\mathrm{L}}, \tag{9.31}$$

which can be rewritten so as to highlight the signal's likelihood ratio,

$$\mathcal{L}_q \geqslant \frac{1}{\kappa-1}\left[\frac{\kappa}{\lambda\mu+1-\lambda} - 1\right],$$

the optimal r_{m} is given by (9.30), and the cost of hiring the monitor by

$$C^{\mathrm{L}} = c + \mathcal{C}r_{\mathrm{m}}.$$

Given $p_{\mathrm{L}} = 0$, (9.31) is a necessary and sufficient condition for

$$C^{\mathrm{L}} < C^{\mathrm{IL}},$$

and so the optimal policy is to offer liquidity to the active monitor.

Since (9.31) is the necessary and sufficient condition for the optimal contract to be liquid, we can finally derive the following comparative statics results:

The optimal contract for the active monitor is more likely to be liquid if

- *the frequency of attractive reinvestment opportunities (λ) or/and the value of these opportunities (μ) is/are high,*
- *the intermediate signal is informative ($\mathcal{L}_q$ high),*
- *monitoring capital is not too scarce (κ low).*

The first two implications are intuitive. The third is perhaps less so; to see why the active monitor's claim is more likely to be liquid when monitoring capital is not too scarce, recall that part of the monitor's benefit from liquidity is returned by him in the form of a contribution to the initial investment. But this effect plays a minor role if monitoring capital is scarce.

Speculative monitoring (the presence of an intermediate signal) is needed in order to provide the active monitor with an exit option. And the more precise the corresponding information, the better the case for liquidity. This result explains why monitors' exit strategies are often associated with an IPO or a sale to a large buyer. In either case, the floating or sale of securities creates an early performance measurement, i.e., a valuation of assets in place; the rationale for it is the same as in Chapter 8: speculative monitoring enables an assessment of performance before the actual profits accrue. Interestingly, venture capital contracts may include "drag-along" covenants that allow the general partner to force exit by limited partners and possibly the entrepreneur in the case where he finds a buyer; and often require that all convertible debt be converted prior to putting up the firm for sale or an IPO. These contractual features may be interpreted as ways of increasing the volume of equity put up for sale, thereby increasing the incentive of the buyer or of investors in an IPO to engage in careful speculative monitoring. Similar covenants can be found in shareholder agreements, which include joint ventures.[49]

48. If this were not the case, then $r_{\mathrm{m}} = R_{\mathrm{m}} = 0$ would be optimal, which obviously violates (IC).

49. See Chemla et al. (2004) for a theoretical analysis of these and other rights specified in shareholder agreements.

Finally, the demand for speculative monitoring leads to a violation of the pecking order (see Application 3 in Chapter 6): it is important to float high-information-intensity securities such as equity in order to stimulate information acquisition by the market.

9.6 Exercises

Exercise 9.1 (low-quality public debt versus bank debt). Consider the model of Section 9.2.1, except that the project has a positive NPV even if the entrepreneur misbehaves.

As usual, the entrepreneur is risk neutral and protected by limited liability. She has assets A and must finance an investment of fixed size $I > A$. The project yields R in the case of success and 0 in the case of failure. The probability of success is p_H if the entrepreneur behaves (no private benefit) and p_L if she misbehaves (private benefit B). Investors are risk neutral and demand a 0 rate of return.

Instead of assuming that the project has positive NPV only in the case of good behavior, suppose that

$$p_H R > p_L R + B > I.$$

Suppose further that there is a competitive supply of monitors and abundant monitoring capital. At private cost c, a monitor can reduce the entrepreneur's private benefit of misbehavior from B to b. Assume that

$$p_H \frac{B-b}{\Delta p} > c > (\Delta p)R - p_H \frac{b}{\Delta p}$$

and

$$(\Delta p)R > c + B.$$

Show that there exist thresholds $A_1 < A_2 < A_3$ such that

- if $A \geqslant A_3$, the firm issues high-quality public debt (public debt that has a high probability of being repaid);
- if $A_3 > A \geqslant A_2$, the firm borrows from a monitor (and from uninformed investors);
- if $A_2 > A \geqslant A_1$, the firm issues junk bonds (public debt that has a low probability of being repaid);
- if $A_1 > A$, the firm does not invest.

Exercise 9.2 (start-up and venture capitalist exit strategy). There are three periods, $t = 0, 1, 2$. The rate of interest in the economy is equal to 0, and everyone is risk neutral. A start-up entrepreneur with initial cash A and protected by limited liability wants to invest in a fixed-size project. The cost of investment, incurred at date 0, is $I > A$. The project yields, at date 2, $R > 0$ with probability p and 0 with probability $1 - p$. The probability of success is $p = p_H$ if the entrepreneur works and $p = p_L = p_H - \Delta p$ ($\Delta p > 0$) if the entrepreneur shirks. The entrepreneur's effort decision is made at date 0. Left unmonitored, the entrepreneur obtains private benefit B if she shirks and 0 otherwise. If monitored (at date 0), the private benefit from shirking is reduced to $b < B$.

There is a competitive industry of venture capitalists (monitors). A venture capitalist (general partner) has no fund to invest at date 0 and incurs private cost $c_A > 0$ when monitoring the start-up and 0 otherwise (the subscript "A" refers to "active monitoring"). The twist is that the venture capitalist wants his money back at date 1, before the final return, which is realized at date 2 (technically, the venture capitalist has preferences $c_0 + c_1$, while the entrepreneur and the uninformed investors have preferences $c_0 + c_1 + c_2$, where c_t is the date-t consumption). Assume that

$$I - p_H\left(R - \frac{B}{\Delta p}\right) > A > I - p_H\left(R - \frac{b + c_A}{\Delta p}\right).$$

(i) Assume first that the financial market learns (for free) at date 1 whether the project will be successful or fail at date 2. Note that we are then in the standard two-period model, in which the outcome can be verified at date 1 (one can, for example, organize an IPO at date 1, at which the shares in the venture are sold at a price equal to their date-2 dividend).

Show that the entrepreneur cannot be financed without hiring a venture capitalist. Write the two incentive constraints in the presence of a venture capitalist and show that financing is feasible. Show that the entrepreneur's utility is $p_H R - I - [p_H c_A / \Delta p]$.

(ii) Assume now that at date 1 a speculator (yet unknown at date 0) will be able to learn the (date-2) realization of the venture's profit by incurring private cost c_P, where the subscript "P" refers to "passive monitoring."

At date 0, the venture capitalist is given s shares. The date-0 contract with the venture capitalist specifies that these s shares will be put for sale at date 1 in a "nondiscriminatory auction" with reservation price P. That is, shares are sold to the highest bidder at a price equal to the highest of the unsuccessful bids, but no lower than P. If left unsold, the venture capitalist's shares are handed over for free to the date-0 uninformed investors (the limited partners) in the venture.

(a) Find conditions under which it is an equilibrium for the speculator (provided he has monitored and received good news) to bid R for shares, and for uninformed arbitrageurs to bid 0 (or less than P).

(b) Write the condition on (s, P) under which the speculator is indifferent between monitoring and not monitoring. Writing the venture capitalist's incentive constraint, show that P satisfies

$$\frac{R-P}{P}=\frac{c_{\mathrm{P}}}{c_{\mathrm{A}}}\frac{\Delta p}{p_{\mathrm{H}}}.$$

How should the venture capital contract be structured if these conditions are not satisfied?

Exercise 9.3 (diversification of intermediaries). Consider two identical entrepreneurs. Both are risk neutral, are protected by limited liability, have a project of fixed size I, and must borrow $I-A$ in order to finance their project. Each project, if undertaken, yields R with probability p and 0 with probability $1-p$. The probability of success is p_{H} if the entrepreneur behaves (receives no private benefit) and p_{L} if she misbehaves (receives private benefit B). The two projects are statistically independent. The rate of interest in the economy is 0.

There is also a competitive supply of monitors, call them venture capitalists. Venture capitalists have no cash. Monitoring a firm involves a nonmonetary cost c for the venture capitalist. The entrepreneur's private benefit from misbehaving is then reduced from B to $b<B$. Assume that

$$I-A>\max\left\{p_{\mathrm{H}}\left(R-\frac{B}{\Delta p}\right), p_{\mathrm{H}}\left(R-\frac{b+c}{\Delta p}\right)\right\}.$$

(i) Show that the entrepreneurs cannot obtain financing without uniting forces (on a stand-alone basis, with or without monitoring).

(ii) Consider now the following structure: the two firms are monitored by the same venture capitalist. By analogy with Diamond's diversification reasoning (see Chapter 4), argue that the venture capitalist is paid a reward (R_{m}) only if the two firms succeed. Show that if

$$p_{\mathrm{H}}\left(R-\frac{b+c p_{\mathrm{H}}/(p_{\mathrm{H}}+p_{\mathrm{L}})}{\Delta p}\right)>I-A,$$

then financing can be arranged.

Exercise 9.4 (the advising monitor model with capital scarcity). Work out the model of Section 9.2.5, but assume that monitors have no capital ($I_{\mathrm{m}}=0$).

Find conditions under which the enlisting of a monitor facilitates financing, or conversely requires a stronger balance sheet.

Exercise 9.5 (random inspections). This exercise investigates a different way of formalizing monitoring. Rather than limiting the set of options available to the entrepreneur, the monitor *ex post* inspects, and, when finding evidence of misbehavior, takes a corrective action.

The timing is described in Figure 9.4.

The model is the standard one, with risk-neutral entrepreneur and investors. The entrepreneur is protected by limited liability and the investors demand a rate of return equal to 0.

At private cost c, the monitor can learn the choice of effort. If the entrepreneur has behaved, the firm is on the right track (as long as the entrepreneur stays on to finish the project), and there is no action to take. By contrast, if the entrepreneur misbehaves, the best policy is to kick her out, in which case she will enjoy neither her private benefit B nor any reward in the case of success. The remedial action (which includes firing the entrepreneur) raises the probability of success to $p_{\mathrm{L}}+\nu$, where $\nu>0$ and $p_{\mathrm{L}}+\nu<p_{\mathrm{H}}$.

In questions (i) and (ii), *one will assume that the entrepreneur and the monitor are rewarded solely as a function of the final outcome* (they get R_{b} and R_{m} in the case of success, and 0 in the case of failure).

Assume that $\nu R_{\mathrm{m}}>c$ and $(\Delta p)R_{\mathrm{b}}<B$, and that the monitor has no cash (so $I_{\mathrm{m}}=0$).

(i) Show that in equilibrium the entrepreneur and the monitor play mixed strategies: the entrepreneur misbehaves with probability $x\in(0,1)$, and the monitor fails to monitor with probability $y\in(0,1)$.

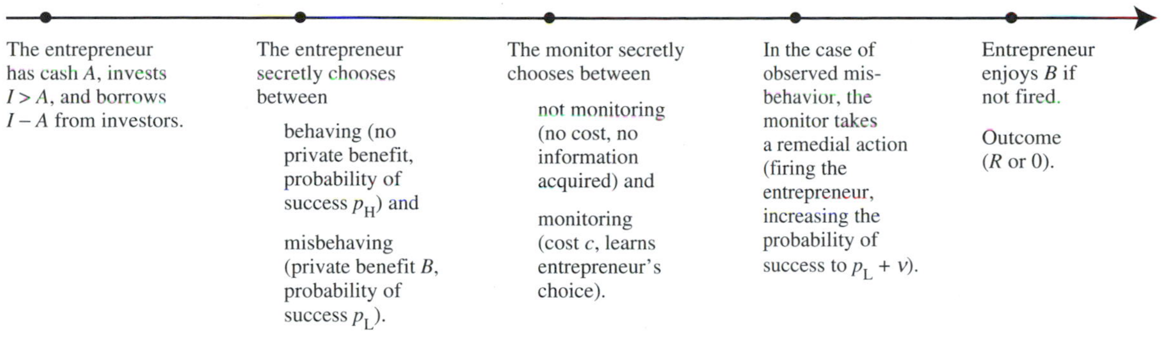
The entrepreneur has cash A, invests I > A, and borrows I − A from investors.
The entrepreneur secretly chooses between
behaving (no private benefit, probability of success p_H) and
misbehaving (private benefit B, probability of success p_L).
The monitor secretly chooses between
not monitoring (no cost, no information acquired) and
monitoring (cost c, learns entrepreneur's choice).
In the case of observed mis-behavior, the monitor takes a remedial action (firing the entrepreneur, increasing the probability of success to $p_L + \nu$).
Entrepreneur enjoys B if not fired.
Outcome (R or 0).

Figure 9.4

(ii) Write the entrepreneur's utility and the uninformed investors' income as functions of R_{m} and R_{b}. What is the optimal financing arrangement?

(iii) In view of Chapter 8, is the performance-based contract studied in (i) and (ii) optimal?

Exercise 9.6 (monitor's junior claim). A risk-neutral entrepreneur protected by limited liability has a fixed-size project that yields R^{S} in the case of success and $R^{\mathrm{F}} \in (0, R^{\mathrm{S}})$ in the case of failure. Her cash on hand A is smaller than the investment cost I.

As in Section 9.2, there are three versions of the project: good (probability of success p_{H}, no private benefit), bad (probability of success p_{L}, private benefit b), Bad (probability of success p_{L}, private benefit B). A risk-neutral monitor can at private cost c rule out the Bad version. Monitoring capital is scarce; actually consider the polar case in which the monitor has no cash on hand (and is protected by limited liability).

As usual, uninformed investors are risk neutral and demand a rate of return equal to 0; one will also assume that funding can be secured only if the entrepreneur is monitored and is induced to choose the good version.

Compute $R_{\mathrm{m}}^{\mathrm{S}}$ and $R_{\mathrm{m}}^{\mathrm{F}}$, the monitor's compensations in the cases of success and failure, respectively. Show that

$$R_{\mathrm{m}}^{\mathrm{F}} = 0.$$

Exercise 9.7 (intertemporal recoupment). An entrepreneur has a sequence of two projects to be undertaken at $t = 1, 2$, respectively. There is no discounting between the two periods. The only link between the two projects is that the second project can be undertaken only if the first has been. Each project is as described in Section 9.2, and has three versions: good (probability of success p_{H}, no private benefit), bad (probability of success p_{L}, private benefit b), Bad (probability of success p_{L}, private benefit B). A risk-neutral monitor can at private cost c rule out the Bad version.

There is no scarcity of monitoring capital, in the sense that a monitor is willing to participate as long as his rate of return (which includes his monitoring cost) exceeds 0. As usual, uninformed investors are risk neutral and demand a rate of return equal to 0; one will also assume that funding can be secured only if the entrepreneur is monitored and is induced to choose the good version.

A project yields R in the case of success and 0 in the case of failure.

Assume that the entrepreneur has no cash on hand ($A = 0$) and that the investment costs for the two projects, I_1 and I_2, satisfy

$$I_1 + c > p_{\mathrm{H}}\left(R - \frac{b}{\Delta p}\right) > I_2 + c$$

(the second project can for example be viewed as a continuation project, involving a lower investment cost),

$$I_1 + I_2 + 2c < 2p_{\mathrm{H}}\left(R - \frac{b}{\Delta p}\right),$$

and

$$p_{\mathrm{H}}R - I_1 - c > 0.$$

Consider two situations depending on whether there is competition among potential monitors:

Concentrated lending market. There is a single potential monitor. This monitor furthermore has full bargaining power, i.e., makes a take-it-or-leave-it contract offer (or offers) to the borrower.

Competitive lending market. There are multiple potential monitors, who compete for the borrower's business.

(i) *Long-term contracts.* First, assume that a contract covers the two periods; characterize the outcome under concentrated and competitive lending, and show that in either case the borrower receives funding for both investments.

(ii) *Short-term contracts.* suppose now that the only contracts that a monitor can sign are one-period (spot) lending contracts, in which the monitor is compensated through a claim on the current profit only. Show that the borrower secures funding only in a concentrated market.

References

Admati, A. and P. Pfleiderer. 1994. Robust financial contracting and the role of venture capitalists. *Journal of Finance* 49:371–402.

Admati, A., P. Pfleiderer, and J. Zechner. 1994. Large shareholder activism, risk sharing and financial market equilibrium. *Journal of Political Economy* 102:1087–1130.

Aghion, P. and J. Tirole. 1997. Formal and real authority in organizations. *Journal of Political Economy* 105:1–29.

Aghion, P., P. Bolton, and J. Tirole. 2004. Exit options in corporate finance: liquidity versus incentives. *Review of Finance* 8:1–27.

Barclay, M. and C. Holderness. 1989. Private benefits from control of public corporations. *Journal of Financial Economics* 25:371–395.

Berger, A., N. Miller, M. Petersen, R. Rajan, and J. Stein. 2005. Does function follow organizational form? Evidence from the lending practices of large and small banks. *Journal of Financial Economics* 76:237–269.

Berglöf, E. 1994. A control theory of venture capital finance. *Journal of Law, Economics, & Organization* 10:247–267.

Besanko, D. and G. Kanatas. 1993. Credit market equilibrium with bank monitoring and moral hazard. *Review of Financial Studies* 6:213–232.

Bhide, A. 1993. The hidden costs of stock market liquidity. *Journal of Financial Economics* 34:31–51.

Biais, B. and C. Gollier. 1997. Trade credit and credit rationing. *Review of Financial Studies* 10:903–937.

Black, B. and R. Gilson. 1998. Venture capital and the structure of capital markets: banks vs stock markets. *Journal of Financial Economics* 47:243–277.

Bolton, P. and M. Dewatripont. 2004. *Contract Theory*. Cambridge, MA: MIT Press.

Bolton, P. and E. von Thadden. 1998. Blocks, liquidity, and corporate control. *Journal of Finance* 53:1–25.

Boot, A. 2000. Relationship banking: what do we know? *Journal of Financial Intermediation* 9:7–25.

Bottazzi, L., M. Da Rin, and T. Hellmann. 2005. What role of legal systems in financial intermediation? Theory and evidence. Mimeo, Università Bocconi.

Burkart, M. and T. Ellingsen. 2004. In-kind finance: a theory of trade credit. *American Economic Review* 94:569–590.

Burkart, M., D. Gromb, and F. Panunzi. 1997. Large shareholders, monitoring and the value of the firm. *Quarterly Journal of Economics* 112:693–728.

——. 1998. Why higher takeover premia protect minority shareholders. *Journal of Political Economy* 106:172–204.

Cantillo, M. and J. Wright. 2000. How do firms choose their lenders? An empirical investigation. *Review of Financial Studies* 13:155–189.

Casamatta, C. 2003. Financing and advising: optimal financial contracts with venture capitalists. *Journal of Finance* 58:2059–2086.

Cestone, G. 2004. Venture capital meets contract theory: risky claims or formal control? Mimeo, Universitat Autònoma de Barcelona.

Chemla, G., M. Habib, and A. Ljungqvist. 2004. An analysis of shareholder agreements. Mimeo, Imperial College, London, University of Zurich, and New York University.

Coffee, J. 1991. Liquidity versus control: the institutional investor as corporate monitor. *Columbia Law Review* 91: 1278–1328.

Crémer, J. 1995. Arm's-length relationships. *Quarterly Journal of Economics* 104:275–295.

Crémer, J. and R. McLean. 1985. Optimal selling strategies under uncertainty for a discriminating monopolist when demands are interdependent. *Econometrica* 53:345–361.

Dessi, R. 2005. Start-up finance, monitoring and collusion. *RAND Journal of Economics* 36:255–274.

Diamond, D. 1984. Financial intermediation and delegated monitoring. *Review of Economic Studies* 51:393–414.

——. 1991. Monitoring and reputation: the choice between bank loans and directly placed debt. *Journal of Political Economy* 99:689–721.

Farrell, J. and N. T. Gallini. 1988. Second-sourcing as a commitment: monopoly incentives to attract competition. *Quarterly Journal of Economics* 103:673–694.

Faure-Grimaud, A. and D. Gromb. 2004. Public trading and private incentives. *Review of Financial Studies* 17:985–1014.

Fudenberg, D. and J. Tirole. 1990. Moral hazard and renegotiation in agency contracts. *Econometrica* 58:1279–1320.

Fulghieri, P. and D. Larkin. 2001. Information production, dilution costs, and optimal security design. *Journal of Financial Economics* 61:3–42.

Gompers, P. and J. Lerner. 1999. *The Venture Capital Cycle*. Cambridge, MA: MIT Press.

Greenbaum, S., G. Kanatas, and I. Vennezia. 1989. Equilibrium loan pricing under the bank client relationship. *Journal of Banking and Finance* 13:221–235.

Grossman, S. and O. Hart. 1980. Takeover bids, the free rider problem, and the theory of the corporation. *Bell Journal of Economics* 11:42–64.

Hellmann, T. 1998. The allocation of control rights in venture capital contracts. *RAND Journal of Economics* 29:57–76.

Hellwig, M. 1991. Banking, financial intermediation and corporate finance. In *European Financial Integration* (ed. A. Giovannini and C. Mayer). Cambridge University Press.

Hermalin, B. and M. Weisbach. 1998. Endogenously chosen boards of directors and their monitoring of the CEO. *American Economic Review* 88:96–118.

Hirschman, A. O. 1970. *Exit, Voice, and Loyalty*. Cambridge, MA: Harvard University Press.

Holmström, B. 1979. Moral hazard and observability. *Bell Journal of Economics* 10:74–91.

——. 1982. Moral hazard in teams. *Bell Journal of Economics* 13:324–340.

Holmström, B. and J. Tirole. 1997. Financial intermediation, loanable funds, and the real sector. *Quarterly Journal of Economics* 112:663–692.

Hoshi, T., A. Kashyap, and D. Scharfstein. 1990a. Bank monitoring and investment: evidence from the changing structure of Japanese corporate banking relationships. In *Asymmetric Information, Corporate Finance, and Investment* (ed. R. Glenn Hubbard). University of Chicago Press.

——. 1990b. The role of banks in reducing the costs of financial distress in Japan. *Journal of Financial Economics* 27:67–88.

——. 1991. Corporate structure, liquidity and investment: evidence from Japanese industrial groups. *Quarterly Journal of Economics* 106:33–60.

Jain, N. 2001. Monitoring costs and trade credit. *Quarterly Review of Economics and Finance* 41:89–110.

James, C. 1987. Some evidence on the uniqueness of bank loans. *Journal of Financial Economics* 19:217–235.

Jéhiel, P. and B. Moldovanu. 2000. Auctions with downstream interaction among buyers. *RAND Journal of Economics* 31:768–791.

——. 2001. Efficient design with interdependent valuations. *Econometrica* 69:1237–1259.

Joskow, P. and J. Tirole. 2000. Transmission rights and market power on electric power networks. *RAND Journal of Economics* 31:450–501.

Kahn, Ch. and A. Winton. 1998. Ownership structure, liquidity demand, and shareholder monitoring. *Journal of Finance* 53:99–129.

Kaplan, S., F. Martel, and P. Strömberg. 2003. How do legal differences and learning affect financial contracts? Mimeo, University of Chicago.

Klemperer, P. 1995. Competition when consumers have switching costs: an overview with applications to industrial organization, macroeconomics, and international trade. *Review of Economic Studies* 62:515–540.

Laffont, J. J. and D. Martimort. 2002. *The Theory of Incentives: The Principal–Agent Model*. Princeton University Press.

Laffont, J.-J. and J. C. Rochet. 1997. Collusion in organizations. *Scandinavian Journal of Economics* 99:485–495.

La Porta, R., F. Lopez-de-Silanes, A. Shleifer, and R. Vishny. 1998. Law and finance. *Journal of Political Economy* 106:1113–1155.

Lerner, J. 1995. Venture capitalists and the oversight of private firms. *Journal of Finance* 50:301–318.

——. 1999. *Venture Capital and Private Equity: A Casebook*. New York: John Wiley.

Lerner, J. and A. Schoar. 2005. Does legal enforcement affect financial transactions? The contractual channel in private equity. *Quarterly Journal of Economics* 120:223–246.

Lummer, S. L. and J. McConnell. 1989. Further evidence on the bank lending process and the capital-market response to bank loan agreements. *Journal of Financial Economics* 25:99–122.

Maskin, E. 1977. Nash equilibrium and welfare optimality. Mimeo, MIT. (Published in *Review of Economic Studies* (1999) 66:23–38.)

Maskin, E. and J. Moore. 1999. Implementation and renegotiation. *Review of Economic Studies* 66:39–56.

Maug, E. 1998. Large shareholders as monitors: is there a trade-off between liquidity and control? *Journal of Finance* 53:65–98.

Morrison, A. 2002. Credit derivatives, disintermediation and investment decisions. Mimeo, Merton College, University of Oxford.

Padilla, J. and M. Pagano. 1997. Endogenous communication among lenders and entrepreneurial incentives. *Review of Financial Studies* 10:205–236.

Pagano, M. and A. Roell. 1998. The choice of stock ownership structure: agency costs, monitoring, and the decision to go public. *Quarterly Journal of Economics* 113:187–225.

Petersen, M. and R. Rajan. 1994. The benefits of lending relationships: evidence from small business data. *Journal of Finance* 49:3–37.

——. 1995. The effect of credit market competition on lending relationships. *Quarterly Journal of Economics* 110:407–443.

Plummer, C. 1987. *QED Report on Venture Capital Financial Analysis*. Palo Alto, CA: QED Research.

Rajan, R. 1992. Insiders and outsiders: the choice between relationship and arm's length debt. *Journal of Finance* 47:1367–1400.

Repullo, R. and J. Suarez. 2000. Entrepreneurial moral hazard and bank monitoring: a model of the credit channel. *European Economic Review* 44:1931–1950.

Repullo, R. and J. Suarez. 2004. Venture capital finance: a security design approach. *Review of Finance* 8:75–108.

Roe, M. 1990. Political and legal restraints on ownership and control of public companies. *Journal of Financial Economics* 27:7–41.

——. 1994. *Strong Managers, Weak Owners: The Political Roots of American Corporate Finance.* Princeton University Press.

Sahlman, W. 1990. The structure and governance of venture-capital organizations. *Journal of Financial Economics* 27: 473–521.

Salanié, B. 2005. *The Economics of Contracts. A Primer*, 2nd edn. Cambridge, MA: MIT Press.

Scheepens, J. 1996. Financial intermediation and corporate finance: an analysis of agency problems and optimal contracts. PhD Dissertation, Tilburg University.

Schmidt, K. 2003. Convertible securities and venture capital finance. *Journal of Finance* 58:1139–1166.

Sharpe, S. 1990. Asymmetric information, bank lending, and implicit contracts: a stylized model of customer relationships. *Journal of Finance* 55:1069–1087.

Shepard, A. 1987. Licensing to enhance demand for new technologies. *RAND Journal of Economics* 18:360–368.

Shleifer, A. and R. Vishny. 1986. Large shareholders and corporate control. *Journal of Political Economy* 94:461–488.

Tirole, J. 1986. Hierarchies and bureaucracies. *Journal of Law, Economics, & Organization* 2:181–214.

——. 1992. Collusion and the theory of organizations. In *Advances in Economic Theory: Proceedings of the Sixth World Congress of the Econometric Society* (ed. J.-J. Laffont), Volume 2, pp. 151–206. Cambridge University Press.

Von Thadden, E. L. 2004. Asymmetric information, bank lending, and implicit contracts: the winner's curse. *Finance Research Letters* 1:11–23.

Winton, A. 1993. Limitation of liability and the ownership structure of the firm. *Journal of Finance* 48:487–512.

PART IV

Security Design: The Control Right View

10

Control Rights and Corporate Governance

10.1 Introduction

Covenants can only go so far in determining a firm's future course of action. New information accrues and circumstances that were not clearly conceptualized at the onset arise after the initial funding has been secured. The firm therefore needs a governance structure that will elicit the parties' information and act on it to select a range of short-term and long-term decisions over which parties may have dissonant preferences: day-to-day management, choice of personnel, refinancing and dividend distribution, investments, mergers and acquisitions, and so forth.

This chapter takes a look at the design of decision processes and in particular at a special class of decision processes, namely, "decision rights" or "control rights." By "control right," I mean the right for a party (or group of parties) to affect the course of action in certain circumstances once the firm has gotten started.[1,2] Despite their simplicity, control rights come in many guises: they can be contingent ("debtholders receive control if covenant X is violated"; "the venture capitalist surrenders control rights to the entrepreneur if certain financial or nonfinancial performance criteria are met"). They cover certain decisions, but not others. And they may be induced by another control right: control over decision A (the primary control right) may implicity grant some control over decision B (i.e., an induced control right) even if, formally, one has no control over the latter decision. That is, one can use one's control right over decision A as a bargaining chip to obtain concessions along dimension B. For example, when a class of investors has gatekeeping power over the issuing of senior claims and therefore may control financing (the primary right stems from covenants such as "investor Y cannot be diluted without his assent" or "the holders of short-term debt can force liquidation if the payments are not made on time"), the need to secure the assent of the holders of such rights gives the latter a control over future decisions that is sometimes as strong as that provided by an explicit control right.[3] These examples as well as the fact that some types of shares carry special voting rights also demonstrate that charters, contracts, and the law may disconnect cash-flow rights and control rights.

In a sense, we already touched on the issue of control rights when we discussed active monitoring in Chapter 9. We assumed that the active monitor could reduce the extent of moral hazard by ruling out some egregious forms of managerial misbehavior. Conditional on the active monitor being informed,

1. In general, decision processes are much more complex than just giving someone the right to decide. For example, in politics, a complex web of sequential rights (gatekeeping power by committees, bicameral enacting process, presidential or judicial review, etc.) is often used to produce new legislation.

2. I will not dwell here on the issues of whether control rights are best formalized in a complete or an incomplete contract setting or what an incomplete contract is exactly (see Maskin and Tirole (1999a,b) and Tirole (1999) for discussions of these issues). The distinction is irrelevant for what follows.

It is worth reminding the reader, though, that complete contracting does not mean that the future course of action is described in the initial contract (otherwise, the notion of control right would be meaningless). For one thing, the parties' preferences over known alternative actions may not be known *ex ante*; furthermore, future actions may not be describable when designing the contract. A control right allocated to one of the two parties is a simple way to elicit this information. Complete contracting simply means that the parties write an optimal contract given their limited knowledge of their future preferences and of the set of future alternatives.

The impact of the allocation of control rights received its first formal analysis in Grossman and Hart's (1986) and Hart and Moore's (1990) models of incomplete contracts (see also Williamson's (1985) less formal approach).

3. To give another example, it is often said that an independent regulatory agency is never really independent if Congress controls its budget. The argument is that Congress can threaten to substantially reduce the agency's budget in order to influence decisions that it is otherwise formally unable to control.

there was no issue as to whom the control right should go to, though: interference by the monitor increased *both* the NPV and the pledgeable income. It was trivially optimal to let the monitor interfere, and there was therefore no interesting allocation of the control right. This chapter studies the more interesting situation in which there is a real tradeoff.

Section 10.2 analyzes the allocation of (formal) control rights between insiders and outsiders. Its main theme is that when a firm is constrained in its ability to secure financing, the allocation of control between insiders and outsiders does not just reflect who desires control most; that is, control is not necessarily allocated to the party who will use it in the collectively most efficient way. In the presence of financing constraints, the allocation of control serves another purpose because it affects the extent to which the insiders can "commit" to return the funds to the investors. The design of a corporate governance structure should not only aim at efficiency, but should also keep an eye on its impact on pledgeable income. This logic implies that firms with severe financing problems are not able to avoid granting rights to their investors, including rights that decrease overall value.

Section 10.2 first makes this key point in the context of a single decision right. It then extends the analysis to multiple and contingent rights. Like collateral pledging, the allocation of control should be contingent on measures of performance. Indeed, contingent control boosts managerial incentives and raises pledgeable income. It is further shown that the allocation of multiple control rights follows a rule of relative willingness to pay for these rights, and that firms with stronger balance sheets can afford to relinquish fewer rights to investors. The theoretical predictions in the matters of contingent rights and multiple rights are supported by existing empirical evidence. Finally, Section 10.2 analyzes the relationship between control rights and specific investments, a relationship that was a key focus in the first formal papers on control rights (see, in particular, Grossman and Hart 1986; Hart and Moore 1990). It is shown that investor control reduces entrepreneurial initiative and may even reduce pledgeable income.

Section 10.3 argues that corporate behavior cannot be fully understood by looking solely at the formal allocation of control rights, and that it often requires examining who is actually in control. In all organizations, players who have no formal control often have an important impact on decision making. In the corporate governance context, management controls many decisions that are in principle bestowed upon the board of directors or the general assembly of shareholders; and large minority shareholders often influence the final outcome even though they do not hold enough voting shares to formally control it. The issue of real control is central to a discussion of corporate governance; in particular, the extent of control by management hinges on the alignment of its incentives with investors' goals and on the existence of informed investors and their ability to interfere with decision making. Section 10.3 argues that private information is an important source of real control. Namely, managers (or large minority blockholders) are able to influence decision making because they are better informed than shareholders and directors.

We should abstain from assuming that managers (or large minority blockholders) actually decide on corporate policies. An important theme in Section 10.3 is that the ability of informed parties to manipulate decisions depends on how trustworthy they appear to uninformed parties; trustworthiness in turn depends on the informed party's incentives and their alignment with the uninformed parties' interests. For example, the extent of managerial control can be shown to increase with the strength of the balance sheet. Another important theme of that section is that managerial control depends on corporate governance; for example, the presence of monitors (see Chapter 9) affects the extent of managerial control. Finally, the degree of informational asymmetry is endogenous, which further stresses the need for a clear distinction between formal and real control.

Section 10.4 returns to the allocation of formal control, now among outsiders. For example, how should control be allocated between equityholders and debtholders? To answer this question, one must first ask, what is the point of creating multiple classes of securities? After all, the creation of several classes of securities is bound to generate conflicts of interest. For example, equityholders, if given the right to decide, may engage in asset substitution, that is, may expropriate debtholders by taking excessive risk. And, as we have seen in Chapter 2, debt covenants can only go so far in limiting excessively risky behavior by shareholders. This apparently simple question will lead us to a general discussion of security design, and to several hypotheses as to why, contrary to the Modigliani–Miller theory, it may matter.

10.2 Pledgeable Income and the Allocation of Control Rights between Insiders and Outsiders

10.2.1 The Aghion–Bolton Model

The importance of control rights in corporate finance was first noted by Aghion and Bolton (1992), and substantially developed by Hart (1995a) and Hart and Moore (1989);[4] for the purpose of this chapter, we can rephrase their finding in the following way: *the transfer of control rights to investors increases the pledgeable income and facilitates financing.* Or, to put it differently, control rights may substitute for necessarily limited cash-flow rights.

To illustrate this in the simplest possible way, let us return to the basic (fixed-size) model of Chapter 3: to finance her project, the entrepreneur must borrow the difference between the investment cost I and her net worth A. The project succeeds (and then yields R) with probability p, where $p = p_{\mathrm{H}}$ if she behaves and p_{L} if she misbehaves (and then takes private benefit B); otherwise the project fails and yields nothing. Let us further introduce the possibility of taking an interim action that

(i) raises the probability of success uniformly by $\tau > 0$ (so the probability of success becomes $p_{\mathrm{H}}+\tau$ or $p_{\mathrm{L}}+\tau$, depending on the entrepreneur's behavior, if the action is taken, and remains p_{H} or p_{L} if the status quo action is selected);[5] and
(ii) engenders private cost $\gamma > 0$ for the entrepreneur (or, more generally, the firm's insiders[6]).

For example, the interim action could consist in switching to a more routine but also more profitable strategy,[7] severing a long-time relationship with a collaborator, firing workers, or divesting a division that management is eager to run. There is then a tradeoff between profitability and insiders' welfare. We assume that this interim action cannot be contracted upon at the initial (financing) stage. By contrast, the parties can contract on who is entitled to decide.[8] The choices of p (the moral-hazard dimension) and of the interim action both exhibit a potential conflict of interest between entrepreneur and investors. Unlike for the moral-hazard dimension, though, the choice of the interim action need not be delegated to the entrepreneur.

We look at whether the choice between this action and the status quo action is to be allocated either to investors or to insiders. The modified timing is described in Figure 10.1, where we indicate with bold letters the modification to the basic fixed-investment model of Chapter 3.

The assumption that the profit-enhancing action is orthogonal to managerial moral hazard, i.e., raises the probability of success uniformly, simplifies the analysis since it does not affect the incentive compatibility condition: if the profit-enhancing action is to be taken, then the incentive constraint becomes

$$[(p_{\mathrm{H}}+\tau)-(p_{\mathrm{L}}+\tau)]R_{\mathrm{b}} \geqslant B$$

4. See also Hart (2001) for a clear exposition of the importance of control rights for financial contracting.

5. Needless to say, τ must not be "too large," i.e., $p_{\mathrm{H}}+\tau \leqslant 1$.

6. The quid pro quo between management and employees may induce the former to internalize some of the latter's concerns. See, for example, Pagano and Volpin (2005) for some modeling and implications of this quid pro quo.

7. Think of an academically oriented software or biotech entrepreneur whose choice of research orientation affects her future job market opportunities or her intrinsic motivation on the job.

8. As discussed in footnote 2, if the interim action and the status quo are identified at the contract design stage, the contract can simply specify which course of action will be selected. In contrast, suppose that *either* the payoffs attached to the various actions known at the initial date are not yet known at this date *or* that the actions cannot even be described *ex ante*. In that case, the players' interim information about the actions and their payoffs must be elicited at the interim stage. It turns out that in this model a focus on control rights is not restrictive, although the optimal (complete) contract may involve a randomization over who will have the control right (which does not affect the qualitative implications derived below).

For other and more sophisticated examples of situations in which the optimal complete contract takes the form of a simple institution, see, for example, Aghion and Tirole (1997), Che and Hausch (1999), Hart and Moore (1999), Maskin and Tirole (1999b), Nöldeke and Schmidt (1998), Segal (1995, 1999), and Tirole (1999). A broad and very useful framework for the analysis of the limits on the effectiveness of complete contracts when these can be renegotiated was developed by Segal and Whinston (2002), building on Maskin and Moore (1999) and Green and Laffont (1992, 1994).

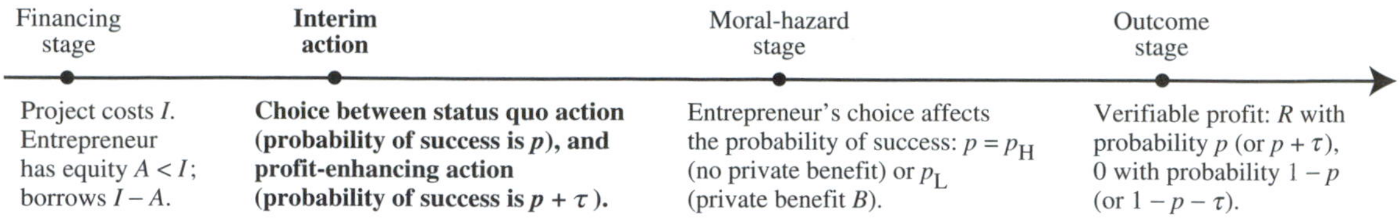
Financing stage
Interim action
Moral-hazard stage
Outcome stage
Project costs I. Entrepreneur has equity A < I; borrows I − A.
Choice between status quo action (probability of success is p), and profit-enhancing action (probability of success is p + τ).
Entrepreneur's choice affects the probability of success: p = pH (no private benefit) or pL (private benefit B).
Verifiable profit: R with probability p (or p + τ), 0 with probability 1 − p (or 1 − p − τ).

Figure 10.1 Control rights.

or

$$(p_{\mathrm{H}} - p_{\mathrm{L}})R_{\mathrm{b}} \geqslant B,$$

where R_{b} is the borrower's reward in the case of success. Note that τ does not enter the incentive constraint. For this reason, it does not matter whether the action is selected before (as in Figure 10.1) or after the managerial moral-hazard stage.

Let us first focus on the interesting case in which the profit-enhancing action reduces aggregate welfare and is thus *first-best* suboptimal:

$$\tau R < \gamma.$$

Suppose that the control right is given to the investors. Because they share part of the profit and bear none of the cost, they indeed select the profit-enhancing action, resulting in pledgeable income:

$$(p_{\mathrm{H}} + \tau)\left[R - \frac{B}{(p_{\mathrm{H}} + \tau) - (p_{\mathrm{L}} + \tau)}\right] = (p_{\mathrm{H}} + \tau)\left[R - \frac{B}{\Delta p}\right].$$

Because investors do not earn supranormal profits in a competitive capital market (they break even), the NPV is also the entrepreneur's welfare when raising funds. This NPV must account for both the increase τ in the probability of success and the entrepreneur's cost γ associated with the interim action:

$$U_{\mathrm{b}} = \mathrm{NPV} = (p_{\mathrm{H}} + \tau)R - I - \gamma.$$

The reader may wonder whether the entrepreneur and the investors would not want to renegotiate from the profit-enhancing action to the total-surplus-maximizing, status quo action after the investment has been sunk and before the interim action is selected. That is, would the Coase Theorem not imply that the two parties should not anticipate the profit-enhancing action? There is, however, no renegotiation since the entrepreneur has no money to compensate investors for the loss of value on their claims.[9]

Suppose in contrast that the entrepreneur does not relinquish control. Because $R_{\mathrm{b}} \leqslant R$, $\tau R_{\mathrm{b}} < \gamma$, and therefore the entrepreneur does not pick the profit-enhancing action. In words, the entrepreneur bears the entire cost and gets only part of the benefits of the profit-enhancing action. The pledgeable income is, as in Chapter 3,

$$p_{\mathrm{H}}\left(R - \frac{B}{\Delta p}\right),$$

and the NPV (i.e., the entrepreneur's payoff) is

$$p_{\mathrm{H}}R - I > (p_{\mathrm{H}} + \tau)R - I - \gamma.$$

As expected, allocating control to investors reduces the NPV by $\gamma - \tau R > 0$. But it increases pledgeable income by $\tau[R - (B/\Delta p)]$.

Suppose now that

$$p_{\mathrm{H}}\left(R - \frac{B}{\Delta p}\right) < I - A < (p_{\mathrm{H}} + \tau)\left(R - \frac{B}{\Delta p}\right).$$

Then the entrepreneur has insufficient cash on hand and can raise funds only by relinquishing the control right to the investors.[10] This first-best suboptimal

9. The entrepreneur might, of course, keep enough wealth (keep some of her cash on hand A or even receive money from investors at the financing stage) in order to be able to compensate investors for surrendering control over the interim action. But then, why would the entrepreneur not just keep the control right in the first place (which is what we study next)? Giving the control right to investors to then buy it back does not alter the basic constraint that the entrepreneur is facing: she must allow investors to break even on average! We leave it to the reader to make this loose reasoning more rigorous.

10. Note that we allow only a "0/1 allocation" of the control right. Optimally, the entrepreneur would want to relinquish control stochastically under the set of inequalities just stated: that is, to give control to investors with probability x, and to retain control with probability $1-x$, such that $(p_{\mathrm{H}} + x\tau)(R - B/\Delta p) = I - A$. A continuous allocation of control is far fetched in the situation considered here, but is less so once we consider the extensions developed later in the chapter. First, the existence of multiple control rights (Section 10.2.2) provides for a more continuous allocation of control (see Exercise 10.9 for a limit case of many control rights). Second, the entrepreneur's real authority

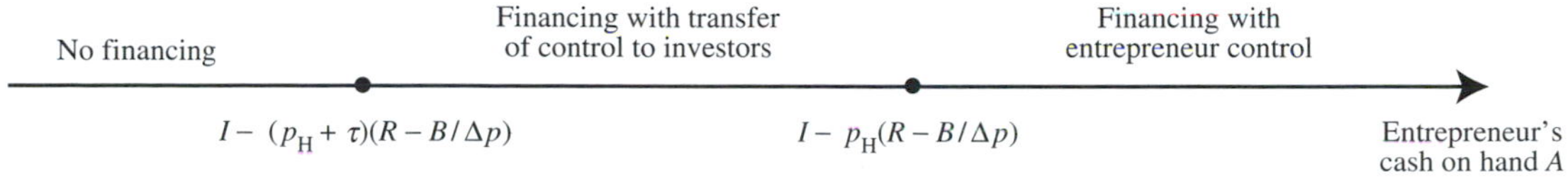

Figure 10.2

choice can thus be second-best optimal once imperfections in the credit market are accounted for.

Note the strong analogy with the strategy of costly collateral pledging under moral hazard. In Section 4.3 we noted that an entrepreneur who has insufficient pledgeable income may want to boost pledgeable income by pledging collateral that has more value to her than to the investors. Costly collateral pledging was thus first-best suboptimal (reduced the NPV), but was second-best optimal, as it allowed the entrepreneur to raise funds. Here, as in Section 4.3, the entrepreneur cannot commit to return the full value of the project to the investors and so there may not be enough pledgeable income to attract financing. Allocating control to investors enables the entrepreneur to commit, albeit in an inefficient way, to return money to investors.

This reasoning actually provides us with an *argument in favor of shareholder value* (see Section 1.8), or more precisely in favor of "investor value," since the model does not distinguish between different types of investor: a substantial initial investment by investors requires sufficient pledgeable income and therefore may force the entrepreneur to relinquish a right even when this reduces value in a first-best sense.[11]

Figure 10.2 summarizes the analysis so far.

Lastly, we note that the allocation of control is a trivial issue when investor control is first-best optimal, that is, when

$$\tau R > \gamma.$$

In this case, investor control increases both the NPV from $p_H R - I$ to $(p_H + \tau)R - I - \gamma$ and the pledgeable income from $p_H(R - B/\Delta p)$ to $(p_H + \tau)(R - B/\Delta p)$. In words, giving control to investors both facilitates financing and, when financing occurs, increases the utility of the entrepreneur, who gains more in reduced investors' stake than she loses through the loss in control.[12]

Reinterpretation (going public). As usual, the investment model can be reinterpreted as one in which the firm already operates, but must borrow in order to finance growth prospects. The prediction in this context is that the entrepreneur may have to surrender control in order to be able to finance growth. One important channel through which entrepreneurs relinquish control is the going-public process. Entrepreneurs often issue new shares with voting rights and thereby lose the control majority in their firm.[13] Conversely, entrepreneurs often prefer to sacrifice growth and keep control over operating, investment, and personnel decisions (for example, staying private may enable them to select their heirs as successors; not being able to select one's heir is akin to the cost γ in the model).

(Section 10.3) varies more continuously, especially if one considers an environment that is uncertain at the date at which rights are allocated but less so at the date at which decisions are taken; in this context, the composition of the board (with more or less independent members) also provides for a more continuous allocation of control (as in Hermalin and Weisbach 1988).

11. Hart (1995b) makes a similar argument when discussing the possibility of a statutory rule requesting companies to have worker representatives on the board. He observes that such a rule may discourage a company from setting up in the first place, given that it may no longer lay off workers in the event of an adverse demand shock (p. 687).

12. Note, furthermore, that allocating control to the entrepreneur is not credible anyway: because entrepreneur control results in a first-best inefficient action, there are gains to transferring control to investors at the interim stage. Furthermore, investors have cash to compensate the entrepreneur for the loss of control. Hence, entrepreneur control is always renegotiated away. This is a key difference with the case of investor control when $\gamma > \tau R$, for which investor control was inefficient but not renegotiated away as long as the entrepreneur invests her cash on hand in the project.

13. Share dilution is not the only way entrepreneurs lose control when they go public. As Boot et al. (2005) note, they also lose control in more insidious ways, due to the regulations they must abide by (restrictions on board composition, information disclosure, shareholder voting rights, and so forth).

In that paper, the cost γ of going public is modeled in a different way relative to this chapter: Boot et al. assume that the entrepreneur and the investors have different priors (heterogeneous beliefs) about profitability, but that there is no adverse selection (each party knows the other party's beliefs, and they just "agree to disagree"). Thus, the investors' preferred action is viewed as suboptimal by the entrepreneur, who is willing to incur costs in order to retain control.

10.2.2 Multiple Control Rights

In practice, there are *multiple control rights* to be divided between insiders and outsiders: product design, day-to-day management, long-term strategic decisions, hiring decisions, mergers, alliance building, etc. The analysis above is straightforwardly generalized.[14] The intuition derived from the single-control-right analysis suggests, and this section confirms, that, in the presence of multiple control rights, it is always optimal for the entrepreneur to abandon *all* rights for which investor control is first-best optimal as well as, possibly, *some* rights for which it is not. Again, the optimal split of rights accounts not only for the value (NPV) impact of the allocation, but also for its impact on pledgeable income.

More formally, and generalizing the framework of Section 10.2.1 to multiple rights, suppose there are K dimensions of decision making and therefore K rights to allocate. Each right $k \in \{1, \dots, K\}$ is characterized by the uniform increase $\tau_k > 0$ in the probability of success and the cost $\gamma_k > 0$ borne by insiders if the course of action is altered in dimension k. The governance structure is now defined by the allocation $x \equiv \{x_1, \dots, x_K\}$ of formal control rights, where $x_k = 1$ if investors obtain the control of decision k and $x_k = 0$ if the entrepreneur retains control.

Let us maximize the NPV (that is, the entrepreneur's utility) subject to being able to secure financing and to the entrepreneur's incentive compatibility constraint:

$$\max_{\{R_b, x\}} \left\{ \left[p_H + \sum_k \tau_k x_k \right] R - I - \sum_k \gamma_k x_k \right\}$$

s.t.

$$\left[p_H + \sum \tau_k x_k \right] [R - R_b] \geqslant I - A,$$

$$R_b \geqslant \frac{B}{\Delta p}.$$

The solution to this program has the following features in the interesting case in which the financing constraint is binding:[15] there exists a threshold $\theta < 1$ such that investors receive control over decision k if and only if their *relative willingness* to pay for that right exceeds the threshold, that is, if and only if[16]

$$\frac{\tau_k R}{\gamma_k} \geqslant \theta.$$

As one would expect, it is optimal for the entrepreneur to abandon to investors those rights that matter most to them and for which investor control will not create large negative externalities on the entrepreneur.[17] Conversely, the entrepreneur should keep control over decisions that matter most to her and are unlikely to have a substantial negative

14. See Aghion and Tirole (1997) for the derivation in a different context.

15. Let μ denote the shadow price of the financing constraint. In the interesting case in which μ is strictly positive, then $R_b = B/\Delta p$, and the derivative of the Lagrangian with respect to x_k is equal to $[\tau_k R - \gamma_k] + \mu \tau_k [R - B/\Delta p]$. The first term is just the (first-best) efficiency of taking the profitability-enhancing stance on decision k, while the second term reflects the benefits in terms of relaxing the financing constraint. Clearly, $x_k = 1$ only if

$$\frac{\tau_k R}{\gamma_k} \geqslant \frac{1}{1 + \mu(1 - B/R\Delta p)}.$$

Note that $R \geqslant B/\Delta p$ (otherwise, the entrepreneur could not borrow) and so the threshold is smaller than 1.

The financing constraint is in general not satisfied with equality if the x_k are constrained to take values 0 or 1. In order not to leave a rent to investors, the entrepreneur must in general make the allocation of the marginal right (that is, the right k_0 with the lowest ratio $\tau_k R/\gamma_k$ among the rights granted to the investors) random ($0 < x_{k_0} < 1$).

The less interesting case, in which the investor breakeven constraint is not binding ($\mu = 0$), admits solution

$$x_k = 1 \quad \text{if and only if } \tau_k R > \gamma_k$$

(ignoring the nongeneric case in which $\tau_k R = \gamma_k$ for some k). That is, the allocation of control is always efficient.

16. This condition is presented in its simpler form; we leave it to the reader to check that it is equivalent to ordering, for the various rights, the investors' benefit from control divided by the entrepreneur's benefit from control and setting a cutoff over which investors receive control.

17. As in the case of a single control right, we briefly discuss the possibility of renegotiation: might an allocation of rights that is not first-best efficient be renegotiated before the control rights are exercised? The only rights for which the allocation is not first-best efficient (i.e., those with $\theta \leqslant \tau_k R/\gamma_k < 1$) are rights that are given to investors. Let us first assume that the entrepreneur has committed her cash on hand A and borrowed only what is needed to fund the investment cost, $I - A$ (it turns out to be optimal to do so). Then the entrepreneur no longer has any means of payment after securing financing, the entrepreneur has no way to compensate the investors for relinquishing these rights. In other words, there are potential gains from trade *ex post*, but these gains cannot be reaped in the absence of compensating transfer (technically, utility is "nontransferable").

As we noted in the single-control-right case, though, the entrepreneur could keep some cash so as to be able to renegotiate and "reacquire" some control rights that are initially allocated to investors, but for which investor control is first-best inefficient (control rights for which the initial allocation yields the first-best efficient exercise are not renegotiated since renegotiation cannot deliver *ex post* gains from trade). But then, such control rights could be directly allocated to the entrepreneur. The two constraints in the maximization of the NPV would still need to be satisfied (in net terms for R_b), and so the entrepreneur cannot do better by creating scope for renegotiation. We conclude that the optimal allocation of rights obtained above is not renegotiated.

impact on profitability. To give a trivial illustration of this, consider the CEO's decision over what to eat for lunch at the headquarters' dining room. Shareholders may have a preference for a fish diet, because it reduces the CEO's probability of heart attack during her tenure very slightly relative to meat. Yet, one would expect $\tau_k R$ to be very small relative to γ_k and so the choice would be left to the CEO. The same applies to most so-called "personal decisions."

The entrepreneur's incentive constraint is then binding ($R_b = B/\Delta p$). Intuitively, the entrepreneur prefers to pay investors in the "efficient" currency (cash, which is one-for-one) than in the "inefficient" one (control rights, whose transfer involves a deadweight loss). The conclusions are again analogous to those reached in Chapter 4 as to the allocation of costly collateral. There, we saw that the entrepreneur prefers to pledge collateral that investors value relatively most; and, of course, money is the best collateral.[18]

An important implication of this analysis is that, ceteris paribus, *firms with stronger balance sheets* (say, with a higher A; see Section 3.2.2 for a broader definition of balance-sheet strength) *abandon fewer rights*. This prediction fits with the evidence. Firms with strong balance sheets (high initial equity, strong collateral, safe income stream) obtain financing on markets, where they relinquish only a few control rights by including some covenants. Firms with intermediate balance sheets relinquish a few more control rights through more restrictive and extensive covenants when they deal with banks. Firms with weak balance sheets, such as high-tech start-ups which have little equity, collateral, and guaranteed income, relinquish most control rights to, say, venture capitalists.

Lerner et al. (2003) analyze the assignment of what industry practitioners perceive to be the five key control rights in alliances between small biotechnology (R&D) firms and pharmaceutical corporations in the United States: (1) "management of clinical trials" (the alliance may seek regulatory approval on a given bioengineered product for a variety of uses, some of which may compete with the pharmaceutical company's existing products); (2) "control of the initial manufacturing process";[19] (3) "control of manufacturing after product approval" (the move of the production to the pharmaceutical company's facilities requires an extensive and time-consuming review by the Food and Drug Administration); (4) "retention of all sales categories for financing firm" (who gets the right to control marketing by disease or country); and (5) "ability to exclude the R&D firm from all aspects of the marketing process."[20]

Lerner et al. find that the R&D firm retains more control rights when it is in a stronger financial position; and that projects that are in their early stages and are thereby presumably subject to more significant agency costs are associated with more control rights transferred to the pharmaceutical company. Lastly, contracts signed at times when little external financing can be raised in public equity markets assign the most control rights to the pharmaceutical company. All three observations fit well with the theoretical prediction.

10.2.3 Contingent Rights

Control rights are often contingent on some observable event. For instance, a start-up entrepreneur loses some of her control rights when failing to meet some targets. Kaplan and Strömberg (2003, 2004) provide evidence that founders obtain or retain more control rights as performance improves and, relatedly, have more control rights in later-stage financings (which occur only if previous performance was satisfactory, because poor performance in early stages may interrupt refinancing).

18. A second parallel with collateral pledging is that in both cases the inefficiency is not renegotiated away.

19. A drug is approved in the United States not as a matter of general principle, but rather only as manufactured in a particular facility. To get approval in another manufacturing facility requires an extensive review process. As a result, whichever party in an alliance in whose facility the drug is manufactured has an important advantage over his partner: even if the other party has the contractual right to terminate the alliance and to manufacture the drug in its own facility, it will be quite costly for that party to do so.

20. The smaller biotech company, seeking to develop its skills as a marketing organization (which many perceive as an essential step in becoming a fully integrated pharmaceutical firm), is often given the right to sell the drug alongside the pharmaceutical firm. In some cases, this means that the two firms' sales representatives sell the drug independently in the same territory; in others, that the biotech company's sales force plays a support role (e.g., they hire salesmen who provided technical backup to the pharmaceutical firm's "frontline" sales force); in yet others, the firms' sales forces take the lead in different market niches (e.g., the biotech firm's sales force might take the lead while selling to the military).

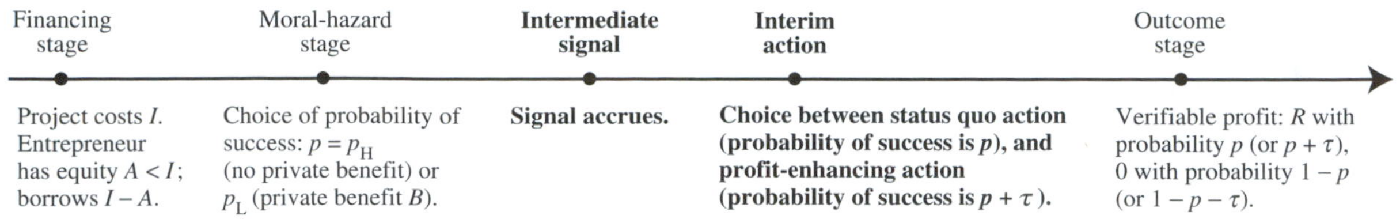
Financing stage
Moral-hazard stage
Intermediate signal
Interim action
Outcome stage
Project costs I. Entrepreneur has equity $A < I$; borrows $I - A$.
Choice of probability of success: $p = p_{\rm H}$ (no private benefit) or $p_{\rm L}$ (private benefit B).
Signal accrues.
Choice between status quo action (probability of success is p), and profit-enhancing action (probability of success is $p + \tau$).
Verifiable profit: R with probability p (or $p + \tau$), 0 with probability $1 - p$ (or $1 - p - \tau$).

Figure 10.3 Contingent control right.

The transfer of control rights is often made contingent on verifiable variables. For example, the venture capitalist obtains voting control if the firm's EBIT (earnings before interest and taxes) falls below some amount, or obtains board control if the firm's "net worth," here measured by the cumulative cash flow to date, falls below some threshold.[21] The transfer of control may also be contingent on nonfinancial performance variables: tests of product functionality, approval of the new drug by the Federal Drug Administration, or patent approval. One mechanism for the transfer of control is the automatic conversion provisions (see Black and Gilson 1998; Kaplan and Strömberg 2003); for example, the venture capitalist loses his superior control, voting, board, and liquidation rights when the firm completes a "successful" IPO (its stock sells at a price above some prespecified threshold) and his convertible preferred stock and debt are then converted into common stock.

Contingent control rights resemble multiple ones: the rights to control the same decision in multiple states of nature are de facto multiple rights (one right per state). An important insight is, however, specific to contingent rights: if the right is contingent on some measure of performance, it can act as a reward and relax the incentive constraint. The allocation of the control right then contributes directly and indirectly to securing financing, where the indirect effect refers to the motivational impact of the threat of losing control in case of bad performance. In general, *making control rights contingent enhances managerial incentives and boosts borrowing capacity.*

To illustrate this, consider the choice of a close collaborator for a software entrepreneur or a restaurant owner. Suppose that hiring a friend (or a family member) of the entrepreneur provides for a more pleasant work environment for the entrepreneur, while hiring a stranger with slightly better qualifications or a sharper profit focus would increase the probability of success. It may then make sense to let the entrepreneur pick her close collaborator, and if targets are not met (e.g., short-term losses are registered) to authorize the investors to replace the collaborator. Venture capital contracts discussed above provide another motivation.

Suppose that the control right is exercised after the entrepreneur's choice of effort and after a signal about entrepreneurial performance accrues (see Figure 10.3).

The signal can be high (H) or low (L). For effort i (high if the entrepreneur behaves or low if the entrepreneur misbehaves), the probability of signal j is σ_{ij}. As in Chapter 8, let us simplify the analysis by assuming that the signal is a sufficient statistic for learning about entrepreneurial effort; that is, the final outcome conveys no further information (beyond that contained in the signal) about the choice of effort. We know that the entrepreneur should be rewarded only as a function of the realization of the signal.[22] Let $R_{\rm b}$ denote the entrepreneur's reward in the case of a high signal (the reward is optimally set equal to 0 in the case of a low signal).

With *noncontingent* investor control, the entrepreneur's incentive compatibility constraint is

$$(\sigma_{\rm HH} - \sigma_{\rm LH})R_{\rm b} \geqslant B,$$

since she bears cost γ regardless of the realization of the signal. So, with a noncontingent control right

21. Note that earnings and cumulative cash flows are verifiable accounting variables. Market values cannot be used as contingencies for unlisted companies.

22. We could, therefore, have omitted the signal and made the allocation of the control right contingent on the outcome; this requires, however, that the decision is taken after the outcome is realized, which is less natural unless the outcome itself stands for an intermediate performance.

allocated to the investors,[23] the pledgeable income is

$$(p_{\mathrm{H}} + \tau)R - \sigma_{\mathrm{HH}}\left[\frac{B}{\sigma_{\mathrm{HH}} - \sigma_{\mathrm{LH}}}\right].$$

With *contingent* control, the entrepreneur both is rewarded and retains control in the case of a high signal (i.e., she both receives R_{b} and avoids cost γ when the signal is high), and so the incentive constraint becomes

$$(\sigma_{\mathrm{HH}} - \sigma_{\mathrm{LH}})(R_{\mathrm{b}} + \gamma) \geqslant B.$$

A contingent control right thus yields pledgeable income

$$(p_{\mathrm{H}} + \sigma_{\mathrm{HL}}\tau)R - \sigma_{\mathrm{HH}}\left[\frac{B}{\sigma_{\mathrm{HH}} - \sigma_{\mathrm{LH}}} - \gamma\right].$$

Contingent control therefore increases the pledgeable income and facilitates financing relative to noncontingent control allocated to investors if and only if

$$\sigma_{\mathrm{HH}}\gamma > (1 - \sigma_{\mathrm{HL}})\tau R \quad \text{or} \quad \gamma > \tau R.$$

This is nothing but the condition under which investor control is first-best suboptimal. This is no "coincidence": starting from noncontingent control, allocating control to the entrepreneur in the case of a good signal increases, in that state, her payoff (in absolute terms but also relatively to the low signal case) by γ but reduces the expected revenue by τR. This explains why first-best suboptimality is also the condition under which contingent control increases pledgeable income in this simple model.

Finally, note the strong analogy with the treatment of contingent collateral in Section 4.3.4, where we show that collateral is optimally pledged in the case of failure. This analogy is not fortuitous. When investor control destroys value, allocating control to investors is like allocating collateral that is valued more highly by the borrower than by the investors. In both cases, a contingent allocation boosts borrower incentives and reduces the agency cost.

10.2.4 Control Rights and the Protection of Noncontractible Investments

The analysis so far has focused on the connection between the allocation of control and the entrepreneur's borrowing capacity. The literature on control rights, in contrast, has often emphasized the relationship between the protection of specific investments, i.e., investments that are valuable only if they are used in the context of a specific relationship between two parties, and asset ownership, where asset ownership confers the right to determine the use of the asset (see, primarily, the work of Grossman and Hart (1986) and Hart and Moore (1990), as well as that by Klein et al. (1978) and Williamson (1985)).[24]

A typical environment in that literature involves a bilateral relationship between a "buyer" and a "seller" who sink noncontractible relationship-specific investments.[25] There are two key themes:

• Having control over assets that are used to create value within the relationship allows their owner to threaten to take the assets away and deal with a third party (another seller if the owner is a buyer, another buyer if the owner is a seller). The existence of such "outside options"[26] enables the owner to bargain for a larger share of the total surplus if the two parties need to renegotiate during the course of their relationship. That is, the allocation of control affects the sharing of the pie in the event of future renegotiation.

• The sharing of the surplus matters in particular if one or two parties to the relationship sink specific investments. The specific-investment-based theory of asset ownership has repeatedly stressed that asset ownership boosts the owner's incentive to invest.[27]

23. A *noncontingent* control right allocated to the entrepreneur yields a lower pledgeable income.

24. Applications of the specific-investment theory of control rights to cash-constrained entrepreneurs and innovation include Aghion and Tirole (1994) and Lerner and Malmendier (2005).

25. In applications, who is the "buyer" and who is the "seller" is sometimes a matter of convention. The theory is, however, often motivated by examples of a supplier of an input (e.g., automobile parts) to a downstream producer (e.g., car manufacturer).

26. A corporate finance example of the exercise of an outside option is the replacement of the current CEO by a new CEO by the board of directors. (Who is the "buyer" and who is the "seller" are questions of semantics (see previous footnote). The board of directors acts on behalf of investors who are the suppliers of capital. The CEO is the supplier of managerial skills and effort.)

27. We have shown earlier in the chapter that lenders have more incentive to invest in the firm if they receive the control rights. A difference with the result mentioned here is that Section 10.2.1 assumed that the lenders' specific investment $(I - A)$ can be contracted upon. The holdup literature, in contrast, assumes that specific investments cannot be contracted upon, but in general does not rely on the existence of cash constraints.

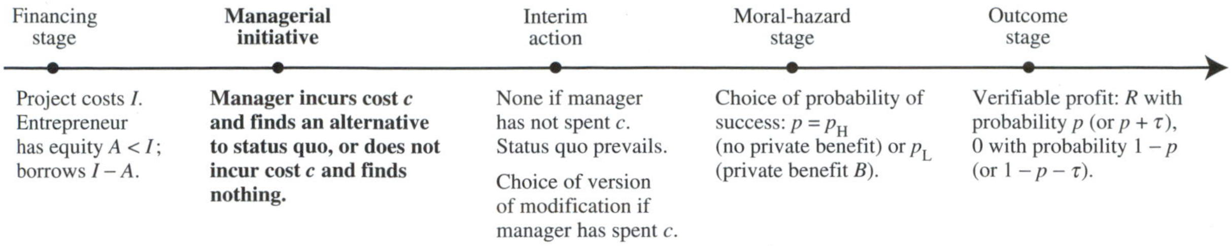
Financing stage
Managerial initiative
Interim action
Moral-hazard stage
Outcome stage
Project costs I. Entrepreneur has equity A < I; borrows I − A.
Manager incurs cost c and finds an alternative to status quo, or does not incur cost c and finds nothing.
None if manager has not spent c. Status quo prevails.
Choice of version of modification if manager has spent c.
Choice of probability of success: p = p_H (no private benefit) or p_L (private benefit B).
Verifiable profit: R with probability p (or p + τ), 0 with probability 1 − p (or 1 − p − τ).

Figure 10.4

This section, in contrast, ignores threats of trading with alternative parties;[28] rather, it analyzes the impact of the allocation of control on the borrower's incentive to come up with improvements to the original project. (Section 10.3 will further the analysis of managerial initiative by stressing the role of informational asymmetries rather than that of the allocation of control.)

Suppose that, in the model of Section 10.2.1, the idea leading to a potential modification of the initial project does not come out of the blue, but rather necessitates managerial initiative. As indicated in Figure 10.4, the borrower must sink some unobservable, private cost c in order to come up with an alternative to the status quo. For simplicity, only the borrower can find a relevant alternative.

In the absence of managerial initiative (the borrower does not spend c), the status quo prevails: the probability of success is $p = p_{\text{H}}$ or $p = p_{\text{L}}$ depending on the borrower's later behavior. Managerial initiative results in the possibility of modifying the initial project. This possibility becomes common knowledge as it arises.[29] The modification, however, comes in two versions.

Borrower-friendly version: relative to the status quo, the modification increases the probability of success by τ_{b} and creates a private benefit $-\gamma_{\text{b}} > 0$ for the borrower;

Lender-friendly version: the modification increases the probability of success by τ_{l} and creates a private benefit $-\gamma_{\text{l}}$ for the borrower, with $\tau_{\text{l}} > \tau_{\text{b}} > 0$ and $(-\gamma_{\text{b}}) > (-\gamma_{\text{l}}) > 0$.

Note that the insiders' "cost" from the profit-enhancing action is now a benefit. This assumption guarantees that the entrepreneur is made better off when coming up with a possible modification, even though the latter becomes common knowledge (and thereby could hurt the entrepreneur in the absence of this assumption).

At the interim action stage, the choice of version may be the object of renegotiation if both parties can benefit from it. That is, if the privately optimal choice of version by the party in control is collectively inefficient (and so there are potential gains from renegotiation) and if the other party has the means to compensate the former for the change of version, then renegotiation occurs. Note that, since there are only two versions, it does not matter whether the interim action (the choice of version) becomes contractible at the interim stage or not: renegotiation can indifferently take the form of a transfer of control or of the specification of a particular version if feasible. We will assume that the entrepreneur then has the bargaining power (makes a take-it-or-leave-it offer to investors).[30]

Let us make the following three assumptions.

• In the relevant range of rewards R_{b} (i.e., rewards that are consistent with the investors' breakeven condition), the borrower ranks the borrower-friendly version over the lender-friendly version (from our previous assumptions, both are preferred to the status quo):

$$\tau_{\text{b}} R_{\text{b}} - \gamma_{\text{b}} > \tau_{\text{l}} R_{\text{b}} - \gamma_{\text{l}} > 0.$$

28. While much of the literature has focused on the interaction between control and outside options, there have also been a number of contributions analyzing the allocation of control when control rights do not boost the value of these outside options; recent entries along the latter line include Aghion et al. (2004) and Hart and Moore (2004).

29. If only because the borrower has to exposit it if she wants investors to act upon it or to renegotiate.

30. This is indeed an assumption, since it is not implied by the fact that investors are competitive (and therefore have no bargaining power) *ex ante*.

We already know that lenders prefer the lender-friendly version to the borrower-friendly version, and the latter to the status quo:

$$\tau_l > \tau_b > 0$$

(and so the lenders benefit from managerial initiative even if the borrower-friendly version is implemented). Thus, both parties want to move away from the status quo, but they disagree on the version.

• Investor control is *ex post* (first best) optimal and initiative is desirable:

$$\tau_l R - \gamma_l > \tau_b R - \gamma_b > c.$$

• For expositional simplicity, we focus on contracts that specify an incentive-compatible stake $R_b \geqslant B/\Delta p$. As footnotes will indicate as we proceed through the analysis, this focus involves no loss of generality. (Furthermore, the reader may ignore *ex post* moral hazard by setting $B = 0$ if (s)he wants. This section is primarily focused on the agency cost associated with noncontractible managerial initiative.)

Even though investor control is ex post efficient, we will show that investor control may not be desirable, and that, for given stakes, investors may even be worse off from having control.

First, note that if the borrower comes up with a potential modification, the selected version is always the efficient, lender-friendly one:

Investor control. Investors, when having control, choose the lender-friendly version, which is not renegotiated because there are no gains to renegotiation. The borrower demonstrates initiative if and only if[31]

$$\tau_l R_b - \gamma_l \geqslant c.$$

As usual, the entrepreneur's utility is equal to the total value minus what is appropriated by the investors. So, we can rewrite this condition in terms of a comparison between the increase in NPV brought about by initiative, $(\tau_l R - \gamma_l) - c$, and the investors' "free-riding benefit," $\tau_l(R - R_b)$, namely, the extra rent that they automatically enjoy when the borrower spends c:

$$(\tau_l R - \gamma_l) - c \geqslant \tau_l(R - R_b).$$

Entrepreneur control. Without initiative, the entrepreneur obtains $p_H R_b$.

With initiative, the entrepreneur can use her control over versioning to offer to choose the lender-friendly version against a higher stake $R'_b > R_b$ in the case of success.[32] Knowing that the borrower chooses the borrower-friendly version if they refuse the offer, the lenders accept to renegotiate as long as[33]

$$(p_H + \tau_l)(R - R'_b) \geqslant (p_H + \tau_b)(R - R_b).$$

The borrower thus chooses the highest value R'_b such that this inequality is satisfied. And so the borrower obtains utility

$$\begin{aligned}(p_H + \tau_l)R'_b - \gamma_l - c \\ &= (p_H + \tau_l)R - \gamma_l - (p_H + \tau_b)(R - R_b) - c.\end{aligned}$$

The borrower demonstrates initiative if and only if this utility exceeds $p_H R_b$, which can be written as[34]

$$(\tau_l R - \gamma_l) - c \geqslant \tau_b(R - R_b).$$

31. How would this analysis be altered if $R_b < B/\Delta p$? In the absence of initiative, the contract might be renegotiated to be incentive compatible ($R'_b \geqslant B/\Delta p$) with $p_H(R - R'_b) = p_L(R - R_b)$ (recall that the borrower has the bargaining power in renegotiation). Similarly, under borrower initiative, the contract might be renegotiated to R''_b such that $(p_H + \tau_l)(R - R''_b) = (p_L + \tau_l)(R - R_b)$. Furthermore, renegotiation occurs in the absence of initiative if it occurs in its presence. Suppose, first, that there is renegotiation in both cases. The borrower then spends c if and only if

$$(p_H + \tau_l)R''_b - \gamma_l - c \geqslant p_H R'_b \quad \text{or} \quad (\tau_l R - \gamma_l) - c \geqslant \tau_l(R - R_b),$$

which is the same condition as when $R_b \geqslant B/\Delta p$. If renegotiation fails in the presence of initiative, but occurs in its absence, then the incentive to demonstrate initiative is even smaller.

32. The entrepreneur could also ask for a lump-sum (not performance-based) payment over and above R_b. This does not alter the analysis when $R_b \geqslant B/\Delta p$ and is dominated if $R_b < B/\Delta p$.

33. The borrower would like to threaten to choose the status quo ($\tau = 0$) if the investors refuse to renegotiate, so as to force the latter to make even more concessions. This threat, however, is not credible, as it is indeed in the borrower's interest to choose the borrower-friendly version when the renegotiation has failed.

34. Again, let us check that this condition is unaltered if the initial contract specifies a stake that is not incentive compatible: $R_b < B/\Delta p$. In the absence of initiative, the contract may be renegotiated to an incentive-compatible level R'_b such that $p_H(R - R'_b) = p_L(R - R_b)$, in which case the borrower's utility becomes $p_H R'_b$.

In the presence of initiative, the contract may be renegotiated to R''_b such that $(p_H + \tau_l)(R - R''_b) = (p_L + \tau_b)(R - R_b)$. As in footnote 31, one can sequentially consider the situation in which renegotiation occurs in both cases, and that in which it occurs only in the absence of initiative. In the former case, for example, the borrower's utility is then $(p_H + \tau_l)R - \gamma_l - (p_L + \tau_b)(R - R_b) - c$. The borrower is willing to spend c provided that $(\tau_l R - \gamma_l) - c \geqslant \tau_b(R - R_b)$.

To sum up, total value in the absence or presence of initiative is unaffected by the allocation of control since under borrower control there is renegotiation to implement the version that yields the highest NPV.[35] What is altered by the allocation of control is the extent of investor free riding on the borrower's initiative: for all R_b,

$$\tau_b(R - R_b) < \tau_l(R - R_b).$$

Put differently, *the borrower appropriates more of the return on her noncontractible investment when she has control over the decision.*[36]

Finally, we show that entrepreneur control may *increase* pledgeable income and thereby facilitate financing.[37] Focusing on initiative-inducing contracts (which, as noted in footnote 36, also solve *ex post* moral hazard if B is small enough),[38] investor control is inconsistent with borrower initiative and funding if

$$(p_H + \tau_l)(R - R_b) < I - A \tag{10.1}$$

for all R_b such that $\tau_l R_b - y_l \geqslant c$.

By contrast, entrepreneur control is consistent with borrower initiative and funding provided that

$$(p_H + \tau_b)(R - R_b) \geqslant I - A \tag{10.2}$$

for some R_b such that $(\tau_l R - y_l) - c \geqslant \tau_b(R - R_b)$.

35. This is actually a general result: renegotiation always leads to an *ex post* efficient outcome when the party under whose control the outcome is efficient has cash, that is, is not wealth constraint (and there is no asymmetry of information).

36. Note that if *ex post* moral hazard is small, i.e., B satisfies

$$\frac{c + y_l}{\tau_l} > \frac{c - (\tau_l - \tau_b)R + y_l}{\tau_b} > \frac{B}{\Delta p},$$

the stakes R_b that generate initiative are also *ex post* incentive compatible, i.e., satisfy $(\Delta p)R_b \geqslant B$.

37. Note the strong analogy with the basic moral-hazard model first developed in Section 3.2. There, we saw that an increase in the entrepreneur's stake directly hurts investors, but indirectly benefits them through enhanced managerial effort. Here, and similarly, entrepreneurial control directly hurts investors, but boosts entrepreneurial initiative. Like that of a higher managerial compensation, the net effect of entrepreneur control may be to boost pledgeable income, that is, to benefit investors.

38. With an *ex ante* competitive capital market, the lenders obtain no surplus, and so the entrepreneur receives the NPV. The issue is therefore how to induce initiative while generating enough pledgeable income to secure funding.

Finally, we could consider the case in which investors have (at least some) bargaining power at the renegotiation stage. Investors would still break even because the extra gains from renegotiation (which exist provided that the entrepreneur keeps enough motivation to demonstrate initiative) are competed away in the *ex ante* capital market.

Conditions (10.1) and (10.2) are consistent provided that

$$(p_H + \tau_l)\left(R - \frac{c + y_l}{\tau_l}\right) < (p_H + \tau_b)\left(\frac{\tau_l R - y_l - c}{\tau_b}\right)$$

$$\iff \quad \tau_l R - y_l > c,$$

which is the condition that initiative increases NPV.

Remark (ex post efficient investor control). We have assumed that investor control is *ex post* efficient. The analysis of the case in which entrepreneur control is *ex post* efficient is similar, with the following twist: when investors have control and therefore choose the inefficient version in the absence of renegotiation, renegotiation may not result in the efficient transfer of control to the entrepreneur (or, equivalently, an agreement on the efficient version). Indeed, the entrepreneur has no cash. She can offer a reduction of her stake from R_b to $R'_b \geqslant 0$, but this reduction (a) may not be sufficient to compensate investors or/and (b) may demotivate the entrepreneur (if $(\Delta p)R'_b < B$). Thus, renegotiation may be inefficient, unlike in the case considered here.

Remark (another perverse effect of investor control). Exercise 10.5 develops a different reason why investor control may make financing more difficult. In that exercise, the investors' exercise of control occurs simultaneously or after the entrepreneur's choice of effort and demotivates the entrepreneur by engaging in "damage control" (increasing the probability of success in the case of misbehavior at a private cost to the entrepreneur). The entrepreneur is then more tempted to misbehave; her stake must therefore be increased, which leads to a reduction in pledgeable income.

10.3 Corporate Governance and Real Control

Often players without formal control rights actually enjoy substantial control over their organizations.[39] To give two standard examples in the corporate finance area, it is well-known that boards of directors often rubber-stamp the top management's decisions, and that large minority shareholders often

39. This section is influenced by my joint work with Philippe Aghion (Aghion and Tirole 1997) on formal versus real authority.

decide for the majority group of smaller ones. The allocation of formal control thus cannot be the full story: there is "separation between ownership and control."

Leading theories in corporate finance do not always make a clear distinction between formal and real control. Rather, they often assume that *management* has the formal right to select various decisions such as long-term investments, dividends and retained earnings, new debt and other securities issues, the CEO's successor, and takeover defenses. These assumptions are, for the most part, factually inaccurate: in practice, management needs to refer to higher authorities (board, general assembly) for permission concerning many of these decisions.[40] The assumptions are also partly nonintuitive. To the extent that the governance structure is in charge of controlling management, it would seem that management would face strong conflicts of interest, in particular when making decisions that affect the firms's corporate governance.

This is not to say that management does not have a substantial influence on such decisions in practice. It does. Managers enjoy much power, though, in part because they have proprietary information that often enables them to get their way. So, while shareholders have formal control over a number of decisions, managers often have real control.

If managers end up making the decisions in the end, would it not be appropriate to assume directly, in "reduced form," that they have formal control? The answer is, in general, "no." By presuming that management decides, one is unable to analyze two key aspects of the corporate governance debate:

- first, the allocation of formal control rights (why must management defer to shareholders for some decisions, but not others? how is the allocation of control rights influenced by the firm's balance sheet?); and
- second, the impact of corporate governance institutions on managerial effective/real control over decisions (when formal control is given to investors, as is the case for many key decisions, the extent of actual control enjoyed by management is a function of the presence and incentives of active monitors, of the divergence of objectives among investors, and so forth).

It is preferable to start from first principles and then derive the conditions under which management gets its way either by procedural design or by lack of alternative for its principals.

10.3.1 Heuristics

To illustrate the benefits of starting from first principles, let us discuss the *extent* of real control by management. Assume that a number of actions are available, but that an action away from the status quo and chosen at random would have disastrous consequences. Only one action besides the status quo is "relevant" and it is *ex ante* unknown which action that is. Indeed, all actions *ex ante* look alike. Formal control belongs to investors (this can be justified, for example, by assuming that there is another action, which is preferred to all others by the entrepreneur and is disastrous for investors, i.e., it does not generate enough pledgeable income for the investors to break even).

Let us generalize the model of Section 10.2.1 slightly by assuming that

(a) the values of the increase, τ, in the probability of success and the cost, γ, to the insiders are random and unknown at the date of contracting;

(b) these values can be positive or negative,

$$\tau \gtrless 0 \quad \text{and} \quad \gamma \gtrless 0.$$

A negative τ means a profit-decreasing action, and a negative γ refers to a private benefit for the entrepreneur (beyond B, that obtained by shirking). Assume that the initial contract, besides allocating formal control to investors, specifies a compensation R_b for the entrepreneur in the case of success.

Suppose in a first step that the entrepreneur learns which is the relevant action as well as its payoff characteristics $\{\tau, \gamma\}$ at the interim stage, and that investors learn nothing. The entrepreneur can propose the action to investors (the description of the action, by itself, reveals no information about the values of τ and γ as all actions are identical in the

40. For example, corporate charter defenses (including staggered boards, supermajority rules, and so forth) require shareholder ratification. Poison pill plans may be adopted without shareholder approval, but they must still be approved by the board of directors (and can later be removed by shareholders through a vote). For an institutional background on takeovers, see Section 1.5, as well as Jarrell et al. (1988) and Shleifer and Vishny (1988).

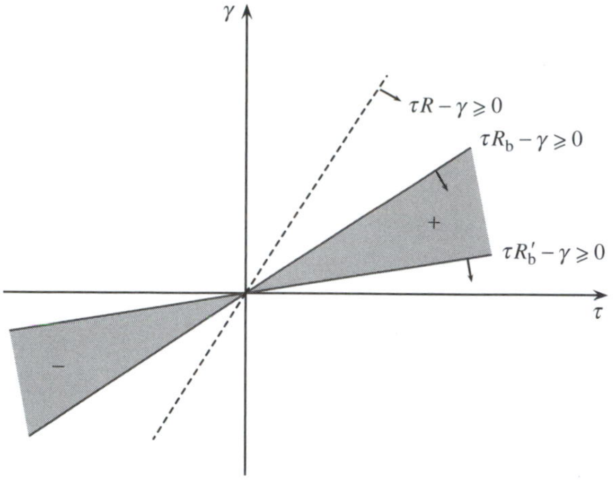

Figure 10.5

eyes of investors), and will do so if the action yields the entrepreneur a payoff superior to the status quo action, that is, if

$$\tau R_b - \gamma \geqslant 0.$$

Should investors then rubber-stamp the entrepreneur's proposal (without knowing τ and γ) or refuse to go along with it, resulting in a deadlock? Since they bear or receive none of the private cost or benefit γ, investors try to figure out whether the proposed action is on average profit enhancing. To this purpose their only piece of information is that it is in the interest of the entrepreneur to recommend the action, i.e., that the entrepreneur prefers the action to the status quo. Investors therefore rubber-stamp if and only if

$$E(\tau \mid \tau R_b - \gamma \geqslant 0) \geqslant 0. \qquad (10.3)$$

Condition (10.3) implies that the key to managerial real control is congruence. As we now show, *the higher the power of the managerial incentive scheme, the more likely it is that investors will go along with the entrepreneur's proposal:* for any joint distribution of $\{\tau, \gamma\}$, the left-hand side is positive when the entrepreneur's stake is R_b provided it is positive for some stake $R_b' < R_b$. To see this, it suffices to represent the set defined by $\tau R_b \geqslant \gamma$ in the $\{\tau, \gamma\}$-space. An increase in the entrepreneur's stake from R_b' to R_b adds to this set only points with $\tau > 0$ and subtracts only points with $\tau < 0$ in Figure 10.5.

We can now discuss the impact of the strength of the balance sheet on the separation of ownership and control. We measure this strength by the entrepreneur's cash on hand A. As discussed in Chapter 3, other measures of balance-sheet strength include the two measures of moral hazard—the private benefit B and the likelihood ratio $\Delta p / p_H$—and the market interest rate when it is not exogenously fixed.[41] These other indicators would lead to the same conclusions. A firm with a strong balance sheet (a high A) must pay back less to investors; thus R_b is large and so the entrepreneur enjoys much real control over decisions.[42] Conversely, a firm with a weak balance sheet (a low A) has a low R_b and therefore a low congruence between the entrepreneur and investors. This will result in frequent deadlocks, as one would expect.

This brings us to a discussion of active monitoring. When deadlocks are frequent, an active monitor who can bring further information to bear on the decision, may break deadlocks and therefore be particularly helpful, as argued by Burkart et al. (1997) (who, citing Franks et al. (1996), note that ownership concentration in the United Kingdom increases during periods of financial difficulty).

Suppose that an active monitor collects at a cost a signal σ_m about the quality of the entrepreneur's proposal, and that this active monitor has interests that are congruent with those of other investors, so that his recommendation to rubber-stamp or veto the entrepreneur's proposal is trusted by the latter. The signal σ_m contains information about the values of τ and γ (technically, it refines the investors' information partition). Thus, combined with the information conveyed by the fact that the entrepreneur recommends moving away from the status quo, it allows investors to make a better-informed decision.

41. Collateral and income prospects are other indicators of the strength of a balance sheet.

42. In the model, there is a single decision and so the entrepreneur enjoys either full or no control over this decision. More generally, we could envision multiple decisions with different characteristics (different joint distributions over τ and γ), or equivalently a single decision to be taken in different states of nature (some information about the joint distribution over τ and γ could be learned by investors after the initial financing stage but before they choose whether to rubber-stamp the proposal). There would then be a broader range of degrees of real control.

The criterion for rubber-stamping the proposal is[43]

$$E(\tau \mid \tau R_b - \gamma \geqslant 0,\ \sigma_m) \geqslant 0.$$

In the next subsection, we will refer to the existence of such a monitor as "relationship lending" (see Chapter 9). By contrast, the absence of a monitor will be referred to as an "arm's-length relationship."

When the monitor does not have a majority of voting shares and has a conflict of interest with the other investors (for example, because the decision may affect one of his affiliated entities, or because the monitor certified the initial financing to the other investors in the first place and may want to try to cover up his mistake or else because the monitor may collude with the entrepreneur), the other investors should assess their relative congruence with the entrepreneur and the monitor for the type of decision at stake.

10.3.2 Strength of the Balance Sheet and Corporate Governance

This section provides a formal analysis of the question just posed: is a firm with a strong balance sheet more or less likely to resort to relationship lending?

10.3.2.1 Determinants of Trust and Monitoring

We first demonstrate two results:

(i) A stronger balance sheet leads to a less conflictual relationship with (more rubber-stamping by) arm's-length lenders.
(ii) Relationship lending is associated with a weak balance sheet.

To show this, suppose that the firm has enough pledgeable income under an arm's-length relationship provided that investors have control (otherwise an arm's-length relationship is not an option, making result (i) vacuous).

43. While I am unaware of general results to this effect, it is straightforward to construct robust examples where, say, a small reduction in net worth calls for the presence of an active monitor. The next subsection studies one such environment. Here note simply that, for a continuous joint distribution over $\{\tau, \gamma\}$, the pledgeable income is continuous in R_b (with or without active monitoring). In contrast, in the absence of active monitoring, the NPV jumps down when $E(\tau \mid \tau R_b - \gamma \geqslant 0) = 0$ and R_b decreases slightly. So, under regularity conditions, if active monitoring is almost optimal before R_b decreases, then it becomes strictly optimal after the decrease.

Arm's-length relationship. In the absence of active monitoring, the entrepreneur's net utility (also equal to the NPV) is

$$U_b = p_H R - I$$

if managerial proposals are turned down (deadlock), and

$$U_b^+(R_b) = p_H R - I + E(\tau R - \gamma \mid \tau R_b - \gamma \geqslant 0) \times \Pr(\tau R_b - \gamma \geqslant 0)$$

if they are embraced (rubber-stamping). Because managerial proposals are accepted when

$$E(\tau(R - R_b) \mid \tau R_b - \gamma \geqslant 0) \geqslant 0,$$
$$U_b^+(R_b) > U_b, \quad \text{for all such } R_b.$$

Put differently, rubber-stamping cannot hurt investors who always have the option not to go along with the entrepreneur's recommendation; and it always benefits the entrepreneur, who makes a recommendation only if its acceptance benefits her. *Because rubber-stamping requires mutual consent, the action can only increase value in expectation,* if not necessarily in each of its realizations. Let $\bar{R}_b$ denote the minimum managerial stake such that investors trust managerial proposals; it is defined by

$$E(\tau \mid \tau \bar{R}_b - \gamma \geqslant 0) = 0;$$

we assume that $B/\Delta p < \bar{R}_b < R$.[44]

The investors' gross payoff (see Figure 10.6) as a function of R_b is

$$\mathcal{P}(R_b) = p_H(R - R_b) + \max\{0, E(\tau(R - R_b) \mid \tau R_b - \gamma \geqslant 0) \times \Pr(\tau R_b - \gamma \geqslant 0)\}.$$

The first term on the right-hand side of this equation is the only term in the deadlock region; it decreases linearly with R_b. The second term's variation with R_b is complex, but it can easily be shown that this second term increases with R_b when investors have a weak preference for rubber-stamping, that is, in the left part of the no-deadlock region in Figure 10.6. Accordingly, the pledgeable income need not be a monotonic function of entrepreneurial compensation.

44. If $\bar{R}_b < B/\Delta p$, then investors always go along with managerial proposals in the relevant range ($R_b \geqslant B/\Delta p$). The analysis is then straightforward.

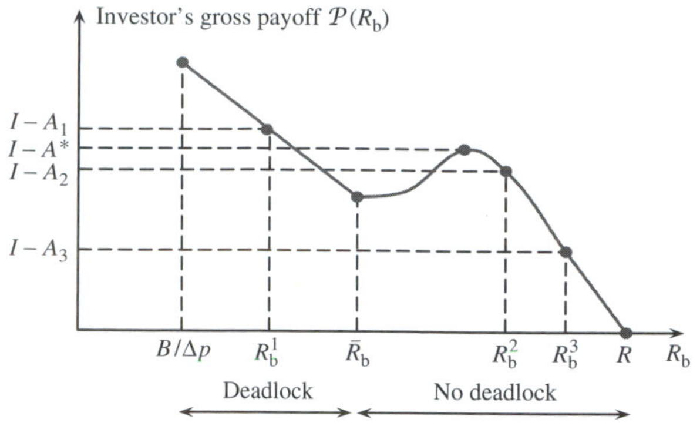

Figure 10.6

The borrower's stake R_b is the highest value $R_b^*(A)$ that enables investors to break even. If two stakes lead to the same expected investor income, the higher of the two makes the entrepreneur better off both because it directly yields her more income in the case of success and because it gives her more real authority. So, for example, for initial wealth A_2, the stake is R_b^2. The value $R_b^*(A)$ is an increasing function of A. As seen in Figure 10.6, managerial proposals are accepted only when $R_b \geqslant \bar{R}_b$.

The borrower's utility is $U_b^+ = U_b^+(R_b^*(A))$ for $A \geqslant A^*$, and is increasing in A. For $A < A^*$, the borrower's net utility, U_b, is independent of A. This proves result (i).

Relationship lending. Relationship lending may be beneficial for two reasons. The first, emphasized in Chapter 9, is that a tight relationship with a large investor reduces moral hazard and may be the only way for the firm to harness sufficient pledgeable income and thereby secure financing. The second, stressed here, is that relationship lending facilitates decision making in a situation in which investors are suspicious of the borrower's motivation.

To simplify the analysis, let us assume that an active monitor, by spending monitoring cost c, has access to the same information as the borrower concerning potential project modifications. More precisely, to prepare for his monitoring task, the monitor must spend the cost c upfront, that is, before being presented with a proposed modification; he can then assess the modification's profitability once the entrepreneur comes up with a suggestion. Provided that the monitor is given enough of a stake in success to be incentivized to learn about such modifications, the initial project is amended when $\tau \geqslant 0$. The borrower's utility in the presence of an active monitor (and assuming there is no scarcity of monitoring capital and so the total cost of employing an active monitor is c)[45] is

$$U_b^a = p_H R - I + [E(\tau R - \gamma \mid \tau \geqslant 0) \cdot \Pr(\tau \geqslant 0) - c].$$

This utility is independent of A. In contrast, we have seen that under an arm's-length relationship, U_b^+ is increasing in A. For A large (close to I), an arm's-length relationship is optimal. More generally there exists A^{**} such that an arm's-length relationship is optimal if and only if[46] $A \geqslant A^{**}$. This proves result (ii).

10.3.2.2 Application to Disclosure

The same logic implies that the entrepreneur will need to supply more information to investors as the balance sheet deteriorates and this deterioration is observed by investors (an unobserved degradation by definition does not raise concerns with investors).

Disclosure may be formalized in two ways: an overall "*ex ante*" disclosure policy and an "*ex post*" spontaneous disclosure, where "*ex post*" refers to a situation in which the entrepreneur already knows the proposal's characteristics (τ, γ). For simplicity, let us restrict attention to the case of *ex ante* disclosure.[47] Suppose that setting up a disclosure mechanism costs c (transaction costs, involuntary

45. Recall from Chapter 9 that monitors, even if they are competitive, may enjoy a rent. That is, their return may exceed that justified by their contribution to the initial investment and the monitoring cost. We have assumed that monitors have enough cash on hand that they do not enjoy such scarcity rents.

46. If $U_b^a < p_H R - I$, then $A^{**} = I - p_H(R - B/\Delta p)$; $A^{**} \in (A^*, I)$ if $U_b^a > U_b$.

47. *Ex post* disclosure could, for example, be modeled as in Dewatripont and Tirole (2005). In that paper, the agent with private information (the entrepreneur here) can at a cost disclose decision-relevant information that, also at a cost, can be assessed by the decision maker (here the investors); she can also disclose "cues" (information that has no direct bearing on the decision at hand, but is useful to assess the congruence between the two parties). In particular, the informed agent can either disclose information (provide information that helps the decision maker to assess his payoff from the proposed course of action), or put no effort into communication and rely on the decision maker to rubber-stamp the proposal. Communication does not increase monotonically with congruence. The agent with private information does not disclose information when congruence is high: she knows that the decision maker will rubber-stamp and therefore takes him for granted. By contrast, the agent discloses information when congruence is lower.

disclosure of strategic information to competitors and so forth), but supplies investors with useful information to evaluate the managerial proposals. Adopting a disclosure policy is then equivalent, in the previous analysis, to going for relationship lending, rather than keeping an arm's-length relationship. We can thus conclude that firms that need to raise funds or renegotiate existing loans will engage in more disclosure when having an (observably) weaker balance sheet. Put differently, firms will disclose more in bad times than in good times.

10.3.2.3 Managerial Initiative

Let us now assume that ideas for a new course of action do not arise exogenously; rather, they require entrepreneurial initiative. Initiative can be measured by the probability that the entrepreneur comes up with a proposed change in the course of action; this probability is now endogenous and smaller than 1, and can be expected to be influenced by the presence of a monitor who collects information about the investors' benefit from moving away from the status quo. In general, the monitor will collect more information if he has a higher stake in the firm. The following result (due to Burkart et al. 1997) can also be obtained.

(iii) Entrepreneurial initiative decreases with the ownership share of the monitor when the entrepreneur has real authority in the absence of monitoring.

The intuition for this result, developed in more detail in Section 10.6, is that an increase in the monitor's share enhances the latter's incentive to acquire information about the profitability of the entrepreneur's proposal. If the entrepreneur enjoys real authority in the absence of monitoring, the resulting increase in the intensity of monitoring results in a higher likelihood that the proposal be overturned or modified and thus in a lower payoff associated with coming up with proposals in the first place.[48]

Note that result (iii) relies on the interests of the entrepreneur and the investors being *ex post* dissonant with regards to the monitoring decision, that is, on the entrepreneur having real authority in the absence of monitoring and therefore losing control over the decision on when the active monitor becomes informed. By contrast, if the entrepreneur does not enjoy real authority in the absence of monitoring (her suggestions are rejected), then monitoring necessarily *enhances* initiative, because monitoring creates at least some probability that a suggestion be accepted.[49]

10.3.3 Private Benefits of Large Shareholders

Students of corporate finance are sometimes surprised by the frequent assertion that a holder of a large minority stake (10 or 20%, say) "controls" the firm. Relatedly, large blocks (which, incidentally, are seldom broken up) sell at a premium relative to the market price of individual shares, as was shown by Barclay and Holderness (1989) for blocks of at least 5% of common stocks listed on the New York Stock Exchange or the American Stock Exchange. Formal control is normally associated with a majority of voting rights, and the conventional wisdom regarding large minority blockholdings must be associated with a different channel of control.

There are several reasons why a block share may be valuable in firms without a majority shareholder. First, when shareholders' interests diverge, coalitions must be formed in order for the board to make a decision. A large blockholder may be uniquely placed to be part of this coalition and may derive

48. The reader will here note the analogy with the treatment of specific investments and the allocation of control rights in Section 10.2.4.

A well-known paper stressing the potentially negative impact of a principal's information on an agent's effort is Crémer (1995), who emphasizes a different reason why monitoring may reduce an agent's effort (see also Riordan's (1990) early work on the topic). In Crémer's multiperiod model, a principal has more difficulty in committing to a threat of kicking out the agent in a case of poor performance when he is better informed about the underpinnings of this performance. The framework is one of moral hazard, unknown agent ability and noncommitment: the agent exerts effort that together with an unknown ability (plus perhaps exogenous noise) results in a first-stage observable performance. The principal may then keep the agent or fire her. The principal may or may not become informed about the agent's ability at the end of the first stage. If he becomes informed, the decision over whether to retain the agent depends only on this observed ability and therefore not on performance, which reduces the agent's incentive to exert effort in the first place. Thus, being informed may well hurt the principal in a noncommitment environment.

49. This point is reminiscent of the discussion in Section 9.4 as to whether the presence of an active monitor facilitates refinancing. There, we saw that if refinancing is a sure thing when starting with an arm's-length relationship, then the presence of an informed monitor necessarily reduces the probability of refinancing, while the reverse holds if an arm's-length relationship does not allow refinancing.

some benefits, e.g., a cash transfer or an increase in ownership stake, in the formation of a majority coalition (Zwiebel 1995). Similarly, a large blockholder may be courted by the raider in a takeover attempt. Second, there may be a serious failure of corporate governance. For example, a large shareholder may collude with management to let the management pursue value-decreasing policies in exchange for, say, below-market transfer prices with a subsidiary of the large shareholder or an access to the firm's knowhow.[50] Third, the large shareholder may enjoy "control amenities" (prestige and perks attached to sitting on the board, etc.).

We are here interested in a fourth possible reason: even when corporate governance functions properly, the large blockholder may enjoy real authority, in the same way that the manager enjoys real authority. As one would expect, the large blockholder will have a higher impact on decision making if his interests are better aligned with those of majority shareholders. Conversely, high potential private benefits and low ownership share make it unlikely that the large shareholder will be able to convince other shareholders to go against managerial policy choices (see Exercise 10.3). Furthermore, they make the large shareholder unlikely to represent a useful counterpower to the manager if his interests are aligned with her own; for, the large blockholder will then tend to second managerial proposals to his own benefit.

10.4 Allocation of Control Rights among Securityholders

10.4.1 Potential Rationales for the Multiplicity of Securities

Part III distinguished between informed investors (active or passive monitors) and uninformed investors; because monitors are subject to moral hazard themselves, they may face income streams that differ from those of other investors. But there is a sense in which we have still been considering a single class of securities: we have introduced no reason why one should design different classes of securities with different control rights. In the case in which control rights are relevant (active monitoring), it was optimal to achieve as much congruence among the active monitor and other investors as is consistent with incentives to monitor. That is, there was no gain attached to artificially creating conflicting goals and externalities from decision making among investors. In practice, though, we observe claims, such as outside equity and debt, with very conflicting interests and different control rights. The cost of such security designs is obvious: those investors in control may not internalize the welfare of other investors. The divergence of objectives creates externalities. For example, it is well known that shareholders may want to select negative-NPV actions that increase risk and "expropriate" debtholders, and that costly covenants and exit options protecting debtholders (short-term debt, convertible debt) must be put in place so as to limit the importance of this phenomenon (Jensen and Meckling 1976). The puzzle is thus to find the benefits, not the costs, of the coexistence of multiple securities. Explaining the coexistence of multiple securities with differentiated control rights is one of the main challenges currently facing corporate finance theory.

From a broad perspective, there are several possible explanations for the multiplicity of securities. Each probably has some relevance, but none is immune to criticism.

10.4.1.1 Investors' Demand for Specific Securities

Investors do not have identical preferences as to the characteristics of securities. They may for example face different tax treatments or marginal rates, or have different liquidity needs. Thus, they may demand differentiated securities. An important contribution along this line, reviewed in Chapter 12, is due to Gorton and Pennacchi (1990). Consider an economy with "short-term" and "long-term" investors. The difference between the two categories of investors is that short-term investors anticipate buying a house, facing possible unemployment, or being sick, say, and are therefore likely to be forced to sell their assets. Unlike long-term investors, short-term investors are concerned about losing money to better-informed traders in the market when they resell their assets (as in Kyle (1985) for example). They will thus be eager to buy "low-information-intensity

50. The idea is that the large shareholder fails to perform the role of an active monitor in exchange for a favor from management (see Chapter 9 for a model of this type of collusion).

securities," that is, securities for which private information held by speculators is less likely to be an important factor. In a nutshell, AAA bonds (which by definition are unlikely to default, and on whose payoff there is therefore little asymmetric information) will probably be resold on the market at a fair value, while the stock of a firm will be subject to substantial adverse selection in the market and will therefore probably sold at a discount. Assuming that the speculative monitoring considerations discussed in Chapter 8 are minor for this firm, it pays the firm to tailor the securities to the needs of its clientele: issue stocks for long-term investors and bonds for those with more pressing liquidity needs.

While this explanation for the multiplicity of securities seems to make sense, more work is still required to make it tight. In particular, it is unclear whether security design and repackaging for the clientele's benefit should be performed at the firm's level or at that of an intermediary. Could one not obtain the benefits of congruence among investors at the firm's level and create the benefits from diversity for investors through unbundling at the intermediary's level?[51] A different issue related to the existence of intermediaries is whether they could not bundle high-information-intensity assets from different firms in order to create the low-information-intensity securities desired by short-term investors? This bundling is actually performed on a routine basis for example by closed-end funds offering market indices such as the S&P 500, which are less subject to asymmetric information than individual stocks (see Subrahmanyam 1991; Gorton and Pennacchi 1993).

10.4.1.2 Liquidity Management

Another important dimension of security design is the timing of the firm's liquidity needs. A high-tech start-up usually generates little or no income for a long time and must therefore be financed mainly through equity; as we saw in Chapter 5, short- and medium-term debt would create serious liquidity problems and would result in inefficiencies. In contrast, a firm in a mature industry with large cash flows and few investment needs should be subject to substantial leverage in order to ensure that the firm disgorges the excess cash.

More generally, because refinancing is subject to the same credit rationing problems as the initial financing, the firm's future liquidity must be carefully planned at the initial stage. Different securities have different impacts on the firm's available liquidity. Short-term debt drains liquidity whereas equity does not: while stockholdings are liquid at the level of the individual investor, they are illiquid for the collectivity of investors as a whole since an investor must resell his/her shares to another investor, without any flow of money out of the firm. Long-term debt in this respect is somewhat akin to equity, which explains why it is often proposed (in prudential regulation, for example) that part of long-term debt be counted as equity, even though long-term debt has very different cash-flow and control-rights characteristics compared with equity.

Liquidity management represents an important dimension of security design. But per se it does not explain the multiplicity of securities. The firm could equivalently replace this array of securities (short-term debt, equity, etc.) with different cash-draining characteristics by a single, composite one which would have the same timing and amount of liquidity demands on the firm. Thus, liquidity management can offer a clue as to the multiplicity of securities only if it is combined with one of the last two explanations, which we now describe.

10.4.1.3 Monitoring

Another, relatively unexplored, approach to explaining the multiplicity of claims would focus on the multidimensional nature of monitoring, together with a conflict of interest between the various monitoring tasks (otherwise the multiple monitoring tasks could be performed by the same monitor).[52] For instance, it may be optimal to separate the monitoring of moral hazard along the first- and second-order stochastic dominance dimensions. Monitoring

51. Alternatively, the firm could issue multiple securities, but allocate control rights to a "neutral" group of investors, whose payoff would be representative of all other investor claims combined.

52. See Dewatripont and Tirole (1999) for a theoretical perspective on the rationale for advocacy in a situation in which an agent must perform conflicting tasks (which echoes on the output side Holmström and Milgrom's (1991) work on multitask effort substitution on the input side). These remarks borrow from discussions with Mathias Dewatripont.

of first-order stochastic dominance (profit enhancement) usually requires compensating the monitor with a claim on profit that puts heavy weight on the upside. Such claims, however, may discourage the monitor from paying attention to risk taking. Similarly, it may be odd to ask a monitor in charge of preventing distress to also monitor that the firm maintains the resale value of its collateral in the case of distress.

To sum up, multitask monitoring may give rise to the creation of conflicting claims for different active monitors; yet, per se, it will not explain the multiplicity of claims offered to *uninformed* investors (e.g., corporate bonds and equities held by small investors). In this respect, it would be interesting to analyze the coexistence of multidimensional speculative monitoring as well.

The structure of return flows associated with a security is not the only factor impacting the monitoring of the firm by the holders of this security. The liquidity/resellability of the claim also plays a major role, as already discussed in Section 9.5 in the case of active monitors. Chapter 11 will return to this aspect in the context of *potential* active monitors. This chapter will discuss takeovers and the concomitant incentive for potential acquirers to spot value-enhancing actions.

10.4.1.4 Control Rights: Multiple Securities as a Disciplining Device

The return structure of a claim determines its holder's monitoring focus on some aspects of management as well as the intensity of monitoring, as we just saw. But the return also determines the holder's choice of intervention if control rights are bundled with the return stream. Thus security design also matters from a control rights perspective. Now, as we already observed, decision making that is efficient from the investors' perspective would seem to call for a congruence between the rights holders and the other investors in order to prevent externalities. So, allocating control to claimholders who do not represent the collective interest of all investors in the firm would seem to make little sense unless this allocation serves to discipline management. We develop this theme in Section 10.4.2.

10.4.2 Security Design as a Disciplining Device

As we just discussed, designing securities with different return streams is bound to generate conflicts of interest among different securityholders. It is therefore *a priori* unclear why, provided one has reached the conclusion that investors should be given a specific control right (see Section 10.2), this control right should be allocated to a specific class of investors (e.g., shareholders or debtholders) whose interests are not representative of those of the community of investors as a whole. Put differently, the Aghion–Bolton model does not explain the coexistence of multiple claims (e.g., debt and equity) with different control rights.

Control, however, is often exerted by investors whose claim makes them unrepresentative of the community of investors as a whole. For example, during "normal times" equityholders have control, while in "bad times" debtholders acquire control, if only through their threat of liquidating the firm or through that of calling the entire principal due. Interestingly, control in normal (bad) times goes to securityholders who care more (less) about the upside than about the downside. Why do certain control rights go to certain cash flow claims? Somehow, such biases in policy preferences must serve one of several possible incentive purposes. This section investigates a specific one: security design disciplines management through a carrot-and-stick mechanism.

A carrot-and-stick view of security design is developed in Dewatripont and Tirole (1994) on the coexistence of debt and equity, and by Berglöf and von Thadden (1994) on the coexistence of short- and long-term debt. The basic idea of these papers is straightforward and builds on the contingent-control insight of Section 10.2.3. Managers' welfare in general depends on their firm's course of action as well as on their monetary compensation scheme. That is, interim decisions by investors should be treated as part of the managerial incentives package. But, while the carrot-and-stick theory of control in Section 10.2.3 emphasized the contingent allocation of control between insiders and outsiders, the carrot-and-stick view of security design emphasizes the contingent allocation of control among outsiders.

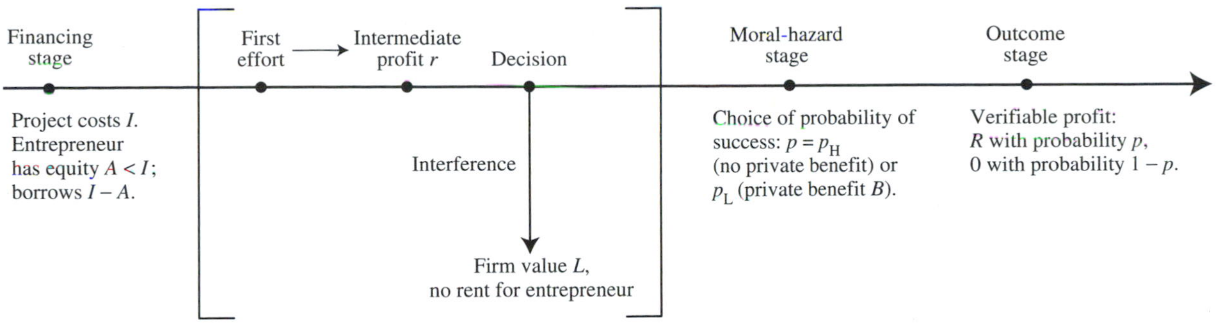
Financing stage
Project costs I. Entrepreneur has equity A < I; borrows I − A.
First effort
Intermediate profit r
Decision
Interference
Firm value L, no rent for entrepreneur
Moral-hazard stage
Choice of probability of success: p = p_H (no private benefit) or p_L (private benefit B).
Outcome stage
Verifiable profit: R with probability p, 0 with probability 1 − p.

Figure 10.7 Multiple securities as a disciplining device.

The carrot and the stick are provided by allocations of control to investors who are more or less congruent with management. In particular, allocating control to "tough investors"—namely, investors whose preferences (as implied by their cash flow claim) have little congruence with those of managers—when interim managerial performance is weak and to "soft investors"—namely, investors whose preferences are less dissonant with those of management—when interim managerial performance is satisfactory creates good incentives for management.

Let us consider debtholders. The fact that they do not benefit from the upside makes them conservative, inclined to liquidate assets, downsize, encourage routine management, and more generally interfere to make the firm's return safer. Debtholder control is feared by managers and should arise when the firm's performance is poor. In contrast, equityholders, who are compensated on the upside, are somewhat less likely than debtholders to interfere with management[53] (although they still have substantial conflicts of interest with management) and should receive control in good times.

To illustrate the carrot-and-stick idea, let us enrich the basic model of Chapter 3 by adding an intermediate date and performance, and a decision over whether to "continue" or "interfere" in the firm's management after this intermediate performance is observed. The timing is summarized in Figure 10.7, where the new building block relative to the standard model is in bold characters.

53. Or they might interfere equally but not take actions that are as painful for management.

After the financing stage ("date 0"), the entrepreneur exerts a first effort, that (possibly stochastically) determines a "date-1" or intermediate performance. This performance (short-term profit/EBIT, functionality test, drug approval, etc.) is verifiable. For concreteness, assume this is a short-term profit $r \in \{r_L, r_H\}$ with $r_L < r_H$; but as some of the examples suggest, the intermediate performance measurement may refer to a nonmonetary variable as well.

A decision must then be made as to whether to let the entrepreneur "continue" with her selected course of action or to "interfere." In the case of continuation, the "date-2" operations are as in the basic model. The entrepreneur is subject to moral hazard and must therefore be given a minimum share of the final cake R in the case of eventual success. In the case of interference, the investors can recoup a value L and the entrepreneur receives no rent or, more generally, a lower rent than under continuation.

To make things interesting, let us assume that what constitutes "continuation" and "interference" cannot be contracted upon at the financing stage.[54] This may be because "interference" can take many forms: reduction in the riskiness of the project or refusal to invest in new activities, downsizing, enhanced oversight by an active monitor, reduction in the entrepreneur's scope of authority, firing of the entrepreneur, reorganization, liquidation, and so

54. If the actions can be described, managerial incentives are not altered, but security design is irrelevant. Indeed, the initial contract can specify the course of action contingently on "date-1" performance. In a sense, and as we will see later, the design of securities with dissonant objectives serves to implement or approach the optimal state-contingent course of action.

forth. The inability to describe precisely the decision *ex ante* will, as in previous sections, lead to an allocation of control rights. Ruling out entrepreneur control, say because it would lead to a shortage of pledgeable income, we focus on the allocation of control to different classes of investors.

Abstracting from the details of this formulation, *the first key assumption is that different courses of action have different impacts on the entrepreneur's welfare.* This assumption implies that the entrepreneur is not indifferent as to who will receive control rights, and hence that a contingent allocation of control rights can be used to discipline the entrepreneur. This first assumption delivers a theory of security design in which contingent control rights covary with cash-flow rights.

The second key assumption, which underlies the specific security design, namely, the allocation of control to equityholders in normal times and to debtholders in bad times, is that the course of action least preferred by the entrepreneur (which we labeled "interference") produces a less risky cash flow.[55] As we will see, this assumption will imply that the entrepreneur can be punished by allocating control to a class of investors with a conservative slant.

Returning to our model, let us assume that

$$p_{\mathrm{H}}\left(R - \frac{B}{\Delta p}\right) > L.$$

That is, when the entrepreneur is held to her incompressible share, $R_{\mathrm{b}} = B/\Delta p$, interference reduces the income that can be pledged to the investors (it is "inefficient" even from the point of view of pledgeable income).

The reason why the decision in general is part of the incentives package is again the scarcity of pledgeable income. Paying the entrepreneur a bonus for a high intermediate profit r_{H} over and above her "quasi-rent" (her expected share in the final profit) under continuation reduces the pledgeable income. Offering the entrepreneur the prospect of this continuation quasi-rent, $p_{\mathrm{H}}R_{\mathrm{b}}$ (where, as earlier, $R_{\mathrm{b}} \geqslant B/\Delta p$ is the entrepreneur's reward in the case of final success), for a high first-period profit and of interference for a low first-period r_{L} profit may well be a cheaper way to provide the same incentives, in the sense that it delivers a higher pledgeable income (note again, the analogy with the treatment of contingent control in Section 10.2.3). There is, of course, a cost of doing so. In this model, interference is costly for the investors as long as $p_{\mathrm{H}}(R - R_{\mathrm{b}}) > L$. Thus, the threat of interference reduces both the project's NPV (since $p_{\mathrm{H}}R > L$) and, for a given date-1 entrepreneurial behavior, pledgeable income. However, if the entrepreneur can control the first-period profit fairly well (there is little noise in first-period performance), the probability of interference conditional on a high first-period effort is low and so is the cost of basing the first-period incentives on the threat of interference.

To implement this contingent continuation decision, the entrepreneur can issue a level of short-term debt d exceeding the low first-period profit and smaller than or equal to the high first-period profit: $r_{\mathrm{L}} < d \leqslant r_{\mathrm{H}}$. If short-term debt is paid back from date-1 income, then equityholders, whose only potential income is an amount $R_{\mathrm{E}} > 0$ in the case of final success (if the firm continues), have control. They choose to continue because (a) debtholders have priority, and so total (short- plus long-term) debt $d + D$ must first be paid in full out of the payoff L under interference before shareholders can receive any income, and (b) debtholders are better off when being paid in full. Because by assumption the investors' total income (debt plus equity) is greater under continuation than under interference, the shareholders' income is *a fortiori* larger under continuation.

In contrast, in the case of distress (the short-term debt is not paid back entirely), the whole debt (short-term debt d and long-term debt $D = R - R_{\mathrm{E}} - R_{\mathrm{b}}$) becomes due. Assume for simplicity that the low intermediate profit is equal to 0, so that none of d is repaid and so $(d+D)$ remains due. Debtholders, who have priority over the reorganization value L and receive $(d+D)$ in the case of continuation and success and 0 otherwise, want to interfere if $p_{\mathrm{H}}(d + D) < L$.

Exercise 10.1 studies this general logic in more detail. The following example makes the accounting particularly simple. Suppose that a high (respectively, low) intermediate effort deterministically yields profit r_{H} (respectively, $r_{\mathrm{L}} = 0$), and that a low intermediate income yields private benefit B_0

55. In this model, this reduced riskiness is extreme, since the value L is taken to be deterministic.

(over and above the private benefit, B, if any, potentially enjoyed under continuation). Assume further that there is just enough pledgeable income to allow funding in the case of a high intermediate effort and continuation,

$$r_H + p_H\left(R - \frac{B}{\Delta p}\right) = I - A;$$

and that the threat of termination suffices to discipline management at the intermediate stage when the entrepreneur's reward in the case of success is set at its minimal incentive-compatible level,

$$B_0 \leqslant p_H R_b = p_H\left(\frac{B}{\Delta p}\right).$$

The NPV is then $r_H + p_H R - I$.

To implement this outcome and receive funding, the entrepreneur can issue short-term debt $d = r_H$ (and, say, no long-term debt, although this is not important), and give control to debtholders in the case of nonrepayment. Provided that

$$p_H d < L,$$

debtholders prefer not to roll over their debt when they are not repaid, as they receive $\min\{d, L\}$ by interfering. And so the entrepreneur receives no income when the firm's short-term profit is low. We also check that shareholders prefer not to interfere when they have control, i.e., when the short-term debt has been reimbursed, since

$$p_H\left(R - \frac{B}{\Delta p}\right) > \max\{L - d, 0\},$$

which results from the assumption that investors' total income is large in the absence of interference.

It is important to point out what the multiplicity of claims accomplishes. Suppose there were a single claim ("100% equity"). When deciding whether to interfere, the investors would compare $p_H(R - R_b)$ and L, and therefore would always continue provided R_b is not too large (or always interfere otherwise) *regardless of the intermediate performance*. Because it would be noncontingent, the exercise of the control right would then have no disciplining impact on the date-1 effort. Indeed, the reader will here recognize an illustration of the *soft-budget-constraint problem* studied in Chapter 5. The control right is exercised with a forward-looking perspective while its use as a disciplining device requires it to be backward looking; or, put differently, the date-1 profit does not affect future prospects and therefore does not change the incentives of the securityholders as a whole.[56]

Finally, the key property of the carrot-and-stick scheme is that the incentives of the controlling investors be made contingent on some measure of performance. This is naturally accomplished as above by transferring control from one class of securityholder to another. Alternatively, and equivalently, a single class of securityholders might retain control, but its returns stream would be adjusted as a function of the measure of entrepreneurial performance so as to duplicate the contingent incentives of the control-transfer mechanism.[57]

10.4.3 The Investors' Coalition Conundrum: Is Modigliani–Miller Back?

A crucial assumption for the theory just described, as for other potential theories of the multiplicity of securities, is that the securityholders do not undo the multiplicity.

In the context of control rights, the carrot-and-stick argument requires that whoever is in control does not renegotiate with other securityholders. In the theory of debt and equity discussed above, debtholders exert a negative externality on shareholders when they interfere. In the absence of full repayment of the short-term debt, debtholders who have control interfere even though the continuation value from the point of view of debtholders *and* equityholders, $p_H(R - R_b)$, exceeds the liquidation proceeds, L. Debtholders could, for example, design

56. Symmetrically, the same reasoning can be used to derive a security-design version of investor promises to refinance projects or retain management when the firm returns cash to investors (see, for example, the Bolton–Scharfstein model in Sections 3.8, 4.7, and 7.2, as well as Section 11.4 in the next chapter). Suppose that $p_H(R - B/\Delta p) < L$. Because the entrepreneur has minimum stake $B/\Delta p$ in the case of success, investors, taken together, are better off interfering. However, to induce managers to exert effort earlier in the relationship, it may be optimal not to interfere when the intermediate performance is high. Giving control to equityholders in such times and to debtholders (or unbiased investors for that matter) in bad times may provide the required carrot and stick.

57. This more complex implementation may make sense in situations in which a proper exercise of control requires substantial investments in information acquisition by a controlling claimholder. The contingent return-stream scheme then economizes on information acquisition costs relative to the control-transfer scheme described in this section.

a debt-for-equity swap that benefits all investors, since total investor payoff is higher under continuation; or shareholders could inject more funds and repay some of the debt so as to make debtholders willing to continue.

Were all securityholders to renegotiate and gains from trade between them to be realized (that is, were the Coase Theorem to apply), we would be back to the single-claim, noncontingent control case and the theory would have no content. The anticipation of continuation regardless of debt repayment would undermine the entrepreneur's *ex ante* incentive. This is actually a more general result: the investors' net gain to continuing is independent of first-period performance,[58] and so a performance-contingent pattern of investor control cannot be used to discipline the entrepreneur if securities are renegotiated and investors therefore behave in a united way.

In the carrot-and-stick theory, the entrepreneur would no longer fear debtholder control, since debtholders would internalize the negative impact of liquidation or conservative interference on shareholders after negotiating with them. This point is completely general and needs to be confronted by any theory of security design based on the allocation of control rights: while the allocation of control rights between insiders and outsiders matters, security design is irrelevant as long as securityholders re-form the broad coalition when they are about to interfere. Is Modigliani and Miller's result of irrelevance of security design back?

One of two assumptions is usually made to avoid this strong implication of the Coase Theorem. The first is that for some reason (transaction costs associated with investor dispersion,[59] asymmetric information among investors,[60] or cash constraints) renegotiation does not work well or does not happen at all. This failure of renegotiation among investors creates *ex post* inefficiencies, but preserves the *ex ante* commitment created by the multiplicity of securities.

Mathias Dewatripont has remarked[61] that there is a tension between, on the one hand, the existence of multiple securities and, on the other, the practice of facilitating renegotiation involving dispersed securityholders, such as exchange offers and the nomination of bondholder trustees in the case of corporate bonds, as well as the premise of much work on the economics of bankruptcy that efficient renegotiation should be facilitated. Or, put differently, why should one bother designing multiple securities if the desired outcome is that produced by a 100% equity firm?

Two innovative proposals for bankruptcy law reforms are due to Bebchuk (1988) and Aghion et al. (1992). Both papers offer market-based mechanisms for the reorganization of financially distressed firms.[62] Under both recapitalization processes, most senior creditors are turned into equityholders. In Bebchuk's scheme junior creditors are given options to buy senior creditors' shares at a strike price that induces them to exercise the options if the value of shares exceeds what is due to senior creditors. Similarly, former equityholders receive options to buy the shares at an even higher strike price, respecting the claims' initial priority. The Aghion et al. scheme adds a second stage, in which managers and other parties can propose a reorganization scheme to the residual owners. Without going into the details of these two schemes, let us make two points. First,

58. This independence relies on the absence of serial correlation of profits. The theory can be extended to allow for a serial correlation.

59. Investor dispersion is particularly problematic for public debt. In the United States, public debt restructuring almost always takes the form of a package of new securities plus cash in exchange for the original public debt, as the 1939 Trust Indenture Act requires unanimous consent to modify principal, interest, or maturity of public debt. See Gertner and Scharfstein (1991) for an analysis of workouts of distressed firms with outstanding bank debt and public debt. In an analysis of distressed junk bond issuers in the United States, Asquith et al. (1994) shows that public debt restructuring is crucial for avoiding bankruptcy even when bank debt is restructured; real debt relief tends to come from subordinated public creditors, since banks rarely forgive principal or provide new financing outside formal bankruptcy proceedings.

60. Berkovitch and Israel (1999) emphasize the role of asymmetric information among investors in a bankruptcy context.

61. At the Nobel foundation conference on corporate finance (Stockholm, August 1995).

62. There has been much recent debate about the virtues of various bankruptcy codes (see, for example, Davydenko and Franks (2004) for an international comparison of the effects of bankruptcy codes). For example, Chapter 11 in the United States has been criticized for giving too much control and bargaining power to managers, who usually initiate the bankruptcy process, and for allowing firms that should be liquidated to continue losing money for a couple of years. Chapter 11 stops payments to creditors including secured ones while managers continue to run day-to-day operations and prepare a reorganization plan to propose to the court. New financing can acquire seniority over existing creditors under court approval.

these schemes are attempts at respecting the priority of claims while eliciting market information about the relative merits of liquidation and various forms of ownership and continuation. In that sense, they represent formal mechanisms of renegotiation among investors (and possibly management).[63] Second, they take financial distress as given and attempt to achieve *ex post* efficient outcomes once the firm is in distress. They do not adopt an *ex ante* viewpoint explaining the design of a capital structure that leads to distress. Further research should clarify the consistency of the various theoretical and institutional pieces of the security design puzzle.[64]

The alternative approach to reestablishing the commitment value afforded by the existence of multiple securities with contingent control rights is to assume that the entrepreneur is somehow brought into the renegotiation process and that her post-renegotiation utility increases with her utility in the absence of renegotiation. The key modeling element is then the description of the concession made by the entrepreneur.[65] In Bolton and Scharfstein (1996) the entrepreneur has observable, but nonverifiable, savings. The investors cannot directly put their hands on the savings, but may be more demanding when they know that the entrepreneur is able to make a concession.[66] Alternatively, and in a situation in which the entrepreneur has private information about the existence of potential profit-enhancing actions, the entrepreneur may offer courses of action that she would not normally volunteer (as in Sections 10.2 and 10.3 the entrepreneur's stake in profit does not compensate for the private cost of undertaking the action) in order to prevent a deadlock in bargaining.

63. In that sense, they belong to the general class of mechanisms eliciting the various parties' information to achieve efficient outcomes (Maskin 1977).

64. See Berglöf et al. (2003) for an analysis integrating security design and bankruptcy procedures.

65. Because the latter is by assumption cash constrained *ex ante* (this is why she borrows in the first place) as well as (in an optimal design) *ex post*, this concession must be of a different nature. For example, it may be the revelation by the entrepreneur of hard information about a first-best suboptimal profit-enhancing action.

66. Furthermore, Bolton and Scharfstein derive a role for multiple creditors by introducing two complementary assets held as securities by two creditors. In the case of default, each creditor decides whether to liquidate his own asset. A buyer of the assets therefore needs to agree with both in order to realize the full value of the liquidated firm (the equivalent of L in this section). Having two creditors rather than one holding the two assets as collateral increases the bargaining power vis-à-vis the buyer under the Shapley value, but under Bolton and Scharfstein's assumptions this increased bargaining power, which tends to discourage the buyer from showing up in the first place, reduces the expected liquidation value when the entrepreneur has no hidden cash. In contrast, having two creditors also forces the entrepreneur to concede more when she has hidden cash. This increases pledgeable income.

Supplementary Sections

10.5 Internal Capital Markets

This supplementary section is concerned with a *specific control right*: *the ability to decide and contract on future financing decisions*. The right over the refinancing decision matters when future cash infusions are not perfectly planned at the onset, or else if the initial plans are subject to renegotiation. While covenants on indebtedness or on dividend distributions always limit the extent to which certain categories of debtholders can be diluted (see Chapter 2), firms may keep varying degrees of freedom concerning their ability to secure new funds.

At one end of the spectrum, the abandonment of the control right over the refinancing decision is starkly exemplified by the case of divisions, which cannot turn to the capital market but must rather get headquarters' approval. Of course, many more control rights are relinquished by divisions besides that over refinancing. This is also partly true for start-ups, that not only see their staged financing controlled by the venture capitalist, but must also conform to other controls as well. Still another example is provided by highly levered companies; if leverage is so high that the company is unable to face its debt obligations, creditors can threaten to liquidate the firm, and thereby acquire de facto, although not de jure, control over the firm's access to the capital market.[67]

We can formalize the impact of the allocation of this specific control right through its effect on the

67. The content of this right depends, of course, on the creditors' ability to use covenants in order to limit other forms of indebtedness, such as leasing contracts, trade credit, or off-balance-sheet exposures, and to control risk management.

bargaining power in future refinancing stages: an entrepreneur who has not surrendered the control right can play future investors off against each other. This gives the entrepreneur lots of bargaining power in such negotiations. In contrast, a division (or an independent entity that has surrendered the control right) will face a monopoly supplier of funds in the future.

10.5.1 Harnessing Pledgeable Income through Exclusivity: How Internal Capital Markets Facilitate Initial Funding

We first build on Section 9.4 by considering a two-stage financing decision in which, relative to their respective investment costs, the second stage generates plenty of pledgeable income while the first generates little. We can assign the difference between these two stages to differences in income (one may have in mind that the firm takes time to develop a decent product or must build a brand-name or goodwill) or, equivalently and as we will do here, to differences in investment costs.

There are two dates, $t = 1, 2$, and no discounting between the periods. The fixed-investment projects at dates 1 and 2 have respective investment costs I_1 and I_2 (the assumptions to follow imply that $I_1 > I_2$). The two projects may or may not be related (the projects are related if the first corresponds to an "inception" stage and enables the second, "follow-up" stage); for the sake of exposition, let us assume that they are not, and so the second project can be realized without the first. The entrepreneur has initial wealth A at date 1. Except for the investment cost, the two projects are identical. They yield R with probability p and 0 with probability $1 - p$. The probability of success is p_H (if the entrepreneur behaves), or p_L (if she misbehaves, in which case she gets private benefit B). Let us assume that each project has positive NPV ($p_H R > I_t$ for $t = 1, 2$) and that

$$I_2 < p_H\left(R - \frac{B}{\Delta p}\right) < I_1 - A \tag{10.4}$$

and

$$2p_H\left(R - \frac{B}{\Delta p}\right) > (I_1 + I_2) - A. \tag{10.5}$$

Thus, the first project cannot be funded on a stand-alone basis; the second project generates enough pledgeable income not only for stand-alone finance (condition (10.4)), but also to compensate for the shortage of pledgeable income on the first project (condition (10.5)). We also assume that a project's NPV is negative if the entrepreneur misbehaves: $p_L R + B < I_2 (< I_1)$.

We make the assumption (without endogenizing it) that the entrepreneur can (1) sign a financing contract with date-1 lenders, and (2), if she wants to, assign a control right over the date-2 refinancing decision to a particular lender. The internal capital market (ICM) case will refer to the situation in which such an exclusive right is contracted for, and the external capital market (ECM) case to that in which the entrepreneur keeps entire freedom on the date-2 refinancing decision, and all date-1 liabilities can be levied only on date-1 income (if any).[68] As usual, we assume that the capital market is competitive.

External capital market. Under an ECM, at date 2, the entrepreneur is able to borrow as condition (10.4) implies that the pledgeable income exceeds the date-2 investment cost. Because the entrepreneur faces a competitive capital market at date 2, she obtains the entire value of date-2 borrowing:

$$V_2 = p_H R - I_2.$$

This implies that date-1 lenders are not able to put their hands on any of the date-2 pie: viewed from the point of view of date 1, V_2 is the equivalent of a private benefit or nonpledgeable income. Because the date-1 pledgeable income $p_H[R - (B/\Delta p)]$ is smaller than the date-1 net investment cost $I_1 - A$, the first project does not receive financing (note that the entrepreneur does not value at date 1 cash (that is, retained earnings) more than current consumption, because the date-2 project is financed regardless of the level of retained earnings). The ECM therefore leads to inefficient credit rationing at date 1.

Internal capital market. Suppose now that the entrepreneur receives date-1 financing from a lender, to whom she gives control over the date-2 refinancing decision. At date 2, the entrepreneur and the lender then bargain over the sharing of the

68. Under an ECM, one may have in mind that either the entrepreneur makes project 1 a stand-alone corporate entity, or that the same entity implements the two projects but the entrepreneur keeps the right to decide on the date-2 refinancing decision.

date-2 return. Let $(1-\theta)$ and θ denote the bargaining powers of the entrepreneur and the lender in that negotiation. One may have in mind that with probability θ (respectively, $1-\theta$) the lender (respectively, the borrower) chooses the date-2 contract. If the lender were to choose the date-2 financing arrangement ($\theta = 1$), he would give the minimum needed for incentive purposes, $R_b^2 = B/\Delta p$ in the case of success and 0 in the case of failure, to the entrepreneur and keep an expected

$$p_H\left(R - \frac{B}{\Delta p}\right) - I_2$$

for himself. That is, he would appropriate the date-2 NPV, $p_H R - I_2$, except for the minimum incentive payment, $p_H B/\Delta p$, to the entrepreneur. In contrast, if the entrepreneur were to choose ($\theta = 0$), the outcome would be that under a date-2 competitive capital market, and so the lender would receive no surplus. More generally, for $0 \leqslant \theta \leqslant 1$, the lender receives

$$\theta\left[p_H\left(R - \frac{B}{\Delta p}\right) - I_2\right].$$

And hence, if

$$-\left[(I_1 - A) - p_H\left(R - \frac{B}{\Delta p}\right)\right] + \theta\left[p_H\left(R - \frac{B}{\Delta p}\right) - I_2\right] \geqslant 0,$$

allocating the control right over the refinancing decision to a lender enables financing at the initial round. From condition (10.5), this will obtain if θ is sufficiently high.

In short, an internal capital market, as for other control rights transferred to investors, increases the pledgeable income and facilitates financing.

10.5.2 A Dark Side of Internal Capital Markets

The models of Gertner et al. (1994), Scharfstein and Stein (2000) and Brusco and Panunzi (2005) embody, in different ways, the idea that an ICM exposes the entrepreneur to a "holdup" and thereby stifles initiative.

This holdup problem is the flip side of the benefit of ICMs just analyzed. Indeed, the idea in the previous section was precisely that an ICM organizes such a holdup so as to allow the lender to recoup his first-period losses. But because the date-2 entrepreneurial surplus is smaller than when she faces a date-2 competitive capital market, the entrepreneur has dulled incentives to invest at date 1. To illustrate this in the simplest manner, suppose that the very existence of the date-2 follow-up project requires a private investment cost C sunk by the entrepreneur at date 1, where

$$p_H \frac{B}{\Delta p} < C < V_2. \tag{10.6}$$

Suppose further that $\theta = 1$ (the lender has all the bargaining power under an ICM). The first inequality in (10.6) implies that the entrepreneur has no incentive to invest under an ICM: when the lender has full bargaining power, the entrepreneur receives the minimum incentive payment ($p_H(B/\Delta p)$ in expectation), which is not sufficient to compensate her for her investment. The second inequality in (10.6), however, implies that such an investment is both socially optimal and privately optimal for the entrepreneur under an ECM (under which she appropriates the entire surplus).

This holdup cost of ICMs is closely related to the industrial organization literature on the dulled incentives of parties to a long-term relationship who do not own productive assets (Grossman and Hart 1986; Klein et al. 1978; Williamson 1975) and to the treatment of relationship banking in Chapter 9.

10.5.3 Other Aspects of Internal Capital Markets

The literature on ICMs has emphasized a number of other important features.

10.5.3.1 High-Intensity Monitoring

An internal capital market almost always involves a large and possibly unique lender (although logically this would not need to be the case). As Alchian (1969) and Williamson (1975) have stressed, internal capital markets are therefore usually associated with high-intensity monitoring. This feature, as we have discussed in Chapter 9, has both costs and benefits. Suppose that there is uncertainty about the date-2 profitability for investors and that the presence of a large lender creates an active monitor and reduces the asymmetry of information between the entrepreneur and financiers at date 2. This reduced uncertainty may in some cases facilitate refinancing. On the other hand, we also know that too much information may also be detrimental, because it may stifle the entrepreneur's initiative (see Section 10.6) or else induce her to try to exploit a soft budget constraint (see von Thadden 1995).

10.5.3.2 Allocation among Divisions

In contrast with venture capital and leverage buyout practices (see Sections 1.6.2 and 2.4.1), headquarters do operate cross-subsidies among divisions of a conglomerate. For example, Lamont (1997), studying the impact of the 1986 drop in the oil price in companies with oil interests, shows that these companies did cut investment across the board, including in nonoil-related divisions. Shin and Stulz (1998) similarly show that investment in one division is generally related to the cash flow of other divisions.

This redistribution of liquidity among divisions has both a bright and a dark side. On the bright side, the better information held by headquarters relative to the capital market makes it more likely that ICMs do a good job at picking winners, especially if the firm operates in related lines of business (Stein 1997): this is the multiple-division version of the high-intensity monitoring argument just discussed.

Also on the bright side, the headquarters may play the role of liquidity pools. In Chapter 15, we will stress that the stand-alone provision of liquidity by productive entities is an inefficient way to proceed, because liquidity is costly and lucky entities, that is, those which turn out to have low liquidity needs, may end up with liquidity that they do not need. The usual way to avoid this waste of liquidity is to have it centralized in financial institutions (banks) that then redispatch the liquidity as needed through the mechanism of credit lines (i.e., options to draw on a liquidity pool). But conglomerate headquarters may perform a similar function by redistributing the conglomerate's cash flow among the divisions. Furthermore, as stressed by Brusco and Panunzi (2005), this redispatching may build on information collected by the headquarters about the divisions' prospects.

Faure-Grimaud and Inderst (2004) compare the sensitivity of investment to cash flow of focused firms and conglomerate divisions. External redispatching of liquidity by the financial sector under project finance (focused firms) cannot duplicate internal redispatching of liquidity within the conglomerate, since it is assumed that the same entrepreneur runs the divisions and therefore the information structure varies across institutions (so the analysis is akin to a multistage-financing version of the comparison between the Diamond diversified conglomerate and the project-finance standalone entity in Section 4.2). A key result of the Faure-Grimaud–Inderst analysis is that conglomerate divisions exhibit a reduced (re)investment–cash-flow sensitivity relative to focused firms performing the same activity, as better-performing diversions cross-subsidize the underperforming ones. They also show that, even though the average probability of refinancing per unit (divisions or focused firm) is higher in a conglomerate, "winner picking" implies that this need not be so at the individual unit's level: if division B has (even slightly) better continuation prospects than division A, then the conglomerate's liquidity will tend to be channeled to division B, and division A will benefit less from generating cash flow than it would if it were run as a focused firm. This redispatching is *ex post* efficient but may dull *ex ante* incentives to produce cash flow.

On the dark side, the competition between the divisions for corporate funding (stressed, for example, by Stein (1997)) may have perverse effects, such as excessive lobbying (Rajan et al. 2000; Scharfstein and Stein 2000). Similarly, collusion between specific divisions and the headquarters may lead to inefficient cross-subsidizations of weak divisions by stronger ones.

10.5.3.3 Product-Market Dimension

Being part of a large firm has implications for product-market competition. For example, Cestone and Fumagalli (2005) show that (endogenous) cross-subsidies from the most profitable to the least profitable divisions serves as a commitment device if these least profitable divisions are also those that face more aggressive competitors. For the interaction between finance and product markets, we refer to the analysis in Chapter 7.

Finally, there is a growing empirical literature on the efficiency of ICMs in allocating investment. The literature so far has pointed at the existence of an impact of ICMs on the investment pattern and showed that the concern about weak divisions receiving too much capital at the expense of strong ones should be taken seriously. Measuring cross-subsidization is not easy for several reasons, including the facts that conglomerate divisions and stand-alone entities are likely to have different attributes and that apparently unrelated divisions of a conglomerate may be hit by common shocks, such as those affecting a regional economy (Chevalier 2004). We refer to Stein (2003, pp. 145–152) for a careful review of the relevant considerations.

10.6 Active Monitoring and Initiative

As discussed in Section 10.3, high-intensity monitoring has the potential to stifle entrepreneurial initiative. This supplementary section studies the mechanics behind this reduction in managerial initiative, and echoes some of Section 9.2.2's analysis of the externalities attached to monitoring.

As in Sections 10.2 and 10.3, we assume that at the interim stage, a change in the course of action away from the status quo can be implemented, but that this change requires information. Here, we suppose that there are $n > 2$ possible changes in the course of action, and that a random (i.e., uninformed) choice among the n actions proves disastrous (in expectation) to both the entrepreneur and the investors.

The n actions are *ex ante* (i.e., in the absence of information) identical. To formalize the above considerations, we assume that $(n-2)$ of them end up giving a large negative payoff, that we denote "$-\infty$," to both parties. Therefore only two actions are relevant. One action increases the probability of success by

$$\tau > 0$$

relative to the status quo, while the other does not change the probability of success.

Also, one action imposes a cost

$$\gamma > 0$$

on insiders while the other imposes no such cost.

Preferences are said to be *congruent* if the action that raises the probability of success imposes no cost on insiders, and *dissonant* otherwise. The *ex ante* probability of congruence is denoted $\xi \in [0,1]$.[69] Of course, the choice of terminology for the "dissonance" case embodies the assumption that the entrepreneurial stake, R_b, in the case of success is low enough that the entrepreneur would not want to propose an investor-value-enhancing action that would impose cost γ:

$$\gamma > \tau R_b, \tag{10.7}$$

a condition that we will later impose (as we know, this assumption requires that the entrepreneur's net worth be small enough that she has to borrow and therefore reimburse a large enough amount). The payoffs attached to the n actions are summarized in Table 10.1.

Table 10.1

$-\infty$	$\cdots$	τ	$\cdots$	0	$\cdots$	$-\infty$
$-\infty$	$\cdots$	0	$\cdots$	γ	$\cdots$	$-\infty$
Congruence (ξ)						
$-\infty$	$\cdots$	τ	$\cdots$	0	$\cdots$	$-\infty$
$-\infty$	$\cdots$	γ	$\cdots$	0	$\cdots$	$-\infty$
Dissonance ($1-\xi$)						

For example, the entrepreneur might be a biotechnology or computer science professor running a start-up. The status quo is the strategy defined by the start-up's initial business plan. The professor/entrepreneur may or may not propose a change in the course of action. Such a change may affect the probability of success of the venture; and it may impact the entrepreneur's "outside" (nonventure) payoff, namely, her ability to return to academia in the case of failure, the enhancement of her academic CV, or her capability in alternative ventures. There may or may not be congruence between the venture's commercial goals and the entrepreneur's objectives outside the venture.

Let us assume that

$$\tau R > \gamma > \tau\left[R - \frac{I-A}{p_H + \tau}\right]. \tag{10.8}$$

69. Thus, the state of nature can be described by the occurrence or nonoccurrence of congruence (a binary variable) as well as by the mapping of payoffs to action names (all permutations are equally likely).

The first inequality in (10.8) says that in the case of dissonance, enhancing investor value is first-best efficient. The second inequality implies (10.7); for, were the investor-value-enhancing action always selected, the lenders would receive R_l in the case of success, satisfying the breakeven condition

$$(p_H + \tau)R_l = I - A.$$

More generally, investors must get at least this value in the case of success, implying that the borrower receives, in the case of success,

$$R_b \leqslant R - R_l = R - \frac{I - A}{p_H + \tau}.$$

Hence, the entrepreneur does not recommend a change in the course of action if preferences turn out to be dissonant.

Any investor can learn the realization of the payoff matrix (which includes the identity of the relevant actions, as described in Table 10.1) with probability x at private cost $c_m(x)$ satisfying $c_m(0) = 0$, $c'_m(0) = 0$, $c'_m > 0$, $c''_m > 0$, $c_m(1) = +\infty$. The entrepreneur can learn the realization of the payoff matrix with probability y at private cost $c_b(y)$ satisfying $c_b(0) = 0$, $c'_b(0) = 0$, $c'_b \geqslant 0$, $c''_b \geqslant 0$. (We do not assume that $c_b(1) = +\infty$ since we will initially consider the case in which the entrepreneur learns this realization for free ($c_b(1) = 0$) as a byproduct of her running the firm.)

Thus, each party either perfectly learns the identity of the two relevant actions and the payoffs attached to them, or learns nothing at all (in which case (s)he does not want to choose or propose an action at random as this would have negative consequences in expectation).

Lastly, we assume that the control right is given to the investors. This assumption can be rationalized in several ways. First, and as emphasized in this chapter, there may not be enough pledgeable income, and thus transferring control to investors may (in cases (b) and (c) below) be necessary to secure funding. Second, the left inequality in (10.8) implies that investor control is optimal even if there is no shortage of pledgeable income (up to the caveat discussed in (c) below).[70] That is, investor control is optimal even if there is enough pledgeable income to secure funding under entrepreneur control.

70. Third, one could add a third relevant action that, in contrast with the other two, would always be common knowledge and for which entrepreneur control would drastically lower value.

(a) *Fully informed entrepreneur, dispersed ownership.* Cases (a) and (b) assume that the entrepreneur learns the payoff matrix for free as a byproduct of her running the firm; they therefore cannot address the question of the impact of monitoring on entrepreneurial initiative.

Furthermore, case (a) presumes a dispersed (atomistic) ownership. This implies that individual investors have too small a stake to be willing to spend any monitoring cost. The investors are thus uninformed, and, because the entrepreneur only recommends an action that either increases or does nothing to the probability of success, rubber-stamp entrepreneurial suggestions when they arise.

Thus, under dispersed ownership, the entrepreneur has real, although no formal, authority.

(b) *Fully informed entrepreneur, large investor.* Maintaining the assumption that the entrepreneur is always fully informed, suppose now that a large investor holds a fraction R_m/R of the shares, that is, has stake R_m in the case of success.

The large monitor chooses monitoring intensity x (recall that x is this probability of learning payoffs), so as to equate his marginal monitoring cost $c'_m(x)$ with his marginal private benefit. To compute the latter, note that monitoring only turns out to be beneficial to the investors when preferences are dissonant. In that case, which has probability $1 - \xi$, the entrepreneur does not recommend the investor-value-enhancing action. The marginal benefit of monitoring for the large investor is therefore $(1 - \xi)\tau R_m$. Thus

$$c'_m(x) = (1 - \xi)\tau R_m. \tag{10.9}$$

Let us now compute the optimal monitoring level, assuming that pledgeable income is sufficient to secure funding for the monitoring level maximizing NPV (in Exercise 10.4 a shortage of pledgeable income leads either to increased monitoring or to no funding at all). This level is given by

$$\max_{\{x\}}\{p_H R - I + [\xi(\tau R) + (1 - \xi)x(\tau R - y)] - c_m(x)\}$$

or

$$c'_m(x) = (1 - \xi)(\tau R - y). \tag{10.10}$$

Comparing (10.9) and (10.10), the optimal monitoring level is obtained when

$$\tau R_{\rm m} = \tau R - \gamma$$

or

$$\frac{R_{\rm m}}{R} = \frac{\tau R - \gamma}{\tau R}.$$

Because, by assumption, $\gamma > \tau R_{\rm b}$ (otherwise preferences would always be congruent), the large investor must not hold all the outside (nonentrepreneurial) shares:

$$\frac{R_{\rm m}}{R} + \frac{R_{\rm b}}{R} < 1.$$

This result is another illustration of the overmonitoring principle analyzed in Chapter 9. At the margin, an increase in the large investor's monitoring intensity exerts two externalities: a positive one on other investors and a negative one on the entrepreneur. Only the latter exists if the large investor holds all external shares, resulting in overmonitoring.

(c) *Large investor and entrepreneurial initiative.* Lastly, let us assume that the entrepreneur's information level is endogenous. Her private cost of learning the payoff matrix with probability y (and learning nothing with probability $1 - y$) is $c_{\rm b}(y)$, where now $c_{\rm b}(1) = +\infty$ (so as to guarantee an interior solution for the choice of y). The variable y measures the entrepreneur's degree of initiative. We look for a Nash equilibrium (x^*, y^*) of the information-acquisition game between the entrepreneur and the large investor when they have stakes $R_{\rm b}$ and $R_{\rm m}$, respectively.

Learning the actions' payoffs benefits the entrepreneur only if (a) the large investor is uninformed (which has probability $1 - x$), since otherwise the large investor selects the investor-value-enhancing action anyway, and (b) given our maintained assumption that $\tau R_{\rm b} < \gamma$, preferences are congruent (which has probability ξ). Hence,

$$c_{\rm b}'(y^*) = (1 - x^*)\xi[\tau R_{\rm b}]. \qquad (10.11)$$

Note in particular that an increase in the equilibrium monitoring intensity x^* reduces entrepreneurial initiative y^*.

Monitoring benefits investors if either the entrepreneur is uninformed (which has probability $1 - y^*$) or the entrepreneur is informed and preferences are

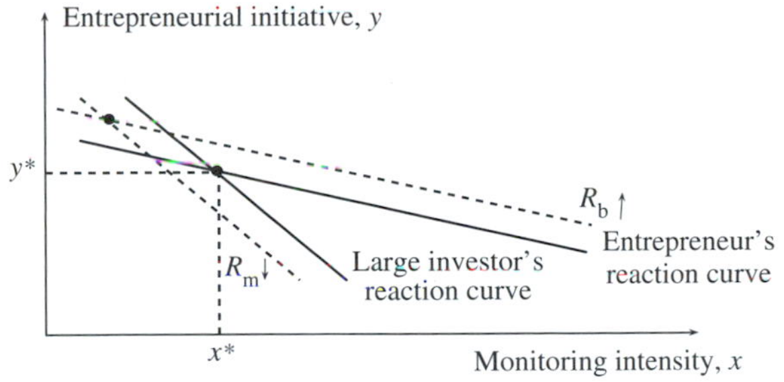

Figure 10.8

dissonant (which has probability $y^*(1 - \xi)$). Hence,

$$c_{\rm m}'(x^*) = [y^*(1 - \xi) + (1 - y^*)][\tau R_{\rm m}]. \qquad (10.12)$$

We will assume that the Nash equilibrium is stable,[71] as depicted in Figure 10.8.

As shown by Burkart et al. (1997), there are two ways, depicted in Figure 10.8, to boost entrepreneurial initiative at the contract design stage (both of which may reduce pledgeable income and thus may not be consistent with securing financing). The first is, of course, to raise the entrepreneur's stake $R_{\rm b}$. The second is to reduce the large investor's stake $R_{\rm m}$ so as to increase the impact of the entrepreneur's acquired information. Both policies increase y^* and reduce x^*.

Cestone (2004) builds on Burkart et al. by adding an advisory role for the monitor (see Chapter 9). In her model, a venture capitalist has a dual monitoring function: he tries to prevent decisions that are unfavorable to investors and he brings managerial support to the start-up entrepreneur. A high-powered incentive scheme, i.e., a large cash-flow stake for the venture capitalist, has two effects in this multitask environment: it encourages the venture capitalist to provide more advice to the entrepreneur, which is unambiguously beneficial; but it also may induce overmonitoring, since interference kills initiative. This latter effect implies that it may be optimal to turn control rights to the entrepreneur when giving high-powered incentives to the venture capitalist. Put differently, the venture capitalist's control rights and cash-flow rights need not covary: the venture capitalist may have control and limited (but

71. Stability means that the entrepreneur's reaction curve is flatter than the large investor's, or $c_{\rm b}'' c_{\rm m}'' > \xi^2 \tau^2 R_{\rm b} R_{\rm m}$.

nonnegligible) cash-flow rights, or no control and more extensive cash-flow rights. Cestone notes that venture capitalists usually lose their control rights when their preferred stocks are converted into common stocks.

10.7 Exercises

Exercise 10.1 (security design as a disciplining device). Go through the analysis in Section 10.4.2 more formally. The date-1 income is r with probability p_H^1 (if the entrepreneur exerts a high effort at date 1) or p_L^1 (if the entrepreneur exerts a low effort at date 1), and 0 otherwise. The entrepreneur enjoys date-1 private benefit B_0 when shirking and 0 otherwise. Let R_b^* be defined by

$$I - A - p_H^1 r - (1 - p_H^1)L = p_H^1[p_H(R - R_b^*)],$$

and assume that

$$R_b^* \geqslant \frac{B}{\Delta p},$$

$$p_H(R - R_b^*) > L,$$

and

$$(p_H^1 - p_L^1)[p_H R_b^*] \geqslant B_0.$$

(i) Interpret those conditions.

(ii) Describe an optimal incentive scheme and security design.

(iii) Suppose that $R_b^* = B/\Delta p$. Argue that a short-term bonus (a payment in the case of date-1 profit r) is suboptimal. Argue more generally that there is no benefit in having such a payment.

Exercise 10.2 (allocation of control and liquidation policy). This exercise considers the allocation of a control right over liquidation. As described in Figure 10.9, the framework has three dates: date 0 (financing and investment), date 1 (choice of liquidation), and date 2 (payoff in the case of continuation). There is moral hazard in the case of continuation. As usual, there is universal risk neutrality, the entrepreneur is protected by limited liability, and the investors demand a rate of return equal to 0.

One will assume that the variables (p_L, p_H, R, B) in the case of continuation are known *ex ante*. As usual, misbehaving (choosing probability p_L) yields a private benefit $B > 0$ to the entrepreneur. Let

$$\rho_0 \equiv p_H\left(R - \frac{B}{\Delta p}\right)$$

and

$$\rho_1 \equiv p_H R.$$

In contrast, the liquidation proceeds L and the fallback option U_b^0 for the entrepreneur may be *ex ante* random, even though they become common knowledge at date 1 before the liquidation decision. Lastly, L is fully pledgeable to investors while none of U_b^0 is.

(i) Solve for the optimal complete (state-contingent) contract, assuming that a court is able to directly verify $\omega \equiv (L, U_b^0)$ (and the profit in the case of success) and to enforce the contract specifying the probability of continuation $x(\omega) \in [0,1]$ and the allocation of L and R between the investors and the entrepreneur.

(ii) Assume from now on that,

$$\text{for all } \omega, \quad U_b^0 \leqslant \rho_1 - \rho_0.$$

That is, in the absence of a "golden parachute" given to the entrepreneur in the case of liquidation, the entrepreneur always prefers to continue. Compare the sets Ω^{FB} and Ω^{SB} of states of nature in which continuation is optimal in the absence and presence of financing constraint. How does Ω^{SB} vary with the entrepreneur's net worth A? (A diagram will help.)

(iii) From now on, assume that the court observes neither L nor U_b^0. Only the entrepreneur and the investors do. The remaining questions look at how far one can go toward the implementation of the optimal full-observability contract described in (i) using a simple allocation of the control right concerning liquidation.

One will focus on the case in which Ω^{SB} (see question (ii)) is strictly included in Ω^{FB}, and so inefficient liquidation is required.

Suppose first that the entrepreneur has the control right and that renegotiation occurs once ω is realized. Argue that

$$\Omega^{EN} = \Omega^{FB},$$

where Ω^{EN} is the set of states of nature over which continuation occurs under entrepreneur control.

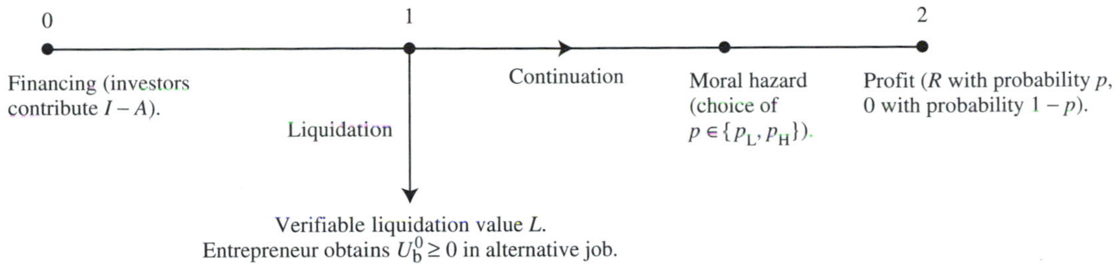

Figure 10.9

Conclude that the project is then not financed.

(iv) *Investor control.* Perform the analysis of question (iii) in the case of investor control in the absence of a golden parachute (the initial contract does not provide for any compensation for the entrepreneur in the case of liquidation). Suppose that the entrepreneur does not keep any savings. Show that

$$\Omega^{\mathrm{IN}} \subset \Omega^{\mathrm{SB}},$$

where Ω^{IN} is the set of states of nature over which continuation occurs under investor control. Is the project financed?

(v) *Investor control with golden parachute.* Argue that a positive golden parachute ($r_b > 0$ given to the entrepreneur in the case of liquidation) is optimal when investors have control.

Exercise 10.3 (large minority blockholding). Consider the active monitor model (see Chapter 9). The firm yields R in the case of success and 0 in the case of failure. The entrepreneur, large shareholder, and small shareholders have shares s_1, s_2, and s_3, respectively, where $s_1+s_2+s_3 = 1$. (To complete the model's description, one can, as in Chapter 9, assume that $s_1 R \geqslant b/\Delta p$ and $s_2 R \geqslant c/\Delta p$, using the notation of this chapter.) The small shareholders have formal control (one share bears one voting right and $s_3 > \frac{1}{2}$).

The project can be modified in a countable number of ways ($k = 0, 1, \dots$). Option 0 consists in "not modifying the project" (this option is known to everyone). Options 1 through ∞ do modify the project; all but two of them have disastrous consequences for all parties (so taking a modification at random is dominated by the status quo option 0). The two relevant modifications are such that one increases the probability of success by $\tau > 0$ and the other reduces it by $\mu > 0$. One involves a private cost $\gamma > 0$ or a private benefit $-\gamma$ for the entrepreneur, with $(\tau + \mu)s_1 R < \gamma$, and the other no such cost. Lastly, an action may involve a private benefit ξ for the large blockholder (or one of his subsidiary). There are three states of nature, as shown in Table 10.2. In each state of nature, the left-hand payoffs correspond to the (uninformed) investor-friendly modification and the right-hand payoffs to the (uninformed) investor-hostile modification.

Table 10.2 Probabilities: β (state 1); $(1-\beta)\kappa$ (state 2); $(1-\beta)(1-\kappa)$ (state 3).

	State 1		State 2		State 3	
Impact on probability of success	τ	$-\mu$	τ	$-\mu$	τ	$-\mu$
Private cost for entrepreneur	0	$-\gamma$	0	γ	0	γ
Private benefit for large blockholder	0	0	0	0	0	ξ

The timing goes as follows:

(1) The entrepreneur learns the two relevant modifications and their impact on payoffs, and makes a proposal to shareholders.
(2) The large blockholder learns the relevant modifications and their impact on payoffs, and either seconds the entrepreneur's recommendation for a modification or makes a counterproposal.
(3) Majority shareholders decide between the status quo and the recommendation(s).

(i) Predict the outcome in each state of nature.

(ii) Add a fourth state of nature in which the entrepreneur and large shareholder see eye-to-eye and both prefer a value-decreasing action (say, the payoffs in state 4 are as in state 2, except that for the second relevant action, "y" becomes "$-y$" and the large shareholder receives ξ). What would you predict?

Exercise 10.4 (monitoring by a large investor). Section 10.6 assumed that the entrepreneur does not have enough pledgeable income to recommend the investor-value-enhancing action in the case of dissonance, but has enough pledgeable income to induce (through the choice of the large investor's share) the level of monitoring that maximizes the NPV and still receive funding.

Suppose instead that pledgeable income is low so that the level of pledgeable income is not sufficient to attract funding when the NPV-maximizing monitoring level is induced. Go through the steps of case (b) ("fully informed entrepreneur, large investor") assuming that there is no scarcity of monitoring capital (on this, see Section 9.2), and show that the monitoring level x is given by

$$p_{\mathrm{H}}\left[R - \frac{B}{\Delta p}\right] + [\xi + (1-\xi)x]\tau R = I - A + c_{\mathrm{m}}(x)$$

and

$$c'_{\mathrm{m}}(x) > (1-\xi)(\tau R - y).$$

Exercise 10.5 (when investor control makes financing more difficult to secure). The general thrust of control rights theory is that investors are reassured, and so are more willing to lend, if they have control rights over the firm. The purpose of this exercise is to build a counterexample in which investor control is self-defeating and jeopardizes financing.

(i) An entrepreneur has cash A and wants to invest $I > A$ into a (fixed-size) project. The project yields $R > 0$ with probability p and 0 with probability $1 - p$. The probability of success is p_{H} if the entrepreneur behaves and $p_{\mathrm{L}} = p_{\mathrm{H}} - \Delta p$ ($\Delta p > 0$) if the entrepreneur misbehaves. The entrepreneur receives private benefit $B > 0$ in the latter case, and 0 in the former case. All parties are risk neutral, the entrepreneur is protected by limited liability, and the rate of interest in the economy is 0.

What is the necessary and sufficient condition for the entrepreneur to be able to obtain financing from investors?

(ii) Now add a control right. This control right can raise the expected revenue in the case of misbehavior, but does nothing in the case of good behavior; namely, the holder of the control right can select an action ("damage control") that raises the probability of success from p_{L} to $p_{\mathrm{L}} + \nu$ ($\nu > 0$) in the case of misbehavior, but keeps p_{H} constant. This interim action imposes a cost $\gamma > 0$ on the entrepreneur. (If the action is not selected, the probabilities of success are as in question (i), and there is no private cost γ.) The choice of action is simultaneous (say) with the entrepreneur's choice of effort.

First assume "entrepreneur control" (the entrepreneur is given the right to select this action or not). Write the two incentive constraints for the entrepreneur to behave. Show that, compared with question (i), the pledgeable income remains the same if $\nu B/(\Delta p) \leqslant \gamma$, and is decreased otherwise.

(iii) Next consider "investor control." Assume that when indifferent, the investors select the dominant strategy, i.e., the damage-control action (alternatively, one can assume that the action raises p_{H} as well, to $p_{\mathrm{H}} + \varepsilon$, where ε is arbitrarily small). Show that the financing condition is now

$$p_{\mathrm{H}}\left[R - \frac{B}{\Delta p - \nu}\right] \geqslant I - A.$$

Conclude that investor control, besides reducing NPV, may also make it more difficult for the entrepreneur to secure financing.

Exercise 10.6 (complementarity or substitutability between control and incentives). This exercise pursues the agenda set in Exercise 10.5 by considering various forms of complementarity and substitutability between the exercise of control rights and managerial incentives. It therefore relaxes the assumption of separability between the two.

(i) An entrepreneur has cash A and wants to invest $I > A$ into a (fixed-size) project. The project yields $R > 0$ with probability p and 0 with probability $1 - p$. The probability of success is p_{H} if the entrepreneur behaves and $p_{\mathrm{L}} = p_{\mathrm{H}} - \Delta p$ ($\Delta p > 0$) if the entrepreneur misbehaves. The entrepreneur receives private benefit $B > 0$ in the latter case, and 0 in the former case. All parties are risk neutral, the entrepreneur is protected by limited liability, and the rate of interest in the economy is 0.

What is the necessary and sufficient condition for the entrepreneur to be able to obtain financing from investors?

(ii) Now consider the possibility that a profit-enhancing action be chosen. For reasons of simplicity (but not for the sake of realism!), assume that this action is chosen simultaneously with effort. This action raises the probability of success to

- $p_H + \tau_H$ if the entrepreneur behaves, and
- $p_L + \tau_L$ if the entrepreneur misbehaves.

The action is indeed profit enhancing ($\tau_L, \tau_H > 0$) and is

- complementary with effort if $\Delta\tau \equiv \tau_H - \tau_L > 0$,
- substitutable with effort if $\Delta\tau < 0$.

The action further inflicts a disutility γ on the manager, where

$$\max(\tau_L, \tau_H) \cdot R < \gamma.$$

Lastly, assume that the high effort must be induced in order for financing to occur.

Write the pledgeable income under investor control and entrepreneur control. When does investor control increase the pledgeable income (and therefore facilitate financing)?

Exercise 10.7 (extent of control). A simple variation on the basic model of Section 10.2.1 involves a choice between limited investor control and extended investor control, rather than between entrepreneur control and investor control. Suppose, in the model of Section 10.2.1, that entrepreneur control is out of the picture (after you finish the exercise, you may want to think about a sufficient condition for this to be case), but that there are two degrees of investor control:

Limited. The action taken then increases the probability of success by $\tau_A > 0$ and inflicts cost $\gamma_A > 0$ on insiders.

Extended (investors have control over a wide set of actions). The selected action then increases the probability of success by $\tau_B > \tau_A$ and inflicts cost $\gamma_B > \gamma_A$ on insiders.

Assume that

$$\tau_A R - \gamma_A > \tau_B R - \gamma_B.$$

Find conditions under which limited or extended investor control prevails.

Exercise 10.8 (uncertain managerial horizon and control rights). This exercise considers the allocation of control between investors and management when the entrepreneur has an uncertain horizon.

We consider the fixed-investment model. The investment cost is I and the entrepreneur has only $A < I$. The entrepreneur is risk neutral and protected by limited liability; the investors are risk neutral and demand rate of return equal to 0. The profit is equal to R in the case of success and is 0 in the case of failure. In the absence of profit-enhancing action, the probability of success is p; when the profit-enhancing action is taken this probability becomes $p + \tau$, where $\tau > 0$, but the action imposes a nonmonetary cost on insiders, γ, where

$$\gamma > \tau R.$$

As usual, $p = p_H$ if the entrepreneur behaves (no private benefit) and $p = p_L$ if she misbehaves (private benefit B).

The twist relative to Chapter 10 is that the entrepreneur may not be able to run the project to completion: with probability λ, she must quit the firm for exogenous reasons. She learns this after the investment is sunk, but before the moral-hazard stage. If the entrepreneur quits (which will have probability λ), a new and *cashless* manager will be brought in. This manager is also risk neutral and protected by limited liability and has the same private benefit, probabilities of success, and payoff in the case of success as the entrepreneur.

Figure 10.10 summarizes the timing.

Let x and y in $[0, 1]$ denote the probabilities that investors receive control when the entrepreneur and the replacement manager are in charge, respectively. And assume that

$$(p_H + \tau)\frac{B}{\Delta p} \geqslant \gamma$$

(interpret this assumption), and that

$$\rho_1 \equiv p_H R > I > \rho_0^+ \equiv (p_H + \tau)\left(R - \frac{B}{\Delta p}\right).$$

(i) Assuming that incentives must be provided for good behavior (by either the entrepreneur or the replacement manager), write down the following.

- The entrepreneur's utility. (Hint: this utility is slightly different from the project's social value. Why?)
- The pledgeable income and the breakeven condition.

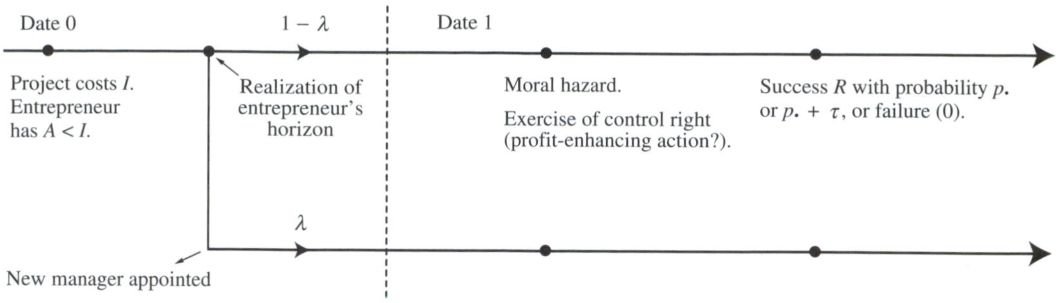

Figure 10.10

(ii) Argue that $y = 1$. Find the conditions under which the project is undertaken. (Warning. Two conditions must be fulfilled: investors must be willing to finance it, and the entrepreneur must be willing to go ahead with it.)

Exercise 10.9 (continuum of control rights). This exercise extends the analysis of Section 10.2.2 to a continuum of control rights. As in Section 10.2.2, consider a risk-neutral entrepreneur protected by limited liability. The entrepreneur has cash on hand A and wants to finance a project with cost $I > A$. The project yields R if it succeeds and 0 if it fails. Investors are risk neutral and demand a rate of return equal to 0. There is a continuum of control rights, where the decision attached to a control right can be thought of as a modification relative to the initial project and is characterized by the pair (t, g): $t \gtrless 0$ is the increase in the probability of success and $g \gtrless 0$ is the private cost borne by the entrepreneur if the decision is taken (the modification is made). Let $F(t, g)$ denote the continuous joint distribution over the space of control rights and $E_F[\cdot]$ the expectations with respect to distribution F.

The probability of success is

$$p + \tau \equiv p + E_F[tx(t, g)],$$

where $x(t, g) = 1$ if the decision (t, g) is taken and 0 otherwise. Similarly, let

$$y \equiv E_F[gx(t, g)].$$

Moral hazard is modeled in the usual way: $p = p_H$ if the entrepreneur behaves (no private benefit) and $p = p_L$ if the entrepreneur misbehaves (and receives private benefit B). Assume that the project can be funded only if the entrepreneur is provided with the incentive to behave.

(i) Solve for the optimal policy $x(\cdot, \cdot)$, assuming that the investors' breakeven constraint is binding (which it is for A small enough or I large enough).

(ii) Show that, as A decreases, τ and y increase.

(iii) Discuss the implementation of the optimal $x(\cdot, \cdot)$ function.

(iv) Consider the degenerate case in which g is the same for all control rights ($g > 0$). Show that

$$\frac{d^2 y}{d\tau^2} > 0.$$

References

Aghion, P. and P. Bolton. 1992. An incomplete contracts approach to financial contracting. *Review of Economic Studies* 59:473–493.

Aghion, P., M. Dewatripont, and P. Rey. 2004. Transferable control. *Journal of the European Economic Association* 2: 115–138.

Aghion, P., O. Hart, and J. Moore. 1992. The economics of bankruptcy reform. *Journal of Law, Economics, & Organization* 8:523–546.

Aghion, P. and J. Tirole. 1994. On the management of innovation. *Quarterly Journal of Economics* 109:1185–1209.

——. 1997. Formal and real authority in organizations. *Journal of Political Economy* 105:1–29.

Alchian, A. 1969. Corporate management and property rights. In *Economic Policy and the Regulation of Corporate Securities* (ed. H. Manne). Washington, D.C.: American Enterprise Institute.

Asquith, P., R. Gertner, and D. Scharfstein. 1994. Anatomy of financial distress: an examination of junk-bond issuers. *Quarterly Journal of Economics* 109:625–658.

Barclay, M. and C. Holderness. 1989. Private benefits from control of public corporations. *Journal of Financial Economics* 25:371–395.

Bebchuk, L. 1988. A new approach to corporate reorganizations. *Harvard Law Review* 101:775–804.

Berglöf, E. and E. L. von Thadden. 1994. Short-term versus long-term interests: a model of capital structure with multiple investors. *Quarterly Journal of Economics* 109:1055–1084.

Berglöf, E., G. Roland, and E. L. von Thadden. 2003. Optimal debt design and the role of bankruptcy. Mimeo, University of Mannheim, Stockholm School of Economics, and University of California, Berkeley.

Berkovitch, E. and R. Israel. 1999. Optimal bankruptcy laws across different economic systems. *Review of Financial Studies* 12:347–377.

Black, B. and R. Gilson. 1998. Venture capital and the structure of capital markets: banks vs stock markets. *Journal of Financial Economics* 47:243–277.

Bolton, P. and D. Scharfstein. 1996. Optimal debt structure and the number of creditors. *Journal of Political Economy* 104:1–25.

Boot, A., R. Gopalan, and A. Thakor. 2005. The entrepreneur's choice between private and public ownership. *Journal of Finance*, in press.

Brusco, S. and F. Panunzi. 2005. Reallocation of corporate resources and managerial incentives in internal capital markets. *European Economic Review* 49:659–681.

Burkart, M., D. Gromb, and F. Panunzi. 1997. Large shareholders, monitoring and the value of the firm. *Quarterly Journal of Economics* 112:693–728.

Cestone, G. 2004. Venture capital meets contract theory: risky claims or formal control? Mimeo, Universitat Autònoma de Barcelona.

Cestone, G. and C. Fumagalli. 2005. The strategic impact of resource flexibility in business groups. *RAND Journal of Economics* 36:193–214.

Che, Y.-K. and D. Hausch. 1999. Cooperative investments and the value of contracting: Coase vs Williamson. *American Economic Review* 89:125–147.

Chevalier, J. 2004. What do we know about cross-subsidization? Evidence from merging firms. *Advances in Economic Analysis & Policy* 4(1), Article 3. (Available at http://www.bepress.com/bejeap/advances/vol4/iss1/art3.)

Crémer, J. 1995. Arm's length relationships. *Quarterly Journal of Economics* 104:275–295.

Davydenko, S. and J. Franks. 2004. Do bankruptcy codes matter? A study of defaults in France, Germany and the UK. Mimeo, London Business School.

Dessein, W. 2002. Authority and communication in organizations. *Review of Economic Studies* 69:811–838.

Dewatripont, M. and J. Tirole. 1994. A theory of debt and equity: diversity of securities and manager–shareholder congruence. *Quarterly Journal of Economics* 109:1027–1054.

Dewatripont, M. and J. Tirole. 1999. Advocates. *Journal of Political Economy* 107:1–39.

——. 2005. Modes of communication. *Journal of Political Economy*, in press.

Faure-Grimaud, A. and R. Inderst. 2005. Conglomerate entrenchment under optimal financial contracting. *American Economic Review* 95:850–861.

Franks, J., C. Mayer, and L. Renneboog. 1996. The role of large share stakes in poorly performing companies. Mimeo, London Business School.

Gertner, R. and D. Scharfstein. 1991. A theory of workouts and the effects of reorganization law. *Journal of Finance* 46:1184–1222.

Gertner, R., D. Scharfstein, and J. Stein. 1994. Internal versus external capital markets. *Quarterly Journal of Economics* 109:1211–1230.

Gorton, G. and G. Pennacchi. 1990. Financial intermediaries and liquidity creation. *Journal of Finance* 45:49–71.

——. 1993. Security baskets and index-linked securities. *Journal of Business* 66:1–27.

Green, J. and J. J. Laffont. 1992. Renegotiation and the form of efficient contracts. *Annales d'Economie et de Statistique* 25/26:123–150.

——. 1994. Non verifiability, costly renegotiation and efficiency. *Annales d'Economie et de Statistique* 36:81–95.

Grossman, S. and O. Hart. 1986. The costs and benefits of ownership: a theory of lateral and vertical integration. *Journal of Political Economy* 94:691–719.

Hart, O. 1995a. *Firms, Contracts, and Financial Structure*. Oxford University Press.

——. 1995b. Corporate governance: some theory and implications. *Economic Journal* 105:678–689.

——. 2001. Financial contracting. *Journal of Economic Literature* 34:1079–1100.

Hart, O. and J. Moore. 1989. Default and renegotiation: a dynamic model of debt. Mimeo, MIT and LSE. (Published in *Quarterly Journal of Economics* (1998) 113:1–42.)

——. 1990. Property rights and the nature of the firm. *Journal of Political Economy* 98:1119–1158.

——. 1998. Cooperatives vs outside ownership. Mimeo, Harvard University and LSE.

——. 1999. Foundations of incomplete contracts. *Review of Economic Studies* 66:115–138.

——. 2004. Agreeing now to agree later: contracts that rule out but do not rule in. Mimeo, Harvard and LSE.

Hermalin, B. and M. Weisbach. 1998. Endogenously chosen boards of directors and their monitoring of the CEO. *American Economic Review* 88:96–118.

Holmström, B. and P. Milgrom. 1991. Multi-task principal-agent analyzes: incentive contracts, asset ownership, and job design. *Journal of Law, Economics, & Organization* 7(Special Issue):24–52.

Jarrell, G., J. Brickley, and J. Netter. 1988. The market for corporate control: the empirical evidence since 1980. *Journal of Economic Perspectives* 2:49–68.

Jensen, M. and W. R. Meckling. 1976. Theory of the firm, managerial behaviour, agency costs and ownership structure. *Journal of Financial Economics* 3:305–360.

Kaplan, S. and P. Strömberg. 2003. Financial contracting theory meets the real world: an empirical analysis of venture capital contracts. *Review of Economic Studies* 70:281–315.

——. 2004. Characteristics, contracts, and actions: evidence from venture capitalist analyses. *Journal of Finance* 59:2177–2210.

Klein, B., R. Crawford, and A. Alchian. 1978. Vertical integration, appropriable rents and the competitive contracting process. *Journal of Law and Economics* 21:297–326.

Kyle, A. 1985. Continuous auctions and insider trading. *Econometrica* 53:1315–1335.

Lamont, O. 1997. Cash flow and investment: evidence from internal capital markets. *Journal of Finance* 52:83–109.

Lerner, J. and U. Malmendier. 2005. Contractibility and the design of research agreements. Mimeo, Harvard University and Stanford University.

Lerner, J., H. Shane, and A. Tsai. 2003. Do equity financing cycles matter? Evidence from biotechnology alliances. *Journal of Financial Economics* 67:411–446.

Maskin, E. 1977. Nash equilibrium and welfare optimality. Mimeo, MIT. (Published in *Review of Economic Studies* (1999) 66:23–38.)

Maskin, E. and J. Moore. 1999. Implementation and renegotiation. *Review of Economic Studies* 66:39–56.

Maskin, E. and J. Tirole. 1999a. Unforeseen contingencies and incomplete contracts. *Review of Economic Studies* 66: 83–114.

——. 1999b. Two remarks on property rights. *Review of Economic Studies* 66:139–150.

Nöldeke, G. and K. Schmidt. 1998. Sequential investments and options to own. *RAND Journal of Economics* 29:633–653.

Pagano, M. and P. Volpin. 2005. Shareholder protection, stock market development, and politics. Marshall Lecture, European Economic Association, Amsterdam, August 27.

Rajan, R., H. Servaes, and L. Zingales. 2000. The cost of diversity: the diversification discount and inefficient investment. *Journal of Finance* 55:35–80.

Riordan, M. 1990. What is vertical integration? In *The Firm as a Nexus of Treaties* (ed. M. Aoki, B. Gustafsson, and O. Williamson). London: Sage.

Scharfstein, D. and J. Stein. 2000. The dark side of internal capital markets: divisional rent-seeking and inefficient investment. *Journal of Finance* 55:2537–2564.

Segal, I. 1995. Essays on commitment, renegotiation, and incompleteness of contracts. PhD thesis, Harvard University.

——. 1999. Complexity and renegotiation: a foundation for incomplete contracts. *Review of Economic Studies* 66:57–82.

Segal, I. and M. Whinston. 2002. The Mirrlees approach to mechanism design with renegotiation (with applications to hold-up and risk sharing). *Econometrica* 70:1–45.

Shin, H. H. and R. Stulz. 1998. Are internal capital markets efficient? *Quarterly Journal of Economics* 113:531–552.

Shleifer, A. and R. Vishny. 1988. Value maximization and the acquisition process. *Journal of Economic Perspectives* 2:7–20.

Stein, J. 1997. Internal capital markets and the competition for corporate resources. *Journal of Finance* 52:111–133.

——. 2002. Information production and capital allocation: decentralized vs. hierarchical firms. *Journal of Finance* 57: 1891–1921.

——. 2003. Agency, information and corporate investment. In *Handbook of the Economics of Finance* (ed. G. Constantinides, M. Harris, and R. Stulz). Amsterdam: North-Holland.

Subrahmanyam, A. 1991. A theory of trading in stock index futures. *Review of Financial Studies* 4:17–51.

Tirole, J. 1999. Incomplete contracts: where do we stand? *Econometrica* 67:741–781.

Von Thadden, E. L. 1995. Long term contracts, short term investment and monitoring. *Review of Economic Studies* 62:557–575.

Williamson, O. 1975. *Markets and Hierarchies: Analysis of Antitrust Implications.* New York: Free Press.

——. 1985. *The Economic Institutions of Capitalism: Firms, Markets, Relational Contracting.* New York: Free Press.

Zwiebel, J. 1995. Corporate conservatism and relative compensation. *Journal of Political Economy* 103:1–25.

11
Takeovers

11.1 Introduction

This chapter focuses on the transfer of ownership of firms, and in particular on the market for corporate control, in which a new company or managerial team takes control of a firm and replaces its existing management or at least manages the firm's assets differently.

Although the main focus will be on hostile takeovers (takeovers that are not welcomed by the incumbent management), we must realize that hostile takeovers represent only a small fraction of actions leading to a managerial turnover (since turnover may simply result from a decision of the board of directors) or to a merger or acquisition (friendly acquisitions negotiated with management and approved by the board of directors).[1]

We refer to Chapter 1 for a broad discussion of the market for corporate control. The current chapter looks at the rationale and the mechanics of takeovers. It analyzes the two common motivations advanced for the existence of takeovers: the benefits accruing from a new management team with fresh ideas, superior efficiency, or, more simply, the willingness to abandon past, mistaken strategies (the "*ex post* rationale"), and the disciplining effect on incumbent management of the hovering threat of a takeover in the case of poor performance (the "*ex ante* rationale"). Firms may facilitate takeovers in order to enjoy these "new blood" and "disciplining" benefits; they, however, want to limit (and appropriate some of) the rents enjoyed by acquirers. Much of the literature on takeovers focuses on this tradeoff between efficiency and rent extraction. Sometimes, though, there is no efficiency component to takeovers. For example, the raider may want to build an empire; or he may want to suppress a product that cannibalizes or will cannibalize the sales of one of his own products; or else he may want to transfer assets or intermediate goods at a good price to one of his divisions. That is, such a raider reduces shareholder value, but is willing to acquire the firm in order to enjoy control benefits.

The chapter proceeds in two stages. First, Sections 11.2–11.4 abstract from specific institutions and study the general tradeoff between efficiency and rent extraction. This mechanism-design approach to takeovers will be called the "pure theory of takeovers," and will serve as a benchmark for the more positive analysis. It is also used in Section 11.3 to analyze whether private incentives to facilitate or deter takeovers coincide with social ones and whether takeovers should be regulated.

Much of the literature, on the other hand, focuses on the impact of country- and time-specific institutions concerning voting rules, disclosure regulations, and takeover defenses (such as greenmail, poison pills, supermajority or fair-price amendments, and dual-class votes) on the likelihood and efficiency of takeovers. Sections 11.5–11.8 will therefore recast this "positive theory of takeovers" as a study of the implementation (or nonimplementation) of the economic rationale for takeovers.

11.2 The Pure Theory of Takeovers: A Framework

Consider the following situation. A firm knows that, with some probability, a new management team ("the raider") that is able to manage the firm as well as and possibly better than incumbent management will appear in the future. Importantly, this raider is not part of the initial financial arrangement that creates the firm. In particular, we rule out options

1. Of course, some "friendly mergers" occur under the threat of a takeover, and so it is hard to allocate mergers and acquisitions into friendly and hostile groups.

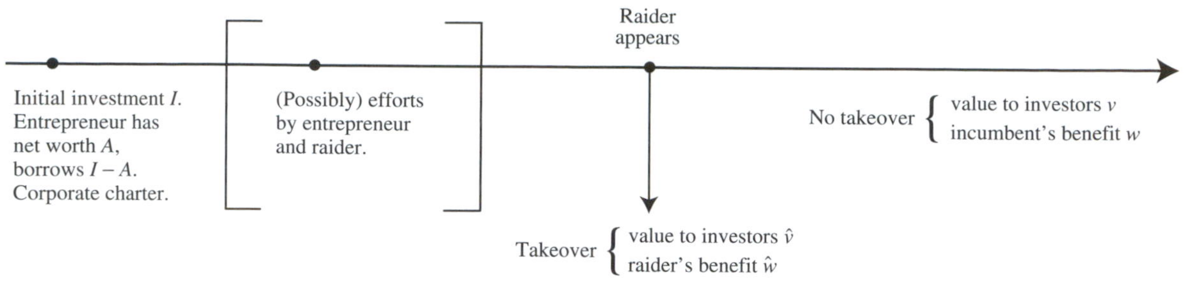

Figure 11.1

that allow a corporate entity (a potential raider) to acquire control of the firm in the future.[2] Put differently, the future raider is not yet identified, or else there are several potential raiders and it is too complex to design option contracts for each of them.

Figure 11.1 describes the timing of events. In the absence of takeover, the firm keeps being run by the incumbent management. Investors receive expected value v and the incumbent entrepreneur receives expected surplus w.

In the event of a takeover, a raider obtains control of the firm.[3] Let $\hat{v}$ and $\hat{w}$ denote the expected value to investors[4] and the raider's expected surplus under raider management.

Fixed-investment example. In the fixed-investment model (see Section 3.2),

$$v = p_H(R - R_b) \quad \text{and} \quad w = p_H R_b,$$

where R is the profit in the case of success (there is no profit if the project fails), R_b is the entrepreneur's stake, and p_H the probability of success.[5] The values $\hat{v}$ and $\hat{w}$ may differ from those under incumbent management through the probability, $\hat{p}_H$, of success. Or $\hat{w}$ may differ from w because the raider enjoys a private benefit just from heading the firm.

The initial "corporate charter" defines the terms under which the raider can take control.[6] The first question that the charter design must address is that of whether the transfer of control to the would-be raider should be made easy or hard. That is, for what values of $\hat{v}$ and $\hat{w}$ should a transfer occur? A second question is raised when the entrepreneur takes actions prior to the appearance of the raider: what impact does a takeover-friendly or -hostile charter have on the incumbent management's incentives? Similarly, the raider may need to sink a fixed cost to identify the target and define a corporate strategy for this target: what impact does the charter have on the raider's incentive to commit such resources? We now examine these questions in sequence. Indeed, we ignore the effort stage (indicated in brackets in Figure 11.1) in a first step.

11.3 Extracting the Raider's Surplus: Takeover Defenses as Monopoly Pricing

We assume that the corporate charter is unconstrained; in particular, the law does not require it

2. An illustration of such a forward contract is provided by the 1997 agreement between a consortium formed by Mannesman, AT&T, and Unisource on one side, and Deutsche Bahn on the other to create a new telecommunications company, initially controlled by Deutsche Bahn with an option for the consortium to acquire control in 1999 (see Nöldeke and Schmidt (1998) for more details).

3. Like most of the literature on takeovers, we formalize control as an all-or-nothing phenomenon. As will be discussed in Section 11.5.5, large shareholders do have an influence on the firm's decision making even when they do not have a control majority. The higher their ownership share, the more intense is their monitoring (Burkart et al. 1998, Chapter 9), and the more real authority they enjoy (Chapter 10).

4. We are interested in the impact of the raid on the investors (the increase or decrease from v to $\hat{v}$) and on incumbent management (the removal of the surplus w). It should be kept in mind, though, that takeovers may affect other "stakeholders" (e.g., the workers through the breach of implicit contracts, as in Shleifer and Summers (1988)), the creditors, or the Treasury.

5. Assuming that R_b, the entrepreneur's stake in the case of success, satisfies the incentive constraint. So, if B represents the benefit from shirking, and p_L the associated probability of success,

$$R_b \geqslant \frac{B}{p_H - p_L}.$$

6. Needless to say, this view of the corporate charter is exceedingly narrow. But much of the focus in this chapter is on the raider's ability to acquire control and its consequences. Hence, a focus on the transaction price is not unwarranted for our purposes.

to account for the interests of economic agents who are not parties to this initial contract. Under this assumption, the corporate charter stands for the interests of the firm's constituency (entrepreneur and investors) at the date at which it is designed. It has no reason to reflect the interests of parties, such as a raider, that will later become associated with the firm. Rather, it is likely to attempt to capture the latter's surplus. To exploit this monopoly power over future buyers, the charter optimally "taxes" these acquirers.[7]

We will make the following assumptions:

- The raider does not face credit rationing. Thus, he can pay up to the full value $\hat{v} + \hat{w}$ (investor value and private surplus).
- $\hat{v}$, in a first step, is publicly known at the date at which the charter is drawn. By contrast, $\hat{w}$ is private information of the raider at the date of takeover. From the point of view of the target, $\hat{w}$ is distributed according to density $h(\hat{w})$ and cumulative distribution function $H(\hat{w})$ and is private information to the raider.

We will also initially assume that the entrepreneur (incumbent manager) does not face credit rationing (think of this as coming from a high initial net worth) and therefore aims at maximizing the firm's NPV. Later, we will see how the charter is amended if the entrepreneur lacks pledgeable income at the charter design stage.

11.3.1 Incumbent Manager Is Not Credit Constrained

Suppose that the firm can commit to a sale price P to a potential raider.[8] Such a commitment is tantamount to selecting a cutoff value $\hat{w}^*$ for the raider's surplus such that

$$\hat{v} + \hat{w}^* = P.$$

The probability of a sale is then

$$1 - H(\hat{w}^*) = 1 - H(P - \hat{v}).$$

The entrepreneur's utility is equal to the NPV:

$$U_b = -I + (v + w)H(\hat{w}^*) + (\hat{v} + \hat{w}^*)[1 - H(\hat{w}^*)].$$

Maximizing this utility with respect to $\hat{w}^*$ (which, as we have seen, is equivalent to maximizing the NPV over the sale price P) yields first-order condition (assuming an interim solution)

$$\frac{P - (v + w)}{P} = \frac{(\hat{v} + \hat{w}^*) - (v + w)}{\hat{v} + \hat{w}^*} = \frac{1}{\eta}, \tag{11.1}$$

where

$$\eta \equiv \frac{h(\hat{w}^*)(\hat{v} + \hat{w}^*)}{(1 - H(\hat{w}^*))}$$

is the raider's elasticity of demand.

We thus obtain the standard monopoly pricing formula: the "Lerner index"—that is, the relative markup over marginal cost—is equal to the inverse elasticity of demand. The "cost" of "supplying a takeover" to a raider is just the opportunity cost of the forgone surplus $(v + w)$. To see that η is indeed an elasticity of demand, note that the probability of takeover

$$1 - H(\hat{w}^*) = 1 - H(P - \hat{v})$$

defines a "demand for takeovers" $D(P)$. And so $D'(P) = -h(P - \hat{v}) = -h(\hat{w}^*)$. Thus, η is equal to $-D'P/D$, which is the standard definition of an elasticity.

Let

$$\hat{w}^* = \hat{w}^{\mathrm{m}}$$

(where "m" stands for "monopoly") denote the solution to (11.1).[9]

Needless to say, monopoly pricing induces a social inefficiency. As Bebchuk and Zingales (2000) put it, future buyers do not sit at the table at the charter design stage. Their surplus is therefore not internalized and the resulting purchase price is excessive and leads to a socially suboptimal volume

7. The following is closely related to the idea pioneered by Diamond and Maskin (1979) and Aghion and Bolton (1987), according to which two parties to a commercial transaction have an incentive to write long-term contracts with penalties for breach in order to force new partners to a transaction with one of the two parties to offer better terms of trade.

8. We will assume that the raider pays in cash. In practice, though, the raider may pay in equity or debt securities of his own firm. Payments in equity or risky debt raise another issue: the shareholders of the target firm may not know the value of the payment offer made by the raider; that is, they face adverse selection (see Chapter 6) and may be concerned that the bidding firm is overvalued.

But asymmetric information can operate both ways (Fishman 1989): if the target's shareholders have superior information about the value of their firm and the target's size is not negligible with respect to the acquirer's size, then a payment in equities can mitigate the adverse-selection problem by having the target's shareholders share the post-takeover profits.

9. A sufficient condition for the program to be strictly quasi-concave is that the hazard rate $h/[1 - H]$ be strictly increasing (a property satisfied by almost all usual distributions).

of takeovers.[10] Like any monopolist, the entrepreneur trades off a higher price P against the risk of forgoing profitable trading opportunities. From the point of view of society, though, P is a transfer, and so monopoly pricing results in a suboptimally low volume of takeovers.

Remark (other welfare considerations). We identify only one force giving rise to inefficient levels of takeovers. Other forces are in play. For example, and as we earlier discussed, the raider may be subject to an agency problem. Its management may push for this takeover because it gains from building an empire or because it has private information about the poor health of the bidding firm and is trying to "gamble for resurrection";[11] in such cases, the bidder's management exerts its "real control" (see Chapter 10) to reduce the bidder's value. A proper analysis of real and formal authority in the bidding firm is then needed in order to make assertions about the welfare impact of takeover defenses.

11.3.2 Incentive to Prepare a Raid

The preceding analysis neglected the impact of the corporate charter on the potential raider's incentive to design a business plan for the firm. Suppose, for instance, that the raider needs to invest cost c to be able to formulate a strategy for the firm. That is, by paying c, he creates a value pair $(\hat{v}, \hat{w})$, where $\hat{w}$ is drawn from the distribution H. His *ex post* gain is then $\hat{v} + \hat{w} - P = \hat{w} - \hat{w}^{\text{m}}$ if $\hat{v} + \hat{w} \geqslant P$ and 0 otherwise. Under monopoly pricing, the raider then prepares a raid if and only if

$$\int_{\hat{w}^{\text{m}}}^{\infty} (\hat{w} - \hat{w}^{\text{m}})\, \text{d}H(\hat{w}) \geqslant c. \tag{11.2}$$

If inequality (11.2) is not satisfied, then the firm must reduce the sale price P below $\hat{v} + \hat{w}^{\text{m}}$, so as to encourage the raider to participate.

10. The conclusion would be different if the potential raider could be part of the initial charter design. It would then make sense to build an option for the raider to acquire the firm at a lower price (say, the "marginal cost" $v + w$), in exchange for an up-front payment for this option. The Coase Theorem would then obtain: there would be a socially efficient volume of takeovers.

See Burkart (1996) for an earlier discussion of the regulation of takeovers.

11. Such strategies are sometimes perceived as coming from "managerial overconfidence," but need not be associated with hubris.

11.3.3 Incumbent Manager Is Credit Constrained

Let us return to the situation in which the raider's participation in the process is not an issue; but let us now assume that the entrepreneur (who, as usual, receives the NPV) must adjust her policy so as to let her investors break even. Let us illustrate the main finding in the context of the fixed-investment model developed in Section 3.2 and discussed in Section 11.2 ($v + w = p_{\text{H}}R$): the entrepreneur chooses R_{b} and $\hat{w}^*$ so as to solve

$$\max_{\{R_{\text{b}}, \hat{w}^*\}} \{-I + (v + w)H(\hat{w}^*) + (\hat{v} + \hat{w}^*)[1 - H(\hat{w}^*)]\}$$

s.t.

$$vH(\hat{w}^*) + (\hat{v} + \hat{w}^*)[1 - H(\hat{w}^*)] \geqslant I - A,$$

$$v = p_{\text{H}}(R - R_{\text{b}}),$$

$$w = p_{\text{H}}R_{\text{b}},$$

$$(\Delta p)R_{\text{b}} \geqslant B.$$

If the first constraint, the investors' breakeven constraint, is nonbinding, then $\hat{w}^* = \hat{w}^{\text{m}}$. The interesting case is when the entrepreneur has a weak balance sheet, as, say, measured by a low value of A. The breakeven constraint is then binding and has a strictly positive shadow price. The quest for pledgeable income then mandates that the entrepreneur takes as small a share in profit as is consistent with incentives:

$$R_{\text{b}} = \frac{B}{\Delta p}.$$

Taking the minimal incentive-compatible stake is a costless way (in terms of NPV, which depends only on $v + w = p_{\text{H}}R$, and not on R_{b}) of creating pledgeable income. We now show that the entrepreneur also resorts to a more costly way of creating pledgeable income, namely, a below-monopoly-level acquisition price. Letting $\mu > 0$ denote the shadow price of the investor breakeven constraint, the first-order condition with respect to $\hat{w}^*$ yields

$$\frac{(\hat{v} + \hat{w}^*) - (v + w/(1 + \mu))}{\hat{v} + \hat{w}^*} = \frac{1}{\eta}. \tag{11.3}$$

This implies that $\hat{w}^* < \hat{w}^{\text{m}}$.

The quest for pledgeable income leads to a higher occurrence of takeovers. Or, anticipating our later discussion of the implementation of P through takeover defenses, a weaker initial balance sheet calls for more limited takeover defenses. The intuition for this result is that unlike the investor value, v, under incumbent management, and the resale price, $P = \hat{v} + \hat{w}^*$, the entrepreneur's surplus, w, is nonpledgeable. This is why it receives weight only $1/(1+\mu)$ in the opportunity cost of takeovers in formula (11.3).

To sum up, we obtain here another illustration of the concessions made by firms to investors in their quest for pledgeable income. In this respect, there is little difference between a higher probability of takeover, costly collateral pledging, the enrollment of speculative and active monitors, and the transfer of control rights to investors. All these policies sacrifice NPV to boost pledgeable income.

11.3.4 Unknown Value Enhancement

We have heretofore assumed that the payoff to investors under raider management was known; only the raider's surplus was subject to uncertainty. Let us now assume that $\hat{v}$ is also unknown.

An important difference between $\hat{v}$ and $\hat{w}$ is that a measure of $\hat{v}$ (the realization of the random variable whose mean is $\hat{v}$) is available *ex post*. We now show that this observation implies that *partial* sales are in general optimal.

To illustrate this in a simple way, suppose as before that $\hat{w}$ is unknown and is distributed according to a uniform distribution on $[0,1]$:

$$\hat{w} \sim U[0,1].$$

Assume further that $\hat{v}$ is independent of $\hat{w}$.

For simplicity, we treat the case in which the entrepreneur is not credit constrained.

Let us consider the following *thought experiment*: suppose that, contrary to our assumption, $\hat{v}$ were actually known (as has been the case until now). The entrepreneur would then maximize the NPV. Using the fact that the distribution of $\hat{w}$ is uniform, $H(\hat{w}) = \hat{w}$, the optimal $\hat{w}^*$ solves

$$\max\{-I + (v+w)\hat{w}^* + (\hat{v} + \hat{w}^*)(1-\hat{w}^*)\}$$

or

$$\hat{w}^{\mathrm{m}} = \tfrac{1}{2}(1 + v + w - \hat{v}) \iff P = \tfrac{1}{2}(1 + v + w + \hat{v}).$$

Let us now return to the situation in which only the raider knows $\hat{v}$ (and of course $\hat{w}$). Then the entrepreneur cannot increase the NPV relative to the situation of the thought experiment. But it turns out that, despite the imperfect knowledge about $\hat{v}$, the same NPV as in the thought experiment can be obtained: suppose that only half of the shares are put up for sale to the raider,[12] and that the price for this block of shares is set at the following level:

$$P = \tfrac{1}{2}(1 + v + w).$$

The raider then purchases the block if and only if the investor value for half of the shares plus the raider's (entire) surplus exceeds the sale price:

$$\tfrac{1}{2}\hat{v} + \hat{w} \geqslant P$$

or

$$\hat{w} \geqslant \tfrac{1}{2}(1 + v + w - \hat{v}).$$

In a sense, a partial sale can be used as a *metering* device that allows the firm to benefit from part of the investor value increases brought about by the raider.

11.4 Takeovers and Managerial Incentives

Let us now turn to the impact of a takeover prospect on managerial incentives to raise profitability. The popular debate assigns both a positive and a negative incentive impact to takeovers. On the one hand, the market for corporate control is meant to keep incumbent managers on their toes by threatening them with the prospect of takeover in case of poor managerial performance (Manne 1965). Thus, takeovers are good for governance. Jensen (1988) has been a strong advocate of this perspective. On the other hand, takeovers are asserted to induce managers to adopt a short-term, "myopic" perspective. Because similar ideas have been developed in previous chapters, I will present a very informal account of the main arguments.

11.4.1 Takeover-Induced Myopia

Let us start with a simple version of the "myopia" argument.[13] Return to the fixed-investment model.

12. I here finesse the issue of control. If the raider requires control to implement his policy, assume that the block sold to the raider has a majority of voting rights. In general, this may require different classes of shares with different voting rights (see Section 11.6 for a discussion of dual-class shares).

13. More sophisticated versions can, for example, be found in Bebchuk and Stole (1992), Laffont and Tirole (1988), Schnitzer (1992), and Stein (1988, 1989).

Suppose that the probability that the project is successful under incumbent management is $p + \tau$, where p is equal to p_{H} or p_{L} depending on whether the incumbent management later works or shirks, and τ is some pre-takeover-stage investment by the entrepreneur. Let $\gamma(\tau)$ denote the (convex) private cost to the entrepreneur of choosing τ. Assume that the choice of τ is unobservable by other parties. In particular, the incumbent manager's (actual, as opposed to anticipated) choice of τ affects neither the raider's willingness to pay for the firm (at the date of the raid) nor the acquisition price. Letting R_{b} denote the entrepreneur's stake in success and H the probability of no takeover taking place, the entrepreneur chooses τ so as to maximize

$$\tau R_{\mathrm{b}} H - \gamma(\tau).$$

In general, this choice involves two distortions relative to the socially optimal level. First, when retained, the entrepreneur receives less than the full pie ($R_{\mathrm{b}} < R$) and therefore has a suboptimal incentive to raise the probability of success. This is another version of the standard effect identified in Section 3.2: the quest for pledgeable income forces the entrepreneur to give some of the return to investors, which dulls entrepreneurial incentives.

More interestingly, incentives are also dulled by the prospect of a takeover ($H < 1$); the entrepreneur invests less if the probability that she will reap the fruits of the investment decreases. Whether this induces a social cost depends on the transferability of the investment τ. If τ is not transferred to a new team (e.g., it corresponds to some noncodified knowledge accumulated by the entrepreneur), then this second reduction in incentives is not distortive, since the investment pays off privately and socially with probability H only. In contrast, if the investment is transferable (so τ corresponds to the choice of a better project, to a better maintenance of the equipment, etc.), a new factor of underinvestment is the positive externality of investment on the raider.[14]

Here managerial myopia—the tendency to excessively privilege the present over the future—takes the form of an underinvestment in future profitability, as the benefits will partly go to the new managerial team. Alternatively, and closely related, managerial myopia might consist in "sabotaging" the profit of the raider so as to decrease the likelihood of a takeover;[15] or, along the lines of the analysis of Chapter 7, in sacrificing long-run payoff in order to "posture," that is, to obtain good short-term results and appear efficient to investors.

11.4.2 Takeovers and Managerial Discipline

Conversely, the takeover threat may induce the entrepreneur to work harder. The analysis is similar to that of Section 10.4.2. There, we argued that contingent interference may be an instrument of managerial discipline. The basic point is that performance-related rewards and punishments cannot consist in solely monetary rewards. In particular, to the extent that managers derive rents from their position, a sanction for poor performance may require taking that position away. This strategy was analyzed in Section 10.4.2 in the context of a liquidation or downsizing of assets in the case of poor intermediate performance—but the key feature of this policy is not the form of interference per se, but the fact that the manager enjoys lower rents from office or loses them altogether. The same can be accomplished, perhaps at a lower cost, through the replacement of the incumbent team by a new team.

Bertrand and Mullainathan (2003) analyze the impact on corporate behavior of the passage of laws restricting takeovers of firms incorporated in a given state in the United States. Among other things, they compare plants located in the same state but belonging to firms incorporated in different states. For example, they can look at changes in two plants located in New York but belonging to firms incorporated in Delaware and California when an antitakeover law is passed in Delaware, which enables them to filter out state-specific shocks. They find that wages, and in particular white-collar ones, increase significantly when an antitakeover law is passed. By contrast, the passage of an antitakeover law does not affect firm size overall (it leads to fewer

14. In the case of transferable investments, the value of H depends not only on the price P demanded for the acquisition but also on the equilibrium value τ^*. The entrepreneur's investment is then given in a rational expectations equilibrium by $R_{\mathrm{b}} H(P, \tau^*) = \gamma'(\tau^*)$.

15. An example of such behavior is entrenchment, in which the incumbent team invests in assets that it knows how to run, but the future managerial team will have little expertise in managing.

plant destructions and fewer plant creations). They conclude that the evidence is consistent with the idea that takeover protection enables managers to enjoy a "quiet life," but does not support empire-building theories.

A final note: facilitating takeovers per se may not improve managerial incentives. A takeover-friendly charter in general makes a takeover more likely both when performance is good and when it is poor. The net effect on managerial incentives for good performance is *a priori* unclear, unless takeover incentives put us in a range in which takeovers are only a threat when performance is poor. Ideally, for incentive purposes, one would want takeovers to be facilitated when performance is poor and discouraged when performance is good.

11.5 Positive Theory of Takeovers: Single-Bidder Case

The pure theory of takeovers focuses on the price the firm would want to charge the raider in an acquisition and on the associated likelihood of a takeover. It does not elicit the mechanism through which this price will actually come about.

In contrast, the positive theory of takeovers takes as given some common institutions and looks at how they impact the likelihood of a takeover and the price paid by the raider. Much of the literature analyzes tender offers. Assuming that there exists a single bidder, in a (stylized) tender offer, the raider makes a price offer and shareholders then individually decide whether to tender their shares. This is in sharp contrast with the analysis in Section 11.3, in which the acquisition price was set by the firm rather than by the raider; we will see, however, that the firm's charter can influence the tender offer price, and so the firm can indirectly select the price.

Offers may be *restricted* (to a certain percentage of outstanding shares) or *unrestricted* (the raider purchases all tendered shares, regardless of their number). Similarly, offers may be *conditional* on the raider's acquiring a certain percentage of the shares (e.g., a simple majority stake of 51%) or *unconditional.*

In a first step we will assume that all shares carry equal voting rights and that the raider needs a simple majority or, more generally, a fraction $\kappa \in (0,1)$ of the shares in order to gain control, replace the incumbent management, and implement the new policy. That is, a raider who purchases only a minority of shares or, more generally, a fraction less than κ of the shares is on the same footing as any other investor, and neither delivers investor value $\hat{v}$ nor enjoys rent $\hat{w}$ from control.[16] Later on, we introduce dual-class shares, some with a voting right, some without.

We say that the raider *enhances value* (to investors) if

$$\hat{v} > v.$$

The case $\hat{v} < v$ corresponds to a "*value-decreasing raider.*" We focus on the case in which the value enhancement or decrease is symmetric information.[17]

11.5.1 Value-Enhancing Raider: The Grossman–Hart Analysis

Grossman and Hart (1980) identified a simple free-rider incentive in the shareholders' response to a tender: if the investor value of the firm under raider management exceeds that under incumbent management, tendering becomes a "public good" to which no one wishes to contribute, but everyone hopes others will. To illustrate this point, while minimizing notation, let us normalize to 1 the value added by the raider's taking over:

$$\hat{v} - v \equiv 1.$$

And let us redefine P as the *premium* over v offered by the raider. That is, the raider offers price $v + P$. The relevant range for P is $[0, 1]$. A negative-premium offer is always rejected, while premia above 1 are accepted but wasteful for the raider.

We will assume that there is a continuum, of mass 1, of shareholders. The assumption of a continuum finesses the issue of a shareholder's potentially

16. Like the entire literature, we do not allow the raider to enjoy real authority when he purchases a fraction of shares that is lower than κ. This assumption is a strong one, especially when the raider is value enhancing. Indeed, with $v < \hat{v}$, shareholders might be inclined to listen to his suggestions!

To study this, one would need to combine the study of the emergence of share concentration (Section 9.3), that of real authority (Section 10.3), and this section. I am not aware of any research along these lines.

17. A number of papers have extended the theory to allow for the raider's having private information about what he plans to do with the target. This work is reviewed in Hirshleifer's (1992, 1995) surveys on mergers and acquisitions.

being "pivotal," i.e., affecting the outcome through his tendering choice. A shareholder will therefore compare the takeover premium that is offered by the raider to the expected value enhancement, taking the probability of takeover as exogenous to his tendering choice and equal to its equilibrium value. Later, we will consider a (potentially large, but) finite number of shares, and will study the robustness of this first-cut analysis.

Consider an unrestricted, unconditional offer, and assume that the raider needs to acquire a fraction $\kappa \in (0,1)$ of the shares to gain control. We claim that the probability of takeover success must be equal to the premium:

$$\beta \equiv \Pr(\text{takeover success}) = P.$$

If this probability exceeded P, then each shareholder would be better off holding on to his share, since

$$\beta\hat{v} + (1-\beta)v > v + P;$$

and so the takeover would fail with probability 1, a contradiction. Similarly, for a probability of success smaller than P, all would be better off tendering and thus the takeover would succeed. So the equilibrium probability of takeover success must equal the premium. The fraction of shares tendered must be exactly equal to κ. The mechanics of how the probability of a successful takeover comes out as $\beta = P$ remains mysterious at this stage of the analysis, which only derives necessary conditions for equilibrium. Section 11.5.3 will show how this probability emerges in the presence of a large, but finite, number of shareholders. Leaving aside any private surplus $\hat{w}$, the profit made by the raider on the takeover attempt is

$$\pi = \kappa[\beta \cdot 1 - P] = 0.$$

That is, the raider is unable to derive any benefit from the value enhancement.[18] Free riding by shareholders fully captures the raider's value enhancement.[19] It may thereby discourage a potential raider from setting up a raid.

Remark (free riding and the incentive to go public). Zingales (1995) argues that the free-rider benefits associated with dispersed shareholdings are a reason why firms may want to go public rather than keeping a concentrated ownership, which may not allow them to appropriate as much of the surplus of future acquirers.

11.5.2 Positive Raider Surplus despite Free Riding

11.5.2.1 Private Benefit from Control

When the raider derives a private surplus $\hat{w}$ from control, then he gets to keep this surplus and optimally bids $P = 1$. To see this, note that the raider's profit when offering premium P is

$$\pi = \kappa[\beta - P] + \beta\hat{w} = P\hat{w}.$$

The raider strictly prefers to bid the maximum premium: $P = 1$. Thus, a tender offer mechanism fully extracts the raider's investor value enhancement under shareholder free riding, and captures none of the raider's private surplus. Dispersed shareholders are good at extracting increases, $\hat{v} - v$, in share value. They, however, can capture none of the raider's private benefit $\hat{w}$. By contrast, a large shareholder of the target company can extract some of the raider's private benefit provided that (a) he has sufficient bargaining power in the negotiation with the raider, and (b) the raider has cash on hand to finance the acquisition and therefore can pay more than the value of shares to gain access to his private benefit (if the acquisition is externally financed, the raider's private benefit cannot be captured since financiers are not willing to pay more than the value of shares) (see Burkart 1995; Zingales 1995).

Let us turn to three further mechanisms that enable the raider to capture some of the value enhancement.

11.5.2.2 Toehold

Raiders often have substantial toeholds when making a tender offer.[20] Suppose that the raider already owns a fraction $\theta < \kappa$ of the shares when making

18. If $\hat{w} > 0$, the raider enjoys $\hat{w}$ with probability $\beta = P$ (see below).

19. Burkart et al. (2005) analyzes takeovers of companies owned by a set of atomistic shareholders and one minority blockholder. The blockholder has more incentives to tender his shares than atomistic bidders.

20. They can secretly purchase shares prior to a tender offer. U.S. regulations require the purchaser of shares combining to a block of at least 5% of shares to file an "SEC 13d" report within 10 days of the acquisition. So the raider can purchase more shares in those 10 days. Raiders therefore own on average 14% of target firms. More than half of the bidders have toeholds (see, for example, Betton and Eckbo (2000) for more detail).

a tender offer. Assuming, again, that $\hat{w} = 0$, the raider's profit for premium P is

$$\pi(P) = (\kappa - \theta)(\beta - P) + \theta\beta,$$

where β is, as earlier, the probability of takeover success and must in equilibrium be equal to P. Hence,

$$\pi(P) = \theta P.$$

The optimal bid is then $P = 1$, yielding profit

$$\pi = \theta.$$

Thus, the raider fully appropriates the value added to the toehold shares.[21]

11.5.2.3 Dilution

Grossman and Hart (1980) discuss another mechanism through which raiders may be given incentives to prepare a raid. Suppose that, having gained control, the raider is able to capture a fraction ϕ between 0 and 1 of the gains made by the shareholders who have not tendered their shares. This, in a sense, amounts to a partial expropriation of minority shareholders, and therefore may conflict with laws protecting the latter. For example, one may have in mind that the raider forces the firm to purchase some supplies at an inflated price from one of the raider's affiliates. This amounts to increasing $\hat{w}$ while decreasing $\hat{v}$. Namely, starting from the absence of private benefit, dilution creates one equal to $\hat{w} = \phi(\hat{v} - v) = \phi$, while $\hat{v} - v = 1$ becomes $(1 - \phi)(\hat{v} - v) = 1 - \phi$.

Again a fraction κ of the shares is tendered (assuming no toehold). The new probability of takeover success β when the premium is P is given by the shareholders' indifference between tendering and not tendering:

$$P = (1 - \phi)\beta(P).$$

The raider's profit is then (for $P \leqslant 1 - \phi$)

$$\begin{aligned}\pi(P) &= \beta(P)[\kappa \cdot 1 + (1 - \kappa)\phi] - \kappa P \\ &= \beta(P)\phi.\end{aligned}$$

As in the case of a toehold, the optimal tender offer for the raider induces a sure success. That is,

$$P = 1 - \phi$$

and

$$\pi = \phi.$$

Thus, the raider appropriates the value of the dilution on untendered shares as well as from tendered shares (through the threat of dilution if the shareholder does not tender).

Dilution, however, may not be feasible to the extent that a controlling shareholder often has a fiduciary duty to minority shareholders; for example, the tunneling of assets by the raider to affiliated entities would be unlawful in the United States. Müller and Panunzi (2004) point out that in the 1980s merger wave, raiders often practiced dilution in a more subtle way by setting up acquisition subsidiaries.

Under such "bootstrap acquisitions," before making a public tender offer, the raider organizes a highly leveraged shell company (the acquisition subsidiary) that is assetless, obtains a loan commitment from lenders by pledging the future cash flows of the target firm as a security for its debt, and will be merged with the target firm if the majority of shareholders tender their shares. Importantly, the cash from the loan is used to pay the tendered shares and to compensate the raider, but does not go to the new merged entity. The minority shareholders thus bear (some of) the debt once the acquisition subsidiary is merged with the target, but do not receive the proceeds of debt issuance. In a sense, the raider sells claims on the value enhancement, $\hat{v} - v$, by buying rights on v.

Suppose, as earlier, that the raider makes an unrestricted and unconditional tender offer.[22] Let D denote the shell company's debt[23] and assume that $0 \leqslant D \leqslant 1$. As earlier, let P denote the takeover premium offered by the raider and $\beta(P)$ the probability of takeover success. In equilibrium, a fraction κ of the shares is tendered. The shareholders' indifference equation is $P = \beta(1 - D)$. Because the proceeds of the debt D serve to pay the acquired shares and compensate the raider, the latter's utility is $\pi = [D - \kappa P] + \beta[\kappa(1 - D)] = D$.

21. The role of toeholds in encouraging takeover attempts in a free-rider environment was stressed by, among others, Shleifer and Vishny (1986a,b) and Hirshleifer and Titman (1990).

22. Müller and Panunzi assume that the offer is conditional on a fraction at least equal to κ being tendered. We look at unconditional offers only for consistency with the rest of the section.

23. This debt, for expositional simplicity, is assumed to be safe. Otherwise the tendering indifference equation derived below is slightly different.

The reader can check that the raider cannot prevent free riding if the acquisition subsidiary is financed through equity rather than debt. Also, (s)he should note the strong similarity with the study of commitment through the use of third parties in Chapter 7.

11.5.2.4 Takeover Defenses

Takeover defenses come in many guises,[24] and, except for the common feature that they make it harder for a raider to acquire a firm, are hard to summarize concisely. Let us illustrate their role in the case of poison pills, more specifically in the most common form of a "flip-over plan" under which the holders of shares are entitled to purchase new shares at a substantial discount after a hostile takeover.[25] For computational simplicity, let us assume a simple majority rule ($\kappa = \frac{1}{2}$) and that the new shares carry no voting rights.[26] In the case of takeover success, the 50% of shares kept by the initial shareholders are worth $\hat{v} + \Delta$ (with $\Delta > 0$), while the 50% acquired by the raider are worth $\hat{v} - \Delta$ to him due to the dilution.[27] Letting, as before, β denote the probability of success and P the premium over v, shareholders are indifferent between tendering and keeping their shares if and only if

$$\beta(\hat{v} + \Delta) + (1 - \beta)v = v + P$$

or

$$\beta = \frac{P}{1 + \Delta}.$$

The raider's profit is then

$$\begin{aligned}\pi &= \beta\hat{w} + \tfrac{1}{2}[\beta(\hat{v} - \Delta) + (1 - \beta)v - (v + P)] \\ &= \beta(\hat{w} - \Delta).\end{aligned}$$

Assuming that $\hat{w} > \Delta$ (otherwise the raider makes no offer), it is optimal for the raider to succeed for certain ($\beta = 1$) by choosing

$$P = 1 + \Delta.$$

The poison pill further raises the purchase price. In contrast with the dilution of initial shareholders by the raider considered in Grossman and Hart, poison pills allow a dilution of the raider by initial shareholders.

Poison pills thereby allow the firm to adjust the purchase price paid by the raider. Suppose, for example, that the raider's benefit from control, $\hat{w}$, is known (the distribution H is a spike at $\hat{w}$).[28] In the absence of a poison pill, $P = 1$ and the raider's surplus is $\hat{w}$. The optimal poison pill then yields dilution $\Delta^* = \hat{w}$.

11.5.3 Value-Enhancing Raider: Pivotal Tendering

A series of papers by Bagnoli and Lipman (1988), Holmström and Nalebuff (1992), Gromb (1995), and Segal (1999) have carefully analyzed strategic behavior among shareholders facing a tender offer. Let us assume that there are n shares, $a \leqslant n$ of the shares carrying a voting right, and that the raider must possess $k \leqslant a$ shares in order to exercise control (so $\kappa = k/a$). Each share carries a cash-flow right equal to $1/n$th of the investor payoff (v under incumbent management, $\hat{v}$ under raider management). Lastly, we assume in a first step that each shareholder owns one share.

It can be shown that assuming that the raider does not bid for the nonvoting shares involves no loss of generality. Intuitively, the raider and the shareholders have the same valuation for the nonvoting shares. Hence, no trade of nonvoting shares between them can benefit both, or, put differently, any sale of nonvoting shares to the raider must occur at a price equal to the expectation of their *ex post* value. For the same reason, "nonvoting shares" could also stand for "debt": the raider has no incentive to acquire the firm's outstanding debt.

Note that the raider can appropriate the entire value enhancement (at least on the voting shares) if *conditional* offers are feasible. Indeed, suppose that he makes an unrestricted offer at an arbitrarily small

24. See, for example, Malatesta (1992) and Section 1.5. Malatesta and Walking (1988) is among the classic references on poison pills.

25. Here we assume that the poison pill cannot be removed. Bebchuk and Hart (2001) allow the tender offer to be accompanied by a proxy vote contest over the redemption of the poison pill.

Also, the threshold that triggers the exercise of the option to buy new shares may be smaller than 50%.

26. If the new shares carry a voting right, the analysis is basically unchanged.

27. For example, suppose that the holders of untendered shares are entitled to one extra share per share for free. Then the raider has only one-third of the cash rights. Then $\Delta = \frac{1}{3}\hat{v}$.

28. And $v + w < \hat{v} + \hat{w}$.

premium

$$P = \varepsilon$$

for the a shares, conditional on all voting shares being tendered. It is then an equilibrium for all shareholders to tender;[29] for, each obtains $(v + \varepsilon)$ by tendering, and only v if he does not tender (and thereby defeats the tender offer). Thus, shareholder unanimity strengthens the raider to the point that the free-rider problem completely disappears! Only the value enhancement on the nonvoting shares is not appropriated by the raider.

Second, assume that conditional offers are forbidden or are not credible.[30] Let us look at voting shares and let P, as earlier, denote the premium over v offered by the raider. We will focus on the *symmetric, mixed-strategy equilibrium*, in which each shareholder tenders his share with a probability x to be determined.[31] Let m denote the (random) number of voting shares tendered overall.

Consider shareholder $i \in \{1, \dots, a\}$. Let m_{-i} denote the number of voting shares tendered by other shareholders. Because these play a mixed strategy, m_{-i} is a random variable. The probability that the takeover succeeds if shareholder i does not tender his share is $\Pr(m_{-i} \geqslant k)$. In order for shareholder i to be indifferent between tendering his voting share and not tendering it, it must be the case that he obtains the same utility from both strategies, or

$$P = \Pr(m_{-i} \geqslant k) \cdot 1. \qquad (11.4)$$

The raider's profit π is most easily computed by noticing that the expected value enhancement (on voting shares) is equal to $a[\Pr(m \geqslant k) \cdot 1]/n$ and that this value enhancement is necessarily shared between raider and shareholders. The latter obtain P/n each since one of their optimal strategies is to tender. Hence,

$$\frac{a}{n} \Pr(m \geqslant k) = \frac{a}{n} P + \pi$$

or

$$\pi = [\Pr(m \geqslant k) - \Pr(m_{-i} \geqslant k)] \frac{a}{n} = \binom{a-1}{k-1} x^k (1-x)^{a-k} \frac{a}{n}.$$

From equation (11.4), we know that there is a one-to-one increasing mapping between $P \in [0, 1]$ and x spanning the full support $[0, 1]$: increasing the premium raises the probability of tendering. Thus, maximizing π with respect to P is equivalent to maximizing π with respect to x (and then using equation (11.4) to compute the optimal premium). A simple computation (take the derivative of the logarithm of π) yields the optimal probability of tendering (i.e., the raider's optimal tradeoff between a high probability of takeover success and a low premium paid to shareholders):

$$x^* = \frac{k}{a}.$$

We can now return to Grossman and Hart's analysis of the free-rider problem. The raider's profit, replacing x by its optimal value, is

$$\pi = \binom{a-1}{k-1} \left(\frac{k}{a}\right)^k \left(1 - \frac{k}{a}\right)^{a-k} \frac{a}{n}.$$

Bagnoli and Lipman (1988) and Holmström and Nalebuff (1992) show that when the number of shares a becomes large,[32] the raider's profit converges to 0 (at speed $1/\sqrt{a}$). Intuitively, the probability that any shareholder is pivotal, that is, of *exactly* $k - 1$ other shareholders tendering their shares, becomes very small. Hence, for shareholders to be indifferent between tendering their share or not, it must be the case that the probability of takeover success be very close to the premium.

29. This is not the only equilibrium. There are other equilibria in which the takeover fails (e.g., if all refuse to tender their share, there is no individual impact of not tendering one's share). However, these alternative equilibria rely on weakly dominated strategies (tendering one's share either has no impact or benefits the shareholder if the others also tender their share). The equilibrium we focus on is the only one that is robust to the elimination of weakly dominated strategies.

30. The terms of the offer could later be relaxed if the conditions set in the offer are not satisfied.

31. The equilibrium is far from being unique. For example, there are pure-strategy ones in which k shareholders tender and $a - k$ do not tender for $P \in (0, 1)$. These equilibria resemble the one prevailing under a conditional offer: each of the k shareholders tendering their share is pivotal, and makes the takeover attempt fail if he does not tender his share. And, for the same reason, the raider fully appropriates the value enhancement on the voting shares.

There are also mixed equilibria, in which a set of shareholders tenders for certain, another set does not tender for certain, and a third set randomizes over the tendering decision (as in the mixed-strategy equilibrium).

32. Keeping a/n constant (e.g., equal to 1, if all shares carry a voting right).

Whatever the number of shares, the nonvoting shares trade at a premium with respect to voting shares equal to[33]

$$\Pr(m \geqslant k \mid x = x^*) - \Pr(m_{-i} \geqslant k \mid x = x^*) > 0.$$

The holders of nonvoting shares are the ultimate free riders. Holders of voting and nonvoting shares have conflicting interests. Nonvoting shareholders, whose interest lies solely in the success of the takeover, are hurt by the free-riding behavior of voting shareholders, and therefore prefer supermajority rules and a low number of voting shares. In contrast, voting shareholders prefer a large number of voting shares and the simple majority rule, because these reduce the probability that they are pivotal and allow them to be less pressured by the raider.

As Gromb (1995) points out, the optimal charter in this environment has *one-share–all-votes*. That is, the firm optimally issues many shares, only one of which has a voting right. The raider purchases this share at an arbitrarily small premium,[34] but the important point is that the takeover occurs with probability 1 (as under the unanimity rule) and so all nonvoting shares (which represent almost the entire value of the firm) free ride on the surefire value enhancement.

Remark (other free-riding securityholders). Nonvoting shareholders are not the only free riders. Along similar lines, holders of risky debt benefit when a value-enhancing raid succeeds. Their claim is similar to that of nonvoting shares to the extent that it carries no voting right and benefits from value-enhancing takeovers (Israel 1992).[35]

Remark (sequential offers). This analysis, like the rest of the chapter, has assumed that the raider makes a single, once-and-for-all tender offer. One may wonder whether the possibility of making new tender offers after an unsuccessful one alleviates or aggravates the free-riding problem. Harrington and Prokop (1993) generalize the analysis with a finite number of shareholders, each holding one share, to a discrete-time, infinite-horizon environment. As long as he has not yet acquired k shares, the raider makes a new unconditional offer each period; and so he acquires new shares until he finally obtains control of the firm.[36] Two key results emerge:

- The raider's payoff is strictly lower than that predicted by static (one-shot-offer) equilibria. The anticipation of a higher tender offer in the future makes shareholders more inclined to hold onto their share. The free-rider problem is exacerbated by the lack of price commitment and the raider must offer a higher premium than in the static context.
- As readers familiar with the Coase (1972) conjecture[37] will intuit, the raider's expected profit converges to 0 as the time period between offers goes to 0. Thus, even with a small number of shareholders (so free riding is limited in a static context), the raider must leave almost all the surplus to shareholders.

11.5.4 Multiple Shares per Shareholder

As Holmström and Nalebuff (1992) point out, the previous analysis hinges crucially on each shareholder holding a single share. Dividing a share into N shares, each with value $1/N$ of the value of the original share, affects the holders of voting shares' incentive to tender. The basic idea is that shareholder's act of tendering a share makes takeover success more likely and thereby raises the profitability of all shares that the same shareholder does not tender. This weakens the shareholders' incentive to free ride and enables the raider to capture a substantial fraction of the pie.

33. Furthermore, when the number a of voting shares increases, fixing k, the value of these shares increases, while that of nonvoting shares decreases. And when the threshold k increases, keeping a constant, the value of voting shares decreases while that of nonvoting shares increases.

34. This is clear under the maintained assumption of a tender offer. Of course, the owner of the voting share might try to bargain over the price of the share; but due to the others' free riding the two have little surplus to share anyway. So the assumption we make about the credibility of a tender offer (that is, of a lack of bargaining power of the owner of the voting share) is without consequence for the final outcome.

35. Of course, for this to hold, it must be the case that the value enhancement is not accompanied by an increase in risk.

36. The equilibrium concept is the generalization of the static one in this section: the paper focuses on symmetric equilibria, or more precisely on symmetric Markov perfect equilibria. If m_t denotes the number of shares held by the raider at the beginning of period t and P_t the takeover price (or premium), each of the remaining $(a - m_t)$ shareholders tenders his share with probability $x_t = x(m_t, P_t)$.

37. See, for example, Fudenberg and Tirole (1991, Chapter 10) for an exposition.

Start from the situation in which there are a voting shares, k of which must be acquired by the raider to gain control. Each shareholder holds exactly one share. Now subdivide shares N times: each shareholder now holds N shares, and there is a total of aN voting shares. Let kN denote the new number of shares that the raider must acquire; so the percentage of shares to be acquired is kept constant.

Again, we look for the symmetric equilibrium. Each shareholder withholds $M < N$ shares, tenders $N - M - 1$ shares, and randomizes over the tendering decision of the Mth share.[38] The number of shares tendered must be approximately kN in order for this randomization to be rational.

For N large, whenever the raider offers a premium P, $0 < P < 1$, the percentage of shares tendered is almost deterministic, by the law of large numbers. Furthermore, by now familiar reasoning, it must be close to k/a; otherwise all shares would be tendered, inducing each shareholder to keep his shares, or vice versa.[39] Furthermore, the support of the distribution of the number of shares tendered (that is, the range of uncertainty faced by an outside observer as to the number of tendered shares) has size exactly equal to a, since each of the a shareholders randomizes on only one share. So the support is smaller than a shareholder's number of untendered shares for N large.

Next, let us deduce from this that the probability that the takeover is successful converges to 1 as N goes to ∞. If this probability of success were bounded away from 1, then any shareholder could make it exactly 1 by tendering a more shares, which is a small number relative to the M shares not tendered, where, recall, M/N is close to $(a-k)/a$. Hence, each shareholder would have the ability to raise the probability of success substantially by tendering a negligible (for N large) incremental fraction of his shares. This raises the profitability of the "inframarginal shares" (the $M \simeq [1-(k/a)]N$ shares withheld for certain). Hence, if m is the (random) number of shares tendered,

$$\Pr(m \geqslant kN) \to 1 \quad \text{as } N \to \infty.$$

The raider's profit is then approximately

$$\pi \simeq \frac{kN}{aN}[\Pr(m \geqslant kN) - P] \simeq \frac{k}{a}[1 - P].$$

The raider's optimal strategy is to choose P arbitrarily small, yielding raider profit

$$\pi \simeq \frac{k}{a}.$$

Thus, Holmström and Nalebuff (1992), focusing on the symmetric, mixed-strategy equilibrium, show that it makes a substantial difference whether shares are divisible or not.[40] With one share per shareholder, the probability of being pivotal is infinitesimal for a large number of shareholders/shares, and so everyone behaves as a perfect free rider, as in Grossman and Hart (1980). When shareholders have a lot of shares, then each can be pivotal and has an incentive to boost the probability of a takeover in order to raise the profitability of his inframarginal untendered shares. This reduces free riding and lets the raider make a (nonnegligible) profit. For example, the raider appropriates half of the value added in case of a simple majority rule,

$$\frac{k}{a} = \frac{1}{2}$$

and makes even more for supermajority rules.

One may wonder how the Holmström–Nalebuff analysis is modified in the presence of some exogenous noise (for instance, about the number of shareholders who will be informed about and/or care to participate in the tender offer, or about those (here none) who enter separate sale agreements with the raider); one could conjecture with Hirshleifer (1995) that such extra noise would make it unlikely that

38. In fact, he can be indifferent with regards only to a single share: the benefit from the increase in the probability of takeover success brought about by tendering a share declines with the number of shares tendered (the number of "inframarginal" shares not tendered is then smaller).

39. More formally, letting m denote the (random) number of shares tendered, for any $\varepsilon > 0$, and $\eta > 0$, there exists N_0 such that, for all $N > N_0$, $\Pr(x(N)-\varepsilon < m/aN < x(N)+\varepsilon) > 1-\eta$, where $x(N)$ is the expected fraction of shares tendered. So, if, for example, $k/a > x(N)+\varepsilon$, then tendering all of one's shares is optimal as long as $P > \eta$ (since the probability of a successful takeover is bounded above by η), a contradiction; and similarly for $k/a < x(N) - \varepsilon$. Choosing $\eta < \min(P, 1-P)$, we see that $x(N)$ must converge to k/a.

40. Holmström and Nalebuff also look at similar equilibria for asymmetric initial shareholdings, in which shareholders with more shares tender more.

shareholders would perceive themselves as pivotal. That is, noise should reinstate free riding by lowering the individual shareholder's prospect of being pivotal and should substantially reduce the raider's profit. The validity of this conjecture is confirmed in the discussion below.

11.5.5 Discussion

Grossman and Hart's (1980) intuition for free riding builds on the idea that with a large number of shareholders, each feels that (s)he is nonpivotal, i.e., will not influence the outcome of the takeover attempt. Each shareholder therefore refuses to sell as long as the premium does not match the subsequent value enhancement; and so the raider is unable to benefit from the value enhancement he brings along. A number of papers in various fields of economics (in particular, Fudenberg et al. 1998) have studied environments with many small players and exogenous uncertainty (as opposed to the endogenous uncertainty arising in the mixed-strategy equilibria studied above) and derived conditions under which it is indeed optimal for economic agents to behave in the large-number limit as if they individually had no impact on aggregate outcomes. Segal (1999, Section 7) derives an interesting general result along this line; in an application to takeovers he assumes that there is probability ε that a shareholder does not receive the raider's offer or is unable to respond, and that the product of ε times the number of shareholders goes to ∞ as the latter number goes to ∞ (a condition that is trivially satisfied if, for example, ε is independent of the number of shareholders). This creates a fair amount of uncertainty as to the (absolute) number of shares that are being tendered; and so each shareholder rationally anticipates that (s)he is not going to affect the outcome of the tender offer. This reasoning is actually quite general, and, as Segal shows, applies to any arbitrary voluntary mechanism (conditional bids, etc.) and not only to the unconditional, unrestricted mechanism considered here. Segal thereby provides a useful argument in support of Grossman and Hart's free-riding prediction.

Segal (1999) brings another argument against the idea that individual shareholders should feel very concerned that their tendering decision will have a strong impact on their payoff. Even if the shareholder actually turns out to be pivotal (provide the raider with a majority of votes when tendering), the change in payoff may be largely overpredicted by the discontinuous payoff function presumed in the takeover literature, as the reader may have suspected from previous material covered in the book. Provided that the raider's offer is not conditional and so he acquires the shares that are tendered, his intensity of active monitoring in general increases continuously with the raider's shareholding (see Chapter 9); so the expected benefits of curbing managerial moral hazard will move rather continuously. A similar point can be made more generally for shareholders' payoffs under raider's real authority (Chapter 10). Overall, the literature on takeovers takes too narrow a view of "control." Finally, a toehold will encourage the raider to buy more shares in the future, resulting in the eventual transfer of formal authority to the raider.

11.6 Value-Decreasing Raider and the One-Share–One-Vote Result

Let us return to the simplifying case of a continuum of shares and now assume that the raider lowers investor value:

$$\hat{v} < v.$$

Such a raider is necessarily interested in control benefits $\hat{w}$. (Our treatment here follows that of Grossman and Hart (1988). Harris and Raviv (1988) obtain related results.)

For a positive premium ($P \geqslant 0$), it is a (weakly) dominant strategy to tender; similarly, when $P \leqslant \hat{v} - v$, then not tendering is a (weakly) dominant strategy for all shareholders. Hence, let us consider the relevant range in which

$$\hat{v} - v < P < 0.$$

The first observation is that shareholders face a *coordination problem* in their tendering decision. Collectively, they are better off if the takeover fails for certain than if it succeeds for certain (since $P < 0$); furthermore, each has more incentive to tender if the others also do.[41] Contrast this with the

41. Technically, the tendering game exhibits a "strategic complementarity." We will encounter a similar situation when discussing bank runs in Section 12.3.

case of value-increasing raiders, for which we saw that each has *less* incentive to tender his share when the probability of takeover success increases, and therefore when others are more likely to tender their share.

In the *trust equilibrium*, each shareholder trusts other shareholders not to tender, and so does not tender himself. This equilibrium yields the highest possible payoff to shareholders. In the *suspicion equilibrium* (or "panic equilibrium"), all tender believing that others will tender as well. They all cut their losses by obtaining $v + P$ rather than $\hat{v}$. This is the worse possible outcome for the shareholders.

While these two equilibria coexist, it can be argued that the trust equilibrium Pareto-dominates any other equilibrium (from the point of view of shareholders), and so should be a kind of "focal point." Furthermore, as Grossman and Hart (1988) note, the suspicion equilibrium would disappear if a friendly arbitrageur (who would leave the incumbent team in control) were to come and overbid (that is, bid $v + P'$, with $P' > P$). The shareholders would then be individually and collectively better off tendering their shares to the friendly arbitrageur than selling them to the raider.

Charter design can also rule out shareholder panics of the suspicion equilibrium kind by requiring unanimity ($k = a$). Then, a raider cannot succeed unless $P \geqslant 0$. Of course, we have seen that the unanimity rule is detrimental to shareholders when confronted with a value-enhancing raider, since it then allows the raider to capture the entire value enhancement. The unanimity rule is shareholder friendly for value-decreasing raids for the same reason it is shareholder hostile for value-enhancing raids: it makes every shareholder pivotal, i.e., responsible for the success or failure of the raid.

Next, ruling out the unanimity rule and assuming away panics, the raider is constrained to offer

$$P \geqslant 0$$

if he wants to take control of the firm. The raider can then obtain control by offering $P = 0$. What is the optimal charter? As we have noted earlier, a tender mechanism cannot capture the raider's surplus. The latter is equal to $\hat{w}$ minus the number of shares acquired times the value loss $(v - \hat{v})$. The shareholders' loss is equal to $(v - \hat{v})$ times the number of shares not acquired by the raider. Thus the firm wants the value-decreasing raider to acquire as many shares as possible.

Suppose, for example, that there are two classes of shares: class A (with one vote each) and class B (without voting rights).[42] The raider will not be interested in class-B shares (which do not help him obtain control and for which he loses $v - \hat{v}$ per share) and will attempt to acquire only class-A shares. So he will acquire all class-A shares if he is forced to make an unrestricted offer within a given class, or will bid for the minimum number of class-A shares needed for control (e.g., 51% under the simple majority rule) if he can make restricted offers. Either way, class-B shares lose $v - \hat{v}$ each, unlike the class-A shares that are purchased at price v and lose nothing. The optimal corporate charter is therefore to have no class-B shares at all (for any given majority rule on class-A shares).

More generally, assuming that all shares are associated with equal cash-flow rights (rights to the revenue stream) and fixing the number of voting rights (a say) and a majority rule ($k \leqslant a$ rights are needed to have control), it is optimal for the firm to endow each voting share with the same number of voting rights, provided that the raider can make offers for each class of shares.[43] Thus, as Grossman and Hart (1988) show, the one-share-one-vote charter is optimal when facing a value-decreasing raider, as it

42. We keep assuming that there is no large owner of voting shares. In practice, dual-class shares are often issued so as to allow owners or founders to retain control. For example, as of 2004, the Ford family had 40% of voting rights in the Ford corporation with only 4% of total equity (cash flow) rights. The class B shares in Berkshire Hathaway (Warren Buffet's firm) have 3/20 of the voting rights of class A shares. Another well-known case in point is Google, in which founders and top executives maintained control at the IPO by retaining shares that carry 10 votes. Needless to say, such dual-class structures tend to make their owners entrenched and may be taken on by investor activists such as CalPERS, the large Californian pension fund.

43. Let m_i denote the number of shares with $i = 0, 1, \ldots$ voting rights, with $\sum_i m_i i = a$. Then the raider solves

$$\min\Big\{\sum_i n_i\Big\} \quad \text{s.t. } \sum_i n_i i \geqslant k \text{ and } n_i \leqslant m_i.$$

So there exists i_0 such that $n_i = m_i$ for $i > i_0$ and $n_i = 0$ for $i < i_0$.

In turn, the firm ought to maximize over $\{m_{\bullet}\}$ and i_0:

$$\max\Big\{\sum_{i \geqslant i_0} m_i\Big\} \quad \text{s.t. } \sum_{i \geqslant i_0} m_i i = k$$

(there is no loss of generality in assuming that $n_{i_0} = m_{i_0}$). The solution to this program is to have $m_i = 0$ for $i \geqslant 2$.

forces the raider to acquire the maximum number of shares.

Remark (a reinterpretation with multiple value-enhancing raiders). The environment with the single value-decreasing raider studied here can be reinterpreted as a multiple-raider environment in which the "value-decreasing raider" actually increases investor value to $\hat{v}_1 > v$, but less so than the other raider who delivers $\hat{v}_2 > \hat{v}_1$: suppose that the former, let us call him the "low-value raider," enjoys private benefit from control, $\hat{w}_1 > 0$, while the latter, the "high-value raider," does not, $\hat{w}_2 = 0$. The low-value raider may then overbid the high-value one in their contest for control of the firm. The one-share–one-vote rule again forces the low-value raider to acquire as many shares as possible at the value $\hat{v}_2$ that would have been created by the high-value raider. This remark leads us to the next topic of this chapter: bidding contests.

11.7 Positive Theory of Takeovers: Multiple Bidders

The analysis thus far has assumed that there was a single relevant bidder. A large literature, surveyed by Hirshleifer (1995), extends the analysis to competitive bidding.[44] For conciseness, I will not attempt to review this literature, and will content myself with a few themes.

Some of the literature focuses on revelations by bidders, through takeover bids, of information about share value under their management. In Fishman (1988), two raiders have independent valuations $\hat{v}_1$ and $\hat{v}_2$.[45] The highest bidder buys all the shares (there is no free riding; equivalently, the winner can perfectly dilute shareholders who held on to their share). Bidder 1 knows $\hat{v}_1$ and selects a premium P. Bidder 2, observing P, must then decide whether to pay a fixed cost c_2 in order to learn $\hat{v}_2$; if he does so, he learns $\hat{v}_2$ and enters a bidding contest with bidder 1 (and gets $\hat{v}_2 - \hat{v}_1 - c_2$ if $\hat{v}_2 \geqslant \hat{v}_1$ and $-c_2$ otherwise). Fishman derives conditions under which the first bidder finds it advantageous to bid a positive premium $P > 0$, despite the fact that $P > 0$ amounts to wasting money if bidder 2 does not compete (either does not acquire information, or finds out that $\hat{v}_2 \leqslant P$). Conversely, in this signaling equilibrium, a low-premium bid by the first bidder is more likely to attract competition. Empirically, a second bidder does indeed seem less likely to appear and compete after a high-premium bid than after a low-premium one (Jennings and Mazzeo 1993).

Another strand of the literature on bidding contests looks at the impact of toeholds. The theoretical work of Burkart (1995) and Singh (1998) shows that a toehold increases the bidder's chance of winning a takeover contest.[46] Consider a battle between bidder 1 (with privately known value $\hat{v}_1$ to shareholders, say) having accumulated a toehold, and bidder 2 (with privately known value $\hat{v}_2$ to shareholders) with no such toehold; the bidding contest is as an ascending auction, in which the winner buys all outstanding shares at the price at which the loser abandoned.[47] Even if he loses, bidder 1 gains from forcing bidder 2 to raise his bid since that will raise the capital gain on the toehold. Bidder 2 has no such incentive. Hence, ceteris paribus, bidder 1 bids more on average.

Bulow et al. (1999) extend the Burkart–Singh analysis to the case of "common values" in order to obtain stronger effects (with private values, that is, when $\hat{v}_i$ carries no information that can help predict $\hat{v}_j$, a small toehold has only a small effect). Each bidder has private information about the target's profitability (which, say, is the same under either management).[48] Common values, as usual, give rise to a winner's curse. Bulow et al.'s point is that the winner's curse is very severe for bidder 2 when bidder 1 has a toehold. The toehold makes bidder 1 more aggressive, and so bidder 2 winning is particularly

44. See, for example, Hirshleifer and Png (1989) and Dewatripont (1993). In Burkart et al. (2000) a minority block is initially held by an incumbent shareholder and the rest of shares dispersed among small shareholders. When the raider appears, the incumbent and the raider may negotiate privately either to trade the block or to enter into a standstill agreement (the raider then pledges not to buy new shares); if renegotiation fails, the two wage a public tender contest. Burkart et al. find a tendency toward block trades and low ownership by the raider despite the fact that the higher concentration of ownership created by a public tender generates more monitoring and a higher firm value; the reason for this result is that the two parties do not internalize the small shareholders' welfare in their bilateral negotiation.

45. There is no "common value" element.

46. This prediction is consistent with the available empirical evidence (Betton and Eckbo 2000; Walking 1985).

47. Free-rider problems are ruled out.

48. In the Bulow et al. model, $\hat{w}_1 = \hat{w}_2 = 0$. And $\hat{v}_1 = \hat{v}_2 = v(t_1, t_2)$, where t_1 and t_2 are the private information held by bidders 1 and 2.

bad news about the actual valuation of the target. This makes bidder 2 bid more conservative, which in turn reduces the winner's curse for bidder 1, and so forth.

Bulow et al. also show that, for a takeover contest characterized by a first-price, sealed-bid auction, the bidder with the larger toehold is more likely to win, but the winner's curse is less powerful.[49]

11.8 Managerial Resistance

Managers usually resist hostile takeover attempts in several ways. Not only do they routinely advise shareholders against tendering their shares, but they also lobby both "*ex ante*" (in the absence of takeover threat) and "*ex post*" (after a raider arrives) for takeover defenses. Recall that takeover defenses must be approved by shareholders, as in the case of corporate charter defenses such as supermajority rules or staggered boards,[50] or by the board, as in the case of poison pills.[51] In response to a takeover, the firm may also threaten the raider with litigation to gain time, may sell some of the assets desired by the raider to a third party, increase debt prior to the bid, acquire another firm to create antitrust problems for the bidder, or may agree to "greenmail," that is, repurchase the raider's current block of shares at a hefty price in exchange for a standstill agreement, under which the raider promises not to seek control of the firm in the future.

It is not clear why managers should have a say in such decisions. They face an obvious conflict of interest: a successful takeover is likely to result in the loss of employment and the control of their rents. On the basis of Chapter 10, it would be hard to make a case in favor of any *formal* right held by management in this area!

However, we know from Chapter 10 that managers may enjoy substantial *real* authority from their superior information. For example, management may have information indicating that

- the raider's success would lead to a reduction in the target's value;
- the raid is value enhancing, but the offer made by the raider is too low (the target is underpriced).

In the former case, the takeover should be prevented; in the latter case, takeover defenses should more mildly push the raider's price up.[52]

No general theory of managerial resistance based on this notion of real control is available, and so we can only conjecture what its main ingredients could be. We know from Chapter 10 that management is more likely to influence the board and the general assembly if its interests are better aligned with those of shareholders. Indeed, this alignment is often the stated rationale for golden parachutes. The fact that managers receive large golden parachutes after dismissal not only raises redistributive concerns as these managers often receive indecent amounts of money, but also seems to be at odds with incentive theory because managers that add little value (v is low) are more likely to be replaced in the wake of a takeover. The efficiency rationale for a golden parachute is that it acts as a counterweight for the rents from control and thereby reduces the managers' natural bias in favor of strong takeover defenses. Furthermore, and following the analysis in Chapter 10, one would expect the managers' real authority to increase with managerial stockholdings;[53] indeed, managers with large stockholdings are less likely to oppose takeovers (Walking and Long 1984).

11.9 Exercise

Exercise 11.1 (takeover defenses). Extend the analysis of takeover defenses in Section 11.5.2 to the case in which the new shares created by the flip-over plan carry a voting right.

49. In the case of symmetric toeholds, the expected sale price is higher in an ascending auction than in a first-price auction (see Singh (1998) for the case of private values and Bulow et al. (1999) for common values).

50. For example, one-third of board members comes up for reelection each year, which implies that even a successful raider cannot take immediate control of the board.

51. We do not, of course, consider here statutory defenses, which are not controlled by the firm.

52. For example, in Bagwell (1991) and Stulz (1988), repurchasing shares in an environment with an upward-sloping supply of shares (say, because shareholders have different capital gains bases) forces the raider to increase his bid.

53. Managerial stockholdings, if they are substantial and carry voting rights, however, also reduce the number of shares that can be tendered by independent shareholders.

References

Aghion, P. and P. Bolton. 1987. Contracts as a barrier to entry. *American Economic Review* 77:388–401.

Bagnoli, M. and B. Lipman. 1988. Successful takeovers without exclusion. *Review of Financial Studies* 1:89–110.

Bagwell, L. 1991. Share repurchase and takeover deterrence. *RAND Journal of Economics* 22:72–88.

Bebchuk, L. and O. Hart. 2001. Takeover bids vs. proxy fights in contests for corporate control. National Bureau of Economic Research, Working Paper 7203.

Bebchuk, L. and L. Stole. 1992. Do short-term objectives lead to under- or over-investment in long-term projects? *Journal of Finance* 48:719–729.

Bebchuk, L. and L. Zingales. 2000. Ownership structures and the decision to go public. In *Concentrated Corporate Ownership* (ed. R. Morck), pp. 55–75. University of Chicago Press.

Bertrand, M. and S. Mullainathan. 2003. Enjoying the quiet life? Corporate governance and managerial preferences. *Journal of Political Economy* 111:1043–1075.

Betton, S. and E. B. Eckbo. 2000. Toeholds, bid jumps, and expected payoffs in takeovers. *Review of Financial Studies* 13:841–882.

Bulow, J., M. Huang, and P. Klemperer. 1999. Toeholds and takeovers. *Journal of Political Economy* 107:427–454.

Burkart, M. 1995. Initial shareholdings and overbidding in takeover contests. *Journal of Finance* 50:1491–1515.

——. 1996. Economics of takeover regulation. Mimeo, Stockholm School of Economics.

Burkart, M., D. Gromb, and F. Panunzi. 1998. Why higher takeover premia protect minority shareholders. *Journal of Political Economy* 106:172–204.

——. 2000. Agency conflicts in public and negotiated transfers of corporate control. *Journal of Finance* 55:647–677.

——. 2005. Monitoring blocks and takeover premia. Mimeo, Stockholm School of Economics, London Business School, and Università Bocconi. *Journal of Institutional and Theoretical Economics*, in press.

Coase, R. 1972. Durability and monopoly. *Journal of Law and Economics* 15:143–149.

Dewatripont, M. 1993. The leading shareholder strategy, takeover contests and stock price dynamics. *European Economic Review* 37:983–1004.

Diamond, P. and E. Maskin. 1979. An equilibrium analysis of search and breach of contracts. I. Steady states. *Bell Journal of Economics* 10:282–316.

Fishman, M. 1988. A theory of pre-emptive takeover bidding. *RAND Journal of Economics* 19:88–101.

——. 1989. Preemptive bidding and the role of medium of exchange in acquisitions. *Journal of Finance* 44:41–58.

Fudenberg, D. and J. Tirole. 1991. *Game Theory.* Cambridge, MA: MIT Press.

Fudenberg, D., D. Levine, and W. Pesendorfer. 1998. When are non-anonymous players negligible? *Journal of Economic Theory* 79:46–71.

Gromb, D. 1995. Is one share-one vote optimal? Mimeo, Ecole Polytechnique, Paris.

Grossman, S. and O. Hart. 1980. Takeover bids, the free rider problem, and the theory of the corporation. *Bell Journal of Economics* 11:42–64.

Grossman, S. and O. Hart. 1988. One share/one vote and the market for corporate control. *Journal of Financial Economics* 20:175–202.

Harrington, J. and J. Prokop. 1993. The dynamics of the free-rider problem in takeovers. *Review of Financial Studies* 6: 851–882.

Harris, M. and A. Raviv. 1988. Corporate control contests and capital structure. *Journal of Financial Economics* 20: 55–88.

Hirshleifer, D. 1992. Takeovers. In *The New Palgrave Dictionary of Money and Finance* (ed. P. Newman, M. Milgate, and J. Eatwell). New York: Macmillan.

——. 1995. Mergers and acquisitions: strategic and informational issues. In *Handbook in Operations Research and Management Science* (ed. R. Jarrow, V. Maksimovic, and W. Ziemba), Volume 9, Chapter 26. Amsterdam: North-Holland.

Hirshleifer, D. and I. Png. 1989. Facilitation of competing bids and the price of a takeover target. *Review of Financial Studies* 2:587–606.

Hirshleifer, D. and S. Titman. 1990. Share tendering strategies and the success of hostile takeover bids. *Journal of Political Economy* 98:295–324.

Holmström, B. and B. Nalebuff. 1992. To the raider goes the surplus? A reexamination of the free-rider problem. *Journal of Economics and Management Strategy* 1:37–62.

Israel, R. 1992. Capital and ownership structures and the market for corporate control. *Review of Financial Studies* 5:181–188.

Jennings, R. H. and M. A. Mazzeo. 1993. Competing bids, target management resistance and the structure of takeover bids. *Review of Financial Studies* 5:883–910.

Jensen, M. 1988. Takeovers: their causes and consequences. *Journal of Economic Perspectives* 2:21–48.

Laffont, J.-J. and J. Tirole. 1988. Repeated auctions of incentive contracts, investment and bidding parity, with an application to takeovers. *RAND Journal of Economics* 19: 516–537.

Malatesta, P. 1992. Takeover defences. In *The New Palgrave Dictionary of Money and Finance* (ed. P. Newman, M. Milgate, and J. Eatwell). London: Macmillan.

Malatesta, P. and R. Walking. 1988. Poison pill securities: stockholder wealth, profitability, and ownership structure. *Journal of Financial Economics* 20:347–376.

Manne, H. 1965. Mergers and the market for corporate control. *Journal of Political Economy* 73:110–120.

Müller, H. and F. Panunzi. 2004. Tender offers and leverage. *Quarterly Journal of Economics* 119:1217–1248.

Nöldeke, G. and K. Schmidt. 1998. Sequential investments and options to own. *RAND Journal of Economics* 29:633–653.

Schnitzer, M. 1992. Breach of trust in takeovers and the optimal corporate charter. PhD dissertation, Chapter 4, Bonn University.

Segal, I. 1999. Contracting with externalities. *Quarterly Journal of Economics* 114:337–388.

Shleifer, A. and L. Summers. 1988. Breach of trust in hostile takeovers. In *Corporate Takeovers: Causes and Consequences* (ed. A. Auerbach), pp. 33–56. University of Chicago Press.

Shleifer, A. and R. Vishny. 1986a. Large shareholders and corporate control. *Journal of Political Economy* 94:461–488.

——. 1986b. Greenmail, white knights, and shareholders' interest. *RAND Journal of Economics* 17:293–309.

Singh, R. 1998. Takeover bidding with toeholds: the case of the owner's curse. *Review of Financial Studies* 11:679–704.

Stein, J. 1988. Takeover threats and managerial myopia. *Journal of Political Economy* 96:61–80.

——. 1989. Efficient capital markets, inefficient firms: a model of myopic corporate behavior. *Quarterly Journal of Economics* 104:655–669.

Stulz, R. 1988. Managerial control of voting rights: financing policies and the market for corporate control. *Journal of Financial Economics* 20:25–54.

Walking, R. 1985. Predicting tender offer success: a logistic analysis. *Journal of Financial and Quantitative Analysis* 20:461–478.

Walking, R. and M. Long. 1984. Agency theory, managerial welfare, and takeover bid resistance. *RAND Journal of Economics* 15:54–68.

Zingales, L. 1995. Inside ownership and the decision to go public. *Review of Economic Studies* 62:425–448.

PART V

Security Design: The Demand Side View

12

Consumer Liquidity Demand

12.1 Introduction

As studied in Chapter 5, corporations and financial intermediaries secure their liquidity on the asset side of their balance sheet through lines of credit and the hoarding of liquid assets. They also manage their liquidity on the liability side. Short-term debt drains liquidity much more than long-term debt or securities, such as preferred equity and common equity, that embody a valuable option of not being forced to pay (preferred or common equity) dividends if times get rough.

By assuming that investors' utility is represented by the present discounted value of their consumptions (with a discount rate normalized at 0), we have ignored their own liquidity demand. In practice, consumers face personal shocks and value the flexibility of being able to realize their assets when they need to. For example, ignoring differences in rates of return, they value demand deposits over and above savings that are locked in for a few months or years.[1] They hoard substantial amounts of liquid assets in order to insure against shocks. They are willing to sacrifice returns in order to make sure they will have enough money to buy a house or a car when the opportunity arises, to send their children to (more or less expensive) college, or to protect themselves against illness or unemployment. Thus, consumers compete with corporations for the available stock of liquidity.[2] Consumer liquidity demand has been the focus of a large and interesting literature, starting with the seminal papers of Bryant (1980) and Diamond and Dybvig (1983).

This chapter looks at three aspects of consumer liquidity demand:

(i) The role that financial institutions may play as (a) liquidity pools and (b) insurers. We will see that the first role, which prevents the waste associated with individual securing of liquidity (duplication of costly liquidity provision) is primordial, while the second, which aims at flattening the term structure of interest rates in order to reduce the cost of impatience, is more fragile as it is exposed to opportunistic arbitrage by financial markets.

(ii) The runs that may occur on financial intermediaries with (efficiently) limited liquid assets on their balance sheet.

(iii) The design of a menu of securities that fits the individual profiles—short term versus long term—of investors.

12.2 Consumer Liquidity Demand: The Diamond–Dybvig Model and the Term Structure of Interest Rates

12.2.1 Insuring against Liquidity Shocks

The Diamond–Dybvig model depicts the optimal contract between a financial intermediary and a consumer who faces uncertainty as to the timing of her consumption. The model, in its simplest and most common form, has three periods, $t = 0, 1, 2$.[3]

Consumer preferences. Consumers are *ex ante* identical. For notational simplicity, let us assume that they have no demand for consumption at date 0, and therefore invest their entire date-0 resources, 1 per consumer. More generally, their savings are

1. Unless they are worried about a time-inconsistency problem and do not want to be exposed to the temptation to consume (see, for example, Laibson 1997).

2. This competition has been little studied in the literature unfortunately.

3. Good alternative expositions of the Diamond–Dybvig model can be found in Bond and Townsend (1995), Freixas and Rochet (1997), and Gorton and Winton (2003).

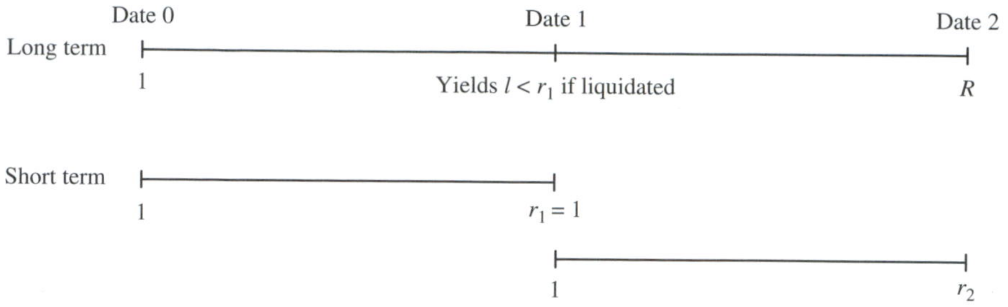

Figure 12.1 Liquid and illiquid investments.

equal to 1 per consumer. They have no further resources at dates 1 and 2, and have state-contingent preferences over date-1 and date-2 consumptions, c_1 and c_2, given by

$$\left.\begin{aligned} &u(c_1) \quad \text{if impatient (probability } \lambda\text{)}, \\ &u(c_2) \quad \text{if patient (probability } 1-\lambda\text{)}, \end{aligned}\right\} \tag{12.1}$$

where the function u is increasing and *strictly* concave, and $u'(0) = \infty$. Consumers do not know at date 0 whether they will be impatient ("face a liquidity shock") or not. They learn at date 1 their "type" (patient or impatient).[4] In the simplest version of this model there is no aggregate uncertainty, and so exactly a fraction λ of consumers will want to consume at date 1.

The specification of consumer preferences embodied in (12.1) is a simple-minded way of formalizing the idea that the consumer does not know when she will need money.[5]

Technology. Date-0 resources are invested in short-term (liquid) and long-term projects. Short-term projects yield r_1 at date 1 per unit of date-0 investment. Similarly, 1 unit of investment (in a short-term project) at date 1 yields r_2 at date 2. Long-term projects yield $R > 1$ at date 2 per unit of date-0 investment, and nothing at date 1. Liquidity is costly as long-term projects have a higher yield:

$$r_1 r_2 < R.$$

In words, an investor with a long-term perspective, that is, one who would be unconcerned by the possibility of a liquidity shock ($\lambda = 0$), would invest in the long-term asset rather than in a short-term asset that she would roll over at date 1 (see Figure 12.1).

Without loss of generality, let us assume that

$$r_1 = 1.$$

This production function defines a *technological yield curve.* Let r_{LT} denote the per-period return on the long-term asset:

$$(1 + r_{\text{LT}})^2 = R \quad \text{or} \quad r_{\text{LT}} = \sqrt{R} - 1.$$

In comparison, a short-term investment at date 0 yields rate of interest

$$r_{\text{ST}} = r_1 - 1 = 0 < r_{\text{LT}}.$$

The technological yield curve is upward sloping.

Liquidating a long-term investment at date 1 yields a salvage value l per unit of date-0 investment. In this section, we will assume for simplicity that this salvage value is equal to 0, but more generally it will be assumed to be lower than $r_1 = 1$ (if $l \geqslant 1$, the long-term asset dominates and there is never any investment in short-term assets).

Lastly, the representative investor must decide how to allocate her savings between short-term investment i_1 and long-term investment i_2:

$$i_1 + i_2 = 1.$$

12.2.2 Self-Provision of Liquidity Is Inefficient

As is the case for corporate liquidity demand and for a related reason, self-provision of liquidity—a consumer's investing in liquid assets solely to cover her own liquidity shock—is wasteful. If the consumer happens not to face a liquidity shock, the costly liquidity that she has hoarded is wasted. Somehow,

4. These types are also called "late dier" and "early dier" in the literature.

5. For example, most of the insights derived below still hold if the consumer has utility $u(c_1 + c_2)$ when patient, provided that the rate of return between dates 1 and 2 (called r_2 below) exceeds 1: $r_2 \geqslant 1$.

the community of consumers should be able to use the law of large numbers to reduce their investment in liquid assets while enjoying the same amount of liquidity.

Autarky. To demonstrate the inefficiency of an "autarky situation" (as it is called in the literature), suppose that, as announced earlier,

$$l = 0,$$

and that the representative consumer invests i_1 and i_2 in short- and long-term assets. Then, because $r_1 = 1$,

$$c_1 = i_1 \quad \text{and} \quad c_2 = r_2 i_1 + R i_2 = R - c_1(R - r_2). \tag{12.2}$$

As the consumption c_1 when the depositor is impatient grows from 0 to 1, the date-2 consumption enjoyed by the patient incarnation falls from R to r_2.

The representative consumer therefore maximizes her expected utility:

$$\max_{\{c_1\}}\{\lambda u(c_1) + (1-\lambda)u(R - c_1(R - r_2))\}. \tag{12.3}$$

Indeed, the optimization with respect to $\{i_1, i_2\}$ can be reduced to one over the date-1 consumption, since c_1 determines the investment in short-term assets needed and therefore the investment in long-term assets as well. This optimization yields either an interior or a corner solution:

$$\left.\begin{aligned} &\text{either} \quad \frac{\lambda u'(c_1)}{(1-\lambda)u'(c_2)} = R - r_2 \\ &\text{or} \quad c_1 = 1 \quad \left(\text{if } \frac{\lambda u'(1)}{(1-\lambda)u'(r_2)} > R - r_2\right). \end{aligned}\right\} \tag{12.4}$$

It is easy to check that the fraction invested in liquid assets $i_1 = c_1$ grows when the probability λ of facing a liquidity shock increases and when the "technological premium" associated with a long-term investment, $R - r_2$, decreases. Note, in particular, that everything is invested in the short-term asset when this premium is low or when the probability of a liquidity shock is high.

The benefits from pooling liquidity: mutual funds. The autarky outcome studied above precludes any resale. We have emphasized the excessive investment in liquid assets (possibly to the level of the consumer's entire savings). The flip side of the same coin is that any investment in the long-term asset is thrown away (as $l = 0$) when the consumer turns out to be impatient. Somehow the opening of date-1 resale markets should generate gains from trade. Long-term assets held by impatient consumers are very attractive to patient consumers, who could use their own liquid assets to purchase the impatient consumers' long-term assets.

Along these lines let us show that a mutual fund enables consumers to enjoy the same date-1 consumption as under autarky, and a much larger date-2 return. Let $(\bar{c}_1, \bar{c}_2)$ denote the consumptions under autarky (they solve (12.2) and (12.4)). Let the consumers invest in a mutual fund with short- and long-term investments:

$$i_1 = \lambda\bar{c}_1 \quad \text{and} \quad i_2 = 1 - \lambda\bar{c}_1.$$

That is, they invest less in short-term assets and more into long-term ones than under autarky. This mutual fund distributes dividends equal to $i_1 r_1 = i_1$ at date 1, and $i_2 R$ at date 2. At date 1, the impatient consumers resell their share of the mutual fund to patient consumers, who compete with their scarce resources (the dividends they receive at date 1) for this valuable asset. The date-1 mutual fund price p is such that the patient consumers' resources, $(1-\lambda)i_1$, equal the value of the shares sold by the impatient ones:

$$(1-\lambda)i_1 = \lambda p.$$

The impatient consumers then consume

$$c_1 = i_1 + p = \frac{i_1}{\lambda} = \bar{c}_1.$$

At date 2, the patient consumers each consume

$$c_2 = \frac{i_2 R}{1-\lambda},$$

since they end up holding not only their initial shares, but also the shares of the impatient consumers and therefore own $1/(1-\lambda)$ shares of the fund each. It is easily checked that

$$c_2 = \frac{[1-\lambda\bar{c}_1]R}{1-\lambda} > \bar{c}_2 = R - \bar{c}_1(R - r_2).$$

These computations show that the resaleability of assets allows consumers to economize on liquidity provision and thereby increases their welfare.

Let us next compute the mutual fund's optimal portfolio: because

$$i_1 = \lambda c_1 \quad \text{and} \quad i_2 = \frac{(1-\lambda)c_2}{R}, \tag{12.5}$$

the optimal portfolio solves

$$\max_{\{c_1\}} \left\{\lambda u(c_1) + (1-\lambda)u\left(\frac{(1-\lambda c_1)R}{1-\lambda}\right)\right\}, \tag{12.6}$$

yielding

$$\frac{u'(c_1)}{u'(c_2)} = R. \tag{12.7}$$

Note that the optimal mutual fund does not fully insure consumers against liquidity shocks ($c_1 < c_2$). It is optimal to take advantage of the upward-sloping yield curve and sacrifice some insurance. We will come back to this point shortly.

Comparison with corporate liquidity demand. To sum up, and as we have already noted, an important analogy between corporate liquidity demand (Chapter 5) and consumer liquidity demand (this chapter) is that corporations and consumers alike must obtain some insurance against liquidity shocks. Such insurance is costly when long-term investments have higher returns than short-term ones. Accordingly, liquidity ought to be hoarded sparingly and dispatched properly. When shocks are not perfectly correlated among economic actors (corporations, consumers), liquidity can be pooled and fewer low-yield investments are needed in comparison with the situation in which these actors self-provide liquidity. Or, put differently, autarky results in an overprovision of liquidity.

Consumer and corporate liquidity demands, however, differ in at least two respects:

- A key theme of corporate liquidity demand is that investments in short- and long-term assets, while competing for scarce resources at date 0, are later on *complements*, as liquidity enables long-term assets to bear their fruits. There is no such complementarity in the consumer liquidity demand model.
- *A consumer* consumes the cash that she receives, and *does not create any pledgeable income* (in the notation of Chapter 5, $\rho_0 = 0$). This observation has several consequences. First, the consumers' total investment is equal to their savings or "cash on hand" ($i_1 + i_2 = A = 1$ here), while firms can invest more than their cash on hand ($i_1 + i_2 > A$).[6] In particular, the only way for consumers to satisfy their liquidity needs is to invest in real, low-yield, short-term assets. By contrast, Chapter 15 will show that, under some circumstances, the private sector may create enough "inside liquidity" and avoid having to invest in low-yield assets.

12.2.3 Optimal Liquidity Insurance

The mutual fund is only one of many ways available for pooling liquidity. Another familiar financial institution through which consumers pool their liquidity is the bank. Demand deposits allow consumers to choose the timing of withdrawals. A bank, of course, does not hold an amount of liquid assets equal to the level of demand deposits. Rather, it uses the law of large numbers to economize on liquid assets, as it knows that only a fraction of consumers will withdraw their deposits at any point in time.

More generally, one may wonder about the nature of the "optimal insurance scheme." The first point to note is that it is optimal to *match* the maturities of investments and consumptions. Given that there is no aggregate uncertainty and so one can predict exactly the levels of investment that are needed for date-contingent consumptions, investing $i_1 > \lambda c_1$ and rolling over the unneeded income ($i_1 - \lambda c_1$) is dominated by investing "just what is needed" for date-1 consumption ($i_1 = \lambda c_1$) and investing the rest in the higher-yield long-term asset. And so (12.5) holds.

6. For instance, the two-shock model of Section 5.3.1 can be rewritten by adapting the notation slightly to facilitate the comparison with the consumer liquidity demand. Recall that the entrepreneur chooses investment scale I that, if the liquidity shock is met at date 1, yields total income $\rho_1 I$ and pledgeable income $\rho_0 I$ (with $\rho_0 < \rho_1$). With probability λ, the firm must pay $x\rho I$ to salvage a fraction x of its assets. With probability $1-\lambda$, it faces no shock at the intermediate stage. Letting $i_2 = I$ and $i_1 = \lambda x \rho i_2$, the breakeven and NPV conditions were given by

$$i_1 + i_2 - A = [\lambda x + (1-\lambda)]\rho_0 i_2$$

and

$$U_b = [\lambda x + (1-\lambda)]\rho_1 i_2 - (1 + \lambda x \rho) i_2.$$

Recall from Chapter 5 that, at the optimum, $x = 1$ if $\rho(1-\lambda) < 1$ and $x = 0$ if $\rho(1-\lambda) > 1$. In particular, i_1 and i_2 may both be positive, while in the optimal mutual-fund policy of the risk-neutral version of Diamond–Dybvig (the consumer's expected utility is $\lambda c_1 + (1-\lambda)c_2$), $i_2 = 1$ as long as $R > 1$ (concave versions of production technologies can also be studied so as to facilitate the comparison with the Diamond–Dybvig model with risk-averse consumers).

The optimal allocation must then solve (12.6), yielding, again, a solution characterized by (12.7). Let (c_1^*, c_2^*) solve (12.7) and $c_2^* = (1 - \lambda c_1^*)R/(1 - \lambda)$.

Implementation by a deposit contract. The optimal allocation can be implemented by a bank deposit contract provided that the rate of interest received by the consumer on this deposit depends on the date at which she withdraws. Namely, the consumer receives rates of interest r_{ST}^* and r_{LT}^* on deposits withdrawn at dates 1 and 2, such that

$$1 + r_{\mathrm{ST}}^* = c_1^* \quad \text{and} \quad (1 + r_{\mathrm{LT}}^*)^2 = c_2^*.$$

Let us follow Diamond and Dybvig (1983) and most of the subsequent literature in assuming that the consumers' coefficient of relative risk aversion exceeds 1:

$$\left| \frac{cu''(c)}{u'(c)} \right| > 1 \quad \text{for all } c.$$

This assumption is empirically reasonable (see, for example, Gollier 2001, Chapter 2). Equation (12.7),

$$\frac{u'(c_1^*)}{u'(c_2^*)} = R,$$

can then be shown to imply that[7]

$$1 < c_1^* < c_2^* < R. \tag{12.8}$$

We have

$$r_{\mathrm{ST}}^* > r_{\mathrm{ST}} \quad \text{and} \quad r_{\mathrm{LT}}^* < r_{\mathrm{LT}}.$$

In words, *the optimal insurance scheme flattens the yield curve relative to the technological yield curve.*

Note that, while the optimal insurance scheme flattens the yield curve relative to the technological one, no prediction can be made concerning its slope. If risk aversion is low (the coefficient of relative risk aversion is close to 1), the yield curve is close to the technological yield curve and is therefore upward sloping. In contrast, if risk aversion is very high (the coefficient of relative risk aversion goes to infinity), then consumptions at the two dates are almost equalized and so the yield curve is downward sloping (the interest on long-term deposits is compounded and yet does not exceed the short-term deposit interest rate).

We have not yet wondered about whether this deposit contact is "incentive compatible." For example, would the patient consumers not want to withdraw at date 1 and reinvest the proceeds in the date-1 short-term technology yielding r_2? Indeed if $r_2 > 1$, and risk aversion is large, then $c_1^* r_2 > c_2^*$ from our previous analysis, and so it is indeed in the interest of patient consumers to feign impatience, cash out, and reinvest. Let us therefore assume at this stage that the bank is able to observe who is patient and who is not, or, equivalently, is able to prevent reinvestment elsewhere. This assumption is unrealistic, especially in a decentralized market economy, but it has the pedagogical merit of separating insurance concerns from incentive compatibility issues in a first step. Let us be "patient" and delay the discussion of incentive compatibility for a more general treatment in the next section.

More general preferences: suboptimality of mutual funds (advanced). The equivalence between mutual funds and demand deposits breaks down for more general specifications of preferences. Suppose with Jacklin (1987) that the representative consumer's preferences are more generally given by

$$\begin{aligned} &u^{\mathrm{I}}(c_1^{\mathrm{I}}, c_2^{\mathrm{I}}) \quad \text{with probability } \lambda \text{ (impatient)},\\ &u^{\mathrm{P}}(c_1^{\mathrm{P}}, c_2^{\mathrm{P}}) \quad \text{with probability } 1 - \lambda \text{ (patient)}. \end{aligned}$$

To make sense of the terminology, one can imagine that the impatient type has a higher marginal rate of substitution between date-1 and date-2 consumptions $((\partial u/\partial c_1)/(\partial u/\partial c_2))$ than the patient type.

Ignoring again incentive compatibility questions, the optimal allocation then chooses investments and consumptions so as to solve

$$\max_{\{c_1^{\mathrm{I}}, c_2^{\mathrm{I}}, c_1^{\mathrm{P}}, c_2^{\mathrm{P}}\}} \{\lambda u^{\mathrm{I}}(c_1^{\mathrm{I}}, c_2^{\mathrm{I}}) + (1 - \lambda) u^{\mathrm{P}}(c_1^{\mathrm{P}}, c_2^{\mathrm{P}})\}$$

$$\text{s.t.} \tag{12.9}$$

$$[\lambda c_1^{\mathrm{I}} + (1 - \lambda) c_1^{\mathrm{P}}] + \frac{[\lambda c_2^{\mathrm{I}} + (1 - \lambda) c_2^{\mathrm{P}}]}{R} = 1,$$

since $i_1 = \lambda c_1^{\mathrm{I}} + (1 - \lambda) c_1^{\mathrm{P}}$ is needed to deliver the total date-1 consumption and $i_2 = [\lambda c_2^{\mathrm{I}} + (1 - \lambda) c_2^{\mathrm{P}}]/R$ is what it takes to deliver the total date-2 consumption.

7. To show this, note that the assumption on the coefficient of relative risk aversion says that the function $cu'(c)$ is decreasing. Hence, $Ru'(R) < 1 \cdot u'(1)$, and so at the feasible allocation $\{c_1 = 1,\ c_2 = R\}$, $u'(c_1)/u'(c_2) = u'(1)/u'(R) > R$. To obtain (12.8), one must increase c_1 above 1, and concomitantly reduce c_2 below R. To conclude, recall that $R > 1$ and (12.7) imply that $c_1^* < c_2^*$.

At the optimal allocation, marginal utilities are equalized across types:

$$\frac{\partial u^{\mathrm{I}}}{\partial c_1^{\mathrm{I}}} = \frac{\partial u^{\mathrm{P}}}{\partial c_1^{\mathrm{P}}} \quad \text{and} \quad \frac{\partial u^{\mathrm{I}}}{\partial c_2^{\mathrm{I}}} = \frac{\partial u^{\mathrm{P}}}{\partial c_2^{\mathrm{P}}}.$$

Furthermore,

$$\frac{\partial u^{\theta}}{\partial c_1^{\theta}} \bigg/ \frac{\partial u^{\theta}}{\partial c_2^{\theta}} = R \quad \text{for } \theta \in \{\mathrm{I}, \mathrm{P}\}.$$

In contrast, a mutual fund mechanism equalizes only marginal rates of substitution: if p denotes the price (in terms of date-1 consumption) of shares in the date-2 dividend, then each type $\theta \in \{\mathrm{I}, \mathrm{P}\}$ faces a date-1 budget constraint,

$$c_2^{\theta} - i_2 R = (i_1 - c_1^{\theta})\left(\frac{i_2 R}{p}\right),$$

and maximizes $u^{\theta}(c_1^{\theta}, c_2^{\theta})$ subject to this constraint. Thus marginal rates of substitution are equalized:

$$\frac{\partial u^{\mathrm{I}}}{\partial c_1^{\mathrm{I}}} \bigg/ \frac{\partial u^{\mathrm{I}}}{\partial c_2^{\mathrm{I}}} = \frac{\partial u^{\mathrm{P}}}{\partial c_1^{\mathrm{P}}} \bigg/ \frac{\partial u^{\mathrm{P}}}{\partial c_2^{\mathrm{P}}}.$$

But, in general, the mutual fund scheme contains no mechanism to redistribute across types. The consumer enters date 1 with the same budget (dividend plus resale value) regardless of her type. This insurance shortage must be remedied through a different scheme, in which the consumer gets the solution to (12.9), $(c_1^{\mathrm{I}}, c_2^{\mathrm{I}})$ when impatient and $(c_1^{\mathrm{P}}, c_2^{\mathrm{P}})$ when patient. Assuming $c_1^{\mathrm{I}} > c_1^{\mathrm{P}}$ and $c_2^{\mathrm{I}} < c_2^{\mathrm{P}}$, this can be accomplished by a combination of long-term savings that are locked in until maturity and deliver c_2^{I} at date 2, together with a deposit contract that offers the option of withdrawing the total amount c_1^{I} at date 1 versus withdrawing the smaller amount c_1^{P} in exchange for return $[c_2^{\mathrm{P}} - c_2^{\mathrm{I}}]$ at date 2.

Even if we rule out reinvestments outside the bank offering such contracts, it is no longer clear that the optimal allocation is incentive compatible, that is, that type $\theta \in \{\mathrm{I}, \mathrm{P}\}$ prefers $(c_1^{\theta}, c_2^{\theta})$ to $(c_1^{\theta'}, c_2^{\theta'})$ for $\theta' \neq \theta$ (while this created no difficulty with the more special preferences studied earlier). (Noninnocuous) conditions need to be imposed to guarantee that the optimal allocation is incentive compatible (see Jacklin 1987).

Interbank lending. As shown by Bhattacharya and Gale (1987), interbank lending performs a useful pooling function when banks suffer idiosyncratic shocks in their depositors' withdrawal rates. Thus, suppose that there are two *ex ante* identical banks. The fraction of impatient depositors will be high (λ_{H}) in one bank and low (λ_{L}) in the other. So there is no aggregate uncertainty. The average withdrawal rate is $\lambda = \frac{1}{2}(\lambda_{\mathrm{H}} + \lambda_{\mathrm{L}})$. But there is idiosyncratic risk: no one knows at date 0 which bank will face the high withdrawal rate.

The banks can reach the efficient outcome by granting each other credit lines. They invest $i_1 = \lambda c_1^*$ and $i_2 = (1 - \lambda)c_2^*/R$ per consumer each and redispatch the liquid asset between the two when the shocks accrue. The liquidity-poor bank (with withdrawal rate $\lambda_i = \lambda_{\mathrm{H}}$) can transfer some of the claim to the proceeds $i_2 R$ on its long-term investment to the liquidity-rich bank (with withdrawal rate $\lambda_i = \lambda_{\mathrm{L}}$) in exchange for $\frac{1}{2}(\lambda_{\mathrm{H}} - \lambda_{\mathrm{L}})c_1^*$ at date 1.[8]

12.2.4 Financial Markets and the Jacklin Critique

A common theme in the economics of information and incentives is that markets conflict with the optimal provision of insurance (e.g., Pauly 1974; Helpman and Laffont 1975; Bernheim and Whinston 1986). Jacklin's (1987) critique of the Diamond–Dybvig model fits within this overall theme.

In a nutshell, Jacklin argues that financial markets' ability to arbitrage the implicit cross-subsidy in favor of the impatient relative to the technological yield curve undermines the overall insurance mechanism.

Suppose that a consumer initially bypasses the insurance system and invests her entire savings in the high-yield long-term asset ($i_2 = 1$). This strategy clearly delivers the highest possible payoff if the consumer turns out to be patient, since then

$$c_2 = R > c_2^*.$$

But what if the consumer ends up being impatient? The trick is then to sell the claim to the long-term payoff to the patient consumers, who use their ability to withdraw their deposits at the bank in order to finance the purchase. Normalize the number

8. The analysis by Bhattacharya and Gale (1987) is much broader than reported here. In particular, it also deals with situations in which banks are imperfectly informed about each other's solvency (investment in or return on the long-term assets, or the number of withdrawing depositors).

of shares issued by the consumer at one (divisible) share. A patient consumer can withdraw an amount c_1^* from the bank and is willing to pay price p per share for α shares such that

$$c_1^* = \alpha p,$$

as long as she gets at least as much consumption at date 2 as when she leaves her money at the bank:

$$\alpha R \geqslant c_2^*.$$

That is, the consumer who has invested in the long-term asset can obtain price p for the claim on this asset, such that

$$p = \frac{c_1^* R}{c_2^*} > c_1^*.$$

In effect, this opportunistic consumer free rides on the banks' costly provision of liquidity. She can have her cake and eat it too.

More generally, the same reasoning shows that any insurance scheme is undone by financial markets as long as $c_2 < R$. Hence, in the presence of financial markets, the best feasible allocation is

$$\hat{c}_1 = 1 \quad \text{and} \quad \hat{c}_2 = R. \tag{12.10}$$

Financial markets force the yield curve back to the technological yield curve. The reader will find in Allen and Gale (1997) useful complements on free riding and the underprovision of liquidity.

Remark (differential access to financial markets). Diamond (1997) studies the intermediate case in which some consumers have access to financial markets (as in Jacklin 1987) while others do not (as in Diamond and Dybvig 1983). Suppose, for instance, that everyone is *ex ante* identical. At date 1, the consumer learns her type. But there are now three types rather than two: an impatient type (receives c_1) and two patient types. In Diamond's terminology, those with access to financial markets are "type 2A," while those with no such access (who cannot reinvest the money they withdraw at date 1) are "type 2B." The bank is unable to tell the different types apart. The date-0 optimal contract offers return c_1 if the consumer withdraws at date 1 and c_2^{B} at date 2 if the consumer does not, where

$$1 < c_1 < c_2^{\mathrm{B}} < R.$$

In equilibrium, patient consumers with no access to financial markets just consume c_2^{B}. Patient consumers with such access withdraw c_1 and reinvest in one of these long-term investment vehicles yielding R; they consume[9]

$$c_2^{\mathrm{A}} = c_1 R > R.$$

The extent of flattening of the bank's yield curve relative to the technological yield curve then depends on the fraction of consumers with no access to financial markets. If this fraction is important, extensive cross-subsidies *à la* Diamond–Dybvig are doable; if not, then the bank must offer a steep yield curve, close to the technological yield curve.

12.2.5 Economizing on Liquidity by Rolling over Deposits

Let us ignore the Jacklin critique and address another potential enrichment of the Diamond–Dybvig model. By not describing the economy as an ongoing one, Diamond and Dybvig overestimate the need for low-yield liquid assets, at least in a relatively stationary context. The idea is that if investments by incoming generations of consumers (new investors) offset the disinvestments by earlier generations of investors facing liquidity needs, then no asset needs to be liquidated and everything can be invested in the high-yield long-term asset.

Following Qi (1994), consider an overlapping-generations (OLG) version of the Diamond–Dybvig model in which:

- a new generation ("generation t") invests its savings (1 per individual) at date t, and lives up to date $t+2$;
- members of this generation learn at date $t+1$ whether their utility function is $u(c_{t+1}^t)$ (probability λ) or $u(c_{t+2}^t)$ (probability $1-\lambda$), where c_τ^t is generation t's consumption at date τ;
- the population is constant; and
- the technology is similar to that described above: 1 unit of "long-term investment" yields $R > 1$ two periods later; 1 unit of "short-term investment" yields 1 one period later.

9. One can envision that this arbitrage is enabled by financial entities that invest in the long-term asset and resell it at cost (1) at date 1 to these type-2A consumers.

Table 12.1 The OLG structure.

	t	$t+1$	$t+2$	$t+3$	$t+4$
Generation t	invests 1	$u(c^t_{t+1})$ (prob. λ)	$u(c^t_{t+2})$ (prob. $1-\lambda$)		
Generation $t+1$		invests 1	$u(c^{t+1}_{t+2})$ (prob. λ)	$u(c^{t+1}_{t+3})$ (prob. $1-\lambda$)	
Generation $t+2$			invests 1	$u(c^{t+2}_{t+3})$ (prob. λ)	$u(c^{t+2}_{t+4})$ (prob. $1-\lambda$)

Table 12.1 summarizes the timing.

Consider a bank that in *steady state* offers consumption profile $\{c_1$ (for the impatient), c_2 (for the patient)$\}$ so as to maximize the depositors' expected utility:

$$\max\{\lambda u(c_1) + (1-\lambda)u(c_2)\}. \tag{12.11}$$

This bank needs not invest in low-yield short-term investments. At period $t+2$, say, it can employ the return R on the generation t's deposits invested in high-yield assets, to honor the deposit withdrawal by generation t's patient types and generation $t+1$'s impatient types. Thus, the budget constraint is

$$\lambda c_1 + (1-\lambda)c_2 \leqslant R. \tag{12.12}$$

Note that the maximization of (12.11) subject to (12.12) yields perfect insurance:

$$c_1 = c_2 = R.$$

This allocation, which exhibits a downward-sloping yield curve, however, is not incentive compatible if patient consumers can withdraw and reinvest in a similar bank (or the same bank under a different name). Such arbitrage indeed imposes that

$$(c_1)^2 \leqslant c_2. \tag{12.13}$$

That is, if the consumer can withdraw and reinvest, the yield curve must be either flat ($(c_1)^2 = c_2$) or upward sloping ($(c_1)^2 < c_2$). Given that the optimal yield curve in the absence of constraint (12.13) is downward sloping, *the constrained optimal yield curve is flat*:

$$(c_1)^2 = c_2,$$

which implies

$$c_2 > R > c_1 > 1.$$

This analysis requires that there be no aggregate uncertainty and that the economy be in a steady state. In particular, Qi (1994) looks at how a bank can get started. We refer to the paper for more detail.

While highly stylized, this OLG analysis captures an important aspect of reality. Banks make heavy use of the facts that demand deposits are rolled over, and that, to honor the promises made in previous deposit agreements, they can attract new deposits rather than liquidate their long-term assets. The same strategy plays an important role on the equity side as well. For example, the underlying assets in a closed-end mutual fund (whose shares are sold on the open market) are not liquidated when an investor wants to sell her share. Rather, this share is transferred to another investor.

Allen and Gale (1997, 2000, Chapter 6) analyze an OLG model with a safe and a risky asset. The safe asset can be accumulated over time. Financial markets allow cross-sectional risk-sharing opportunities to be exploited, but may provide insufficient intertemporal risk smoothing. An intermediated system fares better in the latter dimension. However, the intertemporal smoothing provided by a long-lived intermediary is fragile as arbitrage opportunities undermine the insurance it offers.

12.3 Runs

12.3.1 Depositor Panics

A substantial fraction of the literature on consumer liquidity demand, starting with Bryant (1980) and Diamond and Dybvig (1983), is preoccupied by the possibility of bank runs.[10] A basic hazard faced by financial institutions performing a maturity transformation function is the risk that depositors run for exit even when they do not actually experience liquidity needs. A run may occur when long-term assets are liquidated in order to honor the withdrawal demands. Thus, if other depositors withdraw, even a patient depositor has an incentive to withdraw since

10. Early analysis of bank runs can be found in Bagehot (1873) and Kindelberger (1978). Other useful references include Fulghieri and Rovelli (1998), Gale and Vives (2002), and Rochet and Vives (2004).

the financial institution then becomes an empty shell.

To understand the mechanics of bank runs, consider the technology described in the previous section, with

$$l = r_1 = r_2 = 1 \quad \text{and} \quad R > 1.$$

That is, a unit long-term investment yields R if carried to its maturity, but only 1 if it is liquidated at date 1. The short-term technology in each period is a storage technology that transforms 1 unit of good in a given period into 1 unit of good in the following period. The long-term investment here dominates the short-term investment, and we will therefore focus on investment policies in which the bank invests solely in the long-term asset:

$$i_1 = 0 \quad \text{and} \quad i_2 = 1.$$

The representative consumer, as before, saves 1 at date 0 and learns her type at date 1; with probability λ, the consumer is impatient and has utility $u(c_1)$, and with probability $1 - \lambda$, the consumer is patient and has utility $u(c_2)$. We assume that a patient consumer who withdraws at date 1 has access to the storage technology and can thus consume at date 2 what she withdrew at date 1.[11]

Consider the Diamond–Dybvig allocation (letting L denote the fraction of the long-term asset that is liquidated at date 1):

$$\max_{\{c_1,c_2,L\}} \{\lambda u(c_1) + (1-\lambda)u(c_2)\}$$

s.t.

$$\lambda c_1 = L,$$

$$(1-\lambda)c_2 = R(1-L).$$

This program is equivalent to

$$\max_{\{c_1\}} \left\{\lambda u(c_1) + (1-\lambda)u\left(\left(\frac{1-\lambda c_1}{1-\lambda}\right)R\right)\right\},$$

yielding, as earlier,

$$\frac{u'(c_1)}{u'(c_2)} = R,$$

and so, provided that the consumers' coefficient of relative risk aversion exceeds 1,

$$1 < c_1^* < c_2^* < R.$$

11. Alternatively, we could assume that the patient consumer has utility $u(c_1 + c_2)$.

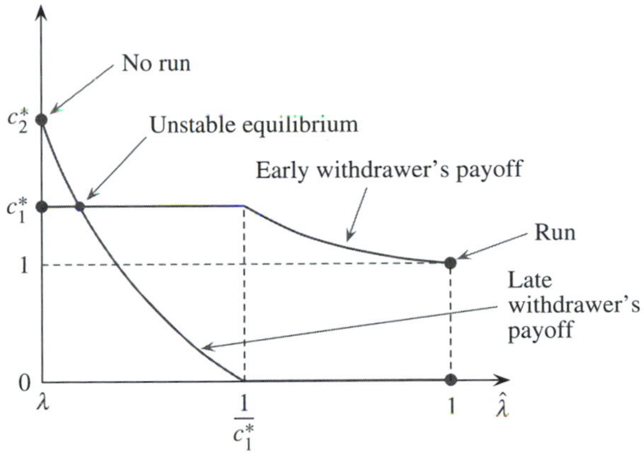

Figure 12.2 Incentive to run.

Let $\hat{\lambda} \geqslant \lambda$ denote the fraction of consumers who withdraw at date 1 (so $\hat{\lambda} = \lambda + (1-\lambda)x$, where x is the fraction of patient consumers who run on the bank). Because $c_1^* < c_2^*$, the Diamond–Dybvig outcome $\hat{\lambda} = \lambda$ is an equilibrium. But this equilibrium is not unique.

A consumer receives

$$\min\left\{c_1^*, \frac{1}{\hat{\lambda}}\right\} \qquad \text{if she withdraws at date 1,}$$

$$\max\left\{\left(\frac{1-\hat{\lambda}c_1^*}{1-\hat{\lambda}}\right)R, 0\right\} \qquad \text{if she does not.}$$

To see this, note that the bank keeps liquidating long-term investments as long as it cannot honor the withdrawal requests. If $\hat{\lambda}c_1^* < 1$, then all such requests are satisfied, and the fraction $(1-\hat{\lambda})$ of consumers who did not run receives the return R on the remaining long-term investment $(1-\hat{\lambda}c_1^*)$, which is less than $c_2^* = [(1-\lambda c_1^*)/(1-\lambda)]R$.

The payoffs are represented as functions of $\hat{\lambda}$ for $\hat{\lambda} \geqslant \lambda$ in Figure 12.2.

An interesting property of the strategic interaction among depositors is that the incentive to run (the difference between the consumptions when withdrawing at date 1 and waiting) increases with the number of other consumers who withdraw (at least as long as $\hat{\lambda} < 1/c_1^*$, since beyond this value, a late withdrawer receives nothing anyway). This game exhibits "strategic complementarities" (my running increases your incentive to run). And indeed there is exactly one other stable equilibrium, in which all consumers withdraw at date 1. This "bad or panic equilibrium" yields a low consumption for both the patient and the impatient types.[12]

Large depositor. Suppose now that a fraction $\mu > 0$ of deposits is held by a large depositor.[13] The fraction $1-\mu$ is held by atomistic depositors (previously we had $\mu = 0$). Let us further assume that the large depositor has a single incarnation (patient or impatient), which, if we assume, as we will do, that the total fractions of "impatient and patient deposits" are fixed at levels λ and $1-\lambda$, respectively, requires that $\mu \leqslant \min(\lambda, 1-\lambda)$.[14] How is the analysis affected?[15]

Suppose first that the large depositor turns out to be impatient. Then the analysis is unaltered, since the only strategies of interest are those of the patient depositors, who face a real choice between withdrawing and leaving their deposits at the bank.

In contrast, the analysis is changed when the large depositor is patient. On the one hand, the no-run equilibrium still exists (since $c_1^* < c_2^*$). On the other hand, the panic equilibrium may disappear. A run can occur *only if* the large depositor does not find it in her interest to keep her money in the bank, or

$$1 \geqslant \frac{1-\hat{\lambda}c_1^*}{1-\hat{\lambda}}R \quad \text{with } \hat{\lambda} = 1-\mu.$$

Put differently, the risk of a run disappears if

$$(1-\mu)(Rc_1^* - 1) < R - 1.$$

In particular, for μ close to $(1-\lambda)$ (most of the "patient deposits" are held by the large depositor), this latter condition is verified (from $c_1^* < c_2^*$), and so there is no panic equilibrium. More generally, *the panic equilibrium is less likely to exist, the larger the fraction of deposits held by a large player.* This is easily understood: panics are generated by a lack of coordination. This coordination problem is less likely to be an issue if deposits are concentrated in large part in a single hand (it is no longer an issue with a single patient depositor).

12.3.2 Antirun Policies

As was recognized by Diamond and Dybvig and the subsequent literature, there are various ways to prevent bad equilibria from happening.

12.3.2.1 Suspension of Convertibility

One policy for preventing runs is a suspension of convertibility (Gorton 1985, 1988). Before the design of deposit insurance schemes, suspensions of convertibility occurred frequently. For example, the American banking system suspended convertibility eight times between 1814 and 1907.

The idea behind a suspension of convertibility is straightforward. Suppose that the bank announces that it will stop honoring demand deposit withdrawal once level λ is reached. Patient depositors then know that there will be enough long-term investment around at date 2 to honor their date-2 claim c_2^*. And so they have no incentive to run.[16]

Suspensions of convertibility are, of course, no panacea. They raise a moral-hazard problem on the bank's side. The run may actually be triggered by bad news about the bank's fundamentals (we will come back to this). In this case, the bank, if given the right to suspend convertibility may use this right to stop outflows even when its management, rather than a pure depositor panic, is the culprit for the run. This is why suspensions of convertibility are better entrusted to the central bank (or at the country level with the International Monetary Fund), even though these solutions are not without hazard either.

12.3.2.2 Credit Line and Lender of Last Resort

Second, the bank may have an explicit or implicit credit line with another financial institution or the central bank that protects it against a run. Again, if patient consumers know that long-term assets will not be forced to liquidation by a run, they have no reason to worry and therefore do not withdraw their deposits.

---

12. As indicated in the figure, there is a third equilibrium with $\lambda < \mathring{\lambda} < 1$. This equilibrium is, however, unstable: suppose that a slightly higher fraction than $\mathring{\lambda}$ withdraws. Then everyone else wants to withdraw.

13. To make things comparable, assume that the consumptions "c_t" of that depositor are consumptions per unit of deposit.

14. More generally, we could avoid this restrictive assumption, and assume that the large depositor suffers a liquidity shock corresponding to a (random) fraction of her deposits.

15. Large depositors are considered in Corsetti et al. (2002) and (in a version closer to that adopted here) Ventura (2001).

16. See Green and Lin (2003) and Peck and Shell (2003) for studies of more general contingent withdrawal contracts, in which the amount that can be withdrawn depends on the number of consumers who have already withdrawn.

Of course, in the case of a private sector arrangement, the credit line mechanism can protect only against a run on a single bank or a small number of banks. To avoid a run on a single bank, it suffices that each bank stand ready to liquidate a small amount of its long-term assets to come to the rescue of the endangered bank (or to hoard a little more liquidity than needed if $l < 1$).

However, such arrangements cannot protect the banking sector as a whole. If runs occur simultaneously on all banks, liquidity must be provided from elsewhere (the central bank or abroad).

12.3.2.3 Interbank and Other Liquidity Markets

Alternatively, banks can make up for temporary shortfalls in liquidity by borrowing liquidity in the interbank market. A solvent bank, with fully pledgeable income Ri_2 in the model, can credibly promise to repay any date-1 loan that is destined only to honor the deposit withdrawals.

While "bank runs" have a negative connotation and much thought has been given to how to avoid them, another strand of the literature, initiated by Calomiris and Kahn (1991), emphasizes the benefits of creating competition in monitoring. The possibility of a bank run keeps depositors (or, presumably, at least large ones) on their toes. They are then induced to collect information about the bank's performance. There is then a tradeoff between the inefficiency generated by liquidations and the disciplining benefit associated with the monitoring of banking moral hazard.[17]

12.4 Heterogenous Consumer Horizons and the Diversity of Securities

In the Diamond–Dybvig model, consumers are identical *ex ante* (although not *ex post*), and a single claim fits them all. In practice, consumers are heterogenous in several respects, including their savings horizon, or, to use the terminology of this chapter, the frequency of liquidity shocks. Gorton and Pennacchi (1990) provide an interesting extension of the Diamond–Dybvig model that allows for such heterogeneity.

Their study is motivated by the long-standing advice given by bankers to their clients: "If you save for the long term, invest in equities; if you are looking for liquidity, invest in debt instruments." The alleged "liquidity" benefits of debt in this advice does not quite refer to the possibility that equities cannot be resold quickly in well-functioning markets. Rather, it refers to the fear of trading against better-informed traders in such markets.

A useful innovation of the Gorton–Pennacchi model is to employ the consumer-liquidity-demand model to refine our understanding of market microstructure. In traditional models of markets microstructures (say, Kyle 1985), trade is driven by the presence of apparently irrational "liquidity traders" who trade assets without regard to their return. These liquidity traders generate value for the other traders and thereby give rise to trading volume.[18] The Diamond–Dybvig model allows the model to endogenize liquidity trading by explicitly modeling preference shocks that give rise to a demand for altering one's portfolio. The benefit of this "rationalization" of liquidity trading is not purely aesthetic. As we will see, it shows that liquidity trading in equities is highly responsive to the set of securities that are offered in the market.

The Gorton–Pennacchi model is similar to Diamond and Dybvig's, with two twists. First, the payoff of the long-term investment is uncertain and is not commonly observed at date 1. Second, the number of impatient consumers is also random and unobservable. In contrast, consumers are risk neutral, which eliminates the insurance focus that is so prominent in the Diamond–Dybvig literature.

There are three dates ($t = 0, 1, 2$).

Consumers. Consumers all have date-0 savings equal to 1, but are *ex ante* heterogenous with respect to their consumption horizon. More precisely, there are two categories of consumer.

17. See Chapters 8 and 9 for a discussion of the variety of ways in which incentives for monitoring can be designed.

18. Another approach is to assume that investors are risk-averse and learn over time news about their tastes or about the value of the components of their existing portfolios, and therefore want to rebalance these portfolios. This approach is much more complex (and depends on the set of futures and derivative markets allowed). Much of the microstructure literature therefore relies on the irrational-liquidity-traders approach.

Potential liquidity traders, in proportion α, have the following preferences:

$$u(c_1, c_2) = c_1 \quad \text{with probability } \tilde{\lambda},$$
$$u(c_1, c_2) = c_1 + c_2 \quad \text{with probability } 1 - \tilde{\lambda}.$$

As in Diamond and Dybvig, these consumers learn their preferences at date 1; the realized fraction of liquidity traders, $\tilde{\lambda}$, takes two possible values, λ_L or λ_H, with $\lambda_H > \lambda_L$. The realization of $\tilde{\lambda}$ is unobservable.

Long-term investors, in proportion $1 - \alpha$, have the following preferences:

$$u(c_1, c_2) = c_1 + c_2 \quad \text{with probability } 1.$$

That is, long-term investors take a long-term perspective and never need money at date 1 (they are happy to get the return from their savings at date 2).

Technology. On the technology side, we will assume that the savings are invested in a long-term asset yielding a random $\tilde{R}$ at date 2, where $\tilde{R} = R_L$ or $R_H > R_L$. This long-term return is publicly observable only at date 2 (when realized).

States of nature. Let us now turn to the probability distribution over the state of nature $(\tilde{\lambda}, \tilde{R})$.[19] In principle, there are four possible states of nature as each of these variables can take on two values. To simplify the computations, we will make two innocuous assumptions. First, $\tilde{\lambda}$ and $\tilde{R}$ are perfectly correlated in the following way. There are only two states of nature:

$$(\lambda_L, R_L) \quad \text{with probability } q_L,$$
$$(\lambda_H, R_H) \quad \text{with probability } q_H,$$

with $q_L + q_H = 1$. Second, potential liquidity traders that are revealed patient do not have cash at date 1 to participate in the date-1 asset market. Only long-term investors (and possibly some newly arrived arbitrageurs, also with utility function $c_1 + c_2$) have date-1 resources to buy the shares sold by the impatient investors. (The second assumption is just meant to shorten the analysis by not having to consider the inferences drawn by the patient liquidity traders about the state of nature from the observation that they individually are patient. The first assumption focuses the analysis on those two states of nature in which the asset price may not reveal publicly the state of nature. The reader can alternatively assume four states of nature and follow the lines of Section 8.3 to check that the analysis in no way hinges on these two assumptions.)

Speculator. To formalize the idea that small investors may "lose their shirt" when disposing of the asset at date 1, let us assume that an informed trader, called the speculator, appears at date 1, who learns the state of nature and may buy as many shares as he likes (he has a large enough date-1 endowment). The speculator cannot engage in short sales; neither can any other economic agent. The speculator also has preferences $c_1 + c_2$. He places at date 1 an order flow. The date-1 arbitrageurs (long-term investors or newly arrived arbitrageurs) observe only the *total* order flow, that is, the impatient investors' sales minus the speculator's purchase, but cannot decompose this order flow to figure out exactly how much is demanded by the speculator (otherwise they could infer the state of nature from the speculator's order flow, as we shall see shortly).

12.4.1 Trading Losses in the Stock Market

When informed that the state is L, the speculator knows that the long-term payoff is R_L and since the asset price P necessarily lies in the interval $[R_L, R_H]$, the speculator does not buy and so stays out of the market. The order flow is then equal to the impatient consumers' sales:

$$\alpha\lambda_L.$$

When learning that the state is H, the speculator buys a quantity $b > 0$ of shares. The dilemma facing the speculator is that a high demand reveals that the state is high, leading arbitrageurs to raise their own demand until the price is R_H and so there is no profit opportunity. More formally, the order flow is now

$$\alpha\lambda_H - b.$$

The only value of purchases by the speculator that does not reveal that the payoff is R_H is

$$b = \alpha(\lambda_H - \lambda_L).$$

19. Formally, the state of nature also includes the identity of those among potential liquidity traders who will face a liquidity shock. Because there is no aggregate uncertainty in this respect, we omit this description from that of the state of nature.

The equilibrium involves full pooling. Arbitrageurs learn nothing about the state of nature, and their posterior belief that the state is H is still q_H. And so the market price of shares at date 2 is always

$$P = q_H R_H + q_L R_L.$$

This pooling gives rise to adverse selection in the stock market. Arbitrageurs (who, after all, are not forced to trade) are not affected by this adverse selection, as they discount the price to reflect the asymmetry of information. The victims of adverse selection are the impatient consumers or liquidity traders, who sell at a price reflecting the *ex ante* expectation, even though the high state is more likely *per unit of sale* (the liquidity traders sell more in the high state).

The speculator makes (*ex ante*) expected profit,

$$\pi = q_H[\alpha(\lambda_H - \lambda_L)][R_H - P].$$

That is, the speculator trades only in the high state (probability q_H). He then trades as much as is consistent with not revealing his information ($\alpha(\lambda_H - \lambda_L)$), and makes profit $R_H - P$ per share purchased. The speculator's profit can be rewritten as

$$\pi = \alpha(\lambda_H - \lambda_L)q_H q_L(R_H - R_L).$$

Note, in particular, that this profit grows with the fraction of potential liquidity traders and with the uncertainty about the extent of their actual liquidity trading.

To confirm that the speculator feeds off the potential liquidity traders, let us compute the latter's expected loss:

$$\begin{aligned} q_H\lambda_H(R_H - P) - q_L\lambda_L(P - R_L) &= (\lambda_H - \lambda_L)q_H q_L(R_H - R_L) \\ &= \frac{\pi}{\alpha}. \end{aligned}$$

The speculator's profit is indeed equal to a potential liquidity trader's expected loss times the number (α) of such traders.

12.4.2 Debt as a Low-Information-Intensity Security and the Equity Premium

As in Chapter 8, the liquidity traders' loss can be interpreted as generating an equity premium. In order for potential liquidity traders to hold the stock, they must be enticed by a date-0 price discount, or equivalently an equity premium (a higher return). There are (at least) two equivalent versions that can be offered for depicting this phenomenon in the context of this bare-bones model. First, potential liquidity traders demand to pay less than the expected return. Namely, the price discount per share is equal to π/α so that the issuer must price shares at $q_H R_H + q_L R_L - (\pi/\alpha)$ in order to arouse interest from liquidity traders. Second, were the stock sold solely to the long-term investors (which requires that they have enough savings to purchase all the shares), the price would jump by π/α to $q_H R_H + q_L R_L$.

This equity premium observation (which is not specific to the Gorton–Pennacchi model, and is rather a general implication of the logic of market microstructure) also fits well with the well-known fact that the return on equity grows with the holding length. As popular wisdom commands, the stock market is more appealing to long-term investors than to short-term ones.

Let us push the comparison with the analysis of Chapter 8 a bit further. Speculation (the acquisition of private information about returns in order to profit from trading securities) is here a purely *parasitical* activity. It is even socially wasteful if either the speculator incurs a cost (presumably smaller than π) in order to acquire the information, or if the potential liquidity traders are discouraged from buying the security because they will "lose their shirt" and do not find an alternative and substitutable security to invest in.

The perspective on speculation provided by Gorton and Pennacchi is therefore quite different from the Holmström and Tirole (1993) view exposited in Chapter 8. There, even though we stressed that there could be excessive speculation, we emphasized the benefits of market monitoring. We argued that speculators' greed creates a measure of the value of assets in place, and therefore allows firms to assess the performance of their management. In other words, market monitoring is an integral part of the firms' governance mechanism. We will later return to this discussion.

Returning to the Gorton–Pennacchi model, we observed that potential liquidity traders are willing to pay less than long-term investors for the shares. This suggests that it is in the interest of the security designers to introduce a security that is better suited to their needs, and thereby offer a menu of securities. Indeed, suppose that

$$\alpha(q_H R_H + q_L R_L) \leqslant R_L. \qquad (12.14)$$

This condition is more likely to be satisfied when the projects have sufficient guaranteed income or collateral (R_L) and when there are few potential liquidity traders. The security designers[20] can then offer a fraction α (or more generally a fraction between α and $R_L/[q_H R_H + q_L R_L]$) of securities with *safe* payoff $q_H R_H + q_L R_L$ (or slightly less[21]) at date 2. The residual claim on the long-term projects is then sold to the public in equity shares. The safe debt security appeals to potential liquidity traders because it is not affected by adverse selection. Its final payoff is independent of the state of nature and is therefore common knowledge. Thus, as long as condition (12.14) holds, the equity premium, or equivalently the profit that can be enjoyed by an informed speculator, vanishes.

In contrast, if

$$\alpha(q_H R_H + q_L R_L) > R_L,$$

there are too many potential liquidity traders in the market to accommodate entirely with a safe claim. They must bear some of the risk and therefore the equity premium reappears.

12.4.3 A Broader Perspective

The issuance of debt illustrates a broader strategy already alluded to in Chapter 8: investors who may be forced to sell fear that they will be trading against better-informed players and try to avoid this likely loss by purchasing securities that are less exposed to this risk. This flight to low-information-intensity securities takes multiple forms, and debt is only one of these.

Another way of limiting costly trade with speculators is to buy bundles of indices on the grounds that they are less exposed to asymmetric information "thanks to the law of large numbers": stock index futures, closed-end mutual funds, real-estate investment trusts, etc. The general idea is that even though one may be poorly informed about the value of a particular firm, one is on average better informed about that of a bundle of firms as an overappreciation of a firm's value tends to be compensated by an underappreciation of another (see Subrahmanyam 1991; Gorton and Pennacchi 1993). This is easily illustrated in the context of "continuum of firms" with independent date-2 profit realizations. The per-firm *ex post* value of the index is then a deterministic $q_H R_H + q_L R_L$, and so potential liquidity traders can enjoy liquidity without any sacrifice in return.

There is some empirical support for this view. For example, the bid–ask spread (which in part measures the extent of the adverse-selection problem) for the index is about one-tenth of that in individual stocks. Furthermore, the spectacular development of index funds in the last two decades points to the benefits of such bundling.

This evolution toward debt and bundles of equity claim is privately rational for (at least short-term) investors. It is also socially desirable if one subscribes to the view of Gorton and Pennacchi. On the other hand, it also jeopardizes the role of financial markets as a monitoring device,[22] and therefore has potentially detrimental effects. The cost involved in turning companies public and in spinning off divisions to have them listed individually are evidence of a demand for market monitoring. An important research topic is therefore to combine the negative and positive aspects of market monitoring and to analyze whether the investors' private incentives will in the future affect the relevant tradeoffs.[23]

20. We can assume that these security designers correspond to the corporate entities that invest in the long-term projects. Alternatively, these corporate entities could issue just stocks, and financial markets could perform the repackaging of these stocks by stripping the debt component from the stocks and offering it as a safe debt derivative instrument. As long as financial markets are competitive and efficient, the initial stocks would not include an equity premium, due to the expectation of subsequent repackaging.

21. In order to make sure that the long-term investors are not attracted to buy the debt security.

22. At least of the speculative/passive type studied in Chapter 8; concerning *active* monitoring (see Chapter 9), index funds do have some influence as they are not swayed by business ties.

23. While this section has assumed that trading costs are governed by adverse selection in asset markets, another relevant consideration is the existence of transaction costs. Favero et al. (2005) analyze a Diamond–Dybvig model in which consumers can buy or sell at date 1 some assets with heterogeneous and exogenously determined transaction costs. Consumers can only trade the set of primary assets (and so, as in standard microstructure theory, consumers cannot economize on transaction costs by trading asset bundles or derivatives).

Supplementary Sections

12.5 Aggregate Uncertainty and Risk Sharing

The analysis of interest rates in Section 12.2 focused on the term structure and neglected the allocation of the interest rate risk in an economy by assuming that there was no aggregate risk. In practice, interest rate risk is a serious issue, and financial institutions have developed various instruments, such as interest rate swaps, to reallocate the risk among economic agents. Ultimately, someone—consumers, banks, corporations, or other agents—must bear the risk. A question confronting both the private sector and public policy (e.g., through the regulatory treatment of value at risk in banking institutions) is who should actually bear it.

To start analyzing interest rate risk, Hellwig (1994) extends the Diamond-Dybvig model to allow for an uncertain realization at date 1 of the date-2 return on short-term investment r_2. The randomness of r_2 is a metaphor for a more general uncertainty about the rate of return on new investments in the economy.[24]

Consumers' preferences are as described in Section 12.2: facing known probability λ of a liquidity shock, their expected utility is

$$E[\lambda u(c_1) + (1-\lambda)u(c_2)],$$

where c_1 denotes the consumer's date-1 consumption in the state of nature in which she is impatient, c_2 the date-2 consumption when she is patient, and the expectation will refer to the impact of aggregate uncertainty on these consumptions. The utility function u's coefficient of relative risk aversion $(-cu''/u')$ exceeds 1.[25]

A consumer's date-0 savings, equal to 1, are allocated between the short- and long-term investments:

$$i_1 + i_2 = 1.$$

Technology is described as in Diamond and Dybvig except for the aggregate uncertainty about r_2. A unit of short-term (liquid) investment sunk at date 0 yields r_1 at date 1. A unit of short-term investment sunk at date 1 yields r_2 at date 2. The value of r_2 is publicly learned at date 1. A unit of long-term (illiquid) investment sunk at date 0 yields R at date 2, and $l < r_1$ if liquidated at date 1. To keep the model as closely related to Diamond and Dybvig as possible, let us assume that liquidating the long-term project never delivers a higher return that the long-term project itself:

$$lr_2 < R \quad \text{for all realizations of } r_2. \tag{12.15}$$

The random variable r_2 is assumed to have a continuous distribution with support included in $[0, R/l)$.

12.5.1 Socially Optimal Insurance

The first-best outcome is a choice of investments i_1, i_2 and (r_2-contingent) consumptions c_1 and c_2 and liquidation level L solving

$$\max_{\{i_1,i_2,c_1(\cdot),c_2(\cdot)L(\cdot)\}} \{E[\lambda u(c_1) + (1-\lambda)u(c_2)]\}$$

s.t.

$$\lambda c_1 \leqslant r_1 i_1 + lL \quad \text{for all } r_2,$$

$$(1-\lambda)c_2 \leqslant R(i_2 - L) + r_2(r_1 i_1 + lL - \lambda c_1) \quad \text{for all } r_2,$$

$$i_1 + i_2 = 1,$$

$$0 \leqslant L \leqslant i_2 \quad \text{for all } r_2.$$

The first constraint expresses the fact that impatient consumers' consumption must be financed from the

The main point of the Favero et al. paper is to analyze the impact of transaction costs on asset pricing and to estimate the model in the euro area. (Other recent papers analyzing the impact of transaction costs on asset pricing in general equilibrium models include Acharya and Pedersen (2005), Eisfeldt (2003), and Vayanos (2004).)

24. An early paper on the sharing of long-term aggregate risk in Bryant-Diamond-Dybvig models is Jacklin and Bhattacharya (1988). In their basic model, the date-2 return R of the long-term asset is random and no information about R is revealed before date 2. Agents have more general preferences than posited here, in that their valuation for the income stream (c_1, c_2) is

$$u(c_1) + \beta_t u(c_2),$$

where $\beta_t = \beta_1$ for the impatient consumers and $\beta_t = \beta_2 > \beta_1$ for the patient ones. In the absence of interim information about R, a "deposit contract" can be written as $\{c_{1t}, c_{2t}(R)\}$, where $t = 1$ for the impatient types and $t = 2$ for the patient ones. Jacklin and Bhattacharya then introduce a date-1 signal about return R. As in, for example, Hirshleifer (1971) and Laffont (1985), interim information accrual may reduce welfare.

25. This assumption will be used in the "second-best analysis." See below.

return on the date-0 investment in liquid assets, plus, possibly, the liquidation of some of the long-term assets. As we will see, this constraint may or may not be binding. The second constraint says that the consumption of the patient consumers stems from the return on the unliquidated long-term asset, plus, possibly the leftover from period 1 reinvested at rate r_2; it is obviously binding since there is no point wasting resources.

We will say that there is *earmarking* (or matching of the term structures of investments and consumptions) if long-term investments serve to finance long-term consumption and short-term investments to finance short-term consumption:

$$c_1 = \frac{r_1 i_1}{\lambda} \quad \text{and} \quad c_2 = \frac{R i_2}{1 - \lambda}.$$

Note that, under an earmarking policy, returns on deposits are guaranteed; in other words, consumptions at dates 1 and 2 are *immunized* against interest rate shocks (they are not contingent on r_2).

Is it optimal to immunize depositors against interest rate risk? From the first-order conditions associated with the first-best program, it can be shown that it is never optimal to liquidate the long-term investment ($L = 0$). Intuitively, the liquid investment always yields more than the illiquid one when it comes to generating date-1 income.

If reinvestment takes place at date 1 (i.e., $r_1 i_1 > \lambda c_1$), the consumptions must solve the following *ex post* program (for a given r_2):

$$\max_{\{c_1, c_2\}} \{\lambda u(c_1) + (1 - \lambda) u(c_2)\}$$

$$\text{s.t.} \tag{12.16}$$

$$\lambda c_1 + \frac{(1 - \lambda) c_2}{r_2} = r_1 i_1 + \frac{R i_2}{r_2}.$$

We have written the constraint so as to highlight the role of $1/r_2$ as the relevant discount factor between dates 1 and 2 and the expression of the present discounted value of the endowment (on the right-hand side). Thus, if reinvestment occurs, then

$$u'(c_1) = r_2 u'(c_2). \tag{12.17}$$

Insights. Let us now state the results and then give their interpretations and intuition:

(a) As depicted in Figure 12.3, earmarking is optimal for low-interest-rate realizations ($r_2 \leqslant r_2^*$) and reinvestment for high-interest-rate realizations ($r_2 > r_2^*$).

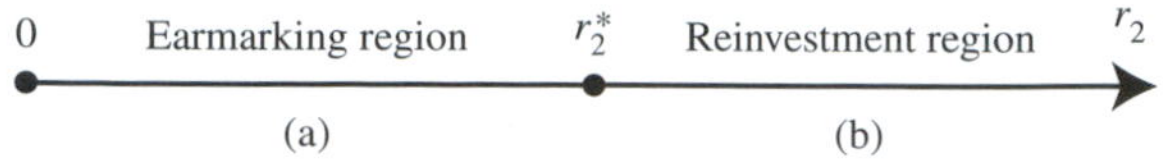

Figure 12.3 Incidence of interest rate risk: (a) $c_1 = r_1 i_1/\lambda$, $c_2 = R i_2/(1 - \lambda)$; (b) $c_1 < r_1 i_1/\lambda$, $c_2 > R i_2/(1 - \lambda)$, and $u'(c_1) = r_2 u'(c_2)$.

(b) The level of investment i_1 in liquid assets at date 0 exceeds the level that would prevail if reinvestment opportunities did not exist or more generally always had a low return ("r_2 small").

To forge intuition about these results, let us begin with (a). One should think of the interest rate risk as creating an *option value* in this first-best world: if r_2 is large, then the date-1 consumption can be reduced in order to take advantage of the favorable reinvestment opportunities. This implies imposing some sacrifice on the impatient types to benefit the patient types. The impatient consumers are, of course, unhappy when the interest rate turns out to be high at date 1. But this is part of a deal a consumer is happy to accept at date 0. Conclusion (b) follows directly from the presence of an option value, which makes liquid investments more valuable.

12.5.2 Incentive Compatibility

Let us now assume more realistically that the patient consumers can feign impatience and reinvest their withdrawal elsewhere at rate r_2. The incentive to do so will, of course, depend heavily on the realization of r_2. A high-interest rate then becomes a double-edged sword. It offers investors an option value, but it also incentivizes them to behave opportunistically and to abuse the insurance deal.

The second-best solution is obtained by solving the first-best program to which is appended the incentive compatibility constraint:

$$r_2 c_1 \leqslant c_2 \quad \text{for all } r_2. \tag{12.18}$$

This incentive compatibility condition creates a second rationale for a negative dependence of c_1 on r_2: generous terms on short-term deposits encourage opportunistic withdrawals. We refer to Hellwig's paper for a full treatment of the second-best solution when r_2 exceeds 1 with probability 1. Two striking results (c) and (d) are as follows.

(c) In the reinvestment region, the impatient consumers bear the entire *valuation risk* of long-term investment while the patient consumers bear the entire *rollover risk* of short-term investment. In particular, no one is immunized against interest rate risk.

To see this, return to the first-best *ex post* program (12.16). We noted that the budget constraint corresponds to an income equal to the sum of the dividend on the liquid investment and the date-1 discounted dividend on the illiquid one. Condition (12.17) reflected a desire to provide some insurance to benefit the impatient type. This insurance, however, is undermined by the incentive compatibility condition: (12.17) together with $r_2 > 1$ implies that $c_1 < c_2$; the assumption that the coefficient of relative risk aversion exceeds 1 then implies that $c_1 u'(c_1) > c_2 u'(c_2)$ and so (12.17) yields $r_2 c_1 > c_2$. We thus conclude that (12.18) is binding:

$$r_2 c_1 = c_2.$$

This in turn implies that the two types can be given the same income $r_1 i_1 + (R i_2 / r_2)$ at date 1 (assuming there is no liquidation. The same is true if there is liquidation); and so

$$c_1 = r_1 i_1 + \frac{R i_2}{r_2} \quad \text{and} \quad c_2 = r_2(r_1 i_1) + R i_2. \tag{12.19}$$

These expressions make it clear that the impatient types fully bear the valuation (or execution) risk on the long-term asset and are hurt when the interest rate rises; conversely, the patient types fully bear the risk of rolling over the short-term return $(r_1 i_1)$ and benefit from increases in the interest rate.

(d) Liquidation may become optimal.

To obtain a rough intuition as to why this may be the case, note that (12.18) suggests reducing c_1 and therefore first-period investment i_1. On the other hand, when r_2 is low, reinvestment does not pay off and incentive compatibility is not an issue. It may be optimal to increase c_1 beyond i_1/λ by liquidating some of the long-term investment provided that l is not too low. Thus, liquidation, if it occurs at all, is associated with low-interest-rate episodes. The second-best result according to which, in the reinvestment region, the impatient consumers bear the valuation risk and the patient ones the rollover risk extends to the case in which liquidation is optimal.

12.6 Private Signals and Uniqueness in Bank Run Models

As discussed in Section 12.3, a large literature in the last two decades has stressed the multiplicity of equilibria associated with deposit contracts. A recent and interesting strand of the literature, starting with Morris and Shin (1998), argues that the multiplicity tends to disappear provided that the economic agents receive private signals about the return to being patient and that their posterior beliefs have wide enough support.[26]

Morris and Shin's work is meant to address international financial crises.[27] As we will see, it captures some aspects of banking crises but not others. Like the bank run literature, it embodies a strategic complementarity: if other investors act in one way (say, run), that makes me more eager to act in that particular way (also run). But it also assumes that investors are better off when a run succeeds, while in banking models runs destroy the investors' value.

12.6.1 The Speculators' Game

Morris and Shin's stylized model of currency crises goes as follows: investors (also called speculators) can be thought of as being foreign investors. The central bank of a country has a level of foreign reserves θ unknown to investors. The central bank behaves mechanistically: it spends reserves to ward off speculation as long as there are some left. If S is the

26. Morris and Shin (1998) build their analysis on Carlsson and van Damme's (1993) work on global games. Earlier papers showing that private information together with a wide enough support allowing for the existence of dominant strategies, eliminates the multiplicity of equilibria in timing or bidding games include Fudenberg and Tirole (1986) on wars of attrition, Klemperer and Meyer (1989) on second-price auctions in supply-and-demand schedules, and Maskin and Riley (1986) on first-price auctions. See Frankel et al. (2003) for state-of-the-art results on unique strategy profiles surviving iterative dominance in games with strategic complementarities and slightly noisy payoff signals.

27. The version presented here is drawn from Corsetti et al. (2002).

Table 12.2 Payoffs in speculation game.

	Individual investor attacks	Individual investor does not attack
Attack succeeds ($S \geqslant \theta$)	$1 - c$	0
Attack fails ($S < \theta$)	$-c$	0

mass of financial resources mobilized by investors, then the currency collapses if and only if

$$S \geqslant \theta.$$

(This is meant to be a reduced form for a situation in which the country initially maintains a peg, and, if speculation is successful, the peg is abandoned and the currency devalued.) The level of investors' resources that can be mobilized to attack the currency is normalized to 1 (there is mass 1 of small investors[28]). And so $S \in [0, 1]$. In contrast, θ may exceed 1, in which case speculation against the currency is always unsuccessful, or be negative (say, because the country has contracted previous senior debts), in which case attacks always succeed regardless of their magnitude.

Assume that an investor individually pays a fixed cost $c \in (0, 1)$ when attacking the currency, and gains 1 when the attack is successful and he has been part of it.[29] The investors' decisions whether to attack the currency are simultaneous. An individual investor's contingent payoff is described in Table 12.2.

While the level of reserves θ is unknown, investors receive a signal as to its value. This signal y is equal to the true value plus noise:

$$y = \theta + \sigma\eta,$$

where η has mean 0 and σ measures (the inverse of) the precision of the signal. The variable η has cumulative distribution F with continuous density on, say, $(-\infty, +\infty)$.

In the public signal case, η is the same for all investors, who therefore have the same information. In the private signal case, each investor receives his own signal; that is, η is i.i.d. across investors. (We could, of course, study the more general case in which investors receive both a public and a private signal. The results would be intermediate between those derived below.)

28. See Corsetti et al. (2004) for the study of a similar game when there is a large investor.

29. In general, payoffs under successful and unsuccessful speculative attacks depends on the *ex post* exchange rate, which in turn depends on the size of the speculative attack and the government response to it. The speculation game may exhibit strategic complementarities or strategic substitutabilities (see Pathak and Tirole 2005).

12.6.1.1 Public Signal

Under a public signal, the outcome resembles that in standard coordination games. There is a range $[\underline{y}, \bar{y}]$ of public signals for which there are multiple equilibria.

The *no-run* equilibrium exists provided that an individual investor does not find it profitable to attack the currency when others do not (and so the currency collapses only if $\theta \leqslant 0$):

$$(1 - c)\Pr(\theta \leqslant 0 \mid y) - c\Pr(\theta > 0 \mid y) \leqslant 0,$$

or

$$(1 - c)[1 - F(y/\sigma)] - cF(y/\sigma) \leqslant 0,$$

or else

$$F(y/\sigma) \geqslant 1 - c. \tag{12.20}$$

Equation (12.20), taken as an equality, defines a unique $\underline{y}$. And so it is an equilibrium for no one to attack as long as $y \geqslant \underline{y}$.

Similarly, a *run equilibrium* exists provided that an individual investor prefers attacking when the others attack (and so the currency collapses whenever $\theta \leqslant 1$):

$$(1 - c)\Pr(\theta \leqslant 1 \mid y) - c\Pr(\theta > 1 \mid y) \geqslant 0$$

or

$$1 - c \geqslant F\left(\frac{y - 1}{\sigma}\right). \tag{12.21}$$

Condition (12.21), taken as an equality, defines a threshold $\bar{y} > \underline{y}$, such that a run equilibrium exists if and only if $y \leqslant \bar{y}$.

Note that this "run equilibrium" cannot be called a "panic equilibrium." Indeed, when $y \in [\underline{y}, \bar{y}]$ investors are better off coordinating on an attack. In a sense, "panicking" corresponds to "staying put."

12.6.1.2 Private Signals

Let us now assume that investor i ($i \in [0, 1]$) receives signal

$$y_i = \theta + \sigma\eta_i,$$

and the noises are i.i.d. A simple "revealed preference" argument shows that in equilibrium investor i attacks the currency if and only if this signal lies below some threshold y_i^* (this is because the investor's net expected payoff to attacking the currency is decreasing in the signal). Let us look for a symmetric equilibrium (this is actually not restrictive): $y_i^* = y^*$.

The amount of resources involved in the attack is then

$$S(\theta) = F\left(\frac{y^* - \theta}{\sigma}\right),$$

and the currency collapses if and only if

$$S(\theta) \geqslant \theta.$$

Because S is decreasing in θ, the currency collapses if and only if $\theta \leqslant \theta^*$, where

$$F\left(\frac{y^* - \theta^*}{\sigma}\right) = \theta^*. \tag{12.22}$$

Second, investor i attacks the currency if and only if

$$(1-c)\Pr(\theta \leqslant \theta^* \mid y_i) - c\Pr(\theta > \theta^* \mid y_i) \geqslant 0.$$

And so y^* is defined by

$$1 - c = F\left(\frac{y^* - \theta^*}{\sigma}\right). \tag{12.23}$$

Combining (12.22) and (12.23), we obtain

$$\theta^* = 1 - c. \tag{12.24}$$

Thus, θ^* and y^* are uniquely determined. The uniqueness of equilibrium enhances predictive power.[30] When the investors' information is precise (σ close to 0), then y^* converges to θ^*.

12.6.2 The Depositors' Game

The bank run literature bears some resemblance to the analysis of the speculators' game in the previous subsection. But it differs from it in that runs are inefficient from the point of view of investors.[31] Another key difference is that, unlike the games considered in Carlsson and van Damme and by Morris and Shin, the game does not quite exhibit strategic complementarities: as Figure 12.2 demonstrates, the net incentive to withdraw is not an increasing function of the number of other consumers who withdraw.

Let us return to the bank run model of Section 12.3, assuming that $l = 1$. Recall that if depositors are entitled to withdraw some arbitrary level $\bar{c}_1$ at date 1, and fraction $\hat{\lambda} \geqslant \lambda$ of depositors exercise this option, the consumptions of the early and late withdrawers are

$$c_1(\hat{\lambda}) = \min\left\{\bar{c}_1, \frac{1}{\hat{\lambda}}\right\}$$

and

$$c_2(\hat{\lambda}, R) = \max\left\{\frac{1 - \hat{\lambda}\bar{c}_1}{1 - \hat{\lambda}}R, 0\right\}.$$

Patient consumers have utility $c_1 + c_2$, and therefore choose the highest of the two. Let us extend the model of Section 12.3 in two respects:

- the date-2 return R is random and drawn from some cumulative distribution on $[0, \infty)$;
- this return is unobserved, but each depositor $i \in [0, 1]$ observes a private signal

  $$y_i = R + \sigma\eta_i,$$

  where the noises $\{\eta_i\}_{i\in[0,1]}$ have mean 0 and are i.i.d. across depositors; they are drawn from some cumulative distribution F with continuous density f.

We maintain the assumption that the bank offers a deposit contract, that is, the option to withdraw some fixed amount $\bar{c}_1$ at date 1.

A (symmetric) equilibrium is then defined by a threshold y^* such that depositor i, when patient, withdraws if and only if $y_i \leqslant y^*$, and a fraction $\lambda^*(y^*, R)$ of withdrawing depositors,[32] with

$$\lambda^*(y^*, R) = \lambda + (1 - \lambda)F\left(\frac{y^* - R}{\sigma}\right). \tag{12.25}$$

It must also be the case that a depositor with signal y^* is indifferent between withdrawing and not withdrawing:

$$E[c_1(\lambda^*(y^*, R))] = E[c_2(\lambda^*(y^*, R), R)], \tag{12.26}$$

where expectations are taken with respect to the random variable R.

30. Angeletos et al. (2005) study a framework that is similar to that of Morris and Shin, but allow for a publicly observed policy choice by the policy maker before investors decide whether to attack. As in Morris and Shin, the equilibrium would be unique if the policy choice were exogenous. However, the endogeneity and observability of the policy reintroduce multiple equilibria in this model.

31. This distinction between the speculators' game and the depositors' game is drawn from Ventura (2001).

32. Thus $\lambda^*(y^*, R)$ is the counterpart of $S(\theta)$ in the speculators' game.

Goldstein and Pauzner (2005) analyze a related model (the technology succeeds or fails at date 2 and the probability of success is drawn from a continuous distribution). Their key insight is that while the depositor game does not exhibit strategic complementarities, it satisfies a weaker property (that they label "one-sided strategic complementarities"), namely, that the net incentive to withdraw increases with the number of withdrawing agents whenever this incentive is negative (see Figure 12.2).

They generalize the uniqueness result under this weaker property. They are then able to perform comparative statics exercises. For example, the probability of a bank run increases continuously with the degree of risk sharing offered by the intermediary.

12.7 Exercises

Exercise 12.1 (Diamond–Dybvig model in continuous time). Following von Thadden (1997), suppose that the representative consumer in the Diamond–Dybvig model has wealth 1 at date 0 and will need to consume at a time $t \in [0,1]$. Namely, the date of the liquidity shock, instead of taking two possible values (periods 1 and 2 in Diamond–Dybvig), belongs to an interval. It is distributed according to cumulative distribution function $F(t)$ ($F(0) = 0$, $F(1) = 1$) with continuous density $f(t)$. The representative consumer's expected utility is therefore

$$U = \int_0^1 u(c(t))f(t)\,dt,$$

where $c(t)$ is her consumption if the liquidity shock occurs at time t.

On the technological side, suppose that one can at any point in time invest in "trees" that then grow until they are harvested. One unit of investment liquidated at maturity m yields $R(m)$. So an investment made at τ and "harvested" at $t \geqslant \tau$ yields $R(t-\tau)$ per unit. We assume that $R(0) = 1$, $\dot{R} > 0$ (where a dot indicates a time derivative), and $\dot{R}/R$, the instantaneous technological rate of return, is increasing in m. This implies in particular that a series of short-term investments yields less than a long-term investment with equivalent total length.

The choice is thus not about an allocation of investment at the initial date, and the exercise focuses entirely on the insurance aspects. Under autarky, the representative consumer receives expected utility

$$\int_0^1 u(R(t))f(t)\,dt.$$

A bank offers a deposit contract in which a depositor chooses the date of withdrawal and obtains $c(t)$ if she withdraws at time $t \in [0,1]$. The depositors' liquidity shocks are i.i.d.

(i) Assume first that the realization of each depositor's liquidity shock is observable by the bank (so there is no incentive compatibility issue). Show that in the optimal insurance policy

$$u'(c(t))R(t)$$

is independent of t.

(ii) Assuming that the coefficient of relative risk aversion exceeds 1, conclude that there is "front loading,"

$$\frac{\dot{c}(t)}{c(t)} < \frac{\dot{R}(t)}{R(t)},$$

and so

$$c(t) > R(t) \quad \text{for } t < t^*$$

and

$$c(t) < R(t) \quad \text{for } t > t^* \text{ for some } t^* \in (0,1).$$

(iii) Show that the "first-best outcome" described above is not incentive compatible, in the sense that depositors may want to withdraw early and reinvest in the technology themselves.

Exercise 12.2 (Allen and Gale (1998) on fundamentals-based panics). Consider the Diamond–Dybvig model developed in Section 12.2 and add randomness in the payoff of the long-term asset. Consumers are Diamond–Dybvig consumers: they invest 1 at date 0, and learn at date 2 whether they are impatient (their utility is $u(c_1)$) or patient (their utility is $u(c_2)$). The probability of being impatient is λ.

The liquid or short-term technology yields one-for-one in each period: $r_1 = r_2 = 1$. The illiquid, long-term technology yields a random R (the same for all illiquid investments). The cumulative distribution is $F(R)$ and the density $f(R)$ on $[0,\infty)$. Liquidating the long-term asset yields nothing ($l = 0$).

One assumes

$$E(R) > 1.$$

The realization of R is publicly observed at date 1.

(i) Compute the socially optimal insurance contract $\{c_1(R), c_2(R)\}$, ignoring incentive compatibility (the ability of patient types to disguise as impatient ones). Note that this contract is incentive compatible.

(ii) Consider now a deposit contract. Consumers are promised, if they withdraw at date 1, a fixed payment $\bar{c}_1$, or a share of i_1 if total withdrawal demand exceeds i_1. The date-2 income is shared among depositors who did not withdraw at date 1. Long-term assets are never liquidated. One will denote by $x(R) \in [0, 1]$ the fraction of patient consumers who "join the run" (declare they are impatient, and store the money they have withdrawn from the bank).

Show that a judicious choice of $\bar{c}_1$ succeeds in implementing the social optimum described in (i).

Exercise 12.3 (depositors' game with a public signal). Consider the depositors' game of Section 12.6.2, except that the depositors receive the same signal:

$$y = R + \sigma\eta.$$

Determine the range of signals over which there exist multiple equilibria.

Exercise 12.4 (random withdrawal rate). Consider a three-date Diamond–Dybvig economy ($t = 0, 1, 2$). Consumers are *ex ante* identical; they save 1 at date 0. At date 1, consumers learn their preferences. A fraction λ has utility $u(c_1)$ and a fraction $(1 - \lambda)$ has utility $u(c_2)$.

At date 0, the consumers put their savings in a bank. They later cannot withdraw and invest in financial markets, so the Jacklin critique does not apply. That is, incentive compatibility issues are ignored in this exercise (a patient depositor cannot masquerade as an impatient one). The bank invests the per-depositor savings into short- and long-term projects: $i_1 + i_2 = 1$. The long-term technology yields (per unit of investment) $R > 1$ at date 2, but only $l < 1$ if liquidated at date 1. The short-term technology yields 1 (so $r_1 = r_2 = 1$).

(i) • Show that the optimal allocation (c_1, c_2) satisfies

$$u'(c_1) = Ru'(c_2).$$

• Suppose that $u(c) = c^{1-\gamma}/(1 - \gamma)$ with $\gamma > 1$. How do i_1 and i_2 vary with γ?

(ii) Suppose now that there is macroeconomic uncertainty, in that λ is unknown: $\lambda = \lambda_L$ with probability β and $\lambda = \lambda_H$ with probability $1 - \beta$, where $0 < \lambda_L < \lambda_H < 1$. Set up the optimal program (let y_ω and z_ω denote the fraction of short-term investment that is *not* rolled over, and the fraction of long-term investment that is liquidated, respectively, in state of nature $\omega \in \{L, H\}$). What does the solution look like for $l = 0$ and l close to 1? (Showoffs: characterize the solution for a general l!)

References

Acharya, V. V. and L. H. Pedersen. 2005. Asset pricing with liquidity risk. *Journal of Financial Economics* 77:375–410.

Allen, F. and D. Gale. 1997. Financial markets, intermediaries and intertemporal smoothing. *Journal of Political Economy* 105:523–546.

——. 1998. Optimal financial crises. *Journal of Finance* 53: 1245–1283.

——. 2000. *Comparing Financial Systems*. Cambridge, MA: MIT Press.

Angeletos, G. M., C. Hellwig, and A. Pavan. 2005. Coordination and policy traps. Mimeo, MIT, UCLA, and Northwestern University.

Bagehot, W. 1873. *Lombard Street: A Description of the Money Market*. London: H. S. King.

Bernheim, D. and M. Whinston. 1986. Common agency. *Econometrica* 54:923–942.

Bhattacharya, S. and D. Gale. 1987. Preference shocks, liquidity and central bank policy. In *New Approaches to Monetary Economics* (ed. W. Barnett and K. Singleton), pp. 69–88. Cambridge University Press.

Bond, P. and R. Townsend. 1995. Diamond–Dybvig models of banking. Teaching Notes for Money and Banking Course, University of Chicago.

Bryant, J. 1980. A model of reserves, bank runs, and deposit insurance. *Journal of Banking and Finance* 43:749–761.

Calomiris, C. and C. Kahn. 1991. The role of demandable debt in structuring optimal banking arrangements. *American Economic Review* 81:497–513.

Carlsson, H. and E. van Damme. 1993. Global games and equilibrium selection. *Econometrica* 61:989–1018.

Corsetti, G., A. Dasgupta, S. Morris, and H. Shin. 2004. Does one Soros make a difference? The role of a large trader in currency crises. *Review of Economic Studies* 71:87–113.

Corsetti, G., P. Pesenti, and N. Roubini. 2002. The role of large players in currency crises. In *Preventing Currency Crises in Emerging Markets* (ed. S. Edwards and J. Frankel). NBER and Chicago University Press.

Diamond, D. 1997. Liquidity, banks, and markets. *Journal of Political Economy* 105:928–956.

Diamond, D. and P. Dybvig. 1983. Bank runs, deposit insurance, and liquidity. *Journal of Political Economy* 91:401–419.

Eisfeldt, A. 2003. Smoothing with liquid and illiquid assets. Mimeo, Northwestern University.

Favero, C., M. Pagano, and E. von Thadden. 2005. Valuation, liquidity and risk in government bond markets. Mimeo, Università Bocconi.

Frankel, D., S. Morris, and A. Pauzner. 2003. Equilibrium selection in global games with strategic complementarities. *Journal of Economic Theory* 108:1–44.

Freixas, X. and J. C. Rochet. 1997. *Microeconomics of Banking.* Cambridge, MA: MIT Press.

Fudenberg, D. and J. Tirole. 1986. A theory of exit in duopoly. *Econometrica* 54:943–960.

Fulghieri, P. and R. Rovelli. 1998. Capital markets, financial intermediaries, and liquidity supply. *Journal of Banking and Finance* 22:1157–1179.

Gale, D. and X. Vives. 2002. Dollarization, bailouts, and the stability of the banking system. *Quarterly Journal of Economics* 117:467–502.

Goldstein, I. and A. Pauzner. 2005. Demand deposit contracts and the probability of bank runs. *Journal of Finance* 60:1293–1327.

Gollier, C. 2001. *The Economics of Risk and Time.* Cambridge, MA: MIT Press.

Gorton, G. 1985. Bank suspension of convertibility. *Journal of Monetary Economics* 15:117–134.

——. 1988. Banking panics and business cycles. *Oxford Economic Papers* 40:751–782.

Gorton, G. and G. Pennacchi. 1990. Financial intermediaries and liquidity creation. *Journal of Finance* 45:49–71.

——. 1993. Security baskets and index-linked securities. *Journal of Business* 66:1–27.

Gorton, G. and A. Winton. 2003. Financial intermediation. In *Handbook of the Economics of Finance* (ed. G. Constantinides, M. Harris, and R. Stulz). Amsterdam: North-Holland.

Green, E. and P. Lin. 2003. Implementing efficient allocations in a model of financial intermediation. *Journal of Economic Theory* 109:1–23.

Hellwig, M. 1994. Liquidity provision, banking, and the allocation of interest rate risk. *European Economic Review* 38:1363–1390.

Helpman, E. and J. J. Laffont. 1975. On moral hazard in general equilibrium theory. *Journal of Economic Theory* 10:8–23.

Hirshleifer, J. 1971. The private and social value of information and the reward to inventive activity. *American Economic Review* 61:561–574.

Holmström, B. and J. Tirole. 1993. Market liquidity and performance monitoring. *Journal of Political Economy* 101:678–709.

Jacklin, C. 1987. Demand deposits, trading restrictions, and risk sharing. In *Contractual Arrangements for Intertemporal Trade* (ed. E. Prescott and N. Wallac), Chapter II, pp. 26–47. Minneapolis, MN: University of Minnesota Press.

Jacklin, C. and S. Bhattacharya. 1988. Distinguishing panics and information based bank runs: welfare and policy implications. *Journal of Political Economy* 96:569–592.

Kindelberger, C. 1978. *Manias, Panics, and Crashes.* New York: John Wiley.

Klemperer, P. and M. Meyer. 1989. Supply function equilibria in oligopoly under uncertainty. *Econometrica* 57:1243–1277.

Kyle, A. 1985. Continuous auctions and insider trading. *Econometrica* 53:1315–1335.

Laffont, J. J. 1985. On the welfare analysis of rational expectations equilibria with asymmetric information. *Econometrica* 53:1–29.

Laibson, D. 1997. Golden eggs and hyperbolic discounting. *Quarterly Journal of Economics* 112:443–478.

Maskin, E. and J. Riley. 1986. Uniqueness of equilibrium in sealed high bid auctions. Mimeo, MIT and UCLA. (Published in *Games and Economic Behavior* (2003) 45:395–409.)

Morris, S. and H. S. Shin. 1998. Unique equilibrium in a model of self-fulfilling currency attacks. *American Economic Review* 88:587–597.

Pathak, P. and J. Tirole. 2005. Pegs, risk management, and financial crises. Mimeo, Harvard University and IDEI.

Pauly, M. V. 1974. Overinsurance and public provision of insurance: the roles of moral hazard and adverse selection. *Quarterly Journal of Economics* 88:44–62.

Peck, J. and K. Shell. 2003. Equilibrium bank runs. *Journal of Political Economy* 111:103–123.

Qi, J. 1994. Bank liquidity and stability in an overlapping generations model. *Review of Financial Studies* 7:389–417.

Rochet, J. C. and X. Vives. 2004. Coordination failures and the lender of last resort: was Bagehot right after all? *Journal of the European Economic Association* 2:1116–1147.

Subrahmanyam, A. 1991. A theory of trading in stock index futures. *Review of Financial Studies* 4:17–51.

Vayanos, D. 2004. Flight to quality, flight to liquidity, and the pricing of risk. National Bureau of Economic Research Working Paper 10327.

Ventura, J. 2001. Some thoughts on the role of large investors in currency crises: a comment to Corsetti et al. Mimeo, MIT.

Von Thadden, E. L. 1997. The term-structure of investment and the banks' insurance function. *European Economic Review* 41:1355–1374.

PART VI

Macroeconomic Implications and the Political Economy of Corporate Finance

13

Credit Rationing and Economic Activity

13.1 Introduction

In the first issue of *Econometrica* (1933), Irving Fisher stressed the key role of credit constraints in amplifying and protracting the ongoing recession. The combination of nonindexed debt contracts and deflation, he argued, redistributed wealth from borrowers to creditors; furthermore, the reduction in the firms' cash flows and the fall in collateral values increased leverage and reduced investment, thereby exacerbating the recession. Fisher's prescient concern about what are now called balanced sheet effects has received substantial empirical, microeconomic, and macroeconomic support since his time. For example, numerous contributions have established links between high leverage ratios, falling asset prices, and low investment and economic activity (see, for example, King (1994) and Bernanke et al. (1999) for an overview).

While this "balance-sheet channel" refers to the influence of firms' balance sheets on their investment and production, the "lending channel," in contrast, focuses on the impact of the strength of financial intermediaries' balance sheets on firms' activity. At the microeconomic level, firms with weak balance sheets (often, small firms) depend on monitoring and certification by financial intermediaries (banks and insurance companies) to secure access to funds. They are thus hurt when banks' and insurance companies' real or regulatory solvency declines. Similarly, the market for initial public offerings of technology companies closed after the Internet and communications company stocks collapsed in 2000; venture capitalists (the intermediaries monitoring and certifying start-ups) were then deprived of an exit strategy and consequently lacked funds to finance new start-ups. It took a couple of years for technology finance to start recovering.

At the macroeconomic level, economists, starting with Bernanke (1983), have documented the contractionary impact on loans of a tight monetary policy (an increase in the federal funds rate) and a concomitant increase in commercial paper issues (showing that the contraction is related to a reduction in loan supply rather than to a decrease in loan demand). Related observations point at the negative impact of bank panics on macroeconomic activity (Friedman and Schwartz 1963) and at the incidence of the tax associated with bank reserves requirements on bank borrowers rather than on depositors (Fama 1985; James 1987).

This chapter provides a theoretical analysis of the balance-sheet channel (Section 13.2) and of the lending channel (Section 13.3). Sections 13.4 and 13.5 study the dynamic linkages in infinite-horizon models with successive generations. Section 13.4 focuses on dynamic complementarities due to net worth accumulation and shows how short-term balance sheet effects can have a long-term impact on the welfare of either individual families or whole countries. Section 13.5, in contrast, looks at dynamic lending substitutabilities and investigates the negative effect of today's investment on future prices and thereby on future investment.

13.2 Capital Squeezes and Economic Activity: The Balance-Sheet Channel

This section analyses the impact of interest rates on economic activity when the corporate sector faces credit constraints. It revisits the basic moral-hazard and adverse-selection models of Chapters 3 and 6, and generalizes them by endogenizing the rate of interest. Taking the interest rate as exogenous (and normalizing it to 0 without loss of generality) was fine until now, since we were focusing on the institutions of corporate finance. Moving to a macroeconomic framework, however, requires endogenizing the rate of interest, unless the savings function is perfectly elastic at some fixed interest rate, such as the interest rate on the world financial markets.

Namely, letting r denote the (real) rate of interest, we posit a savings function $S(r)$, increasing in r. This function can be derived from investors' preferences: let date 0 denote the date at which they lend and date 1 the date at which their claims on firms pay off, with associated consumptions c_0 and c_1; and let investors' preferences be given by

$$U(c_0, c_1) = u(c_0) + c_1,$$

where $u(\cdot)$ is increasing and concave. This formulation is handy since it preserves risk neutrality with respect to returns (and thus the concomitant simplicity) while making the saving function imperfectly elastic. The saving function is then obtained from

$$\max_{\{c_0, c_1\}} \{u(c_0) + c_1\}$$

s.t.

$$c_0 + \frac{c_1}{1+r} = y,$$

where y denotes income. This program is equivalent to[1]

$$\max_{\{c_0\}} \{u(c_0) + (1+r)(y - c_0)\},$$

yielding

$$u'(c_0(r)) = 1 + r.$$

Because u is concave ($u'' < 0$), date-0 consumption decreases with the rate of interest. Savings, $S(r) = y - c_0(r)$, in contrast, increase with the rate of interest.

The extreme case of a perfectly elastic savings function, in which the interest rate is fixed at some exogenous level and is given by a "storage technology," or some "international rate," or else by fully linear investors' preferences ($c_0 + c_1/(1+r)$), provides a special case of savings function relative to this more general environment.

The theme of this section, the aim of which is primarily to introduce basic material, is that an increase in the rate of interest has a negative impact on investment. It is not very surprising, you might say, that when the price of a factor of production (here capital) increases, the use made of this factor of production decreases. It holds whether or not firms face financial constraints. The interesting insight is that interest rates may have very sharp effects in a corporate finance world, as credit constraints exacerbate their impact. Indeed, a small increase in the interest rate may trigger a complete collapse of lending and a discontinuous reduction in welfare.

13.2.1 Moral Hazard

Let us first revisit the basic, fixed-investment model of Section 3.2.

Consider a set of risk-neutral entrepreneurs, technically a continuum of mass 1 of them. Each has

- a project requiring fixed investment I, and owns assets or net worth A;
- a utility function of consumptions c_0 and c_1 at dates 0 and 1 equal to $U(c_0, c_1) = c_0 + c_1$; entrepreneurs are protected by limited liability (in particular, $c_1 \geqslant 0$).

The entrepreneurs' particular utility function is in no way crucial. What is required more generally is that the entrepreneurs not be more impatient than the savers,[2] because otherwise the direction of lending might be reversed, with limited interest for our purpose. In this spirit, we will assume that the equilibrium rate of interest is positive ($r > 0$).

If undertaken, the project either succeeds, that is, yields verifiable income $R > 0$, or fails and yields no income. The probability of success, p, depends on the entrepreneur's behavior: it is equal to p_H if the entrepreneur works and $p_L = p_H - \Delta p$ if she shirks. Shirking yields a private benefit $B > 0$ to the entrepreneur (this private benefit is counted as part of c_1).

We allow for one dimension of heterogeneity: entrepreneurs differ in their assets A. Namely, A, which recall is an index of a firm's strength of

1. We assume an interior equilibrium. This is indeed the case if $u'(0) > 1 + r > u'(y)$.

2. So, for example, in the extreme case in which the savings function is perfectly elastic at some interest rate r, entrepreneurs could have preferences

$$c_0 + \frac{c_1}{1+r}$$

without any change in the analysis.

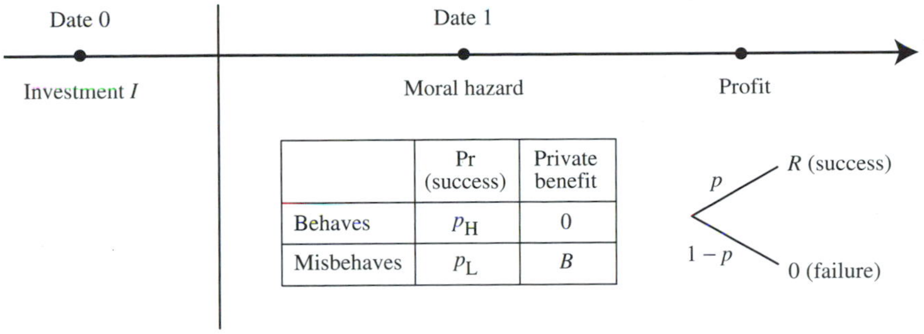

Figure 13.1

balance sheet, is distributed in the population of entrepreneurs according to the continuous cumulative distribution function $G(A)$ with support $[\underline{A}, \bar{A}]$ and density $g(A)$. The upper bound $\bar{A}$ in principle can exceed I; firms with assets $A \geqslant I$ do not need to borrow in order to invest and are therefore net savers; needless to say, those "borrowers" do not preoccupy us. For simplicity, we will therefore assume that $\bar{A} \leqslant I$.

The timing is the familiar one (see Figure 13.1), except that we have now got to be careful about dates since the interest rate may now differ from 0.[3]

We assume that the project has positive NPV if and only if the entrepreneur behaves. That is, in the relevant range for interest rates,

$$p_H R > (1+r)I > p_L R + B.$$

To solve for the macroeconomic equilibrium, we proceed as in Section 3.2. Conditional on the entrepreneur receiving funding, the optimal contract allocates the profit in the case of success between borrower (R_b) and lenders (R_l),

$$R = R_b + R_l,$$

and gives 0 to both in the case of failure (recall that the entrepreneur is risk neutral and therefore must receive the harshest punishment in the case of failure, namely, 0 under limited liability). The incentive compatibility constraint is

$$(\Delta p)R_b \geqslant B,$$

and so the maximum expected income that can be pledged to investors without destroying incentives—the pledgeable income—is equal to

$$p_H\left(R - \frac{B}{\Delta p}\right).$$

A necessary and sufficient condition[4] for an entrepreneur with assets A to receive financing is

$$p_H\left(R - \frac{B}{\Delta p}\right) \geqslant (1+r)(I-A).$$

Let $A^*(r)$ (an increasing function) be the smallest level of cash on hand A that enables funding:

$$p_H\left(R - \frac{B}{\Delta p}\right) = (1+r)[I - A^*(r)].$$

The financial market clears when corporate net investment, $\mathcal{I}(r)$, is equal to investors' savings; $\mathcal{I}(r)$ is given by

$$\mathcal{I}(r) \equiv \int_{A^*(r)}^{\bar{A}} (I-A)g(A)\,\mathrm{d}A - \int_{\underline{A}}^{A^*(r)} Ag(A)\,\mathrm{d}A$$
$$= (1 - G(A^*(r)))I - A^{\mathrm{e}},$$

where

$$A^{\mathrm{e}} \equiv \int_{\underline{A}}^{\bar{A}} Ag(A)\,\mathrm{d}A$$

is the average entrepreneur wealth. Market clearing means that

$$\mathcal{I}(r) = S(r).$$

This equilibrium is depicted by point a in Figure 13.2.

The comparative statics are straightforward. Consider, first, an exogenous reduction in the savings rate. That is, the savings curve moves up in Figure 13.2. Unsurprisingly, the equilibrium shifts to

3. Locating the moral-hazard stage at date 1 rather than date 0 is just an accounting convention, and has no impact on the results.

4. This condition is necessary since the NPV is negative and so someone has to lose if the contract induces shirking. It is easy to see that it is also sufficient. See Section 3.2 for more details.

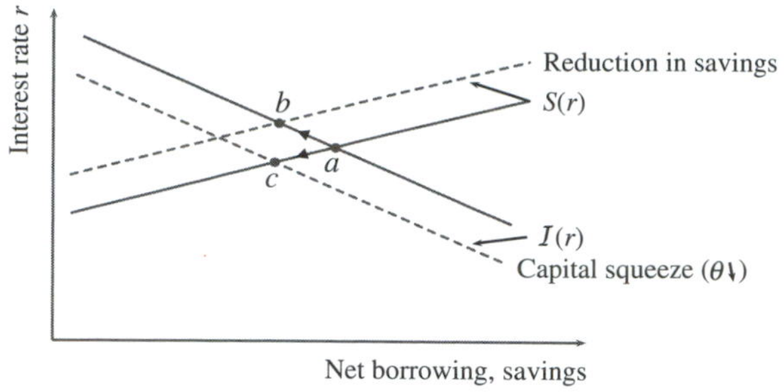

Figure 13.2

point b, with lower investment and an increase in the interest rate.

Let us next look at a deterioration in the firms' balance sheets. The proper way to formalize an overall change in the distribution of the balance sheets is to assume that the distribution of assets A is indexed by a parameter θ, $G(A \mid \theta)$, and that an increase in θ corresponds to an improvement of the distribution in the sense of first-order stochastic dominance:

$$G_\theta(A \mid \theta) < 0 \quad \text{for } \underline{A} < A < \bar{A},$$

where a subscript here denotes a partial derivative ($\partial G/\partial\theta \equiv G_\theta$). Intuitively, when θ increases, the distribution puts more weight on the upper tail and less on the lower tail.[5]

Net borrowing $\mathcal{I}(r,\theta)$ is affected by a capital squeeze (θ decreases) in the following way:

$$\mathcal{I}_\theta = -G_\theta(A^*(r))I - \frac{\mathrm{d}A^{\mathrm{e}}}{\mathrm{d}\theta}.$$

Thus a capital squeeze has two effects:

Eviction (indirect effect). The number of firms that are unable to raise funds because of the weakness of their balance sheet, $G(A^*(r) \mid \theta)$, increases as θ decreases. The firms that are evicted from the pool of borrowers are the marginal firms, which borrowed $I - A^*(r)$. The decrease in the demand for funds corresponds to the first term in the expression of $\mathcal{I}_\theta$;

Greater needs (direct effect). Because

$$A^{\mathrm{e}}(\theta) = \int_{\underline{A}}^{\bar{A}} A\,\mathrm{d}G(A \mid \theta) = \bar{A} - \int_{\underline{A}}^{\bar{A}} G(A \mid \theta)\,\mathrm{d}A$$

(after an integration by parts), $\mathrm{d}A^{\mathrm{e}}(\theta)/\mathrm{d}\theta > 0$. Hence, a capital squeeze reduces the entrepreneurs' average net worth.

Thus, the $\mathcal{I}(\cdot)$ curve may shift outward or (as depicted in Figure 13.2) inward. (As we will observe, this indeterminacy is removed in the variable-investment version.) For example, if the eviction effect dominates, a capital squeeze moves the equilibrium in Figure 13.2 from point a to point c, with a lower level of net borrowing and a lower interest rate.

The investment level, equal to I times the fraction of firms that have access to funding,

$$1 - G(A^*(r) \mid \theta),$$

in contrast is unambiguously reduced by a capital squeeze.[6]

Remark (on redistribution). The literature has emphasized that wealth redistribution has an ambiguous impact on efficiency (leaving aside redistributive aspects of course). While this point has often been made in more sophisticated growth models (e.g., of the type reviewed in Sections 13.4 and 13.5), the basic idea can be conveyed in the static version. A redistribution of wealth, namely, a change in the distribution of wealth levels A keeping total entrepreneur wealth, A^{e}, constant,[7] affects in an ambiguous way the number of firms that make it to the borrowing threshold. For example, suppose that there are two

5. See, for example, Mas Colell et al.'s (1995) textbook for an exposition of first-order stochastic dominance.

Note that, because $G(\bar{A} \mid \theta) = 1$ and $G(\underline{A} \mid \theta) = 0$ for all θ,

$$G_\theta(\bar{A} \mid \theta) = G_\theta(\underline{A} \mid \theta) = 0.$$

A special case is that in which θ is a uniform shift in A (each A becomes $A+\theta$): $G(A \mid \theta) = H(A-\theta)$, where H is a cumulative distribution function. (This case involves a "moving support." And so if $\theta \in [\underline{\theta}, \bar{\theta}]$, the inequality $G_\theta \leqslant 0$ is weak over two ranges in $[\underline{A} + \underline{\theta}, \bar{A} + \bar{\theta}]$.)

6. Its total derivative with respect to θ is (I times)

$$-G_\theta(A^*(r) \mid \theta) - g(A^*(r) \mid \theta)\frac{\mathrm{d}A^*}{\mathrm{d}r}\frac{\mathrm{d}r}{\mathrm{d}\theta}.$$

By definition, $G_\theta < 0$. Also, $\mathrm{d}A^*/\mathrm{d}r > 0$ (a higher interest rate leads to the eviction of marginal firms). Finally,

$$S'(r)\,\mathrm{d}r = \mathcal{I}_r\,\mathrm{d}r + \mathcal{I}_\theta\,\mathrm{d}\theta.$$

And so

$$\frac{\mathrm{d}}{\mathrm{d}\theta}[1 - G(A^*(r) \mid \theta)] = \left(-G_\theta S' + g\frac{\mathrm{d}A^*}{\mathrm{d}r}\frac{\mathrm{d}A^{\mathrm{e}}}{\mathrm{d}\theta}\right)\Big/\left(S' + gI\frac{\mathrm{d}A^*}{\mathrm{d}r}\right) > 0.$$

7. The literature often considers a specific form of wealth redistribution, namely, a mean-preserving decrease in risk for the distribution G (so the parameter θ is now a parameter of second-order stochastic dominance rather than one of first-order stochastic dominance).

For a mean-preserving spread,

$$\frac{\mathrm{d}A^{\mathrm{e}}}{\mathrm{d}\theta} = \int_{\underline{A}}^{\bar{A}} A\,\mathrm{d}G_\theta(A \mid \theta) = 0 \quad \text{and} \quad \int_{\underline{A}}^{A} G_\theta(A \mid \theta) \geqslant 0 \quad \text{for all } A.$$

But $\mathcal{I}_\theta = -G_\theta(A \mid \theta)I$ can *a priori* have any sign.

levels of wealth, A_L and A_H, in the population and that the savings function is perfectly elastic, so that the rate of interest r and the threshold $A^*(r)$ are exogenously determined. A wealth-redistribution policy brings these to A'_L and A'_H, where $A_L < A'_L \leqslant A'_H < A_H$. If the threshold lies between A'_H and A_H, then the wealth redistribution eliminates the entrepreneurial class and reduces efficiency. If it lies between A_L and A'_L, then wealth redistribution allows everyone to be an entrepreneur and increases efficiency.[8]

Variable-investment variant. The same exercise can be performed for a variable investment scale (Section 3.4). The entrepreneur selects a scale $I \in [0, \infty)$. Profit in the case of success (RI) is proportional to investment; there is still no profit in the case of failure. Misbehavior, which, as in the fixed-investment model, reduces the probability of success from p_H to p_L, yields private benefit, BI, proportional to investment, to the entrepreneur. We assume that, in the relevant range of interest rates, the following inequalities, where the magnitudes are expressed per unit of investment, hold:

$$p_H R > 1 + r > \max\left\{p_L R + B, p_H\left(R - \frac{B}{\Delta p}\right)\right\}.$$

The first inequality says that investing is a positive-NPV proposition if incentives are in place. The second inequality says, first, that the NPV is negative if the entrepreneur is induced to misbehave ($1 + r > p_L R + B$), and, second, that the pledgeable income per unit of investment does not cover interest and principal on the loan ($1 + r > p_H(R - B/\Delta p)$)—this assumption, as in Section 3.4, will guarantee that the optimal investment is finite in this constant-returns-to-scale model.

Letting R_b denote the entrepreneur's reward in the case of success (it is 0 in the case of failure), the incentive compatibility constraint is

$$(\Delta p) R_b \geqslant BI,$$

yielding pledgeable income

$$p_H RI - p_H\Big\{\min_{\{R_b \geqslant BI/\Delta p\}} R_b\Big\} \equiv p_H\left(R - \frac{B}{\Delta p}\right)I,$$

and so the investors' breakeven condition (which, due to the competitiveness of the capital market, holds with equality) is

$$p_H\left(R - \frac{B}{\Delta p}\right)I = (1 + r)(I - A).$$

As in Section 3.4, the investment scale is a multiplier of assets:

$$I = \frac{A}{1 - p_H(R - B/\Delta p)/(1 + r)}.$$

Note that

- an increase in the rate of interest reduces the scale of investment,
- all firms are identical up to their scale, and so the distribution of assets among entrepreneurs is irrelevant here (unlike in the fixed-investment case) for a given level of total assets $A^e = \int_{\underline{A}}^{\bar{A}} Ag(A)\,dA$.

Indeed, net borrowing for a distribution indexed by parameter θ is

$$\begin{aligned} \mathcal{I}(r, \theta) &\equiv \int_{\underline{A}}^{\bar{A}} (I - A) g(A \mid \theta)\,dA \\ &= \frac{p_H(R - B/\Delta p)}{(1 + r) - p_H(R - B/\Delta p)} A^e(\theta), \end{aligned}$$

where

$$A^e(\theta) \equiv \int_{\underline{A}}^{\bar{A}} Ag(A \mid \theta)\,dA.$$

As in the fixed-investment version, let us assume that θ is a parameter of first-order stochastic dominance: $G_\theta < 0$. Integrating by parts, and using $G_\theta(\bar{A} \mid \theta) = G_\theta(\underline{A} \mid \theta) = 0$,[9]

$$\frac{dA^e(\theta)}{d\theta} = -\int_{\underline{A}}^{\bar{A}} G_\theta(A \mid \theta)\,dA > 0.$$

Hence, in the variable-investment variant, the investment is scaled down when a firm has lower assets and $\mathcal{I}$ unambiguously shifts inward with a capital squeeze (θ decreases), as depicted in Figure 13.2. Furthermore, as in the case of a fixed investment size, a reduction in savings leads to a higher rate of interest and a smaller investment.[10]

13.2.2 Adverse Selection

As we studied in Chapter 6, adverse selection (the presence of entrepreneurial private information at

8. This mechanism is not the only cause of ambiguity. See Aghion and Bolton (1997) for a more complete discussion.

9. Since $G(\bar{A} \mid \theta) = 1$ and $G(\underline{A} \mid \theta) = 0$ for all θ.

10. Note also that a mean-preserving spread in the distribution of net worths has no impact on investment.

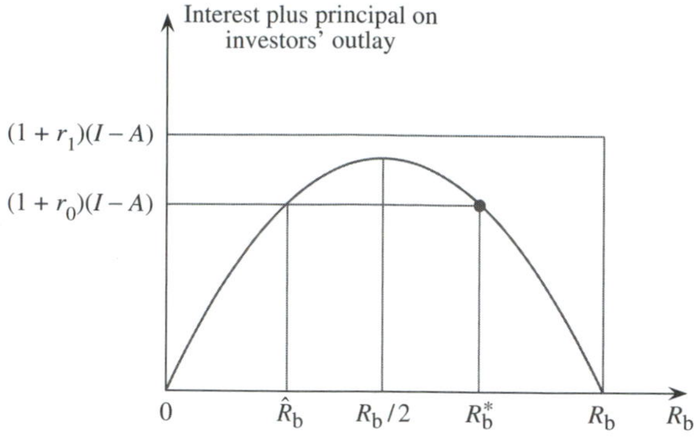

Figure 13.3

the initial financing stage) is another factor conducive to credit rationing. Under adverse selection, the impact of an interest rate increase may be dramatic, as we will shortly see. The increased debt burden may create a serious deterioration of the pool of loan applicants.[11] Conversely, a small improvement in lending conditions may have a substantial impact on economic activity; along these lines, Mankiw (1986) argues that small government interventions (e.g., subsidized loans to students, farmers, and homeowners) can make a big difference.

This section (building on Chapter 6) offers two illustrations of the potentially strong impact of interest rates on activity in the presence of adverse selection. Both illustrations use the fixed-investment version of the model.

(a) *Impact of factor price on behavior: asymmetric information on private benefits.* Let us assume that all borrowers have the same fixed-investment technology and the same level of assets $A < I$. The source of heterogeneity is the level of private benefit B obtained by the entrepreneur when misbehaving. The latter is distributed in the population of entrepreneurs on the interval $[0, \bar{B}]$ according to cumulative distribution function $H(B)$ (with $H(0) = 0$, $H(\bar{B}) = 1$).

Investors would want to screen out "bad types," namely, those with high private benefits from misbehaving. Unfortunately (and as was observed in Exercise 6.1), such types cannot be screened out since their surplus from the lending relationship is at least equal to that of entrepreneurs with a lower private benefit.

Suppose that investors are willing to finance the project of a representative entrepreneur ("representative" from the point of view of investors, as entrepreneurs all look alike). The entrepreneur contributes A and the investors $I - A$. They share the profit in the case of success in proportions R_b and $R - R_b$, respectively. Provided that $\bar{B}$ is sufficiently large, the entrepreneur behaves if $B < B^*(R_b)$ and misbehaves if $B > B^*(R_b)$, where $B^*(R_b)$ is given by

$$(\Delta p) R_b = B^*(R_b). \tag{13.1}$$

The investors' breakeven condition is then

$$\hat{p}(R_b)[R - R_b] = (1 + r)(I - A), \tag{13.2}$$

where

$$\hat{p}(R_b) \equiv p_H H(B^*(R_b)) + p_L[1 - H(B^*(R_b))] \tag{13.3}$$

is the expected probability of success (as assessed by investors).

The key point is that this average probability of success is increasing in R_b: the lower the debt burden (the higher R_b is), the more accountable the entrepreneur is. An increase in the interest rate r increases the debt burden for a given $\hat{p}$ (see equation (13.2)): R_b decreases, making the entrepreneur less accountable (see equation (13.1): B^* decreases), which in turn increases the debt burden, and so forth. This vicious circle may lead to a discontinuous drop (collapse, breakdown) in lending.

Example. Suppose that $p_L = 0$, $\bar{B} = 1$, and H is uniform on $[0, 1]$: $H(B) = B$. Then $H(B^*) = B^* = (\Delta p) R_b = p_H R_b$, and so

$$\hat{p}(R_b) = p_H B^* + p_L(1 - B^*) = p_H^2 R_b.$$

The investors' breakeven condition is

$$p_H^2 R_b (R - R_b) = (1 + r)(I - A).$$

The possibility of collapse is illustrated in Figure 13.3. When the interest rate is equal to r_0, there are two possible equilibria, $\hat{R}_b$ and R_b^*. Both satisfy the investors' breakeven condition. The socially optimal one is the one that is preferred by entrepreneurs and yields entrepreneurial stake R_b^*. (It is also

11. See, for example, Jaffee and Russell (1976), Stiglitz and Weiss (1981), and Mankiw (1986), who, in the tradition of Akerlof (1970), demonstrate the dramatic impact of adverse selection in the market for loans.

the only stable equilibrium: starting from entrepreneurial stake $\hat{R}_b$, a small increase in R_b raises $\hat{p}$ proportionally more than $(R - R_b)$ decreases, and so investors' profit increases, increasing R_b further, and so forth.) A small increase in r_1 completely shuts down the credit market.[12]

(b) *Impact on the pool of applicants: asymmetric information about profitability.* Still in the fixed-investment model, assume now that loan applicants differ in their probability of success rather than in their private benefit. So B is the same for all entrepreneurs, but the probability of success is

$$p + \tau;$$

that is, the probability of success is $p_H + \tau$ if the entrepreneur behaves and $p_L + \tau$ if she misbehaves. As usual, the benefit of this separable form is that incentives can be separated from adverse selection, since the incentive constraint,

$$[(p_H + \tau) - (p_L + \tau)]R_b \geqslant B,$$

for a contract $\{R_b$ in the case of success, 0 in the case of failure$\}$ is independent of τ.

The profitability parameter τ is distributed according to some cumulative distribution function $H(\tau)$ with density $h(\tau)$ on $[\underline{\tau}, \bar{\tau}]$ (we keep the same notation $H(\cdot)$ for the distribution of the privately known parameter, here τ). Let[13]

$$\tau^+(\tau) \equiv E(\tilde{\tau} \mid \tilde{\tau} \geqslant \tau) = \frac{\int_\tau^{\bar{\tau}} \tilde{\tau} h(\tilde{\tau})\, d\tilde{\tau}}{1 - H(\tau)}$$

and

$$\tau^-(\tau) \equiv E(\tilde{\tau} \mid \tilde{\tau} < \tau) = \frac{\int_{\underline{\tau}}^{\tau} \tilde{\tau} h(\tilde{\tau})\, d\tilde{\tau}}{H(\tau)}$$

denote the truncated means. For example, $\tau^+(\tau)$ is the expectation of $\tilde{\tau}$ conditional on $\tilde{\tau}$ exceeding τ.

To simplify the exposition, we will assume that the entrepreneur has no cash on hand:

$$A = 0.$$

But we will allow for a general reservation utility $\bar{U}_b(\tau)$ for the entrepreneur. Until now, we have mostly assumed that the reservation utility is type-independent:

$$\bar{U}_b(\tau) = \bar{U}_b \quad \text{for all } \tau$$

(and have normalized the reservation utility to be 0: $\bar{U}_b = 0$).

We will also be interested in situations in which the utility corresponding to the "outside option," $\bar{U}_b$, increases with τ, and possibly steeply so (the case in which $\bar{U}_b$ increases little with τ is qualitatively similar to that in which it is constant). For example, a talented researcher may have excellent academic prospects (the outside option) when contemplating switching careers and raising funds for a start-up. Or, if the financing helps the firm strengthen its productive capacity or expand, a firm with a good project has a better "outside option" (not being refinanced).[14]

Remark (absence of reward for failure). In the discussion of the incentive constraint above, we assumed that the entrepreneur receives 0 in the case of failure. This is indeed what moral-hazard considerations dictate. But adverse selection only reinforces the optimality of the absence of reward in the case of failure, since such rewards tend to "screen in" low-profitability entrepreneurs. Hence, competitive investors are wary of such contracts.[15] The absence

12. This insight is less interesting than the previous observation that moral hazard increases with the rate of interest; for, the possibility that the market shuts down completely as the interest rate increases slightly also arises under symmetric information: when B is known, and in the absence of other sources of heterogeneity, the market for loans shuts down when r reaches r^*, where

$$(1 + r^*)(I - A) = p_H\left(R - \frac{B}{\Delta p}\right).$$

The basic point, though, is that the introduction of heterogeneity (here with respect to the private benefit) does not eliminate discontinuous market breakdowns.

13. It is well-known that τ^+ and τ^- both grow with τ, at a rate between 0 and 1 as long as the distribution's hazard rates $h/(1 - H)$ and h/H are, respectively, increasing and decreasing (see, for example, An 1998).

14. For a state-of-the-art study of contracting under type-dependent outside options, see Jullien (2000).

15. Suppose that type τ selects a scheme $\{R_b^S(\tau), R_b^F(\tau)\}$ describing the rewards in the cases of success and failure. Assuming that contracts inducing misbehavior yield a negative NPV, and therefore focusing without loss of generality on contracts that do not induce shirking ($R_b^S(\tau) - R_b^F(\tau) \geqslant B/\Delta p$ for all τ), type τ will choose the contract that is most appropriate for the type, and so solves

$$\max_{\hat{\tau} \in [\underline{\tau}, \bar{\tau}]} \{(p_H + \tau)R_b^S(\hat{\tau}) + (1 - p_H - \tau)R_b^F(\hat{\tau})\}.$$

A simple revealed-preference argument (write the two inequalities saying that type τ prefers $\{R_b^S(\tau), R_b^F(\tau)\}$ to $\{R_b^S(\tau'), R_b^F(\tau')\}$ and conversely for type τ' and add up the two inequalities) yields

$$(\tau' - \tau)[[R_b^S(\tau') - R_b^F(\tau')] - [R_b^S(\tau) - R_b^F(\tau)]] \geqslant 0$$

for all (τ, τ').

Note, finally, that incentive compatibility in the choice of contracts implies that a borrower cannot get more for both realizations than

of reward in the case of failure implies that a contract is solely described by the reward R_b in the case of success.

Case 1. High-profitability entrepreneurs are more eager to receive funding. Assume in a first step that the reservation utility does not depend on type (or more generally does not grow fast with the entrepreneur's type):

$$\bar{U}_b(\tau) = \bar{U}_b.$$

Then, for a given R_b, only entrepreneurs with type $\tau \geqslant \tau^*(R_b)$ apply for funding, where

$$[p_H + \tau^*(R_b)]R_b = \bar{U}_b, \qquad (13.4)$$

because the utility from the project, $(p_H + \tau)R_b$, is increasing in profitability. The investors' expected income is then

$$[p_H + \tau^+(\tau^*(R_b))](R - R_b).$$

And so the investors' breakeven condition for a given market rate of interest r is[16]

$$[p_H + \tau^+(\tau^*(R_b))](R - R_b) = (1 + r)(I - A). \quad (13.5)$$

Note that the left-hand side of (13.5) decreases with R_b. Thus, keeping the pool of applicants constant, an increase in the interest rate leads to an increased stake demanded by investors (R_b decreases[17]), which in turn improves the pool of applicants (τ^* increases).

Case 2. Low-profitability entrepreneurs are more eager to receive funding. Suppose now that $\bar{U}_b(\tau)$ is "steeply increasing" (meaning: it is increasing faster than the utility obtained from receiving funding[18]). The contract R_b then attracts the *worst* types:

$$\tau \leqslant \tau^*(R_b),$$

where

$$[p_H + \tau^*(R_b)]R_b = \bar{U}_b(\tau^*(R_b)). \qquad (13.6)$$

The investors' breakeven condition is then given by

$$[p_H + \tau^-(\tau^*(R_b))](R - R_b) = (1 + r)(I - A). \quad (13.7)$$

An increase in the rate of interest now has a drastically different impact. As in case 1, the direct effect is to increase the debt burden $(R - R_b)$. But condition (13.6), together with the fact that $\bar{U}_b(\cdot)$ is steeply increasing, implies that τ^* decreases (the pool of applicants worsens), which lowers τ^-, leading to a further increase in $(R - R_b)$. This spiral may lead to a complete collapse of the credit market.[19]

The two cases are illustrated in Figure 13.4.

13.3 Loanable Funds and the Credit Crunch: The Lending Channel

13.3.1 A "Double-Decker" Model

As was discussed in the introduction to this chapter, firms in the productive sector may not be hit solely by their own capital shortage (the *balance-sheet channel*), but also by a weakness in the balance sheets of the financial institutions that lend to them (the *lending channel*).

A credit crunch refers to a situation in which the banks' equity has fallen to a low level and so banks are capital constrained and cannot lend as much

---

another borrower:

$$R_b^S(\tau') < R_b^S(\tau) \quad \text{if } R_b^F(\tau') > R_b^F(\tau).$$

And so contracts that offer a higher reward for failure (and so by incentive compatibility embody a smaller wedge $R_b^S(\cdot) - R_b^F(\cdot)$) attract lower-profitability types.

16. We are a bit informal here. To be more rigorous, we need to specify whether the entrepreneur selects R_b or investors compete to obtain the entrepreneur's business (the answer is the same for both cases). For example, if the investors compete, for the candidate equilibrium described by (13.4) and (13.5), an investor offering a lower R_b would not interest the entrepreneur, while one offering a higher $R_b' > R_b$ would attract a worse pool of applicants, namely, those with type $\tau \geqslant \tau'$, where $\tau' < \tau^*$ is given by $(p_H + \tau')R_b' = \bar{U}_b$. Hence, this investor would have both a smaller stake *and* a lower probability of success.

17. At least as long as the entrepreneur's reward is sufficient to deter shirking.

18. Again, we are a bit informal here, since the latter utility grows with τ at rate R_b, where R_b is endogenous. It is straightforward to be more careful (note in particular that $R_b \leqslant R$), but we leave this to the reader for the sake of conciseness.

19. Let us illustrate the possibility of a collapse. Suppose that τ is distributed uniformly on $[0, \bar{\tau}]$. And so $\tau^-(\tau^*) = \frac{1}{2}\tau^*$. Let $\bar{U}_b(\tau) = K\tau$, where $K \geqslant R$ (and so the reservation utility grows faster with τ than the utility from being funded, which itself grows at rate $R_b < R$).

Then, for a given $R_b \in [B/\Delta p, R]$, the threshold $\tau^*(R_b)$ under which the entrepreneur applies for funding is given by

$$[p_H + \tau^*(R_b)]R_b = K\tau^*(R_b).$$

The investors' breakeven condition is therefore

$$\left[p_H + \frac{p_H R_b}{2(K - R_b)}\right](R - R_b) = (1 + r)(I - A).$$

It is straightforward to construct examples in which a small increase in the interest rate shuts down a hitherto sizeable loan market.

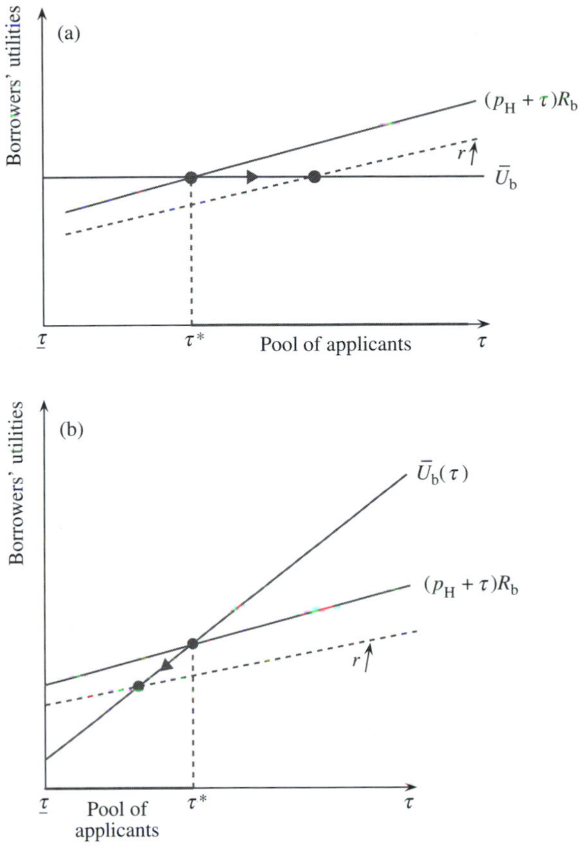

Figure 13.4 (a) Case 1; (b) case 2.

as the opportunities offered to them would warrant.[20] But, of course, the phenomenon has broader applicability: whenever borrowers need to resort to what was labeled "informed capital" in Chapter 9, namely, investors who play a monitoring or certification function, a weakness in the balance sheet of the latter translates into difficult times for the former. For example, a capital shortage at the venture capitalists' level translates one tier down into an increased difficulty for start-ups to raise funds.

This discussion suggests taking a "double-decker" view of credit rationing: the same logic that limits the availability of credit for the "real sector" firms also limits, one tier above, the ability of financial institutions to lend to these firms. Our treatment, which basically combines the partial equilibrium analysis of monitoring of Chapter 9 with the equilibrium approach of Section 13.1, follows Holmström and Tirole (1997).[21]

We thus consider three risk-neutral groups of economic agents: borrowers (firms), monitors (banks), and ordinary (uninformed) investors.

We will assume that each group is composed of a continuum of members, and so market power issues do not arise. The description of equilibrium will distinguish between two rates of interest or rates of return:

(i) the rate demanded by investors—we will let γ denote one plus this rate of interest (so $\gamma = 1 + r$ in the notation of Section 13.1); and

(ii) the rate demanded by monitors on their own invested funds—we will let χ denote one plus this rate of interest.

In equilibrium,

$$\chi > \gamma$$

for two reasons: the first is that monitors must be compensated for their monitoring cost, a cost not incurred by ordinary investors. Because monitors can always decide to invest as ordinary investors, it must be the case that they indeed get a superior return if they are induced to monitor (more on this below). Second, and more interestingly, χ may embody a scarcity rent. If the demand for monitoring is large compared with the supply, then banks are able to extract quasi-rents by charging a high rate of interest.[22]

As in Section 13.1, we consider both the fixed- and the variable-investment variants.

13.3.2 Fixed Investment Size

Entrepreneurs. There is a continuum of entrepreneurs/firms of mass 1. Each has one potential project of size I, yielding profit R in the case of success and 0 in the case of failure. As in Chapter 9, we

20. In the case of banks, capital adequacy requirements set by the Basel Committee and enforced by National Regulatory Authorities directly or indirectly (through the fear of a later constraint) constrain the amount that poorly capitalized banks can lend. Similar regulations apply to insurance companies (see, for example, Dewatripont and Tirole 1994).

21. See also Repullo and Suarez (2000), who look at the impact of monetary shocks (modeled as shifts in the riskless interest rate).

22. This is unrelated to the exercise of market power, since we have assumed there was none.

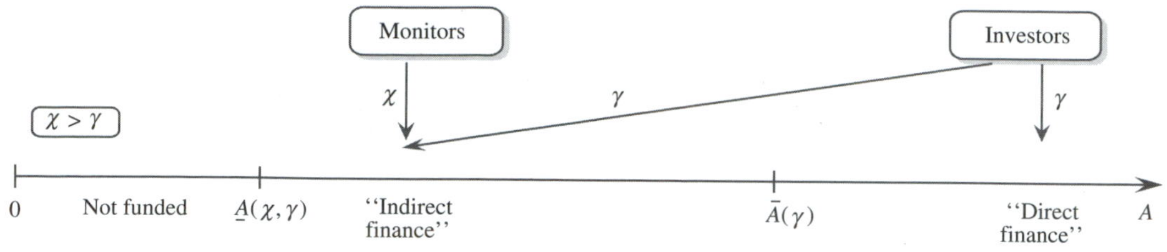

Figure 13.5 Certification.

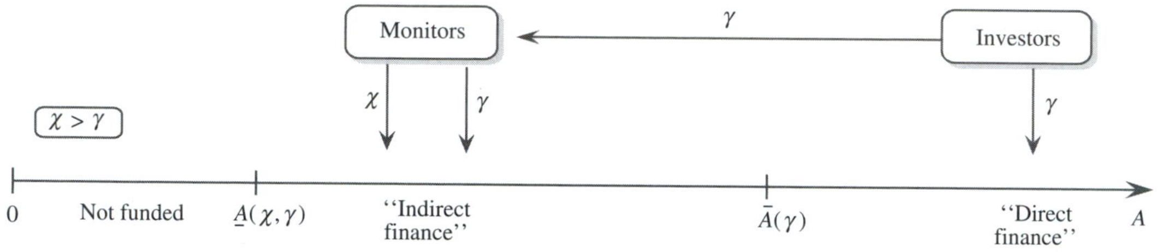

Figure 13.6 Intermediation.

assume that there are three versions of the project:

	good	bad	Bad
Pr(success)	$p_{\rm H}$	$p_{\rm L}$	$p_{\rm L}$
Private benefit	0	b	B

with $p_{\rm H} = p_{\rm L} + \Delta p > p_{\rm L}$ and $B > b > 0$.

Only the good version (good behavior) delivers a positive NPV when financed by uninformed investors:

$$p_{\rm H}R - \gamma I > 0 > [p_{\rm L}R - \gamma I] + B.$$

Entrepreneurial heterogeneity can be modeled in a number of ways. Let us assume here that entrepreneurs differ in their net worth, A. Net worth is distributed according to cumulative distribution $G(A)$ on $[0, \infty)$.

There are two categories of (risk-neutral) investors:

Monitors (financial intermediaries, banks). As in Chapter 9, a monitor can at monitoring cost c rule out the Bad project (the one with high private benefit B). As for the entrepreneur's private benefit, the monitor's cost c, if any, is incurred in the second period. There is a continuum of monitors, with total net worth $K_{\rm m}$ (the distribution, under some assumptions, turns out to be irrelevant). They demand rate of return χ on their (own-account) investment.

Uninformed investors are individually small; they therefore free-ride in the monitoring activity and remain uninformed. As stated above, they demand expected rate of return γ.

We will say that the entrepreneur resorts to "direct or uninformed" finance if she borrows solely from uninformed investors, and to "indirect or informed" finance if a monitor is enlisted as well.

We can consider two cases:

- Exogenous interest rate: uninformed investors have access to a "storage facility" yielding γ units of good for each unit of investment. Their savings are completely elastic at interest rate $(\gamma - 1)$.
- Endogenous interest rate: the uninformed investors' savings are equal to $S(\gamma)$, where S is increasing in γ.

Let us begin with the case of an exogenous interest rate. The market equilibrium can be described in either of two equivalent ways: certification (Figure 13.5) and intermediation (Figure 13.6).

Intermediation occurs when the monitor collects funds from uninformed investors and offers to entrepreneurs bundled loans using both their own capital and the money collected from uninformed investors. For example, banks collect deposits from depositors and lend these as well as bank capital to firms. By contrast, a venture capitalist or a lead investment bank put their own funds into the borrowers' ventures, which then attract (at a different rate of return) the funds of less informed investors (junior partners, say). It is clear that the choice of denomination, in our simple-minded model, is a pure matter of accounting of investment flows and has no real economic implication.

Without a monitor, the borrower, when financed, obtains NPV

$$U_b^* \equiv \frac{p_H R}{\gamma} - I.$$

The entrepreneur's ability to raise uninformed finance as usual depends on her ability to generate enough pledgeable income to reimburse the uninformed investors' initial outlay. Let the revenue R in the case of success be shared between the borrower (R_b) and the uninformed investors (R_u).

The financing condition,

$$p_H R_u \geqslant \gamma(I - A),$$

and the incentive compatibility condition,

$$(\Delta p)R_b \geqslant B$$

(where we use the fact that the borrower prefers the Bad project to the bad project when misbehaving), must both be satisfied. And so

$$p_H\left(R - \frac{B}{\Delta p}\right) \geqslant \gamma(I - A)$$

or

$$A \geqslant \bar{A}(\gamma) \equiv I - \frac{p_H}{\gamma}\left[R - \frac{B}{\Delta p}\right].$$

When $A < \bar{A}(\gamma)$, the entrepreneur cannot obtain financing, at least in the absence of a monitor. The cutoff $\bar{A}(\gamma)$ increases with γ.

With a monitor, we will use the certification paradigm, which is conceptually slightly simpler. The revenue in the case of success is then divided among borrower (R_b), uninformed investors (R_u), and monitor (R_m). On the investment side, the borrower brings A, the monitor I_m, and the uninformed investors $I_u = I - A - I_m$.

Note that by definition of the rate of return χ demanded by the monitor, the following accounting identity prevails:

$$p_H R_m = \chi I_m.$$

Similarly,

$$p_H R_u = \gamma I_u.$$

The entrepreneur's net utility, given that she could invest A at the market rate of return γ, is then

$$\begin{aligned} U_b &= \frac{p_H(R - R_m - R_u)}{\gamma} - A \\ &= \frac{p_H R - \chi I_m - \gamma I_u}{\gamma} - A \\ &= \frac{p_H R - (\chi - \gamma) I_m}{\gamma} - I. \end{aligned}$$

Recall our intuition that χ exceeds γ. One reason for this, as we have noted, is that the monitor could choose to be an uninformed investor in other firms and economize the monitoring cost c; so

$$\chi I_m - c \geqslant \gamma I_m \quad \text{or} \quad \chi - \gamma \geqslant c/I_m.$$

We thus conclude that $U_b^* > U_b$ and so the entrepreneur is better off dispensing with a monitor if she can afford to, i.e., if $A \geqslant \bar{A}(\gamma)$; and that for $A < \bar{A}(\gamma)$, she will want to minimize the monitor's capital involvement I_m.

Suppose that

$$(\Delta p)R_b < B$$

(otherwise the entrepreneur would not need to be monitored), but

$$(\Delta p)R_b \geqslant b,$$

so that, when monitored, the entrepreneur is induced to behave. The monitor's incentive compatibility constraint is then

$$(\Delta p)R_m \geqslant c.$$

This minimum stake in turn requires a minimum investment:

$$I_m \geqslant I_m(\chi) \equiv \frac{p_H c}{(\Delta p)\chi}.$$

Note that the minimum acceptable rate of return for monitors (given by $(\chi - \gamma)I_m = c$) satisfies $\chi = p_H\gamma/p_L$.

The entrepreneur can leverage the presence of a monitor to obtain financing if and only if the present discounted income that can be pledged to the uninformed investors exceeds their initial outlay, or

$$\frac{p_H(R - (b + c)/\Delta p)}{\gamma} \geqslant I - A - I_m(\chi),$$

or

$$A \geqslant \underline{A}(\gamma, \chi),$$

where $\underline{A}(\gamma,\chi)$ is increasing in γ and χ. Because $\chi > \gamma$,

$$\underline{A}(\gamma,\chi) < \bar{A}(\gamma)$$

if and only if $c < \bar{c}$ (with some $\bar{c} > 0$),[23] which we will assume. It must also be the case that entrepreneurs prefer to enlist a monitor and receive funding rather than just invest their net wealth in other firms, i.e., that their net utility is positive:

$$\frac{p_{\rm H}R - (\chi - \gamma)p_{\rm H}c/(\Delta p)\chi}{\gamma} \geqslant I. \tag{13.8}$$

If the monitor obtains no rent from monitoring ($(\chi - \gamma)I_{\rm m} = c$), then condition (13.8) boils down to

$$p_{\rm H}R - c \geqslant \gamma I. \tag{13.9}$$

When the monitor receives a rent ($(\chi - \gamma)I_{\rm m} > c$), condition (13.8) is more stringent than (13.9). Note, however, that if (13.8) were violated, then there would be no demand for monitoring capital and so monitors could not obtain rents after all. Inequality (13.9) is then the relevant condition.

To complete the description of equilibrium, we equate supply of and demand for informed capital:

$$K_{\rm m} \geqslant [G(\bar{A}(\gamma)) - G(\underline{A}(\gamma,\chi))]I_{\rm m}(\chi), \tag{13.10}$$

with inequality only if $(\chi - \gamma)I_{\rm m}(\chi) = c$.

When the interest rate is endogenous, the rates of return γ and χ must also clear the savings market:[24]

$$\begin{aligned} S(\gamma) = &\int_{\bar{A}(\gamma)}^{\infty} (I - A)\,\mathrm{d}G(A) \\ &+ \int_{\underline{A}(\gamma,\chi)}^{\bar{A}(\gamma)} [I - A - I_{\rm m}(\chi)]\,\mathrm{d}G(A) \\ &- \int_0^{\underline{A}(\gamma,\chi)} A\,\mathrm{d}G(A). \end{aligned} \tag{13.11}$$

Note that entrepreneurs who have assets A in excess of investment I, if any,[25] do not need to borrow and actually reinvest the surplus $A - I$ in other firms. The equilibrium rates of return (γ,χ) are then given by (13.10) and (13.11).

Turning to comparative statics (in the broadest framework in which the rate of return received by uninformed investors is endogenous), we can consider the impact of three types of recession:

(a) *Industrial recession (balance-sheet channel).* The distribution $G(A)$ shifts toward lower values of A (that is, $G(A)$ increases for all A). As in Section 13.2, the distribution G is indexed by a parameter θ of first-order stochastic dominance: $G(A \mid \theta)$ with $\partial G/\partial\theta < 0$. An industrial recession corresponds to a decrease in θ, i.e., to a less favorable distribution.

(b) *Credit crunch (lending channel).* $K_{\rm m}$ decreases.

(c) *Shortage of savings.* γ increases (in the perfectly elastic case) or S decreases.

It is easily shown (see Holmström and Tirole 1997) that *in the three types of capital squeeze, aggregate investment goes down and the threshold* ($\underline{A}(\gamma,\chi)$) *over which firms can raise financing increases.*

In particular, firms with weak balance sheets ($\underline{A} \leqslant A < \bar{A}$), which need access to intermediaries in order to raise financing, are hurt by a credit crunch: as monitoring capital $K_{\rm m}$ shrinks, the intermediaries demand a higher rate of return, χ, which squeezes out the marginal firms (with A just above $\underline{A}$) and hurts the others.[26] Firms with strong balance sheets, in contrast, are not directly affected since their financing does not depend on access to intermediaries. They may even gain in a credit crunch to the extent that the reduced demand for uninformed capital by weaker firms may lower the uninformed investors' rate of return. Concretely, banks may become greedier, while the rate of interest on bonds may fall.[27]

23. If $\bar{A} \leqslant \underline{A}$, then there is excess supply of monitoring capital and so $\chi = p_{\rm H}\gamma/p_{\rm L}$; thus $\bar{c}(\Delta p) = p_{\rm H}(B - b)$.

24. Again, the entrepreneurs who do not receive funding save. Holmström and Tirole (1997) implicitly assumed that those who do not get funding do not save, an assumption at odds with the assumption that those entrepreneurs who have cash on hand $A > I$ do save their excess cash (we are grateful to Flavio Toxvaerd for pointing this out to us). The results are qualitatively identical for the various assumptions that can be made about idle entrepreneur wealth.

25. Section 13.2.1 assumed for simplicity that the upper bound on A was lower than I. This assumption is really not crucial, as shown here.

26. Relatedly, Davies and Ioannidis (2003), looking at the behavior of bond issuance and bank lending in the United States between 1970 and 1999, find that securities issuance often does not offset a decline in bank lending, and thereby confirm that the different sources of finance are not substitutable.

27. Needless to say, stronger firms may not benefit from a credit crunch for reasons that are not modeled here. For example, productive activities may exhibit strategic complementarities, as has been emphasized in many macroeconomic models (e.g., Diamond 1982; Shleifer 1986; Cooper and John 1988; Matsuyama 1991).

Lastly, from (13.11), it is apparent that monitors enjoy a rent ($(\chi - \gamma)I_{\rm m} > c$) if and only if $K_{\rm m}$ lies below some threshold. Above that threshold, there is excess supply of monitoring capital and the monitors' rate of return is determined by their indifference between investing in firms they monitor and investing in a portfolio of other firms that they do not monitor.[28]

13.3.3 Variable Investment Size

For the sake of completeness, let us investigate the case of constant-returns-to-scale production. For investment I, a firm's income is RI in the case of success, and 0 in the case of failure; the private benefit is BI if left unmonitored and bI if monitored, in the case of entrepreneurial misbehavior (yielding probability of success $p_{\rm L}$), and 0 in the case of good behavior (yielding probability of success $p_{\rm H}$). The monitoring cost is also proportional to investment: cI. The cost of this constant-returns-to-scale modeling is that there are no longer firms with weak and strong balance sheets: firms are homogeneous up to a scaling factor (namely, their individual net worth A). As a corollary, only total entrepreneurial capital,

$$K_{\rm b} \equiv \int_0^\infty A\,{\rm d}G(A),$$

matters for the determination of equilibrium interest rates and activity, not its distribution among entrepreneurs.

Letting K denote total investment, and decomposing it among the contributions of borrowers, monitors, and uninformed investors,

$$K = K_{\rm b} + K_{\rm m} + K_{\rm u},$$

let

$$\mathfrak{r}_{\rm m} \equiv \frac{K_{\rm m}}{K_{\rm m} + K_{\rm u}} \quad \text{and} \quad \mathfrak{r}_{\rm b} \equiv \frac{K_{\rm b}}{K}.$$

The ratio of the monitors' own funds to total outside finance, $\mathfrak{r}_{\rm m}$, can be interpreted as the solvency ratio of the monitor under the intermediation paradigm.[29] And $\mathfrak{r}_{\rm b}$ is the equity ratio of the borrowers.

We leave it to the reader to check that

$$\begin{array}{c}\text{a \textit{credit crunch}}\\ \text{(reduction in } K_{\rm m})\end{array} \begin{cases} \text{decreases } \gamma, \\ \text{increases } \chi, \\ \text{decreases } \mathfrak{r}_{\rm m}, \\ \text{increases } \mathfrak{r}_{\rm b}; \end{cases}$$

$$\begin{array}{c}\text{a \textit{collateral squeeze}}\\ \text{(a decrease in } K_{\rm b})\end{array} \begin{cases} \text{decreases } \gamma, \\ \text{decreases } \chi, \\ \text{increases } \mathfrak{r}_{\rm m}, \\ \text{decreases } \mathfrak{r}_{\rm b}.^{30} \end{cases}$$

Discussion. This simple model leaves a number of questions open. First, the equivalence of certification and intermediation, while a convenient feature, ought to be reexamined in broader setups. In practice, intermediation gives the intermediary more leeway in allocating the uninformed investors' funds. This leeway, unlike in this model, may aggravate moral hazard. On the other hand, the monitor can more easily enjoy the benefits of diversification under intermediation than under project finance, an issue which again does not arise in this basic model. Second, we have modeled intermediaries as being homogeneous, perhaps up to a scaling factor. In practice, there is a continuum of intermediaries with different monitoring intensities and accordingly with different stakes in the success of the firms they monitor.[31] Furthermore, the demand for various types of monitoring capital moves around with the economic cycle; in particular, firms that have gone through difficult times or face dim prospects need to resort to higher-intensity monitoring.

Third, and more importantly for the sake of this chapter, the story told here is inherently static. Comparative statics was performed on inherited levels of monitoring and entrepreneurial capitals. In practice,

28. We earlier stated that the distribution of $K_{\rm m}$ among intermediaries is irrelevant under some assumptions. Note, first, that individual intermediaries must invest $I_{\rm m}(\chi)$ in each of the monitored firms. One possibility is, thus, that each intermediary has capital equal to a multiple of $I_{\rm m}(\chi)$. If this "integer condition" is not satisfied, then some monitoring capital may be wasted. The analysis then becomes more cumbersome, but is not substantially altered. Second, and in reference to Section 4.2, if some individual intermediaries have more than $I_{\rm m}(\chi)$ and are each able to monitor multiple firms, then we implicitly rule out any ability to diversify. One may have in mind that intermediaries are specialized, in that the shocks faced by the firms they monitor are perfectly correlated (see Chapter 4). Again, this assumption is made for analytical convenience, and does not affect the analysis in a qualitative way.

29. The ratio $\mathfrak{r}_{\rm m}$ is a crude version of the Cooke ratio in banking regulation.

30. For completeness, a savings squeeze increases γ, decreases χ, increases $\mathfrak{r}_{\rm m}$ and $\mathfrak{r}_{\rm b}$.

31. An introduction to this issue can be found in Holmström and Tirole (1997).

there are subtle dynamic interactions between the two, with interesting leads and lags. A key item on the research agenda is to come up with a tractable dynamic version of this "double-decker model."

13.4 Dynamic Complementarities: Net Worth Effects, Poverty Traps, and the Financial Accelerator

This section returns to the "single-tier" structure (that is, it ignores monitoring and the issue of scarcity of monitoring capital studied in Section 13.3). It introduces dynamics and shows that corporate finance considerations lead to strong hysteresis effects[32] where there would be none in an (Arrow–Debreu) framework without agency cost.

13.4.1 Sources of Dynamic Complementarities

Two main sources of hysteresis have been studied in the literature.

Retained earnings/balance sheet effects. A firm coming out of a recession (with low profitability at date t) tends to lack resources to finance new investments. In the absence of agency cost, this lack of resources would have no impact on refinancing,[33] as forward-looking investors and managers would optimally focus on prospects and arrange the financing of positive-NPV projects. Not so in the presence of an agency cost. The latter creates scope for credit rationing, which implies that current profitability affects future investment and future activity (as we already observed in Chapter 5).

For example, if we assume that investments depreciate in one period and that the contracts between the firm and its investors are short-term contracts, in which the investors are repaid for their date-t investment out of the date-t profit (a strong assumption, as we noted in Chapter 5), and letting A_t, I_t, and y_t denote the assets, investment, and profit at date t, the mechanics of hysteresis can be schematically described in the following way:

$$y_t \to A_{t+1} \to I_{t+1} \to y_{t+1} \to A_{t+2} \to \cdots .$$

32. A hysteresis effect refers to the lagging of an effect behind its cause.

33. Unless the firm's low profitability at date t conveys negative information about its profitability at dates $t+1, t+2, \dots$.

New entrepreneurs' opportunities. Rather than focusing on balance sheet effects of *existing* firms, some models trace the source of hysteresis to the impact of existing activity on *would-be* entrepreneurs through factor prices. For example, these potential entrepreneurs may offer their labor to the incumbent firms before accumulating enough wealth to become entrepreneurs themselves. This idea is most easily analyzed in an overlapping-generations framework. In the two papers that initiated the literature on the topic—by Bernanke and Gertler (1989), the seminal formal study of the financial accelerator, and by Banerjee and Newman (1991, 1993)—the young work and thereby accumulate wealth, which they can use to start their own firm when they are older. A higher level of investment and activity at date t raises the demand for labor and thereby the wage w_t of laborers, who then have more resources, which facilitates their access to funding at date $t+1$. In Aghion and Bolton (1997), Piketty (1997), and Matsuyama (2000), by contrast, the effect operates through the interest rate rather than through wages.[34]

Relatedly, the literature has also emphasized the possibility that credit rationing traps either individuals (or families) or entire societies in poverty. We will accordingly provide examples of such individual and collective poverty traps.[35]

13.4.2 Dynamics of Wealth Distribution: A Tale of Two Families

First we provide an example of an individual (family) poverty trap. To develop this example, we will need the following preamble.

13.4.2.1 The Warm-Glow Model

We study long-lived lineages of short-lived family members. Parents become entrepreneurs if they

34. There are, of course, other reasons why current activity may affect the new entrepreneurs' ability to raise funding. For example, a high level of activity may increase tax receipts and boost public investment in infrastructure and thereby improve the profitability of new private investments. Or there may be spillovers and accumulation of social capital. But such sources of hysteresis are not related to corporate finance considerations (unless, say, the public infrastructure investment affects corporate governance, e.g., reduces B in the model).

35. See also Banerjee (2003) and Matsuyama (2005) for excellent discussions of poverty traps, including ones that are not based on credit rationing.

have sufficient funds, earn income, and finally leave wealth as a bequest to their children, who may then use this wealth to undertake projects of their own, and so forth. What motivates parents to leave money to their children is an important modeling choice. Parents who internalize the welfare of their children must also, at least indirectly, internalize that of their grandchildren, that of their great-grandchildren, and thus that of all members of the lineage. Their choice of bequest then resembles that of liquidity management by a long-lived individual unable to secure long-term finance (i.e., facing a sequence of short-term borrowing deals) (see Section 4.7.2). Such liquidity management is complex. For the purposes of this section, we first bypass the difficulty in a somewhat ad hoc way by using the warm-glow model, which enables us to discuss dynamics without worrying about dynamic programming. Namely, suppose that the following conditions hold.

- Individuals live for one period. An individual living at date t has exactly one heir who lives at date $t+1$, and so on.
- Individuals are "altruistic" in a rather specific way. Rather than caring about the utility of their heirs, they derive utility from the bequest they make to their heirs. We will assume that a generation-t individual derives utility from her own consumption c_t and from the bequest $\mathcal{L}_t$ to her heir.[36] Assume further that the utility function is a Cobb–Douglas utility function:

$$\left(\frac{c_t}{1-a}\right)^{1-a}\left(\frac{\mathcal{L}_t}{a}\right)^{a},$$

where $a \in (0,1)$ is the (impure) altruism parameter.[37]

Then the utility from income y_t is (taking logs)

$$\log U_t(y_t) = \max_{\{c_t,\mathcal{L}_t\}} \{(1-a)\log c_t + a\log \mathcal{L}_t\}$$

s.t.

$$c_t + \mathcal{L}_t = y_t.$$

This yields

$$c_t = (1-a)y_t \quad \text{and} \quad \mathcal{L}_t = ay_t,$$

and so

$$U_t(y_t) = y_t.$$

This formulation is particularly convenient since it allows us to keep our risk-neutral framework.

13.4.2.2 Lineages of Entrepreneurs in the Warm-Glow Model

Let us now consider a "warm-glow lineage" in which each generation t is a would-be entrepreneur, who

- is born with some exogenous endowment $\hat{A}$, to which is added the bequest $\mathcal{L}_{t-1}$ made by generation $t-1$;
- invests this total asset either in a storage technology yielding an interest rate equal to 0 (i.e., preserving the wealth) or in a fixed-size project as described in Section 13.2.1; and
- finally uses the proceed of this investment (her "income") for consumption c_t and bequest $\mathcal{L}_t$ to the next generation.

The timing is summarized in Figure 13.7.

Let us assume that the intraperiod rate of interest in the economy is equal to 0.[38]

As in the rest of the book, the private benefit B obtained by misbehaving is expressed in terms of money. So in the case of misbehavior the entrepreneur's utility from income y_t and private benefit B is $y_t + B$. As usual, we will assume that investment has a positive NPV if and only if the entrepreneur is induced to behave:

$$p_{\mathrm{H}}R > I > p_{\mathrm{L}}R + B.$$

It will also prove convenient to assume that success is a sure thing in the case of good behavior:[39]

$$p_{\mathrm{H}} = 1.$$

36. We do not use the notation "B_t" for bequest in order not to create confusion with private benefits. Rather, we build on the French terminology for bequest ("legs").

37. This modeling borrows from Aghion and Bolton (1997), Andreoni (1989), Banerjee (2002), Banerjee and Newman (1991, 1993), Galor and Zeira (1993), Matsuyama (2000, 2002), and Piketty (1997). See Bénabou and Tirole (2005) and the references therein for a discussion of the various motives behind altruistic and prosocial behaviors.

38. For example, there might be outside investors demanding a rate of interest equal to 0; or else there are enough would-be entrepreneurs who do not make it to entrepreneurship and are indifferent between using the storage technology and lending to entrepreneurs at rate of interest equal to 0.

39. If we did not make this assumption, then, under the assumptions made below, the fraction of entrepreneurs in the population would converge to 0 as t goes to ∞ since failing entrepreneurs would deprive their heirs of the opportunity to become entrepreneurs (to avoid this, one could for example assume that $\hat{A}$ is stochastic).

Of course, when $p_{\mathrm{H}} = 1$, the limited liability assumption cannot be motivated by large risk aversion for negative incomes. Relatedly, stiff

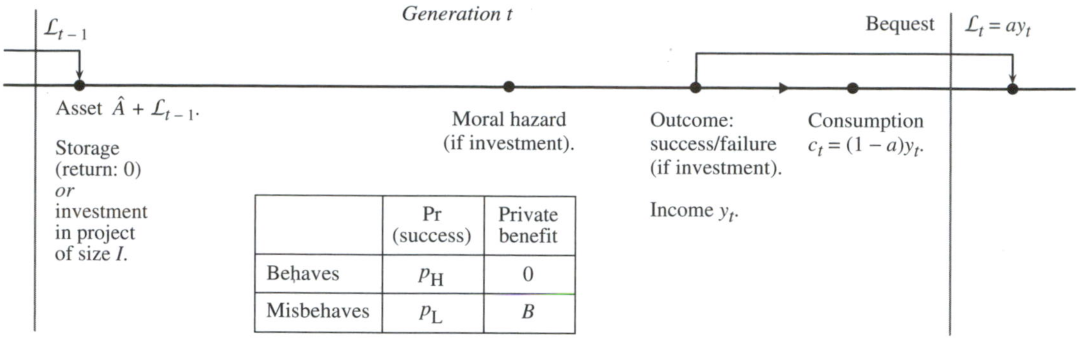

Figure 13.7

Lastly, let $\bar{A}$ be defined (as in equation (13.4)) by the equality between the pledgeable income and the investors' outlay:

$$p_H\left(R - \frac{B}{\Delta p}\right) = I - \bar{A}$$

or (using $p_H = 1$)

$$\bar{A} = I - \left(R - \frac{B}{\Delta p}\right).$$

The role of the following assumption will become clear shortly.

Assumption 13.1.

$$\frac{\hat{A} + a(R - I)}{1 - a} > \bar{A} > \frac{\hat{A}}{1 - a}.$$

(a) *Lineage stuck in a poverty trap.* Suppose that generation t receives bequest

$$\mathcal{L}_{t-1} < \bar{A} - \hat{A}.$$

Generation t's total wealth is then insufficient to have access to funds. Generation t must therefore invest $[\hat{A} + \mathcal{L}_{t-1}]$ into the low-return storage technology, and so

$$y_t = \hat{A} + \mathcal{L}_{t-1}.$$

With warm-glow preferences, bequests to generation $t + 1$ are

$$\mathcal{L}_t = ay_t = a(\hat{A} + \mathcal{L}_{t-1}),$$

and so generation $t + 1$ starts with

$$\hat{A} + \mathcal{L}_t = (1 + a)\hat{A} + a\mathcal{L}_{t-1} < (1 + a)\hat{A} + a(\bar{A} - \hat{A})$$

or

$$\hat{A} + \mathcal{L}_t < \hat{A} + a\bar{A} < \bar{A}$$

from Assumption 13.1.

The dynasty's total wealth per generation converges to $A_\infty < \bar{A}$, given by

$$A_\infty = \hat{A} + aA_\infty \quad \text{or} \quad A_\infty = \frac{\hat{A}}{1 - a} < \bar{A}.$$

The lineage is stuck in a poverty trap.

(b) *Rich, entrepreneurial lineage.* By contrast, suppose that generation t's initial wealth exceeds $\bar{A}$:

$$\mathcal{L}_{t-1} > \bar{A} - \hat{A} \quad \text{or} \quad A_t \equiv \hat{A} + \mathcal{L}_{t-1} > \bar{A}.$$

Generation t has enough pledgeable income to offset the inventors' outlay $I - (\hat{A} + \mathcal{L}_{t-1})$. Under risk neutrality, generation t selects the highest NPV solution and therefore prefers becoming an entrepreneur to investing in the storage technology. The NPV is then

$$p_H R - I = R - I > 0,$$

and so the entrepreneur's end-of-period income after reimbursing lenders is

$$y_t = (R - I) + A_t$$

(recall that the capital market is competitive, and so the entire NPV goes to the entrepreneur).

Generation $(t + 1)$'s total wealth at the beginning of period $t + 1$ is therefore

$$A_{t+1} = \hat{A} + a(R - I + A_t).$$

Note that

$$A_{t+1} > \hat{A} + a(R - I + \bar{A}) > \bar{A}$$

from Assumption 13.1.

jail sentences for defaulting entrepreneurs would be optimal and solve the moral-hazard problem. Thus, the case $p_H = 1$ is best viewed as an approximation of economies in which p_H is large, but smaller than 1.

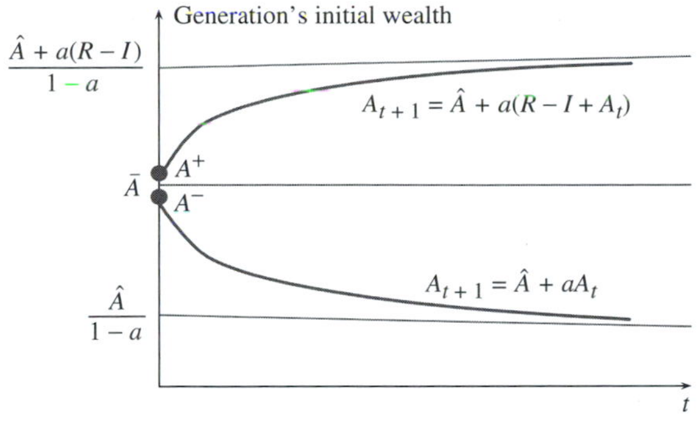
Generation's initial wealth
$\frac{\hat{A}+a(R-I)}{1-a}$
$A_{t+1}=\hat{A}+a(R-I+A_t)$
A^+
$\bar{A}$
A^-
$A_{t+1}=\hat{A}+aA_t$
$\frac{\hat{A}}{1-a}$
t

Figure 13.8

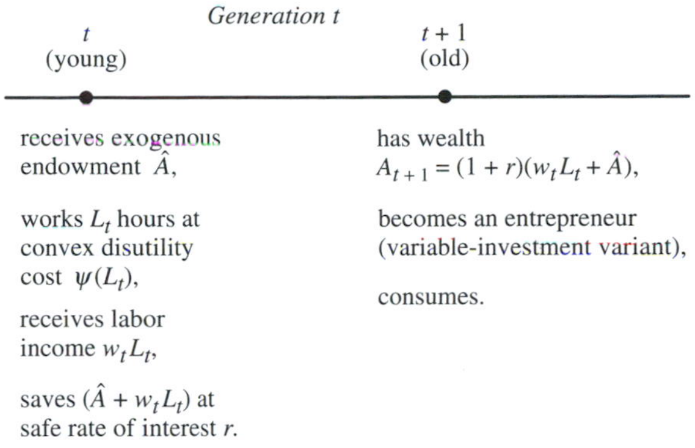
Generation t
t
(young)
$t+1$
(old)
receives exogenous endowment $\hat{A}$,
works L_t hours at convex disutility cost $\psi(L_t)$,
receives labor income w_tL_t,
saves $(\hat{A}+w_tL_t)$ at safe rate of interest r.
has wealth $A_{t+1}=(1+r)(w_tL_t+\hat{A})$,
becomes an entrepreneur (variable-investment variant),
consumes.

Figure 13.9

Hence, future generations also have the opportunity to become entrepreneurs.

The lineage's beginning-of-period wealth converges to A_∞, where

$$A_\infty = \hat{A} + a(R - I + A_\infty)$$

or

$$A_\infty = \frac{\hat{A} + a(R-I)}{1-a}.$$

Figure 13.8 illustrates cases (a) and (b) and shows that a small difference in initial wealth (points A^- and A^+, respectively, in Figure 13.8) can make a big difference: for the current generation (as we know from Chapter 3) and even more for further generations.

Note, finally, that in the Arrow–Debreu world of no agency cost ($B = 0$), long-term incomes of different lineages would converge to $[\hat{A} + a(R - I)]/(1 - a)$ regardless of the lineage's initial wealth (rather than diverge as in Figure 13.8). A stronger investor protection, for example, reduces the dependency on wealth and generates a more equal long-run income distribution.

Discussion of the warm-glow assumption. The warm-glow model does not depict true altruism since each generation does not perfectly internalize the welfare of the next generation. Rather, individuals are portrayed as deriving utility from feeling or looking generous; they care about what they give rather than about how useful this gift is to the next generation.

This impure-altruism assumption turns out to be rather important for the treatment above. By contrast, consider pure altruism: generation $(t-1)$ cares directly about generation t's welfare, U_t, rather than about the bequest $\mathcal{L}_{t-1}$. Then, starting at point A^- in Figure 13.8, a small increase in the bequest moving generation t's initial wealth to point A^+ increases U_t discontinuously, and so we would expect generation $(t-1)$ to increase its bequest so as to enable generation t to have access to financing. (This reasoning assumes that generations $t, t+1, \ldots$ still have warm-glow utilities. If they themselves are truly altruistic, the analysis has to be modified slightly, because the incentive compatibility constraints are a bit different—on this, see also the treatment in Section 4.7—but the basic insight is unaltered.)

13.4.3 Collective Poverty Traps

As was pointed out earlier, hysteresis due to financial imperfections may occur at the level of a society, and not only at that of a family. We here pursue the wage conduit (Banerjee and Newman 1993).

Consider an overlapping-generations model in which

- a generation lives for two periods,
- young agents work and accumulate wealth,
- old agents are entrepreneurs and consume.

The timing for generation t is described in Figure 13.9, which is rather self-explanatory. A few further details, though:

- The rate of interest, r, from one period to the next is exogenous.
- The technology available to (old) entrepreneurs is the variable-investment model of Section 3.4,

reviewed in Section 13.2 (with as usual $p_H R > 1 > p_H(R - B/\Delta p)$). Investment, effort, outcome, and consumption all occur within period $t+1$.

- Producing output requires 1 unit of labor per unit of investment (the technology is a Leontief one, in which factors are combined in fixed proportions).
- The population is constant. Hence, the number of young and old agents are equal at any given point in time.
- Generation t's utility is $-\psi(L_t) + c_{t+1}$, where c_{t+1} is its consumption when old.
- The disutility of labor satisfies $\psi(0) = \psi'(0) = 0$, $\psi' > 0$, $\psi'' > 0$.

The assumption that more investment requires more labor (one-for-one in this example) drives hysteresis: a higher wealth accumulation in the past together with capital market imperfections raises investment, and therefore increases the demand for labor and the wage as well. A higher wage results in higher wealth accumulation, more investment, and so forth.

Let us focus on *steady states*.

Consider first an entrepreneur. A generation-t agent becomes an entrepreneur at date $t+1$. She then invests I_{t+1} and receives the NPV:

$$U_{\mathrm{b}}^{t+1} = [p_H R - (1+w)]I_{t+1},$$

since now the unit cost includes the wage, w, per unit of investment.

The investment I_{t+1} is determined by the investors' breakeven condition:

$$(1+w)I_{t+1} - A_{t+1} \equiv p_H\left(R - \frac{B}{\Delta p}\right)I_{t+1},$$

where

$$A_{t+1} = (1+r)(wL_t + \hat{A})$$

is the wealth when old. Hence, the entrepreneur expected date-$(t+1)$ consumption is

$$U_{\mathrm{b}}^{t+1} = \left[\frac{p_H R - (1+w)}{(1+w) - p_H(R - B/\Delta p)}\right]A_{t+1}.$$

As expected, a higher labor cost w reduces both the NPV per unit of investment (the numerator in the fraction) and the borrowing capacity (through the denominator).

Let us now solve for the labor supply. The marginal cost at t, $\psi'(L_t)$, must equal the marginal benefit at $t+1$:

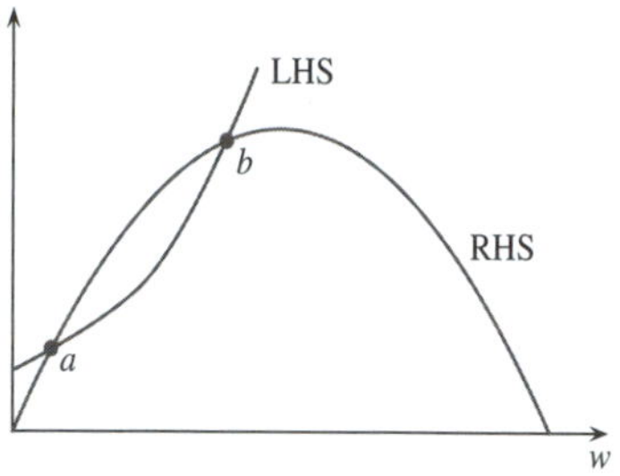

Figure 13.10

$$\frac{\mathrm{d}U_{\mathrm{b}}^{t+1}}{\mathrm{d}L_t} = \left[\frac{\mathrm{d}U_{\mathrm{b}}^{t+1}}{\mathrm{d}A_{t+1}}\right]\left[\frac{\mathrm{d}A_{t+1}}{\mathrm{d}L_t}\right].$$

Because

$$\frac{\mathrm{d}A_{t+1}}{\mathrm{d}L_t} = (1+r)w,$$

$$\psi'(L_t) = \left[\frac{p_H R - (1+w)}{(1+w) - p_H(R - B/\Delta p)}\right](1+r)w.$$

In steady state, and because the technology is a Leontief one,

$$L_t = L = I = I_{t+1},$$

and so

$$\psi'\left(\frac{(1+r)\hat{A}}{1 - wr - p_H(R - B/\Delta p)}\right) = \frac{p_H R - (1+w)}{(1+w) - p_H(R - B/\Delta p)}(1+r)w. \quad (13.12)$$

The left-hand side (LHS) of condition (13.12), is increasing in w (from a positive level at $w = 0$). Its right-hand side (RHS) is concave. The steady-state equilibria are depicted (for the case $\psi''' > 0$) in Figure 13.10.

In Figure 13.10, there are two steady-state equilibria (there can be more generally). The wage and activity are higher in equilibrium b than in equilibrium a.[40] Cycles can also exist.

More on the literature. Matsuyama (2004) shows that heterogeneous technologies may be conducive

40. It is unclear in the absence of further assumptions whether, as long as they belong to the increasing part of the RHS, equilibria with higher wages dominate those with lower ones. For, a generation maximizes $\{-\psi(L) + (\mathrm{RHS})(L + \hat{A}/w)\}$ over L. Hence,

$$\frac{\mathrm{d}U_{\mathrm{b}}^{t+1}}{\mathrm{d}w} = \left(L + \frac{\hat{A}}{w}\right)\frac{\mathrm{d(RHS)}}{\mathrm{d}w} - \frac{\hat{A}(\mathrm{RHS})}{w^2}.$$

The second term represents the reduced multiplier on the agents' exogenous endowment.

to the existence of multiple steady-state equilibria and of cycles. In his model, as in Banerjee and Newman, economic agents accumulate wealth by supplying their labor in the first period of their life. Their wage income is then saved for the second period of their life, in which they can become lenders or entrepreneurs. Entrepreneurs produce units of physical capital, which, combined with labor, produce a final output. Matsuyama's model is built so that, despite credit market imperfections, there exists a unique equilibrium (similar to the neoclassical growth model equilibrium) when entrepreneurs face a unique production technology. Matsuyama then introduces a choice of technology in order to analyze composition effects. Suppose, for example, that there exist two technologies: a high-return/low-pledgeable-income technology and a low-return/high-pledgeable-income one. Multiple steady-state equilibria may then coexist: in a low-capital-intensity steady state, the wage of the young is low; and so their net worth when they build on that wage to become entrepreneurs is small. They consequently invest in a low-return/high-pledgeable-income technology that produces little capital. The dearth of capital generates a low wage for the next generation; and so forth. Matsuyama also demonstrates the possibility of credit cycles.

Aghion et al. (1999) explore the interest rate conduit and show how it may lead to real activity cycles. When entrepreneurs' borrowing capacity is low relative to savings, the interest rate falls. Entrepreneurs then need to reimburse less to allow investors to recoup interest and principal on their loans. Entrepreneurs then rebuild their net worth and increase their investments. This raises the demand for loans and puts pressure on the interest rate, increasing the entrepreneurs' debt burden, and so forth.[41]

13.5 Dynamic Substitutabilities: The Deflationary Impact of Past Investment

Section 13.4 emphasized dynamic complementarities: past investment raises the net worth of existing or would-be entrepreneurs, and thereby relaxes their current borrowing constraint, boosting investment today. Such dynamic complementarities can arise either at the level of families or at the country level.

By fixing the output price, though, the analysis of Section 13.4 neglected an obvious source of dynamic substitutability: in any given industry, an investment glut yesterday has a depressing effect on product prices and discourages investment today. This basic effect operates whether today's entrepreneurs are credit rationed or not; but under some circumstances, the contractionary impact is stronger when firms are credit rationed.

13.5.1 Heuristics

To obtain some first intuition as to how past investment crowds out current investment, let us start with a static model, with first a fixed investment, and then variable investment.

13.5.1.1 Fixed Investment Size

Consider, thus, the fixed-investment model. There is a mass 1 of entrepreneurs. At investment cost I, an entrepreneur can produce R units of a good with probability p (and 0 units with probability $1 - p$). The final price per unit of output is P. Presumably, P depends on past industry investment, but we do not need to go into detail at this stage. The probability of success is p_{H} if the entrepreneur behaves (no private benefit) and $p_{\text{L}} = p_{\text{H}} - \Delta p$ if she misbehaves (private benefit B). We assume that the output realizations are independent across entrepreneurs (there is no aggregate uncertainty); this assumption is consistent with the assumption made above that the output price is deterministic.

Entrepreneurs are risk neutral and are protected by limited liability. The distribution of assets in the population of entrepreneurs is given by the cumulative distribution function $G(A)$ on $[0, \infty)$. Investors are risk neutral and demand rate of return equal to 0. Assume that it is optimal to provide the entrepreneurs with incentives to behave.

Varying P, let us compare the level of *aggregate* investment under credit rationing ($B > 0$) and in its absence ($B = 0$), and show that the first- and second-best levels of investment are as depicted in Figure 13.11.

41. See Aghion et al. (2004) for further work on cycles driven by the interest rate conduit.

Further examples of cycles created by credit rationing are investigated in the next section and in Chapter 14.

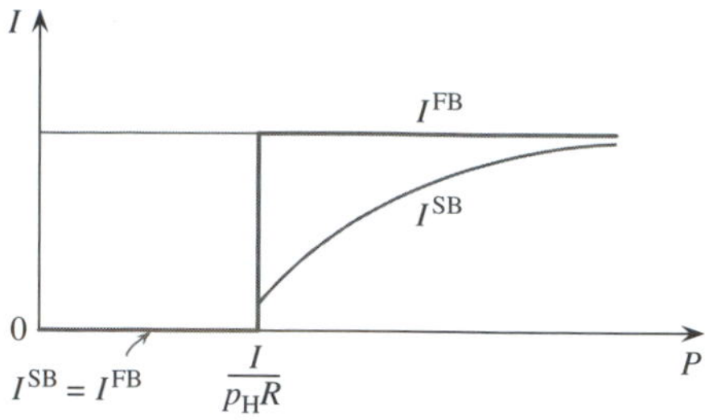

Figure 13.11

Conditional on receiving financing, an entrepreneur's incentive constraint is

$$(\Delta p)R_b \geqslant B,$$

and so the financing condition can be written as $A \geqslant \bar{A}$, where

$$p_H\left[PR - \frac{B}{\Delta p}\right] = I - \bar{A}.$$

The fraction of entrepreneurs who are able to raise funds is

$$X \equiv 1 - G\left(I - p_H\left[PR - \frac{B}{\Delta p}\right]\right), \qquad (13.13)$$

or, equivalently, total investment is[42]

$$I^{SB} = XI,$$

as long as the NPV is positive, i.e., as long as

$$p_H PR - I \geqslant 0.$$

In the positive-NPV range ($P \geqslant I/p_H R$), aggregate investment increases with P as long as $B > 0$. Whether the impact of P on aggregate investment increases with B depends on the derivative of the density. But, as is easily seen in Figure 13.11, *aggregate investment is always more responsive to the output price under credit rationing than with no (or little) credit rationing*, since investment does not move with the output price in this range in the absence of credit rationing.

This illustrates the *net worth effect*: when industry profitability increases, boosting both the pledgeable income and the NPV, and for a given investment level (which is the case here since projects have a fixed size), more and more firms pass the solvency test and get access to financing. This explains the higher responsiveness of investment under financial constraints in the positive-NPV region. As far as investment is concerned, a unit increase in P is tantamount to a uniform increase $p_H R$ in net worths (A).

To complete this analysis, we can now endogenize the product price by assuming the existence of a prior "fraction"[43] X_0 of similar firms that were able to raise financing in the past. The output price is then a decreasing function of total output, $p_H(X_0 + X)R$:[44]

$$P = P(p_H(X_0 + X)R) \quad \text{with } P' < 0. \qquad (13.14)$$

An equilibrium is then a "level of investment" XI, where X is obtained from (13.13) and (13.14):

$$X = 1 - G\left(I - p_H\left(P(p_H(X_0 + X)R)R - \frac{B}{\Delta p}\right)\right).$$

Note that as X_0 grows, X must decrease (a crowding-out effect (if X increased, then P would decrease, and so X would decrease after all)) but $X_0 + X$ must increase (there is less than full crowding out (if $X_0 + X$ decreased, then P would increase, and X would increase after all)).

The increased sensitivity of investment under credit rationing, however, is not a general conclusion, as can also be seen from Figure 13.11. A small increase in P from the negative-NPV to the positive-NPV region raises the first-best investment dramatically, but the second-best one less so as not all firms get on board. The effect in force here will become clear in the variable-investment version that we study now.

13.5.1.2 Variable Investment Size

Next consider the variable-investment model of Section 3.4: the number of units of output produced in the case of success is RI, the private benefit in the case of misbehavior BI. To be incentivized to behave, an entrepreneur with investment size I must receive R_b in the case of success, such that

$$(\Delta p)R_b \geqslant BI.$$

42. "SB" refers to the "second best," that is, to the situation in which agency costs ($B > 0$) lead to credit rationing. By contrast, "FB" will refer to the "first best," that is, to a situation in which there are no agency costs ($B = 0$) and therefore no credit rationing.

43. If previous-generation entrepreneurs have mass exceeding 1, then X_0 can be greater than 1.

44. We slightly abuse notation by using the same letter P for the price function and its realization.

For a given output price P, an entrepreneur with assets A can borrow up to the level at which pledgeable income is equal to investors' outlay:

$$p_H\left(PR - \frac{B}{\Delta p}\right)I = I - A$$

or

$$I = \frac{A}{1 + (p_H B/\Delta p) - p_H PR}.$$

Assuming, without loss of generality,[45] that all entrepreneurs have the same net worth A, let us analyze the impact of a prior level of investment I_0 on current investment. Total output is then $p_H R(I_0 + I)$. Because

$$P = P(p_H R(I_0 + I)), \quad \text{with } P' < 0,$$

$$I = I^{SB} = \frac{A}{1 + (p_H B/\Delta p) - p_H P(p_H R(I_0 + I))R}. \tag{13.15}$$

By the same reasoning as in the fixed-investment version, condition (13.15) implies that previous investment partially crowds out current investment:

$$-1 < \frac{\partial I^{SB}}{\partial I_0} < 0.$$

Let us now compare this sensitivity to that obtained in the absence of credit rationing. In this first-best benchmark, firms maximize their NPV, regardless of their solvency:

$$\max_I \{(p_H PR - 1)I\}.$$

Competitive equilibrium in this constant-returns-to-scale environment implies that unit revenue is equal to unit cost, or

$$p_H P(p_H R(I_0 + I))R = 1. \tag{13.16}$$

Thus, in the absence of credit constraint, past investment fully crowds out current investment:

$$\frac{\partial I}{\partial I_0} = -1.$$

This is due to what might be labeled a *hindering effect of credit rationing*: because part of the benefit from investment expansion accrues to the entrepreneurs and is therefore nonpledgeable, investors are less keen than entrepreneurs to expand as the market becomes more profitable. And so credit rationing may make investment relatively less responsive to market conditions.

Exercise 13.3 pursues this analysis in the intermediate context of variable investment and decreasing returns to scale.

13.5.2 Investment Glut and Dearth Cycles

Let us embed these ideas into a full-fledged dynamic model with overlapping generations of entrepreneurs. The analysis in this section follows that of Suarez and Sussman (1997). The model for each generation is taken to be the constant-returns-to-scale variable-size version.

Generation-t entrepreneurs have mass 1 and are born with net worth A each. They live for two periods, t and $t + 1$. The representative generation-t entrepreneur invests I_t at date t. Production occurs, with an output proportional to I_t, at dates t and $t + 1$. We make the following assumption.

Assumption 13.2 (time to build). *At date t, only a fraction $\theta < 1$ of investment I_t is operational. The output is $\theta R I_t$ with probability p_1 and 0 with probability $1 - p_1$. By contrast, the investment becomes fully operational and yields RI_t with probability p_2 and 0 with probability $1 - p_2$ in the second period of its life (that is, at date $t + 1$). The investment fully depreciates (is useless) after $t + 1$.*

Assumption 13.2 expresses the existence of a time to build if $p_2 \geqslant p_1$ (otherwise, expected output could be greater in the first period of the investment). We therefore assume that, in the absence of moral hazard,

$$p_1 = p_2 = p_H.$$

Let us now introduce moral hazard. Quite generally, a generation-t entrepreneur may misbehave at date t (reduce p_1) and at date $t + 1$ (reduce p_2). The reader can follow the steps of the analysis in Section 4.2 to solve for this general case. Because this does not affect the results, we will look at the slightly simpler case of "increasing moral hazard." That is, reflecting the fact that the future is more foreseeable and contractible at short horizons, we assume that moral hazard is more substantial in the second period. Indeed, we assume this in an extreme form: there is no moral hazard in the first period of production, $p_1 = p_H$, and so the date-t income,

45. Recall that with constant returns to scale, all firms are identical up to a scale factor. Put differently, only total net worth matters.

$(p_H \theta R I_t)P_t$, where P_t is the date-t output price, is fully pledgeable to investors. By contrast, date-$(t+1)$ production involves an agency cost: $p_2 \in \{p_L, p_H\}$. The project yields RI_t with probability p_L (the private benefit is then BI_t) or p_H (there is no private benefit). To incentivize the entrepreneur, the latter must receive R_b in case of period-$(t+1)$ success, where

$$(\Delta p)R_b \geqslant BI_t,$$

with $\Delta p \equiv p_H - p_L$.

The financing condition for the generation-t representative entrepreneur is that the pledgeable income exceeds the investors' outlay. If β denotes the discount factor between periods (for investors and entrepreneurs), this condition can be written as

$$\left[p_H \theta R P_t + \beta p_H \left(R P_{t+1} - \frac{B}{\Delta p}\right)\right] I_t \geqslant I_t - A,$$

and so, provided that the NPV per unit of investment is positive, i.e.,

$$(\theta P_t + \beta P_{t+1}) p_H R > 1,$$

the date-t investment is given by

$$\begin{aligned} I_t &\equiv \frac{A}{[1 + \beta p_H B/\Delta p] - [(\theta P_t + \beta P_{t+1}) p_H R]} \\ &\equiv \mathcal{I}(\theta P_t + \beta P_{t+1}), \quad \text{with } \mathcal{I}' > 0. \end{aligned} \tag{13.17}$$

For the sake of comparison, the investment in the absence of credit rationing would maximize the NPV, and so, under constant returns to scale, the unit revenue must be equal to the unit cost in competitive equilibrium:[46]

$$(\theta P_t + \beta P_{t+1}) p_H R = 1. \tag{13.18}$$

In either case (credit rationing or lack thereof), the output price is given by an inverse demand function for the good:[47]

$$P_t = P((\theta I_t + I_{t-1}) p_H R), \quad \text{with } P' < 0. \tag{13.19}$$

The interesting case arises when we make the following assumption.

46. For the moment, we ignore the possibility that investment at date t be equal to 0.

47. Consumers/investors have intertemporal utility

$$\sum_{t \geqslant 0} \beta^t [c_t + \phi(z_t)],$$

where z_t is their consumption of the good in question, c_t is their consumption of numeraire, and ϕ is increasing and concave. Then the inverse demand function is given by $P(z_t) \equiv \phi'(z_t) = P_t$.

Assumption 13.3. $\beta < \theta$.

This assumption states that enough of the investment becomes operational in the first period of its life that the "short-term" price (P_t) matters more than the "long-term" price (P_{t+1}) in the determination of the generation-t investment I_t, whether there is credit rationing ((13.17) holds) or not ((13.18) holds).

Let us show that, under this assumption, the dynamic equilibrium is stationary in the absence of credit rationing, but that it may take the form of an investment (and output) cycle under credit rationing.

13.5.2.1 Absence of Credit Rationing

Let P^* be the stationary price that satisfies the free-entry condition (13.18),

$$(\theta + \beta) P^* p_H R = 1,$$

and let $\hat{P}_t \equiv P_t - P^*$ and $\hat{P}_{t+1} \equiv P_{t+1} - P^*$.

Equation (13.18) yields

$$\hat{P}_{t+1} = -\frac{\theta}{\beta} \hat{P}_t,$$

and, because $\theta/\beta > 1$, a nonstationary price series would diverge. Thus, the only equilibrium with positive investment in each period[48] is a stationary one:

$$P_t = P^* \quad \text{for all } t.$$

13.5.2.2 Credit Rationing

Under credit rationing, investment is given by (13.17). A *two-period cycle*[49] $\{(I^+, P^+), (I^-, P^-)\}$ satisfies

$$I^+ = \mathcal{I}(\theta P^+ + \beta P^-) > I^- = \mathcal{I}(\theta P^- + \beta P^+),$$
$$P^+ = P((\theta I^+ + I^-) p_H R) > P^- = P((\theta I^- + I^+) p_H R).$$

48. There also exists a cycle in which investment occurs every other period. That is, $I_t = I^+$ and $P_t = P^+$ in even periods, say, and $I_t = 0$ and $P_t = P^-$ in odd periods, where

$$(\theta P^+ + \beta P^-) p_H R = 1,$$
$$P^+ \equiv P(\theta I p_H R) > P^- \equiv P(I p_H R).$$

Note that, because $\theta > \beta$,

$$(\theta P^- + \beta P^+) p_H R < 1,$$

and so there is indeed no investment in odd periods.

49. By Sarkovskii's Theorem (see, for example, Theorem 4.3 in Grandmont 1985) cycles of order 2 are in general the "easiest to obtain," then come other cycles with an even period, and finally cycles with an odd-period, three-period cycles being the last to appear.

Such a cycle exists provided that the price and investment functions are "reactive" enough.[50]

13.6 Exercises

Exercise 13.1 (improved governance). There are two dates, $t = 0, 1$, and a continuum of mass 1 of firms. Firms are identical except for the initial wealth A initially owned by their entrepreneur. A is distributed according to continuous cumulative distribution $G(A)$ with density $g(A)$ on $[0, I]$.

Each entrepreneur has a fixed-size project, and must invest I, and therefore borrow $I - A$, at date 0 in order to undertake it. Those entrepreneurs who do not invest themselves, invest their wealth in other firms. The savings function of nonentrepreneurs (consumers) is an increasing function $S(r)$, where r is the interest rate, with $S(r) = 0$ for $r < 0$ (so total savings equal $S(r)$ plus the wealth of unfinanced entrepreneurs). Entrepreneurs have utility $c_0 + c_1$ from consumptions c_0 and c_1.

A project, if financed, yields $R > 0$ at date 1 with probability p and 0 with probability $1 - p$. The probability of success is p_{H} if the entrepreneur works and $p_{\mathrm{L}} = p_{\mathrm{H}} - \Delta p$ if she shirks. The entrepreneur obtains private benefit B by shirking and 0 otherwise. Assume $p_{\mathrm{H}}R > I > p_{\mathrm{H}}(R - B/\Delta p)$, that financing cannot occur if the entrepreneur is provided with incentives to misbehave, and that the equilibrium interest rate is strictly positive.

(i) What is the pledgeable income? Write the financing condition.

(ii) Give the expression determining the market rate of interest. How does this interest rate change when improved investor protection lowers B?

Exercise 13.2 (dynamics of income inequality). (This exercise builds on the analysis of Section 13.4 and on Matsuyama (2000).)

50. Let $\hat{P}^+ \equiv P^+ - P^{**}$ and $\hat{P}^- \equiv P^- - P^{**}$, where P^{**} is the steady-state price corresponding to equations (13.17) and (13.19). The local mapping from, say, $\hat{P}^+$ into itself around $\hat{P}^+ = 0$ has slope

$$\left[\frac{P'\mathcal{I}'(p_{\mathrm{H}}R)(\theta(1+\beta))}{1 - P'\mathcal{I}'(p_{\mathrm{H}}R)(\theta^2 + \beta)}\right]^2.$$

Because $P'\mathcal{I}' < 0$ and $\theta^2 + \beta < \theta(1+\beta)$ from Assumption 13.3, this slope is greater than 1 provided $P'\mathcal{I}'$ is sufficiently large at P^{**}.

(i) Consider the "warm-glow" model: generations are indexed by $t = 0, 1, \dots, \infty$. Each generation lives for one period; each individual has exactly one heir. A generation-t individual has utility from consumption c_t and bequest $\mathcal{L}_t$ equal to

$$\left(\frac{c_t}{1-a}\right)^{1-a}\left(\frac{\mathcal{L}_t}{a}\right)^a$$

with $0 < a < 1$.

What is the individual's utility from income y_t?

(ii) Consider the entrepreneurship model of Section 13.4, with two twists:

- variable-size investment (instead of a fixed-size one),
- intraperiod rate of interest r (so investors demand $(1 + r)$ times their outlay, in expectation); r is assumed constant for simplicity.

One will assume that $p_{\mathrm{H}} = 1$ and that each generation t is born with endowment $\hat{A}$ (to which is added bequest $\mathcal{L}_{t-1}$, so $A_t = \hat{A} + \mathcal{L}_{t-1}$). See Figure 13.12.

A successful project delivers $RI \geqslant (1 + r)I$, an unsuccessful one 0. The private benefit from misbehaving, BI, is also proportional to investment.

Let

$$\rho_1 \equiv R \quad \text{and} \quad \rho_0 \equiv R - \frac{B}{\Delta p}.$$

Assume that

$$a(\rho_1 - \rho_0) < 1 - \frac{\rho_0}{1 + r}.$$

Show that each dynasty's long-term wealth converges to

$$A_\infty \equiv \frac{\hat{A}}{1 - a(\rho_1 - \rho_0)/(1 - \rho_0/(1 + r))},$$

regardless of its initial total wealth A_0 (that is, $\hat{A}$ plus the bequest from generation -1, if any).

(iii) Now assume that there is a minimal investment scale $\underline{I} > 0$ below which nothing can be produced. For $I \geqslant \underline{I}$, the technology is as above (constant returns to scale, profit RI in the case of success, private benefit BI in the case of misbehavior, etc.).

Compute the threshold A_0^* under which the dynasty remains one of lenders (at rate r) and never makes it to entrepreneurship.

What is the limit wealth A_∞^{L} of these poor dynasties? (The limit wealth of dynasties starting with $A_0 \geqslant A_0^*$ is still A_∞.)

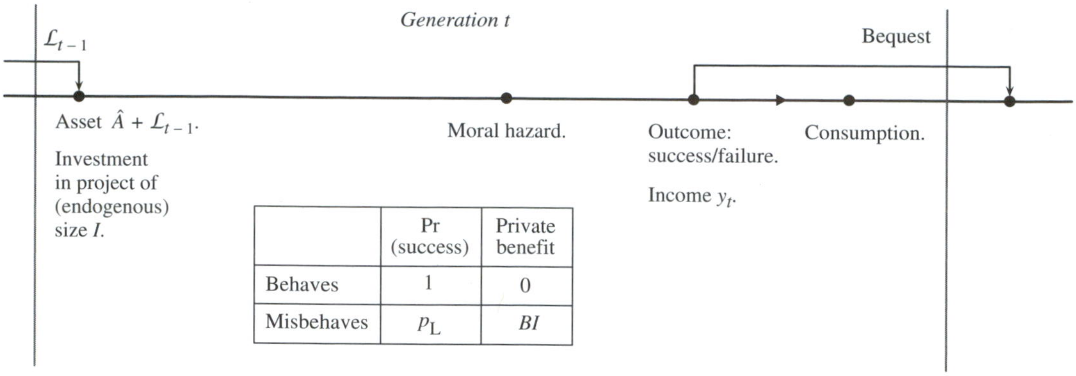

Figure 13.12

(iv) Finally, close the model by assuming that investors are domestic investors and by describing the equilibrium in the loan market. Focus on *steady states*. Show that multiple steady states may coexist:

- one in which everyone (investors, entrepreneurs) has the same wealth and

$$\rho_1 = 1 + r,$$

- others, with unequal wealth distribution, in which $\rho_1 > 1 + r$, a fraction κ of the population is poor (lends), and a fraction $1 - \kappa$ is rich (borrows to undertake projects).

Exercise 13.3 (impact of market conditions with and without credit rationing). This analysis pursues that of Section 13.5.1. There, we compared the sensitivity of investment with the output price (or installed-base investment) in the presence or absence of credit rationing, focusing on either the fixed-investment variant or the constant-returns-to-scale variant. We now assume decreasing returns to scale.

The representative entrepreneur (there is a unit mass of such entrepreneurs) has initial wealth A, is risk neutral and protected by limited liability, and invests $I + K$, where I is the scale of investment and K a fixed cost that is unrelated to scale. We assume that $K \geqslant A$, and so investors are unable to finance by themselves even a small investment.

An entrepreneur is successful with probability p and fails with probability $1 - p$. We assume that the shocks faced by the entrepreneurs are independent.

This hypothesis is consistent with the assumption made below that the output price is deterministic. When successful, the entrepreneur produces $R(I)$ units of a good (with $R(0) = 0$, $R' > 0$, $R'' < 0$, $R'(0) = \infty$, $R'(\infty) = 0$); an entrepreneur who fails produces nothing. For concreteness, let

$$R(I) = I^{\alpha}, \quad \text{with } 0 < \alpha < 1.$$

As usual, the probability of success is endogenous: $p \in \{p_L, p_H\}$. Misbehavior, $p = p_L$ (respectively, good behavior, $p = p_H$), brings about private benefit BI (respectively, no private benefit). To prevent moral hazard, the entrepreneur must receive reward R_b in the case of success, such that

$$(\Delta p) R_b \geqslant BI.$$

The product sells at price P per unit. Presumably, investors are risk neutral and demand rate of return 0.

Suppose that the fixed cost K is "not too large" (so that the entrepreneur wants to invest in the absence of credit rationing), and that

$$\frac{p_H B}{\Delta p} < \frac{1 - \alpha}{\alpha}.$$

(i) Derive the first- and second-best investment levels as functions of P. Show that they coincide for $P \geqslant P_0$ for some P_0.

(ii) Using a diagram, argue that there exists a region of output prices in which the second-best investment is more responsive than the first-best investment to the output price.

(iii) How would you analyze the impact of the existence of an installed-base level of investment I_0?

References

Aghion, P. and P. Bolton. 1997. A theory of trickle-down growth and development. *Review of Economic Studies* 64: 151–172.

Aghion, P., P. Bacchetta, and A. Banerjee. 2004. Financial development and the instability of open economies. *Journal of Monetary Economics* 51:1077–1106.

Aghion, P., A. Banerjee, and T. Piketty. 1999. Dualism and macroeconomic volatility. *Quarterly Journal of Economics* 114:1359–1397.

Akerlof, G. 1970. The market for lemons, qualitative uncertainty and the market mechanism. *Quarterly Journal of Economics* 84:488–500.

An, M. 1998. Logconcavity versus logconvexity: a complete characterization. *Journal of Economic Theory* 80:350–369.

Andreoni, J. 1989. Giving with impure altruism: applications to charity and Ricardian equivalence. *Journal of Political Economy* 97:1447–1458.

Banerjee, A. 2003. Contracting constraints, credit markets, and economic development. In *Advances in Economic Theory: Proceedings of the Eighth World Congress of the Econometric Society* (ed. M. Dewatripont, L. Hansen, and S. Turnovski), pp. 1–46. Cambridge University Press.

Banerjee, A. V. and A. F. Newman. 1991. Risk-bearing and the theory of income distribution. *Review of Economic Studies* 58:211–255.

——. 1993. Occupational choice and the process of development. *Journal of Political Economy* 101:274–298.

Bénabou, R. and J. Tirole. 2005. Incentives and prosocial behavior. Mimeo, Princeton University and IDEI, Toulouse.

Bernanke, B. 1983. Nonmonetary effects of the financial crisis in the propagation of the great depression. *American Economic Review* 80:257–276.

Bernanke, B. and M. Gertler. 1989. Agency costs, net worth and business fluctuations. *American Economic Review* 79: 14–31.

Bernanke, B., M. Gertler, and S. Gilchrist. 1999. The financial accelerator in a quantitative business cycle framework. In *Handbook of Macroeconomics* (ed. J. Taylor and M. Woodford), Volume 1C, Chapter 21. Amsterdam: North-Holland.

Cooper, R. and A. John. 1988. Coordinating coordination failures in Keynesian models. *Quarterly Journal of Economics* 102:441–464.

Davis, P. and C. Ioannidis. 2003. Does the availability of bank borrowing and bond issuance smooth overall corporate financing? Mimeo, Brunel University.

Dewatripont, M. and J. Tirole. 1994. *The Prudential Regulation of Banks.* Cambridge, MA: MIT Press.

Diamond, P. 1982. Aggregate demand in search equilibrium. *Journal of Political Economy* 90:881–894.

Fama, E. 1985. What's different about banks? *Journal of Monetary Economics* 15:29–39.

Fisher, I. 1933. The debt-deflation theory of great depressions. *Econometrica* 1:337–357.

Friedman, M. and A. Schwartz. 1963. *A Monetary History of the United States, 1870–1960.* Princeton University Press.

Galor, O. and Zeira, J. 1993. Income distribution and macroeconomics. *Review of Economic Studies* 60:35–52.

Grandmont, J. M. 1985. On endogenous competitive business cycles. *Econometrica* 53:995–1046.

Holmström, B. and J. Tirole. 1997. Financial intermediation, loanable funds, and the real sector. *Quarterly Journal of Economics* 112:663–692.

Jaffee, D. and T. Russell. 1976. Imperfect information, uncertainty, and credit rationing. *Quarterly Journal of Economics* 90:651–666.

James, C. 1987. Some evidence on the uniqueness of bank loans. *Journal of Financial Economics* 19:217–235.

Jullien, B. 2000. Participation constraints in adverse selection models. *Journal of Economic Theory* 93:1–47.

King, M. 1994. Debt deflation: theory and evidence. *European Economic Review* 38:419–445.

Mankiw, G. 1986. The allocation of credit and financial collapse. *Quarterly Journal of Economics* 101:455–470.

Mas Colell, A., M. Whinston, and J. Green. 1995. *Microeconomic Theory.* Oxford University Press.

Matsuyama, K. 1991. Increasing returns, industrialization and indeterminacy of equilibrium. *Quarterly Journal of Economics* 106:617–650.

——. 2000. Endogenous inequality. *Review of Economic Studies* 67:743–760.

——. 2002. Good and bad investment: an inquiry into the causes of credit cycles. Mimeo, Northwestern University.

——. 2004. Credit traps and credit cycles. Mimeo, Northwestern University.

——. 2005. Poverty trap. In *New Palgrave Dictionary of Economics* (ed. S. Durlauf and L. Blume), 2nd edn. Palgrave Macmillan.

Piketty, T. 1997. The dynamics of the wealth distribution and the interest rate with credit rationing. *Review of Economic Studies* 64:173–189.

Repullo, R. and J. Suarez. 2000. Entrepreneurial moral hazard and bank monitoring: a model of the credit channel. *European Economic Review* 44:1931–1950.

Shleifer, A. 1986. Implementation cycles. *Journal of Political Economy* 94:1163–1190.

Stiglitz, J. and A. Weiss. 1981. Credit rationing in markets with imperfect information. *American Economic Review* 71:393-410.

Suarez, I. and O. Sussman. 1997. Endogenous cycles in a Stiglitz-Weiss economy. *Journal of Economic Theory* 76: 47–71.

14

Mergers and Acquisitions, and the Equilibrium Determination of Asset Values

14.1 Introduction

Capital reallocations across firms serve several purposes. First, and foremost, they move assets from low-productivity uses to higher-productivity ones. There is indeed much empirical evidence in support of the view that capital transactions reflect capital productivity differences between the seller and the acquirer (see, for example, Maksimovic and Phillips 2001; Schoar 2002). Second, and as stressed in several chapters in this book,[1] asset sales may be driven by managerial discipline and concerns surrounding the creation of pledgeable income: management is forced to part with the assets in bankruptcy or when the firm is short of liquidity.

Capital reallocations across firms occur either wholesale, through mergers and acquisitions (M&As) in which the transfer of financial claims brings along that of the underlying assets, or piecewise, through the sale of property, plant, and equipment (the latter transactions tend to be smaller, but dominate M&As because they are also more frequent). Eisfeldt and Rampini's (2003) empirical work shows that such capital reallocations are procyclical even though the gains to capital reallocation, as measured by the cross-sectional deviation of capital productivity, are countercyclical.

This chapter analyzes demand and supply in the market for corporate assets. It studies the determinants of secondary market asset prices and thereby the two-way interaction between *ex ante* borrowing capacity and *ex post* transaction prices. The possibility for the lenders to seize the borrowers' assets in the case of distress or merely to resell these assets in less strenuous times enhances the latter's borrowing capacity. Thus, an important step in credit analysis is the assessment of the value of collateral. Lenders must figure out how much they will recoup from the sale of secured assets (or, occasionally, from managing the assets themselves). Shareholders must similarly extrapolate the return that they will obtain by letting the firm be partly or fully acquired by another corporate entity.

A proper analysis of the return attached to financial claims on the firm must reflect the observation that the relevant collateral value for the lenders is not the average value of the asset over all possible states of nature; for, collateral is seized in the case of distress and so the relevant value of the assets for the lenders is their resale value in bad states of nature.[2] This resale value may differ from the average value because of a correlation between the conditions that gave rise to distress and the external demand for the assets.[3] When distress is caused by industry-wide conditions rather than by firm-idiosyncratic shocks, the assets are unlikely to yield much profit to potential buyers and therefore to fetch a high price. Relatedly, the lenders ought to anticipate the business cycle. A secured loan with maturity of two years may generate a seizure of the

1. See, in particular, the material on collateral pledging in Chapter 3, on liquidity in Chapter 5, and on contingent rights in Chapter 10.

2. Similarly, from the point of view of the borrower's incentives, the relevant value of the assets is their value for the borrower in good states of nature.

3. Another reason why the resale value may differ from the average value is that the borrower may privately receive signals that indicate the imminence of distress. The borrower then has low incentives to maintain assets in good condition as there is a high probability that the assets will be transferred to the lenders. Loan agreements generally impose covenants on the maintenance of secured assets, but they cannot fully prevent some amount of asset depletion just before distress. Asset values may therefore be low in the case of distress for this reason. See Exercise 4.1 for an analysis of credit rationing when assets can be depleted just before distress.

collateralized assets two years from now. The value of the assets as collateral thus depends on the state of the economy two years from now. The stakes involved in properly forecasting asset values can be high. For example, London commercial real estate rental rates fell by 40% between 1990 and 1992, and similar (although more moderate) shocks have occurred in most developed countries. Banks which have tried to seize real estate of companies in distress have found that they were getting low collateral values.

This chapter discusses two innovative contributions by Shleifer and Vishny (1992) and Kiyotaki and Moore (1997), and follow-up work, that go beyond these simple observations by explicitly modeling the feedback between collateral value and investment. Those are equilibrium models: investment depends on collateral value (as in Chapter 4), but in turn a firm's collateral value depends on the level of investment and financial choices by other firms (the firm's environment).

In Shleifer and Vishny (1992), studied in Section 14.2, the relevant environment is the *industry*. Assets are fairly specialized and have value only to other firms in the industry, which have invested in knowledge and are able to operate them. The value of collateral, and thus a firm's borrowing capacity, then hinges on whether there will be other firms in the industry standing by to purchase the assets in the case of distress.[4] In turn, these other firms' value of collateral and incentive to invest depend on whether the firm under consideration is investing. Shleifer and Vishny thus demonstrate the existence of a strategic complementarity[5] between the firms' investments. Consequently, a firm's very existence may enhance the value of other firms' assets and raise these firms' incentives to be present in the industry.

This leads us to a broader discussion of (a) the possibility that firms build, perhaps excessive, "financial muscle," an issue that does not arise in the basic model; (b) other investment design choices by firms that may later enter M&A deals. On the latter issue, it is shown that, for the same reasons that investment decisions are strategic complements, those relative to asset riskiness are strategic substitutes.[6] Intuitively, a firm's incentive to pursue a safe policy increases if profitable acquisitions brought about by the risky choices made by others are in sight; and conversely, the presence of potential buyers alleviates the cost of distress and raises the payoff to risky strategy choices.

In Kiyotaki and Moore's (1997) paper, covered in Section 14.3, the relevant environment is the *economy as a whole*. Assets are perfectly redeployable, that is, nonspecialized, in contrast with Shleifer and Vishny's contribution. To understand the main points, it is useful to make a distinction between *the productive value of assets and their value as collateral*. As discussed above, the assets' value as collateral depends on the state of the economy when the loan matures. Hence, the firm's current borrowing capacity and investment are contingent on the value of the secured assets in the future. Conversely, an increase in the economy-wide level of investment raises the demand for the assets and therefore their price, if the assets are used in the production process. Because high asset prices allow high investments and high investments raise asset prices, there is scope for multiple equilibria (as in Shleifer and Vishny) and cycles. Finally, the section relaxes the Kiyotaki–Moore assumption that productive assets are the only store of value. Their analysis is generalized through the introduction of an alternative store of value (such as Treasury bonds); when in sufficient quantity, the latter eliminates the self-fulfilling prophecies just described.

Our rendering of these contributions takes substantial liberties with the original models.[7] We hope that their spirit has been preserved in the process.

4. Schleifer and Vishny motivate their analysis by noting that failing airlines in the mid 1980s sold their gates, routes, and airplanes at much higher prices than those who failed in the late 1980s, because few airlines wanted to purchase the facilities in the difficult environment of the late 1980s.

5. Two decision variables are strategic complements if a player's choice of a higher level for his decision variable induces an increase in the other player's decision variable (the "reaction curves" are upward sloping).

6. Two decision variables are strategic substitutes if a player's choice of a higher level for his decision variable incentivizes the other player to reduce the level of his own decision variable (the "reaction curves" are downward sloping).

7. For one thing, the modeling is different. For example, we use the standard credit rationing model (in the version developed in Chapter 3), while both contributions assume that profits are not verifiable.

14.2 Valuing Specialized Assets

14.2.1 A Roadmap on Vulture–Carrion Models

Section 4.3.1 on redeployability took the resale price P of assets in distress as given. In practice, and as was discussed in the introduction to the chapter, the resale price depends on whether there are buyers standing by ready to repurchase the assets. This in turn depends on whether other firms that would be potential candidates to purchase the assets (i) have indeed accumulated the knowledge necessary to manage the assets and (ii) have the "financial muscle" to buy the assets.

This section thus focuses on assets (such as equipment, intellectual property, or commercial real estate properties not easily convertible into residential real estate) that have liquidation value only if they are acquired by another firm. What makes such assets interesting is that potential buyers may themselves be financially constrained. The acquisition price then depends on the acquirer's financial structure.

To fix ideas, suppose that firm 1 is in distress and, for the moment, firm 2 is the only possible buyer of its assets. There is scope for an acquisition of firm 1's assets by firm 2 as long as a sellout benefits firm 1's investors. It may be that firm 1's management demonstrated insufficient expertise in running these assets, or else that the activity in which they are employed encountered an adverse shock (a metaphor for the latter situation is that of an airline company, firm 1, owning planes and operating a shuttle between two cities newly connected by a high-speed train).

A negotiation then ensues between the two firms. Firm 2's management can tap its investors and raise funds to acquire firm 1's assets. Investors, though, will not want to bring more funds than what they will receive from their firm's expansion; using a now familiar terminology, they will not accept contributing more than the increase in pledgeable income[8] brought about by the acquisition (they may pay less if firm 2 has power in the negotiation and bargains the price down below the value to investors); put differently, firm 2's investors are never willing to pay the full value of the acquired assets because some of the benefits from acquisitions go to firm 2's insiders:[9] the assets' sale consequently occurs at a discount and leaves a surplus to the acquiring management. This in turn implies that inefficiencies may result: firm 1's *ex ante* investment choices may not be optimal from the point of view of the industry, since they do not internalize the surplus that firm 1 will leave on the table when in distress (see Section 14.2.3).

When firm 2 is the sole acquirer, as in the next subsection, this is the end of the story. Firm 2's management has no incentive to hoard reserves, i.e., build financial muscle, in order to be able to purchase firm 1's assets if the latter enters distress. Its monopsony power secures its ability to acquire the assets, and building financial muscle can only weaken its bargaining position.

Contrast this with the case considered in Section 14.2.5, of multiple potential buyers (firms $2, 3, \dots$) competing to acquire firm 1's assets. If those buyers content themselves with returning to the capital market for more funds when the acquisition opportunity arises, the resale price, by the same logic, will not exceed the increase in pledgeable income brought about by the acquisition. However, because the acquirers' management derives a surplus from the acquisition and because being able to bid more than the pledgeable value of the acquired assets helps buying them, firms $2, 3, \dots$ have an incentive to hoard cash in order to outbid each other. This build-up of financial muscle and the resulting bidding raises the acquisition price; it is, however, wasteful from the point of view of the potential acquirers, who could have employed the hoarded cash for other ends (like their own investment).

We will assume throughout this section that the acquiring firm's investors are well-informed as to the value of the acquisition target and that they exert proper governance. A new set of issues arises when their management has superior information about the acquisition's impact on securities' values. Whether management is able to cajole investors into potentially costly acquisitions then depends on the factors that were studied in Section 10.3.

8. ρ_0 per unit of investment in the notation of this book.

9. $\rho_1 - \rho_0$ per unit of investment in the notation of this book.

14.2.2 Industry-Wide Shocks and Distress Sales: The Shleifer–Vishny Model

This subsection, building on Shleifer and Vishny (1992), endogenizes the resale price in the two-firm, continuous-investment version of the model of Section 4.3.1. Let us restate the key ingredients of this model.

Investment and redeployability. There are two firms in the industry. The "industry" is here defined as a group of symmetric firms using the same equipment/assets. For simplicity, we assume that the two firms do not compete in the same product market (see below for a discussion of this hypothesis). Each firm is run by an entrepreneur, who has initial cash A_i.

Initially, firm i invests I_i, and therefore borrows $I_i - A_i$ from some *ex ante* competitive lender ("lender i"). Then, there is a costless "learning period." At the end of the learning period, each firm learns whether it is "productive" (which has probability x), or "unproductive," i.e., "in distress" (which has probability $1 - x$). Being unproductive means that the firm will always be unsuccessful regardless of whether the entrepreneur behaves. For example, there may be no demand for the firm's output. Its assets are then useless if left in place. A productive firm is described as in the variable-investment model of Section 3.4 (which, incidentally, corresponds to the case $x = 1$).

If both firms are productive, each manages its initial investment. Firm i's profit is either 0 or RI_i. Borrower i's private benefit is 0 (if she behaves) or BI_i (if she does not). The associated probabilities of success are p_H and p_L, respectively.

If firm j is in distress, it sells its assets, which now have no internal use.[10] We assume that potential buyers outside the industry do not have the knowledge to operate these assets. Only firm i (if it itself is not in distress) can buy it. There has been no initial contract that would specify the transfer price in the case of distress. Rather, this transfer price is determined through bargaining after distress occurs. We will later determine the per-unit transfer price P. The entrepreneur in firm i then manages $(I_1 + I_2)$ units of assets, and obtains private benefit 0 (if she behaves) or $B(I_1 + I_2)$ (if she does not). Similarly, the income is either 0 or $R(I_1 + I_2)$. Probabilities of success are p_H if the entrepreneur behaves and p_L if she does not. Firm i has just grown bigger through the acquisition.

As usual, we assume that in the absence of adverse shock ($x = 1$), projects are viable only if the borrower behaves,

$$\rho_1 \equiv p_H R > 1 > p_L R + B, \tag{14.1}$$

and we make a further assumption guaranteeing that loans are finite (even for x close to 1):

$$p_H R < 1 + \frac{p_H B}{\Delta p} \quad \text{or} \quad \rho_0 \equiv p_H\left(R - \frac{B}{\Delta p}\right) < 1. \tag{14.2}$$

(The reader will here recognize inequalities (3.7)–(3.9).)

Loan agreements. Lender i and entrepreneur i secretly sign at the start a loan agreement specifying the amount of the loan $I_i - A_i$ and the stake R_{bi} of entrepreneur i in the case of success (in the absence of purchase of firm j's assets). Two remarks are in order here. First, the other parties (lender j and entrepreneur j, $j \neq i$) in equilibrium anticipate correctly the loan agreement, even though they do not observe it. Second, it can be checked that entrepreneur i and lender i cannot sign better contracts than those which will be considered here (more precisely, we are looking for a Nash equilibrium in which each loan agreement belongs to this class, and no loan agreement can be improved upon by a loan agreement inside or outside this class).

Summary of timing. The timing is summarized in Figure 14.1 (where "MH$_i$" stands for "moral hazard in firm i").

Correlation of shocks. The shocks affecting the demands for the two products may be correlated. We allow for an arbitrary level of correlation. The conditional probabilities (given firm i's state) that firm j is productive or in distress are stated in Table 14.1.

For consistency, the parameters must be such that the probability that firm j is productive is x:

$$x\mu + (1-x)(1-\nu) = x \Leftrightarrow x(1-\mu) = (1-x)(1-\nu). \tag{14.3}$$

Let us illustrate this correlation structure with two polar cases that we will use later on.

10. In particular, the entrepreneur in firm j cannot enjoy private benefit BI_j by keeping the assets.

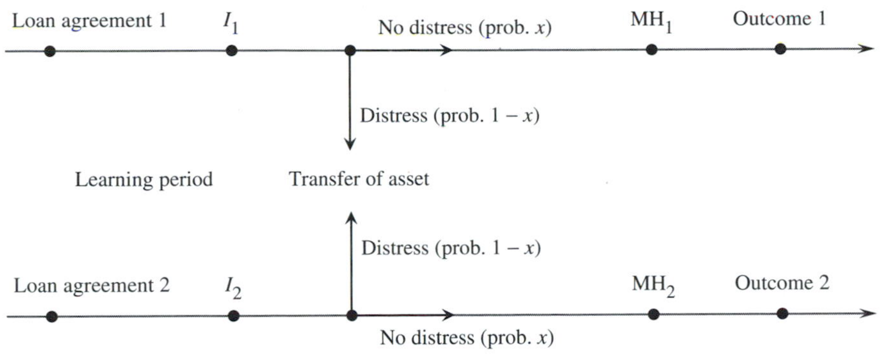

Figure 14.1

Table 14.1

when firm i is	Conditional probability that firm j is productive	in distress
productive (prob. x)	μ	$1 - \mu$
in distress (prob. $1 - x$)	$1 - \nu$	ν

Nonconcurrent risks. In the first polar case, at most one firm is in distress. Put differently, if firm i is in distress then firm j is not: $\nu = 0$. The consistency condition (14.3) then implies $\mu = (2x - 1)/x$ (which naturally requires that $x \geqslant \frac{1}{2}$).[11]

Identical shock. The other polar case is that of perfectly correlated environments. There are only two states of nature: either both firms are productive or both are in distress. This corresponds to $\mu = \nu = 1$.

We now solve for equilibrium. First, we must endogenize the resale price assuming that the firms have invested I_1 and I_2 and distress occurs in one of the firms.

Transfer price. If both firms are in distress (which has probability $(1 - x)\nu$), the four participants (entrepreneurs, lenders) receive no *ex post* revenue. If neither is in distress (which has probability $x\mu$), no sale occurs and the model is the standard variable-investment one.

So let us consider the more interesting case in which *firm 1*, say, *is in distress and firm 2 is not.* We then assume that *lender 1 makes a take-it-or-leave-it offer to lender 2* (see the third remark below for more general bargaining powers). Let P denote the per-unit price demanded by lender 1.

Note that lender 2 must adjust entrepreneur 2's incentive scheme to account for the increased investment and therefore for the increased private benefit from not behaving (now equal to $B(I_1 + I_2)$ instead of BI_2). Assume that entrepreneur 2's incentive compatibility constraint is binding in the absence of a purchase ($(\Delta p)R_{b2} = BI_2$), which actually turns out to be optimal. Then, lender 2 must raise entrepreneur 2's income in the case of success by δR_{b2} such that[12]

$$(\Delta p)(\delta R_{b2}) = BI_1.$$

So, entrepreneur 2's rent increases by $[p_H B/\Delta p]I_1$ and the transfer price is

$$PI_1 = p_H\left[R - \frac{B}{\Delta p}\right]I_1 = \rho_0 I_1.$$

The transfer price is simply the pledgeable income:

$$P = \rho_0.$$

The per-unit pledgeable income can be called the "competitive price" since this price would obtain if there were multiple acquirers bidding competitively for the assets (but see Section 14.2.5). From (14.2), we see that

$$P < 1.$$

11. There are really only three states of nature here, since the state in which both firms are in distress has probability 0. One way to represent this stochastic environment is to envision an underlying random variable ω uniformly distributed on $[0, 1]$. If $\omega \leqslant 1 - 2(1 - x)$, both firms are productive; if $1 - 2(1 - x) < \omega \leqslant 1 - (1 - x) = x$, firm 1 is in distress and firm 2 is productive; if $\omega > x$, firm 2 is in distress and firm 1 is productive.

Nonconcurrent risks generalize the situation in which the environments are perfectly negatively correlated (which corresponds to $x = \frac{1}{2}$).

12. The new incentive constraint is $(\Delta p)(R_{b2} + \delta R_{b2}) \geqslant B(I_2 + I_1)$.

So, the asset is sold at a discount even though the seller has the bargaining power. In this sense, the asset market exhibits some degree of *illiquidity*. Indeed, while reallocation of assets is here efficient as assets in the firm in distress have a zero productivity, it could be inefficient in an environment in which productivity does not fall to 0, but is still lower than the productivity following a reallocation to the other firm (see Exercise 14.4).[13]

Entrepreneur 2 is able to manage more assets because firm 1 is willing to sell its sunk investment I_1 at a discount (its opportunity cost is then equal to 0.) Because firm 1 has the bargaining power, lender 2 actually gains nothing from firm 1's distress, while entrepreneur 2 pockets the extra agency rent $p_H BI_1/\Delta p = (\rho_1 - \rho_0)I_1$.

Entrepreneurs' expected utility. Suppose entrepreneur i maximizes her net utility. As usual, the lenders' zero-profit condition implies that the borrower receives the full surplus associated with investment:

$$U_{bi} = [xp_H RI_i - I_i] + [(1-x)(1-\nu)PI_i] + \left[x(1-\mu)\frac{p_H B}{\Delta p} I_j\right]. \quad (14.4)$$

The first term in brackets in the expression of U_{bi} corresponds to the case in which distress sales are impossible. The second term comes from lender i's revenue from the sales of assets if only firm i is in distress. The third term represents the expected windfall gain from firm j's distress.

We can rewrite (14.4) as

$$U_{bi} = [x\rho_i + (1-x)(1-\nu)\rho_0 - 1]I_i + [x(1-\mu)(\rho_1 - \rho_0)]I_j. \quad (14.5)$$

So let

$$\alpha \equiv x\rho_1 + (1-x)(1-\nu)\rho_0 - 1$$

and

$$\kappa \equiv x(1-\mu)(\rho_1 - \rho_0) > 0.$$

Using (14.4), we can rewrite borrower i's net utility U_{bi} as

$$U_{bi} = \alpha I_i + \kappa I_j. \quad (14.6)$$

Borrowing capacity. Because lender i expects no surplus from the purchase of firm j's assets when the latter is in distress, lender i's expected profit is

$$xp_H(RI_i - R_{bi}) + (1-x)(1-\nu)PI_i - (I_i - A_i) = 0,$$

where R_{bi} is borrower i's income when firm i does not purchase firm j's assets and is successful. Incentive compatibility requires that

$$(\Delta p)R_{bi} \geqslant BI_i,$$

and, as usual, this inequality is satisfied with equality in order to maximize pledgeable income and therefore debt capacity. Using these two equations, firm i's maximal investment is

$$I_i = kA_i,$$

where

$$k = \frac{1}{1 - \rho_0[x + (1-x)(1-\nu)]}. \quad (14.7)$$

Note that the multiplier k (whose denominator is positive since $\rho_0 < 1$) coincides with that given by expression (3.12) when $\nu = 0$ (firm j is never in distress when firm i is—the case of nonconcurrent risks). In particular, that the assets must be sold at a discount when firm i is in distress does not affect the firm's debt capacity even though it reduces the borrower's individual incentive to invest (see the expression of α). The intuition for this result is that the discount is a mere transfer of rent from one entrepreneur to the other and does not affect the lenders' profit.

We also see that the multiplier decreases with ν. That is, *a firm's borrowing capacity decreases with the degree of correlation between firms.* A higher correlation means that the assets are less redeployable.

As we noted, the correlation of shocks reduces the desirability of investment ($\partial\alpha/\partial\nu < 0$). Let ν^* denote the level of ν (if it exists) such that $\alpha = 0$.[14] We consider two cases:

(a) *Low correlation* ($\nu < \nu^*$). Then $\alpha > 0$ and the firms invest up to their borrowing capacity:

13. Two different contributions to the literature have examined the efficiency of the reallocation process, both in an infinite-horizon context. Vayanos (1998) posits transaction costs and derives the price kernel in such an environment. In Eisfeldt (2004), illiquidity stems from asymmetric information between the seller and the buyer (the secondary market for assets suffers from a lemons problem *à la* Akerlof (1970)—see Chapter 6). In her model, economic agents have fewer reasons in good times to trade for informational (rather than efficiency) motives and so the secondary market is less subject to adverse selection, that is, liquidity is procyclical.

14. If α is positive (respectively, negative) for all ν, adopt the convention that $\nu^* = 1$ (respectively, $\nu^* = 0$).

$I_i = kA_i$. While each firm's investment is independent of the existence of the other firm, each firm derives a positive externality from this existence in the form of asset redeployability.

(b) *High correlation* ($\nu > \nu^*$). Then $\alpha < 0$, and no firm invests, even though coordinated investment could be profitable (if $\alpha + \kappa > 0$).

The latter conclusion hinges on the possibility for a firm "not in the business" (that is, that has not invested) to take over and operate the assets of the other firm. Suppose in contrast that an entrepreneur can operate the other firm's equipment only if she herself has invested "enough" (this assumption is consistent with the view that outsiders cannot operate equipment). Namely, she must invest at least $I_i \geqslant \underline{I} > 0$ herself, where $\underline{I} \leqslant kA_i$ for all i. So, we assume that the third term in brackets in the expression of U_{bi} in equation (14.4) ($[x(1-\mu)(\rho_1 - \rho_0)]I_j$) is multiplied by 1 if $I_i \geqslant \underline{I}$ and by 0 if $I_i < \underline{I}$.

Then there exists $\nu^{**} > 0$ (ν^{**} is such that $\alpha+\kappa = 0$) such that, for all $\nu \in [\nu^*, \nu^{**}]$, *two pure-strategy equilibria exist*:

- the good equilibrium ("coordinated one," "vulture equilibrium") in which both firms invest $\underline{I}$ only because that will allow them to get a good deal if the other firm falls in distress;
- the bad equilibrium in which neither invests.[15]

Remark (decreasing returns to scale). Investment externalities are here positive. A firm's investment allows it to stand by to purchase the other firm's assets if the latter is in distress. On the other hand, if (due to entrepreneurial limited attention, for example) returns to investment were decreasing rather than constant,[16] investment externalities could become *negative*, as a more active firm is less eager to take on new tasks. That is, the transfer price a firm in distress can get for its assets is lower, the higher the level of existing investment by the other firm.

Remark (product-market competition). If the firms competed in the product market, the absence of correlation would reduce on average the intensity of competition, and raise the incentive to invest (as it would in the absence of financing constraints[17]).

Remark (alternative distributions of bargaining power). The analysis above, and the rest of Section 14.2 unless otherwise stated, assumes that the acquired firm's investors have full bargaining power and thereby can charge a price equal to the acquiring investors' willingness to pay ($P = \rho_0$). More generally, depending on the two parties' relative bargaining powers, the transaction price can fall anywhere in the range between 0 (the acquired firm's opportunity cost) and ρ_0 (the acquiring firm's investors' willingness to pay).

Allowing for more general distributions of bargaining power does not affect the qualitative results (see Exercise 14.2). Quantitatively, a firm benefits more from the other firm's investment since it purchases it when in distress at an even bigger discount; the same effect also implies that one's own investment is less profitable. So, relative to the case $P = \rho_0$, α decreases and κ increases ($\alpha + \kappa$ remains constant). The other key point is that firm i's borrowing capacity depends on firm j's investment if $P < \rho_0$: the prospect of a cheap acquisition raises the investors' willingness to lend. We therefore conclude that, whenever $P < \rho_0$, investments are strategic complements even in the absence of threshold (minimum) investment. On the other hand, the value of firm i's collateral decreases by $(\rho_0 - P)I_i$ in the case of a transaction. In *symmetric* equilibrium (for $A_1 = A_2 = A$), the two effects cancel, and the borrowing capacity is independent of the distribution of bargaining power.

14.2.3 Underdeveloped Resale Markets

This subsection makes the simple point that in the absence of *ex ante* coordination, the volume of acquisitions is likely to be suboptimal even if financial markets are frictionless. The intuition can be grasped from the treatment in Section 14.2.2, on which we will build: distress creates an *acquisition opportunity* and thereby a windfall surplus for other

15. Entrepreneurs always (weakly) prefer the other entrepreneur to invest, because the latter's investment may create an opportunity for asset acquisition.

16. See Exercise 3.5 for a formalization.

17. This does not imply that, ignoring asset resale benefits, industry profit decreases with the extent of correlation. In particular, in the presence of a threshold investment, $\underline{I}$, a small increase in correlation may transform the industry structure from duopoly to monopoly.

corporate entities. If the competitive price ($P = \rho_0$) obtains, the management of the acquiring firm derives a per-unit-of-investment surplus $\rho_1 - \rho_0$ from the transaction; the windfall surplus is even larger if the acquiring firm has some bargaining power (it is, per unit, $(\rho_1 - \rho_0) + (\rho_0 - P) = \rho_1 - P$). This *ex post* externality generates an *ex ante* externality if we allow firms to determine their probability of distress through investment design choices.

To illustrate this (general) point in a simple manner, let us make the following three assumptions:

- *Nonconcurrent risks.* The two firms are never simultaneously in distress ($\nu = 0$, $\mu = (2x-1)/x$).
- *Ex ante riskiness choice.* Each firm can configure its investment in two ways: (a) the *risky* version considered up to now, in which scale I_i involves up-front cost I_i, but ends up being productive only with probability x; and (b) the *safe* version, scale I_i involves higher up-front cost XI_i, where $X > 1$, but is never in distress. Thus, firms can select to pay more up front and reduce (actually, eliminate) the risk of distress.
- *Symmetry.* $A_1 = A_2 = A$.

We maintain the assumption that the acquired firm's investors have the bargaining power and so $P = \rho_0$ in the case of a transaction.

Coordinated solution. Let us first investigate investment design when firms coordinate *ex ante.*[18] Intuitively, the risky design choice for both is collectively optimal since assets are always productive for at least one of the firms under nonconcurrent risks; thus there is no risk that the assets end up not being used. And the investment cost is lower for a given scale. To check that risky choices are optimal, note that, with the risky design, the per-entrepreneur utility is

$$U_b^r = (\rho_1 - 1)I,$$

where I is given by the investors' breakeven condition:

$$\rho_0 I = I - A.$$

And so

$$U_b^r = \frac{\rho_1 - 1}{1 - \rho_0} A.$$

Compare this with the safe choice for both. The firms then operate "in autarky" since they need not transfer assets to each other. The formulae are the same as in the risky case (which are those given in Section 3.4), except that the unit investment cost is X rather than 1:[19]

$$U_b^s = \frac{\rho_1 - X}{X - \rho_0} A < U_b^r.$$

Similarly, it is easily shown that it is suboptimal to have one of the two firms select the safe design.

Lack of ex ante coordination. Let us now show that it may be individually rational for each firm to select the safe design when, as in the Shleifer–Vishny model, firms do not coordinate their investment choices. Suppose, therefore, that in equilibrium both entrepreneurs adopt the safe design and therefore obtain utility

$$U_b^s = \frac{\rho_1 - X}{X - \rho_0} A.$$

If a firm deviates and chooses the risky design, its utility becomes (using $P = \rho_0$)

$$U_b = [x\rho_1 + (1-x)\rho_0 - 1]I,$$

where its investment, I, is obtained from the investors' breakeven condition:

$$\rho_0 I = I - A$$

(the investors receive ρ_0 per unit of investment regardless). And so

$$U_b = \frac{[\rho_1 - (1-x)(\rho_1 - \rho_0)] - 1}{1 - \rho_0} A.$$

Hence, $U_b^s > U_b$ (firms strictly prefer the safe design) if and only if

$$(1-x)(X - \rho_0) > X - 1,$$

a condition that holds, for instance, if X is close to 1. More generally, if the latter inequality holds, both firms' choosing the safe option is the only equilibrium.

The lack of coordination therefore yields an inefficiently low volume (here a complete absence) of transactions.

To reach efficiency, the firms must contract *ex ante.* Either they contractually obligate each other

18. We here focus on coordination of investment designs. They could further agree *ex ante* on a resale price P *ex post*, but in a symmetric outcome, the choice of P does not affect borrowing capacity or NPV (see Exercise 14.2).

19. The NPV per entrepreneur is $U_b^s = (\rho_1 - X)I$, and the investors' breakeven condition is $\rho_0 I = XI - A$.

to choose the risky design or they provide incentives that induce each to make this choice. An example of the latter approach consists in giving each party a *put* option at price $P = \rho_1$ (or slightly lower).[20] Note that this option requires each firm i to hoard liquidity at least equal to $(\rho_1 - \rho_0)I$, where I is the per-firm investment, since investors will not want *ex post* to contribute more than $\rho_0 I$ for the acquisition of firm j's assets (see Chapter 5 for a treatment of liquidity management). Each solution faces its own difficulties: it may be hard to specify *ex ante* the exact design choice. And the put option, for example, creates moral hazard in quality choices (initial investment quality and maintenance).

14.2.4 Risk Attitudes as Strategic Substitutes

Building on Perotti and Suarez (2002), let us pursue the investigation of risk attitudes begun in the previous subsection. The general point is that risk attitudes give rise to strategic substitutabilities: a firm is more prone to take risks if the other does not, and conversely. Intuitively, choosing a risky strategy is more appealing if one is more likely to find an acquirer for the assets when one falls into distress, i.e., if the other firm chooses a safe strategy. Conversely, the safe strategy has more appeal if there are more frequent opportunities for an acquisition, i.e., if the other firm chooses a risky strategy. This strategic substitutability did not arise in the nonconcurrent risk version of Section 14.2.3 since firms were never simultaneously in distress. Introducing a positive probability of simultaneous distress under risky choices creates a strategic substitutability in riskiness choices. For conciseness, we will make this general point in the context of the risky/safe choice model introduced in Section 12.2.3, but in the specific, polar case of *identical shock*: if both firms choose the risky strategy, then either both firms are productive or both are in distress ($\mu = \nu = 1$).

Let y_i denote the probability that firm i chooses the risky strategy. So $y_i = 1$ if it chooses the risky strategy and $y_i = 0$ if it chooses the safe strategy.

At the financing stage each firm contracts with its investors on its choice of strategy; financing contracts are simultaneous, and so firms do not observe their rival's choice of strategy (they can only anticipate its equilibrium value). We continue to assume that asset sales take place at per-unit price $P = \rho_0$. Let us first compute the firms' borrowing capacities. Recall that, from $P = \rho_0$, the borrowing capacity does not depend on acquisition opportunities. And so the breakeven condition is

$$[x + (1 - x)(1 - y_j)]\rho_0 I_i = I_i - A_i \quad \text{if firm } i \text{ chooses the risky strategy,}$$

$$\rho_0 I_i = X I_i - A_i \quad \text{if firm } i \text{ chooses the safe strategy.}$$

Borrower i's utility (i.e., firm i's NPV) is

$$\begin{aligned} U_{bi}(y_i, y_j, I_j(y_i^*)) &= y_i[x\rho_1 + (1 - x)(1 - y_j)\rho_0 - 1] \\ &\quad \times \left[\frac{A_i}{1 - [x + (1 - x)(1 - y_j)]\rho_0}\right] \\ &\quad + (1 - y_i)[\rho_1 - X]\left[\frac{A_i}{X - \rho_0}\right] \\ &\quad + (1 - y_i)y_j(1 - x)(\rho_1 - \rho_0)I_j(y_i^*), \end{aligned}$$

where

$$I_j(y_i^*) = \left[\frac{A_j}{1 - [x + (1 - x)(1 - y_i^*)]\rho_0}\right].$$

The first term in the expression of U_{bi} is the NPV gross of the potential acquisition for the risky choice ($y_i = 1$), the second its counterpart for the safe choice ($y_i = 0$), and the third the windfall gain from a possible acquisition (which occurs with probability $(1 - y_i)y_j(1 - x)$). When strategies are chosen simultaneously, firm j's investment I_j depends on the anticipated (i.e., equilibrium) choice y_i^* and not on the actual decision y_i of firm i (recall that investment I_j is independent of y_i due to the assumption that the target firm has the bargaining power in an M&A).

Strategic substitutability is equivalent to

$$\frac{\partial}{\partial y_j}\left(\frac{\partial U_{bi}}{\partial y_i}\right) < 0,$$

which indeed holds; it is due to two effects:[21]

20. Let us say that the manager decides *ex post* whether to sell the firm's assets to the other firm, and the proceeds of the sale mostly go to investors (at most $\rho_1 - \rho_0$ per unit goes to management, otherwise the manager might decide to sell the assets even when the firm is not in distress).

21. Beware: when computing $\partial U_{bi}/\partial y_i$, one should take $I_j(y_i^*)$ as given. The reason for this is that we are computing firm i's reaction curve (how y_i optimally reacts to y_j and I_j).

- the "rescue effect," which corresponds to the cross derivative of the first of the three terms in the expression of U_{bi}: $y_j = 0$ increases both the NPV and the pledgeable income when the risky strategy is selected by firm i;
- the "acquisition opportunity effect," which corresponds to the cross derivative of the third term.

It can be checked that an equilibrium with differentiated strategies exists under some parameter configurations.[22]

As in Section 14.2.3, the equilibrium risk choices need not be efficient and *ex ante* coordination may be needed to achieve an industry optimum.

14.2.5 Financial Muscle

14.2.5.1 Two Motivations for Building Financial Muscle

We have not yet needed to discuss how liquidity management interacts with mergers and acquisitions. For two distinct reasons, a corporate entity may hoard liquidity in order to purchase assets in the future, or, put differently, may not content itself with going back to the financial market in order to seize acquisition opportunities, unlike in the environments considered in the last three subsections.

First, the acquiring firm may compete with other potential acquirers. Having extra cash on hand beyond what can be raised through seasoned offerings may help win the bidding war. This motivation is illustrated below, where we emphasize the collective wastefulness of financial muscle.

Second, the acquiring firm may need to reinvest in order to make the acquired assets operational for its own use. This motivation is also illustrated below, where it is further noted that when the selling firm has bargaining power, a Williamsonian holdup problem may arise (see Williamson 1975, 1985). Building financial muscle in order to be able to retool acquired assets is akin to a specific investment. This (sunk) investment may be expropriated through haggling over the transfer price P. This may discourage the potential acquirer from hoarding financial muscle when the latter involves an opportunity cost (the hoarded liquidity could be used for alternative purposes). We consequently note that firms may acquire insufficient financial muscle.

14.2.5.2 Bidding for Assets: Too Little or Too Much Financial Muscle?

Let us now investigate (building on Holmström and Tirole (2005)) whether potential acquirers accumulate (collectively) too little or too much financial muscle. For the sake of simplicity we will assume that there are two distinct classes of firms: safe firms, which are never in distress, and risky firms, which may become distressed, in which case they may be purchased by the safe firms.[23]

14.2.5.3 Bilateral Monopoly: Is Liquidity Hoarding Held Up?

Let us first describe the model in the case of a single risky firm and a single safe firm. The two firms choose investment sizes J and I, respectively. To simplify notation without altering the basic insights, the two firms are identical, except for the probability of distress, which is 0 for the safe firm and $1-x$ for the risky one. Both are run by risk-neutral entrepreneurs with initial cash on hand A each and protected by limited liability. The timing is summarized in Figure 14.2.

We further assume that when buying the J units of asset from the risky firm when the latter is in distress, the safe firm must pay a known retooling cost ρJ to adapt these assets to its own production process. Letting P denote the unit acquisition price, the total cost of the acquisition is thus $(P+\rho)J$. To limit

22. Suppose symmetric net worths ($A_1 = A_2 = A$). An equilibrium in which one chooses the safe strategy and the other the risky one exists if and only if

$$\frac{\rho_1 - X}{X - \rho_0} + (1-x)\left(\frac{\rho_1 - \rho_0}{1-\rho_0}\right) \geqslant \frac{x\rho_1 - 1}{1 - x\rho_0}$$

and

$$\frac{x\rho_1 + (1-x)\rho_0 - 1}{1-\rho_0} \geqslant \frac{\rho_1 - X}{X - \rho_0}.$$

Eliminating the term $(\rho_1 - X)/(X - \rho_0)$, it is easily shown that these two inequalities are satisfied for $X \in [\underline{X}, \bar{X}]$ with $\underline{X} > 1$.

23. For conciseness, we rule out the purchase of distressed firms' assets by risky, but intact, firms. In the first application of the model, in which there is a single risky firm, this question obviously does not arise. To endogenize this assumption when there are multiple risky firms, one can assume either that the risky firms' shocks are correlated, and so they fall into distress at the same time; or else (contrary to what is assumed below for notational simplicity) that the expected return on their investment is higher than that of safe firms, and so risky firms have more incentives to invest themselves than to hoard reserves to purchase assets from other firms.

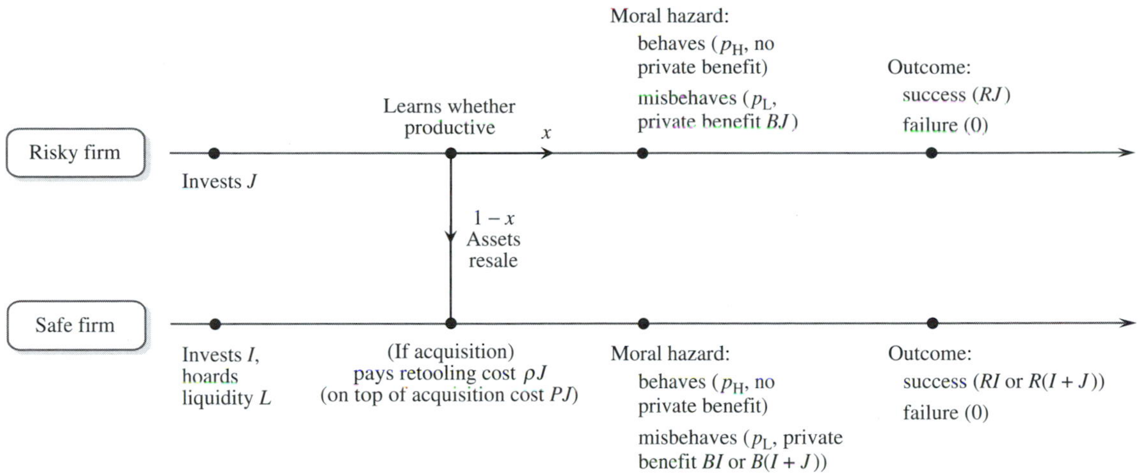

Figure 14.2

the number of cases to be considered, we assume that $\rho \leqslant \rho_0$.

The treatment of the bilateral monopoly case, compared with the simpler competitive asset resale market case considered below, involves conceptually difficult, but interesting, twists. As we want to allow for a wide range of bargaining powers, let us assume that in the case of distress of the risky firm:

- with probability z, the risky firm makes a take-it-or-leave-it resale offer to the safe firm;
- with probability $1-z$, the safe firm makes a take-it-or-leave-it purchase offer.

Thus z is a measure of the selling firm's bargaining power.

Bargaining and the choice of financial muscle. The case in which the safe firm makes the offer is a no-brainer: it offers 0 (or just above), the opportunity cost of the risky firm's assets when in distress. By contrast, the situation in which the risky firm makes the offer requires more thinking. Let us assume that the amount of liquidity L hoarded by the safe firm (say, the credit line that the firm secures from its bank[24]) is *not* observed by the risky firm. We look for conditions under which the following is an equilibrium:

- the risky firm demands per-unit price ρ_0 for its assets;
- the safe firm, anticipating this and knowing that it will be able to raise $\rho_0 J$ on the asset market, hoards liquidity $L = \rho J$.

Making offer ρ_0 is clearly optimal for the seller since $\rho_0 J$ is the pledgeable income on the acquired assets and thus the upper bound on what new investors are willing to contribute in a seasoned offering.

Let us next investigate whether it is indeed in the safe firm's interest to hoard liquidity. Let $y = 1$ if it hoards the necessary amount (ρJ) and $y = 0$ if it does not. Noting that liquidity is not needed to acquire the assets when the acquirer makes the offer (since $\rho \leqslant \rho_0$), the safe firm's NPV is then

$$U_b^s = (\rho_1 - 1)I + (1-x)[z[\rho_1 - (\rho_0 + \rho)]y + (1-z)(\rho_1 - \rho)]J.$$

The second term on the right-hand side is the expected gain from acquisitions, and uses the fact that the total acquisition cost is $(\rho_0 + \rho)J$ when the seller makes the offer and only ρJ when the acquirer makes the offer.

24. We adopt the convention that the safe firm's entrepreneur can raise ρ_0 in a seasoned security offering, to which L is added to form total available cash. Alternatively, and as we discussed in Chapter 5, one could ban seasoned offerings and provide the firm with a bigger credit line.

The safe firm's investors must break even, and so

$$\rho_0 I + (1-x)[z[\rho_0 - (\rho_0+\rho)]y + (1-z)(\rho_0-\rho)]J = I - A.$$

The investors' breakeven condition yields the investment level I:

$$I = \frac{A + [(1-z)(\rho_0-\rho) - z\rho y](1-x)J}{1-\rho_0}.$$

Note that hoarding liquidity ($y = 1$) reduces the investment scale. Substituting into the NPV equation,

$$U_b^s = (\rho_1 - 1)\frac{A + [(1-z)(\rho_0-\rho) - z\rho y](1-x)J}{1-\rho_0} + (1-x)[z[\rho_1 - (\rho_0+\rho)]y + (1-z)(\rho_1-\rho)]J.$$

We conclude that it is an equilibrium for the safe firm to hoard liquidity to purchase assets if and only if U_b^s is increasing in y, or

$$\rho_1 - (\rho_0+\rho) \geqslant \frac{(\rho_1-1)\rho}{1-\rho_0}$$

or

$$1 \geqslant \rho_0 + \rho.$$

We thus obtain the simple result that the potential acquirer builds the necessary financial muscle if and only if the total per unit cost of acquisition when the acquired firm has bargaining power is lower than the safe firm's own cost of investment. The potential acquirer simply compares the costs of the two alternative approaches to investing: internal growth and acquisitions. Intuitively, when the seller has the bargaining power, 1 unit of hoarded liquidity allows the purchase of $1/\rho$ units of distressed assets (the remaining cost, ρ_0 per unit when the seller has the bargaining power, is self-financing to the extent that it can be raised through a secondary offering). But it also has opportunity cost $1/(1-\rho_0)$ since 1 unit of assets allows the financing of $1/(1-\rho_0)$ units of investment. In the "make-or-buy" choice, the buy option is attractive if

$$\frac{1}{1-\rho_0} < \frac{1}{\rho}.$$

Note that this inequality is always satisfied if ρ_0 is small: the opportunity cost of hoarding liquidity and thereby reducing the net worth that can be used for one's own investment is then small as the multiplier is close to 1.

In this simple model the equilibrium is in general not unique: there are lots of other self-fulfilling equilibria in which the firm hoards $L^* \neq \rho J$ and the seller demands P^* such that $P^* + \rho = L^* + \rho_0$. The seller does not want to demand more than $P > P^*$ because being too greedy prevents the potential acquirer from buying the assets. Conversely, the potential acquirer is willing to hoard $L = L^*$, as long as $P^* + \rho \leqslant 1$ (note that ρ_0 is in the interior of the range of equilibrium prices).[25]

Equilibrium selection. Exercise 14.3 describes one appealing way of breaking this indeterminacy: adding *ex ante* uncertainty about the level of the retooling cost. Namely, the retooling cost $\tilde{\rho}$ is, as the liquidity shock in Chapter 5, drawn from a cumulative distribution function $F(\tilde{\rho})$; Exercise 14.3 further assumes that the safe firm's entrepreneur privately observes its realization. It shows that

(i) the safe firm is granted a credit line that allows it to withstand all shocks $\tilde{\rho} \leqslant \rho^*$ for some cutoff ρ^*;

(ii) the equilibrium credit line and the acquisition price P demanded by the seller satisfy

$$P + \rho^* = 1$$

(in words, in (the unique) equilibrium, the costs of investment in the make-or-buy choice are equalized!);

(iii) when the distribution of $\tilde{\rho}$ converges to a spike at ρ (is close to the deterministic specification posited earlier), then P converges to $1 - \rho$. Interestingly, this solution is the *competitive* solution described below! Furthermore, the probability of striking a deal converges to 1.

Intuitively, hoarding reserves that are left unused is costless to the acquirer (as long as the latter returns these reserves to the investors when unused). The seller then knows that the acquirer will hoard reserves that are sufficient to support (from his point of view) efficient continuations, that is, whenever $\rho \leqslant 1 - P$, where P is the anticipated price. And P is determined by the standard monopoly tradeoff

25. Relatedly, the potential acquirer has an incentive to claim that it has shallow pockets ($L = 0$) so as to force the seller to make a low offer. It is, however, difficult to "prove" shallow pockets since the bank and the firm may contract for a secret credit line.

between being greedy/running the risk of not selling and ensuring a sale by charging a low price.

Let us finally turn to a brief analysis of externalities. In this uncertain retooling cost version, *for a given investment* J by the risky firm, the efficient volume of trade occurs whenever the assets are sold at their opportunity cost, i.e., are given away ($P = 0$). Except in the limit in which the retooling cost is highly predictable (result (iii) above), the volume of trade is suboptimally low. This inefficiency could be alleviated by

(i) either an *ex ante* agreement between the two firms mandating a costless transfer of assets in the case of distress;[26]

(ii) or an *ex ante* agreement between the two parties that the acquirer builds more financial muscle than he would build to maximize his own profit.[27]

In a nutshell, the seller is too greedy (like in any monopoly problem) and the buyer too stingy.

Another set of externalities arises when considering the investment level J. An increase in J augments the value of the acquisition opportunity for the safe firm. The safe firm therefore might want (perhaps in exchange for an option to freely acquire assets in the case of distress) to subsidize J's investment. Alternatively, it might want to commit to hoard more liquidity than it does when acting in a noncooperative way, since an increase in financial muscle raises the risky firm's revenue in distress and boosts its investment.

14.2.5.4 Make-or-Buy Decision in a Competitive Environment: Excessive Financial Muscle

Let us now consider the case with many risky firms and many safe firms. We assume that the risky (respectively, safe) firms are all identical and as described previously. The productivity shocks encountered by the risky firms are independent and so, by the law of large numbers, the equilibrium is deterministic. We no longer need to describe bargaining: asset transfers occur at some per-unit market price P.

26. Provided that distress can be verified in court. Otherwise, when in distress, the risky firm might continue to operate and engage in a war of attrition in order to force the acquirer to pay a positive price.

27. Of course, an increase in L induces an increase in P. But the pass-through coefficient is smaller than 1 (see Exercise 14.3).

Building on the previous analysis, and now calling $\mathcal{J}$ the total amount purchased by the representative safe firm, the latter's NPV is

$$U_{\mathrm{b}}^{\mathrm{s}} = (\rho_1 - 1)I + [\rho_1 - (P + \rho)]\mathcal{J},$$

where ρ is the (deterministic) per-unit retooling cost. The investors' breakeven condition is

$$\rho_0 I + [\rho_0 - (P + \rho)]\mathcal{J} = I - A.$$

And so

$$U_{\mathrm{b}}^{\mathrm{s}} = (\rho_1 - 1)\frac{A - (P + \rho - \rho_0)\mathcal{J}}{1 - \rho_0} + [\rho_1 - (P + \rho)]\mathcal{J}.$$

The derivative of $U_{\mathrm{b}}^{\mathrm{s}}$ with respect to $\mathcal{J}$ must be equal to 0 in a competitive equilibrium, which yields the condition of indifference between making and buying:

$$P + \rho = 1.$$

It can be argued that (fixing the risky firms' total investment) the safe firms collectively invest too much in financial muscle. Indeed they would be better off if they could agree not to hoard any liquidity at all. This buyer cartel would then acquire the distressed assets for free. Cartelization would not, of course, result in a Pareto-improvement as the sellers would suffer from a concerted lack of buyer financial muscle.

Pareto-improving concerted reductions in liquidity hoarding do arise in Holmström and Tirole (2005), who

- consider a symmetric version of this model (all firms are risky), without retooling cost;
- assume that liquidity is costly to hoard (hoarding L costs $g(L)$, with $g'(0) = 1$ and $g'' > 0$).

Over a range of parameters, firms invest too little and hoard too much liquidity (indeed, because here hoarding, and not only using, liquidity is costly, the collectively optimal amount of hoarding is equal to 0).

14.3 General Equilibrium Determination of Asset Values, Borrowing Capacities, and Economic Activity: The Kiyotaki–Moore Model

The paper by Shleifer and Vishny explores one determinant of the value of collateral, namely, the correlation among shocks affecting a group of firms within which assets can be redeployed. It demonstrates the linkage between firms' borrowing capacities and investments through the demand for secured assets in the case of distress. The Kiyotaki and Moore (1997) paper also focuses on the equilibrium value of assets as collateral, but with an emphasis on the forecast of *future* economy-wide activity and firms' borrowing capacity. In Kiyotaki and Moore, uncertainty about the demand for assets plays no role; actually, there is a large number (an infinity) of firms among which assets can be redeployed; these firms face independent shocks, and "by the law of large numbers" the economy follows a deterministic path. A firm's borrowing capacity at date t depends, positively, on the value of assets at date $t+1$ (because assets are used as collateral), and, negatively, on the assets' rental rate at date t (because assets are used as inputs into production). In turn, the borrowing capacity determines investment and therefore the productive use of the asset, which affects the rental rate. The economy can have multiple steady states, some with high asset value, rental rate, borrowing capacities, and economic activity, and others with lower values of each of these variables. The economy may also exhibit cycles, fluctuating between a state of high activity and high asset value and a state of low activity and low asset value.

14.3.1 The Model

To study the interaction between economic activity and asset value, it is convenient to use an infinite-horizon model. For simplicity, the rate of time preference of the agents in the economy (lenders and entrepreneurs) determines the rate of interest (although not, as we will see, the price of assets):

Preferences. The horizon is infinite: $t = 0, 1, 2, \dots$. All agents have linear preferences:

$$\sum_{t \geqslant 0} \beta^t c_t,$$

where c_t is their date-t consumption and β is the discount factor ($\beta = 1/\gamma$ and $\gamma = 1 +$ interest rate).

Goods. There are two goods: durable and nondurable. The durable good will be labeled "real estate" and the nondurable one the "good." There are A units of real estate in the economy. Real estate neither depreciates nor expands and can be used as commercial or residential real estate. Real estate is the only store of value from one period to the next. There is no transaction cost involved in affecting real estate to one use or another.

The perishable consumption good lasts at most one period. This good is received as an endowment at the beginning of the period and can either be consumed immediately or invested. If invested, it may yield more units of the good (or none) at the end of the period, but these units will need to be consumed because the good cannot be stored until the next period.

Agents. There is the usual "mismatch between ideas and resources." There are two classes of agents (there is a continuum of agents in each class). *Entrepreneurs* can operate productive activities. They, however, receive no endowment of the good, and therefore they must borrow the entire amount of their investment. On the other hand, they can own real estate that they held or purchased in the previous period and use it as collateral. Indeed, we will look for an equilibrium in which entrepreneurs own the entire stock of real estate.

Lenders or investors receive a (large) endowment of date-t good at the beginning of period t. They consume some of it immediately and lend the rest to entrepreneurs against a claim on end-of-period income and possibly collateralized assets.

Production technology. Consider an entrepreneur with a units of real estate at the start of date t. Let this entrepreneur invest (and therefore borrow) i units of date-t good. (We use lowercase letters at the firm level, and will later use uppercase ones when we aggregate at the economy level.) Production requires using λi units of commercial real estate during the period.

The remaining real estate $(a - \lambda i)$ can be rented as residential real estate at rental rate r_t. Let $D_{\mathrm{R}}(r_t)$ denote the aggregate demand for residential real estate (from lenders or third parties, say).[28] We assume

28. It is straightforward to endogenize this demand function. For example, one could assume that agents have intertemporal utilities

$$\sum_{t \geqslant 0} \beta^t [c_t + \Phi(z_t)],$$

where z_t is their date-t consumption of residential real estate, and $\Phi(z_t)$ is the gross surplus they derive from this consumption ($\Phi' > 0$, $\Phi'' < 0$, $\Phi'(0) = \infty$, $\Phi'(\infty) = 0$). The individual demand for residential

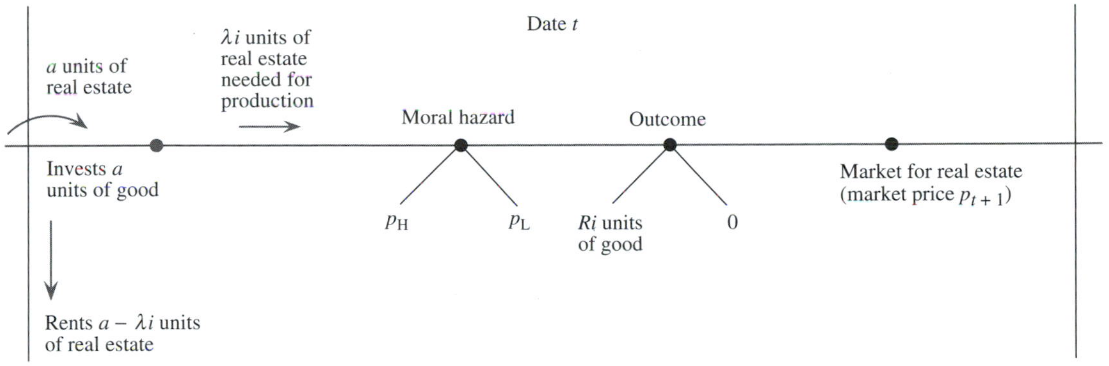

Figure 14.3

that this demand is downward sloping. Rental therefore generates a flow of income $(a - \lambda i)r_t$.

The entrepreneur either succeeds and obtains Ri units of date-t good at the end of the period or fails and obtains 0. The probability of success is p. There is moral hazard. The entrepreneur can either work, in which case she enjoys no private benefit and the probability of success is p_H, or shirk, in which case she enjoys private benefit Bi and the probability of success is p_L. Let $\Delta p = p_H - p_L > 0$.

Loan agreements. The contract between an entrepreneur and her lenders is a within-period contract. The entrepreneur receives R_b units of good in the case of success and 0 otherwise. Let us also adopt the conventions that (i) lenders receive the residential real estate income $(a - \lambda i)r_t$, and (ii) assets a at the end of the period go to the entrepreneur in the case of success and to the lenders in the case of failure. These conventions impose no loss of generality.

End-of-period market for real estate. At the end of period t, owners of real estate (successful entrepreneurs, investors who have seized the collateral) can sell (or buy more) real estate at price p_{t+1} on a competitive market. The proceeds of the sale are immediately consumed because the good is perishable.

The timing is summarized in Figure 14.3. We will look for an equilibrium in which investors do not carry real estate from one period to the next. When they seize assets, they sell them immediately to successful entrepreneurs, who thus spend part of their income expanding (and consume the rest).

real estate is then $z_t = (\Phi')^{-1}(r_t)$, and total demand is obtained by aggregation of individual demands.

Remark (entrepreneur selection). Entrepreneurs who fail disappear (they receive no endowment and have no asset, so will be unable to borrow); their continuation utility is equal to 0. So, ownership of the stock A of assets is more and more concentrated over time among entrepreneurs. If one does not like this conclusion, one can assume parthenogenesis; an "entrepreneur" is a dynasty of entrepreneurs. Each entrepreneur has several children, among whom she distributes the assets (the distribution of assets has no effect in this model because of the linearity).

Remark (no-agency-cost case). In the absence of credit market imperfections (that is, if there were no moral hazard), credit would not be rationed to entrepreneurs, and, given constant returns to scale, the rental rate would need to adjust so that investment yields zero profit; so, $r_t = r$, where

$$p_H R - 1 - \lambda r = 0.$$

The economy would be in steady state, and so the phenomena of multiple equilibria and cycles investigated below are entirely due to credit rationing.

14.3.2 Borrowing Capacities and Asset Values in Equilibrium

In this model there is no aggregate uncertainty. The path of the economy will be characterized by the price and rental rate of real estate (p_t, r_t).

We look for an equilibrium in which the "continuation valuation" $V_t(a)$ (expected present discounted consumption from date t on) of an entrepreneur owning a units of real estate at the beginning of date t is proportional to a:

$$V_t(a) = v_t a. \tag{14.8}$$

Arbitrage among successful entrepreneurs on the real estate market at the end of period t then implies that

$$p_{t+1} = \beta v_{t+1}. \tag{14.9}$$

The borrowing capacity of an entrepreneur with assets a at the start of period t is given, as usual, by the two conditions that the entrepreneur is induced to work and that the investors break even:

$$(\Delta p)(R_{\rm b} + p_{t+1}a) = Bi \tag{IC$_{\rm b}$}$$

and

$$p_{\rm H}(Ri - R_{\rm b}) + (1 - p_{\rm H})p_{t+1}a + (a - \lambda i)r_t = i. \tag{IC$_{\rm l}$}$$

So

$$i = k_t a, \tag{14.10}$$

where the multiplier is given by

$$k_t \equiv \frac{p_{t+1} + r_t}{1 - [p_{\rm H}R - \lambda r_t - p_{\rm H}B/\Delta p]} = \frac{p_{t+1} + r_t}{(1 + \lambda r_t) - \rho_0}, \tag{14.11}$$

where, as usual, $\rho_0 \equiv p_{\rm H}(R - B/\Delta p)$. Furthermore, the zero-profit condition for the investors implies that the entrepreneur receives the expected profit from the date-t production. Because of the arbitrage condition, we can always assume, *for the purpose of computing the valuation function* $V_t(a)$, that, if the entrepreneur succeeds at date t, she sells her assets at the end of the period:

$$\begin{aligned} V_t(a) &= [p_{t+1} + r_t]a + [p_{\rm H}R - \lambda r_t - 1]i \\ &= v_t a = \left[\frac{\rho_1 - \rho_0}{(1 + \lambda r_t) - \rho_0}\right][p_{t+1} + r_t]a, \end{aligned} \tag{14.12}$$

where $\rho_1 \equiv p_{\rm H}R$. Using (14.9) and (14.12), we obtain

$$\begin{aligned} p_t &= \left[\frac{p_{\rm H}B/\Delta p}{1 - [p_{\rm H}R - \lambda r_t - p_{\rm H}B/\Delta p]}\right]\beta(p_{t+1} + r_t) \\ &= \frac{\rho_1 - \rho_0}{[(1 + \lambda r_t) - \rho_0]}\beta(p_{t+1} + r_t). \end{aligned} \tag{14.13}$$

Note that

$$k_t = \frac{\Delta p}{\beta p_{\rm H}B}p_t = \frac{p_t}{\beta(\rho_1 - \rho_0)}. \tag{14.14}$$

The multiplier is proportional to the price of real estate! This may sound counterintuitive because high real estate prices increase production costs. But one should recall that assets are in equilibrium held by the entrepreneurs, who, first, are *net* suppliers of real estate services, and, second, can use highly valued assets as collateral to boost their borrowing capacity.

The second equilibrium condition (besides equation (14.13)) is obtained from the *equilibrium in the real estate market*. The demand for residential use is equal to the supply. Total investment in the economy is $I_t = k_t A$, and thus

$$\begin{aligned} D_{\rm R}(r_t) &= A - \lambda I_t \\ &= A - \lambda k_t A, \end{aligned}$$

or, using (14.14),

$$\begin{aligned} D_{\rm R}(r_t) &= \left[1 - \frac{\lambda \Delta p}{\beta p_{\rm H}B}p_t\right]A \\ &= \left[1 - \frac{\lambda p_t}{\beta(\rho_1 - \rho_0)}\right]A. \end{aligned} \tag{14.15}$$

Existence of this equilibrium imposes conditions on the parameters. First, it must be the case that real estate is more productively held by entrepreneurs than by investors, that is, its rate of return must not exceed that implied by discount factor β (i.e., $(1 - \beta)/\beta$), or equivalently

$$p_t \geqslant \beta(p_{t+1} + r_t).$$

From (14.13) and recalling that $\rho_1 = p_{\rm H}R$ we must therefore have

$$p_{\rm H}R \geqslant 1 + \lambda r_t. \tag{14.16}$$

That is, the marginal productivity of investment gross of agency cost must be positive. On the other hand, the multiplier k_t must be positive, meaning that the marginal productivity of investment net of the agency cost is negative:

$$p_{\rm H}R < 1 + \lambda r_t + \frac{Bp_{\rm H}}{\Delta p}. \tag{14.17}$$

Lastly, the total net supply of real estate should be positive:

$$p_t \leqslant \frac{\beta p_{\rm H}B}{\lambda \Delta p}. \tag{14.18}$$

14.3.3 Dynamic Analysis

The dynamic system is defined by (14.13) and (14.15). From (14.15), we obtain an increasing function,

$$r_t = \mathcal{R}(p_t), \tag{14.19}$$

on $[0, \bar{p}]$, where the upper bound $\bar{p}$ is defined by $\bar{p} = \beta p_H B/\lambda\Delta p$. Note that by choosing $D_R(\cdot)$ judiciously, one can generate any increasing function $\mathcal{R}(\cdot)$. Substituting (14.19) into (14.13), one obtains

$$p_t = \frac{p_H B/\Delta p}{1 - [p_H R - \lambda\mathcal{R}(p_t) - p_H B/\Delta p]} \times \beta[p_{t+1} + \mathcal{R}(p_t)]. \quad (14.20)$$

It is also easy to show that in the relevant range (defined by (14.16)-(14.18)), equation (14.13) implies that p_t is increasing in $r_t = \mathcal{R}(p_t)$. This implies that the mapping from p_t into p_{t+1} defined by (14.20) can have a fairly arbitrary slope. Indeed, p_{t+1} decreases with p_t if the slope of $\mathcal{R}(\cdot)$ is big enough. Figure 14.4 illustrates the possibilities.

First, one notes that there may exist several steady-state equilibrium prices (four of them, indicated by an asterisk, in Figure 14.4). Interestingly, *economic activity, investment, leverage* (from (14.14)), *real estate price*, and *rental rate all covary across steady states.* Second, there may exist cycles such as the $\{p_1, p_2\}$ cycle in Figure 14.4. The economy then alternates between a state of high activity and high asset price and a state of low activity and low asset price.[29]

To recap, we have seen that (i) current economic activity depends on the firms' current borrowing capacity and therefore on the future market price of durable investments (here real estate), (ii) the latter depends on future activity (or borrowing capacity), (iii) consequently, economic activity in the present and in the future are linked through the mechanism of borrowing capacity and asset value, and (iv) this creates a covariation of several economic variables, and further may generate cycles and multiple equilibria.

14.3.4 Adding a Competing Store of Value

Let us conclude the study of the Kiyotaki-Moore model with the following point, which will serve as an introduction to the next chapter. The possibility of multiple steady states and cycles in the Kiyotaki-

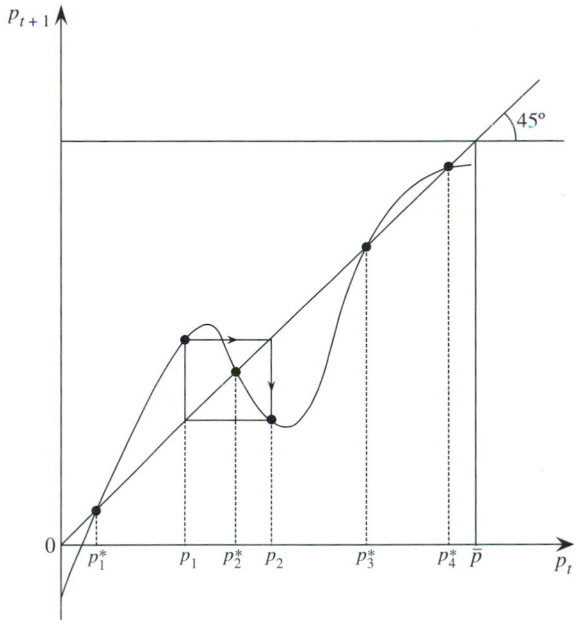

Figure 14.4

Moore model hinges on the dual role of the assets as inputs into the production process and as stores of value, i.e., liquidity instruments that help the (successful) entrepreneurs "bridge" the periods (store their retained earnings in order to reinvest later).[30] If we introduce into the economy another store of value that is not directly used in the production process (for example, Treasury bonds, as discussed in the next chapter), the productive asset (real estate here) now competes with the alternative store of value and loses part or all of its value as a bridge across periods.

To see this, let us introduce a *pure store of value* in quantity L. One unit of this pure store of value delivers 1 unit of nonstorable consumption good in each period, forever.

Dynamics. Letting q_{t+1} denote the price of the pure store of value at the end of period t (by analogy with p_{t+1}, the price of real estate at the end of period t), and l the individual holding of the store of value by the representative (surviving) entrepreneur, we can generalize the previous analysis. The date-t

29. See Freixas and Rochet (1997) for more on cycles in such models. For more on cycles in credit-constrained economies in a closed and an open context, respectively, see Aghion et al. (1999, 2004) as well as Sections 13.4 and 13.5.

30. In this sense, Kiyotaki and Moore's paper is related to the Woodford (1990) paper discussed in the next chapter.

borrowing capacity becomes[31]

$$i = \frac{(p_{t+1} + r_t)a + (q_{t+1} + 1)l}{(1 + \lambda r_t) - \rho_0},$$

where the numerator is the value of assets held by the entrepreneur at the beginning of date t and the denominator is as usual the difference between the unit production cost and the unit pledgeable income.

The valuation function is

$$V_t(a, l) = \left[\frac{\rho_1 - \rho_0}{(1 + \lambda r_t) - \rho_0}\right] \times [(p_{t+1} + r_t)a + (q_{t+1} + 1)l].$$

Thus, whether they are held solely by the entrepreneurs or jointly by entrepreneurs and consumers (a question that we will briefly analyze below), the two assets (real estate and pure store of value) must command the same return, and this rate of return must be at least equal to the one that consumers are willing to accept:

$$\frac{p_{t+1} + r_t}{p_t} = \frac{q_{t+1} + 1}{q_t} \geqslant \frac{1}{\beta}.$$

This equalization of rates of return is obvious if consumers hold part of those assets: the rates of return must then be equal to the inverse of the discount factor (i.e., $1/\beta$). But, from the optimization condition at the end of period $t - 1$, rate-of-return equalization holds even if all assets are held by entrepreneurs. Indeed, the latter allocate their wealth $p_t a + q_t l$ so as to solve

$$\max\{\beta V_t(a, l) - p_t a - q_t l\}.$$

As earlier, the rental rate for real estate is given by

$$D_R(r_t) = A - \lambda I_t.$$

The difference between this and the earlier treatment is that the aggregate investment I_t is now larger due to the availability of the alternative store of value. In particular, if the pure store of value is entirely held by the entrepreneurs, which, starting from the equilibrium for $L = 0$ studied in Section 14.3.3, requires that L not be too large,[32] then

$$I_t = \frac{(p_{t+1} + r_t)A + (q_{t+1} + 1)L}{(1 + \lambda r_t) - \rho_0}.$$

Glut of stores of value. To illustrate the impact of an alternative store of value in the Kiyotaki–Moore model, suppose that L is large and so stores of value are in part held by consumers. Then the rate of return on the stores of value must be equal to the consumers' rate of discount:

$$\frac{p_{t+1} + r_t}{p_t} = \frac{q_{t+1} + 1}{q_t} = \frac{1}{\beta},$$

and so

$$q_t = q = \frac{\beta}{1 - \beta}$$

(in contrast, p_t increases over time as the economy grows and thus the industrial use of real estate drives the rental rate r_t up).

Suppose that entrepreneurs at date 0 start with a small amount of assets.[33] Then, as long as the NPV is strictly positive, that is, as long as

$$\rho_1 > 1 + \lambda r_t,$$

successful entrepreneurs do not want to consume. They accumulate assets until their firms are wealthy enough that their investment and the concomitant demand for commercial real estate drives the rental rate to its steady-state value r^* and the NPV to 0:

$$\rho_1 = 1 + \lambda r^*.$$

To see why successful entrepreneurs indeed hoard assets until the economy reaches its steady state, note that, for $\rho_1 > 1 + \lambda r_t$,

$$q_t < \beta\left[\frac{\rho_1 - \rho_0}{(1 + \lambda r_t) - \rho_0}\right](q_{t+1} + 1),$$

31. The date-t investors' breakeven condition becomes

$$p_H\left[Ri - \frac{Bi}{\Delta p} + p_{t+1}a + q_{t+1}l\right] + (1 - p_H)[p_{t+1}a + q_{t+1}l] + ar_t + l = [1 + \lambda r_t]i.$$

32. This is the case whenever

$$\frac{p_{t+1} + r_t}{p_t} = \frac{q_{t+1} + 1}{q_t} < \frac{1}{\beta},$$

where

$$D_R(r_t) = A - \lambda\frac{(p_{t+1} + r_t)A + (q_{t+1} + 1)L}{(1 + \lambda r_t) - \rho_0}.$$

To see when this holds, one can *a contrario* assume that

$$\frac{p_{t+1} + r_t}{p_t} = \frac{q_{t+1} + 1}{q_t} = \frac{1}{\beta}$$

and

$$D_R(r_t) > A - \lambda\frac{(p_{t+1} + r_t)A + (q_{t+1} + 1)L}{(1 + \lambda r_t) - \rho_0}.$$

This latter set of conditions holds if and only if $L > \bar{L}$ for some $\bar{L} > 0$. Conversely, the former set holds if and only if $L < \bar{L}$.

33. But not equal to 0; otherwise, having no endowment in each period, they would never "get started."

and so an entrepreneur with retained earnings, say, 1 unit of pure store of value, at the end of period $t-1$ is better off saving it, which will allow her to borrow $(q_{t+1}+1)/[(1+\lambda r_t)-\rho_0]$ and enjoy payoff $\rho_1-\rho_0$ on each unit of investment, rather than selling it at price q_t and consume the proceeds.

The steady-state values (indexed by an asterisk) are then given by

$$\begin{aligned} \rho_1 &= 1+\lambda r^*, \\ p^* &= \frac{\beta}{1-\beta} r^*, \\ q^* &= \frac{\beta}{1-\beta}, \\ D_R(r^*) &= A-\lambda I^*. \end{aligned}$$

The economy converges to the steady state in finite time, and its path is uniquely determined. This result illustrates the role played by the Kiyotaki–Moore assumption that there is no (or, more generally, little) alternative store of value.[34]

The next chapter analyzes the equilibrium determinants of the quantity of stores of value in the economy and emphasizes the theme (touched upon in this subsection) that an increase in the volume of stores of value (liquidity) reduces liquidity premia and interest rates and benefits the productive sector.

14.4 Exercises

Exercise 14.1 (investment externalities in an industry with decreasing returns to scale). Suppose that the entrepreneur's limited attention, say, induces decreasing returns to scale. Income in the case of success is $R(I)$, where $R'>0$, $R''<0$, $R'(0)=\infty$, $R'(\infty)=0$. Redo the analysis of the Schleifer–Vishny model with this modification, and determine the sign of the investment externality.

Exercise 14.2 (alternative distributions of bargaining power in the Shleifer–Vishny model). Perform the analysis of Section 14.2.2 for an arbitrary unit price $P\in[0,\rho_0]$ of resale of a distressed firm's assets to a productive one. (Assume that bargaining occurs between the two firms' investors, and that the acquiring firm's investors then redesign their managerial incentives. Thus the per-unit surplus ρ_0-P goes to the acquiring firm's investors.)

Exercise 14.3 (liquidity management and acquisitions). Consider the model of Section 14.2.5 when the retooling cost is random. Suppose that this retooling cost is drawn from cumulative distribution function $F(\rho)$ on $[0,\infty)$, with density $f(\rho)$ and monotonic hazard rate ($f(\rho)/F(\rho)$ is decreasing). The level of the retooling cost is privately observed by the potential acquirer (the safe firm). The timing is as described in Figure 14.2.

Assume that the safe firm's entrepreneur and investors *ex ante* secretly agree on an investment level I and a credit line L. This credit line can be used if needed for the acquisition by the entrepreneur and completed by the liquidity, $\rho_0 I$, that can be raised through a seasoned offering that dilutes the initial investors. (Fixing a credit line L of this sort is indeed an optimal policy.)

One will assume that the seller always has the bargaining power ($z=1$ in the notation of Section 14.2.5) and therefore sets price P. Lastly, let ρ^* denote the equilibrium threshold for the retooling cost (that is, assets in equilibrium are acquired and retooled if and only if $\rho\leqslant\rho^*$).

(i) Write the entrepreneur's optimal liquidity management (to this end, follow the steps described in Chapter 5). Show that given (anticipated) equilibrium price P, the threshold ρ^* satisfies the "indifference between make and buy" equation:

$$P+\rho^*=1.$$

(ii) Write the objective function of the risky firm when in distress. Compute the equilibrium price P. Note that $P<1$. What happens to P if for some reason the anticipated level L increases?

(iii) Suppose that the cumulative distribution function $F(\rho)$ converges to a spike at $\bar{\rho}$.[35] Show that

$$P+\bar{\rho}=1,$$

and that $F(\rho^*)$ converges to 1.

34. Comparing this steady state with one that prevails when $L=0$, the rental rate is larger due to the large investment afforded by the introduction of the pure store of value.

35. While still satisfying the monotone hazard rate property.

Exercise 14.4 (inefficiently low volume of asset reallocations). This exercise applies the logic of corporate risk management developed in Chapter 5 to show that, even with frictionless resale markets, there will be an inefficiently low volume of transactions in the secondary market.

There are three dates, $t = 0, 1, 2$, and at least two firms $i = 1, 2$.

Firm 1, the firm of interest, is managed by a risk-neutral entrepreneur, who owns initial wealth A at date 0 and is protected by limited liability. This firm invests at a variable investment level $I \in [0, \infty)$. The per-unit profitability of investment is random and learned at date 1. The investment yields RI with probability $p + \tau$ and 0 with probability $1 - (p + \tau)$. The random variable τ is drawn from a continuous distribution. The variable p is equal to p_H if the entrepreneur behaves (no private benefit) and p_L if the entrepreneur misbehaves (private benefit BI). Let

$$\rho_1 = (p_H + \tau)R$$

and

$$\rho_0 = (p_H + \tau)\left(R - \frac{B}{\Delta p}\right) \equiv \rho_1 - \Delta\rho$$

denote the random continuation per-unit NPV and pledgeable income when the entrepreneur behaves and the realization of profitability is τ. The distribution on τ induces a cumulative distribution function $F(\rho_0)$ on $[\underline{\rho}_0, \bar{\rho}_0]$.

At date 1, the firm may either continue or resell assets I to firm 2 (or to a competitive market). Firm 2 has a known level $\hat{\rho}_0$ of per-unit pledgeable income per unit of investment (its NPV per unit of investment is in general larger than this).

Firms 1 and 2 do not contract with each other at date 0. Rather, investors in firm 1 make a take-it-or-leave-it offer to firm 2 at date 1 if firm 1's initial contract specifies that assets ought to be reallocated.

Assume for simplicity that the contract between firm 1's investors and the entrepreneur can be contingent on the realization of ρ_0.

Show that at the optimal contract assets are resold whenever $\rho_0 < \rho_0^*$, where

$$\rho_0^* < \hat{\rho}_0,$$

and so the volume of asset reallocations is inefficiently low.

References

Aghion, P., P. Bacchetta, and A. Banerjee. 2004. Financial development and the instability of open economies. *Journal of Monetary Economics* 51:1077–1106.

Aghion, P., A. Banerjee, and T. Piketty. 1999. Dualism and macroeconomic volatility. *Quarterly Journal of Economics* 114:1321–1358.

Akerlof, G. 1970. The market for lemons, qualitative uncertainty and the market mechanism. *Quarterly Journal of Economics* 84:488–500.

Eisfeldt, A. 2004. Endogenous liquidity in asset markets. *Journal of Finance* 59:1–29.

Eisfeldt, A. and A. Rampini. 2003. Capital reallocation and liquidity. Mimeo, Northwestern University.

Freixas, X. and J. C. Rochet. 1997. *Microeconomics of Banking.* Cambridge, MA: MIT Press.

Holmström, B. and J. Tirole. 2005. Inside and outside liquidity (Wicksell Lectures). Mimeo, MIT and IDEI, Toulouse.

Kiyotaki, N. and J. Moore. 1997. Credit cycles. *Journal of Political Economy* 105:211–248.

Maksimovic, V. and G. Phillips. 2001. The market for corporate assets: who engages in mergers and asset sales and are there efficiency gains? *Journal of Finance* 56:2019–2065.

Perotti, E. and J. Suarez. 2002. Last bank standing: what do I gain if you fail? *European Economic Review* 46:1599–1622.

Schoar, A. 2002. Effects of corporate diversification on productivity. *Journal of Finance* 57:2379–2403.

Shleifer, A. and R. Vishny. 1992. Liquidation values and debt capacity: a market equilibrium approach. *Journal of Finance* 47:1343–1366.

Vayanos, D. 1998. Transactions costs and asset prices: a dynamic equilibrium model. *Review of Financial Studies* 11:1–58.

Williamson, O. 1975. *Markets and Hierarchies: Analysis of Antitrust Implications.* New York: Free Press.

——. 1985. *The Economic Institutions of Capitalism.* New York: Free Press.

Woodford, M. 1990. Public debt as private liquidity. *American Economic Review, Papers and Proceedings* 80:382–388.

15

Aggregate Liquidity Shortages and Liquidity Asset Pricing

15.1 Introduction

15.1.1 The Investors' Commitment Problem and the Demand for Stores of Value

As stressed repeatedly throughout this book, agency problems deprive firms of a proper access to finance. Despite the many strategies designed to boost pledgeable income, firms often cannot invest as much and under the same conditions as they would if they did not need outside funding.

This chapter shows that agency may generate an additional source of inefficiency. Namely, production plans that generate a positive present discounted value (PDV) of *pledgeable* (i.e., investor) income, estimated at the investors' intertemporal marginal rate of substitution (IMRS), may not be feasible.

This new departure from the Arrow–Debreu paradigm arises when firms face sequential financing needs and agency will in the future continue to create a wedge between value and pledgeable income, that is, when refinancing is not a foregone conclusion.

A key difference between credit rationing at the initial financing stage and credit rationing at later refinancing stages is that the latter can be planned and addressed.

In Chapter 5, though, we assumed either (a) that investors could commit to refinance the firm out of their own future income as specified in the initial contract or, alternatively, (b) that stores of value could be set aside that could be called upon to allow investors to fulfill their contractual refinancing obligations. By contrast, in a world in which investors cannot pledge their future human capital (or, for some of them, are not yet born), investors may be unable to commit to inject new funds as required in the future unless there exists in the economy a sufficient quantity of stores of value that enable investor commitment.

In an *efficient production plan*, each entrepreneur maximizes her utility subject to the investors' intertemporal budget constraint: the PDV of investors' income net of investments, assessed at the investors' IMRS, must be nonnegative.

An efficient production plan may require a transfer of wealth across states of nature or across time: the firm may need cash injections in the future in adverse states of nature, while being a source of cash for the investors in more favorable ones; or the firm may have excess cash in some period that it would like to carry over to later periods if earnings and investment opportunities are asynchronized.

Two kinds of stores of value or liquid assets allow firms to transfer wealth across states of nature or across time:

Inside liquidity, namely, liquidity created by the corporate sector through the issuance of claims on its future cash flow—equity and debt claims in firms that other firms can use as stores of value and resell when funds are needed. Among other things, this chapter asks whether the corporate sector as a whole creates enough stores of value on its own.

Outside liquidity, namely, liquidity generated "outside" the corporate sector—land or other natural resources, or rents already existing in the economy;[1] or, as will be discussed in Section 15.3.3, government-created liquidity such as Treasury securities.

1. The distinction between inside and outside liquidity is not as clear cut as it would seem. In practice, some of the existing rents have been created by the corporate sector. In the end, though, what matters is the total amount of stores of value that can be harnessed to operate the future wealth transfers.

15.1.2 Chapter Outline

Section 15.2 analyzes transfers of wealth across states of nature. To measure inside liquidity, it embeds the corporate-liquidity-demand framework of Chapter 5 in a general equilibrium setting. As in Chapter 5, a borrowing firm anticipates the accrual of liquidity needs later on. Concerned about being rationed by the credit market in the future, it optimally demands some insurance against it; that is, it secures liquidity that it will be able to use in adverse circumstances. As we just discussed, Chapter 5, however, assumed either that current investors were able to commit to bring the funds even when reinvesting augments their losses, or that there existed a sufficient amount of stores of value to allow investors to abide by their promise.

Section 15.2 therefore raises the sufficiency question: does the volume of equity and debt claims on the corporate sector suffice to resolve the investors' commitment problem and thereby to allow entrepreneurs to achieve their efficient production plan? A simple and general self-sufficiency result emerges: even in the absence of outside stores of value, efficient production plans can be implemented provided that (a) the liquidity needs are independently distributed across firms (there is no aggregate shock), and (b) the existing liquidity is pooled among firms and dispatched through a system of credit lines (liquidity is not wasted).

Section 15.3, in contrast, shows that aggregate uncertainty creates scope for a shortage of inside liquidity even if it is pooled and dispatched properly. This lack of self-sufficiency introduces a role for outside liquidity and generates liquidity premia (i.e., a market return below the interest rate predicted by the IMRS) for assets that are used as stores of value. Asset prices are then determined not solely by the assets' stochastic yields and the consumers' IMRS, but also by their consumption or supply of liquidity services.

Finally, Section 15.4 shows that similar insights arise even in the absence of aggregate uncertainty provided that firms have asynchronized income and projects and are at times net lenders, so that they must transfer wealth forward in time.

Most of this chapter, except the end of Section 15.4, will focus on a three-period setting: $t = 0, 1, 2$. All economic agents (entrepreneurs, investors) will have preferences over consumption streams $\{c_0, c_1, c_2\}$ such that $c_t \geqslant 0$ for all t:

$$U = c_0 + c_1 + c_2.$$

In particular, the investors' IMRS is equal to 1, i.e., consumers demand a rate of return equal to 0. Any return above or below 0 will therefore be attributable to a liquidity service or consumption. (The end of Section 15.4 will consider an extension to the infinite-horizon setting, with the natural generalization of preferences: $U = \sum_t \beta^t c_t$ with discount factor $\beta < 1$; the IMRS is then equal to β.)

(This chapter borrows particularly heavily from my joint work with Bengt Holmström (see Holmström and Tirole 1996, 1998, 2001, 2002, 2005) and from the many discussions about the literature that I have had with him.)

15.2 Moving Wealth across States of Nature: When Is Inside Liquidity Sufficient?

This section argues that the corporate sector as a whole creates enough liquidity to sustain an efficient production plan provided that

- the corporate sector is a net borrower,
- there is no economy-wide shock, and
- liquidity is dispatched properly within the corporate sector.

The third assumption will be discussed in this section, while the first and the second will be relaxed in Sections 15.4 and 15.3, respectively.

15.2.1 The Sufficiency Result

15.2.1.1 Model

We first illustrate the sufficiency result in the context of the two-shock, variable-investment version of Section 15.3.1,[2] and then point at the generality of the result.

There are three periods, $t = 0, 1, 2$. Investors are risk neutral and the market rate of interest in the economy is 0. The economy is also populated by a

2. Although the reader may want to return to Section 5.3.1 in order to refresh his/her memory, the presentation here is entirely self-contained.

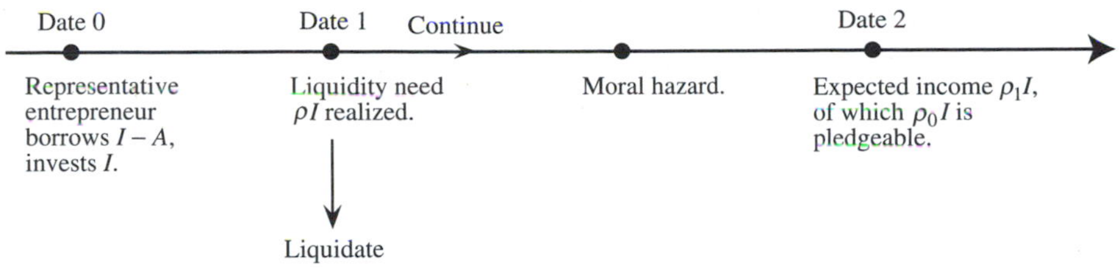

Figure 15.1

large number—technically a continuum of mass 1—of *ex ante* identical, risk-neutral entrepreneurs. The representative entrepreneur at date 0 has wealth A, borrows $I - A$, and invests I. At date 1, a given firm faces liquidity shock ρI, with

$$\rho = \begin{cases} \rho_L & \text{with probability } 1 - \lambda \text{ (healthy firm),} \\ \rho_H > \rho_L & \text{with probability } \lambda \text{ (firm in distress).} \end{cases}$$

The firm can continue only if it finds funds to defray its liquidity shock; otherwise, it is liquidated. We normalize the liquidation value at 0.

In the case of continuation, the firm's date-2 expected income is denoted by $\rho_1 I$, of which only $\rho_0 I < \rho_1 I$ is pledgeable to investors (see Figure 15.1).[3]

15.2.1.2 Efficient Allocation

Let us assume that

$$\rho_L < \rho_0 < \rho_H < \rho_1 \tag{15.1}$$

and

$$(1 - \lambda)(\rho_H - \rho_L) < 1. \tag{15.2}$$

Let us first discuss condition (15.1). Note that a firm can, at date 1, raise ρ_0 per unit of investment by returning to the capital market and by issuing new claims on date-2 profit (i.e., by diluting the claims of the date-0 investors in the firm). The inequality $\rho_H > \rho_0$ means that in the bad (high-shock) state of nature, the "wait-and-see" policy of returning to the capital market if needed will not suffice to cover the high realization of the liquidity shock. The condition $\rho_H < \rho_1$ means that continuation is *ex post* socially desirable even in the case of a high liquidity shock. Lastly, we assume that $\rho_L < \rho_0$. Otherwise the liquidity shock would always exceed the pledgeable income and so investors could never recoup their date-0 investment and would not lend, which would violate the net-borrowing assumption.

As was stressed in Chapter 5, there is a trade-off between investment scale and continuation. That continuation in the high-liquidity-shock state is *ex post* socially desirable ($\rho_1 > \rho_H$) does not imply that it is *ex ante* optimal for the entrepreneur. Continuation in the high-liquidity-shock state is costly to investors ($\rho_H > \rho_0$), making them less eager to fund investment at a given investment scale and forcing the entrepreneur to reduce investment size. Condition (15.2) implies, as we will show, that the high liquidity shock is small enough and sufficiently frequent that the entrepreneur is willing to accept a lower investment scale in exchange for being able to continue when $\rho = \rho_H$.

Because investors lose money (even abstracting from any contribution to the initial investment) in the event of an adverse shock ($\rho_H > \rho_0$), they would never by themselves refinance the firm at date 1 in that state of nature. Let us in a first step ignore this difficulty (which is, however, central to the insights of this chapter), and assume that somehow investors can commit to any probability x in $[0, 1]$ of continuation in the adverse state of nature and that they do not demand an extra return for this (that is, they just want to recoup the extra loss $x(\rho_H - \rho_0)I$ induced by continuation in that state). One can, for example, imagine that there exists in the economy a sufficient quantity of stores of value that in exchange for 1 unit of good at date 0 deliver 1 unit of good at date 1.[4]

3. The wedge between date-2 value and pledgeable income can, as in Chapter 5, be motivated by moral-hazard considerations: the firm yields RI with probability p and 0 with probability $1 - p$. The probability p of success is equal to p_H if the entrepreneur behaves and $p_L = p_H - \Delta p$ if she misbehaves. Letting BI denote the entrepreneur's private benefit in the case of misbehavior, the entrepreneur must be given reward R_b in the case of success such that $(\Delta p)R_b \geqslant BI$, and so $\rho_1 \equiv p_H R$ and $\rho_0 = p_H[R - B/\Delta p]$.

4. Or, for that matter, at date 2, since consumers at date 1 are willing to pay 1 for an asset that yields 1 at date 2.

The investors' outlay at date 0 is equal to $I - A$, their expected outlay at date 1 is $((1-\lambda)\rho_L + \lambda\rho_H x)I$, and their expected income is $(1-\lambda+\lambda x)\rho_0 I$. Hence, the investors' breakeven constraint is

$$[1 + (1-\lambda)\rho_L + \lambda\rho_H x]I - A \leqslant [1-\lambda+\lambda x]\rho_0 I.$$

The *efficient allocation* is defined as the one that maximizes the representative entrepreneur's utility subject to the constraint that investors break even at their IMRS. Note that such an allocation is efficient given the existence of an agency cost (put differently, it is "constrained efficient"). This efficient allocation solves

$$\max_{\{I,x\}}\{(1-\lambda+\lambda x)(\rho_1 - \rho_0)I\}$$

s.t.

$$[1 + (1-\lambda)\rho_L + \lambda\rho_H x]I - A \leqslant [1-\lambda+\lambda x]\rho_0 I.$$

Using the investors' breakeven constraint (satisfied with equality), we can compute I as a function of x:

$$I = \frac{1}{(1 + (1-\lambda)\rho_L + \lambda\rho_H x) - (1-\lambda+\lambda x)\rho_0} A.$$

And so the efficient allocation is given by

$$\max_{\{x\}}\left\{\frac{(1-\lambda+\lambda x)(\rho_1-\rho_0)}{(1 + (1-\lambda)\rho_L + \lambda\rho_H x) - (1-\lambda+\lambda x)\rho_0} A\right\}.$$

As in Chapter 5, consider the "unit cost of effective investment," that is, the average cost of bringing 1 unit of investment to completion. If x is the probability of continuation at date 1 in the high-shock state, then the total—investment plus reinvestment—cost per unit of initial investment is $1 + (1-\lambda)\rho_L + \lambda\rho_H x$, yielding a total probability of continuation[5] equal to $1-\lambda+\lambda x$. And so the unit cost of effective investment is

$$c(x) \equiv \frac{1 + (1-\lambda)\rho_L + \lambda\rho_H x}{1-\lambda+\lambda x}.$$

The program yielding the efficient allocation becomes

$$\max_{\{x\}}\left\{\frac{(\rho_1-\rho_0)A}{c(x)-\rho_0}\right\}.$$

The optimal x must therefore minimize $c(x)$, which, together with condition (15.2), implies that

$$x = 1.$$

5. Alternatively, x could denote the fraction of the initial investment that is not liquidated (i.e., $1 - x$ is the downsizing intensity).

Let us now write the investors' breakeven constraint for the policy of never liquidating:

$$[(1-\lambda)(\rho_0 - \rho_L) + \lambda(\rho_0 - \rho_H)]I = I - A$$

or

$$(\rho_0 - \bar{\rho})I = I - A,$$

where

$$\bar{\rho} \equiv (1-\lambda)\rho_L + \lambda\rho_H$$

is the expected liquidity shock per unit of investment.

Lastly, we assume that

$$\rho_1 > 1 + \bar{\rho},$$

and so entrepreneurs prefer investing to consuming A (the project's NPV is positive).

To sum up, the efficient allocation is given by

$$x = 1 \quad \text{and} \quad I = \frac{A}{(1+\bar{\rho}) - \rho_0}.$$

15.2.1.3 The Sufficiency Result

Next we assume that investors cannot pledge their future earnings and therefore cannot directly commit to reinject cash at date 1 in the firm when they lose money on this reinjection ($\rho_H > \rho_0$); we ask whether the efficient allocation can nevertheless be implemented.

Assume that the shocks are drawn independently across firms, and so there is no macroeconomic uncertainty. Because the corporate sector is a net borrower,

$$I - A > 0,$$

the investors' breakeven condition implies that investors' profit in the healthy firms (those facing a low shock at date 1) more than offsets the loss that they incur in the others:

$$(1-\lambda)(\rho_0 - \rho_L) > \lambda(\rho_H - \rho_0). \qquad (15.3)$$

We can define (gross) *inside* liquidity as the value, $(1-\lambda)(\rho_0-\rho_L)I$, of healthy firms. Condition (15.3) states that the (gross) inside liquidity exceeds the net refinancing need, $\lambda(\rho_H - \rho_0)I$, of firms facing a high liquidity shock (and so the net amount of inside liquidity, namely, the difference between gross outside liquidity and the net refinancing need, is positive).

Put differently, the corporate sector's long-term investments create enough stores of value in the form of tradable rights to pledgeable date-2 profits that the policy that is optimal when the future is discounted at the investors' rate of time preference can be implemented:

- in the absence of outside stores of value,
- without any need for the corporate sector to create inefficient stores of value.[6]

The reasoning is completely general: as long as the corporate sector is a net borrower, the net value of investors' date-1 claims on the corporate sector must be strictly positive, which implies that reinvestments can be financed through the value of existing shares.

As we will see, this property need not hold in the presence of an aggregate shock.

15.2.2 Wasting Inside Liquidity

The sufficiency result by itself only states that the corporate sector produces enough inside liquidity to support its optimal reinvestment policy. It is silent on *how* the latter can be implemented.

Let us first point out that the "natural implementation," namely, the policy that consists in each firm holding the stock index, that is, a representative portfolio of claims on all firms in the economy, in general does not work. The date-1 value of the index is

$$(\rho_0 - \bar{\rho})I.$$

To see this, note that the corporate sector will return $\rho_0 I$ to investors at date 2. The average reinvestment cost, however, is $((1-\lambda)\rho_L + \lambda\rho_H)I = \bar{\rho}I$, which must be financed at date 1 by issuing new shares on the corporate sector date-2 income and thereby diluting existing shareholders.

Thus, if all firms hold equal shares in the index,[7] those with a high liquidity shock can meet it by reselling shares if and only if[8]

$$(\rho_H - \rho_0)I \leqslant (\rho_0 - \bar{\rho})I$$

or

$$\rho_H + \bar{\rho} \leqslant 2\rho_0. \qquad (15.4)$$

If $\rho_H + \bar{\rho} > 2\rho_0$, then holding the stock index does not allow the firms facing the high liquidity shock to continue.[9]

Why does this "self-provision" of liquidity result in a waste of liquidity? Firms that face a low liquidity shock at date 1 have excess cash for two reasons: first (reasoning in terms of per unit of investment), they can raise up to ρ_0 when they need only ρ_L; second, they have invested in the stock index, with resulting value $\rho_0 - \bar{\rho}$. This excess liquidity is, of course, not fully wasted as the extra profit is partly reappropriated by distressed firms that own a fraction of the stock index and therefore own part of the healthy firms. Still, healthy firms do have excess liquidity. At date 1, they either redistribute the excess cash to or invest it on behalf of their owners; they have no incentive to invest in distressed firms, in which the reinvestment cost exceeds the pledgeable income.

Readers familiar with the treatment of corporate liquidity demand in Chapter 5, on the one hand, and with the Diamond–Dybvig model of consumer liquidity demand of Chapter 12, on the other, will intuit the rational response to this potential waste: in order to force healthy firms to redispatch cash to distressed ones at date 1, firms must at date 0 pool their liquidity and organize a system of (or akin to) *credit lines*. For example,[10] shares are deposited with one (or an arbitrary number of) financial institutions; each firm is then entitled to draw on a credit line up to a cap of $\rho_H I$.[11] The financial institution can raise the cash needed to honor the credit lines by selling at date 1 shares it holds in firms to date-1 investors.[12] From the net-borrower assumption, the

6. For example, such inefficient inside liquidity could take the form of short-term investments that deliver less than 1 unit of good at date 1 per unit of investment at date 0.

7. Implementing the optimal policy would be even more difficult with unequal shares, since the firms with fewer-than-average shares would have a harder time satisfying (15.4) below.

8. A related way to derive the same inequality goes as follows. The stock index *at the end of date* 1, as we noted, has value $\rho_0 I$. And so the total value for investors of a firm that holds the index is its own value plus the index, or $2\rho_0 I$. However, it must sell some of this stake to meet its liquidity shock $\rho_i I$, where $i \in \{L, H\}$. Hence, the firm's pledgeable wealth at the end of date 1, $2\rho_0 I - E(\rho_i I) = (2\rho_0 - \bar{\rho})I$, must exceed the high liquidity need, $\rho_H I$.

9. Or forces them to downsize if part of the investment can be abandoned without impacting the rest of the investment.

10. We assume that firms cannot misuse their credit lines, say, by demanding more than what they need and investing at date 1 in inefficient projects; see Holmström and Tirole (2005) for an analysis of what happens when they can engage in such misuse. Also, there is some indeterminacy here as to the way in which the efficient allocation can be collectively implemented. The key feature shared by these implementations is the centralized dispatch of liquidity.

11. Healthy firms draw only $\rho_L I$.

12. As will be discussed in more detail below, we assume that individual investors have at date 1 cash on hand that they can use to buy shares in the firms. That cash, however, cannot be committed in the

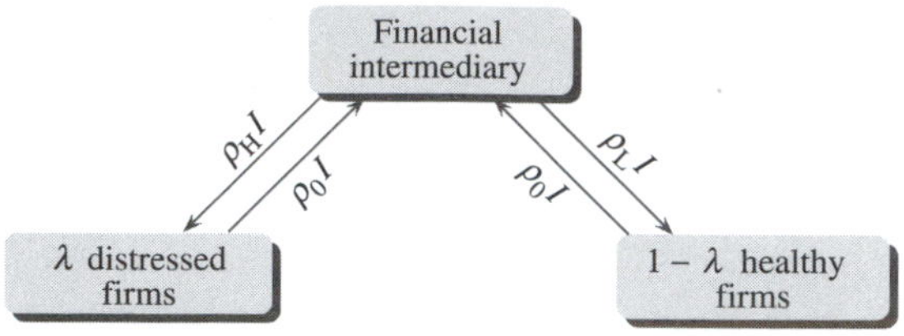

Figure 15.2

proceeds of such sales can cover the financing of the credit lines:[13]

$$(1-\lambda)(\rho_0 - \rho_L)I > \lambda(\rho_H - \rho_0)I$$

(see Figure 15.2).

Discussion. The implications of a self-provision of liquidity have been investigated in detail in an international context by Caballero and Krishnamurthy (2001, 2003, 2004a,b). Their models are richer than the one presented here, in (at least) two ways. First, they involve two goods (tradables, nontradables) rather than one; a liquidity shortage can then be interpreted as a lack of international liquidity (technically, a shortfall in tradables) for the country. Second, the supply of liquidity is not fixed, but increases with its price; namely, firms can create liquidity by investing in (low-yield) short-term investments (on this see Chapter 12).

Caballero and Krishnamurthy, for example, consider settings in which domestic borrowers must borrow in dollars (tradables) at date 0 to produce pesos (nontradables) at date 2. A fraction of firms experience a high liquidity shock at date 1, formalized as the need to reinject dollar-denominated investment into the firm. Each firm thus makes two uses of dollars at date 0: long-term investment and reserves for a possible date-1 liquidity shock. Caballero and Krishnamurthy show that, from a social viewpoint, firms (which do not coordinate their liquidity provision) overinvest in the illiquid asset and underinvest in reserves (hence, the use of "underinsurance" in the title of their 2003 paper). Healthy firms resell their extra dollars at date 1 to distressed ones who pledge nontradable collateral in exchange. But they need not appropriate the full surplus of continuation and so, at date 0, there is underinvestment in reserves.[14]

In practice, liquidity may be wasted in other ways. For example, a lack of coordination may result in too many asset sales in a recession. One may have in mind here banks disposing of their large commercial and residential real estate portfolios when their capital adequacy becomes insufficient. With a downward-sloping demand for the corresponding assets, such "fire sales" depress the price; put differently, the sellers could be better off agreeing to limit the amount of asset sales in bad times.[15]

Lorenzoni (2003) develops a setting in which there is no firm-specific uncertainty and thus only an aggregate shock (so wasting liquidity by failing to pool it is not an issue) and in which financiers can write detailed state-contingent contracts with entrepreneurs. Workers (risk-neutral ones), however, are hired after the aggregate shock is realized. While wages are determined *ex post* through the labor market clearing equation and therefore are state contingent (they are lower in recessions), their evolution does not mimic an optimal *ex ante* labor contract. Put differently, workers *ex post* do share some of the risk with firms, but they do not contribute in the *ex ante* optimal way to the optimal sharing of risk in the economy (here, the efficient provision of liquidity to firms, due to worker risk neutrality). This reasoning is reminiscent of the observation that investors *ex post* do not provide the *ex ante* socially efficient volume of funds to a firm that has not planned its liquidity management. Under worker risk neutrality,

form of credit lines granted by the consumers to the firms at date 0 either because consumers "were not yet born" or because their date-1 cash comes from labor income and human capital is inalienable.

13. Alternatively, the intermediary can grant a credit line equal to $(\rho_H - \rho_0)I$ per firm, and allow the firm to raise further income by issuing new securities. Firms in distress raise $\rho_0 I$ by diluting their owner and complement this amount by drawing on the credit line. Healthy firms do not need to draw on the credit line and may just issue enough securities to raise $\rho_L I$.

14. Another contribution that builds on self-provision of liquidity (but in a closed-economy context) is Kiyotaki and Moore (2001), which develops an infinite-horizon model in which a store of value commands a liquidity premium. In each period only a fraction of entrepreneurs have an investment opportunity. In order to be able to borrow and invest, credit-rationed entrepreneurs must carry net worth from the previous period through holding stores of value (a bit like in the Kiyotaki–Moore model reviewed in Section 14.3). Entrepreneurs self-provide their liquidity, i.e., they do not pool. This waste of liquidity creates a shortage of liquidity even in the absence of aggregate liquidity shock.

15. The analysis is similar to that of the impact of cartelization of the asset resale market on pledgeable income (see the analysis in Exercise 4.16).

an *ex ante* labor contract is a way of committing "funds" in the form of a substantial wage reduction during hard times in exchange for a rent (relative to a spot labor market outcome) for the workers in good times. Lorenzoni shows that the firms' balance sheet may be overexposed to the aggregate shock.

Yet another way in which liquidity may be wasted is when consumers themselves demand liquidity. For example, consumers may demand liquid assets more when fearing unemployment. But the consumer demand for liquidity drains the liquidity available to corporations, which may need to lay workers off in a recession. To avoid this, complex coordination between firms and their employees might be needed.[16]

15.3 Aggregate Liquidity Shortages and Liquidity Asset Pricing

15.3.1 Aggregate Shocks and the Value of Outside Liquidity

Suppose now that liquidity shocks are perfectly correlated across firms in the model of Section 15.2 (that firms face the same shock is the starkest way of introducing an aggregate shock; Exercise 15.3 studies the more general case of imperfectly correlated shocks). In this polar case, and in the absence of outside liquidity, firms cannot continue when $\rho = \rho_H > \rho_0$:

$$x = 0.$$

We will assume that the entrepreneurs prefer investing to consuming even if the investment is liquidated in the bad state of nature, i.e., that, per unit of investment, the expected output $(1-\lambda)\rho_1$ exceeds the sum of the initial investment cost, 1, and the expected reinvestment cost, $(1-\lambda)\rho_L$:

$$(1-\lambda)\rho_1 > 1 + (1-\lambda)\rho_L.$$

(This positive-NPV assumption is more stringent than the previous one: $\rho_1 > 1 + \bar{\rho}$.)

Because all firms are valueless in the bad state of nature, distressed firms cannot meet liquidity shocks by selling (even indirectly through a financial intermediary) shares in healthy ones.

The problem is that money cannot be moved across states of nature at date 1. The corporate sector has a high value in the good state of nature (when $\rho = \rho_L$) but, according to the continuation strategy defined in Section 15.2, is a "sink" in the bad state of nature (when $\rho = \rho_H$). In the latter state, investors are unwilling to bring more than $\rho_0 I$ when $\rho_H I$ would be needed.

The key source of inefficiency is the inability of investors to commit to transfer the large profit that they can make in the good state of nature to subsidize firms in the bad state of nature. This inability of investors to commit to refinancing firms in a recession may have two sources:

- consumers with income to invest at date 1 are not yet born at date 0, or
- consumers with income to invest at date 1 are already present at date 0, but they are unable to pledge their future income (say, the income derived from their human capital) at dates 1 and 2.

In practice, two factors may lead to a less drastic conclusion:

(a) First, there may be alternative stores of value. There may exist exogenous or outside stores of value (e.g., land). Alternatively, the corporate sector itself may create stores of value, for example by investing in "inefficient projects" that have a low yield, but support reinvestment in the more efficient projects in a recession.

(b) Second, the government's regalian power of taxation may help harness the investors' otherwise unpledgeable income in the bad state of nature at date 1.

Here we introduce outside stores of value into the picture. For simplicity, there are L^S such stores of value. A store of value yields 1 unit of good at date 1 for certain. Its date-0 price is q; because the market rate of interest is equal to 0 and investors can buy the store of value,

$$q \geqslant 1.$$

Furthermore, if $q = 1$, then the corporate sector is able to implement its efficient allocation. If $q > 1$, then the corporate sector must hold all stores of value.[17]

16. For more on the waste of liquidity, see Holmström and Tirole (2005).

17. This is, of course, extreme. We could allow consumers to face liquidity shocks themselves (as in Chapter 12) and hold some of the liquid assets.

In the bad state of nature, the representative firm continues with probability x. Equivalently, a fraction $1-x$ of its investment is liquidated. For ease of exposition, we will work under the latter interpretation.

The liquidity need in the bad state, $\rho_H xI$, must not exceed the sum of the amount $\rho_0 xI$, which can be raised by returning to the capital market at date 1, and of the income L associated with a date-0 purchase of outside liquidity in amount L. And so

$$(\rho_H - \rho_0)xI \leqslant L.$$

The investors' breakeven constraint condition states that the total investor date-0 outlay to pay for illiquid and liquid assets should be recouped from the pledgeable income:

$$[I + qL] - A \leqslant L + (1-\lambda)(\rho_0 - \rho_L)I + \lambda(\rho_0 - \rho_H)xI.$$

To make things interesting, we will assume that L^S is not so large that $q = 1$ (we will later provide a condition for this to be the case). $q > 1$ only if firms compete with each other for the scarce liquidity. The date-0 price q adjusts to the level at which the demand for liquid assets is equal to the supply:

$$L = L^S.$$

Let

$$U_b = [(1-\lambda)(\rho_1 - \rho_L) + \lambda(\rho_1 - \rho_H)x]I - (q-1)(\rho_H - \rho_0)xI - I \quad (15.5)$$

denote the representative borrower's utility or net present value, given that an amount of liquidity $L = (\rho_H - \rho_0)xI$ is required to bring a fraction x of investment to completion in the bad state of nature.

The investors' breakeven constraint can be rewritten as

$$[(1-\lambda)(\rho_0 - \rho_L) + \lambda(\rho_0 - \rho_H)x]I - (q-1)(\rho_H - \rho_0)xI \geqslant I - A. \quad (15.6)$$

This constraint yields the investment level I as a function of x and q. Substituting into (15.5),

$$U_b = \frac{\rho_1 - c(x,q)}{c(x,q) - \rho_0} A,$$

where

$$c(x,q) = \frac{1 + (1-\lambda)\rho_L + \lambda\rho_H x + (q-1)(\rho_H - \rho_0)x}{1 - \lambda + \lambda x}$$

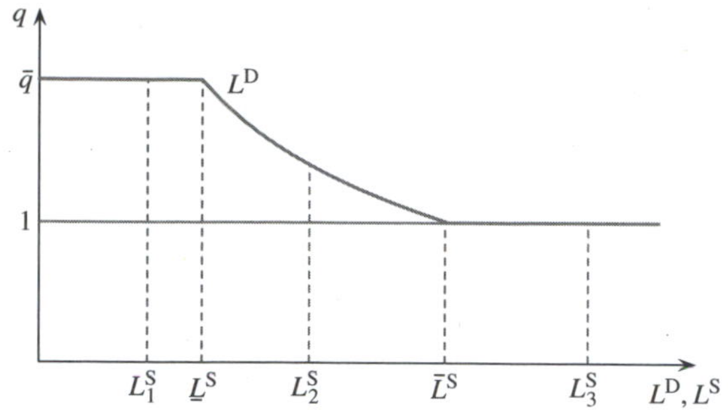

Figure 15.3

is the cost of effective investment, that is, the average cost of bringing 1 unit of investment to completion. Let $\bar{q}$ be given by

$$\frac{\partial c}{\partial x}(x, \bar{q}) = 0$$

$$\iff \quad (1-\lambda)(\rho_H - \rho_L) + \frac{(1-\lambda)}{\lambda}(\rho_H - \rho_0)(\bar{q} - 1) = 1.$$

Then

$$\begin{aligned} x &= 1 && \text{if } q < \bar{q} \\ &= 0 && \text{if } q > \bar{q} \\ &\in [0,1] && \text{if } q = \bar{q}. \end{aligned}$$

For $q < \bar{q}$, the demand for liquid assets is given by

$$L^D = (\rho_H - \rho_0)I = \frac{\rho_H - \rho_0}{c(1,q) - \rho_0} A.$$

The equilibrium in the market for liquidity is depicted in Figure 15.3, where

$$\bar{L}^S \equiv \frac{(\rho_H - \rho_0)A}{1 + \bar{\rho} - \rho_0}$$

is the lowest amount of outside liquidity such that the market clearing price for liquidity is $q = 1$.

Figure 15.3 illustrates the three regions. When liquidity is very scarce ($L^S = L_1^S$ for example), there is liquidation ($x < 1$); the price of liquid assets is then the highest price, $\bar{q}$, that firms are willing to pay in order to hold this liquidity and be able to salvage their assets in the bad state of nature. As the supply of liquidity L^S increases, x increases. Once x reaches 1, the price of liquid assets adjusts. A lower price increases the firms' borrowing capacity and, indirectly, the demand for liquid assets, which are a complementary input into the production process. This region is illustrated by $L^S = L_2^S$ in

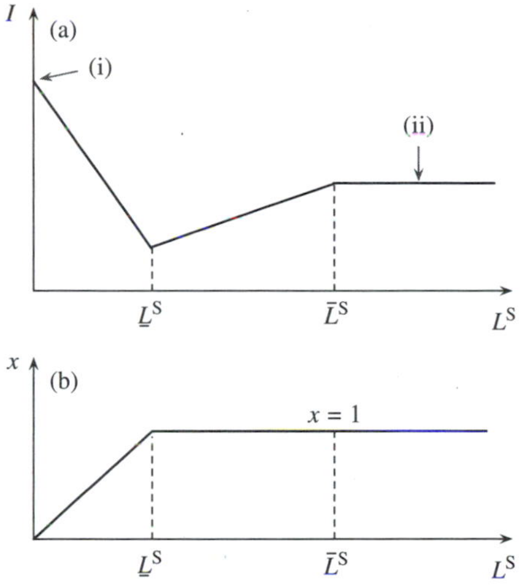

Figure 15.4 (a) (i) $I = A/(1 + (1-\lambda)\rho_L - (1-\lambda)\rho_0)$; (ii) $I = A/(1 + \bar{\rho} - \rho_0)$.

Figure 15.3. Finally, for $L^S \geqslant \bar{L}^S$ (for instance $L^S = L_3^S$ in Figure 15.3), there is an excess supply of liquidity. The market price is then $q = 1$, and the excess liquidity, $L^S - \bar{L}^S$, is absorbed by individual investors, who demand a rate of return equal to 0.

Does liquidity crowd investment in or out? Figure 15.4 illustrates the relationship between liquid and illiquid assets: a higher stock of liquid assets first depresses and then boosts corporate investment.[18]

Whether liquid assets crowd in or out illiquid ones depends on whether the entrepreneurs are willing to invest without continuing in the adverse state of nature ($(1-\lambda)\rho_1 > 1 + (1-\lambda)\rho_L$) or not. In the former case, which we have just analyzed, the purchase of liquid assets first comes at the expense of investment: liquid assets *crowd out* illiquid ones. For larger amounts of liquidity ($L \geqslant \bar{L}_S$), $x = 1$ and liquid assets and investment are necessarily *complements*: a larger stock of liquid assets lowers the liquidity premium $(q-1)$ and thereby the cost of investment.[19]

When investing yields a negative NPV per unit of investment when the investment is liquidated in the adverse state ($(1-\lambda)\rho_1 < 1 + (1-\lambda)\rho_L$), entrepreneurs invest only if they can complement their illiquid investment with liquidity. In this case, liquid and illiquid investments are always *complements* (see Exercise 15.4).

Remark (using foreign liquidity). It might appear that a shortage of liquidity at the domestic level could be compensated by resorting to international liquidity. After all, aggregate shocks are likely to be smaller in relative size at the world level than at a country's level. For example, Thai banks and firms could obtain liquidity through a credit line from a consortium of international banks or by holding shares in the U.S. S&P500 index. This resort to international liquidity is unfortunately limited by the country's own pledgeability problem (also called the "shortage of international collateral"). Thus the conclusions reached in this section carry over to an environment of capital account liberalization.[20]

15.3.2 Liquidity Asset Pricing

The analysis in the previous subsection focused on the pricing of safe claims, namely, claims that deliver a constant yield at date 1 regardless of the state of the economy. We now note that risky claims can also be priced out by invoking the value of their "liquidity service" (or disservice).[21]

In our example, there are only two aggregate states of nature: $\omega \in \{\mathrm{L}, \mathrm{H}\}$. Let $m(\omega)$ denote (one plus) the liquidity service of the safe claim, i.e., the marginal utility of one more unit of good available at date 1 in state of nature ω. Because there is no demand for liquidity in the good state of nature,

$$m_L = 1.$$

By contrast, 1 unit of good available in the bad state of nature generally has a value in excess of 1:

$$m_H \geqslant 1.$$

18. For $L^S < \underline{L}^S$, $x < 1$ and $q = \bar{q}$. Investment is then given by

$$[1 + (1-\lambda)\rho_L - (1-\lambda)\rho_0]I + [(\bar{q}-1) + \lambda]L^S = A.$$

For $L^S \in [\underline{L}^S, \bar{L}^S]$, $x = 1$ and $q \leqslant \bar{q}$. Furthermore,

$$L^S = (\rho_H - \rho_0)I \quad \text{and} \quad I = \frac{A}{1 + \bar{\rho} + (q-1)(\rho_H - \rho_0) - \rho_0}.$$

19. Note that our choice of consumer preferences $(c_0 + c_1 + c_2)$ implies that stores of value cannot crowd out investment through an increase in the rate of interest demanded by consumers. An elastic savings function would add a factor of substitutability between stores of value and investment as in Diamond (1965) and Tirole (1985).

20. On this, see Caballero and Krishnamurthy (2001, 2003, 2004a,b) and Holmström and Tirole (2002).

21. For more details, see Holmström and Tirole (2002, 2005).

m_{H} can be computed from the price of the safe asset:

$$q = E[m(\omega) \cdot 1] = 1 - \lambda + \lambda m_{\mathrm{H}},$$

and so

$$q - 1 = \lambda(m_{\mathrm{H}} - 1). \qquad (15.7)$$

The liquidity premium, $q - 1$, is equal to the product of the probability λ that the asset will perform a liquidity service and the net value, $m_{\mathrm{H}} - 1$, of this service.

$m(\omega)$ is the liquidity asset pricing model (LAPM) analog of the stochastic discount factor in the consumption-based capital asset pricing model (CCAPM).[22] Like the stochastic discount factor, it allows a systematic pricing of assets with arbitrary return streams. Using the expression of m_{H} given in (15.7), one can then find the date-0 price, per unit of expected return, of an arbitrary asset i with flow return $\{y^i(\omega)\}_{\{\omega=L,H\}}$:

$$q^i = \frac{E[m(\omega)y^i(\omega)]}{E[y^i(\omega)]}.$$

Consider, for example, the representative firm with investment I whose shares are acquired by a financial institution that also hoards liquid assets and grants the firm the right to draw enough liquidity in order to continue in the bad state of nature. From the point of view of the financial institution, this firm yields

$$y^{\mathrm{firm}}(L) = (\rho_0 - \rho_{\mathrm{L}})I \quad \text{and} \quad y^{\mathrm{firm}}(H) = -(\rho_{\mathrm{H}} - \rho_0)I.$$

Hence, its price is

$$\begin{aligned} q^{\mathrm{firm}} &= \frac{[(1-\lambda)(\rho_0 - \rho_{\mathrm{L}}) - \lambda(\rho_{\mathrm{H}} - \rho_0)m_{\mathrm{H}}]I}{[(1-\lambda)(\rho_0 - \rho_{\mathrm{L}}) - \lambda(\rho_{\mathrm{H}} - \rho_0)]I} \\ &= 1 - \frac{\lambda(\rho_{\mathrm{H}} - \rho_0)(m_{\mathrm{H}} - 1)}{E[y^{\mathrm{firm}}(\omega)/I]} \\ &= 1 - \frac{(q-1)[(\rho_{\mathrm{H}} - \rho_0)I]}{E[y^{\mathrm{firm}}(\omega)]}. \end{aligned}$$

Because it consumes rather than supplies liquidity in the bad state of nature, the firm is valued below par, that is, it exhibits an equity premium. In this simple model, the equity premium is perfectly negatively correlated with the liquidity premium $q - 1$, as q varies between 1 and $\bar{q}$ (due to variations in the supply of outside liquidity, say).

22. For expositions of the CCAPM, see, in particular, Campbell et al. (1996), Cochrane (2005), and Duffie (2001).

15.3.3 Government Provision of Outside Liquidity

We saw that, whenever liquidity is properly dispatched within the corporate sector, the failure to achieve the efficient allocation stems from the investors' inability to promise income to the corporate sector in the bad state of nature.[23] In that state of nature and under condition (15.2), continuation is desirable, but the corporate sector is *ex post* unable to convince investors to bring cash, as only part of the benefits from continuation can be returned to them.

The government's unique ability to tax consumers can make up for the latter's inability to pledge money to the corporate sector. Ideally, the government would like to boost the corporate sector's solvency in the bad state of nature by taxing consumers and transferring the proceeds to the corporate sector. Such a policy need not be to the detriment of consumers, though: the government can tax the corporate sector in the good state of nature and thereby compensate (in expectation) consumers for the loss they incur in the bad state of nature. But optimal liquidity provision is *contingent* liquidity provision: the government must operate a redistribution from the households to corporations in those states of nature in which the latter encounter hardship.

In practice, the creation of outside liquidity by the government takes a variety of other forms, among which only a richer model can distinguish. One has the government issue Treasury bonds (at date 0 in our model). These bonds are akin to the stores of value studied in Section 15.3.1, in that they can be used by the corporate sector to overcome the high liquidity shock. The government can create liquidity and thereby affect the allocation because it has access to consumers' date 1 (and 2) endowments and can thereby back the bond issue through this tax "collateral."

It is also important to stress that liquidity is created by forcing consumers to redistribute toward the corporate sector in bad times. Were the coupons of the Treasury bonds financed through a corporate tax, the Treasury bonds would do nothing to boost

23. This feature underlies the non-Ricardian properties discussed below.

the corporate sector solvency in bad times: the logic of this argument elaborates on that underlying the result that an investment subsidy financed through a corporate income tax has no effect on investment (see Exercise 3.19).

Other ways in which the government creates liquidity and supports economic activity in bad times include a countercyclical monetary policy; deposit insurance premia that are not indexed to the business cycle (banks are riskier in a recession and therefore market-based deposit insurance premia would then adjust upwards) and use of the discount window; publicly provided unemployment insurance (in a recession, layoffs are more frequent and workers remain unemployed for a longer period of time, so a market-based, private layoff insurance scheme would yield high premia in recessions); implicit guarantees to private pension funds; and so forth.

These injections of liquidity are either discretionary (e.g., countercyclical monetary policy) or part of an automatic stabilization mechanism (e.g., nonindexed deposit insurance premia). As Sundaresan and Wang (2004) point out, explicit preannouncements of liquidity provision are rare because the timing of liquidity crises is uncertain. These authors, though, identify one episode in which the government offered state-contingent liquidity: the century change date. There was a fear that a Y2K computer bug might provoke widespread difficulties and a severe liquidity crisis. Sundaresan and Wang first present evidence for the United States of high liquidity premia associated with this concern. They then describe and assess how private sector concerns were partially alleviated by the central bank's provision of state-contingent liquidity. For example, the Federal Reserve auctioned off call options on the ability to borrow from the discount window at dates around January 1, 2000, at a strike set at 150 basis points above the prevailing Federal funds rate; other auctions related to the right to enter overnight repo transactions with the New York Fed at a preset strike price (also 150 basis points above the prevailing Federal funds rate).

Finally, this informal treatment of government creation of outside liquidity misses a discussion of the cost of this creation. For example, taxing consumers involves a deadweight loss of taxation.[24] Clearly, the government must engage in a cost-benefit analysis when choosing how much liquidity to create. The market for liquid assets may help guide the government in this respect, as liquidity premia reflect the corporate demand for stores of value and their scarcity. Similarly, along the intertemporal dimension, the design of the term structure of public debt can be guided by the liquidity premia embodied in the bonds of various maturities.

15.4 Moving Wealth across Time: The Case of the Corporate Sector as a Net Lender

Historically, the enabling of transfers of wealth by stores of value was first stressed in environments where wealth had to be moved across periods rather than across states of nature. It has, for example, figured prominently in the overlapping generations (OLG) literature,[25] in which consumers want to save some of the income earned when young for their old-age consumption. To give this older literature a corporate finance connotation, let us follow Woodford (1990) in assuming that entrepreneurs' income and investment opportunities are asynchronized.

We still consider three dates, $t = 0, 1, 2$. Assume a continuum of mass 1 of identical entrepreneurs. The representative entrepreneur is, as earlier, born with endowment A at date 0. She no longer has any meaningful investment opportunity at that date, however. By contrast, she anticipates that she will at date 1 have a variable-investment-size project: by investing $I \in [0, \infty)$ at date 1, the entrepreneur will create an expected income equal to $\rho_1 I$ at date 2, of which only $\rho_0 I$ is pledgeable to date-1 investors. As in Section 3.4, we assume that

$$\rho_1 > 1 > \rho_0,$$

so that investment has a positive NPV, but pledgeable income per unit of investment is lower than unity.

24. The size of the deadweight loss may further depend on whether taxes are levied during the recession (in which case they may impose further hardships on households, who may be laid off by their firm) or delayed through the use of government borrowing.

25. First developed by Allais (1947), Samuelson (1958), and Diamond (1965).

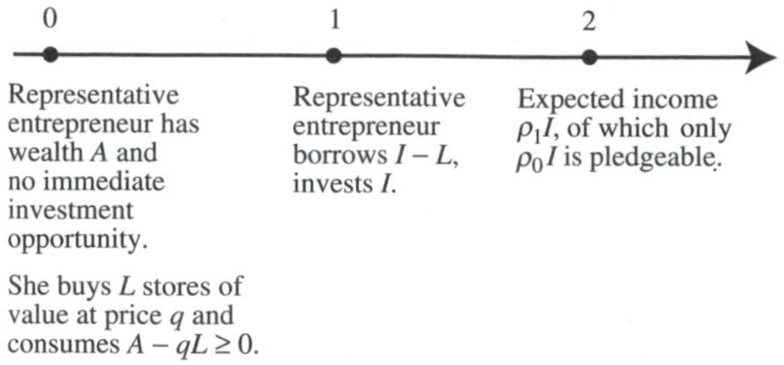
0
1
2
Representative entrepreneur has wealth A and no immediate investment opportunity.
She buys L stores of value at price q and consumes A − qL ≥ 0.
Representative entrepreneur borrows I − L, invests I.
Expected income ρ1I, of which only ρ0I is pledgeable.

Figure 15.5

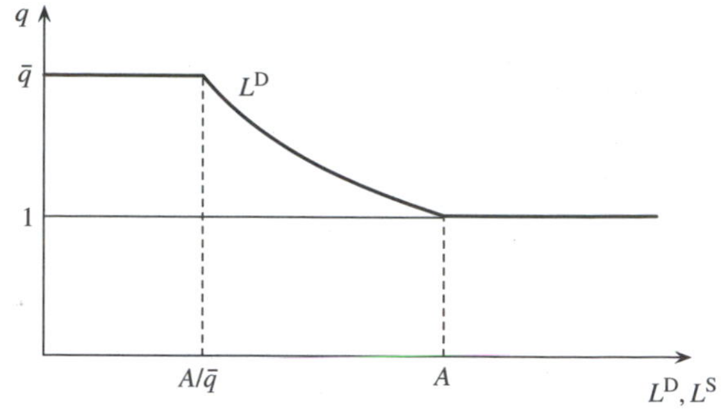
q
q̄
1
L^D
A/q̄
A
L^D, L^S

Figure 15.6

We further assume that there exist L^S stores of value at date 0, each of which deliver 1 unit of good at date 1.

The timing is summarized in Figure 15.5.

We obtain the equilibrium outcome by working backwards in time. Assume that, at date 1, the representative entrepreneur has wealth L (she has then consumed $A - qL$ at date 0). The analysis is identical to that of Section 3.4, for that level of net worth. The entrepreneur's borrowing capacity is determined by the date-1 investors' breakeven constraint:

$$I - L = \rho_0 I \quad \Longleftrightarrow \quad I = \frac{L}{1 - \rho_0}.$$

The NPV—which, due to the breakeven condition, goes to the entrepreneur—corresponds to the nonpledgeable part:

$$(\rho_1 - \rho_0)I = \frac{\rho_1 - \rho_0}{1 - \rho_0} L.$$

Turning now to the market for liquid assets at date 0, note that the representative entrepreneur's intertemporal utility is

$$[A - qL] + \left[\frac{\rho_1 - \rho_0}{1 - \rho_0} L\right],$$

where L must satisfy $qL \leqslant A$.

Qualitatively, there can be two equilibrium configurations.

Excess liquidity: $L = A \leqslant L^S$ and $q = 1$. When there is a large number of stores of value ($L^S \geqslant A$), the latter command no liquidity premium. Entrepreneurs save their entire endowment and invest it at date 1.

Scarce liquidity: because entrepreneurs are willing to pay up to

$$\bar{q} \equiv \frac{\rho_1 - \rho_0}{1 - \rho_0} > 1$$

per unit of liquidity, as L^S falls below A, the price first adjusts so as to clear the supply and the demand for liquidity,

$$A = qL^S,$$

until L^S reaches the level $A/\bar{q}$. As L^S falls further, the price of liquidity stabilizes at the entrepreneurs' willingness to pay $\bar{q}$ (see Figure 15.6).

In the region in which liquidity is very scarce ($L^S < A/\bar{q}$), *financial development*, interpreted as an increase in the extent of pledgeability ρ_0 (keeping ρ_1 constant), makes liquidity more valuable and raises its price (that is, $\bar{q}$ increases).

Creation of liquid instruments by the corporate sector. Suppose now that $L^S = 0$, but that each entrepreneur can, at date 0 and at increasing and convex cost $C(L)$, create L units of income at date 1. The privately optimal investment is given by[26]

$$C'(L) = \bar{q} = \frac{\rho_1 - \rho_0}{1 - \rho_0}.$$

Note, in particular, that the marginal unit of inside liquidity thus created has a negative return ($1/\bar{q} < 1$). Indeed, if $C'(0) \geqslant 1$, all units of liquidity have a negative return. Yet, each entrepreneur is willing to invest in these inefficient projects in order to benefit from the attractive investment opportunities at date 1.

Infinite-horizon versions. There are at least two ways of extending these ideas to infinite-horizon settings. First, we can follow Woodford (1990) in assuming multiple categories of infinitely lived entrepreneurs. Woodford's model has two groups of entrepreneurs. A group-1 entrepreneur receives an endowment A (of a nondurable good) in each

26. Provided that $C'(0) < \bar{q} < C'(C^{-1}(A))$.

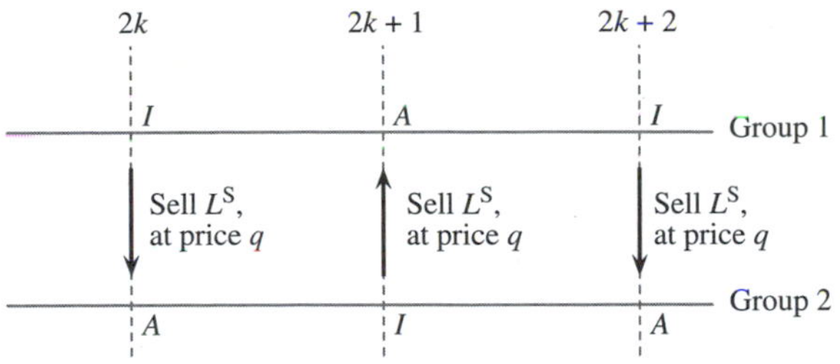

Figure 15.7

odd period; she has investment opportunities only in even periods. A group-2 entrepreneur in contrast receives endowment A (of a nondurable good) in each even period and has investment opportunities in odd periods.

For expositional simplicity, Woodford assumes that the return on investment is immediate (accrues at the period in which the investment is made), and that none of it is pledgeable ($\rho_0 = 0$).

The only means of transferring wealth from periods of endowment to periods of investment is ownership of a store of value. There are L^S consols or consol bonds[27], each yielding 1 unit of nondurable good per period, forever.

In equilibrium, group-1 entrepreneurs purchase the store of value from group 2 in odd periods; and vice versa in even periods (see Figure 15.7).

All have preferences

$$\sum_{0}^{\infty} \beta^t c_t,$$

where $\beta < 1$ is the discount factor and $c_t \geqslant 0$ is consumption. In a period with an investment opportunity, investing I yields $\rho_1 I$ (of which, recall, nothing is pledgeable). We assume that $\beta\rho_1 > 1$, so delaying consumption in order to invest is worthwhile. Focusing for conciseness on the case in which there are few consols, the price of consols, q, is given by

$$q = \beta(1 + q)\rho_1,$$

since one consol purchased at date t yields dividend 1 and generates resale price q, and this net worth $(1 + q)$ enables the entrepreneur to invest at the same level (due to $\rho_0 = 0$), yielding $(1 + q)\rho_1$.

27. A bond is a consol bond if it does not have a maturity and pays a fixed coupon perpetually.

Note, in particular, that the rate of return on consols, $1/q$, is smaller than the agents' rate of preference $(1 - \beta)/\beta$: the liquid asset sells at a *discount*.[28]

An alternative approach is to posit an OLG structure. In order to facilitate comparison with the Woodford model, let us assume that investment I yields $\rho_1 I$ within the same period and that none of this income is pledgeable to investors.[29]

Generation t (G_t) comprises a unit mass of entrepreneurs. G_t's representative entrepreneur receives exogenous and nondurable endowment A and can use it either to consume at date t or to purchase L_t consols from generation G_{t-1}, which will enable her to invest at $t + 1$ (see Figure 15.8). There are L^S consols in the economy, each delivering 1 unit of perishable good per period, forever. In equilibrium, L_t must be equal to L^S for all t.

Let β denote the discount factor between the two periods of a generation's life. G_t's representative entrepreneur's utility from consumption (c_t, c_{t+1}) at dates t and $t + 1$ is thus $u_t = c_t + \beta c_{t+1}$.

Focusing again on the case in which there are few consols, the market price of a consol is given by the same condition as in the Woodford model:

$$q = \beta(1 + q)\rho_1.$$

Every generation but the first has utility $u_t = A$, since it is in equilibrium indifferent between buying consols and consuming the endowment. The initial generation (that born with the consols, which start delivering income at date 1, say) has utility $u_0 = A + \beta(1 + q)L^S\rho_1 = A + qL^S$.[30]

28. Put differently, the rate of interest on a consol, r^c, is given by $q \equiv 1/r^c$. The rate of time preference, r, satisfies $\beta \equiv 1/[1 + r]$. And so $r^c < r$.

29. This total lack of pledgeability makes the analogy with the Allais-Samuelson-Diamond OLG model particularly striking. For, an old consumer in this model consumes but cannot borrow.

30. Under the OLG structure and under certain circumstances, all generations can be made better off through a sequence of transfers from each generation to the previous one. Suppose, for example, that $L^S = 0$, and so all generations including the initial one have utility $u_t = A$. Suppose that the initial generation sells a "bubble" (i.e., an asset paying no dividend and with rate of return equal to the market rate of interest) $b = A$ to the second generation, and so forth. Then each generation but the first has utility $u_t = \beta\rho_1 A > A$. The first generation also gains as it gets $u_0 = A + \beta\rho_1 A$. (With consols $L^S > 0$, the feasibility of such schemes depends on the rate of growth of the economy and on whether the consols appear over time or are capitalized at the initial date (see, for example, Tirole 1985).)

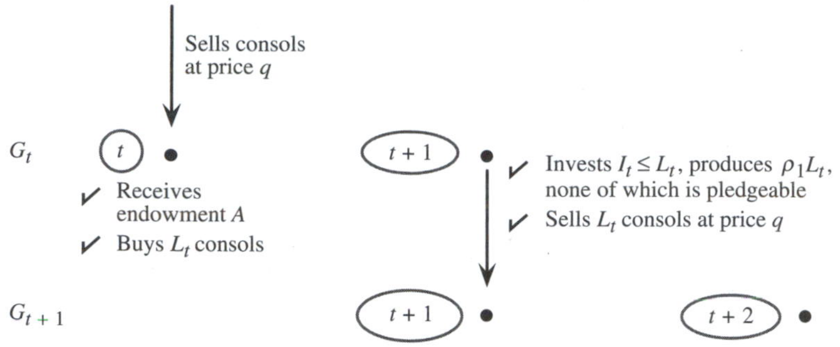

Figure 15.8

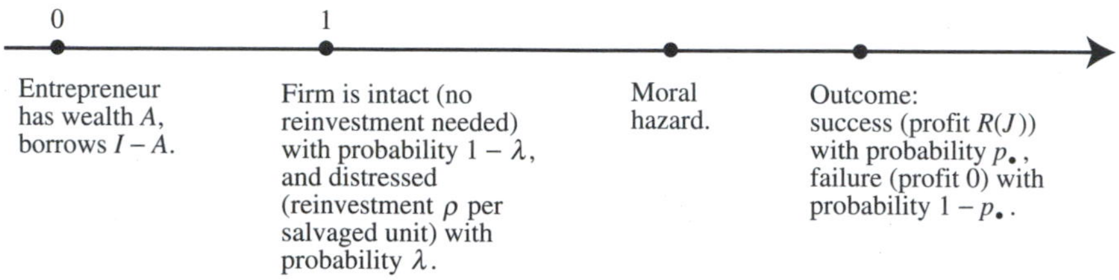

Figure 15.9

15.5 Exercises

Exercise 15.1 (downsizing and aggregate liquidity). Consider the variable-investment model with *decreasing* returns to scale and a liquidity shock. There is a unit mass of identical entrepreneurs. The timing for a given entrepreneur is in Figure 15.9.

At date 1, an amount J, $0 \leqslant J \leqslant I$, is rescued. In the absence of a liquidity shock (event has probability $1-\lambda$), of course $J = I$. But in the face of a liquidity shock (which has probability λ), the investment is downsized to $J \leqslant I$ (the cost of continuation is then ρJ). The shock is verifiable. Let $R(J)$ denote the profit in the case of success.

The moral-hazard stage is described as it usually is: the probability of success is p_{H} if the entrepreneur works and $p_{\mathrm{L}} = p_{\mathrm{H}} - \Delta p$ if she shirks. The entrepreneur obtains private benefit BJ by misbehaving and 0 otherwise. Investors and entrepreneur are risk neutral, and the latter is protected by limited liability.

Economic agents do not discount the future (which does not imply that rates of interest are always 0!).

From now on, use J for the amount that is salvaged when there is a liquidity shock (as we noted, the corresponding amount is I in the absence of shock).

Assume that $R(0) = 0$, $R' > 0$, $R'' < 0$, $R'(0) = \infty$, $R'(\infty) = 0$.

(i) Assume that there is plenty of liquidity in the economy, so that the firms have access to a store of value (by paying $q = 1$ at date 0, they receive 1 at date 1).

Show that downsizing occurs in the case of a liquidity shock,

$$J^* < I^*,$$

if and only if

$$\rho > \frac{1}{1-\lambda}.$$

(Hints: (1) write the incentive constraints (the sharing rule can be adjusted to the realization of the shock) and infer the pledgeable income; (2) maximize the entrepreneur's utility (employ the usual trick) subject to the investors' breakeven condition, ignoring the constraint $J \leqslant I$; let μ denote the shadow price of the constraint; (3) derive the stated result.)

(ii) Suppose that the liquidity shocks are *perfectly correlated.*

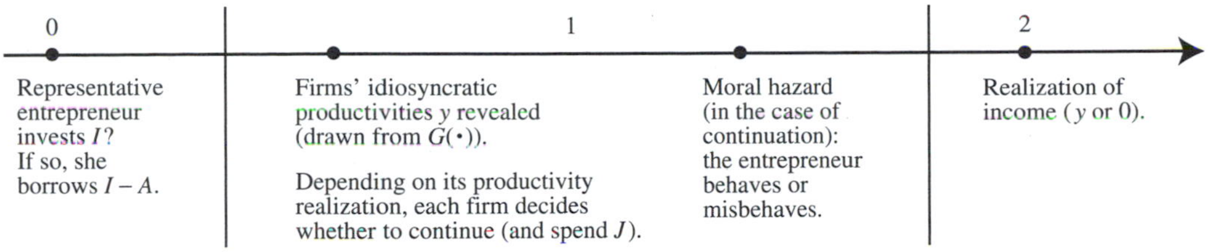

Figure 15.10

- What is the minimal number L^* of outside stores of value (delivering 1 unit of good each at date 1) needed to support the allocation described in (i)?
- Argue that if $L < L^*$, then $q > 1$ and $J < I$ *a fortiori* if $\rho > 1/(1-\lambda)$.

  Derive the equations giving the liquidity premium $(q-1)$ under these assumptions.

(iii) Suppose now that the liquidity shocks are independent across firms.

- Argue that (provided that the entrepreneurs borrow at date 0) there is enough liquidity to support the allocation derived in (i).
- Suppose that each entrepreneur holds the stock index. When will this provide enough liquidity? How can one prevent this potential waste of liquidity?

Exercise 15.2 (news about prospects and aggregate liquidity). Consider an economy with a continuum of identical risk-neutral entrepreneurs. The representative entrepreneur has a fixed-size investment project costing I, and limited personal wealth $A < I$. The project, if undertaken, will deliver a random but verifiable income $y \in [0,1]$, with cumulative distribution function $G(y)$ and density $g(y)$, provided that a reinvestment J is made after y is learned, but before y is produced. The project yields nothing if it is interrupted.

Moreover, in the case of "continuation" (that is, if J is sunk), and regardless of the value of y, the entrepreneur may behave, in which case income is y for certain, or misbehave, in which case income is y with probability p_L and 0 with probability $1-p_L$. The entrepreneur, who is protected by limited liability, obtains private benefit B when misbehaving (and no private benefit otherwise). Let

$$\mathcal{R} \equiv \frac{B}{1-p_L}$$

(one will assume that B is small enough that, in the relevant range, it is worth inducing the entrepreneur to behave in the case of continuation).

The timing is summarized in Figure 15.10.

The rate of interest in the economy is equal to 0.

(i) Compute the NPV and the investors' net income as functions of the threshold y^* for continuation.

(ii) Let $y_0^* \equiv J$ and $y_1^* = J + \mathcal{R}$.

Define A_0^* and A_1^* by

$$I - A_k^* \equiv \int_{y_k^*}^{1} y\,\mathrm{d}G(y) - [1 - G(y_k^*)][J + \mathcal{R}],$$

for $k \in \{0,1\}$.

• What are the date-0 investment policy (investment/no investment) and the date-1 reinvestment policy (the threshold y^*) as functions of A? (Hint: distinguish three regions $A \geqslant A_0^*$, $A \leqslant A_1^*$, and $A_1^* < A < A_0^*$.)

• Argue that, for $A > A_1^*$, the entrepreneur must arrange at date 0 for her firm's date-1 liquidity.

(iii) • Is there enough inside liquidity if productivities are drawn *independently* from the distribution $G(\cdot)$? Why?

(iv) Suppose, in contrast, that there is a macroeconomic shock θ that is revealed at the beginning of date 1. (One will denote by $E_\theta[\cdot]$ the date-0 expectations over the random variable θ.) Let $y^*(\theta)$ denote the state-contingent threshold.

• Write the date-0 financing constraint.

• Show that the optimal threshold when liquidity is abundant is actually state independent: there exists y^* such that

$$y^*(\theta) = y^* \quad \text{for all } \theta.$$

• Show that the second-best allocation can be implemented when there are at least

$$\min_{\{\theta\}} \int_{y^*}^{1} (y - J - \mathcal{R})\,\mathrm{d}G(y \mid \theta)$$

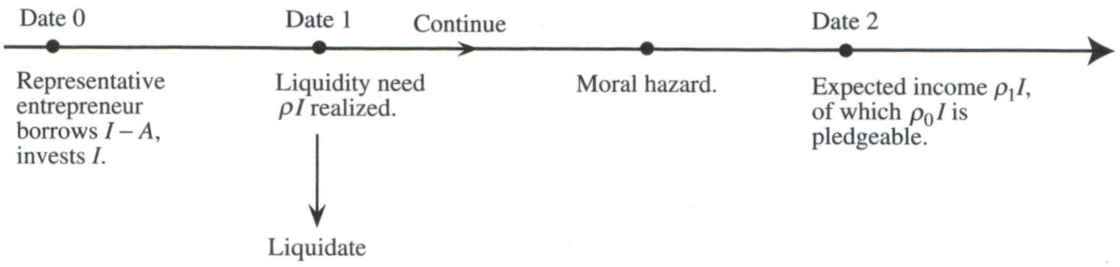
Date 0
Date 1
Continue
Date 2
Representative entrepreneur borrows $I - A$, invests I.
Liquidity need ρI realized.
Moral hazard.
Expected income $\rho_1 I$, of which $\rho_0 I$ is pledgeable.
Liquidate

Figure 15.11

units of outside liquidity delivering 1 unit of good for certain at date 1.

• What would happen if there were few such stores of value?

Exercise 15.3 (imperfectly correlated shocks). This exercise extends the analysis of Section 15.3 to allow for imperfect correlation among the shocks faced by the firms. As in Section 15.3.1, there is a mass 1 of *ex ante* identical entrepreneurs. Each entrepreneur has a constant-returns-to-scale project. An investment of size I at date 0 yields $\rho_1 I$ at date 2, of which $\rho_0 I$ is pledgeable, provided that the liquidity shock ρI is met at date 1. ρ is equal to ρ_L with probability $(1-\lambda)$ and ρ_H with probability λ, with $\rho_L < \rho_0 < \rho_H < \rho_1$ and $(1-\lambda)(\rho_H - \rho_0) < 1$. As usual, entrepreneurs and investors are risk neutral, and the latter demand a rate of return equal to 0 (see Figure 15.11).

The new feature is that shocks are imperfectly correlated: for a fraction $1-\theta$ of entrepreneurs, shocks are drawn independently ($\theta = 0$ in Section 15.2.1). A fraction θ of entrepreneurs face the same shock, ρ_L with probability $(1-\lambda)$ and ρ_H with probability λ ($\theta = 1$ in Section 15.3.1).

There is no outside store of value, and the long-term projects are the only investment projects available to the corporate sector.

Show that the private sector is self-sufficient (i.e., the efficient allocation can be implemented using the inside liquidity created by the long-term projects) if and only if $\theta \leqslant \theta^*$, where

$$(1-\theta^*)(I-A) = \theta^*(\rho_H - \rho_0)I,$$

where I is independent of θ.

Exercise 15.4 (complementarity between liquid and illiquid assets). Go through the analysis of Section 15.3.1 assuming that entrepreneurs do not want to invest in projects that are discontinued in the adverse state of nature:

$$(1-\lambda)\rho_1 < 1 + (1-\lambda)\rho_L.$$

Show that an increase in the supply L^S of liquid assets increases the investment I in illiquid ones.

References

Allais, M. 1947. *Economie et Intérêt.* Paris: Imprimerie Nationale.

Caballero, R. and A. Krishnamurthy. 2001. International and domestic collateral constraints in a model of emerging market crises. *Journal of Monetary Economics* 48:513–548.

——. 2003. Excessive dollar debt: financial development and underinsurance. *Journal of Finance* 58:867–893.

——. 2004a. A "vertical" analysis of monetary policy in emerging markets. Mimeo, MIT.

——. 2004b. Smoothing sudden stops. *Journal of Economic Theory* 119:104–127.

Campbell, J., A. W. Lo, and C. MacKinlay. 1996. *The Econometrics of Financial Markets.* Princeton University Press.

Cochrane, J. 2005 *Asset Pricing*, 2nd edn. Princeton University Press.

Diamond, P. 1965. National debt in a neo-classical growth model. *American Economic Review* 55:1126–1150.

Duffie, D. 2001. *Dynamic Asset Pricing Theory*, 3rd edn. Princeton University Press.

Holmström, B. and J. Tirole. 1996. Modeling aggregate liquidity. *American Economic Review, Papers & Proceedings* 86:187–191.

——. 1998. Private and public supply of liquidity. *Journal of Political Economy* 106:1–40.

——. 2001. LAPM: a liquidity-based asset pricing model. *Journal of Finance* 56:1837–1867.

——. 2002. Domestic and international supply of liquidity. *American Economic Review* 92:42–45.

——. 2005. *Inside and Outside Liquidity.* Mimeo, MIT and IDEI, Toulouse. Cambridge, MA: MIT Press, in press.

Kiyotaki, N. and J. Moore. 2001. Liquidity and asset prices. Mimeo, Edinburgh University and London School of Economics.

Lorenzoni, G. 2003. The costs of credit booms. Mimeo, Princeton University.

Samuelson, P. 1958. An exact consumption-loan model of interest with or without the contrivance of money. *Journal of Political Economy* 66:467–482.

Sundaresan, S. M. and Z. Wang. 2004. Public provision of private liquidity: evidence from the millennium date change. Mimeo, Columbia Business School.

Tirole, J. 1985. Asset bubbles and overlapping generations. *Econometrica* 53:1071–1100 (reprint 1499–1528).

Woodford, M. 1990. Public debt as private liquidity. *American Economic Review, Papers & Proceedings* 80:382–388.

16

Institutions, Public Policy, and the Political Economy of Finance

16.1 Introduction

Our analysis of financial design has taken the legal, regulatory, social, and political environment as given. We now investigate the determinants of public policies regarding corporate finance. To set the scene, we begin with a few reminders concerning public policy and its normative and positive rationales.

(a) *A large array of policies affecting corporate financing.* The interaction between public policy and corporate financing starts with the various laws and regulations that affect the borrowers' ability to pledge income to the investors. Those rules impact the latter's formal and real control over the firms through voting procedures (one-share–one-vote, proxy by mail, ability to call extraordinary shareholder meetings), board composition, and transparency requirements (disclosure rules, regulation of auditors' or analysts' conflicts of interest); they protect minority shareholders (by limiting controlling shareholders' tunneling ability or ordering mandatory dividends) or creditor rights; and they may shield contracting commitments from borrower opportunism (depending on the efficiency and probity of the court system) or from government intervention into private contracting (debt moratoria, mingling in mergers and acquisitions).[1]

It would, however, be a mistake to restrict attention to rules that explicitly govern the contracting relationship between investors and borrowers, as most public policies influence corporate profitability and pledgeable income: tax, labor, and environmental laws; competition policy; prudential and other regulations with regards to financial intermediaries (capital adequacy and risk management regulations, banking bailouts, promotion of bank competition[2]); policies affecting savings (interest rate regulation) and the macroeconomy; and open-economy policies (trade and capital account liberalization, exchange rate management).

(b) *Rationales and determinants of public policy.* An influential view, developed, for example, in North (1981), distinguishes between the (positive) role of the government as an enabler of private contracting through the provisions of a legal, regulatory, and enforcement environment, and the (negative) role of the government when expropriating private wealth on behalf of powerful interest groups.[3]

Needless to say, this view is overly simplistic for two reasons. First, redistribution, when it operates from the rich to the poor, is a most legitimate objective, even though one can argue about whether the redistribution is best performed through specific policies (such as employment protection, minimum wage, or codetermination) rather than through a progressive income taxation.[4] Second, efficiency-

1. An interesting question is whether the regulatory infrastructure could not be provided by the private sector itself. A number of rules could, of course, be set by the contracting parties themselves, offering more flexibility for financial design; in this view, the government can content itself with (a) the design of some "default rules" that economize on transaction costs for parties whose preferred contractual design is rather ordinary, (b) the enforcement of private contracting arrangements. We will later come back to rationales for government intervention.

2. See Kroszner and Strahan (1999) for an analysis of the politics of the relaxation of bank branching restrictions in the United States.

3. North calls the latter the "predatory theory of the state."

4. In the celebrated model of Atkinson and Stiglitz (1976), the least distortive means of achieving (an arbitrary amount of) redistribution is income taxation. The Atkinson–Stiglitz result implies that redistribution should not be a concern in any other policy dimension. It rests on a number of strong assumptions, such as the perfect observability

enhancing government intervention is not limited to the provision of a contract-enhancing infrastructure. The restrictive view exposited above assumes that if the parties' contracts are enforceable, then they will contract efficiently; that is, the Coase Theorem (1960) will apply. As is well-known, though, private contracts may be inefficient for several reasons. First, the absence of some stakeholders at the bargaining table leads to a failure to internalize their welfare and therefore to contract-generated externalities;[5] we already encountered this rationale when discussing limits on antitakeover devices in Chapter 11. Second, efficient contracting generally requires symmetric information; as discussed in Chapter 6, private information held by the contracting parties may lead to suboptimal or inefficient contracting.[6] Proponents of the view that private contracting inefficiencies may call for government intervention have also put forth the possibility of socially undesirable bargaining positions[7] and, more in accord with supporters of a more laissez-faire approach, the transaction-cost savings of regulation.[8]

(c) *Contracting and property rights institutions.* The chapter's organization reflects a basic distinction between contracting and property rights institutions.[9]

Contracting institutions (analyzed in Section 16.2) will refer to the policy environment that prevails when borrowers, investors, and other stakeholders—most notably the employees—contract. As discussed above, this policy environment includes not only the laws and regulations that govern contracts between borrowers and investors, but other policy variables as well, such as taxes, labor laws, or macroeconomic policies, which also affect pledgeable income and value.

Property rights institutions (studied in Sections 16.3 and 16.4), in contrast, will refer to the permanence of the contracting institutions. Because their relationship is often long lasting, stakeholders cannot take it for granted that the contracting environment in force at the date of contracting will remain unaltered. Public policies may be modified in the future either because of the time inconsistency of public policy (the fact that governments in general would like to commit to future policies that they would have no incentives to abide by when the time comes), as studied in Section 16.3, or because of changes in government, the relative power of interest groups, or the composition of dominant political alliances, as studied in Section 16.4.

When contractual institutions are not remanent, stakeholders must project into the future to forecast how they will evolve over time. In particular, the

---

of income, the identity of tastes (individuals differ in their ability to earn money, but their preferences are separable between their labor input and the basket of goods and services they consume), and the absence of externalities.

5. This is the standard rationale for antitrust enforcement (to protect consumers against undue monopolization or the abuse of market power) and environmental regulation.

6. Aghion and Hermalin (1990) more generally argue that adverse selection provides a rationale for certain types of government intervention into private contracting.

7. As in the cases of duress or unequal expertise. Another argument, of a behavioral nature, stresses individuals' time-inconsistency problems; their desire for instant gratification or avoidance of costly conflict may push them to accept terms of contracting that their "long-term self" would not sign up for. This is the rationale behind cooling-off periods, which allow consumers to cancel certain types of purchases within, say, a week of the purchase.

Our discussion of possible rationales for government intervention is closely related to Shavell's discussion of "legal overriding of contracts" (2004, Chapter 13). Shavell first mentions "harmful externalities" and "losses in welfare to the contracting parties." In the latter category, he includes (a) the possibility for courts to override terms of the contracts that are inconsistent with the court's interpretation of the contract, (b) losses due to asymmetric information at the date of contracting, and (c) misleading representations (as when a person buys food that is mislabeled), including in some cases a lack of disclosure. Shavell then discusses "paternalism" as another oft-cited reason why it may not be optimal to enforce contracts. Paternalism may relate to the prohibition of the sale of things that are deemed inalienable (such as human organs, babies, or voting rights) or to undesirable consumptions (of certain drugs, of pornography for children). Shavell argues (properly in my view) that, once one digs deeper and derives justifications for such paternalism, one is led to consider one of the previous rationales for the legal overriding of contracts (externalities, asymmetric information, individual's time inconsistency, etc.) and so paternalism is not a rationale on its own.

8. A standard illustration is supplied by the fact that very few people read the small print, if any, on the parking ticket when they park their car in a public parking space, or go through the terms of the license of the software they install on their computers. Clearly, it could not be efficient to enforce all contracting provisions in such circumstances, as this would force consumers to devote a wasteful amount of time to protect themselves against exploitative clauses (not to mention the anxiety created by the possibility of mistake).

Transaction costs of contracting can also be reduced by the provision of standard-form agreements (as we already noted), and by the courts' completing incomplete terms "in the spirit of the contract."

9. The definitions given here differ slightly from those found in the literature, most notably in Acemoglu and Johnson (2003). Acemoglu and Johnson define "contracting institutions" as those supporting private contracts, and "property rights institutions" as those constraining the expropriation by government and elite.

credibility of contractual institutions hinges on the cost for governments to renege on their promises or on changing the previous administration's policies. Constitutional provisions, judicial reviews, the outright devolution of decision making to independent bodies,[10] and reputational concerns of entrenched, long-lasting governments all tend to insulate policy from interest group pressure and to make contracting institutions longer lasting.[11] Stakeholders must also anticipate how political majorities may evolve and which interest groups future governments will want to pander to.

16.2 Contracting Institutions

16.2.1 Roadmap

This section focuses on the borrower–investor relationship and analyzes the two parties' preferences over contracting institutions. It first assumes that there are no externalities among borrowers, an assumption which in particular rules out competition for savings (that is, the investors supply funds elastically for a given rate of return).

A key theme of the book has been that borrowers must usually make concessions to investors in order to attract financing. Indeed, most interesting issues in financial design stem from a basic conflict between value and pledgeable income. Borrowers often sacrifice value in order to boost pledgeable income. When pressed to produce return to attract investors, borrowers first offer them a large debt repayment or a higher share of profits. This policy is, however, limited by entrepreneurial moral hazard and must be supplemented by costly concessions.[12] Value is sacrificed until investors get a sufficient rate of return, i.e., until the pledgeable income allows them to recoup their initial outlay.

Importantly, the weaker the firm's balance sheet, the more extensive the concessions made to investors. For example, the weaker the balance sheet (the parentheses refer to the relevant sections, numbered within chapters), the lower the scale of operations (3.4), the higher the amount of costly collateral pledged to investors (4.2), the more restricted the entrepreneur's exit options (4.4), the shorter the debt maturity (5.2), the higher the need for speculative and active monitoring (8.2 and 9.2), the more numerous the control rights conceded to investors (10.2) and, among investors, to creditors (10.4), and the weaker the antitakeover defenses (11.3).

This observation leads to a "topsy-turvy principle" concerning borrowers' preferences over contracting institutions. From an "*ex ante* perspective," firms with weak balance sheets benefit most from strong contracting institutions, which allow them to have access to financing and then to reduce the number of costly concessions that they must make to investors. Once they have raised funds, though, firms with a weak balance sheet often become the most vocal advocates of a weakening in contracting institutions, as they do not want to abide by the concessions that they have made to attract funding in the first place.

Section 16.2.2 provides a few illustrations of this logic. Section 16.2.3 then synthesizes them in a general model. Finally, Section 16.2.4 adds externalities among borrowers to the picture by allowing them to compete either for savings or in the product market.

We will develop these arguments within the fixed-investment model, and will take cash on hand (net worth) as an indicator of the strength of the borrowers' balance sheet (as discussed earlier in the book, there are other indicators, such as those arising from a heterogeneity in opportunities for misbehavior, which lead to similar results).

10. Such as the judiciary or independent agencies (regulatory agencies or central banks).

11. There is a legitimate question as to the desirability of commitment in the realm of public policy. On the one hand, commitment protects stakeholders against expropriation of their specific investments and thereby induces them to invest. On the other hand, a lack of commitment allows more flexibility to react to changes in the environment (when policies cannot be contractually indexed on these changes); it also allows an incoming administration to undo bad public policies chosen by a previous administration that was captured by interest groups (see, for example, the mechanism-design approach in Laffont and Tirole (1993, Chapter 16), which provides conditions under which regulatory flexibility is desirable despite the fact that it allows the regulator to partially expropriate the regulated firm's investment).

Faure-Grimaud and Martimort (2003) analyze the possibility of collusion between interest groups and regulatory agencies in a dynamic setup in which political principals change over time. They show that regulatory independence stabilizes policies by making it harder for a new majority to overrule previous policies and make them more responsive to its own preferences. Independence thus moderates the swings associated with changes in political majorities.

12. Recall that with a dichotomous effort (behavior, misbehavior), pledging a higher share to investors is costless as long as the entrepreneur keeps a sufficient stake to be induced to behave. When effort is continuous, in contrast, the dilution of the entrepreneur's stake always reduces effort away from the efficient level and therefore itself constitutes a costly concession.

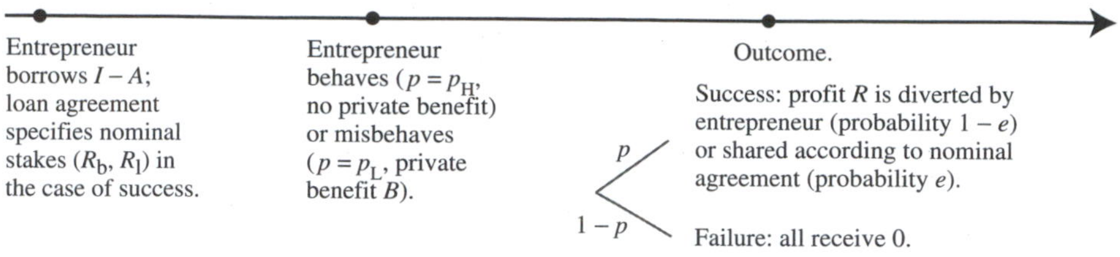
Entrepreneur borrows $I - A$; loan agreement specifies nominal stakes (R_b, R_l) in the case of success.
Entrepreneur behaves ($p = p_H$, no private benefit) or misbehaves ($p = p_L$, private benefit B).
Outcome.
p
$1 - p$
Success: profit R is diverted by entrepreneur (probability $1 - e$) or shared according to nominal agreement (probability e).
Failure: all receive 0.

Figure 16.1

16.2.2 Contracting Institutions, Financial Structure, and Attitudes toward Reform

The illustrations build on the fixed-investment model of Section 3.2: risk-neutral entrepreneurs are protected by limited liability and have a project of size I and cash on hand A, and so must borrow $I - A$. The population of entrepreneurs in the economy is described by the cumulative distribution function $G(A)$; that is, entrepreneur heterogeneity stems from differences in net worth.[13] The project, if funded, yields profit R with probability p and 0 with probability $1 - p$, where p is subject to entrepreneurial moral hazard: $p = p_H$ (the entrepreneur receives no private benefit) or $p = p_L = p_H - \Delta p$ (the entrepreneur receives private benefit B). The market rate of return is, for the moment, normalized at 0; that is, investors stand ready to supply funds as long as they recoup their investment in expectation. We will assume throughout that it is optimal to provide the entrepreneur with an incentive to behave. The project has positive NPV if the entrepreneur behaves, $p_H R > I$, but not if she misbehaves, $I > p_L R + B$.

The first illustration, which follows Acemoglu and Johnson (2003)[14] closely and is developed in Section 16.2.2.1, analyzes this basic model in an imperfect-enforcement environment, where only a fraction of the investors' nominal claim on the final profit is actually returned to investors. Weak enforcement is represented as a reduction in the pledgeable income and in a first step is assumed per se not to destroy value (i.e., it reduces the piece going to investors, not the size of the cake). The other three illustrations are summarized in the text and are treated in more detail in the supplementary section; they extend this imperfect-enforcement model by introducing costly concessions to investors (costly collateral pledging, short-term debt and control rights).

16.2.2.1 Weak Contract Enforcement Impairs Funding Ability

As usual, we let R_l and R_b denote the lenders' and borrower's claims on the final profit in the case of success. Suppose that the investors' claim $R_l = R - R_b$ is enforced only with probability e; relatedly, a fraction of profit could be diverted in all impunity by the entrepreneur.[15] The parameter is a measure of the strength of enforcement. In practice, it is affected by laws,[16] regulations such as those on transparency and minority shareholder protection and by the efficacy and expediency of courts. With imperfect enforcement, we must distinguish between the nominal or contractual entrepreneurial stake R_b in success, and the actual stake, which, with probability $1 - e$, is equal to R and exceeds the contractual stake. We assume that the entrepreneur chooses her effort before knowing whether she will be able to divert income in the case of success (see Figure 16.1).

On the one hand, given nominal stakes (R_b, R_l), an imperfect enforcement makes investors less eager

13. As we just noted, we could alternatively measure the strength of balance sheets through a heterogeneity in benefits from misbehavior or other relevant variables.

14. See also Bolton and Rosenthal (2002) for a theoretical analysis of government intervention in debt contracts.

15. The two interpretations give slightly different expressions since the investors in expectation receive eR_l in the former and $\max\{eR, R_l\}$ in the latter. But the results are very similar for both interpretations.

16. A case in point (studied by Kroszner 1999) is the repudiation by the United States of the gold indexation clause in long-term (private and public) contracts during the Great Depression (the law was passed by Congress on June 5, 1933, and then upheld by the Supreme Court). The debt burden of borrowers would have been 69% (the extent of the devaluation) higher if gold clauses had been enforced.

to lend than when $e = 1$; indeed, they recoup their initial outlay if and only if

$$p_H e R_l \geqslant I - A. \tag{16.1}$$

On the other hand, the entrepreneur, again for given nominal stakes, appropriates a higher fraction of the return, and so has stronger incentives to behave; the incentive compatibility condition is now

$$(\Delta p)[eR_b + (1-e)R] \geqslant B. \tag{16.2}$$

Rewriting the investors' breakeven condition (16.1), a necessary condition for financing is that

$$p_H e R - p_H e R_b \geqslant I - A,$$

or, using the incentive constraint (16.2),

$$p_H e R - p_H \left[\frac{B}{\Delta p} - (1-e)R\right] \geqslant I - A$$

$$\Leftrightarrow \quad p_H\left[R - \frac{B}{\Delta p}\right] \geqslant I - A. \tag{16.3}$$

The reader will here recognize condition (3.3), obtained for $e = 1$. Intuitively, imperfect enforcement implies an extra *ex post* transfer from investors to the entrepreneurs, and this transfer can *ex ante* be undone (reappropriated by the investors) by lowering the nominal reward R_b. Because the *ex post* transfer involves no deadweight loss, the necessary condition for financing is unchanged.

This, however, does not imply that the contracting institutions (here described by the enforcement level e) are irrelevant; the necessary condition (16.3) is also sufficient if and only if one can find a nominal reward $R_b \geqslant 0$ satisfying (16.1) and (16.2). Two cases need to be considered. If $(1-e)R < B/\Delta p$ (which holds when e is close to 1), then, from (16.2), incentive compatibility requires $R_b > 0$ anyway. The necessary and sufficient condition for financing is then (16.3). In other words, small changes in contracting institutions (i.e., in the parameter e) are neutral.

We will focus on the other case by making the following assumption.

Assumption 16.1. $(1-e)R > B/\Delta p$.

This condition, which holds for lower levels of enforcement,[17] states that the entrepreneur is incentivized even in the absence of nominal reward ($R_b = 0$). Under this condition, the breakeven condition, combined with $R_l \leqslant R$, imposes that

$$p_H e R \geqslant I - A$$

or

$$A \geqslant \bar{A}(e),$$

where the threshold,[18]

$$\bar{A}(e) \equiv I - p_H e R, \tag{16.4}$$

is a decreasing function of e: *the stronger the enforcement, the more firms that have access to financing.* The fraction of firms that receive funding is equal to $[1 - G(\bar{A}(e))]$.

Conditional on receiving funding, the borrower's utility is independent of the level of enforcement, since the lack of enforcement involves no deadweight loss and therefore does not impact the NPV:

$$U_b \equiv p_H R - I.$$

Remark. Jappelli et al. (2005) provide empirical evidence of the impact of the quality of contract enforcement on the access to funding. They first develop a theoretical model in which lenders' ability to recoup collateral depends on the efficiency of court enforcement.[19] An improvement in judicial efficiency opens up the credit market to borrowers with little collateral; and so, again, borrowers with weak balance sheets benefit *ex ante* from better corporate institutions. Jappelli et al. then test the model using judicial data for twenty-seven Italian districts.[20] Proxies for court (in)efficiency are taken to be the length of trials and the number of civil suits pending per inhabitant. Judicial districts with better legal enforcement also display more lending and fewer credit constraints.

The topsy-turvy principle. We have assumed that there is commitment as to the level of enforcement. That is, e is determined prior to the investors' funding decision. Let us investigate the political forces that may (a) *ex ante* affect the determination of e and (b) *ex post* create a lobby for a revision of contracting institutions. For expositional simplicity, we

17. Recall that $p_H R > I > p_L R + B$, and so $R > B/\Delta p$.

18. Note that $\bar{A}(e)$ exceeds the value $\bar{A}$ given by $p_H(R - B/\Delta p) = I - \bar{A}$ due to Assumption 16.1.

19. The fraction of the cash flow that can be recouped by investors also depends on the efficiency of the court system in Jappelli et al.

20. See also their paper for references of empirical studies performed on other countries.

will confine our attention to a dichotomous choice between weak institutions ($e = e_W$) and strong institutions ($e = e_S$), where

$$e_W < e_S.$$

From an *ex ante* perspective (that is, prior to the funding decisions), a move from weak institutions to strong ones benefits "borrowers with weak balance sheets," namely, those with

$$\bar{A}(e_S) \leqslant A < \bar{A}(e_W),$$

who receive funding only under strong institutions. "Borrowers with very weak balance sheets," i.e., "nonborrowers" ($\bar{A} < \bar{A}(e_S)$), are indifferent because they never have access to financing. "Borrowers with strong balance sheets" ($\bar{A} \geqslant \bar{A}(e_W)$) are also unaffected by the reform. (Actually, borrowers with strong balance sheets would suffer from institutions being strong rather than weak if savings were not perfectly elastic, so that the entry of entrepreneurs with weak balance sheets would compete the interest rate up. Conversely, borrowers with very weak balance sheets, who really are savers, would benefit from strong institutions if the interest rate were not rigid. See Section 16.2.4.)

Ex post (after investments are made), though, entrepreneurs with initial cash on hand A, provided they receive funding, reimburse $R_1(A)$, given by

$$p_H e R_1(A) = I - A.$$

Thus firms with weak balance sheets reimburse more, regardless of the level of enforcement. This implies that firms with weak balance sheets *ex post* have more incentives to lobby for a weak enforcement. They suffer from time inconsistency as they need a strong enforcement *ex ante* and have a deep interest in a weak enforcement *ex post*. By contrast, firms with a strong balance sheet do not benefit *ex ante* (and, as we noted, even lose if savings are elastic) from strong institutions and are less hurt by strong institutions *ex post*.

16.2.2.2 Contracting Institutions and Concessions (Collateral, Liability Maturity, Control Rights)

The previous simple illustration did not offer scope for costly concessions, that is, payments to investors in "inefficient currencies." Consequently, weak contracting institutions either had no impact or prevented funding altogether. The next three illustrations, developed in the supplementary section, show, among other things, that weak institutions destroy value in a "more continuous way," by forcing the firms to make inefficient concessions. For conciseness, the treatment in the text of these illustrations covers only the key ideas.

• The second illustration enriches the first by allowing the borrower to pledge assets and not only income to investors. In the *costly collateral* model, investors value the assets that they foreclose less than the borrower does, and so the borrower pledges as little collateral as is needed to attract financing. Consequently, firms with weak balance sheets pledge more collateral to make up for the dearth of pledgeable income. Furthermore, and as in Section 4.2, it is efficient to pledge in a contingent rather that unconditional fashion: the collateral is turned over to the investors only if the firm fails.

When investor *claims on income* are better enforced, pledgeable income is more abundant, and so less collateral needs to be pledged: firm value is raised for those borrowers who had (and still have) access to financing. Furthermore, some borrowers who were previously unable to commit enough collateral to attract funds gain access to financing.

When investor *claims on assets* are better enforced (that is, when the probability that investors are indeed able to seize the assets in the case of failure increases), less collateral needs to be pledged in order to boost pledgeable income by a given amount, and again more borrowers get access to financing.

Ex ante, firms with weak balance sheets benefit most from a better enforcement of investor claims on income or assets because better contracting institutions either allow them to gain access to financing or allow them to pledge fewer assets. Once the funds have been raised, though, these weak-balance-sheet firms become the strongest advocates of a relaxation of the enforcement of investor claims, as they have pledged more income and/or more assets to investors.

• The third illustration investigates the impact of contracting institutions on the *maturity structure of liabilities*. Recall from Section 5.2 that firms with weak balance sheets must not only allocate a bigger share of final profit to their investors, but must also issue more short-term debt. Short maturities, while appealing to investors, induce inefficient liquidity shortages and early liquidations. In that sense, they represent a concession to investors.

When investor claims on long-term profit are better enforced, there is more pledgeable income, and so borrowers can contract for more liquidity (less short-term debt) with investors. As a result, firm value increases. The impact on the level of short-term debt, in contrast, is ambiguous. As discussed in Chapter 5, liquidity results from a combination of retained earnings[21] (for cash-rich firms) and the ability to conduct a seasoned offering. With stronger enforcement, a seasoned offering raises more cash, and so, while the contracted-for amount of liquidity increases, the net impact on target retained earnings, and thus on short-term debt, is *a priori* unclear.

The topsy-turvy principle again holds. Firms with weak balance sheets have a particularly short maturity and high risk of illiquidity; hence, they are *ex ante* the primary beneficiaries of a better enforcement. But they become particularly eager to see enforcement relaxed as time goes by.

• The fourth illustration investigates the impact of contracting institutions on *governance*. Recall from Section 10.2 that firms with weak balance sheets must relinquish more control rights to assuage investors. When investor claims on income are better enforced, fewer control rights need be relinquished and borrower utility increases. Furthermore, firms with weak balance sheets *ex ante* benefit most from the better enforcement of investor cash-flow rights, as they value the marginal control rights that they relinquish highly. Similarly, when investor control rights are better enforced, borrowers with weak balance sheets *ex ante* benefit most. As usual, the profile of borrowers' preferences over enforcement as a function of the strength of their balance sheet is reversed once funding has been secured.

21. We abuse terminology slightly by letting "retained earnings" denote the difference between short-term profit and short-term debt (there is no difference between a short-term debt payment and a dividend in the model of Section 5.2).

16.2.3 The Broader Picture

More generally, the borrower makes concessions $c = (c_1, \dots, c_n)$ in order to get investors on board. Concessions may be the investors' income claim, the amount of collateral, the level of short-term liabilities, or the extent of investor control, as in the illustrations above, or any other concession reviewed in this book. The contracting institutions are summarized by a vector $e = (e_1, \dots, e_{\mathrm{m}})$; examples of components of e include, as we have seen, the enforcement of equity and debt claims or that of control rights. But more generally, e stands for all variables that are exogenous to the firm and yet affect pledgeable income and possibly firm value.

The pledgeable income can then be written as[22] $\mathcal{P}(c, e)$, where, in the relevant range,

$$\frac{\partial \mathcal{P}}{\partial c_i} > 0, \quad i = 1, \dots, n \text{ (concessions help attract funding)},$$

$$\frac{\partial \mathcal{P}}{\partial e_j} > 0, \quad j = 1, \dots, m.$$

The investors' breakeven condition is then

$$\mathcal{P}(c, e) \geqslant I - A.$$

The firm's *value gross of investment* can be written $\mathcal{V}(c, e)$, where, in the relevant range,

$$\frac{\partial \mathcal{V}}{\partial c_i} < 0, \quad i = 1, \dots, n.$$

(The NPV is then $\mathcal{V}(c, e) - I$.) When the contracting environment is formalized as the degree of enforcement of cash-flow rights, affecting *ex post* transfers between investors and borrower (Section 16.2.2.1),

$$\frac{\partial \mathcal{V}}{\partial e_j} = 0, \quad j = 1, \dots, m.$$

More generally, though, an investor-friendly contracting environment increases or decreases the NPV for a given design of concessions. A stricter enforcement of investors' claims on costly collateral pledges, for instance, reduces the NPV, ceteris paribus.[23] Or, to take an example not yet alluded to,

22. Here we keep assuming that investment is fixed, and so we omit I in the expression of $\mathcal{P}$. As we note below, this involves no loss of generality.

23. Of course, and as we will see in Section 16.5.1, the borrower may reduce the amount of collateral pledged accordingly so as to keep the same expected value of the pledge as the contracting environment changes.

an investor-friendly environment may create transaction costs or penalize the firm in its competitive environment,[24] as when it involves disclosure of information to investors ($\partial \mathcal{V}/\partial e_j < 0$). Conversely, when we broaden the range of applications of the theory to tax or labor laws, the borrower may benefit from an investor-friendly environment ($\partial \mathcal{V}/\partial e_j > 0$).[25]

Remark (variable investment). While we have apparently stuck to the fixed-investment-size environment, the modeling above actually allows for variable investment size *as long as investment moderation is modeled as a concession.*

To see this, let $\mathcal{P}(I, c, e)$ and $\mathcal{V}(I, c, e)$ denote more generally pledgeable income and value (and so $\mathcal{P} - (I - A)$ is the investors' net profit); suppose that the borrower, ceteris paribus, prefers a larger investment than the investors would want, as has been the case in the models we have considered in the book:

$$\frac{\partial((\mathcal{V} - I) - (\mathcal{P} - (I - A)))}{\partial I} > 0.$$

This inequality has an *ex post* version:

$$\frac{\partial(\mathcal{V} - \mathcal{P})}{\partial I} > 0.$$

Once funding is secured, the entrepreneur receives in expectation the gross value of investment minus what is returned to investors. Indeed, in the relevant range, we have the fundamental equation of credit rationing: at the margin an extra unit of investment increases social value but cannot be funded,

$$\frac{\partial \mathcal{V}}{\partial I} > 1 > \frac{\partial \mathcal{P}}{\partial I}. \tag{16.5}$$

(Suppose that the marginal value of investment and the marginal pledgeable income both exceed 1. Then increasing investment marginally benefits the borrower and facilitates financing. Similarly, if both values are below 1, the two parties benefit from a reduction in investment.) Thus we can view (a low) investment as a concession, $c_{n+1} \equiv -I$, as long as we redefine the pledgeable income in *ex ante* (or net) terms, $\mathcal{P}^{\mathrm{n}} \equiv \mathcal{P} - (I - A)$, with $\partial \mathcal{V}/\partial c_{n+1} < 0$ and $\partial \mathcal{P}^{\mathrm{n}}/\partial c_{n+1} > 0$ in the relevant range.

We are now in a position to examine the impact of a change in the contracting environment on firm value. Treating its components as well as concessions as continuous variables, the borrower solves

$$\max_{\{c\}} \mathcal{V}(c, e)$$

s.t.

$$\mathcal{P}(c, e) \geqslant I - A.$$

And so if μ denotes the shadow price of the financing constraint,

$$\frac{\partial \mathcal{V}}{\partial c_i} + \mu \frac{\partial \mathcal{P}}{\partial c_i} = 0 \quad \text{for all } i.$$

The impact of a change in a component of the contracting environment is

$$\frac{\mathrm{d}\mathcal{V}}{\mathrm{d}e_j} = \frac{\partial \mathcal{V}}{\partial e_j} + \mu \frac{\partial \mathcal{P}}{\partial e_j}.$$

The first term on the right-hand side of this latter equation is the *direct (or cost) effect*; as we observed, this direct effect is equal to 0 if the enforcement relates to cash-flow rights and is a mere transfer between investors and borrower. The second, and more interesting, term is the *enabling effect* (a better enforcement allows the borrower to make fewer costly concessions).

A special case. Let us assume (as in Section 16.2.2.1) that there is no direct effect:

$$\mathcal{V}(c, e) = \mathcal{V}(c).$$

We will furthermore focus on single-dimensional c and e. Figure 16.2 illustrates the funding decision.

In Figure 16.2, the *relevant range* refers to concessions that lie between c^{FB} (the first-best level, which maximizes $\mathcal{V}$) and $c_1^*(e)$ (the concession that maximizes pledgeable income).[26] The figure illustrates the financing decision for three types of firm:

24. For example, the disclosure of information to investors as to the firm's strategy in the market may benefit competitors. It then reduces value even if it raises pledgeable income on balance.

25. One may have in mind, for example, a decrease in wage-related taxes, an increase in R&D investment subsidies, or the provision of communications or telecommunications infrastructures that benefit corporations.

26. For example, in the costly collateral pledging illustration, the first-best level was 0 and the one preferred by investors was the maximum feasible level of collateral. In the maturity liability illustration, the concession referred to (minus) the cutoff liquidity shock that could be withstood by the firm; the first-best cutoff level was (using the usual notation; see also the supplementary section) ρ_1, while the one that maximizes pledgeable income was ρ_0. In the control rights illustration, the first-best level of control rights, derived in the supplementary section, was given by $y'(\tau^{\mathrm{FB}}) = R$; and investors wanted as many control rights as possible.

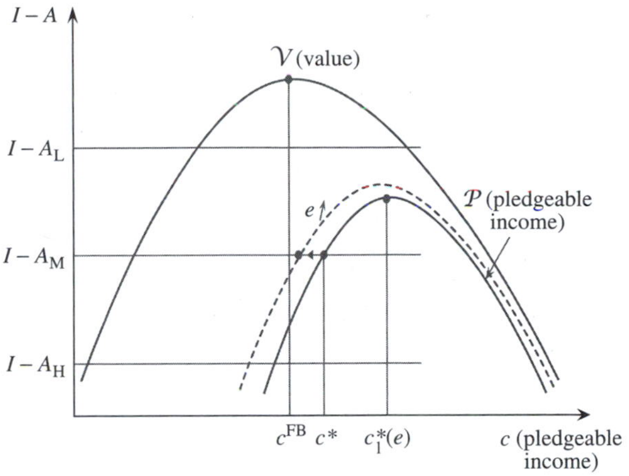

Figure 16.2

A_L ("very weak balance sheet"), A_M ("weak balance sheet"), and A_H ("strong balance sheet"), with $A_L < A_M < A_H$. The firm with cash on hand A_L cannot make concessions that guarantee enough pledgeable income to investors to allow them to recoup their initial outlay. The firm with cash on hand A_H can secure financing without sacrificing value ($c = c^{FB}$). Finally, the firm with cash on hand A_M must make concession c^* and sacrifice some value in order to attract financing.

The dashed curve shows the impact of an increase in enforcement e: pledgeable income increases and the firm's cash on hand A_M is able to make fewer concessions; and so firm value increases. Firms with strong balance sheets are unaffected, and a few marginal firms with very weak balance sheets gain access to funding.

16.2.4 Externalities among Borrowers

We have already alluded to the fact that the analysis above neglected interactions among borrowers. These interactions can occur either in the input markets (for example, competition for savings or labor) or in the output market. (Section 16.3 will study a third form of interactions, namely, through the impact of private contracting choices on future government policies.)

Competition for savings. We have assumed that investors supply funds perfectly elastically to borrowers as long as they receive a nonnegative rate of return. Let us now introduce an upward-sloping savings function, while preserving investor risk neutrality. That is, investors have utility function

$$u(c_0) + c_1,$$

where c_0 and c_1 are their consumptions at the date of funding and at the date at which investors receive their return.[27] The function u is increasing and concave. Assuming that y is the investors' date-0 endowment and letting r denote the market rate of interest, the savings function is given by[28]

$$u'(y - S(r)) = 1 + r.$$

Note that $S'(r) > 0$.

For simplicity, we keep assuming that entrepreneurs have utility function $c_0 + c_1$ from consumption stream $\{c_0, c_1\}$ and we will restrict attention to positive interest rates so that entrepreneurs who do not receive funding save their cash on hand (this assumption is not important). Finally, and also for simplicity, we will focus on the special case of no direct effect of the degree of enforcement on the NPV.

Using the general formulation exposited above, let $\bar{A}(e, r)$ and $\underline{A}(e, r)$ be defined by[29]

$$\mathcal{P}(c^{FB}, e) = (1 + r)(I - \bar{A}(e, r))$$

and

$$\mathcal{P}(c_1^*(e), e) = (1 + r)(I - \underline{A}(e, r)).$$

Note that $\underline{A}(e, r) < \bar{A}(e, r)$ and that both are decreasing in e.[30]

Thus, firms with cash on hand $A < \underline{A}(e, r)$ do not have access to funding, those with $\underline{A}(e, r) \leqslant A < \bar{A}(e, r)$ receive financing but must make inefficient concessions, and those with $A \geqslant \bar{A}(e, r)$ secure "first-best funding."

Consider a distribution $G(A)$ of firms with $G(0) = 0$ and $G(I) = 1$ (for simplicity, this hypothesis does

27. The notation $\{c_0, c_1\}$ for consumptions is used here only. It is not to be confused with that for concessions.

28. The investor solves $\max_{\{c_0, c_1\}}\{u(c_0) + c_1\}$, where

$$c_1 = (1 + r)(y - c_0) = (1 + r)S.$$

29. The cutoff type's utility, as measured at date 1, is then

$$U_b(\underline{A}(e, r)) = \mathcal{V}(c_1^*(e)) - [1 + r(e)]I \geqslant 0,$$

where $c_1^*(e)$ is the concession made by $\underline{A}(e, r)$ and $r(e)$ the equilibrium rate of interest.

30. This is obvious from $\bar{A}(e, r)$. For $\underline{A}(e, r)$, recall that $\mathcal{P}$ is by definition maximized at $c_1^*(e)$ and so $\mathrm{d}\mathcal{P}/\mathrm{d}e = \partial\mathcal{P}/\partial e$.

not alter the analysis). The date-0 equilibrium interest rate is determined in the market for funds:

$$S(r) = \int_{\underline{A}(e,r)}^{I} (I - A)\,dG(A) - \int_{0}^{\underline{A}(e,r)} A\,dG(A).$$

And so the interest rate r increases with the level of enforcement e (as more firms get access to financing).[31]

A borrower's net utility, as measured at date 1, is given by[32]

$$U_b = \mathcal{V}(c) - (1 + r)I.$$

And so

$$\frac{dU_b}{de} = \mathcal{V}'(c^*(e))\frac{dc^*}{de} - \left(\frac{dr}{de}\right)I.$$

Firms with strong balance sheets ($A \geqslant \bar{A}(e,r)$) are hurt by an improvement in contracting institutions since $c^* = c^{FB}$ and so $\mathcal{V}' = 0$. They simply see their cost of capital increase. The utility of entrepreneurs of firms with weak balance sheets ($\underline{A}(e,r) \leqslant A < \bar{A}(e,r)$) is more indeterminate: their cost of capital has increased, but better enforcement allows them to make fewer concessions to investors ($dc^*/de < 0$), which benefits the entrepreneur (as $\mathcal{V}' < 0$). And, of course, the entrepreneurs in firms with very weak balance sheets ($A < \underline{A}(e,r)$) are better off: the marginal firms gain access to funding, while the others remain net lenders and therefore benefit from an increase in the rate of interest.

Competition in the product market. In their paper on the politics of financial development in the twentieth century, Rajan and Zingales (2003) emphasize the potential hostility of incumbents to financial development. The idea is that better contracting institutions result in entry by firms with little cash on hand and thereby breed competition for incumbents.

Suppose indeed that (i) entry reduces the incumbent's expected profit,[33] and (ii) entrants have much less cash than incumbents (they could alternatively have a weaker reputation, a greater investment need, or whatever feature calls for more pledgeable income). Incumbents may then oppose an improvement in contracting institutions so as to hinder entrants' access to capital and thereby to deter entry.

Competition for labor. In Biais and Mariotti (2003), entrepreneurs with strong balance sheets can invest irrespective of the degree of investor protection. They favor a soft bankruptcy law, which may preclude liquidation and thereby reduce the pledgeable income and the funding ability of firms with weaker balance sheets. A soft bankruptcy law thereby reduces labor demand and the workers' wage. Firms that still obtain funding thus benefit in two ways: a reduced wage bill and a lower probability of liquidation brought about by this reduction in the wage bill.[34]

16.3 Property Rights Institutions

16.3.1 Overview

As we discussed in the introduction to this chapter, there is a natural distinction between policies and their persistence. Section 16.2 looked at the consequences of the contractual environment on corporate financing.[35] The contracting institutions define the set of feasible contracts that can govern the relationship among borrowers, investors, and other stakeholders. The firm's policy environment may evolve over time for two reasons: the first, studied in Section 16.4, is associated with (endogenous) shifts in political power; the second is the standard time-inconsistency issue, the object of this section.

As is well-known, a government, even if it has stable preferences over interest groups and therefore outcomes, may in general want to alter its policies as the various parties (borrowers, investors, and other stakeholders) sink their investments. Typically, the government tends to be much less respectful "*ex post*" than "*ex ante*" of the interest of groups that it does not try to pander to; put differently, it would

31. Note that the interest rate is the expected return demanded by investors. If the investors' claim is interpreted as debt (on this, see Chapter 3), then the *nominal* interest rate (equal to the ratio of the debt claim over the loan, minus 1), may vary in an ambiguous way with the efficiency of the court system as it factors in the probability of repayment (see Jappelli et al. 2005).

32. One way of obtaining this expression is as follows: the borrower could lend A and obtain return $(1 + r)A$. Instead, she receives $\mathcal{V} - \mathcal{P}$ from the undertaking, where $\mathcal{P} = (1 + r)(I - A)$. Thus,

$$U_b = [\mathcal{V} - (1 + r)(I - A)] - [(1 + r)A] = \mathcal{V} - (1 + r)I.$$

33. See Chapter 7 for the link between product-market competition and corporate financing.

34. Biais and Mariotti actually show that overall welfare may be higher under a soft bankruptcy law.

35. It also took an initial, very incomplete stab at the persistence issue by showing how borrowers' preferences changed as they received financing, depending on the strength of their balance sheet.

often like to promise not to expropriate in the future the investments made by these less favored groups, but it is unable later on to abide by its promise. The anticipation of reneging in turn discourages less favored groups from sinking investments.[36] For example, a government may *ex ante* be eager to facilitate the access of firms to funding by wealthy domestic or foreign investors. Once lending has occurred, though, the government's policy choices put less weight on attracting funds and more weight on other stakeholders, including borrowers.

More generally, time inconsistency may arise even if investors receive the same weight as, or even a higher weight than, borrowers in the government's objective function; for, the government may *ex ante* want to promise to *ex post* implement inefficient (i.e., value-reducing) policies that boost pledgeable income and thereby *ex ante* enable firms' access to funding. Once investment has been attracted, though, the rationale for costly policies has disappeared and so it becomes optimal for the government to adopt a less investor-friendly policy. Anticipating this incentive, investors are therefore more reluctant to lend in the first place than they would be, were the government able to commit to a policy long term.[37]

Even though governments cannot commit without devolving all their regalian powers, they can adopt policies that alleviate the time-inconsistency problem. In particular, we will argue that the strategy of providing a "shield" for investors in general, and those least favored by the government in particular, facilitates funding and we will offer a couple of practical applications of this idea.

For simplicity, much of our analysis focuses on the borrower–investors relationship, but the general principles will obviously apply to a broader spectrum of stakeholders.

This section's general points can be summarized in the following way.

• The incentives of policy makers are, except in some instances of targeted interventions (such as the public bailout of a private company), determined by economy-wide considerations; for, the corporate laws and regulation, the tax and labor environments, and the many other policy dimensions that were discussed in the introduction to this chapter apply not to a single firm, but to a larger set of firms, sometimes to all firms.

Technically, this situation gives rise to *common-agency externalities*.[38] One can view the state as a common "agent" who takes discretionary actions—public policies. The multiple "principals" are the "borrower–investors" pairs,[39] whose welfare is affected by the public policies. In structuring a financial contract, the borrower and investors do not take into account the general equilibrium effect of contract designs on policy, and therefore tend to exert externalities on other borrowers and investors. This abstract principle will take a more concrete form when we investigate specific examples below.

• The remanence of the contracting environment, i.e., the extent of time inconsistency, depends crucially on how the policy risk is allocated among stakeholders. *Time consistency is enhanced when some match between stakeholders' exposure to policy risk and political constituencies is achieved.* Put differently, property rights institutions are more sturdy if those who bear the political risk are also politically influential. This implies that, from a social viewpoint, fragile claims should be shifted toward those who have influence over politics in order to minimize the risk of expropriation; this incentive to

36. Policy makers' time inconsistency figures prominently in many fields of economics, such as monetary and fiscal policy (e.g., Kydland and Prescott 1977; Barro and Gordon 1983; Rogoff 1985; Persson et al. 1987; Calvo 1996; Athey et al. 2005), international trade (Matsuyama 1990; Tornell 1991; Bagwell and Staiger 2000), sovereign debt management (e.g., Bulow and Rogoff 1989a,b), and utility regulation (e.g., Laffont and Tirole 1993, Chapters 9, 10, 16, and the references therein). It is also an important issue in corporate finance, since investments often bear fruit over long horizons.

37. These considerations will be studied in the context of a three-period framework in which the government chooses its policy after firms get access to funding. But the time-inconsistency problem arises even under the more realistic assumption that funding is an ongoing activity. At any point in time there is an "installed base" of investors' investment in the firms, whose supply is therefore inelastic. And so the government is not concerned about the impact of funding on past funding; rather, its policy choices are guided by the elasticity of *marginal* (new) funding.

38. The theory of common agency was developed in contributions in a moral-hazard context by Pauly (1974) and Bernheim and Whinston (1986a,b), among others, and in an adverse-selection context by Martimort (1991) and Stole (1990).

39. Or, more generally, all parties to a private contract. Workers and other stakeholders can be appended without modifying the argument.

match exposure to policy risk and politically influential groups, however, does not exist at the individual financial arrangement level.[40]

16.3.2 Basics of Time Inconsistency in Corporate Finance

To illustrate the time-inconsistency issue, we employ the variable-investment model of Section 3.4.

Entrepreneurs. There is a continuum of risk-neutral entrepreneurs protected by limited liability. The representative entrepreneur has cash on hand A and borrows $I - A$ in order to reach investment size I. Risk-neutral investors demand a rate of return equal to 0.

The project succeeds (yields profit RI) with probability $p + \tau$ and fails (yields nothing) with probability $1 - (p + \tau)$.[41] The component p is chosen by the entrepreneur. The latter may behave, and receive no private benefit, and then $p = p_{\rm H}$; or she misbehaves and receives private benefit BI, in which case $p = p_{\rm L} = p_{\rm H} - \Delta p$.

Government policy and incidence. The component $\tau \geqslant 0$, in contrast, is chosen by the government. This profit-friendly action involves cost $\hat{\gamma}(\tau)I$, also proportional to investment, with $\hat{\gamma}(0) = \hat{\gamma}'(0) = 0$, $\hat{\gamma}' > 0$, and $\hat{\gamma}'' > 0$.

The incidence of the cost $\hat{\gamma}(\tau)I$, that is, the way this cost is allocated between borrowers and lenders, falls on both parties: a share $\sigma_{\rm b}$ (respectively, $\sigma_{\rm l}$) is borne by the borrowers (respectively, the lenders), where $\sigma_{\rm b} + \sigma_{\rm l} = 1$. We can make one of two alternative assumptions on how the incidence operates. Suppose, for instance, that the profit-enhancing action (τ) is a better transportation infrastructure or court system. The question is whether the corresponding cost ($\hat{\gamma}(\tau)I$) is borne by the parties as part of participating in a financing agreement or in another incarnation (say, as a taxpayer); for example, the cost of the transportation infrastructure might be financed through a tax on capital, in which case the investors would pay it only if they invest in firms, or through an income tax, in which case they would pay it regardless of their investment in the firm. As we will show, up to a couple of twists, the choice of assumption is rather inconsequential for the analysis. We will first assume that $\sigma_k\hat{\gamma}(\tau)I$ ($k = {\rm b}, {\rm l}$) is borne by the parties when and only when they enter a financing agreement of size I, and later we make the opposite assumption, that they bear these costs as citizens.

Government objective function. The government's objective function puts weights $w_{\rm b}$ and $w_{\rm l}$ on the borrower's and the lenders' welfares, respectively.[42]

Timing. Figure 16.3 summarizes the timing. As usual, the separable form for the probability function ensures that it does not matter whether policy τ is chosen before or after the entrepreneur chooses her effort.

We are obviously particularly interested in the case in which the government cannot commit to a policy. In this case, the initial choice (stage (i)) is irrelevant.

40. The analysis in this section builds on Tirole (2003), where the model is framed in a capital-account-liberalization context and it is argued that ignoring political economy considerations can lead to incorrect policy making by international financial institutions such as the International Monetary Fund.

41. As usual, we will assume that probabilities lie in $[0, 1]$ in the relevant range of parameters.

42. This reduced form will suffice for our purposes. One may just assume that the politicians in power put weights $w_{\rm b}$ and $w_{\rm l}$ on the two political constituencies. These weights may result from bargaining and alliance building among interest groups, as in Section 16.4. Alternatively, they could be endogenized through the political economy process. There are two broad approaches in this respect.

The first approach assumes that the politician is driven by reelection concerns. For example, in Maskin and Tirole (2004), the politician uses policy choices to signal his/her congruence with political constituencies that are unaware of his/her true preferences (see also the older literature initiated by Barro (1973) and Ferejohn (1986): this literature abstracts from informational asymmetries and uses the voters' indifference between candidates to reward or punish incumbents as a function of their past behavior). Policy choices may also reflect the voting elasticities, i.e., how sensitive various constituencies' voting behavior is to the candidate's attractiveness, as in the "Ramsey model of political choices" developed by Lindbeck and Weibull (1987) (this model formally applies only to the choice of political platforms, but its main thrust carries over to the policy choices made by incumbents in office).

The second approach (which is not necessarily inconsistent with the first) focuses on the quid pro quo between interest groups and policy makers. Grossman and Helpman (1994) formalize such capture of policy makers as a symmetric-information bidding contest among interest groups, as in Bernheim and Whinston (1986a). Laffont and Tirole (1991, 1993) use a three-tier (principal–supervisor–agent) framework in which the general electorate's imperfect knowledge about the consequences of policy choices (or about policy choices themselves) both motivates the existence of government decision making and affects the extent to which interest groups can effectively capture the policy process.

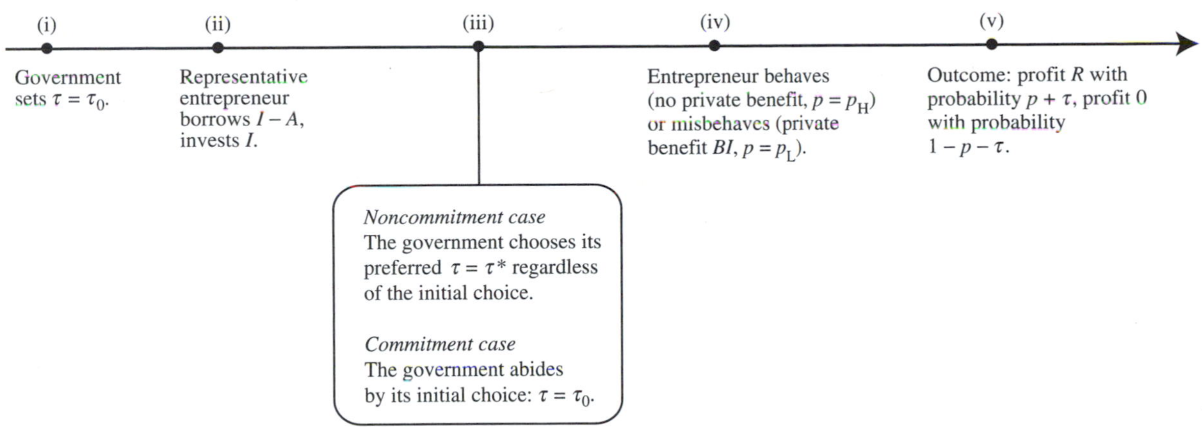
(i)
(ii)
(iii)
(iv)
(v)
Government sets $\tau = \tau_0$.
Representative entrepreneur borrows $I - A$, invests I.
Entrepreneur behaves (no private benefit, $p = p_H$) or misbehaves (private benefit BI, $p = p_L$).
Outcome: profit R with probability $p + \tau$, profit 0 with probability $1 - p - \tau$.
Noncommitment case
The government chooses its preferred $\tau = \tau^*$ regardless of the initial choice.
Commitment case
The government abides by its initial choice: $\tau = \tau_0$.

Figure 16.3

Borrowing capacity. When facing policy τ, the representative entrepreneur's borrowing capacity is obtained in the usual fashion. The entrepreneur behaves if and only if her stake in the case of success, R_b, is sufficient to induce her to forgo the private benefit:

$$[(p_H + \tau) - (p_L + \tau)]R_b \geqslant BI;$$

and so an amount $(p_H + \tau)BI/\Delta p$ is not pledgeable to investors. The investors are willing to finance the firm at level I if and only if they recoup their investment in expectation. And so, remembering that the market rate of interest is equal to 0, the investors' breakeven constraint is given by

$$(p_H + \tau)\left(R - \frac{B}{\Delta p}\right)I - \sigma_1 \hat{\gamma}(\tau) I = I - A,$$

where use is made of the assumption that the incidence falls on investors in proportion to the firm's investment (under the alternative assumption that they bear the cost as taxpayers rather than as stakeholders in the firm, the term $\sigma_1 \hat{\gamma}(\tau) I$ on the left-hand side disappears because the investors' tax burden is then not contingent on whether they invest in the firm). We will assume all along that, in the relevant range, the pledgeable income per unit of investment $((p_H + \tau)[R - B/\Delta p] - \sigma_1 \hat{\gamma}(\tau))$ is smaller than 1; otherwise, the entrepreneurs' borrowing capacity would be infinite in this constant-returns-to-scale model. Similarly, we will assume that the NPV is positive and so entrepreneurs want to invest $((p_H + \tau)R - 1 - \hat{\gamma}(\tau) > 0)$.

It will prove convenient to change variables. Let a denote the proportional increase in expected revenue brought about by the public policy[43]

$$a \equiv \frac{\tau}{p_H} \quad \text{and} \quad \gamma(a) \equiv \hat{\gamma}(p_H a).$$

As usual, let

$$\rho_0 \equiv p_H\left(R - \frac{B}{\Delta p}\right) \quad \text{and} \quad \rho_1 \equiv p_H R.$$

The borrowing constraint can be rewritten as

$$(1 + a)\rho_0 I - \sigma_1 \gamma(a) I = I - A$$

or

$$I = I(a) = \frac{A}{1 + \sigma_1 \gamma(a) - (1 + a)\rho_0}. \tag{16.6}$$

We will think of a as an "investor-friendly action." In this perspective, we will focus on a range of parameters such that $\rho_0 > \sigma_1 \gamma'(a)$. Otherwise, a would not be an investor-friendly action and investment would decrease with a.

Borrowers' utility. Because investors break even, the representative borrower's net utility is equal to the project's NPV:[44]

$$U_b = [(p_H + \tau)R - 1 - \hat{\gamma}(\tau)]I;$$

43. The variable a thus defined resembles the enforcement variable e in Section 16.2 in that both variables are profit friendly and are determined exogenously at the level of the firm.

44. A different derivation is

$$\begin{aligned} U_b &= [(p_H + \tau)R_b - \sigma_b \hat{\gamma}(\tau) I] - A \\ &= (p_H + \tau)(RI - R_l) - \sigma_b \hat{\gamma}(\tau) I - A \\ &= (p_H + \tau)RI - \sigma_l \hat{\gamma}(\tau) I - (I - A) - \sigma_b \hat{\gamma}(\tau) I - A \\ &= [(p_H + \tau)R - 1 - \hat{\gamma}(\tau)]I. \end{aligned}$$

note that the borrower *ex ante* bears the full incidence, as she must compensate investors not only for their contribution, $I - A$, to investment, but also for the subsequent cost $\sigma_b \hat{\gamma}(\tau) I$ that will be imposed upon them by the government's policy. Changing variables,

$$U_b = [(1+a)\rho_1 - 1 - \gamma(a)]I(a). \tag{16.7}$$

Ex post, in contrast, the borrower has transferred shares to investors and so her utility is

$$\begin{aligned} U_b^{ex\ post} &= (p_H + \tau)R_b - \sigma_b \hat{\gamma}(\tau) I \\ &= \left[(p_H + \tau)\frac{B}{\Delta p} - \sigma_b \hat{\gamma}(\tau)\right] I \\ &= [(1+a)(\rho_1 - \rho_0) - \sigma_b \gamma(a)]I. \end{aligned}$$

Noncommitment. Suppose, first, that the government chooses its policy after investments are sunk. Investment then depends on the anticipated or equilibrium value a^* of the policy,

$$I = I(a^*),$$

and not on the realized policy a, which has not yet been chosen. (Of course, in a rational expectations equilibrium, $a = a^*$; but we need to allow for the possibility that $a \neq a^*$ in order to study government incentives.)

For policy a and weights w_b and w_l on the borrowers and the lenders,[45] the government's *ex post* objective function is

$$\begin{aligned} W^{ex\ post}&(a, a^*) \\ &= [w_b[(1+a)(\rho_1 - \rho_0) - \sigma_b \gamma(a)] \\ &\qquad + w_l[(1+a)\rho_0 - \sigma_l \gamma(a)]]I(a^*). \end{aligned}$$

And so

$$\frac{dW^{ex\ post}}{da} = 0$$

yields policy $a = a^*$, given by

$$\gamma'(a^*) = \frac{w_b(\rho_1 - \rho_0) + w_l \rho_0}{w_b \sigma_b + w_l \sigma_l}. \tag{16.8}$$

Commitment. Let us now solve the benchmark case of commitment. Investors, having a perfectly elastic supply of funds, enjoy no rent *ex ante* (in contrast, as we have seen, they have quasi-rents *ex post*). And so the government's objective function is

$$\begin{aligned} W^{ex\ ante} &= w_b U_b + w_l \cdot 0 \\ &= w_b[(1+a)\rho_1 - 1 - \gamma(a)]I(a). \end{aligned}$$

The optimal commitment policy solves

$$\frac{dW^{ex\ ante}}{da} = 0$$

or $a = a^C$ ("C" for "commitment"), given by

$$\gamma'(a^C) = \rho_1 + \frac{U_b(a^C) I'(a^C)}{I^2(a^C)}. \tag{16.9}$$

Because $U_b > 0$ (otherwise the entrepreneur would not invest) and $I' > 0$,

$$\gamma'(a^C) > \rho_1.$$

That is, the optimal policy is even more profit friendly than it would be in the absence of credit rationing or for a fixed investment ($\gamma' = \rho_1$). The reason for this is that the prospect of an investor-friendly policy helps entrepreneurs attract funds: it has an *enabling effect.*

Let us now compare the commitment and noncommitment policies. Rewriting (16.9), one has

$$\gamma'(a^C) = \gamma'(a^*) + \underbrace{\frac{(w_b - w_l)(\rho_0 - \rho_1 \sigma_l)}{w_b \sigma_b + w_l \sigma_l}}_{\text{rent-shifting effect}} + \underbrace{\frac{U_b(a^C) I'(a^C)}{I^2(a^C)}}_{\text{enabling effect}}. \tag{16.10}$$

The enabling effect (discussed above) by itself implies that the equilibrium policy is not investor friendly enough ($a^* < a^C$), regardless of the weights on the two groups. This effect is the only source of divergence between the commitment and noncommitment outcomes when the government's welfare function weighs the two groups equally ($w_b = w_l$).

The second source of divergence comes from the fact that investors have no stake *ex ante* but have quasi-rents *ex post*: in order to attract funding, borrowers shift quasi-rents (namely, $(1+a)\rho_0 I$) to investors.

For example, if the government puts more weight on borrowers ($w_b > w_l$), then the rent-shifting effect

45. Again we assume that the government's weights on the two groups are stable. A large literature, starting with Persson and Svensson (1989), Tabellini and Alesina (1990), and Aghion and Bolton (1991), has investigated how a government may try to constrain future ones with different preferences.

indicates the existence of opportunism against investors under noncommitment (a positive rent-shifting effect) if and only if

$$\frac{\rho_0}{\rho_1} > \sigma_1,$$

that is, if and only if the fraction of cash-flow rights held by investors exceeds the fraction of the cost they bear.

Under the same condition, the government is *ex post* too investor friendly (ignoring the enabling effect) if it puts more weight on lenders ($w_b < w_l$).

Alternative assumption on incidence. If we make the alternative assumption that the cost of the policy is socialized and so the borrowers and the lenders bear costs as citizens rather than as parties to the agreement, i.e., $\sigma_b \hat{\gamma}(\tau)\bar{I}$ and $\sigma_l \hat{\gamma}(\tau)\bar{I}$, respectively, where $\bar{I}$ is the representative entrepreneur's investment (rather than the investment of the firm in question) the conclusions are even starker. We only sketch the analysis as it closely follows the previous one.

The financing condition is now

$$I = I(a) = \frac{A}{1-(1+a)\rho_0},$$

and the borrower's *ex ante* utility is

$$U_b = [(1+a)\rho_1 - 1]I(a) - \sigma_b \gamma(a)\bar{I}$$

(where, in equilibrium, $\bar{I} = I(a)$).

The *ex post* social welfare function $W^{ex\ post}(a, a^*)$ is unchanged, and so a^* is still given by condition (16.8).

The *ex ante* social welfare function is now written as

$$W^{ex\ ante} = w_b[(1+a)\rho_1 - 1 - \sigma_b \gamma(a)]I(a) + w_l[-\sigma_l \gamma(a)]I(a).$$

The difference between this and the previous assumption on incidence is that investors bear

$$\sigma_l \gamma(a) I(a)$$

as citizens anyway, and so they have no way of shifting this cost to borrowers through a demand for a higher share of income claims. The comparison between a^C and a^* is now given by

$$\gamma'(a^C) = \gamma'(a^*) + \underbrace{\frac{(w_b - w_l)\rho_0}{w_b\sigma_b + w_l\sigma_l}}_{\text{rent-shifting effect}} + \underbrace{\left(\frac{w_b[(1+a^C)\rho_1 - 1 - \sigma_b\gamma(a^C)]}{w_b\sigma_b + w_l\sigma_l} - \frac{w_l\sigma_l\gamma(a^C)}{w_b\sigma_b + w_l\sigma_l}\right)\frac{I'(a^C)}{I(a^C)}}_{\text{enabling effect}}. \tag{16.11}$$

When $w_b = w_l$, a^C does not depend on the assumption made on incidence: conditions (16.10) and (16.11) give the same expression for a^C.

This is no longer so under unequal weights:

- When $w_b > w_l$ and $\sigma_l > 0$, then the rent-shifting effect is higher in (16.11) than in (16.10) and so is the enabling effect for any a^C; hence, the latter assumption on incidence calls for an even higher a^C, because the investors, as we noted, are unable to pass the cost of the policy through to borrowers.

- The opposite conclusion holds when $w_b < w_l$. Interestingly, suppose that the government cares only about investors ($w_b = 0$). Then

$$a^C = 0 < a^*.$$

The reason for this is that *ex ante* investors have nothing to gain from a profit-enhancing policy: they compete away the resulting gains by accepting a higher investment level from borrowers; and they must bear $\sigma_l \gamma(a) I(a)$ as citizens. Hence, the government would like to protect them by being as profit unfriendly as possible. This policy, however, is time inconsistent: *ex post*, the investors have acquired a stake in the firms and the government is forced to support these claims. (An analogy would be that of a nationwide union opposing the introduction of pension funds, knowing well that once these funds are in place, the workers will have a stake in the corporate sector's profitability, and so the union will have to accept agreements and policies that are more corporate friendly.)

16.3.3 Shield Economics

Earlier we claimed that, from a social viewpoint, policy risk should be shifted to politically influential actors. Let us provide a few illustrations of this principle. For concreteness, let us assume that the costs attached to the government's policy are borne by the contracting parties (first assumption on incidence) and that the noncommitment outcome does not support enough investment from the government's point of view:

$$a^{\mathrm{C}} > a^*.$$

Assume that there are two types of investors: type-1, or politically connected, investors, with weight w_{l_1}, and type-2, or less connected, investors, with weight w_{l_2}, where

$$w_{l_1} > w_{l_2}.$$

Interpretation 1 (nationality). In this interpretation, type-1 investors are domestic investors and type-2 investors foreign investors.

Interpretation 2 (social class). Another interpretation involves rich and poor investors. The government puts more weight on poor (type-1) investors than on rich (type-2) investors, either because it is concerned about social justice or (more prosaically or sometimes more realistically) because the poor are more likely than the rich to be politically pivotal.

Let θ_1 and θ_2 denote the shares of investor cash-flow rights held by type-1 and type-2 investors, respectively ($\theta_1 + \theta_2 = 1$). Condition (16.8) generalizes to

$$y'(a^*) = \frac{w_{\mathrm{b}}(\rho_1 - \rho_0) + (w_{l_1}\theta_1 + w_{l_2}\theta_2)\rho_0}{w_{\mathrm{b}}\sigma_{\mathrm{b}} + (w_{l_1}\theta_1 + w_{l_2}\theta_2)\sigma_1}.$$

Let us analyze what happens to policy when more of the claims on corporate income are held by type-1 investors and fewer are held by type-2 investors (θ_1 increases). Then a^* increases if and only if

$$\rho_0 > \sigma_1 y'(a^*),$$

which is nothing but the statement that a is an investor-friendly action. A stronger ownership by type-1 investors, keeping investors' cash-flow rights constant, then increases a^* towards the commitment outcome. Put differently, *the time-consistency problem is alleviated by aligning stake ownership and the politically influential investor group.*

Application 1: Home Bias or Portfolio Diversification?

In interpretation 1, type-1 investors are domestic investors and type-2 investors foreign investors. Under (frictionless!) capital mobility and assuming risk neutrality, investors are *individually* indifferent as to where to invest. Consequently, small transaction costs associated with investing abroad or small tax incentives for home investment create a strong home bias. Conversely, a small amount of risk aversion calls for international portfolio diversification, i.e., investing very little domestically.[46] This suggests that θ_1 may vary. For a government suffering from not being able to commit to investor-friendly policies, a home bias (θ_1 high) is a boon, as it makes the commitment not to expropriate investors a bit more credible (see Tirole 2003; Wagner 2001).

Application 2: Pension Funds

Let us sketch a highly stylized model of pension funds politics.[47] At the initial date (stages (i) and (ii) in the timing), there are two classes, the poor (type-1 investors) and the rich (type-2 investors). Only the rich have money to invest. The government would like to guarantee some fixed amount of pension benefits (for stage (v) in the timeline in Figure 16.3) for the poor. There are two ways of doing so.

(1) "*Pay as you go*": the government will tax the rich at the final date to deliver the target retirement benefits to the poor.
(2) "*Pension funds*": the government taxes the rich at the initial date and puts the money on behalf of the poor into pension funds, i.e., shares in the entrepreneurs' firms. The poor receive the income attached to these shares at the end.

Under a pay-as-you-go system, $\theta_1 = 0$ (the poor do not own shares). Under the pension fund system, $\theta_1 > 0$. Because $w_{l_1} > w_{l_2}$, the government at stage (iii) chooses a higher a^* under a pension-fund

46. Domestic investors might even want to short their country to the extent that their human capital is positively correlated with the country's index (i.e., they are more likely to lose their job or see their career halt precisely when the country faces a recession).

47. This model, among other things, abstracts from key issues related to the overlapping-generations aspect of savings and retirement benefits.

system.[48] In other words, *the pension funds system, like the home bias, is an indirect commitment to support an investment-friendly environment.*

Biais and Perotti (2002) put forth a related idea. They argue that privatization policies, especially those providing incentives for a wide range of citizens to hold shares in the privatized firms (as was the case in the United Kingdom and in France), build popular (or at least median voter) support for investor protection. Relatedly, Pagano and Volpin (2005c) develop a political economy model in which there is a two-way interaction between investor protection and the size of the stock market. Better investor protection allows firms to issue more equity; in turn, a large stock market expands the shareholder base and creates political support for shareholder protection (there may therefore exist multiple equilibria). Pagano and Volpin further present evidence on panel data for forty-seven countries over the period 1993–2002 that is consistent with the theory.

Application 3: Who Should Hold Equity?

Finally, and by the same principle, one can argue that *providing politically influential investors with an incentive to hold equity rather than debt is also an indirect commitment to support an investment-friendly environment.* According to this reasoning, if equity is more exposed to political risk than are debt claims, foreigners or the rich should hold debt. The point can be made in two different, but similar, ways. First, one can follow Section 3.4 and generalize the variable-investment model to allow for a salvage value of assets: the profit is then $R^{F}I$ for a failing firm and $R^{S}I = (R^{F} + R)I$ for a successful firm. The safe claim on income $R^{F}I$ is debt, and the claim on the risky income RI is equity. As long as investors are either risk neutral or are able to diversify their portfolio, the prices of claims adjust so that individual investors are indifferent between holding debt and holding equity (both yield a zero return in our model). Once the concern for government expropriation of investors (through a low a) arises, it is socially optimal for the politically less influential groups to hold debt, and to leave equity, which is exposed to policy risk, to more favored investors. Put differently, the government should encourage, perhaps through tax incentives or regulations, equity holding by its most favored investors.

An exception to this reasoning arises when a denotes a policy affecting the enforcement of debt claims (consider, for instance, a policy affecting the creditors' ability to seize collateral in bankruptcy). The analysis is then obviously reversed.

Finally, another way of making the same point consists in looking at the allocation of savings between corporate equity and Treasury bonds. If there is little or no risk of default on sovereign bonds and provided that time inconsistency leads to too little investment from the government's viewpoint, it is socially desirable, ceteris paribus, that investors with little political clout hold the bonds rather than equity.

48. Suppose, for instance, that $\sigma_1 = 0$. Then

$$y'(a^*) = \rho_1 - \rho_0 + \frac{w_{l_1}\theta_1 + w_{l_2}\theta_2}{w_b}\rho_0.$$

And so an increase in θ_1 from 0 to a positive value leads to a higher a^*.

16.4 Political Alliances

Contracting and property rights institutions are fashioned by political alliances. These alliances are not cast in stone, though. Rather, they are endogenous and furthermore are policy contingent.

To illustrate these points, we enlarge the set of relevant stakeholders to include workers besides entrepreneurs and investors, and look at two specific issues: rules regarding dismissals and those regarding takeovers or creditor rights. The first illustration is in the spirit of the contribution by Pagano and Volpin (2005a); the second is in the spirit of work by Perotti and von Thadden (2001) and Pagano and Volpin (2005b).

16.4.1 Rules Regulating Dismissals: When Managers Side with Investors

Consider the following environment.

Entrepreneurs. There is a continuum of entrepreneurs of mass 1. Each entrepreneur has a project of fixed size I, which requires hiring N workers. As usual, the entrepreneur has limited wealth A, is risk neutral, and is protected by limited liability. She may further engage in moral hazard: the project yields R with probability p and 0 with probability $1-p$, where

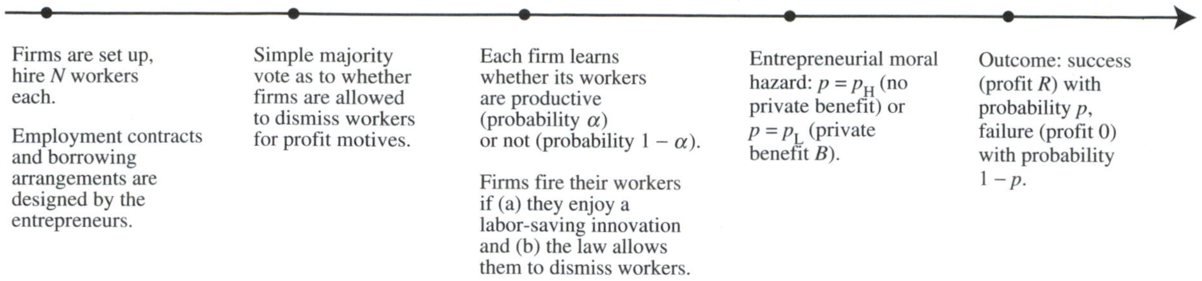
Firms are set up, hire N workers each.
Employment contracts and borrowing arrangements are designed by the entrepreneurs.
Simple majority vote as to whether firms are allowed to dismiss workers for profit motives.
Each firm learns whether its workers are productive (probability α) or not (probability 1 − α).
Firms fire their workers if (a) they enjoy a labor-saving innovation and (b) the law allows them to dismiss workers.
Entrepreneurial moral hazard: p = p_H (no private benefit) or p = p_L (private benefit B).
Outcome: success (profit R) with probability p, failure (profit 0) with probability 1 − p.

Figure 16.4

$p = p_{\mathrm{H}}$ (no private benefit) or $p = p_{\mathrm{L}} = p_{\mathrm{H}} - \Delta p$ (private benefit B).

The distribution of cash on hand in the population of entrepreneurs is given by $G(A)$. This heterogeneity in wealth will deliver a smooth labor demand function by firms. For simplicity, entrepreneurs do not become workers when their project does not receive funding.

At the intermediate date (see Figure 16.4 for a description of the timing), there may or may not be a (firm-specific) innovation that makes workers useless. If the labor-saving innovation accrues (which has probability $1 - \alpha$), the same stochastic profit can be obtained without keeping the N workers employed. With probability α, the firm needs to keep the N workers in order to produce. The shocks are independent and identically distributed (i.i.d.) across firms.

Workers, if they are retained, are given efficiency wage $\bar{w} > 0$, regardless of the technological mutation. This efficiency wage could be endogenized through the introduction of worker moral hazard.[49] Let

$$w \equiv N\bar{w}$$

denote the wage bill.

Workers. There is a continuum of mass N of cashless[50] workers. Workers either find a job in a firm or they become self-employed. In the latter case, their income is normalized at 0 (so $\bar{w}$ also measures the rent associated with being employed in a firm). Like other economic agents, workers are risk neutral.

Investors. There is a continuum of investors with mass NH, where $H < 1$ (there are fewer investors than workers). Investors are risk neutral and willing to lend any amount as long as they receive a rate of return equal to 0.

(a) *Private labor contracts are enforced.* Suppose, first, that firms can offer any employment contract they want to workers and that such contracts, if agreeable at the initial date with workers, are later enforced. Let us further assume that some workers in equilibrium remain self-employed (see below for a sufficient condition). It is in the interest of borrowers to offer workers wage $\bar{w}$ and keep the option to dismiss them (employment-at-will contract). Employed workers then obtain $\bar{w}$ with probability α and 0 with probability $1 - \alpha$, which is more than they get, 0, when self-employed. Borrowers take advantage of the existence of a "reserve army" of workers to offer employment-at-will contracts without severance pay in the case of dismissal.

Given this employment contract, a borrower with cash on hand A can raise funds if and only if

$$I - A \leqslant \alpha[p_{\mathrm{H}}[R - B/\Delta p] - N\bar{w}] + (1 - \alpha)[p_{\mathrm{H}}(R - B/\Delta p)]$$

or, letting $\rho_0 \equiv p_{\mathrm{H}}(R - B/\Delta p)$ and using the definition of the wage bill ($w \equiv N\bar{w}$),

$$I - A \leqslant \rho_0 - \alpha w. \tag{16.12}$$

(The investors foot the wage bill w at the intermediate stage either through a credit line or a dilution right (see Chapter 5). In either case they are worse off in the state of nature in which workers have to be retained by the firm.)

49. As in, for example, the efficiency-wage models of Calvo and Wellisz (1978) and Shapiro and Stiglitz (1984).

50. Thus, workers cannot post a bond with firms in order to bid for their future quasi-rent.

The number of workers employed in corporations is

$$N[1 - G(I + \alpha w - \rho_0)].$$

This number is lower than N (there is a reserve army of self-employed workers), for example, if

$$I + \alpha w > \rho_0$$

(i.e., if a cashless entrepreneur cannot raise funds) and the density around $A = 0$ is positive. The number of self-employed workers is equal to $NG(I + \alpha w - \rho_0)$.

(b) *Vote on dismissal regulation at the intermediate stage.* Suppose now that after investments have been sunk and workers hired in firms, a vote takes place as to whether firms are allowed to dismiss workers (see Figure 16.4). The simple majority rule governs the outcome of the vote.[51]

For expositional simplicity (this involves no restriction in the analysis), let us assume that N is large, so that we can ignore the entrepreneurs' votes when determining the winning majority.

Let us investigate the preferences of the three other categories of economic agent:

Employed workers obviously prefer to vote against dismissals and receive $\bar{w}$ for certain rather than only with probability α.

Investors vote against a dismissal regulation.

Self-employed workers are here indifferent. For concreteness, we will assume that they vote against a dismissal regulation. This would be the case, for example, if they had even a small amount of savings, so that they would be congruent with investors.[52] Assuming a different voting pattern for self-employed workers would not affect the analysis qualitatively.

Let us assume that

$$1 - G(I + \alpha w - \rho_0) > G(I + \alpha w - \rho_0) + H, \quad (16.13)$$

where H, recall, is the ratio of investors to workers. Then a majority votes in favor of prohibiting dismissals. This implies that our maintained hypothesis that private employment contracts are enforceable is unwarranted.

Thus, suppose to the contrary that, at the investment stage, economic agents expect that layoffs will later be prohibited. The investors' breakeven condition is altered by the fact that the wage bill w is incompressible. Only firms with cash on hand A such that

$$I - A \leqslant \rho_0 - w$$

are able to fund that investment. The number of workers is therefore smaller than earlier and is now equal to

$$N[1 - G(I + w - \rho_0)].$$

If

$$1 - G(I + w - \rho_0) > G(I + w - \rho_0) + H, \quad (16.14)$$

then dismissal regulation is indeed the equilibrium outcome.

If neither (16.13) nor (16.14) hold, the only possible equilibrium expectation is that an anti-dismissal law will be voted for with probability z, $0 < z < 1$; for this to be the case, though, no majority in favor of or against the dismissal regulation can emerge:[53]

$$1 - G(I + [\alpha + (1 - \alpha)z]w - \rho_0) = G(I + [\alpha + (1 - \alpha)z]w - \rho_0) + H. \quad (16.15)$$

Note the stabilizing mechanism: the expectation that layoffs will be regulated reduces the entrepreneurs' access to funding; firms create fewer jobs, and so the political support for the law decreases.

We simplified the analysis by assuming that entrepreneurs are too few to have a political weight.

51. The determination of policy by simple majority voting is a blatant oversimplification of actual public decision making. A large literature (see, in particular, Persson and Tabellini 2000, 2003) has studied how political institutions shape public policies.

52. Alternatively, in a slight extension of the model in which product prices depended on the cost of production, they, as consumers, would be in favor of cost minimization.

53. The reader may wonder how this probability z (which is the only possible equilibrium outcome) can emerge in reality. Introducing a bit of noise answers this question. Suppose, for example, that the distribution $G(A)$ is not perfectly known at the initial date. Rather, it is indexed by an unknown parameter θ drawn from some smooth distribution $K(\theta)$. Suppose, for instance, that θ is a parameter of first-order stochastic dominance: $G_\theta(A \mid \theta) < 0$ (a higher θ means a more favorable distribution of wealth). Then

$$z = 1 - K(\theta^*)$$

(a majority is in favor of a dismissal regulation when $\theta > \theta^*$, i.e., when lots of firms have access to funding and therefore few workers are self-employed) and

$$1 - G(I + [\alpha + (1 - \alpha)z]w - \rho_0 \mid \theta^*) = G(I + [\alpha + (1 - \alpha)z]w - \rho_0 \mid \theta^*) + H.$$

When $\theta \neq \theta^*$ (i.e., with probability 1), a strict majority for or against the regulation emerges. Note that the noise in the distribution can be "arbitrarily small."

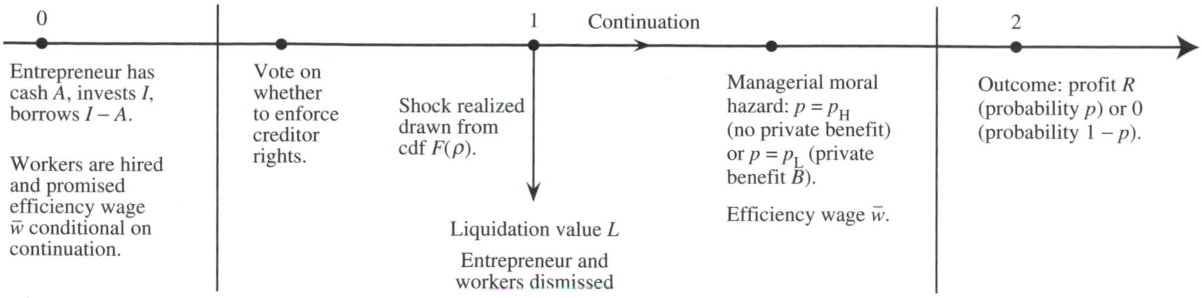

Figure 16.5

Adding them to the determination of the winning majority does not change the overall picture. It is, however, interesting to see whether managers are congruent or dissonant with workers on this policy dimension.

Entrepreneurs *ex ante* are, of course, against regulating dismissals, as this regulation reduces both pledgeable income and value.[54] *Ex post*, though, their preferences depend on how reimbursements are structured. If investors foot the wage bill entirely, then entrepreneurs are *ex post* not affected by the regulation. By contrast, if the wage bill is financed at least in part through a dilution of all claims, entrepreneurs vote against the regulation. This indeterminacy is an artefact of the modeling in that (almost all) firms that receive funding have extra cash. If we add an extra "margin" (choice of liquidity, allocation of control rights, and so forth), this indeterminacy disappears. For example, when the firms must content themselves with limited liquidity in order to attract investors, entrepreneurs *ex post* strictly prefer no regulation.[55]

Lastly, note that entrepreneurs might vote differently if the regulation came together with some fiscal benefits.

16.4.2 Rules Regulating Takeovers or Creditor Rights: When Managers Side with Employees

Let us next consider (*ex post*) attitudes toward the enforcement of laws concerning takeovers or creditor rights. As we saw in Chapters 4, 5, and 11, the ability of investors to liquidate the firm in the case of distress or to sell the firm to a more efficient managerial team facilitates financing. Consider the familiar timing described in Figure 16.5.

The firm faces a random liquidity shock ρ with cumulative distribution function $F(\rho)$ at date 1. It can continue only if it spends ρ. Otherwise, the firm is liquidated and the liquidation value, L, is pledgeable to investors; L could alternatively be interpreted as the price at which the firm is sold to a raider (see Chapter 11). We assume for the moment that the investors' claim L on income is enforceable as specified by the contract.

As in the previous subsection, there are N workers per firm who in the case of continuation must each be paid efficiency wage $\bar{w}$, for total wage bill $w = N\bar{w}$.

54. The NPV is equal to

$$U_b = \rho_1 - [\alpha + (1-\alpha)z]w - I$$

when funded, where, as usual, $\rho_1 = p_H R$.

55. To see this, suppose, as in Chapter 5, that the firm faces a liquidity shock ρ with distribution $F(\rho)$ at the intermediate stage, and that this shock must be withstood in order to continue. Whether workers are made obsolete by a labor-saving innovation and whether a regulation has been voted for is known to the firm when it must cover liquidity demand ρ. It is then optimal to have two thresholds: ρ^* when workers are dismissed and ρ^*_w when they are not. The NPV is then

$$U_b(\rho^*, \rho^*_w) = [\alpha + (1-\alpha)z]\Big[F(\rho^*_w)(\rho_1 - w) - \int_0^{\rho^*_w} \rho \, dF(\rho)\Big] + (1-\alpha)(1-z)\Big[F(\rho^*)\rho_1 - \int_0^{\rho^*} \rho \, dF(\rho)\Big] - I.$$

The investors' breakeven condition can be written as

$$I - A = [\alpha + (1-\alpha)z]\Big[F(\rho^*_w)(\rho_0 - w) - \int_0^{\rho^*_w} \rho \, dF(\rho)\Big] + (1-\alpha)(1-z)\Big[F(\rho^*)\rho_0 - \int_0^{\rho^*} \rho \, dF(\rho)\Big].$$

The reader will check that maximizing the NPV subject to the breakeven condition yields $\rho^*_w = \rho^* - w$. Hence, the entrepreneurs are better off even *ex post* when there is no regulation: because the liquidity needs are reduced by w (the shock is really ρ instead of $\rho + w$), the firm is more likely to be liquidated.

Letting $\rho_0 \equiv p_{\mathrm{H}}[R-(B/\Delta p)]$, the investors' breakeven condition, which we will assume is binding, is

$$I - A = F(\rho^*)(\rho_0 - w) - \int_0^{\rho^*} \rho \,\mathrm{d}F(\rho) + [1 - F(\rho^*)]L,$$

where ρ^* is the cutoff (the firm continues if and only if $\rho \leqslant \rho^*$). Letting $\rho_1 \equiv p_{\mathrm{H}}R$, the NPV is

$$U_{\mathrm{b}} = F(\rho^*)(\rho_1 - w) - \int_0^{\rho^*} \rho \,\mathrm{d}F(\rho) + [1 - F(\rho^*)]L - I.$$

Recall from Chapter 5 that the optimal cutoff satisfies

$$\rho_0 - [w + \rho^* + L] \leqslant 0 < \rho_1 - [w + \rho^* + L]$$

if the budget constraint is binding. That is, at the cutoff, the net pledgeable income, $\rho_0 - (w + \rho)$, is smaller than the opportunity cost L of continuation; the net value, $\rho_1 - (w + \rho)$, in contrast is greater than this opportunity cost.

Suppose now that investors' rights to L are no longer enforced: they cannot foreclose L (or sell the firm to a raider). Consider a shock ρ such that

$$\rho > \rho^* \quad \text{and} \quad \rho + w < \rho_0;$$

such shocks may exist if $\rho_0 - (w + \rho^*) > 0$.[56] Investors are deprived of their earlier right to liquidate and collect proceeds L (a right that was conferred on them since $\rho > \rho^*$); furthermore, the pledgeable income (ρ_0) exceeds the cost of continuing ($\rho + w$) and so investors are better off letting the firm continue when they cannot seize L.

Hence, with positive probability, managers and workers who both receive a quasi-rent in the case of continuation are *ex post* in favor of a law restricting creditors' rights (or takeovers[57]). Needless to say, we could then perform an analysis similar to that of Section 16.4.1 and thereby see how political majorities endogenously emerge in favor of or against such regulations.

56. Let μ denote the shadow price of the investors' breakeven constraint. Simple computations show that

$$\rho^* = \frac{\rho_1 + \mu\rho_0}{1 + \mu} - (w + L)$$

and so

$$\rho_0 - (w + \rho^*) = L - \frac{\rho_1 - \rho_0}{1 + \mu}.$$

And so, if, for example, $L \geqslant \rho_1 - \rho_0$, the condition in the text is satisfied (since, generally, one must account for the fact that μ is a decreasing function of L).

57. The political alliance between management and employees is particularly stressed in Hellwig (2000), an early paper in this literature.

Remark (related literature). Perotti and von Thadden (2004) emphasize how the law reallocates control rights between shareholders (who benefit from risky choices) and creditors (who want to play it safe). In their model, workers side with creditors, since the latter's choice is not about liquidation, but rather between a risky and a safe ongoing strategy for the firm. Put differently, their jobs are less jeopardized by a safe but relatively unprofitable conservative strategy.

In Cespa and Cestone (2002), a firm faces a takeover threat that would remove management. Stakeholders may collude with management so as to reduce the probability of takeover in exchange for managerial concessions benefitting the stakeholders. Collusion is less likely when governance rules are weak since management may be able to use antitakeover defenses and prevent the takeover without colluding with stakeholders. Stakeholders may then favor an active market for corporate control. Stakeholders and small shareholders thus have congruent views on corporate governance, but disagree on issues for which profitability conflicts with stakeholder welfare.

In Pagano and Volpin (2005b), the motivation of workers on the job is provided by either managerial monitoring or high wages. Because managers bear the entire cost of monitoring workers and share with investors the financial cost of high wages, they have a bias towards granting high wages to workers. At the same time, committing to pay high wages makes the company less appealing to potential raiders and thereby protects the rents that managers can extract from corporate control. This creates an implicit alliance between workers and managers to reduce the occurrence of takeovers.

Supplementary Sections

16.5 Contracting Institutions, Financial Structure, and Attitudes toward Reform

This part of the supplementary sections demonstrates in more detail than Section 16.2 how enforcement affects collateral pledging, liquidity, and the allocation of control rights, and how preferences regarding enforcement vary across borrowers.

16.5.1 Contracting Institutions and Collateral Pledging

Relative to the first illustration, we add an extra dimension of contracting: the entrepreneur can pledge an amount C,

$$0 \leqslant C \leqslant C^{\max},$$

of collateral in the case of failure (as in Section 4.3.4, it is not optimal to pledge collateral in the case of success). Collateral pledging is costly to the extent that investors value collateral C at only βC, where $\beta < 1$. We assume that the pledge is enforced with probability $\hat{e} < 1$ (the law and the judicial systems presumably have an important say in the determination of $\hat{e}$). The probability of nondiversion of profits is still e.

The NPV of a project that is funded is equal to the NPV in the absence of collateral pledging, $p_{\mathrm{H}}R - I$, minus the deadweight loss, $(1-\beta)C$, incurred when investors seize the collateral, which has probability $(1-p_{\mathrm{H}})\hat{e}$:

$$U_{\mathrm{b}} = p_{\mathrm{H}}R - I - (1-p_{\mathrm{H}})(1-\beta)\hat{e}C.$$

The funding condition becomes

$$p_{\mathrm{H}}eR_{\mathrm{l}} + (1-p_{\mathrm{H}})\hat{e}\beta C \geqslant I - A,$$

while the incentive compatibility constraint can be written as

$$(\Delta p)[[eR_{\mathrm{b}} + (1-e)R] + \hat{e}C] \geqslant B.$$

This incentive constraint is, from Assumption 16.1, irrelevant.[58]

First, note that if $A \geqslant \bar{A}(e)$, where $\bar{A}(e)$ is given by (16.4), the firm can borrow without pledging collateral. It thereby obtains the highest feasible NPV, $p_{\mathrm{H}}R - I$. And so, for $A \geqslant \bar{A}(e)$,

$$C(A) = 0 \quad \text{and} \quad U_{\mathrm{b}}(A) = p_{\mathrm{H}}R - I.$$

When $A < \bar{A}(e)$, the firm must pledge collateral.

To cut the number of cases to be considered, let us assume that borrowers cannot pledge an amount of collateral so large that the NPV becomes negative.

58. Recall that Assumption 16.1 states that $(1-e)R > B/\Delta p$, and so the incentive constraint holds for any $R_{\mathrm{b}}, C \geqslant 0$.

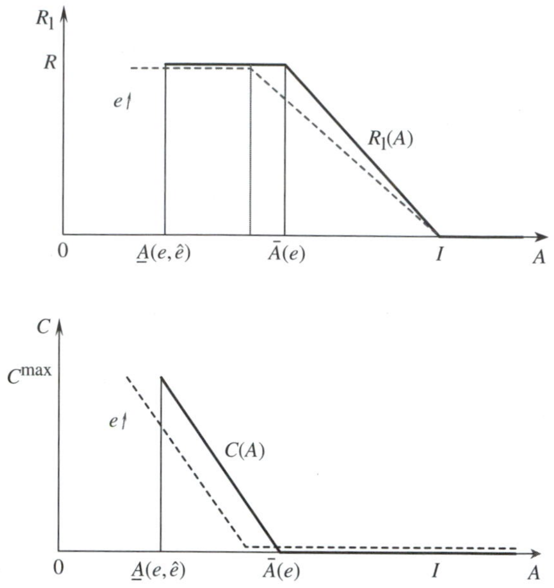

Figure 16.6

Assumption 16.2. $p_{\mathrm{H}}R - I - (1-p_{\mathrm{H}})(1-\beta)\hat{e}C^{\max} \geqslant 0.$

Borrowers minimize the deadweight loss and therefore choose the lowest C that is consistent with the investors' breakeven condition. The latter reveals that optimally $R_{\mathrm{l}} = R$ when $A < \bar{A}(e)$ (pledging income is cheaper than pledging assets) and so

$$p_{\mathrm{H}}eR + (1-p_{\mathrm{H}})\hat{e}\beta C(A) = I - A,$$

as long as $C(A) \leqslant C^{\max}$, or

$$A \geqslant \underline{A}(e,\hat{e}),$$

where

$$p_{\mathrm{H}}eR + (1-p_{\mathrm{H}})\hat{e}\beta C^{\max} = I - \underline{A}(e,\hat{e}).$$

Figures 16.6 and 16.7 describe the comparative statics of the optimal contract when contracting institutions $(e,\hat{e})$ change.

Claims on income. When entrepreneurs have more difficulty diverting profits (e increases in Figure 16.6), funding is more widely available (as earlier), and less collateral is pledged. Thus, a stronger enforcement of income claims raises NPV even when funds are available.

Claims on assets. When courts and the law make it easier for borrowers to seize assets ($\hat{e}$ increases in

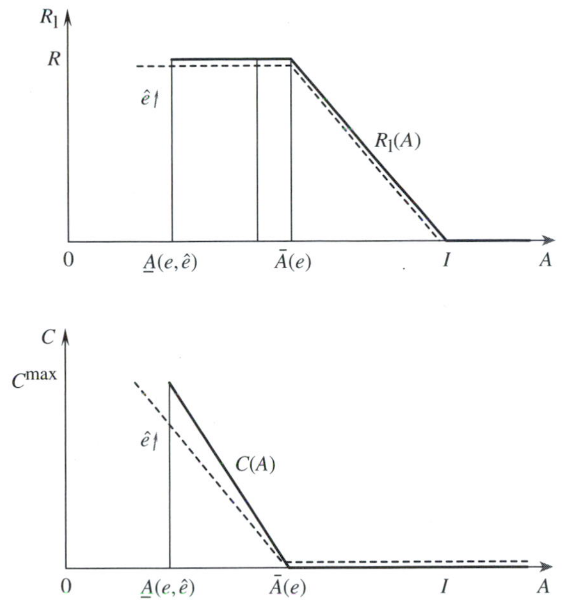

Figure 16.7

Figure 16.7), funds are more widely available. Hence, financing is facilitated. By contrast, conditional on receiving financing, a change in the enforcement of claims on assets has no impact on NPV, because all that matters for NPV and pledgeable income is the expected amount of collateral seized ($\hat{e}C$).

We can again illustrate the topsy-turvy principle. Firms with weak balance sheets benefit the most from a stronger enforcement of claims on income and on assets because they either gain access to funding or else need to pledge a lower amount of collateral to attract investors.

From an *ex post* perspective, though, firms with weak balance sheets have issued more claims on income (R_l) and more claims on collateral (C). They are therefore the strongest advocates for weaker contracting institutions.

16.5.2 Contracting Institutions and Liability Maturity Structure

To analyze the impact of contracting institutions on liability maturity, let us add imperfect enforcement to the canonical model of debt maturity developed in Section 5.2.

The timing is summarized in Figure 16.8.

As indicated in bold in the figure, imperfect enforcement is modeled as two indices of diversion, $1-e$ and $1-\mathring{e}$. That is, the investors recoup the long-term profit with probability e and the short-term profit with probability $\mathring{e}$.

For the moment, we assume that diversion is infeasible in the short run:

$$\mathring{e} = 1.$$

We will later observe that the ability to divert money in the short term is likely to be less problematic than the ability to do so in the long term.

Letting, as in Section 5.2, $F(\rho)$ denote the cumulative distribution of liquidity shocks, and ρ^* the cutoff under which continuation is funded, and maintaining Assumption 16.1,[59] and assuming that the firm pledges the entire income R in the case of success (Assumption 16.1 implies that such pledging is consistent with incentive compatibility), the pledgeable income is

$$\begin{aligned}\mathcal{P}(\rho^*, e) &= r + \int_0^{\rho^*} (\hat{\rho}_0 - \rho)\,\mathrm{d}F(\rho) \\ &= r + F(\rho^*)\hat{\rho}_0 - \int_0^{\rho^*} \rho\,\mathrm{d}F(\rho),\end{aligned}$$

where

$$\hat{\rho}_0 \equiv e p_{\mathrm{H}} R$$

is the date-2 pledgeable income under imperfect enforcement.

The borrower's utility (the NPV) is

$$\begin{aligned}U_{\mathrm{b}}(\rho^*) &= r + \int_0^{\rho^*} (\rho_1 - \rho)\,\mathrm{d}F(\rho) - I \\ &= r + F(\rho^*)\rho_1 - \int_0^{\rho^*} \rho\,\mathrm{d}F(\rho) - I.\end{aligned}$$

Firms with strong balance sheets. $U_{\mathrm{b}}(\rho^*)$ is maximized when the continuation policy is efficient: $\rho^* = \rho_1$. And so,

$$\text{if } \mathcal{P}(\rho_1, e) \geqslant I - A, \text{ then } \rho^* = \rho_1.$$

This optimal liquidity management can be implemented (see Section 5.2) through

- a dilution right, and

59. Recall that this assumption states that

$$(1-e)R > \frac{B}{\Delta p}$$

and guarantees that the incentive compatibility constraint is satisfied even if the entrepreneur is granted no nominal stake in the final profit.

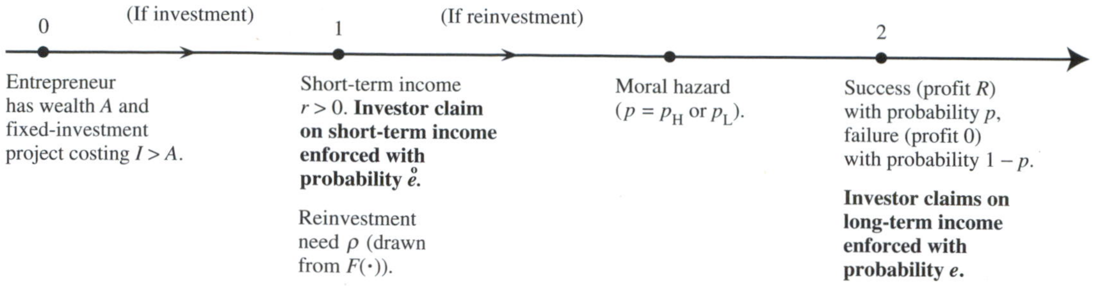

Figure 16.8

- a short-term debt level d (a credit line if negative) leaving enough cash in the firm to make up for credit rationing:

$$\hat{\rho}_0 + [r - d] = \rho^* = \rho_1.$$

That is, the firm can raise up to the pledgeable income of continuation, $\hat{\rho}_0$, by raising new securities. Date-1 cash on hand, $r - d$, complements dilution to provide the firm with enough liquidity. Note that for firms with strong balance sheets, the short-term debt increases with the quality of enforcement. This is due to the fact that a better enforcement makes it easier to return to the capital market at date 1.

Lastly, note that the utility of entrepreneurs with strong balance sheets is not affected by a small change in the strength of enforcement.

Firms with weak balance sheets. As in the case of perfect enforcement, firms with weaker balance sheets (provided that they receive funding) must content themselves with less liquidity, i.e., must issue more short-term debt. That is, if

$$\mathcal{P}(\rho_1, e) > I - A \geqslant \mathcal{P}(\hat{\rho}_0, e),$$

then

$$\hat{\rho}_0 < \rho^* < \rho_1.$$

The cutoff ρ^* is given by

$$r + F(\rho^*)\hat{\rho}_0 - \int_0^{\rho^*} \rho \, \mathrm{d}F(\rho) = I - A.$$

One has

$$\frac{\partial \rho^*}{\partial \hat{\rho}_0} = \frac{F(\rho^*)}{f(\rho^*)(\rho^* - \hat{\rho}_0)} > 0.$$

A weaker enforcement calls for a lower amount of liquidity and therefore for a larger probability of early termination (ρ^* increases with e).

As for firms with strong balance sheets, optimal liquidity management can be implemented through a combination of short-term debt d and dilution rights, where

$$\rho^* = \hat{\rho}_0 + [r - d].$$

The weaker the balance sheet, the higher the amount of short-term debt.

The impact of enforcement on the level of short-term debt is in general ambiguous. If the density of ρ is constant or decreasing (F is concave), though, then $F(\rho^*) > f(\rho^*)(\rho^* - \hat{\rho}_0)$ and so short-term debt decreases when enforcement improves. In other words, the "*pledgeability effect*" (the fact that the firm need no longer substitute short-term debt for (the lack of) pledgeable long-term income) dominates the "*seasoned offering effect*" (an increase in the quality of enforcement implies that the firm can raise more money in the capital market at date 1 and therefore needs fewer retained earnings). Only the latter effect exists for firms with strong balance sheets.

Who gains most from a stronger enforcement? Recall that firms with strong balance sheets are not affected by the strength of enforcement. By contrast, for a firm with a weak balance sheet,

$$\frac{\mathrm{d}U_\mathrm{b}}{\mathrm{d}e} = \frac{\mathrm{d}U_\mathrm{b}}{\mathrm{d}\rho^*}\frac{\partial \rho^*}{\partial \hat{\rho}_0}\frac{\partial \hat{\rho}_0}{\partial e} = \frac{\rho_1 - \rho^*}{\rho^* - \hat{\rho}_0} F(\rho^*)(p_\mathrm{H} R) > 0.$$

After the liquidity need has been met, though, these firms have pledged $R_\mathrm{l} = R$, while firms with strong balance sheets have promised $R_\mathrm{l} < R$.[60]

60. We assume here that the strong-balance-sheet firms return the entire short-term profit to investors, and enjoy the "slack" in the investors' participation constraint through a nominal claim on long-term income. The point holds more generally if this slack translates into both a claim on short-term income and one on long-term income.

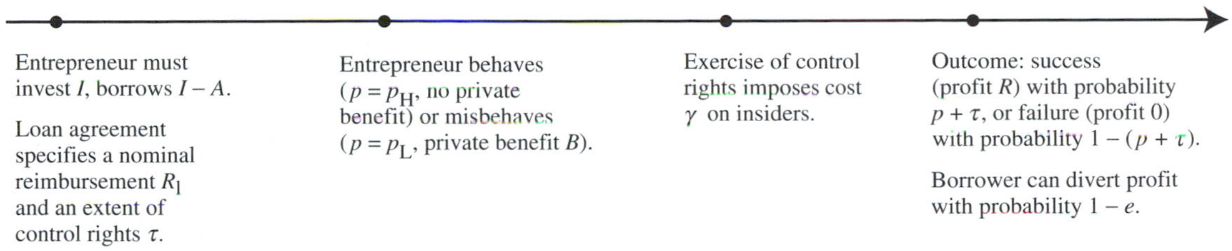
Entrepreneur must invest I, borrows $I - A$.
Loan agreement specifies a nominal reimbursement R_1 and an extent of control rights τ.
Entrepreneur behaves ($p = p_H$, no private benefit) or misbehaves ($p = p_L$, private benefit B).
Exercise of control rights imposes cost γ on insiders.
Outcome: success (profit R) with probability $p + \tau$, or failure (profit 0) with probability $1 - (p + \tau)$.
Borrower can divert profit with probability $1 - e$.

Figure 16.9

Hence, the topsy-turvy principle holds: the firms with the weak balance sheet are *ex post* the most vocal lobbyists in favor of a weakening in enforcement.

Remark (enforcement of claims on intermediate cash flow). We assumed that date-1 income could not be diverted. What happens if $\mathring{e} < 1$? Without supplying a complete analysis, let us note that date-1 diversion may not be as costly to the firms (from an *ex ante* viewpoint) as date-2 diversion. To see this, let the contract specify that if d is not paid to investors at date 1, then the firm is liquidated.[61] If $\rho \leqslant \rho^*$ and $r < (1 - e)p_H R$, the borrower has no incentive to divert date-1 income.[62] By contrast, imperfect enforcement is costly when $\rho > \rho^*$, since the borrower then has nothing to lose (this results in a reduction of pledgeable income equal to $[1 - F(\rho^*)](1 - \mathring{e})r$). The reader familiar with Section 4.7 and with the Bolton and Scharfstein (1990) model will here recognize the theme that the carrot of continuation (or the stick of early termination) alleviates concerns about early diversion of cash by the borrower.

16.5.3 Contracting Institutions and Control Rights

As in Chapter 10, we now assume that the concession takes the form of control rights allocated to investors. To simplify the exposition, we consider the continuum of control rights version. This version can be summarized (see Exercise 10.9) by the total increase, $\tau \geqslant 0$, in the probability of success and the total cost, $\gamma(\tau)$, for the insiders attached to these control rights, with $\gamma(0) = 0$, $\gamma' > 0$, $\gamma'' > 0$.

Figure 16.9 illustrates the timing with imperfect enforcement of claims on income (recall that, given separability of the production function, it does not matter whether moral hazard occurs before or after the exercise of control rights).

In Figure 16.9, we assume that there is no uncertainty as to whether investors will be able to exercise their control rights. The analysis with imperfect enforcement of control rights is more complex and will be briefly discussed later on.

The borrower's utility is then

$$U_b(\tau) = (p_H + \tau)R - \gamma(\tau) - I;$$

and the investors' breakeven condition is

$$(p_H + \tau)eR \geqslant I - A.$$

We keep making Assumption 16.1 so as to shorten the exposition (recall that the incentive compatibility constraint is then automatically satisfied).

Let τ^{FB} denote the first-best allocation of control rights:

$$\gamma'(\tau^{FB}) = R.$$

Because the transfer of control rights to investors is costly while that of income (by assumption) creates no deadweight loss, the entrepreneur first gives cash-flow rights and limited control rights ($\tau = \tau^{FB}$) to investors; if this does not create enough pledgeable income to allow investors to recoup their investment, the entrepreneur gives all cash-flow rights (R) as well as extended control rights ($\tau > \tau^{FB}$) to investors.

And so, if $A \geqslant \bar{A}(e)$, where

$$(p_H + \tau^{FB})eR = I - \bar{A}(e),$$

61. More generally, one would want the liquidation decision itself to be subject to enforcement problems.

62. The reader may wonder whether the contract is renegotiation-proof, as the investors might want to refinance anyway when $\rho < \hat{\rho}_0$. But for weak long-term enforcement ($\hat{\rho}_0$ close to 0), this is not an issue.

the borrower relinquishes only those control rights that are efficiently allocated to investors.

Firms with weak balance sheets must surrender more control rights, i.e.,

$$\tau(A) > \tau^{\mathrm{FB}},$$

where

$$[p_{\mathrm{H}} + \tau(A)]eR = I - A.$$

It can further be shown[63] that *firms with weaker balance sheets benefit more, from an ex ante viewpoint, from an enhanced enforcement of claims on income* (an increase in e); for, a weak enforcement forces the firm to make up for pledgeable income by surrendering very costly control rights to investors.[64]

Finally, let us briefly discuss the enforcement of the exercise of control rights, focusing on firms with weak balance sheets, which transfer all cash-flow rights (R) as well as extended control rights ($\tau > \tau^{\mathrm{FB}}$) to investors. Suppose that, with probability $1 - e'$ with $e' < 1$, the investors do not get to exercise their control rights. Rather, entrepreneurs choose *ex post* the level of τ. This results in an expected increase in the probability of success $\tau_{\mathrm{b}}(e) < \tau^{\mathrm{FB}}$, and expected cost for insiders $\gamma_{\mathrm{b}}(e) = \gamma(\tau_{\mathrm{b}}(e))$. It is still optimal for the entrepreneur to allocate all cash-flow rights to investors. Then[65]

$$\gamma'(\tau_{\mathrm{b}}(e)) = (1 - e)R.$$

The investors' breakeven condition for firms with weak balance sheets becomes[66]

$$[p_{\mathrm{H}} + e'\tau(A) + (1 - e')\tau_{\mathrm{b}}(e)]eR = I - A.$$

A weaker enforcement of control rights (e' decreases) forces the firm to relinquish more control rights and hurts borrowers.[67] Furthermore, firms with weak balance sheets suffer more from a weaker enforcement of control rights.[68]

A weaker enforcement of claims on income has two opposite effects: first, the standard, direct effect of lowering pledgeable income; second, an increased-accountability effect—because the borrower receives more of the final profit, her exercise of control rights when those of investors are not protected becomes more congruent with investors' preferences (τ_{b} decreases with e). This increased-accountability effect raises the pledgeable income, but it cannot, however, make a weak enforcement of income claims a good thing; for, if it dominated the direct effect, then the borrower could achieve the same outcome under strong enforcement by giving a smaller income claim to investors.[69]

16.6 Property Rights Institutions: Are Privately Optimal Maturity Structures Socially Optimal?

Another illustration of the common-agency externalities (discussed in Section 16.3) is provided by the choice of liability maturity structures. This section investigates whether the maturity structure that is optimal for individual firms is socially optimal when the government cannot commit to future policies, that is, whether the government could increase welfare by encouraging shorter or longer maturity structures.[70]

63.
$$\frac{\mathrm{d}U_{\mathrm{b}}}{\mathrm{d}e} = [\gamma'(\tau(A)) - R]\,\frac{p_{\mathrm{H}} + \tau(A)}{e},$$
and so
$$\frac{\partial}{\partial A}\left(\frac{\mathrm{d}U_{\mathrm{b}}}{\mathrm{d}e}\right) < 0$$
since $\gamma'' > 0$ and $\tau' < 0$.

64. *Ex post*, in contrast, firms with weak balance sheets have more to gain from a lack of enforcement of claims on income since they, being subject to a stricter governance, are successful with a higher probability. (Also, firms with very strong balance sheets pledge $R_{\mathrm{l}} < R$ and so have weaker incentives to lobby for repudiation.)

65. We also assume that the events in which investors' control rights and claims on income are not enforced are not correlated. This is probably an unreasonable assumption, but the analysis is straightforwardly extended to allow for correlation.

66. The NPV's new expression is
$$U_{\mathrm{b}} = [p_{\mathrm{H}} + e'\tau(A) + (1 - e')\tau_{\mathrm{b}}(e)]R - [e'\gamma(\tau(A)) + (1 - e')\gamma(\tau_{\mathrm{b}}(e))] - I.$$

67. Simple computations, making use of the investors' breakeven condition, show that
$$\frac{\partial U_{\mathrm{b}}}{\partial e'} = \gamma'(\tau(A))[\tau(A) - \tau_{\mathrm{b}}(e)] - [\gamma(\tau(A)) - \gamma(\tau_{\mathrm{b}}(e))] > 0$$
since γ is convex.

68.
$$\frac{\partial}{\partial A}\left(\frac{\partial U_{\mathrm{b}}}{\partial e'}\right) = \gamma''(\tau(A))\,\frac{\mathrm{d}\tau}{\mathrm{d}A}\,[\tau(A) - \tau_{\mathrm{b}}(e)] < 0.$$

69. Namely, comparing e_{W} and e_{S}, $e_{\mathrm{W}} < e_{\mathrm{S}}$, consider giving claim $R_{\mathrm{l}} < R$ to investors, such that
$$(1 - e_{\mathrm{W}})R = (1 - e_{\mathrm{S}})R + e_{\mathrm{S}}(R - R_{\mathrm{l}}).$$
The investors' and the borrower's stakes are then unchanged.

70. An interesting question is whether the government is indeed capable of manipulating the firms' maturity structure. Suppose, for instance, that the government levies a tax on short-term debt repayments. The firms in general can evade this tax without altering their liquidity management: they can offset short-term debt repayment by

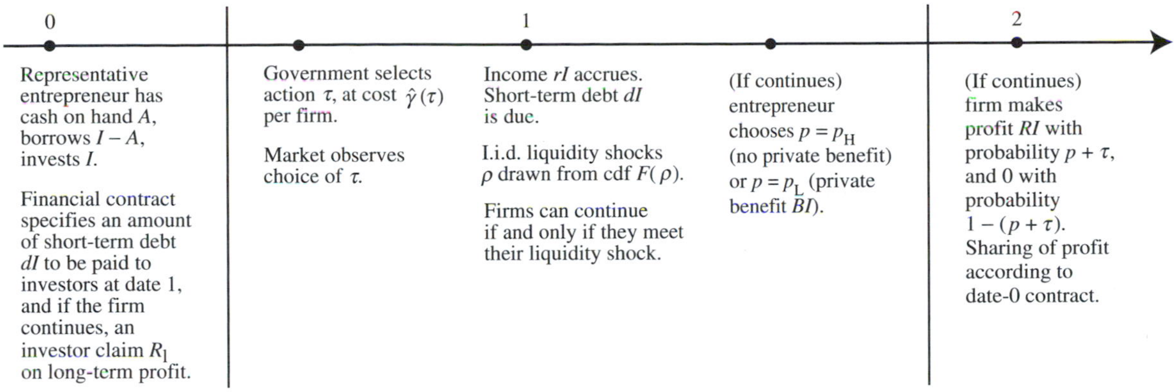

Figure 16.10

Let us return to the optimal-maturity-structure model of Section 5.2, but with a variable investment size, and append an interim government action as we did in the Section 16.3.3. The timing is summarized in Figure 16.10.

The new feature is the introduction of a firm-specific, investment-proportional liquidity shock $\rho I \in [0, \infty)$ that must be covered by the firm in order to continue. This shock is not known at date 0 and is distributed according to cumulative distribution function $F(\rho)$ with density $f(\rho)$. We assume that the distribution has a monotone hazard rate:[71]

$$\frac{f(\rho)}{F(\rho)} \text{ is decreasing.}$$

Recall from Chapter 5 that, in order to meet their liquidity shocks, firms can use their "retained earnings" $[r - d]I$, i.e., what is not distributed to investors at date 1. They can further dilute initial investors by issuing new claims in a seasoned offering.

The model is otherwise that of the Section 16.3.2. The government selects a level τ of profit-friendly policy, at cost $\hat{\gamma}(\tau)$ per firm that has invested. The probability of success of firms that are not liquidated is then $p + \tau$ ($p_H + \tau$ in equilibrium). As earlier, it is convenient to change variable and let

$$a \equiv \frac{\tau}{p_H} \quad \text{and} \quad \gamma(a) \equiv \hat{\gamma}(p_H a).$$

The (per-unit-of-investment) continuation value is then $(1 + a)\rho_1$ and the (per-unit-of-investment) continuation pledgeable income $(1 + a)\rho_0$, with

$$\rho_1 \equiv p_H R \quad \text{and} \quad \rho_0 \equiv p_H\left(R - \frac{B}{\Delta p}\right).$$

For simplicity (but this is not crucial at all), we will assume that the cost $\gamma(a)I$ per continuing firm is entirely borne by the entrepreneur whose firm continues.

Lastly, we assume that the government cares solely about entrepreneurs:

$$w_I = 0.$$

This assumption makes government opportunism particularly salient. While the government would like to *ex ante* commit to be investor friendly so as to enable its corporate friends to raise funds, it finds it hard to abide by its promise later on. That is, the time-consistency problem is severe.

The key feature of the timing described in Figure 16.10 is that the policy choice is made before firms need to refinance. A policy that is less investor friendly (a lower τ, or equivalently a lower a) makes it more difficult for firms to raise funds in a seasoned offering. Hence, more firms are liquidated. The threat of liquidation and the fact that entrepreneurs enjoy quasi-rents (namely, $(1 + a)(\rho_1 - \rho_0)I$ when their firm continues) imposes some discipline on the government. The harder question, though, is,

reducing dilution rights, keeping the reinvestment policy constant. (If dilution rights reach the zero level, investors must further check that the entrepreneur does not use the full retained earnings to finance continuation.) Provided that investors can control dilution rights (and that excess cash in the firm is not wasted), short-term debt repayments can always be deferred while keeping total liquidity payments constant.

71. This monotone-hazard-rate condition is satisfied by most familiar distributions (e.g., uniform, normal, logistic, chi-squared, exponential, and Laplace) and is usually made in order to guarantee the quasi-concavity of objective functions in maximization problems.

How does the firms' maturity structure impact this discipline?

As in Section 5.2, we first derive the optimal cutoff ρ^* under which the initial contract lets the firm continue, and then consider implementation of the optimal contract through a liability maturity structure.

Let a^* denote the equilibrium value of the government's policy. At date 0, entrepreneurs and investors anticipate this value and so the investors' breakeven condition is

$$I - A = \left[r + F(\rho^*)(1 + a^*)\rho_0 - \int_0^{\rho^*} \rho \, dF(\rho)\right] I.$$

The representative entrepreneur's utility is equal to the NPV:

$$U_b(\rho^*) \equiv \left[r + F(\rho^*)[(1 + a^*)\rho_1 - \gamma(a^*)] - \int_0^{\rho^*} \rho \, dF(\rho) - 1\right] I,$$

where we use the assumption that the cost of the government policy is borne by continuing entrepreneurs.[72]

Following the steps of the analysis of Chapter 5, the cutoff that maximizes value is given by

$$\rho^* = (1 + a^*)\rho_1 - \gamma(a^*);$$

the cutoff that maximizes pledgeable income is (provided that γ is not too large) smaller:

$$\rho^* = (1 + a^*)\rho_0.$$

The optimal cutoff, obtained by using the investors' breakeven constraint to determine I as a function of ρ^* and substituting into the NPV equation, therefore satisfies[73]

$$(1 + a^*)\rho_0 < \rho^* < (1 + a^*)\rho_1 - \gamma(a^*).$$

As in Chapter 5, the optimal contract can be implemented through a combination of

- short-term debt d^*I due at date 1 (or the availability of a credit line, if $d^*I < 0$), and
- dilution rights, i.e., the ability to conduct a seasoned offering, with

$$\rho^* = [r - d^*] + (1 + a^*)\rho_0. \qquad (16.16)$$

The first term on the right-hand side is the financial cushion created by the partial distribution of short-term earnings to investors. The second term represents the maximum that can be collected by returning to the capital market at date 1.

Let us now turn to the government's optimal policy at date 1. Let a denote the actual choice of policy (we will be primarily interested in small deviations around the equilibrium policy a^* since we want to determine the first-order condition for this policy). A deviation by the government away from the equilibrium policy changes the amount that firms can raise through a seasoned offering. Namely, they can raise $(1 + a)\rho_0 I$. And so the new cutoff is

$$\rho^*(a) = [r - d^*] + (1 + a)\rho_0$$

or

$$\rho^*(a) = \rho^* + (a - a^*)\rho_0.$$

Remembering that the government aims at maximizing the entrepreneurs' aggregate welfare ($w_1 = 0$), the date-1 choice of a solves

$$\max_{\{a\}}\{F(\rho^*(a))[(1 + a)(\rho_1 - \rho_0) - \gamma(a)]I\},$$

where

- the investment I is fixed at date 1;
- due to the quasi-rent transfer, the entrepreneurs' financial stake in their firms is only $(1 + a)(\rho_1 - \rho_0)I$;
- by assumption, the total cost of the policy is $\gamma(a)I$ per continuing firm and is borne by entrepreneurs.

Taking the first-order condition (in log derivatives) and imposing the equilibrium condition ($a = a^*$):

$$\frac{\gamma'(a^*) - (\rho_1 - \rho_0)}{(1 + a)(\rho_1 - \rho_0) - \gamma(a^*)} = \frac{f(\rho^*)}{F(\rho^*)}\rho_0. \qquad (16.17)$$

(The monotone-hazard-rate assumption and the convexity of $\gamma(\cdot)$ further imply that the (log of the) government's objective is quasi-concave.)

72. Note that γ is only in the NPV equation, not in the breakeven condition, since the entrepreneur incurs this cost whether she shirks or not.

73. As in Chapter 5, the optimal cutoff minimizes the unit cost of bringing on average 1 unit of investment to completion:

$$\rho^* \text{ minimizes } c(\rho^*) = \frac{1 - r + \int_0^{\rho^*} \rho \, dF(\rho)}{F(\rho^*)}.$$

As usual, constant returns to scale imply that the range of allowable parameters must be restricted so that there is investment and this investment is not infinite.

We are now in a position to state the main result. Using the monotone-hazard-rate assumption, conditions (16.16) and (16.17) imply that

$$\frac{\mathrm{d}a^*}{\mathrm{d}\rho^*} < 0 \quad \text{or} \quad \frac{\mathrm{d}a^*}{\mathrm{d}d^*} > 0.$$

A shortening of the liability maturity structure (an increase in the firms' level of short-term debt) disciplines the government. Intuitively, more short-term debt makes the firms more fragile as the cushion they accumulate by not fully distributing short-term profits shrinks. They become more dependent on returning to the capital market, which forces the government to make investor claims on firms more valuable.

This increase in discipline is often a good thing from an *ex ante* viewpoint. Investors are not affected since (a) they always break even at date 0, and (b) we assumed that the incidence of the government policy was entirely on entrepreneurs. A sufficient condition for entrepreneurs to be made better off is that the density f be nonincreasing.[74]

Remark (endogenous uncertainty about government policy). The government's policy is perfectly predictable in the deterministic model described above; and so a deterministic amount of debt is *one* way of implementing the optimal management of liquidity. Suppose in contrast that the government's policy is random as $\gamma(a) = \gamma_0(a) + \varepsilon a$, where ε is a random variable that is learned by the government at date 1 (before choosing policy a). The analysis above can easily be generalized (see Tirole 2003). The key difference is that deterministic debt is no longer optimal. Rather, we have the following two points:

- The optimal debt is (negatively and linearly) indexed on the stock index, $d^* = d_0 - d_1 a$, in order to take advantage of the new information about the firm's prospects: if the government adopts a value- and investor-friendly policy (because it learns that this policy is cheap), then the firm should take advantage of this. Dilution rights become more valuable, but they are optimally complemented by a lengthening of the maturity structure.
- State-contingent debt makes the government policy more investor friendly, precisely because it increases the firms' reinvestment sensitivity to public policy.

16.7 Exercises

The first exercise is inspired by a paper by Gertler and Rogoff (1990).

Exercise 16.1 (borrowing abroad). Consider a small country with a mass 1 of identical entrepreneurs. There is a single (tradable) good. The representative entrepreneur has initial wealth A and a variable-investment constant-returns-to-scale project. A project of size $I \in [0, \infty)$ at date 1 yields at date 2 verifiable revenue RI with probability p and 0 with probability $1 - p$. The probability p is not subject to moral hazard. There is moral hazard, though: instead of investing I in the firm, the entrepreneur can invest it abroad and get private return μI, where $\mu < 1$. The investors are unable to seize the return from this alternative investment. Everyone is risk neutral, has discount factor 1 (i.e., has utility equal to the undiscounted sum of consumptions at dates 1 and 2), and the entrepreneur is protected by limited liability.

One will assume that

$$pR > 1 > pR - \mu.$$

(i) Compute the representative entrepreneur's borrowing capacity and utility. Show that the outcome is the same as in a situation in which the entrepreneur cannot divert funds and invest them abroad,

74. From an *ex ante* point of view, and for an arbitrary policy a, let $I(a, \rho^*)$ be defined by the breakeven condition:

$$I - A = rI + F(\rho^*)(1 + a)\rho_0 I - \left[\int_0^{\rho^*} \rho \, \mathrm{d}F(\rho)\right] I.$$

The representative entrepreneur's utility can be expressed as

$$U_\mathrm{b}(a, \rho^*) \equiv F(\rho^*)[(1 + a)(\rho_1 - \rho_0) - \gamma(a)]I(a, \rho^*) - A.$$

The optimal contract maximizes $U_\mathrm{b}(a, \rho^*)$ over ρ^* for a given a. Around the equilibrium values (ρ^*, a^*), and making use of the government's first-order condition and of the optimality condition for ρ^* ($\rho^* = c(\rho^*)$, see footnote 73),

$$\frac{\mathrm{d}\log(U_\mathrm{b} + A)}{\mathrm{d}\rho^*} \propto \left[\frac{F(\rho^*)}{f(\rho^*)} - [\rho^* - (1 + a)\rho_0]\right] \frac{\mathrm{d}a^*}{\mathrm{d}\rho^*},$$

where "$\propto$" means "proportional to." So, if $f' \leqslant 0$ (a condition that is more stringent than the monotone-hazard-rate condition, $f'F \leqslant f^2$),

$$\frac{F(\rho^*)}{f(\rho^*)} \geqslant \rho^*.$$

Because $\mathrm{d}a^*/\mathrm{d}\rho^* < 0$,

$$\frac{\mathrm{d}\log(U_\mathrm{b} + A)}{\mathrm{d}\rho^*} < 0.$$

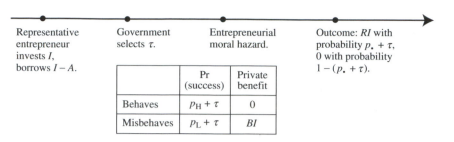

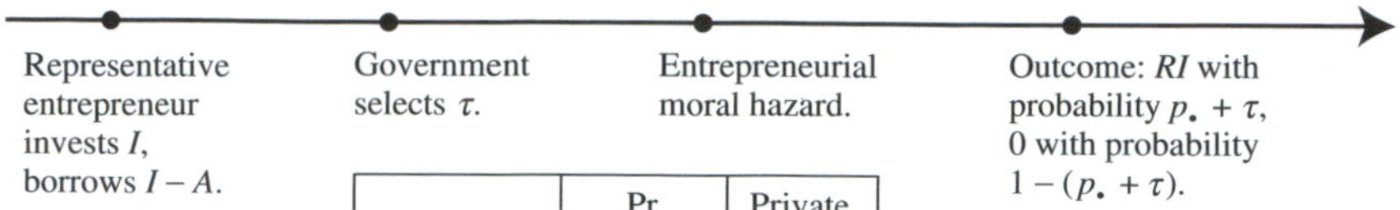
Representative entrepreneur invests I, borrows $I - A$.
Government selects τ.
Entrepreneurial moral hazard.
Outcome: RI with probability $p_{\bullet} + \tau$, 0 with probability $1 - (p_{\bullet} + \tau)$.

	Pr (success)	Private benefit
Behaves	$p_H + \tau$	0
Misbehaves	$p_L + \tau$	BI

Figure 16.11

but can enjoy a private benefit per unit of investment $B = \mu$. Explain why.

(ii) Adopt the convention that the payment to investors, R_l, is a debt payment. Suppose that the entrepreneurs' projects are independent and that the government imposes a per-unit-of-income tax on successful projects and offers a guarantee/compensation σ on private debt (so τRI is the tax on successful projects and σR_l is the investors' payoff in the case of bankruptcy). Show that the borrowing capacity and entrepreneur utility are the same as in (i).

In contrast, compute the impact on entrepreneurs when the government starts at date 1 with an inherited public debt outstanding to foreign lenders equal to D ($\leqslant A$) per entrepreneur and must finance it through an income tax on successful projects.

(iii) Coming back to question (i), suppose that the government can through its governance institutions or other policies affect the return μ on investments abroad. There are two levels $\mu_L < \mu_H$ (where both levels satisfy the conditions in (i)). The choice between the two levels involves no cost (but affects behavior!). The government's objective function is to maximize the representative entrepreneur's welfare.

Assuming that all borrowing is foreign borrowing, what is the representative entrepreneur's utility when

(a) the government can commit to μ before foreign investors invest;

(b) the government chooses μ after they have invested (but before the entrepreneurs select their action)?

(iv) Suppose now that the output RI (in the case of success) is in terms of a nontradable good (but the endowment A and the investment I are in tradable goods). Another sector of the economy (the "export sector") will receive $\mathcal{R}$ in tradable goods at date 2. All domestic agents have utility from date-2 consumptions c and c^* of nontradable and tradable goods equal to $c + c^*$ (so the two goods are perfect substitutes for domestic residents, while foreigners consume only the tradable good). Define the date-2 exchange rate $e \geqslant 1$ as the price of tradables in terms of nontradables. Compute the borrowing capacity and the exchange rate. (One will, for example, assume that funds fraudulently invested abroad cannot be reimported and must be consumed abroad. So they yield μ rather than $e\mu$.)

Exercise 16.2 (time-consistent government policy). Consider a unit mass of identical entrepreneurs with variable-investment projects. The timing is summarized in Figure 16.11.

The cost of the policy for the country is $\gamma(\tau)I$ (where $\gamma'(0) = 0$, $\gamma'(\tau) > 0$, for $\tau > 0$, $\gamma'(1 - p_H) = \infty$, $\gamma'' > 0$).

All investors are domestic investors (there are no foreign lenders and, when choosing τ, the government maximizes social welfare, equal to entrepreneurs' welfare plus investors' welfare).

Assume that

$$(p_H + \tau)R > 1 > (p_H + \tau)\left(R - \frac{B}{\Delta p}\right)$$

in the relevant range of values of τ, and that it is never optimal to induce entrepreneurs to misbehave. Everyone is risk neutral, and the entrepreneurs are protected by limited liability.

(i) • Show that, when expecting policy τ, entrepreneurs invest

$$I(\tau) = \frac{A}{1 - (p_H + \tau)(R - B/\Delta p)}.$$

• What is the equilibrium value τ^*?

Table 16.1

	Date 0	Date 1		
	Government selects g^* (commitment)	Government selects g^* (noncommitment)		
nt			SI	Exchange rate determined
t	Entrepreneur borrows $I - A$	Entrepreneur takes private benefit BI, or none	Outcome RI or 0	

(ii) What value would the government choose if it selected τ *before* entrepreneurs borrow?

(iii) Informally explain how your answer to (i) would change if investors were foreign investors and the government discounted their welfare relative to that of domestic residents.

Exercise 16.3 (political economy of exchange rate policies). Consider a country that has liberalized its capital account. There are two goods: a tradable good (the only one consumed by foreigners) and a nontradable good.

• The only investors are foreign investors, with preferences over date-0 and date-1 consumptions

$$c_0^* + c_1^*,$$

where an asterisk refers to the tradable good.

• The country is populated by a unit mass of domestic entrepreneurs endowed with a constant-returns-to-scale technology. The representative entrepreneur (1) invests I units of tradables in equipment (where I is endogenous), (2) produces RI units of tradables in the case of success, and 0 in the case of failure, and SI units of nontradables for certain. We assume that firms' outcomes are independent (there is no macroeconomic shock).

The model is a variation on the standard variable-investment model:

- Each entrepreneur is initially endowed with A units of tradables (her only wealth), borrows $I - A$.
- There is moral hazard. The probability of success in the tradable-good activity is p_H if the entrepreneur behaves, and p_L otherwise. The entrepreneur receives private benefit BI in *tradables* by misbehaving and 0 otherwise.
- An entrepreneur's utility is $c_1 + u(c_1^*) + v(g^*)$, where c_1 is the consumption of nontradables, c_1^* the consumption of the tradable good, and g^* the level of public good supplied by the government. u and v are concave.

We add a government. The government has international reserves $\mathcal{R}^*$, of which it consumes g^* to produce a public good. The rest, $\mathcal{R}^* - g^*$, is dumped on the currency market at the end. So, e, the price of tradables in terms of nontradables, is given *ex post* by

$$p_H RI + \mathcal{R}^* - g^* = c_1^*(e) + d^* + \frac{d}{e},$$

where I is the representative entrepreneur's investment, d^* is the entrepreneurs' average reimbursed debt in tradables and d is the average reimbursed debt in nontradables. The government cares only about the welfare of entrepreneurs, i.e., does not internalize that of the foreigners.

The timing is summarized in Table 16.1, where "t" and "nt" stand for "tradables" and "nontradables," respectively.

Consider financing contracts in which

- investors receive $R_l^* = RI - R_b^*$ in tradables in the case of success, and 0 in the case of failure;
- investors have nominal claims R_l^S and R_l^F in nontradables in the cases of success and failure, respectively.

(i) Relate (d, d^*) and (R_l^*, R_l^S, R_l^F).

(ii) Fixing an expected exchange rate e, determine the investment I of the representative entrepreneur in this constant-returns-to-scale model assuming that $\rho_0 \equiv p_H(R - B/\Delta p) < 1 - (S/e)$ in the relevant range.

Show that $R_l^F = SI$ and that

$$I = \frac{A}{1 - [(S/e) + \rho_0]}.$$

(iii) Compare the exchange rate and the welfare of entrepreneurs when the government chooses

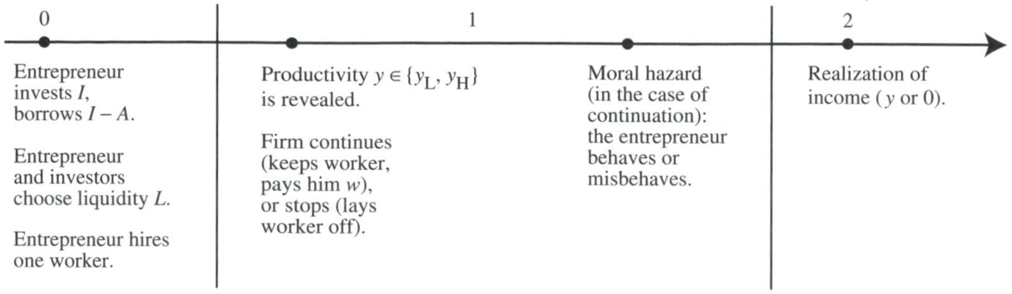

Figure 16.12

g^* after the private sector borrows abroad ("noncommitment") and when the government can commit to g^* before entrepreneurs borrow abroad ("commitment").

Assume that the exchange rate depreciates as government expenditures g^* grow. Show that $v'(g^*) > e$ under commitment (underspending) and $v'(g^*) < e$ under noncommitment (overspending).

(iv) Show that there is an externality among borrowers when the government cannot commit.

Exercise 16.4 (time consistency and the soft budget constraint). A firm is run by a risk-neutral entrepreneur with wealth A, and has a fixed-size project with investment cost I. The project, if undertaken at date 0, will deliver a verifiable income, $y \in \{y_L, y_H\}$ in the case of success and 0 in the case of failure, at date 2, provided that one worker is employed in the firm. The project yields nothing if it is interrupted (the worker is laid off). $y = y_H$ with probability ρ and $y = y_L < y_H$ with probability $1 - \rho$.

Moreover, in the case of "continuation" and regardless of the value of y, the entrepreneur may behave (the income is y for certain, the entrepreneur receives no private benefit) or misbehave (the income is y with probability p_L and 0 with probability $1 - p_L$, the entrepreneur receives private benefit B). The entrepreneur is protected by limited liability. Let

$$\mathcal{R} \equiv \frac{B}{1 - p_L}.$$

(One will assume that B is small enough that it is worth inducing the entrepreneur to behave in the case of continuation.) The (risk-neutral) worker is paid w in the case of continuation and 0 otherwise. He obtains unemployment benefit paid by the state $w_u < w$ when laid off. We take w and w_u as given. (Note: they could be endogenized through some efficiency wage and incentive-to-search stories, but take these as exogenous for this exercise.)

Assume that the interest rate in the economy is 0 and that

$$w < y_L < w + \mathcal{R}$$

and

$$I - A \leqslant \rho(y_H - w - \mathcal{R}) + (1 - \rho)(y_L - w - \mathcal{R}).$$

(i) Write the firm's NPV depending on whether the firm continues ($x = 1$) or stops ($x = 0$) when productivity is low ($y = y_L$). Show that $x^* = 1$. Assuming a perfectly functioning capital market at date 1, what is the amount of liquidity that is needed to complement capital market refinancing?

(ii) Introduce a government that can at date 1 bring a subsidy $s \geqslant 0$ to the firm (it is a pure subsidy: the government takes no ownership stake in exchange). The shadow cost of public funds is λ, and so the cost of subsidy s for the taxpayers is $(1 + \lambda)s$. The government maximizes total welfare (entrepreneur, investors, worker, taxpayers). Assuming that

$$\lambda[(w - w_u) + \mathcal{R}] \leqslant (1 + \lambda)y_L$$

and that the government selects its subsidy at date 1 (having observed the realization of y), what is the liquidity L chosen by entrepreneur and investors at date 0?

How would the government (contingent) choice of s be affected if the government could commit to s at date 0, before the investors and the entrepreneur write their contract?

References

Acemoglu, D. and S. Johnson. 2003. Unbundling institutions. National Bureau of Economic Research Working Paper 9934.

Aghion, P. and P. Bolton. 1991. Government debt and the risk of default. In *Capital Markets and Debt Management* (ed. R. Dornbusch and M. Draghi). Cambridge, MA: MIT Press.

Aghion, P. and B. Hermalin. 1990. Legal restrictions on private contracts can enhance efficiency. *Journal of Law, Economics, & Organization* 6:381–409.

Athey, S., A. Atkeson, and P. Kehoe. 2005. The optimal degree of discretion in monetary policy. *Econometrica* 73: 1431–1475.

Atkinson, A. B. and J. Stiglitz. 1976. The design of tax structure: direct and indirect taxation. *Journal of Public Economics* 6:55–75.

Bagwell, K. and R. Staiger. 2000. GATT-think. Mimeo, Columbia University, and University of Wisconsin.

Barro, R. 1973. The control of politicians: an economic model. *Public Choice* 14:19–42.

Barro, R. and D. Gordon. 1983. Rules, discretion and reputation in a model of monetary policy. *Journal of Monetary Economics* 12:101–121.

Bernheim, D. and M. Whinston. 1986a. Menu auctions, resource allocation, and economic influence. *Quarterly Journal of Economics* 101:1–33.

——. 1986b. Common agency. *Econometrica* 54:923–942.

Biais, B. and T. Mariotti. 2003. Credit, wages and bankruptcy laws. IDEI Working Paper 231, Toulouse.

Biais, B. and E. Perotti. 2002. Machiavellian privatization. *American Economic Review* 92:240–258.

Bolton, P. and H. Rosenthal. 2002. Political intervention in debt contracts. *Journal of Political Economy* 110:1103–1134.

Bolton, P. and D. Scharfstein. 1990. A theory of predation based on agency problems in financial contracting. *American Economic Review* 80:93–106.

Bulow, J. and K. Rogoff. 1989a. A constant recontracting model of sovereign debt. *Journal of Political Economy* 97: 155–178.

——. 1989b. Multilateral negotiations for rescheduling developing country debt: a bargaining theoretic framework. In *Analytical Issues in Debt* (ed. J. Frenkel, M. Dooley, and P. Wickham). Washington, D.C.: IMF.

Calvo, G. A. 1996. *Money, Exchange Rates, and Output.* Cambridge, MA: MIT Press.

Calvo, G. A. and S. Wellisz. 1978. Supervision, loss of control, and the optimal size of the firm. *Journal of Political Economy* 86:943–952.

Cespa, G. and G. Cestone. 2002. Stakeholder activism and the "congruence of interests" between small shareholders and stakeholders. Mimeo, Universitat Pompeu Fabra.

Coase, R. 1960. The problem of social cost. *Journal of Law and Economics* 3:1–44.

Faure-Grimaud, A. and D. Martimort. 2003. Regulatory inertia. *RAND Journal of Economics* 34:413–437.

Ferejohn, J. 1986. Incumbent performance and electoral control. *Public Choice* 50:5–26.

Grossman, G. and E. Helpman. 1994. Protection for sale. *American Economic Review* 84:833–850.

Gertler, M. and K. Rogoff. 1990. North–South lending and endogenous domestic capital market inefficiencies. *Journal of Monetary Economics* 26:245–266.

Hellwig, M. 2000. On the economics and politics of corporate finance and corporate control. In *Corporate Governance: Theoretical and Empirical Perspectives* (ed. X. Vives), Chapter 3. Cambridge University Press.

Jappelli, T., M. Pagano, and M. Bianco. 2005. Courts and banks: effect of judicial costs on credit market performance. *Journal of Money, Credit, and Banking* 37:223–244.

Kroszner, R. 1999. Is it better to forgive than to receive? Repudiation of the gold indexation clause in long-term debt during the Great Depression. Working Paper, University of Chicago.

Kroszner, R. and P. Strahan. 1999. What drives deregulation? Economics and politics of the relaxation of bank branching restrictions. *Quarterly Journal of Economics* 114:1437–1467.

Kydland, F. and E. Prescott. 1977. Rules rather than discretion: the inconsistency of optimal plans. *Journal of Political Economy* 85:473–491.

Laffont, J. J. and J. Tirole. 1991. The politics of government decision making: a theory of regulatory capture. *Quarterly Journal of Economics* 106:1089–1127.

——. 1993. Commitment and political accountability. In *A Theory of Incentives in Procurement and Regulation*, Chapter 16. Cambridge, MA, and London: MIT Press.

La Porta, R., F. Lopez-de-Silanes, A. Shleifer, and R. Vishny. 1997. Legal determinants of external finance. *Journal of Finance* 52:1131–1150.

——. 1998. Law and finance. *Journal of Political Economy* 107:1113–1155.

Lindbeck, A. and J. Weibull. 1987. Balanced-budget redistribution as the outcome of political competition. *Public Choice* 52:273–297.

Martimort, D. 1991. Multi principaux avec sélection adverse. Mimeo, Institut d'Economie Industrielle, Toulouse.

Maskin, E. and J. Tirole. 2004. The politician and the judge: accountability in government. *American Economic Review* 94:1034–1054.

Matsuyama, K. 1990. Perfect equilibria in a trade liberalization game. *American Economic Review* 80:480–492.

North, D. 1981. *Structure and Change in Economic History.* New York: W. W. Norton.

Pagano, M. and P. Volpin. 2005a. The political economy of corporate governance. *American Economic Review* 95: 1005–1030.

——. 2005b. Workers, managers, and corporate control. *Journal of Finance* 60:841–868.

——. 2005c. Shareholder protection, stock market development, and politics. Presented as the Marshall Lecture, European Economic Association Meeting, August 27, 2005.

Pauly, M. V. 1974. Overinsurance and public provision of insurance: the roles of moral hazard and adverse selection. *Quarterly Journal of Economics* 88:44–62.

Perotti, E. and E. L. von Thadden. 2001. The political economy of bank- and market dominance. Mimeo, University of Amsterdam and University of Lausanne.

Persson, M., T. Persson, and L. Svensson. 1987. Time consistency of fiscal and monetary policy. *Econometrica* 55: 1419–1432.

Persson, T. and L. Svensson. 1989. Why a stubborn conservative would run a deficit: policy with time inconsistent preferences. *Quarterly Journal of Economics* 65:325–346.

Persson, T. and G. Tabellini. 2000. *Political Economics: Explaining Economic Policy.* Cambridge, MA: MIT Press.

——. 2003. *The Economic Effect of Constitutions.* Cambridge, MA: MIT Press.

Rajan, R. and L. Zingales. 2003. The great reversals: the politics of financial development in the 20th century. *Journal of Financial Economics* 69:5–50.

Rogoff, K. 1985. The optimal degree of commitment to an intermediate monetary target. *Quarterly Journal of Economics* 100:1169–1190.

Shapiro, C. and J. Stiglitz. 1984. Equilibrium unemployment as a worker discipline device. *American Economic Review* 74:433–444.

Shavell, S. 2004. *Foundations of Economic Analysis of Law.* The Belknap Press of the Harvard University Press.

Stole, L. 1990. Mechanism design under common agency. Mimeo, Department of Economics, MIT.

Tabellini, G. and A. Alesina. 1990. Voting on the budget deficit. *American Economic Review* 80:37–49.

Tirole, J. 2003. Inefficient foreign borrowing: a dual- and common-agency perspective. *American Economic Review* 93:1678–1702.

Tornell, A. 1991. Time inconsistency of protectionist programs. *Quarterly Journal of Economics* 106:963–974.

Wagner, W. 2001. International diversification, governmental incentives, and the home bias in portfolio investment. Mimeo, Tilburg University.

PART VII

Answers to Selected Exercises, and Review Problems

Answers to Selected Exercises

Exercise 3.1 (random financing). (i) The investors' breakeven condition is

$$xI - A \leqslant x p_{\mathrm{H}}(R - R_{\mathrm{b}}).$$

Because the NPV is negative if the entrepreneur has an incentive to shirk, R_{b} must satisfy

$$(\Delta p)R_{\mathrm{b}} \geqslant B.$$

The investors' breakeven condition (which will be satisfied with equality under a competitive capital market) is then

$$x\left[p_{\mathrm{H}}\left(R - \frac{B}{\Delta p}\right) - I\right] \geqslant -A$$

or

$$x\bar{A} \leqslant A.$$

(ii) The NPV is equal to

$$U_{\mathrm{b}} = x(p_{\mathrm{H}}R - I)$$

and so maximizing U_{b} is tantamount to maximizing x. Hence,

$$x^* = \frac{A}{\bar{A}}.$$

The probability that the project is undertaken grows from 0 to 1 as the borrower's net worth grows from 0 to $\bar{A}$.

Exercise 3.2 (impact of entrepreneurial risk aversion). (i) When $p_{\mathrm{H}} < 1$, the entrepreneur must receive at least c_0 in the case of failure, because the probability of failure is positive even in the case of good behavior. Because of risk neutrality above c_0, it is optimal to give the entrepreneur exactly c_0 in the case of failure. Let R_{b} denote the reward in the case of success.

The incentive constraint is

$$(\Delta p)(R_{\mathrm{b}} - c_0) \geqslant B. \qquad \text{(IC)}$$

The pledgeable income is

$$p_{\mathrm{H}}R - (1 - p_{\mathrm{H}})c_0 - p_{\mathrm{H}} \min_{\{\mathrm{IC}\}} R_{\mathrm{b}} = p_{\mathrm{H}}\left(R - \frac{B}{\Delta p}\right) - c_0.$$

To allow financing, this pledgeable income must exceed $I - A$. Hence, $\bar{A} = I + c_0 - p_{\mathrm{H}}(R - B/\Delta p)$.

When $p_{\mathrm{H}} = 1$, the pledgeable income is then $p_{\mathrm{H}}R$ (if $c_0 > 0$, deviations can be punished harshly by giving the entrepreneur, say, 0 in the case of failure).

(ii) Let $R_{\mathrm{b}}^{\mathrm{S}}$ and $R_{\mathrm{b}}^{\mathrm{F}}$ denote the rewards in the cases of success and failure, respectively. The incentive constraint is

$$(\Delta p)[u(R_{\mathrm{b}}^{\mathrm{S}}) - u(R_{\mathrm{b}}^{\mathrm{F}})] \geqslant B.$$

The optimal contract solves

$$\max U_{\mathrm{b}} = p_{\mathrm{H}}u(R_{\mathrm{b}}^{\mathrm{S}}) + (1 - p_{\mathrm{H}})u(R_{\mathrm{b}}^{\mathrm{F}})$$

s.t.

$$p_{\mathrm{H}}R - p_{\mathrm{H}}R_{\mathrm{b}}^{\mathrm{S}} - (1 - p_{\mathrm{H}})R_{\mathrm{b}}^{\mathrm{F}} \geqslant I - A,$$

$$(\Delta p)[u(R_{\mathrm{b}}^{\mathrm{S}}) - u(R_{\mathrm{b}}^{\mathrm{F}})] \geqslant B,$$

and (if limited liability is imposed)

$$R_{\mathrm{b}}^{\mathrm{F}} \geqslant 0.$$

It must also be the case that the solution to this program exceeds the utility, $u(A)$, obtained by the entrepreneur if the project is not financed. The entrepreneur's incentive compatibility constraint is binding; otherwise, the solution to this program would give full insurance to the entrepreneur, which would violate the incentive compatibility condition. We refer to Holmström[1] and Shavell[2] for general considerations on this moral-hazard problem.

Exercise 3.3 (random private benefits). (i) $B^* = p_{\mathrm{H}}(R - r_1)$.

1. Holmström, B. 1979. Moral hazard and observability. *Bell Journal of Economics* 10:74–91.

2. Shavell, S. 1979. Risk sharing and incentives in the principal and agent relationship. *Bell Journal of Economics* 10:55–73.

(ii) The investors' expected income is

$$p_{\mathrm{H}}^2 \frac{r_1(R - r_1)}{R} I = \frac{B^*(p_{\mathrm{H}}R - B^*)}{R} I.$$

The borrowing capacity is such that this expected income is equal to the investors' initial investment, $I - A$. Thus

$$I = kA,$$

where

$$k = \frac{1}{1 - B^*(p_{\mathrm{H}}R - B^*)/R}.$$

The borrowing capacity is maximized for

$$B^* = \tfrac{1}{2} p_{\mathrm{H}} R,$$

or, equivalently,

$$r_1 = \tfrac{1}{2} R.$$

(iii) Using the fact that investors break even, the entrepreneur's expected utility is

$$\left(p_{\mathrm{H}} \frac{B^*}{R} R + \int_{B^*}^{R} \frac{B}{R} \, \mathrm{d}B\right) I = \frac{p_{\mathrm{H}} B^* + \frac{1}{2} R - (B^*)^2/2R}{1 - B^*(p_{\mathrm{H}}R - B^*)/R} A.$$

At the optimum,

$$\tfrac{1}{2} p_{\mathrm{H}} R < B^* < p_{\mathrm{H}} R.$$

Recall that $B^* = p_{\mathrm{H}}R$ maximizes the return per unit of investment as it eliminates shirking, while $B^* = \frac{1}{2} p_{\mathrm{H}} R$ maximizes borrowing capacity.

(iv) When B is verifiable, the entrepreneur's expected utility is still

$$\left(p_{\mathrm{H}} B^* + \frac{R}{2} - \frac{(B^*)^2}{2R}\right) I.$$

For a given B^*, the contract should specify

$$r_1(B) \begin{cases} = R - B/p_{\mathrm{H}} & \text{if } B < B^* \text{ (recall that } p_{\mathrm{L}} = 0), \\ > R - B/p_{\mathrm{H}} & \text{if } B > B^*. \end{cases}$$

The maximal investment is then

$$I = \frac{A}{1 - p_{\mathrm{H}} B^* + (B^*)^2/2R}.$$

Borrowing capacity is maximized at $B^* = p_{\mathrm{H}}R$. Because this threshold also maximizes per-unit expected income, it is clearly optimal overall.

Exercise 3.4 (product-market competition and financing). (i) Because the two projects are statistically independent, there is no point making an entrepreneur's reward contingent on the outcome of the other firm's performance. (Technically, this result is a special case of the "sufficient statistics" results of Holmström[3] and Shavell[4]. This result states that an agent's reward should be contingent only on variables that the agent can control—a sufficient statistic for the vector of observable variables relative to effort—and not on extraneous noise.) So, let $R_{\mathrm{b}}^{\mathrm{S}}$ and $R_{\mathrm{b}}^{\mathrm{F}}$ denote an entrepreneur's reward in the cases of success and failure. As usual,

$$(\Delta p)(R_{\mathrm{b}}^{\mathrm{S}} - R_{\mathrm{b}}^{\mathrm{F}}) \geqslant B \quad \text{and} \quad R_{\mathrm{b}}^{\mathrm{F}} = 0.$$

Let $x \in [0, 1]$ denote the probability that the rival firm invests. Then the expected income is

$$p_{\mathrm{H}}[x p_{\mathrm{H}} D + (1 - x p_{\mathrm{H}}) M].$$

The pledgeable income is equal to this expression minus $p_{\mathrm{H}} B/\Delta p$.

At best, the other firm is not financed, and $R = M$ in the case of success. The threshold $\underline{A}$ is given by

$$I - \underline{A} = p_{\mathrm{H}}\left(M - \frac{B}{\Delta p}\right).$$

(ii) At worst, the rival firm is financed. So, the expected return in the case of success is

$$p_{\mathrm{H}} D + (1 - p_{\mathrm{H}}) M.$$

So,

$$I - \bar{A} = p_{\mathrm{H}}\left(p_{\mathrm{H}} D + (1 - p_{\mathrm{H}}) M - \frac{B}{\Delta p}\right).$$

(iii) One of the firms gets funding while the other does not (obvious). There also exists a third, mixed-strategy equilibrium, in which each firm gets funded with positive probability.

(iv) If only one firm receives financing, then

$$R_{\mathrm{b}}^{\mathrm{F}} = c_0$$

(as long as $p_{\mathrm{H}} < 1$, so that there is always a probability of failing even when the entrepreneur works), and

$$R_{\mathrm{b}}^{\mathrm{S}} = c_0 + \frac{B}{\Delta p},$$

which yields the minimum net worth given in the statement of the question.

(v) Suppose now that both entrepreneurs receive financing. Consider the following reward scheme for

3. Holmström, B. 1979. Moral hazard and observability. *Bell Journal of Economics* 10:74–91.

4. Shavell, S. 1979. Risk sharing and incentives in the principal and agent relationship. *Bell Journal of Economics* 10:55–73.

the entrepreneur:

$$R_\mathrm{b} < c_0 \quad \text{if the firm fails and the rival firm succeeds,}$$

$$R_\mathrm{b} = c_0 \quad \text{otherwise.}$$

There is no longer moral hazard: as long as the other entrepreneur works, shirking yields probability Δp that the other entrepreneur succeeds while this entrepreneur fails (recall that the two technologies are perfectly correlated), resulting in a large (infinite) punishment. If

$$D > M - \frac{B}{\Delta p},$$

then product-market competition facilitates financing! Correlation enables benchmarking provided that both firms secure financing.

Exercise 3.5 (continuous investment and decreasing returns to scale). (i) The incentive constraint is, as in the model of Section 3.4,

$$(\Delta p)R_\mathrm{b} \geqslant BI. \tag{IC}$$

The pledgeable income is

$$p_\mathrm{H}\Big[R(I) - \min_{\{\mathrm{IC}\}} R_\mathrm{b}\Big] = p_\mathrm{H}\Big[R(I) - \frac{BI}{\Delta p}\Big].$$

Thus the entrepreneur selects I to solve

$$\max \mathrm{NPV} = \max U_\mathrm{b} = p_\mathrm{H}R(I) - I$$

s.t.

$$p_\mathrm{H}\Big[R(I) - \frac{BI}{\Delta p}\Big] \geqslant I - A. \tag{BB}$$

Clearly, if $I = I^*$ satisfies (BB) (A is high), then it solves this program. The shadow price of the budget constraint is then $\mu = 0$.

So suppose A is small enough that (BB) is not satisfied at $I = I^*$. Then I is determined by (BB) (since the objective function is concave). In that region, by the envelope theorem

$$\frac{\mathrm{d}U_\mathrm{b}}{\mathrm{d}A} = v = [p_\mathrm{H}R'(I) - 1]\frac{\mathrm{d}I}{\mathrm{d}A} = \frac{1}{(p_\mathrm{H}B/\Delta p)/(p_\mathrm{H}R' - 1) - 1}.$$

So v decreases with A.

Exercise 3.6 (renegotiation and debt forgiveness). (i) Suppose that $R_\mathrm{b} < BI/(\Delta p)$.

In the absence of renegotiation, the entrepreneur will shirk and obtain utility

$$BI + p_\mathrm{L}R_\mathrm{b},$$

and the lender's expected revenue is

$$p_\mathrm{L}(RI - R_\mathrm{b}).$$

Renegotiation must be mutually advantageous. So a necessary condition for renegotiation is that total surplus increases. A renegotiation toward a stake $\hat{R}_\mathrm{b} < BI/(\Delta p)$ does not affect surplus and thus is a mere redistribution of wealth between the investors and the entrepreneur. So renegotiation, if it happens, must yield stake

$$\hat{R}_\mathrm{b} \geqslant \frac{BI}{\Delta p}$$

for the entrepreneur. It constitutes a Pareto-improvement if the following two conditions are satisfied:

$$p_\mathrm{H}\hat{R}_\mathrm{b} \geqslant BI + p_\mathrm{L}R_\mathrm{b}$$

and

$$p_\mathrm{H}(RI - \hat{R}_\mathrm{b}) \geqslant p_\mathrm{L}(RI - R_\mathrm{b}).$$

The second inequality, together with the incentive constraint, implies that

$$(\Delta p)RI - p_\mathrm{H}\frac{BI}{\Delta p} + p_\mathrm{L}R_\mathrm{b} \geqslant 0.$$

Conversely, if this condition is satisfied, then the two parties can find an $\hat{R}_\mathrm{b}$ that makes them both better off.

Note that the standard assumptions

$$p_\mathrm{H}\Big[RI - \frac{BI}{\Delta p}\Big] \geqslant I - A$$

and

$$I \geqslant p_\mathrm{L}RI + BI$$

imply that

$$(\Delta p)RI - p_\mathrm{H}\frac{BI}{\Delta p} + A - BI \geqslant 0.$$

So, if $A > BI$ and R_b is small enough, the condition for renegotiation may not be satisfied.

(ii) The "project" consists in creating incentives for the entrepreneur. It creates NPV equal to $(\Delta p)RI$, does not involve any new investment, and the entrepreneur can bring an amount of money $\hat{A} \equiv p_\mathrm{L}R_\mathrm{b}$ that is the forgone expected income.

For this fictitious project, the pledgeable income is

$$(\Delta p)RI - p_{\mathrm{H}}\frac{BI}{\Delta p}$$

and the investors' outlay is

$$0 - \hat{A}.$$

Hence, it is "financed" if and only if

$$(\Delta p)RI - p_{\mathrm{H}}\frac{BI}{\Delta p} \geqslant -p_{\mathrm{L}}R_{\mathrm{b}}.$$

Exercise 3.7 (strategic leverage). (i) • The NPV, if the project is funded, is

$$(p_{\mathrm{H}} + \tau)R - I(\tau).$$

So, if $A \geqslant A^*$, $\tau = \tau^*$.

• For $A < A^*$, the pledgeable income can be increased by reducing τ below τ^*:

$$\frac{\mathrm{d}}{\mathrm{d}\tau}\left[(p_{\mathrm{H}}+\tau)\left(R-\frac{B}{\Delta p}\right)-[I(\tau)-A]\right] = R-\frac{B}{\Delta p}-I'(\tau).$$

Let τ^{**} be defined by

$$I'(\tau^{**}) = R - \frac{B}{\Delta p}.$$

The pledgeable income decreases with τ for $\tau \geqslant \tau^{**}$. The borrower can raise funds if and only if $A > A^{**}$, with

$$(p_{\mathrm{H}} + \tau^{**})\left(R - \frac{B}{\Delta p}\right) = I(\tau^{**}) - A^{**}.$$

The quality of investment increases with A (for $A > A^{**}$) and is flat beyond A^*. For $A \in [A^{**}, A^*]$,

$$[p_{\mathrm{H}} + \tau(A)]\left[R - \frac{B}{\Delta p}\right] = I(\tau(A)) - A.$$

For $A \geqslant A^*$, $\tau(A) = \tau^*$.

(ii) • Define $\hat{\tau}$ by

$$I'(\hat{\tau}) = [1 - (p_{\mathrm{H}} + \hat{\tau})]R.$$

($\hat{\tau}$ maximizes a firm's NPV given that the other firm's choice is $\hat{\tau}$.) Borrower i's incentive compatibility constraint is $(\Delta p)(1-q_j)R_{\mathrm{b}} \geqslant B$, where R_{b} is her reward in the case of income R. So the pledgeable income is

$$(p_{\mathrm{H}} + \tau)\left[(1 - q_j)R - \frac{B}{\Delta p}\right].$$

$(\hat{\tau}, \hat{\tau})$ is a symmetric Nash equilibrium if and only if

$$(p_{\mathrm{H}} + \hat{\tau})\left[[1 - (p_{\mathrm{H}} + \hat{\tau})]R - \frac{B}{\Delta p}\right] \geqslant I(\hat{\tau}) - A.$$

This equation yields $\hat{A}$.

• "Natural monopoly case." Let $\tau(A)$ be defined as in subquestion (i). Consider a candidate equilibrium in which borrower 1 selects $\tau(A)$ and borrower 2 does not raise funds. That is,

$$A \leqslant \min_{\tau}\left\{I(\tau)-(p_{\mathrm{H}}+\tau)\left[(1-(p_{\mathrm{H}}+\tau(A)))R-\frac{B}{\Delta p}\right]\right\}.$$

(iii) • $(\tilde{q}, \tilde{q})$ is a symmetric Nash equilibrium for $A = \tilde{A}$.

• By choosing $q_1 = \tilde{q} + \varepsilon$, borrower 1 deters entry by borrower 2.

Exercise 3.8 (equity multiplier and active monitoring). (i) See Section 3.4.

(ii) Suppose that monitoring at level c is to be induced. Two incentive compatibility constraints must be satisfied:

$$(\Delta p)R_{\mathrm{m}} \geqslant cI \quad \text{and} \quad (\Delta p)R_{\mathrm{b}} \geqslant b(c)I.$$

Because there is no scarcity of monitoring capital, the monitor contributes I_{m} to the project and breaks even:

$$I_{\mathrm{m}} = p_{\mathrm{H}}R_{\mathrm{m}} - cI = p_{\mathrm{H}}\frac{c}{\Delta p}I - cI.$$

The equity multiplier, k, is given by

$$p_{\mathrm{H}}(R - R_{\mathrm{b}} - R_{\mathrm{m}})I = I - A - I_{\mathrm{m}}$$

or

$$p_{\mathrm{H}}\left[R - \frac{b(c) + c}{\Delta p}\right]I = I - A - p_{\mathrm{H}}\frac{c}{\Delta p}I + cI,$$

that is,

$$I = k(c)A,$$

where

$$k(c) = \frac{1}{1 + c - p_{\mathrm{H}}[R - b(c)/\Delta p]} = \frac{1}{1 - \rho_0 + c + (p_{\mathrm{H}}/\Delta p)[b(c) - B]}.$$

The project's NPV (which includes the monitoring cost) is equal to

$$\rho_1 I - I - cI = (\rho_1 - 1 - c)k(c)A.$$

The borrower maximizes $(\rho_1 - 1 - c)k(c)$ since the other parties receive zero utility and she therefore receives the project's NPV.

Exercise 3.9 (concave private benefit). (i) Suppose that the NPV per unit of investment is positive:

$$p_{\mathrm{H}}R > 1$$

(otherwise there is no investment).

The entrepreneur's utility is equal to the NPV,

$$U_b = (p_H R - 1)I,$$

and so the entrepreneur chooses the highest investment that is consistent with the investors' breakeven constraint

$$p_H\left(RI - \frac{B(I)}{\Delta p}\right) = I - A.$$

Because $\lim_{I\to\infty} B'(I) = B$ and $p_H(R - (B/\Delta p)) < 1$, this upper limit indeed exists.

(ii) The shadow price is given by

$$v = \frac{dU_b}{dA} = (p_H R - 1)\frac{dI}{dA} = \frac{1}{(p_H B'(I)/(p_H R - 1)) - 1}.$$

Hence v increases with A (since $B'' < 0$ and $dI/dA > 0$).

Exercise 3.10 (congruence, pledgeable income, and power of incentive scheme). (i) Either $R_b \geqslant B/(\Delta p)$ and the entrepreneur always behaves well. The NPV is

$$\text{NPV}^1 = p_H R - I + (1-x)B$$

and the financing condition

$$p_H\left(R - \frac{B}{\Delta p}\right) \geqslant I - A. \tag{1}$$

Or $R_b < B/(\Delta p)$. The NPV is then

$$\text{NPV}^2 = x(p_L R + B) + (1-x)(p_H R + B) - I < \text{NPV}^1,$$

and the financing condition ($R_b = 0$ then maximizes the pledgeable income) is

$$[xp_L + (1-x)p_H]R \geqslant I - A. \tag{2}$$

The pledgeable income is increased only if x is sufficiently low. The high-powered incentive scheme is always preferable if (1) is satisfied; otherwise, the parties may content themselves with a low-powered scheme (provided (2) is satisfied).

(ii) Suppose that the menu offers (R_b^S, R_b^F) when interests are divergent and $(\hat{R}_b^S, \hat{R}_b^F)$ when interests are aligned. The state (divergent/congruent) is not observed by the investors and so this menu must be incentive compatible (the entrepreneur must indeed prefer the incentive scheme tailored to the state of nature she faces).

The interesting case is when the incentive scheme in the divergent state is incentive compatible ($(\Delta p)\times(R_b^S - R_b^F) \geqslant B$; otherwise, setting all rewards equal to 0 is obviously optimal).

In the congruent state, the entrepreneur must not pretend interests are divergent, and so

$$p_H \hat{R}_b^S + (1-p_H)\hat{R}_b^F \geqslant p_H R_b^S + (1-p_H)R_b^F.$$

So one might as well take $\hat{R}_b^S = R_b^S$ and $\hat{R}_b^F = R_b^F$. This choice yields incentive compatibility in the congruent state and maximizes the pledgeable income.

Exercise 3.11 (retained-earnings benefit). (i) Let us assume away any discounting for notational simplicity. The assumption on $\underline{B}^2$ implies that retained earnings are always needed to finance the second project, as

$$p_H^2\left(R^2 - \frac{B^2}{\Delta p^2}\right) < I^2 \quad \text{for all } B^2.$$

The borrower's utility is, as a function of date-1 earnings R_b^1,

$$U_b(R_b^1) = \begin{cases} R_b^1 & \text{if the second project is not financed,} \\ R_b^1 + \text{NPV}^2 & \text{otherwise,} \end{cases}$$

where

$$\text{NPV}^2 = p_H^2 R^2 - I^2$$

is independent of B^2.

Let $\hat{R}_b^1(B^2)$ denote the required level of retained earnings when the date-2 private benefit turns out to be B^2:

$$p_H^2\left(R^2 - \frac{B^2}{\Delta p^2}\right) = I^2 - \hat{R}_b^1(B^2).$$

This equation also defines a threshold $\hat{B}^2(R_b^1)$.

Thus, the expected utility is

$$E[U_b(R_b^1)] = R_b^1 + F(\hat{B}^2(R_b^1))[\text{NPV}^2].$$

The shadow value of retained earnings is therefore

$$\mu = \frac{d[E[U_b(R_b^1)]]}{dR_b^1} = 1 + f(\hat{B}^2(R_b^1))\left[\frac{d\hat{B}^2}{dR_b^1}\right][\text{NPV}^2].$$

(ii) The date-1 incentive compatibility constraint is

$$(\Delta p^1)[R_b^1 + F(\hat{B}^2(R_b^1))[\text{NPV}^2]] \geqslant B^1.$$

The pledgeable income,

$$p_H^1\left[R^1 - \min_{\{\text{IC}^1\}} R_b^1\right],$$

is therefore larger than in the absence of a second project. It is therefore more likely to exceed $I^1 - A^1$, where A^1 is the entrepreneur's initial wealth.

Exercise 3.12 (investor risk aversion and risk premia). (i) This condition says that the risk-free rate is normalized at 0. In other words, investors are willing to lend 1 unit at date 0 against a safe return of 1 unit at date 1.

(ii) With a competitive capital market, the financing condition becomes

$$p_H q_S R_l \geqslant I - A.$$

With a risk-neutral entrepreneur, the incentive compatibility constraint is unchanged:

$$(\Delta p) R_b \geqslant B.$$

Thus, enough pledgeable income can be harnessed provided that

$$p_H\left[R - \frac{B}{\Delta p}\right] \geqslant \frac{I - A}{q_S}. \tag{1}$$

Comparing condition (1) with condition (3.3) in Chapter 3, we conclude that obtaining financing is easier for a countercyclical firm than for a procyclical one, ceteris paribus.

(iii) The entrepreneur maximizes her utility subject to the investors' being willing to lend

$$\max_{\{R_b^F, R_b^S\}} \{p_H R_b^S + (1 - p_H) R_b^F\} \tag{2}$$

s.t.

$$q_S p_H (R - R_b^S) + q_F (1 - p_H)(-R_b^F) \geqslant I - A, \tag{3}$$

$$(\Delta p)(R_b^S - R_b^F) \geqslant B, \tag{4}$$

$$R_b^F \geqslant 0. \tag{5}$$

Letting μ_1, μ_2, and μ_3 denote the shadow prices of the constraints, the first-order conditions are

$$p_H[1 - \mu_1 q_S] + \mu_2(\Delta p) = 0 \tag{6}$$

and

$$(1 - p_H)[1 - \mu_1 q_F] - \mu_2(\Delta p) + \mu_3 = 0. \tag{7}$$

• First, note that for $q_S \neq q_F$ at least one of constraints (4) and (5) must be binding: if $\mu_2 = \mu_3 = 0$, (6) and (7) cannot be simultaneously satisfied.

• Conversely, (4) and (5) cannot be simultaneously binding, except when condition (1) is satisfied with exact equality.

• Suppose that constraint (4) is not binding ($\mu_2 = 0$), which, from what has gone before, implies that $R_b^F = 0$. Then $\mu_1 = 1/q_S$, and (7) can be satisfied only if

$$q_F > q_S.$$

• In contrast, suppose that constraint (5) is not binding ($\mu_3 = 0$). Constraints (6) and (7) taken together imply that

$$q_S > q_F.$$

To sum up, the maximum punishment result ($R_b^F = 0$) carries over to procyclical firms, because the incentive effect compounds with the "marginal rates of substitution" effect (the investors value income in the case of failure relatively more compared with the entrepreneur). But it does not in general hold for countercyclical firms. Then the investors care more about the payoff in the case of success, and the entrepreneur should keep marginal incentives equal to $B/\Delta p$ and select $R_b^F > 0$ (since the firm's income is equal to 0 in the case of failure, this requires the firm to hoard some claim at date 0 so as to be able to pay the entrepreneur even in the case of failure).

Entrepreneurial risk aversion changes the incentive constraint (4) and the objective function (2). It may be the case that $R_b^F > 0$ even for a procyclical firm.

Exercise 3.13 (lender market power). (i) If $A \geqslant I$, then the "borrower" does not need the lender and just obtains the NPV ($U_b = V$). So let us assume that $A < I$. The lender must respect two constraints. First, the standard incentive compatibility constraint:

$$(\Delta p) R_b \geqslant B. \tag{IC$_b$}$$

Second, her net utility must be nonnegative:

$$U_b = p_H R_b - A \geqslant 0. \tag{IR$_b$}$$

The lender maximizes

$$U_l = p_H[R - R_b] - (I - A)$$

subject to these two constraints.

Let us first ignore (IC$_b$). The lender sets $R_b = A/p_H$ and thus

$$U_b = 0.$$

The lender appropriates the entire surplus ($U_l = V$) as long as $R_b = A/p_H$ satisfies the incentive

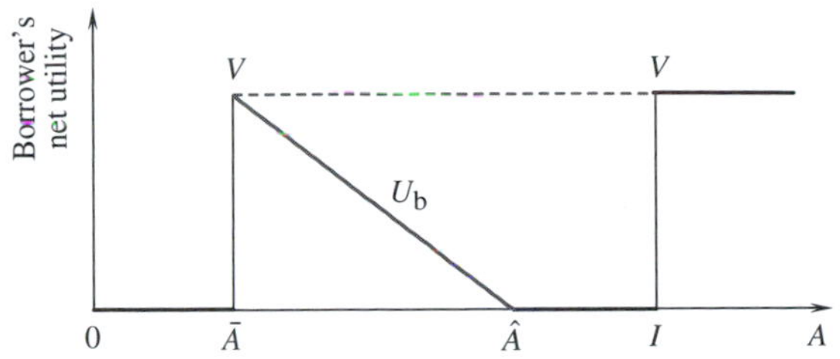

Figure 1

constraint, or

$$(\Delta p)\frac{A}{p_H} \geqslant B \quad \Longleftrightarrow \quad A \geqslant \hat{A}.$$

For $A \in [\bar{A}, \hat{A})$, the lender cannot capture the borrower's surplus without violating the incentive constraint; then the borrower's net utility

$$U_b = p_H \frac{B}{\Delta p} - A$$

is decreasing in A.

Lastly, the lender is willing to lend as long as

$$U_l = V - U_b \geqslant 0 \quad \text{or} \quad A \geqslant \bar{A}.$$

The borrower's net utility is as represented in Figure 1.

The borrower is "better off" (from the relationship) if she is either very rich (she does not need the lender) or poor (she cannot be expropriated by the lender)—although, of course, not too poor!

(ii) The lender solves

$$\max U_l = p_H(RI - R_b) - (I - A)$$

s.t.

$$(\Delta p)R_b \geqslant BI, \qquad (\text{IC}_b)$$

$$p_H R_b \geqslant A. \qquad (\text{IR}_b)$$

If (IC_b) were not binding, (IR_b) would have to be binding (U_l is decreasing in R_b) and

$$U_l = (p_H R - 1)I$$

would yield $I = \infty$, violating (IC_b), a contradiction.

If (IR_b) were not binding, (IC_b) would have to be binding, and

$$U_l = \left(p_H\left(R - \frac{B}{\Delta p}\right) - 1\right)I + A,$$

and so $I = 0 = R_b$, contradicting (IR_b).

Hence, the two constraints are binding, and so

$$I = \frac{1}{p_H B/\Delta p} A.$$

Recall that, in the presence of a competitive market,

$$I^* = \frac{1}{1 - p_H(R - B/\Delta p)} A,$$

and so

$$I < I^*.$$

With variable-size investment, lender market power leads to a contraction of investment.

Exercise 3.14 (liquidation incentives). (i) Technically, the realization of y is a "sufficient statistic" for inferring the effort chosen by the entrepreneur. Rewarding the entrepreneur as a function not only of y, but also of the realization of the final profit amounts to introducing into the incentive scheme noise over which the entrepreneur has no control. (We leave it to the reader to start with a general incentive scheme and then show that without loss of generality the reward can be made contingent on y only.)

Second, it is optimal to liquidate if and only if $y = \underline{y}$. Hence, one can define expected profits:

$$R^S \equiv \bar{y}R \quad \text{and} \quad R^F \equiv L,$$

where "success" ("S") now refers to a good signal, "failure" ("F") to a bad signal, and R^S and R^F denote the associated continuation profits.

We are now in a position to apply the analysis of Section 3.2. Let R_b^S denote the entrepreneur's reward in the case of a good signal ($y = \bar{y}$) and 0 that in the case of a bad signal. Incentive compatibility requires that

$$(\Delta p)R_b^S \geqslant B.$$

The NPV is

$$U_b \equiv p_H \bar{y}R + (1 - p_H)L - I,$$

and the pledgeable income is

$$\mathcal{P} \equiv p_H \bar{y}R + (1 - p_H)L - p_H \frac{B}{\Delta p}.$$

Financing is then feasible provided that $A \geqslant \bar{A}$, where

$$p_H\left(\bar{y}R - \frac{B}{\Delta p}\right) + (1 - p_H)L = I - \bar{A}.$$

(ii) Truth telling by the entrepreneur requires that

$$\bar{y}R_b \geqslant L_b \geqslant \underline{y}R_b.$$

The entrepreneur's other incentive compatibility constraint (that relative to effort) is then

$$(\Delta p)(\bar{y}R_b - L_b) \geqslant B.$$

The investors' payoff is then

$$p_H\bar{y}(R - R_b) + (1 - p_H)(L - L_b).$$

As expected, it is highest when L_b and R_b are as small as is consistent with the incentive constraints:

$$L_b = \underline{y}R_b \quad \text{and} \quad (\Delta p)(\bar{y}R_b - L_b) = B.$$

And so the pledgeable income is

$$p_H\bar{y}(R - R_b) + (1 - p_H)(L - L_b)$$

for these values of L_b and R_b. Simple computations show that the financing condition amounts to

$$p_H\bar{y}R + (1 - p_H)L - [p_H\bar{y} + (1 - p_H)\underline{y}]\frac{B}{(\Delta p)(\Delta y)} \geqslant I - A$$

or

$$A \geqslant \bar{A} + \underline{y}\frac{B}{(\Delta p)(\Delta y)}.$$

Exercise 3.15 (project riskiness and credit rationing). The managerial minimum reward (consistent with incentive compatibility) is the same for both variants:

$$\frac{B}{\Delta p^A} = \frac{B}{\Delta p^B}.$$

And so the investors' breakeven condition can be written (with obvious notation) as

$$I - A \leqslant p_H^A\left(R^A - \frac{B}{\Delta p}\right) \quad \text{for variant A}$$

and

$$I - A \leqslant p_H^B\left(R^B - \frac{B}{\Delta p}\right) \quad \text{for variant B}.$$

Because $p_H^A > p_H^B$, the safer project (project A) is financed for a smaller range of cash on hand A. That is, the safe project is more prone to credit rationing. Intuitively, the nonpledgeable income is higher for a safe project, since the entrepreneur has a higher chance to be successful and thus to receive the incentive payment $B/\Delta p$.

This, however, assumes that good behavior is needed for funding either variant. Let us relax this assumption. Good behavior boosts the pledgeable income (as well as the NPV, for that matter) more when the payoff in the case of success is high, that is, for the risky project. Thus, suppose that the following conditions hold:

$$I - A > p_H^B\left(R^B - \frac{B}{\Delta p}\right),$$

$$I - A > p_L^B R^B,$$

$$I - A \leqslant p_L^A R^A,$$

$$I < p_L^A R^A + B.$$

The first two inequalities state that the risky variant cannot receive financing whether good behavior or misbehavior is induced by the managerial compensation scheme (note, for example, that the second inequality is automatically satisfied if p_H^B is close to its lowest feasible value Δp). The third states that the risky project generates enough pledgeable income when the cash-flow rights are allocated entirely to investors. Finally, the fourth inequality guarantees that the safe project's NPV is positive.

To check that these inequalities are not inconsistent, assume, for example, that $A = 0$ and $p_L^A R^A = I$ (or just above); then

$$p_L^B R^B = \frac{p_L^B/p_L^A}{p_H^B/p_H^A} I < I.$$

Lastly, for B large enough, the first inequality is satisfied. We conclude that the risky project may be more prone to credit rationing if high-powered incentives are not necessarily called for.

Exercise 4.15 investigates a different notion of project risk, in which a safe project yields a higher liquidation value and a lower long-term payoff and is less prone to credit rationing than a risky project.

Exercise 3.16 (scale versus riskiness tradeoff). The risky project's NPV is

$$U_b^r = (x\rho_1 - 1)I.$$

The investors' breakeven condition can be written as

$$x\rho_0 I = I - A.$$

And so

$$U_b^r = \frac{x\rho_1 - 1}{1 - x\rho_0}A = \frac{\rho_1 - 1/x}{1/x - \rho_0}A.$$

Note that this is the same formula as obtained in Section 3.4.2, except that the expected cost of bringing

1 unit of investment to completion is $1/x$ rather than 1.

Turn now to the safe project. The NPV is then

$$U_b^s = (\rho_1 - X)I,$$

and the investors' breakeven condition is

$$\rho_0 I = XI - A.$$

Hence,

$$U_b^s = \frac{\rho_1 - X}{X - \rho_0} A.$$

The expected cost of bringing 1 unit of investment to completion is now X.

Thus the safe project is strictly preferred to the risky one if and only if

$$X < \frac{1}{x} \quad \text{or} \quad xX < 1.$$

Exercise 3.17 (competitive product market interactions). The representative firm's investment must satisfy

$$p_H\left[PR - \frac{B}{\Delta p}\right]i \geqslant i - A, \qquad (1)$$

since the manager's reward in the case of success, R_b, must satisfy

$$(\Delta p)R_b \geqslant Bi.$$

The representative entrepreneur wants to borrow up to her borrowing capacity as long as the NPV per unit of investment is positive:

$$p_H PR \geqslant 1. \qquad (2)$$

In equilibrium $i = I$ and $P = P(p_H RI)$. Let I^* (the optimal level from an individual firm's viewpoint) be given by

$$p_H RP^* = 1 \quad \text{and} \quad P^* = P(p_H RI^*).$$

Two cases must therefore be considered, depending on whether A is (a) large or (b) small:

(a) if

$$p_H[P^*R - B/\Delta p]I^* \geqslant I^* - A,$$

then the borrowing constraint is not binding and $I = I^*$;

(b) if

$$p_H[P^*R - B/\Delta p]I^* < I^* - A,$$

then (1) is binding, and so

$$I = \frac{A}{1 - p_H[RP(p_H RI) - B/\Delta p]}.$$

Exercise 3.18 (maximal incentives principle in the fixed-investment model). Recall that, because the investors break even, the entrepreneur's expected payoff when the project is financed is nothing but the project's NPV. The entrepreneur's expected payoff is therefore independent of the way the investment is financed. The financing structure just serves the purpose of guaranteeing good behavior by the entrepreneur. Let R_b^S and R_b^F denote the (nonnegative) rewards of the borrower in the cases of success (R^S) and failure (R^F), respectively. The incentive constraint can be written as

$$(\Delta p)(R_b^S - R_b^F) \geqslant B. \qquad (\text{IC}_b)$$

This constraint implies that setting R_b^F at its minimum level (0) provides the entrepreneur with maximal incentives. So, the incentive constraint becomes

$$(\Delta p)R_b^S \geqslant B.$$

The pledgeable income is equal to total expected income minus the borrower's minimum stake consistent with incentives to behave:

$$p_H R^S + (1 - p_H)R^F - p_H \frac{B}{\Delta p} = p_H\left(R - \frac{B}{\Delta p}\right) + R^F.$$

Thus the project is financed if and only if

$$p_H\left(R - \frac{B}{\Delta p}\right) \geqslant I - (A + R^F). \qquad (1)$$

As one would expect, the minimum income R^F plays the same role as cash or collateral. It is really part of the borrower's net worth.

The optimum contract can be implemented through a *debt contract*: let D, $R^F < D < R^S$, be defined by

$$p_H D + (1 - p_H)R^F = I - A. \qquad (\text{IR}_l)$$

That is, the borrower owes D to the lenders. In the case of failure (R^F), the borrower defaults and the lenders receive the firm's cash, R^F. Equation (IR_l) then guarantees that the lenders break even.

In this fixed-investment version of the model, the debt contract is, however, in general not uniquely optimal: a small reward $R_b^F > 0$ for the borrower in the case of failure would still be consistent with (IC_b) and (IR_l) as long as condition (IR_l) is satisfied with strict inequality. By contrast, the standard debt contract is uniquely optimal in the variable-investment version of the model as it maximizes the borrower's borrowing capacity (see Section 3.4.3).

Exercise 3.19 (balanced-budget investment subsidy and profit tax). The total investment subsidy is sI and the profit tax tRI. Budget balance then requires

$$p_{\mathrm{H}} tRI = sI.$$

The amount of income that is pledgeable to investors is

$$p_{\mathrm{H}}\left[R - tR - -\frac{B}{\Delta p}\right] I,$$

and so the breakeven constraint is

$$p_{\mathrm{H}}\left[(1-t)R - \frac{B}{\Delta p}\right] I = (1-s)I - A.$$

Adding up the two equalities yields

$$p_{\mathrm{H}}\left[R - \frac{B}{\Delta p}\right] I = I - A$$

or

$$I = \frac{A}{1-\rho_0}.$$

Finally, the entrepreneur receives the NPV, $(\rho_1 - 1)I$, since both the investors and the government make no surplus.

Exercise 3.20 (variable effort, the marginal value of net worth, and the pooling of equity). (i) Let R_{b} denote the entrepreneur's reward in the case of success. The entrepreneur is residual claimant when she does not need to borrow:

$$R_{\mathrm{b}} = R.$$

And so she maximizes

$$\max_{p}\{pR - \tfrac{1}{2}p^2 - I\}$$

yielding

$$p = R$$

and

$$U_{\mathrm{b}} = \tfrac{1}{2}R^2 - I > 0.$$

(ii) More generally,

$$p = R_{\mathrm{b}}.$$

The investors' breakeven condition is

$$p(R - R_{\mathrm{b}}) \geqslant I - A$$

or

$$R_{\mathrm{b}}(R - R_{\mathrm{b}}) \geqslant I - A.$$

Only the region $R_{\mathrm{b}} \geqslant \frac{1}{2}R$ is relevant: were R_{b} to be smaller than $\frac{1}{2}R$, then $\hat{R}_{\mathrm{b}} = R - R_{\mathrm{b}}$ would yield the same pledgeable income, but a higher utility to the entrepreneur.

The highest pledgeable income is obtained when $R_{\mathrm{b}} = \frac{1}{2}R$. Thus a necessary condition for financing is that $A \geqslant A_1$, where

$$\tfrac{1}{4}R^2 = I - A_1.$$

It must further be the case that the project's NPV be positive. That is, for the (maximum) value of R_{b} satisfying

$$R_{\mathrm{b}}(R - R_{\mathrm{b}}) = I - A,$$

then

$$U_{\mathrm{b}} = R_{\mathrm{b}}R - I - \tfrac{1}{2}R_{\mathrm{b}}^2 - A \geqslant 0.$$

So, using the breakeven constraint to rewrite the NPV, let

$$U_{\mathrm{b}} = V(A) = \max_{\{R_{\mathrm{b}}\}}\{R_{\mathrm{b}}R - \tfrac{1}{2}R_{\mathrm{b}}^2 - I\}$$

s.t.

$$R_{\mathrm{b}}(R - R_{\mathrm{b}}) \geqslant I - A.$$

This yields the shadow price of equity, $V'(A)$:

$$V'(A) = [R - R_{\mathrm{b}}(A)]\left[\frac{\mathrm{d}R_{\mathrm{b}}(A)}{\mathrm{d}A}\right] > 0,$$

where $R_{\mathrm{b}}(A)$ is given by the investors' breakeven condition. For $A > I$, we can define $V(A) = (\frac{1}{2}R^2) - I$. And so $V'(A) = 0$ (note that we discuss net utilities, so the no-agency-cost benchmark is a shadow price of cash on hand equal to 0; this benchmark is equal to 1 for gross utilities). When $A > I$, the entrepreneur is residual claimant and exerts the socially optimal effort. For $A < I$, $V'(A) > 0$, but $V'(I) = 0$: a local increase in the entrepreneur's compensation just below R has only a second-order effect.

Furthermore,

$$V''(A) < 0.$$

Let $A_2 < I$ satisfy

$$V(A_2) = 0.$$

Then

$$\bar{A} = \max\{A_1, A_2\}.$$

(iii) Let $I \equiv I_{\mathrm{L}}$. That is, we fix I_{L} and the corresponding $V(\cdot)$ function. In the absence of an *ex ante* arrangement between the two entrepreneurs, each receives a *net* utility:

$$\tfrac{1}{2}V(A)$$

(the gross utility is $\frac{1}{2}(V(A) + A)$). For, because $R_{\mathrm{b}}R - \frac{1}{2}R_{\mathrm{b}}^2$ is concave, it is optimal for both to have the same reward if they both invest. Thus the strategy consisting in (a) pooling cash on hand, (b) investing, and (c) setting identical reward schemes and investment, yields, for each entrepreneur,

$$V(A - \tfrac{1}{2}(I_{\mathrm{H}} - I_{\mathrm{L}})).$$

Alternatively, the two can pool resources but only the low-investment-cost project will be funded. The expected net utility of each is then

$$\tfrac{1}{2}V(\max(2A, I_{\mathrm{L}})),$$

since, if $2A \geqslant I_{\mathrm{L}}$, the low-investment-cost entrepreneur is residual claimant.

Note that

$$\tfrac{1}{2}V(\max(2A, I_{\mathrm{L}})) > \tfrac{1}{2}V(A),$$

so pooling is always optimal.

The lucky entrepreneur cross-subsidizes the unlucky entrepreneur if and only if

$$V(A - \tfrac{1}{2}(I_{\mathrm{H}} - I_{\mathrm{L}})) > \tfrac{1}{2}V(\max(2A, I_{\mathrm{L}})).$$

The unlucky entrepreneur cross-subsidizes the lucky one if this inequality is violated. Finally, because

$$V(A) > \tfrac{1}{2}V(\max(2A, I_{\mathrm{L}})),$$

the cross-subsidization is from the lucky to the unlucky for I_{H} below some threshold.

Exercise 3.21 (hedging or gambling on net worth?). (i) Letting R_{b} denote the entrepreneur's stake in success (and 0 in failure), the incentive compatibility constraint is

$$(\Delta p)R_{\mathrm{b}} \geqslant B.$$

Financing is feasible if and only if

$$p_{\mathrm{H}}\left(R - \frac{B}{\Delta p}\right) \geqslant I - A.$$

The entrepreneur's date-1 *gross* utility is

$$[p_{\mathrm{H}}R - I] + [A - \bar{A}] \quad \text{if } A \geqslant \bar{A}$$

and

$$A \quad \text{if } A < \bar{A}.$$

- If $A_0 \geqslant \bar{A}$, the entrepreneur's date-0 expected gross utility is

$$U_{\mathrm{b}}^{\mathrm{h}} = [p_{\mathrm{H}}R - I] + A_0$$

if she hedges.

By contrast, and letting $F(\varepsilon)$ denote the cumulative distribution of ε, her expected utility becomes

$$\begin{aligned} U_{\mathrm{b}}^{\mathrm{g}} &= [1 - F(\bar{A} - A_0)][[p_{\mathrm{H}}R - I] + m^{+}(\bar{A})] \\ &\quad + F(\bar{A} - A_0)m^{-}(\bar{A}) \\ &< U_{\mathrm{b}}^{\mathrm{h}}, \end{aligned}$$

where

$$\begin{aligned} m^{+}(\bar{A}) &\equiv E[A \mid A \geqslant \bar{A}], \\ m^{-}(\bar{A}) &\equiv E[A \mid A < \bar{A}], \\ [1 - F(\bar{A} - A_0)]m^{+}(\bar{A}) &+ F(\bar{A} - A_0)m^{-}(\bar{A}) = A_0. \end{aligned}$$

- If $A_0 < \bar{A}$, then

$$U_{\mathrm{b}}^{\mathrm{h}} = A_0 < U_{\mathrm{b}}^{\mathrm{g}}.$$

(ii) *Ex post* the entrepreneur chooses p so as to solve

$$\max_{\{p\}}\{pR_{\mathrm{b}} - \tfrac{1}{2}p^2\},$$

and so

$$p = R_{\mathrm{b}}.$$

The pledgeable income is

$$\mathcal{P} = R_{\mathrm{b}}(R - R_{\mathrm{b}})$$

and the NPV, i.e., the entrepreneur's expected *net* utility, in the case of financing is

$$U_{\mathrm{b}} = R_{\mathrm{b}}R - I.$$

Without loss of generality, assume that $R_{\mathrm{b}} \geqslant \frac{1}{2}R$ (if $R_{\mathrm{b}} < \frac{1}{2}R$, $\hat{R}_{\mathrm{b}} = R - R_{\mathrm{b}}$ yields the same $\mathcal{P}$ and a higher U_{b}).

Assume that $I - A_0 < \frac{1}{4}R^2$. This condition means that the entrepreneur can receive funding if she hedges (the highest pledgeable income is reached for $R_{\mathrm{b}} = \frac{1}{2}R$). She also receives funding even in the absence of hedging provided that the support of ε is small enough (the lower bound is smaller than $\frac{1}{4}R^2 - (I - A_0)$ in absolute value). Let

$$V(A) \equiv R_{\mathrm{b}}(A)R - I,$$

where $R_{\mathrm{b}}(A)$ is the largest root of

$$R_{\mathrm{b}}(R - R_{\mathrm{b}}) = I - A.$$

One has

$$\frac{\mathrm{d}V}{\mathrm{d}A} = R\frac{\mathrm{d}R_{\mathrm{b}}}{\mathrm{d}A} = \frac{R}{2R_{\mathrm{b}}(A) - R} > 0$$

and

$$\frac{\mathrm{d}^2V}{\mathrm{d}A^2} = -\frac{2R}{(2R_{\mathrm{b}}(A) - R)^2}\frac{\mathrm{d}R_{\mathrm{b}}}{\mathrm{d}A} < 0.$$

Hence, V is concave and so

$$V(A_0) > E[V(A_0 + \varepsilon)].$$

The entrepreneur is better off hedging.

(iii) The investment is given by the investors' breakeven condition:

$$p_H\left[RI - \frac{B(I)}{\Delta p}\right] = I - A.$$

This yields investment $I(A)$, with $I' > 0$ and $I'' < 0$ if $B'' > 0$, $I'' > 0$ if $B'' < 0$. The *ex ante* utility is

$$U_b^h = (p_H R - 1)E[I(A_0 + \varepsilon)]$$

in the absence of hedging. And so $U_b^h > U_b^g$ if $B'' > 0$ and $U_b^h < U_b^g$ if $B'' < 0$.

(iv) When the profit is unobservable by investors, there is no pledgeable income and so

$$I = A.$$

And so

$$U_b^h = R(A_0) \quad \text{and} \quad U_b^g = E[R(A_0 + \varepsilon)] < R(A_0)$$

since R is concave.

(v) Quite generally, in the absence of hedging the realization of ε generates a distribution $G(I)$ over investment levels $I = I(\varepsilon)$ and over cash used in the project $\mathcal{A}(\varepsilon) \leqslant A_0 + \varepsilon$ such that

$$\mathcal{P}(I(\varepsilon)) \geqslant I(\varepsilon) - \mathcal{A}(\varepsilon),$$

where $\mathcal{P}$ is the pledgeable income. And so

$$E[\mathcal{P}(I)] \geqslant E[I] - A_0.$$

Drawing I from distribution $G(\cdot)$ regardless of the realization of ε and keeping $A_0 - E[\mathcal{A}(\varepsilon)]$ makes the entrepreneur as well off.

In general, the entrepreneur can do strictly better by insulating her investment from the realization of ε (in the constant-returns-to-scale model of Section 3.4, though, she is indifferent between hedging and gambling).

Consider, for example, the case $A_0 < \bar{A}$ in subquestion (i). Then we know that gambling is optimal. The probability that the project is financed is

$$1 - F(\bar{A} - A_0) \quad \text{and} \quad [1 - F(\bar{A} - A_0)]\bar{A} < A_0.$$

This last inequality states that there is almost surely "unused cash": either $A_0 + \varepsilon < \bar{A}$ and then there is no investment, or $A_0 + \varepsilon > \bar{A}$ and then there is "excess cash" $[A_0 + \varepsilon - \bar{A}]$.

Consider therefore the date-0 contract in which the date-1 income $r = A_0 + \varepsilon$ is pledged to investors. The probability of funding is then X, which allows investors to break even:

$$A_0 = X\left[I - p_H\left(R - \frac{B}{\Delta p}\right)\right] = X\bar{A}.$$

Clearly,

$$X > 1 - F(\bar{A} - A_0),$$

and so the entrepreneur's date-0 expected gross utility has increased from

$$[1 - F(\bar{A} - A_0)](p_H R - I) + A_0$$

to

$$X(p_H R - I) + A_0.$$

Of course, this is not quite a fair comparison, since we have allowed random funding under hedging and not under gambling. But, because there is excess cash in states of nature in which $A > \bar{A}$, the same result would hold even if we allowed for random funding under gambling: when $A < \bar{A}$, the project could be funded with probability $x(A) = A/\bar{A}$. The total probability of funding under gambling would then be

$$\int_0^{\bar{A}-A_0} \frac{A\,\mathrm{d}F(A - A_0)}{\bar{A}} + [1 - F(\bar{A} - A_0)]$$
$$< \frac{\int_0^{\bar{A}-A_0} A\,\mathrm{d}F(A - A_0) + \int_{\bar{A}-A_0}^{\infty} A\,\mathrm{d}F(A - A_0)}{\bar{A}} = \frac{A_0}{\bar{A}}.$$

For more on liquidity and risk management, see Chapter 5.

Exercise 4.1 (maintenance of collateral and asset depletion just before distress). (i) When $c = 0$ (no moral hazard on maintenance), the pledgeable income is equal to (A plus)

$$p_H\left(R - \frac{B}{\Delta p}\right).$$

Consider $c > 0$. First, suppose that the entrepreneur receives R_b in the case of success, and r_b in the case of good maintenance. That is, the two incentives are not linked together. The IC constraints are

$$(\Delta p)R_b \geqslant B \quad \text{and} \quad r_b \geqslant c.$$

The pledgeable income is (A plus)

$$p_H\left(R - \frac{B}{\Delta p}\right) - c.$$

However, and as in Diamond's (1984) model (see Section 4.2), it is optimal to link the two incentives. Let us look for conditions that guarantee that the entrepreneur both exerts effort to raise the probability of success and maintains the collateral. We just saw that it is optimal to reward the entrepreneur only if the project is successful *and* the asset has been maintained. Let $R_b > 0$ denote this reward. There are three potential incentive compatibility constraints:

- {work, maintain} $\succeq$ {shirk, maintain}

$$p_H R_b - c \geqslant p_L R_b - c + B$$

or

$$(\Delta p) R_b \geqslant B.$$

- {work, maintain} $\succeq$ {shirk, do not maintain}

$$p_H R_b - c \geqslant B.$$

Note that this second constraint does not bind if the first constraint is satisfied, since by assumption $p_L B/(\Delta p) \geqslant c$.

- {work, maintain} $\succeq$ {work, do not maintain}

$$p_H R_b - c \geqslant 0.$$

This third constraint is not binding either.

The necessary and sufficient condition for financing is

$$p_H\left(R - \frac{B}{\Delta p}\right) \geqslant I - A,$$

and the NPV is

$$U_b = [p_H R - I] + [A - c].$$

(ii) The decision over whether to maintain the collateral now depends on the realization of the signal about the eventual outcome of the project. The entrepreneur stops maintaining the asset when learning that the project will fail. When no signal accrues, the conditional probability of success (assuming that the entrepreneur has chosen probability of success $p \in \{p_L, p_H\}$) is

$$\frac{p}{p + (1-p)(1-\xi)}.$$

The borrower maintains the asset if and only if

$$\frac{p}{p + (1-p)(1-\xi)}(R_b + A) \geqslant c.$$

The *ex ante* incentive compatibility condition (relative to the choice of p) is then (for c not too large)

$$p_H(R_b + A - c) + (1 - p_H)(1 - \xi)(-c) \geqslant p_L(R_b + A - c) + (1 - p_L)(1 - \xi)(-c) + B.$$

The interpretation of the term $(\Delta p)\xi c$ in the inequality in the statement of question (ii) is that if the entrepreneur works, she reduces the probability of receiving a signal that enables her to avoid maintenance benefitting the lenders.

(iii) • Suppose, first, that the entrepreneur does not pledge the assets. Then the condition for financing is the familiar one (with the value of collateral, A, being nonpledgeable to investors):

$$p_H\left(R - \frac{B}{\Delta p}\right) \geqslant I.$$

• If the entrepreneur pledges the assets in the case of failure, then the financing condition becomes

$$p_H\left[R - \left(\frac{B}{\Delta p} + \xi c - A\right)\right] + (1 - p_H)(1 - \xi)A \geqslant I.$$

Not pledging the asset in the case of failure facilitates financing if

$$p_H \xi c > [p_H + (1 - p_H)(1 - \xi)]A,$$

which is never satisfied if $A > c$. Note that (1) the NPVs differ (the NPV is higher in the absence of pledging since the asset is then always maintained) and (2) more generally one should consider pledging only part of the asset.

Exercise 4.2 (diversification across heterogeneous activities). (i) Under specialization, the entrepreneur's net utility is (see Section 3.4)

$$U_b^i = \frac{\rho_1^i - 1}{1 - \rho_0^i} A \quad \text{for activity } i.$$

So, the entrepreneur prefers the low-NPV, low-agency-cost activity α if and only if

$$\frac{\rho_1^\alpha - 1}{1 - \rho_0^\alpha} > \frac{\rho_1^\beta - 1}{1 - \rho_0^\beta}. \tag{1}$$

(ii) Let R_2 denote the entrepreneur's reward if both activities succeed ($R_1 = R_0 = 0$). The entrepreneur must prefer behaving in both activities to misbehaving in both:

$$(p_H^2 - p_L^2) R_2 \geqslant B^\alpha I^\alpha + B^\beta I^\beta. \tag{2}$$

Now if the ratios I^α/I^β and B^α/B^β are sufficiently close to 1, a case we will focus on in the rest of the question, then the entrepreneur does not want to misbehave in a single activity either (the proof is similar to that in Section 4.2).

The entrepreneur solves

$$\max_{\{I^\alpha,I^\beta\}} \{(\rho_1^\alpha - 1)I^\alpha + (\rho_1^\beta - 1)I^\beta\}$$

s.t.

$$\rho_1^\alpha I^\alpha + \rho_1^\beta I^\beta - \frac{p_H^2}{p_H^2 - p_L^2}[B^\alpha I^\alpha + B^\beta I^\beta] \geqslant I^\alpha + I^\beta - A. \quad (3)$$

In contrast, the specialization solution solves the same program but with $p_H^2/[p_H^2 - p_L^2]$ replaced by $p_H/[p_H - p_L]$, which is bigger. Let

$$\tilde{\rho}_0^i \equiv p_H R^i - \frac{p_H^2}{p_H^2 - p_L^2} B^i > \rho_0^i.$$

Diversification reduces the agency cost. If

$$\frac{\rho_1^\alpha - 1}{1 - \tilde{\rho}_0^\alpha} < \frac{\rho_1^\beta - 1}{1 - \tilde{\rho}_0^\beta},$$

then the optimum is to have

$$I^\beta > I^\alpha.$$

But $I^\alpha = 0$ is not optimal. We need to reintroduce the incentive constraint according to which the entrepreneur does not want to shirk in activity β only (the one that yields the highest total private benefit): condition (2) (satisfied with equality so as to maximize borrowing capacity, and now labeled (2′)),

$$(p_H + p_L)(\Delta p)R_2 = B^\alpha I^\alpha + B^\beta I^\beta, \quad (2')$$

does not imply

$$p_H(\Delta p)R_2 \geqslant B^\beta I^\beta \quad (4)$$

if the ratio I^α/I^β is too small. Conditions (2′) and (4) (satisfied with equality) together define the optimal ratio I^α/I^β.

Exercise 4.4 ("value at risk" and benefits from diversification). Let R_0, R_1, and R_2 denote the entrepreneur's reward contingent on 0, 1, and 2 successes, respectively. The NPV (given that the entrepreneur will never receive rewards strictly above $\bar{R}$, we can reason on the risk-neutral zone in $u(\cdot)$ and use the NPV) is

$$2[p_H R - I].$$

To see whether the two projects can be financed simultaneously, minimize the nonpledgeable part of this NPV,

$$\tfrac{1}{4}[1+\alpha]R_2 + \tfrac{1}{2}[1-\alpha]R_1 + \tfrac{1}{4}[1+\alpha]R_0, \quad (1)$$

while providing incentives. To compute the entrepreneur's expected compensation above, note that the probability of two successes is

Pr(project 1 succeeds | work on project 1)
× Pr(project 2 succeeds | work on project 2 and success in project 1)

or $\frac{1}{2}[\frac{1}{2}(1+\alpha)]$. And so forth.

(i) The two incentive constraints are

$$\tfrac{1}{4}[1+\alpha]R_2 + \tfrac{1}{2}[1-\alpha]R_1 + \tfrac{1}{4}[1+\alpha]R_0 \geqslant 2B + R_0 \quad (2)$$

and

$$\tfrac{1}{4}[1+\alpha]R_2 + \tfrac{1}{2}[1-\alpha]R_1 + \tfrac{1}{4}[1+\alpha]R_0 \geqslant B + \tfrac{1}{2}R_1 + \tfrac{1}{2}R_0. \quad (3)$$

(ii) If $\bar{R}$ is large, one can then reward the entrepreneur only in the upper tail:

$$R_2 = \frac{8B}{1+\alpha}.$$

This value minimizes (1) subject to (2), and also satisfies (3).

(iii) When $\bar{R} < (8B)/(1+\alpha)$, the entrepreneur can no longer be rewarded solely in the upper tail to satisfy (2). Note that $R_0 = 0$ is optimal from (2) and (3). (2) can be satisfied by $\{R_2 = \bar{R},\ R_1 \leqslant \bar{R},\ R_0 = 0\}$ if and only if

$$\tfrac{1}{8}(3-\alpha)\bar{R} \geqslant B. \quad (4)$$

The question is then whether (3) is also satisfied.

• For *positive correlation* ($\alpha > 0$), increasing R_1 makes (3) harder to satisfy. Hence, minimizing the nonpledgeable income requires choosing the lowest R_1 that satisfies (2). This value satisfies (3) if and only if $B \geqslant (\frac{1}{2}R_1)$, or, after substitutions,

$$B \leqslant \tfrac{1}{4}\bar{R},$$

which is more constraining than (4).

• For *negative correlation* ($\alpha < 0$), increasing R_1 makes it easier to satisfy (3). While it is still optimal to set $R_2 = \bar{R}$, the binding constraint may now be (3) (and thus the nonpledgeable income exceeds $2B = 2p_H B/\Delta p$ here). Financing may be feasible even though it would not be so if project correlation were positive (but $\frac{1}{4}(1-\alpha)\bar{R}$ must exceed B).

Exercise 4.5 (liquidity of entrepreneur's claim). The entrepreneur's incentive constraint when the liquidity shock is observed by investors is

$$(1-\lambda)(\Delta p)R_\mathrm{b} \geqslant B.$$

The NPV is

$$U_\mathrm{b} = \mathrm{NPV} = \lambda(\mu-1)r_\mathrm{b} + p_\mathrm{H}R - I,$$

while the breakeven constraint is

$$\lambda(\mu_0-1)r_\mathrm{b} + p_\mathrm{H}R - (1-\lambda)p_\mathrm{H}R_\mathrm{b} \geqslant I - A.$$

As in the text, it is optimal to compensate the entrepreneur by providing her with liquidity (since $\mu > 1$) once R_b is equal to $B/(1-\lambda)\Delta p$. The level of liquidity, r_b^*, given to the entrepreneur is set by the breakeven constraint

$$\lambda(1-\mu_0)r_\mathrm{b}^* + [I-A] = p_\mathrm{H}\left(R - \frac{B}{\Delta p}\right).$$

It increases when more of the proceeds of reinvestment become pledgeable.

(ii) If λ is a choice variable, the entrepreneur faces multiple tasks. She solves

$$\begin{aligned}\max_{\{\lambda\in\{0,\bar{\lambda}\},\, p\in\{p_\mathrm{L},p_\mathrm{H}\}\}} & U_\mathrm{b}(p,\lambda) \\ &= \{\lambda[\mu-\mu_0]r_\mathrm{b} + (1-\lambda)pR_\mathrm{b} \\ &\qquad - \lambda c + B\mathbf{1}_{\{p=p_\mathrm{L}\}}\}.\end{aligned}$$

The NPV is

$$U_\mathrm{b} = \mathrm{NPV} = \lambda(\mu-1)r_\mathrm{b} + p_\mathrm{H}R - I - \lambda c.$$

For a given contract $(R_\mathrm{b}, r_\mathrm{b})$ the entrepreneur chooses

$$\lambda = \bar{\lambda} \quad \text{if } (\mu-\mu_0)r_\mathrm{b} - pR_\mathrm{b} \geqslant c.$$

Note that, for $p = p_\mathrm{H}$, the entrepreneur does not "oversearch" for new investment opportunities as long as

$$(\mu-\mu_0)r_\mathrm{b} - p_\mathrm{H}R_\mathrm{b} \leqslant (\mu-1)r_\mathrm{b} \iff (1-\mu_0)r_\mathrm{b} \leqslant p_\mathrm{H}R_\mathrm{b}.$$

Suppose that one wants to implement $p = p_\mathrm{H}$. Then

- either $\lambda = 0$, and then the outcome is the same as in the absence of a liquidity shock;
- or, more interestingly, $\lambda = \bar{\lambda}$ (which implies *a fortiori* that $\lambda = \bar{\lambda}$ if the entrepreneur deviates and chooses $p = p_\mathrm{L}$):

$$U_\mathrm{b}(p_\mathrm{H},\bar{\lambda}) \geqslant U_\mathrm{b}(p_\mathrm{L},\bar{\lambda}) \iff (1-\bar{\lambda})(\Delta p)R_\mathrm{b} \geqslant B.$$

Furthermore,

$$U_\mathrm{b}(p_\mathrm{H},\bar{\lambda}) \geqslant U_\mathrm{b}(p_\mathrm{H},0) \iff (\mu-\mu_0)r_\mathrm{b} - p_\mathrm{H}R_\mathrm{b} \geqslant c.$$

Hence, $R_\mathrm{b} = B/[(1-\bar{\lambda})(\Delta p)]$, and so an added constraint with respect to subquestion (i) is

$$(\mu-\mu_0)r_\mathrm{b} \geqslant c + p_\mathrm{H}\frac{B}{(1-\bar{\lambda})\Delta p}.$$

Exercise 4.6 (project size increase at an intermediate date). Consider first the entrepreneur's date-1 behavior when the size has been doubled. If the entrepreneur has worked on the initial project, and using the perfect correlation between the two projects, the incentive constraint is

$$p_\mathrm{H}\mathcal{R}_\mathrm{b} \geqslant p_\mathrm{L}\mathcal{R}_\mathrm{b} + B.$$

If she shirked on the first project, then it is optimal to shirk again.

The date-0 incentive constraint is then

$$\begin{aligned}(1-\lambda)&p_\mathrm{H}R_\mathrm{b} + \lambda p_\mathrm{H}\mathcal{R}_\mathrm{b} \\ &\geqslant B + (1-\lambda)p_\mathrm{L}R_\mathrm{b} + \lambda[p_\mathrm{L}\mathcal{R}_\mathrm{b} + B].\end{aligned}$$

To obtain the nonpledgeable income, minimize the left-hand side of the latter inequality subject to the incentive constraints, yielding

$$\mathcal{R}_\mathrm{b} = \frac{B}{\Delta p} \quad \text{and} \quad R_\mathrm{b} = \frac{B}{(1-\lambda)\Delta p}.$$

Thus the nonpledgeable income is

$$(1+\lambda)p_\mathrm{H}\frac{B}{\Delta p}.$$

Exercise 4.7 (group lending and reputational capital). (i) By assumption,

$$p_\mathrm{H}\left(R - \frac{B}{\Delta p}\right) < p_\mathrm{H}\left(R - \frac{B}{(1+a)\Delta p}\right) < I - A.$$

Under individual borrowing, the pledgeable income is $p_\mathrm{H}[R-(B/\Delta p)]$, and so individual borrowing is not feasible. Under group lending, let R_b denote the borrower's individual reward when both succeed. They get 0 when at least one of them fails. The idea is that a borrower is punished "twice" for her failure: she gets no reward and also suffers from the other borrower's not receiving a reward. The incentive constraint is then

$$p_\mathrm{H}(\Delta p)[(1+a)R_\mathrm{b}] \geqslant B, \qquad (\mathrm{IC_b})$$

yielding pledgeable income per borrower

$$\mathcal{P} = p_H R - p_H^2 \Big[\min_{\{IC_b\}} R_b \Big] = p_H \Big[R - \frac{B}{(1+a)\Delta p} \Big].$$

Hence, group lending is not feasible either.

(ii) If both players are altruistic with $a = \frac{1}{2}$, they both cooperate in the unique equilibrium of the "stage-2" game. They have payoff $\frac{3}{2}$, since they enjoy the monetary gain of the other agent. More precisely, the utilities in the stage-2 game are as follows:

		Agent 1	
		C	D
Agent 2	C	$\frac{3}{2}, \frac{3}{2}$	$-1, 1$
	D	$1, -1$	$-\frac{3}{2}, -\frac{3}{2}$

Cooperating is a dominant strategy ($\frac{3}{2} > 1$ and $-1 > -\frac{3}{2}$), and so both cooperate.

If both agents are selfish ($a = 0$), the payoffs given in the statement of the question are those of a standard prisoner's dilemma and both agents defect.

(iii) The structure of payoffs is such that the altruistic agent gets nothing in the second stage if she misbehaves in the first stage. Consider the incentive constraint facing altruistic agents:

$$p_H(\Delta p)(1+a)R_b + \tfrac{3}{2}\delta \geqslant B$$

with $a = \frac{1}{2}$. The pledgeable income per borrower is

$$p_H\Big(R - \frac{2B}{3\Delta p} + \frac{\delta}{\Delta p}\Big).$$

The financing is secured if

$$p_H\Big(R - \frac{2B}{3\Delta p} + \frac{\delta}{\Delta p}\Big) \geqslant I - A.$$

From this, the minimum discount factor to secure financing is

$$\delta_{\min} = \frac{\Delta p}{p_H}(I - A) - (\Delta p)R + \tfrac{2}{3}B > 0,$$

by assumption. The intuition is that the altruistic agent behaves in order to separate herself from the selfish agent and to build a reputation for being altruistic. The term $\delta/\Delta p$ reflects the gain from reputation and can be interpreted as the borrower's "social collateral."

Exercise 4.9 (borrower-friendly bankruptcy court). (i) • Monetary returns, such as L and r, that are not subject to moral hazard (or adverse selection) are optimally pledged to investors if financing is a constraint. This increases the income that is returned to investors without creating bad incentives for the entrepreneur.

• The entrepreneur's incentive constraint is (for a given realization of r)

$$[p_H(r) - p_L(r)]R_b \geqslant B \quad \text{or} \quad (\Delta p)R_b \geqslant B.$$

Condition (1) in the statement of the question says that continuation always maximizes social (total) value. However, systematic continuation (continuation for all r) generates too little pledgeable income to permit financing (right-hand side of condition (2) in the statement); on the other hand, systematic liquidation would generate enough pledgeable income (left-hand side of (2)).

Financing requires liquidating inefficiently. Intuitively, there is then no point giving $R_b(r) > B/\Delta p$ for some rs in the case of continuation. The difference serves no incentive purpose and can be used to boost pledgeable income, allowing for more frequent continuation (in other words, it is more efficient to compensate the management with continuation rather than with money as long as incentives are sufficient). (Note: to prove this, generalize the optimization program in subquestion (ii) to allow for a choice of $R_b(r)$ for $r \geqslant r^*$.)

(ii) • The borrower solves

$$\max \text{NPV} = \max_{\{r^*\}} \Big\{ E[r] + \int_{r^*}^{\bar{r}} \rho_1(r) f(r)\,dr + \int_0^{r^*} L f(r)\,dr \Big\}$$

s.t.

$$E[r] + \int_{r^*}^{\bar{r}} \rho_0(r) f(r)\,dr + \int_0^{r^*} L f(r)\,dr \geqslant I - A.$$

Clearly, r^* is the lowest value that satisfies the breakeven constraint. Condition (2) in the statement of the question implies that $0 < r^* < \bar{r}$. And, of course, $L \geqslant \rho_0(r^*)$.

(iii) • With a short-term debt contract, $d = r^*$, the firm will be able to repay its debt and continue if $r \geqslant r^*$. If $r < r^*$, the lenders are entitled to use default to liquidate. The investors do not want to renegotiate since $L > \rho_0(r^*)$.

• $dr^*/dA < 0$. A lower amount of equity calls for more pledgeable income.

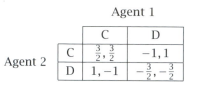

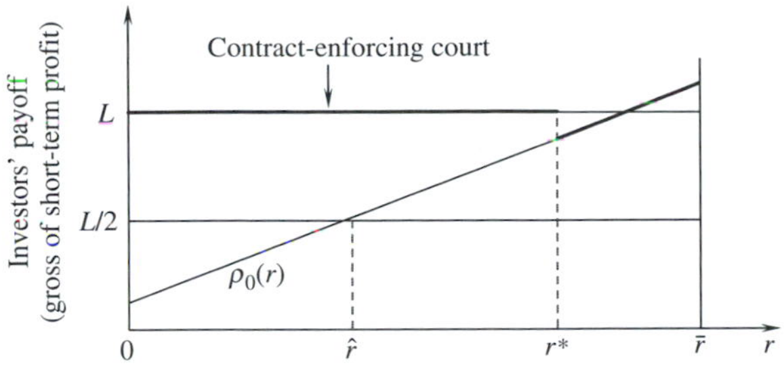

Figure 2

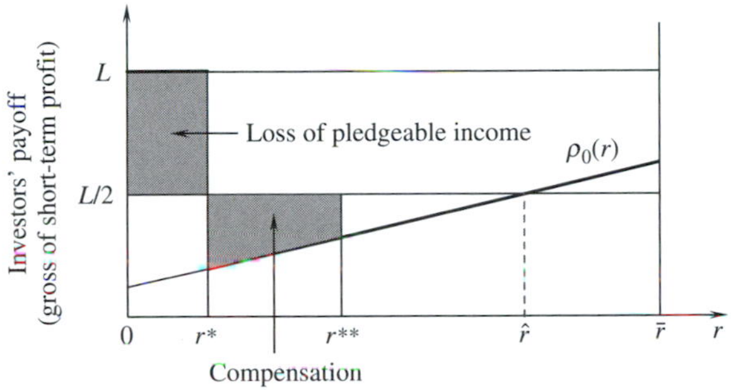

Figure 3

(iv) • Were the court to enforce the financial contract (previous questions), then the investors get (besides the short-term profit) L for $r < r^*$ and $\rho_0(r)$ for $r \geqslant r^*$. If $r^* > \hat{r}$, then the borrower-friendly court uniformly (weakly) reduces the available income whatever the continuation policy, as shown in Figure 2. Hence, investors, who just broke even, lose money and financing is no longer feasible.

(v) • A decrease in the investors' payoff (besides the short-term profit) from L to $\frac{1}{2}L$ over $[0, r^*]$ must be compensated by an increase in bankruptcy (see Figure 3). So, no bankruptcy occurs on some interval $[0, r^{**}]$ with $r^* < r^{**} \leqslant \bar{r}$, if this permits financing at all.

From an *ex ante* viewpoint, the lenders are not hurt since they break even regardless of the bankruptcy regime. The borrower suffers from poor enforcement (a simple way to check this is to note that, with a contract-enforcing court, she could choose to return only $\frac{1}{2}L$ to investors in the case of liquidation). See Chapter 16 for an in-depth study of who are the losers and who are the winners when public policies are modified.

Exercise 4.10 (benefits from diversification with variable-investment projects). (i) The analysis follows the lines of Section 3.4. The incentive constraint on project i with size I^i is

$$(\Delta p)R_{\mathrm{b}}^i \geqslant BI^i,$$

where R_{b}^i is the entrepreneur's reward in the case of success in project i; and so the pledgeable income is $\rho_0 I^i$.

The entrepreneur allocates A^i to project i, where

$$A^1 + A^2 = A.$$

Her total utility is

$$U_{\mathrm{b}} = \sum_i [(\rho_1 - 1)I^i] = \sum_i \left[(\rho_1 - 1)\left(\frac{A^i}{1-\rho_0}\right)\right] = \frac{\rho_1 - 1}{1 - \rho_0}A.$$

It does not really matter how the entrepreneur allocates her wealth between the two projects. In particular, there is no benefit to having a second project.

(ii) As in the case of fixed-investment projects, it is optimal to reward the entrepreneur only if the two projects succeed ($R_2 > 0$, $R_1 = R_0 = 0$). The two incentive constraints are

$$p_{\mathrm{H}}^2 R_2 \geqslant p_{\mathrm{H}} p_{\mathrm{L}} R_2 + \max_{i \in \{1,2\}} \{BI^i\}$$

and

$$p_{\mathrm{H}}^2 R_2 \geqslant p_{\mathrm{L}}^2 R_2 + B(I^1 + I^2).$$

Let

$$I \equiv I^1 + I^2.$$

Then

$$U_{\mathrm{b}} = \mathrm{NPV} = \sum_i [p_{\mathrm{H}} R I^i - I^i] = (\rho_1 - 1)I$$

and the financing condition becomes

$$p_{\mathrm{H}} R I - p_{\mathrm{H}}^2 R_2 \geqslant I - A.$$

Thus, everything depends only on total investment I, except for the first incentive constraint. For a given I, this constraint is relaxed by taking

$$I^1 = I^2 = \tfrac{1}{2}I.$$

The rest of the analysis proceeds as in Section 4.2. The first incentive constraint is satisfied if the second is. And so

$$U_{\mathrm{b}} = \frac{\rho_1 - 1}{1 - \rho_0'}A.$$

Exercise 4.11 (optimal sale policy). (i) The entrepreneur maximizes NPV,

$$\int_{s^*}^{1} (sR)f(s)\,ds + F(s^*)L,$$

subject to the investors' breakeven constraint:

$$\int_{s^*}^{1} s\left(R - \frac{B}{\Delta p}\right)f(s)\,ds + F(s^*)L \geqslant I - A, \qquad (\mu)$$

where use is made of the fact that the proceeds L from the sale should go to investors in order to maximize pledgeable income. One finds

$$s^*\left[\frac{R + \mu(R - B/\Delta p)}{1 + \mu}\right] = L.$$

Note that $s^*R = L$ if financing is not a constraint (A large), and

$$s^*\left[R - \frac{B}{\Delta p}\right] < L.$$

The optimal s^* trades off maximizing NPV (which would call for $s^* = L/R$) and pleasing investors (which would lead to $s^* = L/[R - (B/\Delta p)]$).

(Showoffs: we have assumed that it is optimal to induce the entrepreneur to exert effort when the firm is not liquidated. A sufficient condition for this to be the case is

$$(s - \Delta p)R \leqslant \max\left\{L, \left(s - \frac{B}{\Delta p}\right)R\right\};$$

that is, the pledgeable income is always lowest under continuation and shirking. To see this, consider state-contingent probabilities $x(s)$ of continuation and working, $y(s)$ of continuation and shirking, and $z(s)$ of liquidation.

Solve

$$\max_{\{x(\cdot),y(\cdot),z(\cdot)\}} \left\{\int_{\underline{s}}^{\bar{s}} [x(s)(sR) + y(s)[(s - \Delta p)R] + z(s)L]f(s)\,ds\right\}$$

s.t.

$$\int_{\underline{s}}^{\bar{s}} \left[x(s)\left[\left(s - \frac{B}{\Delta p}\right)R\right] + y(s)[(s - \Delta p)R] + z(s)L\right]f(s)\,ds \geqslant I - A$$

and $x(s) + y(s) + z(s) = 1$ for all s.)

(ii) Endogenizing $R_b(s) \geqslant B/\Delta p$ for $s \geqslant s^*$ (where the threshold may differ from the one obtained in (a)), the expression for the NPV is unchanged. The breakeven constraint becomes

$$\int_{s^*}^{1} s[R - R_b(s)]f(s)\,ds + F(s^*)L \geqslant I - A.$$

The derivative with respect to $R_b(s)$ is negative and so

$$R_b(s) = B/\Delta p \quad \text{as long as } \mu > 0.$$

(iii) It is optimal to sell if $s = s_1$. Let R_b^* ($> B/\Delta p$ from the assumption made) be defined by

$$s_2(R - R_b^*) = I - A.$$

If

$$B_0 \leqslant s_2 R_b^*,$$

then the "career concerns" incentives are sufficient to prevent first-stage moral hazard. The only possible issue is then renegotiation. That is, if $s_1[R - B/\Delta p] > L$, the two parties are tempted to renegotiate.

If in contrast

$$B_0 > s_2 R_b^*,$$

then even in the absence of renegotiation, there is first-stage moral hazard. Financing becomes infeasible.

Exercise 4.12 (conflict of interest and division of labor). (i) The incentive constraints are

$$\begin{aligned} p_H R_b + (1 - p_H)\hat{R}_b - c &\\ \geqslant p_L R_b + (1 - p_L)\hat{R}_b - c + B &\quad \text{(no shirking on project choice)}\\ \geqslant p_H R_b &\quad \text{(no shirking on maintenance)}\\ \geqslant p_L R_b + B &\quad \text{(no shirking on either dimension).} \end{aligned}$$

The first two constraints can be rewritten as

$$(\Delta p)(R_b - \hat{R}_b) \geqslant B \quad \text{and} \quad \hat{R}_b \geqslant \frac{c}{1 - p_H}.$$

The third,

$$(\Delta p)R_b + (1 - p_H)\hat{R}_b \geqslant B + c,$$

is guaranteed by the other two.

(ii) The nonpledgeable income is

$$\min_{\{IC\}}\{p_H R_b + (1 - p_H)\hat{R}_b\} = p_H \frac{B}{\Delta p} + \frac{c}{1 - p_H}.$$

The financing condition is

$$p_H R + (1 - p_H)L - p_H \frac{B}{\Delta p} - \frac{c}{1 - p_H} \geqslant I - A.$$

(iii) The agent in charge of maintenance is given $\hat{R}_b$ conditional on failure and proper maintenance, and 0 otherwise. Her incentive constraint is

$$(1 - p_H)\hat{R}_b \geqslant c.$$

So when given $\hat{R}_b = c/(1 - p_H)$, this agent exerts care in maintaining the asset and receives no rent.

The entrepreneur's incentive constraint then becomes

$$(\Delta p)R_b \geqslant B.$$

The nonpledgeable income is now

$$p_H \frac{B}{\Delta p} + (1 - p_H)\hat{R}_b = p_H \frac{B}{\Delta p} + c.$$

For more on the division of labor when multiple tasks are in conflict, see Dewatripont and Tirole (1999) as well as Review Problem 9.[5]

Exercise 4.14 (diversification and correlation). (i) The two incentive constraints are

$$p_H^2 R_2 \geqslant p_L^2 R_2 + 2B \quad \text{and} \quad p_H^2 R_2 \geqslant p_H p_L R_2 + B.$$

The first constraint can be rewritten as

$$p_H^2 R_2 \geqslant \frac{2p_H^2 B}{(p_H + p_L)\Delta p}. \qquad \text{(IC)}$$

The second constraint is satisfied if the first is. The pledgeable income is

$$2p_H R - \min_{\{IC\}}\{p_H^2 R_2\},$$

hence the result.

(ii) The entrepreneur receives $p_H R_2$ by behaving on both projects. When misbehaving (either on one or the two projects), the entrepreneur receives expected income $p_L R_2$. And so she might as well misbehave in both. The incentive constraint is then

$$p_H R_2 \geqslant p_L R_2 + 2B. \qquad \text{(IC)}$$

And so the pledgeable income is

$$2p_H R - \min_{\{IC\}}\{p_H R_2\} = 2p_H R - 2p_H \frac{B}{\Delta p}.$$

This yields the financing condition.

(iii) The incentive constraints are

$$[xp_H + (1 - x)p_H^2]R_2 \geqslant [xp_L + (1 - x)p_L^2]R_2 + 2B$$

and

$$[xp_H + (1 - x)p_H^2]R_2 \geqslant [xp_L + (1 - x)p_L p_H]R_2 + B.$$

The second turns out to be satisfied if the first is. The financing condition becomes

$$p_H\left[R - \left[\frac{1 - (1 - x)(1 - p_H)}{1 - (1 - x)(1 - p_L - p_H)}\right]\frac{B}{\Delta p}\right] \geqslant I - A.$$

Ex ante (before financing), $x = 0$ facilitates financing. *Ex post* (after the investors have committed their funds), the entrepreneur's payoff,

$$[xp_H + (1 - x)p_H^2]R_2,$$

is increasing in x and so $x = 1$. Note that the NPV is independent of x:

$$U_b = NPV = 2[p_H R - I].$$

Exercise 4.15 (credit rationing and the bias towards less risky projects). (i) Note, first, that the incentive compatibility constraint is the same regardless of the choice of project specification: letting R_b denote the entrepreneur's reward in the case of success (as usual, there is no point rewarding the entrepreneur in the case of failure), the incentive compatibility constraints are

$$(p_H^s - p_L^s)R_b \geqslant B$$
$$\iff (p_H^r - p_L^r)R_b \geqslant B$$
$$\iff (\Delta p)R_b \geqslant B.$$

The pledgeable income is therefore

$$\mathcal{P}^s = xp_H^s\left(R - \frac{B}{\Delta p}\right) + (1 - x)L^s$$

for the safe variant, and

$$\mathcal{P}^r = xp_H^r\left(R - \frac{B}{\Delta p}\right) + (1 - x)L^r$$

for the risky one.

Because $\mathcal{P}^s > \mathcal{P}^r$, choosing the safe variant facilitates funding. Lastly, $\bar{A}$ is defined by

$$\mathcal{P}^r \equiv I - \bar{A}.$$

The NPV is otherwise the same for both variants. Hence, U_b is the same provided the project is funded.

(ii) The entrepreneur having discretion over the choice of projects adds an extra dimension of moral hazard. Providing her with "high-powered incentives" (R_b in the case of success, 0 in the case of failure) is ideal for encouraging good behavior in the case of continuation, but it also pushes the

5. Dewatripont, M. and J. Tirole. 1999. Advocates. *Journal of Political Economy* 107:1–39.

entrepreneur to take risks, as[6]

$$xp_{\rm H}^{\rm r}R_{\rm b} > xp_{\rm H}^{\rm s}R_{\rm b}.$$

More generally, any incentive scheme that addresses the *ex post* moral-hazard problem ($(\Delta p)(R_{\rm b}^{\rm S} - R_{\rm b}^{\rm F}) \geqslant B$) encourages the choice of the risky variant unless the entrepreneur receives a reward (only) when the collateral value is high ($L^{\rm s}$). But such a reward further reduces pledgeable income and may jeopardize financing altogether when $A < \bar{A}$, but $\mathcal{P}^{\rm s} \geqslant I - A$.

Exercise 4.16 (fire sale externalities and total surplus-enhancing cartelizations). (i) The representative entrepreneur's borrowing capacity i is determined by the investors' breakeven condition:

$$[x\rho_0 + (1-x)P]i = i - A,$$

where

$$\rho_0 \equiv p_{\rm H}\left(R - \frac{B}{\Delta p}\right)$$

is the pledgeable income per unit of investment in the absence of distress.

Because it is individually optimal to resell all assets when in distress, $J = (1-x)I$, and so

$$P = P((1-x)I).$$

Furthermore, in equilibrium $i = I$, and so

$$I = \frac{A}{1 - [x\rho_0 + (1-x)P((1-x)I)]}.$$

The representative firm's NPV (or utility) is

$$U_{\rm b} = [x\rho_1 + (1-x)P((1-x)I) - 1]I$$

for the value of I just obtained.

(ii) In the case of cartelization, specifying that at most $z < 1$ can be resold on the market, and so $J \equiv (1-x)zI$, these expressions become

$$I = \frac{A}{1 - [x\rho_0 + (1-x)zP((1-x)zI)]}$$

and

$$U_{\rm b} = [x\rho_1 + (1-x)zP((1-x)zI) - 1]I.$$

6. Note that the choice of the risky project is perfectly detected in the case of liquidation, since liquidation then yields only $L^{\rm r}$ instead of the (higher) level $L^{\rm s}$. The entrepreneur is, however, protected by limited liability and therefore cannot be punished for the wrong choice of project. (For the reader interested in contract theory: if we endogenized limited liability through large risk aversion below 0, we would need to assume that the safe project yields the low liquidation value $L^{\rm r}$ at least with positive probability. Otherwise, the entrepreneur could be threatened with a negative income in the case of low liquidation value and there would be no moral hazard in the choice of project.)

Let

$$H(z,I) \equiv (1-x)zP((1-x)zI).$$

Then

$$\frac{\partial H}{\partial z} = (1-x)[P + JP'].$$

Hence, H decreases with z if and only if the elasticity of demand is greater than 1.

Let us check that an elasticity of demand greater than 1 is consistent with the stability condition (incidentally, the same reasoning applies to the more general case in which only a fraction z of the assets are put up for sale). Simple computations show that

$$\frac{{\rm d}i}{{\rm d}I} = \frac{(1-x)^2 i^2 P'}{A},$$

and that the conditions

$$\frac{{\rm d}i}{{\rm d}I} > -1 \quad \text{and} \quad P + JP' < 0$$

are consistent if and only if

$$1 > x\rho_0 + 2(1-x)P.$$

This latter condition is not guaranteed by the fact that investment is finite ($1 > x\rho_0 + (1-x)P$), but is satisfied when x is large enough.

When the elasticity of demand exceeds 1,

$$I = \frac{A}{1 - [x\rho_0 + H(z,I)]}$$

decreases with z, and

$$U_{\rm b} = [x\rho_1 + H(z,I) - 1]I$$

decreases with z for two reasons: both the NPV per unit of investment and the investment decrease.

Simple computations show that

$$[A - J^2P']\,{\rm d}I = (1-x)I^2[P + JP']\,{\rm d}z,$$

and so ${\rm d}I/{\rm d}z < 0$.

(iii) Let $\hat{\rho}_1 \equiv x\rho_1 + (1-x)zP$. The change in total surplus is given by

$${\rm d}(U_{\rm b} + S^{\rm n}) = [(1-x)[P\,{\rm d}z + z\,{\rm d}P]I + (\hat{\rho}_1 - 1)\,{\rm d}I] - (1-x)I\,{\rm d}P,$$

where the first term (in brackets) on the RHS measures the change in the entrepreneur's utility and the second term the change in buyer surplus. And so

$${\rm d}(U_{\rm b} + S^{\rm n}) = (1-x)PI\,{\rm d}z + (\hat{\rho}_1 - 1)\,{\rm d}I.$$

The term $(1-x)PI\,\mathrm{d}z$ corresponds to a better utilization of distressed assets (which are valued P by the marginal buyer) when $\mathrm{d}z > 0$, while the second term (the original one from the point of view of welfare analysis) stands for the social surplus created by an increase in borrowing capacity (associated with $\mathrm{d}z < 0$).

The total surplus increases when z decreases as long as

$$\hat{\rho}_1 - 1 \geqslant \frac{1-\hat{\rho}_0-(1-x)^2z^2(A/(1-\hat{\rho}_0))P'}{\eta-1},$$

where $\hat{\rho}_0 \equiv x\rho_0 + (1-x)zP$ and $\eta \equiv -P'J/P$.

Note that $\hat{\rho}_1$ can be increased without bound (by increasing ρ_1 keeping ρ_0 constant, i.e., by increasing B for a given ρ_0) without altering any other variable. So for $\hat{\rho}_1$ sufficiently large, total surplus increases.

Exercise 4.17 (loan size and collateral requirements). When collateral is pledged only in the case of failure, the NPV (also equal to the entrepreneur's utility) is

$$U_b = p_H R(I) - I - (1-p_H)[C - \phi(C)].$$

The entrepreneur's incentive compatibility constraint can be written as

$$(\Delta p)[R_b + C] \geqslant BI,$$

where R_b denotes the entrepreneur's reward in the case of success. The investors' breakeven constraint is

$$p_H[R(I) - R_b] + (1-p_H)\phi(C) \geqslant I - A,$$

or, if the incentive constraint is binding,

$$p_H\left[R(I) - \frac{BI}{\Delta p} + C\right] + (1-p_H)\phi(C) \geqslant I - A.$$

Maximizing U_b with respect to I and C subject to this latter constraint yields

$$p_H R'(I) - 1 = \frac{\mu}{1+\mu}\left(\frac{p_H B}{\Delta p}\right)$$

and

$$\phi'(C) = \frac{1}{1+\mu} - \frac{\mu}{1+\mu}\frac{p_H}{1-p_H},$$

where μ is the shadow price of the investors' breakeven constraint. As the balance sheet deteriorates, μ increases, I decreases, and C increases. Borrowing increases if the agency cost decreases; the impact of A on net borrowing $(I - A)$ is more ambiguous.

Exercise 5.1 (long-term contract and loan commitment). (i) The entrepreneur wants to carry on both projects as often as possible as this maximizes NPV. The pledgeable income in a contract that pays $R_b = B/p_H\Delta p$ in the case of two successes and continues in the case of first success is

$$p_H(p_H R - I) + \left(p_H R - I - p_H\frac{B}{\Delta p}\right);$$

hence, if it is weakly larger than 0, then the investors break even and the second project is financed if the first one was successful. If it is strictly larger than 0, then with investors breaking even, the entrepreneur has some additional income; it is optimal to take it in the form of a stochastic loan commitment in period 1.

(ii) Intuitively, ξ weakly increases in R, p_H and decreases in B, I, and p_L (as long as p_L is not too large). The optimal ξ is such that

$$(p_H + \xi(1-p_H))\left(p_H R - I - p_H\frac{B}{\Delta p}\right) + \left(p_H R - I - \left(p_H\frac{B}{\Delta p} - (1-\xi)(\Delta p)p_H\frac{B}{\Delta p}\right)\right) = 0$$

or $\xi = 1$ if the solution to the previous equation exceeds 1.

(iii) The contract is renegotiation proof. Indeed, either $p_H R - I - p_H B/\Delta p < 0$ and then the lenders will not invest in the second project unless obliged to, or $\xi = 1$ and then the borrower wants to carry on the second project.

(iv) The described sequence of short-term contracts is behaviorally equivalent to the optimal long-term contract from (i).

Exercise 5.2 (credit rationing, predation, and liquidity shocks). (i) The incentive constraint is

$$(\Delta p)R_b \geqslant B_1.$$

Hence, expected pledgeable income is

$$\rho_0^1 = p_H\left(R_1 - \frac{B_1}{\Delta p}\right).$$

The entrepreneur receives funding if and only if

$$\rho_0^1 \geqslant I_1 - A.$$

(ii) • The competitor preys if the entrepreneur waits until date 1 to secure funding for the date-1 investment.

• To prevent predation, the entrepreneur can (publicly) secure at date 0 a credit line equal to $(I_1 - \rho_0^1 - a)$, or else obtain a guarantee that the date-1 project will be funded.

• Such long-term contracts are not renegotiated because they are *ex post* efficient (social surplus is maximized if the date-1 project is undertaken, as $p_H R_1 > I_1$).

(iii) • The condition implies that unconditional financing of the two projects and date-0 shirking cannot allow investors to break even.

• x^* is given by

$$(\Delta q)(1 - x^*)\left(\frac{p_H B_1}{\Delta p}\right) \geqslant B_0.$$

• Suppose that $\rho_0^1 > I_1$. In states of nature where the initial contract specifies that the date-1 project is not financed, investors can offer to finance the project. They and the entrepreneur then get an extra rent (for example, $\rho_0^1 - I_1$ and $p_H B_1/\Delta p$ if the investors make a take-it-or-leave-it renegotiation offer).

(iv) Termination is no longer a threat under renegotiation. The only way to induce the entrepreneur to behave at date 0 and date 1 is to give her, in the case of success at date 1, $R_b = B_1/\Delta p$ if profit is equal to a, and $\mathcal{R}_b > R_b$ if it is equal to A, such that

$$(\Delta q) p_H (\mathcal{R}_b - R_b) \geqslant B_0.$$

This reduces the date-1 pledgeable income from ρ_0^1 to

$$\rho_0^1 - q_H p_H (\mathcal{R}_b - R_b) = \rho_0^1 - q_H \frac{B_0}{\Delta q}.$$

The condition in the statement of the exercise then implies that funding cannot be secured at date 0.

Exercise 5.3 (asset maintenance and the soft budget constraint). (i) Assume that the financiers can commit not to renegotiate the initial contract. The optimal contract for the entrepreneur maximizes the NPV,

$$U_b = \left\{\int_0^{\bar{L}} \left[F(\rho^*(L))\rho_1 - \int_0^{\rho^*(L)} \rho f(\rho)\,d\rho - 1 + [1 - F(\rho^*(L))]L\right] g(L)\,dL\right\} I,$$

subject to the financing constraint,

$$\left\{\int_0^{\bar{L}} \left[F(\rho^*(L))\rho_0 - \int_0^{\rho^*(L)} \rho f(\rho)\,d\rho + [1 - F(\rho^*(L))]L - \Delta(L)\right] g(L)\,dL\right\} I \geqslant I - A,$$

and the incentive compatibility constraint for maintenance,

$$\left\{\int_0^{\bar{L}} [F(\rho^*(L))(\rho_1 - \rho_0) + \Delta(L)]\ell(L) g(L)\,dL\right\} I \geqslant B_0 I,$$

where

$$\ell(L) \equiv \frac{g(L) - \tilde{g}(L)}{g(L)}$$

is the likelihood ratio, and $\rho_1 - \rho_0 \equiv B/\Delta p$.

Letting μ and ν denote the shadow prices of these two constraints, one gets the formulae in the statement of the question by differentiating with respect to $\rho^*(L)$ and $\Delta(L)$.

(ii) The function $\rho^*(\cdot)$ obtained under commitment has slope exceeding -1 (except for very large L, for which the slope is equal to -1). This slope can be positive or negative. The soft-budget-constraint problem arises when ρ is smaller than $\rho_0 - L$ (allowing for negative values of ρ), i.e., for L small.

Exercise 5.4 (long-term prospects and the soft budget constraint). Go through the same steps as in Exercise 5.3, replacing "ρ_1" by "$\rho_1 + R_L$," "ρ_0" by "$\rho_0 + R_L$," eliminating the liquidation values, and making the functions $\rho^*(\cdot)$ and $\Delta(\cdot)$ functions of R_L instead of L. One finds

$$\rho^*(R_L) = R_L + \frac{\rho_1 + \nu\rho_0}{1+\nu} + \frac{\mu(\rho_1 - \rho_0)}{1+\nu}\ell(R_L)$$

and

$$\Delta^*(R_L) = 0 \quad \text{if } \nu\ell(R_L) < \nu$$

(and if $\Delta^*(R_L) > 0$, then $\rho^*(R_L) = \rho_1 + R_L$).

Exercise 5.5 (liquidity needs and pricing of liquid assets). (i) The borrower's utility, conditional on receiving funds, is equal to the project's NPV. Letting $(x_L, x_H) \in \{0,1\}^2$ denote the probabilities of continuation in low- and high-liquidity shock states, we have

$$U_b = (1-\lambda)(\rho_1 - \rho_L)x_L + \lambda(\rho_1 - \rho_H)x_H - (I - A) - (q-1)(\rho_H - \rho_0)x_H.$$

Funding is feasible if

$$(1-\lambda)(\rho_0-\rho_L)x_L+\lambda(\rho_0-\rho_H)x_H \geqslant I-A+(q-1)(\rho_H-\rho_0)x_H.$$

For, the borrower needs no liquidity in order to cover the low shock: because $\rho_0 > \rho_L$, the investors are willing to let their claim be diluted in order to continue. In contrast, the borrower needs to hoard $(\rho_H - \rho_0)$ Treasury bonds if $x_H = 1$, in order to make up the shortfall between the liquidity shock and what can be raised on the capital market by diluting existing claimholders.

Clearly, $x_L = 1$ as this both raises the borrower's objective function and relaxes the financing constraint. In contrast, $x_H = 1$ raises the objective function as long as $(q-1)(\rho_H-\rho_0) \leqslant \lambda(\rho_1-\rho_H)$ but reduces the pledgeable income. If condition (2) in the statement of the exercise is satisfied, then $x_H = 1$ is indeed optimal. Otherwise $x_H = 0$ is optimal given the financing constraint. (Note that, were we to allow $0 \leqslant x_H \leqslant 1$, that is, randomized liquidation, an $x_H \in (0,1)$ could be optimal when condition (2) is violated.)

(ii) Suppose neither (2) nor (3) is binding. Then each firm hoards $(\rho_H - \rho_0)$ Treasury bonds. But then there is excess demand for Treasury bonds as $T < \rho_H - \rho_0$.

Next, note that, for λ small, condition (2) cannot bind. Hence, (3) must bind:

$$q-1=\lambda\frac{\rho_1-\rho_H}{\rho_H-\rho_0}.$$

(iii) The new asset yields no liquidity premium since it yields no income in the bad state, and so $q' = 1 - \lambda$.

Exercise 5.6 (continuous entrepreneurial effort; liquidity needs). (i) The entrepreneur chooses probability of success p such that

$$\max_p \{pR_b - \tfrac{1}{2}p^2\}.$$

Hence,

$$p = R_b.$$

The breakeven constraint is

$$p(R-R_b) = I-A \quad \text{or} \quad R_b(R-R_b) = I-A.$$

Note that this equation is satisfied for $R_b = \frac{1}{2}R$.

(ii) The investors' breakeven condition is

$$I-A+\int_0^{\rho^*}\rho f(\rho)\,\mathrm{d}\rho = F(\rho^*)R_b(R-R_b).$$

The entrepreneur maximizes

$$F(\rho^*)R_b^2$$

subject to the breakeven condition.

Exercise 5.7 (decreasing returns to scale). (i) The optimal policy maximizes the entrepreneur's expected utility, which is equal to the NPV,

$$U_b = rI + F(\rho^*)p_H R(I) - \bigg(\int_0^{\rho^*}\rho f(\rho)\,\mathrm{d}\rho\bigg)I - I,$$

subject to the investors' breakeven constraint,

$$rI + F(\rho^*)p_H\bigg(R(I)-\frac{BI}{\Delta p}\bigg) \geqslant I-A+\bigg(\int_0^{\rho^*}\rho f(\rho)\,\mathrm{d}\rho\bigg)I. \qquad (\mathrm{IR_l})$$

Let us assume that this constraint is binding. Taking the first-order conditions with respect to I and ρ^*, we obtain, after some manipulations,

$$p_H\bigg[R'(I)-\frac{R(I)}{I}\bigg] = \frac{1-r-\int_0^{\rho^*}(\rho^*-\rho)f(\rho)\,\mathrm{d}\rho}{F(\rho^*)}. \qquad (1)$$

(ii) The right-hand side of (1) is decreasing in the cutoff ρ^*. The left-hand side of (1) is decreasing in I. Thus ρ^* and I comove positively. From ($\mathrm{IR_l}$), when the balance sheet deteriorates (A decreases), both I and ρ^* decrease. This implies, in particular, that the firm issues more short-term debt.

Exercise 5.8 (multistage investment with interim accrual of information about prospects). (i) • Start with variant (a) (uncertainty about τ). The optimal contract specifies a cutoff τ^* above which the firm should reinvest I_1.

The NPV (also equal to the entrepreneur's utility under a competitive capital market) is, for a given τ^*,

$$U_b(\tau^*) = \int_{\tau^*}^{\bar{\tau}}[(p_H+\tau)R - I_1]f(\tau)\,\mathrm{d}\tau - I_0.$$

As usual, the incentive constraint (in the case of continuation) requires a minimum stake R_b in the case of success for the entrepreneur. R_b must satisfy

$$(\Delta p)R_b \geqslant B.$$

So the pledgeable income

$$\mathcal{P}(\tau^*) = \int_{\tau^*}^{\bar{\tau}} \left[(p_H + \tau)\left(R - \frac{B}{\Delta p}\right) - I_1\right] f(\tau)\, d\tau.$$

Financing requires that

$$\mathcal{P}(\tau^*) \geqslant I_0 - A.$$

U_b and $\mathcal{P}$ are maximized at τ_1^* and τ_0^* such that

$$(p_H + \tau_1^*)R = I_1$$

and

$$(p_H + \tau_0^*)\left(R - \frac{B}{\Delta p}\right) = I_1,$$

respectively. The entrepreneur is more eager to continue than the investors.

If $\mathcal{P}(\tau_1^*) \geqslant I_0 - A$, then the firm has deep pockets and the first-best continuation threshold τ_1^* is consistent with financing. So $\mathcal{P}(\tau_1^*) \equiv I_0 - A_1$. Otherwise, continuation must be less frequent as A declines:

$$\mathcal{P}(\tau^*) = I_0 - A.$$

But at the level A_0 at which

$$\mathcal{P}(\tau_0^*) = I_0 - A_0,$$

there is no longer the possibility to increase pledgeable income at the expense of value. For $A < A_0$, financing cannot be secured.

• The analysis of variant (b) proceeds similarly, with

$$U_b(R^*) = \int_{R^*}^{\infty} [p_H R - I_1] g(R)\, dR - I_0,$$

$$\mathcal{P}(R^*) = \int_{R^*}^{\infty} \left[p_H\left(R - \frac{B}{\Delta p}\right) - I_1\right] g(R)\, dR - I_0,$$

$$p_H R_1^* = I_1,$$

$$p_H\left(R_0^* - \frac{B}{\Delta p}\right) = I_1.$$

(ii) For $A = A_0$, the entrepreneur must give the entire pledgeable income in order to secure funding. So, she only takes

$$R_b = \frac{B}{\Delta p}$$

in the case of continuation, and

$$\mathcal{R} = (p_H + \tau)\frac{B}{\Delta p} = \frac{B}{(\Delta p)R} y,$$

where $B/(\Delta p)R < 1$ in variant (a), and $\mathcal{R} = p_H B/\Delta p$ in variant (b).

Exercise 5.9 (the priority game: uncoordinated lending leads to a short-term bias). (i) The first-best allocation maximizes the NPV:

$$\max_{\{I_1\}}\{r - I_1 + [p + \tau(I_1)]R\},$$

yielding

$$\tau'(I_1^*)R = 1.$$

Note that $I_1^* < r$ by assumption, and so an amount $(r - I_1^*)$ can be distributed at date 1. The date-1 payouts, r_b and r_l to borrower and lenders, and the date-2, success-contingent payouts, R_b and R_l, must satisfy

$$r_b + r_l + I_1^* = r,$$

$$R_b + R_l = R,$$

$$I = r_l + [p + \tau(I_1^*)]R_l.$$

This yields one degree of freedom.

(ii) Suppose that the entrepreneur secretly proposes the following contract to a (representative) lender: the lender's short-term claim increases by δr_l in exchange for the transfer of his long-term claim to the entrepreneur (by assumption, the entrepreneur is not allowed to defraud other investors of their short- or long-term claims). The lender is willing to accept this deal as long as

$$\delta r_l \geqslant [p + \tau(I_1)](\delta R_l).$$

Deepening investment decreases:

$$\delta I_1 = -\delta r_l.$$

The entrepreneur's interim utility increases by

$$\delta U_b = [\tau'(I_1)(-\delta r_l)]R_b + [p + \tau(I_1)](\delta R_b)$$
$$= [-\tau'(I_1)R_b + 1](\delta r_l) > 0$$

when $I_1 = I_1^*$, since $\tau'(I_1^*)R = 1$ and $R_b < R$.

Note that the incentive to sacrifice the long-term profitability by increasing short-term debt decreases as R_b increases. Thus, it is optimal for the borrower to hold the smallest possible short-term claim ($r_b = 0$) and the largest long-term claim consistent with the investors' breakeven constraint and the collusion-proof constraint:

$$I = r - I_1 + [p + \tau(I_1)](R - R_b)$$

and

$$\tau'(I_1)R_b = 1,$$

where $I_1 < I_1^*$.

Exercise 5.10 (liquidity and deepening investment). (i) Let R_b denote the entrepreneur's reward in the case of success (she optimally receives 0 in the case of failure). The incentive constraint, as usual, is

$$(\Delta p)R_b \geqslant B.$$

The necessary and sufficient condition for financing is that the pledgeable income exceeds the investors' outlay:

$$p_H\Big(R - \frac{B}{\Delta p}\Big) \geqslant I - A.$$

(ii) The incentive compatibility condition is not affected by a deepening investment:

$$[(p_H + \tau) - (p_L + \tau)]R_b \geqslant B \iff (\Delta p)R_b \geqslant B.$$

The investors' breakeven condition is

$$[F(\rho^*)(p_H + \tau) + [1 - F(\rho^*)]p_H](R - R_b) \geqslant I - A + \int_0^{\rho^*} \rho f(\rho)\,d\rho.$$

(iii) The NPV (or borrower's utility) is

$$U_b \equiv [F(\rho^*)(p_H + \tau) + [1 - F(\rho^*)]p_H]R - I - \int_0^{\rho^*} \rho f(\rho)\,d\rho.$$

This NPV is maximized at

$$\rho^* = \tau R = \hat{\rho}_1.$$

Because

$$R_b \geqslant \frac{B}{\Delta p},$$

the first best is implementable only in Case 1, which follows.

Case 1:

$$[F(\hat{\rho}_1)(p_H + \tau) + [1 - F(\hat{\rho}_1)]p_H]\Big(R - \frac{B}{\Delta p}\Big) \geqslant I - A + \int_0^{\hat{\rho}_1} \rho f(\rho)\,d\rho$$

$$\iff [1 + \mu F(\hat{\rho}_1)]\rho_0 \geqslant I - A + \int_0^{\hat{\rho}_1} \rho f(\rho)\,d\rho.$$

Case 2: if

$$[1 + \mu F(\hat{\rho}_0)]\rho_0 < I - A + \int_0^{\hat{\rho}_0} \rho f(\rho)\,d\rho,$$

financing is infeasible.

Case 3: in the intermediate case, ρ^* is given by

$$[1 + \mu F(\rho^*)]\rho_0 = I - A + \int_0^{\rho^*} \rho f(\rho)\,d\rho.$$

(iv) Whenever $\rho^* > \hat{\rho}_0$ (which is the generic case, conditional on financing), the firm must hoard liquidity in order to avoid credit rationing at the intermediate stage. The investors' maximal return on the deepening investment, $\mu\rho_0$, is smaller than the total value, $\mu\rho_1$, of this reinvestment.

Exercise 5.11 (should debt contracts be indexed to output prices?). (i) For a given policy $\rho^*(P)$, the NPV is

$$U_b = \bar{P}r + E[F(\rho^*(P))p_H PR] - I - E\Big[\int_0^{\rho^*(P)} \rho f(\rho)\,d\rho\Big],$$

where expectations are taken with respect to the random price P. The investors' breakeven constraint is

$$\bar{P}r + E\Big[F(\rho^*(P))\Big[p_H\Big(PR - \frac{B}{\Delta p}\Big)\Big]\Big] \geqslant I - A + E\Big[\int_0^{\rho^*(P)} \rho f(\rho)\,d\rho\Big].$$

Let μ denote the shadow price of the budget constraint (we assume that $\mu > 0$). Then, taking the derivative of the Lagrangian with respect to $\rho^*(P)$ yields

$$\rho^*(P) = p_H PR - \Big(\frac{\mu}{1+\mu}\Big)\frac{p_H B}{\Delta p}.$$

(ii) To implement the optimal policy through a state-contingent debt $d(P)$, one must have

$$\rho^*(P) = [Pr - d(P)] + \Big[p_H\Big(PR - \frac{B}{\Delta p}\Big)\Big]$$

or

$$d(P) = Pr - \ell_0,$$

where

$$\ell_0 \equiv \frac{1}{1+\mu}\Big(p_H \frac{B}{\Delta p}\Big).$$

Exercise 6.1 (privately known private benefit and market breakdown). (i) If the borrower's private benefit B were common knowledge, then, if financed, the borrower would receive R_b in the case of success, with

$$R_b \geqslant \frac{B}{\Delta p},$$

so as to induce her to behave. The project would be funded if and only if the pledgeable income exceeded the investment cost:

$$p_H\Big(R - \frac{B}{\Delta p}\Big) \geqslant I.$$

Suppose that the borrower offers a contract specifying that she will receive R_b in the case of success and 0 in the case of failure (offering to receive more than 0 in the case of failure would evidently raise suspicion, and can indeed be shown not to improve the borrower's welfare). There are three possible cases:

(a) $R_b \geqslant B_H/\Delta p$ induces the borrower to work regardless of her type, and thus creates an information insensitive security for the lenders, who obtain

$$p_H(R - R_b) - I \leqslant p_H\left(R - \frac{B_H}{\Delta p}\right) - I < 0$$

using (1). So, such high rewards for the borrower cannot attract financing.

(b) $R_b < B_L/\Delta p$ induces the borrower to shirk regardless of her type. The lenders' claim is again information insensitive, and from (2) fails to attract financing.

(c) $B_L/\Delta p \leqslant R_b < B_H/\Delta p$: suppose that, in equilibrium, the good borrower offers a contract with a reward in this range, and that this attracts financing.[7] A bad borrower must then "pool" and offer the same contract: if she were to offer a different contract, her type would be revealed to the capital market and her project would not be funded. Furthermore, she receives utility from the project being funded at least equal to that of a good borrower (she receives the same payoff conditional on working and a higher payoff conditional on shirking). So, she is better off pooling with the good borrower than not being funded.

We conclude that equilibrium is necessarily a pooling equilibrium. It either involves no funding at all or funding of both types. From the study of cases (a) and (b), we also know that, in the case of funding, the good type behaves and the bad one misbehaves.

(ii) A necessary condition for funding is thus that

$$[\alpha p_H + (1 - \alpha)p_L](R - R_b) \geqslant I.$$

Since $R_b \geqslant B_L/\Delta p$, there cannot be any lending if

$$\alpha < \alpha^*,$$

where

$$[\alpha^* p_H + (1 - \alpha^*)p_L]\left(R - \frac{B_L}{\Delta p}\right) = I.$$

Thus, if the proportion of good borrowers is smaller than $\alpha^* \in (0, 1)$, there is no lending at all. Bad borrowers drive out good ones and the loan market breaks down.

Suppose, next, that the proportion of good borrowers is high: $\alpha > \alpha^*$. The borrower may now be able to receive financing. Suppose that the borrower, regardless of her type, offers to receive R_b^* in the case of success and 0 in the case of failure, where

$$[\alpha p_H + (1 - \alpha)p_L](R - R_b^*) = I.$$

Because $\alpha > \alpha^*$, $R_b^* > B_L/\Delta p$ and so the good borrower behaves. The investors' breakeven condition is therefore satisfied. It is an equilibrium for both types to offer contract $\{R_b^*, 0\}$ and for the capital market to fund the project.[8]

(iii) • The pooling equilibrium (which exists whenever $\alpha \geqslant \alpha^*$) exhibits no market breakdown. Indeed, there is *more lending under adverse selection than under symmetric information.*[9]

• It involves an externality between the two types of borrower. The good type obtains reward

$$R_b^* = R - I/[\alpha p_H + (1 - \alpha)p_L]$$

in the case of success below that, $R - I/p_H$, that she would obtain under symmetric information. The good type thus *cross-subsidizes* the bad type, who would not receive any funding under symmetric information.

• The project's NPV conditional on being funded falls from $p_H R - I$ to $[\alpha p_H + (1 - \alpha)p_L]R - I$ due to asymmetric information. The *quality of lending* is thus affected by adverse selection.

Exercise 6.2 (more on pooling in credit markets). A loan agreement specifying reward R_b in the case of success, and 0 in the case of failure, induces a proportion $H(R_b\Delta p)$ of borrowers to behave. This proportion is endogenous and increases with R_b. Thus

7. The reasoning can easily be extended to allow mixed strategies by the borrower and the capital market.

8. A more formal analysis of equilibrium behavior and of the equilibrium set can be performed along the lines of Section 6.4. We prefer to stick to a rather informal presentation at this stage.

9. This result and the following two can be found, for example, in de Meza and Webb's (1987) early contribution on the topic. (De Meza, D. and D. Webb. 1987. Too much investment: a problem of asymmetric information. *Quarterly Journal of Economics* 102:281–292.)

the lender's expected profit is

$$U_l = H(R_b\Delta p)p_H(R-R_b)+(1-H(R_b\Delta p))p_L(R-R_b).$$

Because $p_H > p_L$ so with only high-quality types, the level of R_b that satisfies the breakeven constraint of lenders could be larger than R_b when they face distribution H of borrowers. Thus, there is an externality among different types of borrowers.

Under a uniform distribution on $[0,\bar{B}]$ and for $p_L = 0$, the level of R_b maximizing pledgeable income is given by

$$\begin{aligned} 0 &= h(R_b\Delta p)p_H(R-R_b)\Delta p \\ &\quad - h(R_b\Delta p)p_L(R-R_b)\Delta p \\ &\quad - H(R_b\Delta p)p_H - (1-H(R_b\Delta p))p_L \\ &= h(R_b\Delta p)(R-R_b)(\Delta p)^2 - H(R_b\Delta p)\Delta p - p_L \\ &= \frac{1}{\bar{B}}(R-R_b)p_H^2 - \frac{R_b}{\bar{B}}p_H^2 \end{aligned}$$

or

$$R_b = \tfrac{1}{2}R.$$

Thus the pledgeable income is

$$\mathcal{P}(R_b) = \frac{1}{\bar{B}}\frac{p_H^2}{4}R^2,$$

and is smaller than I for $\bar{B}$ large enough.

Exercise 6.3 (reputational capital). (i) In this one-period adverse-selection problem, the bad type is always more eager to go on with a project than the good type. Thus, we may only have a pooling equilibrium. The assumptions imply that if we induce the bad type to work, or if we do not induce the good type to work, then the pledgeable income will not cover investment expenses. So, the only chance to receive funding is to induce the good type to work and the bad type to shirk. Under this type of contract, the pledgeable income is

$$\begin{aligned} [\alpha p_H + (1-\alpha)p_L]\Big(R - \frac{b}{\Delta p}\Big) \\ = (p_H - (1-\alpha)\Delta p)\Big(R - \frac{b}{\Delta p}\Big). \end{aligned}$$

(ii) First, note that the good type always works in the first period as $b < A\Delta p_1$.

In a pooling equilibrium, the bad type would always work. But then, the updated belief on the probability of the good type would still be α in period 2, and from the first inequality of the last displayed set of inequalities, and the result in (i), the project would not be financed in period 2. But this implies that the bad type would be better off shirking in period 1. So there is no pooling equilibrium.

In a separating equilibrium, the bad type would not work in period 1. Then, after a success in period 1, the updated belief on the probability of the good type would be α_S, and conditional on success in period 1 the project would be financed in period 2 (by the last assumed inequality) and the payoff to the borrower in the case of success would be

$$R - \frac{I-A}{p_H - (1-\alpha_S)\Delta p}.$$

That, however, means that the bad type strictly prefers to work in period 1. Thus, there is no separating equilibrium.

The semiseparating equilibrium requires that the bad type is indifferent between working and shirking in period 1, that is,

$$B = (\Delta p_1)\Big[p_L\Big(R - \frac{I-A}{p_H - (1-\alpha_S')\Delta p}\Big) + B\Big].$$

This determines the updated belief α_S' on the probability of the good type conditional on success in period 1, and thus determines the probability of the bad type working in period 1.

Exercise 6.5 (asymmetric information about the value of assets in place and the negative stock price reaction to equity offerings with a continuum of types). (i) The investors receive R_l in the case of success and 0 in the case of failure. The entrepreneur therefore issues equity if and only if

$$(p+\tau)(R-R_l) \geqslant pR \quad\Longleftrightarrow\quad \tau R \geqslant (p+\tau)R_l$$

and so there indeed exists a cutoff $p^* \in [\underline{p},\bar{p}]$ such that the entrepreneur issues equity if and only if $p \leqslant p^*$.

(ii) The investors' breakeven condition is therefore

$$[E[p \mid p \leqslant p^*] + \tau]R_l = I \quad\text{or}\quad R_l = \frac{I}{m^-(p^*)+\tau}.$$

If interior, the cutoff satisfies

$$\tau R = (p^*+\tau)R_l \quad\text{or}\quad \frac{\tau R}{I} = \frac{p^*+\tau}{m^-(p^*)+\tau}.$$

Note also that $p^* > \underline{p}$: if p^* were equal to $\underline{p}$, then $m^-(p^*) = p^*$ and so types $\underline{p}$ and just above would be strictly better off issuing equity. The condition

$(m^-)' \leqslant 1$ does not suffice to guarantee uniqueness, though. Uniqueness, however, prevails if $(m^-)'$ is bounded away from 1 (for example, $(m^-)' = \frac{1}{2}$ in the case of a uniform distribution) and if $\tau R/I$ is close to 1.

For $p^* = \bar{p}$, $m^-(p^*) = E[p]$ (the prior expectation). And so the condition stated in (ii) ensures that the cutoff is interior.

Finally, if there are multiple equilibria, the one with the highest p^* yields the lowest stigma for equity issues since

$$R_1 = \frac{I}{m^-(p^*) + \tau}$$

is then smallest among equilibria.

For a uniform density, the equilibrium is, as we noted, unique, and, if interior, is given by

$$[\tfrac{1}{2}(p^* + \underline{p}) + \tau]\tau R = (p^* + \tau)I.$$

(ii) Let us now look at the stock price reaction. The market value prior to the announcement of the equity issue is equal to total value (given that investors will break even on average):

$$\begin{aligned} V_0 &= E(p)R + F(p^*)[\tau R - I] \\ &= [F(p^*)m^-(p^*) + [1 - F(p^*)]m^+(p^*)]R \\ &\quad + F(p^*)[\tau R - I]. \end{aligned}$$

The *ex post* value of shares upon an announcement is

$$V_1 = [m^-(p^*) + \tau]R - I.$$

And so

$$\begin{aligned} V_0 - V_1 = {} & [1 - F(p^*)] \\ & \times [m^+(p^*)R - [[m^-(p^*) + \tau]R - I]]. \end{aligned}$$

In the case of an interior equilibrium,

$$\begin{aligned} V_0 - V_1 = {} & [1 - F(p^*)]R \\ & \times \left[m^+(p^*) - \frac{p^*}{p^* + \tau}(m^-(p^*) + \tau)\right]. \end{aligned}$$

But

$$\frac{m^+(p^*)}{p^*} > 1 > \frac{m^-(p^*) + \tau}{p^* + \tau}.$$

Hence,

$$V_0 - V_1 > 0.$$

(iv) Let

$$H(p^*, \tau) \equiv \frac{\tau R}{I}[m^-(p^*) + \tau] - [p^* + \tau].$$

At the Pareto-dominant, interior equilibrium,

$$H_{p^*} < 0$$

(where the subscript denotes a partial derivative). Furthermore, and using the fact that $H = 0$ at an equilibrium,

$$H_\tau = [m^-(p^*) + \tau]\frac{R}{I} + \frac{p^* - m^-(p^*)}{m^-(p^*) + \tau} > 0.$$

Hence, p^* increase with τ. So does the volume $[1 - F(p^*)]I$.

Exercise 6.6 (adverse selection and rating). (i) • Condition (1) means that the pledgeable income of a good (bad) borrower exceeds (is lower than) the investors' investment $I - A$. The pledgeable income is equal to the expected income, $p_H R$, minus the entrepreneur's incompressible share, $p_H b/\Delta p$ (or $p_H B/\Delta p$).

• To see that no lending occurs in equilibrium, note that the bad type (type B) always derives a (weakly) higher surplus from being financed than a good type (type b). Hence, contracts that provide financing to a good type will also provide financing to a bad one (pooling behavior).

Condition (1) implies that one cannot offer a breakeven contract that induces the bad type to work. So any breakeven contract must induce misbehavior by the bad type. But condition (2) in turn implies that pooling contracts with stakes for the borrower in the interval $[b/\Delta p, B/\Delta p)$ generate a loss for the investors.

(ii) • In a separating equilibrium the good type chooses x and then offers R_b, and the bad type, which is recognized, chooses $x = 0$ and, from condition (1), receives no funding. Were the bad type to mimic the good type, she would get funding with probability $1 - x$; for, either the signal reveals the type and then she gets no funding, or the signal reveals nothing and the investors still believe they face a good type (we here use the fact that the equilibrium is separating).

Letting R_b^G denote the good type's "full information" (with net capital $A - rx$) contract (given by $p_H(R - R_b^G) = I - A + rx$), it must be the case that the bad type does not want to mimic the good type and prefers to keep her capital A instead. That is,

$$A \geqslant (1 - x)[p_L R_b^G + B] + x(A - rx)$$

or

$$A \geqslant x(A - rx) + (1 - x)\Big[p_{\mathrm{L}}\Big(R - \frac{I - A + rx}{p_{\mathrm{H}}}\Big) + B\Big],$$

which yields the condition in the question. This condition is satisfied with equality at the separating equilibrium (see the chapter).

Exercise 6.7 (endogenous communication among lenders). (i) First, consider date 1. The assumption $[\alpha p + (1-\alpha)q]R - I + \delta[\alpha p + (1-\alpha)q](R - I) < 0$ implies that a foreign bank would not lend at date 1 even if it faced no competition at date 1 and it remained a monopoly at date 2 and hence could offer $R_{\mathrm{b}} = 0$ in either period (with probability $\alpha p + (1 - \alpha)q$, the borrower would be known to be successful at date 2).

Thus, only the local bank will lend at date 1. Furthermore, the condition

$$qR - I + \delta q(R - I) < 0$$

implies that it would not lend to a bad type even if it faced no competition in either period. Hence, the local bank lends only to the good type. It offers $R_{\mathrm{b}}^{1} = 0$.

In the absence of information sharing, foreign banks do not know whether the borrower succeeded at date 1, and therefore at date 2 (they put probability p on the borrower's being successful at date 2).

Note that the foreign banks do not want to make offers to the local borrower at date 2: suppose that they offer $R_{\mathrm{b}} < R$. Either the borrower will succeed and then the local, incumbent bank will offer a bit more ($R_{\mathrm{b}} + \varepsilon$), or it will fail and then the incumbent will not bid. Hence, a foreign bank can win the contest for the local firm only if the latter will fail. Hence, they do not bid, and the incumbent bank bids $R_{\mathrm{b}}^{2} = 0$ if the borrower is successful (and does not finance otherwise). The local bank's profit (and thus each bank's profit since banks do not make profits in foreign markets) is

$$\pi^{\mathrm{ns}} = \alpha[pR - I + \delta p(R - I)],$$

where "ns" means "no sharing."

The borrower's *ex ante* utility is

$$U_{\mathrm{b}}^{\mathrm{ns}} = 0.$$

Suppose now that banks share their information. They are then Bertrand competitors at date 2 and make no profit at that date. But the local bank still lends at date 1 if the borrower's type is p: the profits and utilities are

$$\pi^{\mathrm{s}} = \alpha[pR - I] \quad \text{and} \quad U_{\mathrm{b}}^{\mathrm{s}} = \delta\alpha p(R - I).$$

Hence, banks do not want to share their information.

(ii) Suppose now that α is endogenous. Then $C(\alpha)$ needs to be subtracted from the borrower's previous utility (which is now a gross utility) in order to obtain the net utility.

In the absence of information sharing, the borrower is held up by the local bank, and so

$$\alpha^{\mathrm{ns}} = \pi^{\mathrm{ns}} = U_{\mathrm{b}}^{\mathrm{ns}} = 0.$$

Under information sharing, the borrower's investment is given by

$$\max_{\alpha}\{\delta\alpha p(R - I) - C(\alpha)\},$$

and so, for an interior solution,

$$C'(\alpha^*) = \delta p(R - I).$$

Then

$$\pi^{\mathrm{s}} = \alpha^*[pR - I] > \pi^{\mathrm{ns}}$$

and

$$U_{\mathrm{b}}^{\mathrm{s}} = \delta\alpha^* p(R - I) - C(\alpha^*).$$

Exercise 6.8 (pecking order with variable investment). (i) The separating program is

$$\max_{\{R_{\mathrm{b}}^{\mathrm{S}}, R_{\mathrm{b}}^{\mathrm{F}}\}} \{p_{\mathrm{H}} R_{\mathrm{b}}^{\mathrm{S}} + (1 - p_{\mathrm{H}}) R_{\mathrm{b}}^{\mathrm{F}}\}$$

s.t.

$$[p_{\mathrm{H}}(R^{\mathrm{S}} I - R_{\mathrm{b}}^{\mathrm{S}}) + (1 - p_{\mathrm{H}})(R^{\mathrm{F}} I - R_{\mathrm{b}}^{\mathrm{F}})] \geqslant I - A, \quad (\mathrm{IR_l})$$

$$q_{\mathrm{H}} R_{\mathrm{b}}^{\mathrm{S}} + (1 - q_{\mathrm{H}}) R_{\mathrm{b}}^{\mathrm{F}} \leqslant \tilde{U}_{\mathrm{b}}^{\mathrm{SI}}, \quad (\mathrm{M})$$

$$(\Delta p)(R_{\mathrm{b}}^{\mathrm{S}} - R_{\mathrm{b}}^{\mathrm{F}}) \geqslant BI. \quad (\mathrm{IC_b})$$

Note that ($\mathrm{IC_b}$) implies that the bad borrower works if she mimics the good one.

(ii) The key observation is that the solution to the separating program satisfies

$$R_{\mathrm{b}}^{\mathrm{F}} = 0.$$

That is, the good borrower receives nothing in the case of failure. In particular, if $R^{\mathrm{F}} I$ stands for the salvage value of the leftover assets, this salvage value is entirely transferred to the investors in the case of failure.

The proof of this observation is instructive. Suppose that $R_b^F > 0$. Consider a small increase $\delta R_b^S > 0$ in the borrower's reward in the case of success and a small decrease $\delta R_b^F < 0$ in her reward in the case of failure such that

$$p_H(\delta R_b^S) + (1 - p_H)(\delta R_b^F) = 0.$$

This change alters neither the objective function nor the investors' profit from the good borrower (see (IR_l)), but it relaxes the moral-hazard constraint (IC_b), and interestingly the mimicking constraint[10] as well since $q_H < p_H$. In words, a good borrower, who has a higher probability of success, cares relatively more about her income in the case of success and relatively less about her income in the case of failure than a bad borrower.

(iii) Because the weak monotonic-profit assumption is satisfied, Proposition 6.2 in the supplementary section implies that the separating allocation is the unique perfect Bayesian equilibrium allocation if and only if prior beliefs lie below some threshold α^*.

Exercise 6.9 (herd behavior). Entrepreneur 1, who moves first, chooses his best project, regardless of the state of nature. The investors then attach probability of success

$$m = \alpha p + (1 - \alpha)q$$

to the project. They are willing to go along with compensation R_b^1 such that

$$m(R - R_b^1) = I.$$

Now consider entrepreneur 2. In the unfavorable environment, she has no choice but choosing the strategy that gives a probability of success. Suppose now that she herds with entrepreneur 1 in the favorable environment. Her overall probability of success when she selects the same strategy as entrepreneur 1 is

$$\theta p + (1 - \theta)r.$$

So let R_b^U and R_b^F denote the second entrepreneur's compensation in the case of success depending on whether the environment is unfavorable or favorable, respectively:

$$q(R - R_b^U) = I \quad \text{and} \quad [\theta p + (1 - \theta)r](R - R_b^F) = I.$$

Herding behavior requires that

$$rR_b^F \geqslant pR_b^U$$

or

$$r\left[R - \frac{I}{\theta p + (1 - \theta)r}\right] \geqslant p\left[R - \frac{I}{q}\right].$$

This condition requires in particular that, despite herding, the choice of the same strategy by both entrepreneurs is sufficiently good news about the environment ($\theta p + (1 - \theta)r > q$) and therefore brings about much better financing terms for entrepreneur 2. It is satisfied, for example, if the project is hardly creditworthy in the unfavorable environment ($qR \simeq I$) and r is not too small.

Exercise 6.10 (maturity structure). In this simple example the good borrower can costlessly separate from the bad one by not hoarding any liquidity (i.e., setting short-term debt $d = r$). Because $\rho_0^G > \rho$, the good borrower knows that she will be able to find sufficient funds by going to the capital market at date 1 and diluting existing external claims. By contrast, the project will be stopped at date 1 for the bad borrower in the absence of liquidity hoarding, which would not be the case if the borrower resorted to hoarded liquidity rather than to the capital market to meet the liquidity shock.

This example is very special but it conveys the basic intuition: going back to the capital market is less costly for a good borrower than for a bad one if information about the firm's quality accrues in between. What is special about the example is that signaling by not hoarding liquidity is costless to the good borrower. Suppose that the liquidity shock is random and may exceed ρ_0^G. Then we know from Chapter 5 that it is optimal for the good borrower to hoard liquidity under symmetric information. So, signaling may involve insufficient continuation in general.

10. The mimicking constraint can be shown to be binding. If it were not binding, the solution to the separating program would be the good borrower's full information contract. The borrower would thus obtain reward $BI^G/\Delta p$ in the case of success, and 0 in the case of failure, where I^G is determined by the good borrower's symmetric-information debt capacity. But then

$$q_H R_b^S + (1 - q_H)R_b^F = q_H BI^G/\Delta p > \tilde{U}_b^{SI} = q_H BI^B/\Delta p,$$

where I^B is determined by the bad borrower's symmetric-information debt capacity. Because under symmetric information a good borrower can borrow more than a bad one, $I^G > I^B \geqslant 0$, and so (M) must be binding after all.

Exercise 7.1 (competition and vertical integration). (i) • The project can be financed because there is enough pledgeable income from condition (1).

• Feasible contracts:

$$R_1^{\mathrm{F}} + \theta_1 M \geqslant I \quad \text{and} \quad (\Delta p)(1-\theta_1)M \geqslant B.$$

For example, the debt contract,

$$R_1^{\mathrm{F}} = R^{\mathrm{F}} \quad \text{and} \quad \theta_1 = (I - R^{\mathrm{F}})/M$$

(which amounts to a debt $\mathcal{D} = I$), is an optimal contract. To obtain it as the unique optimal contract, one could, for example, add variable investment.

(ii) • The entrepreneur obtains

$$U_{\mathrm{b}} = R^{\mathrm{F}} + M - I$$

under an exclusive contract with the supplier.

By contrast, the industry profit when the rival obtains the enabling technology is

$$2(R^{\mathrm{F}} + D - I) + K < R^{\mathrm{F}} + M - I$$

from condition (2) and the profit-destruction effect. Because neither the supplier's nor the rival's rent (which is 0 under exclusivity) can decrease, the entrepreneur cannot gain from nonexclusivity.

• The supplier will not find it profitable to supply the enabling technology to the rival if and only if

$$R_1^{\mathrm{F}} + \theta_1 M \geqslant R_1^{\mathrm{F}} + \theta_1 D + \left[R^{\mathrm{F}} + \left(D - \frac{B}{\Delta p}\right) - (I-K)\right] \quad (3)$$

or

$$\theta_1(M - D) \geqslant R^{\mathrm{F}} + \left(D - \frac{B}{\Delta p}\right) - (I - K).$$

The term in square brackets in (3) is the difference between the rival's pledgeable income and the extra investment cost $I - K$. The solution is thus to offer enough equity to the supplier. Note that the borrower can always achieve this while maintaining borrower incentives: $(\Delta p)(1-\theta_1)D \geqslant B$. (If the borrower chose effort *after* observing the supplier's action, the incentive constraint would become $(\Delta p)(1-\theta_1)M \geqslant B$.)

Remark. For some parameter values an optimal debt/equity mix might involve a larger expected payment for the supplier than the investment I, but that is not a problem as the entrepreneur may demand a lump-sum payment equal to the difference up front, thus leaving the supplier with no rent.

Exercise 7.2 (benefits from financial muscle in a competitive environment). (i) • If $\rho > \rho_0(R)$, then the entrepreneur will not be able to withstand the liquidity shock if it occurs. Hence, it needs a liquidity cushion, perhaps in the form of a credit line.

• The NPV is

$$(1-\lambda)[\rho_1(R)] + \lambda[\rho_1(R) - \rho]z - I,$$

where $z = 1$ if the firm withstands the liquidity shock, and $z = 0$ otherwise. Hence,

(a) $z = 0$ if $\rho \geqslant \rho_1(R)$;

(b) $z = 1$ if $\rho < \rho_1(R)$ and there is enough pledgeable income to "secure a credit line,"

$$\rho_0(R) \geqslant I - A + \lambda\rho$$

or

$$(1-\lambda)\rho_0(R) - (I - A) \geqslant \lambda[\rho - \rho_0(R)]; \quad (5)$$

(c) $z = 0$ if (5) is not satisfied and

$$(1-\lambda)\rho_0(R) \geqslant I - A;$$

(d) no investment takes place if

$$(1-\lambda)\rho_0(R) < I - A.$$

(ii) • *Simultaneous choices*: under simultaneous choices, there is no commitment effect. Condition (1) and question (i) imply that the incumbent does not want to withstand her liquidity shock regardless of the existence of the entrant. The left inequality in (2) then implies that the entrant has enough pledgeable income to obtain financing if the incumbent does not build financial muscle (and wants to be financed from (3)); while the right inequality prevents the incumbent from investing ($I - A > \rho_0(C) > (1-\lambda)\rho_0(C)$).

• *Sequential choices*: suppose now that the incumbent chooses her financial structure first. The analysis of the simultaneous choice case shows that the incumbent cannot obtain financing without financial muscle. By contrast, condition (2) shows that the incumbent deters entry if she commits to withstand her liquidity shock. Condition (4) then implies that the incumbent has enough pledgeable income in a monopoly situation even if she withstands the costly liquidity shock.

Exercise 7.3 (dealing with asset substitution). (i) • The liquidation value L_0 is fully pledgeable. By contrast, only $R - R_b$ is pledged in the case of success, where

$$p_H R_b \geqslant p_L R_b + B.$$

Hence, the left-hand side of (1) is the pledgeable income.

• With a competitive capital market, the entrepreneur's utility is the NPV:

$$U_b^* = (1-x)L_0 + x p_H R - I.$$

• Optimal contracts must satisfy

$$(1-x)(L_0 - r_b) + x p_H (R - R_b) = I - A,$$

with

$$R_b \geqslant B/\Delta p.$$

For $A = \bar{A}$ the optimal contract is necessarily a debt contract ($r_b = 0$).

(ii) • Interpretation of equation (2). The NPV is

$$(1-x)L + x[p_H + \tau(L)]R - I.$$

Hence, $L = L_0$ maximizes the NPV, which is then equal to U_b^*.

• Consider a "step-function" contract: in the case of liquidation, the entrepreneur receives

$$\begin{aligned} &0 \quad \text{if } L < L_0, \\ &r_b \quad \text{if } L \geqslant L_0. \end{aligned}$$

Furthermore, the entrepreneur receives $R_b = B/\Delta p$ in the case of continuation and success (this value minimizes both the nonpledgeable income and the incentive to cut down on maintenance to raise future profit). With this incentive scheme, the entrepreneur's utility

$$(1-x)r_b(L) + x[p_H + \tau(L)]R_b$$

is maximized either at $L = L_0$ or at $L = 0$. One therefore needs

$$(1-x)r_b + x p_H \frac{B}{\Delta p} \geqslant x[p_H + \tau(0)]\frac{B}{\Delta p}.$$

The threshold for financing that does not encourage asset substitution is given by

$$I - A^* = (1-x)(L_0 - r_b) + x p_H \left(R - \frac{B}{\Delta p}\right),$$

where r_b is given by the first inequality satisfied with equality.

Exercise 7.4 (competition and preemption). Let us first compute the first date $t_l < t_0$ at which lenders are willing to finance an entrepreneur who will later on be a monopolist:

$$I - \mathrm{e}^{-r(t_0 - t_l)} A = \mathrm{e}^{-r(t_0 - t_l)} p_H \left(M - \frac{B}{\Delta p}\right).$$

Thus no financing is feasible before date t_l.

Next, compute the earliest date $t_b < t_0$ at which the entrepreneur prefers to invest (as a monopolist) rather than just consuming her endowment:

$$\text{NPV} = \mathrm{e}^{-r(t_0 - t_b)} p_H M - I = 0,$$

where the NPV is computed from date t_b on.

The condition in the statement of the question,

$$p_H M \gtrless p_H \left(M - \frac{B}{\Delta p}\right) + A,$$

is equivalent to

$$t_b \gtrless t_l.$$

Note that $t_b < t_l$ if $A = 0$.

(a) If $t_b \geqslant t_l$, then the equilibrium involves rent equalization, as in Fudenberg and Tirole (1985)[11]. Only one entrepreneur invests, and this at date t_b. (See Fudenberg and Tirole (1985) for a more rigorous description of the strategies.) This entrepreneur does not enjoy any rent relative to the entrepreneur who does not invest.

(b) If $t_b < t_l$, then we are back to a situation similar to the static game. Entrepreneurs are unable to invest before t_l, even though, starting from t_b, they would like to preempt their rival. (Again, we refer to Fudenberg and Tirole (1985) for more details about this type of situation.)

Exercise 7.5 (benchmarking). (i) Let us write the NPV, the breakeven constraint, and the incentive constraint. First, the NPV accounts for deadweight losses due to negative incomes:

$$\begin{aligned} U_b &= \text{NPV} \\ &= \rho[p_H D - (1-p_H)\theta b_2] \\ &\quad + (1-\rho)[p_H^2 D + p_H(1-p_H)(M - \theta b_1) \\ &\qquad - (1-p_H)^2 \theta b_2] - I. \end{aligned}$$

11. Fudenberg, D. and J. Tirole. 1985. Preemption and rent equalization in the adoption of new technology. *Review of Economic Studies* 52:383–401.

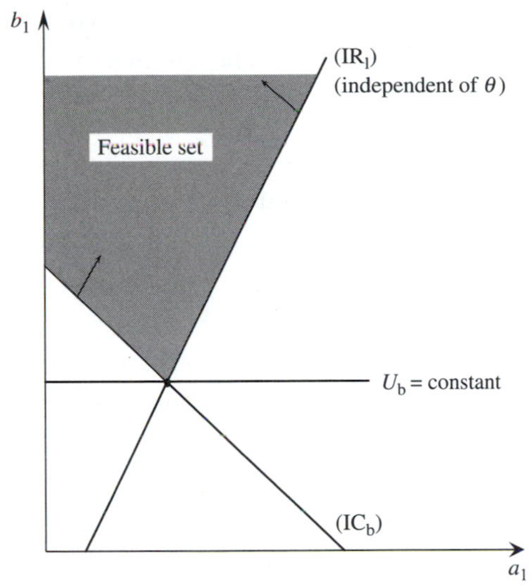

Figure 4

The breakeven constraint is

$$\rho[p_H(D-a_2)+(1-p_H)b_2] + (1-\rho)[p_H^2(D-a_2)+p_H(1-p_H)(M-a_1+b_1) + (1-p_H)^2b_2] \geqslant I-A. \tag{IR$_1$}$$

Lastly, the incentive constraint is

$$\rho[a_2+(1+\theta)b_1] + (1-\rho)[p_H[a_2+(1+\theta)b_1] + (1-p_H)[a_1+(1+\theta)b_2]] \geqslant \frac{B}{\Delta p}. \tag{IC$_b$}$$

To show that one can set $a_2 = b_2 = 0$ without loss of generality, write the Lagrangian and the first-order condition. Equivalently, if $a_2 > 0$, we can decrease a_2 and increase a_1 so as to keep both (IR_1) and (IC_b) unchanged, and note that these two variables do not enter into the expression of the NPV; while, if $b_2 > 0$, we can decrease it and increase b_1 so that (IR_1) and the NPV are kept intact, but (IC_b) is then not binding.

The diagrammatic representation of the problem in the (a_1, b_1)-space is as in Figure 4.

(ii) • When ρ tends to 1: b_1 going to infinity has almost no cost in terms of NPV. Thus (IC_b) becomes costless to satisfy, as in Section 7.1.1 in the case of perfect correlation.

• When θ goes to 0, then punishments are almost costless, and so again (IC_b) can be satisfied without jeopardizing (IR_1). Again there is basically no agency cost (as in the case in which firms have a large amount of collateral that the lenders value almost as much as the borrower).

Exercise 7.7 (optimal contracts in the Bolton–Scharfstein model). Consider a more general long-term contract in which the entrepreneur's reward contingent on different events is r_b^S if date-0 profit is D but there is no refinancing at date 1 (with probability z^S); and, if refinanced, R_b^{SS} (R_b^{FS}) when the entrepreneur succeeds in both periods (when she fails at date 0, but succeeds at date 1, respectively). When reinvesting at date 1, to "commit to" high effort, the entrepreneur should keep a high enough stake, i.e., R_b^{SS} and $R_b^{FS} \geqslant B/\Delta p$.

Fixing the continuation policy z^S and z^F, as long as the high effort is guaranteed the predation deterrence constraint is not affected by this enrichment of the contract space:

$$D \geqslant (z^S - z^F)(M-D). \tag{PD}$$

The date-0 incentive compatibility constraint and investor's breakeven constraint, however, need to be modified:

$$z^S R_b^{SS} + (1-z^S)r_b^S \geqslant B_0 + p_L[z^S R_b^{SS} + (1-z^S)r_b^S] + (1-p_L)z^F R_b^{FS}$$
$$\iff (\Delta p)[z^S R_b^{SS} - z^F R_b^{FS} + (1-z^S)r_b^S] \geqslant B_0 \tag{IC$'$}$$

and

$$I - A \leqslant z^S(D + D - R_b^{SS} - I) + (1-z^S)(D - r_b^S)$$
$$\iff I - A \leqslant D + z^S(D - I - R_b^{SS}) - (1-z^S)r_b^S. \tag{IR$'$}$$

The entrepreneur's expected utility is

$$U_b = z^S R_b^{SS} + (1-z^S)r_b^S - A = \mathrm{NPV} = D - I + z^S(D-I),$$

as usual, when (IR$'$) is binding.

As in Section 7.1.2, suppose (PD) is binding. (IC$'$) is binding; for, if it were not, z^F could be increased to relax (PD) without violating (IC$'$).

Then one can show that

- $R_b^{SS} \geqslant R_b^{FS}$ ($\geqslant B/\Delta p$): if $R_b^{SS} < R_b^{FS}$, then R_b^{FS} could be reduced so as to relax (IC$'$), which would contradict the fact that (IC′) is binding. And so $R_b^{FS} = B/\Delta p$.

- $r_b^S = 0$: suppose $z^S \in (0,1)$ and $r_b^S > 0$ (if $z^S = 1$, we could simply set $r_b^S = 0$). From (PD) being binding, the incentive constraint can be written as

$$z^S(R_b^{SS} - R_b^{FS}) + (1 - z^S)r_b^S + \frac{D}{M - D}R_b^{FS} = \frac{B_0}{\Delta p}.$$

Keeping z^S unchanged, we can decrease r_b^S and increase R_b^{SS} so that $z^S R_b^{SS} + (1 - z^S)r_b^S$ remains the same, i.e., in the case of date-0 success, one rewards the entrepreneur only in the case of continuation. There is no loss of generality in doing so since no constraint is affected, nor is the entrepreneur's objective function.

Exercise 7.8 (playing the soft-budget-constraint game vis-à-vis a customer). (i) At date 2, given success and in the absence of a date-1 contract, the customer would offer a purchasing price equal to 0 (or any arbitrarily small but positive amount) and the entrepreneur would accept. In this event, the entrepreneur and the investors get zero profit. Therefore, by playing wait-and-see, the customer would enjoy expected payoff $p_L v$, since the entrepreneur would shirk under this strategy. The same outcome prevails if the customer offers $R = 0$ at date 1.

Given that the entrepreneur has obtained funding at date 0, to induce a high probability of success at date 1 the customer needs to offer a price $R = R_l + B/\Delta p$. This is more profitable for the customer than offering a contract that is not incentive compatible:

$$p_H\left(v - R_l - \frac{B}{\Delta p}\right) > p_L v.$$

When this inequality holds, the NPV is

$$p_H\left(R_l + \frac{B}{\Delta p}\right) - I,$$

which is smaller than $(\Delta p)v - I$. On the other hand, if the condition above is violated, it is optimal for the customer to offer $R = 0$. But in this case the entrepreneur shirks and the project is not financed at date 0.

(ii) Suppose now that the entrepreneur issues short-term debt r_1 at date 0. At time 1 the customer has to cover r_1 in order for the firm to continue. It is as if date 1 were an initial financing stage at which the customer finances an investment with size r_1. The short-term debt can be chosen such that the customer refinances the project only if the entrepreneur works, i.e.,

$$p_L v < r_1.$$

Then, to induce the high effort, the customer offers a transfer price $R = B/\Delta p$, on top of r_1. The customer gets

$$p_H\left(v - \frac{B}{\Delta p}\right) - r_1.$$

By assumption $p_H(v - B/\Delta p) > p_L v$. It is possible to extract the full surplus from the customer by setting $r_1 = p_H(v - B/\Delta p)$. This amount is greater than $I - A$ by assumption and so investors are willing to finance the project at date 0. The entrepreneur then gets

$$p_H\frac{B}{\Delta p} - A + [r_1 - (I - A)],$$

which is equal to the NPV, $p_H v - I$. This is intuitive since both the initial investors and the customer get zero profit.

Exercise 7.9 (optimality of golden parachutes). Consider the following class of contract: when the entrepreneur reports a signal $s \in \{r, q\}$, the probability of continuation is z^s. She is paid R_b^s in the case of continuation and success, and T^s in the case of termination. In the latter event, the investors get $L_l^s = L - T^s \leqslant L$.

In the case of continuation, in order to overcome the moral-hazard problem, both R_b^r and R_b^q must exceed $B/\Delta p$. For the q-type entrepreneur, the (NM) constraint is now

$$z^r(q_H - \tau)R_b^r + (1 - z^r)T^r \leqslant z^q q_H R_b^q + (1 - z^q)T^q. \qquad \text{(NM′)}$$

The investors' breakeven condition is

$$\begin{aligned} I - A \leqslant\ & \alpha[z^r r_H(R - R_b^r) + (1 - z^r)(L - T^r)] \\ & + (1 - \alpha)[z^q q_H(R - R_b^q) + (1 - z^q)(L - T^q)] \end{aligned}$$

and the entrepreneur gets expected payoff

$$\begin{aligned} U_b &= \alpha[z^r r_H R_b^r + (1 - z^r)T^r] \\ &\qquad + (1 - \alpha)[z^r q_H R_b^r + (1 - z^q)T^q] - A \\ &= \text{NPV} \\ &= \alpha[z^r r_H R + (1 - z^r)L] \\ &\qquad + (1 - \alpha)[z^q q_H R + (1 - z^q)L] - I, \end{aligned}$$

under the investors' breakeven condition.

We claim that the following properties hold.

• (NM′) is binding. Otherwise, we could decrease either R_b^q or T^q and increase the pledgeable income unless $R_b^q = B/\Delta p$ and $T^q = 0$. But, in the latter case, from (NM′) being slack, we must have $z^q > 0$, then from $L > q_H(R - B/\Delta p)$ the pledgeable income can be increased by reducing z^q.

• $R_b^r = B/\Delta p$: if $R_b^r > B/\Delta p$, decreasing it boosts pledgeable income and relaxes (NM′).

• $T^r = 0$: suppose $T^r > 0$ and $z^r < 1$ (when $z^r = 1$, we can simply set $T^r = 0$). Following the logic of Section 7.2.1, a simultaneous change of T^r and z^r that keeps the pledgeable income constant must satisfy

$$\left[r_H\left(R - \frac{B}{\Delta p}\right) - L + T^r\right] dz^r = (1 - z^r)\, dT^r.$$

By doing so, the LHS of (NM′) changes by an amount equal to

$$\left[r_H\left(R - \frac{B}{\Delta p}\right) - L + (q_H - \tau)\frac{B}{\Delta p}\right] dz^r;$$

(NM′) is relaxed by a simultaneous decrease of T^r and z^r. (If $z^r = 0$, we could instead decrease T^r to relax (NM′) and increase the pledgeable income.)

Incorporating these findings, the program becomes

$$\begin{aligned}
&\max\{\text{NPV} = \alpha[L + z^r(r_H R - L)] \\
&\qquad\qquad + (1-\alpha)[L + z^q(q_H R - L)] - I\} \\
&\text{s.t.}\quad z^r(q_H - \tau)\frac{B}{\Delta p} = z^q q_H R_b^q + (1 - z^q)T^q, \quad \text{(NM′)} \\
&I - A = \mathcal{P} = \alpha\{L + z^r[r_H(R - B/\Delta p) - L]\} \\
&\qquad + (1-\alpha)\{L + z^q[q_H(R - R_b^q) - L] \\
&\qquad\qquad - (1 - z^q)T^q\}. \\
&\qquad\qquad\qquad\qquad \text{(IR′)}
\end{aligned}$$

• When $q_H R > L$, it is optimal not to adopt the golden parachute policy, $T^q = 0$: suppose $T^q > 0$. First, note that to satisfy (NM′) as an equality, $T^q < q_H B/\Delta p \leqslant q_H R_b^q$ as long as $\tau > 0$. Therefore, an increase in z^q relaxes (NM′) and increases the NPV. Consider a simultaneous change in z^q and T^q that leaves (NM′) unchanged:

$$(q_H R_b^q - T^q)\, dz^q = -(1 - z^q)\, dT^q.$$

Since $T^q < q_H R_b^q$, a decrease in T^q comes with an increase in z^q, which increases the NPV. This change is feasible since the pledgeable income is increased:

$$\begin{aligned}
d\mathcal{P} &\approx [q_H(R - R_b^q) - L + T^q]\, dz^q - (1 - z^q)\, dT^q \\
&= (q_H R - L)\, dz^q > 0.
\end{aligned}$$

• When $q_H R < L$, a golden parachute is optimal, $T^q > 0$ and $z^q = 0$. From $T^q < q_H R_b^q$, the relevant part in the pledgeable income can be written as

$$L + z^q[q_H R - L - (q_H R_b^q - T^q)] - T^q,$$

therefore decreasing z^q raises both the pledgeable income and the NPV. At the optimum $z^{q*} = 0$, and the optimal T^q is determined by (NM′):

$$T^{q*} = z^r(q_H - \tau)\frac{B}{\Delta p}.$$

It is also easy to check for both cases that the (NM) constraint of the r-type entrepreneur is not binding.

Exercise 7.10 (delaying income recognition). We look for a "pooling equilibrium" in which the entrepreneur keeps a low profile ($\hat{y}_1 = 0$) when successful ($y_1 = R_1$). To this end, let us compute the posterior probability α_{LB} (where "LB" stands for "late bloomer") that the entrepreneur has high ability at date 2 (H_2) following (reported) profit 1 at date 1 and (actual and reported) profit R_2 at date 2:

$$\alpha_{LB} = \Pr(H_2 \mid (0, R_2)) = \frac{A + B}{C + D},$$

where $A = \alpha\rho[r + r\tau]$, $B = (1-\alpha)(1-\rho)(r + q\tau)$, $C = \alpha[\rho r + (1-\rho)q + r\tau]$, and $D = (1-\alpha)[(1-\rho)r + \rho q + q\tau]$. The numerator represents the probability that the entrepreneur has ability H_2 and succeeds at date 2: with probability $\alpha\rho$, she had high ability at date 1 and still has high ability and so has average probability of success $r + r\tau$ (due to the date-1 hidden savings made when she is successful at date 1, which has probability r); with probability $(1-\alpha)(1-\rho)$ she had low ability at date 1 (and therefore had hidden savings with probability q) and became expert in the task (and so has probability of success $r + q\tau$). The denominator represents the total probability of date-2 success in this pooling equilibrium, and is computed in a similar way.

By contrast, the probability that the entrepreneur has type H_2 when she fails at date 2 is

$$\alpha_F = \frac{E + F}{G + H} < \alpha_{LB},$$

where $E = \alpha\rho[1-(r+r\tau)]$, $F = (1-\alpha)(1-\rho)[1-r-q\tau]$, $G = \alpha[1-(\rho r+(1-\rho)q+r\tau)]$, and $H = +(1-\alpha)[1-[(1-\rho)r+\rho q+q\tau]]$.

Suppose now that the entrepreneur reports $\hat{y}_1 = R_1$. Let

$$\alpha_{\mathrm{EB}} \equiv \Pr(H_2 \mid (R_1, R_2)) = \frac{I}{J+K}$$

(where $I = [\alpha\rho r + (1-\alpha)(1-\rho)q]r$, $J = [\alpha\rho r + (1-\alpha)(1-\rho)q]r$, and $K = [\alpha(1-\rho)r + (1-\alpha)\rho q]q$) and

$$\beta_{\mathrm{EB}} \equiv \Pr(H_2 \mid (R_1, 0)) = \frac{M}{N+O}$$

(where $M = [\alpha\rho r + (1-\alpha)(1-\rho)q](1-r)$, $N = [\alpha\rho r + (1-\alpha)(1-\rho)q](1-r)$, and $O = [\alpha(1-\rho)r + (1-\alpha)\rho q](1-q)$) denote the posterior beliefs when such an "early bloomer" (EB) succeeds and fails at date 2, respectively. It can be checked that a good report at date 1 improves one's reputation for an arbitrary date-2 performance,

$$\alpha_{\mathrm{EB}} > \alpha_{\mathrm{LB}} \quad \text{and} \quad \beta_{\mathrm{EB}} > \alpha_{\mathrm{F}},$$

and that

$$\alpha_{\mathrm{LB}} > \beta_{\mathrm{EB}}.$$

Intuitively, a late success is more telling than an early one if either the type has a reasonable probability to evolve or if an early success confirms what one already knows, namely, that the entrepreneur has high ability.

Now assume that

$$\alpha_{\mathrm{EB}} > \alpha_{\mathrm{LB}} > \hat{\alpha} > \beta_{\mathrm{EB}} > \alpha_{\mathrm{F}}.$$

Then, the entrepreneur keeps her job at date 3 if and only if she succeeds at date 2. Keeping a low profile at date 1 when $y_1 = R_1$ is then the optimal strategy because it increases the probability of date-2 success by τ.

Exercise 8.1 (early performance measurement boosts borrowing capacity in the variable-investment model). In the variable-investment model, the private benefit of shirking is BI, and the income in the case of success RI. Using the notation of Section 8.2.2, the incentive compatibility constraint is

$$(\sigma_{\mathrm{HH}} - \sigma_{\mathrm{LH}})R_{\mathrm{b}} \geqslant BI,$$

where R_{b} is the entrepreneur's reward in the case of success. The borrowing capacity is then given by the investors' breakeven constraint:

$$p_{\mathrm{H}}RI - \sigma_{\mathrm{HH}}\frac{BI}{\sigma_{\mathrm{HH}} - \sigma_{\mathrm{LH}}} = I - A.$$

And so

$$\begin{aligned} U_{\mathrm{b}} = \sigma_{\mathrm{HH}}R_{\mathrm{b}} - A &= (p_{\mathrm{H}}R - 1)I \\ &= \frac{\rho_1 - 1}{1 - (\rho_1 - \sigma_{\mathrm{HH}}B/(\sigma_{\mathrm{HH}} - \sigma_{\mathrm{LH}}))}A. \end{aligned}$$

In the absence of an intermediate signal, the expression is the same except that $\sigma_{\mathrm{HH}}/[\sigma_{\mathrm{HH}} - \sigma_{\mathrm{LH}}]$ is replaced by $p_{\mathrm{H}}/[p_{\mathrm{H}} - p_{\mathrm{L}}]$.

Exercise 8.2 (collusion between the designated monitor and the entrepreneur). When the signal is high, there is no collusion. In the absence of collusion, the entrepreneur obtains $\hat{R}_{\mathrm{b}}$ since it is in the interest of the monitor to exercise his options. Furthermore, the entrepreneur cannot receive more than $\hat{R}_{\mathrm{b}}$ from the assumption that the entrepreneur cannot receive income without being detected.

Suppose therefore that the signal is low. In the absence of collusion, the entrepreneur and the monitor both receive 0. Suppose that the entrepreneur instead offers to tunnel resources to the monitor. For a given choice of τ, the monitor agrees to collude if and only if his loss from exercising the options is compensated by the diverted resources:

$$s[p_{\mathrm{H}} - (\nu_{\mathrm{L}} - \tau)]R < T(\tau).$$

There is no collusion provided that

$$H(s) \equiv \max_{\{\tau\}}\{T(\tau) - s[p_{\mathrm{H}} - (\nu_{\mathrm{L}} - \tau)R]\} \leqslant 0.$$

Because $\partial H/\partial s < 0$, there is no collusion provided that s exceeds some threshold.

Exercise 9.1 (low-quality public debt versus bank debt). Consider the three possible financing options.

High-quality public debt. Such debt has probability p_{H} of being reimbursed. As usual, the incentive constraint is

$$(\Delta p)R_{\mathrm{b}} \geqslant B,$$

$$p_{\mathrm{H}}\left(R - \frac{B}{\Delta p}\right) \geqslant I - A,$$

and so such financing is doable only if

$$\Longrightarrow \quad A_3 = I - p_{\mathrm{H}}\left(R - \frac{B}{\Delta p}\right).$$

The entrepreneur's utility is then the NPV:

$$U_b^3 = p_H R - I > 0.$$

Low-quality public debt. Such debt corresponds to the case in which the entrepreneur has too low a stake to behave; and this debt is repaid with probability p_L:

$$(\Delta p)R_b < B \quad \text{and} \quad p_L(R - R_b) = I - A.$$

Hence,

$$A_1 = I - p_L R.$$

The entrepreneur's utility is then

$$U_b^1 = p_L R + B - I > 0.$$

Monitoring. Follow the treatment in Chapter 9. To secure such financing with stake R_m for the monitor:

$$(\Delta p)R_m \geqslant c \quad \text{and} \quad p_H R_m - c = I_m.$$

And so a necessary and sufficient condition is

$$p_H\left(R - \frac{b}{\Delta p}\right) - c \geqslant I - A,$$

yielding threshold

$$A_2 = I + c - p_H\left(R - \frac{b}{\Delta p}\right),$$

and NPV

$$U_b^2 = p_H R - I - c.$$

Summing up, under the assumptions made in the statement of the exercise:

$$U_b^3 > U_b^2 > U_b^1 > 0 \quad \text{and} \quad A_3 > A_2 > A_1.$$

So, financing is arranged as described in the statement of the question.

(A similar framework is used by Morrison[12], except that the monitor is risk averse (which makes it more costly to hire). Morrison allows the monitor to contract with a "protection seller" in the credit derivative market in order to pass the default risk on to this third party and to thereby obtain insurance. This reduces the monitor's incentive to monitor.)

Exercise 9.2 (start-up and venture capitalist exit strategy). (i) When the date-2 payoff can be verified at date 1, and there is no active monitor, the entrepreneur's reward, R_b, in the case of success must ensure incentive compatibility and allow investors to recoup their date-0 outlay:

$$(\Delta p)R_b \geqslant B \quad \text{and} \quad p_H(R - R_b) \geqslant I - A.$$

Because

$$I - p_H\left(R - \frac{B}{\Delta p}\right) > A,$$

these two conditions are mutually inconsistent.

Suppose, in contrast, that an active monitor receives R_A in the case of success. We now have two incentive compatibility conditions and one breakeven condition:

$$(\Delta p)R_b \geqslant b,$$
$$(\Delta p)R_A \geqslant c_A,$$

and

$$p_H(R - R_b - R_A) \geqslant I - A.$$

Because

$$A > I - p_H\left(R - \frac{b + c_A}{\Delta p}\right),$$

these inequalities are consistent. The second and the third inequalities then bind, and so the NPV for the entrepreneur (which is equal to the total value created by the project minus the rent received by the monitor) is

$$p_H R_b - A = p_H\left[R - \frac{c_A}{\Delta p}\right] - I.$$

(ii) The conditions are

$$p_H s[R - P] \geqslant c_P$$

(the speculator makes money when he acquires information and exercises his call option in the case of good news),

$$(\Delta p)sP \geqslant c_A$$

(this is the previous IC constraint with $R_A = sP$), and

$$P \geqslant p_H R$$

(the speculator cannot make money by refusing to monitor and purchasing the shares at price P).

Ignoring the last constraint yields the condition in the statement of the exercise. The third constraint requires that

$$\frac{c_A}{c_P} \geqslant \frac{1 - p_H}{p_H(\Delta p)}.$$

If this condition is not satisfied, the speculator does not have enough incentives to acquire the information when only the shares of the active monitor are

12. Morrison, A. 2002. Credit derivatives, disintermediation and investment decisions. Mimeo, Merton College, University of Oxford.

brought to the market at date 1. This means that the active monitor should be granted the right to "drag along" the shares (or some of the shares) of the limited partners in order to ensure the stock receives enough attention.

Exercise 9.3 (diversification of intermediaries). (i) Straightforward. Follows the lines of Chapters 3 and 4.

(ii) Similar to Chapter 4's treatment of diversification.

The venture capitalist obtains R_m if both projects succeed. The incentive constraints are

$$p_H^2 R_m \geqslant p_H p_L R_m + c \quad \text{(no shirking on monitoring one firm)}$$
$$\geqslant p_L^2 R_m + 2c \quad \text{(no shirking on monitoring both firms).}$$

As usual, it can be checked that only the latter constraint is binding. So

$$R_m \geqslant \frac{2c}{(\Delta p)(p_H + p_L)}.$$

The nonpledgeable income (aggregated over the two firms) is

$$2\left[p_H \frac{b}{\Delta p} + p_H \left(\frac{p_H}{p_H + p_L}\right) \frac{c}{\Delta p}\right].$$

Exercise 9.4 (the advising monitor model with capital scarcity). The entrepreneur's utility when enlisting a monitor is now equal to the NPV minus the rent derived by the monitor:

$$U_b^m = (p_H + q_H)\left(R - \frac{c}{\Delta q}\right) - I.$$

Note that U_b^m may no longer exceed

$$U_b^{nm} = p_H R - I,$$

even when $(\Delta q)R > c$.

Funding with a monitor on board is feasible if and only if

$$(p_H + q_H)\left(R - \frac{B}{\Delta p} - \frac{c}{\Delta q}\right) \geqslant I - A.$$

The presence of a monitor facilitates funding if and only if

$$(p_H + q_H)\left(R - \frac{B}{\Delta p} - \frac{c}{\Delta q}\right) > p_H\left(R - \frac{B}{\Delta p}\right)$$

or

$$q_H R > c + p_H \frac{c}{\Delta q} + q_H \frac{B}{\Delta p}.$$

The left-hand side is the increase in expected revenue; the right-hand side is the sum of the monitoring cost and the extra rents for the two agents.

Exercise 9.5 (random inspections). (i) Suppose first that the entrepreneur behaves with probability 1; then there is no gain from monitoring and so $y = 1$. But, in the absence of monitoring, the entrepreneur prefers to misbehave:

$$(\Delta p)R_b < B,$$

a contradiction. Conversely, suppose that the entrepreneur misbehaves with probability 1; because

$$\nu R_m > c,$$

the monitor monitors for certain ($y = 0$). But then the entrepreneur prefers to behave as

$$p_H R_b > 0.$$

Hence, the entrepreneur must randomize. For her to be indifferent between behaving and misbehaving, it must be the case that

$$p_H R_b = y(p_L R_b + B) + (1 - y) \cdot 0$$

or

$$y = \frac{p_H R_b}{p_L R_b + B}.$$

Similarly, the monitor must randomize. Indifference between monitoring and not monitoring implies that

$$(1 - x)p_H R_m + x(p_L + \nu)R_m - c = (1 - x)p_H R_m + x p_L R_m$$

or

$$x\nu R_m = c \iff x = \frac{c}{\nu R_m}.$$

(ii) Assume that $p_H(R - B/\Delta p) < I - A$, so that financing is not feasible in the absence of a monitor. As usual, one should be careful here: because the monitor has no cash and thus cannot be asked to contribute to the investment and gets a rent, the borrower's utility differs from the NPV,

$$U_b = (1 - x)p_H R_b + xy(B + p_L R_b) - A$$
$$= p_H R_b - A,$$

using the indifference condition for the entrepreneur. The uninformed investors' breakeven condition is

$$\mathcal{P} \equiv (1-x)p_H(R - R_b - R_m) + x[yp_L(R - R_b - R_m) + (1-y)(p_L + \nu)(R - R_m)] \geqslant I - A.$$

Note that $y = 0$ maximizes $\mathcal{P}$. First, if $x > 0$, a smaller y increases the amount of money returned to uninformed investors when correcting misbehavior. Second, it raises managerial discipline (reduces the level of R_b necessary to obtain incentive compatibility); indeed R_b can be taken equal to 0! (Note this would no longer hold if the entrepreneur could capture private benefit $b \in (0, B]$ before being fired.) The pledgeable income is then

$$\mathcal{P} = [(1-x)p_H + x(p_L + \nu)]\left[R - \frac{c}{x\nu}\right].$$

Noting that $\partial\mathcal{P}/\partial x > 0$ at $x = 0$ and $\partial\mathcal{P}/\partial x < 0$ at $x = 1$, the pledgeable income is maximized for x between 0 and 1. (The optimum does not, of course, involve $R_b = 0$. We are just computing what it takes to obtain financing.)

(iii) We know from Chapter 8 that the entrepreneur is best rewarded on the basis of a sufficient statistic for her performance. Here, the monitor's information is not garbled by exogenous noise, unlike the final outcome. Hence, it would in principle be better to reward the management on the basis of information disclosed (in an incentive-compatible way) by the monitor. We leave it to the reader to derive the optimal contract when one allows the monitor to report on his observation of the entrepreneur's choice of effort.

Exercise 9.6 (monitor's junior claim). Let R_b^S and R_b^F denote the entrepreneur's rewards in the cases of success and failure. We are interested in situations in which the entrepreneur would choose the Bad project if left unmonitored:

$$(\Delta p)(R_b^S - R_b^F) < B.$$

Under monitoring, incentive compatibility requires that

$$(\Delta p)(R_b^S - R_b^F) \geqslant b,$$

where $\Delta p \equiv p_H - p_L$.

Similarly, the monitor's compensation scheme must satisfy

$$(\Delta p)(R_m^S - R_m^F) \geqslant c.$$

The uninformed investors are willing to lend if and only if

$$p_H(R^S - R_b^S - R_m^S) + (1-p_H)(R^F - R_b^F - R_m^F) \geqslant I - A.$$

Finally, the borrower's utility is

$$p_H R_b^S + (1-p_H)R_b^F.$$

It is therefore in the borrower's interest to minimize the monitor's rent,

$$p_H R_m^S + (1-p_H)R_m^F - c,$$

subject to his incentive constraint,

$$(\Delta p)(R_m^S - R_m^F) \geqslant c.$$

This yields

$$R_m^F = 0 \quad \text{and} \quad R_m^S = \frac{c}{\Delta p}.$$

A necessary and sufficient condition for the borrower to have access to financing is

$$p_H\left(R^S - \frac{b+c}{\Delta p}\right) + (1-p_H)R^F \geqslant I - A.$$

Exercise 9.7 (intertemporal recoupment). (i) *Long-term contracts.* The potential NPV is

$$V = 2p_H R - (I_1 + I_2) - 2c.$$

Under *competition among monitors*, the borrower can obtain V, for example, by proposing a contract specifying that the selected monitor at date t, $t = 1, 2$, contributes I_m^t and receives R_m^t in the case of success (and 0 in the case of failure) such that

$$p_H(R_m^1 + R_m^2) = I_m^1 + I_m^2 + 2c,$$
$$(\Delta p)R_m^t = c.$$

(The reader familiar with Sections 4.2 and 4.7 will notice that considering two incentive constraints, one per period, is in general not optimal. More on this later. However, we here show that the upper bound on the borrower's utility can be reached, and so we do not need to enter the finer analysis of "cross-pledging.")

Similarly, giving a stake R_b^t in the case of success (and 0 in the case of failure) such that

$$(\Delta p)R_b^t \geqslant b$$

suffices (but is not necessary) to ensure borrower incentive compatibility.

Uninformed investors are then willing to finance the rest of the investments provided that

$$\sum_{t=1}^{2} p_{\mathrm{H}}[R - R_{\mathrm{b}}^{t} - R_{\mathrm{m}}^{t}] \geqslant \sum_{t=1}^{2} [I_t - I_{\mathrm{m}}^{t}]$$

or

$$p_{\mathrm{H}}[2R - R_{\mathrm{b}}^{1} - R_{\mathrm{b}}^{2}] \geqslant I_1 + I_2 + 2c.$$

The second condition in the statement of the exercise ensures that this condition can be met while satisfying the entrepreneur's incentive compatibility.

Under *monopoly in monitoring*, the same reasoning applies, with a few twists. First, the entrepreneur is rewarded only in the case of two successes. From Chapter 4, we know that she then gets R_{b} such that

$$[(p_{\mathrm{H}})^2 - (p_{\mathrm{L}})^2]R_{\mathrm{b}} \geqslant 2b.$$

(Two remarks. First, we do not allow termination to be used as a disciplining device. It is not renegotiation-proof anyway. Second, one can check that the monitor's incentive scheme can be designed so as to induce monitoring in both periods.) Second, the monitor then receives the NPV minus the entrepreneur's rent, i.e.,

$$V - \frac{(p_{\mathrm{H}})^2}{(p_{\mathrm{H}})^2 - (p_{\mathrm{L}})^2} 2b = V - 2\left(\frac{p_{\mathrm{H}}}{p_{\mathrm{H}} + p_{\mathrm{L}}}\right)\left(\frac{p_{\mathrm{H}}b}{\Delta p}\right).$$

(ii) *Short-term contracts.* Under competition, each monitor obtains no profit at date 2. The condition

$$I_1 + c > p_{\mathrm{H}}\left(R - \frac{b}{\Delta p}\right)$$

implies that no lending is feasible at date 1.

Under *monopoly*, the monitor will secure

$$p_{\mathrm{H}}\left(R - \frac{b}{\Delta p}\right) - I_2 - c > 0$$

at date 2, if he helps the firm obtain funding at date 1. His intertemporal profit is then

$$2p_{\mathrm{H}}\left(R - \frac{b}{\Delta p}\right) - (I_1 + I_2) - 2c > 0$$

(which is smaller than that under commitment because of the absence of cross-pledging across periods).

Exercise 10.1 (security design as a disciplining device). (i) R_{b}^{*} is the maximal entrepreneurial stake in the firm's payoff in the case of continuation that is consistent with the investors' breaking even. The entire short-term income (r in the case of success and L in the case of failure) is pledged to investors, and the project continues only in the case of date-1 success. The three conditions say that if the entrepreneur is rewarded R_{b}^{*} in the case of date-2 success, then

- $R_{\mathrm{b}}^{*} \geqslant B/\Delta p$: her date-2 incentive compatibility constraint is satisfied;
- $p_{\mathrm{H}}(R - R_{\mathrm{b}}^{*}) > L$: interference reduces the investors' income; and
- $(p_{\mathrm{H}}^{1} - p_{\mathrm{L}}^{1})[p_{\mathrm{H}}R_{\mathrm{b}}^{*}] \geqslant B_0$: the entrepreneur's date-1 incentive compatibility constraint is also satisfied.

(ii) From the definition of R_{b}^{*}, the project is financed, and from the three conditions, high efforts in both periods are guaranteed. Although there is an efficiency loss in terminating the project in the case of date-1 failure, this relaxes the date-1 incentive constraint and is optimal if p_{H}^{1} is large enough, that is, if the probability of interference is low enough.

The incentive scheme offered to the entrepreneur is that she is rewarded R_{b}^{*} if and only if she is successful in both periods; and the project is terminated if the date-1 income is equal to 0.

To implement this incentive scheme, the entrepreneur can issue two kinds of securities with different cash flow and control rights:

- short-term debt $d \in (0, \min\{L/p_{\mathrm{H}}, r\})$; debtholders receive control if d is not repaid at date 1; and
- long-term equities associated with control at time 1 if d is paid, and the following cash-flow rights: at date 1 equityholders receive the residual revenue ($r - d$ in the case of a date-1 success, and $\max\{0, L - d\}$ in the case of a date-1 failure); at date 2 they receive $R - R_{\mathrm{b}}^{*}$ in the case of success.

Debtholders interfere and terminate the project if there is no date-1 income, since

$$p_{\mathrm{H}}d < \min\{L, d\}.$$

Equityholders, when in control, do not interfere and so the project continues.

(iii) Suppose $R_{\mathrm{b}}^{*} = B/\Delta p$, and all three conditions still hold. Now if the entrepreneur is also paid

$r_b \in (0, r]$ in the case of date-1 success, the date-1 incentive constraint is relaxed:

$$(p_H^1 - p_L^1)[r_b + p_H R_b^*] \geqslant B_0.$$

But given that it is satisfied for $r_b = 0$, there is no benefit to boosting incentives in this way. Indeed, a positive r_b reduces the pledgeable income. The breakeven constraint of investors becomes more stringent:

$$I - A \leqslant p_H^1(r - r_b) + (1 - p_H^1)L + p_H^1[p_H(R - R_b^*)].$$

A positive r_b is not optimal as it makes the financing more difficult to arrange but has no incentive effect.

In general, a short-term bonus reduces the pledgeable income, while incentives are best provided by vesting the manager's compensation.

Exercise 10.2 (allocation of control and liquidation policy). (i) As usual, if financing is a binding constraint it is optimal to give 0 to the entrepreneur in the case of failure and to allocate the entire liquidation value L to investors in the case of liquidation. This increases the pledgeable income without perverse incentive effects or destruction of value. The entrepreneur maximizes her expected utility,

$$U_b = E_\omega[x(L, U_b^0)p_H R_b + [1 - x(L, U_b^0)]U_b^0],$$

subject to the incentive constraint,

$$(\Delta p)R_b \geqslant B,$$

and the investors' breakeven constraint,

$$E_\omega[x(L, U_b^0)p_H(R - R_b) + [1 - x(L, U_b^0)]L] \geqslant I - A.$$

The interesting case is when both the incentive and the participation constraints are binding. Let us rewrite the program as

$$\max E_\omega[x(L, U_b^0)(\rho_1 - \rho_0) + [1 - x(L, U_b^0)]U_b^0]$$

s.t.

$$E_\omega[x(L, U_b^0)\rho_0 + [1 - x(L, U_b^0)]L] = I - A.$$

Let $\mu \geqslant 1$ denote the multiplier of the participation constraint. We obtain

$$x^{SB}(\omega) = 1 \quad \text{if and only if } \rho_1 - U_b^0 \geqslant -(\mu - 1)\rho_0 + \mu L,$$

where "SB" stands for "second best."

As one would expect, continuation is less desirable when the liquidation value and the entrepreneur's alternative employment become more attractive (and, because of the difficulty of attracting

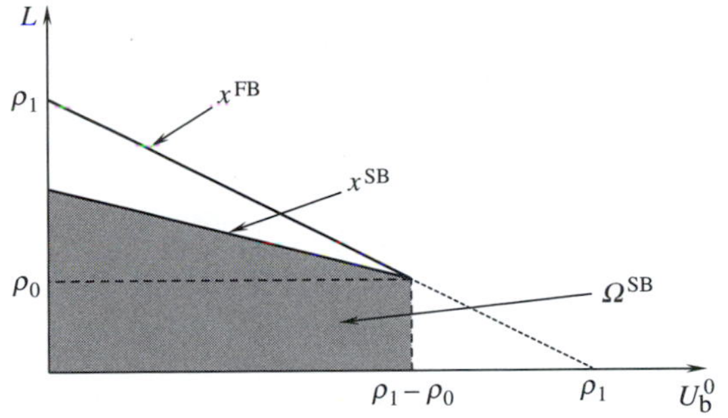

Figure 5

financing, the liquidation value receives a higher weight than the entrepreneur's fallback option).

(ii) The first-best continuation rule is given by

$$x^{FB}(\omega) = 1 \quad \text{if and only if } \rho_1 - U_b^0 \geqslant L$$

(that is, $\mu = 1$). Ω^{SB} is included in Ω^{FB}, as described in Figure 5. More generally, Ω^{SB} shrinks as A decreases (μ increases).

(To show this, note that for $L < \rho_0$, everyone prefers to continue. So the interesting region is $L > \rho_0$.)

(iii) When the entrepreneur has control, the entrepreneur can guarantee himself $\rho_1 - \rho_0$ by choosing to continue. Second, renegotiation always leads to the first-best efficient outcome:

(a) *Continuation is first-best efficient.* If the initial contract makes the entrepreneur want to continue in the absence of renegotiation, there is nothing to renegotiate about (a necessary condition for renegotiation is the existence of gains from trade). If the entrepreneur prefers to liquidate (because of the existence of a golden parachute), the investors will want to compensate the entrepreneur to induce him to continue (the split of the gains from renegotiation depend on the relative bargaining powers).

(b) *Liquidation is first-best efficient.* Again, if the entrepreneur prefers to liquidate in the absence of renegotiation there is nothing to renegotiate about. Otherwise, the investors will "bribe" the entrepreneur to liquidate.

So

$$\Omega^{EN} = \Omega^{FB}.$$

Compare the investors' return with the pledgeable income derived in question (i). In Ω^{SB} and outside

Ω^{FB}, the decision rule is unchanged, and the investors cannot get more than ρ_0 and L, respectively. In $\Omega^{FB} - \Omega^{SB}$, the investors get at most ρ_0, while they were getting $L > \rho_0$. Thus, the project cannot be financed.

(iv) Under investor control, and in the absence of a golden parachute,

$$x^{IN}(\omega) = 1 \quad \text{if and only if } \rho_0 \geqslant L.$$

If $\rho_0 < L$, then investors cannot get more than under liquidation (there is no way the entrepreneur can compensate them). If $\rho_0 > L$, but $p_H R_l < L$, then the entrepreneur can offer a reduction of her stake in the case of success (while keeping $R_b \geqslant B/\Delta p$).

The project is financed since the investors get the same amount as in (i), except when $L > \rho_0$ and $\omega \in \Omega^{SB}$ for which they get more (L instead of ρ_0).

(v) In the absence of renegotiation, the investors liquidate if and only if

$$L - r_b \geqslant \rho_0.$$

The policy is renegotiated (toward liquidation) if

$$(\rho_1 - \rho_0) - U_b^0 \leqslant L - \rho_0 < r_b.$$

In contrast, if

$$(\rho_1 - \rho_0) - U_b^0 > L - \rho_0 > r_b,$$

then there is no renegotiation and there is (inefficient relative to the first best) liquidation.

A *small* golden parachute increases the NPV while continuing to satisfy the financing constraint (an alternative would be to ask the investors to finance more than $I - A$ and let the entrepreneur save so as to be able to "bribe" the investors to induce continuation).

Exercise 10.3 (large minority blockholding). If $\xi < (\tau + \mu)s_2 R$, then the large shareholder and the uninformed (majority) investors have aligned interests. The majority shareholders therefore always follow the large shareholder's recommendation.

Let us therefore assume that $\xi > (\tau + \mu)s_2 R$. Let us look for an equilibrium in which the entrepreneur makes her suggestion "truthfully" (just announces her preferred modification). In state 2, the large shareholder seconds the entrepreneur's proposal. He makes a counterproposal in states 1 and 3.

The majority shareholders then go along with the joint proposal (in state 2). In the case of disagreement, the majority shareholders select the entrepreneur's proposal, that of the large shareholder, or the status quo so as to solve

$$\max\{-\beta\mu + \tau(1-\kappa), \beta\tau - \mu(1-\beta)(1-\kappa), 0\}.$$

Note that in the equilibrium under consideration both the entrepreneur and the minority blockholder have incentives to report their preferences truthfully (and that there are other equilibria where this is not the case).

Exercise 10.4 (monitoring by a large investor). Let

$$U_b(x) \equiv p_H R + [\xi + (1-\xi)x][\tau R - \gamma] - c_m(x) - I$$

denote the NPV (the NPV is equal to the borrower's utility because there is no scarcity of monitoring capital, and therefore no rent to be left to the monitor). Let

$$\mathcal{P}(x) \equiv [p_H + [\xi + (1-\xi)x]\tau]\left(R - \frac{B}{\Delta p}\right) - c_m(x)$$

denote the income that can be pledged to investors given that (a) the entrepreneur's stake must exceed $B/\Delta p$ in order to elicit good behavior, and (b) the monitor's expected income must compensate him for his monitoring cost. Concerning the last point, the monitor's reward R_m in the case of success and investment contribution I_m must satisfy the following breakeven and incentive conditions:

$$p_H R_m = I_m + c_m(x) \quad \text{and} \quad (1-\xi)\tau R_m = c_m'(x).$$

Note that

$$U_b(x) - \mathcal{P}(x) = [\xi + (1-\xi)x]\left(\tau\frac{B}{\Delta p} - \gamma\right) + \text{constant},$$

and so is decreasing in x.

If there is a shortage of pledgeable income, the optimal monitoring level given by (10.11) and maximizing the NPV,

$$c_m'(x^*) = (1-\xi)(\tau R - \gamma),$$

is no longer adequate. Indeed

$$U_b'(x^*) = 0 \quad \Longrightarrow \quad \mathcal{P}'(x^*) > 0.$$

Thus, the monitoring intensity must increase beyond x^*:

$$c_m'(x) > (1-\xi)(\tau R - \gamma).$$

If funding is feasible, then x is given by (the smallest value satisfying)

$$\mathcal{P}(x) = I - A.$$

Let $\hat{x}$ ($> x^*$) be defined by

$$c'_{\rm m}(\hat{x}) \equiv (1-\xi)\tau\Big(R - \frac{B}{\Delta p}\Big).$$

Because the pledgeable income no longer increases above $\hat{x}$, funding is feasible only if

$$\mathcal{P}(\hat{x}) \geqslant I - A.$$

Exercise 10.5 (when investor control makes financing more difficult to secure). (i) The incentive constraint is as usual

$$p_{\rm H}R_{\rm b} \geqslant p_{\rm L}R_{\rm b} + B, \qquad (1)$$

yielding pledgeable income

$$\mathcal{P}_1 \equiv p_{\rm H}\Big(R - \frac{B}{\Delta p}\Big).$$

The entrepreneur can receive funding if and only if

$$\mathcal{P}_1 \geqslant I - A.$$

(ii) Assume entrepreneur control. Either

$$\nu R_{\rm b} \leqslant \gamma,$$

and then the entrepreneur does not engage in damage control when shirking. The relevant incentive constraint remains (1), or

$$\nu R_{\rm b} > \gamma,$$

and the incentive constraint becomes

$$p_{\rm H}R_{\rm b} \geqslant (p_{\rm L} + \nu)R_{\rm b} + B - \gamma. \qquad (2)$$

If

$$\nu\Big(\frac{B}{\Delta p}\Big) \leqslant \gamma,$$

then the incentive constraint is unchanged when $R_{\rm b} = B/\Delta p$, and so the pledgeable income (the maximal income that can be pledged to investors while preserving incentive compatibility) is still $\mathcal{P}_1$.

(iii) Under investor control, the damage-control action is selected, and so the incentive constraint becomes

$$p_{\rm H}R_{\rm b} - \gamma \geqslant (p_{\rm L} + \nu)R_{\rm b} + B - \gamma \qquad (3)$$

or

$$(\Delta p - \nu)R_{\rm b} \geqslant B.$$

The new pledgeable income is

$$\mathcal{P}_2 = p_{\rm H}\Big(R - \frac{B}{\Delta p - \nu}\Big),$$

and is smaller than under entrepreneur control.

Exercise 10.6 (complementarity or substitutability between control and incentives). (i) As usual, this condition is

$$p_{\rm H}\Big(R - \frac{B}{\Delta p}\Big) \geqslant I - A.$$

(ii) Under *entrepreneur control*, the profit-enhancing action is not chosen in combination with the high effort since

$$(p_{\rm H} + \tau_{\rm H})R_{\rm b} - \gamma < p_{\rm H}R_{\rm b}$$

(since $\tau_{\rm H}R_{\rm b} < \tau_{\rm H}R < \gamma$).

Thus, to induce the high effort, $R_{\rm b}$ must satisfy $(\Delta p)R_{\rm b} \geqslant B$.

But then it is also optimal for the entrepreneur not to misbehave and choose the profit-enhancing action simultaneously:

$$\begin{aligned}(p_{\rm L} + \tau_{\rm L})R_{\rm b} + B - \gamma &\leqslant p_{\rm H}R_{\rm b} + \tau_{\rm L}R_{\rm b} - \gamma \\ &< p_{\rm H}R_{\rm b},\end{aligned}$$

since $R_{\rm b} < R$. The analysis is therefore the same as in (i).

Under *investor control*, it is a dominant strategy for the investors to select the profit-enhancing action. Hence, the manager's incentive constraint becomes

$$(p_{\rm H} + \tau_{\rm H})R_{\rm b} \geqslant (p_{\rm L} + \tau_{\rm L})R_{\rm b} + B$$

or

$$(\Delta p + \Delta\tau)R_{\rm b} \geqslant B.$$

The pledgeable income increases with investor control if and only if

$$(p_{\rm H} + \tau_{\rm H})\Big(R - \frac{B}{\Delta p + \Delta\tau}\Big) > p_{\rm H}\Big(R - \frac{B}{\Delta p}\Big).$$

This condition is necessarily satisfied if $\Delta\tau \geqslant 0$ (complementarity or separability). But it may fail if $\Delta\tau$ is sufficiently negative.

Exercise 10.7 (extent of control). The NPV is larger under limited investor control:

$$(p_{\rm H} + \tau_{\rm A})R - \gamma_{\rm A} > (p_{\rm H} + \tau_{\rm B})R - \gamma_{\rm B}.$$

We will assume that these NPVs are positive.

So the entrepreneur will grant limited control as long as this suffices to raise funds, i.e.,

$$(p_H + \tau_A)\left(R - \frac{B}{\Delta p}\right) \geqslant I - A.$$

If this condition is not satisfied, the entrepreneur must grant extended control in order to obtain financing. Financing is then feasible provided that

$$(p_H + \tau_B)\left(R - \frac{B}{\Delta p}\right) \geqslant I - A.$$

Lastly, note that

$$\tau_A R - \gamma_A \geqslant 0$$

is a sufficient condition for ruling out entrepreneurial control (but entrepreneurial control may be suboptimal even if this condition is not satisfied; for, it may conflict with the investors' breakeven condition).

Exercise 10.8 (uncertain managerial horizon and control rights). (i) The assumption

$$(p_H + \tau)\left(\frac{B}{\Delta p}\right) \geqslant \gamma$$

means that the new manager is willing to take on the job even if control is allocated to investors. Because his reward R_b must satisfy

$$(\Delta p)R_b \geqslant B,$$

regardless of who has control, the new manager receives rent

$$(p_H + \tau y)\left(\frac{B}{\Delta p}\right) - \gamma y$$

(smaller than the rent, $p_H B/\Delta p$, that he would receive if he were given control rights).

The entrepreneur's utility is (if the project is undertaken)

$$U_b = (1-\lambda)[(p_H + \tau x)R - \gamma x] + \lambda(p_H + \tau y)\left(R - \frac{B}{\Delta p}\right) - I.$$

The financing condition is

$$(1-\lambda)(p_H + \tau x)\left(R - \frac{B}{\Delta p}\right) + \lambda(p_H + \tau y)\left(R - \frac{B}{\Delta p}\right) \geqslant I - A.$$

(ii) Clearly, $y = 1$ both maximizes U_b and facilitates financing.

Also, a necessary condition for U_b to be positive is that λ not be too big.

Letting $\rho_0 \equiv p_H[R - B/\Delta p]$, if financing is feasible for $x = 0$: $(1-\lambda)\rho_0 + \lambda\rho_0^+ \geqslant I - A$, then $x = 0$ is optimal. The entrepreneur invests if and only if $U_b \geqslant 0$, or

$$(1-\lambda)\rho_1 + \lambda\rho_0^+ \geqslant I.$$

If $(1-\lambda)\rho_0 + \lambda\rho_0^+ < I - A$, then, in order to obtain financing, the entrepreneur must set x in the following way:

$$(1-\lambda)\rho_0 + \lambda\rho_0^+ + \tau x\left(R - \frac{B}{\Delta p}\right) = I - A.$$

Financing then occurs if and only if $U_b \geqslant 0$ for this value of x.

Exercise 10.9 (continuum of control rights). (i) Let R_b denote the entrepreneur's reward in the case of success. The entrepreneur maximizes her utility, which is equal to the NPV,

$$\max_{\{x(\cdot,\cdot)\}} \{[p_H + E_F[tx(t,g)]]R - I - E_F[gx(t,g)]\},$$

subject to the constraint that investors break even,

$$[p_H + E_F[tx(t,g)]][R - R_b] \geqslant I - A,$$

and to the incentive compatibility constraint,

$$(\Delta p)R_b \geqslant B.$$

Clearly, $R_b = B/\Delta p$ if the investors' breakeven constraint is binding. Let μ denote the shadow price of this constraint. Writing the Lagrangian and taking the derivative with respect to $x(t,g)$ for all t and g yields

$$x(t,g) = 1 \iff tR - g + \mu\left[t\left(R - \frac{B}{\Delta p}\right)\right] \geqslant 0.$$

This defines a straight line through the origin in the (t,g)-space under which $x = 1$ and over which $x = 0$.

(ii) When A decreases, more pledgeable income must be harnessed. So the straight line must rotate counterclockwise (add $t > 0$ realizations and subtract $t < 0$ ones). In the process, both τ and γ increase.

(iii) If $x(t,g) = 1$ and $t > 0$, the control right can be given to investors. If $x(t,g) = 1$ and $t < 0$ (which implies $g < 0$: the decision yields a private benefit to the entrepreneur), then the control can be allocated to the entrepreneur. Because

$$|g| > |t|R > |t|R_b,$$

the entrepreneur chooses $x(t,g) = 1$. Furthermore, $x(t,g) = 1$ is not renegotiated since it is first-best efficient.

One proceeds similarly for $x(t,g) = 0$.

(iv) Assume that g is the same for all rights and is positive. The optimal rule becomes

$$t \geqslant t^* = \frac{g}{R + \mu(R - B/\Delta p)}.$$

Let $H(t)$ denote the cumulative distribution function over t:

$$\gamma \equiv g[1 - H(t^*)],$$

$$\tau \equiv \int_{t^*}^{\infty} t\,\mathrm{d}H(t).$$

Hence,

$$\frac{\mathrm{d}\gamma}{\mathrm{d}\tau} = \frac{g}{t^*} \quad \text{and} \quad \frac{\mathrm{d}^2\gamma}{\mathrm{d}\tau^2} > 0.$$

One can, as earlier, envision that τ increases as A decreases, for example.

Exercise 12.1 (Diamond–Dybvig model in continuous time). To provide consumption $c(t)$ to consumers whose liquidity need arises between t and $t + \mathrm{d}t$ (in number $f(t)\,\mathrm{d}t$), one must cut $x(t)\,\mathrm{d}t$, where

$$x(t)R(t)\,\mathrm{d}t = c(t)f(t)\,\mathrm{d}t.$$

Together with the fact that the total number of trees per representative depositor is 1, this implies that the first-best contract solves

$$\max\left\{\int_0^1 u(c(t))f(t)\,\mathrm{d}t\right\}$$

s.t.

$$\int_0^1 \frac{c(t)}{R(t)} f(t)\,\mathrm{d}t \leqslant 1.$$

The first-order condition is then, for each t,

$$\left[u'(c(t)) - \frac{\mu}{R(t)}\right] f(t) = 0,$$

where μ is the shadow price of the constraint.

(ii) Take the (log-) derivative of the first-order condition:

$$u'(c(t))R(t) = \mu \implies c\frac{u''}{u'}\frac{\dot{c}}{c} + \frac{\dot{R}}{R} = 0.$$

Because the coefficient of relative risk aversion exceeds 1,

$$\frac{\dot{c}}{c} < \frac{\dot{R}}{R}.$$

Note that, from the constraint, the average c/R is equal to 1. The existence of t^* follows (drawing a diagram may help build intuition).

(iii) Suppose that a depositor who has not yet suffered a liquidity shock withdraws at date τ. Reinvesting in the technology, she will obtain $c(\tau)R(t - \tau)$ if the actual date of the liquidity shock is $t > \tau$. Withdrawing is a "dominant strategy" (that is, yields more regardless of the future events) if

$$c(\tau)R(t - \tau) > c(t) \quad \text{for all } t > \tau.$$

The log-derivative of $(c(\tau)R(t - \tau)/c(t))$ with respect to t is, for τ close to 0,

$$\frac{\dot{R}(t-\tau)}{R(t-\tau)} - \frac{\dot{c}(t)}{c(t)} \simeq \frac{\dot{R}(t)}{R(t)} - \frac{\dot{c}(t)}{c(t)} > 0.$$

We thus conclude that the first-best outcome is not incentive compatible.

Exercise 12.2 (Allen and Gale (1998)[13] on fundamentals-based panics). (i) Let i_1 and i_2 denote the investments in the short- and long-term technologies. The social optimum solves

$$\max E[\lambda u(c_1(R)) + (1 - \lambda)u(c_2(R))]$$

s.t.

$$\lambda c_1(R) \leqslant i_1,$$

$$(1 - \lambda)c_2(R) \leqslant (i_1 - \lambda c_1(R)) + Ri_2,$$

$$i_1 + i_2 = 1.$$

This yields

(a) $c_1(R) = c_2(R) = i_1 + Ri_2$

$$\text{for } R \leqslant \frac{(1-\lambda)i_1}{\lambda i_2} = R^*,$$

(b) $c_1(R) = c_1(R^*)$,

and

$$c_2(R) = \frac{Ri_2}{1-\lambda} \geqslant c_1(R) \quad \text{for } R \geqslant R^*.$$

For low long-term payoffs, $\lambda c_1(R) < i_1$ and the impatient types share risk with the patient types, as their short-term investment can be rolled over to

13. Allen, F. and D. Gale. 1998. Optimal financial crises. *Journal of Finance* 53:1245–1283.

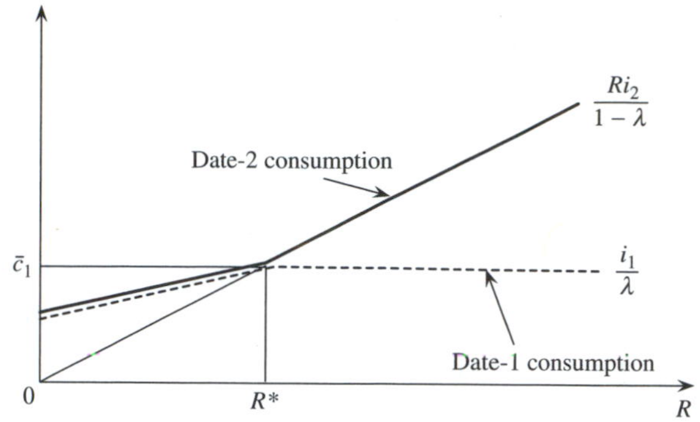

Figure 6

give some income to the latter. In contrast, high long-term payoffs (for which $\lambda c_1(R) = i_1$) are enjoyed solely by the patient types, who have no means of sharing the manna from heaven with the impatient types.

The optimal allocation is depicted in the Figure 6.

(ii) Let

$$\bar{c}_1 \equiv \frac{i_1}{\lambda}.$$

Suppose that the deposit contract promises

$$\min\{\bar{c}_1, i_1/(\lambda + (1-\lambda)x)\}$$

and that a fraction $x(R)$ of the patient depositors withdraw at date 1. For $R \leqslant R^*$, we claim that the following equations characterize the equilibrium:

$$[\lambda + (1-\lambda)x(R)]c_1 = i_1,$$

$$\frac{Ri_2}{(1-\lambda)(1-x(R))} = c_2,$$

$$c_1 = c_2.$$

First, note that, for $R > 0$, $x(R) = 1$ is not an equilibrium behavior, as patient consumers could consume an infinite amount by not withdrawing. Similarly, for $R < R^*$, $x(R) = 0$ is not part of an equilibrium because $Ri_2/(1-\lambda)$ is smaller than i_1/λ. Hence, a fraction in $(0,1)$ of patient consumers must withdraw at date 1. This implies that patient consumers are indifferent between withdrawing and consuming, or

$$c_1 = c_2.$$

Exercise 12.4 (random withdrawal rate). (i) This follows along standard lines. Asset maturities should match those of consumptions, $\lambda c_1 = i_1$ and $(1-\lambda)c_2 = i_2 R$:

$$\max_{c_1}\left\{\lambda u(c_1) + (1-\lambda)u\left(\frac{1-\lambda c_1}{1-\lambda}R\right)\right\}$$

implies

$$u'(c_1) = Ru'(c_2).$$

For CRRA utility, $c_1/c_2 = R^{-1/\gamma}$. So i_1 grows and i_2 decreases as risk aversion (γ) increases.

(ii) The optimal program solves

$$\max_{\{i_1,i_2,y.,z.\}}\left\{\beta\left[\lambda_L u\left(\frac{i_1 y_L + i_2 z_L \ell}{\lambda_L}\right) + (1-\lambda_L)u\left(\frac{i_1(1-y_L) + i_2 R(1-z_L)}{1-\lambda_L}\right)\right] + (1-\beta)\left[\lambda_H u\left(\frac{i_1 y_H + i_2 z_H \ell}{\lambda_H}\right) + (1-\lambda_H)u\left(\frac{i_1(1-y_H) + i_2 R(1-z_H)}{1-\lambda_H}\right)\right]\right\}.$$

Clearly, $z_\omega > 0 \Rightarrow y_\omega = 1$ and $y_\omega < 1 \Rightarrow z_\omega = 0$.

Also, $y_L = 1$ implies $y_H = 1$, and $z_H = 0$ implies $z_L = 0$.

For $\ell = 0$, the optimum has $z_\omega = 0$. It may be optimal to roll over some of i_1 in state L. For ℓ close to 1, i_2 serves to finance date-1 consumption in state H.

Exercise 13.1 (improved governance). (i) The pledgeable income is $p_H(R - B/\Delta p)$. The financing constraint is

$$(1+r)(I-A) \leqslant p_H\left(R - \frac{B}{\Delta p}\right).$$

(ii) The cutoff A^* is given by

$$(1+r)(I-A^*) = p_H\left(R - \frac{B}{\Delta p}\right).$$

Market equilibrium:

$$\left[S(r) + \int_0^{A^*(r)} Ag(A)\,dA\right] = \int_{A^*(r)}^{I} (I-A)g(A)\,dA$$

or, equivalently,

$$S(r) + \int_0^I Ag(A)\,dA = [1 - G(A^*(r))]I.$$

(Note that entrepreneurs with weak balance sheets, $A < A^*$, would demand a zero rate of interest from their preferences. However, they receive the equilibrium market rate.)

Because A^* increases with the interest rate and with the quality of investor protection (here, $-B$), an increase in investor protection raises the equilibrium interest rate.

Exercise 13.2 (dynamics of income inequality). (i) See Section 13.3:

$$U_t(y_t) = y_t.$$

(ii) The incentive constraint is

$$(\Delta p)R_b^t \geqslant BI_t,$$

and so the pledgeable income is

$$p_H\left(R - \frac{B}{\Delta p}\right)I_t = \rho_0 I_t,$$

yielding an investment level given by

$$\rho_0 I_t = (1+r)(I_t - A_t) \quad \text{or} \quad I = \frac{A_t}{1 - \rho_0/(1+r)}.$$

A project's NPV is

$$[p_H R - (1+r)]I_t = [\rho_1 - (1+r)]I_t.$$

By assumption, $\rho_1 \geqslant 1 + r$, and so entrepreneurs prefer to invest in a project rather than lending their assets. Income is

$$y_t = [\rho_1 - \rho_0]I_t,$$

and so

$$A_{t+1} = a\frac{\rho_1 - \rho_0}{1 - \rho_0/(1+r)}A_t + \hat{A},$$

which converges to A_∞ as t tends to ∞.

(iii) The threshold is given by

$$\frac{A_0^*}{1 - \rho_0/(1+r)} = \underline{I}.$$

The limit wealth of poor dynasties is the limit point of the following first-order difference equation:

$$A_{t+1} = a(1+r)A_t + \hat{A}$$

or

$$A_\infty^{\mathrm{L}} = \frac{\hat{A}}{1 - a(1+r)}.$$

(iv) • If $\rho_1 = 1 + r$, individuals are indifferent between being investors and becoming entrepreneurs. Note that wealths are equalized at

$$A_\infty = \frac{\hat{A}}{1 - a\rho_1},$$

corresponding to investment

$$I_\infty = \frac{A_\infty}{1 - \rho_0/(1+r)} = \frac{\rho_1 \hat{A}}{(1 - a\rho_1)(\rho_1 - \rho_0)}.$$

Equilibrium in the loan market requires that

$$\kappa A_\infty = (1-\kappa)(I_\infty - A_\infty)$$

or

$$\kappa(\rho_1 - \rho_0) = (1-\kappa)\rho_0.$$

• If $\rho_1 > (1+r)$, then lenders must be unable to become entrepreneurs and so have wealth A_∞^{L}. Thus

$$\kappa A_\infty^{\mathrm{L}} = (1-\kappa)(I_\infty - A_\infty),$$

where I_∞ was derived in question (ii).

Exercise 13.3 (impact of market conditions with and without credit rationing). (i) The representative entrepreneur's project has NPV (equal to the entrepreneur's utility)

$$U_b = p_H PR(I) - I - K,$$

and the scale of investment I can be financed as long as the pledgeable income exceeds the investors' initial outlay:

$$\mathcal{P}(I) \equiv p_H\left[PR(I) - \frac{BI}{\Delta p}\right] \geqslant I + K - A$$

(this is the financing condition).

In the absence of any financing constraint (i.e., when $B = 0$), the representative entrepreneur would choose a first-best (FB) policy:

$$p_H PR'(I^{\mathrm{FB}}) = 1 \quad \text{or} \quad p_H P\alpha(I^{\mathrm{FB}})^{\alpha-1} = 1,$$

provided that the fixed cost K is not too large, i.e., $K \leqslant p_H PR(I^{\mathrm{FB}}) - I^{\mathrm{FB}}$. (Otherwise, the optimal investment is equal to 0.)

When does the financing constraint bind?

Simple computations show that

$$\mathcal{P}(I^{\mathrm{FB}}) - I^{\mathrm{FB}} = (1-\alpha)\left[\frac{1}{\alpha} - \frac{p_H B/\Delta p}{1-\alpha}\right]I^{\mathrm{FB}}.$$

Let us assume that the agency cost is not too large:

$$\frac{p_H B}{\Delta p} < \frac{1-\alpha}{\alpha}$$

(otherwise the financing constraint is necessarily binding).

Because I^{FB} is increasing in the product price P, the financing constraint is binding for low prices, as illustrated in Figure 7, where I^{SB} denotes the solution to the financing condition (taken with equality).

(ii) Thus, there is at least some region (to the left of P_0 in the figure) in which the expansionary impact of the product price (the contractionary impact of past investment) is stronger in the presence of credit rationing, i.e., when the presence of B makes the financing condition binding.

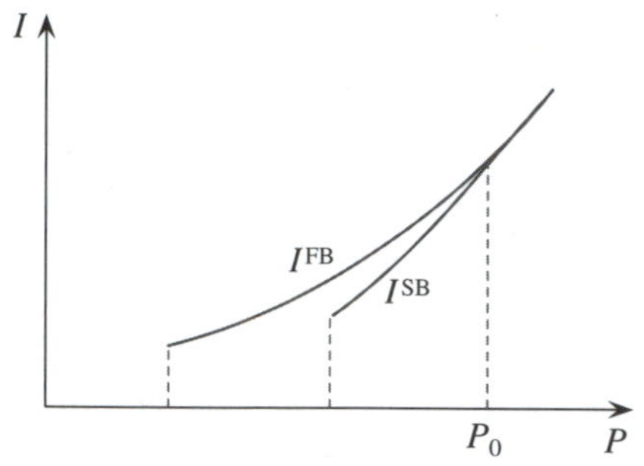

Figure 7

(iii) To conclude this brief analysis, we can now endogenize the product price by assuming the existence of a prior investment I_0 by, say, a mass 1 of the previous generation of entrepreneurs. Then, P is a decreasing function of total effective investment, i.e., total output:

$$P = P(p_H[R(I) + R(I_0)]), \quad \text{with } P' < 0.$$

When I_0 increases, I must decrease (if I increases, then P decreases, and so I decreases after all): this is the crowding-out effect; furthermore, total output must increase (if it decreased, then P would increase and so would I; and thus $p_H[R(I) + R(I_0)]$ would increase after all).

Exercise 14.2 (alternative distributions of bargaining power in the Shleifer–Vishny model). Entrepreneur i's utility (or, equivalently, firm i's NPV) is

$$\begin{aligned} U_{bi} &= [x\rho_1 + (1-x)(1-\nu)P - 1]I_i \\ &\quad + x(1-\mu)[(\rho_1 - \rho_0) + (\rho_0 - P)]I_j \\ &\equiv \hat{\alpha} I_i + \hat{\kappa} I_j, \end{aligned}$$

where

$$\hat{\alpha} = \alpha - (1-x)(1-\nu)(\rho_0 - P)$$

and

$$\hat{\kappa} = \kappa + x(1-\mu)(\rho_0 - P).$$

Recalling that $(1-x)(1-\nu) = x(1-\mu)$, note that $\hat{\alpha} + \hat{\kappa} = \alpha + \kappa$, as it should be from the fact that a change in bargaining power induces a mere redistribution of wealth for given investments.

Firm i's borrowing capacity is now given by

$$\begin{aligned} &[x\rho_0 + (1-x)(1-\nu)P]I_i \\ &\quad + x(1-\mu)(\rho_0 - P)I_j = I_i - A_i \end{aligned}$$

or

$$I_i = \frac{A_i + x(1-\mu)(\rho_0 - P)I_j}{\begin{array}{r} 1 + (1-x)(1-\nu)(\rho_0 - P) \\ -\rho_0[x + (1-x)(1-\nu)] \end{array}}.$$

In *symmetric* equilibrium ($A_1 = A_2 = A$; $I_1 = I_2 = I$),

$$I = \frac{A}{1 - \rho_0[x + (1-x)(1-\nu)]}$$

is independent of P.

Exercise 14.3 (liquidity management and acquisitions). (i) Suppose that the acquirer expects price demand P for the assets when the risky firm is in distress (which has probability $1-x$). The NPV for a given cutoff ρ^* is given by

$$U_b^s = (\rho_1 - 1)I + (1-x)J\int_0^{\rho^*} [\rho_1 - (P + \rho)]\,dF(\rho).$$

The borrowing capacity in turn is given by

$$\rho_0 I + (1-x)J\int_0^{\rho^*} [\rho_0 - (P+\rho)]\,dF(\rho) = I - A.$$

And so

$$\begin{aligned} U_b^s &= (\rho_1 - 1)\frac{A - (1-x)J\int_0^{\rho^*}[(P+\rho) - \rho_0]\,dF(\rho)}{1-\rho_0} \\ &\quad + (1-x)J\int_0^{\rho^*} [\rho_1 - (P+\rho)]\,dF(\rho). \end{aligned}$$

Maximizing with respect to ρ^* and simplifying yields

$$\rho^* = 1 - P.$$

And so

$$\rho_0 + L^* = P + \rho^* = 1.$$

(ii) Anticipating that the safe firm has extra liquidity L^*, the seller chooses price P so as to solve

$$\max_P \{F(\rho_0 + L^* - P)P\},$$

since the acquirer can raise funds only when $P + \rho \leqslant \rho_0 + L^*$.

The derivative of this objective function is

$$-f(\rho^*)P + F(\rho^*) = -f(1-P)P + F(1-P).$$

Note that this derivative is positive at $P = 0$ and negative at $P = 1$. Furthermore, $-P + F(1-P)/f(1-P)$ is a decreasing function of P from the monotone hazard rate condition and so the equilibrium price is unique and belongs to $(0, 1)$.

Suppose next that L increases for some reason (and that this is observed by the seller). The first-order condition then becomes

$$-P + \frac{F(\rho_0 + L - P)}{f(\rho_0 + L - P)} = 0$$

and so

$$-\left[1 + \left(\frac{F}{f}\right)'\right]\frac{\mathrm{d}P}{\mathrm{d}L} + \left(\frac{F}{f}\right)' = 0.$$

Because $(F/f)' > 0$,

$$0 < \frac{\mathrm{d}P}{\mathrm{d}L} < 1.$$

This implies that the cutoff, and thus the probability of a sale, increases despite the price adjustment.

(iii) Suppose that the distribution F converges to a spike at $\bar{\rho}$. Consider thus a sequence $F_n(\rho)$ with

$$\lim_{n\to\infty} F_n(\rho) = 0 \quad \text{for } \rho < \bar{\rho}$$

and

$$\lim_{n\to\infty} F_n(\rho) = 1 \quad \text{for } \rho > \bar{\rho}.$$

Let us give an informal proof of the result stated in (iii) of the question. Choosing a price P that triggers a cutoff that is smaller than $\bar{\rho}$ and does *not* converge with n to $\bar{\rho}$ would yield (almost) zero profit, and so choosing an alternative price that leads to a cutoff a bit above $\bar{\rho}$ would yield a higher profit. Conversely, if the cutoff is above $\bar{\rho}$ and does *not* converge to $\bar{\rho}$, then $Pf_n \simeq 0$ and $F_n \simeq 1$, and so the first-order condition is not satisfied. (This proof is loose. A proper proof must consider a subsequence having the former or latter property.)

Exercise 14.4 (inefficiently low volume of asset reallocations). At the optimum, firm 1's assets are resold in the secondary market if and only if

$$\rho_0 < \rho_0^*.$$

Furthermore, it is optimal for the contract to specify that the proceeds from the sale to firm 2 go to the investors in firm 1 (so as to maximize the pledgeable income). And so the investment I is given by the investors' breakeven constraint:

$$\left[F(\rho_0^*)\hat{\rho}_0 + \int_{\rho_0^*}^{\bar{\rho}_0} \rho_0 \, \mathrm{d}F(\rho_0)\right] I = I - A,$$

which yields

$$I = I(\rho_0^*).$$

The entrepreneur's utility is

$$\begin{aligned} U_\mathrm{b} &= \mathrm{NPV} \\ &= \left[F(\rho_0^*)\hat{\rho}_0 + \int_{\rho_0^*}^{\bar{\rho}_0} (\rho_0 + \Delta\rho)\, \mathrm{d}F(\rho_0)\right] I(\rho_0^*). \end{aligned}$$

The optimal cutoff maximizes U_b and satisfies

$$\hat{\rho}_0 - \Delta\rho < \rho_0^* < \hat{\rho}_0.$$

Exercise 15.1 (downsizing and aggregate liquidity). (i) The incentive constraint is

$$(\Delta p) R_\mathrm{b}^0 \geqslant BI$$

in the case of no shock, and

$$(\Delta p) R_\mathrm{b}^\rho \geqslant BJ$$

in the presence of a liquidity shock.

So the pledgeable incomes are $p_\mathrm{H}(R(I) - BI/\Delta p)$ and $p_\mathrm{H}(R(J) - BJ/\Delta p)$, respectively.

The investors' breakeven constraint is

$$(1-\lambda) p_\mathrm{H}\left[R(I) - \frac{BI}{\Delta p}\right] + \lambda\left[p_\mathrm{H}\left[R(J) - \frac{BJ}{\Delta p}\right] - \rho J\right] \geqslant I - A. \quad (1)$$

The entrepreneur's utility is equal to the NPV:

$$U_\mathrm{b} = (1-\lambda) p_\mathrm{H} R(I) + \lambda[p_\mathrm{H} R(J) - \rho J] - I. \quad (2)$$

Let μ denote the shadow price of constraint (1). Maximizing U_b subject to (1) (and ignoring the constraint $J \leqslant I$) yields first-order conditions with respect to I and J:

$$[(1-\lambda) p_\mathrm{H} R'(I) - 1][1+\mu] - \mu(1-\lambda) p_\mathrm{H} \frac{B}{\Delta p} = 0$$

or

$$p_\mathrm{H} R'(I) = \frac{1}{1-\lambda} + \frac{\mu}{1+\mu} p_\mathrm{H} \frac{B}{\Delta p}, \quad (3)$$

and

$$\lambda[p_\mathrm{H} R'(J) - \rho][1+\mu] - \lambda\mu p_\mathrm{H} \frac{B}{\Delta p} = 0$$

or

$$p_\mathrm{H} R'(J) \equiv \rho + \frac{\mu}{1+\mu} p_\mathrm{H} \frac{B}{\Delta p}. \quad (4)$$

Comparing (3) and (4), one observes that ignoring the constraint $J \leqslant I$ is justified if and only if

$$\rho > \frac{1}{1-\lambda},$$

that is, when the cost of continuation in the state of nature with a liquidity shock exceeds the cost of one more unit of investment in the state without. This simple comparison comes from the fact that the per-unit agency cost is the same in both states of nature. Let (I^*, J^*) denote the solution (obtained from (1), (3), and (4)).

(ii) • Under perfect correlation, no inside liquidity is available. So, in order to continue in the case of a liquidity shock, each firm requires

$$L = \rho J^*.$$

Hence, $L^* = \rho J^*$.

• If $L < L^*$, then

$$J = \frac{L}{\rho} < J^*. \tag{5}$$

• The solution is obtained by solving the modified program in which the extra cost associated with the liquidity premium, $(q-1)\rho J$, is subtracted in U_b (in (2)), and added to the right-hand side of (1), yielding a modified investor breakeven constraint—let us call it (1′). Equation (3) is unchanged, while (4) becomes

$$p_H R'(J) = \rho\left(1 + \frac{q-1}{\lambda}\right) + \frac{\mu}{1+\mu} p_H \frac{B}{\Delta p}. \tag{4'}$$

So $J < I$ *a fortiori*.

The liquidity premium is obtained by solving (1′), (3), (4′), and (5).

(iii) • Under independent shocks, exactly a fraction λ of firms incur no shock. Assuming $q = 1$ for the moment, (1) yields (provided $I > A$)

$$V = (1-\lambda)p_H\left[R(I) - \frac{BI}{\Delta p}\right] + \lambda p_H\left[R(J) - \frac{BJ}{\Delta p}\right]$$
$$> \lambda\rho J. \tag{6}$$

V is the value of the stock index after the shocks have been met. And so the corporate sector, as a whole, can by issuing new claims raise enough cash to meet average shock $\lambda\rho J$. So there is, in principle, no need for outside liquidity.

• This, however, assumes that liquidity is not wasted. If each entrepreneur holds the stock index, then, when facing a liquidity shock, the entrepreneur can raise $p_H[R(J) - BJ/\Delta p]$ by issuing new claims on the firm.

Meeting the liquidity shock then requires that

$$p_H\left[R(J) - \frac{BJ}{\Delta p}\right] + [V - \lambda\rho J] \geqslant \rho J$$

or

$$(1-\lambda)p_H\left[R(I) - \frac{BI}{\Delta p}\right] \geqslant (1+\lambda)\left[\rho J - p_H\left[R(J) - \frac{BJ}{\Delta p}\right]\right],$$

which is not guaranteed.

It is then optimal to pool the liquidity, for example, through a credit line mechanism.

Exercise 15.2 (news about prospects and aggregate liquidity).

(i) $$\text{NPV} = \int_{y^*}^{1} y\,dG(y) - [1 - G(y^*)]J - I.$$

Investors' net income

$$= \int_{y^*}^{1} y\,dG(y) - [1 - G(y^*)][J + \mathcal{R}] - [I - A].$$

(ii) • The NPV is maximized for $y^* = y_0^* = J$. So, if

$$\int_J^1 y\,dG(y) - [1 - G(J)][J + \mathcal{R}] \geqslant I - A \iff A \geqslant A_0^*,$$

then $y^* = J$.

Otherwise, by concavity of the NPV, the contract raises y^* so as to attract investment:

$$\int_{y^*}^{1} y\,dG(y) - [1 - G(y^*)][J + \mathcal{R}] = I - A.$$

The pledgeable income can no longer be increased when $y^* = y_1^* = J + \mathcal{R}$.

So, for $A < A_1^*$, no financing is feasible.

• If $A > A_1^*$, then $y^* < J + \mathcal{R}$. Hence, for $y^* \leqslant y < J + \mathcal{R}$, investors have negative profit from continuation, and the firm cannot obtain financing just by going back to the capital market.

(iii) If productivities are drawn independently, the financing constraint,

$$\int_{y^*}^{1} y\,dG(y) - [1 - G(y^*)][J + \mathcal{R}] = I - A,$$

implies

$$\int_{y^*}^{1} y\,dG(y) - [1 - G(y^*)][J + \mathcal{R}] > 0,$$

and so, *collectively*, firms have enough income to pledge when going back to the capital market.

(iv) • Suppose, in a first step, that there exists a large enough quantity of stores of value, and so

$q = 1$ (there is no liquidity premium). Then the breakeven condition can be written as

$$E_\theta\left[\int_{y^*(\theta)}^1 (y - J - \mathcal{R})\,\mathrm{d}G(y \mid \theta)\right] \geqslant I - A.$$

- Maximize

$$E_\theta\left[\int_{y^*(\theta)}^1 (y - J)\,\mathrm{d}G(y \mid \theta)\right] - I$$

subject to the financing constraint (let μ denote the multiplier of the latter). Then

$$y^*(\theta) - J + \mu[y^*(\theta) - J - \mathcal{R}] = 0$$
$$\Longrightarrow\ y^*(\theta) = J + \frac{\mu}{1+\mu}\mathcal{R}.$$

- The lowest amount of pledgeable income,

$$\min_{\{\theta\}} \int_{y^*}^1 (y - J - \mathcal{R})\,\mathrm{d}G(y \mid \theta),$$

may be negative. It must then be complemented by an equal number of stores of value delivering one for certain, say.

- If there are not enough stores of value, then they trade at a premium ($q > 1$).

Exercise 15.3 (imperfectly correlated shocks). A shortage of liquidity may occur only if the fraction θ of correlated firms faces the high shock (the reader can follow the steps of Section 15.2.1 to show that in the other aggregate state there is no liquidity shortage).

The liquidity need is then, in aggregate,

$$[\theta + (1-\theta)\lambda](\rho_H - \rho_0)I.$$

The net value of shares in the healthy firms is

$$(1-\theta)(1-\lambda)(\rho_0 - \rho_L)I.$$

Using the investors' breakeven condition and the assumption that liquidity bears no premium:

$$[(1-\lambda)(\rho_0 - \rho_L) - \lambda(\rho_H - \rho_0)]I = I - A.$$

And so the corporate sector is self-sufficient if

$$(1-\theta)(1-\lambda)(\rho_0 - \rho_L)I \geqslant [\theta + (1-\theta)\lambda](\rho_H - \rho_0)I$$

or

$$(1-\theta)(I - A) \geqslant \theta(\rho_H - \rho_0)I.$$

Exercise 15.4 (complementarity between liquid and illiquid assets). The NPV per unit of investment is equal to

$$(1 - \lambda + \lambda x)\rho_1$$
$$- [1 + (1-\lambda)\rho_L + [\lambda\rho_H + (q-1)(\rho_H - \rho_0)]x].$$

We know that this NPV is negative for $x = 0$. Thus, either its derivative with respect to x is nonpositive,

$$\lambda\rho_1 \leqslant \lambda\rho_H + (q-1)(\rho_H - \rho_0),$$

and then there is no investment ($I = 0$). The absence of corporate investment implies that there is no corporate demand for liquidity, and so $q = 1$, which contradicts the fact that $\rho_1 > \rho_H$. Hence, the derivative with respect to x must be strictly positive:

$$\lambda\rho_1 > \lambda\rho_H + (q-1)(\rho_H - \rho_0),$$

implying that $x = 1$.

For a low supply of liquid assets, this in turn implies that

(a) investment is limited by the amount of liquid assets,

$$L^S = (\rho_H - \rho_0)I;$$

(b) the entrepreneurs compete away the benefits associated with owning liquid assets, and so they are indifferent between investing in illiquid and liquid assets and not investing at all,

$$\rho_1 = 1 + \bar{\rho} + (\bar{\bar{q}} - 1)(\rho_H - \rho_0).$$

Furthermore, for a low supply of liquid assets, entrepreneurs do not borrow as much as their borrowing capacity would allow them to. This borrowing capacity, denoted $\bar{I}$, is given by

$$\rho_0\bar{I} = [1 + \bar{\rho} + (\bar{\bar{q}} - 1)(\rho_H - \rho_0)]\bar{I} - A$$
$$= \rho_1\bar{I} - A.$$

When L^S reaches $\underline{L}^S$, given by

$$\underline{L}^S \equiv \frac{\rho_H - \rho_0}{\rho_1 - \rho_0}A,$$

then $I = \bar{I}$. For $L^S > \underline{L}^S$, q decreases with L^S and investment,

$$I = \frac{A}{1 + \bar{\rho} + (q-1)(\rho_H - \rho_0) - \rho_0} = \frac{L^S}{\rho_H - \rho_0},$$

increases until $L^S = \bar{L}^S$ (i.e., $q = 1$), after which it is no longer affected by the supply of liquid assets.

Exercise 16.1 (borrowing abroad). (i) Investing abroad is inefficient since $\mu < 1$. So it is optimal to prevent investment abroad. Letting R_l denote the return to investors in the case of success, the incentive compatibility constraint is

$$p(RI - R_l) \geqslant \mu I.$$

The breakeven constraint is

$$pR_l = I - A.$$

The NPV,

$$U_b = (pR - 1)I,$$

is maximized when I is maximized subject to the incentive compatibility and breakeven constraints, and so

$$I = \frac{A}{1 - (pR - \mu)}, \quad \text{and so } U_b = \frac{pR - 1}{1 - (pR - \mu)} A.$$

This is a reinterpretation of the basic model with

$$p_H = p, \quad p_L = 0, \quad B = \mu.$$

Investing abroad brings the probability of success of the domestic investment down to 0. And because investors are unable to grab any of the diverted funds, their proceeds are but a private benefit for the entrepreneur.

(ii) One has

$$p[(1 - \tau)RI - R_l] \geqslant \mu I$$

and

$$pR_l + (1 - p)\sigma R_l = I - A.$$

The government's breakeven constraint is

$$p\tau RI = (1 - p)\sigma R_l.$$

The borrowing capacity is unchanged, because the pledgeable income is unaffected.

In contrast, when public debt D (per entrepreneur) is financed through corporate taxes,

$$p\tau RI = D,$$

then

$$I = \frac{A - D}{1 - (pR - \mu)}$$

and

$$U_b = \frac{pR - 1}{1 - (pR - \mu)}(A - D).$$

(iii) In the case of government commitment, $\mu = \mu_L$ maximizes U_b. In the absence of commitment, suppose that investors expect $\mu = \mu_L$. Then the entrepreneurs receive

$$p(RI - R_l) = \mu_L I \quad \text{if } \mu = \mu_L$$

and

$$\max(p(RI - R_l), \mu_H I) = \mu_H I \quad \text{if } \mu = \mu_H.$$

Hence, $\mu = \mu_H$. And U_b is decreased.

(iv) The exchange rate is given at date 2 by

$$e\mathcal{R} = pR_l.$$

(Assuming that there is no excess supply of tradables $\mathcal{R}$; otherwise $e \equiv 1$.) One has

$$p(RI - R_l) = \mu I$$

and

$$\frac{pR_l}{e} = I - A.$$

Then

$$I = \mathcal{R} + A = \frac{A}{1 - (pR - \mu)/e}.$$

$e \geqslant 1$ is equivalent to $(1 + A/\mathcal{R})(pR - \mu) \geqslant 1$.

Exercise 16.2 (time-consistent government policy). (i) The incentive constraint is

$$[(p_H + \tau) - (p_L + \tau)]R_b \geqslant BI.$$

And so the investors' breakeven condition is

$$(p_H + \tau)\left(R - \frac{B}{\Delta p}\right)I = I - A.$$

This yields $I(\tau)$.

The government maximizes

$$[(p_H + \tau)R - \gamma(\tau)]I.$$

Hence,

$$\gamma'(\tau^*) = R.$$

(ii) $\max_\tau\{[(p_H + \tau)R - 1 - \gamma(\tau)]I\}$

$$\Longrightarrow \; [\gamma'(\tau^c) - R]I = [(p_H + \tau)R - 1 - \gamma(\tau^c)]\frac{dI}{d\tau}.$$

(iii) $\tau < \tau^*$ then.

Exercise 16.3 (political economy of exchange rate policies). (i) $d^* = p_H R_1^*$ and $d = p_H R_1^S + (1-p_H)R_1^F$.

(ii) The entrepreneur's incentive constraint (expressed in tradables) is

$$(\Delta p)\left[R_b^* + \frac{R_b^S - R_b^F}{e}\right] \geqslant BI.$$

The foreign investors' breakeven constraint can be written as

$$d^* + \frac{d}{e} = p_H R_1^* + \frac{p_H R_1^S + (1-p_H)R_1^F}{e} \geqslant I - A.$$

And so, adding up these two inequalities,

$$p_H\left(R - \frac{B}{\Delta p}\right)I + \frac{p_H SI + (1-p_H)R_1^F - p_H R_b^F}{e} \geqslant I - A.$$

Thus, if the NPV per unit of investment is positive (which we will assume), it is optimal to set

$$R_b^F = 0 \quad \text{and} \quad R_1^F = SI.$$

The investment is therefore

$$I(e) = \frac{A}{1 - [(S/e) + \rho_0]}. \tag{1}$$

It decreases as the exchange rate depreciates because part of the firm's production is in nontradables.

(iii) *Commitment.* Suppose, first, that the government chooses g^* *before* entrepreneurs borrow abroad.

The representative entrepreneur has expected utility

$$[SI - d] + p_H R_b^* + \max_{c_1^*}[u(c_1^*) - ec_1^*] + v(g^*).$$

In the end, the entrepreneur's average consumption of nontradables is

$$SI$$

and the (average and individual) consumption of tradables is

$$\mathcal{R}^* - g^* + [p_H R - 1]I + A$$

since the NPV, $(p_H R - 1)I + SI$, must accrue to them from the investors' breakeven condition.

Hence, the government chooses g^* so as to solve

$$\max_{g^*}\{SI + u(\mathcal{R}^* - g^* + [p_H R - 1]I + A) + v(g^*)\}$$

subject to (1) and the market-clearing equation,

$$p_H RI(e) + \mathcal{R}^* - g^* = c_1^*(e) + [I(e) - A]. \tag{2}$$

The first-order condition is (using $u' = e$)

$$v'(g^*) = e\left[1 - \left[\frac{S}{e} + (p_H R - 1)\right]\frac{\mathrm{d}I}{\mathrm{d}e}\frac{\mathrm{d}e}{\mathrm{d}g^*}\right] > e.$$

Noncommitment. Under noncommitment, investment is fixed at some level $\bar{I}$ at the date at which g^* is chosen. So the government solves

$$\max_{g^*}\left\{S\bar{I} + u\left(\mathcal{R}^* - g^* + p_H R\bar{I} - d^* - \frac{d}{e}\right) + v(g^*)\right\}$$

and so

$$v'(g^*) = e\left[1 - \frac{d}{e^2}\frac{\mathrm{d}e}{\mathrm{d}g^*}\right] < e.$$

(iv) Note that under noncommitment g^* increases as the debt expressed in nontradables, d, increases. Overspending imposes a negative externality on foreigners when their claims are in nontradables and therefore can be depreciated.

Each borrower would be better off if the other borrowers issued fewer claims in nontradables. But each borrower also has an individual incentive to use nontradables as collateral so as to maximize borrowing capacity.

Review Problems

Review Problem 1 (knowledge questions). Answer the following subquestions:

(a) How does theory account for the sensitivity of investment to cash flow? What does it predict concerning the impact of balance-sheet strength on this sensitivity?

(b) What are the costs and benefits of issuing senior debt?

(c) Describe the main ingredients and conclusions of a model of signaling and term structure of debt.

(d) Explain the control approach to the diversity of securities.

(e) Why does the initial owner issue several securities (rather than just 100% equity) in the Gorton–Pennachi paper?

(f) Discuss the costs and benefits of a liquid market for stocks. According to your discussion, are subsidiaries more or less likely to be publicly traded?

(g) When does diversification boost borrowing capacity? Why?

(h) What determines the allocation of formal control rights between an entrepreneur and investors?

(i) What is a credit crunch? Who suffers most from a credit crunch?

(j) Explain a firm's demand for liquidity.

(k) How does corporate liquidity demand affect the pricing of assets in general equilibrium?

(l) Explain briefly but precisely the logic and conclusions of the Shleifer and Vishny (1992) *Journal of Finance* model of endogenous value of collateral.

(m) True or false?

- Speculators acquire too little information.
- Financial markets destroy insurance opportunities in the Diamond and Dybvig (1983) model.
- Firms with the strongest balance sheets suffer more from a credit crunch.
- The "cross-pledging"/diversification benefit is highest when the borrower can secretly choose the extent of the correlation between her different activities.
- Speculative monitoring boosts pledgeable income by improving performance measurement.

(m) What is the relationship between corporate finance and "poverty traps"? What are the sources of dynamic complementarity and substitutability in macroeconomic models with credit-constrained firms?

(n) What is market timing? What is the theoretical take on this notion?

(o) Discuss briefly the implications of the entrepreneur's having private information when issuing claims (type of securities issued, etc.).

(p) Explain the theory of free cash flow.

(q) Is there a liquidity–accountability tradeoff?

(r) Borrowers often sacrifice *value* (in the sense of NPV) so as to increase the income that can be pledged to the investors and to thereby obtain financing. Give *four* illustrations of this general phenomenon.

(s) Give the intuition for the existence of a corporate demand for liquidity, and why it is optimal to hoard *some* liquidity but *not enough* to allow for all reinvestments smaller than the continuation NPV.

(t) Consider an adverse-selection context in which the borrower has two possible types. What is the low-information-intensity optimum? When is the equilibrium unique?

(u) "In the pure theory of takeovers, the latter are more likely when the incumbent is credit constrained at the initial stage": true or false? Why?

(v) Are borrowers with weak or strong balance sheets the stronger supporters of strong contracting institutions? Do their preferences in the matter change over the firm's life cycle? Give some examples.

(w) Discuss property rights institutions. Are there externalities in the allocation of investors among existing securities?

(x) Give a couple of reasons why a monitor may overmonitor.

(y) How can an entrant in a market reduce the probability of predation by an incumbent?

(z) Define the notion of financial muscle. When do firms accumulate too much or too little financial muscle in the context of mergers and acquisitions?

Review Problem 2 (medley). An entrepreneur, who has no cash and no assets, wants to finance a project which costs $I > 0$. The project yields R with probability p and 0 with probability $1 - p$. A loan contract specifies a reward R_{b} for the entrepreneur if the income is R and 0 if the income is 0. If financed, the probability of success (that is, income R) depends on the (noncontractible) effort $e \in \{\underline{e}, \bar{e}\}$ chosen by the entrepreneur: it is equal to p_{H} if $e = \bar{e}$ and p_{L} if $e = \underline{e}$, where

$$1 > p_{\mathrm{H}} > p_{\mathrm{L}} = 0.$$

The entrepreneur enjoys private benefit $B > 0$ if $e = \underline{e}$ and 0 if $e = \bar{e}$. There is a competitive loan market and the economy's rate of interest is equal to 0.

(i) Show that the project is financed if and only if

$$p_{\mathrm{H}}R \geqslant B + I. \qquad (1)$$

Interpret condition (1).

Subquestions (ii)–(iv) modify subquestion (i) in a single direction

(ii) (Debt overhang.) Suppose that before this project comes up the entrepreneur owes debt $D > 0$ to some initial creditors. This debt is senior and cannot be diluted. Furthermore, the initial debtholders cannot be reached before the investment is financed. Show that (1) must be replaced by

$$p_{\mathrm{H}}R \geqslant B + I + p_{\mathrm{H}}D. \qquad (2)$$

If (2) is not satisfied, what should be done to prevent this debt overhang problem?

(iii) (Inalienability of human capital.) Suppose (*à la* Hart and Moore 1994[14]; see also Section 4.5) that, just before income R is realized (which can happen only if $e = \bar{e}$ and there is a "good state of nature"), both parties learn that the project is about to be successful (provided that the entrepreneur completes it, which she can do at no additional cost). The entrepreneur can then force her lenders to renegotiate "*à la* Nash," that is, to split the pie, because she is indispensable for the completion of the project. How is the analysis in question (i) modified?

(iv) (Intermediation.) Suppose that (1) is not satisfied but $p_{\mathrm{H}}R > I$. Introduce a monitoring technology: the entrepreneur can go to a bank. By spending $c > 0$, the bank can catch the entrepreneur if $e = \underline{e}$ and reverse the decision to $e = \bar{e}$; in this case the entrepreneur is punished: she receives no income and does not enjoy her private benefit. There is no scarcity of monitoring capital (and therefore no rent for the monitor in equilibrium). All borrowing is from the monitor; that is, there are no uninformed investors (unlike in Chapter 9). So $I_{\mathrm{m}} = I$ and $R_{\mathrm{b}} + R_{\mathrm{m}} = R$, where I_{m} and R_{m} denote the monitor's investment contribution and stake in success (if the entrepreneur does not misbehave, otherwise the monitor appropriates the entire return).

The bank and the entrepreneur choose simultaneously whether to monitor (for the bank), and whether to select $\bar{e}$ (for the entrepreneur). The expected-payoff matrix for this game is thus

	$\bar{e}$	$\underline{e}$
M	$(p_{\mathrm{H}}R_{\mathrm{m}} - c, p_{\mathrm{H}}(R - R_{\mathrm{m}}))$	$(p_{\mathrm{H}}R - c, 0)$
DNM	$(p_{\mathrm{H}}R_{\mathrm{m}}, p_{\mathrm{H}}(R - R_{\mathrm{m}}))$	$(0, B)$

where P is the payment to the bank, "M" is "Monitor," "DNM" is "Do not monitor," and where the first payoff is that of the bank.

- Show that the equilibrium is in mixed strategies: the entrepreneur chooses $\underline{e}$ with probability $z = c/(p_{\mathrm{H}}R)$. The bank does not monitor with probability $y = p_{\mathrm{H}}(R - R_{\mathrm{m}})/B$.
- Argue that the project is financed if and only if

$$p_{\mathrm{H}}R \geqslant c + I. \qquad (3)$$

- Suppose that (3) is satisfied but not (1). Show that the entrepreneur's expected payoff is

$$(p_{\mathrm{H}}R - c - I)\left(\frac{p_{\mathrm{H}}R}{p_{\mathrm{H}}R - c}\right) < p_{\mathrm{H}}R - I.$$

14. Hart, O. and J. Moore. 1994. A theory of debt based on the inalienability of human capital. *Quarterly Journal of Economics* 109:841–880.

Review Problem 3 (project choice and monitoring). Consider the fixed-investment model with two alternative projects: the two projects have the same investment cost I and the same payoffs, R in the case of success and 0 in the case of failure. The entrepreneur has initial wealth A and must collect $I - A$ from risk-neutral investors who demand a rate of return equal to 0. Project 1 has probability of success p_{H} if the entrepreneur works and $p_{\mathrm{L}} = p_{\mathrm{H}} - \Delta p$ if she shirks. Similarly, the probabilities of success are q_{H} and $q_{\mathrm{L}} = q_{\mathrm{H}} - \Delta q$ for project 2, where

$$\Delta q = \Delta p.$$

Project 1 (respectively, 2) delivers private benefit B (respectively, b) when the entrepreneur shirks; no private benefit accrues in either project if the entrepreneur works. We assume that project 1 has a higher probability of success

$$p_{\mathrm{H}} > q_{\mathrm{H}},$$

and that

$$p_{\mathrm{H}}\left(R - \frac{B}{\Delta p}\right) < q_{\mathrm{H}}\left(R - \frac{b}{\Delta p}\right) < I.$$

Assume that *at most one project* can be implemented (because, say, the entrepreneur has limited attention), and (except in question (ii)) that the investors can verify which project, if any, is implemented.

(i) Divide the set of possible net worths A, $[0, \infty)$, into three regions $[0, \bar{A}_q)$, $[\bar{A}_q, \bar{A}_p)$, and $[\bar{A}_p, \infty)$ and show that the equilibrium investment policies in these regions are "not invest," "invest in project 2," and "invest in project 1." Verify that

$$\bar{A}_p - \bar{A}_q = (p_{\mathrm{H}} - q_{\mathrm{H}})R - \frac{[p_{\mathrm{H}}B - q_{\mathrm{H}}b]}{\Delta p}.$$

(ii) In this question *only*, suppose that the investors cannot verify which project the entrepreneur is choosing (they only observe success/failure). Argue that nothing is altered if $A \geqslant \bar{A}_p$. Show that if $A \in [\bar{A}_q, \bar{A}_p)$, then financing may be jeopardized unless the entrepreneur must incur private cost ψ in order to substitute project 1 for project 2, where $\psi \geqslant B - (q_{\mathrm{H}} - p_{\mathrm{L}})b/(\Delta p)$.

(iii) Suppose now that the private benefit of shirking on project 1 can be reduced from B to b by using an active monitor. This active monitor has private cost c of monitoring and demands monetary rate of return χ (where $\chi \geqslant p_{\mathrm{H}}/p_{\mathrm{L}}$): $p_{\mathrm{H}}R_{\mathrm{m}} = \chi I_{\mathrm{m}}$.

What is the cost M of hiring the active monitor? Assuming $(B - b)/(\Delta p) > M$, solve for the equilibrium policies as in question (i), assuming that

$$q_{\mathrm{H}}R < p_{\mathrm{H}}R - M < q_{\mathrm{H}}R + (p_{\mathrm{H}} - q_{\mathrm{H}})\frac{b}{\Delta p}.$$

(iv) Ignoring active monitoring, suppose now that both projects can be implemented simultaneously (at cost $2I$) and that they are statistically independent. Assume that $q_{\mathrm{L}} = 0$, that only total profit is observed, that the entrepreneur is rewarded only in the case of overall success ($R_2 > 0$, $R_1 = R_0 = 0$), and that "work" must be induced on both projects. Describe the three incentive compatibility constraints and argue that one of them is irrelevant. Distinguish two cases depending on

$$\frac{B}{B + b} \gtrless \frac{q_{\mathrm{H}}}{p_{\mathrm{H}}}.$$

Determine the threshold $\bar{A}_{pq}$ over which the entrepreneur can thus diversify.

Review Problem 4 (exit strategies). An entrepreneur has cash A and wants to finance a project involving investment cost $I > A$. The project yields R with probability p and 0 with probability $1 - p$. The entrepreneur may either behave and enjoy no private benefit, in which case the probability of success is p_{H}, or misbehave and enjoy private benefit B, in which case the project fails *for certain* ($p_{\mathrm{L}} = 0$).

Assume that $p_{\mathrm{H}}R > I$ and $B < I$ (the NPV is positive if and only if the entrepreneur behaves).

(i) Define the notion of pledgeable income. Show that the entrepreneur can obtain financing if and only if

$$p_{\mathrm{H}}R - I \geqslant B - A. \tag{1}$$

Show that the entrepreneur's utility is

$$U_{\mathrm{b}} = p_{\mathrm{H}}R - I. \tag{2}$$

(ii) Suppose now that the entrepreneur, with probability λ ($0 < \lambda < 1$), has an interesting outside investment opportunity. To profit from this opportunity, the entrepreneur must receive cash (exactly) equal to $r > 0$ before the final outcome on the initial project is realized. With probability $1 - \lambda$, no such opportunity arises. Whether the opportunity arises is *not* observable by the investors (so the entrepreneur can "fake" a liquidity need and strategically exit). If the opportunity arises and the entrepreneur is able to invest r in it, the entrepreneur receives μr, where $\mu > 1$. This payoff is also unobservable by investors. The timing is as follows:

Stage 0. The investors bring $I - A$ (provided they are willing to finance the project), and investment occurs.

Stage 1. The entrepreneur chooses between p_H and p_L.

Stage 2. The entrepreneur privately learns whether she faces an investment opportunity (and therefore needs cash r in order not to forgo the opportunity).

Stage 3. The project's outcome (R or 0) is publicly observed. The entrepreneur receives μr if she faced an investment opportunity (and only r if she faked an investment opportunity) at stage 2 *and* invested r.

Consider a contract in which the entrepreneur is offered a *choice* for stage 2 between

(a) receiving r at stage 2 and nothing at stage 3, and
(b) receiving nothing at stage 2 and R_b in the case of success (and 0 in the case of failure) at stage 3.

(This class of contracts is actually optimal.) The menu is designed so that she chooses option (a) at stage 2 if and only if she has an investment opportunity.

- Show that the incentive constraint at stage 1 is

$$(1 - \lambda)(p_H R_b - r) \geqslant B.$$

To prove this, argue that, were the entrepreneur to misbehave, she would always select option (a), while, if she behaves, then necessarily $p_H R_b > r$.

(iii) Keeping within the framework of question (ii) and assuming that

$$\mu r \geqslant r + \frac{B}{1 - \lambda}, \qquad (3)$$

show that the project is financed if and only if

$$p_H R - I \geqslant B - A + r \qquad (4)$$

and the entrepreneur's utility is then

$$U_b^L = p_H R - I + \lambda(\mu - 1)r \qquad (5)$$

(the superscript "L" stands for the fact that the entrepreneur has a liquid claim).

Compare (4) and (5) with (1) and (2), and conclude on the desirability and feasibility of liquid compensation contracts. What is the interpretation of (3)?

(iv) Suppose now that, at some cost c, a signal can be obtained at stage 2. So, if the entrepreneur claims she needs cash r at stage 2 (which has probability λ), a signal is obtained, which takes one of two values: good or bad. The probability of a good signal is q_H if the entrepreneur has behaved and $q_L < q_H$ if she misbehaved. The entrepreneur receives r at stage 2 only if the good signal accrues. Option (b) is unchanged. Show that the project is financed if and only if

$$p_H R + \lambda q_H(\mu - 1)r - B - q_L[\lambda\mu + 1 - \lambda]r \geqslant I - A + c.$$

(Show that the incentive constraint is $\lambda q_H \mu r + (1 - \lambda)p_H R_b \geqslant B + q_L[\lambda\mu + 1 - \lambda]r$.) What is U_b? What do you infer about the desirability of acquisition of this signal?

Review Problem 5 (property rights institutions and international finance). Consider a country with a continuum of identical firms (of mass 1). The representative firm is described as in Section 3.4. That is, it has initial wealth A and has a variable-investment project. As usual, let

$$\rho_0 \equiv p_H\left(R - \frac{B}{\Delta p}\right) < 1 < \rho_1 \equiv p_H R.$$

To finance their investment, the domestic firms must borrow from domestic residents and from foreign investors. Domestic residents have limited savings $S_D < \rho_0 A/(1 - \rho_0)$. Foreign investors have unlimited amounts of money to lend at the market rate of return. The rate of return demanded by foreigners and domestic residents is 0.

After the financing has been secured, the country's government chooses a tax rate $t \geqslant 0$ on income received by *investors.* This tax rate does not apply to the entrepreneurs and does not discriminate between domestic and foreign investors.

To close the model, assume that the government transforms tax proceeds $t\mathcal{I}$ (for an amount of investor income $\mathcal{I}$) into $B_0(t)\mathcal{I}$, where

$$B_0' > 0, \quad B_0'' < 0, \quad \text{and} \quad B_0'(0) = 1.$$

(That is, tax collection is wasteful here.) Assume that these benefits $B_0(t)\mathcal{I}$ are returned to entrepreneurs

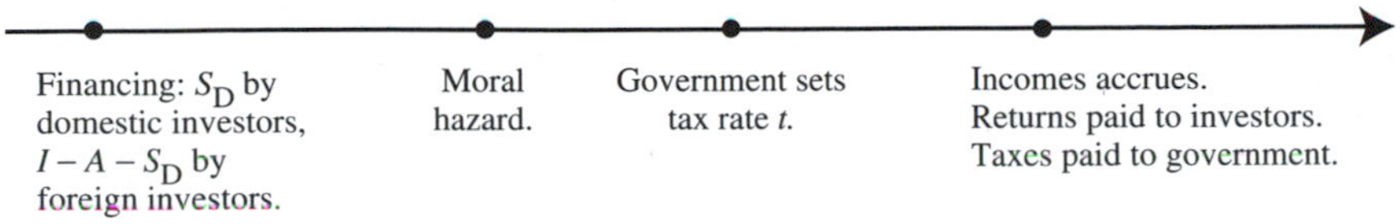

Figure 1

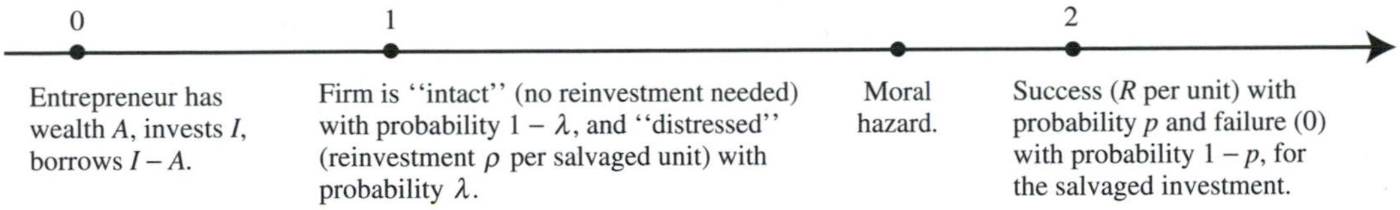

Figure 2

in proportion to the tax income collected. Thus the representative entrepreneur's equilibrium NPV is

$$(\rho_1 - 1)I - t^* \rho_0 I + B_0(t^*)\rho_0 I.$$

The government maximizes the sum of the welfares of the entrepreneurs and of the domestic investors, and puts no weight on foreign investors (see Figure 1).

(i) Solve for a rational expectation equilibrium (I^*, t^*, θ^*), where I^* is the representative entrepreneur's investment, t^* is the equilibrium tax rate, and θ^*, equal to $S_D/(I^* - A)$, is the fraction of external financing brought by domestic residents.

(ii) How does the entrepreneur's welfare change with domestic savings S_D?

(iii) What tax rate would prevail if the government were able to commit on the tax rate before the financing stage?

(iv) How would your answer to question (i) change if the government were still unable to commit to a tax rate and furthermore could discriminate between domestic and foreign investors?

Review Problem 6 (inside liquidity). Consider the variable-investment model with two possible values of liquidity shocks (0 and ρ per unit of investment). The timing is described in Figure 2.

Investors and entrepreneurs are risk neutral, the entrepreneur is protected by limited liability and the rate of interest in the economy is 0. If the firm is in distress (suffers a liquidity shock), a reinvestment $\rho x I$ allows it to salvage a fraction $x \in [0, 1]$ of the investment (so there is no constraint to salvage all or nothing, even though, as we will see, the solution will be a "corner solution").

Continuation is subject to moral hazard. The probability of success is p_H if the entrepreneur behaves and p_L is she misbehaves. The private benefit of misbehaving is BxI. The project yields RxI in the case of success and 0 in the case of failure. Let

$$\rho_0 \equiv p_H\left(R - \frac{B}{\Delta p}\right) < c$$
$$\equiv \min\left\{1 + \lambda\rho, \frac{1}{1-\lambda}\right\} < \rho_1 \equiv p_H R.$$

In the first two questions, one will assume that there is a costless outside store of value (there are assets that at per-unit cost $q = 1$ at date 0 yield a return equal to 1 at date 1).

(i) Show that, when choosing x, the entrepreneur can borrow up to

$$I = \frac{A}{(1 + \lambda\rho x) - [1 - \lambda + \lambda x]\rho_0}.$$

(ii) Compute the borrower's utility and show that

$$x = 1 \quad \text{if and only if } (1 - \lambda)\rho \leqslant 1$$

(and $x = 0$ otherwise).

(Hint: write the borrower's utility as a function of the "average unit cost of preserved investment.")

(iii) Suppose now that there is no outside store of value. There is mass 1 of (*ex ante* identical) entrepreneurs. The only liquidity in the economy is the inside liquidity created by the securities issued by the firms. One will assume that $\rho_0 < \rho < 1/[1 - \lambda]$. Is there enough liquidity if the firms' liquidity shocks are perfectly correlated? If not, what is the level of the liquidity shortage?

(iv) Consider question (iii) except that the liquidity shocks faced by the entrepreneurs are independently distributed. Show that the firms' holding the stock index may not be optimal. What should be done?

Review Problem 7 (monitoring). (i) A borrower has assets A and must find funds $I-A$. The project yields R or 0 and the borrower is protected by limited liability. Shirking yields probability of success p_L and private benefit B, while working yields probability of success $p_H = p_L + \Delta p > p_L$ and private benefit 0. Assume that

$$I - A > p_H\left(R - \frac{B}{\Delta p}\right).$$

There is one potential monitor, who, at private cost $c(x)$ ($c' > 0$, $c'' > 0$, $c'(0) = 0$), can with probability x reduce the private benefit of shirking from B to $b < B$. The borrower learns what her private benefit is (that is, whether monitoring was successful) before choosing his effort.

Compute the optimal fraction α of the final return R in the case of success that should be held by the large monitor. Show that if the large monitor holds all outside shares (i.e., all shares not belonging to the borrower), there is overmonitoring. Explain.

(ii) Suppose that initially the large monitor is not around, but it is known that one will appear (before the borrower selects her effort decision). So outside shares are initially held by small, uninformed shareholders. (The timing is: at date 0, the borrower issues the securities to the small, uninformed investors. Between dates 0 and 1, the potential large monitor appears and may try to purchase shares from the initial investors; at date 1, the monitoring and effort decisions are selected. The return, if any, accrues at date 2.)

Suppose that the large shareholder makes a tender offer (bid P) for a fraction or all the investors' shares (the tender offer is unrestricted and unconditional: the large shareholder purchases all shares that are tendered to him at the price offer P).

• One usually believes that the supply function in competitive financial markets is perfectly elastic. Show that the "supply function" $\alpha(P)$ (the number of shares tendered) is here upward sloping.

Give the intuition for this result.

• Compute the large shareholder's *ex ante* payoff for arbitrary bids P.

• Conclude. Is the borrower able to raise funds at date 0?

(iii) • Discuss *informally* the implications of question (ii). How would private benefits of control of large shareholders affect the analysis?

Review Problem 8 (biotechnology research agreements). Lerner and Malmendier[15] study biotechnology research collaborations. Almost all such contracts in their sample specify termination rights. These may be conditional on specific events (50% of the contracts in their sample of 584 biotechnology research agreements) or at the complete discretion of the financier (39%). The financing firm may in the case of termination acquire broader licensing rights than it would have in the case of continuation. These broad licensing rights can be viewed as costly collateral pledging that both increase the income of the financier and boost the R&D firm's incentive to achieve a good performance on the project.[16] Lerner and Malmendier's empirical finding is that such an assignment of termination and broad licensing rights is more likely when it is hard to specify a lead product candidate in the contract (and so entrepreneurial moral hazard is particularly important) and when the R&D firm is highly constrained financially. This review problem builds on their analysis.

There are three dates, $t = 0, 1, 2$, and two players, a biotechnology entrepreneur or borrower and a financier (pharmaceutical company).

At date 0, the risk-neutral biotechnology entrepreneur has a project involving initial investment cost I. The entrepreneur has initial wealth A, and so the (risk-neutral) financier must contribute $I - A$. The market rate of interest in the economy is 0 and the capital market is competitive. If the research activity is noncontractible, the entrepreneur exerts unobservable date-0 effort $e = 0$ or 1. (When it is contractible, then necessarily $e = 1$.) A high effort is to be interpreted as focusing on the project while a

15. Lerner, J. and U. Malmendier. 2005. Contractibility and the design of research agreements. AFA 2005 Philadelphia Meeting. (Available at http://ssrn.com/abstract=642303.)

16. See Section 4.3.4 for the theoretical foundations of this assertion.

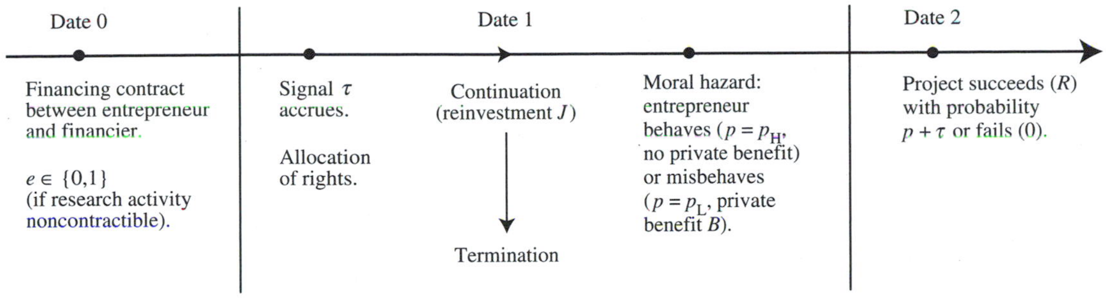
Date 0
Date 1
Date 2
Financing contract between entrepreneur and financier.
e ∈ {0,1} (if research activity noncontractible).
Signal τ accrues.
Allocation of rights.
Continuation (reinvestment J)
Termination
Moral hazard: entrepreneur behaves (p = p_H, no private benefit) or misbehaves (p = p_L, private benefit B).
Project succeeds (R) with probability p + τ or fails (0).

Figure 3

low effort corresponds to paying more attention to alternative or adjacent activities, whose value is C_e if they are later pursued by the entrepreneur and only βC_e with $\beta < 1$ if they are seized and pursued by the financier. These payoffs are noncontractible and will accrue to the owner (entrepreneur or financier) of the corresponding rights. Furthermore,

$$C_0 > C_1.$$

At date 1, a publicly observed signal $\tau \in [\underline{\tau}, \bar{\tau}]$ accrues. The cumulative distribution is $F(\tau)$ if $e = 1$ and $G(\tau)$ if $e = 0$, with densities $f(\tau)$ and $g(\tau)$ satisfying the monotone likelihood ratio property:

$$\frac{f(\tau)}{g(\tau)} \text{ is increasing in } \tau.$$

Contingent on the realization of the signal, the project can be terminated or continued. Termination yields 0 on this specific project (while the value of the alternative activities, C_e or βC_e depending on the owner, are independent of the signal). Continuation requires the financier to reinvest J into the project. Success brings a verifiable profit R, failure yields no profit. The probability of success at date 2 is then $p + \tau$. Regardless of the signal τ, p is determined by entrepreneurial moral hazard at date 1: if the entrepreneur behaves, she receives no private benefit and $p = p_H$; if she misbehaves, she receives private benefit $B > 0$ and $p = p_L = p_H - \Delta p$, where $\Delta p > 0$.

The timing is summarized in Figure 3.

We assume that at date 0 the entrepreneur offers a contract to the financier (nothing hinges on this assumption about relative bargaining power). A financing *contract* specifies[17]

- $e = 1$ if the research activity is contractible and contingent on the realization of the signal τ;
- a probability $x(\tau)$ of continuation;
- a probability $y(\tau)$ that the entrepreneur keeps the rights on the adjacent activities;
- a reward $R_b(\tau)$ for the entrepreneur in the cases of continuation and success.

We assume that the entrepreneur is protected by limited liability and so the latter reward must be nonnegative. Because the entrepreneur is risk neutral, there is no loss of generality in assuming that the entrepreneur receives no reward if either the project is interrupted at date 1 or if it fails at date 2.

Assumption 1. *The project has positive maximum NPV relative to that, C_0, obtained in the absence of financing if and only if $e = 1$. Let τ^{FB} be defined by*

$$[p_H + \tau^{FB}]R = J,$$

then

$$\int_{\tau^{FB}}^{\bar{\tau}} [(p_H + \tau)R - J]\,dF(\tau) + C_1 - I > C_0,$$

$$\int_{\tau^{FB}}^{\bar{\tau}} [(p_H + \tau)R - J]\,dG(\tau) + C_0 - I < C_0.$$

(i) Suppose, first, that the research activity is contractible: the contract can specify $e = 1$ and so there is no moral hazard at date 0. Show that the optimal contract falls into one of the four following regions, as A decreases: (1) high payment, no reversion, first-best termination; (2) termination rights for the financier; (3) termination and reversion rights for the financier; and (4) no funding.

(ii) Solve for the optimal contract when the effort is noncontractible.

17. At the optimum contract, x and y will take values 0 or 1 only.

Review Problem 9 (conflict of interest in multitasking). An R&D entrepreneur has an idea for a new product. To market this product, the entrepreneur must first develop a technology. The technology, if developed, then allows the product to be marketed, yielding profit R. No profit is made if no technology is developed.

There are two possible and independent research strategies. Each is described as follows. The probability that the entrepreneur succeeds in developing the technology is p_H if she behaves (and then receives no private benefit) and $p_L = p_H - \Delta p$ if she misbehaves (and then receives private benefit B). Assume all along that the incentive contract must induce good behavior. Each research strategy involves investment cost $I < p_H R$. The technologies are substitutes (the profit is R whether one or two technologies have been developed). They are independent in that the success or failure of one technology conveys no information about the likelihood of success of the other.

The entrepreneur has cash on hand A and is risk neutral and protected by limited liability. The investors are risk neutral and the market rate of interest is equal to 0.

(i) Suppose that the entrepreneur and the investors decide that the entrepreneur will pursue a single research strategy. Show that the project can be funded if and only if

$$p_H\left(R - \frac{B}{\Delta p}\right) \geqslant I - A.$$

(ii) Suppose that

$$p_H(1 - p_H)R > I.$$

Interpret this inequality.

Consider funding the two research strategies. The investment cost is then equal to $2I$. Assume that the *managerial reward R_b can be contingent only on the firm's profit* (which is equal to R whether one or two technologies have been developed). Thus, R_b cannot be made contingent on the market of successfully developed substitute technologies.

Show that the nonpledgeable income is equal to

$$[1 - (1 - p_H)^2]\frac{B}{(1 - p_H)\Delta p}.$$

What is the necessary and sufficient condition for investors to be willing to finance the two research strategies?

(iii) Show that the entrepreneur (who owns the research strategies) may want to hire a second and identical entrepreneur to perform the second research strategy, even if it means leaving an agency rent to the new entrepreneur (this will be shown to occur whenever $A < p_H B/\Delta p$). One will assume that the entrepreneurs are rewarded on the basis of their own profit and that if both technologies succeed, each "division" receives R with probability $\frac{1}{2}$.

Answers to Selected Review Problems

Review Problem 2 (medley). (i) The incentive constraint is

$$(p_H - p_L)R_b \geqslant B$$

or, since $p_L = 0$,

$$p_H R_b \geqslant B.$$

Hence the nonpledgeable income is equal to B and the pledgeable income is

$$p_H R - B.$$

Because the entrepreneur has no cash ($A = 0$), this pledgeable income must exceed the investment cost I.

(ii) (Debt overhang.) Assume that $D < R$ (otherwise, new investors will never receive any income). The income that can be pledged to new investors is

$$p_H(R - D) - B.$$

Hence condition (2) must hold in the absence of renegotiation with initial lenders. The only way to raise funds if (2) is violated is to renegotiate the initial lender's debt to a level $R_l \leqslant d$, where $d \in (0, D)$ satisfies

$$p_H(R - d) = B + I.$$

(iii) (Inalienability of human capital.) The threat of renegotiation implies that the borrower can demand $\frac{1}{2}R$ whenever R is about to accrue. And so a new constraint must be added to the funding program:

$$R_b \geqslant \tfrac{1}{2}R.$$

Let R_b^* denote the borrower's stake in the absence of negotiation (i.e., in question (i)):

$$p_H(R - R_b^*) = I$$

with

$$p_H R_b^* \geqslant B$$

for incentive compatibility.

Either $R_b^* \geqslant \frac{1}{2}R$ and there is no renegotiation, and the outcome is as in question (i), or $R_b^* < \frac{1}{2}R$, and then rewards that allow investors to recoup their initial outlay (i.e., $R_b \leqslant R_b^*$ are renegotiated up to $\frac{1}{2}R$ just before success. Anticipating this, investors do not want to lend:

$$p_H(R - \tfrac{1}{2}R) - I < p_H(R - R_b^*) - I = 0.$$

(iv) (Intermediation.) The entrepreneur works if she is monitored with probability 1; but then the monitor does not want to monitor. Conversely, if the entrepreneur works with probability 1, the monitor does not monitor and the entrepreneur shirks if $p_H R_b < B$, which we will assume (we will assume that (1) is not satisfied). Hence the equilibrium must be in mixed strategies. Let us first write the monitor's indifference equation:

$$(1 - z)(p_H R_m) + z(p_H R) - c = (1 - z)p_H R_m$$

$(= I_m = I)$. Hence

$$z p_H R = c.$$

Similarly, y is given by the entrepreneur's indifference equation:

$$p_H(R - R_m) = yB.$$

The monitor is willing to finance I if and only if

$$(1 - z)p_H R_m = \left(1 - \frac{c}{p_H R}\right) p_H R_m \geqslant I$$

or, because $R_m \leqslant R$,

$$p_H R \geqslant c + I.$$

Finally, consider the entrepreneur's utility. There are two ways of writing it. First,

$$\begin{aligned} U_b = p_H(R - R_m) &= p_H R - \frac{I}{1 - z} \\ &= p_H R - \frac{I}{1 - c/p_H R}. \end{aligned}$$

Alternatively, U_b is equal to the NPV:

$$U_b = \text{NPV} = p_H R - yz(p_H R - B) - (1-y)c - I.$$

Replacing z and yB by the values found above, we have

$$U_b = p_H R - c - I + \frac{c}{p_H R} p_H (R - R_m)$$

or

$$\left(1 - \frac{c}{p_H R}\right) U_b = p_H R - c - I,$$

which gives the same expression as previously.

Review Problem 3 (project choice and monitoring). (i) The incentive constraints for projects 1 and 2 are

$$(\Delta p) R_b \geqslant B \quad \text{and} \quad (\Delta p) R_b \geqslant b,$$

respectively. The cutoff levels of cash on hand for the two projects are given by

$$p_H\left(R - \frac{B}{\Delta p}\right) = I - \bar{A}_p$$

and

$$q_H\left(R - \frac{b}{\Delta p}\right) = I - \bar{A}_q.$$

(ii) • Suppose that $A \geqslant \bar{A}_p$. Then, choosing project 2 instead of project 1 yields, to the entrepreneur,

$$\max\{q_H R_b, q_L R_b + b\} < \max\{p_H R_b, p_L R_b + B\}.$$

• In contrast, if $A \in [\bar{A}_q, \bar{A}_p)$, then the entrepreneur gets

$$\max\{p_H R_b, p_L R_b + B\} = p_L R_b + B$$

(minus the private cost, ψ, of substituting the project), since

$$q_H(R - R_b) = I - A \geqslant I - \bar{A}_p = p_H\left(R - \frac{B}{\Delta p}\right),$$

and so

$$R_b < \frac{B}{\Delta p}.$$

The issue is moot if

$$\max_{\{A \in [\bar{A}_q, \bar{A}_p)\}} \{p_L R_b + B - q_H R_b\} = (p_L - q_H)\frac{b}{\Delta p} + B \leqslant \psi.$$

(iii) • $p_H R_m = \chi I_m$ and $(\Delta p) R_m = c$ imply

$$M = p_H R_m - I_m = c + p_L R_m - I_m$$
$$= c + \left(p_L - \frac{p_H}{\chi}\right)\frac{c}{\Delta p}.$$

• The first inequality in the condition stated in the question says that the NPV is higher when monitored in project 1 than when unmonitored in project 2. So for $A < \bar{A}_p$, the entrepreneur would prefer project 1 monitored to project 2. The second inequality states that pledgeable income is higher under project 2. So we now have four regions:

$$\begin{aligned} [0, \bar{A}_q)&: \text{ no project,} \\ [\bar{A}_q, \bar{A}_p^m)&: \text{ project 2,} \\ [\bar{A}_p^m, \bar{A}_p)&: \text{ project 1 monitored,} \\ [\bar{A}_p, \infty)&: \text{ project 1 unmonitored.} \end{aligned}$$

(iv) • Incentive constraints

$$p_H q_H R_2 \geqslant \begin{cases} p_H q_L R_2 + b = b, & (1) \\ p_L q_H R_2 + B, & (2) \\ p_L q_L R_2 + B + b = B + b. & (3) \end{cases}$$

(1) is obviously nonbinding.
If (3) is binding, then the pledgeable income is

$$(p_H + q_H)R - [B + b].$$

If (2) is binding, it is

$$(p_H + q_H)R - p_H \frac{B}{\Delta p}.$$

The new NPV is $(p_H + q_H)R - 2I$.

• In the latter case, the financing condition is

$$(p_H + q_H)R - p_H \frac{B}{\Delta p} > I - A$$

or

$$\left[p_H\left[R - \frac{B}{\Delta p}\right] - [I - A]\right] + q_H R - I \geqslant 0.$$

• In the former case, the financing condition is

$$(p_H + q_H)R - (B + b) \geqslant 2I - A.$$

Review Problem 4 (exit strategies). (i) Pledgeable income: maximum income that can be promised to investors without destroying incentives. Incentive constraint is

$$(\Delta p) R_b \geqslant B.$$

And so

$$p_H R - p_H R_b = p_H R - B \geqslant I - A$$

for $p_L = 0$. The borrower's expected utility is

$$U_b = \text{NPV} = p_H R - I.$$

(ii) • The incentive constraint is

$$(1 - \lambda) p_H R_b + \lambda \mu r \geqslant B + [\lambda \mu + (1 - \lambda)] r$$

or

$$(1-\lambda)(p_H R_b - r) \geqslant B.$$

• If $p_H R_b < r$, then option (a) is optimal regardless of the existence of an opportunity. There is then no incentive to behave.

(iii) • The investors are willing to finance if and only if

$$p_H R - (1-\lambda)p_H R_b - \lambda r \geqslant I - A,$$

or, using the incentive constraint,

$$p_H R - \left(r + \frac{B}{1-\lambda}\right)(1-\lambda) - \lambda r \geqslant I - A,$$

or

$$p_H R - I \geqslant B - A + r. \qquad (1)$$

• (5) is just the NPV.

• From (4), financing is harder to obtain if option (a) (the liquidity option) is available, unless r is small. But the entrepreneur's welfare is higher provided the entrepreneur can get financing.

(iv) • The incentive constraint is

$$\lambda[q_H \mu r] + (1-\lambda)p_H R_b \geqslant B + q_L(\lambda\mu + 1 - \lambda)r.$$

• The pledgeable income is

$$p_H R - \lambda q_H r - (1-\lambda)p_H R_b,$$

and must exceed total net outlay by investors $(I + c - A)$. To obtain the condition in question (iv), replace $(1-\lambda)p_H R_b$ using the incentive constraint.

• The entrepreneur's utility is then

$$U_b = p_H R - I + \lambda q_H(\mu - 1)r - c.$$

• When $q_H = q_L = 1$, we obtain the same answers as in question (iii), as one should.

• In the case of a perfect signal ($q_H = 1$, $q_L = 0$), the financing condition is then

$$p_H R - I \geqslant B - A - \lambda(\mu - 1)r + c.$$

Review Problem 5 (property rights institutions and international finance). (i) Let θ^* denote the fraction of claims held by domestic residents. The government maximizes total domestic surplus:

$$\max_t \{B_0(t) - \theta^* t\}$$

or

$$B_0'(t^*) = \theta^* = \frac{S_D}{I^* - A}.$$

The financing constraint becomes

$$(1 - t^*)\rho_0 I = I - A;$$

hence,

$$I^* = \frac{A}{1 - (1 - t^*)\rho_0}.$$

(ii) An increase in S_D raises θ^* and I^*, and lowers t^*.

(iii) It would be optimal to commit to $t = 0$.

(iv) The government would fully tax foreigners and not tax domestic residents. Hence,

$$I^* - A = S_D.$$

There is no tax on domestic investors, who obtain a rate of return exceeding 0.

Review Problem 6 (inside liquidity). (i) The investors' breakeven constraint is

$$[1 + \lambda\rho x]I - A = [(1-\lambda) + \lambda x]\rho_0 I.$$

Hence,

$$I = \frac{A}{[1 + \lambda\rho x] - [1 - \lambda + \lambda x]\rho_0}.$$

(ii) The NPV is

$$U_b = [(1 - \lambda + \lambda x)\rho_1 - (1 + \lambda\rho x)]I$$
$$= \frac{\rho_1 - c(x)}{c(x) - \rho_0}A,$$

where

$$c(x) = \frac{1 + \lambda\rho x}{1 - \lambda + \lambda x}$$

is the average cost per unit of preserved investment. Minimizing $c(x)$ yields $x = 1$ if and only if

$$(1-\lambda)\rho \leqslant 1.$$

(iii) There is a shortage of liquidity equal to $(\rho - \rho_0)I$.

(iv) The date-1 value of the average share in the index is $(1-\lambda)\rho_0 I$ (assuming that the investors' stake in the distressed firms has been diluted). And so, if $\rho - \rho_0 > (1-\lambda)\rho_0$, the index does not bring enough liquidity to the distressed firms.

The solution is a liquidity pool (e.g., a system of credit lines with a bank: see Chapter 15).

Review Problem 7 (monitoring). (i) • The large monitor chooses x so as to maximize

$$[x p_H + (1-x)p_L]\alpha R - c(x).$$

And so

$$c'(x) = (\Delta p)\alpha R.$$

The NPV is maximal when x solves

$$\max\{xp_{\rm H}R + (1-x)(p_{\rm L}R + B) - c(x)\}$$

or

$$c'(x) = (\Delta p)R - B,$$

corresponding to

$$\alpha = 1 - \frac{B/\Delta p}{R} < 1 - \frac{R_{\rm b}}{R}.$$

• Explanation: when the large monitor holds all outside shares, there is no externality of monitoring on the small investors and a negative externality on the borrower.

(ii) • Suppose α shares are tendered. Then

$$x^*(\alpha) = (c')^{-1}((\Delta p)\alpha R),$$

an increasing function of α.

Therefore,

$$P(\alpha) = [x^*(\alpha)p_{\rm H} + [1 - x^*(\alpha)]p_{\rm L}]R.$$

$\alpha(P)$ is the inverse function and is increasing.

A higher price is consistent with more shares being tendered, as this generates more monitoring and thus a higher value per share.

• The large shareholder's profit for a given P is

$$\max_x\{[xp_{\rm H} + (1-x)p_{\rm L}]\alpha(P)R - c(x) - P\alpha(P)\}$$
$$= -c(x^*(\alpha(P))), \quad \text{in equilibrium.}$$

• Thus there is no monitoring, and the borrower cannot raise funds.

(iii) • The large shareholder needs to be able to *dilute* (see Chapter 11). Burkart et al. (1998)[18] look at takeover bids with such dilution and show that the upward-sloping supply curve arises *on* the equilibrium path (and not only off the path as above).

• Possible explanations: overpayment by empire builders; informed trade; benefits from control (gain access to production technology, below-market transfer prices to large shareholder's subsidiary, etc.).

Review Problem 8 (biotechnology research agreements). In the case of continuation, the incentive compatibility constraint is

$$(p_{\rm H} + \tau)R_{\rm b}(\tau) \geqslant (p_L + \tau)R_{\rm b}(\tau) + B$$

and so

$$R_{\rm b}(\tau) \geqslant \underline{R}_{\rm b} \equiv \frac{B}{\Delta p}.$$

(i) *Contractible research activity.* Let us first assume that the contract can specify $e = 1$, and so there is no moral hazard at date 0.

The optimal contract maximizes the entrepreneur's utility $U_{\rm b}$ (also equal to the NPV, since the entrepreneur chooses the contract so as leave no surplus to the financier) subject to the financier's breakeven constraint and the incentive constraint:

Program I:

$$U_{\rm b} = \max_{\{x(\cdot),y(\cdot),R_{\rm b}(\cdot)\}} \{E[x(\tau)[(p_{\rm H}+\tau)R - J] + y(\tau)C_1 + [1-y(\tau)]\beta C_1] - I\}$$

s.t.

$$E[x(\tau)[(p_{\rm H}+\tau)[R - R_{\rm b}(\tau)] - J] + [1-y(\tau)]\beta C_1] \geqslant I - A,$$

$$R_{\rm b}(\tau) \geqslant B/\Delta p \quad \text{for all } \tau.$$

Let μ denote the shadow price of the investors' breakeven constraint, $\theta(\tau)$ the shadow price of the incentive constraint, and L the Lagrangian:

$$\frac{\partial L}{\partial x(\tau)} = (p_{\rm H}+\tau)R - J + \mu[(p_{\rm H}+\tau)[R - R_{\rm b}(\tau)] - J],$$

$$\frac{1}{C_1}\frac{\partial L}{\partial y(\tau)} = (1-\beta) - \mu\beta,$$

$$\frac{\partial L}{\partial R_{\rm b}(\tau)} = -\mu x(\tau)(p_{\rm H}+\tau) + \theta(\tau).$$

The solution to Program I is characterized by three thresholds: $A_{\rm L} \leqslant A_{\rm M} \leqslant A_{\rm H}$.[19]

• *High-payment region.* When $A > A_{\rm H}$ (financially unconstrained entrepreneur), then $\mu = 0$. The continuation rule is the first-best, efficient continuation rule,

$$x(\tau) = 1 \quad \text{if and only if } (p_{\rm H}+\tau)R \geqslant J \iff \tau \geqslant \tau^{\rm FB},$$

and there is no reversion,

$$y(\tau) = 1 \quad \text{for all } \tau.$$

Because of risk neutrality, there is some indeterminacy as to the level of $R_{\rm b}(\tau)$. One can, for example,

18. Burkart, M., D. Gromb, and F. Panunzi. 1998. Why higher takeover premia protect minority shareholders. *Journal of Political Economy* 106:172–204.

19. We use weak inequalities because some regions may not exist once the entrepreneur's participation constraint (that the entrepreneur may prefer not to be financed rather than face drastic conditions) $U_{\rm b} \geqslant C$ is taken into account. Also the rights reversion region may not exist even in the absence of this constraint (I believe).

take it to be constant and equal to some $R_b > \underline{R}_b$ (over $[\tau^{FB}, \bar{\tau}]$). Furthermore, R_b decreases as A decreases and is equal to $\underline{R}_b$ when $A = A_H$.

For $A < A_H$, $\mu > 0$ and $R_b(\tau) = \underline{R}_b$ for all τ. There exists a cutoff τ^* such that

$$x(\tau) = 1 \quad \text{if and only if } \tau \geqslant \tau^*$$

and

$$(p_H + \tau^*)\left(R - \frac{B}{\Delta p}\right) < J < [p_H + \tau^*]R$$

(the biotech entrepreneur accepts a less frequent continuation so as to please the pharmaceutical company; note that, at the cutoff value, the latter still incurs a loss).

- *Termination region.* When $A_M < A < A_H$,

$$\tau^* > \tau^{FB}, y(\tau) = 1 \quad \text{and} \quad R_b = \underline{R}_b.$$

The cutoff τ^* increases as A decreases, while μ increases. The pharmaceutical company is less and less keen on refinancing as A decreases, but does not need to be granted inefficient reversion rights.

For $A = A_M$, $\mu = (1 - \beta)/\beta$.

- *Termination-and-rights reversion.* When $A_L < A < A_M$,

$$R_b = \underline{R}_b.$$

Reversion rights are used in order to secure financing. In the absence of date-0 moral hazard there is some indeterminacy as to the state of nature in which reversion occurs (only the expressed amount of reversion is determined). However, with (an arbitrarily small amount of) date-0 moral hazard, MLRP implies (see below) that it is strictly optimal to set

$$y(\tau) = \begin{cases} 1 & \text{for } \tau \geqslant \tau^{**}, \\ 0 & \text{for } \tau < \tau^{**}, \end{cases}$$

for some τ^{**}. Let us therefore focus on such a cutoff rule.

As A decreases, τ^{**} increases (reversion becomes more frequent).

- *No-financing region.* $A < A_L$.

(ii) *Noncontractible research activity.* When the initial contract cannot specify the nature of the research activity, there is moral hazard. From Assumption 1, the contract must ensure that the entrepreneur selects $e = 1$. The optimal contract is then obtained by solving the following program.

Program II. This equals Program I plus the *ex ante* incentive compatibility constraint:

$$\int_{\underline{\tau}}^{\bar{\tau}} [x(\tau)(p_H + \tau)R_b(\tau) + y(\tau)C_1]\,dF(\tau)$$
$$\geqslant \int_{\underline{\tau}}^{\bar{\tau}} [x(\tau)(p_H + \tau)R_b(\tau) + y(\tau)C_0]\,dG(\tau).$$

Let L^{II} denote the Lagrangian of the new program, and λ the Kuhn–Tucker multiplier of the *ex ante* (IC) constraint. The first-order conditions are

$$\begin{aligned} \frac{\partial L^{II}}{\partial x(\tau)} = \Big\{&[(p_H + \tau)R - J] \\ &+ \mu[(p_H + \tau)(R - R_b(\tau)) - J] \\ &+ \lambda[(p_H + \tau)R_b(\tau)]\left[1 - \frac{g(\tau)}{f(\tau)}\right]\Big\} f(\tau), \end{aligned}$$

$$\begin{aligned} \frac{\partial L^{II}}{\partial y(\tau)} = \Big\{&(1 - \beta)C_1 - \mu\beta C_1 \\ &+ \lambda\left[C_1 - C_0\frac{g(\tau)}{f(\tau)}\right]\Big\} f(\tau), \end{aligned}$$

$$\begin{aligned} \frac{\partial L^{II}}{\partial R_b(\tau)} = \Big\{&-\mu x(\tau)(p_H + \tau) \\ &+ \lambda x(\tau)(p_H + \tau)\left[1 - \frac{g(\tau)}{f(\tau)}\right] \\ &+ \theta(\tau)\Big\} f(\tau), \end{aligned}$$

where all Kuhn–Tucker multipliers, μ, λ, and $\theta(\tau)$, are nonnegative.

As in part (i), optimization over probabilities yields corner solutions: for each τ, $x(\tau), y(\tau) \in \{0, 1\}$; also $R_b(\tau) \in \{B/\Delta p, R\}$. Furthermore, from MLRP, both $1 - g(\tau)/f(\tau)$ and $C_1 - C_0 g(\tau)/f(\tau)$ increasing in τ. An optimal contract can be described as follows: (i) $x(\tau) = 1$ if and only if $\tau \in [\tau^*, \bar{\tau}]$, otherwise $x(\tau) = 0$; (ii) there exists $\tau^B \in [\tau^*, \bar{\tau}]$ such that $R_b(\tau) = R$ over $(\tau^B, \bar{\tau}]$ and $R_b(\tau) = B/\Delta p$ otherwise; and (iii) $y(\tau) = 1$ if and only if $\tau \in [\tau^{**}, \bar{\tau}]$, otherwise $y(\tau) = 0$.

Depending on the values of μ and λ, four cases can be distinguished. We omit the analysis for $\mu = \lambda = 0$ and $\mu > 0 = \lambda$, because the optimal contract then takes the same form as in the corresponding cases in part (i); if $\mu = 0$ the borrower's reward $R_b(\tau)$ is chosen in $\{B/\Delta p, R\}$ here.

To facilitate discussion, let $\hat{\tau} \in (\underline{\tau}, \bar{\tau})$ satisfy $f(\hat{\tau}) = g(\hat{\tau})$. From MLRP and

$$\int_{\underline{\tau}}^{\bar{\tau}} [f(\tau) - g(\tau)]\,d\tau = 0,$$

we know that $\hat{\tau}$ exists if $f(\tau)/g(\tau)$ is continuous. For simplicity we will assume so. Again from MLRP we have for all $\tau \geqslant \hat{\tau}$, $f(\tau) \geqslant g(\tau)$, and for all $\tau \leqslant \hat{\tau}$, $f(\tau) \leqslant g(\tau)$.

• $\mu = 0 < \lambda$, this is likely to be the case when, for example, A is large so that the investors' participation is not an issue, but C_1 is small relative to C_0 and so *ex ante* (IC) poses a problem.

Since, at $\tau = \bar{\tau}$, $f(\bar{\tau}) > g(\bar{\tau})$ and $(p_H + \bar{\tau})R > J$, we must have $x(\bar{\tau}) = 1$. This in turn implies that

$$\frac{\partial L^{\mathrm{II}}}{\partial R_b(\tau)}\bigg|_{\tau=\bar{\tau}} = \left\{\lambda(p_H + \bar{\tau})\left[1 - \frac{g(\bar{\tau})}{f(\bar{\tau})}\right] + \theta(\bar{\tau})\right\} f(\bar{\tau}) > 0,$$

and therefore $\tau^B < \bar{\tau}$. Also we must have $\tau^B \geqslant \hat{\tau}$. To boost *ex ante* incentives, the entrepreneur is provided with a high stake (the whole R) in the specific project when the signal is very favorable ($\tau > \tau^B \geqslant \hat{\tau}$).

To determine τ^*, it must lie between τ^{FB} and $\hat{\tau}$, when they are not equal. The tradeoff here is between NPV and *ex ante* incentives: either $\tau^{FB} < \hat{\tau}$ and $\tau^{FB} < \tau^* < \hat{\tau}$, from NPV concerns the specific project should continue more often ($\tau^{FB} < \tau^*$), but reducing τ^* harms *ex ante* incentives; or $\tau^{FB} > \hat{\tau}$ and $\tau^{FB} > \tau^* > \hat{\tau}$, and then increasing NPV calls for a higher τ^*, but this again has an adverse effect on *ex ante* incentives. Note that as λ gets larger, i.e., as *ex ante* (IC) becomes more stringent, τ^* moves toward $\hat{\tau}$.

To determine τ^{**}, whether reversion is used ($\tau^{**} > \underline{\tau}$) is determined by the sign of the FOC at $\underline{\tau}$,

$$\frac{\partial L^{\mathrm{II}}}{\partial y(\tau)}\bigg|_{\tau=\underline{\tau}} = \left\{(1-\beta)C_1 + \lambda\left[C_1 - C_0\frac{g(\underline{\tau})}{f(\underline{\tau})}\right]\right\} f(\underline{\tau}).$$

If it is positive (which is possible because $C_1 - C_0 g(\underline{\tau})/f(\underline{\tau}) < 0$), then reversion is employed in order to boost incentives. This is more likely to be the case as λ gets larger, i.e., as *ex ante* (IC) gets more stringent.

• μ and $\lambda > 0$, both (IR) and *ex ante* (IC) are binding.

As above, for the derivative with respect to $R_b(\tau)$, if $\tau^B < \bar{\tau}$ it must be the case that

$$\frac{\partial L^{\mathrm{II}}}{\partial R_b(\tau)}\bigg|_{\tau=\bar{\tau}} = \left\{-\mu(p_H + \bar{\tau}) + \lambda(p_H + \bar{\tau})\left[1 - \frac{g(\bar{\tau})}{f(\bar{\tau})}\right]\right\} f(\bar{\tau}) > 0.$$

Again we must have $\tau^B > \hat{\tau}$. And, as suggested by the intuition, this range shrinks or expands (τ^B increases or decreases) when (IR) or *ex ante* (IC) becomes more stringent, respectively.

For τ^*, the optimal value lies between $\min\{\tau^{FB}, \hat{\tau}\}$ and $\max\{\hat{\tau}, \tau^{\mathcal{P}}\}$, where $\tau^{\mathcal{P}} > \tau^{FB}$ and is defined by $(p_H + \tau^{\mathcal{P}})(R - B/\Delta p) \equiv J$. When A decreases, μ is larger, the concern over pledgeable income becomes more important, and the optimal threshold moves toward $\tau^{\mathcal{P}}$. On the other hand, when C_0 increases and *ex ante* (IC) becomes more important, τ^* moves toward $\hat{\tau}$.

For τ^{**}, the strictly negative term $-\mu\beta C_1$ in the FOC shows that a binding (IR) induces the use of reversion in order to boost pledgeable income. For the reversion at any τ, $y(\tau) = 0$, increases the investor's return by βC_1, and this contributes to the project value with a coefficient μ. On the other hand, from *ex ante* incentive concern, $y(\tau) = 1$ only for those τ high enough so that $C_1 - C_0 g(\tau)/f(\tau) \geqslant 0$. There may not exist any τ satisfying this condition. In this case, both (IR) and *ex ante* (IC) require τ^{**} to increase. The two forces work together and in opposition to the NPV concern (the term $(1-\beta)C_1$) in determining the optimal threshold. But if such τ exist (and this will be an interval $[\tau^C, \bar{\tau}]$, where τ^C satisfies $C_1 - C_0 g(\tau^C)/f(\tau^C) = 0$), then the optimal contract should reflect the incentive value of assigning $y(\tau) = 1$ over the range $[\tau^C, \bar{\tau}]$. The NPV and *ex ante* (IC) considerations both demand less reversion, which goes against the concern over pledgeable income (reflected by $-\mu\beta C_1$).

Note that in both cases, and when $\hat{\tau} > \tau^{\mathcal{P}}$, it is possible to have optimal $\tau^* > \tau^{\mathcal{P}}$. This, however, is not renegotiation-proof and therefore we need to add a binding renegotiation-proofness constraint $\tau^* = \tau^{\mathcal{P}}$. This constraint imposes a restriction on the entrepreneur's ability to rely on $x(\tau)$ to curb *ex ante* incentives, and therefore the optimal contract will have reversion and a high payment (τ^B) to boost *ex ante* incentives.

Review Problem 9 (conflict of interest in multitasking). (i) The derivations are in Section 3.2. Use the incentive constraint

$$(\Delta p)R_b \geqslant B$$

to infer that the pledgeable income is

$$\mathcal{P}_1 \equiv p_H\left(R - \frac{B}{\Delta p}\right).$$

(ii) The inequality

$$p_H(1 - p_H)R > I$$

says that, *in the absence of agency costs*, pursuing the two research strategies is profitable (with probability $1 - p_H$ the first strategy fails; the expected payoff of the second strategy is then $p_H R$).

Let R_b denote the entrepreneur's reward if the final profit is R (she receives 0 if the profit is 0). The incentive constraints are

$$[1 - (1 - p_H)^2]R_b \geqslant [p_H + (1 - p_H)p_L]R_b + B$$

and

$$[1 - (1 - p_H)^2]R_b \geqslant [1 - (1 - p_L)^2]R_b + 2B.$$

The first constraint can be rewritten as

$$(1 - p_H)(\Delta p)R_b \geqslant B.$$

It is easy to check that this latter condition implies that the second incentive constraint is satisfied.

So the nonpledgeable income is

$$[1 - (1 - p_H)^2]\frac{B}{(1 - p_H)(\Delta p)}.$$

The two research strategies can be funded if and only if the pledgeable income $\mathcal{P}_2$ exceeds the net investment cost $2I - A$:

$$\mathcal{P}_2 \equiv [1 - (1 - p_H)^2]\left[R - \frac{B}{(1 - p_H)\Delta p}\right] \geqslant 2I - A.$$

Suppose that $\mathcal{P}_1 = I - A$ (or just above) and so the project can be funded with a single research strategy. Then

$$\begin{aligned}\mathcal{P}_2 - (2I - A) &= [\mathcal{P}_2 - (2I - A)] - [\mathcal{P}_1 - (I - A)] \\ &= [p_H(1 - p_H)R - I] - \frac{p_H}{1 - p_H}\frac{B}{\Delta p}.\end{aligned}$$

The first term on the right-hand side represents the increase in the NPV while the second term stands for the increase in the agency cost. There is no way to obtain funding for the two research strategies if the increase in NPV is small.

(iii) With two agents, each pursuing a research strategy, the individual incentive constraints can be written as

$$(\Delta p)(1 - \tfrac{1}{2}p_H)R_b \geqslant B.$$

The nonpledgeable income per agent is

$$p_H(1 - \tfrac{1}{2}p_H)R_b = p_H\left(\frac{B}{\Delta p}\right).$$

Financing is feasible if

$$\begin{aligned}\hat{\mathcal{P}}_2 &= [1 - (1 - p_H)^2]R - 2p_H\frac{B}{\Delta p} \\ &= \mathcal{P}_1 + p_H(1 - p_H)R - p_H\frac{B}{\Delta p} \\ &\geqslant 2I - 2A\end{aligned}$$

(since the new entrepreneur can be asked to contribute A).

Note that

$$\hat{\mathcal{P}}_2 - (2I - 2A) = (p_H(1 - p_H)R - I) - \left(p_H\frac{B}{\Delta p} - A\right).$$

The right-hand side measures the increase in the NPV of the entrepreneur who owns the research strategies. It represents the difference between

- the increase in expected profit, net of the investment cost,
  $$p_H(1 - p_H)R - I,$$
- and the rent to be left to the new entrepreneur,
  $$p_H\frac{B}{\Delta p} - A.$$

Note that, unless $A = 0$, it may be possible that

$$\hat{\mathcal{P}}_2 > 2I - 2A$$

(and the NPV is then strictly positive) and

$$\mathcal{P}_2 < 2I - A,$$

since

$$\hat{\mathcal{P}}_2 - (2I - 2A) > \mathcal{P}_2 - (2I - A).$$

Index

absolute-priority rule, 55, 138
accounting-based performance measures, 22, 29, 59, 118, 123, 180, 299, 306, 338, 340, 344, 353, 376, 378, 407, 625
accounting, creative, *see* creative accounting
acquisitions, 5, 9, 17, 20, 29, 43, 50–51, 88, 100, 367, 425, 498–99, 503, 507, 515, 618
  bootstrap, 433
active monitoring, *see* monitoring, active
adverse selection, 2–4, 26, 52, 102, 113–14, 182, 220–21, 237–76, 306, 333, 341, 350, 355, 358, 391, 405, 427, 459–60, 475, 477, 502, 536, 586, 596, 598
advisory monitoring models, 364
affirmative covenants, 80, 104
alliances, 64, 92, 393, 536, 551
alternative risk transfer, 216
arm's length finance, 333
Arrow-Debreu model, 1, 484
AS model, 333, 335
asset substitution, *see also* gambling, risk taking, 85, 87, 161–63, 165, 314, 323–24, 389, 602
authority, 65–68, 79, 240, 334, 407
  formal, 84, 239, 398, 416, 428
  real, 9, 35, 84, 204, 239, 398, 402–4, 416, 428, 431, 441

bailouts, 220, 535
balance sheet, 3–6, 86–87, 99, 100, 117
  and collateral, 169
  and control rights, 390
  and credit rationing, 117
  and debt maturity, 204, 558
  and group lending, 180
  and liquidity, 174–75
  and monitoring, 359
  and takeovers, 428
  channel, 5, 471, 478, 482
bank
  debt, 47, 52, 55, 88–89, 342, 379, 410
  loans, 47, 80–82, 84, 88–91, 93, 96, 101
  runs, 5, 454–55, 457, 463, 465–66
bankruptcy, *see also* Chapter 7, Chapter 11, 1, 8, 15, 20, 25–27, 29, 51–54, 77, 79, 87, 92, 103, 113, 132, 141, 167, 190–91, 199, 256, 410–11, 497, 544, 551, 564, 586–87
behavioral corporate finance, 9
benchmarking, 3, 29, 122–23, 180, 278, 283–87, 310–11, 324, 573, 602
block shareholder, 4, 37, 40, 53
board of directors, 9, 18–20, 25, 29–30, 33, 37, 63, 65, 84, 239, 254, 258, 334, 395, 425
bond covenant, 87
Brander–Lewis model, 289, 296, 298, 319, 321, 325
bubble, 8, 9, 95, 102, 123, 177, 529

call option, 21, 23, 46, 77, 342–43, 353, 527, 607
capital
  adequacy, 83, 375, 479, 522, 535
  asset pricing model (CAPM), 219
  market, internal, *see* internal capital market
  structure, 76, 82, 102–3, 132, 199, 411
CAPM, *see* capital asset pricing model
career concerns, 26, 63, 278, 283, 306–7, 310–11, 321, 336, 588
carrot and stick, 186, 225, 406–7, 409–10, 559
cartelization, 165–66, 194, 509, 522, 590
cash-flow rights, 40, 51, 54, 75, 91, 387, 389, 408, 417, 434, 541, 559–60, 578, 610
certification, *see also* monitoring, 91–93, 246, 249–51, 358, 375, 471, 479–81, 483
Chapter 7, 52
Chapter 11, 20, 26, 52, 87, 410
Coase Theorem, 53, 64, 390, 410, 428, 536
collateral, 2, 3, 6, 7, 51, 55, 60, 75–77, 80–82, 88, 90, 92, 99, 102–4, 164, 251
collusion, 20, 28, 42, 46, 182, 262, 293, 321, 336, 338, 343, 349, 353, 356, 359, 362–64, 414, 537, 555, 594, 606
commercial paper, 81–83, 88–89, 101, 216, 333–34, 471
competition
  bank, 535
  between legal environments, 36
  between monitors, 457, 609–10
  for corporate funding, 414

competition (*continued*)
    for labor, 544
    for savings, 537, 543
    in lending, 4
    international, 49
    product-market, *see* product-market competition
conglomerates, 9, 36, 47, 414–15
    break-up of, 49
contracting institutions, 5, 54–56, 536–41, 544, 556–57, 559
control rights, 4, 6, 9, 25, 27, 36, 51, 53, 59, 64, 75–76, 80, 84, 91–93
    and balance-sheet strength, 401
    and block shareholders, 403
    and competition, 286
    and contracting institutions, 559
    and shareholder value, 391
    and specific investments, 395
    contingent, 388, 393–94, 497
    multiple, 392
convertible
    bonds, 77, 248, 351
    debt, 77, 95, 137, 316, 351, 378, 404
corporate social responsibility, 56, 58, 60
costly
    collateral pledging, 3, 92, 123, 130, 143, 170–71, 204, 251, 325, 391, 429, 537–38, 542, 630
    state verification, 113, 131, 138, 141–43
covenants, 2, 20, 47, 53, 60, 64, 76–77, 79–80, 82, 84–92, 99, 103–6
    negative, 60, 80, 84, 88, 103, 119
    positive, 60, 84–85
creative accounting, 86, 283, 299–300
credit
    analysis, 82–83, 87, 102–3, 116, 127, 165, 184, 274, 497
    crunch, 5, 90, 478, 482–83, 625
    cycles, 489
    line, 95, 205
creditor rights, 54–55, 535, 551, 554
cross
    -pledging, 157–59, 163, 180, 192, 609–10, 625
    -subsidization, 3, 48, 237–38, 242–43, 247, 249–50, 254, 414–15, 581
currencies, 203, 214, 216, 305, 343, 393, 463–65, 540, 565
    efficient, 203, 294, 305

deadlock, 29, 59, 64, 400–1, 411
debt
    demandable, 337–38, 350–53
    forgiveness, 114, 126, 140, 146, 205, 227
    maturity, 3, 80, 232, 537, 557
    overhang, 114, 125–26, 179, 205, 224, 297, 626
default, 36, 48, 76, 80–83, 86–87, 89, 103–4
deposit insurance, 99, 527
Diamond–Dybvig model, 447, 450, 452–53, 455, 457, 460–61, 466–67, 521, 615, 625
dilution, 85, 91, 119, 205
disclosure, 31, 66, 89, 92, 105, 181, 241, 246, 249–50, 333, 345, 402–3, 425, 535–36, 542
dissipative signal, 3, 239, 249, 303
dividend smoothing, 313–14
dividends, *see also* payout policy, 1, 7, 8, 29, 46, 51, 55, 64, 76–78, 85, 95, 97–98, 100–1, 119, 141, 187, 199, 204–5, 225, 238–40, 257–60, 313–14, 351, 379, 399, 411, 447, 449, 452, 463, 529, 535, 541
dual-class shares, 40, 429, 431, 439

earnings
    before interest and taxes, 91, 394, 407
    manipulation, 283, 299, 304–5, 307
EBIT, *see* earnings before interest and taxes
empire building, 9, 163
Employee Stock Ownership Plan (ESOP), 45
equity
    offering, 3, 8, 97, 100–1, 237, 244–46, 262, 275, 597
    premium, 337, 349, 459–60, 526
exchange offer, 52, 227, 410
executive
    compensation, 18, 24, 29, 35, 41, 49
    turnover, 25–26, 171
exit
    and voice, 334
    strategy, 248, 356, 379, 471, 607

fiduciary duty, 37, 58, 62, 433
financial
    fragility, 10
    intermediaries, 5, 79, 83, 166, 357, 447, 471, 480, 535
    muscle, 3, 5, 166, 286, 321–23, 498–99, 506, 508–9, 601, 626
fire sale, 82, 165–66, 194, 522, 590
foreign exchange, 10, 77, 214
forward markets, 217
free cash flow, 50–51, 119, 199, 225, 258
free rider, 436–37

gambling, 24, 53, 85, 152–53, 214, 217, 307, 309, 315–17, 581–82
GJ model, 333
going public, 92, 244, 246, 391
golden parachute, 19, 45, 304–5, 307, 326, 419, 441, 604–5, 611–12
greenmail, 46, 425, 441
growth prospects, 93, 96, 199, 206, 225

herd behavior, 9, 278, 307, 310, 600
holdup, 53, 93, 157, 177, 257, 297, 356, 372, 374, 395, 413, 506
hubris, 9, 50, 428

ICM, *see* capital market, internal
implicit incentives, 15, 20–21, 26, 62–63, 171
inalienability of human capital, 177, 626
information sharing, 122, 249, 276–77, 599
initial public offering (IPO), 8, 48, 54, 89–95, 123, 176–77, 237, 240, 250–51, 262, 264, 356, 367–69, 375, 378–79, 394, 439, 471
initiative, 42, 93, 360–61, 373, 396–98, 403, 413–17
inside liquidity, 5, 450, 517–18, 520–21, 528, 531–32, 620, 629
insider trading, 17, 21, 44, 341–42, 345
intermediation, 166, 480, 483, 626
internal capital market, 9, 20, 33, 52, 78, 95–96, 98, 411–15
investment banking, 28, 48, 95, 251
investment-cash-flow sensitivity, *see* sensitivity of investment to cash flow
investor
  activism, 15, 36, 38, 41–42, 356, 362
  protection, 54–56, 94, 333, 359, 487, 493, 544, 616
IPO, *see* initial public offering (IPO)
irrelevance result, *see* Modigliani–Miller Theorem

Jacklin critique, 452–53, 467
junior debt, 76, 246

large blockholder, 42, 355, 369, 371, 375, 403–4, 419
lemons problem, 81, 237, 244, 249, 502
lender market power, 116, 149, 576–77
lending channel, 5, 471, 478, 482
leveraged buyout (LBO), 31, 40, 43–44, 47, 49, 90, 295
likelihood ratio
  monotone, 132
liquidity
  aggregate, 522, 530–31, 619–20
  asset pricing model (LAPM), 526
  demand, 5, 199–200, 375, 405, 447–48, 450, 454, 521
    consumer, 5, 447, 450, 454, 521, 554
    firm, 199–200, 405, 448, 450, 521, 554
  management, 2, 8, 153, 200, 203, 205, 209, 215–16, 219, 226–29, 405, 485, 505–6, 515, 557–58, 560, 618
  premium, 231, 522, 525–26, 528, 531, 593, 620
  ratio, 212
  redispatching, 414, 452, 521
  trading, 40, 337, 346, 348–49, 367, 457, 459
liquidity-accountability tradeoff, 172, 625
loan commitment, 81, 86, 89, 200, 216, 229, 433, 591
low-information-intensity securities, 3, 5, 248–49, 405, 460

M&As, *see* mergers and acquisitions
management buyout (MBO), 43, 47–49
managerial myopia, 301, 430
marked-to-market accounting, 300
market
  breakdown, 3, 237, 239, 249, 269–70, 273, 477, 596
  timing, 9, 94, 101–2, 238, 244
  value accounting, 45
maximal insider incentives, 132–33
mergers and acquisitions, 5, 28, 43–44, 50–51, 102, 166, 257, 387, 431, 497, 506, 535, 626
mezzanine finance, 76
microfinance, 180
Modigliani–Miller Theorem, 1–3, 8, 77–78, 84, 102, 389, 409
monitoring
  active, 4, 27–28, 42, 47, 90, 147, 343, 355, 359–70, 387, 400–1, 404, 537, 574, 627
  delegated, 90, 335, 357
  market, 176, 337–38, 343–45, 349–51, 359, 459–60
  passive, 4, 333, 337–38, 350, 355, 375
monotonic reimbursement, 133–34, 271

one-share-one-vote, 54, 439–40, 535
option
  in the money, 24, 308–9
  out of the money, 23–24, 309
outside liquidity, 5, 517–18, 523–24, 526–27, 532, 620
overborrowing, 119–21
overconfidence, 428
overmonitoring, 42, 356, 359–61, 365–66, 417, 630

payout policy, 3, 8, 61, 75, 78, 95–98, 100, 141, 187, 199, 257–58, 270, 305, 313, 594
pecking order, 176, 238, 247, 278, 379, 599
poison pill, 4, 45–46, 399, 425, 434, 441
posturing, 307
poverty trap, 5, 484, 486, 625
preferred stock, 76, 91, 177, 199, 342, 394, 418
priority, 52, 54–55, 76–77, 80, 87–88, 91, 103, 114–15, 121, 138, 233, 408, 410–11, 594
privately
  held equity, 47, 90
  placed debt, 81, 83–84, 88–89
product-market competition, 3, 15, 20, 28–29, 98, 145–46, 229, 283, 286, 289, 296, 310, 321, 414, 503, 537, 544, 572–73
project finance, 158–60, 183, 192, 244, 275, 414, 419, 483

property rights institutions, 6, 54, 536, 544–45, 551, 560, 626, 628
provisions for loan losses, 299
proxy fights, 17, 20, 25, 37–38, 41–42, 45, 51, 333–34, 336, 355

quest for pledgeable income, 157, 286, 428–29

rating agency, 19, 27–28, 77, 79, 83, 114, 250, 276, 335
ratings, 83, 88–89, 251, 257, 276
redeployability, 164–65, 194, 499–500, 503
relationship
 banking, 177, 251, 355, 369, 413
 lending, 80, 181, 476
relative performance evaluation, *see* benchmarking, 22, 122, 285, 310
renegotiation, *see* soft budget constraint
reorganization, 6, 25, 45, 52–54, 87, 311, 407–8, 410
reputation, 20, 22, 37, 57, 79, 83, 88, 91–92, 95, 121–22, 144, 179, 181, 205, 216, 250, 276, 306, 336, 369, 544, 606
reputational capital, 91, 122, 179, 190, 274–75
retained earnings/retentions, 3, 95–98, 102, 128, 143, 148, 167, 185–86, 200, 218–19, 225, 238, 246, 255, 258, 290, 313, 399, 513, 515, 541, 558, 561, 575
risk
 management, 3, 22, 29, 52, 66, 153, 162, 199–200, 213–17, 219, 234, 299, 411, 535, 582
 taking, 17, 61, 77, 85, 119, 283, 299, 307, 314–16, 318, 337, 406

Sarbanes–Oxley Act, 16, 19, 28, 32, 34–35, 305
seasoned
 equity offerings (SEOs), 8, 9, 90, 100, 240, 262
 offerings, 219, 235, 237, 239, 264, 275, 366, 506–7, 515, 541, 558, 561–62
security design, 2, 3, 240, 290–91, 389, 404–8, 410–11, 418, 610
senior debt, 76, 85, 91, 326, 464, 625–26
sensitivity of investment to cash flow, 2, 3, 100, 124, 128, 216, 220, 224–25, 291, 294, 414, 625
SEO, *see* seasoned equity offerings (SEOs)
share repurchases, 8, 78, 85, 97, 100, 204, 257, 314
shareholder
 activism, 17, 333
 rights, 42
 value, 4, 16, 20, 23, 25, 46–47, 56–57, 59–62, 64, 102, 391, 425
short-termism, *see* managerial myopia

soft budget constraint, 3, 89, 119, 179, 201, 213, 215, 220–24, 230–31, 297–98, 325, 361, 409, 414, 566, 592, 604
specific investment, 164, 177–79, 297, 388, 395, 506, 537
speculation, 333, 335, 343, 345, 351, 459, 463–64
stakeholder society, 15–16, 56–60, 62–64
standard debt contract, 113, 132, 134, 138–40, 248, 271, 579
start-up, 36, 47, 90–91, 96, 123, 177, 199, 239, 362, 375, 379, 393, 405, 411, 415, 417, 471, 477, 479, 607
stock price reaction, negative, 3, 46, 50, 101, 237–38, 245, 262, 275–76, 313, 597
stores of value, 5, 8, 513–15, 517–20, 522–23, 525–26, 528, 531–32, 620–21
subordinated debt, 76, 333
sufficient statistic, 122–23

takeover
 defenses, 45, 425, 428, 434, 441
 managerial resistance, 441
takeovers, 3, 4, 15, 17, 20, 25–27, 31–32, 35–36, 41, 43–51, 53, 55, 57–58, 60, 90, 93
tender offer, 17, 29, 37, 43, 45, 366–69, 431–37, 630
time
 consistency, 545, 566
 inconsistency, 536, 540, 545, 551
toehold, 45, 371, 432–33, 438, 440–41
trade credit, 80–82, 88, 95, 99, 101, 299, 355, 411
tradeoff theory, 8
Treasury bond, 133, 173, 177, 231, 352, 498, 513, 526, 551, 593
tunneling, 343, 353, 356, 362–63, 433, 535

underpricing, 3, 91, 93, 239–40, 262–64, 272
underwriting, 28, 81, 88, 93–95, 241, 250, 262, 335, 375

venture capital, 26, 68, 79, 90–92, 98, 123, 176–77, 251, 375, 378, 380, 414
vertical integration, 64, 286, 322, 601

warranties, 80, 104
whistleblowing, 34
window dressing, 300
winner picking, 414
winner's curse, 93, 240, 262, 368, 370–72, 440–41
workout, 52–53, 410

yardstick competition, *see also* benchmarking, 22
yield curve, 450–51, 453–54
 technological, 448, 451–52